Delphi™ 4

Developer's Guide

Xavier Pacheco
Steve Teixeira

SAMS

201 West 103rd Street
Indianapolis, Indiana 46290

DELPHI™ 4 DEVELOPER'S GUIDE

Copyright © 1998 by Sams Publishing

International Standard Book Number: 0-672-31284-0

Library of Congress Catalog Card Number: 98-84680

Printed in the United States of America

First Printing: August, 1998

01 00 99 98   4   3   2   1

Trademarks

WARNING AND DISCLAIMER

EXECUTIVE EDITOR
Brian Gill

AQUISITIONS EDITOR
Ron Gallagher

DEVELOPMENT EDITOR
Tony Amico

MANAGING EDITOR
Jodi Jensen

PROJECT EDITOR
Dana Rhodes Lesh

COPY EDITORS
Margaret Berson
Geneil Breeze
Bart Reed
Hugh Vandivier

INDEXER
Rebecca Salerno

TECHNICAL EDITORS
Danny Thorpe
Alain Tadros
Anders Ohlsson

SOFTWARE DEVELOPMENT SPECIALIST
Dan Scherf

PRODUCTION
Marcia Deboy
Jenny Earhart
Cynthia Fields
Susan Geiselman

OVERVIEW

CONTENTS

PART III COMPONENT-BASED DEVELOPMENT 465

20 KEY ELEMENTS OF THE VISUAL COMPONENT LIBRARY 467

APPENDIXES

FOREWORD

When I speak with other Delphi developers, one of the questions I'm most often asked is how we came up with the idea to create Delphi. Believe it or not, it all started with one simple line of code written on the whiteboard one day in a Turbo Pascal R&D meeting:

```
Button.Caption := 'OK';
```

Although this line of code might seem simple to even the greenest Delphi programmer, it was quite groundbreaking at the time. This was the early 1990s, when writing a real application in Windows meant wading through a nasty swap of window procedures, messages, callbacks, handles, and pointers. Windows frameworks such as OWL and MFC were becoming popular, but they did little to hide the complexity of Windows and certainly didn't approach the simplicity illustrated by that one line of code on the whiteboard. We had the line of code—now all we needed was the development environment that made it real.

We knew that the current version of Turbo Pascal wasn't up to the task, so we went about reinventing Pascal to fit our needs. We added a number of new features to the language, such as a reference object model, properties, class references, method pointers, and Runtime Type Information (RTTI). Then we went about creating a new class library to take advantage of the new language elements. As we added classes such as TWindow (later renamed TForm), TEdit, and TButton to this library, we knew that that line of code on the whiteboard was becoming a reality. This was a very exciting time. We were like kids with a new toy.

Of course, as this yet-unnamed tool grew from an experiment into a product, there were others in the company who couldn't wait to get their hands on each new build. Notable among these early Delphi hackers were Steve and Xavier. They have been with the product since the very early days; their years of experience with Delphi come through loud and clear in each code listing and paragraph of *Delphi 4 Developer's Guide*.

By the way, it wasn't until the last minute that we decided to call this product *Delphi*. Delphi was one of the product code names, and we liked it so much that it stuck. Some other interesting facts about the product:

- It was Danny Thorpe who thought up the name *Delphi*. We were brainstorming for code names that alluded to the unique database capabilities of the tool, and Danny suggested *Delphi* because it was the place you go to commune with the database oracles.

- We actually used several code names for the Delphi 1 project in an effort to keep the project as quiet as possible. These included Wasabi, AppBuilder, Mango, and Visual Foo. Despite what you might have heard, VBK (for *Visual Basic Killer*), although popular with a certain former company president and the press, was never a Delphi code name.

- Where does T come from? The *T* stands for *type* and is put in front of almost all types in the Visual Component Library (VCL). This originated from the naming convention used for MacApp from Apple. We first adopted this convention with Turbo Vision, the application framework that came with Turbo Pascal 6.

- One contribution of the aforementioned president to Delphi was that the help hints on the palette don't show the leading T.

Reading through *Delphi 4 Developer's Guide* reminds me of those early days of Delphi. It's written by folks who are clearly excited about Delphi, and as such, it captures some of the excitement that we felt in creating something truly unique. I know this book will soon become an indispensable part of your software development library.

Chuck Jazdzewski
Chief Architect, Borland Delphi
Inprise Corporation
June 1998

ABOUT THE AUTHORS

Xavier Pacheco is the president and chief consultant of XAPWARE Technologies, Inc., where he specializes in Delphi client/server development and training. Xavier has coauthored three Delphi books, regularly writes for Delphi periodicals, and contributes to the Delphi newsgroups as a TeamB member. Xavier enjoys spending time with his wife, Anne, and his daughter, Amanda. Xavier and Anne live in Colorado where they enjoy outdoor activities among the Rocky Mountains. You can reach Xavier at `xavier@xapware.com`.

Steve Teixeira is an R&D engineer at Inprise Corporation, where he works on the Borland Delphi and Borland C++Builder products. Steve has coauthored three books on Delphi, is a regular contributor to several Delphi periodicals, and has spoken at numerous industry conferences.

When he isn't programming or writing, Steve likes to spend time with his family, play basketball, and enjoy the outdoors. Steve lives in Ben Lomond, California, with his wife and son.

You can reach Steve at `steixeira@inprise.com`.

DEDICATION

For Anne

—Xavier Pacheco

For C.J.

—Steve Teixeira

ACKNOWLEDGMENTS

We need to thank those without whose help this book would never have been written. In addition to our thanks, we also want to point out that any errors you find in the book are our own, in spite of everyone's efforts.

We'd first like to thank our technical reviewer, Danny Thorpe. Danny is one of the best reviewers in the business, and a way-awesome Delphi programmer. Danny always goes the extra mile by not only checking for technical accuracy but also pointing out better algorithms or providing additions to the text. In fact, some of the truly insightful nuggets of wisdom you'll find throughout the book are Danny's words.

In addition to Danny, both Anders Ohlsson and Alain "Lino" Tadros came in at the last minute to help with the technical review when the load got heavy. It's no stretch to say that this book wouldn't have been completed on schedule if it weren't for their efforts, so thanks, guys!

Next, huge thanks to Nick Hodges and Louis Kleiman. Nick, the Web Wiz, wrote Chapter 30, "Internet-Enabling Your Applications with WebBroker." Louis had the you-know-what touch while writing Chapter 31, "MIDAS Development."

Thanks to Chuck Jazdzewski for providing the foreword. Chuck generously found the time to write the foreword despite the intense time demands on the chief architect of Delphi during ship time.

While writing *Delphi 4 Developer's Guide*, we received advice and tips from a number of our friends and coworkers. These people include Charlie Calvert, Mark Duncan, Josh Dahlby, Roland Bouchereau, Scott Frolich, Jason Sprenger, Bill Fisher, Jeff Peters, Ellie Peters, David Streever, Rich Jones, and others whose names we can't recall.

Finally, thanks to the gang at Sams—Brian Gill, Tony Amico, Ron Gallagher, Dana Lesh, and the zillions of behind-the-scenes people that we never meet but without whose help this book would not be a reality.

Special Thanks from Xavier

I can never be thankful enough for God's abundant blessings, the greatest of which is His Son, Jesus Christ—my Savior. I thank God for my wife, Anne, whose love, patience, and understanding I will always need. Thank you, Anne, for your support and encouragement and mostly for your prayers and commitment to our Holy Father. I am thankful for my daughter, Amanda, and the joy she brings. Amanda, you are truly a blessing to my life.

Special Thanks from Steve

Many heartfelt thank-yous go to my loving wife, Helen, who provided me with the emotional support and intermittent shouts of "TComponent!" that helped me get through the book. Thank you, C.J., for helping me keep all the demands of life in proper perspective.

TELL US WHAT YOU THINK!

As the reader of this book, *you* are our most important critic and commentator. We value your opinion and want to know what we're doing right, what we could do better, what areas you'd like to see us publish in, and any other words of wisdom you're willing to pass our way.

As the executive editor for the Programming team at Macmillan Computer Publishing, I welcome your comments. You can fax, email, or write me directly to let me know what you did or didn't like about this book—as well as what we can do to make our books stronger.

Please note that I cannot help you with technical problems related to the topic of this book, and that due to the high volume of mail I receive, I might not be able to reply to every message.

When you write, please be sure to include this book's title and author as well as your name and phone or fax number. I will carefully review your comments and share them with the author and editors who worked on the book.

Fax: 317-817-7070

E-mail: prog@mcp.com

Mail: Executive Editor
         Programming
         Macmillan Computer Publishing
         201 West 103rd Street
         Indianapolis, IN 46290 USA

INTRODUCTION

Can you believe that it's been nearly four years since we began work on the first edition of *Delphi Developer's Guide*? At the time, we were just a couple developers working in Borland's language support department looking for a new software challenge. We had an idea for a book that made a point of avoiding things you could learn in product documentation in favor of showing proper coding practices and a few cool techniques. We also figured our experience in developer support would enable us to answer developers' questions before they were even asked. We pitched the idea to the people at Sams Publishing, and they loved it. Then began the many grueling months of manuscript development, programming, late nights, programming, and I think we missed a few deadlines because we were so busy programming. Finally, the book was finished.

Our expectations were modest. At first, we were just hoping we would break even. However, after several months of robust sales, we thought that our concept of a no-nonsense developer's guide was just what the doctor (or in this case, the developers) ordered. Our feelings were legitimized when you, the reader, voted *Delphi Developer's Guide* to the Delphi Informant Reader's Choice Award for best Delphi book.

I think our publisher slipped something into the water because we couldn't stop writing. We released *Delphi 2 Developer's Guide* the next year and completed a manuscript for *Delphi 3 Developer's Guide* (which was unfortunately never published) the year after that. What you have in your hands is our latest work, *Delphi 4 Developer's Guide*, and we think you'll find it an even more valuable resource than any previous edition.

Currently, Steve is an R&D engineer for Delphi and C++Builder at Inprise Corporation (formerly Borland International), and Xavier runs his own Delphi consulting and training firm, XAPWARE Technologies, Inc. We feel that our unique combination of experience "in the trenches" in Borland's developer support department, our real-world experience as developers, and inside knowledge of the Delphi product all add up to one darn good Delphi book.

Simply stated, if you want to develop applications in Delphi, this is the book for you. Our goal is to show you not just how to develop applications using Delphi, but how to develop applications the right way. Delphi is a very unique tool that enables you to drastically reduce the time it takes to develop applications while still offering a level of performance that meets or exceeds that of most C++ compilers on the market. This book shows you how to get the best of these two worlds by demonstrating effective use of Delphi's design-time environment and proper techniques for code reuse and by showing you how to write good, clean, efficient code.

This book is divided into five parts. Part I, "Essentials for Rapid Development," provides you with a strong foundation in the important aspects of Delphi and Win32 programming. Part II, "Advanced Techniques," builds upon those foundations by helping you build small but useful applications and utilities that help to expand your knowledge of more in-depth programming topics. Part III, "Component-Based Development," discusses Visual Component Library (VCL) component development and development using the Component Object Model (COM). Part IV, "Database Development," takes you through database development in Delphi, from local tables to SQL databases and multitier solutions. Part V, "Rapid Database Application Development," brings together much of what you learned in the previous parts in order to build larger-scale real-world applications.

CHAPTERS ON THE CD?

No doubt you've seen the table of contents by now, and you might have noticed that there are several chapters that appear only on the CD and are not in the printed book. The reason for this is simple: We wrote more material than could be bound into a single book. Faced with this problem, we had several choices. We could have split *Delphi 4 Developer's Guide* into two books, but we chose not to do so primarily because it would be more expensive for readers to obtain the material. Another option was to leave out some chapters entirely, but we felt that this would create some obvious gaping holes in the book's coverage. The choice we made, of course, was to put some chapters on the CD. This allowed us to balance the forces of coverage, convenience, and cost. It's important to remember that the chapters on the CD are not "extras" but full-fledged parts of the book. They were written, reviewed, and edited with the same care and close attention to detail as the rest of the book.

WHO SHOULD READ THIS BOOK

As the title of this book says, this book is for developers. So if you're a developer and you use Delphi, you should have this book. In particular, however, this book is aimed at three groups of people:

- Delphi developers who are looking to take their craft to the next level.
- Experienced Pascal, BASIC, or C/C++ programmers who are looking to hit the ground running with Delphi.
- Programmers who are looking to get the most out of Delphi by leveraging the Win32 API and some of Delphi's less obvious features.

CONVENTIONS USED IN THIS BOOK

The following typographic conventions are used in this book:

- Code lines, commands, statements, variables, program output, and any text you see onscreen appear in a `monospaced` typeface.

- Anything that you type also appears in a `monospaced` typeface.

- Placeholders in syntax descriptions appear in *`italic monospace`*. Replace the placeholder with the actual filename, parameter, or whatever element it represents.

- *Italics* highlight technical terms when they first appear in the text and sometimes are used to emphasize important points.

- Procedures and functions are indicated by open and close parentheses after the procedure or function name. Although this is not standard Pascal syntax, it helps to differentiate them from properties, variables, and types.

Within each chapter, you will encounter several Notes, Tips, and Cautions that help to highlight the important points and aid you in steering clear of the pitfalls.

You will find all the source code and project files on the CD-ROM accompanying this book, as well as source samples that we could not fit in the book itself. Also, take a look at the components and tools in the directory `\THRDPRTY`, where you'll find some powerful trial versions of third-party components.

UPDATES TO THIS BOOK

Updates, extras, and errata information for this book are available via the Web. Visit `http://www.xapware.com/ddg` for the latest news.

GETTING STARTED

People sometimes ask us what drives us to continue to write Delphi books. It's hard to explain, but whenever we meet with other developers and see their obviously well-used and bookmarked ratty-looking copies of *Delphi Developer's Guide*, it somehow makes it worthwhile.

Now it's time to relax and have some fun programming with Delphi. We'll start slow but progress into the more advanced topics at a quick but comfortable pace. Before you know it, you'll have the knowledge and technique required to truly be called a Delphi guru.

ESSENTIALS FOR RAPID DEVELOPMENT

PART

I

In This Part

WINDOWS PROGRAMMING IN DELPHI 4

IN THIS CHAPTER

This chapter explains how to use the Delphi 4 Integrated Development Environment (IDE) and how programming Microsoft Windows and Windows NT with Delphi is different from programming with other languages and development environments. This chapter is intended for readers who are new to the Delphi programming environment. If you already have some experience programming in a previous version of Delphi, much of this chapter will be review for you. However, you might want to at least skim this chapter because it discusses the history of Delphi and introduces many of the basic concepts you'll use throughout the book.

A LITTLE HISTORY

Delphi is, at heart, a Pascal compiler. Delphi 4 is the next step in the evolution of the same Pascal compiler that Borland has been developing since Anders Hejlsberg wrote the first Turbo Pascal compiler more than 14 years ago. Pascal programmers throughout the years have enjoyed the stability, grace, and, of course, the compile speed that Turbo Pascal offers. Delphi 4 is no exception—its compiler is the synthesis of more than a decade of compiler experience and a state-of-the-art 32-bit optimizing compiler. You'll be happy to find that Delphi 4 is as stable, graceful, and quick as any of its predecessors.

Delphi 1

In the early days of DOS, programmers had a choice between productive-but-slow BASIC, or efficient-but-complex assembly language. Turbo Pascal, which offered the simplicity of a structured language and the performance of a real compiler, bridged that gap. Windows 3.1 programmers faced a similar choice—a choice between a powerful yet unwieldy language such as C++, or an easy-to-use but limiting language such as Visual Basic. Delphi 1 answered that call by offering a radically different approach to Windows development: visual development, compiled executables, DLLs, databases, you name it—a visual environment without limits. Delphi 1 was the first Windows development tool to combine a visual development environment, an optimizing native-code compiler, and a scalable database access engine. It defined the phrase *Rapid Application Development (RAD)*.

Delphi 2

A year later, Delphi 2 provided all these same benefits under the modern 32-bit operating systems of Windows 95 and Windows NT. Additionally, Delphi 2 extended productivity with additional features and functionality not found in version 1, such as a 32-bit compiler that produces faster applications, an enhanced and extended object library, revamped database support, improved string handling, OLE support, Visual Form Inheritance, and compatibility with 16-bit Delphi projects. Delphi 2 became the yardstick by which all other RAD tools are measured.

Delphi 3

During the development of Delphi 1, the Delphi development team was preoccupied with simply creating and releasing a groundbreaking development tool. For Delphi 2, the development team had its hands full primarily with the tasks of moving to 32-bit (while maintaining almost complete backward compatibility) and adding new database and client/server features needed by corporate IT. While Delphi 3 was being created, the development team had the opportunity to expand the tool set in order to provide an extraordinary level of breadth and depth for solutions to some of the sticky problems faced by Windows developers. In particular, Delphi 3 made it easy to use the notoriously complicated technologies of COM and ActiveX, World Wide Web application development, "thin client" applications, and multitier database architectures. Delphi 3's Code Insight helped to make the actual code writing process a bit easier, although for the most part, the basic methodology for writing Delphi applications was the same as in Delphi 1.

Delphi 4

Delphi 4 focuses on making Delphi development easier. The new Module Explorer enables you to browse and edit units from a convenient graphical interface, and new code navigation and class completion features enable you to focus on the meat of your applications with a minimum amount of busy work. The IDE has been redesigned with dockable toolbars and windows to make your development more convenient, and the debugger has been greatly improved. Secure in its position as the preeminent RAD tool, this release extends Delphi's reach into the enterprise with outstanding multitier support using technologies like MIDAS, DCOM, and CORBA.

WHAT IS DELPHI?

Delphi is a RAD and database development tool for Microsoft Windows and Windows NT. As mentioned earlier, Delphi combines the ease of use of a visual development environment, the speed and power of an optimizing 32-bit compiler, and the data-management capabilities provided by a tightly integrated, scalable database engine. Although none of these technologies is unique in its own right, Delphi 4 is unique in that it seamlessly integrates these three primary technologies into one development environment.

The Delphi 4 Product Family

Delphi 4 comes in four flavors designed to fit a variety of needs: Delphi 4 Standard, Delphi 4 Professional, Delphi 4 Client/Server Suite, and Delphi 4 Enterprise. Each of these versions is targeted at a different type of developer.

Delphi 4 Standard is the entry-level version. It provides everything you need to start writing applications with Delphi, and it's ideal for hobbyists and students who want to break into Delphi programming on a budget. This version includes the following features:

- Optimizing 32-bit Object Pascal compiler
- Visual Component Library (VCL), which includes new Windows 95 controls and 100 components standard on the Component Palette
- *Package* support, which enables you to create small executables and component libraries
- An object-oriented Form Designer, which supports visual form inheritance and linking
- Delphi 1, which is included for 16-bit Windows development
- Database components and connectivity for Paradox and dBASE tables
- Virtual data set architecture, which allows you to incorporate your own database engines into VCL
- Full support for Win32 API, including COM, using ActiveX controls, multi-threading, and various Microsoft and third-party software development kits (SDKs)

Delphi 4 Professional is intended for use by professional developers who don't require client/server features. If you are a professional developer building and deploying applications or Delphi components, this product is designed for you. The Professional edition includes everything in the Standard edition plus the following:

- More than 30 additional components on the Component Palette, including additional data-aware components
- One-step ActiveX control and ActiveForm creation
- QuickReports reporting tool for integrating custom reports into your applications
- TeeChart graphing and charting components for data visualization
- Single-user Local InterBase Server (LIBS), enabling you to do SQL-based client/server development without being connected to a network
- Enhanced database functionality, including Database Explorer tool, data repository, support for ODBC data sources, and low-level Borland Database Engine (BDE) API access
- Web Deployment feature for easy distribution of ActiveX content via the Web.
- InstallSHIELD Express application-deployment tool
- Open Tools API for developing components that integrate tightly within the Delphi 4 environment, and an interface for PVCS version control

- Internet Solutions Pack ActiveX controls for developing Internet-aware applications

- Visual Component Library (VCL) and runtime library (RTL) source code

- WinSight32 tool for browsing window and message information

Delphi 4 Client/Server Suite is targeted toward corporate client/server developers. If you are developing applications that communicate with SQL database servers, this edition contains all the tools necessary to take you through the client/server application development cycle. The Client/Server Suite includes everything included in the other two Delphi 4 editions plus the following:

- WebBroker technologies, including wizards and components that make ISAPI, NSAPI, WinSock, and CGI development easy

- Development license for MIDAS (Multitier Distributed Application Services) applications, providing an unprecedented level of ease for multitier application development

- DecisionCube components, which give you the capability for visual, multidimensional analysis of data

- Native drivers for InterBase, Oracle, Microsoft SQL Server, Sybase, Informix, and DB2 database servers, and a license for unlimited redistribution of these drivers

- SQL Database Explorer, which enables you to browse and edit server-specific metadata

- SQL Monitor, which enables you to view SQL communications to and from the server so that you can debug and fine-tune your SQL application performance

- Data Pump Expert for rapid upsizing

- Four-user InterBase for Windows NT license

- Integrated PVCS version control

- Visual Query Builder

Delphi 4 Enterprise was created for use by large organizations building multitier applications for the enterprise. This package fills the needs of solutions-oriented developers concerned with things like 24x7 application reliability, scalability, and load balancing in heterogeneous environments. This edition of Delphi is usually sold as a bundle with training, support, and enterprise-level system distributed application management and connectivity tools such as AppMinder, Entera, VisiBroker ORB, and SAP/Connect.

Visual Development Environment

Delphi 4 enables you to create applications by interactively selecting components from a Component Palette and dropping them onto a form. The real beauty of this visual IDE is that Delphi 4 actually generates code for you as you drag and drop visual components onto your form. This approach to programming is similar to that of Microsoft's Visual Basic and a host of others. However, what truly sets Delphi apart from the crowd in this respect is that you can use true object-oriented programming techniques to extend any Delphi components to suit your own needs. If you like everything about the functionality of a particular component but the way it's drawn onscreen doesn't suit you, for example, you can create a descendant component that incorporates a new method for the component to draw itself. Not only can you use and extend the Delphi variety of components, but also you can use industry-standard ActiveX controls.

A key element to the Delphi IDE is *Visual Form Inheritance* (VFI). VFI enables you to dynamically descend from any of the other forms in your project or in the Gallery. What's more, changes made to the base form from which you descend will cascade and reflect in its descendants. You'll find more information on this important feature in Chapter 4, "Application Frameworks and Design Concepts."

Optimizing 32-Bit Compiler

One thing that has traditionally separated Delphi from similar visual development tools is its native code compiler that generates fast, efficient code. If you're moving up from Delphi 1, you should know that Delphi 4's 32-bit compiler incorporates a host of internal optimizations that can boost the performance of your calculation-intensive 16-bit applications by as much as two to five times, just by recompiling! The Delphi compiler also provides hints, which help you write cleaner code; warnings, which help you avoid potential bugs; and multiple error messages, which enable you to correct multiple errors in each compile pass.

Additionally, the Delphi compiler and the Borland C++ compiler share the same back-end code-generation engine. One advantage of this setup is that it gives you the capacity to create and use standard .obj files in your Delphi applications.

Scalable Database Access

Delphi is an ideal tool to design database client applications that communicate with a variety of local or remote databases. The Standard edition of Delphi can connect to local and networked Paradox, dBASE, Access, and FoxPro tables, whereas the Professional edition contains ODBC and InterBase drivers, and the Client/Server Suite edition comes with SQLLinks drivers for a variety of networked SQL database servers. If you're a database developer, this spells smooth scalability from local to remote databases. If you're a "regular programmer," this means that you finally have a database engine built seamlessly into your development environment of choice and no longer have to rely on a third-party database library when you need the data-management capability of a true database in your applications.

Additional tools provided with Delphi for the database programmer include the *Database Explorer*, which enables you to drag and drop new tables to your Delphi application and to interactively browse and edit server metadata, and SQL Monitor, which enables you to view SQL conversations between client and server for debugging and performance optimization.

The Language and the Library

The underlying language of Delphi is an object-oriented version of Pascal that Borland calls *Object Pascal*. Object Pascal provides a number of productivity-enhancing additions to the Pascal language, including:

- *Exception handling*, which enables you to detect and gracefully recover from runtime errors
- *Runtime Type Information* (RTTI), which enables you to determine the type of an object at runtime rather than compile time
- *Interface* support, which makes COM development easy and enables you to build robust application foundations
- Unlimited-length *strings*, which enable you to write string-handling code without having to worry about size limitations or allocation nightmares
- Currency data type for more accurate monetary calculations
- C++-style *assertions*, which help you to write more robust code
- Variant data type, which enables you to leverage technologies such as OLE that involve "untyped" data and late type binding

Visual Component Library (VCL) is Delphi's object-oriented class framework. Similar to today's other major Windows frameworks, Object Windows Library (OWL) and Microsoft Foundation Classes (MFC), VCL provides an object-oriented cushion around the often hairy Win32 API. VCL's major advantage over these other frameworks is its close integration with the visual development environment. Each of the components that you drag and drop from the Component Palette to a form is a VCL element or control.

THE DELPHI 4 IDE

The Delphi 4 IDE is divided into four main portions: the main window, the Form Designer, the Object Inspector, and the Code Editor.

The Main Window

Think of the *main window* as the control center for the Delphi 4 IDE. The main window has all the standard functionality of the main window of any other Windows program. It consists of three parts: the main menu, the toolbars, and the Component Palette. As in any Windows program, you go to the main menu when you need to open, create, or save new projects, forms, units, or files. You also use the main menu when you need to cut, copy, paste, or bring up another programming tool such as Turbo Debugger or version control. The toolbar provides pushbutton access to all the main menu options. Figure 1.1 shows the entire Delphi 4 IDE.

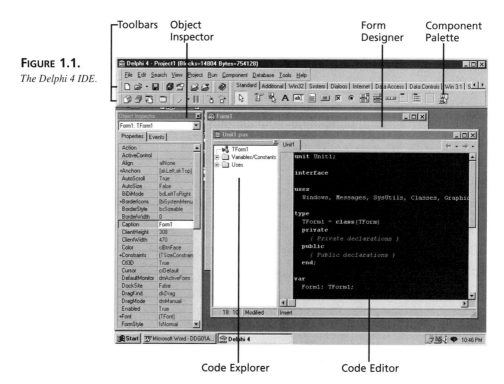

FIGURE 1.1.

The Delphi 4 IDE.

The Delphi Toolbars

Figure 1.2 shows a closer look at Delphi's toolbars. Each toolbar button corresponds to some function in the IDE, such as opening a file or building a project. Notice that each of the buttons on the toolbars and Component Palette offers a *ToolTip*. These are little "bubbles" that contain a description of the function of a particular button. You activate the ToolTip by leaving the mouse cursor on a button for more than a second or two.

Standard toolbar ┌─Custom toolbar

FIGURE 1.2.

The Delphi 4 toolbars.

View
toolbar

Debug
toolbar

There are four separate toolbars in the IDE: View, Standard, Debug, and Custom. Figure 1.2 shows the default button configuration for these toolbars, but you can add or remove buttons by selecting Customize from the local menu on a toolbar. This brings up the Customize dialog box, shown in Figure 1.3. You add buttons by dragging them from this dialog box and dropping them on the toolbar. To remove a button, simply drag it off the toolbar.

FIGURE 1.3.

The Customize dialog box.

IDE toolbar customization doesn't stop at configuring which buttons are shown. You can also relocate each of the toolbars, the Component Palette, and menus within the main window. To do so, click on the raised gray bars on the right side of a toolbar and drag it around the main window. If you drag the mouse outside the confines of the main window while doing this, you'll see yet another level of customization: The toolbars can be undocked from the main window and can reside in their own floating tool windows. Figure 1.4 shows undocked toolbars.

The Form Designer

The Form Designer begins as an empty window, ready for you to turn it into a Windows application. Consider the Form Designer your artist's canvas for creating Windows applications; here is where you determine how your applications will be represented visually to your users. You interact with the Form Designer by selecting components from the Component Palette and dropping them onto your form. After you have a particular component on the form, you can use the mouse to adjust the position or size of the component. You can control the appearance and behavior of these components by using the Object Inspector and Code Editor.

Figure 1.4.

Undocked toolbars.

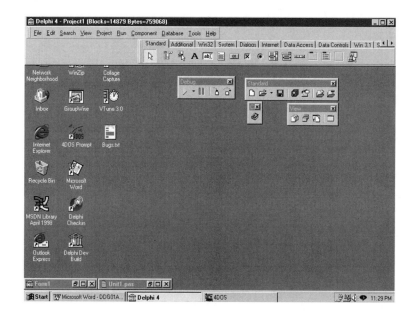

The Object Inspector

With the Object Inspector, you can modify a form's or component's properties or enable your form or component to respond to different events. *Properties* are data such as height, color, and font that determine how an object appears onscreen. *Events* are portions of code executed in response to occurrences within your application. A mouse-click message and a message for a window to redraw itself are two examples of events. The Object Inspector window uses the standard Windows *notebook tab* metaphor in switching between component properties or events; just select the desired page from the tabs at the top of the window. The properties and events displayed in the Object Inspector reflect whichever form or component currently has focus in the Form Designer.

One of the most useful tidbits of knowledge that you as a Delphi programmer should know is that the help system is tightly integrated with the Object Inspector. If you ever get stuck on a particular property or event, just press the F1 key, and WinHelp comes to the rescue.

The Code Editor

The Code Editor is where the actual programming—in the strictest sense—occurs. It is where you type the code that dictates how your program behaves, and where Delphi inserts the code that it generates based on the components in your application. The top of the Code Editor window contains *notebook tabs*, where each tab corresponds to a different source-code module or file. Each time you add a new form to your application, a new unit is created and added to the set of tabs at the top of the Code Editor. You also can add units to your application that don't represent forms, and they will end up as a tab at the top of the Code Editor.

The Code Explorer

New to Delphi 4 is the Code Explorer, which provides a tree-style view of the unit shown in the Code Editor. The Code Explorer enables you to easily navigate units and add new elements or rename existing elements in a unit. Figure 1.5 shows the Code Explorer.

FIGURE 1.5.

The Code Explorer.

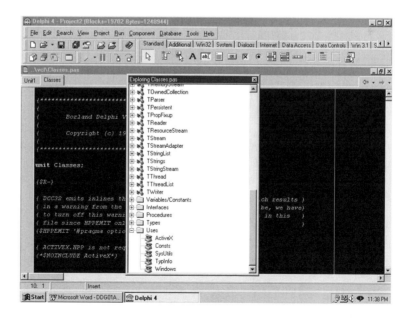

THE SOURCE CODE GENERATOR

The Delphi IDE generates Object Pascal source code for you as you work with the visual components of the Form Designer. The simplest example of this capability is starting a new project. Select File | New | Project in the main window, to see a new form in the Form Designer and that form's source code skeleton in the Code Editor. The source code to the new form's unit is shown in Listing 1.1.

LISTING 1.1. A PROGRAM SKELETON.

```
unit Unit1;

interface

uses
  Windows, Messages, SysUtils, Classes, Graphics, Controls, Forms,
Dialogs;

type
  TForm1 = class(TForm)
  private
    { Private declarations }
  public
    { Public declarations }
  end;

var
  Form1: TForm1;

implementation

{$R *.DFM}

end.
```

It's important to note that the source code module associated with any form is stored in a unit. Although every form has a unit, not every unit has a form. If you're not familiar with how the Pascal language works and what exactly a *unit* is, see Chapter 2, "The Object Pascal Language," which discusses the Object Pascal language for those who are new to Pascal from C, C++, Visual Basic, or another language.

Taking a unit skeleton one piece at a time, the top portion

```
TForm1 = class(TForm)
 private
   { Private declarations }
 public
   { Public declarations }
 end;
```

indicates that the form object itself is an object derived from TForm, and the space in which you can insert your own public and private variables is labeled clearly. Don't worry about what *object*, *public*, or *private* means right now. Chapter 2 discusses Object Pascal in more detail.

The following line is very important:

```
{$R *.DFM}
```

The $R directive in Pascal is used to load an external resource file. This line links the .dfm (which stands for Delphi form) file into the executable. The .dfm file contains a binary representation of the form you created in the Form Designer. The * symbol in this case isn't intended to represent a wildcard; it represents the file having the same name as the current unit. So, for example, if the preceding line was in a file called UNIT1.PAS, the *.DFM would represent a file by the name of UNIT1.DFM.

The application's project file is worth a glance, too. A project filename ends in .dpr (which stands for Delphi project) and is really nothing more than a Pascal source file with a funny extension. The project file is where the main portion of your program (in the Pascal sense) lives. Unlike other versions of Pascal with which you might be familiar, most of the "work" of your program is done in units rather than in the main module. Here's the project file from the sample application:

```
program Project1;

uses
  Forms,
  Unit1 in 'Unit1.pas' {Form1};

{$R *.RES}

begin
  Application.Initialize;
  Application.CreateForm(TForm1, Form1);
  Application.Run;
end.
```

As you add more forms and units to the application, they appear in the uses clause of the project file. Notice, too, that after the name of a unit in the uses clause, the name of the related form appears in comments. If you ever get confused about which units go with which forms, you can regain your bearings by selecting View | Project Manager to bring up the Project Manager window.

> **NOTE**
>
> Each form has exactly one unit associated with it, and you can also have other "code-only" units that are not associated with any form. In Delphi, you work mostly within your program's units, and you will rarely edit your project's .dpr file.

CREATING A SMALL APPLICATION

The simple act of plopping a component such as a button onto a form causes code for that element to be generated and added to the form object:

```
TForm1 = class(TForm)
  Button1: TButton;
private
  { Private declarations }
public
  { Public declarations }
end;
```

Now, as you can see, the button is an instance variable of the TForm1 class. When you refer to the button in contexts outside TForm1 later in your source code, you must remember to address it as part of the scope of TForm1 by saying Form1.Button1. Scoping is explained in more detail in Chapter 2.

When this button is selected in the Form Designer, you can change its behavior through the Object Inspector. Suppose that, at design time, you want to change the width of the button to 100 pixels, and at runtime, you want to make the button respond to a press by doubling its own height. To change the button width, move over to the Object Browser window, find the Width property, and change the value associated with Width to 100. Note that the change doesn't take effect in the Form Designer until you press Enter or move off the Width property. To make the button respond to a mouse click, select the Events page on the Object Inspector window to reveal the list of events to which the button can respond. Double-click in the column next to the OnClick event, and Delphi generates a procedure skeleton for a mouse-click response and whisks you away to that spot in the source code—in this case, a procedure called TForm1.Button1Click(). All that's left to do is insert the code to double the button's width between the begin..end of the event's response method:

```
Button1.Height := Button1.Height * 2;
```

To verify that the "application" compiles and runs, press the F9 key on your keyboard and watch it go!

NOTE

Delphi maintains a reference between generated procedures and the controls to which they correspond. When you compile or save a source code module, Delphi scans your source code and removes all procedure skeletons for which you haven't entered any code between the begin and end. This means that if you didn't write any code between the begin and end of the TForm1.Button1Click()procedure, for example, Delphi would have removed the procedure from your source code. The bottom line here is this: Don't delete procedures that Delphi has created; just delete your code and let Delphi remove the procedures for you.

After you have fun making the button really big on the form, terminate your program and go back to the Delphi IDE. Now is a good time to mention that you could have generated a response to a mouse click for your button just by double-clicking a control after dropping it onto the form. Double-clicking a component automatically invokes its associated component editor. For most components, this response generates a handler for the first of that component's events listed in the Object Inspector.

WHAT'S SO GREAT ABOUT EVENTS, ANYWAY?

If you have ever developed Windows applications the traditional way, without a doubt you'll find the ease of use of Delphi events a welcome alternative to manually catching Windows messages, cracking those messages, and testing for window handles, control IDs, WParams, LParams, and so on. If you don't know what all that means, that's okay; Chapter 5, "Understanding Messages," covers messaging internals.

A Delphi event is often triggered by a Windows message. The OnMouseDown event of a TButton, for example, is really just an encapsulation of the Windows WM_xBUTTONDOWN messages. Notice that the OnMouseDown event gives you information such as which button was pressed and the location of the mouse when it happened. A form's OnKeyDown event provides similar useful information for key presses. For example, here's the code that Delphi generates for an OnKeyDown handler:

```
procedure TForm1.FormKeyDown(Sender: TObject; var Key: Word;
 Shift: TShiftState);
begin
end;
```

All the information you need about the key is right at your fingertips. If you're an experienced Windows programmer, you'll appreciate that there aren't any LParams or

WParams, inherited handlers, translates, or dispatches to worry about. This goes way beyond "message cracking" as you might know it because one Delphi event can represent several different Windows messages as it does with OnMouseDown (which handles a variety of mouse messages), and each of the message parameters is passed in as easy-to-understand parameters. Chapter 5 gets into the gory details of how Delphi's internal messaging system works.

CONTRACT-FREE PROGRAMMING

Arguably the biggest benefit that Delphi's event system has over the standard Windows messaging system is that all events are contract-free. *Contract-free* means to the programmer that you never are *required* to do anything inside your event handlers. Unlike standard Windows message-handling, you don't have to call an inherited handler or pass information back to Windows after handling an event.

Of course, the downside to the contract-free programming model that Delphi's event system provides is that it doesn't always give you the power or flexibility that directly handling Windows messages gives you. You're at the mercy of those who designed the event as far as what level of control you'll have over your application's response to the event. For example, you can modify and kill keystrokes in an OnKeyPress handler, but an OnResize handler provides you only with a notification that the event occurred—you have no power to prevent or modify the resize.

Never fear, though. Delphi doesn't prevent you from working directly with Windows messages. It's not as straightforward as the event system because message handling assumes that the programmer has a greater level of knowledge of what Windows expects from every handled message. You have complete power to handle all Windows messages directly by using the message keyword. You find out much more about writing Windows message handlers in Chapter 5.

The great thing about developing applications with Delphi is that you can use the high-level, easy stuff (such as events) when it suits you, and still have access to the low-level stuff whenever you need it.

TURBO PROTOTYPING

After hacking Delphi for a little while, you'll probably notice that the learning curve is especially mild. In fact, even if you're new to Delphi, you'll find that writing your first project in Delphi pays immediate dividends in the forms of a short development cycle and a robust application. Delphi excels in the one facet of application development that has been the bane of many a Windows programmer: user interface (UI) design.

Sometimes the designing of the UI and the general layout of a program is referred to as *prototyping*. In a nonvisual environment, prototyping an application often takes longer than writing the application's implementation, or what is called the *back end*. Of course, the back end of an application is the whole objective of the program in the first place, right? Sure, an intuitive and visually pleasing UI is a big part of the application, but what good would it be, for example, to have a communications program with pretty windows and dialog boxes but no capacity to send data through a modem? As it is with people, so it is with applications; a pretty face is nice to look at, but it has to have substance to be a regular part of our lives. Please, no comments about back ends.

Delphi enables you to use its custom controls to whip out nice-looking UIs in no time flat. In fact, you'll find that after you become comfortable with Delphi's forms, controls, and event-response methods, you'll cut huge chunks off the time you usually take to develop application prototypes. You'll also find that the UIs you develop in Delphi look just as nice as—if not better than—those designed with traditional tools. Often, what you "mock up" in Delphi, turns out to be the final product.

EXTENSIBLE COMPONENTS AND ENVIRONMENT

Because of the object-oriented nature of Delphi, in addition to creating your own components from scratch, you can also create your own customized components based on stock Delphi components. Chapter 21, "Writing Delphi Custom Components," shows you how to take some existing Delphi components and extend their behavior to create new components. Additionally, Chapter 7, "Using ActiveX Controls with Delphi," describes how to incorporate ActiveX controls into your Delphi applications.

In addition to allowing you to integrate custom components into the IDE, Delphi provides the capability to integrate entire subprograms, called *experts*, into the environment. Delphi's Expert Interface enables you to add special menu items and dialog boxes to the IDE to integrate some feature that you feel is worthwhile. An example of an expert is the Database Form Expert located on the Delphi Database menu. Chapter 26, "Using Delphi's Open Tools API," outlines the process for creating experts and integrating them into the Delphi IDE.

SUMMARY

By now you should have an understanding of the Delphi 4 product line and the Delphi IDE, and you should know enough about Delphi to create a small project. The next several chapters explore the specific elements of Delphi in greater detail. Before you continue, make sure that you have a grasp of elements of the Delphi IDE and how to navigate around that environment.

THE OBJECT PASCAL LANGUAGE

IN THIS CHAPTER

This chapter sets aside the visual elements of Delphi in order to provide you with an overview of Delphi's underlying language—Object Pascal. To begin with, you'll receive an introduction to the basics of the Object Pascal language such as language rules and constructs. Later on, you will learn about some of the more advanced aspects of Object Pascal such as classes and exception handling. Because this isn't a beginner's book, it assumes that you have some experience with other high-level computer languages such as C, C++, or Visual Basic, and it compares Object Pascal language structure to that of those other languages. By the time you're finished with this chapter, you will understand how programming concepts such as variables, types, operators, loops, cases, exceptions, and objects work in Pascal as compared to C++ and Visual Basic.

Even if you have some recent experience with Pascal, you'll find this chapter useful, as this is really the only point in the book where you learn the nitty-gritty of Pascal syntax and semantics.

COMMENTS

As a starting point, you should know how to make comments in your Pascal code. Object Pascal supports three types of comments: curly brace comments; paren/asterisk comments; and C++-style double slash comments. Examples of each type of comment follow:

```
{ Comment using curly braces }
(* Comment using paren and asterisk *)
// C++-style comment
```

The two types of Pascal comments are virtually identical in behavior. The compiler considers the comment to be everything between the open-comment and close-comment delimiters. For C++-style comments, everything following the double backslash until the end of the line is considered a comment.

NOTE

You cannot nest comments of the same type. Although it is legal syntax to nest Pascal comments of different types inside one another, we don't recommend the practice:

```
{ (* This is legal *) }
(* { This is legal } *)
(* (* This is illegal *) *)
{ { This is illegal } }
```

NEW PROCEDURE AND FUNCTION FEATURES

Because procedures and functions are a fairly universal topic as far as programming languages are concerned, we won't go into too much detail here. We just want to fill you in on a few new or little-known features.

Parentheses

Although not new to Delphi 4, one of the lesser-known features of Object Pascal is that parentheses are optional when calling a procedure or function that takes no parameters. Therefore the following syntax examples are both valid:

```
Form1.Show;
Form1.Show();
```

Granted, this feature isn't one of those things that sends chills up and down your spine, but it's particularly nice for those who split their time between Delphi and languages like C++ or Java, where parentheses are required. If you're not able to spend 100% of your time in Delphi, this feature means you don't have to remember to use different function-calling syntax for different languages.

Overloading

Delphi 4 introduces the concept of function overloading, that is, the ability to have multiple procedures or functions of the same name with different parameter lists. All overloaded methods are required to be declared with the overload directive as shown following:

```
procedure Hello(I: Integer); overload;
procedure Hello(S: string); overload;
procedure Hello(D: Double); overload;
```

Note that the rules for overloading methods of a class are slightly different and are explained in the section "Method Overloading." Although this is one of the features most requested by developers since Delphi 1, the phrase that comes to mind is, "Be careful what you wish for." Having multiple functions and procedures with the same name (on top of the traditional ability to have functions and procedures of the same name in different units) can make it more difficult to predict the flow of control and debug your application. Because of this, overloading is a feature you should employ judiciously. You don't have to avoid it; just don't overuse it.

Default Value Parameters

Also new to Delphi 4 are default value parameters, that is, the ability to provide a default value for a function or procedure parameter and not have to pass that parameter when calling the routine. In order to declare a procedure or function that contains default value parameters, follow the parameter type with an equal sign and the default value as shown in the following example:

```
procedure HasDefVal(S: string; I: Integer = 0);
```

The `HasDefVal()` procedure can be called in one of two ways. First, you can specify both parameters:

```
HasDefVal('hello', 26);
```

Second, you can specify only parameter `S` and use the default value for `I`:

```
HasDefVal('hello');  // default value used for I
```

You must follow several rules when using default value parameters:

- Parameters having default values must appear at the end of the parameter list. Parameters without default values may not follow parameters with default values in a procedure or function's parameter list.
- Default value parameters must be of an ordinal, pointer, or set type.
- Default value parameters must be passed by value or as `const`. They may not be reference, `out`, or untyped parameters.

One of the biggest benefits of default value parameters is in adding functionality to existing functions and procedures without sacrificing backward compatibility. For example, suppose you sell a unit that contains a revolutionary function called `AddInts()` that adds two numbers:

```
function AddInts(I1, I2: Integer): Integer;
begin
  Result := I1 + I2;
end;
```

In order to keep up with the competition, you feel you must update this function so that it has the capability for adding three numbers. However, you're loathe to do so because adding a parameter will cause existing code that calls this function to not compile. Thanks to Delphi 4 and default parameters, you can enhance the functionality of `AddInts()` without compromising compatibility:

```
function AddInts(I1, I2: Integer; I3: Integer = 0);
begin
  Result := I1 + I2 + I3;
end;
```

VARIABLES

You might be used to declaring variables off the cuff: "I need another integer, so I'll just declare one right here in the middle of this block of code." If that has been your practice, you're going to have to retrain yourself a little in order to use variables in Object Pascal. Object Pascal requires you to declare all variables up front in their own section before you begin a procedure, function, or program. Perhaps you used to write free-wheeling code like this:

```
void foo(void)
{
  int x = 1;
  x++;
  int y = 2;
  float f;
  //... etc ...
}
```

In Object Pascal, any such code must be tidied up and structured a bit more to look like this:

```
Procedure Foo;
var
  x, y: Integer;
  f: Double;
begin
  x := 1;
  inc(x);
  y := 2;
  //... etc ...
end;
```

> **NOTE**
>
> Object Pascal—like Visual Basic, but unlike C and C++—is not a case-sensitive language. Upper- and lowercase are used for clarity's sake, so use your best judgment, as the style used in this book indicates. If the identifier name is several words mashed together, remember to capitalize for clarity. For example, the following name is unclear and difficult to read:
>
> ```
> procedure thisprocedurenamemakesnosense;
> ```
>
> This code is quite readable, however:
>
> ```
> procedure ThisProcedureNameIsMoreClear;
> ```
>
> For a complete reference on the coding style guidelines used for this book, see Chapter 6, "Delphi 4 Developer's Guide Coding Standards Document," on the CD-ROM accompanying this book.

You might be wondering what all this structure business is and why it's beneficial. You will find, however, that Object Pascal's structured style lends itself to code that is more readable, maintainable, and less buggy than the more scattered style of C++ or Visual Basic.

Notice how Object Pascal enables you to group more than one variable of the same type together on the same line with the following syntax:

```
VarName1, VarName2 : SomeType;
```

Remember that when you're declaring a variable in Object Pascal, the variable name precedes the type, and there is a colon between the variables and types. Note that the variable initialization is always separate from the variable declaration.

A language feature introduced in Delphi 2.0 enables you to initialize global variables inside a var block. Examples demonstrating the syntax for doing so are shown following:

```
var
  i: Integer = 10;
  S: string  = 'Hello world';
  D: Double  = 3.141579;
```

NOTE

Preinitialization of variables is only allowed for global variables and not variables that are local to a procedure or function.

TIP

The Delphi compiler sees to it that all global data is automatically zero-initialized. When your application starts, all integer types will hold 0, floating-point types will hold 0.0, pointers will be nil, strings will be empty, and so forth. Therefore, it is not necessary to zero-initialize global data in your source code.

CONSTANTS

Constants in Pascal are defined in a const clause, which behaves similarly to C's const keyword. Here is an example of three constant declarations in C:

```
const float ADecimalNumber = 3.14;
const int i = 10;
const char * ErrorString = "Danger, Danger, Danger!";
```

The major difference between C constants and Object Pascal constants is that Object Pascal, like Visual Basic, does not require you to declare the constant's type along with the value in the declaration. The Delphi compiler automatically allocates proper space for the constant based on its value, or, in the case of scalar constants such as Integers, the compiler keeps track of the values as it works, and space never is allocated:

```
const
  ADecimalNumber = 3.14;
  i = 10;
  ErrorString = 'Danger, Danger, Danger!';
```

> **NOTE**
>
> Space is allocated for constants as follows: Integer values are "fit" into the smallest type allowable (10 into a ShortInt, 32000 into a SmallInt, and so on). Alphanumeric values fit into char or the currently defined (by $H) string type. Floating-point values are mapped to the extended data type, unless the value contains 4 or fewer decimal places explicitly, in which case it is mapped to a Comp type. Sets of Integer and char are of course stored as themselves.

Optionally, you can also specify a constant's type in the declaration. This provides you with full control over how the compiler treats your constants:

```
const
  ADecimalNumber: Double = 3.14;
  I: Integer = 10;
  ErrorString: string = 'Danger, Danger, Danger!';
```

Object Pascal permits the usage of compile-time functions in const and var declarations. These routines include: Ord(), Chr(), Trunc(), Round(), High(), Low(), and SizeOf(). For example, all of the following code is valid:

```
type
  A = array[1..2] of Integer;

const
  w: Word = SizeOf(Byte);

var
  i: Integer = 8;
  j: SmallInt = Ord('a');
  L: Longint = Trunc(3.14159);
  x: ShortInt = Round(2.71828);
  B1: Byte = High(A);
  B2: Byte = Low(A);
  C: char = Chr(46);
```

CAUTION

The behavior of 32-bit Delphi type-specified constants is different than that in 16-bit Delphi 1.0. In Delphi 1.0, the identifier declared wasn't treated as a constant but as a preinitialized variable called a `typed constant`. However, in Delphi 2 and later, type-specified constants have the capability of being truly constant. Delphi provides a backward compatibility switch on the Compiler page of the Project I Options dialog, or you can use the $J compiler directive. By default, this switch is enabled for compatibility with Delphi 1.0 code, but you're best served not to rely on this capability, as the implementers of the Object Pascal language are trying to move away from the notion of assignable constants.

If you try to change the value of any of these constants, the Delphi compiler emits an error explaining that it's against the rules to change the value of a constant. Because constants are read-only, Object Pascal optimizes your data space by storing those constants that merit storage in the application's code pages. If you're unclear about the notions of code and data pages, see Chapter 3, "The Win32 API."

NOTE

Object Pascal does not have a preprocessor as C and C++ do. There is no concept of a macro in Object Pascal and, therefore, no Object Pascal equivalent for C's `#define` for constant declaration. Although you may use Object Pascal's `$define` compiler directive for conditional compiles similar to C's `#define`, you cannot use it to define constants. Use `const` in Object Pascal where you would use `#define` to declare a constant in C or C++.

OPERATORS

Operators are the symbols in your code that enable you to manipulate all types of data. For example, there are operators for adding, subtracting, multiplying, and dividing numeric data. There are also operators for addressing a particular element of an array. This section explains some of the Pascal operators and describes some of the differences between the C and Visual Basic counterparts.

Assignment Operators

If you're new to Pascal, Delphi's assignment operator is going to be one of the toughest things to get used to. To assign a value to a variable, use the `:=` operator as you would C or Visual Basic's = operator. Pascal programmers often call this the *gets* or *assignment* operator, and the expression

```
Number1 := 5;
```

is pronounced either "Number1 gets the value 5," or "Number1 is assigned the value 5."

Comparison Operators

If you've already programmed in Visual Basic, you should be very comfortable with Delphi's comparison operators because they are virtually identical. These operators are fairly standard throughout programming languages, so they are covered only briefly in this section.

Object Pascal uses the = operator to perform logical comparisons between two expressions or values. Object Pascal's = operator is analogous to C's == operator, so a C expression that would be written like

```
if (x == y)
```

would be written like this in Object Pascal:

```
if x = y
```

> **NOTE**
>
> Remember that in Object Pascal, the := operator is used to assign a value to a variable, and the = operator compares the values of two operands.

Delphi's *not-equal-to* is <>, and its purpose is identical to C's != operator. To determine whether two expressions are not equal, use this code:

```
if x <> y then DoSomething
```

Logical Operators

Pascal uses the words and and or as logical *and* and *or* operators, whereas C uses the && and ¦¦ symbols, respectively, for these operators. The most common use of the and and or operators is as part of an if statement or loop, such as in the following two examples:

```
if (Condition 1) and (Condition 2) then
  DoSomething;

while (Condition 1) or (Condition 2) do
  DoSomething;
```

Pascal's logical *not* operator is not, which is used to check a comparison for a false condition. It is analogous to C's ! operator. It is also often used as a part of if statements:

```
if not (condition) then (do something);    // if condition is false then...
```

Table 2.1 provides an easy reference of how Pascal operators map to corresponding C and Visual Basic operators.

TABLE 2.1. ASSIGNMENT, COMPARISON, AND LOGICAL OPERATORS.

Operator	Pascal	C	Visual Basic
Assignment	:=	=	=
Comparison	=	==	=
Not equal to	<>	!=	<>
Less than	<	<	<
Greater than	>	>	>
Less than or equal to	<=	<=	<=
Greater than or equal to	>=	>=	>=
Logical and	and	&&	and
Logical or	or	||	or
Logical not	not	!	not

Arithmetic Operators

You should already be familiar with most Object Pascal arithmetic operators because they generally are similar to those used in C, C++, and Visual Basic. Table 2.2 illustrates all the Pascal arithmetic operators and their C and Visual Basic counterparts.

TABLE 2.2. ARITHMETIC OPERATORS.

Operator	Pascal	C	Visual Basic
Addition	+	+	+
Subtraction	-	-	-
Multiplication	*	*	*
Floating-point division	/	/	/
Integer division	div	/	/
Modulus	mod	%	Mod

You may notice that the main difference between Pascal and other languages is that Pascal has different division operators for floating-point and integer math. The `div` operator automatically truncates any remainder when dividing two integer expressions.

NOTE

Remember to use the correct division operator for the types of expressions with which you are working. The Object Pascal compiler gives you an error if you try to divide two floating-point numbers with the integer `div` operator or two integers with the floating-point `/` operator, as the following code illustrates:

```
var
  i: Integer;
  r: Real;
begin
  i := 4 / 3;        // This line will cause a compiler error
  f := 3.4 div 2.3;  // This line also will cause an error
end;
```

Many other programming languages don't distinguish between integer and floating-point division. Instead, they always perform floating-point division and then convert the result back to an integer when necessary. This can be rather expensive in terms of performance. The Pascal `div` operator is faster and more specific.

Bitwise Operators

Bitwise operators are operators that enable you to modify individual bits of a given variable. Common bitwise operators enable you to shift the bits to the left or right or to perform bitwise *and*, *not*, *or*, and *exclusive or* (*xor*) operations with two numbers. The Shift+left and Shift+right operators are `shl` and `shr`, respectively, and they are much like C's `<<` and `>>` operators. The remainder of Pascal's bitwise operators are easy enough to remember: and, not, or, and xor. Table 2.3 lists the bitwise operators.

TABLE 2.3. BITWISE OPERATORS.

Operator	Pascal	C	Visual Basic
And	and	&	And
Not	not	~	Not
Or	or	¦	Or
Xor	xor	^	Xor
Shift+left	shl	<<	None
Shift+right	shr	>>	None

Increment and Decrement Procedures

Increment and decrement procedures generate optimized code for adding one or subtracting one from a given integral variable. Pascal doesn't really provide honest-to-gosh increment and decrement operators similar to C's ++ and − operators, but Pascal's `Inc()` and `Dec()` procedures compile optimally to one machine instruction.

You can call `Inc()` or `Dec()` with one or two parameters. For example, the following two lines of code increment and decrement `variable`, respectively, by one, using the `inc` and `dec` assembly instructions:

```
Inc(variable);

Dec(variable);
```

Compare the following two lines, which increment or decrement `variable` by 3 using the `add` and `sub` assembly instructions:

```
Inc(variable, 3);

Dec(variable, 3);
```

Table 2.4 compares the increment and decrement operators of different languages.

NOTE

With compiler optimization enabled, the `Inc()` and `Dec()` procedures often produce the same machine code as *variable* := *variable* + 1 syntax, so use whichever you feel more comfortable with for incrementing and decrementing variables.

TABLE 2.4. INCREMENT AND DECREMENT OPERATORS.

Operator	Pascal	C	Visual Basic
Increment	`Inc()`	++	None
Decrement	`Dec()`	−	None

OBJECT PASCAL TYPES

One of Object Pascal's greatest features is that it is strongly typed, or *typesafe*. This means that actual variables passed to procedures and functions must be of the same type as the formal parameters identified in the procedure or function definition. You will not see any of the famous compiler warnings about suspicious pointer conversions that C programmers have grown to know and love. This is because the Object Pascal compiler will not permit you to call a function with one type of pointer when another type is specified in the function's formal parameters (although functions that take untyped `Pointer` types accept any type of pointer). Basically, Pascal's strongly typed nature enables it to perform a sanity check of your code—to ensure you're not trying to put a square peg in a round hole.

A Comparison of Types

Delphi's base types are similar to those of C and Visual Basic. Table 2.5 compares and contrasts the base types of Object Pascal with those of C/C++ and Visual Basic. You may want to earmark this page because this table provides an excellent reference for matching types when calling functions in non-Delphi Dynamic Link Libraries (DLLs) or object files (OBJs) from Delphi or the reverse.

TABLE 2.5. A PASCAL-TO-C/C++-TO-VISUAL BASIC 32-BIT TYPE COMPARISON.

Visual Type of Variable	*Pascal*	*C/C++*	*Basic*
8-bit signed integer	`ShortInt`	`char`	*None*
8-bit unsigned integer	`Byte`	`BYTE,` `unsigned short`	*None*
16-bit signed integer	`SmallInt`	`short`	`Short`
16-bit unsigned integer	`Word`	`unsigned short`	*None*
32-bit signed integer	`Integer,` `Longint`	`int, long`	`Integer`
32-bit unsigned integer	`Cardinal,` `LongWord`	`unsigned long`	*None*
64-bit signed integer	`Int64`	`__int64`	*None*
4-byte floating point	`Single`	`float`	`Single`
6-byte floating point	`Real48`	*None*	*None*
8-byte floating point	`Double`	`double`	`Double`
10-byte floating point	`Extended`	`long double`	*None*
64-bit currency	`currency`	*None*	`Currency`
16-byte variant	`Variant,` `OleVariant,` `TVarData`	`VARIANT` `Variant†,` `OleVariant†`	*(Default)*

continues

TABLE 2.5. CONTINUED

Type of Variable	*Pascal*	*C/C++*	*Visual Basic*
1-byte character	Char	char	None
2-byte character	WideChar	WCHAR	
Fixed length-byte string	ShortString	*None*	*None*
Dynamic string	AnsiString	AnsiString†	$
Null-terminated string	PChar	char *	*None*
Null-terminated wide string	PWideChar	LPCWSTR	*None*
Dynamic 2-byte string	WideString	WideString†	*None*
1-byte Boolean	Boolean, ByteBool	*(Any 1-byte)*	*None*
2-byte Boolean	WordBool	*(Any 2-byte)*	Boolean
4-byte Boolean	BOOL, LongBool	BOOL	*None*

† Borland C++Builder class that emulates the corresponding Object Pascal type.

NOTE

If you are porting 16-bit code from Delphi 1.0, be sure to bear in mind that the size of both the Integer and Cardinal types has increased from 16 to 32 bits. Actually, that's not quite accurate: Under Delphi 2 and 3 the Cardinal type was treated as an unsigned 31-bit integer in order to preserve arithmetic precision (because Delphi 2 and 3 lacked a true unsigned 32-bit integer to which results of integer operations could be promoted). Under Delphi 4, Cardinal is a true unsigned 32-bit integer.

CAUTION

In Delphi 1, 2, and 3, the Real type identifier specified a 6-byte floating-point number, which is a type unique to Pascal and generally incompatible with other languages. In Delphi 4, Real is an alias for the Double type. The old 6-byte floating-point number is still there, but it is now identified by Real48. You can also force the Real identifier to refer to the 6-byte floating-point number using the {$REALCOMPATIBILITY ON} directive.

Characters

Delphi provides three character types:

AnsiChar   This is the standard 1-byte ANSI character that programmers have grown to know and love.

WideChar   This character is 2 bytes in size and represents a Unicode character.

Char   This is currently identical to AnsiChar, but Borland warns that the definition may change in a later version of Delphi to a WideChar.

Keep in mind that because a character is no longer guaranteed to be one byte in size, you shouldn't hard-code the size into your applications. Instead, you should use the SizeOf()function where appropriate.

> **NOTE**
>
> The SizeOf() standard procedure returns the size, in bytes, of a type or instance.

A Multitude of Strings

Strings are variable types used to represent groups of characters. Every language has its own spin on how string types are stored and used. Pascal has several different string types to suit your programming needs:

- AnsiString, the default string type for Object Pascal, is comprised of AnsiChar characters and allows for virtually unlimited lengths. It is also compatible with null-terminated strings.

- ShortString remains in the language primarily for backward compatibility with Delphi 1.0. Its capacity is limited to 255 characters.

- WideString is similar in functionality to AnsiString except that it is comprised of WideChar characters.

- PChar is a pointer to a null-terminated Char string—like C's char * or lpstr types.

- PAnsiChar is a pointer to a null-terminated AnsiChar string.

- PWideChar is a pointer to a null-terminated WideChar string.

By default, when you declare a string variable in your code as shown in the following example, the compiler assumes that you are creating an AnsiString:

```
var
  S: string;    // S is an AnsiString
```

Alternatively, you can cause variables declared as `strings` to instead be of type `ShortString` using the $H compiler directive. When the value of the $H compiler directive is negative, `string` variables are `ShortStrings`, and when the value of the directive is positive (the default), `string` variables are `AnsiStrings`. The following code demonstrates this behavior:

```
var
  {$H-}
  S1: string;  // S1 is a ShortString
  {$H+}
  S2: string;  // S2 is an AnsiString
```

The exception to the $H rule is that a `string` declared with an explicit size (limited to a maximum of 255 characters) is always a `ShortString`:

```
var
  S: string[63];    // A ShortString of up to 63 characters
```

The `AnsiString` Type

The `AnsiString`, or "long string," type was introduced to the language in Delphi 2.0. It exists primarily as a result of widespread Delphi 1.0 customer demand for an easy-to-use string type without the intrusive 255-character limitation. `AnsiString` is that and more.

Although `AnsiStrings` maintain an almost identical interface as their predecessors, they are dynamically allocated and garbage-collected. Because of this, `AnsiString` is sometimes referred to as a *lifetime-managed* type. Object Pascal also automatically manages allocation of string temporaries as needed, so you needn't worry about allocating buffers for intermediate results as you would in C/C++. Additionally, `AnsiStrings` are always guaranteed to be null-terminated, which makes them compatible with the null-terminated strings used by the Win32 API. The `AnsiString` type is actually implemented as a pointer to a string structure in heap memory. Figure 2.1 shows how an `AnsiString` is laid out in memory.

FIGURE 2.1.

An `AnsiString` in memory.

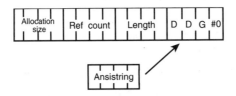

CAUTION

The complete internal format of the long string type is left undocumented by Borland, and Borland reserves the right to change the internal format of long strings with future releases of Delphi. The information here is intended mainly to help you understand how AnsiStrings work, and you should avoid being dependent on the structure of an AnsiString in your code.

Developers moving from Delphi 1 to Delphi 2 who avoided the implementation of details of string were able to migrate their code with no problems. Developers who wrote code that depended on the internal format (such as the 0th element in the string being the length) had to modify their code for Delphi 2.

As Figure 2.1 illustrates, AnsiStrings are reference counted, which means that several strings may point to the same physical memory. String copies, therefore, are very fast because it is merely a matter of copying a pointer rather than copying the actual string contents. When two or more AnsiStrings share a reference to the same physical string, the Delphi memory manager uses a copy-on-write technique, which enables it to wait until a string is modified to release a reference and allocate a new physical string. The following example illustrates these concepts:

```
var
  S1, S2: string;
begin
  // store string in S1, ref count of S1 is 1
  S1 := 'And now for something... ';
  S2 := S1;          // S2 now references S1.  Ref count of S1 is 2.
  // S2 is changed, so it is copied to its own
  // memory space, and ref count of S1 is decremented

  S2 := S2 + 'completely different!';
```

LIFETIME-MANAGED TYPES

In addition to AnsiString, Delphi provides several other types that are lifetime-managed. These types include dynamic arrays, WideString, Variant, OleVariant, interface, and dispinterface. You'll learn more about each of these types later in this chapter. For now, we'll focus on the question: What exactly are lifetime-managed types and how do they work?

Lifetime-managed types, sometimes called "garbage-collected" types, are types that potentially consume some particular resource while in use and release the resource automatically when they fall out of scope. Of course, the variety of resource used depends on the type involved. For example, an AnsiString consumes memory for the character string while in use, and the memory occupied by the character string is released when it leaves scope.

For global variables, this process is fairly straightforward: as a part of the finalization code generated for your application, the compiler inserts code to ensure that each lifetime-managed global variable is cleaned up. Because all global data is zero-initialized when your application loads, each lifetime-managed global variable will always initially contain a zero, empty, or other value indicating the variable is "unused." This way, the finalization code won't attempt to free resources unless they are actually used in your application.

Whenever you declare a local lifetime-managed variable, the process is slightly more complex: first, the compiler inserts code to ensure that the variable is initialized to zero when the function or procedure is entered. Next, the compiler generates a try..finally exception-handling block, which it wraps around the entire function body. Finally, the compiler inserts code in the finally block to clean up the lifetime-managed variable (exception handling is explained in more detail in the section "Structured Exception Handling"). With this in mind, consider the following procedure:

```
procedure Foo;
var
  S: string;
begin
  // procedure body
  // use S here
end;
```

Although this procedure looks simple, if you take into account the code generation by the compiler behind the scenes, it would actually look like this:

```
procedure Foo;
var
  S: string;
begin
  S := '';
  try
    // procedure body
    // use S here
  finally
    // clean up S here
  end;
end;
```

String Operations

You can concatenate two `strings` by using the + operator or the `Concat()` function. The preferred method of string concatenation is the + operator because the `Concat()` function exists primarily for backward compatibility. The following example demonstrates the use of + and `Concat()`:

```
{ using + }
var
  S, S2: string
begin
  S:= 'Cookie ':
  S2 := 'Monster';
  S := S + S2;    { Cookie Monster }
end.

{ using Concat() }
var
  S, S2: string;
begin
  S:= 'Cookie ';
  S2 := 'Monster';
  S := Concat(S, S2);    { Cookie Monster }
end.
```

NOTE

Always use single quotation marks (*'A String'*) when working with string literals in Object Pascal.

TIP

`Concat()` is one of many "compiler magic" functions and procedures (like `ReadLn()` and `WriteLn()`, for example) that don't have an Object Pascal definition. Because such functions and procedures are intended to accept an indeterminate number of parameters or optional parameters, they cannot be defined in terms of the Object Pascal language. Because of this, the compiler provides a special case for each of these functions and generates a call to one of the "compiler magic" *helper functions* defined in the `System` unit. These helper functions are generally implemented in assembly language in order to circumvent Pascal language rules.

In addition to the "compiler magic" string support functions and procedures, there are a variety of functions and procedures in the `SysUtils` unit designed to make working with strings easier. Search for "String-handling routines (Pascal-style)" in the Delphi online help system.

continues

> Furthermore, you'll find some very useful home-brewed string utility functions and procedures in the StrUtils unit in the \Source\Utils directory on the CD-ROM accompanying this book.

Length and Allocation

When first declared, an AnsiString has no length and therefore no space allocated for the characters in the string. To cause space to be allocated for the string, you can assign the string to a literal or another string, or you can use the SetLength()procedure, as shown here:

```
var
  S: string;         // string initially has no length
begin
  S := 'Doh!';       // allocates at least enough space for string literal
  { or }
  S := OtherString   // increases ref count of OtherString (assume
                     // OtherString already points to a valid string)
  { or }
  SetLength(S, 4);   // allocates enough space for at least 4 chars
end;
```

You can index the characters of an AnsiString like an array, but be careful not to index beyond the length of the string. For example, the following code snippet will cause an error:

```
var
  S: string;
begin
  S[1] := 'a';  // Won't work because S hasn't been allocated!
end;
```

This code, however, works properly:

```
var
  S: string;
begin
  SetLength(S, 1);
  S[1] := 'a';       // Now S has enough space to hold the character
end;
```

Win32 Compatibility

As mentioned earlier, AnsiStrings are always null-terminated, so they are compatible with null-terminated strings. This makes it easy to call Win32 API functions or other functions requiring PChar type strings. All that is required is that you typecast the string as a PChar (typecasting is explained in more detail in the section "Typecasting and Type Conversion"). The following code demonstrates how to call the Win32 GetWindowsDirectory() function, which accepts a PChar and buffer length as parameters:

```
var
  S: string;
begin
  SetLength(S, 256);              // important! get space for string first
  // call function, S now holds directory string
  GetWindowsDirectory(PChar(S), 256);
end;
```

After using an AnsiString where function or procedure expects a PChar, you must manually set the length of the string variable to its null-terminated length. The RealizeLength() function, which also comes from the STRUTILS unit, accomplishes that task:

```
procedure RealizeLength(var S: string);
begin
  SetLength(S, StrLen(PChar(S)));
end;
```

Calling RealizeLength() completes the substitution of a long string for a PChar:

```
var
  S: string;
begin
  SetLength(S, 256);             // important! get space for string first
  GetWindowsDirectory(PChar(S), 256); // call function, S now holds
                                      // directory string
  RealizeLength(S);              // set S length to null length
end;
```

> **CAUTION**
>
> Exercise care when typecasting a string to a PChar variable. Because strings are garbage-collected when they go out of scope, you must pay attention when making assignments such as P := PChar(Str), where the scope (or lifetime) of P is greater than Str.

Porting Issues

When you're porting 16-bit Delphi 1.0 applications, you need to keep in mind a number of issues when migrating to AnsiStrings:

- In places where you used the PString (pointer to a ShortString) type, you should instead use the string type. Remember, an AnsiString is already a pointer to a string.

- You can no longer access the 0th element of a string to get or set the length. Instead, use the Length() function to get the string length, and the SetLength() procedure to set the length.

- There is no longer any need to use StrPas() and StrPCopy() to convert back and forth between strings and PChars. As shown earlier, you can typecast an AnsiString to a PChar. When you want to copy the contents of a PChar to an AnsiString, you can use a direct assignment:

```
StringVar := PCharVar;
```

CAUTION

Remember that you must use the SetLength() procedure to set the length of a long string, whereas the past practice was to directly access the 0th element of a short string to set the length. This issue will arise when you attempt to port 16-bit Delphi 1.0 code to 32 bits.

The ShortString Type

If you're a Delphi veteran, you'll recognize the ShortString type as the Delphi 1.0 string type. ShortStrings are sometimes referred to as Pascal strings or length-byte strings. To reiterate, remember that the value of the $H directive determines whether variables declared as string are treated by the compiler as AnsiString or ShortString.

In memory, the string resembles an array of characters where the 0th character in the string contains the length of the string, and the string itself is contained in the following characters. The storage size of a ShortString defaults to the maximum of 256 bytes. This means that you can never have more than 255 characters in a ShortString (255 characters + 1 length byte = 256). As with AnsiStrings, working with ShortString is fairly painless because the compiler allocates string temporaries as needed, so you don't have to worry about allocating buffers for intermediate results or disposing of them as you do with C.

Figure 2.2 illustrates how a Pascal string is laid out in memory.

FIGURE 2.2.

A ShortString *in memory.*

A ShortString variable is declared and initialized with the following syntax:

```
var
  S: ShortString;
begin
  S := 'Bob the cat.';
end.
```

Optionally, you can allocate fewer than 256 bytes for a ShortString using just the string type identifier and a length specifier, as in the following example:

```
var
  S: string[45];  { a 45-character ShortString }
begin
  S := 'This string must be 45 or fewer characters.';
end.
```

The preceding code causes a ShortString to be created regardless of the current setting of the $H directive. The maximum length you can specify is 255 characters.

Never store more characters to a ShortString than you have allocated memory for. If you declare a variable as a string[8], for example, and try to assign 'a_pretty_darn_long_string' to that variable, the string would be truncated to only eight characters, and you would lose data.

When using an array subscript to address a particular character in a ShortString, you could get bogus results or corrupt memory if you attempt to use a subscript index that is greater than the declared size of the ShortString. For example, suppose that you declare a variable as follows:

```
var
  Str: string[8];
```

If you then attempt to write to the 10th element of the string as follows, you're likely to corrupt memory used by other variables:

```
var
  Str: string[8];
  i: Integer;
```

```
begin
  i := 10;
  Str[i] := 's';  // will corrupt memory
```

You can have the compiler link in special logic to catch these types of errors at runtime by selecting Range Checking in the Options | Project dialog box.

TIP

Although including range-checking logic in your program helps you find string errors, range checking slightly hampers the performance of your application. It's common practice to use range checking during the development and debugging phases of your program, but remove range checking after you become confident in the stability of your program.

Unlike AnsiStrings, ShortStrings are not inherently compatible with null-terminated strings. Because of this, a bit of work is required to be able to pass a ShortString to a Win32 API function. The following function, ShortStringAsPChar(), is taken from the STRUTILS.PAS unit mentioned earlier:

```
func function ShortStringAsPChar(var S: ShortString): PChar;
{ This function null-terminates a string so that it can be passed to
  functions }
{ that require PChar types. If string is longer than 254 chars, then it
  will be truncated to 254. }
begin
  if Length(S) = High(S) then Dec(S[0]); { Truncate S if it's too long }
  S[Ord(Length(S)) + 1] := #0;           { Place null at end of string }
  Result := @S[1];                       { Return "PChar'd" string }
end;
```

CAUTION

The functions and procedures in the Win32 API require null-terminated strings. Do not try to pass a ShortString type to an API function because your program will not compile. Your life will be easier if you use long strings when working with the API.

The WideString Type

The WideString type is a *lifetime-managed* type similar to AnsiString; they are both dynamically allocated, garbage-collected, and they are even assignment-compatible with one another. However, WideString differs from AnsiString in three key respects:

- WideStrings are comprised of WideChar characters rather than AnsiChar characters, making them compatible with Unicode strings.

- WideStrings are allocated using the SysAllocStrLen() API function, making them compatible with OLE BSTR strings.

- WideStrings are not reference counted, so assigning one WideString to another requires the entire string to be copied from one location in memory to another. This makes WideStrings less efficient than AnsiStrings in terms of speed and memory use.

As mentioned earlier, the compiler automatically knows how to convert between variables of AnsiString and WideString type as shown following:

```
var
  W: WideString;
  S: string;
begin
  W := 'Margaritaville';
  S := W;  // Wide converted to Ansi
  S := 'Come Monday';
  W := S;  // Ansi converted to Wide
end;
```

In order to make working with WideStrings feel natural, Object Pascal overloads the Concat(), Copy(), Insert(), Length(), Pos(), and SetLength() routines and the +, =, and <> operators for use with WideStrings. Therefore, the following code is syntactically correct:

```
var
  W1, W2: WideString;
  P: Integer;
begin
  W1 := 'Enfield';
  W2 := 'field';
  if W1 <> W2 then
    P := Pos(W1, W2);
end;
```

As with the AnsiString and ShortString types, you can use array brackets to reference individual characters of a WideString:

```
var
  W: WideString;
  C: WideChar;
begin
  W := 'Ebony and Ivory living in perfect harmony';
  C := W[Length(W)];  // C holds the last character in W
end;
```

2

Null-Terminated Strings

Earlier, this chapter mentioned that Delphi has three different null-terminated string types: PChar, PAnsiChar, and PWideChar. As their names imply, each of these represents a null-terminated string of each of Delphi's three character types. In this chapter, we refer to each of these string types generically as PChar. The PChar type in Delphi exists mainly for compatibility with Delphi 1.0 and the Win32 API, which makes extensive use of null-terminated strings. A PChar is defined as a pointer to a string followed by a null (zero) value (if you're unsure of exactly what a pointer is, read on; pointers are discussed in more detail later in this section). Unlike memory for AnsiStrings and WideStrings, memory for PChars is not automatically allocated and managed by Object Pascal. Therefore, you usually will need to allocate memory for the string to which it points, using one of Object Pascal's memory allocation functions. The theoretical maximum length of a PChar string is just under 4 gigabytes. The layout of a PChar variable in memory is shown in Figure 2.3.

TIP

Because Object Pascal's AnsiString type can be used as a PChar in most situations, you should use this type rather than PChars wherever possible. Because memory management for strings occurs automatically, you greatly reduce the chance of introducing memory corruption bugs into your applications if, where possible, you avoid PChars and the manual memory allocation associated with them.

FIGURE 2.3.
A PChar *in memory.*

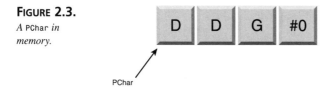

Using PChars

As mentioned earlier, PChar variables require you to manually allocate and free the memory buffers that contain their strings. Normally, you allocate memory for a PChar buffer using the StrAlloc()function, but several other functions can be used to allocate memory for PChars, including AllocMem(), GetMem(), StrNew(), or even the VirtualAlloc()API function. Corresponding functions also exist for many of these functions, which must be used to deallocate memory. Table 2.6 lists several allocation functions and their corresponding deallocation functions.

TABLE 2.6. MEMORY ALLOCATION AND DEALLOCATION FUNCTIONS.

Memory Allocated with...	Must Be Freed with...
AllocMem()	FreeMem()
GlobalAlloc()	GlobalFree()
GetMem()	FreeMem()
New()	Dispose()
StrAlloc()	StrDispose()
StrNew()	StrDispose()
VirtualAlloc()	VirtualFree()

The following example demonstrates memory allocation techniques when working with PChars and strings:

```
var
  P1, P2: PChar;
  S1, S2: string;
begin
  P1 := StrAlloc(64 * SizeOf(Char));   // P1 points to an allocation of 63
                                       // Chars
  StrPCopy(P1, 'Delphi 4 ');           // Copy literal string into P1
  S1 := 'Developer''s Guide';          // Put some text in string S1
  P2 := StrNew(PChar(S1));             // P1 points to a copy of S1
  StrCat(P1, P2);                      // concatenate P1 and P2
  S2 := P1;            // S2 now holds 'Delphi 4 Developer's Guide'
  StrDispose(P1);                      // clean up P1 and P2 buffers
  StrDispose(P2);
end.
```

Notice, first of all, the use of SizeOf(Char) with StrAlloc() when allocating memory for P1. Remember that the size of a Char may change from one byte to two in future versions of Delphi, so you cannot assume the value of Char to always be one byte. SizeOf() ensures that the allocation will work properly no matter how many bytes a character occupies.

StrCat()is used to concatenate two PChar strings. Note here that you cannot use the + for concatenation as you can with long strings and ShortStrings.

The StrNew()function is used to copy the value contained by string S1 into PChar P2. Be careful when using this function. It's common to have memory overwrite errors when using StrNew() because it allocates only enough memory to hold the string. Consider the following example:

```
var
P1, P2: Pchar;
begin
  P1 := StrNew('Hello ');   // Allocate just enoughmemory for P1 and P2
  P2 := StrNew('World');
  StrCat(P1, P2);           // BEWARE: Corrupts memory!
  .
  .
  .
end;
```

> **TIP**
>
> As with other types of strings, Object Pascal provides a decent library of utility functions and procedures for operating on PChars. Search for "String-handling routines (null-terminated)" in the Delphi online help system.
>
> You'll also find some useful null-terminated functions and procedures in the StrUtils unit in the \Source\Utils directory on the CD-ROM accompanying this book.

Variant Types

Delphi 2.0 introduced a powerful data type called the Variant. Variants were brought about primarily in order to support OLE Automation, which uses the Variant type heavily. In fact, Delphi's Variant data type is an encapsulation of the variant used with OLE. Delphi's implementation of variants has also proven to be useful in other areas of Delphi programming, as you will soon learn. Object Pascal is the only compiled language that completely integrates variants as a dynamic data type at runtime, and as a static type at compile time, in that the compiler always knows that it is a variant.

Delphi 3 introduced a new type called OleVariant, which is identical to Variant except that it can only hold Automation-compatible types. In this section we initially focus on the Variant type, and then we discuss OleVariant and contrast it with Variant.

Variants Change Types Dynamically

One of the main purposes of variants is to have a variable whose underlying data type cannot be determined at compile time. This means that a variant can change the type to which it refers at runtime. For example, the following code will compile and run properly:

```
var
  V: Variant;
```

```
begin
  V := 'Delphi 4 is Great!';   // Variant holds a string
  V := 1;                      // Variant now holds an Integer
  V := 123.34;                 // Variant now holds a floating point
  V := True;                   // Variant now holds a boolean
  V := CreateOleObject('Word.Basic'); // Variant now holds an OLE object
end;
```

Variants can support all simple data types, such as Integers, floating-point values, strings, Booleans, date and time, currency, and also OLE Automation objects. Note that variants cannot refer to Object Pascal Objects. Also, variants can refer to a nonhomogeneous array, which can vary in size and whose data elements can refer to any of the preceding data types including another variant array.

The Variant Structure

The data structure defining the Variant type is defined in the System unit and is also shown in the following listing:

```
type
  TVarData = record
    VType: Word;
    Reserved1, Reserved2, Reserved3: Word;
    case Integer of
      varSmallint: (VSmallint: Smallint);
      varInteger:  (VInteger: Integer);
      varSingle:   (VSingle: Single);
      varDouble:   (VDouble: Double);
      varCurrency: (VCurrency: Currency);
      varDate:     (VDate: Double);
      varOleStr:   (VOleStr: PWideChar);
      varDispatch: (VDispatch: Pointer);
      varError:    (VError: Integer);
      varBoolean:  (VBoolean: WordBool);
      varUnknown:  (VUnknown: Pointer);
      varByte:     (VByte: Byte);
      varString:   (VString: Pointer);
      varArray:    (VArray: PVarArray);
      varByRef:    (VPointer: Pointer);
  end;
```

The TVarData structure consumes 16 bytes of memory. The first two bytes of the TVarData structure contain a word value that represents the data type to which the variant refers. The following listing shows the various values that may appear in the VType field of the TVarData record. The next 6 bytes are unused. The remaining 8 bytes contain the actual data or a pointer to the data represented by the variant. Again, this structure maps directly to OLE's implementation of the variant type.

```
{ Variant type codes }
const
  varEmpty    = $0000;
  varNull     = $0001;
  varSmallint = $0002;
  varInteger  = $0003;
  varSingle   = $0004;
  varDouble   = $0005;
  varCurrency = $0006;
  varDate     = $0007;
  varOleStr   = $0008;
  varDispatch = $0009;
  varError    = $000A;
  varBoolean  = $000B;
  varVariant  = $000C;
  varUnknown  = $000D;
  varByte     = $0011;
  varString   = $0100;
  varTypeMask = $0FFF;
  varArray    = $2000;
  varByRef    = $4000;
```

NOTE

As you may notice from the type codes in the preceding listing, a `Variant` cannot contain a reference to a `Pointer` or `class` type.

You'll notice from the `TVarData` listing that the `TVarData` record is actually a *variant record*. Don't confuse this with the `Variant` type. Although the variant record and variant type have similar names, they represent two totally different constructs. Variant records allow for multiple data fields to overlap in the same area of memory like a C/C++ union. This is discussed in more detail in the "Records" section later in this chapter. The `case` statement in the `TVarData` variant record indicates the type of data to which the variant refers. For example, if the `VType` field contains the value `varInteger`, only 4 bytes of the 8 data bytes in the variant portion of the record are used to hold an integer value. Likewise, if `VType` has the value `varByte`, only 1 byte of the 8 are used to hold a byte value.

You'll notice that if `VType` contains the value `varString`, the 8 data bytes don't actually hold the string, but rather, they hold a pointer to this string. This is an important point because you can access fields of a variant directly, as shown following:

```
var
  V: Variant;
begin
  TVarData(V).VType := varInteger;
```

```
  TVarData(V).VInteger := 2;
end;
```

You must understand that in some cases this is a dangerous practice because it is possible to lose the reference to a string or other lifetime-managed entity, which will result in your application leaking memory or other resources. You'll see what we mean by the term "garbage-collected" in the following section.

Variants Are Lifetime-Managed

Delphi automatically handles the allocation and deallocation of memory required of a variant type. For example, examine the following code, which assigns a string to a variant variable:

```
procedure ShowVariant(S: string);
var
  V: Variant
begin
  V := S;
  ShowMessage(V);
end;
```

As discussed earlier in this chapter in the sidebar on lifetime-managed types, several things are going on here that might not be apparent. Delphi first initializes the variant to an unassigned value. During the assignment, it sets its VType field to varString and copies the string pointer into its VString field. It then increases the reference count of string S. When the variant leaves scope, that is, the procedure ends and returns to the code that called it, the variant is cleared, and the reference count of string S is decremented. Delphi does this by implicitly inserting a try..finally block in the procedure as shown following:

```
procedure ShowVariant(S: string);
var
  V: Variant
begin
  V := Unassigned;  // initialize variant to "empty"
  try
    V := S;
    ShowMessage(V);
  finally
    // Now clean up the resources associated with the variant
  end;
end;
```

This same implicit release of resources occurs when you assign a different data type to the variant. For example, examine the following code:

```
procedure ChangeVariant(S: string);
var
  V: Variant
begin
  V := S;
  V := 34;
end;
```

This code boils down to the following pseudo-code:

```
procedure ChangeVariant(S: string);
var
  V: Variant
begin
  Clear Variant V, ensuring it is initialized to "empty"
  try
    V.VType := varString; V.VString := S; Inc(S.RefCount);
    Clear Variant V, thereby releasing reference to string;
    V.VType := varInteger; V.VInteger := 34;
  finally
    Clean up the resources associated with the variant
  end;
end;
```

If you understand what happens in the preceding illustrations, you will see why it is not recommended that you manipulate fields of the TVarData record directly, as shown following:

```
procedure ChangeVariant(S: string);
var
  V: Variant
begin
  V := S;
  TVarData(V).VType := varInteger;
  TVarData(V).VInteger := 32;
  V := 34;
end;
```

Although this may appear to be safe, it is not because it results in the failure to decrement the reference count of string S, probably resulting in a memory leak. As a general rule, don't access the TVarData fields directly, or if you do, be absolutely sure that you know exactly what you're doing.

Typecasting Variants

You can explicitly typecast expressions to type Variant. For example, the following expression

```
Variant(X)
```

results in a variant type whose type code corresponds to the result of the expression X, which must be an integer, real, currency, string, character, or Boolean type.

You can also typecast a variant to that of a simple data type. For example, given the following assignment

```
V := 1.6;
```

where V is a variable of type `Variant`, the following expressions will have the results shown:

```
S := string(V);    // S will contain the string '1.6';
// I is rounded to the nearest Integer value, in this case: 2.
I := Integer(V);
B := Boolean(V);   // B contains False if V contains 0, otherwise B is
                   // True
D := Double(V);    // D contains the value 1.6
```

These results are dictated by certain type-conversion rules applicable to `Variants`. These rules are defined in detail in Delphi's *Object Pascal Language Guide*.

By the way, in the preceding example, it is not necessary to typecast the variant to another data type to make the assignment. The following code would work just as well:

```
V := 1.6;
S := V;
I := V;
B := V;
D := V;
```

What happens here is that the conversions to the target data types are made through an implicit typecast. However, because these conversions are made at runtime, there is much more code logic attached to this method. If you are sure of the type a variant contains, you are better off explicitly typecasting it to that type in order to speed up the operation. This is especially true if the variant is being used in an expression, which we'll discuss next.

Variants in Expressions

You can use variants in expressions with the following operators: +, =, *, /, div, mod, shl, shr, and, or, xor, not, :=, <>, <, >, <=, >=.

When using variants in expressions, Delphi knows how to perform the operations based on the contents of the variant. For example, if two variants V1 and V2 contain integers, the expression V1 + V2 results in the addition of the two integers. However, if V1 and V2 contain strings, the result is a concatenation of the two strings. What happens if V1 and V2 contain two different data types? Delphi uses certain promotion rules in order to perform the operation. For example, if V1 contains the string '4.5' and V2 contains a floating-point number, V1 will be converted to a floating point and then added to V2. The following code illustrates this:

```
var
  V1, V2, V3: Variant;
begin
  V1 := '100';  // A string type
  V2 := '50';   // A string type
  V3 := 200;    // An Integer type
  V1 := V1 + V2 + V3;
end;
```

Based on what we just mentioned about promotion rules, it would seem at first glance that the preceding code would result in the value 350 as an integer. However, if you take a closer look, you'll see that this is not the case. Because the order of precedence is from left to right, the first equation that gets executed is V1 + V2. Because these two variants refer to strings, a string concatenation is performed resulting in the string '10050'. That result is then added to the integer value held by the variant V3. Because V3 is an integer, the result '10050' is converted to an integer and added to V3, giving an end result of 10250.

Delphi promotes the variants to the highest type in the equation in order to successfully carry out the calculation. However, when an operation is attempted on two variants of which Delphi cannot make any sense, an "invalid variant type conversion" exception is raised. The following code illustrates this:

```
var
  V1, V2: Variant;
begin
  V1 := 77;
  V2 := 'hello';
  V1 := V1 / V2;  // Raises an exception.
end;
```

As stated earlier, it is sometimes a good idea to explicitly typecast a variant to a specific data type if you know what that type is and if it is used in an expression. Consider the following line of code:

```
V4 := V1 * V2 / V3;
```

Before a result can be generated for this equation, each operation is handled by a runtime function that goes through several gyrations to determine the compatibility of the types the variants represent. Then the conversions are made to the appropriate data types. This results in a large amount of overhead and code size. A better solution is obviously not to use variants. However, when necessary, you can also explicitly typecast the variants so the data types are resolved at compile time:

```
V4 := Integer(V1) * Double(V2) / Integer(V3);
```

Keep in mind that this assumes you know the data types the variants represent.

Empty and Null

Two special `VType` values for variants merit a brief discussion. The first is `varEmpty`, which means that the variant has not yet been assigned a value. This is the initial value of the variant set by the compiler as it comes into scope. The other is `varNull`, which is different from `varEmpty` in that it actually represents the value *Null* as opposed to a lack of value. This distinction between no value and Null value is especially important when applied to the field values of a database table. In Chapter 27, "Writing Desktop Database Applications," you'll learn how variants are used in the context of database applications.

Another difference is that attempting to perform any equation with a variant containing a `varEmpty` `VType` value will result in an "invalid variant operation" exception. The same is not true of variants containing a `varNull` value, however. When a variant involved in an equation contains a Null value, that value will propagate to the result. Therefore, the result of any equation containing a Null is always Null.

If you want to assign or compare a variant to one of these two special values, the `System` unit defines two variants, `Unassigned` and `Null`, which have the `VType` values of `varEmpty` and `varNull`, respectively.

> **CAUTION**
>
> It may be tempting to use variants instead of the conventional data types because they seem to offer so much flexibility. However, this will increase the size of your code and cause your applications to run more slowly. Additionally, it will make your code more difficult to maintain. Variants are useful in many situations. In fact, the VCL itself uses variants in several places, most notably in the ActiveX and database areas, because of the data type flexibility they offer. Generally speaking, however, you should use the conventional data types instead of variants. Only in situations where the flexibility of the variant outweighs the performance of the conventional method should you resort to using variants. Ambiguous data types beget ambiguous bugs.

Variant Arrays

Earlier we mentioned that a variant can refer to a nonhomogeneous array. Therefore the following syntax is valid:

```
var
  V: Variant;
  I, J: Integer;
begin
  I := V[J];
end;
```

Bear in mind that, although the preceding code will compile, you'll get an exception at runtime because V does not yet contain a variant array. Object Pascal provides several variant array support functions that allow you to create a variant array. These are VarArrayCreate() and VarArrayOf().

VarArrayCreate()

VarArrayCreate() is defined in the System unit as

```
function VarArrayCreate(const Bounds: array of Integer;
  VarType: Integer): Variant;
```

To use VarArrayCreate(), you pass in the array bounds for the array you want to create and a variant type code for the type of the array elements (the first parameter is an open array, which is discussed in the "Passing Parameters" section later in this chapter). For example, the following returns a variant array of integers and assigns values to the array items:

```
var
  V: Variant;
begin
  V := VarArrayCreate([1, 4], varInteger); // Create a 4-element array
  V[1] := 1;
  V[2] := 2;
  V[3] := 3;
  V[4] := 4;
end;
```

If variant arrays of a single type aren't confusing enough, you can pass varVariant as the type code in order to create a variant array of variants! This way, each element in the array has the ability to contain a different type of data. You can also create a multidimensional array by passing in the additional bounds required. For example, the following code creates an array with the bounds [1..4, 1..5];

```
V := VarArrayCreate([1, 4, 1, 5], varInteger);
```

VarArrayOf()

The VarArrayOf() function is defined in the System unit as

```
function VarArrayOf(const Values: array of Variant): Variant;
```

This function returns a one-dimensional array whose elements are given in the `Values` parameter. The following example creates a variant array of three elements with an integer, a string, and a floating-point value:

```
V := VarArrayOf([1, 'Delphi', 2.2]);
```

Variant Array Support Functions and Procedures

In addition to `VarArrayCreate()` and `VarArrayOf()`, there are several other variant array support functions and procedures. These functions are defined in the `System` unit and are also shown following.

```
procedure VarArrayRedim(var A: Variant; HighBound: Integer);
function VarArrayDimCount(const A: Variant): Integer;
function VarArrayLowBound(const A: Variant; Dim: Integer): Integer;
function VarArrayHighBound(const A: Variant; Dim: Integer): Integer;
function VarArrayLock(const A: Variant): Pointer;
procedure VarArrayUnlock(const A: Variant);
function VarArrayRef(const A: Variant): Variant;
function VarIsArray(const A: Variant): Boolean;
```

The `VarArrayRedim()` function allows you to resize the upper bound of the rightmost dimension of a variant array. The `VarArrayDimCount()` function returns the number of dimensions in a variant array. `VarArrayLowBound()` and `VarArrayHighBound()` return the lower and upper bounds of an array, respectively. `VarArrayLock()` and `VarArrayUnlock()` are two special functions, which are described in later detail in the next section.

`VarArrayRef()` is intended to work around a problem that exists in passing variant arrays to OLE automation servers. The problem occurs when you pass a variant containing a variant array to an automation method, like this:

```
Server.PassVariantArray(VA);
```

The array is passed not as a variant array, but rather as a variant containing a variant array—an important distinction. If the server expected a variant array rather than a reference to one, the server will likely encounter an error condition when you call the method with the preceding syntax. `VarArrayRef()` takes care of this situation by massaging the variant into the type and value expected by the server. This syntax for using `VarArrayRef()` is

```
Server.PassVariantArray(VarArrayRef(VA));
```

`VarIsArray()` is a simple Boolean check, which returns `True` if the variant parameter passed to it is a variant array or `False` otherwise.

Initializing a Large Array—`VarArrayLock()`, `VarArrayUnlock()`

Variant arrays are important in OLE Automation, as they provide the only means for passing raw binary data to an OLE automation server (because pointers are not a legal type in OLE automation, as you will learn in Chapter 23, "COM and ActiveX"). However, if used incorrectly, variant arrays can be a rather inefficient means of exchanging data. Consider the following line:

```
V := VarArrayCreate([1, 10000], VarByte);
```

This line creates a variant array of 10,000 bytes. Suppose you have another array (nonvariant) declared of the same size and you want to copy the contents of this nonvariant array to the variant array. Normally, you can only do this by looping through the elements and assigning them to the elements of the variant array, as shown following:

```
begin
  V := VarArrayCreate([1, 10000], VarByte);
  for i := 1 to 10000 do
    V[i] := A[i];
end;
```

The problem with this code is that it is bogged down by the significant overhead required just to initialize the variant array elements. This is due to the assignments to the array elements having to go through the runtime logic to determine type compatibility, location of each element, and so forth. To avoid these runtime checks, you can use the `VarArrayLock()` function and `VarArrayUnlock()` procedure.

`VarArrayLock()` locks the array in memory so that it cannot be moved or resized while it is locked, and it returns a pointer to the array data. `VarArrayUnlock()` unlocks an array locked with `VarArrayLock()` and once again allows the variant array to be resized and moved in memory. After the array is locked, you can employ a more efficient means to initialize the data by using, for example, the `Move()` procedure with the pointer to the array's data. The following code performs the initialization of the variant array shown earlier, but in a much more efficient manner:

```
begin
  V := VarArrayCreate([1, 10000], VarByte);
  P := VarArrayLock(V);
  try
    Move(A, P^, 10000);
  finally
    VarArrayUnlock(V);
  end;
end;
```

Supporting Functions

There are several other support functions for variants that you can use. These functions are declared in the `System` unit and are also listed following:

```
procedure VarClear(var V: Variant);
procedure VarCopy(var Dest: Variant; const Source: Variant);
procedure VarCast(var Dest: Variant; const Source: Variant; VarType:
Integer);
function VarType(const V: Variant): Integer;
function VarAsType(const V: Variant; VarType: Integer): Variant;
function VarIsEmpty(const V: Variant): Boolean;
function VarIsNull(const V: Variant): Boolean;
function VarToStr(const V: Variant): string;
function VarFromDateTime(DateTime: TDateTime): Variant;
function VarToDateTime(const V: Variant): TDateTime;
```

The `VarClear()` procedure clears a variant and sets the `VType` field to `varEmpty`. `VarCopy()` copies the `Source` variant to the `Dest` variant. The `VarCast()` procedure converts a variant to a specified type and stores that result into another variant. `VarType()` returns one of the var*XXX* type codes for a specified variant. `VarAsType()` has the same functionality as `VarCast()`. `VarIsEmpty()` returns `True` if the type code on a specified variant is `varEmpty`. `VarIsNull()` indicates whether or not a variant contains a Null value. `VarToStr()` converts a variant to its string representation (an empty string in the case of a Null or empty variant). `VarFromDateTime()` returns a variant that contains a given `TDateTime` value. `VarToDateTime()` returns the `TDateTime` value contained in a variant.

OleVariant

The `OleVariant` type is nearly identical to the `Variant` type described throughout this section of this chapter. The only difference between `OleVariant` and `Variant` is that `OleVariant` only supports Automation-compatible types. Currently, the only `VType` supported that is not Automation-compatible is `varString`, the code for `AnsiString`. When an attempt is made to assign an `AnsiString` to an `OleVariant`, the `AnsiString` will be automatically converted to an OLE `BSTR` and stored in the variant as a `varOleStr`.

Currency

Delphi 2.0 introduced a new type called `Currency`, which is ideal for financial calculations. Unlike floating-point numbers that allow the decimal point to "float" within a number, `Currency` is a fixed-point decimal type that is hard-coded to a precision of 15 digits before the decimal and 4 digits after the decimal. As such, it is not susceptible to round-off errors as are floating-point types. When porting your Delphi 1.0 projects, it's a good idea to use this type in place of `Single`, `Real`, `Double`, or `Extended` where money is involved.

USER-DEFINED TYPES

Integers, strings, and floating-point numbers often are not enough to adequately represent variables in the real-world problems that programmers must try to solve. In cases like these, you must create your own types to better represent variables in the current problem. In Pascal, these user-defined types usually come in the form of records or objects; you declare these types using the Type keyword.

Arrays

Object Pascal enables you to create arrays of any type of variable (except files). For example, a variable declared as an array of eight integers reads

```
var
  A: Array[0..7] of Integer;
```

This statement is equivalent to the following C declaration:

```
int A[8];
```

It also is equivalent to this Visual Basic statement:

```
Dim A(8) as Integer
```

Object Pascal arrays have a special property that differentiate them from other languages: They don't have to begin at a certain number. You therefore can declare a three-element array that starts at 28, as in the following example:

```
var
  A: Array[28..30] of Integer;
```

Because Object Pascal arrays aren't guaranteed to begin at zero or one, you must use some care when iterating over array elements in a for loop. The compiler provides built-in functions called High() and Low(), which return the lower and upper bounds of an array variable or type. Your code will be less error-prone and easier to maintain if you use these functions to control your for loop as shown following:

```
var
  A: array[28..30] of Integer;
  i: Integer;
begin
  for i := Low(A) to High(A) do  // don't hard-code for loop!
    A[i] := i;
end;
```

> **TIP**
>
> Always begin character arrays at 0. Zero-based character arrays can be passed to functions that require PChar-type variables. This is a special-case allowance that the compiler provides.

To specify multiple dimensions, use a comma-delimited list of bounds:

```
var
  // Two-dimensional array of Integer:
  A: array[1..2, 1..2] of Integer;
```

To access a multidimensional array, use commas to separate each dimension within one set of brackets:

```
I := A[1, 2];
```

Dynamic Arrays

New to Delphi 4 are dynamic arrays. *Dynamic arrays* are dynamically allocated arrays in which the dimensions aren't known at compile time. To declare a dynamic array, just declare an array without including the dimensions:

```
var
  // dynamic array of string:
  SA: array of string;
```

Before you can use a dynamic array, you must use the SetLength() procedure to allocate memory for the array:

```
begin
  // allocate room for 33 elements:
  SetLength(SA, 33);
```

After memory has been allocated, you can access the elements of the dynamic array just like a normal array:

```
SA[0] := 'Pooh likes hunny';
OtherString := SA[0];
```

> **NOTE**
>
> Dynamic arrays are always zero-based.

Dynamic arrays are lifetime managed, so there is no need to free them when you are through using them; they will be released when they leave scope. However, there may come a time when you want to remove the dynamic array from memory before it leaves scope (if it uses a lot of memory, for example). To do this, you need only assign the dynamic array to `nil`:

```
SA := nil;  // releases SA
```

Dynamic arrays are manipulated using reference semantics similar to `AnsiStrings` rather than value semantics like a normal array. A quick test—what is the value of `A1[0]` at the end of the following code fragment:

```
var
  A1, A2: array of Integer;
begin
  SetLength(A1, 4);
  A2 := A1;
  A1[0] := 1;
  A2[0] := 26;
```

The correct answer is 26. This is because the assignment `A2 := A1` doesn't create a new array but instead provides `A2` with a reference to the same array as `A1`. Therefore, any modifications to `A2` will also affect `A1`. If you want to instead make a complete copy of `A1` in `A2`, use the `Copy()` standard procedure:

```
A2 := Copy(A1);
```

After the preceding line of code executes, `A2` and `A1` will be two separate arrays initially containing the same data. Changes to one won't affect the other. You can optionally specify the starting element and number of elements to be copied as parameters to `Copy()` as shown in the following:

```
// copy 2 elements, starting at element one:
A2 := Copy(A1, 1, 2);
```

Dynamic arrays can also be multidimensional. To specify multiple dimensions, add an additional `array of` to the declaration for each dimension:

```
var
  // two-dimensional dynamic array of Integer:
  IA: array of array of Integer;
```

To allocate memory for a multidimensional dynamic array, pass the sizes of the other dimensions as additional parameters to `SetLength()`:

```
begin
  // IA will be a 5 x 5 array of Integer
  SetLength(IA, 5, 5);
```

Access multidimensional dynamic arrays the same way you do normal multidimensional arrays—each element separated by a comma with a single set of brackets:

```
IA[0,3] := 28;
```

Records

A user-defined structure is referred to as a `record` in Object Pascal, and it is the equivalent of C's `struct` or Visual Basic's `Type`. As an example, here is a record definition in Pascal and equivalent definitions in C and Visual Basic:

```
{ Pascal }
Type
  MyRec = record
    i: Integer;
    d: Double;
  end;

/* C */
typedef struct {
  int i;
  double d;
} MyRec;

'Visual Basic
Type MyRec
  i As Integer
  d As Double
End Type
```

When working with records, you use the dot symbol to access its fields, for example:

```
var
  N: MyRec;
begin
  N.i := 23;
  N.d := 3.4;
end;
```

Object Pascal also supports *variant records,* which allow different pieces of data to overlay the same portion of memory in the record. Not to be confused with the `Variant` data type, variant records allow each overlapping data field to be accessed independently. If your background is C/C++, you will recognize variant records as being the same concept as `unions` within C `structs`. The following code shows a variant record in which a `Double`, `Integer`, and `char` all occupy the same memory space:

```
type
  TVariantRecord = record
    NullStrField: PChar;
    IntField: Integer;
```

```
    case Integer of
        0: (D: Double);
        1: (I: Integer);
        2: (C: char);
    end;
```

> **NOTE**
>
> The rules of Object Pascal state that the variant portion of a record cannot be of any lifetime-managed type.

Here is the C++ equivalent of the preceding type declaration:

```
struct TUnionStruct
{
  char * StrField;
  int IntField;
  union
  {
    double D;
    int i;
    char c;
  };
};
```

Sets

Sets are a uniquely Pascal type that have no equivalent in Basic, C, or C++ (although Borland C++Builder does implement a template class called Set, which emulates the behavior of a Pascal set). Sets provide a very efficient means of representing a collection of ordinal, character, or enumerated values. You can declare a new set type using the keywords set of followed by an ordinal type or subrange of possible set values, for example:

```
type
  TCharSet = set of char;      // possible members: #0 - #255

  TEnum = (Monday, Tuesday, Wednesday, Thursday, Friday);
  TEnumSet = set of TEnum;  // can contain any combination of TEnum
members

  TSubrangeSet = set of 1..10; // possible members: 1 - 10
  TAlphaSet = set of 'A'..'z'; // possible members: 'A' - 'z'
```

Note that a set can only contain up to 256 elements. Additionally, the only ordinal types may follow the set of keywords. Therefore, the following declarations are illegal:

```
type
  TIntSet = set of Integer;   // Invalid: too many elements
  TStrSet = set of string;    // Invalid: not an ordinal type
```

Sets store their elements internally as individual bits. This makes them very efficient in terms of speed and memory usage. Sets with fewer than 32 elements in the base type can be stored and operated upon in CPU registers, for even greater efficiency. Sets with 32 or more elements (such as a set of char[nd]255 elements) are stored in memory. To get the maximum performance benefit from sets, keep the number of elements in the set's base type under 32.

Using Sets

Use square brackets when referencing set elements. The following code demonstrates how to declare set-type variables and assign them values:

```
type
  TCharSet = set of char;       // possible members: #0 - #255

  TEnum = (Monday, Tuesday, Wednesday, Thursday, Friday, Saturday,
         ➥Sunday);
  TEnumSet = set of TEnum;   // can contain any combination of TEnum
                             // members

var
  CharSet: TCharSet;
  EnumSet: TEnumSet;
  SubrangeSet: set of 1..10; // possible members: 1 - 10
  AlphaSet: set of 'A'..'z'; // possible members: 'A' - 'z'

begin
  CharSet := ['A'..'J', 'a', 'm'];
  EnumSet := [Saturday, Sunday];
  SubrangeSet := [1, 2, 4..6];
  AlphaSet := [];  // Empty; no elements
end;
```

Set Operators

Object Pascal provides several operators for use in manipulating sets. You can use these operators to determine set membership, union, difference, and intersection.

Membership

Use the in operator to determine whether a given element is contained in a particular set. For example, the following code would be used to determine whether the CharSet set mentioned earlier contains the letter 'S':

```
if 'S' in CharSet then
  // do something;
```

The following code determines whether EnumSet lacks the member Monday:

```
if not (Monday in EnumSet) then
  // do something;
```

Union and Difference

Use the + and - operators or the Include() and Exclude() procedures to add and remove elements to and from a set variable:

```
Include(CharSet, 'a');          // add 'a' to set
CharSet := CharSet + ['b'];     // add 'b' to set
Exclude(CharSet, 'x');          // remove 'z' from set
CharSet := CharSet - ['y', 'z']; // remove 'y' and 'z' from set
```

> **TIP**
>
> When possible, use Include() and Exclude() to add and remove a single element to and from a set rather than the + and - operators. Both Include() and Exclude() constitute only 1 machine instruction each, whereas the + and - operators require 13 + 6n (where n is the size in bits of the set) instructions.

Intersection

Use the * operator to calculate the intersection of two sets. The result of the expression Set1 * Set2 is a set containing all the members that Set1 and Set2 have in common. For example, the following code could be used as an efficient means for determining whether a given set contains multiple elements:

```
if ['a', 'b', 'c'] * CharSet = ['a', 'b', 'c'] then
  // do something
```

Objects

Think of objects as records that also contain functions and procedures. Delphi's object model is discussed in much greater detail later in the "Using Delphi Objects" section of this chapter, so this section covers just the basic syntax of Object Pascal objects. An object is defined as follows:

```
Type
  TChildObject = class(TParentObject);
    SomeVar: Integer;
    procedure SomeProc;
  end;
```

Although Delphi objects are not identical to C++ objects, this declaration is roughly equivalent to the following C++ declaration:

```
class TChildObject : public TParentObject
{
  int SomeVar;
  void SomeProc();
};
```

Methods are defined in the same way as normal procedures and functions (which are discussed in the section "Procedures and Functions"), with the addition of the object name and the dot symbol operator:

```
procedure TChildObject.SomeProc;
begin
  { procedure code goes here }
end;
```

Object Pascal's . symbol is similar in functionality to Visual Basic's . operator and C++'s :: operator. You should note that, although all three languages allow usage of classes, only Object Pascal and C++ allow creation of new classes that behave in a fully object-oriented manner, which we'll describe in the section "Object-Oriented Programming."

> **NOTE**
>
> Object Pascal objects are not laid out in memory the same as C++ objects, so it's not possible to use C++ objects directly from Delphi or the reverse. However, Chapter 13, "Hard Core Techniques," shows a technique for sharing objects between C++ and Delphi.
>
> An exception to this is Borland C++Builder's capability of creating classes that map directly to Object Pascal classes using the proprietary __declspec(delphiclass) directive. Such objects are likewise incompatible with regular C++ objects.

Pointers

A *pointer* is a variable that contains a memory location. You already saw an example of a pointer in the PChar type earlier in this chapter. Pascal's generic pointer type is called, aptly, Pointer. A Pointer is sometimes called an untyped pointer because it contains only a memory address and the compiler doesn't maintain any information on the data to which it points. That notion, however, goes against the grain of Pascal's typesafe nature, so pointers in your code will usually be typed pointers.

> **NOTE**
>
> Pointers are a somewhat advanced topic, and you definitely don't need to master them to write a Delphi application. As you become more experienced, pointers will become another valuable tool for your programmer's toolbox.

Typed pointers are declared by using the ^, or pointer, operator in the Type section of your program. Typed pointers help the compiler keep track of exactly what kind of type a particular pointer points to, enabling the compiler to keep track of what you're doing (and can do) with a pointer variable. Here are some typical declarations for pointers:

```
Type
  PInt = ^Integer;        // PInt is now a pointer to an Integer
  Foo = record            // A record type
    GobledyGook: string;
    Snarf: Real;
  end;
  PFoo = ^Foo;            // PFoo is a pointer to a foo type
var
  P: Pointer;             // Untyped pointer
  P2: PFoo;               // Instance of PFoo
```

> **NOTE**
>
> C programmers will notice the similarity between Object Pascal's ^ operator and C's * operator. Pascal's Pointer type corresponds to C's void * type.

Remember that a pointer variable only stores a memory address. Allocating space for whatever the pointer points to is your job as a programmer. You can allocate space for a pointer by using one of the memory allocation routines discussed earlier and shown in Table 2.6.

> **NOTE**
>
> When a pointer doesn't point to anything (its value is zero), its value is said to be Nil, and it is often called a *Nil* or *Null* pointer.

If you want to access the data that a particular pointer points to, follow the pointer variable name with the ^ operator. This method is known as *dereferencing* the pointer. The following code illustrates working with pointers:

```
Program PtrTest;

Type
  MyRec = record
    I: Integer;
    S: string;
    R: Real;
  end;
  PMyRec = ^MyRec;

var
  Rec : PMyRec;
begin
  New(Rec);       // allocate memory for Rec
  Rec^.I := 10;   // Put stuff in Rec. Note the dereference
  Rec^.S := 'And now for something completely different.';
  Rec^.R := 6.384;
  { Rec is now full }
  Dispose(Rec);   // Don't forget to free memory!
end.
```

WHEN TO USE New()

Use the New() function to allocate memory for a pointer to a structure of a known size. Because the compiler knows how big a particular structure is, a call to New() will cause the correct number of bytes to be allocated—making it safer and more convenient to use than GetMem() or AllocMem(). Never allocate Pointer or PChar variables by using the New() function because the compiler cannot guess how many bytes you need for this allocation. Remember to use Dispose() to free any memory you allocate using the New() function.

You will typically use GetMem() or AllocMem() to allocate memory for structures for which the compiler cannot know the size. The compiler cannot tell ahead of time how much memory you want to allocate for PChar or Pointer types, for example, because of their variable-length nature. Be careful not to try to manipulate more data than you have allocated with these functions, however, because this is one of the classic causes of an Access Violation error. You should use FreeMem() to clean up any memory you allocate with GetMem() or AllocMem(). AllocMem(), by the way, is a bit safer than GetMem() because AllocMem() always initializes the memory it allocates to zero.

One aspect of Object Pascal that may give C programmers some headaches is the strict type checking performed on pointer types. For example, the variables a and b in the following example are not type-compatible:

```
var
  a: ^Integer;
  b: ^Integer;
```

By contrast, the variables a and b in the equivalent declaration in C are type-compatible:

```
int *a;
int *b
```

Object Pascal creates a unique type for each pointer-to-type declaration, so you must create a named type if you want to assign values from a to b as shown following:

```
type
  PtrInteger = ^Integer;   // create named type

var
  a, b: PtrInteger;        // now a and b are compatible
```

Type Aliases

Object Pascal has the ability to create new names, or aliases, for types which are already defined. For example, if you want to create a new name for an Integer called MyReallyNiftyInteger, you can do so using the following code:

```
type
  MyReallyNiftyInteger = Integer;
```

The newly defined type alias is compatible in every way with the type for which it is an alias, which means, in this case, that you can use MyReallyNiftyInteger anywhere you can use Integer.

It is possible, however, to define *strongly typed* aliases that are considered a new, unique type by the compiler. To do this, use the type reserved word in the following manner:

```
type
  MyOtherNeatInteger = type Integer;
```

Using this syntax, the MyOtherNeatInteger type will be converted to an Integer when necessary for purposes of assignment, but MyOtherNeatInteger won't be compatible with Integer when used in var or out parameters. Therefore, the following code is syntactically correct:

```
var
  MONI: MyOtherNeatInteger;
  I: Integer;
begin
```

```
  I := 1;
  MONI := I;
```

But the following code won't compile:

```
procedure Goon(var Value: Integer);
begin
  // some code
end;

var
  M: MyOtherNeatInteger;
begin
  M := 29;
  Goon(M);   // Error: M is not var compatible with Integer
```

In addition to these compiler-enforced type compatibility issues, the compiler also generates runtime type information for strongly typed aliases. This enables you to create unique property editors for simple types, as you will learn in Chapter 22, "Advanced Component Techniques."

TYPECASTING AND TYPE CONVERSION

Typecasting is a technique by which you can force the compiler to view a variable of one type as another type. Because of Pascal's strongly typed nature, you will find that the compiler is very picky about types matching up in the formal and actual parameters of a function call. Hence, you occasionally will be required to cast a variable of one type to a variable of another type to make the compiler happy. Suppose that you need to assign the value of a character to a byte variable:

```
var
  c: char;
  b: byte;
begin
  c := 's';
  b := c;   // compiler complains on this line
end.
```

In the following syntax, a typecast is required to convert c into a byte. In effect, a typecast tells the compiler that you really know what you're doing and want to convert one type to another:

```
var
  c: char;
  b: byte;
begin
  c := 's';
  b := byte(c);   // compiler happy as a clam on this line
end.
```

> **NOTE**
>
> You can typecast a variable of one type to another type only if the data size of the two variables is the same. For example, you cannot typecast a `Double` as an `Integer`. To convert a floating-point type to an integer, use the `Trunc()` or `Round()` functions. To convert an integer into a floating-point value, use the assignment operator: `FloatVar := IntVar`.

Object Pascal also supports a special variety of typecasting between objects using the `as` operator, which is described later in the "Runtime Type Information" section of this chapter.

STRING RESOURCES

Delphi 3 introduced the ability to place string resources directly into Object Pascal source code using the `resourcestring` clause. String resources are literal strings (usually those that are displayed to the user) that are physically located in a resource attached to the application or library rather than embedded in the source code. Your source code references the string resources in place of string literals. By separating strings from source code, you can more easily translate your application by added string resources in a different language. String resources are declared in the form of *identifier = string literal* in the `resourcestring` clause, as shown in the following:

```
resourcestring
  ResString1 = 'Resource string 1';
  ResString2 = 'Resource string 2';
  ResString3 = 'Resource string 3';
```

Syntactically, resource strings can be used in your source code in a manner identical to string constants:

```
resourcestring
  ResString1 = 'hello';
  ResString2 = 'world';

var
  String1: string;

begin
  String1 := ResString1 + ' ' + ResString2;
  .
  .
  .
end;
```

Behind the scenes at compile time, the Delphi compiler places resource strings in a string resource and links that resource to your application. At runtime, references to a resource string result in an implicit call to the LoadString() API function to load the string from the resource into memory.

TESTING CONDITIONS

This section compares if and case constructs in Pascal to similar constructs in C and Visual Basic. It assumes that you have used these types of programmatic constructs before, so it doesn't spend time explaining them to you.

The if Statement

An if statement enables you to determine whether certain conditions are met before executing a particular block of code. As an example, here is an if statement in Pascal, followed by equivalent definitions in C and Visual Basic:

```
{ Pascal }
if x = 4 then y := x;

/* C */
if (x == 4) y = x;

'Visual Basic
If x = 4 Then y = x
```

2

THE OBJECT
PASCAL
LANGUAGE

> **NOTE**
>
> If you have an if statement that makes multiple comparisons, make sure you enclose each set of comparisons in parentheses for code clarity. Do this:
>
> if (x = 7) and (y = 8) then
>
> Don't do this; it causes the compiler displeasure:
>
> if x = 7 and y = 8 then

Use the begin and end keywords in Pascal almost as you would use { and } in C or C++. For example, use the following construct if you want to execute multiple lines of text when a given condition is true:

```
if x = 6 then begin
  DoSomething;
  DoSomethingElse;
  DoAnotherThing;
end;
```

You can combine multiple conditions using the `if..else` construct:

```
if x =100 then
  SomeFunction
else if x = 200 then
  SomeOtherFunction
else begin
  SomethingElse;
  Entirely;
end;
```

Using case Statements

The `case` statement in Pascal works in much the same way as a `switch` statement in C or C++. A case statement provides a means for choosing one condition among many possibilities without a huge `if..else if..else if` construct. Here is an example of Pascal's case statement:

```
case SomeIntegerVariable of
  101 : DoSomething;
  202 : begin
      DoSomething;
      DoSomethingElse;
    end;
  303 : DoAnotherThing;
  else DoTheDefault;
end;
```

> **NOTE**
>
> The selector type of a `case` statement must be an ordinal type. It's illegal to use a nonordinal type, such as a string, as a `case` selector.

Here is the C `switch` statement equivalent to the preceding example:

```
switch (SomeIntegerVariable)
{
  case 101: DoSomeThing; break;
  case 202: DoSomething;
            DoSomethingElse; break
  case 303: DoAnotherThing; break;
  default: DoTheDefault;
}
```

LOOPS

A *loop* is a construct that enables you to repeatedly perform some type of action. Pascal's loop constructs are very similar to what you should be familiar with from your experience with other languages, so this chapter doesn't spend any time teaching you about loops. This section describes the various loop constructs you can use in Pascal.

The `for` Loop

A `for` loop is ideal when you need to repeat an action a predetermined number of times. Here is an example, albeit not a very useful one, of a `for` loop that adds the loop index to a variable 10 times:

```
var
  I, X: Integer;
begin
  X := 0;
  for I := 1 to 10 do
    inc(X, I);
end.
```

The C equivalent of the preceding example is as follows:

```
void main(void) {
  int x, i;
  x = 0;
  for(i=1; i<=10; i++)
    x += i;
}
```

Here is the Visual Basic equivalent of the same concept:

```
X = 0
For I = 1 to 10
  X = X + I
Next I
```

> **CAUTION**
>
> A caveat to those familiar with Delphi 1.0: assignments to the loop control variable are no longer allowed due to the way the loop is optimized and managed by the 32-bit compiler.

The `while` Loop

Use a `while` loop construct when you want some part of your code to repeat itself while some condition is true. A `while` loop's conditions are tested before the loop is executed, and a classic example for the use of a `while` loop is to repeatedly perform some action on a file as long as the end of the file is not encountered. Here is an example that demonstrates a loop that reads one line at a time from a file and writes it to the screen:

```
Program FileIt;

{$APPTYPE CONSOLE}

var
  f: TextFile;   // a text file
  s: string;
begin
  AssignFile(f, 'foo.txt');
  Reset(f);
  while not EOF(f) do begin
    readln(f, S);
    writeln(S);
  end;
  CloseFile(f);
end.
```

Pascal's while loop works basically the same as C's while loop or Visual Basic's Do While loop.

repeat..until

The repeat..until loop addresses the same type of problem as a while loop but from a different angle. It repeats a given block of code until a certain condition becomes True. Unlike a while loop, the loop code always is executed at least once because the condition is tested at the end of the loop. Repeat..until is roughly equivalent to C's do..while loop.

For example, the following code snippet repeats a statement that increments a counter until the value of the counter becomes greater than 100:

```
var
  x: Integer;
begin
  X := 1;
  repeat
    inc(x);
  until x > 100;
end.
```

The Break() Procedure

Calling Break() from inside a while, for, or repeat loop causes the flow of your program to skip immediately to the end of the currently executing loop. This method is useful when you need to leave the loop immediately because of some circumstance that may arise within the loop. Pascal's Break() procedure is analogous to C's Break and Visual Basic's Exit statement. The following loop uses Break() to terminate the loop after five iterations:

```
var
  i: Integer;
begin
  for i := 1 to 1000000 do
  begin
    MessageBeep(0);              // make the computer beep
    if i = 5 then Break;
  end;
end;
```

The `Continue()` Procedure

Call `Continue()` inside a loop when you want to skip over a portion of code and the flow of control to continue with the next iteration of the loop. Note in the following example that the code after `Continue()` is not executed in the first iteration of the loop:

```
var
  i: Integer;
begin
  for i := 1 to 3 do
  begin
    writeln(i, '. Before continue');
    if i = 1 then Continue;
    writeln(i, '. After continue');
  end;
end;
```

PROCEDURES AND FUNCTIONS

As a programmer, you should already be familiar with the basics of procedures and functions. A procedure is a discrete program part that performs some particular task when it is called and then returns to the calling part of your code. A function works the same except that a function returns a value after its exit to the calling part of the program.

If you're familiar with C or C++, consider that a Pascal procedure is equivalent to a C or C++ function that returns void, whereas a function corresponds to a C or C++ function that has a return value.

Listing 2.1 demonstrates a short Pascal program with a procedure and a function.

LISTING 2.1. EXAMPLE OF FUNCTIONS AND PROCEDURES.

```
Program FuncProc;

{$APPTYPE CONSOLE}

procedure BiggerThanTen(i: Integer);
```

continues

LISTING **2.1.** CONTINUED

```
{ writes something to the screen if I is greater than 10 }
begin
  if I > 10 then
    writeln('Funky.');
end;

function IsPositive(I: Integer): Boolean;
{ Returns True if I is 0 or positive, False if I is negative }
begin
  if I < 0 then
    Result := False
  else
    Result := True;
end;

var
  Num: Integer;
begin
  Num := 23;
  BiggerThanTen(Num);
  if IsPositive(Num) then
    writeln(Num, 'Is positive.')
  else
    writeln(Num, 'Is negative.');
end.
```

> **NOTE**
>
> The local variable `Result` in the `IsPositive()` function deserves special attention. Every Object Pascal function has an implicit local variable called `Result` that contains the return value of the function. Note that unlike C and C++, the function doesn't terminate as soon as a value is assigned to `Result`.
>
> You also can return a value from a function by assigning the name of a function to a value inside the function's code. This is standard Pascal syntax, and a holdover from previous versions of Borland Pascal.
>
> Be careful to note, too, that the implicit Result variable is not allowed when the compiler's Extended Syntax option is disabled in the Project | Options | Compiler dialog or using the {$X-} directive.

Passing Parameters

Pascal enables you to pass parameters by value or by reference to functions and procedures. The parameters you pass can be of any base or user-defined type, or open array (open arrays are discussed later in this chapter). Parameters also can be constant if their values will not change in the procedure or function.

Value Parameters

Value parameters are the default mode of parameter passing. When a parameter is passed by value, it means that a local copy of that variable is created, and the function or procedure operates on the copy. Consider the following example:

```
procedure Foo(s: string);
```

When you call a procedure in this way, a copy of string s will be made, and Foo() will operate on the local copy of s. This means that you can choose the value of s without having any effect on the variable passed into Foo().

Reference Parameters

Pascal enables you to pass variables to functions and procedures by reference; parameters passed by reference are also called *variable parameters*. Passing by reference means that the function or procedure receiving the variable can modify the value of that variable. To pass a variable by reference, use the keyword var in the procedure's or function's parameter list:

```
procedure ChangeMe(var x: longint);
begin
  x := 2;  { x is now changed in the calling procedure }
end;
```

Instead of making a copy of x, the var keyword causes the address of the parameter to be copied so that its value can be directly modified.

Using var parameters is equivalent to passing variables by reference in C++ using the & operator. Like C++'s & operator, the var keyword causes the address of the variable to be passed to the function or procedure rather than the value of the variable.

Constant Parameters

If you don't want the value of a parameter passed into a function to change, you can declare it with the const keyword. The const keyword not only prevents you from modifying the value of the parameters, but it also generates more optimal code for strings and records passed into the procedure or function. Here is an example of a procedure declaration that receives a constant string parameter:

```
procedure Goon(const s: string);
```

Open Array Parameters

Open array parameters provide you with the capability for passing a variable number of arguments to functions and procedures. You can either pass open arrays of some homogenous type or constant arrays of differing types. The following code declares a function that accepts an open array of integers:

```
function AddEmUp(A: array of Integer): Integer;
```

You may pass variables, constants, or constant expressions to open array functions and procedures. The following code demonstrates this by calling `AddEmUp()` and passing a variety of different elements:

```
var
  i, Rez: Integer;
const
  j = 23;
begin
  i := 8;
  Rez := AddEmUp([i, 50, j, 89]);
```

In order to work with an open array inside the function or procedure, you can use the `High()`, `Low()`, and `SizeOf()` functions to obtain information about the array. To illustrate this, the following code shows an implementation of the `AddEmUp()` function that returns the sum of all the numbers passed in A:

```
function AddEmUp(A: array of Integer): Integer;
var
  i: Integer;
begin
  Result := 0;
  for i := Low(A) to High(A) do
    inc(Result, A[i]);
end;
```

Object Pascal also supports an `array of const`, which allows you to pass heterogeneous data types in an array to a function or procedure. The syntax for defining a function or procedure that accepts an `array of const` is as follows:

```
procedure WhatHaveIGot(A: array of const);
```

You could call the preceding function with the following syntax:

```
WhatHaveIGot(['Tabasco', 90, 5.6, @WhatHaveIGot, 3.14159, True, 's']);
```

The compiler implicitly converts all parameters to type `TVarRec` when they are passed to the function or procedure accepting the `array of const`. `TVarRec` is defined in the `System` unit as follows:

```
type
PVarRec = ^TVarRec;
  TVarRec = record
    case Byte of
      vtInteger:     (VInteger: Integer; VType: Byte);
```

```
      vtBoolean:     (VBoolean: Boolean);
      vtChar:        (VChar: Char);
      vtExtended:    (VExtended: PExtended);
      vtString:      (VString: PShortString);
      vtPointer:     (VPointer: Pointer);
      vtPChar:       (VPChar: PChar);
      vtObject:      (VObject: TObject);
      vtClass:       (VClass: TClass);
      vtWideChar:    (VWideChar: WideChar);
      vtPWideChar:   (VPWideChar: PWideChar);
      vtAnsiString:  (VAnsiString: Pointer);
      vtCurrency:    (VCurrency: PCurrency);
      vtVariant:     (VVariant: PVariant);
      vtInterface:   (VInterface: Pointer);
      vtWideString:  (VWideString: Pointer);
      vtInt64:       (VInt64: PInt64);
  end;
```

The VType field indicates what type of data the TVarRec contains. This field can have any one of the following values:

```
const
  { TVarRec.VType values }
  vtInteger    = 0;
  vtBoolean    = 1;
  vtChar       = 2;
  vtExtended   = 3;
  vtString     = 4;
  vtPointer    = 5;
  vtPChar      = 6;
  vtObject     = 7;
  vtClass      = 8;
  vtWideChar   = 9;
  vtPWideChar  = 10;
  vtAnsiString = 11;
  vtCurrency   = 12;
  vtVariant    = 13;
  vtInterface  = 14;
  vtWideString = 15;
  vtInt64      = 16;
```

As you might guess, because array of const in the code allows you to pass parameters regardless of their type, they can be difficult to work with on the receiving end. As an example of how to work with array of const, the following implementation for WhatHaveIGot() iterates through the array and shows a message to the user indicating what type of data was passed in which index:

```
procedure WhatHaveIGot(A: array of const);
var
  i: Integer;
```

```
    TypeStr: string;
begin
  for i := Low(A) to High(A) do
  begin
    case A[i].VType of
      vtInteger    : TypeStr := 'Integer';
      vtBoolean    : TypeStr := 'Boolean';
      vtChar       : TypeStr := 'Char';
      vtExtended   : TypeStr := 'Extended';
      vtString     : TypeStr := 'String';
      vtPointer    : TypeStr := 'Pointer';
      vtPChar      : TypeStr := 'PChar';
      vtObject     : TypeStr := 'Object';
      vtClass      : TypeStr := 'Class';
      vtWideChar   : TypeStr := 'WideChar';
      vtPWideChar  : TypeStr := 'PWideChar';
      vtAnsiString : TypeStr := 'AnsiString';
      vtCurrency   : TypeStr := 'Currency';
      vtVariant    : TypeStr := 'Variant';
      vtInterface  : TypeStr := 'Interface';
      vtWideString : TypeStr := 'WideString';
      vtInt64      : TypeStr := 'Int64';
    end;
    ShowMessage(Format('Array item %d is a %s', [i, TypeStr]));
  end;
end;
```

SCOPE

Scope refers to some part of your program in which a given function or variable is
known to the compiler. A global constant is in scope at all points in your program, for
example, whereas a variable local to some procedure only has scope within that procedure. Consider Listing 2.2.

LISTING 2.2. AN ILLUSTRATION OF SCOPE.

```
program Foo;

{$APPTYPE CONSOLE}

const
  SomeConstant = 100;

var
  SomeGlobal: Integer;
  R: Real;

procedure SomeProc(var R: Real);
```

```
var
  LocalReal: Real;
begin
  LocalReal := 10.0;
  R := R - LocalReal;
end;

begin
  SomeGlobal := SomeConstant;
  R := 4.593;
  SomeProc(R);
end.
```

SomeConstant, SomeGlobal, and R have global scope—their values are known to the compiler at all points within the program. Procedure SomeProc() has two variables in which the scope is local to that procedure: R and LocalReal. If you try to access LocalReal outside of SomeProc(), the compiler displays an unknown identifier error. If you access R within SomeProc(), you will be referring to the local version, but if you access R outside that procedure, you will be referring to the global version.

UNITS

Units are the individual source code modules that make up a Pascal program. A unit is a place for you to group functions and procedures that can be called from your main program. To be a unit, a source module must consist of at least three parts:

- A unit statement. Every unit must have as its first line a statement saying that it is a unit and identifying the unit name. The name of the unit always must match the filename. For example, if you have a file named FooBar, the statement would be

  unit FooBar;

- The interface part. After the unit statement, a unit's next functional line of code should be the interface statement. Everything following this statement, up to the implementation statement, is information that can be shared with your program and with other units. The interface part of a unit is where you declare the types, constants, variables, procedures, and functions that you want to make available to your main program and to other units. Only declarations—never procedure bodies—can appear in the interface. The interface statement should be one word on one line:

  interface

- The implementation part. This follows the interface part of the unit. Although the implementation part of the unit contains primarily procedures and functions, it is also where you declare any types, constants, or variables that you do not want to make available outside of this unit. The `implementation` part is where you define any functions or procedures that you declared in the interface part. The `implementation` statement should be one word on one line:

```
implementation
```

Optionally, a unit can also include two other parts:

- An `initialization` part. This portion of the unit, which is located near the end of the file, contains any initialization code for the unit. This code will be executed before the main program begins execution, and it executes only once.

- A `finalization` part. This portion of the unit, which is located in between the `initialization` and `end.` of the unit, contains any cleanup code that executes when the program terminates. The `finalization` section was introduced to the language in Delphi 2.0. In Delphi 1.0, unit finalization was accomplished by adding a new exit procedure using the `AddExitProc()` function. If you are porting an application from Delphi 1.0, you should move your exit procedures into the finalization part of your units.

> **NOTE**
>
> When several units have `initialization`/`finalization` code, execution of each section proceeds in the order in which the units are encountered by the compiler (the first unit in the program's uses clause, then the first unit in that unit's uses clause, and so on). Also, it's a bad idea to write initialization and finalization code that relies on such ordering because one small change to the uses clause can cause some difficult-to-find bugs!

The uses Clause

The uses clause is where you list the units that you want to include in a particular program or unit. For example, if you have a program called `FooProg` that uses functions and types in two units, `UnitA` and `UnitB`, the proper uses declaration is as follows:

```
Program FooProg;

uses UnitA, UnitB;
```

Units can have two uses clauses: one in the `interface` section and one in the `implementation` section.

Here is code for a sample unit:

```
Unit FooBar;
```

```
interface

uses BarFoo;

  { public declarations here }

implementation

uses BarFly;

  { private declarations here }

initialization
  { unit initialization here }
finalization
  { unit clean-up here }
end.
```

Circular Unit References

Occasionally, you will have a situation where UnitA uses UnitB and UnitB uses UnitA. This is called a circular unit reference. The occurrence of a circular unit reference is often an indication of a design flaw in your application, and you should avoid structuring your program with a circular reference. The optimal solution is often to move a piece of data that both UnitA and UnitB need to use out to a third unit. However, as with most things, sometimes you just can't avoid the circular unit reference. In such a case, move one of the uses clauses to the implementation part of your unit and leave the other one in the interface part. This usually solves the problem.

PACKAGES

Delphi *packages* enable you to place portions of your application into separate modules, which can be shared across multiple applications. If you already have an existing investment in Delphi 1 or 2 code, you'll appreciate that you can take advantage of packages without any changes to your existing source code.

Think of a package as a collection of units stored in a separate DLL-like module (a Delphi Package Library, or DPL file). Your application can then link with these "packaged" units at runtime rather than compile/link time. Because the code for these units resides in the DPL file rather than in your EXE or DLL, the size of your EXE or DLL can become very small. Four types of packages are available for you to create and use:

1. Runtime package. This type of package contains units required at runtime by your application. When compiled to depend on a particular runtime package, your application will not run in the absence of that package. Delphi's VCL30.DPL is an example of this type of package.

2. Design package. This type of package contains elements necessary for application design such as components, property and component editors, experts. It can be installed into Delphi's component library using the Component|Install Package menu item. Delphi's `DCL*.DPL` packages are examples of this type of package. This type of package is described in more detail in Chapter 21, "Writing Delphi Custom Components."

3. Runtime and Design package. This package serves both of the purposes listed in items 1 and 2. Creating this type of package makes application development and distribution a bit simpler, but this type of package is less efficient because it must carry the baggage of design support even in your distributed applications.

4. Neither runtime nor design package. This rare breed of package is intended to be used only by other packages and is not intended to be referenced directly by an application or used in the design environment.

Using Delphi Packages

Package-enabling your Delphi applications is easy. Simply check the *Build with Runtime Packages* check box in the Project|Options|Packages dialog. The next time you build your application after selecting this option, your application will be linked dynamically to runtime packages rather than having units linked statically into your EXE or DLL. The result will be a much more svelte application (although bear in mind that you will have to deploy the necessary packages with your application).

Package Syntax

Packages are most commonly created using the Package Editor, which you invoke by choosing the File|New|Package menu item. This editor generates a Delphi Package Source (DPK) file, which will be compiled into a package. The syntax for this DPK file is quite simple, and it is in the following format:

```
package PackageName

requires Package1, Package2, ...;

contains Unit1, Unit2, ...;

end.
```

Packages listed in the `requires` clause are required in order for this package to load. Typically, packages containing units used by units listed in the `contains` clause are listed here. Units listed in the `contains` clause will be compiled into this package. Note that units listed here must not also be listed in the `contains` clause of any of the packages listed in the `requires` clause. Note also that any units used by units in the `contains` clause will be implicitly pulled into this package (unless they are contained in a required package).

OBJECT-ORIENTED PROGRAMMING

Volumes have been written on the subject of object-oriented programming (OOP). Often, OOP seems more like a religion than a programming methodology, spawning arguments about its merits (or lack thereof) passionate and spirited enough to make the Crusades look like a slight disagreement. We're not orthodox OOPists, and we're not going to get involved in the relative merits of OOP; we just want to give you the lowdown on a fundamental principle on which Delphi's Object Pascal Language is based.

OOP is a programming paradigm that uses discrete objects—containing both data and code—as application building blocks. Although the OOP paradigm doesn't necessarily lend itself to easier-to-write code, the result of using OOP traditionally has been easy-to-maintain code. Having objects' data and code together simplifies the process of hunting down bugs, fixing them with minimal effect on other objects, and improving your program one part at a time. Traditionally, an OOP language contains implementations of at least three OOP concepts:

Encapsulation	Deals with combining related data fields and hiding the implementation details. The advantages of encapsulation include modularity and isolation of code from other code.
Inheritance	The capability to create new objects that maintain the properties and behavior of ancestor objects. This concept enables you to create object hierarchies such as VCL—first creating generic objects and then creating more specific descendants of those objects that have more narrow functionality.
	The advantage of inheritance is the sharing of common code. Figure 2.4 presents an example of inheritance—how one root object, `fruit`, is the ancestor object of all fruits, including the melon. `melon` is the ancestor of all melons, including a watermelon. You get the picture.
Polymorphism	Literally, polymorphism means "many shapes." Calls to methods of an object variable will call code appropriate to whatever instance is actually in the variable.

FIGURE 2.4.

An illustration of inheritance.

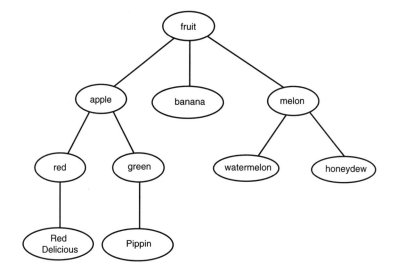

A NOTE ON MULTIPLE INHERITANCE

Object Pascal does not support multiple inheritance of objects as C++ does. *Multiple inheritance* is the concept of a given object being derived from two separate objects, creating an object that contains all the code and data of the two parent objects.

To expand on the analogy presented in Figure 2.4, multiple inheritance enables you to create a candy apple object by creating a new object that inherits from the apple class and some other class called candy. Although this functionality seems useful, it often introduces more problems and inefficiencies into your code than it solves.

Object Pascal provides two approaches to solving this problem. The first solution is to make one class *contain* the other class. You'll see this solution throughout Delphi's VCL. To build upon the candy apple analogy, you would make the candy object a member of the apple object. The second solution is to use *interfaces* (you'll learn more about interfaces in the section "Interfaces"). Using interfaces, you could essentially have one object that supports both a candy and an apple interface.

You should understand the following three terms before you continue to explore the concept of objects:

field   Also called *field definitions* or *instance variables*, fields are data variables contained within objects. A field in an object is just like a field in a Pascal record. In C++, fields sometimes are referred to as *data members*.

method   The name for procedures and functions belonging to an object. Methods are called *member functions* in C++.

property   A property is an entity that acts as an accessor to the data and code contained within an object. Properties insulate the end user from the implementation details of an object.

2

THE OBJECT
PASCAL
LANGUAGE

NOTE

It generally is considered bad OOP style to access an object's fields directly. This is because the implementation details of the object may change. Instead, use accessor properties, which allow a standard object interface without becoming embroiled in the details of how the objects are implemented. Properties are explained in the section "Properties."

Object-Based Versus Object-Oriented

In some tools, you manipulate entities (objects), but you cannot create your own objects. OCX controls in Visual Basic 4 are a good example of this. Although you can use an OCX control in your applications, you cannot create one, and you cannot inherit one OCX control from another in Visual Basic. Environments such as these often are called *object-based environments*.

Delphi is a fully object-oriented environment. This means that you can create new objects in Delphi either from scratch or based on existing components. This includes all Delphi objects, be they visual, nonvisual, or even design-time forms.

USING DELPHI OBJECTS

As mentioned earlier, objects (also called *classes*) are entities that can contain both data and code. Delphi objects also provide you with all the power of object-oriented programming in offering full support of inheritance, encapsulation, and polymorphism.

Declaration and Instantiation

Of course, before using an object, you must have declared an object using the `class` keyword. As described earlier in this chapter, objects are declared in the type section of a unit or program:

```
type
  TFooObject = class;
```

In addition to an object type, you usually also will have a variable of that class type, or *instance*, declared in the var section:

```
var
  FooObject: TFooObject;
```

You create an instance of an object in Object Pascal by calling one of its *constructors*. A constructor is responsible for creating an instance of your object and allocating any memory or initializing any fields necessary so that the object is in a usable state upon exiting the constructor. Object Pascal objects always have at least one constructor called Create()—although it is possible for an object to have more than one constructor. Depending on the type of object, Create() can take different numbers of parameters. This chapter focuses on the simple case where Create() takes no parameters.

Unlike C++, object constructors in Object Pascal are not called automatically, and it is incumbent on the programmer to call the object constructor. The syntax for calling a constructor is as follows:

```
FooObject := TFooObject.Create;
```

Notice that the syntax for a constructor call is a bit unique. You are referencing the Create() method of the object by the type rather than the instance as you would with other methods. This may seem odd at first, but it does make sense. FooObject, a variable, is undefined at the time of the call, but the code for TFooObject, a type, is static in memory. A static call to its Create() method is therefore totally valid.

The act of calling a constructor to create an instance of an object is often called *instantiation*.

NOTE

When an object instance is created using the constructor, the compiler will ensure that every field in your object is initialized. You can safely assume that all numbers will be initialized to 0, all pointers to Nil, and all strings will be empty.

Destruction

When you are finished using an object, you should deallocate the instance by calling its Free() method. The Free() method first checks to ensure that the object instance is not Nil, and then it calls the object's *destructor* method, Destroy(). The destructor, of course, does the opposite of the constructor; it deallocates any allocated memory and performs any other housekeeping required in order for the object to be properly removed from memory. The syntax is simple:

```
FooObject.Free;
```

Unlike the call to `Create()`, the object instance is used in the call to the `Free()` method. Remember never to call `Destroy()` directly but instead to call the safer `Free()` method.

CAUTION

In C++, the destructor of an object declared statically is called automatically when your object leaves scope, but you must call the destructor for any dynamically allocated objects. The rule is the same in Object Pascal, except that all objects are implicitly dynamic in Object Pascal, so you must follow the rule of thumb that anything you create, you must free. The exception to this rule is that when your object is owned by other objects (as described in Chapter 20, "Key Elements of the Visual Component Library"), it will be freed for you.

You might be asking yourself how all these methods got into your little object. You certainly didn't declare them yourself, right? Right. The methods just discussed actually come from the Object Pascal's base `TObject` object. In Object Pascal, all objects are always descendants of `TObject` regardless of whether or not they are declared as such. Therefore, the declaration

```
Type TFoo = Class;
```

is equivalent to the declaration

```
Type TFoo = Class(TObject);
```

Methods

Methods are procedures and functions belonging to a given object. Methods are those things that give an object behavior rather than just data. Two important methods of the objects you create are the constructor and the destructor methods, which we just covered. You can also create custom methods in your objects to perform a variety of tasks.

Creating a method is a two-step process. You first must declare the method in the object type declaration, and then you must define the method in the code. The following code demonstrates the process of declaring and defining a method:

```
type
  TBoogieNights = class
    Dance: Boolean;
```

```
    procedure DoTheHustle;
  end;

procedure TBoogieNights.DoTheHustle;
begin
  Dance := True;
end;
```

Note that when defining the method body, you have to use the fully qualified name, as you did when defining the DoTheHustle method. It's important also to note that the object's Dance field can be accessed directly from within the method.

Method Types

Object methods can be declared as static, virtual, dynamic, or message. Consider the following example object:

```
TFoo = class
  procedure IAmAStatic;
  procedure IAmAVirtual; virtual;
  procedure IAmADynamic; dynamic;
  procedure IAmAMessage(var M: TMessage); message wm_SomeMessage;
end;
```

Static Methods

IAmAStatic is a static method. The *static* method is the default method type, and it works similarly to a regular procedure or function call. The compiler knows the address of these methods, and so, when you call a static method, it is able to link that information into the executable statically. Static methods execute the fastest; however they do not have the ability to be overridden to provide *polymorphism*.

Virtual Methods

IAmAVirtual is a virtual method. *Virtual* methods are called in the same way as static methods, but because virtual methods can be overridden, the compiler does not know the address of a particular virtual function when you call it in your code. The compiler, therefore, builds a Virtual Method Table (VMT) that provides a means to look up function addresses at runtime. All virtual method calls are dispatched at runtime through the VMT. An object's VMT contains all its ancestor's virtual methods as well as the ones it declares, so virtual methods use more memory than dynamic methods, although they execute faster.

Dynamic Methods

IAmADynamic is a dynamic method. *Dynamic* methods are basically virtual methods with a different dispatching system. The compiler assigns a unique number to each dynamic method and uses those numbers, along with method addresses, to build a Dynamic Method Table (DMT). Unlike the VMT, an object's DMT contains only the dynamic methods that it declares, and that method relies on its ancestor's DMTs for the rest of its dynamic methods. Because of this, dynamic methods are less memory intensive than virtual methods, but they take longer to call because you may have to propagate through several ancestor DMTs before finding the address of a particular dynamic method.

Message Methods

IAmAMessage is a message-handling method. The value after the message keyword dictates what message the method will respond to. Message methods are used to create an automatic response to Windows messages, and you generally don't call them directly. Message handling is discussed in detail in Chapter 5, "Understanding Messages."

Overriding Methods

Overriding a method is Object Pascal's implementation of the OOP concept of polymorphism. It enables you to change the behavior of a method from descendant to descendant. Object Pascal methods can be overridden only if they are first declared as virtual or dynamic. To override a method, just use the override directive instead of virtual or dynamic in your descendant object type. You could override the IAmAVirtual and IAmADynamic methods as in the following example:

```
TFooChild = class(TFoo)
  procedure IAmAVirtual; override;
  procedure IAmADynamic; override;
  procedure IAmAMessage(var M: TMessage); message wm_SomeMessage;
end;
```

The override directive replaces the original method's entry in the VMT with the new method. If you had redeclared IAmAVirtual and IAmADynamic with the virtual or dynamic keyword instead of override, you would have created new methods rather than overriding the ancestor methods. Also, if you attempt to override a static method in a descendant type, the static method in the new object completely replaces the method in the ancestor type.

Method Overloading

Like regular procedures and functions, methods can be overloaded so that a class can contain multiple methods of the same name with differing parameter lists. Overloaded methods must be marked with the overload directive, although the use of the directive on the first instance of a method name in a class hierarchy is optional. The following code example shows a class containing three overloaded methods:

```
type
  TSomeClass = class
    procedure AMethod(I: Integer); overload;
    procedure AMethod(S: string); overload;
    procedure AMethod(D: Double); overload;
  end;
```

Reintroducing Method Names

Occasionally, you may want to add a method to one of your classes to replace a method of the same name in an ancestor of your class. In this case, you don't want to override the ancestor method but instead obscure and completely supplant the base class method. If you simply add the method and compile, you will see that the compiler will produce a warning explaining that the new method hides a method of the same name in a base class. To suppress this error, use the reintroduce directive on the method in the ancestor class. The following code example demonstrates proper use of the reintroduce directive:

```
type
  TSomeBase = class
    procedure Cooper;
  end;

  TSomeClass = class
    procedure Cooper; reintroduce;
  end;
```

Self

An implicit variable called Self is available within all object methods. Self is a pointer to the class instance that was used to call the method. Self is passed by the compiler as a hidden parameter to all methods.

Properties

It may help to think of properties as special accessor fields that enable you to modify data and execute code contained within your class. For components, properties are those things that show up in the Object Inspector window when published. The following example illustrates a simplified Object with a property:

```
TMyObject = class
private
  SomeValue: Integer;
  procedure SetSomeValue(AValue: Integer);
public
  property Value: Integer read SomeValue write SetSomeValue;
end;
```

```
procedure TMyObject.SetSomeValue(AValue: Integer);
begin
  if SomeValue <> AValue then
    SomeValue := AValue;
end;
```

TMyObject is an object that contains the following: one field—an integer called
SomeValue, one method—a procedure called SetSomeValue, and one property called
Value. The sole purpose of the SetSomeValue procedure is to set the value of the
SomeValue field. The Value property doesn't actually contain any data. Value is an
accessor for the SomeValue field; when you ask Value what number it contains, it reads
the value from SomeValue. When you attempt to set the value of the Value property,
Value calls SetSomeValue to modify the value of SomeValue. This is useful for two reasons: First, it allows you to present the user of the class with a simple variable without
making them worry about the class's implementation details. Second, you can allow the
user to override accessor methods in descendant classes for polymorphic behavior.

Visibility Specifiers

Object Pascal offers you further control over the behavior of your objects by enabling
you to declare fields and methods with directives such as protected, private, public,
published, and automated. The syntax for using these keywords is as follows:

```
TSomeObject = class
private
  APrivateVariable: Integer;
  AnotherPrivateVariable: Boolean;
protected
  procedure AProtectedProcedure;
  function ProtectMe: Byte;
public
  constructor APublicContructor;
  destructor APublicKiller;
published
  property AProperty read APrivateVariable write APrivateVariable;
end;
```

You can place as many fields or methods as you want under each directive. Style dictates
that you should indent the specifier the same as you indent the class name. The meanings
of these directives follow:

> private   These parts of your object are accessible only to code in the same
> unit as your object's implementation. Use this directive to hide
> implementation details of your objects from users and to prevent
> users from directly modifying sensitive members of your object.

protected	Your object's `protected` members can be accessed by descendants of your object. This capability enables you to hide the implementation details of your object from users while still providing maximum flexibility to descendants of your object.
public	These fields and methods are accessible anywhere in your program. Object `constructors` and `destructors` always should be `public`.
published	Runtime Type Information (RTTI) to be generated for the published portion of your objects enables other parts of your application to get information on your object's published parts. The Object Inspector uses RTTI to build its list of properties.
automated	The automated specifier is obsolete but remains for compatibility with Delphi 2. Chapter 23 has more details on this.

Here, then, is code for the `TMyObject` class that was introduced earlier, with directives added to improve the integrity of the object:

```
TMyObject = class
private
  SomeValue: Integer;
  procedure SetSomeValue(AValue: Integer);
published
  property Value: Integer read SomeValue write SetSomeValue;
end;

procedure TMyObject.SetSomeValue(AValue: Integer);
begin
  if SomeValue <> AValue then
    SomeValue := AValue;
end;
```

Now, users of your object will not be able to modify the value of `SomeValue` directly, and they will have to go through the interface provided by the property `Value` to modify the object's data.

"Friend" Classes

The C++ language has a concept of *friend classes*—that is, classes that are allowed access to the private data and functions in other classes. This is accomplished in C++ using the `friend` keyword. Although, strictly speaking, Object Pascal doesn't have a similar keyword, it does allow for similar functionality. All objects declared within the same unit are considered "friends" and are allowed access to the private information located in other objects in that unit.

Inside Objects

All class instances in Object Pascal are actually stored as 32-bit pointers to class instance data located in heap memory. When you access fields, methods, or properties within a class, the compiler automatically performs a little bit of hocus-pocus that generates the code to dereference that pointer for you. So, to the untrained eye, a class appears as a static variable. What this means, however, is that unlike C++, Object Pascal offers no reasonable way to allocate a class from an application's data segment rather than from the heap.

TObject: The Mother of Objects

Because everything descends from TObject, every class has some methods that it inherits from TObject, and you can make some special assumptions about the capabilities of an object. Every class has the ability, for example, to tell you its name, type, or even whether it is inherited from a particular class. The beauty of this is that you, as an applications programmer, don't have to care what kind of magic the compiler does to makes this happen. You can just take advantage of the functionality it provides!

TObject is a special object because its definition comes from the System unit, and the Object Pascal compiler is "aware" of TObject. The following code illustrates the definition of the TObject class:

```
type
  TObject = class
    constructor Create;
    procedure Free;
    class function InitInstance(Instance: Pointer): TObject;
    procedure CleanupInstance;
    function ClassType: TClass;
    class function ClassName: ShortString;
    class function ClassNameIs(const Name: string): Boolean;
    class function ClassParent: TClass;
    class function ClassInfo: Pointer;
    class function InstanceSize: Longint;
    class function InheritsFrom(AClass: TClass): Boolean;
    class function MethodAddress(const Name: ShortString): Pointer;
    class function MethodName(Address: Pointer): ShortString;
    function FieldAddress(const Name: ShortString): Pointer;
    function GetInterface(const IID: TGUID; out Obj): Boolean;
    class function GetInterfaceEntry(const IID: TGUID): PInterfaceEntry;
    class function GetInterfaceTable: PInterfaceTable;
    function SafeCallException(ExceptObject: TObject;
      ExceptAddr: Pointer): HResult; virtual;
    procedure AfterConstruction; virtual;
    procedure BeforeDestruction; virtual;
    procedure Dispatch(var Message); virtual;
```

```
    procedure DefaultHandler(var Message); virtual;
    class function NewInstance: TObject; virtual;
    procedure FreeInstance; virtual;
    destructor Destroy; virtual;
  end;
```

You'll find each of these methods documented in Delphi's online help system.

In particular, note the methods that are preceded by the keyword `class`. Prepending the `class` keyword to a method enables it to be called like a normal procedure or function without actually having an instance of the class of which the method is a member. This is a juicy bit of functionality that was borrowed from C++'s `static` functions. Be careful, though, not to make a class method depend on any instance information, or you'll get a compiler error.

Interfaces

Perhaps the most significant addition to the Object Pascal language in the recent past is the native support for *interfaces*, which was introduced in Delphi 3. Simply put, an interface defines a set of functions and procedures that can be used to interact with an object. The definition of a given interface is known to both the implementer and the client of the interface—acting as a contract of sorts for how an interface will be defined and used. A class can implement multiple interfaces, providing multiple known "faces" by which a client can control an object.

As its name implies, an interface defines only, well, an interface by which object and clients communicate. This is similar in concept to a C++ PURE VIRTUAL class. It is the job of a class that supports an interface to implement each of the interface's functions and procedures.

In this chapter you'll learn about the language elements of interfaces. For information on using interfaces within your applications, see Chapter 23.

Defining Interfaces

Just as all Delphi classes implicitly descend from `TObject`, all interfaces are implicitly derived from an interface called `IUnknown`. `IUnknown` is defined in the `System` unit as follows:

```
type
  IUnknown = interface
    ['{00000000-0000-0000-C000-000000000046}']
    function QueryInterface(const IID: TGUID; out Obj): Integer; stdcall;
    function _AddRef: Integer; stdcall;
    function _Release: Integer; stdcall;
  end;
```

As you can see, the syntax for defining an interface is very similar to that of a class. The primary difference is that an interface can optionally be associated with a Globally Unique Identifier (GUID), which is unique to the interface. The definition of IUnknown comes from the Component Object Model (COM) specification provided by Microsoft. This is also described in more detail in Chapter 23.

Defining a custom interface is straightforward if you understand how to create Delphi classes. The following code defines a new interface called IFoo, which implements one method called F1():

```
type
  IFoo = interface
    ['{2137BF60-AA33-11D0-A9BF-9A4537A42701}']
    function F1: Integer;
  end;
```

TIP

The Delphi IDE will manufacture new GUIDs for your interfaces when you use the Ctrl+Shift+G key combination.

The following code defines a new interface, IBar, which descends from IFoo:

```
type
  IBar = interface(IFoo)
    ['{2137BF61-AA33-11D0-A9BF-9A4537A42701}']
    function F2: Integer;
  end;
```

Implementing Interfaces

The following bit of code demonstrates how to implement IFoo and IBar in a class called TFooBar:

```
type
  TFooBar = class(TInterfacedObject, IFoo, IBar)
    function F1: Integer;
    function F2: Integer;
  end;

function TFooBar.F1: Integer;
begin
  Result := 0;
end;

function TFooBar.F2: Integer;
begin
  Result := 0;
end;
```

Note that multiple interfaces can be listed after the ancestor class in the first line of the class declaration in order to implement multiple interfaces. The binding of an interface function to a particular function in the class happens when the compiler matches a method signature in the interface with a matching signature in the class. A compiler error will occur if a class declares that it implements an interface but the class fails to implement one or more of the interface's methods.

If a class implements multiple interfaces that have methods of the same signature, you must alias the same-named methods as shown in the short example following:

```
type
  IFoo = interface
    ['{2137BF60-AA33-11D0-A9BF-9A4537A42701}']
    function F1: Integer;
  end;

  IBar = interface
    ['{2137BF61-AA33-11D0-A9BF-9A4537A42701}']
    function F1: Integer;
  end;

  TFooBar = class(TInterfacedObject, IFoo, IBar)
    // aliased methods
    function IFoo.F1 = FooF1;
    function IBar.F1 = BarF1;
    // interface methods
    function FooF1: Integer;
    function BarF1: Integer;
  end;

function TFooBar.FooF1: Integer;
begin
  Result := 0;
end;

function TFooBar.BarF1: Integer;
begin
  Result := 0;
end;
```

The `implements` Directive

New to Delphi 4 is the `implements` directive, which enables you to delegate the implementation of interface methods to another class or interface. This technique is sometimes called *implementation by delegation*. `Implements` is used as the last directive on a property of class or interface type like this:

```
type
  TSomeClass = class(TInterfacedObject, IFoo)
```

```
    // stuff
    function GetFoo: TFoo;
    property Foo: TFoo read GetFoo imlements IFoo;
    // stuff
  end;
```

The use of `implements` in the preceding code example instructs the compiler to look to the `Foo` property for the methods that implement the `IFoo` interface. The type of the property must be a class that contains `IFoo` methods or an interface of type `IFoo` or a descendant of `IFoo`. You can also provide a comma-delimited list of interfaces following the `implements` directive, in which case the type of the property must contain the methods to implement the multiple interfaces.

The `implements` directive buys you two key advantages in your development: First, it allows you to perform aggregation in a no-hassle manner. Aggregation is a COM concept pertaining to the combination of multiple classes for a single purpose (see Chapter 23 for more information on aggregation). Second, it allows you to defer the consumption of resources necessary to implement an interface until it is absolutely necessary. For example, say there was an interface whose implementation requires allocation of a 1MB bitmap, but that interface is seldom required by clients. You probably wouldn't want to implement that interface all the time "just in case" because that would be a waste of resources. Using `implements`, you could create the class to implement the interface on demand in the property accessor method.

Using Interfaces

A few important language rules apply when you're using variables of interface types in your applications. The foremost rule to remember is that interfaces are a lifetime-managed type. This means they are always initialized to `nil`, they are reference counted, a reference is automatically added when you obtain an interface, and they are automatically released when they leave scope or are assigned the value `nil`. The following code example illustrates the lifetime-management of an interface variable:

```
var
  I: ISomeInterface;
begin
  // I is initialized to nil
  I := FunctionReturningAnInterface;  // ref count of I is incremented
  I.SomeFunc;
  // ref count of I is decremented.  If 0, I is automatically released
end;
```

Another unique rule of interface variables is that an interface is assignment-compatible with classes that implement the interface. For example, the following code is legal using the `TFooBar` class defined earlier:

```
procedure Test(FB: TFooBar)
var

  F: IFoo;
begin

  F := FB;  // legal because FB supports IFoo
  .
  .
  .
```

Finally, the as typecast operator can be used to `QueryInterface` a given interface variable for another interface (this is explained in greater detail in Chapter 23). This is illustrated in the following:

```
var
  FB: TFooBar;
  F: IFoo;
  B: IBar;
begin
  FB := TFooBar.Create
  F := FB;  // legal because FB supports IFoo
  B := F as IBar;  // QueryInterface F for IBar
  .
  .
  .
```

If the requested interface is not supported, an exception will be raised.

STRUCTURED EXCEPTION HANDLING

Structured exception handling (SEH) is a method of error handling that enables your application to recover gracefully from otherwise fatal error conditions. In Delphi 1.0, exceptions were implemented in the Object Pascal language, but starting in Delphi 2.0, exceptions are a part of the Win32 API. What makes Object Pascal exceptions easy to use is that they are just classes that happen to contain information about the location and nature of a particular error. This makes exceptions as easy to implement and use in your applications as any other class.

Delphi contains predefined exceptions for common program-error conditions, such as out of memory, divide by zero, numerical overflow and underflow, and file I/O errors. Delphi also enables you to define your own exception classes as you may see fit in your applications.

Listing 2.3 demonstrates how to use exception handling during file I/O.

LISTING 2.3. FILE I/O USING EXCEPTION HANDLING.

```
Program FileIO;

uses Classes, Dialogs;

{$APPTYPE CONSOLE}

var
  F: TextFile;
  S: string;
begin
  AssignFile(F, 'FOO.TXT');
  try
    Reset(F);
    try
      ReadLn(F, S);
    finally
      CloseFile(F);
    end;
  except
    on EInOutError do
      ShowMessage('Error Accessing File!');
  end;
end.
```

In Listing 2.3, the inner `try..finally` block is used to ensure that the file is closed regardless of whether or not any exceptions come down the pike. What this block means in English is "Hey, program, try to execute the statements between the `try` and the `finally`. If you finish them or run into an exception, execute the statements between the `finally` and the `end`. If an exception does occur, move on to the next exception-handling block." This means that the file will be closed and the error can be properly handled no matter what error occurs.

NOTE

The statements after `finally` in a `try..finally` block execute regardless of whether or not an exception occurs. Make sure that the code in your `finally` block does not assume that an exception has occurred. Also, because the `finally` statement doesn't stop the migration of an exception, the flow of your program's execution will continue on to the next exception handler.

The outer `try..except` block is used to handle the exceptions as they occur in the program. After the file is closed in the `finally` block, the `except` block puts up a message informing the user that an I/O error occurred.

One of the key advantages that exception handling provides over the traditional method of error handling is the ability to distinctly separate the error-detection code from the error-correction code. This is a good thing primarily because it makes your code easier to read and maintain by enabling you to concentrate on one distinct aspect of the code at a time.

The fact that you cannot trap any specific exception by using the `try..finally` block is significant. When you use a `try..finally` block in your code, it means that you don't care what exceptions might occur. You just want to perform some tasks when they do occur to gracefully get out of a tight spot. The `finally` block is an ideal place to free any resources you've allocated (such as files or Windows resources), because it will always execute in the case of an error. In many cases, however, you need some type of error handling that is able to respond differently depending on the type of error that occurs. You can trap specific exceptions by using a `try..except` block, which is again illustrated in Listing 2.4.

LISTING 2.4. A `try..except` EXCEPTION-HANDLING BLOCK.

```
Program HandleIt;

{$APPTYPE CONSOLE}

var
  R1, R2: Double;
begin
  while True do begin
  try
    Write('Enter a real number: ');
    ReadLn(R1);
    Write('Enter another real number: ');
    ReadLn(R2);
    Writeln('I will now divide the first number by the second...');
    Writeln('The answer is: ', (R1 / R2):5:2);
  except
    On EZeroDivide do
      Writeln('You cannot divide by zero!');
    On EInOutError do
      Writeln('That is not a valid number!');
  end;
  end;
end.
```

Although you can trap specific exceptions with the `try..except` block, you also can catch other exceptions by adding the catch-all `else` clause to this construct. The syntax of the `try..except..else` construct follows:

```
try
  Statements
except
  On ESomeException do Something;
else
  { do some default exception handling }
end;
```

> **CAUTION**
>
> When using the `try..except..else` construct, you should be aware that the `else` part will catch *all* exceptions—even exceptions you might not expect, such as out-of-memory or other runtime-library exceptions. Be careful when using the `else` clause, and use the clause sparingly. You should always reraise the exception when you trap with unqualified exception handlers. This is explained in the section "Reraising an Exception."

You can achieve the same effect as a `try..except..else` construct also by not specifying the exception class in a `try..except` block, as shown in this example:

```
try
  Statements
except
  HandleException  // almost the same as else statement
end;
```

Exception Classes

Exceptions are merely special instances of objects. These objects are instantiated when an exception occurs and are destroyed when an exception is handled. The base exception object is called `Exception`, and that object is defined as follows:

```
type
  Exception = class(TObject)
  private
    FMessage: string;
    FHelpContext: Integer;
  public
    constructor Create(const Msg: string);
    constructor CreateFmt(const Msg: string; const Args: array of const);
```

```
constructor CreateRes(Ident: Integer);
constructor CreateResFmt(Ident: Integer; const Args: array of const);
constructor CreateHelp(const Msg: string; AHelpContext: Integer);
constructor CreateFmtHelp(const Msg: string; const Args: array of
➥const; AHelpContext: Integer);
constructor CreateResHelp(Ident: Integer; AHelpContext: Integer);
constructor CreateResFmtHelp(Ident: Integer; const Args: array of
➥const; AHelpContext: Integer);
property HelpContext: Integer read FHelpContext write FHelpContext;
property Message: string read FMessage write FMessage;
end;
```

The important element of the `Exception` object is the `Message` property, which is a string. `Message` provides more information or explanation on the exception. The information provided by `Message` depends on the type of exception that is raised.

When you handle a specific type of exception in an `except` block, that handler also will

CAUTION

If you define your own exception object, make sure that you derive it from a known exception object such as `Exception` or one of its descendants. The reason for this is so that generic exception handlers will be able to trap your exception.

catch any exceptions that are descendants of the specified exception. For example, `EMathError` is the ancestor object for a variety of math-related exceptions, such as `EZeroDivide` and `EOverflow`. You can catch any of these exceptions by setting up a handler for `EMathError` as shown here:

```
try
  Statements
except
  on EMathError do  // will catch EMathError or any descendant
    HandleException
end;
```

Any exceptions that you do not explicitly handle in your program eventually will flow to, and be handled by, the default handler located within the Delphi runtime library. The default handler will put up a message dialog informing the user that an exception occurred. Incidentally, Chapter 4, "Application Frameworks and Design Concepts," will show an example of how to override the default exception handling.

When handling an exception, you sometimes need to access the instance of the exception object in order to retrieve more information on the exception, such as that provided by its `Message` property. There are two ways to do this: use an optional identifier with the `on ESomeException` construct, or use the `ExceptObject()` function.

You can insert an optional identifier in the `on ESomeException` portion of an `except` block and have the identifier map to an instance of the currently raised exception. The syntax for this is to preface the exception type with an identifier and a colon, as follows:

```
try
  Something
except
  on E:ESomeException do
    ShowMessage(E.Message);
end;
```

In this case, the identifier (`E` in this case) becomes the instance of the currently raised exception. This identifier is always of the same type as the exception it prefaces.

You can also use the `ExceptObject()` function, which returns an instance of the currently raised exception. The drawback to `ExceptObject()`, however, is that it returns a `TObject` that you must then typecast to the exception object of your choice. The following example shows the usage of this function:

```
try
  Something
except
  on ESomeException do
    ShowMessage(ESomeException(ExceptObject).Message);
end;
```

The `ExceptObject()` function will return `Nil` if there is no active exception.

The syntax for raising an exception is similar to the syntax for creating an object instance. To raise a user-defined exception called `EBadStuff`, for example, you would use this syntax:

```
Raise EBadStuff.Create('Some bad stuff happened.');
```

Flow of Execution

After an exception is raised, the flow of execution of your program propagates up to the next exception handler until the exception instance is finally handled and destroyed. This process is determined by the call stack and therefore works program-wide (not just within one procedure or unit). Listing 2.5 illustrates the flow of execution of a program when an exception is raised. This listing is the main unit of a Delphi application that consists of one form with one button on the form. When the button is clicked, the

Button1Click() method calls Proc1(), which calls Proc2(), which in turn calls Proc3(). An exception is raised in Proc3(), and you can witness the flow of execution propagating through each try..finally block until the exception is finally handled inside Button1Click().

TIP

When you run this program from the Delphi IDE, you'll be able to see the flow of execution better if you disable the integrated debugger's handling of exceptions by unchecking Tools I Debugger Options I Preferences I Break on Exception.

LISTING 2.5. MAIN UNIT FOR THE EXCEPTION PROPAGATION PROJECT.

```
unit Main;

interface

uses
  SysUtils, Windows, Messages, Classes, Graphics, Controls, Forms, Dialogs,
  StdCtrls;

type
  TForm1 = class(TForm)
    Button1: TButton;
    procedure Button1Click(Sender: TObject);
  private
    { Private declarations }
  public
    { Public declarations }
  end;

var
  Form1: TForm1;

implementation

{$R *.DFM}

type
  EBadStuff = class(Exception);

procedure Proc3;
begin
  try
```

```
      raise EBadStuff.Create('Up the stack we go!');
  finally
    ShowMessage('Exception raised. Proc3 sees the exception');
  end;
end;

procedure Proc2;
begin
  try
    Proc3;
  finally
    ShowMessage('Proc2 sees the exception');
  end;
end;

procedure Proc1;
begin
  try
    Proc2;
  finally
    ShowMessage('Proc1 sees the exception');
  end;
end;

procedure TForm1.Button1Click(Sender: TObject);
const
  ExceptMsg = 'Exception handled in calling procedure. The message is
  ➥"%s"';
begin
  ShowMessage('This method calls Proc1 which calls Proc2 which calls
  ➥Proc3');
  try
    Proc1;
  except
    on E:EBadStuff do
      ShowMessage(Format(ExceptMsg, [E.Message]));
  end;
end;

end.
```

Reraising an Exception

When you need to perform special handling for a statement inside an existing
try..except block and still allow the exception to flow to the block's outer default handler, use a technique called *reraising the exception*. Listing 2.6 demonstrates an example
of reraising the exception.

LISTING 2.6. RERAISING AN EXCEPTION.

```
try              // this is outer block
  { statements }
  { statements }
  ( statements }
  try              // this is the special inner block
    { some statement that may require special handling }
  except
    on ESomeException do
    begin
      { special handling for the inner block statement }
      raise;     // reraise the exception to the outer block
    end;
  end;
except
  // outer block will always perform default handling
  on ESomeException do Something;
end;
```

RUNTIME TYPE INFORMATION

Runtime Type Information (RTTI) is a language feature that gives a Delphi application the capability to retrieve information about its objects at runtime. RTTI is also the key to links between Delphi components and their incorporation into the Delphi IDE, but it isn't just an academic process that occurs in the shadows of the IDE.

Objects, by virtue of being TObject descendants, contain a pointer to their RTTI and have several built-in methods that enable you to get some useful information out of the RTTI. The following table lists some of the TObject methods that use RTTI to retrieve information about a particular object instance.

Function	Return Type	Returns
ClassName()	string	The name of the object's class
ClassType()	TClass	The object's type
InheritsFrom()	Boolean	Boolean to indicate whether class descends from a given class
ClassParent()	TClass	The object ancestor's type
InstanceSize()	word	The size in bytes of an instance
ClassInfo()	Pointer	A pointer to the object's in-memory RTTI

Object Pascal provides two operators, is and as, that allow comparisons and typecasts of objects via RTTI.

The as keyword is a new form of typesafe typecast. It enables you to cast a low-level object to a descendant and will raise an exception if the typecast is invalid. Suppose that you have a procedure to which you want to be able to pass any type of object. This function definition could be defined as

```
Procedure Foo(AnObject: TObject);
```

If you want to do something useful with AnObject later in this procedure, you probably will have to cast it to a descendant object. Suppose that you want to assume that AnObject is a TEdit descendant, and you want to change the text it contains (a TEdit is a Delphi VCL edit control). You can use the following code:

```
(Foo as TEdit).Text := 'Hello World.';
```

You can use the Boolean comparison operator is to check whether two objects are of compatible types. Use the is operator to compare an unknown object to a known type or instance to determine what properties and behavior you can assume about the unknown object. For example, you might want to check to see whether AnObject is pointer-compatible with TEdit before attempting to typecast it:

```
If (Foo is TEdit) then
  TEdit(Foo).Text := 'Hello World.';
```

Notice that you did not use the as operator to perform the typecast in this example. That's because a certain amount of overhead is involved in using RTTI, and because the first line has already determined that Foo is a TEdit, you can optimize by performing a pointer typecast in the second line.

SUMMARY

Quite a bit of material was covered in this chapter. You learned the basic syntax and semantics of the Object Pascal language including variables, operators, functions, procedures, types, constructs, and style. You should also have a clear understanding of OOP, objects, fields, properties, methods, TObject, interfaces, exception handling, and RTTI.

Now that you have the big picture of how Delphi's object-oriented Object Pascal language works, you're ready to move on to more advanced discussions of the Win32 API and the Visual Component Library.

THE WIN32 API

IN THIS CHAPTER

This chapter gives you an introduction to the Win32 API and the Win32 system in general. The chapter discusses the capabilities of the Win32 system and also points out some key differences to the 16-bit implementation of various features. The intent of this chapter is not to document the Win32 system in depth but rather to give you a basic idea of how Win32 operates. By having a basic understanding of the Win32 operation, you'll be able use advanced features provided by the Win32 system whenever the need arises.

OBJECTS—THEN AND NOW

The term *objects* is used for a number of reasons. When we speak of the Win32 architecture, we're not speaking of objects as they exist in object-oriented programming or COM. Objects have a totally different meaning in this context, and to make things more confusing, an object means something different in 16-bit Windows than it does in Win32. We want to make sure that you understand what objects are in Win32.

Basically two types of objects are in the Win32 environment: kernel objects and GDI/USER objects.

Kernel Objects

Kernel objects are native to the Win32 system and include events, file mappings, files, mailslots, mutexes, pipes, processes, semaphores, and threads. The Win32 API includes various functions specific to each kernel object. Before discussing kernel objects in general, we want to discuss processes that are essential to understanding how objects are managed in the Win32 environment.

Processes

A *process* can be thought of as a running application or an application instance. Therefore, several processes can be active at once in the Win32 environment. Each process gets its own 4GB address space for its code and data. Within this 4GB address space, any memory allocations, threads, file mappings, and so on exist. Additionally, any dynamic link libraries (DLLs) loaded by a process are loaded into the address space of the process. We'll say more about the memory management of the Win32 system later in this chapter, in the section "Win32 Memory Management."

Processes are inert. In other words, they execute nothing. Instead, each process gets a *primary thread* that executes code within the context of the process that owns this thread. A process may contain several threads; however, it has only one main or primary thread.

NOTE

A *thread* is an operating system object that represents a path of code execution within a particular process. Every Win32 application has at least one thread—often called the *primary thread* or *default thread*—but applications are free to create other threads to perform other tasks. Threads are covered in greater depth in Chapter 11, "Writing Multithreaded Applications."

When a process is created, the system creates the main thread for it. This thread may then create additional threads, if necessary. The Win32 system allocates CPU time called *time slices* to the threads of the process.

Table 3.1 shows some common process functions of the Win32 API.

TABLE 3.1. PROCESS FUNCTIONS.

Function	Purpose
CreateProcess()	Creates a new process and its primary thread. This function replaces the WinExec() function used in Windows 3.11.
ExitProcess()	Exits the current process, terminating the process and all threads related to that process.
GetCurrentProcess()	Returns a pseudohandle of the current process. A *pseudohandle* is a special handle that can be interpreted as the current process handle. A real handle can be obtained by using the DuplicateHandle()function.
DuplicateHandle()	Duplicates the handle of a kernel object.
GetCurrentProcessID()	Retrieves the current process ID, which uniquely identifies the process throughout the system until the process has terminated.
GetExitCodeProcess()	Retrieves the exit status of a specified process.
GetPriorityClass()	Retrieves the priority class for a specified process. This value and the values of each thread priority in the process determine the base priority level for each thread.
GetStartupInfo()	Retrieves the contents of the TStartupInfo structure initialized when the process was created.
OpenProcess()	Returns a handle of an existing process as specified by a process ID.
SetPriorityClass()	Sets a process's priority class.
TerminateProcess()	Terminates a process and kills all threads associated with that process.
WaitForInputIdle()	Waits until the process is waiting for input from the user.

Some Win32 API functions require an application's instance handle, whereas others require a module handle. In 16-bit Windows, there was a distinction between these two values. This is not true under Win32. Every process gets its own instance handle. Your Delphi 4 applications can refer to this instance handle by accessing the global variable, HInstance. Because HInstance and the application's module handle are the same, you can pass HInstance to Win32 API functions calling for a module handle such as the GetModuleFileName() function, which returns the filename of a specified module. See the following warning for when HInstance does not refer to the module handle of the current application.

> **CAUTION**
>
> HInstance will not be the module handle of the application for code that's compiled into packages. Use MainInstance to refer always to the host application module and HInstance to refer to the module in which your code resides.

Another difference between Win32 and 16-bit Windows has to do with the HPrevInst global variable. In 16-bit Windows, this variable held the handle of a previously run instance of the same application. You could use the value to prevent multiple instances of your application from running. This no longer works in Win32. Each process runs within its own 4GB address space and can't see any other processes. Therefore, HPrevInst is always assigned the value 0. You must use other techniques to prevent multiple instances of your application from running, as shown in Chapter 13, "Hard-Core Techniques."

More on Kernel Objects

There are several kinds of kernel objects. When a kernel object is created, it exists in the address space of the process, and that process gets a handle to that object. This handle can't be passed to other processes or reused by the next process to access the same kernel object. However, a second process can obtain its own handle to a kernel object that already exists, by using the appropriate Win32 API function. For example, the CreateMutex() Win32 API function creates a named or unnamed mutex object and returns its handle. The OpenMutex() Win32 API returns the handle to an existing named mutex object. OpenMutex() passes the name of the mutex whose handle is being requested.

> **NOTE**
>
> Named kernel objects are optionally assigned a null-terminated string name when created with their respective `CreateXXXX()` functions. This name is registered in the Win32 system. Other processes can access the same kernel object by opening it, using the `OpenXXXX()` function, and passing the specified object name.

If you want to share a mutex across processes, you can have the first process create the mutex by using the `CreateMutex()` function. This process must pass a name that will be associated with this new mutex. Other processes must use the `OpenMutex()`function, to which they pass the same name of the mutex used by the first process. `OpenMutex()` will return a handle to the mutex object of the given name. Various security constraints may be imposed on other processes accessing existing kernel objects. Such security constraints are specified when the mutex is initially created with `CreateMutex()`. Look to the online help for these constraints as they apply to each kernel object.

Because multiple processes can access kernel objects, kernel objects are maintained by a usage count. As a second application accesses the object, the usage count is incremented. When it's done with the object, the application should call the `CloseHandle()` function, which decrements the object's usage count.

GDI and User Objects

Objects in 16-bit Windows referred to entities that could be referenced by a handle. This didn't include kernel objects because they didn't exist under 16-bit Windows.

In 16-bit Windows, there are two types of objects: those stored in the GDI and USER local heaps, and those allocated from the global heap. Examples of GDI objects are brushes, pens, fonts, palettes, bitmaps, and regions. Examples of user objects are windows, window classes, atoms, and menus.

There is a direct relationship between an object and its handle. An object's handle is a selector that, when converted into a pointer, points to a data structure describing an object. This structure exists in either the GDI or USER default data segment, depending on the type of object to which the handle referred. Additionally, a handle for an object referring to the global heap is a selector to the global memory segment; therefore, when converted to pointer, it points to that memory block.

A result of this particular design is that objects in 16-bit Windows are sharable. The globally accessible Local Descriptor Table (LDT) stores the handles to these objects. The GDI and USER default data segments are also globally accessible to all applications and DLLs under 16-bit Windows. Therefore, any application or DLL can get to an object used by another application. Do note that objects such as the LDT are only sharable in Windows 3.1. Many applications use this arrangement for different purposes. One example is to enable applications to share memory.

Win32 deals with GDI and USER objects a bit differently, and the same techniques that you used in 16-bit Windows might not be applicable to the Win32 environment.

To begin with, Win32 introduces kernel objects, which we've already discussed. Also, the implementation of GDI and USER objects are different under Win32 than under 16-bit Windows.

Under Win32, GDI objects are not shared like their 16-bit counterparts. GDI objects are stored in the address space of the process rather than in a globally accessible memory block (each process gets its own 4GB address space). Additionally, each process gets its own handle table, which stores handles to GDI objects within the process. This is an important point to remember, because you don't want to be passing GDI object handles to other processes.

Earlier, we mentioned that LDTs are accessible from other applications. In Win32, each process address space is defined by its own LDT. Therefore, Win32 uses LDTs as they were intended to be used: as process-local tables.

CAUTION

Although it's possible that a process could call `SelectObject()` on a handle from another process and successfully use that handle, this would be entirely coincidental. GDI objects have different meanings in different processes, so you don't want to practice this method.

The managing of GDI handles happens in the Win32 GDI subsystem, which includes the validation of GDI objects and the recycling of handles.

USER objects work similarly to GDI objects and are managed by the Win32 USER subsystem. However, any handle tables are also maintained by USER—not in the address space of the process, as with the GDI handle tables. Therefore, objects such as windows, window classes, atoms, and so on are sharable across processes.

MULTITASKING AND MULTITHREADING

Multitasking is a term used to describe an operating system's capability of running multiple applications concurrently. The system does this by issuing time slices to each application. In this sense, multitasking is not true multitasking but rather *task-switching*. In other words, the operating system isn't really running multiple applications at the same time. Instead, it's running one application for a certain amount of time and then switching to another application and running it for a certain amount of time. It does this for each application. To the user it appears as though all applications are running simultaneously because the time slices are small.

This concept of multitasking isn't really a new feature of Windows and has existed in previous versions. The key difference between the Win32 implementation of multitasking and that of earlier versions of Windows is that Win32 uses *preemptive multitasking*, whereas earlier versions use *nonpreemptive multitasking*.

Nonpreemptive multitasking means that the Windows system doesn't schedule time to applications based on the system timer. Applications have to tell Windows that they are finished processing code before Windows can grant time to other applications. This is a problem because a single application can tie up the system with a lengthy process. Therefore, unless the programmers of the application make sure that the application gives up time to other applications, problems can arise for the user.

Under Win32, the system grants CPU time to the threads for each process. The Win32 system manages the time allotted to each thread based on thread priorities. This concept is discussed in greater depth in Chapter 11.

3

THE WIN32 API

> **NOTE**
>
> The Windows NT implementation of Win32 offers the capacity to perform true multitasking on machines with multiple processors. Under these conditions, each application can be granted time on its own processor. Actually, each individual thread can be given CPU time on any available CPU in a multiprocessor machine.

Multithreading is the capability of an application to multitask within itself. This means that your application can perform different types of processing simultaneously. A process can have several threads, and each thread contains its own distinct code to execute. Threads may have dependencies on one another and therefore must be synchronized. For example, it wouldn't be a good idea to assume that a particular thread will finish processing its code when its result will be used by another thread. Thread-synchronization techniques are used to coordinate multiple-thread execution. Threads are discussed in greater depth in Chapter 11.

WIN32 MEMORY MANAGEMENT

The Win32 environment introduces you to the 32-bit flat memory model. Finally, Pascal programmers can declare that big array without running into a compile error:

```
BigArray = array[1..100000] of integer;
```

The following sections discuss the Win32 memory model and how the Win32 system lets you manipulate memory.

Just What Is the Flat Memory Model?

The 16-bit world uses a segmented memory model. Under that model, addresses are represented with a *segment:offset* pair. The *segment* refers to a base address, and the *offset* represents a number of bytes from that base. The problem with this scheme is that it is confusing to the average programmer, especially when dealing with large memory requirements. It is also limiting—data structures larger than 64KB are extremely painful to manage, and thus are avoided.

Under the flat-memory model, these limitations are gone. Each process has its own 4GB address space to use for allocating large data structures. Additionally, an address actually represents a unique memory location.

How Does the Win32 System Manage Memory?

It's not likely that your computer has 4GB installed. How does the Win32 system make more memory available to your processes than the amount of physical memory installed on the computer? Addresses that are 32-bit don't actually represent a memory location in physical memory. Instead, Win32 uses *virtual addresses*.

By using virtual memory, each process can get its own 4GB virtual address space. The upper 2MB area of this address space belongs to Windows, and the bottom 2MB is where your applications reside and where you can allocate memory. One advantage to this scheme is that the thread for one process can't access the memory in another process. The address $54545454 in one process points to a completely different location than the same address in another process.

It's important to note that a process doesn't actually have 4GB of memory but rather has the capability to access a range of addresses up to 4GB. The amount of memory available to a process really depends on how much physical RAM is installed on the machine and how much space is available on disk for a paging file. The physical RAM and the paging file are used by the system to break the memory available to a process into pages. The size of a page depends on the type of system on which Win32 is installed. These pages sizes are 4KB for Intel platforms and 8KB for Alpha platforms. The defunct PowerPC and MIPS platforms used 4KB pages as well. The system then moves pages from the paging file to physical memory and back as needed. The system maintains a page map to translate the virtual addresses of a process to a physical address. We won't get into the hairy details of how all this happens; we just want to familiarize you with the general scheme of things at this point.

A developer can manipulate memory in the Win32 environment in essentially three ways: virtual memory, file-mapping objects, and heaps.

Virtual Memory

Win32 provides a set of low-level functions that enable you to manipulate the virtual memory of a process. This memory exists in one of the following three states:

Free   Memory that is available to be reserved and/or committed.

Reserved   Memory within an address range that is reserved for future use. Memory within this address is protected from other allocation requests. However, this memory cannot be accessed by the process because no *physical* memory is associated with it until it's committed. The `VirtualAlloc()` function is used to reserve memory.

Committed   Memory that has been allocated and associated with physical memory. Committed memory can be accessed by the process. The `VirtualAlloc()` function is used to commit virtual memory.

As stated earlier, Win32 provides various `VirtualXXXX()` functions for manipulating virtual memory, as shown in Table 3.2. These functions are also documented in detail in the online help.

TABLE 3.2. VIRTUAL MEMORY FUNCTIONS.

Function	*Purpose*
`VirtualAlloc()`	Reserves and/or commits pages in a process's virtual address space.
`VirtualFree()`	Releases and/or decommits pages in a process's virtual address space.
`VirtualLock()`	Locks a region of a process's virtual address to prevent it from being swapped to a page file. This prevents page faults with subsequent accesses to that region.

continues

TABLE 3.2. CONTINUED

Function	Purpose
VirtualUnLock()	Unlocks a specified region of memory in a process's address space so that it can be swapped to a page file if necessary.
VirtualQuery()	Returns information about a range of pages in the calling process's virtual address space.
VirtualQueryEx()	Returns the same information as VirtualQuery() except that it allows you to specify the process.
VirtualProtect()	Changes access protection for a region of committed pages in the calling process's virtual address space.
VirtualProtectEx()	Same as VirtualProtect() except that it makes changes to a specified process.

NOTE

The *xxx*EX() routines listed in this table can only be used by a process that has debugging privileges on the other process. It's complicated and rare for anything but a debugger to use these routines.

Memory-Mapped Files

Memory-mapped files (file-mapping objects) allow you to access disk files in the same way that you would access dynamically allocated memory. This is done by mapping all or part of the file to the calling process's address range. After this is done, you can access the file's data by using a simple pointer. Memory-mapped files are discussed in greater detail in Chapter 12, "Working with Files."

Heaps

Heaps are contiguous blocks of memory in which smaller blocks can be allocated. Heaps efficiently manage the allocation and manipulation of dynamic memory. Heap memory is manipulated using various HeapXXXX() Win32 API functions. These functions are listed in Table 3.3 and are also documented in detail in Delphi's online help.

TABLE 3.3. HEAP FUNCTIONS.

Function	Purpose
HeapCreate()	Reserves a contiguous block in the virtual address space of the calling process and allocates physical storage for a specified initial portion of this block
HeapAlloc()	Allocates a block of nonmovable memory from a heap
HeapReAlloc()	Reallocates a block of memory from the heap, allowing you to resize or change the heap's properties
HeapFree()	Frees a memory block allocated from the heap with HeapAlloc()
HeapDestroy()	Destroys a heap object created with HeapCreate()

NOTE

It's important to note that there are several differences in the Win32 implementation of Windows NT and Windows 95. Generally, these differences have to do with security and speed. The Windows 95 memory manager, for instance, is leaner than that of Windows NT (NT maintains more internal tracking information on heap blocks). However, the NT virtual memory manager is generally regarded as much faster than Windows 95.

Be aware of such differences when using the various functions associated with these Windows objects. The online help will point out platform-specific variations of that function's usage. Be sure to refer to the help whenever using such functions.

ERROR HANDLING IN WIN32

Most Win32 API functions return either True or False, indicating that the function was either successful or unsuccessful, respectively. If the function is unsuccessful (the function returns False), you must use the GetLastError() Win32 API function to obtain the error code value for the thread in which the error occurred.

NOTE

Not all Win32 system API functions set error codes that are accessible by GetLastError(). For example, many GDI routines don't set error codes.

This error code is maintained on a per-thread basis, so `GetLastError()` must be called in the context of the thread causing the error. Following is an example of this function's usage:

```
if not CreateProcess(CommandLine, nil, nil, nil, False,
  NORMAL_PRIORITY_CLASS, nil, nil, StartupInfo, ProcessInfo) then
    raise Exception.Create('Error creating process:
➥'+IntToStr(GetLastError));
```

> **TIP**
>
> The Delphi 4 SYSUTILS unit has a standard exception class and utility function to convert system errors into exceptions. These functions are `Win32Check()` and `RaiseLastWin32Error`, which raises an EWin32Error exception. Use these helper routines instead of writing your own result checks.

This code attempts to create a process specified by the null-terminated string `CommandLine`. If the function fails, an exception is raised. This exception displays the last error code that resulted from the function call by getting it from the `GetLastError()` function. You might use a similar approach in your application.

> **TIP**
>
> Error codes returned by `GetLastError()` are typically documented in the online help under the functions that cause the error to occur. So, the error code for `CreateMutex()` would be documented under `CreateMutex()` in the online help.

SUMMARY

This chapter introduced you to the Win32 API. You should now have an idea of the new kernel objects available, as well as how Win32 manages memory. You should also be familiar with the different memory-management features available to you. As a Delphi developer, it isn't necessary that you know all the ins and outs of the Win32 system. However, you should possess a basic understanding of the Win32 system, its functions, and how you can use these functions to maximize your development effort. This chapter provides you with a starting point.

APPLICATION FRAMEWORKS AND DESIGN CONCEPTS

IN THIS CHAPTER

This chapter is about Delphi project management and architecting. It shows you how to use forms properly in your applications as well as how to manipulate their behavioral and visual characteristics. The techniques discussed in this chapter include application startup/initialization procedures, form reuse/inheritance, and user interface enhancement. The text discusses the framework classes that make up Delphi 4 applications: TApplication, TForm, and TScreen. We will then show you why understanding these concepts is essential to properly architecting Delphi applications. Finally, the chapter discusses the requirements your applications must meet to qualify for the Microsoft Windows 95 logo.

UNDERSTANDING THE DELPHI ENVIRONMENT AND PROJECT ARCHITECTURE

You need at least two important elements to properly build and manage Delphi 4 projects. The first is knowing the ins and outs of the development environment with which you create your projects. The second is having a solid understanding of the inherent architecture of the applications created with Delphi 4. This chapter doesn't walk you through the Delphi 4 environment (the Delphi documentation shows you how to work within that environment); instead, this chapter points out features of the Delphi 4 IDE that help you manage your projects more effectively. This chapter will also explain the architecture inherent in all Delphi applications. This will not only allow you to maximize the environment's features but also to properly use a solid architecture instead of fighting it—a common mistake among those who don't understand Delphi project architectures.

Our first suggestion is to become well acquainted with the Delphi 4 development environment. This book assumes that you're already familiar with the Delphi 4 IDE. Second, this book assumes that you've thoroughly read the Delphi 4 documentation (hint). However, you should navigate through each of the Delphi 4 menus and bring up each of its dialog boxes. When you see an option, setting, or action you're unsure of, bring up the online help and read through it. The time you spend doing this can be not only interesting but also insightful (not to mention that you'll learn how to navigate through the online help efficiently).

TIP

The Delphi 4 help system is without a doubt the most valuable and speedy reference you have at your disposal. It would be advantageous to learn how to use it to explore the thousands of help screens available.

Delphi 4 contains help on everything from how to use the Delphi 4 environment to details on the Win32 API and complex Win32 structures. You can get immediate help on a topic by typing the topic in the editor and, with the cursor still on the word you typed, pressing Ctrl+F1. The help screen appears immediately. Help is also available from the Delphi 4 dialog boxes by selecting the Help button or by pressing F1 when a particular component has focus. You can also navigate through Help by simply selecting Help from Delphi 4's Help menu.

FILES THAT MAKE UP A DELPHI 4 PROJECT

A Delphi 4 project is composed of several related files. Some files are created at design time as you define forms. Others aren't created until you compile the project. To manage a Delphi 4 project effectively, you must know the purpose of each of these files. Both the Delphi 4 documentation and the online help give detailed descriptions of the Delphi 4 project files. It's a good idea to review the documentation to ensure that you're familiar with these files before going on with this chapter.

The Project File

The *project file* is created at design time and has the extension .dpr. This file is the main program source file. The project file is where the main form and any automatically created forms are instantiated. You'll seldom have to edit this file except when performing program initialization routines, displaying a splash screen, or performing various other routines that must happen immediately when the program starts. The following code shows a typical project file.

```
program Project1;
uses
  Forms,
  Unit1 in 'Unit1.pas' {Form1};
{$R *.RES}
begin
  Application.Initialize;
  Application.CreateForm(TForm1, Form1);
  Application.Run;
end.
```

Pascal programmers will recognize this file as a standard Pascal program file. Notice that this file lists the form unit Unit1 in the uses clause. Project files list all form units that belong to the project in the same manner. The following line refers to the project's resource file:

```
{$R *.RES}
```

This line tells the compiler to link the resource file that has the same name as the project file and an `.res` extension to this project. The project resource file contains the program icon and version info.

Finally, the `begin..end` block is where the application's main code is executed. In this simple example, the main form, `Form1`, is created. When `Application.Run()` executes, `Form1` is displayed as the main form. You can add code in this block as shown later in this chapter.

Project Unit Files

Units are Pascal source files with a `.pas` extension. There are basically three types of units files: form/data module units, component units, and general purpose units.

- *Form/data module units* are units automatically generated by Delphi 4. There's one unit for each form or data module you create. For example, you can't have two forms defined in one unit and use them both in the Form Designer.

- *Component units* are unit files created by you or Delphi 4 whenever you create a new component.

- *General purpose units* are units you can create for data types, variables, procedures, and classes you want to make accessible to your applications.

Details about units are provided later in this chapter.

Form Files

A *form file* contains a binary representation of a form. Whenever you create a new form, Delphi 4 creates both a form file (with the extension `.dfm`) and a Pascal unit (with the extension `.pas`) for your new form. If you look at a form's unit file, you see the following line:

```
{$R *.DFM}
```

This line tells the compiler to link the corresponding form file (the form file that has the same name as the unit file and a `.dfm` extension) to the project.

You typically don't edit the form file itself (although it's possible to do so). You can load the form file into the Delphi 4 editor so that you can view or edit the text representation of this file. Select File | Open and then select the option to open only form files (`.dfm`). You can also do this by simply right-clicking the Form Designer and selecting View as Text from the pop-up menu. When you open the file, you see the text representation of the form.

Viewing the textual representation of the form is handy because you can see the non-default property settings for the form and any components that exist on it. One way you can edit the form file is to change a component type. For example, suppose that the form file contains this definition for a TButton component:

```
object Button1: TButton
   Left = 8
   Top = 8
   Width = 75
   Height = 25
   Caption = 'Button1'
   TabOrder = 0
 end
```

If you change the line `object Button1: TButton` to `object Button1: TLabel`, you change the component type to a TLabel component. When you view the form, you see a label on the form and not a button.

> **NOTE**
>
> Changing component types in the form file might result in a property read error. For example, changing a TButton (which has a TabOrder property) to a TLabel (which doesn't have a TabOrder property) results in this error. However, there's no need for concern because Delphi will correct the reference to the property the next time the form is saved.

> **CAUTION**
>
> You must be extremely careful when you edit the form file. It's possible to corrupt it, which will prevent Delphi 4 from opening the form later.

Resource Files

Resource files contain binary data, also called *resources*, that are linked to the application's executable file. The .res file automatically created by Delphi 4 contains the project's application icon, the application's version information, and other information. You can add resources to your application by creating a separate resource file and linking it to your project. You can create this resource file with a resource editor such as the Image Editor provided with Delphi 4 or the Resource Workshop.

> **CAUTION**
>
> Don't edit the resource file that Delphi creates automatically at compile time. Doing so will cause any changes to be lost the next time you compile. If you want to add resources to your application, create a separate resource file with a different name from that of your project file. Then link the new file to your project by using the $R directive as shown in the following line:
>
> `{$R MYRESFIL.RES}`

Project Options and Desktop Settings Files

The *project options file* (with the extension .dof) is where the options specified from the Project I Options menu are saved. This file is created when you first save your project; the file is saved again with each subsequent save.

The *desktop options file* (with the extension .dsk) stores the options specified from the Tools I Options menu for the desktop. Desktop option settings differ from project option settings in that project options are specific to a given project; desktop settings apply to the Delphi 4 environment.

> **TIP**
>
> A corrupt .dsk or .opt file can result in unexpected results (such as a GPF) during compilation. If this happens, delete both the .opt and .dsk files. They're regenerated when you save your project and when you exit Delphi 4; the IDE and project will revert to the default settings.

Backup Files

Delphi 4 creates *backup files* for the DPR project file and for any PAS units on the second and any subsequent saves. The backup files contain the last copy of the file before the save was performed. The project backup file has the extension .~dp. Unit backup files have the extension .~pa.

A binary backup of the .dfm form file is also created after you've saved it for the second or subsequent time. This form file backup has a .~df extension.

You harm nothing if you delete any of these files—as long as you realize that you're deleting your last backup. Also, if you find that you prefer not to create these files at all, you can prevent Delphi from creating them by deselecting Create Backup File in the Environment Options dialog box's Display page.

Package Files

Packages are simply DLLs that contain code that can be shared among many applications. However, packages are specific to Delphi in that they allow you to share components, classes, data, and code between modules. This means that you can now reduce the footprint of your applications drastically by using components residing in packages instead of linking them directly into your applications. Later chapters talk much more about packages. Package source files use the extension `.dpk` (short for Delphi package). When compiled, a `.dll` file is created. This `.dll` may be composed of several units or `.dcu` (Delphi compiled units) files, which can be any of the unit types previously mentioned. The binary image of a `.dpk` file containing all included units and the package header has the extension `.dcp` (Delphi compiled package). Don't be concerned if this seems confusing now; we'll explain packages in more detail later.

PROJECT MANAGEMENT TIPS

There are several ways to optimize the development process by using techniques that facilitate better organization and code reuse. The next few sections offer some tips on these techniques.

One Project, One Directory

It's a good idea to manage your projects so that one project's files are separate from other projects' files. Doing so prevents one project from overwriting another project's files.

Notice that each project on the CD-ROM that accompanies this book is in its own directory. You should follow this approach and maintain each of your projects in its own directory.

FILE NAMING CONVENTIONS

It's a good idea to establish a standard file naming convention for the files that make up your projects. You might take a look at the DDG Coding Standards Document included on the CD and used by the authors for the projects contained in this book.

4

APPLICATION
FRAMEWORKS
AND DESIGN

Units for Sharing Code

You can share commonly used routines with other applications by placing such routines in units that can be accessed by multiple projects. Typically, you create a utility directory somewhere on your hard drive and place your units in that directory. When you need to access a particular function that exists in one of the units in that directory, you just place the unit's name in the uses clause of the unit/project file requiring access.

You must also add the utility directory's path to the Search Path on the Directories/Conditionals page in the Project Options dialog box. Doing so ensures that Delphi 4 knows where to find your utility units.

TIP

By using the Project Manager, you can add a unit from another directory to an existing project, which automatically takes care of adding the search path.

To explain how to use utility units, Listing 4.1 shows a small unit, StrUtils.pas, that contains a single string-utility function. In reality, such units would probably contain many more routines, but this suffices as an example. The comments explain the function's purpose.

LISTING 4.1. THE StrUtils.pas UNIT.

```
unit strutils;
interface
function ShortStringAsPChar(var S: ShortString): PChar;
implementation
function ShortStringAsPChar(var S: ShortString): PChar;
{ This function null-terminates a short string so that it can be passed to
  functions that require PChar types. If string is longer than 254 chars,
  then it will be truncated to 254.
}
begin
  if Length(S) = High(S) then Dec(S[0]); { Truncate S if it's too long }
  S[Ord(Length(S)) + 1] := #0;           { Place null at end of string }
  Result := @S[1];                       { Return "PChar'd" string }
end;
end.
```

Suppose that you have a unit, SomeUnit.pas, that requires the use of this function. Simply add StrUtils to the uses clause of the unit in need, as shown here:

```
unit SomeUnit;
interface
...
implementation
uses
  strutils;
...
end.
```

Also, you must ensure that Delphi 4 can find the unit's `StrUtils.pas` by adding it to the search path from the Project | Options menu.

When you do this, you can use the function `ShortStringAsPChar()` anywhere in the `implementation` section of `SomeUnit.pas`. You must place `StrUtils` in the `uses` clause of all units that need access to the `ShortStringAsPChar()` function. It isn't enough to add `StrUtils` to only one unit in a project, or even to the project file (`.dpr`) of the application to make the routine available throughout the entire application.

TIP

Because `ShortStringAsPChar()` is a handy function, it pays to place it in a utility unit where it can be reused by any application so that you don't have to remember how or where you last used it.

Units for Global Identifiers

Units are also useful for declaring global identifiers for your project. As mentioned earlier, a project typically consists of many units—form units, component units, and general purpose units. What if you need a particular variable to be present and accessible to all units throughout the run of your application? The following steps show a simple way to create a unit to store these global identifiers:

1. Create a new unit in Delphi 4.
2. Give the unit a name indicating that it holds global identifiers for the application (for example, `Globals.pas` or `ProjGlob.pas`).
3. Place the variables, types, and so on in the `interface` section of your global unit. These are the identifiers that will be accessible to other units in the application.
4. To make these identifiers accessible to a unit, just add the unit name to the `uses` clause of the unit that needs access (as described earlier in this chapter in the discussion about sharing code in units).

4

**APPLICATION
FRAMEWORKS
AND DESIGN**

Making Forms Know About Other Forms

Just because each form is contained within its own unit doesn't mean that it can't access another form's variables, properties, and methods. Delphi generates code in the form's corresponding .pas file, declaring the instance of that form as a global variable. All that's required is that you add the name of the unit defining a particular form to the uses clause of the unit defining the form needing access. For example, if Form1, defined in UNIT1.PAS, needs access to Form2, defined in UNIT2.PAS, just add UNIT2 to UNIT1's uses clause:

```
unit Unit1;
interface
...
implementation
uses
  Unit2;
...
end.
```

Now UNIT1 can refer to Form2 anywhere in its implementation section.

> **NOTE**
>
> Form linking will automatically include Unit2 in Unit1's uses clause when you compile the project if you refer to the Unit2's form global (call it Form2); all that's necessary is to refer to Form2 somewhere in Unit1.

Multiple Projects Management (Project Groups)

Often, a product is made up of multiple projects (projects that are interdependent on one another). Examples of such projects are the separate tiers in a multitiered application, or DLLs to be used in other projects might be considered part of the overall project, even though DLLs are separate projects themselves.

Delphi 4 introduces an extremely valuable enhancement to managing such project groups. The Project Manager allows you to combine several Delphi projects into one grouping called a project group. We won't go into to the details of using the Project Manager because Delphi's documentation already does this. We do want to emphasize how important it is to organize project groups and how the Project Manager helps you do this.

It's still important that each project lives in its own directory and that all files specific to that project alone reside in the same directory. Any shared units, forms, and so on should be placed in a common directory that is accessed by the separate projects. For example, your directory structure might look something like this:

```
\DDGBugProduct
\DDGBugProduct\BugReportProject
\DDGBugProduct\BugAdminTool
\DDGBugProduct\CommonFiles
```

Given this structure, you have two separate directories for each Delphi project, `BugReportProject` and `BugAdminTool`. However, both of these projects may use forms and units that are common. You would place these files into the `CommonFiles` directory.

Organization is crucial in your development efforts, especially in a team development environment. It's highly recommended that you establish a standard before your team dives into creating a bunch of files that are going to be difficult to manage. You can use Project Manager to help you understand your project management structure.

THE FRAMEWORK CLASSES OF A DELPHI 4 PROJECT

Most Delphi 4 applications have at least one instance of a `TForm`. Also, Delphi 4 VCL applications will have only one instance of a `TApplication` and a `TScreen`. These three classes play important roles in managing the behavior of Delphi 4 projects. The following sections familiarize you with the roles of these classes so that you have the knowledge to modify their default behaviors when necessary.

The `TForm` Class

The `TForm` class is the focal point for Delphi 4 applications. In most cases, the entire application revolves around the main form. From the main form, you can launch other forms, usually as a result of a menu or button-click event. You might want Delphi 4 to create your forms automatically, in which case you don't have to worry about creating and destroying them. You may also choose to create the forms dynamically at runtime.

> **NOTE**
>
> Delphi can create applications that don't use forms such as console apps, services, COM servers, and so on. Therefore, the `TForm` class is not always the focal point of your applications.

You can display the form to the end user by using one of two methods: modal or modeless. The method you choose depends on how you intend the user to interact with the form and other forms concurrently.

Displaying a Modal Form

A *modal form* is displayed so that the user can't access the rest of the application until he or she has dismissed the form. Modal forms are typically associated with dialog boxes, much like the dialog boxes in Delphi 4 itself. In fact, you'll probably use modal forms in most cases. To display a form as modal, simply call its ShowModal() method. The following code shows how you create an instance of a user-defined form, TModalForm, and then display it as a modal form:

```
Begin
  // Create ModalForm instance
  ModalForm := TModalForm.Create(Application);
  try
    if ModalForm.ShowModal = mrOk then      // Show form in modal state
      { do something };                     // Execute some code
  finally
    ModalForm.Free;                         // Free form instance
    ModalForm := nil;                       // Set form variable to nil
  end;
end;
```

This code shows how you would dynamically create an instance of TModalForm and assign it to the variable ModalForm. It's important to note that, if you create a form dynamically, you must remove it from the list of available forms from the Auto-Create list box in the Project Options dialog box. This dialog box is invoked by selecting Project|Options from the menu. If the form instance is already created, however, you can show it as a modal form just by calling the ShowModal() method. The surrounding code can be removed:

```
begin
  if ModalForm.ShowModal = mrOk then    // ModalForm is already created
    { do something }
end;
```

The ShowModal() method returns the value assigned to ModalForm's ModalResult property. By default, ModalResult is zero, which is the value of the predefined constant mrNone. When you assign any nonzero value to ModalResult, the form is closed, and the assignment made to ModalResult is passed back to the calling routine through the ShowModal() method.

Buttons have a ModalResult property. You can assign a value to this property that's passed to the form's ModalResult property when the button is pressed. If this value is anything other than `mrNone`, the form will close, and the value passed back from the `ShowModal()` method will reflect that assigned to `ModalResult`.

You can also assign a value to the form's `ModalResult` property at runtime:

```
begin
  ModalForm.ModalResult := 100; // Assigning a value to ModalResult
  // causing form to close.
end;
```

The following table shows the predefined `ModalResult` values:

Constant	Value
mrNone	0
mrOk	idOk
mrCancel	idCancel
mrAbort	idAbort
mrRetry	idRetry
mrIgnore	idIgnore
mrYes	idYes
mrNo	idNo
mrAll	mrNo+1

Launching Modeless Forms

You can launch a modeless form by calling its `Show()` method. Calling a modeless form differs from the modal method in that the user can switch between the modeless form and other forms in the application. The intent of modeless forms is to allow users to work with different parts of the application at the same time as the form is displayed. The following code shows how you can dynamically create a modeless form:

```
Begin
// Check for an instance of modeless first
  if not Assigned(Modeless) then
    Modeless := TModeless.Create(Application);  // Create form
  Modeless.Show                                 // Show form as non-modal
end;                                            // instance already exists
```

This code also shows how you prevent multiple instances of one form class from being created. Remember that a modeless form allows the user to interact with the rest of the application. Therefore, nothing prevents the user from selecting the menu option again to create another form instance of `TModeless`. It's important that you manage the creation and destruction of forms.

Here's an important note about form instances: When you close a modeless form—either by accessing the system menu or clicking the Close button in the upper-right corner of the form—the form isn't actually freed from memory. The instance of the form still exists in memory until you close the main form (that is, the application). In the preceding code example, the `then` clause is executed only once, provided that the form is not auto-created. From that point on, the `else` clause is executed because the form instance always exists from its previous creation. This is fine if it is the way you want your application to function. But if you want the form to be freed whenever the user closes it, you must provide code for the `OnClose` event handler for the form and set its `Action` parameter to `caFree`. This tells the VCL to free the form when it's closed:

```
procedure TModeless.FormClose(Sender: TObject;
  var Action: TCloseAction);
begin
  Action := caFree;  // Free the form instance when closed
end;
```

The preceding version of the code solves the issue of the form not being freed. There's another issue, however. You might have noticed that this line was used in the first snippet of code showing modeless forms:

```
if not Assigned(Modeless) then
```

This line checks for an instance of `TModeless` referenced by the `Modeless` variable. Actually, this really checks to see that `Modeless` is not `nil`. Although `Modeless` will be `nil` the first time you enter the routine, it won't be `nil` when you enter the routine a second time after having destroyed the form. The reason is because the VCL doesn't set the variable `Modeless` to `nil` when it's destroyed. Therefore, this is something you must do yourself.

Unlike the modal form, you can't determine in code when the modeless form will be destroyed. Therefore, you can't destroy the form inside the routine that creates it. The user can close the form at any moment while running the application. Therefore, setting `Modeless` to `nil` must be a process of the `TModeless` class itself. The best place to do this is in the `OnDestroy` event handler for `TModeless`:

```
procedure TModeless.FormDestroy(Sender: TObject);
begin
  Modeless := nil; // Set the Modeless variable to nil when destroyed
end;
```

This ensures that the `Modeless` variable is set to `nil` every time it's destroyed, preventing the `Assigned()` method from failing. Keep in mind that it's up to you to ensure that only one instance of `TModeless` is created at a time, as shown in this routine.

> **CAUTION**
>
> Avoid the following pitfall when working with modeless forms:
>
> ```
> begin
>   Form1 := TForm1.Create(Application);
>   Form1.Show;
> end;
> ```
>
> This code results in memory unnecessarily being consumed because each time you create a form instance, you overwrite the previous instance referenced by Form1. Although you could refer to each instance of the form created through the Screen.Forms list, the practice shown in the preceding code is not recommended. Passing nil to the Create() constructor will result in no way to refer to the form instance pointer after the Form1 instance variable is overwritten.

The project ModState.dpr on the accompanying CD illustrates using both a modal and modeless form.

Managing a Form's Icons and Borders

TForm has a BorderIcons property, which is a set that may contain the following values: biSystemMenu, biMinimize, biMaximize, and biHelp. By setting any or all of these values to False, you can remove the system menu, the Maximize button, or the Minimize button from the form. All forms have the Windows 95/98 Close button.

You also can change the nonclient area of the form by changing the BorderStyle property. The BorderStyle property is defined as follows:

```
TFormBorderStyle = (bsNone, bsSingle, bsSizeable, bsDialog,
➥bsSizeToolWin, bsToolWindow);
```

The BorderStyle property gives forms the following characteristics:

bsDialog	Nonsizable border, Close button only.
bsNone	No border, nonsizable, no buttons.
bsSingle	Nonsizable border, all buttons available. If only one of the biMinimize or biMaximize buttons is set to False, both buttons appear on the form. However, the button set to False is disabled. If both are False, neither button appears on the form. If the biSystemMenu is False, no buttons appear on the form.
bsSizeable	Sizable border. All buttons available. The same circumstances exist for this option regarding buttons as with the bsSingle setting.

4

APPLICATION FRAMEWORKS AND DESIGN

`bsSizeToolWin`	Sizable border. Close button only and small caption bar.
`bsToolWindow`	Nonsizable border. Close button only and small caption bar.

> **NOTE**
>
> Changes to the `BorderIcon` and `BorderStyle` properties aren't reflected at design time. These changes happen at runtime only. This is also the case with other properties, most of which are found on `TForm`. The reason for this behavior is that it doesn't make sense to change the appearance of certain properties at design time. Take, for example, the `Visible` property. It is difficult to select an invisible control on the form when its `Visible` property is set to `False`.

STICKY CAPTIONS!

You might have noticed that none of the options mentioned allow you to create captionless, resizable forms. Although this isn't impossible, doing so requires a bit of trickery not yet covered. You must override the form's `CreateParams()` method and set the styles required for that window style. The following code snippet does this:

```
unit Nocapu;
interface
uses
  SysUtils, WinTypes, WinProcs, Messages, Classes,
  Graphics, Controls, Forms, Dialogs;
type
  TForm1 = class(TForm)
public
    { override CreateParams method }
    procedure CreateParams(var Params: TCreateParams); override;
end;
var
  Form1: TForm1;
implementation
{$R *.DFM}
procedure TForm1.CreateParams(var Params: TCreateParams);
begin
  inherited CreateParams(Params);  { Call the inherited Params }
  { Set the style accordingly }
  Params.Style := WS_THICKFRAME or WS_POPUP or WS_BORDER;
end;
end.
```

> You'll learn more about the `CreateParams()` method in Chapter 21, "Writing Delphi Custom Components."
>
> You can find an example of a sizable borderless form in the project `NoCaption.dpr` on the CD-ROM that accompanies this book. This demo also illustrates how to capture the `WM_NCHITTEST` message to enable moving the form without the caption by dragging the form.

Take a look at the `BrdrIcon.dpr` project on the CD-ROM. This project shows how you can change the `BorderIcon` and `BorderStyle` properties at runtime so that you see the visual effect. Listing 4.2 shows the main form for this project, which contains the relevant code.

LISTING 4.2. THE MAIN FORM FOR BorderStyle/BorderIcon PROJECT.

```
unit MainFrm;

interface

uses
  SysUtils, Windows, Messages, Classes, Graphics, Controls,
  Forms, Dialogs, StdCtrls, ExtCtrls;

type
  TMainForm = class(TForm)
    gbBorderIcons: TGroupBox;
    cbSystemMenu: TCheckBox;
    cbMinimize: TCheckBox;
    cbMaximize: TCheckBox;
    rgBorderStyle: TRadioGroup;
    cbHelp: TCheckBox;
    procedure cbMinimizeClick(Sender: TObject);
    procedure rgBorderStyleClick(Sender: TObject);
  end;

var
  MainForm: TMainForm;

implementation

{$R *.DFM}

procedure TMainForm.cbMinimizeClick(Sender: TObject);
var
```

continues

4

APPLICATION
FRAMEWORKS
AND DESIGN

LISTING 4.2. CONTINUED

```
  IconSet: TBorderIcons;  // Temp variable to hold values.
begin
  IconSet := [];  // Initialize to an empty set
  if cbSystemMenu.Checked then
    IconSet := IconSet + [biSystemMenu]; // Add the biSystemMenu button
  if cbMinimize.Checked then
    IconSet := IconSet + [biMinimize];   // Add the biMinimize button
  if cbMaximize.Checked then
    IconSet := IconSet + [biMaximize];   // Add the biMaximize button
  if cbHelp.Checked then
    IconSet := IconSet + [biHelp];

  BorderIcons := IconSet;                // Assign result to the form's
end;                                     // BorderIcons property.

procedure TMainForm.rgBorderStyleClick(Sender: TObject);
begin
  BorderStyle := TBorderStyle(rgBorderStyle.ItemIndex);
end;

end.
```

NOTE

Some properties in the Object Inspector affect the appearance of your form; others define behavioral aspects for your form. Experiment with each property that's unfamiliar. If you need to know more about a property, use the Delphi 4 help system to find additional information.

Form Reusability: Visual Form Inheritance

A useful feature of Delphi 4 is a concept known as *visual form inheritance*. In the first version of Delphi, you could create a form and save it as a template, but you didn't have the advantage of true *inheritance* (the capability to access the ancestor form's components, methods, and properties). By using inheritance, all descendant forms share the same code as their ancestor. The only overhead is the methods you add to your descendant forms. Therefore, you also gain the advantage of reducing your application's overall footprint. Another advantage is that changes made to the ancestor code are also applied to its descendants.

THE OBJECT REPOSITORY

Delphi 4 has a project management feature that allows programmers to share forms, dialog boxes, data modules, and project templates. This feature is called the *Object Repository*. By using the Object Repository, developers can share the various objects listed with developers of other projects. Additionally, the Object Repository allows developers to maximize code reuse by allowing them to inherit their objects from objects that exist in the Object Repository. Chapter 4 of the *Delphi 4 User's Guide* covers the Object Repository. It is a good idea to become familiar with this powerful feature.

TIP

In a network environment, you might want to share form templates with other programmers. This is possible by creating a shared repository. In the Environment Options dialog box (select Tools | Environment Options), you can specify the location of a shared repository. Each programmer must map to the same drive that points to this directory location. Then, whenever File | New is selected, Delphi will scan this directory for any shared items in the repository.

Inheriting from Another Form

Inheriting a form from another form is simple because it's completely built into the Delphi 4 environment. To create a form that descends from another form definition, you simply select File | New from Delphi's main menu, which invokes the New Items dialog box. This dialog box actually gives you a view of the objects that exist in the Object Repository (see the earlier sidebar "The Object Repository"). You then select the Forms page, which lists the forms that have been added to the Object Repository.

NOTE

You don't have to go through the Object Repository to get form inheritance. You can inherit from forms that are in your project. Select File | New and then select the Project page. From there, you can select an existing form in your project. Forms shown in the Project page are not in the Object Repository.

The various forms listed are those that have been added previously to the Object Repository. You'll notice that there are three options on how to include the form in your project: Copy, Inherit, and Use.

Choosing Copy adds an exact duplicate of the form to your project. If the form kept in the Object Repository is modified, this won't affect your copied form.

Choosing Inherit causes a new form class derived from the form you selected to be added to your project. This powerful feature allows you to inherit from the class in the Object Repository, so that changes made to the Object Repository's form are reflected by the form in your project as well. This is the option that most developers ought to select.

Choosing Use causes the form to be added to your project as if you had created it as part of the project. Changes you make to the item at design time will appear in all projects that also use the form and any projects that inherit from the form.

The `TApplication` Class

Every form-based Delphi 4 program contains a global variable, `Application`, of the type `TApplication`. `TApplication` encapsulates your program and performs many behind-the-scenes functions that enable your application to work correctly within the Windows environment. Some of these functions are creating your window class definition, creating the main window for your application, activating your application, processing messages, context-sensitive help, menu accelerator key processing, and VCL exception handling.

NOTE

Only form-based Delphi applications contain the global `Application` object. Applications such as console apps don't contain a VCL `Application` object.

You typically won't have to be concerned about the background tasks that `TApplication` performs. However, some situations might necessitate that you delve into the inner workings of `TApplication`.

Because the `TApplication` doesn't appear in the Object Inspector, you can't modify its properties there. But you can choose Project|Options and select the Application page, from which you can set some of the properties for `TApplication`. Mostly, you work with the `TApplication` instance, `Application`, at runtime; that is, you set its property values and assign event handlers to `Application` when the program is running.

TApplication's Properties

TApplication has several properties that you can access at runtime. The following sections discuss some of the properties specific to TApplication and how you can use them to change the default behavior of Application to enhance your project. TApplication's properties are also well documented in the Delphi 4 online help.

The TApplication.ExeName Property

The Application ExeName property holds the full path and filename for the project. Because this is a runtime, read-only property, you can't modify it. But you can read it— or even let your users know where they ran the application from. For example, the following line of code changes a main form's caption to the contents of ExeName:

```
Application.MainForm.Caption := Application.ExeName;
```

TIP

Use the ExtractFileName() function to retrieve the filename from a string containing the full path of a file:

```
ShowMessage(ExtractFileName(Application.ExeName));
```

Use ExtractFilePath() to retrieve the path of a full path string:

```
ShowMessage(ExtractFilePath(Application.ExeName));
```

Finally, use ExtractFileExt() to extract the extension of a filename:

```
ShowMessage(ExtractFileExt(Application.ExeName));
```

The TApplication.MainForm Property

In the preceding section, you saw how to access the MainForm property to change its Caption to reflect the ExeName for the application. MainForm points to a TForm so that you can access any TForm property through MainForm. You can also access properties that you add to your descendant forms, as long as you typecast MainForm accordingly:

```
(MainForm as TForm1).SongTitle := 'The Flood';
```

MainForm is a read-only property. You can specify which form in your application is the main form at design time by using the Forms page in the Project Options dialog box.

The TApplication.Handle Property

The Handle property is an HWND (a window handle, in Win32 API terms). The window handle is the owner of all top-level windows in your application. Handle is what makes

4

APPLICATION FRAMEWORKS AND DESIGN

modal dialogs modal over all windows of your application. You don't have to access `Handle` that often, unless you intend to take over the default behavior of the application in a way that isn't provided by Delphi. You may also refer to the `Handle` property when using Win32 API functions requiring the application's window handle. We'll discuss more about `Handle` later.

The `TApplication.Icon` and `TApplication.Title` Properties

The `Icon` property holds the icon that represents the application when your project is minimized. You can change the application's icon by providing another icon and assigning it to `Application.Icon`, as described in the later section "Adding Resources to Your Project."

The text that appears next to the icon in the application's task button on the Windows 95/98 taskbar is the application's `Title` property. If you're running Windows NT, this text appears just underneath the icon. Changing the title of the task button is simple: just make a string assignment to the `Title` property:

```
Application.Title := 'New Title';
```

Other Properties

The `Active` property is a read-only Boolean property that indicates whether the application has focus and is active.

The `ComponentCount` property indicates the number of components that `Application` contains. Mainly, these components are forms and a `THintWindow` instance if the `Application.ShowHint` property is `True`. `ComponentIndex` is always `-1` for any component that does not have an owner. Therefore, `TApplication.ComponentIndex` is always `-1`. This property mainly applies to forms and components on forms.

The `Components` property is an array of components that belong to the `Application`. There will be `TApplication.ComponentCount` items in the `Components` array. The following code shows how you would add the class names of all components referred to by `ComponentCount` to a `TListBox`:

```
var
  i: integer;
begin
  for i := 0 to Application.ComponentCount - 1 do
    ListBox1.Items.Add(Application.Components[i].ClassName);
end;
```

The `HelpFile` property contains the Windows help filename, which enables you to add online help to your application. It is used by `TApplication.HelpContext` and other help invocation methods.

The `TApplication.Owner` property is always `nil` because `TApplication` can't be owned by any other component.

The `ShowHint` property enables or disables the display of hints for the entire application. The `Application.ShowHint` property overrides the values of any other component's `ShowHint` property. Therefore, if `Application.ShowHint` is `False`, hints are not displayed for any component.

The `Terminated` property is `True` whenever the application has been terminated by closing the main form or by calling the `TApplication.Terminate()` method.

TApplication's Methods

`TApplication` has several methods with which you should be familiar. The following sections discuss some of the methods specific to `TApplication`.

The `TApplication.CreateForm()` Method

The `TApplication.CreateForm()` method is defined as follows:

```
procedure CreateForm(InstanceClass: TComponentClass; var Reference)
```

This method creates an instance of a form with the type specified by `InstanceClass` and assigns that instance to the `Reference` variable. Earlier, you saw how this method was called in the project's `.dpr` file. The code had the following line, which creates the instance of `Form1` of type `TForm1`:

```
Application.CreateForm(TForm1, Form1);
```

The line would have been created automatically by Delphi 4 if `Form1` appeared in the project's auto-create forms list. However, you can call this method elsewhere in your code if you're creating a form that doesn't appear in the auto-create list (in which case the form's instance wouldn't have been created automatically). This approach doesn't differ much from calling the form's own `Create()` method, except that `TApplication.CreateForm()` checks to see whether the `TApplication.MainForm` property is `nil`; if so, `CreateForm()` assigns the newly created form to `Application.MainForm`. Subsequent calls to `CreateForm()` don't affect this assignment. Typically, you don't call `CreateForm()`; you use a form's `Create()` method instead.

The `TApplication.HandleException()` Method

The `HandleException()` method is where the `TApplication` instance displays information about exceptions that occur in your project. This information is displayed with a standard exception message box defined by VCL. You can override this message box by attaching an event handler to the `Application.OnException` event, as shown in the later section "Overriding the Application's Exception Handling."

TApplication's `HelpCommand()`, `HelpContext()`, and `HelpJump()` Methods

The `HelpCommand()`, `HelpContext()`, and `HelpJump()` methods each provide a way for you to interface your projects with the Windows help system provided by the `WINHELP.EXE` program that ships with Windows. `HelpCommand()` allows you to call any of the WinHelp macro commands and macros defined in your help file. `HelpContext()` allows you to launch a help page in the help file specified by the `TApplication.HelpFile` property. The page displayed is based on the value of the `Context` parameter passed to `HelpContext()`. `HelpJump()` is much like `HelpContext()`, except that it takes a `JumpID` string parameter.

The `TApplication.ProcessMessages()` Method

`ProcessMessages()` causes your application to actively retrieve any messages that are waiting for it and then process them. This is useful when you have to perform a process within a tight loop and you don't want your code to prevent you from executing other code (such as processing an abort button). In contrast, `TApplication.HandleMessages()` puts the application into an idle state if there are no messages, whereas `ProcessMessages()` won't put it in an idle state. The `ProcessMessages()` method is used in Chapter 10, "Printing in Delphi."

The `TApplication.Run()` Method

Delphi 4 automatically places the `Run()` method within the project file's main block. You never have to call this method yourself, but you should know where it goes and what it does in case you ever have to modify the project file. Basically, `TApplication.Run()` first sets up an exit procedure for the project, which ensures that all components are freed when the project ends. It then enters a loop that calls the methods to process messages for the project until the application is terminated.

The `TApplication.ShowException()` Method

The `ShowException()` method simply takes an exception class as a parameter and displays a message box with information about that exception. This method comes in handy if you are overriding the `Application`'s exception handling method, as shown in the later section "Overriding the Application's Exception Handling."

Other Methods

`TApplication.Create()` creates the `Application` instance. This method is called internally by Delphi 4; you should never call it.

`TApplication.Destroy()` destroys the `TApplication` instance. This method is called internally by Delphi 4. You should never call this method.

`TApplication.MessageBox()` allows you to display a Windows `MessageBox`. However, this method doesn't require that you pass a window's handle, as the Windows `MessageBox()` function does.

`TApplication.Minimize()` places your application in a minimized state.

`TApplication.Restore()` restores your application to its previous size from a minimized or maximized state.

`TApplication.Terminate()` terminates the execution of your application. `Terminate()`, unlike `Halt()`, is an indirect call to `(PostQuitMessage)` resulting in a graceful shutdown of the application.

> **NOTE**
>
> Use the `TApplication.Terminate()` method to halt an application. `Terminate()` calls the Windows API function `PostQuitMessage()`, which posts a message to your application's message queue. VCL responds by properly freeing objects that have been created in your application. The `Terminate()` method is a clean way to stop your application's process. It's important to note that your application does not terminate at the call to `Terminate()`. Instead, it continues to run until the application returns to its message queue and retrieves the `WM_QUIT` message. `Halt()`, on the other hand, forcibly terminates your application without freeing any objects or shutting down gracefully. Execution does not return from a call to `Halt()`.

TApplication's Events

`TApplication` has several events to which you can add event handlers. These events are not accessible from the Object Inspector, like the events for the form or components on the Component Palette. To add an event handler to the `Application` variable, you must first define the handler as a method. Then you assign that method to the handler at runtime. You see a demonstration of this later in this chapter, when the code for the `Application.OnException` event is provided.

Table 4.1 lists the events associated with `TApplication`.

TABLE 4.1. TApplication EVENTS.

Event	Description
OnActivate	Occurs when the application becomes active; OnDeactivate occurs when the application stops being active (for example, when you switch to another application).
OnException	Occurs when an unhandled exception has occurred; you can add default processing for unhandled exceptions. OnException occurs if the exception makes it all the way up to the application object. Normally, you should allow exceptions to be handled by the default exception handler and not trapped by Application.OnException or lower code. If you must trap an exception, reraise it and make sure that the exception instance carries a full description of the situation so that the default exception handler can present useful information.
OnHelp	Occurs for any invocation of the help system, such as when F1 is pressed or when the following methods are called: HelpCommand(), HelpContext(), and HelpJump().
OnMessage	Enables you to process messages before they're dispatched to their intended controls. OnMessage gets to peek at all messages posted to all controls in the application. Exercise caution when using OnMessage because it could result in a bottleneck.
OnHint	Enables you to display hints associated with controls when the mouse is positioned over the control. An example of this is the status line hints.
OnIdle	Occurs when the application is switched into an idle state. OnIdle is not called continuously. Once in the idle state, an application will not wake up until it receives a message.

You work more with TApplication later in this chapter, as well as in other projects in other chapters.

NOTE

TApplication.OnIdle event is a handy way to perform certain processing when no user interaction is occurring. One common use for the OnIdle event handler is to update menus and speedbuttons based on the status of the application.

The TScreen Class

The TScreen class simply encapsulates the state of the screen on which your application runs. TScreen is not a component that you add to your Delphi 4 forms, nor do you create it dynamically during runtime. Delphi 4 automatically creates a TScreen global variable, called Screen, which you can access from within your application. The TScreen class contains several properties that you'll find useful. These properties are listed in Table 4.2.

TABLE 4.2. TScreen PROPERTIES.

Property	Meaning
ActiveControl	A read-only property that indicates which control on the screen has current focus. As focus shifts from one control to another, ActiveControl is assigned the newly focused control before the OnExit event of the control losing focus finishes.
ActiveForm	Indicates the form that has focus. This property is set when another form switches focus or when the Delphi 4 application gains focus from another application.
Cursor	The cursor shape global to the application. By default, this is set to crDefault. Each windowed component has its own Cursor property that may be modified. However, when the cursor is set to something other than crDefault, all other controls reflect that change until Screen.Cursor is set back to crDefault. Another way to look at this is Screen.Cursor = crDefault means "ask the control under the mouse what cursor should be displayed." Screen.Cursor <> crDefault means "don't ask."
Cursors	A list of all cursors available to the screen device.
DataModuleCount	Number of DataModules belonging to the application.
DataModules	A list of all DataModules belonging to the application.
FormCount	The number of available forms in the application.
Forms	A list of forms available to the application.
Fonts	A list of font names available to the screen device.
Height	The height of the screen device in pixels.
PixelsPerInch	Indicates the relative scale of the system font.
Width	The width of the screen device in pixels.

DEFINING A COMMON ARCHITECTURE—USING THE OBJECT REPOSITORY

Delphi makes it so easy to develop applications that you can get 60 percent into your application development before you realize that you should have spent more time up front on application architecture. A common problem with development is that developers are too anxious to begin coding before they spend the appropriate time really thinking about application design. This alone is one of the biggest contributors to project failure.

Thoughts on Application Architecture

This is not a book on architecture or object-oriented analysis and design. However, we strongly feel that this is one of the most important aspects of application development in addition to requirements, detail design, and everything else that constitutes the initial 80 percent of a product before coding begins. We listed some of our favorite references on topics such as object-oriented analysis in Appendix C, "Suggested Reading." It is in your best interest that you research this topic thoroughly before you roll your sleeves up and start coding.

A few examples of the many issues that come into play when considering application architecture are as follows:

- Does the architecture support code reuse?
- Is the system organized so that modules, objects, and so on are localized?
- Can changes more easily be made to the architecture?
- Are the user interface and back-end localized so that either can be replaced?
- Does the architecture support a team development effort; in other words, can team members easily work on separate modules without overlap?

These are just a few of the things to consider during development.

Volumes have been written on this topic alone, so we won't attempt to compete with that information. We do, however, hope that we've sparked an interest enough to make you learn about it if you aren't already an architecture guru. The following sections illustrate a simple method of architecting a common U/I for database application and how Delphi can help you do that.

Delphi's Inherent Architecture

You'll often hear that you don't have to be a component writer to be a Delphi developer. Although true, it's also true that if you're a component writer, you're a much better Delphi developer.

This is because component writers clearly understand the object model and architecture that Delphi applications inherit just by being Delphi applications. This means that component writers are better equipped to take advantage of this powerful and flexible model in their own applications. In fact, you've probably already heard that Delphi is written in

Delphi. Delphi is an example of an application written with the same inherent architecture that your applications can also use.

Even if you don't intend to write components, you'll be better off if you learn about their architecture anyway. Become thoroughly knowledgeable of the VCL, the Object Pascal model, and the Win32 operating system.

An Architecture Example

To demonstrate the power of form inheritance as well as the use of the Object Repository, you're going to define a common application architecture. The issues you're focusing on are code reusability, flexibility for change, consistency, and facility for team development.

The form class hierarchy, or rather, framework, consists of forms to be used specifically for database applications. These forms are typical of most database applications. The forms should be aware of the state of the database operation (edit, add, or browse). They should also contain the common controls used in performing these operations on a database table such as a toolbar and status bar whose displays and controls change accordingly depending on the form's state. Additionally, they should provide an event, which can be invoked whenever the form mode changes.

This framework should also enable a team to work on isolated parts of an application without having the entire application where there is likelihood of overlapping effort or changes being made to the same files by different programmers.

For now, this framework's hierarchy will contain three levels. This will be expanded on later in the book.

Table 4.3 describes the purpose for each form in the framework.

4

TABLE 4.3. DATABASE FORM FRAMEWORK.

Form Class	*Purpose*
`TChildForm = class(TForm)`	Provides the capability to be inserted as a child to another window.
`TDBModeForm = class(TChildForm)`	Is aware of a database state (browse, insert, edit) and contains an event to be invoked upon state change.
`TDBNavStatForm = class(TDBBaseForm)`	Typical database entry form that is aware of its state and contains the standard navigation bar and status bar to be used by all database applications.

The Child Form (`TChildForm`)

`TChildForm` is a base class for forms that can be launched as independent modal and modeless forms and can become child windows to any other window.

This capability makes it easy for a team of developers to work on separate pieces of an application apart from the overall application. It also provides a nice U/I feature in that the user can launch a form as a separate entity in an application, even though that might not be the normal method of interacting with that form. Listing 4.3 is the source to `TChildForm`. You'll find this and all other forms you place in the Object Repository on the `\OBJREPOS` directory on the CD.

LISTING 4.3. `TChildForm` SOURCE.

```
unit ChildFrm;

interface

uses
  Windows, Messages, SysUtils, Classes, Graphics, Controls,
  Forms, Dialogs, StdCtrls, ExtCtrls, Menus;

type

  TChildForm = class(TForm)
  private
    FAsChild: Boolean;
    FTempParent: TWinControl;
  protected
    procedure CreateParams(var Params: TCreateParams); override;
    procedure Loaded; override;
  public
    constructor Create(AOwner: TComponent); overload; override;
    constructor Create(AOwner: TComponent; AParent: TWinControl);
reintroduce; overload;

    // The method below must be overriden to return either the main menu
    // of the form, or nil.
    function GetFormMenu: TMainMenu; virtual; abstract;
    function CanChange: Boolean; virtual;
  end;

implementation

{$R *.DFM}
constructor TChildForm.Create(AOwner: TComponent);
begin
  FAsChild := False;
  inherited Create(AOwner);
end;
```

```
constructor TChildForm.Create(AOwner: TComponent; AParent: TWinControl);
begin
  FAsChild := True;
  FTempParent := aParent;
  inherited Create(AOwner);
end;

procedure TChildForm.Loaded;
begin
  inherited;
  if FAsChild then
  begin
    align := alClient;
    BorderStyle := bsNone;
    BorderIcons := [];
    Parent := FTempParent;
    Position := poDefault;
  end;
end;

procedure TChildForm.CreateParams(var Params: TCreateParams);
Begin
  Inherited CreateParams(Params);
  if FAsChild then
    Params.Style := Params.Style or WS_CHILD;
end;

function TChildForm.CanChange: Boolean;
begin
  Result := True;
end;

end.
```

This demonstrates a few techniques: first, how to use the overload extensions to the Object Pascal language and second, how to make a form a child of another window.

Providing a Second Constructor

You'll notice that you've declared two constructors for this child form. The first constructor declared is used when the form is created as a normal form. This is the constructor with one parameter. The second constructor, which takes two parameters, is declared as an overloaded constructor. You would use this constructor to create the form as a child window. The parent to the form is passed as the AParent parameter. Notice that you've used the reintroduce directive to suppress the warning you'll get about hiding the virtual constructor.

4

APPLICATION FRAMEWORKS AND DESIGN

The first constructor simply sets the FAsChild variable to False to ensure that the form is created normally. The second constructor sets the value to True and sets FTempParent to the AParent parameter. This value is used later as the parent of the child form in the Loaded() method.

Making a Form a Child Window

To make a form a child window, there are a few things that you need to do. First, you have to make sure that various property settings have been set, which you'll see is done programmatically in TChildForm.Loaded(). In Listing 4.3, you ensure that when the form becomes a child that it doesn't look like a dialog box. You do this by removing the border and any border icons. You also make sure that the form is client-aligned and set the parent to the window referred to by the FTempParent variable. If this form were going to be used as a child only, you could have made these settings at design time. However, this form will also be launched as a normal form, so you set these properties only if the FAsChild variable is True.

You also have to override the CreateParams() method to tell Windows to create the form as a child window. You do this by setting the WS_CHILD style in the Params.Style property.

This base form is not restricted to a database application. In fact, you can use it for any form that you want to have child window capabilities. You'll find a demo of this child form being used as both a normal form and as a child form in the ChildTest.dpr project found in the \Form Framework directory on the CD.

The Database Base Mode Form (TDBModeForm)

The TDBModeForm is a descendant of the TChildForm. Its purpose is to be aware of the state of a table (browse, insert, edit). This form also provides an event that occurs whenever the mode is changed.

Listing 4.4 shows the source code to the TDBModeForm.

LISTING 4.4. TDBModeForm.

```
unit DBModeFrm;

interface

uses
  Windows, Messages, SysUtils, Classes, Graphics, Controls, Forms,
  Dialogs, CHILDFRM;

type
```

```
    TFormMode = (fmBrowse, fmInsert, fmEdit);

    TDBModeForm = class(TChildForm)
    private
      FFormMode      : TFormMode;
      FOnSetFormMode : TNotifyEvent;
    protected
      procedure SetFormMode(AValue: TFormMode); virtual;
      function  GetFormMode: TFormMode; virtual;
    public
      property FormMode: TFormMode read GetFormMode write SetFormMode;
    published
      property OnSetFormMode: TNotifyEvent read FOnSetFormMode write
➥FOnSetFormMode;
    end;

var
  DBModeForm: TDBModeForm;

implementation

{$R *.DFM}

procedure TDBModeForm.SetFormMode(AValue: TFormMode);
begin
  FFormMode := AValue;
  if Assigned(FOnSetFormMode) then
    FOnSetFormMode(self);
end;

function TDBModeForm.GetFormMode: TFormMode;
begin
  Result := FFormMode;
end;

end.
```

The implementation of TDBModeForm is straightforward. Although you're using some techniques we haven't yet discussed, you should be able to follow what's happening here. First, you just defined the enumerated type, TFormMode, to represent the form's state. Then you provided the FormMode property and its read and write methods. The technique for creating the property and read/write methods is discussed further in Chapter 21, "Writing Delphi Custom Components."

A demo using TDBModeForm is in the project FormModeTest.DPR found in the \Form Framework directory on the CD.

The Database Navigation/Status Form (`TDBNavStatForm`)

`TDBNavStatForm` brings the bulk of the functionality of this framework. This form contains the common set of components to be used in our database applications. In particular, it has a navigation bar and status bar that automatically change based on the form's state. For example, you'll see that the Accept and Cancel buttons are initially disabled when the form is in the state of `fsBrowse`. However, when the user places the form in `fsInsert` or `fsEdit` state, the buttons become enabled. The status bar also displays the state the form is in.

Listing 4.5 shows the source code for the `TDBNavStatForm`. Notice that you've eliminated the component list from the listing. You'll see these if you load the demo project for this form.

LISTING 4.5. `TDBNavStatForm`.

```
unit DBNavStatFrm;

interface

uses
  Windows, Messages, SysUtils, Classes, Graphics, Controls, Forms,
  Dialogs, DBMODEFRM, ComCtrls, ToolWin, Menus, ExtCtrls, ImgList;

type
  TDBNavStatForm = class(TDBModeForm)
    { components not included in listing. }
    procedure sbAcceptClick(Sender: TObject);
    procedure sbInsertClick(Sender: TObject);
    procedure sbEditClick(Sender: TObject);
  private
    { Private declarations }
  protected
    procedure Setbuttons; virtual;
    procedure SetStatusBar; virtual;
    procedure SetFormMode(AValue: TFormMode); override;
  public
    constructor Create(AOwner: TComponent); overload; override;
    constructor Create(AOwner: TComponent; AParent: TWinControl);
➥overload;
    procedure SetToolBarParent(AParent: TWinControl);
    procedure SetStatusBarParent(AParent: TWinControl);
  end;

var
  DBNavStatForm: TDBNavStatForm;
```

```
implementation

{$R *.DFM}

{ TDBModeForm3 }

procedure TDBNavStatForm.SetFormMode(AValue: TFormMode);
begin
  inherited SetFormMode(AValue);
  SetButtons;
  SetStatusBar;
end;

procedure TDBNavStatForm.Setbuttons;

  procedure SetBrowseButtons;
  begin
    sbAccept.Enabled  := False;
    sbCancel.Enabled  := False;

    sbInsert.Enabled  := True;
    sbDelete.Enabled  := True;
    sbEdit.Enabled    := True;

    sbFind.Enabled    := True;
    sbBrowse.Enabled  := True;


    sbFirst.Enabled   := True ;
    sbPrev.Enabled    := True ;
    sbNext.Enabled    := True ;
    sbLast.Enabled    := True ;
  end;

  procedure SetInsertButtons;
  begin
    sbAccept.Enabled  := True;
    sbCancel.Enabled  := True;

    sbInsert.Enabled  := False;
    sbDelete.Enabled  := False;
    sbEdit.Enabled    := False;

    sbFind.Enabled    := False;
    sbBrowse.Enabled  := False;

    sbFirst.Enabled   := False;
    sbPrev.Enabled    := False;
```

continues

4

APPLICATION
FRAMEWORKS
AND DESIGN

LISTING 4.5. CONTINUED

```
    sbNext.Enabled    := False;
    sbLast.Enabled    := False;
  end;

  procedure SetEditButtons;
  begin
    sbAccept.Enabled  := True;
    sbCancel.Enabled  := True;

    sbInsert.Enabled  := False;
    sbDelete.Enabled  := False;
    sbEdit.Enabled    := False;

    sbFind.Enabled    := False;
    sbBrowse.Enabled  := True;

    sbFirst.Enabled   := False;
    sbPrev.Enabled    := False;
    sbNext.Enabled    := False;
    sbLast.Enabled    := False;
  end;

begin
  case FormMode of
    fmBrowse: SetBrowseButtons;
    fmInsert: SetInsertButtons;
    fmEdit:   SetEditButtons;
  end; { case }

end;

procedure TDBNavStatForm.SetStatusBar;
begin
  case FormMode of
    fmBrowse: stbStatusBar.Panels[1].Text := 'Browsing';
    fmInsert: stbStatusBar.Panels[1].Text := 'Inserting';
    fmEdit:   stbStatusBar.Panels[1].Text := 'Edit';
  end;

  mmiInsert.Enabled := sbInsert.Enabled;
  mmiEdit.Enabled   := sbEdit.Enabled;
  mmiDelete.Enabled := sbDelete.Enabled;
  mmiCancel.Enabled := sbCancel.Enabled;
  mmiFind.Enabled   := sbFind.Enabled;

  mmiNext.Enabled     := sbNext.Enabled;
  mmiPrevious.Enabled := sbPrev.Enabled;
  mmiFirst.Enabled    := sbFirst.Enabled;
  mmiLast.Enabled     := sbLast.Enabled;

end;
```

```
procedure TDBNavStatForm.sbAcceptClick(Sender: TObject);
begin
  inherited;
    FormMode := fmBrowse;
end;

procedure TDBNavStatForm.sbInsertClick(Sender: TObject);
begin
  inherited;
  FormMode := fmInsert;
end;

procedure TDBNavStatForm.sbEditClick(Sender: TObject);
begin
  inherited;
  FormMode := fmEdit;
end;

constructor TDBNavStatForm.Create(AOwner: TComponent);
begin
  inherited Create(AOwner);
  FormMode := fmBrowse;
end;

constructor TDBNavStatForm.Create(AOwner: TComponent; AParent:
➡TWinControl);
begin
  inherited Create(AOwner, AParent);
  FormMode := fmBrowse;
end;

procedure TDBNavStatForm.SetStatusBarParent(AParent: TWinControl);
begin
  stbStatusBar.Parent := AParent;
end;

procedure TDBNavStatForm.SetToolBarParent(AParent: TWinControl);
begin
  tlbNavigationBar.Parent := AParent;
end;

end.
```

4

APPLICATION
FRAMEWORKS
AND DESIGN

The event handlers for the various TToolButtons basically set the form to its appropriate state. This, in turn, invokes the SetFormMode() methods, which you've overridden to call the SetButtons() and SetStatusBar() methods. SetButtons() enables or disables the buttons accordingly based on the form's mode.

You'll notice that you've also provided two procedures to change the parent of the `TToolBar` and the `TStatusBar` components on the form. This functionality is provided so that when the form is invoked as a child window, you can set the parent of these components to the main form. When you run the demo provided in the \Form Framework directory on the CD, you'll see why this makes sense.

As stated earlier, the `TDBNavStatForm` inherits the functionality to be an independent form, as well as a child window. The demo invokes an instance of `TDBNavStatForm` with the following code:

```
procedure TMainForm.btnNormalClick(Sender: TObject);
var
  LocalNavStatForm: TNavStatForm;
begin
  LocalNavStatForm := TNavStatForm.Create(Application);
  try
    LocalNavStatForm.ShowModal;
  finally
    LocalNavStatForm.Free;
  end;
end;
```

The following code shows how to invoke the form as a child window:

```
procedure TMainForm.btnAsChildClick(Sender: TObject);
begin
  if not Assigned(FNavStatForm) then
  begin
    FNavStatForm := TNavStatForm.Create(Application, pnlParent);
    FNavStatForm.SetToolBarParent(self);
    FNavStatForm.SetStatusBarParent(self);
    mmMainMenu.Merge(FNavStatForm.mmFormMenu);
    FNavStatForm.Show;
    pnlParent.Height := pnlParent.Height - 1;
  end;
end;
```

This code not only invokes the form as a child to the `TPanel`, `pnlParent`, but also sets the form's `TToolBar` and `TStatusBar` to reside on the main form. Additionally, notice the call to the `TMainForm.mmMainMenu.Merge()`. This allows us to merge any menus that reside on the `TDBNavStatForm` instance with the `MainForm`'s main menu. Naturally, when you free the `TDBNavStatForm` instance, you must also call to `TMainForm.mmMainMenu.UnMerge()` as shown in the following code:

```
procedure TMainForm.btnFreeChildClick(Sender: TObject);
begin
  if Assigned(FNavStatForm) then
  begin
    mmMainMenu.UnMerge(FNavStatForm.mmFormMenu);
```

```
    FNavStatForm.Free;
    FNavStatForm := nil;
  end;
end;
```

Take a look at the demo provided on the CD of this form. Figure 4.1 shows this project with both the child form and independent `TDBNavStatForm` instances created. Notice that you've placed a `TImage` component on the form to better display the form as a child.

FIGURE 4.1.

`TDBNavStatForm`
*as a normal form
and as a child
window.*

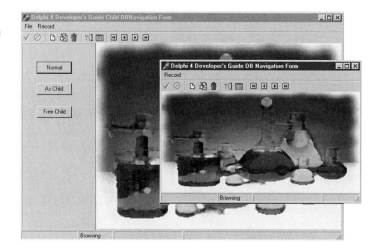

Later, you'll use and expand on this same framework to create a fully functional database application.

MISCELLANEOUS PROJECT MANAGEMENT ROUTINES

The projects that follow are a series of project management routines that have been helpful to many developers using Delphi 4.

Adding Resources to Your Project

Earlier, you learned that the `.res` file is the resource file for your application. You also learned what Windows resources are. You can add resources to your applications by creating a separate `.res` file to store your bitmaps, icons, cursors, and so on.

You must use a resource editor to build a `.res` file. After you create your `.res` file, you simply link it to your application by placing this statement in the application's `.dpr` file:

```
{$R MYFILE.RES}
```

This statement can be placed directly under the following statement, which links the resource file with the same name as the project file to your project:

```
{$R *.RES}
```

If you've done this correctly, you can then load resources from the .res file by using the `TBitmap.LoadFromResourceName()` or `TBitmap.LoadFromResourceID()` method. Listing 4.6 shows the technique for loading a bitmap, icon, and cursor from a resource (.res) file. You can find this project, `Resource.dpr`, on the CD-ROM that accompanies this book. Notice the API functions used here—`LoadIcon()` and `LoadCursor()`—are all documented in the Windows API help.

> **NOTE**
>
> The Windows API provides a function, `LoadBitmap()`, which will load a bitmap as the name implies. However, this function does not return a color palette and therefore does not work for loading 256 color bitmaps. Use `TBitmap.LoadFromResouceName()` or `TBitmap.LoadFromResouceID()` instead.

LISTING 4.6. EXAMPLES OF LOADING RESOURCES FROM AN .res FILE.

```
unit MainFrm;
interface
uses
  Windows, Forms, Controls, Classes, StdCtrls, ExtCtrls;

const
  crXHair = 1; // Declare a constant for the new cursor. This value
type           // must be a positive number. or less than -20.

  TMainForm = class(TForm)
    imgBitmap: TImage;
    btnChemicals: TButton;
    btnClear: TButton;
    btnChangeIcon: TButton;
    btnNewCursor: TButton;
    btnOldCursor: TButton;
    btnOldIcon: TButton;
    btnAthena: TButton;
    procedure btnChemicalsClick(Sender: TObject);
    procedure btnClearClick(Sender: TObject);
    procedure btnChangeIconClick(Sender: TObject);
    procedure btnNewCursorClick(Sender: TObject);
    procedure btnOldCursorClick(Sender: TObject);
    procedure btnOldIconClick(Sender: TObject);
    procedure btnAthenaClick(Sender: TObject);
  end;
```

```
var
  MainForm: TMainForm;

implementation

{$R *.DFM}

procedure TMainForm.btnChemicalsClick(Sender: TObject);
begin
  { Load the bitmap from the resource file. The bitmap must be
    specified in all CAPS! }
  imgBitmap.Picture.Bitmap.LoadFromResourceName(hInstance, 'CHEMICAL');
end;

procedure TMainForm.btnClearClick(Sender: TObject);
begin
  imgBitmap.Picture.Assign(nil); // Clear the image
end;

procedure TMainForm.btnChangeIconClick(Sender: TObject);
begin
  { Load the icon from the resource file. The icon must be
    specified in all CAPS! }
  Application.Icon.Handle := LoadIcon(hInstance, 'SKYLINE');
end;

procedure TMainForm.btnNewCursorClick(Sender: TObject);
begin
  { Assign the new cursor to the Screen's Cursor array }
  Screen.Cursors[crXHair] := LoadCursor(hInstance, 'XHAIR');
  Screen.Cursor := crXHair;  // Now change the cursor
end;

procedure TMainForm.btnOldCursorClick(Sender: TObject);
begin
  // Change back to default cursor
  Screen.Cursor := crDefault;
end;

procedure TMainForm.btnOldIconClick(Sender: TObject);
begin
  { Load the icon from the resource file. The icon must be
    specified in all CAPS! }
  Application.Icon.Handle := LoadIcon(hInstance, 'DELPHI');
end;

procedure TMainForm.btnAthenaClick(Sender: TObject);
begin
  { Load the bitmap from the resource file. The bitmap must be
    specified in all CAPS! }
  imgBitmap.Picture.Bitmap.LoadFromResourceName(hInstance, 'ATHENA');
end;

end.
```

4

APPLICATION
FRAMEWORKS
AND DESIGN

Changing the Screen's Cursor

Probably one of the most commonly used `TScreen` properties is the `Cursor` property, which enables you to change the global cursor for the application. For example, the following code changes the current cursor to an hourglass to indicate that users must wait while a lengthy process executes:

```
Screen.Cursor := crHourGlass
{ Do some lengthy process }
Screen.Cursor := crDefault;
```

`crHourGlass` is a predefined constant that indexes into the `Cursors` array. There are other cursor constants, such as `crBeam` and `crSize`. The existing cursor values range from 0 to -20 (`crDefault` to `crHelp`). Look in the online help for the `Cursors` property to see a list of all available cursors. You can assign these values to `Screen.Cursor` when necessary.

You also can create your own cursors and add them to the `Cursors` property array. To do this, you must first define a constant with a value that doesn't conflict with the already available cursors. Predefined cursor values are from –20 to 0. Application cursors should only use positive ID numbers. All negative cursor ID numbers are reserved by Borland.

```
crCrossHair := 1;
```

You can use any resource editor (such as the Image Editor that ships with Delphi 4) to create your custom cursor. You must save the cursor into a resource (`.res`) file. One important point: You must give your `.res` file a different name than that of your project. Remember that Delphi 4 creates a `.res` file of the same name as your project whenever you compile your project. You don't want Delphi 4 to overwrite the cursor you create. When you compile your project, make sure that the `.res` file is in the same directory as your source files, so that Delphi 4 will link the cursor resource with your application. You tell Delphi 4 to link the `.res` file by placing a statement such as the following into the application's `.dpr` file:

```
{$R CrossHairRes.RES}
```

Finally, you must add the following lines of code to load the cursor, add it to the `Cursors` property, and then switch to that cursor:

```
procedure TMainForm.FormCreate(Sender: TObject);
begin
  Screen.Cursors[crCrossHair] := LoadCursor (hInstance, 'CROSSHAIR');
  Screen.Cursor := crCrossHair;
end;
```

Here you use the `LoadCursor()` Win32 API function to load the cursor. `LoadCursor()` takes two parameters: an instance handle to the module from which you want to get the cursor and the name of the cursor as specified in the `.res` file. Make sure to write the cursor name in the file in FULL CAPS!

`hInstance` refers to the application currently running. Next, assign the value returned from `LoadCursor()` to the `Cursors` property at the location specified by `crCrossHair`, which was previously defined. Finally, assign the current cursor to `Screen.Cursor`.

For an example, locate the project `CrossHair.dpr` on the CD. This project loads and changes to the crosshair cursor created here and placed in the file `CrossHairRes.res`.

You might also want to invoke the Image Editor by selecting Tools | Image Editor and opening the `CrossHairRes.res` file to see how the cursor was created.

Preventing Multiple Instances of a Form from Being Created

If you use `Application.CreateForm()` or `TForm.Create()` in your code to create a form instance, it's a good idea to ensure that no instance of the form is being held by the `Reference` parameter (as described in the earlier section "The `TForm` Class"). The following code fragment shows this:

```
begin
  if not Assigned(SomeForm) then begin
    Application.CreateForm(TSomeForm, SomeForm);
    try
      SomeForm.ShowModal;
    finally
      SomeForm.Free;
      SomeForm := nil;
    end;
  end
  else
    SomeForm.ShowModal;
end;
```

In this code, it's necessary to assign `nil` to the `SomeForm` variable after it has been destroyed. Otherwise, the `Assigned()` method doesn't function properly, and the method fails. This wouldn't work for a modeless form, however. With modeless forms, you can't determine in code when the form is going to be destroyed. Therefore, you must make the `nil` assignment from within the `OnDestroy` event handler of the form being destroyed. This method was described earlier in this chapter.

Adding Code to the `.dpr` File

You can place code in the project's `.dpr` file before you launch your main form. Such code can be initialization code, a splash screen, database initialization—anything you

4

APPLICATION
FRAMEWORKS
AND DESIGN

deem necessary before the main form is displayed. You also have the opportunity to terminate the application before the main form comes up. Listing 4.7 shows a `.dpr` file that prompts the user for a password before granting access to the application. This project is also saved on the CD-ROM as `Initalize.dpr`.

LISTING 4.7. THE `Initialize.dpr` FILE, SHOWING PROJECT INITIALIZATION.

```
program Initalize;

uses
  Forms,
  Dialogs,
  Controls,
  MainFrm in 'MainFrm.pas' {MainForm};

{$R *.RES}

var
  Password: String;
begin
  if InputQuery('Password', 'Enter your password', PassWord) then
    if Password = 'D4DG' then
    begin
      // Other initialization routines can go here.
      Application.CreateForm(TMainForm, MainForm);
    Application.Run;
    end
    else
      MessageDlg('Incorrect Password, terminating program', mtError,
➥[mbok], 0);
end.
```

Overriding the Application's Exception Handling

The Win32 system has a powerful error-handling capability—exceptions. By default, whenever an exception occurs in your project, the `Application` instance automatically handles that exception by displaying to the user a standard error box.

As you build larger applications, you'll start to define exception classes of your own. Perhaps the Delphi 4 default exception handling will no longer suit your needs because you have to perform special processing on a specific exception. In such cases, it will be necessary to override `TApplication`'s default exception handling and replace it with your own custom routine.

You saw that `TApplication` has an `OnException` event handler to which you can add code. When an exception occurs, this event handler is called. There you can perform your special processing so that the default exception message doesn't show.

However, recall that the TApplication object's properties aren't editable from the Object Inspector. You must assign a procedure to those properties at runtime.

> **NOTE**
>
> Event handlers such as OnException, OnClick, and OnCreate are really just pointers to procedures. Actually, there's a little more to them than that. For now, consider them pointers to procedures to which you can assign object methods.

To assign a method to the application's OnException event handler, you must define a method of the type TExceptionEvent (a special procedure definition applicable to the exception event handler). Don't worry about the definition of this procedure for now; you learn about event handlers later in this book. For now, think of it as a procedural pointer. After this procedure has been defined, you just assign it to the application's OnException event handler as shown here:

```
Application.OnException := MainForm.AppOnException;
```

You can do this in the project file after the main form has been created. After this is done, whenever an exception occurs, Application checks to see whether OnException points to anything. If it does, Application calls that event handler instead of performing its own exception handling routine.

Listings 4.8 and 4.9 show you what you need to do to override the application's default exception handling. Listing 4.9 is the project file where a method AppOnException is assigned to the Application.OnException event.

LISTING 4.8. MAIN FORM FOR EXCEPTION OVERRIDE DEMO.

```
unit MainFrm;

interface

uses
  SysUtils, Windows, Messages, Classes, Graphics, Controls,
  Forms, Dialogs, StdCtrls;

type

  ENotSoBadError = class(Exception);
  EBadError      = class(Exception);
  ERealBadError  = class(Exception);
```

continues

4

LISTING 4.8. CONTINUED

```
TMainForm = class(TForm)
    btnNotSoBad: TButton;
    btnBad: TButton;
    btnRealBad: TButton;
    procedure btnNotSoBadClick(Sender: TObject);
    procedure btnBadClick(Sender: TObject);
    procedure btnRealBadClick(Sender: TObject);
  public
    { Define a procedure of the type TExceptionEvent }
    procedure AppOnException(Sender: TObject; E: Exception);
  end;

var
  MainForm: TMainForm;

implementation

{$R *.DFM}

procedure TMainForm.AppOnException(Sender: TObject; E: Exception);
var
  rslt: Boolean;
begin
  if E is EBadError then begin
  { Show a custom message box and prompt for application termination. }
    rslt := MessageDlg(Format('%s %s %s %s %s', ['An', E.ClassName,
        'exception has occured.', E.Message, 'Quit App?']),
        mtError, [mbYes, mbNo], 0) = mrYes;
    if rslt then
      Application.Terminate;
  end
  else if E is ERealBadError then begin // Show a custom message
                                        // and terminate the application.
    MessageDlg(Format('%s %s %s %s %s', ['An', E.ClassName,
        'exception has occured.', E.Message, 'Quitting Application']),
        mtError, [mbOK], 0);
    Application.Terminate;
  end
  else // Perform default exception handling
    Application.ShowException(E);
end;

procedure TMainForm.btnNotSoBadClick(Sender: TObject);
begin
  raise ENotSoBadError.Create('This isn''t so bad!');
end;

procedure TMainForm.btnBadClick(Sender: TObject);
begin
```

```
    raise EBadError.Create('This is bad!');
end;

procedure TMainForm.btnRealBadClick(Sender: TObject);
begin
  raise ERealBadError.Create('This is real bad!');
end;

end.
```

LISTING 4.9. PROJECT FILE FOR EXCEPTION OVERRIDE DEMO.

```
program OnException;

uses
  Forms,
  MainFrm in 'MainFrm.pas' {MainForm};

{$R *.RES}

begin
  Application.Initialize;
  Application.CreateForm(TMainForm, MainForm);
  Application.OnException := MainForm.AppOnException;
  Application.Run;
end.
```

In Listing 4.8, you create three `Exception` descendants. Then the `MainForm.AppOnException()` method (which is used as the `Application.OnException` event handler) uses RTTI to check the type of exception that occurred and performs special processing based on the exception type. The comments in the code discuss the process. You'll also find the project that uses these routines, `OnException.dpr`, on the CD-ROM accompanying this book.

4

> **TIP**
>
> If the Stop on Delphi Exceptions check box is selected in the Language Exceptions page of the Debugger Options dialog box (accessed by selecting Tools | Debugger Options), Delphi 4's IDE debugger reports the exception in its own dialog box before your application has a chance to handle the exception. Although useful for debugging, having this check box selected can be annoying when you want to see how your project handles exceptions. Disable the option to make your project run normally.

Displaying a Splash Screen

Suppose that you want a splash screen for your project, much like the Delphi 4 splash screen. This form can display when you launch your application and can stay visible while your application initializes. Displaying a splash screen is actually simple. Following are the initial steps to create a splash screen:

1. After creating your application's main form, create another form to represent the splash screen. Call this form SplashForm.

2. Use the Project | Options menu to ensure that SplashForm is not in the auto-create list.

3. Assign bsNone to SplashForm's BorderStyle property and [ ] to its BorderIcons property.

4. Place a TImage component onto SplashForm and assign alClient to the image's Align property.

5. Load a bitmap into the TImage component by selecting its Picture property.

Now that you've designed the splash screen, you only have to edit the project's .dpr file to display it. Listing 4.10 shows the project file (.dpr) for which the splash screen is displayed. You'll find this project, Splash.dpr, on the accompanying CD.

LISTING 4.10. A .dpr FILE WITH A SPLASH SCREEN.

```
program splash;

uses
  Forms,
  MainFrm in 'MainFrm.pas' {MainForm},
  SplashFrm in 'SplashFrm.pas' {SplashForm};

{$R *.RES}
begin
  Application.Initialize;
  { Create the splash screen }
  SplashForm := TSplashForm.Create(Application);
  SplashForm.Show;   // Display the splash screen
  SplashForm.Update; // Update the splash screen to ensure it gets drawn

  { This while loop simply uses the TTimer component on the SplashForm
    to simulate a lengthy process. }
  while SplashForm.tmMainTimer.Enabled do
    Application.ProcessMessages;

  Application.CreateForm(TMainForm, MainForm);
  SplashForm.Hide;   // Hide the splash screen
```

```
  SplashForm.Free;   // Free the splash screen
  Application.Run;
end.
```

Notice the while loop:

```
while SplashForm.tmMainTimer.Enabled do
    Application.ProcessMessages;
```

This is simply a way to simulate a long process. A TTimer component was placed on the SplashForm, and its Interval property was set to 3000. When the OnTimer event of the TTimer component occurs, after about three seconds it executes the following line:

```
tmMainTimer.Enabled := False;
```

which will cause the while loop's condition to be False and will jump execution out of the loop.

Minimizing Form Size

To illustrate how to suppress or control form sizing, we've created a project whose main form has a blue background and a panel onto which components are placed. When the user resizes the form, the panel remains centered. The form also prevents the user from shrinking the form smaller than its panel. Listing 4.11 shows the form's unit source code.

LISTING 4.11. THE SOURCE CODE FOR THE TEMPLATE FORM.

```
unit BlueBackFrm;

interface

uses
  SysUtils, Windows, Messages, Classes, Graphics, Controls, Forms,
Dialogs,
  StdCtrls, Buttons, ExtCtrls;

type
  TBlueBackForm = class(TForm)
    pnlMain: TPanel;
    bbtnOK: TBitBtn;
    bbtnCancel: TBitBtn;
    procedure FormResize(Sender: TObject);
  private
    Procedure CenterPanel;
    { Create a message handler for the WM_WINDOWPOSCHANGING message }
    procedure WMWindowPosChanging(var Msg: TWMWindowPosChanging);
```

4

APPLICATION FRAMEWORKS AND DESIGN

continues

LISTING 4.11. CONTINUED

```
        message WM_WINDOWPOSCHANGING;
  end;

var
  BlueBackForm: TBlueBackForm;

implementation
uses Math;
{$R *.DFM}

procedure TBlueBackForm.CenterPanel;
{ This procedure centers the main panel horizontally and
  vertically inside the form's client area
}
begin
  { Center horizontally }
  if pnlMain.Width < ClientWidth then
    pnlMain.Left := (ClientWidth - pnlMain.Width) div 2
  else
    pnlMain.Left := 0;

  { Center vertically }
  if pnlMain.Height < ClientHeight then
    pnlMain.Top := (ClientHeight - pnlMain.Height) div 2
  else
    pnlMain.Top := 0;
end;

procedure TBlueBackForm.WMWindowPosChanging(var Msg:
➡TWMWindowPosChanging);
var
  CaptionHeight: integer;
begin
  { Calculate the caption height }
  CaptionHeight := GetSystemMetrics(SM_CYCAPTION);
  { This procedure does not take into account the width and
    height of the form's frame. You can use
    GetSystemMetrics() to obtain these values. }


  // Prevent window from shrinking smaller then MainPanel's width
  Msg.WindowPos^.cx := Max(Msg.WindowPos^.cx, pnlMain.Width+20);

  // Prevent window from shrinking smaller then MainPanel's width
  Msg.WindowPos^.cy := Max(Msg.WindowPos^.cy,
➡pnlMain.Height+20+CaptionHeight);

  inherited;
end;
```

```
procedure TBlueBackForm.FormResize(Sender: TObject);
begin
  CenterPanel; // Center MainPanel when the form is resized.
end;

end.
```

This form illustrates capturing Windows messages, specifically the WM_WINDOWPOSCHANG-ING message, which occurs whenever the window size is about to be changed. This is an opportune time to prevent take over the resizing of a window. Chapter 5, "Understanding Messages," will delve further into Windows messages. This demo can be found in the project `TempDemo.dpr` on the CD.

Running a Formless Project

The form is the focal point of all Delphi 4 applications. However, nothing prevents you from creating an application that has no form. The `.dpr` file is nothing more than a program file that "uses" units that define the forms and other objects. This program file can certainly perform other programming processes that require no form. To do this, simply create a new project and remove the main form from the project by selecting File | Remove From Project. Your DPR file will look like the following code:

```
program Project1;
uses
 Forms;
{$R *.RES}
begin
  Application.Run;
end.
```

In fact, you can even remove the `uses` clause and the call to `Application.Run`:

```
program Project1;
begin
end.
```

This is a rather useless project, but keep in mind that you can place whatever you want in the `begin..end` block, which would be the starting point of a Win32 console application.

Exiting Windows

One reason you might want to exit Windows from an application is that your application has made some system configuration changes that don't go into effect until the user restarts Windows. Rather than have the user perform that task through Windows, your application can ask the user whether she want to exit Windows; the application can then take care of the dirty work. Keep in mind, however, that requiring a system restart is considered bad form and should be avoided.

Exiting Windows requires the use of one of two Windows API functions: `ExitWindows()` or `ExitWindowsEx()`.

The `ExitWindows()` function is a carryover from 16-bit Windows. In that previous version of Windows, you could specify various options that allowed you to reboot Windows after exiting. However, in Win32, this function just logs the current user out of Windows and enables another user to log on to the next Windows session.

`ExitWindows()` has been replaced by the new function `ExitWindowsEx()`. With this function, you can log off, shut down Windows, or shut down Windows and restart the system (reboot). Listing 4.12 shows the use of both functions.

LISTING 4.12. EXITING WINDOWS USING `ExitWindows()` OR `ExitWindowsEx()`.

```
unit MainFrm;

interface

uses
  SysUtils, Windows, Messages, Classes, Graphics, Controls, Forms,
  Dialogs, StdCtrls, ExtCtrls;

type
  TMainForm = class(TForm)
    btnExit: TButton;
    rgExitOptions: TRadioGroup;
    procedure btnExitClick(Sender: TObject);
  end;

var
  MainForm: TMainForm;

implementation

{$R *.DFM}

procedure TMainForm.btnExitClick(Sender: TObject);
begin
  case rgExitOptions.ItemIndex of
    0: Win32Check(ExitWindows(0, 0)); // Exit and log on as a
                                      // different user.
    1: Win32Check(ExitWindowsEx(EWX_REBOOT, 0));  // Exit/Reboot
    2: Win32Check(ExitWindowsEx(EWX_SHUTDOWN, 0));// Exit to Power Off
    // Exit/Log off/Log on as different user
```

```
   3: Win32Check(ExitWindowsEx(EWX_LOGOFF, 0));
  end;
end;

end.
```

Listing 4.12 uses the value of a radio button to determine which Windows exit option to use. The first option uses `ExitWindows()` to log the user off and restart Windows, asking the user to log on.

The remaining options use the `ExitWindowsEx()` function. The second option exits Windows and reboots the system. The third option exits Windows and shuts down the system so that the user can turn off the computer. The fourth option performs the same task as the first, except that it uses the `ExitWindowsEx()` function.

Both `ExitWindows()` and `ExitWindowsEx()` return `True` if the function is successful and `False` if otherwise. You can use the `Win32Check()` function from `SysUtils.pas` that calls the Win32 API function `GetLastError()` and displays the proper error string in the event of an error.

> **NOTE**
>
> If you are running Windows NT, the `ExitWindowsEx()` function will not shut down the system; this requires a special privilege. You must use the Win32 API function `AdjustTokenPrivleges()` to enable the `SE_SHUTDOWN_NAME` privilege. More information on this topic can be found in the Win32 online help.

You'll find an example of this code in the project `ExitWin.dpr` on the CD accompanying this book.

Preventing Windows Shutdown

Shutting down Windows is one thing, but what if another application performs the same task—that is, calls `ExitWindowsEx()`—while you're editing a file and haven't yet saved the file? Unless you somehow capture the exit request, you risk losing valuable data. It's simple to capture the exit request. All that's required is that you process the `OnCloseQuery` event for the main form in your application. In that event handler, you can place code similar to the following:

```
procedure TMainForm.FormCloseQuery(Sender: TObject; var CanClose:
➥Boolean);
begin
```

```
  if MessageDlg('Shutdown?', mtConfirmation, mbYesNoCancel, 0) = mrYes
then
    CanClose := True
  else
    CanClose := False;
end;
```

By setting `CanClose` to `False`, you tell Windows not to shut down. Another option is to set `CanClose` to `True` only after prompting the user to save a file if necessary. You'll find this demonstrated in the project `NoClose.dpr` on the accompanying CD.

NOTE

If running a formless project, you must subclass the application's window procedure and capture the `WM_QUERYENDSESSION` message that's sent to each application running whenever `ExitWindows()` or `ExitWindowsEx()` is called from any application. If the application returns a nonzero value from this message, that application can end successfully. The application should return zero to prevent Windows from shutting down. You learn more about processing Windows messages in Chapter 5.

THE WINDOWS 95 LOGO REQUIREMENTS

Applications may qualify to license the "Designed for Microsoft Windows 95" logo if certain requirements have been met. Licensing this logo helps users identify your application as one compatible with Windows 95. It also tells users that your software is written to take advantage of the powerful features offered by Windows 95, rather than just run under the Windows 95 operating system. This is important to first-time computer or software users. The following sections outline the requirements for the logo eligibility.

When Do Logo Requirements Apply?

Logo requirements apply to applications, personal computer systems, and hardware and peripheral devices. This chapter is concerned only with the requirements applicable to applications (because that's the focus of this book). For information on the additional requirements, contact Microsoft for an updated list or refer to *Programmer's Guide to Microsoft Windows 95*, published by Microsoft. This information is also contained in the latest release of the Microsoft Developer's Network CD-ROM.

TIP

You'll find a demo Windows 95 logo application in the Projects page of the Object Repository.

Is it necessary that your application qualify for the Windows 95 logo? Absolutely not. However, the intent is to develop applications with interfaces and behaviors consistent throughout the Windows environment. If your application meets these guidelines, your users will find it easier to learn your application if they have experience using other Windows applications. Understandably, what the guidelines promote doesn't always apply to what your application must do; in these cases, it's necessary to go against the rules.

Four types of programs can qualify for the Windows 95 logo:

- *File-based.* Those applications with File Open, Save, and Close menu options.

- *Full-screen applications.* Applications that aren't windowed and can't be minimized within the Windows environment. Such applications include educational and game applications.

- *Utility applications.* Applications such as disk management, virus scanners, system utilities, and so on.

- *Development applications.* Applications or tools used for developing Windows applications such as compilers, linkers, and interpreters.

The following sections describe the requirements for the first three application types; requirements for compilers and linkers don't apply in this book.

Requirements That Apply to All Applications

Five requirements apply to each of the four application types listed in the preceding section. These requirements are as follows:

1. The application must use the Win32 API and be compiled with a 32-bit compiler that generates the correct *Portable Executable* (*PE*) format. The Delphi 4 compiler generates executables of this format.

2. The application must support the Windows 95 shell/user interface. The following requirements must be met:

    - Registers 16×16 pixel and 32×32 pixel icons for file types used in the application, as well as the application's icon.

    - Follows the guidelines presented in *The Windows Interface Guidelines for Software Design*, published by Microsoft Press.

    - Uses the system-defined dialog boxes and controls.

    - Uses the system-defined colors.

    - Mouse button 2 is used only for context menu support. Any other use of this button doesn't meet the requirements.

- Uses the appropriate Windows 95 installation guidelines. By following these guidelines, your applications become visible on the shell. The installation should make use of the Registry where appropriate and should avoid making entries in the WIN.INI or SYSTEM.INI file.

3. The application should be tested on both Windows 95 and Windows NT. If the application is targeted for one platform or the other, it must degrade gracefully to the platform for which it wasn't targeted. The application must run successfully under both operating systems unless architectural differences prevent it from doing so.

4. Support for long filenames is required. The application must use these filenames in the title bars and other controls. The application must not display the file's extension when used within the application.

NOTE

Delphi's file-handling routines all support long filenames.

---

5. The application must be Plug-and-Play-aware. It must know how to respond to messages that result from adding or removing a new device.

Requirements for File-Based Applications

The following requirements apply to file-based applications:

1. Support for the Universal Naming Convention (UNC) for pathnames. By using the UNC, your users can browse and open documents on a network without having to know the file's network path.

NOTE

Delphi's file-handling routines all support the Universal Naming Convention.

---

2. Support for OLE containers and objects. OLE drag and drop, automation, and compound files are also requirements.

3. The application must be able to send mail using the Messaging Application Programming Interface (MAPI) or the Common Messaging Call (CMC) API.

Requirements for Utility-Based Applications

The following requirements apply to the utility-based applications, such as virus protection, file utilities, and so on:

1. The application must use the Win32 API and be compiled with a 32-bit compiler that generates the correct Portable Executable (PE) format. Exceptions to this rule are those utility applications that perform exclusive file-locking functions, interrupts, and components that interface with 16-bit drivers.

2. Supports the Windows 95 shell/user interface. The following requirements must be met:

   • Registers 16×16 pixel and 32×32 pixel icons for file types used in the application, as well as the application's icon.

   • Follows the guidelines presented in *The Windows Interface Guidelines for Software Design*, published by Microsoft Press.

   • Uses the system-defined dialog boxes and controls.

   • Uses the system-defined colors.

   • Mouse button 2 is used only for context menu support. Any other use of this button doesn't meet the requirements.

   • Uses the appropriate Windows 95 installation guidelines. By following these guidelines, your applications become visible on the shell. The installation should make use of the Registry where appropriate and should avoid making entries in the WIN.INI or SYSTEM.INI file.

3. The application should be tested on both Windows 95 and Windows NT. If the application is targeted for one or the other platform, it must degrade gracefully to the platform for which it wasn't targeted. The application must run successfully under both operating systems. An exception to this rule is when the utilities are platform-specific.

4. Support for long filenames is required. The application must use these filenames in the title bars and other controls. The application must not display the file's extension when used within the application.

5. Plug-and-Play and file-based application requirements are recommended by Microsoft but not required. However, support for the UNC *is* required if the utility software accesses networked files.

4

APPLICATION
FRAMEWORKS
AND DESIGN

SUMMARY

This chapter focuses on project management techniques and architectural issues. It discusses the key components that make up most Delphi 4 projects: `TForm`, `TApplication`, and `TScreen`. We demonstrated how you might start designing your applications by first developing a common architecture. The chapter also shows various useful routines for your application. Finally, it discusses the requirements you must follow if your application is to qualify for the Windows 95 logo.

UNDERSTANDING MESSAGES

IN THIS CHAPTER

Although VCL components expose many Win32 messages via Object Pascal events, it's still essential that you, the Win32 programmer, understand how the Windows message system works.

As a Delphi applications programmer, you'll find that the events surfaced by VCL will suit most of your needs; only occasionally will you have to delve into the world of Win32 message handling. As a Delphi component developer, however, you and messages will become very good friends because you have to directly handle many Windows messages and then invoke events corresponding to those messages.

WHAT IS A MESSAGE?

A *message* is a notification of some occurrence sent by Windows to an application. Clicking a mouse button, resizing a window, or pressing a key on the keyboard, for example, causes Windows to send a message to an application notifying the program of what occurred.

A message manifests itself as a *record* passed to an application by Windows. That record contains information such as what type of event occurred and additional information specific to the message. The message record for a mouse-button click message, for example, contains the mouse coordinates at the time the button was pressed. The record type passed from Windows to the application is called a TMsg. TMsg is defined in the Windows unit as shown in the following code:

```
type
  TMsg = packed record
    hwnd: HWND;       // the handle of the Window for which the message is
                      // intended
    message: UINT;    // the message constant identifier
    WParam: WPARAM;   // 32 bits of additional message-specific information
    LParam: LPARAM;   // 32 bits of additional message-specific information
    time: DWORD;      // the time that the message was created
    pt: TPoint;       // the position of the mouse cursor when the message
                      // was created
  end;
```

WHAT'S IN A MESSAGE?

Does the information in a message record look like Greek to you? If so, here's a little insight to what's what:

hwnd   The 32-bit window handle of the window for which the message is intended. The window can be almost any type of screen object because Win32 maintains window handles for most visual objects (windows, dialog boxes, buttons, edits, and so on).

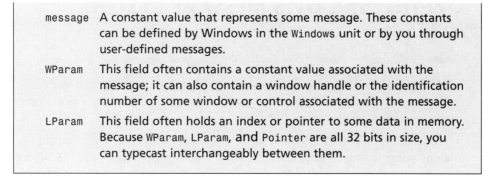

message	A constant value that represents some message. These constants can be defined by Windows in the `Windows` unit or by you through user-defined messages.
WParam	This field often contains a constant value associated with the message; it can also contain a window handle or the identification number of some window or control associated with the message.
LParam	This field often holds an index or pointer to some data in memory. Because `WParam`, `LParam`, and `Pointer` are all 32 bits in size, you can typecast interchangeably between them.

TYPES OF MESSAGES

The Win32 API predefines a constant for each Windows message. These constants are the values kept in the message field of the `TMsg` record. All these constants are defined in Delphi's `Messages` unit; most are also described in the online help. Notice that each of these constants begins with the letters `WM`, which stand for *Windows message*. Table 5.1 lists some of the common Windows messages, along with their meanings and values.

TABLE 5.1. COMMON WINDOWS MESSAGES.

Message Identifier	Value	Tells a Window That...
WM_ACTIVATE	$0006	It's being activated or deactivated.
WM_CHAR	$0102	WM_KEYDOWN and WM_KEYUP messages have been sent for one key.
WM_CLOSE	$0010	It should terminate.
WM_KEYDOWN	$0100	A keyboard key is being pressed.
WM_KEYUP	$0101	A keyboard key has been released.
WM_LBUTTONDOWN	$0201	The user is pressing the left mouse button.
WM_MOUSEMOVE	$0200	The mouse is being moved.
WM_PAINT	$000F	It must repaint its client area.
WM_TIMER	$0113	A timer event has occurred.
WM_QUIT	$0012	A request to shut down the program.

5

HOW THE WINDOWS MESSAGE SYSTEM WORKS

A Windows application's message system has three key components:

- *Message queue*. Windows maintains a message queue for each application. A Windows application must get messages from this queue and dispatch them to the proper windows.
- *Message loop*. The loop mechanism in a Windows program that fetches a message from the application queue and dispatches it to the appropriate window, fetches the next message, dispatches it to the appropriate window, and so on.
- *Window procedure*. Each window in your application has a window procedure that receives each of the messages passed to it by the message loop. The window procedure's job is to take each window message and respond to it accordingly. A window procedure is a callback function; it usually returns a value to Windows after processing a message.

NOTE	

A *callback function* is a function in your program that's called by Windows or some other external module.

Getting a message from point A (some event occurs, creating a message) to point B (a window in your application responds to the message) is a five-step process:

1. Some event occurs in the system.
2. Windows translates this event into a message and places it into the message queue for your application.
3. Your application retrieves the message from the queue and places it in a TMsg record.
4. Your application passes on the message to the window procedure of the appropriate window in your application.
5. The window procedure performs some action in response to the message.

Steps 3 and 4 make up the application's message loop. The message loop is often considered the heart of a Windows program because it's the facility that enables your program to respond to external events. The message loop spends its whole life fetching messages from the application queue and passing them to the appropriate windows in your application. If there are no messages in your application's queue, Windows allows other applications to process their messages. Figure 5.1 shows these steps.

FIGURE 5.1.
*The Windows
message system.*

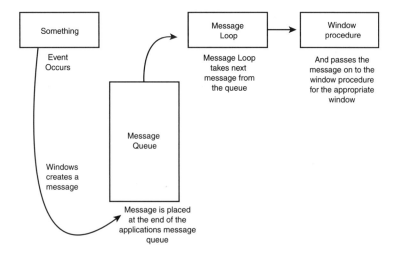

DELPHI'S MESSAGE SYSTEM

VCL handles many of the details of the Windows message system for you. The message loop is built into VCL's Forms unit, for example, so you don't have to worry about fetching messages from the queue or dispatching them to a window procedure. Delphi also places the information located in the Windows TMsg record into a generic TMessage record:

```
type
  TMessage = record
    Msg: Cardinal;
    case Integer of
      0: (
        WParam: Longint;
        LParam: Longint;
        Result: Longint);
      1: (
        WParamLo: Word;
        WParamHi: Word;
        LParamLo: Word;
        LParamHi: Word;
        ResultLo: Word;
        ResultHi: Word);
  end;
```

Notice that TMessage record has a little less information than does TMsg. That's because Delphi internalizes the other TMsg fields; TMessage contains just the essential information you need to handle a message.

5

**UNDERSTANDING
MESSAGES**

It's important to note that the TMessage record also contains a Result field. As mentioned earlier, some messages require the window procedure to return some value after processing a message. With Delphi, you accomplish this process in a straightforward fashion by placing the return value in the Result field of TMessage. This process is explained later in detail in the section "Assigning Message Result Values."

Message-Specific Records

In addition to the generic TMessage record, Delphi defines a message-specific record for every Windows message. The purpose of these message-specific records is to give you all the information the message offers without having to decipher the WParam and LParam fields of a record. All the message-specific records can be found in the Messages unit. As an example, here's the message record used to hold most mouse messages:

```
type
  TWMMouse = record
    Msg: Cardinal;
    Keys: Longint;
    case Integer of
      0: (
        XPos: Smallint;
        YPos: Smallint);
      1: (
        Pos: TSmallPoint;
        Result: Longint);
  end;
```

All the record types for specific mouse messages (WM_LBUTTONDOWN and WM_RBUTTONUP, for example) are simply defined as equal to TWMMouse, as in the following example:

```
TWMRButtonUp = TWMMouse;
TWMLButtonDown = TWMMouse;
```

> **NOTE**
>
> A message record is defined for nearly every standard Windows message. The naming convention dictates that the name of the record is the same as the name of the message with a *T* prepended and without the underscore. For example, the name of the message record type for a WM_SETFONT message is TWMSetFont.
>
> By the way, TMessage works with all messages in all situations but isn't as convenient as message-specific records.

HANDLING MESSAGES

Handling or *processing* a message means that your application responds in some manner to a Windows message. In a standard Windows application, message handling is performed in each window procedure. By internalizing the window procedure, however, Delphi makes it much easier to handle individual messages; instead of having one procedure that handles all messages, each message has its own procedure. Three requirements must be met for a procedure to be a message-handling procedure:

- The procedure must be a method of an object.
- The procedure must take one var parameter of a TMessage or other message-specific record type.
- The procedure must use the message directive followed by the constant value of the message you want to process.

Here's an example of a procedure that handles WM_PAINT messages:

```
procedure WMPaint(var Msg: TWMPaint); message WM_PAINT;
```

> **NOTE**
>
> When naming message-handling procedures, the convention is to give them the same name as the message itself, using camel-capitalization and without the underscore.

As an example, write a simple message-handling procedure for WM_PAINT that processes the message simply by beeping. Start by creating a new, blank project. Then access the Code Editor window for this project and add the header for the WMPaint function to the private section of the TForm1 object:

```
procedure WMPaint(var Msg: TWMPaint); message WM_PAINT;
```

Now add the function definition to the implementation part of this unit. Remember to use the dot operator to scope this procedure as a method of TForm1. Don't use the message directive as part of the function implementation:

```
procedure TForm1.WMPaint(var Msg: TWMPaint);
begin
  Beep;
  inherited;
end;
```

Notice the use of the inherited keyword here. Call inherited when you want to pass the message to the ancestor object's handler. By calling inherited in this example, you pass on the message to TForm's WM_PAINT handler.

> **NOTE**
>
> Unlike normal calls to inherited methods, here you don't give the name of the inherited method. That's because the name of the method is unimportant when it's dispatched. Delphi knows what method to call based on the message value used with the `message` directive in the class interface.

The main unit in Listing 5.1 provides a simple example of a form that processes the `WM_PAINT` message. Creating this project is easy: Just create a new project and add the code for the `WMPaint` procedure to the `TForm` object.

LISTING 5.1. GetMess: A MESSAGE-HANDLING EXAMPLE.

```
unit GMMain;

interface

uses
  SysUtils, Windows, Messages, Classes, Graphics, Controls,
  Forms, Dialogs;

type
  TForm1 = class(TForm)
  private
    procedure WMPaint(var Msg: TWMPaint); message WM_PAINT;
  end;

var
  Form1: TForm1;

implementation

{$R *.DFM}

procedure TForm1.WMPaint(var Msg: TWMPaint);
begin
  MessageBeep(0);
  inherited;
end;

end.
```

Whenever a `WM_PAINT` message comes down the pike, it's passed to the `WMPaint` procedure. The `WMPaint` procedure simply informs you of the `WM_PAINT` message by making some noise with the `MessageBeep()` procedure and then passes the message to the inherited handler.

MessageBeep(): THE POOR-MAN'S DEBUGGER

While we're on the topic of beeping, now is a good time for a slight digression. The MessageBeep() procedure is one of the most straightforward and useful elements in the Win32 API. Its use is simple: Call MessageBeep(), pass a predefined constant, and Windows beeps the PC's speaker (if you have a sound card, it plays a WAV file). Big deal, you say? On the surface it may not seem like much, but MessageBeep() really shines as an aid in debugging your programs.

If you're looking for a quick-and-dirty way to tell whether your program is reaching a certain place in your code—without having to bother with the debugger and breakpoints—MessageBeep() is for you. Because it doesn't require a handle or some other Windows resource, you can use it practically anywhere in your code, and as a wise man once said, "MessageBeep() is for the itch you can't scratch with the debugger." If you have a sound card, you can pass MessageBeep() one of several predefined constants to have it play a wider variety of sounds—these constants are defined under MessageBeep() in the Win32 API Help file.

If you're like the authors and too lazy to type out that whole big, long function name and parameter, you can use the Beep() procedure found in the SysUtils unit. The implementation of Beep() is simply a call to MessageBeep() with the parameter 0.

Message Handling: Not Contract-Free

Unlike responding to Delphi events, handling windows messages is not contract-free. Often, when you decide to handle a message yourself, Windows expects you to perform some action when processing the message. Most of the time, VCL has much of this basic message processing built in—all you have to do is call inherited to get to it. Think of it this way: You write a message handler so that your application will do the things you expect, and you call inherited so that your application will do the additional things Windows expects.

NOTE

The contractual nature of message handling can be more than just calling the inherited handler. With message handlers, you are sometimes restricted in what you can do. For example, in a WM_KILLFOCUS message, you cannot set focus to another control without causing a crash.

To demonstrate the `inherited` elements, try running the program in Listing 5.1 without calling `inherited` in the `WMPaint()` method. Just remove the line that calls `inherited` so that the procedure looks like this:

```
procedure TForm1.WMPaint(var Msg: TWMPaint);
begin
  MessageBeep(0);
end;
```

Because you never give Windows a chance to perform basic handling of the `WM_PAINT` message, the form will never paint itself.

Sometimes there are circumstances in which you don't want to call the inherited message handler. An example is handling the `WM_SYSCOMMAND` messages to prevent a window from being minimized or maximized.

Assigning Message Result Values

When you handle some Windows messages, Windows expects you to return a result value. The classic example is the `WM_CTLCOLOR` message. When you handle this message, Windows expects you to return a handle to a brush with which you want Windows to paint a dialog box or control. (Delphi provides a `Color` property for components that does this for you, so that example is just for illustration purposes.) You can return this brush handle easily with a message-handling procedure by assigning a value to the `Result` field of `TMessage` (or another message record) after calling `inherited`. For example, if you were handling `WM_CTLCOLOR`, you could return a brush handle value to Windows with the following code:

```
procedure TForm1.WMCtlColor(var Msg: TWMCtlColor);
var
  BrushHand: hBrush;
begin
  inherited;
  { Create a brush handle and place into BrushHand variable }
  Msg.Result := BrushHand;
end;
```

The TApplication OnMessage Event

Another technique for handling messages is to use `TApplication`'s `OnMessage` event. When you assign a procedure to `OnMessage`, that procedure is called whenever a message is pulled from the queue and about to be processed. This event handler is called before Windows itself has a chance to process the message. The `Application.OnMessage` event handler is of `TMessageEvent` type and must be defined with a parameter list as shown here:

```
procedure SomeObject.AppMessageHandler(var Msg: TMsg; var Handled:
➥Boolean);
```

All the message parameters are passed to the OnMessage event handler in the Msg parameter. (Note that this parameter is of the Windows TMsg record type described earlier in this chapter.) The Handled field requires you to assign a Boolean value indicating whether you have handled the message.

The first step in creating an OnMessage event handler is to create a method that accepts the same parameter list as a TMessageEvent. For example, here's a method that keeps a running count of how many messages your application receives:

```
var
  NumMessages: Integer;

procedure Form1.AppMessageHandler(var Msg: TMsg; var Handled: Boolean);
begin
  Inc(NumMessages);
  Handled := False;
end;
```

The second and final step in creating the event handler is to assign a procedure to Application.OnMessage somewhere in your code. This can be done in the DPR file after creating the project's forms but before calling Application.Run:

```
Application.OnMessage := Form1.AppMessageHandler;
```

One limitation of OnMessage is that it's executed only for messages pulled out of the queue and not for messages sent directly to the window procedures of windows in your application. Chapter 13, "Hard-Core Techniques," shows techniques for working around this limitation by hooking into the application window procedure.

TIP

OnMessage sees all messages posted to all window handles in your application. This is the busiest event in your application (thousands of messages per second), so don't do anything in an OnMessage handler that takes a lot of time, or you'll slow your whole application to a crawl. Clearly, this is one place where a breakpoint would be a very bad idea.

SENDING YOUR OWN MESSAGES

Just as Windows sends messages to your application's windows, you will occasionally need to send messages between windows and controls within your application. Delphi provides several ways to send messages within your application: the Perform() method (which works independently of the Windows API) and the `SendMessage()` and `PostMessage()` API functions.

The `Perform()` Method

VCL provides the `Perform()` method for all `TControl` descendants; `Perform()` enables you to send a message to any form or control object when given an instance of that object. The `Perform()` method takes three parameters—a message and its corresponding `LParam` and `WParam`—and is defined as follows:

```
function TControl.Perform(Msg: Cardinal; WParam, LParam: Longint):
➥Longint;
```

To send a message to a form or control, use the following syntax:

```
RetVal := ControlName.Perform(MessageID, WParam, LParam);
```

After you call `Perform()`, it doesn't return until the message has been handled. The `Perform()` method packages its parameters into a `TMessage` record and then calls the object's `Dispatch()` method to send the message—bypassing the Windows API messaging system. The `Dispatch()` method is described later in this chapter.

The `SendMessage()` and `PostMessage()` API Functions

Sometimes you need to send a message to a window for which you don't have a Delphi object instance. For example, you might want to send a message to a non-Delphi window, but you have only a handle to that window. Fortunately, the Windows API offers two functions that fit this bill: `SendMessage()` and `PostMessage()`. These two functions are essentially identical, except for one key difference: `SendMessage()`, similar to `Perform()`, sends a message directly to the window procedure of the intended window and waits until the message is processed before returning; `PostMessage()` posts a message to the Windows message queue and returns immediately.

`SendMessage()` and `PostMessage()` are declared as follows:

```
function SendMessage(hWnd: HWND; Msg: UINT; WParam: WPARAM; LParam:
➥LPARAM): LRESULT; stdcall;
function PostMessage(hWnd: HWND; Msg: UINT; WParam: WPARAM; LParam:
➥LPARAM): BOOL; stdcall;
```

- `hWnd` is the window handle for which the message is intended.
- `Msg` is the message identifier.
- `WParam` is 32 bits of additional message-specific information.
- `LParam` is 32 bits of additional message-specific information.

> **NOTE**
>
> Although `SendMessage()` and `PostMessage()` are used similarly, their respective return values are different. `SendMessage()` returns the result value of the message being processed, but `PostMessage()` returns only a `BOOL` that indicates whether the message was placed in the target window's queue.

NONSTANDARD MESSAGES

Until now, discussion has centered on regular Windows messages (those that begin with `WM_XXX`). However, two other major categories of messages merit some discussion: notification messages and user-defined messages.

Notification Messages

Notification messages are messages sent to a parent window when something happens in one of its child controls that may require the parent's attention. Notification messages occur only with the standard Windows controls: button, list box, combo box, and edit control; and with the Windows 95 common controls: tree view, list view, and so on. For example, clicking or double-clicking a control, selecting some text in a control, and moving the scroll bar in a control all generate notification messages.

You can handle notification messages by writing message-handling procedures in the form that contains a particular control. Table 5.2 lists the Win32 notification messages for standard windows controls.

TABLE 5.2. STANDARD CONTROL NOTIFICATION MESSAGES.

Notification	*Meaning*
Button Notification	
`BN_CLICKED`	The user clicked a button.
`BN_DISABLE`	A button is disabled.
`BN_DOUBLECLICKED`	The user double-clicked a button.
`BN_HILITE`	The user highlighted a button.
`BN_PAINT`	The button should be painted.
`BN_UNHILITE`	The highlight should be removed.

continues

TABLE 5.2. CONTINUED

Notification	Meaning
Combo Box Notification	
CBN_CLOSEUP	The list box of a combo box has closed.
CBN_DBLCLK	The user double-clicked a string.
CBN_DROPDOWN	The list box of a combo box is dropping down.
CBN_EDITCHANGE	The user has changed text in the edit control.
CBN_EDITUPDATE	Altered text is about to be displayed.
CBN_ERRSPACE	The combo box is out of memory.
CBN_KILLFOCUS	The combo box is losing the input focus.
CBN_SELCHANGE	A new combo box list item is selected.
CBN_SELENDCANCEL	The user's selection should be canceled.
CBN_SELENDOK	The user's selection is valid.
CBN_SETFOCUS	The combo box is receiving the input focus.
Edit Notification	
EN_CHANGE	The display is updated after text changes.
EN_ERRSPACE	The edit control is out of memory.
EN_HSCROLL	The user clicked the horizontal scroll bar.
EN_KILLFOCUS	The edit control is losing the input focus.
EN_MAXTEXT	The insertion is truncated.
EN_SETFOCUS	The edit control is receiving the input focus.
EN_UPDATE	The edit control is about to display altered text.
EN_VSCROLL	The user clicked the vertical scroll bar.
LBN_DBLCLK	The user double-clicked a string.
List Box Notification	
LBN_ERRSPACE	The list box is out of memory.
LBN_KILLFOCUS	The list box is losing the input focus.
LBN_SELCANCEL	The selection is canceled.
LBN_SELCHANGE	The selection is about to change.
LBN_SETFOCUS	The list box is receiving the input focus.

Internal VCL Messages

VCL has an extensive collection of its own internal and notification messages. Although you don't commonly use these messages in your Delphi applications, Delphi component writers will find them useful. These messages begin with CM_ (for *component message*) or CN_ (for *component notification*), and they are used to manage VCL internals such as focus, color, visibility, window re-creation, dragging, and so on. You can find a complete list of these messages in the Component Writer's portion of the Delphi online help.

User-Defined Messages

At some point, you'll come across a situation in which one of your own applications must send a message to itself, or you have to send messages between two of your own applications. At this point, one question that might come to mind is, "why would I send myself a message instead of simply calling a procedure?" It's a good question, and there are actually several answers. First, messages give you polymorphism without requiring knowledge of the recipient's type. Messages are thus as powerful as virtual methods but more flexible. Also, messages allow for optional handling: If the recipient doesn't do anything with the message, no harm done. Finally, messages allow for broadcast notifications to multiple recipients and "parasitic" eavesdropping, which isn't easily done with procedures alone.

Messages Within Your Application

Having an application send a message to itself is easy. Just use the Perform(), SendMessage(), or PostMessage() function and use a message value in the range of WM_USER + 100 through $7FFF (the value Windows reserves for user-defined messages):

```
const
 SX_MYMESSAGE = WM_USER + 100;

begin
  SomeForm.Perform(SX_MYMESSAGE, 0, 0);
  { or }
  SendMessage(SomeForm.Handle, SX_MYMESSAGE, 0, 0);
  { or }
  PostMessage(SomeForm.Handle, SX_MYMESSAGE, 0, 0);
  .
  .
  .
end;
```

Then create a normal message-handling procedure for this message in the form in which you want to handle this message:

```
TForm1 = class(TForm)
  .
  .
  .
```

```
private
  procedure SXMyMessage(var Msg: TMessage); message SX_MYMESSAGE;
end;

procedure TForm1.SXMyMessage(var Msg: TMessage);
begin
  MessageDlg('She turned me into a newt!', mtInformation, [mbOk], 0);
end;
```

As you can see, there's little difference between using a user-defined message in your application and handling any standard Windows message. The real key here is to start at WM_USER + 100 for interapplication messages and to give each message a name that has something to do with its purpose.

CAUTION

Never send messages with values of WM_USER through $7FFF unless you're sure that the intended recipient is equipped to handle the message. Because each window can define these values independently, the potential for bad things to happen is great unless you keep careful tabs about whom you send WM_USER through $7FFF messages.

Messaging Between Applications

When you want to send messages between two or more applications, it's usually best to use the RegisterWindowMessage() API function in each application. This method ensures that every application uses the same message number for a given message.

RegisterWindowMessage() accepts a null-terminated string as a parameter and returns a new message constant in the range of $C000 through $FFFF. This means that all you have to do is call RegisterWindowMessage() with the same string in each application between which you want to send messages; Windows returns the same message value for each application. The true benefit of RegisterWindowMessage() is that, because a message value for any given string is guaranteed to be unique throughout the system, you can safely broadcast such messages to all windows with fewer harmful side effects. It can be a bit more work to handle this kind of message, though; because the message identifier isn't known until runtime, you can't use a standard message handler procedure, and you must override a control's WndProc() or DefaultHandler() method or subclass an existing window procedure. A technique for handling registered messages is demonstrated in Chapter 13.

> **NOTE**
>
> The number returned by RegisterWindowMessage() varies between Windows sessions and can't be determined until runtime.

Broadcasting Messages

TWinControl descendants can broadcast a message record to each of their owned controls—thanks to the Broadcast() method. This technique is useful when you need to send the same message to a group of components. For example, to send a user-defined message called um_Foo to all of Panel1's owned controls, use the following code:

```
var
  M: TMessage;
begin
  with M do
  begin
    Message := UM_FOO;
    WParam := 0;
    LParam := 0;
    Result := 0;
  end;
  Panel1.Broadcast(M);
end;
```

THE ANATOMY OF A MESSAGE SYSTEM: VCL

There's much more to VCL's message system than handling messages with the message directive. After a message is issued by Windows, it makes a couple of stops before reaching your message-handling procedure (it may make a few more stops afterward). All along the way, you have the power to act on the message.

For posted messages, the first stop for a Windows message in VCL is the Application.ProcessMessage() method, which houses the VCL main message loop. The next stop for a message is the handler for the Application.OnMessage event. OnMessage is called as messages are fetched from the application queue in the ProcessMessage() method. Because sent messages aren't queued, OnMessage won't be called for sent messages.

For posted messages, the DispatchMessage() API is then called internally to dispatch the message to the StdWndProc() function. For sent messages, StdWndProc() will be called directly by Win32. StdWndProc() is an assembler function that accepts the message from Windows and routes it to the object for which the message is intended.

The object method that receives the message is called `MainWndProc()`. Beginning with `MainWndProc()`, you can perform any special handling of the message your program might require. Generally, you handle a message at this point only if you don't want a message to go through VCL's normal dispatching.

After leaving the `MainWndProc()` method, the message is routed to the object's `WndProc()` method and then on to the dispatch mechanism. The dispatch mechanism, found in the object's `Dispatch()` method, routes the message to any specific message-handling procedure that you have defined or that already exists within VCL.

Then the message finally reaches your message-specific handling procedure. After flowing through your handler and the inherited handlers you might have invoked using the `inherited` keyword, the message goes to the object's `DefaultHandler()` method. `DefaultHandler()` performs any final message processing and then passes the message to the Windows `DefWindowProc()` function or other default window procedure (such as `DefMDIProc`) for any Windows-default processing. Figure 5.2 shows VCL's message-processing mechanism.

FIGURE 5.2.

VCL's message system.

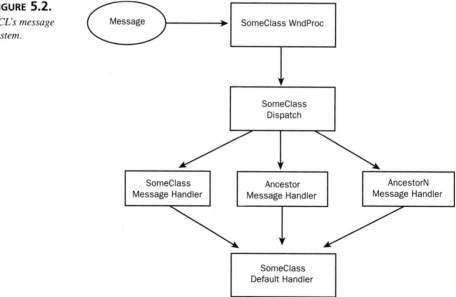

NOTE

You should always call `inherited` when handling messages unless you're absolutely certain that you want to prevent normal message processing.

> **TIP**
>
> Because all unhandled messages flow to `DefaultHandler()`, that's usually the best place to handle interapplication messages in which the values were obtained by way of the `RegisterWindowMessage()` procedure.

To better understand VCL's message system, create a small program that can handle a message at the `Application.OnMessage`, `WndProc()`, message procedure, or `Defaulthandler()` stage. This project is called CatchIt; its main form is shown in Figure 5.3.

FIGURE 5.3.

The main form of the CatchIt message example.

The `OnClick` event handlers for `PostMessButton` and `SendMessButton` are shown in the following code. The former uses `PostMessage()` to post a user-defined message to the form; the latter uses `SendMessage()` to send a user-defined message to the form. To differentiate between post and send, note that the value 1 is passed in the `WParam` of `PostMessage()`; the value 0 (zero) is passed for `SendMessage()`.

```
procedure TMainForm.PostMessButtonClick(Sender: TObject);
{ posts message to form }
begin
  PostMessage(Handle, SX_MYMESSAGE, 1, 0);
end;

procedure TMainForm.SendMessButtonClick(Sender: TObject);
{ sends message to form }
begin
  SendMessage(Handle, SX_MYMESSAGE, 0, 0); // send message to form
end;
```

This application provides the user with the opportunity to "eat" the message in the `OnMessage` handler, `WndProc()` method, message-handling method, or `DefaultHandler()` method. That is, to not trigger the inherited behavior, and to therefore stop the message from fully circulating through VCL's message-handling system. Listing 5.2 shows the completed source code for the main unit of this project, demonstrating the flow of messages in a Delphi application.

LISTING 5.2. THE SOURCE CODE FOR CIMain.PAS.

```pascal
unit CIMain;

interface

uses
  SysUtils, WinTypes, WinProcs, Messages, Classes, Graphics, Controls,
  Forms, Dialogs, StdCtrls, ExtCtrls, Menus;

const
  SX_MYMESSAGE = WM_USER;                   // User-defined message value
  MessString = '%s message now in %s.';    // String to alert user of
                                           // message

type
  TMainForm = class(TForm)
    GroupBox1: TGroupBox;
    PostMessButton: TButton;
    WndProcCB: TCheckBox;
    MessProcCB: TCheckBox;
    DefHandCB: TCheckBox;
    SendMessButton: TButton;
    AppMsgCB: TCheckBox;
    EatMsgCB: TCheckBox;
    EatMsgGB: TGroupBox;
    OnMsgRB: TRadioButton;
    WndProcRB: TRadioButton;
    MsgProcRB: TRadioButton;
    DefHandlerRB: TRadioButton;
    procedure PostMessButtonClick(Sender: TObject);
    procedure SendMessButtonClick(Sender: TObject);
    procedure EatMsgCBClick(Sender: TObject);
    procedure FormCreate(Sender: TObject);
    procedure AppMsgCBClick(Sender: TObject);
  private
    { Handles messages at Application level }
    procedure OnAppMessage(var Msg: TMsg; var Handled: Boolean);
    { Handles messages at WndProc level }
    procedure WndProc(var Msg: TMessage); override;
    { Handles message after dispatch }
    procedure SXMyMessage(var Msg: TMessage); message SX_MYMESSAGE;
    { Default message handler }
    procedure DefaultHandler(var Msg); override;
  end;

var
  MainForm: TMainForm;

implementation

{$R *.DFM}

const
  // strings which will indicate to user whether a message is sent or
  // posted
```

```
    SendPostStrings: array[0..1] of String = ('Sent', 'Posted');

procedure TMainForm.FormCreate(Sender: TObject);
{ OnCreate handler for main form }
begin
  // set OnMessage to my OnAppMessage method
  Application.OnMessage := OnAppMessage;
  // use the Tag property of checkboxes to store a reference to their
  // associated radio buttons
  AppMsgCB.Tag := Longint(OnMsgRB);
  WndProcCB.Tag := Longint(WndProcRB);
  MessProcCB.Tag := Longint(MsgProcRB);
  DefHandCB.Tag := Longint(DefHandlerRB);
  // use the Tag property of radio buttons to store a reference to their
  // associated checkbox
  OnMsgRB.Tag := Longint(AppMsgCB);
  WndProcRB.Tag := Longint(WndProcCB);
  MsgProcRB.Tag := Longint(MessProcCB);
  DefHandlerRB.Tag := Longint(DefHandCB);
end;

procedure TMainForm.OnAppMessage(var Msg: TMsg; var Handled: Boolean);
{ OnMessage handler for Application }
begin
  // check to see if message is my user-defined message
  if Msg.Message = SX_MYMESSAGE then
  begin
    if AppMsgCB.Checked then
    begin
      // Let user know about the message.  Set Handled flag appropriately
      ShowMessage(Format(MessString, [SendPostStrings[Msg.WParam],
        'Application.OnMessage']));
      Handled := OnMsgRB.Checked;
    end;
  end;
end;

procedure TMainForm.WndProc(var Msg: TMessage);
{ WndProc procedure of form }
var
  CallInherited: Boolean;
begin
  CallInherited := True;           // assume we will call the inherited
  if Msg.Msg = SX_MYMESSAGE then   // check for our user-defined message
  begin
    if WndProcCB.Checked then      // if WndProcCB checkbox is checked...
    begin
      // Let user know about the message.
```

continues

LISTING 5.2. CONTINUED

```
    ShowMessage(Format(MessString, [SendPostStrings[Msg.WParam],
      ➥'WndProc'])) ;
    // Call inherited only if we are not supposed to eat the message.
    CallInherited := not WndProcRB.Checked;
   end;
  end;
  if CallInherited then inherited WndProc(Msg);
end;

procedure TMainForm.SXMyMessage(var Msg: TMessage);
{ Message procedure for user-defined message }
var
  CallInherited: Boolean;
begin
  CallInherited := True;          // assume we will call the inherited
  if MessProcCB.Checked then      // if MessProcCB checkbox is checked...
  begin
    // Let user know about the message.
    ShowMessage(Format(MessString, [SendPostStrings[Msg.WParam],
      'Message Procedure'])) ;
    // Call inherited only if we are not supposed to eat the message.
    CallInherited := not MsgProcRB.Checked;
  end;
  if CallInherited then Inherited;
end;

procedure TMainForm.DefaultHandler(var Msg);
{ Default message handler for form }
var
  CallInherited: Boolean;
begin
  CallInherited := True;                   // assume we will call the
inherited
  if TMessage(Msg).Msg = SX_MYMESSAGE then // check for our user-defined
message
  begin
    if DefHandCB.Checked then              // if DefHandCB checkbox is
checked...
    begin
      // Let user know about the message.
      ShowMessage(Format(MessString,
[SendPostStrings[TMessage(Msg).WParam],
        'DefaultHandler'])) ;
      // Call inherited only if we are not supposed to eat the message.
      CallInherited := not DefHandlerRB.Checked;
    end;
  end;
```

```
    if CallInherited then inherited DefaultHandler(Msg);
end;

procedure TMainForm.PostMessButtonClick(Sender: TObject);
{ posts message to form }
begin
  PostMessage(Handle, SX_MYMESSAGE, 1, 0);
end;

procedure TMainForm.SendMessButtonClick(Sender: TObject);
{ sends message to form }
begin
  SendMessage(Handle, SX_MYMESSAGE, 0, 0); // send message to form
end;

procedure TMainForm.AppMsgCBClick(Sender: TObject);
{ enables/disables proper radio button for checkbox click }
begin
  if EatMsgCB.Checked then
  begin
    with TRadioButton((Sender as TCheckBox).Tag) do
    begin
      Enabled := TCheckbox(Sender).Checked;
      if not Enabled then Checked := False;
    end;
  end;
end;

procedure TMainForm.EatMsgCBClick(Sender: TObject);
{ enables/disables radio buttons as appropriate }
var
  i: Integer;
  DoEnable, EatEnabled: Boolean;
begin
  // get enable/disable flag
  EatEnabled := EatMsgCB.Checked;
  // iterate over child controls of GroupBox in order to
  // enable/disable and check/uncheck radio buttons
  for i := 0 to EatMsgGB.ControlCount - 1 do
    with EatMsgGB.Controls[i] as TRadioButton do
    begin
      DoEnable := EatEnabled;
      if DoEnable then DoEnable := TCheckbox(Tag).Checked;
      if not DoEnable then Checked := False;
      Enabled := DoEnable;
    end;
end;

end.
```

> **CAUTION**
>
> Although it's fine to use just the `inherited` keyword to send the message to an inherited handler in message-handler procedures, that technique doesn't work with `WndProc()` or `DefaultHandler()`. With those procedures, you must also provide the name of the inherited procedure or function, as in this example:
>
> ```
> inherited WndProc(Msg);
> ```

You might have noticed that the `DefaultHandler()` procedure is somewhat unusual in that it takes one *untyped* var parameter. That's because `DefaultHandler()` assumes that the first word in the parameter is the message number; it isn't concerned with the rest of the information being passed. Because of this, you typecast the parameter as a `TMessage` so that you can access the message parameters.

THE RELATIONSHIP BETWEEN MESSAGES AND EVENTS

Now that you know all the ins and outs of messages, recall that this chapter began by stating that VCL encapsulates many Windows messages in its event system. Delphi's event system is designed to be an easy interface into Windows messages. Many VCL events have a direct correlation with a WM_*XXX* Windows message. Table 5.3 shows some common VCL events and the Windows message responsible for the event.

TABLE 5.3. VCL EVENTS AND CORRESPONDING WINDOWS MESSAGES.

VCL Event	Windows Message
OnActivate	WM_ACTIVATE
OnClick	WM_XBUTTONDOWN
OnCreate	WM_CREATE
OnDblClick	WM_XBUTTONDBLCLICK
OnKeyDown	WM_KEYDOWN
OnKeyPress	WM_CHAR
OnKeyUp	WM_KEYUP
OnPaint	WM_PAINT
OnResize	WM_SIZE
OnTimer	WM_TIMER

Table 5.3 is a good rule-of-thumb reference when looking for events that correspond directly to messages.

> **TIP**
>
> Never write a message handler when you can use a predefined event to do the same thing. Because of the contract-free nature of events, you'll have fewer problems handling events than you will handling messages.

SUMMARY

By now, you should have a pretty clear understanding of how the Win32 messaging system works and how VCL encapsulates that messaging system. Although Delphi's event system is great, knowing how messages work is essential for any serious Win32 programmer.

If you're eager to learn more about handling Windows messages, check out Chapter 21, "Writing Delphi Custom Components." In that chapter, you will see practical application of the knowledge you gained in this chapter.

DELPHI 4 DEVELOPER'S GUIDE CODING STANDARDS DOCUMENT

Copyright© 1998 Xavier Pacheco and Steve Teixeira

IN THIS CHAPTER

This document describes the coding standards for Delphi programming as used in *Delphi 4 Developer's Guide*. In general, this document follows the often "unspoken" formatting guidelines used by Borland International with a few minor exceptions. The purpose for including this document in *Delphi 4 Developer's Guide* is to present a method by which development teams can enforce a consistent style to the coding that they do. The intent is for every programmer on a team to understand the code being written by other programmers. This is accomplished by making the code more readable by use of consistency.

This document by no means includes everything that might exist in a coding standard. However, it does contain enough detail to get you started. Feel free to use and modify these standards to fit your needs. We don't recommend, however, that you deviate too far from the standards used by Borland's development staff. We recommend this because as you bring new programmers to your team, the standards that they are most likely to be most familiar with are Borland's. Like most coding standards documents, this document will evolve as needed. Therefore, you'll find the most updated version online at `www.xapware.com/ddg`.

This document does not cover *user interface standards*. This is a separate but equally important topic. Enough third-party books and Microsoft documentation cover such guidelines that we decided not to replicate this information but rather to refer you to the Microsoft Developers Network and other sources where that information may be available.

USING ACTIVEX CONTROLS WITH DELPHI

IN THIS CHAPTER

Delphi gives you the great advantage of easily integrating industry-standard ActiveX controls (formerly known as OCX or OLE controls) into your applications. Unlike Delphi's own custom components, ActiveX controls are designed to be independent of any particular development tool. This means that you can count on many vendors to provide a variety of ActiveX solutions that open up a world of features and functionality.

ActiveX control support in 32-bit Delphi works similarly to the way VBX support works in 16-bit Delphi 1. You select an option to add new ActiveX controls from Delphi's IDE main menu or Package Editor and Delphi builds an Object Pascal wrapper for the ActiveX control—which is then compiled into a package and added to the Delphi Component Palette. Once on the palette, the ActiveX control seamlessly merges into the Component Palette along with your other VCL and ActiveX components. From that point, you are just a click and drop away from adding an ActiveX control to any of your applications. This chapter discusses integrating ActiveX controls into Delphi, using an ActiveX control in your application, and shipping ActiveX-equipped applications.

NOTE

Delphi 4 does not support VBX (Visual Basic Extension) controls. If you have a Delphi 1 project that relies on one or more VBX controls, check with the VBX vendor(s) to see whether they supply a comparable ActiveX solution.

ADVANCED TECHNIQUES

IN THIS PART

GRAPHICS PROGRAMMING WITH GDI AND FONTS

IN THIS CHAPTER

In previous chapters, you worked with a property called `Canvas`. `Canvas` is appropriately named because you can think of a window as an artist's blank canvas on which you paint various Windows objects. Each button, window, cursor, and so on is nothing more than a collection of pixels in which the colors have been set to give it some useful appearance. In fact, think of each individual window as a separate surface on which its separate components are painted. To take this analogy a bit further, imagine that you are an artist who requires various tools to accomplish your task. You need a palette from which to choose different colors. You probably will use different styles of brushes, drawing tools, and special artist's techniques as well. Win32 makes use of similar tools and techniques—in the programming sense—to paint the various objects with which users interact. These tools are made available through the Graphics Device Interface, otherwise known as the GDI.

Win32 uses the GDI to paint or draw the images you see on your computer screen. Before Delphi, in traditional Windows programming, programmers worked directly with the GDI functions and tools. Now, the `TCanvas` object encapsulates and simplifies the use of these functions, tools, and techniques. This chapter teaches you how to use `TCanvas` to perform useful graphics functions. You will also see how you can create advanced programming projects with Delphi 4 and the Win32 GDI. We illustrate this by creating a paint program and an animation program.

DYNAMIC LINK LIBRARIES

IN THIS CHAPTER

This chapter discusses Win32 *dynamic link libraries*, otherwise known as *DLLs*. DLLs are a key component to writing any Windows application. This chapter discusses several aspects of using and creating DLLs. It gives you an overview of how DLLs work and discusses how to create and use DLLs. You learn different methods of loading DLLs and linking to the procedures and functions they export. This chapter also covers the use of callback functions and illustrates how to share DLL data among different calling processes.

WHAT EXACTLY IS A DLL?

Dynamic link libraries are program modules that contain code, data, or resources that can be shared among many Windows applications. One of the primary uses of DLLs is to enable applications to load code that executes at runtime instead of linking that code to the application at compile time. Thus, multiple applications can simultaneously use the same code provided by the DLL. In fact, the files KERNEL32.DLL, USER32.DLL, and GDI32.DLL are three DLLs on which Win32 relies heavily. KERNEL32.DLL is responsible for memory, process, and thread management. USER32.DLL contains routines for the user interface that deal with the creation of windows and the handling of Win32 messages. GDI32.DLL deals with graphics. You'll also hear of other system DLLs, such as ADVA-PI32.DLL and COMDLG32.DLL, which deal with object security/Registry manipulation and common dialog boxes, respectively.

Another advantage to using DLLs is that your applications become modular. This simplifies updating your applications because you need to replace only DLLs instead of replacing the entire application. The Windows environment presents a typical example of this type of modularity. Each time you install a new device, you also install a device driver DLL to enable that device to communicate with Windows. The advantage to modularity becomes obvious when you imagine having to reinstall Windows each time you install a new device to your system.

On disk, a DLL is basically the same as a Windows EXE file. One major difference is that a DLL isn't an independently executable file, although it may contain executable code. The most common DLL file extension is .dll. Other file extensions are .drv for device drivers, .sys for system files, and .fon for font resources, which contain no executable code.

DLLs share their code with other applications through a process called *dynamic linking*, discussed later in this chapter. In general, when an application uses a DLL, the Win32 system ensures that only one copy of that DLL resides in memory. It does this by using *memory-mapped files*. The DLL is first loaded into the Win32 system's global heap. It's then mapped into the address space of the calling process. In the Win32 system, each process is given its own 32-bit linear address space. When the DLL is loaded by multiple processes, each process receives its own image of the DLL. Therefore, processes don't share the same physical code, data, or resource as was the case in 16-bit Windows. In Win32, the DLL appears as though it's actually code belonging to the calling process.

This doesn't mean that when multiple processes load a DLL, the physical memory is consumed by each usage of the DLL. The DLL image is placed into each process's address space by mapping its image from the system's global heap to the address space of each process that uses the DLL, at least in the ideal scenario. (See the following sidebar.)

SETTING A DLL'S PREFERRED BASE ADDRESS

DLL code is only shared between processes if the DLL can be loaded into the process address space of all interested clients at the DLL's preferred base address. If the preferred base address and range of the DLL overlaps with something already allocated in a process, the Win32 loader has to relocate the entire DLL image to some other base address. When that happens, none of the relocated DLL image is shared with any other process in the system—each relocated DLL instance consumes its own chunk of physical memory and swap file space.

It is critical that you set the base address of every DLL you produce to a value that does not conflict with or overlap other address ranges used by your application by using the $IMAGEBASE directive.

If your DLL will be used by multiple applications, choose a unique base address that's unlikely to collide with application addresses at the low end of the process virtual address range or common DLLs (like VCL packages) at the high end of the address range. The default base address for all executable files (EXEs and DLLs) is $400000, which means unless you change your DLL base address, it will always collide with the base address of its host EXE and therefore never be shared between processes.

There is another side benefit of base address loading. Because the DLL does not require relocation or fixes (which is usually the case), and because it is stored on a local disk drive, the DLL's memory pages are mapped directly onto the DLL file on disk. The DLL code does not consume any space in the system's page file (a.k.a. swap file). This is why the system's total committed page count and size statistics can be much larger than the system swap file plus RAM.

You'll find detailed information on using the $IMAGEBASE directive by looking up "Image Base Address" in the Delphi 4 online help.

9

DYNAMIC LINK LIBRARIES

Following are some terms that you'll need to know in regard to DLLs:

- Application. A Windows program residing in an `.exe` file.

- Executable. A file containing executable code. Executable files include `.dll` and `.exe` files.

- Instance. When referring to applications and DLLs, an *instance* is the occurrence of an executable. Each instance can be referred to by an *instance handle*, which is assigned by the Win32 system. When an application is run twice, for example, there are two instances of that application and, therefore, two instance handles. When a DLL is loaded, there's an instance of that DLL as well as a corresponding instance handle. The term *instance* as used here should not be confused with the instance of a class.

- Module. In 32-bit Windows, *module* and *instance* can be used synonymously. This differs from 16-bit Windows, in which the system maintains a database to manage modules and provides a module handle for each module. In Win32, each instance of an application gets its own address space, and therefore there's no need for a separate module identifier. However, Microsoft still uses the term in its own documentation. Just be aware that module and instance are one and the same.

- Task. Windows is a multitasking (or task-switching) environment. It must be able to allocate system resources and time to the various instances running under it. It does this by maintaining a task database that maintains instance handles and other necessary information to enable it to perform its task-switching functions. The task is the element to which Windows grants resources and time blocks.

STATIC LINKING VERSUS DYNAMIC LINKING

Static linking refers to the method by which the Delphi compiler resolves a function or procedure call to its executable code. The function's code can exist in the application's `.dpr` file or in a unit. When linking your applications, these functions and procedures become part of the final executable file. In other words, on disk, each function will reside at a specific location in the program's `.exe` file.

A function's location also is predetermined at a location relative to where the program is loaded in memory. Any calls to that function cause program execution to jump to where the function resides, execute the function, and then return to the location from which it was called. The relative address of the function is resolved during the linking process.

This is a loose description of a more complex process that the Delphi compiler uses to perform static linking. However, for the purpose of this book, you don't need to understand the underlying operations that the compiler performs to use DLLs effectively in your applications.

> **NOTE**
>
> Delphi implements a smart linker that automatically removes functions, procedures, variables, and typed constants that never get referenced in the final project. Therefore, functions that reside in large units that never get used don't become a part of your .exe file.

Suppose that you have two applications that use the same function that resides in a unit. Both applications, of course, would have to include the unit in their uses statements. If you ran both applications simultaneously in Windows, the function would exist twice in memory. If you had a third application, there would be a third instance of the function in memory, and you would be using up three times its memory space. This small example illustrates one of the primary reasons for dynamic linking. Through dynamic linking, this function resides in a DLL. Then, when an application loads the function into memory, all other applications that need to reference it can share its code by mapping the image of the DLL into their own process memory space. The end result is that the DLL's function exists only once in memory—theoretically.

With *dynamic linking*, the link between a function call and its executable code is resolved at runtime by using an external reference to the DLL's function. These references can be declared in the application, but usually they're placed in a separate import unit. The import unit declares the imported functions and procedures and defines various types required by DLL functions.

For example, suppose that you have a DLL named MAXLIB.DLL that contains a function:

```
function Max(i1, I2: integer): integer;
```

This function returns the higher of the two integers passed to it. A typical import unit would look like this:

```
unit MaxUnit;
interface
function Max(I1, I2: integer): integer;
implementation
function Max; external 'MAXLIB';
end.
```

You'll notice that although this looks somewhat like a typical unit, it doesn't define the function Max(). The keyword external simply says that the function resides in the DLL of the name that follows it. To use this unit, an application would simply place MaxUnit in its uses statement. When the application runs, the DLL is loaded into memory automatically, and any calls to Max() are linked to the Max() function in the DLL.

This illustrates one of two ways to load a DLL; it's called *implicit loading*, which causes Windows to automatically load the DLL when the application loads. Another method is to *explicitly load* the DLL; this is discussed later in this chapter.

WHY USE DLLS?

There are several reasons for using DLLs, some of which were mentioned earlier. In general, use DLLs to share code or system resources, to hide your code implementation or low-level system routines, or to design custom controls. We discuss these topics in the following sections.

Sharing Code, Resources, and Data with Multiple Applications

Earlier in this chapter, you learned that the most common reason for creating a DLL is to share code. Unlike units, which enable you to share code with different Delphi applications, DLLs enable you to share code with any Windows application that can call functions from DLLs.

Additionally, DLLs provide a way for you to share resources such as bitmaps, fonts, icons, and so on that you normally would put into a resource file and link directly into your application. If you place these resources into a DLL, many applications can make use of them without using up the memory required to load them more often.

In the 16-bit Windows, DLLs had their own data segment, so all applications that used a DLL could access the same data-global and static variables. In the Win32 system, this is a different story. Because the DLL image is mapped to each process's address space, all data in the DLL belongs to that process. One thing worth mentioning here is that although the DLL's data isn't shared between different processes, it's shared by multiple threads within the same process. Because threads execute independently of one another, you must take precautions not to cause conflicts when accessing a DLL's global data.

This doesn't mean that there aren't ways to make multiple processes share data made accessible through a DLL. One technique would be to create a shared memory area (using a memory-mapped file) from within the DLL. Each application using that DLL would be able to read the data stored in the shared memory area. This technique is shown later in the chapter.

Hiding Implementation

In some cases, you might want to hide the details of the routines that you make available from a DLL. Regardless of your reason for deciding to hide your code's implementation, a DLL provides a way for you to make your functions available to the public and not give away your source code in doing so. All you need to do is provide an interface unit to enable others to access your DLL. If you're thinking that this is already possible with Delphi compiled units (DCUs), consider that DCUs apply only to other Delphi applications that are created with the same version of Delphi. DLLs are language independent, so you can create a DLL that can be used by C++, VB, or any other language that supports DLLs.

The Windows unit is the interface unit to the Win32 DLLs. The Win32 API unit source files are included with Delphi 4. One of the files you get is `WINDOWS.PAS`, the source to the Windows unit. In `WINDOWS.PAS`, you find function definitions like the following in the `interface` section:

```
function ClientToScreen(Hwnd: HWND; var lpPoint: TPoint): BOOL; stdcall;
```

The corresponding link to the DLL is in the `implementation` section, as in the following example:

```
function ClientToScreen; external user32 name 'ClientToScreen';
```

This basically says that the procedure `ClientToScreen()` exists in the dynamic-link library `USER32.DLL`, and its name is `ClientToScreen`.

Custom Controls

Custom controls usually are placed in DLLs. These controls aren't the same as Delphi custom components. Custom controls are registered under Windows and can be used by any Windows development environment. These types of custom controls are placed in DLLs to conserve memory by having only one copy of the control's code in memory when multiple copies of the control are being used.

> **NOTE**
>
> The old custom control DLL mechanism is extremely crude and inflexible, which is why Microsoft now uses OLE and ActiveX controls. Such controls are rare.

9

DYNAMIC LINK LIBRARIES

CREATING AND USING DLLS

The following sections take you through the process of actually creating a DLL with Delphi. You'll see how to create an interface unit so that you can make your DLLs available to other programs. You'll also learn how to incorporate Delphi forms into DLLs before going on to using DLLs in Delphi.

Counting Your Pennies (A Simple DLL)

The following DLL example illustrates placing a routine that's a favorite of many computer science professors into a DLL. The routine converts a monetary amount in pennies to the minimum number of nickels, dimes, or quarters needed to match the total number of pennies.

A Basic DLL

Our library contains the `PenniesToCoins()` method. Listing 9.1 shows the complete DLL project.

LISTING 9.1. PenniesLib.dpr, A DLL TO CONVERT PENNIES TO OTHER COINS.

```
library PenniesLib;
{$DEFINE PENNIESLIB}
uses
  SysUtils,
  Classes,
  PenniesInt;

function PenniesToCoins(TotPennies: word; CoinsRec: PCoinsRec): word;
  StdCall;
  begin
  Result := TotPennies;   // Assign value to Result
  { Calculate the values for quarters, dimes, nickels, pennies }
  with CoinsRec^ do
  begin
    Quarters     := TotPennies div 25;
    TotPennies   := TotPennies - Quarters * 25;
    Dimes        := TotPennies div 10;
    TotPennies   := TotPennies - Dimes * 10;
    Nickels      := TotPennies div 5;
    TotPennies   := TotPennies - Nickels * 5;
    Pennies      := TotPennies;
  end;
end;

{ Export the function by name }
exports
  PenniesToCoins;
end.
```

Notice that this library uses the unit `PenniesInt`. We'll discuss this in more detail momentarily.

The exports clause specifies which functions or procedures in the DLL get exported and made available to calling applications.

Defining an Interface Unit

Interface units enable users of your DLL to statically import your DLL's routines into their applications by just placing the import unit's name in their module's uses statement. Interface units also allow the DLL writer to define common structures used by both the library and the calling application. We demonstrate that here with the interface unit. Listing 9.2 shows the source code to PenniesInt.pas.

LISTING 9.2. PenniesInt.pas, THE INTERFACE UNIT FOR PenniesLib.Dll.

```
unit PenniesInt;
{ Interface routine for PENNIES.DLL }

interface
type

  { This record will hold the denominations after the conversions have
    been made }
  PCoinsRec = ^TCoinsRec;
  TCoinsRec = record
    Quarters,
    Dimes,
    Nickels,
    Pennies: word;
  end;

{$IFNDEF PENNIESLIB}
{ Declare function with export keyword }

function PenniesToCoins(TotPennies: word; CoinsRec: PCoinsRec): word;
  StdCall;
{$ENDIF}

implementation

{$IFNDEF PENNIESLIB}
{ Define the imported function }
function PenniesToCoins; external 'PENNIESLIB.DLL' name 'PenniesToCoins';
{$ENDIF}

end.
```

In the type section of this project, you declare the record TCoinsRec as well as a pointer to this record. This record will hold the denominations that will make up the penny amount passed into the `PenniesToCoins()` function. The function takes two parameters—the total amount of money in pennies and a pointer to a `TCoinsRec` variable. The result of the function is the amount of pennies passed in.

`PENNIESINT.PAS` declares the function that the `PENNIESLIB.DLL` exports in its `interface` section. The definition of the `PenniesToCoins()` function is placed in the implementation section. This definition specifies that the function is an external function existing in the `.dll` file `PenniesLib.dll`. It links to the DLL function by the name of the function. Notice that you used a compiler directive `PENNIESLIB` to conditionally compile the declaration of the `PenniesToCoins()` function. You do this because it is not necessary to link this declaration when compiling the interface unit for the library. This allows us to share the interface unit's type definitions with both the library and any applications that intend to use the library. Any changes to the structures used by both only have to be made in the interface unit.

TIP

To define an applicationwide conditional directive, specify the conditional in the Directories/Conditionals page of the Project | Options dialog box. Note that you must rebuild your project for changes to conditional defines to take effect because Make logic doesn't reevaluate conditional defines.

NOTE

The following definition shows one of two ways to import a DLL function:

```
function PenniesToCoins; external 'PENNIESLIB.DLL' index 1;
```

This method is called importing by ordinal. The other method by which you can import DLL functions is by name:

```
function PenniesToCoins; external 'PENNIESLIB.DLL' name
'PenniesToCoins';
```

The by name method uses the name specified after the name keyword to determine which function to link to in the DLL.

The by-ordinal method reduces the DLL's load time because it doesn't have to look up the function name in the DLL's name table. However, this method isn't the preferred method in Win32. Importing by name is the preferred technique so that applications won't be hypersensitive to relocation of DLL entry points as DLLs get updated over time. When you import by ordinal, you are binding to a place in the DLL. When you import by name, you're binding to the function name, regardless of where it happens to be placed in the DLL.

If this were an actual DLL that you planned to deploy, you would provide both `PenniesLib.dll` and `PenniesInt.pas` to your users. This would enable them to use the DLL by defining the types and functions in `PenniesInt.pas` that `PenniesLib.dll` requires. Additionally, programmers using different languages, such as C++, could convert `PenniesInt.pas` to their languages, enabling them to use your DLL in their development environments. You'll find a sample project that uses `PenniesLib.dll` on the CD-ROM that accompanies this book.

Displaying Modal Forms from DLLs

This section shows you how to make modal forms available from a DLL. One reason placing commonly used forms in a DLL is beneficial is that it enables you to extend your forms for use with any Windows application or development environment, such as C++, Visual Basic, and Object PAL.

To do this, remove your DLL-based form from the list of auto-created forms.

We've created such a form that contains a `TCalendar` component on the main form. The calling application will call a DLL function that will invoke this form. When the user selects a day on the calendar, the date will be returned to the calling application.

Listing 9.3 shows the source to `CalendarLib.dpr`, the DLL project file. Listing 9.4 shows the source code for `DllFrm.pas`, the DLL form's unit, which illustrates how to encapsulate the form into a DLL.

LISTING 9.3. LIBRARY PROJECT SOURCE—`CalendarLib.dpr`.

```
unit DLLFrm;

interface

uses
  SysUtils, WinTypes, WinProcs, Messages, Classes, Graphics, Controls,
  Forms, Dialogs, Grids, Calendar;

type

  TDLLForm = class(TForm)
    calDllCalendar: TCalendar;
    procedure calDllCalendarDblClick(Sender: TObject);
  end;

{ Declare the export function }
function ShowCalendar(AHandle: THandle; ACaption: String): TDateTime;
  StdCall;
```

continues

LISTING 9.3. CONTINUED

```
implementation
{$R *.DFM}

function ShowCalendar(AHandle: THandle; ACaption: String): TDateTime;
var
  DLLForm: TDllForm;
begin
  // Copy application handle to DLL's TApplication object
  Application.Handle := AHandle;
  DLLForm := TDLLForm.Create(Application);
  try
    DLLForm.Caption := ACaption;
    DLLForm.ShowModal;
    // Pass the date back in Result
    Result := DLLForm.calDLLCalendar.CalendarDate; finally
    DLLForm.Free;
  end;
end;

procedure TDLLForm.calDllCalendarDblClick(Sender: TObject);
begin
  Close;
end;

end.
```

The main form in this DLL is incorporated into the exported function. Notice that the DLLForm declaration was removed from the interface section and declared inside the function instead.

The first thing that the DLL function does is to assign the AHandle parameter to the Application.Handle property. Recall from Chapter 4 that Delphi projects, including library projects, contain a global Application object. In a DLL, this object is separate from the Application object that exists in the calling application. For the form in the DLL to truly act as a modal form for the calling application, you must assign the handle of the calling application to the DLL's Application.Handle property as we have so illustrated. Not doing so will result in erratic behavior, especially when you start minimizing the DLL's form. Also, as shown, you must make sure to not pass nil as the owner of the DLL's form.

After the form is created, you assign the ACaption string to the Caption of the DLL form. It is then displayed modally. When the form closes, the date selected by the user in the TCalendar component is passed back to the calling function. The form closes after the user double-clicks the TCalendar component.

> **CAUTION**
>
> ShareMem must be the first unit in your library's uses clause and your project's (select View | Project Source) uses clause if your DLL exports any procedures or functions that pass strings or dynamic arrays as parameters or function results. This applies to all strings passed to and from your DLL—even those nested in records and classes. ShareMem is the interface unit to the Borlndmm.dll shared memory manager, which must be deployed along with your DLL. To avoid using Borlndmm.dll, pass string information using PChar or ShortString parameters.
>
> ShareMem is only required when heap-allocated strings or dynamic arrays are passed between modules, and such transfers also transfer ownership of that string memory. Typecasting an internal string to a PChar and passing it to another module as a PChar does not transfer ownership of the string memory to the callee, so ShareMem is not required.
>
> Note that this ShareMem issue applies only to Delphi/BCB DLLs that pass strings or dynamic arrays to other Delphi/BCB DLLs or EXEs. You should never expose Delphi strings or dynamic arrays (as parameters or function results of DLL exported functions) to non-Delphi DLLs or host apps. They won't know how to dispose of the Delphi items correctly.
>
> Also, ShareMem is never required between modules built with packages. The memory allocator is implicitly shared between packaged modules.

This is all that's required when encapsulating a modal form into a DLL. In the next section, we'll discuss displaying a modeless form in a DLL.

DISPLAYING MODELESS FORMS FROM DLLS

To illustrate placing modeless forms in a DLL, we'll use the same calendar form as with the previous section.

When displaying modeless forms from a DLL, the DLL must provide two routines. The first routine must take care of creating and displaying the form. A second routine is required to free the form. Listing 9.4 displays the source code for our illustration of a modeless form in a DLL.

LISTING 9.4. A MODELESS FORM IN A DLL.

```
unit DLLFrm;

interface
```

9

DYNAMIC LINK LIBRARIES

continues

LISTING 9.4. CONTINUED

```
uses
  SysUtils, WinTypes, WinProcs, Messages, Classes, Graphics, Controls,
  Forms, Dialogs, Grids, Calendar;

type

  TDLLForm = class(TForm)
    calDllCalendar: TCalendar;
  end;

{ Declare the export function }
function ShowCalendar(AHandle: THandle; ACaption: String): Longint;
  stdCall;
procedure CloseCalendar(AFormRef: Longint); stdcall;


implementation
{$R *.DFM}

function ShowCalendar(AHandle: THandle; ACaption: String): Longint;
var
  DLLForm: TDllForm;
begin
  // Copy application handle to DLL's TApplication object
  Application.Handle := AHandle;
  DLLForm := TDLLForm.Create(Application);
  Result := Longint(DLLForm);
  DLLForm.Caption := ACaption;
  DLLForm.Show;
end;

procedure CloseCalendar(AFormRef: Longint);
begin
  if AFormRef > 0 then
    TDLLForm(AFormRef).Free;
end;

end.
```

This listing displays the two routines ShowCalendar() and CloseCalendar().
ShowCalendar() is similar to the same function in the modal form example in that it
makes the assignment of the calling application's application handle to the DLL's application handle and creates the form. Instead of calling ShowModal(), however, this routine
calls Show(), and notice that it doesn't free the form. Also, notice that the function
returns a longint value to which you assign the DLLForm instance. This is because a
reference of the created form must be maintained, and it is best to have the calling

application maintain this instance. This would take care of any issues regarding other applications calling this DLL and creating another instance of the form.

In the `CloseCalendar()` procedure, you simply check for a valid reference to the form and invoke its `Free()` method. Here, the calling application should pass back the same reference that was returned to it from `ShowCalendar()`.

When using such a technique, you must be careful that your DLL never frees the form independently of the host. If it does (for example, returning `caFree` in `CanClose()`), the call to `CloseCalendar()` will crash.

Demos of both the modal and modeless forms are on the CD that accompanies this book in the directories `\ModalDLL` and `\ModelessDLL`.

USING DLLS IN YOUR DELPHI APPLICATIONS

Earlier in this chapter, you learned that there are two ways to load or import DLLs: implicitly and explicitly. Both techniques are illustrated in this section with the DLLs just created.

The first DLL created in this chapter included an `interface` unit. You'll use this interface unit in the following example to illustrate implicit linking of a DLL. The sample project's main form has a `TMaskEdit`, a `TButton`, and nine `TLabels`.

In this application, the user enters an amount of pennies, and when clicking the button, the labels will show the breakdown of denominations of change adding up to that amount. This information is obtained from the `PenniesLib.dll` exported function `PenniesToCoins()`.

The main form is defined in the unit `MainFrm.pas` shown in Listing 9.5.

LISTING 9.5. MAIN FORM FOR THE PENNIES DEMO.

```
unit MainFrm;

interface

uses
  SysUtils, WinTypes, WinProcs, Messages, Classes, Graphics, Controls,
  Forms, Dialogs, StdCtrls, Mask;

type

  TMainForm = class(TForm)
    lblTotal: TLabel;
    lblQlbl: TLabel;
```

continues

LISTING 9.5. CONTINUED

```
  lblDlbl: TLabel;
  lblNlbl: TLabel;
  lblPlbl: TLabel;
  lblQuarters: TLabel;
  lblDimes: TLabel;
  lblNickels: TLabel;
  lblPennies: TLabel;
  btnMakeChange: TButton;
  meTotalPennies: TMaskEdit;
  procedure btnMakeChangeClick(Sender: TObject);
end;

var
  MainForm: TMainForm;

implementation
uses PenniesInt;   // Use an interface unit

{$R *.DFM}

procedure TMainForm.btnMakeChangeClick(Sender: TObject);
var
  CoinsRec: TCoinsRec;
  TotPennies: word;
begin
  { Call the DLL function to determine the minimum coins required
    for the amount of pennies specified. }
  TotPennies := PenniesToCoins(StrToInt(meTotalPennies.Text), @CoinsRec);
  with CoinsRec do
  begin
    { Now display the coin information }
    lblQuarters.Caption := IntToStr(Quarters);
    lblDimes.Caption    := IntToStr(Dimes);
    lblNickels.Caption  := IntToStr(Nickels);
    lblPennies.Caption  := IntToStr(Pennies);
  end
end;

end.
```

Notice that MainFrm.pas uses the unit PenniesInt. Recall that PenniesInt.pas includes the external declarations to the functions existing in PenniesLib.dpr. When this application runs, the Win32 system automatically loads PenniesLib.dll and maps it to the process address space for the calling application.

Usage of an `import` unit is optional. You can remove `PenniesInt` from the `uses` statement and place the `external` declaration to `PenniesToCoins()` in the `MainFrm.pas` implementation section, as in the following code:

```
implementation

function PenniesToCoins(TotPennies: word; ChangeRec: PChangeRec): word;
  ➥StdCall external 'PENNIESLIB.DLL';
```

You also would have to define `PChangeRec` and `TChangeRec` again in `MainFrm.pas`, or you can compile your application using the compiler directive `PENNIESLIB`. This technique is fine in the case where you only need access to a few routines from a DLL. In many cases, you'll find that you require not only the external declarations to the DLL's routines but also access to the types defined in the `interface` unit.

> **NOTE**
>
> Many times, when using another vendor's DLL, you won't have a Pascal inter-face unit; instead, you'll have a C/C++ import library. In this case, you have to translate the library to a Pascal equivalent interface unit.

You'll find this demo on the accompanying CD.

Loading DLLs Explicitly

Although loading DLLs implicitly is convenient, it isn't always the most desired method. Suppose that you have a DLL that contains many routines. If it's likely that your application will never call any of the DLL's routines, it would be a waste of memory to load the DLL every time your application runs. This is especially true when using multiple DLLs with one application. Another example is when using DLLs as large objects: a standard list of functions that are implemented by multiple DLLs but do slightly different things, such as printer drivers and file format readers. In this situation, it would be beneficial to load the DLL when specifically requested to do so by the application. This is referred to as *explicitly* loading a DLL.

To illustrate explicitly loading a DLL, we return to the example DLL with a modal form. Listing 9.6 shows the code for the main form of the application that demonstrates explicitly loading this DLL. The project file for this application is on the accompanying CD in the directory `\ModalDLL`.

LISTING 9.6. MAIN FORM FOR CALENDAR DLL DEMO APPLICATION.

```
unit MainFfm;

interface

uses
  SysUtils, WinTypes, WinProcs, Messages, Classes, Graphics, Controls,
  Forms, Dialogs, StdCtrls;

type
  { First, define a procedural data type, this should reflect the
    procedure that is exported from the DLL. }
  TShowCalendar = function (AHandle: THandle; ACaption: String):
➥TDateTime; StdCall;

  { Create a new exception class to refect a failed DLL load }
  EDLLLoadError = class(Exception);

  TMainForm = class(TForm)
    lblDate: TLabel;
    btnGetCalendar: TButton;
    procedure btnGetCalendarClick(Sender: TObject);
  end;

var
  MainForm: TMainForm;

implementation

{$R *.DFM}

procedure TMainForm.btnGetCalendarClick(Sender: TObject);
var
  LibHandle   : THandle;
  ShowCalendar: TShowCalendar;
begin

  { Attempt to load the DLL }
  LibHandle := LoadLibrary('CALENDARLIB.DLL');
  try
    { If the load failed, LibHandle will be zero.
      If this occurs, raise an exception. }
    if LibHandle = 0 then
      raise EDLLLoadError.Create('Unable to Load DLL');
    { If the code makes it here, the DLL loaded successfully, now obtain
      the link to the DLL's exported function so that it can be called. }
    @ShowCalendar := GetProcAddress(LibHandle, 'ShowCalendar');
    { If the function is imported successfully, then set
      lblDate.Caption to reflect the returned date from
      the function. Otherwise, show the return raise an exception. }
```

```
    if not (@ShowCalendar = nil) then
      lblDate.Caption := DateToStr(ShowCalendar(Application.Handle,
➥Caption))
    else
      RaiseLastWin32Error;
  finally
    FreeLibrary(LibHandle); // Unload the DLL.
  end;
end;

end.
```

This unit first defines a procedural data type, `TShowCalendar`, that reflects the definition of the function it will be using from `CalendarLib.dll`. It then defines a special exception, which is raised when there's a problem loading the DLL. In the `btnGetCalendarClick()` event handler, you'll notice the use of three Win32 API functions: `LoadLibrary()`, `FreeLibrary()`, and `GetProcAddress()`.

`LoadLibrary()` is defined this way:

```
function LoadLibrary(lpLibFileName: PChar): HMODULE; stdcall;
```

This function loads the DLL module specified by `lpLibFileName` and maps it into the address space of the calling process. If this function succeeds, it returns a handle to the module. If it fails, it returns the value 0, and an exception is raised. You can look up `LoadLibrary()` in the online help for detailed information on its functionality and possible return error values.

`FreeLibrary()` is defined like this:

```
function FreeLibrary(hLibModule: HMODULE): BOOL; stdcall;
```

`FreeLibrary()` decrements the instance count of the library specified by `LibModule`. It removes the library from memory when the library's instance count is zero. The instance count keeps track of the number of tasks using the DLL.

Here's how `GetProcAddress()` is defined:

```
function GetProcAddress(hModule: HMODULE; lpProcName: LPCSTR): FARPROC;
stdcall
```

`GetProcAddress()` returns the address of a function within the module specified in its first parameter, `hModule`. `hModule` is the `THandle` returned from a call to `LoadLibrary()`. If `GetProcAddress()` fails, it returns `nil`. You must call `GetLastError()` for extended error information.

9

**DYNAMIC LINK
LIBRARIES**

In the `Button1` `OnClick` event handler, `LoadLibrary()` is called to load CALDLL. If it fails to load, an exception is raised. If the call is successful, a call to the window's `GetProcAddress()` is made to get the address of the function `ShowCalendar()`. Prepending the procedural data type variable `ShowCalendar` with the address of operator (`@`) character prevents the compiler from issuing a type mismatch error due to its strict type-checking. After obtaining the address of `ShowCalendar()`, you can use it as defined by `TShowCalendar`. Finally, `FreeLibrary()` is called within the `finally` block to ensure that the library is freed from memory when no longer required.

You can see that the library is loaded and freed each time this function is called. If this function is called only once during the run of an application, it becomes apparent how explicit loading can save much-needed and often limited memory resources. On the other hand, if this function were called frequently, the DLL loading and unloading would add a lot of overhead.

THE DYNAMICALLY LINKED LIBRARY ENTRY/EXIT FUNCTION

You can provide optional entry and exit code for your DLLs when required under various initialization and shutdown operations. These operations can occur during process or thread initialization/termination.

Process/Thread Initialization and Termination Routines

Typical initialization operations are registering Windows classes or initializing global variables, or initializing an entry/exit function. This occurs during the method of entry for the DLL, which is referred to as the `DLLEntryPoint` function. This function is actually represented by the `begin..end` block of the DLL project file. This is the location where you would set up an entry/exit procedure. This procedure must take a single parameter of the type `DWord`.

The global `DLLProc` variable is a procedural pointer to which you can assign the entry/exit procedure. This variable is initially `nil` unless you set up your own procedure. By setting up an entry/exit procedure, you can respond to the events listed in Table 9.1.

TABLE 9.1. DLL ENTRY/EXIT EVENTS.

Event	Purpose
DLL_PROCESS_ATTACH	The DLL is attaching to the address space of the current process when the process starts up or when a call to `LoadLibrary()` is made. DLLs initialize any instance data during this event.

Event	Purpose
DLL_PROCESS_DETACH	The DLL is detaching from the address space of the calling process. This occurs during a clean process exit or when a call to FreeLibrary() is made. The DLL can uninitialize any instance data during this event.
DLL_THREAD_ATTACH	This event occurs when the current process creates a new thread. When this occurs, the system calls the entry-point function of any DLLs attached to the process. This call is made in the context of the new thread and can be used to allocate any thread-specific data.
DLL_THREAD_DETACH	This event occurs when the thread is exiting. During this event, the DLL can free any thread-specific initialized data.

CAUTION

Threads terminated abnormally—by calling TerminateThread()—are not guaranteed to call DLL_THREAD_DETACH.

DLL Entry/Exit Example

Listing 9.7 illustrates how you would install an entry/exit procedure to the DLL's DLLProc variable.

LISTING 9.7. THE SOURCE CODE FOR DLLENTRY.DPR.

```
library DllEntry;
uses
  SysUtils,
  Windows,
  Dialogs,
  Classes;
procedure DLLEntryPoint(dwReason: DWord);
begin
  case dwReason of
    DLL_PROCESS_ATTACH: ShowMessage('Attaching to process');
    DLL_PROCESS_DETACH: ShowMessage('Detaching from process');
    DLL_THREAD_ATTACH:  MessageBeep(0);
    DLL_THREAD_DETACH:  MessageBeep(0);
  end;
end;
begin
```

continues

9

DYNAMIC LINK LIBRARIES

LISTING 9.7. CONTINUED

```
{ First, assign the procedure to the DLLProc variable }
DllProc := @DLLEntryPoint;
{ Now invoke the procedure to reflect that the DLL is attaching to the
  process }
DLLEntryPoint(DLL_PROCESS_ATTACH);
end.
```

The entry/exit procedure is assigned to the DLL's `DLLProc` variable in the `begin..end` block of the .dll project file. This procedure `DLLEntryPoint()` evaluates its word parameter to determine which event is being called. These events correspond to the events listed in Table 9.1. For illustration, we had each event display a message box when the DLL was being loaded and destroyed. When a thread in the calling application is being created/destroyed, a message beep occurs.

To illustrate the use of this DLL, examine the code shown in Listing 9.8.

LISTING 9.8. SAMPLE CODE FOR DLL ENTRY/EXIT DEMO.

```
unit MainFrm;

interface

uses
  Windows, Messages, SysUtils, Classes, Graphics, Controls,
  Forms, Dialogs, StdCtrls, ComCtrls, Gauges;

type

  { Define a TThread descendant }
  TTestThread = class(TThread)
    procedure Execute; override;
  end;

  TMainForm = class(TForm)
    btnLoadLib: TButton;
    btnFreeLib: TButton;
    btnCreateThread: TButton;
    btnFreeThread: TButton;
    lblCount: TLabel;
    procedure btnLoadLibClick(Sender: TObject);
    procedure btnFreeLibClick(Sender: TObject);
    procedure btnCreateThreadClick(Sender: TObject);
    procedure btnFreeThreadClick(Sender: TObject);
    procedure FormCreate(Sender: TObject);
  private
    LibHandle   : THandle;
    TestThread  : TTestThread;
```

```
    Counter    : Integer;
    GoThread   : Boolean;
  end;

var
  MainForm: TMainForm;

implementation

{$R *.DFM}

procedure TTestThread.Execute;
begin
  while MainForm.GoThread do
  begin
    MainForm.lblCount.Caption := IntToStr(MainForm.Counter);
    Inc(MainForm.Counter);
  end;
end;

procedure TMainForm.btnLoadLibClick(Sender: TObject);
{ This procedure loads the library DllEntryLib.DLL }
begin
  if LibHandle = 0 then
  begin
    LibHandle := LoadLibrary('DLLENTRYLIB.DLL');
    if LibHandle = 0 then
      raise Exception.Create('Unable to Load DLL');
  end
  else
    MessageDlg('Library already loaded', mtWarning, [mbok], 0);
end;

procedure TMainForm.btnFreeLibClick(Sender: TObject);
{ This procedure frees the library }
begin
  if not (LibHandle = 0) then
  begin
    FreeLibrary(LibHandle);
    LibHandle := 0;
  end;
end;

procedure TMainForm.btnCreateThreadClick(Sender: TObject);
{ This procedure creates the TThread instance. If the DLL is loaded a
  message beep will occur. }
begin
  if TestThread = nil then
  begin
```

continues

9

**DYNAMIC LINK
LIBRARIES**

LISTING 9.8. CONTINUED

```
    GoThread   := True;
    TestThread := TTestThread.Create(False);
  end;
end;

procedure TMainForm.btnFreeThreadClick(Sender: TObject);
{ In freeing the TThread a message beep will occur if the DLL is loaded. }
begin
  if not (TestThread = nil) then
  begin
    GoThread   := False;
    TestThread.Free;
    TestThread := nil;
    Counter    := 0;
  end;

end;

procedure TMainForm.FormCreate(Sender: TObject);
begin
  LibHandle  := 0;
  TestThread := nil;
end;

end.
```

This project consists of a main form with four TButton components. BtnLoadLib loads the DLL DllEntryLib.dll. BtnFreeLib frees the library from the process. BtnCreateThread creates a TThread descendant object, which in turn creates a thread. BtnFreeThread destroys the TThread object. The lblCount is used just to show the thread execution.

The btnLoadLibClick() event handler calls LoadLibrary() to load DllEntryLib.dll. This causes the DLL to load and be mapped to the process's address space. Additionally, the initialization code in the DLL gets executed. Again, this is the code that appears in the begin..end block of the DLL, which performs the following to set up an entry/exit procedure for the DLL:

```
begin
  { First, assign the procedure to the DLLProc variable }
  DllProc := @DLLEntryPoint;
  { Now invoke the procedure to reflect that the DLL is attaching to the
    process }
  DLLEntryPoint(DLL_PROCESS_ATTACH);
end.
```

This initialization section will only be called once per process. If another process loads this DLL, this section will be called again, except in the context of the separate process—processes don't share DLL instances.

The `btnFreeLibClick()` event handler unloads the DLL by calling `FreeLibrary()`. When this happens, the procedure to which the `DLLProc` points, `DLLEntryProc()`, gets called with the value of `DLL_PROCESS_DETACH` passed as the parameter.

The `btnCreateThreadClick()` event handler creates the `TThread` descendant object. This causes the `DLLEntryProc()` to get called, and the `DLL_THREAD_ATTACH` value is passed as the parameter. The `btnFreeThreadClick()` event handler invokes `DLLEntryProc` again but passes `DLL_THREAD_DETACH` as the value to the procedure.

Although you invoke only a message box when the events occur, you'll use these events to perform any process or thread initialization or cleanup that might be necessary for your application. Later, you'll see an example of using this technique to set up sharable DLL global data. You can look at the demo of this DLL in the project `DLLEntryTest.dpr` on the CD.

EXCEPTIONS IN DLLS

This section discusses issues regarding DLLs and Win32 exceptions.

Capturing Exceptions in 16-Bit Delphi

Back in the 16-bit days with Delphi 1, Delphi exceptions were language-specific. Therefore, if exceptions were raised in a DLL, you were required to capture the exception before it escaped from the DLL so that it wouldn't creep up the calling modules stack, causing it to crash. You had to wrap every DLL entry point with an exception handler, like this:

```
procedure SomeDLLProc;
begin
  try
    { Do your stuff }
  except
    on Exception do
        { Don't let it get away, handle it and don't re-raise it }
  end;
end;
```

This is no longer the case as of Delphi 2. Delphi 4 exceptions map themselves to Win32 exceptions. Exceptions raised in DLLs are no longer a compiler/language feature of Delphi but rather a feature of the Win32 system.

For this to work, however, you must make sure that SysUtils is included in the DLL's uses clause. Not including SysUtils disables Delphi's exception support inside the DLL.

CAUTION

Most Win32 applications are not designed to handle exceptions, so even though Delphi language exceptions get turned into Win32 exceptions, those that you let escape from a DLL into the host application are likely to shut down the application.

If the host application is built with Delphi or C++Builder, this shouldn't be much of an issue, but there is still a lot of raw C and C++ code out there that doesn't like exceptions.

Therefore, to make your DLLs bulletproof, you might still consider using the 16-bit method of protecting DLL entry points with try..except blocks to capture exceptions raised in your DLLs.

NOTE

When a non-Delphi application uses a DLL written in Delphi, it won't be able to utilize the Delphi language-specific exception classes. However, it can be handled as a Win32 system exception given the exception code of $0EEDFACE. The exception address will be the first entry in the ExceptionInformation array of the Win32 system EXCEPTION_RECORD. The second entry contains a reference to the Delphi exception object. Look up EXCEPTION_RECORD in the Delphi online help for additional information.

Exceptions and the Safecall Directive

Safecall functions are used for COM and exception handling. They guarantee that any exception will propagate to the caller of the function. Instead, a Safecall function converts an exception into an HResult return value. Safecall also implies the StdCall calling convention. Therefore, a Safecall function declared as

```
function Foo(i: integer): string; Safecall;
```

really looks like this according to the compiler:

```
function Foo(i: integer): string; HResult; StdCall;
```

The compiler then inserts an implicit `try..except` block that wraps the entire function contents and catches any exceptions raised. The `except` block invokes a call to `SafecallExceptionHandler()` to convert the exception into an `HResult`. This is somewhat similar to the 16-bit method of capturing exceptions and passing back error values.

CALLBACK FUNCTIONS

A *callback function* is a function in your application called by Win32 DLLs or other DLLs. Basically, Windows has several API functions that require a callback function. When calling these functions, you pass in an address of a function defined by your application that Windows can call. If you're wondering how this all relates to DLLs, remember that the Win32 API is really several routines exported from system DLLs. Essentially, when you pass a callback function to a Win32 function, you're passing this function to a DLL.

One such function is the `EnumWindows()` API function, which enumerates through all top-level windows. This function passes the handle of each window in the enumeration to your application-defined callback function. You are required to define and pass the callback function's address to the `EnumWindows()` function. The callback function that you must provide to `EnumWindows()` is defined this way:

```
function EnumWindowsProc(Hw: HWnd; lp: lParam): Boolean; stdcall;
```

We illustrate the use of the `EnumWindows()` function in the `CallBack.dpr` project on the CD accompanying this book and shown in Listing 9.9.

LISTING 9.9. MAINFORM.PAS, SOURCE TO CALLBACK EXAMPLE.

```
unit MainFrm;

interface

uses
  Windows, Messages, SysUtils, Classes, Graphics, Controls,
  Forms, Dialogs, StdCtrls, ComCtrls;

type

  { Define a record/class to hold the window name and class name for
    each window. Instances of this class will get added to ListBox1 }
  TWindowInfo = class
    WindowName,           // The window name
    WindowClass: String;  // The window's class name
  end;
```

9

DYNAMIC LINK LIBRARIES

continues

LISTING 9.9. CONTINUED

```
TMainForm = class(TForm)
  lbWinInfo: TListBox;
  btnGetWinInfo: TButton;
  hdWinInfo: THeaderControl;
  procedure btnGetWinInfoClick(Sender: TObject);
  procedure FormDestroy(Sender: TObject);
  procedure lbWinInfoDrawItem(Control: TWinControl; Index: Integer;
    Rect: TRect; State: TOwnerDrawState);
  procedure hdWinInfoSectionResize(HeaderControl: THeaderControl;
    Section: THeaderSection);
end;

var
  MainForm: TMainForm;

implementation

{$R *.DFM}
function EnumWindowsProc(Hw: HWnd; AMainForm: TMainForm): Boolean;
  stdcall;
{ This procedure is called by the User32.DLL library as it enumerates
  through windows active in the system. }
var
  WinName, CName: array[0..144] of char;
  WindowInfo: TWindowInfo;
begin
  { Return true by default which indicates not to stop enumerating
    through the windows }
  Result := True;
  GetWindowText(Hw, WinName, 144); // Obtain the current window text
  GetClassName(Hw, CName, 144);    // Obtain the class name of the window
  { Create a TWindowInfo instance and set its fields with the values of
    the window name and window class name. Then add this object to
    ListBox1's Objects array. These values will be displayed later by
    the listbox }
  WindowInfo := TWindowInfo.Create;
  with WindowInfo do
  begin
    SetLength(WindowName, strlen(WinName));
    SetLength(WindowClass, StrLen(CName));
    WindowName := StrPas(WinName);
    WindowClass := StrPas(CName);
  end;
  MainForm.lbWinInfo.Items.AddObject('', WindowInfo); // Add to Objects
                                                      // array
end;

procedure TMainForm.btnGetWinInfoClick(Sender: TObject);
begin
```

```
    { Enumerate through all top-level windows being displayed. Pass in the
      call back function EnumWindowsProc which will be called for each
      window }
    EnumWindows(@EnumWindowsProc, 0);
end;

procedure TMainForm.FormDestroy(Sender: TObject);
var
  i: integer;
begin
  { Free all instances of TWindowInfo }
  for i := 0 to lbWinInfo.Items.Count - 1 do
    TWindowInfo(lbWinInfo.Items.Objects[i]).Free
end;

procedure TMainForm.lbWinInfoDrawItem(Control: TWinControl; Index:
➡Integer;
  Rect: TRect; State: TOwnerDrawState);
begin
  { First, clear the rectangle to which drawing will be performed }
  lbWinInfo.Canvas.FillRect(Rect);
  { Now draw the strings of the TWindowInfo record stored at the
    Index'th position of the listbox. The sections of HeaderControl1
    will give positions to which to draw each string }
  with TWindowInfo(lbWinInfo.Items.Objects[Index]) do
  begin
    DrawText(lbWinInfo.Canvas.Handle, PChar(WindowName),
      Length(WindowName), Rect,dt_Left or dt_VCenter);
    { Shift the drawing rectangle over by using the size
      HeaderControl1's sections to determine where to draw the next
      string }
    Rect.Left := Rect.Left + hdWinInfo.Sections[0].Width;
    DrawText(lbWinInfo.Canvas.Handle, PChar(WindowClass),
      Length(WindowClass), Rect, dt_Left or dt_VCenter);
  end;
end;

procedure TMainForm.hdWinInfoSectionResize(HeaderControl:
  THeaderControl; Section: THeaderSection);
begin
  lbWinInfo.Invalidate; // Force ListBox1 to redraw itself.
end;

end.
```

9

**DYNAMIC LINK
LIBRARIES**

This application uses the EnumWindows() function to extract the window name and class name of all top-level windows and adds them to the owner-draw list box on the main form. The main form uses an owner-draw list box to make both the window name and window class name appear in a columnar fashion. First we'll explain the use of the call-back function. Then we'll explain how we created the columnar list box.

Using the Callback Function

You saw in Listing 9.9 that we defined a procedure `EnumWindowsProc()`, which takes a window handle as its first parameter. The second parameter is user-defined data, so you may pass whatever data you deem necessary as long as its size is the equivalent to an integer data type.

`EnumWindowsProc()` is the callback procedure that you will pass to the `EnumWindows()` Win32 API function. It must be declared with the `StdCall` directive to specify that it uses the Win32 calling convention. When passing this procedure to `EnumWindows()`, it will get called for each top-level window whose window handle gets passed as the first parameter. You use this window handle to obtain both the window name and class name of each window. You then create an instance of the `TWindowInfo` class and set its fields with this information. The `TWindowInfo` class instance is then added to the `lbWinInfo.Objects` array. The data in this list box will be used when the list box is drawn to show this data in a columnar fashion.

Notice that, in the main form's `OnDestroy` event handler, you must make sure to clean up any allocated instances of the `TWindowInfo` class.

The `btnGetWinInfoClick()`event handler calls the `EnumWindows()` procedure and passes `EnumWindowsProc()` as its first parameter.

When you run the application and click the button, you'll see that the information is obtained from each window and is shown in the list box.

Drawing an Owner-Draw List Box

The window name and class name of top-level windows are drawn in a columnar fashion in `lbWinInfo` from the previous project. This was done by using a `TListBox` with its `Style` property set to `lbOwnerDraw`. When this style is set as such, the `TListBox.OnDrawItem` event is called each time the `TListBox` is to draw one of its items. You're responsible for drawing the items as we have illustrated in the example.

In Listing 9.9, the event handler `lbWinInfoDrawItem()` contains the code that performs the drawing of list box items. Here, you draw the strings contained in the `TWindowInfo` class instances, which are stored in the `lbWinInfo.Objects` array. These values are obtained from the callback function `EnumWindowsProc()`. You can refer to the code commentary to determine what this event handler does.

CALLING CALLBACK FUNCTIONS FROM YOUR DLLS

Just as you can pass callback function to DLLs, you can also have your DLLs call callback functions. This section illustrates how you can create a DLL whose exported function takes a callback procedure as parameter. Then, based on whether the user passes in a callback procedure, the procedure gets called. Listing 9.10 contains the source code to this DLL.

LISTING 9.10. SOURCE CODE TO THE StrSrchLib.dll, CALLING A CALLBACK DEMO.

```
library StrSrchLib;

uses
  Wintypes,
  WinProcs,
  SysUtils,
  Dialogs;

type
  { declare the callback function type }
  TFoundStrProc = procedure(StrPos: PChar); StdCall;

function SearchStr(ASrcStr, ASearchStr: PChar;  AProc: TFarProc): Integer;
  StdCall;
{ This function looks for ASearchStr in ASrcStr. When if finds ASearchStr,
  the callback procedure referred to by AProc is called if one has been
  passed in. The user may pass nil as this parameter. }
var
  FindStr: PChar;
begin
  FindStr := ASrcStr;
  FindStr := StrPos(FindStr, ASearchStr);
  while FindStr <> nil do
  begin
    if AProc <> nil then
      TFoundStrProc(AProc)(FindStr);
    FindStr := FindStr + 1;
    FindStr := StrPos(FindStr, ASearchStr);
  end;
end;

exports
  SearchStr;
begin

end.
```

The DLL also defines a procedural type, `TFoundStrProc`, for the callback function, which will be used to typecast the callback function when it's called.

The exported procedure `SearchStr()` is where the callback function is called. The commentary in the listing explains what this procedure does.

An example of this DLL's usage is given in the project `CallBackDemo.dpr` in the `\DLLCallBack` directory on the CD. The source to the main form for this demo is shown in Listing 9.11.

LISTING 9.11. MAIN FORM FOR DLL CALLBACK DEMO.

```
unit MainFrm;

interface

uses
  Windows, Messages, SysUtils, Classes, Graphics, Controls,
  Forms, Dialogs, StdCtrls;

type
  TMainForm = class(TForm)
    btnCallDLLFunc: TButton;
    edtSearchStr: TEdit;
    lblSrchWrd: TLabel;
    memStr: TMemo;
    procedure btnCallDLLFuncClick(Sender: TObject);
  end;

var
  MainForm: TMainForm;
  Count: Integer;

implementation

{$R *.DFM}

{ Define the DLL's exported procedure }
function SearchStr(ASrcStr, ASearchStr: PChar; AProc: TFarProc): Integer;
➥StdCall external
  'STRSRCHLIB.DLL';

{ Define the callback procedure, make sure to use the StdCall directive }
procedure StrPosProc(AStrPsn: PChar); StdCall;
begin
  inc(Count); // Increment the Count variable.
end;
```

```
procedure TMainForm.btnCallDLLFuncClick(Sender: TObject);
var
  S: String;
  S2: String;
begin
  Count := 0; // Initialize Count to zero.
  { Retrieve the length of the text on which to search. }
  SetLength(S, memStr.GetTextLen);
  { Now copy the text to the variable S }
  memStr.GetTextBuf(PChar(S), memStr.GetTextLen);
  { Copy Edit1's Text to a string variable so that it can be passed to
    the DLL function }
  S2 := edtSearchStr.Text;
  { Call the DLL function }
  SearchStr(PChar(S), PChar(S2), @StrPosProc);
  { Show how many times the word occurs in the string. This has been
    stored in the Count variable which is used by the callback function }
  ShowMessage(Format('%s %s %d %s', [edtSearchStr.Text, 'occurs', Count,
➥'times.']));
end;

end.
```

This application contains a TMemo control. EdtSearchStr.Text contains a string that will be searched for in memStr's contents. Memstr's contents are passed as the source string to the DLL function SearchStr(), and edtSearchStr.Text is passed as the search string.

The function StrPosProc() is the actual callback function. This function increments the value of a global variable Count, which you use to hold the number of times the search string occurs in memStr's text.

SHARING DLL DATA ACROSS DIFFERENT PROCESSES

Back in the world of 16-bit Windows, DLL memory was handled differently than it is in the 32-bit world of Win32. One often-used trait of 16-bit DLLs is that DLLs share global memory among different applications. In other words, if you declare a global variable in a 16-bit DLL, any application that uses that DLL will have access to that variable, and changes made to that variable by an application will be seen by another application.

In some ways, this behavior can be dangerous because one application can overwrite data on which another application is dependent. In other ways, developers have made use of this characteristic.

In Win32, this sharing of DLL global data no longer exists. Because each application process maps the DLL to its own address space, the DLL's data also gets mapped to that same address space. This results in each application getting its own instance of DLL data. Changes made to the DLL global data by one application won't be seen from another application.

If you're planning on porting a 16-bit application that relies on the sharable behavior of DLL global data, you can still provide a means for applications to share data in a DLL with other applications. The process isn't automatic, and it requires the use of memory-mapped files to store the shared data. Memory-mapped files are covered in Chapter 12, "Working with Files." We'll use them here to illustrate this method; however, you'll probably want to return to this section to review when you have a more thorough understanding of memory-mapped files after reading Chapter 12.

Creating a DLL with Shared Memory

Listing 9.12 shows a DLL project file that contains the code to allow applications using this DLL to share its global data. This global data is stored in the variable appropriately named `GlobalData`.

LISTING 9.12. ShareLib—DLL ILLUSTRATING SHARING GLOBAL DATA.

```
library ShareLib;

uses
  ShareMem,
  Windows,
  SysUtils,
  Classes;
const

  cMMFileName: PChar = 'SharedMapData';

{$I DLLDATA.INC}

var
  GlobalData : PGlobalDLLData;
  MapHandle  : THandle;

{ GetDLLData will be the exported DLL function }
procedure GetDLLData(var AGlobalData: PGlobalDLLData); StdCall;
begin
  { Point AGlobalData to the same memory address referred to by
    GlobalData. }
  AGlobalData := GlobalData;
end;
```

```
procedure OpenSharedData;
var
   Size: Integer;
begin
  { Get the size of the data to be mapped. }
  Size := SizeOf(TGlobalDLLData);

  { Now get a memory-mapped file object. Note the first parameter passes
    the value $FFFFFFFF or DWord(-1) so that space is allocated from the
    system's paging file. This requires that a name for the memory-mapped
    object get passed as the last parameter. }

  MapHandle := CreateFileMapping(DWord(-1), nil, PAGE_READWRITE, 0, Size,
➥cMMFileName);

  if MapHandle = 0 then
    RaiseLastWin32Error;
  { Now map the data to the calling process's address space and get a
    pointer to the beginning of this address }
  GlobalData := MapViewOfFile(MapHandle, FILE_MAP_ALL_ACCESS, 0, 0, Size);
  { Initialize this data }
  GlobalData^.S := 'ShareLib';
  GlobalData^.I := 1;
  if GlobalData = nil then
  begin
    CloseHandle(MapHandle);
    RaiseLastWin32Error;
  end;
end;

procedure CloseSharedData;
{ This procedure un-maps the memory-mapped file and releases the memory-
  mapped file handle }
begin
  UnmapViewOfFile(GlobalData);
  CloseHandle(MapHandle);
end;

procedure DLLEntryPoint(dwReason: DWord);
begin
  case dwReason of
    DLL_PROCESS_ATTACH: OpenSharedData;
    DLL_PROCESS_DETACH: CloseSharedData;
  end;
end;

exports
  GetDLLData;
```

9

DYNAMIC LINK LIBRARIES

continues

LISTING 9.12. CONTINUED

```
begin
  { First, assign the procedure to the DLLProc variable }
  DllProc := @DLLEntryPoint;
  { Now invoke the procedure to reflect that the DLL is attaching
    to the process }
  DLLEntryPoint(DLL_PROCESS_ATTACH);
end.
```

GlobalData is of the type PGlobalDLLData, which is defined in the include file DllData.inc. This include file contains the following type definition. Note that the include file is linked by using the include directive $I.

type

```
  PGlobalDLLData = ^TGlobalDLLData;
  TGlobalDLLData = record
    S: String[50];
    I: Integer;
  end;
```

In this DLL, you use the same process discussed earlier in the chapter to add entry and exit code to the DLL in the form of an entry/exit procedure. This procedure is called DLLEntryPoint(), as shown in the listing. When a process loads the DLL, the OpenSharedData() method is called. When a process detaches from the DLL, the CloseSharedData() method is called.

We won't get too detailed about memory-mapped file usage here because we cover it in more detail in Chapter 12. However, we'll explain the basics of what's going on so that you understand the purpose of this DLL.

Memory-mapped files provide a means for you to reserve a region of address space in the Win32 system to which physical storage gets committed. This is similar to allocating memory and referring to that memory with a pointer. With memory-mapped files, however, you can map a disk file to this address space and refer to the space within the file as though you were just referencing an area of memory with a pointer.

With memory-mapped files, you must first get a handle to an existing file on disk to which a memory-mapped object will be mapped. You then map the memory-mapping object to that file. At the beginning of the chapter, we told you how the system shares DLLs with multiple applications by first loading the DLL into memory and then giving each application its own image of the DLL, so that it appears as though each application has loaded a separate instance of the DLL. In reality, however, the DLL exists in memory only once. This is done by using memory-mapped files. You can use the same process to give access to data files. You just make necessary Win32 API calls that deal with creating and accessing memory-mapped files.

Now, consider this scenario. Suppose that an application, which we'll call App1, creates a memory-mapped file that gets mapped to a file on disk, `MyFile.dat`. App1 can now read and write data in that file. If, while App1 is running, App2 also maps to that same file, changes made to the file by App1 will be seen by App2. Actually, it's a bit more complex; certain flags must be set so that changes to the file are immediately set and so forth. For this discussion, it suffices to say that changes will be realized by both applications because this is possible.

One of the ways in which memory-mapped files can be used is to create a file mapping from the Win32 paging file rather than an existing file. This means that instead of mapping to an existing file on disk, you can reserve an area of memory to which you can refer as though it were a disk file. This prevents you from having to create and destroy a temporary file if all you want to do is to create an address space that can be accessed by multiple processes. The Win32 system manages its paging file, so when memory is no longer required of the paging file, the memory is released.

In the preceding paragraphs, we presented a scenario that illustrated how two applications can access the same file data by using a memory-mapped file. The same can be done between an application and a DLL. In fact, if the DLL creates the memory-mapped file when it's loaded by an application, it will use the same memory-mapped file when loaded by another application. There will be two images of the DLL, one for each calling application, both of which use the same memory-mapped file instance. The DLL can make the data referred to by the file mapping available to its calling application. When one application makes changes to this data, the second application will see these changes because they're referring to the same data, mapped by two different memory-mapped object instances. We use this technique in the example.

In Listing 9.12, `OpenSharedData()` is responsible for creating the memory-mapped file. It uses the `CreateFileMapping()` function to first create the file-mapping object, which it then passes to the `MapViewOfFile()` function. The `MapViewOfFile()` function maps a view of the file into the address space of the calling process. The return value of this function is the beginning of that address space. Now remember, this is the address space of the calling process. For two different applications using this DLL, this address location might be different, although the data to which they refer will be the same.

> **NOTE**
>
> The first parameter to `CreateFileMapping()` is a handle to a file to which the memory-mapped file gets mapped. However, if mapping to an address space of the system paging file, pass the value $FFFFFFFF (which is the same as `DWord(-1)`) as this parameter value. You must also supply a name for the file-mapping object as the last parameter to `CreateFileMapping()`. This is the name that the system uses to refer to this file mapping. If multiple processes create a memory-mapped file using the same name, the mapping objects will refer to the same system memory.

After the call to `MapViewOfFile()`, the variable `GlobalData` refers to the address space for the memory-mapped file. The exported function `GetDLLData()` assigns that memory to which `GlobalData` refers to the `AGlobalData` parameter. `AGlobalData` is passed in from the calling application, and therefore the calling application has read/write access to this data.

The `CloseSharedData()` procedure is responsible for unmapping the view of the file from the calling process and releasing the file-mapping object. This doesn't affect other file-mapping objects or file mappings from other applications.

Using a DLL with Shared Memory

To illustrate the use of the shared memory DLL, we've created two applications that make use of it. The first application, `App1.dpr`, allows you to modify the DLL's data. The second application, `App2.dpr`, also refers to the DLL's data and continually updates a couple of `TLabel` components by using a `TTimer` component. When you run both applications, you'll be able to see the sharable access to the DLL data—App2 will reflect changes made by App1.

Listing 9.13 shows the source code to the APP1 project.

LISTING 9.13. MAIN FORM FOR App1.dpr.

```
unit MainFrmA1;

interface

uses
  Windows, Messages, SysUtils, Classes, Graphics, Controls,
  Forms, Dialogs, StdCtrls, ExtCtrls, Mask;

{$I DLLDATA.INC}

type
```

```
  TMainForm = class(TForm)
    edtGlobDataStr: TEdit;
    btnGetDllData: TButton;
    meGlobDataInt: TMaskEdit;
    procedure btnGetDllDataClick(Sender: TObject);
    procedure edtGlobDataStrChange(Sender: TObject);
    procedure meGlobDataIntChange(Sender: TObject);
    procedure FormCreate(Sender: TObject);
  public
    GlobalData: PGlobalDLLData;
  end;

var
  MainForm: TMainForm;

{ Define the DLL's exported procedure }
procedure GetDLLData(var AGlobalData: PGlobalDLLData); StdCall External
➥'SHARELIB.DLL';

implementation

{$R *.DFM}

procedure TMainForm.btnGetDllDataClick(Sender: TObject);
begin
  { Get a pointer to the DLL's data }
  GetDLLData(GlobalData);
  { Now update the controls to reflect GlobalData's field values }
  edtGlobDataStr.Text := GlobalData^.S;
  meGlobDataInt.Text  := IntToStr(GlobalData^.I);
end;

procedure TMainForm.edtGlobDataStrChange(Sender: TObject);
begin
  { Update the DLL data with the changes }
  GlobalData^.S := edtGlobDataStr.Text;
end;

procedure TMainForm.meGlobDataIntChange(Sender: TObject);
begin
  { Update the DLL data with the changes }
  if meGlobDataInt.Text = EmptyStr then
    meGlobDataInt.Text := '0';
  GlobalData^.I := StrToInt(meGlobDataInt.Text);
end;

procedure TMainForm.FormCreate(Sender: TObject);
begin
  btnGetDllDataClick(nil);
end;

end.
```

9

**DYNAMIC LINK
LIBRARIES**

This application also links in the include file `DllData.inc`, which defines the `TGlobalDLLData` data type and its pointer. The `btnGetDllDataClick()` event handler gets a pointer to the DLL's data, which is accessed by a memory-mapped file in the DLL. It does this by calling the DLL's `GetDLLData()` function. It then updates its controls with the value of this pointer, `GlobalData`. The `OnChange` event handlers for the edit controls change the values of `GlobalData`. Because `GlobalData` refers to the DLL's data, it modifies the data referred to by the DLL's memory-mapped file.

Listing 9.14 shows the source code to the main form for `App2.dpr`.

LISTING 9.14. SOURCE CODE TO MAIN FORM FOR `App2.dpr`.

```
unit MainFrmA2;

interface

uses
  Windows, Messages, SysUtils, Classes, Graphics, Controls, Forms,
  Dialogs, ExtCtrls, StdCtrls;

{$I DLLDATA.INC}

type

  TMainForm = class(TForm)
    lblGlobDataStr: TLabel;
    tmTimer: TTimer;
    lblGlobDataInt: TLabel;
    procedure tmTimerTimer(Sender: TObject);
  public
    GlobalData: PGlobalDLLData;
  end;

{ Define the DLL's exported procedure }
procedure GetDLLData(var AGlobalData: PGlobalDLLData); StdCall External
➥'SHARELIB.DLL';

var
  MainForm: TMainForm;

implementation

{$R *.DFM}

procedure TMainForm.tmTimerTimer(Sender: TObject);
begin
```

```
  GetDllData(GlobalData);  // Get access to the data
  { Show the contents of GlobalData's fields.}
  lblGlobDataStr.Caption := GlobalData^.S;
  lblGlobDataInt.Caption := IntToStr(GlobalData^.I);
end;

end.
```

This form contains two TLabel components, which get updated during the tmTimer's OnTimer event. When the user changes the values of the DLL's data from App1, App2 will reflect these changes.

You can run both applications to experiment with them. You'll find them on this book's CD.

EXPORTING OBJECTS FROM DLLS

It is possible to access an object and its methods even if that object is contained within a DLL. There are some requirements, however, to how that object is defined within the DLL. There are also some limitations as to how the object can be used. The technique we illustrate here is useful in very specific situations. Typically, you can achieve the same functionality by using packages or interfaces.

The following list summarizes the conditions and limitations to achieve exporting an object from a DLL:

1. The calling application can only use methods of the object that have been declared as virtual.
2. The object instances must be created only within the DLL.
3. The object must be defined in both the DLL and calling application with methods defined in the same order.
4. You cannot create a descendant object from the object contained within the DLL.

There might be additional limitations, but these are primary.

To illustrate this technique, we've created a simple, yet illustrative example of an object that we export. This object contains a function that returns the uppercase or lowercase value of a string based on the value of a parameter indicating uppercase or lowercase. This object is defined in Listing 9.15.

LISTING 9.15. OBJECT TO BE EXPORTED FROM A DLL.

```
type

  TConvertType = (ctUpper, ctLower);

  TStringConvert = class(TObject)
{$IFDEF STRINGCONVERTLIB}
  private
    FPrepend: String;
    FAppend : String;
{$ENDIF}
  public
    function ConvertString(AConvertType: TConvertType; AString: String):
String;
      virtual; stdcall; {$IFNDEF STRINGCONVERTLIB} abstract; {$ENDIF}
{$IFDEF STRINGCONVERTLIB}
    constructor Create(APrepend, AAppend: String);
    destructor Destroy; override;
{$ENDIF}
  end;

{ For any application using this class, STRINGCONVERTLIB is not defined
  and therefore, the class definition will be equivalent to:

  TStringConvert = class(TObject)
  public
    function ConvertString(AConvertType: TConvertType; AString: String):
String;
      virtual; stdcall; abstract;
  end;
}
```

Listing 9.15 is actually an include file named StrConvert.inc. The reason for placing this object in an include file is to meet the third requirement in the preceding list—that the object be equally defined in both the DLL and in the calling application. By placing the object in an include file, both the calling application and DLL can include this file. If changes are made to the object, you only have to compile both projects instead of typing the changes twice—once in the calling application and once in the DLL—which is error prone.

Observe the following definition of the ConvertSring() method:

```
function ConvertString(AConvertType: TConvertType; AString: String):
  ➥String; virtual; stdcall;
```

The reason you declare this method as virtual is not so that one can create a descendant object that can then override the ConvertString() method. Instead, it is declared as virtual so that an entry to the ConvertString() method is made in the Virtual Method Table (VMT). We won't go into detail on the VMT here; it is discussed in Chapter 13, "Hard-Core Techniques." For now, think of the VMT as a block of memory that holds pointers to virtual methods of an object. Because of the VMT, the calling application can obtain a pointer to the method of the object. Without declaring the method as virtual, the VMT would not have an entry for the method, and the calling application would have no way of obtaining the pointer to the method. So really, what you have in the calling application is a pointer to the function. Because you've based this pointer on a method type defined in an object, Delphi automatically handles any fix-ups such as passing the implicit self parameter to the method.

Note the conditional define STRINGCONVERTLIB. When exporting the object, the only methods that need redefinition in the calling application are the methods to be accessed externally from the DLL. Also, these methods can be defined as abstract methods to avoid generating a compile-time error. This is valid because at runtime, these methods will be implemented in the DLL code. The commentary shows what the TStringConvert object looks like on the application side.

Listing 9.16 shows the implementation of the TStringConvert object.

LISTING 9.16. IMPLEMENTATION OF THE TStringConvert OBJECT.

```
unit StringConvertImp;
{$DEFINE STRINGCONVERTLIB}

interface
uses SysUtils;
{$I StrConvert.inc}

function InitStrConvert(APrepend, AAppend: String): TStringConvert;
   stdcall;

implementation

constructor TStringConvert.Create(APrepend, AAppend: String);
begin
  inherited Create;
  FPrepend := APrepend;
  FAppend  := AAppend;
end;
```

9

DYNAMIC LINK LIBRARIES

continues

LISTING 9.16. CONTINUED

```
destructor TStringConvert.Destroy;
begin
  inherited Destroy;
end;

function TStringConvert.ConvertString(AConvertType: TConvertType; AString:
➥String): String;
begin
  case AConvertType of
    ctUpper: Result := Format('%s%s%s', [FPrepend, UpperCase(AString),
➥FAppend]);
    ctLower: Result := Format('%s%s%s', [FPrepend, LowerCase(AString),
➥FAppend]);
  end;
end;

function InitStrConvert(APrepend, AAppend: String): TStringConvert;
begin
  Result := TStringConvert.Create(APrepend, AAppend);
end;

end.
```

As stated in the conditions, the object must be created in the DLL. This is done in a standard DLL exported function `InitStrConvert()`, which takes two parameters that are passed to the constructor. We added this to illustrate how you would pass information to an object's constructor through an interface function.

Also, notice that in this unit you declare the conditional directive STRINGCONVERTLIB. The rest of this unit is self-explanatory. Listing 9.17 shows the DLL's project file.

LISTING 9.17. PROJECT FILE FOR THE StringConvertLib.dll.

```
library StringConvertLib;
uses
  ShareMem,
  SysUtils,
  Classes,
  StringConvertImp in 'StringConvertImp.pas';

exports
  InitStrConvert;
end.
```

Generally, this library doesn't contain anything we haven't already covered. Note, however, that you used the ShareMem unit. This unit must be the first unit declared in the library project file as well as in the calling application's project file. This is an extremely important thing to remember.

Listing 9.18 shows an example of how to use the exported object to convert a string to both uppercase and lowercase. You'll find this demo project on the CD as StrConvertTest.dpr.

LISTING 9.18. DEMO PROJECT FOR STRING CONVERSION OBJECT.

```
unit MainFrm;

interface

uses
  Windows, Messages, SysUtils, Classes, Graphics, Controls, Forms,
  Dialogs, StdCtrls;

{$I strconvert.inc}

type


  TMainForm = class(TForm)
    btnUpper: TButton;
    edtConvertStr: TEdit;
    btnLower: TButton;
    procedure btnUpperClick(Sender: TObject);
    procedure btnLowerClick(Sender: TObject);
  private
  public
  end;

var
  MainForm: TMainForm;

function InitStrConvert(APrepend, AAppend: String): TStringConvert;
   stdcall; external 'STRINGCONVERTLIB.DLL';

implementation

{$R *.DFM}

procedure TMainForm.btnUpperClick(Sender: TObject);
var
  ConvStr: String;
  FStrConvert: TStringConvert;
```

continues

9

LISTING 9.18. CONTINUED

```
begin
  FStrConvert := InitStrConvert('Upper ', ' end');
  try
      ConvStr := edtConvertStr.Text;
      if ConvStr <> EmptyStr then
        edtConvertStr.Text := FStrConvert.ConvertString(ctUpper, ConvStr);
  finally
    FStrConvert.Free;
  end;
end;

procedure TMainForm.btnLowerClick(Sender: TObject);
var
  ConvStr: String;
  FStrConvert: TStringConvert;
begin
  FStrConvert := InitStrConvert('Lower ', ' end');
  try
      ConvStr := edtConvertStr.Text;
      if ConvStr <> EmptyStr then
        edtConvertStr.Text := FStrConvert.ConvertString(ctLower, ConvStr);
  finally
    FStrConvert.Free;
  end;
end;

end.
```

SUMMARY

DLLs are an essential part of creating Windows applications while focusing in on code reusability. This chapter covers the reasons for creating or using DLLs. The chapter illustrates how to create and use DLLs in your Delphi applications and shows different methods of loading DLLs. The chapter discusses some of the special considerations you must take when using DLLs with Delphi and shows you how to make DLL data sharable with different applications.

With this knowledge under your belt, you should be able to create DLLs with Delphi and use them in your Delphi applications with ease. DLLs are used more in other chapters.

PRINTING IN DELPHI

IN THIS CHAPTER

Printing in Windows has been the bane of many a Windows programmer. Don't be discouraged, however; Delphi simplifies most of what you need to know for printing. You can write simple printing routines to output text or bitmapped images with little effort. For more complex printing, a few concepts and techniques are all you need to perform any type of custom printing. When you have that, printing isn't so difficult.

> **NOTE**
>
> You'll find a set of reporting components by QuSoft on the QReport page of the Component Palette. The documentation for this tool is located in the file \QUICKRPT\Qrpt2man.doc from the directory where Delphi 4 was installed.
>
> QuSoft's tools are suitable for applications that generate complex reports. However, they limit you from getting to the nuts and bolts of printing at the source-code level, where you have more control over what gets printed. This chapter doesn't cover QuickReports; instead, it covers creating your own reports in Delphi.

Delphi's TPrinter object, which encapsulates the Windows printing engine, does a great deal for you that you would otherwise have to handle yourself.

This chapter teaches you how to perform a whole range of printing operations by using TPrinter. You learn the simple tasks that Delphi has made much easier for generating printouts. You also learn the techniques for creating advanced printing routines that should start you on your way to becoming a printing guru.

WRITING MULTITHREADED APPLICATIONS

IN THIS CHAPTER

The Win32 operating system provides you with the capability to have multiple threads of execution in your applications. Arguably the single most important benefit Win32 has over 16-bit Windows, this feature provides the means for performing different types of processing simultaneously in your application. This is one of the primary reasons for upgrading to a 32-bit version of Delphi, and this chapter gives you all the details on how to get the most out of threads in your applications.

THREADS EXPLAINED

As discussed in Chapter 3, "The Win32 API," a *thread* is an operating system object that represents a path of code execution within a particular process. Every Win32 application has at least one thread—often called the *primary thread* or *default thread*—but applications are free to create other threads to perform other tasks.

Threads provide a means for running many distinct code routines simultaneously. Of course, unless you have more than one CPU in your computer, two threads can't truly run simultaneously. However, each thread is scheduled fractions of seconds of time by the operating system in such a way as to give the feeling that many threads are running simultaneously.

> **TIP**
>
> Threads are not and never will be supported under 16-bit Windows. This means that any 32-bit Delphi code you write using threads will never be backward compatible to Delphi 1. Keep this in mind if you develop applications for both platforms.

A New Type of Multitasking

The notion of threads is much different from the style of multitasking supported under 16-bit Windows platforms. You might hear people talk about Win32 as a *preemptive multitasking* operating system, whereas Windows 3.1 is a *cooperative multitasking* environment.

The key difference here is that under a preemptive multitasking environment the operating system is responsible for managing which thread executes when. When execution of thread one is stopped in order for thread two to receive some CPU cycles, thread one is said to have been *preempted*. If the code that one thread is executing happens to put itself into an infinite loop, it's usually not a tragic situation because the operating system will continue to schedule time for all the other threads.

Under Windows 3.1, the application developer is responsible for giving control back to Windows at points during application execution. Failure of an application to do so causes the operating environment to appear locked up, and you all know what a painful experience that can be. If you take a moment to think about it, it's slightly amusing that the very foundation of 16-bit Windows depends on all applications behaving themselves and not putting themselves into infinite loops, recursion, or any other unneighborly situation.

Writing Multithreaded Applications

CHAPTER 11

271

11

WRITING
MULTITHREADED
APPLICATIONS

It's because all applications must cooperate for Windows to work correctly that this type of multitasking is referred to as *cooperative*.

Common Uses for Threads

It's no secret that threads represent a serious boon for Windows programmers. You can create secondary threads in your applications anywhere that it's appropriate to do some sort of background processing. Calculating cells in a spreadsheet or spooling a word processing document to the printer are examples of situations where a thread would commonly be used. The goal of the developer should be to perform necessary background processing while still providing the best possible response time for the user interface.

The user interface portion of VCL has a built-in assumption that it's being accessed by only one thread at any given time, so it's really not possible to have multiple threads controlling the user interface. VCL requires that all user interface control happens within the context of an application's primary thread (the exception is the thread-safe TCanvas, which is explained later in this chapter). Of course, techniques are available to update the user interface from a secondary thread (which we discuss later), but this limitation essentially forces you to use threads a bit more judiciously than you might do otherwise. The examples given in this chapter show some ideal uses for multiple threads in Delphi applications.

Misuse of Threads

Too much of a good thing can be bad, and that's definitely true in the case of threads. Even though threads can help to solve some of the problems you may have from an application design standpoint, they do introduce a whole new set of problems that have to be dealt with. For example, suppose you're writing an integrated development environment, and you want the compiler to execute in its own thread so the programmer will be free to continue work on the application while the program compiles. The problem here is this: What if you change a file that the compiler is in the middle of compiling? There are a number of solutions to this problem, such as making a temporary copy of the file while the compile continues, or preventing the user from editing not-yet-compiled files. The point is simply that threads are not a panacea; although they solve some development problems, they invariably introduce others. What's more is that bugs due to threading problems are also much, much harder to debug because threading problems are often time-sensitive. Designing and implementing thread-safe code is also more difficult because you have a lot more factors to consider.

THE TThread OBJECT

Delphi encapsulates the API thread object into an Object Pascal object called TThread. Although TThread encapsulates almost all the commonly used thread API functions into one discrete object, there are some points—particularly those dealing with thread synchronization—where you have to use the API. In this section, you learn how the TThread object works and how to use it in your applications.

TThread Basics

The TThread object is found in the Classes unit and is defined as follows:

```
type
  TThread = class
  private
    FHandle: THandle;
    FThreadID: THandle;
    FTerminated: Boolean;
    FSuspended: Boolean;
    FFreeOnTerminate: Boolean;
    FFinished: Boolean;
    FReturnValue: Integer;
    FOnTerminate: TNotifyEvent;
    FMethod: TThreadMethod;
    FSynchronizeException: TObject;
    procedure CallOnTerminate;
    function GetPriority: TThreadPriority;
    procedure SetPriority(Value: TThreadPriority);
    procedure SetSuspended(Value: Boolean);
  protected
    procedure DoTerminate; virtual;
    procedure Execute; virtual; abstract;
    procedure Synchronize(Method: TThreadMethod);
    property ReturnValue: Integer read FReturnValue write FReturnValue;
    property Terminated: Boolean read FTerminated;
  public
    constructor Create(CreateSuspended: Boolean);
    destructor Destroy; override;
    procedure Resume;
    procedure Suspend;
    procedure Terminate;
    function WaitFor: Integer;
    property FreeOnTerminate: Boolean read FFreeOnTerminate
      write FFreeOnTerminate;
    property Handle: THandle read FHandle;
    property Priority: TThreadPriority read GetPriority write SetPriority;
    property Suspended: Boolean read FSuspended write SetSuspended;
    property ThreadID: THandle read FThreadID;
    property OnTerminate: TNotifyEvent read FOnTerminate write
    ➥FOnTerminate;
  end;
```

As you can tell from the declaration, TThread is a direct descendant of TObject and is therefore not a component. You might also notice that the TThread.Execute() method is abstract. This means that the TThread class itself is abstract, meaning that you will never create an instance of TThread itself. You will only create instances of TThread descendants. Speaking of which, the most straightforward way to create a TThread descendant is to select Thread Object from the New Items dialog box provided by the File|New menu option. The New Items dialog is shown in Figure 11.1.

FIGURE 11.1.

The Thread Object item in the New Items dialog box.

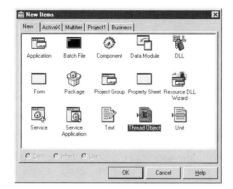

After choosing Thread Object from the New Items dialog box, you'll be presented with a dialog box that prompts you to enter a name for the new object. You could enter TTestThread, for example. Delphi will then create a new unit that contains your object. Your object will initially be defined as follows:

```
type
  TTestThread = class(TThread)
  private
    { Private declarations }
  protected
    procedure Execute; override;
  end;
```

As you can see, the only method that you *must* override in order to create a functional descendant of TThread is the Execute() method. Suppose, for example, that you want to perform a complex calculation within TTestThread. In that case, you could define its Execute() method as follows:

```
procedure TTestThread.Execute;
var
  i: integer;
begin
  for i := 1 to 2000000 do
    inc(Answer, Round(Abs(Sin(Sqrt(i)))));
end;
```

Admittedly, the equation is contrived, but it still illustrates the point in this case because the sole purpose of this equation is to take a relatively long time to execute.

You can now execute this sample thread by calling its Create() constructor. For now, you can do this from a button click in the main form, as shown in the following code (remember to include the unit containing TTestThread into the uses clause of the unit containing TForm1 to avoid a compiler error):

```
procedure TForm1.Button1Click(Sender: TObject);
var
  NewThread: TTestThread;
begin
  NewThread := TTestThread.Create(False);
end;
```

If you run the application and click the button, you'll notice that you can still manipulate the form by moving it or resizing it while the calculation goes on in the background.

> **NOTE**
>
> The single Boolean parameter passed to TThread's Create() constructor is called CreateSuspended, and it indicates whether to start the thread in a suspended state. If this parameter is False, the object's Execute() method will automatically be called following Create(). If this parameter is True, you must call TThread's Resume() method at some point to actually start the thread running. This will cause the Execute() method to be invoked at that time. You would set CreateSuspended to True if you needed to set additional properties on your thread object before allowing it to run. Setting the properties after the thread is running would be asking for trouble.
>
> To go a little deeper, the Create() constructor calls the BeginThread() Delphi RTL function, which calls the CreateThread() API function in order to create the new thread. The value of the CreateSuspended parameter indicates whether to pass the CREATE_SUSPENDED flag to CreateThread().

Thread Instances

Going back to the Execute() method for the TTestThread object, notice that it contains a local variable called i. Consider what might happen to i if you create two instances of TTestThread. Does the value for one thread overwrite the value for the other? Does the first thread take precedence? Does it blow up? The answers are no, no, and no. Win32 maintains a separate stack for each thread executing in the system. This means that as you create multiple instances of the TTestThread object, each one keeps its own copy of i on its own stack. Therefore, all the threads will operate independently of one another in that respect.

An important distinction to make, however, is that this notion of the same variable operating independently in each thread doesn't carry over to global variables. This topic is explored in detail in the "Thread-Local Storage" and "Thread Synchronization" sections, later in this chapter.

Thread Termination

A TThread is considered terminated when the Execute() method has finished executing. At that point, the EndThread() Delphi standard procedure is called, which in turn calls the ExitThread() API procedure. ExitThread() properly disposes of the thread's stack and deallocates the API thread object. This cleans up the thread as far as the API is concerned.

You also need to ensure that the Object Pascal object is destroyed when you're finished using a TThread object. This will ensure that all memory occupied by that object has been properly disposed of. Although this will automatically happen when your process terminates, you might want to dispose of the object earlier so that your application doesn't leak memory as it runs. The easiest way to ensure that the TThread object is disposed of is to set its FreeOnTerminate property to True. This can be done any time before the Execute() method finishes executing. For example, you could do this for the TTestThread object by setting the property in the Execute() method as follows:

```
procedure TTestThread.Execute;
var
  i: integer;
begin
  FreeOnTerminate := True;
  for i := 1 to 2000000 do
    inc(Answer, Round(Abs(Sin(Sqrt(i)))));
end;
```

The TThread object also has an OnTerminate event that's called when the thread terminates. It's also acceptable to free the TThread object from within a handler for this event.

TIP

The OnTerminate event of TThread is called from the context of your application's main thread. This means that you can feel free to access VCL properties and methods from within a handler for this event without using the Synchronize() method, as described in the following section.

It's also important to note that your thread's Execute() method is responsible for checking the status of the Terminated property to determine the need to make an earlier exit. Although this means one more thing you must worry about when working with threads, the flip side is that this type of architecture ensures that the rug isn't pulled out from under you, and that you'll be able to perform any necessary cleanup on thread termination.

To add this code to the `Execute()` method of `TTestThread` is rather simple, and the addition is shown here:

```
procedure TTestThread.Execute;
var
  i: integer;
begin
  FreeOnTerminate := True;
  for i := 1 to 2000000 do begin
    if Terminated then Break;
    inc(Answer, Round(Abs(Sin(Sqrt(i)))));
  end;
end;
```

CAUTION

In case of emergency, you can also use the Win32 API `TerminateThread()` function to terminate an executing thread. You should do this only when no other options exist, such as when a thread gets caught in an endless loop and stops responding. This function is defined as follows:

```
function TerminateThread(hThread: THandle; dwExitCode: DWORD);
```

The `Handle` property of `TThread` provides the API thread handle, so you could call this function with syntax similar to that shown here:

```
TerminateThread(MyHosedThread.Handle, 0);
```

If you choose to use this function, you should be wary of the negative side effects it will cause. First, this function behaves differently under Windows NT and Windows 95/98. Under Windows 95/98, `TerminateThread()` disposes of the stack associated with the thread; under Windows NT, the stack sticks around until the process is terminated. Second, on all Win32 operating systems, `TerminateThread()` simply halts execution wherever it may be and does not allow `try..finally` blocks to clean up resources. This means that files opened by the thread would not be closed, memory allocated by the thread would not be freed, and so forth. Also, DLLs loaded by your process won't be notified when a thread destroyed with `TerminateThread()` goes away, and this may cause problems when the DLL closes. See Chapter 9, "Dynamic Link Libraries," for more information on thread notifications in DLLs.

Synchronizing with VCL

As mentioned several times earlier in this chapter, you should only access VCL properties or methods from the application's primary thread. This means that any code that accesses or updates your application's user interface should be executed from the context of the primary thread. The disadvantages of this architecture are obvious, and this requirement might seem rather limiting on the surface, but it actually has some redeeming advantages that you should know about.

Advantages of a Single-Threaded User Interface

First, it greatly reduces the complexity of your application to have only one thread accessing the user interface. Win32 requires that each thread that creates a window have its own message loop using the GetMessage() function. As you might imagine, having messages coming into your application from a variety of sources can make it extremely difficult to debug. Because an application's message queue provides a means for serializing input—fully processing one condition before moving on to the next—you can depend in most cases on certain messages coming before or after others. Adding another message loop throws this serialization of input out the door, thereby opening up to potential synchronization problems and possibly introducing a need for complex synchronization code.

Additionally, because VCL can depend on the fact that it will be accessed by only one thread at any given time, the need for code to synchronize multiple threads inside VCL is obviated. The net result of this is better overall performance of your application due to a more streamlined architecture.

The Synchronize() Method

TThread provides a method called Synchronize() that allows for some of its own methods to be executed from the application's primary thread. Synchronize() is defined as follows:

```
procedure Synchronize(Method: TThreadMethod);
```

Its Method parameter is of type TThreadMethod (which means a procedural method that takes no parameter), which is defined as follows:

```
type
  TThreadMethod = procedure of object;
```

The method you pass as the Method parameter is the one that's then executed from the application's primary thread. Going back to the TTestThread example, suppose you want to display the result in an edit control on the main form. You could do this by introducing to TTestThread a method that makes the necessary change to the edit control's Text property and calling that method by using Synchronize().

In this case, suppose this method is called GiveAnswer(). Listing 11.1 shows the complete source code for this unit, called ThrdU, which includes the code to update the edit control on the main form.

LISTING 11.1. THE `ThrdU.PAS` UNIT.

```pascal
unit ThrdU;

interface

uses
  Classes;

type
  TTestThread = class(TThread)
  private
    Answer: integer;
  protected
    procedure GiveAnswer;
    procedure Execute; override;
  end;

implementation

uses SysUtils, Main;

{ TTestThread }

procedure TTestThread.GiveAnswer;
begin
  MainForm.Edit1.Text := InttoStr(Answer);
end;

procedure TTestThread.Execute;
var
  I: Integer;
begin
  FreeOnTerminate := True;
  for I := 1 to 2000000 do
  begin
    if Terminated then Break;
    Inc(Answer, Round(Abs(Sin(Sqrt(I)))));
    Synchronize(GiveAnswer);
  end;
end;

end.
```

INSIDE Synchronize()

You already know that the Synchronize() method enables you to execute methods from the context of the primary thread, but up to this point you've treated Synchronize() as sort of a mysterious black box. You don't know *how* it works—you only know that it does. If you'd like to take a peek at the man behind the curtain, read on.

The first time you create a secondary thread in your application, VCL creates and maintains a hidden *thread window* from the context of its primary thread. The sole purpose of this window is to serialize procedure calls made through the Synchronize() method.

The Synchronize() method stores the method specified in its Method parameter in a private field called FMethod and sends a VCL-defined CM_EXECPROC message to the thread window, passing Self (Self being the TThread object in this case) as the lParam of the message. When the thread window's window procedure receives this CM_EXECPROC message, it calls the method specified in FMethod through the TThread object instance passed in the lParam. Remember, because the thread window was created from the context of the primary thread, the window procedure for the thread window is also executed by the primary thread. Therefore, the method specified in the FMethod field is also executed by the primary thread.

To see a more visual illustration of what goes on inside Synchronize(), look at Figure 11.2.

FIGURE 11.2.

A road map of the Synchronize() *method.*

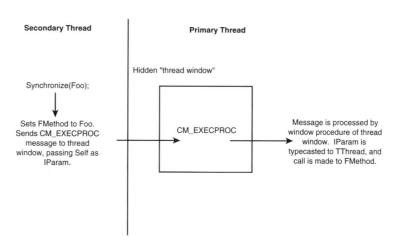

Using Messages for Synchronization

As an alternative to the `TThread.Synchronize()` method, another technique for thread synchronization is to use messages to communicate between threads. You can use the `SendMessage()` or `PostMessage()` API function to send or post messages to windows operating in the context of another thread. For example, the following code could be used to set the text in an edit control residing in another thread:

```
var
  S: string;
begin
  S := 'hello from threadland';
  SendMessage(SomeEdit.Handle, WM_SETTEXT, 0, Integer(PChar(S)));
end;
```

A Demo Application

To fully illustrate how multithreading in Delphi works, you can save the current project as EZThrd. Then you can also put a memo control on the main form so that it resembles that shown in Figure 11.3.

FIGURE 11.3.

The main form of the EZThrd demo.

The source code for the main unit is shown in Listing 11.2.

LISTING 11.2. THE MAIN.PAS UNIT FOR THE EZThRD DEMO.

```
unit Main;

interface

uses
  Windows, Messages, SysUtils, Classes, Graphics, Controls, Forms,
  Dialogs, StdCtrls, ThrdU;

type
  TMainForm = class(TForm)
    Edit1: TEdit;
    Button1: TButton;
    Memo1: TMemo;
```

```
    Label1: TLabel;
    Label2: TLabel;
    procedure Button1Click(Sender: TObject);
  private
    { Private declarations }
  public
    { Public declarations }
  end;

var
  MainForm: TMainForm;

implementation

{$R *.DFM}

procedure TMainForm.Button1Click(Sender: TObject);
var
  NewThread: TTestThread;
begin
  NewThread := TTestThread.Create(False);
end;

end.
```

Notice that after you click the button to invoke the secondary thread, you can still type in the memo control as if the secondary thread doesn't exist. When the calculation is completed, the result will be displayed in the edit control.

Priorities and Scheduling

As mentioned earlier, the operating system is in charge of scheduling each thread some CPU cycles for which it may execute. The amount of time scheduled for a particular thread depends on the priority assigned to the thread. An individual thread's overall priority is determined by a combination of the priority of the process that created the thread—called the *priority class*—and the priority of the thread itself—called the *relative priority*.

Process Priority Class

The *process priority class* describes the priority of a particular process running on the system. Win32 supports four distinct priority classes: Idle, Normal, High, and Realtime. The default priority class for any process, of course, is Normal. Each of these priority classes has a corresponding flag defined in the Windows unit. You can OR any of these flags with the dwCreationFlags parameter of CreateProcess() in order to spawn a process with a specific priority. Additionally, you can use these flags to dynamically adjust the priority class of a given process, as we show in a moment. Furthermore, each priority class can also be represented by a numeric priority level, which is a value between 4 and 24 (inclusive).

Table 11.1 shows each priority class and its corresponding flag and numeric value.

TABLE 11.1. PROCESS PRIORITY CLASSES.

Class	Flag	Value
Idle	IDLE_PRIORITY_CLASS	4
Normal	NORMAL_PRIORITY_CLASS	7–9
High	HIGH_PRIORITY_CLASS	13
Realtime	REALTIME_PRIORITY_CLASS	24

To get and set the priority class of a given process dynamically, Win32 provides the GetPriorityClass() and SetPriorityClass() functions, respectively. These functions are defined as follows:

```
function GetPriorityClass(hProcess: THandle): DWORD; stdcall;
function SetPriorityClass(hProcess: THandle; dwPriorityClass: DWORD):
  BOOL; stdcall;
```

The hProcess parameter in both cases represents a handle to a process. In most cases, you'll be calling these functions in order to access the priority class of your own process. In that case, you can use the GetCurrentProcess() API function. This function is defined as follows:

```
function GetCurrentProcess: THandle; stdcall;
```

The return value of these functions is a pseudohandle for the current process. We say "pseudo" because the function doesn't create a new handle, and the return value doesn't have to be closed with CloseHandle(). It merely provides a handle that can be used to reference an existing handle.

To set the priority class of your application to High, use code similar to the following:

```
if not SetPriorityClass(GetCurrentProcess, HIGH_PRIORITY_CLASS) then
  ShowMessage('Error setting priority class.');
```

> ### CAUTION
>
> In almost all cases, you should avoid setting the priority class of any process to Realtime. Because most of the operating system threads run in a priority class lower than Realtime, your thread will receive more CPU time than the OS itself, and that could cause some unexpected problems.
>
> Even bumping the priority class of the process to High priority class can cause problems if the threads of the process don't spend most of their time idle or waiting for external events (like file I/O). One high-priority thread is likely to drain all CPU time away from lower-priority threads and processes until it blocks on an event or goes idle or processes messages. Preemptive multitasking can easily be defeated by abusing scheduler priorities.

Relative Priority

The other thing that goes into determining the overall priority of a thread is the *relative priority* of a particular thread. The important distinction to make is that priority class is associated with a process and relative priority is associated with individual threads within a process. A thread can have any one of seven possible relative priorities: Idle, Lowest, Below Normal, Normal, Above Normal, Highest, or Time Critical.

TThread exposes a Priority property of an enumerated type TThreadPriority. There's an enumeration in this type for each relative priority:

```
type
  TThreadPriority = (tpIdle, tpLowest, tpLower, tpNormal, tpHigher,
    tpHighest, tpTimeCritical);
```

You can get and set the priority of any TThread object simply by reading from or writing to its Priority property. The following code sets the priority of a TThread descendant instance called MyThread to Highest:

```
MyThread.Priority := tpHighest.
```

Like priority classes, each relative priority is associated with a numeric value. The difference is that relative priority is a signed value which, when added to a process's class priority, is used to determine the overall priority of a thread within the system. It's for this reason that relative priority is sometimes called *delta priority*. The overall priority of a thread can be any value from 1 to 31 (1 being the lowest). There are constants defined in the `Windows` unit that represent the signed value for each priority. Table 11.2 shows how each enumeration in `TThreadPriority` maps to the API constant.

TABLE 11.2. RELATIVE PRIORITIES FOR THREADS.

TThreadPriority	*Constant*	*Value*
tpIdle	THREAD_PRIORITY_IDLE	-15*
tpLowest	THREAD_PRIORITY_LOWEST	-2
tpBelow Normal	THREAD_PRIORITY_BELOW_NORMAL	-1
tpNormal	THREAD_PRIORITY_NORMAL	0
tpAbove Normal	THREAD_PRIORITY_ABOVE_NORMAL	1
tpHighest	THREAD_PRIORITY_HIGHEST	2
tpTimeCritical	THREAD_PRIORITY_TIME_CRITICAL	15*

The reason that the values for the `tpIdle` and `tpTimeCritical` priorities are marked with asterisks is that, unlike the others, these relative priority values are not truly added to the class priority to determine overall thread priority. Any thread that has the `tpIdle` relative priority, regardless of its priority class, has an overall priority of 1. The exception to this rule is the `Realtime` priority class, which, when combined with the `tpIdle` relative priority, has an overall value of 16. Any thread that has a priority of `tpTimeCritical`, regardless of its priority class, has an overall priority of 15. The exception to this rule is the `Realtime` priority class, which, when combined with the `tpTimeCritical` relative priority, has an overall value of 31.

Suspending and Resuming Threads

Recall when you learned about `TThread`'s `Create()` constructor earlier in this chapter. At the time, you discovered that a thread could be created in a suspended state, and that you must call its `Resume()` method in order for the thread to begin execution. As you might guess, a thread can also be suspended and resumed dynamically, using the `Suspend()` method in conjunction with the `Resume()` method.

Timing a Thread

When programming under Windows 3.x, it's pretty common to wrap some portion of code with calls to `GetTickCount()` or `timeGetTime()` to determine how much time a particular calculation may take—something like the following, for example:

```
var
  StartTime, Total: Longint;
begin
  StartTime := GetTickCount;
  { Do some calculation here }
  Total := GetTickCount - StartTime;
```

In a multithreaded environment, it's much more difficult to do because your application may be preempted by the operating system in the middle of the calculation in order to provide CPU cycles to other processes. Therefore, any timing you do that relies on the system time can't provide a true measure of how long it spends crunching the calculation in your thread.

To avoid such problems, Win32 under Windows NT provides a function called `GetThreadTimes()`, which provides quite detailed information on thread timing. This function is declared as follows:

```
function GetThreadTimes(hThread: THandle; var lpCreationTime, lpExitTime,
    lpKernelTime, lpUserTime: TFileTime): BOOL; stdcall;
```

The `hThread` parameter is the handle to the thread for which you want to obtain timing information. The other parameters for this function are passed by reference and are filled in by the function:

lpCreationTime	The time when the thread was created.
lpExitTime	The time when the thread was exited. If the thread is still running, this value is undefined.
lpKernelTime	The amount of time the thread has spent executing operating system code.
lpUserTime	The amount of time the thread has spent executing application code.

Each of the last four parameters is of type `TFileTime`. `TFileTime` is defined in the `Windows` unit as follows:

```
type
  TFileTime = record
    dwLowDateTime: DWORD;
    dwHighDateTime: DWORD;
  end;
```

The definition of this type is a bit unusual, but it's a part of the Win32 API, so here goes: the `dwLowDateTime` and `dwHighDateTime` are combined into a quad word (64-bit) value that represents the number of 100-nanosecond intervals that have passed since January 1, 1601. This means, of course, that if you wanted to write a simulation of English fleet movements as it defeated the Spanish Armada in 1588, the `TFileTime` type would be a wholly inappropriate way to keep track of time. But we digress.

> **TIP**
>
> Because the `TFileTime` type is 64 bits in size, you can typecast a `TFileTime` to an `Int64` type in order to perform arithmetic on `TFileTime` values. The following code demonstrates how to quickly tell whether one `TFileTime` is greater than another:
>
> ```
> if Int64(UserTime) > Int64(KernelTime) then Beep;
> ```

In order to help you work with `TFileTime` values in a manner more native to Delphi, the following functions allow you to convert back and forth between `TFileTime` and `TDateTime` types:

```
function FileTimeToDateTime(FileTime: TFileTime): TDateTime;
var
  SysTime: TSystemTime;
begin
  if not FileTimeToSystemTime(FileTime, SysTime) then
    raise EConvertError.CreateFmt('FileTimeToSystemTime failed. Error code
      %d', [GetLastError]);
  with SysTime do
    Result := EncodeDate(wYear, wMonth, wDay) +
      EncodeTime(wHour, wMinute, wSecond, wMilliseconds)
end;

function DateTimeToFileTime(DateTime: TDateTime): TFileTime;
var
  SysTime: TSystemTime;
begin
  with SysTime do
  begin
    DecodeDate(DateTime, wYear, wMonth, wDay);
    DecodeTime(DateTime, wHour, wMinute, wSecond, wMilliseconds);
    wDayOfWeek := DayOfWeek(DateTime);
  end;
  if not SystemTimeToFileTime(SysTime, Result) then
    raise EConvertError.CreateFmt('SystemTimeToFileTime failed. Error code
      %d', [GetLastError]);
end;
```

> **CAUTION**
>
> Remember that the `GetThreadTimes()` function is implemented only under Windows NT. The function always returns `False` when called under Windows 95 or 98. Unfortunately, Windows 95/98 doesn't provide any mechanism for retrieving thread-timing information.

MANAGING MULTIPLE THREADS

As indicated earlier, although threads can solve a variety of programming problems, they're also likely to introduce new types of problems that you must deal with in your applications. Most commonly, these problems revolve around multiple threads accessing global resources, such as global variables or handles. Additionally, problems can arise when you need to ensure that some event in one thread always occurs before or after some other event in another thread. In this section, you learn how to tackle these problems by using the facilities provided by Delphi for thread-local storage and those provided by the API for thread synchronization.

Thread-Local Storage

Because each thread represents a separate and distinct path of execution within a process, it logically follows that you will at some point want to have a means for storing data associated with each thread. There are three techniques for storing data unique to each thread: The first and most straightforward is local (stack-based) variables. Because each thread gets its own stack, each thread executing within a single procedure or function will have its own copy of local variables. The second technique is to store local information in your TThread descendant object. Finally, you can also use Object Pascal's `thread-var` reserved word to take advantage of operating-system–level thread-local storage.

TThread Storage

Storing pertinent data in the TThread descendant object should be your technique of choice for thread-local storage. It's both more straightforward and more efficient than using `threadvar` (described later). To declare thread-local data in this manner, simply add it to the definition of your TThread descendant as shown here:

```
type
  TMyThread = class(TThread)
  private
    FLocalInt: Integer;
    FLocalStr: String;
    .
    .
    .
  end;
```

> **TIP**
>
> It's about 10 times faster to access a field of an object than to access a thread-var variable, so you should store your thread-specific data in your TThread descendant, if possible. Data that doesn't need to exist for more than the lifetime of a particular procedure or function should be stored in local variables, as those are faster still than fields of a TThread object.

threadvar: API Thread-Local Storage

Earlier we mentioned that each thread is provided with its own stack for storing local variables, whereas global data has to be shared by all threads within an application. For example, say you have a procedure that sets or displays the value of a global variable. When you call the procedure passing a text string, the global variable is set, and when you call the procedure passing an empty string, the global variable is displayed. Such a procedure might look like this:

```
var
  GlobalStr: String;
procedure SetShowStr(const S: String);
begin
  if S = '' then
    MessageBox(0, PChar(GlobalStr), 'The string is...', MB_OK)
  else
    GlobalStr := S;
end;
```

If this procedure is called from within the context of one thread only, there wouldn't be any problems. You'd call the procedure once to set the value of the GlobalStr and call it again to display the value. However, consider what can happen if two or more threads call this procedure at any given time. In such a case, it's possible that one thread could call the procedure to set the string, and then get preempted by another thread that might also call the function to set the string. By the time the operating system gives CPU time back to the first thread, the value of GlobalStr for that thread will be hopelessly lost.

For situations such as these, Win32 provides a facility known as *thread-local storage* that enables you to create separate copies of global variables for each running thread. Delphi nicely encapsulates this functionality with the threadvar clause. Just declare any global variables you want to exist separately for each thread within a threadvar (as opposed to var) clause, and the work is done. A redeclaration of the GlobalStr variable is as simple as this:

```
threadvar
  GlobalStr: String;
```

The unit shown in Listing 11.3 illustrates this very problem. It represents the main unit to a Delphi application that contains only a button on a form. When the button is clicked, the procedure is called to set and then to show GlobalStr. Next, another thread is created, and the value internal to the thread is set and shown again. After the thread creation, the primary thread again calls the SetShowStr to display GlobalStr.

Try running this application with GlobalStr declared as a var and then as a threadvar, and you'll see a difference in the output.

Listing 11.3. The main.pas unit for thread-local storage demo.

```
unit Main;

interface

uses
  Windows, Messages, SysUtils, Classes, Graphics, Controls, Forms,
  Dialogs, StdCtrls;

type
  TMainForm = class(TForm)
    Button1: TButton;
    procedure Button1Click(Sender: TObject);
  private
    { Private declarations }
  public
    { Public declarations }
  end;

var
  MainForm: TMainForm;

implementation

{$R *.DFM}

{ NOTE: Change GlobalStr from var to threadvar to see difference }
var
//threadvar
  GlobalStr: string;

type
  TTLSThread = class(TThread)
  private
    FNewStr: String;
  protected
    procedure Execute; override;
```

continues

LISTING 11.3. CONTINUED

```
public
  constructor Create(const ANewStr: String);
end;

procedure SetShowStr(const S: String);
begin
  if S = '' then
    MessageBox(0, PChar(GlobalStr), 'The string is...', MB_OK)
  else
    GlobalStr := S;
end;

constructor TTLSThread.Create(const ANewStr: String);
begin
  FNewStr := ANewStr;
  inherited Create(False);
end;

procedure TTLSThread.Execute;
begin
  FreeOnTerminate := True;
  SetShowStr(FNewStr);
  SetShowStr('');
end;

procedure TMainForm.Button1Click(Sender: TObject);
begin
  SetShowStr('Hello world');
  SetShowStr('');
  TTLSThread.Create('Dilbert');
  Sleep(100);
  SetShowStr('');
end;

end.
```

NOTE

The demo program calls the Win32 API Sleep() procedure after creating the thread. Sleep() is declared as follows:

```
procedure Sleep(dwMilliseconds: DWORD); stdcall;
```

The Sleep() procedure tells the operating system that the current thread doesn't need any more CPU cycles for another dwMilliseconds milliseconds. Inserting this call into the code has the effect of simulating system conditions where more multitasking is occurring and introducing a bit more "randomness" into the application as to which threads will be executing when.

It's often acceptable to pass zero in the dwMilliseconds parameter. Although that doesn't prevent the current thread from executing for any specific amount of time, it does cause the operating system to give CPU cycles to any waiting threads of equal or greater priority.

Be careful of using Sleep() to work around mysterious timing problems. Sleep() may work around a particular problem on your machine, but timing problems that are not solved conclusively will pop up again on somebody else's machine, especially when their machine is significantly faster or slower or has a different number of processors than your machine.

Thread Synchronization

When working with multiple threads, you'll often need to synchronize the access of threads to some particular piece of data or resource. For example, suppose you have an application that uses one thread to read a file into memory and another thread to count the number of characters in the file. It goes without saying that you can't count all the characters in the file until the entire file has been loaded into memory. However, because each operation occurs in its own thread, the operating system would like to treat them as two completely unrelated tasks. To fix this problem, you must synchronize the two threads so that the counting thread doesn't execute until the loading thread finishes.

These are the types of problems that thread synchronization addresses, and Win32 provides a variety of ways to synchronize threads. In this section, you'll see examples of thread synchronization techniques using critical sections, mutexes, semaphores, and events.

In order to examine these techniques, first take a look at a problem involving threads that need to be synchronized. For the purpose of illustration, suppose that you have an array of integers that needs to be initialized with ascending values. You want to first go through the array and set the values from 1 to 128, and then reinitialize the array with values from 128 to 255. You'll then display the final thread in a list box. An approach to this might be to perform the initializations in two separate threads. Consider the code in Listing 11.4 for a unit that attempts to perform this task.

LISTING 11.4. UNIT THAT ATTEMPTS TO INITIALIZE ARRAY IN THREADS.

```
unit Main;

interface

uses
  Windows, Messages, SysUtils, Classes, Graphics, Controls, Forms,
  Dialogs, StdCtrls;

type
  TMainForm = class(TForm)
    Button1: TButton;
    ListBox1: TListBox;
    procedure Button1Click(Sender: TObject);
  private
    procedure ThreadsDone(Sender: TObject);
  end;

  TFooThread = class(TThread)
  protected
    procedure Execute; override;
  end;

var
  MainForm: TMainForm;

implementation

{$R *.DFM}

const
  MaxSize = 128;

var
  NextNumber: Integer = 0;
  DoneFlags: Integer = 0;
  GlobalArray: array[1..MaxSize] of Integer;

function GetNextNumber: Integer;
begin
  Result := NextNumber;   // return global var
  Inc(NextNumber);        // inc global var
end;

procedure TFooThread.Execute;
var
  i: Integer;
begin
  OnTerminate := MainForm.ThreadsDone;
```

```
  for i := 1 to MaxSize do
  begin
    GlobalArray[i] := GetNextNumber;  // set array element
    Sleep(5);                         // let thread intertwine
  end;
end;

procedure TMainForm.ThreadsDone(Sender: TObject);
var
  i: Integer;
begin
  Inc(DoneFlags);
  if DoneFlags = 2 then       // make sure both threads finished
    for i := 1 to MaxSize do
      { fill listbox with array contents }
      Listbox1.Items.Add(IntToStr(GlobalArray[i]));
end;

procedure TMainForm.Button1Click(Sender: TObject);
begin
  TFooThread.Create(False);   // create threads
  TFooThread.Create(False);
end;

end.
```

Because both threads will execute simultaneously, what happens is that the contents of the array are corrupted as it's initialized. As proof, take a look at the output of this code shown in Figure 11.4.

FIGURE 11.4.

Output from unsynchronized array initialization.

The solution to this problem is to synchronize the two threads as they access the global array so that they don't both dive in at the same time. You can take any of a number of valid approaches to this problem.

Critical Sections

Critical sections provide one of the most straightforward ways to synchronize threads. A critical section is some section of code that allows for only one thread to execute through it at a time. If you wrap the code used to initialize the array in a critical section, other threads will be blocked from entering the code section until the first finishes.

Prior to using a critical section, you must initialize it using the InitializeCriticalSection() API procedure, which is declared as follows:

```
procedure InitializeCriticalSection(var lpCriticalSection:
    TRTLCriticalSection); stdcall;
```

lpCriticalSection is a TRTLCriticalSection record that's passed by reference. The exact definition of TRTLCriticalSection is unimportant, because you'll rarely (if ever) actually look at the contents of one. You'll pass an uninitialized record in the lpCriticalSection parameter, and the record will be filled by the procedure.

> **NOTE**
>
> Microsoft deliberately obscures the structure of the TRTLCriticalSection record because the contents vary from one hardware platform to another, and because tinkering with the contents of this structure can potentially wreak havoc on your process. On Intel-based systems, the critical section structure contains a counter, a field containing the current thread handle, and (potentially) a handle of a system event. On Alpha hardware, the counter is replaced with an Alpha-CPU data structure called a spinlock, which is more efficient than the Intel solution.

When the record is filled, you can create a critical section in your application by wrapping some block of code with calls to EnterCriticalSection() and LeaveCriticalSection(). These procedures are declared as follows:

```
procedure EnterCriticalSection(var lpCriticalSection:
  TRTLCriticalSection); stdcall;
procedure LeaveCriticalSection(var lpCriticalSection:
  TRTLCriticalSection); stdcall;
```

As you might guess, the lpCriticalSection parameter you pass these guys is the same one that's filled in by the InitializeCriticalSection() procedure.

Writing Multithreaded Applications

CHAPTER 11

295

11

WRITING
MULTITHREADED
APPLICATIONS

When you're finished with the TRTLCriticalSection record, you should clean up by calling the DeleteCriticalSection() procedure, which is declared as follows:

```
procedure DeleteCriticalSection(var lpCriticalSection:
    TRTLCriticalSection); stdcall;
```

Listing 11.5 demonstrates the technique for synchronizing the array initialization threads with critical sections.

LISTING 11.5. USING CRITICAL SECTIONS.

```
unit Main;

interface

uses
  Windows, Messages, SysUtils, Classes, Graphics, Controls, Forms, Dialogs,
  StdCtrls;

type
  TMainForm = class(TForm)
    Button1: TButton;
    ListBox1: TListBox;
    procedure Button1Click(Sender: TObject);
  private
    procedure ThreadsDone(Sender: TObject);
  end;

  TFooThread = class(TThread)
  protected
    procedure Execute; override;
  end;

var
  MainForm: TMainForm;

implementation

{$R *.DFM}

const
  MaxSize = 128;

var
  NextNumber: Integer = 0;
  DoneFlags: Integer = 0;
  GlobalArray: array[1..MaxSize] of Integer;
  CS: TRTLCriticalSection;
```

continues

LISTING 11.5. CONTINUED

```
function GetNextNumber: Integer;
begin
  Result := NextNumber;    // return global var
  inc(NextNumber);         // inc global var
end;

procedure TFooThread.Execute;
var
  i: Integer;
begin
  OnTerminate := MainForm.ThreadsDone;
  EnterCriticalSection(CS);           // CS begins here
  for i := 1 to MaxSize do
  begin
    GlobalArray[i] := GetNextNumber;  // set array element
    Sleep(5);                         // let thread intertwine
  end;
  LeaveCriticalSection(CS);           // CS ends here
end;

procedure TMainForm.ThreadsDone(Sender: TObject);
var
  i: Integer;
begin
  inc(DoneFlags);
  if DoneFlags = 2 then
  begin // make sure both threads finished
    for i := 1 to MaxSize do
      { fill listbox with array contents }
      Listbox1.Items.Add(IntToStr(GlobalArray[i]));
    DeleteCriticalSection(CS);
  end;
end;

procedure TMainForm.Button1Click(Sender: TObject);
begin
  InitializeCriticalSection(CS);
  TFooThread.Create(False);  // create threads
  TFooThread.Create(False);
end;

end.
```

After the first thread passes through the call to EnterCriticalSection(), all other threads are prevented from entering that block of code. The next thread that comes along to that line of code is put to sleep until the first thread calls LeaveCriticalSection(). At that point, the second thread is awakened and allowed to take control of the critical section. Figure 11.5 shows the output of this application when the threads are synchronized.

FIGURE 11.5.

Output from
synchronized
array initialization.

Mutexes

Mutexes work very much like critical sections except for two key differences: First, mutexes can be used to synchronize threads across process boundaries. Second, mutexes can be given a string name, and additional handles to existing mutex objects can be created by referencing that name.

TIP

Semantics aside, the biggest difference between critical sections and event objects like mutexes is performance: Critical sections are very lightweight—as few as 10-15 clock cycles to enter or leave the critical section when there are no thread collisions. As soon as there is a thread collision for that critical section, the system creates an event object (a mutex, probably). The cost of using event objects like mutexes is that it requires a round trip into the kernel, which requires a process context switch and a change of ring levels, which piles up to 400 to 600 clock cycles each way. All this overhead is incurred even if your app does not currently have multiple threads, or if no other threads are contending for the resource you're protecting.

The function used to create a mutex is appropriately called CreateMutex(). This function is declared as follows:

```
function CreateMutex(lpMutexAttributes: PSecurityAttributes;
  bInitialOwner: BOOL; lpName: PChar): THandle; stdcall;
```

lpMutexAttributes is a pointer to a TSecurityAttributes record. It's common to pass nil in this parameter, in which case the default security attributes will be used.

bInitialOwner indicates whether the thread creating the mutex should be considered the owner of the mutex when it's created. If this parameter is False, the mutex is unowned.

lpName is the name of the mutex. This parameter can be nil if you don't want to name the mutex. If this parameter is non-nil, the function will search the system for an existing mutex with the same name. If an existing mutex is found, a handle to the existing mutex is returned. Otherwise, a handle to a new mutex is returned.

When you're finished using a mutex, you should close it using the `CloseHandle()` API function.

Listing 11.6 again demonstrates the technique for synchronizing the array initialization threads, except that this time it uses mutexes.

LISTING 11.6. USING MUTEXES FOR SYNCHRONIZATION.

```
unit Main;

interface

uses
  Windows, Messages, SysUtils, Classes, Graphics, Controls, Forms,
  Dialogs, StdCtrls;

type
  TMainForm = class(TForm)
    Button1: TButton;
    ListBox1: TListBox;
    procedure Button1Click(Sender: TObject);
  private
    procedure ThreadsDone(Sender: TObject);
  end;

  TFooThread = class(TThread)
  protected
    procedure Execute; override;
  end;

var
  MainForm: TMainForm;

implementation

{$R *.DFM}

const
  MaxSize = 128;

var
  NextNumber: Integer = 0;
  DoneFlags: Integer = 0;
  GlobalArray: array[1..MaxSize] of Integer;
  hMutex: THandle = 0;
```

Writing Multithreaded Applications

CHAPTER 11

299

11

WRITING
MULTITHREADED
APPLICATIONS

```pascal
function GetNextNumber: Integer;
begin
  Result := NextNumber;   // return global var
  Inc(NextNumber);        // inc global var
end;

procedure TFooThread.Execute;
var
  i: Integer;
begin
  FreeOnTerminate := True;
  OnTerminate := MainForm.ThreadsDone;
  if WaitForSingleObject(hMutex, INFINITE) = WAIT_OBJECT_0 then
  begin
    for i := 1 to MaxSize do
    begin
      GlobalArray[i] := GetNextNumber;   // set array element
      Sleep(5);                          // let thread intertwine
    end;
  end;
  ReleaseMutex(hMutex);
end;

procedure TMainForm.ThreadsDone(Sender: TObject);
var
  i: Integer;
begin
  Inc(DoneFlags);
  if DoneFlags = 2 then     // make sure both threads finished
  begin
    for i := 1 to MaxSize do
      { fill listbox with array contents }
      Listbox1.Items.Add(IntToStr(GlobalArray[i]));
    CloseHandle(hMutex);
  end;
end;

procedure TMainForm.Button1Click(Sender: TObject);
begin
  hMutex := CreateMutex(nil, False, nil);
  TFooThread.Create(False);  // create threads
  TFooThread.Create(False);
end;

end.
```

You'll notice that in this case the `WaitForSingleObject()` function is used to control thread entry into the synchronized block of code. This function is declared as follows:

```pascal
function WaitForSingleObject(hHandle: THandle; dwMilliseconds: DWORD):
  DWORD; stdcall;
```

The purpose of this function is to sleep the current thread up to `dwMilliseconds` milliseconds until the API object specified in the `hHandle` parameter becomes *signaled*. Signaled means different things for different objects. A mutex becomes signaled when it's not owned by a thread, whereas a process, for example, becomes signaled when it terminates. Apart from an actual period of time, the `dwMilliseconds` parameter can also have the value `0`—which means to check the status of the object and return immediately— or `INFINITE`—which means to wait forever for the object to become signaled. The return value of this function can be any one of the values shown in the following table.

Value	*Meaning*
WAIT_ABANDONED	The specified object is a mutex object, and the thread owning the mutex was exited before it freed the mutex. This circumstance is referred to as an *abandoned mutex*; in such a case, ownership of the mutex object is granted to the calling thread, and the mutex is set to nonsignaled.
WAIT_OBJECT_0	The state of the specified object is signaled.
WAIT_TIMEOUT	The timeout interval elapsed, and the object's state is nonsignaled.

Again, when a mutex isn't owned by a thread, it's in the signaled state. The first thread to call `WaitForSingleObject()` on this mutex is given ownership of the mutex, and the state of the mutex object is set to nonsignaled. The thread's ownership of the mutex is severed when the thread calls the `ReleaseMutex()` function, passing the mutex handle as the parameter. At that point, the state of the mutex again becomes signaled.

> **NOTE**
>
> In addition to `WaitForSingleObject()`, the Win32 API also has functions called `WaitForMultipleObjects()` and `MsgWaitForMultipleObjects()`, which enable you to wait for the state of one or more objects to become signaled. These functions are documented in the Win32 API online help.

Semaphores

Another technique for thread synchronization involves using semaphore API objects. *Semaphores* build on the functionality of mutexes while adding one important feature: They offer the capability of resource counting so that a predetermined number of threads can enter synchronized pieces of code at one time. The function used to create a semaphore is `CreateSemaphore()`, and it's declared as follows:

```
function CreateSemaphore(lpSemaphoreAttributes: PSecurityAttributes;
  lInitialCount, lMaximumCount: Longint; lpName: PChar): THandle; stdcall;
```

Writing Multithreaded Applications

CHAPTER 11

301

11

WRITING
MULTITHREADED
APPLICATIONS

Like CreateMutex(), the first parameter to CreateSemaphore() is a pointer to a TSecurityAttributes record to which you can pass Nil for the defaults.

lInitialCount is the initial count of the semaphore object. This is a number between 0 and lMaximumCount. A semaphore is signaled as long as this parameter is greater than zero. The count of a semaphore is decremented whenever WaitForSingleObject() (or one of the other wait functions) releases a thread. A semaphore's count is increased by using the ReleaseSemaphore() function.

lMaximumCount specifies the maximum count value of the semaphore object. If the semaphore is used to count some resources, this number should represent the total number of resources available.

lpName is the name of the semaphore. This parameter behaves the same as the parameter of the same name in CreateMutex().

Listing 11.7 demonstrates using semaphores to perform synchronization of the array initialization problem.

LISTING 11.7. USING SEMAPHORES FOR SYNCHRONIZATION.

```
unit Main;

interface

uses
  Windows, Messages, SysUtils, Classes, Graphics, Controls, Forms,
  Dialogs, StdCtrls;

type
  TMainForm = class(TForm)
    Button1: TButton;
    ListBox1: TListBox;
    procedure Button1Click(Sender: TObject);
  private
    procedure ThreadsDone(Sender: TObject);
  end;

  TFooThread = class(TThread)
  protected
    procedure Execute; override;
  end;

var
  MainForm: TMainForm;
```

continues

LISTING 11.7. CONTINUED

```
implementation

{$R *.DFM}

const
  MaxSize = 128;

var
  NextNumber: Integer = 0;
  DoneFlags: Integer = 0;
  GlobalArray: array[1..MaxSize] of Integer;
  hSem: THandle = 0;

function GetNextNumber: Integer;
begin
  Result := NextNumber;   // return global var
  Inc(NextNumber);        // inc global var
end;

procedure TFooThread.Execute;
var
  i: Integer;
  WaitReturn: DWORD;
begin
  OnTerminate := MainForm.ThreadsDone;
  WaitReturn := WaitForSingleObject(hSem, INFINITE);
  if WaitReturn = WAIT_OBJECT_0 then
  begin
    for i := 1 to MaxSize do
    begin
      GlobalArray[i] := GetNextNumber;   // set array element
      Sleep(5);                          // let thread intertwine
    end;
  end;
  ReleaseSemaphore(hSem, 1, nil);
end;

procedure TMainForm.ThreadsDone(Sender: TObject);
var
  i: Integer;
begin
  Inc(DoneFlags);
  if DoneFlags = 2 then      // make sure both threads finished
  begin
    for i := 1 to MaxSize do
      { fill listbox with array contents }
      Listbox1.Items.Add(IntToStr(GlobalArray[i]));
    CloseHandle(hSem);
  end;
end;
```

```
procedure TMainForm.Button1Click(Sender: TObject);
begin
  hSem := CreateSemaphore(nil, 1, 1, nil);
  TFooThread.Create(False);  // create threads
  TFooThread.Create(False);
end;

end.
```

Because you allow only one thread to enter the synchronized portion of code, the maximum count for the semaphore is 1 in this case.

The `ReleaseSemaphore()` function is used to increase the count for the semaphore. Notice that this function is a bit more involved than its cousin, `ReleaseMutex()`. The declaration for `ReleaseSemaphore()` is as follows:

```
function ReleaseSemaphore(hSemaphore: THandle; lReleaseCount: Longint;
    lpPreviousCount: Pointer): BOOL; stdcall;
```

The `lReleaseCount` parameter enables you to specify the number by which the count of the semaphore will be increased. The old count will be stored in the `longint` pointed to by the `lpPreviousCount` parameter if its value is not `Nil`. A subtle implication of this capability is that a semaphore is never really owned by any thread in particular. For example, suppose the maximum count of a semaphore was 10, and 10 threads called `WaitForSingleObject()` to set the count of the thread to 0 and put the thread in a nonsignaled state. All it takes is one of those threads to call `ReleaseSemaphore()` with 10 as the `lReleaseCount` parameter in order to not only make the thread signaled again, but to increase the count back to 10. This powerful capability can introduce some hard-to-track-down bugs into your applications, so you should use it with care.

Be sure to use the `CloseHandle()` function to free the semaphore handle allocated with `CreateSemaphore()`.

A SAMPLE MULTITHREADED APPLICATION

To demonstrate the usage of `TThread` objects within the context of a real-world application, this section focuses on creating a file search application that performs its searches in a specialized thread. The project is called DelSrch, which stands for *Delphi Search*, and the main form for this utility is shown in Figure 11.6.

FIGURE **11.6.**

*The main form
for the DelSrch
project.*

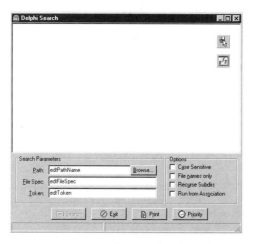

The application works like this. The user chooses a path through which to search and provides a file specification to indicate the types of files to be searched. The user also enters a token to search for in the appropriate edit control. Some option check boxes on one side of the form enable the user to tailor the application to suit his or her needs for a particular search. When the user clicks the Search button, a search thread is created and the appropriate search information—such as token, path, and file specification—is passed to the TThread descendant object. When the search thread finds the search token in certain files, information is appended to the list box. Finally, if the user double-clicks a file in the list box, the user can browse it with a text editor or view it from its desktop association.

Although this is a fairly full-featured application, we'll focus mainly on explaining the application's key search features and how they relate to multithreading.

The User Interface

The main unit for the application is called Main.pas. Shown in Listing 11.8, this unit is responsible for managing the main form and the overall user interface. In particular, this unit contains the logic for owner-drawing the list box, invoking a viewer for files in the list box, invoking the search thread, printing the list box contents, and reading and writing UI settings to an INI file.

LISTING **11.8.** THE Main.pas UNIT FOR THE DELSRCH PROJECT.

```
unit Main;

interface
```

Writing Multithreaded Applications

CHAPTER 11

305

11

WRITING
MULTITHREADED
APPLICATIONS

```
uses
  SysUtils, WinTypes, WinProcs, Messages, Classes, Graphics, Controls,
  Forms, Dialogs, StdCtrls, Buttons, ExtCtrls, Menus, SrchIni,
  SrchU, ComCtrls;


type
  TMainForm = class(TForm)
    lbFiles: TListBox;
    StatusBar: TStatusBar;
    pnlControls: TPanel;
    PopupMenu: TPopupMenu;
    FontDialog: TFontDialog;
    pnlOptions: TPanel;
    gbParams: TGroupBox;
    LFileSpec: TLabel;
    LToken: TLabel;
    lPathName: TLabel;
    edtFileSpec: TEdit;
    edtToken: TEdit;
    btnPath: TButton;
    edtPathName: TEdit;
    gbOptions: TGroupBox;
    cbCaseSensitive: TCheckBox;
    cbFileNamesOnly: TCheckBox;
    cbRecurse: TCheckBox;
    cbRunFromAss: TCheckBox;
    pnlButtons: TPanel;
    btnSearch: TBitBtn;
    btnClose: TBitBtn;
    btnPrint: TBitBtn;
    btnPriority: TBitBtn;
    Font1: TMenuItem;
    Clear1: TMenuItem;
    Print1: TMenuItem;
    N1: TMenuItem;
    Exit1: TMenuItem;
    procedure btnSearchClick(Sender: TObject);
    procedure btnPathClick(Sender: TObject);
    procedure lbFilesDrawItem(Control: TWinControl; Index: Integer;
        Rect: TRect; State: TOwnerDrawState);
    procedure Font1Click(Sender: TObject);
    procedure FormDestroy(Sender: TObject);
    procedure FormCreate(Sender: TObject);
    procedure btnPrintClick(Sender: TObject);
    procedure btnCloseClick(Sender: TObject);
    procedure lbFilesDblClick(Sender: TObject);
    procedure FormResize(Sender: TObject);
    procedure btnPriorityClick(Sender: TObject);
    procedure edtTokenChange(Sender: TObject);
```

continues

LISTING 11.8. CONTINUED

```
    procedure Clear1Click(Sender: TObject);
  private
    procedure ReadIni;
    procedure WriteIni;
    procedure DoOnHint(Sender: TObject);
  public
    Running: Boolean;
    SearchPri: Integer;
    SearchThread: TSearchThread;
    procedure EnableSearchControls(Enable: Boolean);
  end;

var
  MainForm: TMainForm;

implementation

{$R *.DFM}

uses Printers, ShellAPI, StrUtils, FileCtrl, PriU;

procedure PrintStrings(Strings: TStrings);
{ This procedure prints all of the strings in the Strings parameter }
var
  Prn: TextFile;
  I: Integer;
begin
  if Strings.Count = 0 then // Are there strings?
    raise Exception.Create('No text to print!');
  AssignPrn(Prn);                          // assign Prn to printer
  try
    Rewrite(Prn);                          // open printer
    try
      for I := 0 to Strings.Count - 1 do   // iterate over all strings
        WriteLn(Prn, Strings.Strings[I]);  // write to printer
    finally
      CloseFile(Prn);                      // close printer
    end;
  except
    on EInOutError do
      MessageDlg('Error Printing text.', mtError, [mbOk], 0);
  end;
end;

procedure TMainForm.EnableSearchControls(Enable: Boolean);
{ Enables or disables certain controls so options can't be modified }
{ while search is executing. }
begin
  btnSearch.Enabled := Enable;        // enable/disable proper controls
```

Writing Multithreaded Applications

CHAPTER 11

307

11

WRITING
MULTITHREADED
APPLICATIONS

```
    cbRecurse.Enabled := Enable;
    cbFileNamesOnly.Enabled := Enable;
    cbCaseSensitive.Enabled := Enable;
    btnPath.Enabled := Enable;
    edtPathName.Enabled := Enable;
    edtFileSpec.Enabled := Enable;
    edtToken.Enabled := Enable;
    Running := not Enable;                // set Running flag
    edtTokenChange(nil);
    with btnClose do
    begin
      if Enable then
      begin                    // set props of Close/Stop button
        Caption := '&Close';
        Hint := 'Close Application';
      end
      else begin
        Caption := '&Stop';
        Hint := 'Stop Searching';
      end;
    end;
end;

procedure TMainForm.btnSearchClick(Sender: TObject);
{ Called when Search button is clicked.  Invokes search thread. }
begin
  EnableSearchControls(False);         // disable controls
  lbFiles.Clear;                       // clear listbox
  { start thread }
  SearchThread := TSearchThread.Create(cbCaseSensitive.Checked,
      cbFileNamesOnly.Checked, cbRecurse.Checked, edtToken.Text,
      edtPathName.Text, edtFileSpec.Text);
end;

procedure TMainForm.edtTokenChange(Sender: TObject);
begin
  btnSearch.Enabled := not Running and (edtToken.Text <> '');
end;

procedure TMainForm.btnPathClick(Sender: TObject);
{ Called when Path button is clicked.  Allows user to choose new path. }
var
  ShowDir: string;
begin
  ShowDir := edtPathName.Text;
  if SelectDirectory('Choose a search path...', '', ShowDir) then
    edtPathName.Text := ShowDir;
end;
```

continues

LISTING **11.8.** CONTINUED

```pascal
procedure TMainForm.lbFilesDrawItem(Control: TWinControl;
  Index: Integer; Rect: TRect; State: TOwnerDrawState);
{ Called in order to owner draw listbox. }
var
  CurStr: string;
begin
  with lbFiles do
  begin
    CurStr := Items.Strings[Index];
    Canvas.FillRect(Rect);                  // clear out rect
    if not cbFileNamesOnly.Checked then     // if not filename only...
      { if current line is filename... }
      if (Pos('File ', CurStr) = 1) and
        (CurStr[Length(CurStr)] = ':') then
      begin
        Canvas.Font.Style := [fsUnderline]; // underline font
        Canvas.Font.Color := clRed;         // paint red
      end
      else
        Rect.Left := Rect.Left + 15;        // otherwise, indent
    DrawText(Canvas.Handle, PChar(CurStr), Length(CurStr), Rect,
    ➥dt_SingleLine);
  end;
end;

procedure TMainForm.Font1Click(Sender: TObject);
{ Allows user to pick new font for listbox }
begin
  { Pick new listbox font }
  if FontDialog.Execute then
    lbFiles.Font := FontDialog.Font;
end;


procedure TMainForm.FormDestroy(Sender: TObject);
{ OnDestroy event handler for form }
begin
  WriteIni;
end;

procedure TMainForm.FormCreate(Sender: TObject);
{ OnCreate event handler for form }
begin
  Application.OnHint := DoOnHint;  // set up hints
  ReadIni;                         // read INI file
end;

procedure TMainForm.DoOnHint(Sender: TObject);
{ OnHint event handler for Application }
begin
  { Display application hints on status bar }
```

Writing Multithreaded Applications

CHAPTER 11

309

11

WRITING
MULTITHREADED
APPLICATIONS

```delphi
    StatusBar.Panels[0].Text := Application.Hint;
end;

procedure TMainForm.btnPrintClick(Sender: TObject);
{ Called when Print button is clicked. }
begin
  if MessageDlg('Send search results to printer?', mtConfirmation,
    [mbYes, mbNo], 0) = mrYes then
    PrintStrings(lbFiles.Items);
end;

procedure TMainForm.btnCloseClick(Sender: TObject);
{ Called to stop thread or close application }
begin
  // if thread is running then terminate thread
  if Running then SearchThread.Terminate
  // otherwise close app
  else Close;
end;

procedure TMainForm.lbFilesDblClick(Sender: TObject);
{ Called when user double-clicks in listbox. Invokes viewer for }
{ highlighted file. }
var
  ProgramStr, FileStr: string;
  RetVal: THandle;
begin
  { if user clicked on a file.. }
  if (Pos('File ', lbFiles.Items[lbFiles.ItemIndex]) = 1) then
  begin
    { load text editor from INI file.  Notepad is default. }
    ProgramStr := SrchIniFile.ReadString('Defaults', 'Editor', 'notepad');
    FileStr := lbFiles.Items[lbFiles.ItemIndex];       // Get selected
                                                       // file
    FileStr := Copy(FileStr, 6, Length(FileStr) - 5);  // Remove prefix
    if FileStr[Length(FileStr)] = ':' then             // Remove ":"
      DecStrLen(FileStr, 1);
    if cbRunFromAss.Checked then
      { Run file from shell association }
      RetVal := ShellExecute(Handle, 'open', PChar(FileStr), nil, nil,
        SW_SHOWNORMAL)
    else
      { View file using text editor }
      RetVal := ShellExecute(Handle, 'open', PChar(ProgramStr),
        PChar(FileStr), nil, SW_SHOWNORMAL);
    { Check for error }
    if RetVal < 32 then RaiseLastWin32Error;
  end;
end;
```

continues

LISTING 11.8. CONTINUED

```
procedure TMainForm.FormResize(Sender: TObject);
{ OnResize event handler. Centers controls in form. }
begin
 { divide status bar into two panels with a 1/3 - 2/3 split }
  with StatusBar do
  begin
    Panels[0].Width := Width div 3;
    Panels[1].Width := Width * 2 div 3;
  end;
end;

procedure TMainForm.btnPriorityClick(Sender: TObject);
{ Show thread priority form }
begin
  ThreadPriWin.Show;
end;

procedure TMainForm.ReadIni;
{ Reads default values from Registry }
begin
  with SrchIniFile do
  begin
    edtPathName.Text := ReadString('Defaults', 'LastPath', 'C:\');
    edtFileSpec.Text := ReadString('Defaults', 'LastFileSpec', '*.*');
    edtToken.Text := ReadString('Defaults', 'LastToken', '');
    cbFileNamesOnly.Checked := ReadBool('Defaults', 'FNamesOnly', False);
    cbCaseSensitive.Checked := ReadBool('Defaults', 'CaseSens', False);
    cbRecurse.Checked := ReadBool('Defaults', 'Recurse', False);
    cbRunFromAss.Checked := ReadBool('Defaults', 'RunFromAss', False);
    Left := ReadInteger('Position', 'Left', 100);
    Top := ReadInteger('Position', 'Top', 50);
    Width := ReadInteger('Position', 'Width', 510);
    Height := ReadInteger('Position', 'Height', 370);
  end;
end;

procedure TMainForm.WriteIni;
{ writes current settings back to Registry }
begin
  with SrchIniFile do
  begin
    WriteString('Defaults', 'LastPath', edtPathName.Text);
    WriteString('Defaults', 'LastFileSpec', edtFileSpec.Text);
    WriteString('Defaults', 'LastToken', edtToken.Text);
    WriteBool('Defaults', 'CaseSens', cbCaseSensitive.Checked);
    WriteBool('Defaults', 'FNamesOnly', cbFileNamesOnly.Checked);
    WriteBool('Defaults', 'Recurse', cbRecurse.Checked);
    WriteBool('Defaults', 'RunFromAss', cbRunFromAss.Checked);
    WriteInteger('Position', 'Left', Left);
```

```
    WriteInteger('Position', 'Top', Top);
    WriteInteger('Position', 'Width', Width);
    WriteInteger('Position', 'Height', Height);
  end;
end;

procedure TMainForm.Clear1Click(Sender: TObject);
begin
  lbFiles.Items.Clear;
end;

end.
```

Several things worth mentioning happen in this unit. First, you'll notice the fairly small PrintStrings() procedure that's used to send the contents of TStrings to the printer. To accomplish this, the procedure takes advantage of Delphi's AssignPrn() standard procedure, which assigns a TextFile variable to the printer. That way, any text written to the TextFile is automatically written to the printer. When you're finished writing to the printer, be sure to use the CloseFile() procedure to close the connection to the printer.

Also of interest is the use of the ShellExecute() Win32 API procedure to launch a viewer for a file that will be shown in the list box. ShellExecute() not only enables you to invoke executable programs but also to invoke associations for registered file extensions. For example, if you try to invoke a file with a .pas extension using ShellExecute(), it will automatically load Delphi to view the file.

TIP

If ShellExecute() returns a value indicating an error, the application calls RaiseLastWin32Error(). This procedure, located in the SysUtils unit, calls the GetLastError() API function and Delphi's SysErrorMessage() in order to obtain more detailed information about the error and format that information into a string. You can use RaiseLastWin32Error() in this manner in your own applications if you want your users to obtain detailed error messages on API failures.

The Search Thread

The searching engine is contained within a unit called SrchU.pas, which is shown in Listing 11.9. This unit does a number of interesting things, including copying an entire file into a string, recursing subdirectories, and communicating information back to the main form.

LISTING 11.9. THE SrchU.pas UNIT.

```pascal
unit SrchU;

interface

uses Classes, StdCtrls;

type
  TSearchThread = class(TThread)
  private
    LB: TListbox;
    CaseSens: Boolean;
    FileNames: Boolean;
    Recurse: Boolean;
    SearchStr: string;
    SearchPath: string;
    FileSpec: string;
    AddStr: string;
    FSearchFile: string;
    procedure AddToList;
    procedure DoSearch(const Path: string);
    procedure FindAllFiles(const Path: string);
    procedure FixControls;
    procedure ScanForStr(const FName: string; var FileStr: string);
    procedure SearchFile(const FName: string);
    procedure SetSearchFile;
  protected
    procedure Execute; override;
  public
    constructor Create(CaseS, FName, Rec: Boolean; const Str, SPath,
      FSpec: string);
    destructor Destroy; override;
  end;

implementation

uses SysUtils, StrUtils, Windows, Forms, Main;

constructor TSearchThread.Create(CaseS, FName, Rec: Boolean; const Str,
  SPath, FSpec: string);
begin
  CaseSens := CaseS;
  FileNames := FName;
  Recurse := Rec;
  SearchStr := Str;
  SearchPath := AddBackSlash(SPath);
  FileSpec := FSpec;
  inherited Create(False);
end;
```

```
destructor TSearchThread.Destroy;
begin
  FSearchFile := '';
  Synchronize(SetSearchFile);
  Synchronize(FixControls);
  inherited Destroy;
end;

procedure TSearchThread.Execute;
begin
  FreeOnTerminate := True;      // set up all the fields
  LB := MainForm.lbFiles;
  Priority := TThreadPriority(MainForm.SearchPri);
  if not CaseSens then SearchStr := UpperCase(SearchStr);
  FindAllFiles(SearchPath);     // process current directory
  if Recurse then               // if subdirs, then...
    DoSearch(SearchPath);       // recurse, otherwise...
end;

procedure TSearchThread.FixControls;
{ Enables controls in main form. Must be called through Synchronize }
begin
  MainForm.EnableSearchControls(True);
end;

procedure TSearchThread.SetSearchFile;
{ Updates status bar with filename. Must be called through Synchronize }
begin
  MainForm.StatusBar.Panels[1].Text := FSearchFile;
end;

procedure TSearchThread.AddToList;
{ Adds string to main listbox. Must be called through Synchronize }
begin
  LB.Items.Add(AddStr);
end;

procedure TSearchThread.ScanForStr(const FName: string; var FileStr:
➥string);
{ Scans a FileStr of file FName for SearchStr }
var
  Marker: string[1];
  FoundOnce: Boolean;
  FindPos: integer;
begin
  FindPos := Pos(SearchStr, FileStr);
  FoundOnce := False;
  while (FindPos <> 0) and not Terminated do
  begin
    if not FoundOnce then
```

continues

LISTING 11.9. CONTINUED

```pascal
    begin
      { use ":" only if user doesn't choose "filename only" }
      if FileNames then
        Marker := ''
      else
        Marker := ':';
      { add file to listbox }
      AddStr := Format('File %s%s', [FName, Marker]);
      Synchronize(AddToList);
      FoundOnce := True;
    end;
    { don't search for same string in same file if filenames only }
    if FileNames then Exit;

    { Add line if not filename only }
    AddStr := GetCurLine(FileStr, FindPos);
    Synchronize(AddToList);
    FileStr := Copy(FileStr, FindPos + Length(SearchStr),
    ➡Length(FileStr));
    FindPos := Pos(SearchStr, FileStr);
  end;
end;

procedure TSearchThread.SearchFile(const FName: string);
{ Searches file FName for SearchStr }
var
  DataFile: THandle;
  FileSize: Integer;
  SearchString: string;
begin
  FSearchFile := FName;
  Synchronize(SetSearchFile);
  try
    DataFile := FileOpen(FName, fmOpenRead or fmShareDenyWrite);
    if DataFile = 0 then raise Exception.Create('');
    try
      { set length of search string }
      FileSize := GetFileSize(DataFile, nil);
      SetLength(SearchString, FileSize);
      { Copy file data to string }
      FileRead(DataFile, Pointer(SearchString)^, FileSize);
    finally
      CloseHandle(DataFile);
    end;
    if not CaseSens then SearchString := UpperCase(SearchString);
    ScanForStr(FName, SearchString);
  except
    on Exception do
    begin
      AddStr := Format('Error reading file: %s', [FName]);
```

```
        Synchronize(AddToList);
      end;
    end;
end;

procedure TSearchThread.FindAllFiles(const Path: string);
{ procedure searches Path subdir for files matching filespec }
var
  SR: TSearchRec;
begin
  { find first file matching spec }
  if FindFirst(Path + FileSpec, faArchive, SR) = 0 then
    try
      repeat
        SearchFile(Path + SR.Name);             // process file
      until (FindNext(SR) <> 0) or Terminated; // find next file
    finally
      SysUtils.FindClose(SR);                   // clean up
    end;
end;

procedure TSearchThread.DoSearch(const Path: string);
{ procedure recurses through a subdirectory tree starting at Path }
var
  SR: TSearchRec;
begin
  { look for directories }
  if FindFirst(Path + '*.*', faDirectory, SR) = 0 then
    try
      repeat
        { if it's a directory and not '.' or '..' then... }
        if ((SR.Attr and faDirectory) <> 0) and (SR.Name[1] <> '.') and
          not Terminated then
        begin
          FindAllFiles(Path + SR.Name + '\');  // process directory
          DoSearch(Path + SR.Name + '\');      // recurse
        end;
      until (FindNext(SR) <> 0) or Terminated;      // find next
                                                    // directory
    finally
      SysUtils.FindClose(SR);                       // clean up
    end;
end;

end.
```

When created, this thread first calls its FindAllFiles() method. This method uses
FindFirst() and FindNext() to search for all files in the current directory matching the
file specification indicated by the user. If the user has chosen to recurse subdirectories,

the DoSearch() method is then called in order to traverse down a directory tree. This method again makes use of FindFirst() and FindNext() to find directories, but the twist is that it calls itself recursively in order to traverse the tree. As each directory is found, FindAllFiles() is called to process all matching files in the directory.

> **TIP**
>
> The recursion algorithm used by the DoSearch() method is a standard technique for traversing a directory tree. Because recursive algorithms are notoriously difficult to debug, the smart programmer will make use of ones that are already known to work. It's a good idea to save this method so that you can use it with other applications in the future.

To process each file, you'll notice that the algorithm for searching for a token within a file involves using the TMemMapFile object, which encapsulates a Win32 memory-mapped file. This object is discussed in detail in Chapter 12, "Working with Files," but for now you can just assume that this provides an easy way to map the contents of a file into memory. The entire algorithm works like this:

1. When a file matching the file spec is found by the FindAllFiles() method, the SearchFile() method is called and the file contents are copied into a string.

2. The ScanForStr() method is called for each file string. ScanForStr() searches for occurrences of the search token within each string.

3. When an occurrence is found, the filename and/or the line of text is added to the list box. The line of text is added only when the user unchecks the File Names Only check box.

Note that all the methods in the TSearchThread object periodically check the status of the StopIt flag (which is tripped when the thread is told to stop) and the Terminated flag (which is tripped when the TThread object is to terminate).

> **CAUTION**
>
> Remember that any methods within a TThread object that modify the application's user interface in any way must be called through the Synchronize() method, or the user interface must be modified by sending messages.

Adjusting the Priority

Just to add yet another feature, DelSrch enables the user to adjust the priority of the
search thread dynamically. The form used for this purpose is shown in Figure 11.7, and
the unit for this form, `PriU.pas`, is shown in Listing 11.10.

FIGURE 11.7.

*The thread
priority form for
the DelSrch
project.*

LISTING 11.10. THE `PriU.pas` UNIT.

```pascal
unit PriU;

interface

uses
  Windows, Messages, SysUtils, Classes, Graphics, Controls, Forms, Dialogs,
  StdCtrls, ComCtrls, Buttons, ExtCtrls;

type
  TThreadPriWin = class(TForm)
    tbrPriorityTrackBar: TTrackBar;
    Label1: TLabel;
    Label2: TLabel;
    Label3: TLabel;
    btnOK: TBitBtn;
    btnRevert: TBitBtn;
    Panel1: TPanel;
    procedure tbrPriorityTrackBarChange(Sender: TObject);
    procedure btnRevertClick(Sender: TObject);
    procedure FormClose(Sender: TObject; var Action: TCloseAction);
    procedure FormShow(Sender: TObject);
    procedure btnOKClick(Sender: TObject);
    procedure FormCreate(Sender: TObject);
  private
    { Private declarations }
    OldPriVal: Integer;
  public
    { Public declarations }
  end;

var
  ThreadPriWin: TThreadPriWin;

implementation
```

continues

LISTING 11.10. CONTINUED

```
{$R *.DFM}

uses Main, SrchU;

procedure TThreadPriWin.tbrPriorityTrackBarChange(Sender: TObject);
begin
  with MainForm do
  begin
    SearchPri := tbrPriorityTrackBar.Position;
    if Running then
      SearchThread.Priority :=
      ➥TThreadPriority(tbrPriorityTrackBar.Position);
  end;
end;

procedure TThreadPriWin.btnRevertClick(Sender: TObject);
begin
  tbrPriorityTrackBar.Position := OldPriVal;
end;

procedure TThreadPriWin.FormClose(Sender: TObject;
  var Action: TCloseAction);
begin
  Action := caHide;
end;

procedure TThreadPriWin.FormShow(Sender: TObject);
begin
  OldPriVal := tbrPriorityTrackBar.Position;
end;

procedure TThreadPriWin.btnOKClick(Sender: TObject);
begin
  Close;
end;

procedure TThreadPriWin.FormCreate(Sender: TObject);
begin
  tbrPriorityTrackBarChange(Sender);          // initialize thread priority
end;

end.
```

The code for this unit is fairly straightforward. All it does is set the value of the SearchPri variable in the main form to match that of the track bar position. If the thread is running, it also sets the priority of the thread. Because TThreadPriority is an enumerated type, a straight typecast maps the values 1 to 5 in the track bar to enumerations in TThreadPriority.

MULTITHREADING DATABASE ACCESS

Although database programming isn't really discussed until Chapter 27, "Writing Desktop Database Applications," this section is intended to give you some tips on how to use multiple threads in the context of database development. If you're unfamiliar with database programming under Delphi, you might want to look through Chapter 27 before reading on in this section.

The most common request for database applications developers in Win32 is for the capability of performing complex queries or stored procedures in a background thread. Thankfully, this type of thing is supported by the 32-bit Borland Database Engine (BDE) and is fairly easy to do in Delphi.

There are really only two requirements for running a background query through, for example, a TQuery component:

- Each threaded query must reside within its own session. You can provide a TQuery with its own session by placing a TSession component on your form and assigning its name to the TQuery's SessionName property. This also implies that, if your TQuery uses a TDatabase component, a unique TDatabase must also be used for each session.

- The TQuery must not be attached to any TDataSource components at the time the query is opened from the secondary thread. When the query is attached to a TDataSource, it must be done through the context of the primary thread. TDataSource is only used to connect datasets to user interface controls, and user interface manipulation must be performed in the main thread.

To illustrate the techniques for background queries, Figure 11.8 shows the main form for a demo project called BDEThrd. This form enables you to specify a BDE alias, user name, and password for a particular database, and to enter a query against the database. When the Go! button is clicked, a secondary thread is spawned to process the query and the results are displayed in a child form.

FIGURE 11.8.

The main form for the BDEThrd demo.

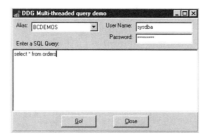

The child form, `TQueryForm`, is shown in Figure 11.9. Notice that this form contains one each of a `TQuery`, `TDatabase`, `TSession`, `TDataSource`, and `TDBGrid`. Therefore, each instance of `TQueryForm` has its own instances of these components.

FIGURE **11.9.**

The child query form for the BDEThrd demo.

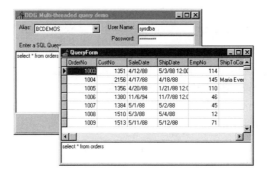

Listing 11.11 shows `Main.pas`, the application's main unit.

LISTING **11.11.** THE `Main.pas` UNIT FOR THE **BDET**HRD DEMO.

```
unit Main;

interface

uses
  Windows, Messages, SysUtils, Classes, Graphics, Controls, Forms,
  Dialogs, Grids, StdCtrls, ExtCtrls;

type
  TMainForm = class(TForm)
    pnlBottom: TPanel;
    pnlButtons: TPanel;
    GoButton: TButton;
    Button1: TButton;
    memQuery: TMemo;
    pnlTop: TPanel;
    Label1: TLabel;
    AliasCombo: TComboBox;
    Label3: TLabel;
    UserNameEd: TEdit;
    Label4: TLabel;
    PasswordEd: TEdit;
    Label2: TLabel;
    procedure Button1Click(Sender: TObject);
    procedure GoButtonClick(Sender: TObject);
    procedure FormCreate(Sender: TObject);
```

```
private
  { Private declarations }
public
  { Public declarations }
end;

var
  MainForm: TMainForm;

implementation

{$R *.DFM}

uses QryU, DB, DBTables;

var
  FQueryNum: Integer = 0;

procedure TMainForm.Button1Click(Sender: TObject);
begin
  Close;
end;

procedure TMainForm.GoButtonClick(Sender: TObject);
begin
  Inc(FQueryNum);    // keep querynum unique
  { invoke new query }
  NewQuery(FQueryNum, memQuery.Lines, AliasCombo.Text, UserNameEd.Text,
    PasswordEd.Text);
end;

procedure TMainForm.FormCreate(Sender: TObject);
begin
  { fill drop-down list with BDE Aliases }
  Session.GetAliasNames(AliasCombo.Items);
end;

end.
```

As you can see, there's not much to this unit. The TCombobox AliasCombo is filled with BDE aliases in the OnCreate handler for the main form using TSession's GetAliasNames() method. When the handler for the Go! button click is in charge of invoking a new query by calling the NewQuery() procedure that lives in a second unit, QryU.pas, notice that it passes a new unique number, FQueryNum, to the NewQuery() procedure with every button click. This number is used to create a unique session and database name for each query thread.

Listing 11.12 shows the code for the QryU.pas unit.

LISTING 11.12. THE QryU.pas UNIT.

```
unit QryU;

interface

uses
  Windows, Messages, SysUtils, Classes, Graphics, Controls, Forms,
  Dialogs, Grids, DBGrids, DB, DBTables, StdCtrls;

type
  TQueryForm = class(TForm)
    Query: TQuery;
    DataSource: TDataSource;
    Session: TSession;
    Database: TDatabase;
    dbgQueryGrid: TDBGrid;
    memSQL: TMemo;
    procedure FormClose(Sender: TObject; var Action: TCloseAction);
  private
    { Private declarations }
  public
    { Public declarations }
  end;

procedure NewQuery(QryNum: integer; Qry: TStrings; const Alias, UserName,
  Password: string);

implementation

{$R *.DFM}

type
  TDBQueryThread = class(TThread)
  private
    FQuery: TQuery;
    FDataSource: TDataSource;
    FQueryException: Exception;
    procedure HookUpUI;
    procedure QueryError;
  protected
    procedure Execute; override;
  public
    constructor Create(Q: TQuery; D: TDataSource); virtual;
  end;

constructor TDBQueryThread.Create(Q: TQuery; D: TDataSource);
begin
  inherited Create(True);        // create suspended thread
  FQuery := Q;                   // set parameters
```

```
    FDataSource := D;
    FreeOnTerminate := True;
    Resume;                        // thread that puppy!
end;

procedure TDBQueryThread.Execute;
begin
  try
    FQuery.Open;                   // open the query
    Synchronize(HookUpUI);         // update UI from main thread
  except
    FQueryException := ExceptObject as Exception;
    Synchronize(QueryError);       // show exception from main thread
  end;
end;

procedure TDBQueryThread.HookUpUI;
begin
  FDataSource.DataSet := FQuery;
end;

procedure TDBQueryThread.QueryError;
begin
  Application.ShowException(FQueryException);
end;

procedure NewQuery(QryNum: integer; Qry: TStrings; const Alias, UserName,
  Password: string);
begin
  { Create a new Query form to show query results }
  with TQueryForm.Create(Application) do
  begin
    { Set a unique session name }
    Session.SessionName := Format('Sess%d', [QryNum]);
    with Database do
    begin
      { set a unique database name }
      DatabaseName := Format('DB%d', [QryNum]);
      { set alias parameter }
      AliasName := Alias;
      { hook database to session }
      SessionName := Session.SessionName;
      { user-defined username and password }
      Params.Values['USER NAME'] := UserName;
      Params.Values['PASSWORD'] := Password;
    end;
    with Query do
    begin
      { hook query to database and session }
      DatabaseName := Database.DatabaseName;
```

continues

LISTING 11.12. CONTINUED

```
      SessionName := Session.SessionName;
      { set up the query strings }
      SQL.Assign(Qry);
    end;
    { display query strings in SQL Memo }
    memSQL.Lines.Assign(Qry);
    { show query form }
    Show;
    { open query in its own thread }
    TDBQueryThread.Create(Query, DataSource);
  end;
end;

procedure TQueryForm.FormClose(Sender: TObject; var Action: TCloseAction);
begin
  Action := caFree;
end;

end.
```

The NewQuery() procedure creates a new instance of the child form TQueryForm, sets up the properties for each of its data-access components, and creates unique names for its TDatabase and TSession components. The query's SQL property is filled from the TStrings passed in the Qry parameter, and the query thread is then spawned.

The code inside the TDBQueryThread itself is rather sparse. The constructor merely sets up some instance variables, and the Execute() method opens the query and calls the HookupUI() method through Synchronize() to attach the query to the data source. You should also take note of the try..except inside the Execute() procedure, which uses Synchronize() to show exception messages from the context of the primary thread.

MULTITHREADED GRAPHICS

We mentioned earlier that VCL isn't designed to be manipulated simultaneously by multiple threads, but this statement isn't entirely accurate. VCL has the capability to have multiple threads manipulate individual graphics objects. Thanks to new Lock() and Unlock() methods introduced in TCanvas, the entire Graphics unit has been made thread safe. This includes the TCanvas, TPen, TBrush, TFont, TBitmap, TMetafile, TPicture, and TIcon classes.

The code for these Lock() methods is similar in that it uses a critical section and the EnterCriticalSection() API function (described earlier in this chapter) to guard access to the canvas or graphics object. After a particular thread calls a Lock() method, that

Writing Multithreaded Applications

CHAPTER 11

325

11

WRITING
MULTITHREADED
APPLICATIONS

thread is free to exclusively manipulate the canvas or graphics object. Other threads waiting to enter the portion of code following the call to `Lock()` will be put to sleep until the thread owning the critical section calls `Unlock()`, which calls `LeaveCriticalSection()` to release the critical section and let the next waiting thread (if any) into the protected portion of code. The following portion of code shows how these methods can be used to control access to canvas:

```
Form.Canvas.Lock;
// code which manipulates canvas goes here
Form.Canvas.Unlock;
```

To further illustrate this point, Listing 11.13 shows the unit `Main` of the MTGraph project—an application that demonstrates multiple threads accessing a form's canvas.

LISTING 11.13. THE `Main.pas` UNIT OF THE MTGRAPH PROJECT.

```
unit Main;

interface

uses
  Windows, Messages, SysUtils, Classes, Graphics, Controls, Forms,
  Dialogs, Menus;

type
  TMainForm = class(TForm)
    MainMenu1: TMainMenu;
    Options1: TMenuItem;
    AddThread: TMenuItem;
    RemoveThread: TMenuItem;
    ColorDialog1: TColorDialog;
    Add10: TMenuItem;
    RemoveAll: TMenuItem;
    procedure FormCreate(Sender: TObject);
    procedure FormDestroy(Sender: TObject);
    procedure AddThreadClick(Sender: TObject);
    procedure RemoveThreadClick(Sender: TObject);
    procedure Add10Click(Sender: TObject);
    procedure RemoveAllClick(Sender: TObject);
  private
    ThreadList: TList;
  public
    { Public declarations }
  end;
```

continues

LISTING 11.13. CONTINUED

```
TDrawThread = class(TThread)
private
  FColor: TColor;
  FForm: TForm;
public
  constructor Create(AForm: TForm; AColor: TColor);
  procedure Execute; override;
end;

var
  MainForm: TMainForm;

implementation

{$R *.DFM}

{ TDrawThread }

constructor TDrawThread.Create(AForm: TForm; AColor: TColor);
begin
  FColor := AColor;
  FForm := AForm;
  inherited Create(False);
end;

procedure TDrawThread.Execute;
var
  P1, P2: TPoint;

  procedure GetRandCoords;
  var
    MaxX, MaxY: Integer;
  begin
    // initialize P1 and P2 to random points within Form bounds
    MaxX := FForm.ClientWidth;
    MaxY := FForm.ClientHeight;
    P1.x := Random(MaxX);
    P2.x := Random(MaxX);
    P1.y := Random(MaxY);
    P2.y := Random(MaxY);
  end;

begin
  FreeOnTerminate := True;
  // thread runs until it or the application is terminated
  while not (Terminated or Application.Terminated) do
  begin
    GetRandCoords;              // initialize P1 and P2
    with FForm.Canvas do
```

Writing Multithreaded Applications

CHAPTER 11

327

11

WRITING
MULTITHREADED
APPLICATIONS

```
    begin
      Lock;                    // lock canvas
      // only one thread at a time can execute the following code:
      Pen.Color := FColor;    // set pen color
      MoveTo(P1.X, P1.Y);     // move to canvas position P1
      LineTo(P2.X, P2.Y);     // draw a line to position P2
      // after the next line executes, another thread will be allowed
      // to enter the above code block
      Unlock;                  // unlock canvas
    end;
  end;
end;

{ TMainForm }

procedure TMainForm.FormCreate(Sender: TObject);
begin
  ThreadList := TList.Create;
end;

procedure TMainForm.FormDestroy(Sender: TObject);
begin
  RemoveAllClick(nil);
  ThreadList.Free;
end;

procedure TMainForm.AddThreadClick(Sender: TObject);
begin
  // add a new thread to the list... allow user to choose color
  if ColorDialog1.Execute then
    ThreadList.Add(TDrawThread.Create(Self, ColorDialog1.Color));
end;

procedure TMainForm.RemoveThreadClick(Sender: TObject);
begin
  // terminate the last thread in the list and remove it from list
  TDrawThread(ThreadList[ThreadList.Count - 1]).Terminate;
  ThreadList.Delete(ThreadList.Count - 1);
end;

procedure TMainForm.Add10Click(Sender: TObject);
var
  i: Integer;
begin
  // create 10 threads, each with a random color
  for i := 1 to 10 do
    ThreadList.Add(TDrawThread.Create(Self, Random(MaxInt)));
end;
procedure TMainForm.RemoveAllClick(Sender: TObject);
```

continues

LISTING 11.13. CONTINUED

```
var
  i: Integer;
begin
  Cursor := crHourGlass;
  try
    for i := ThreadList.Count - 1 downto 0 do
    begin
      TDrawThread(ThreadList[i]).Terminate;  // terminate thread
      TDrawThread(ThreadList[i]).WaitFor;    // make sure thread
                                             // terminates
    end;
    ThreadList.Clear;
  finally
    Cursor:= crDefault;
  end;
end;

initialization
  Randomize;  // seed random number generator
end.
```

This application has a main menu containing four items, as shown in Figure 11.10. The first item, Add Thread, creates a new TDrawThread instance, which paints random lines on the main form. This option can be selected repeatedly in order to throw more and more threads into the mix of threads accessing the main form. The next item, Remove Thread, removes the last thread added. The third item, Add 10, creates 10 new TDrawThread instances. Finally, the fourth item, Remove All, terminates and destroys all TDrawThread instances. Figure 11.10 also shows the result of ten threads simultaneously drawing to the form's canvas.

FIGURE 11.10.

The MTGraph main form.

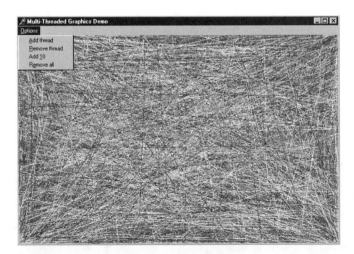

Canvas-locking rules dictate that as long as every user of a canvas locks it before drawing and unlocks it afterward, multiple threads using that canvas will not interfere with each other. Note that all OnPaint events and Paint() method calls initiated by VCL automatically lock and unlock the canvas for you, so existing, normal Delphi code can coexist with new background thread graphics operations.

Using this application as an example, examine the consequences or symptoms of thread collisions if you fail to properly perform canvas locking. If thread 1 sets a canvas's pen color to red and then draws a line, and thread 2 sets the pen color to blue and draws a circle, and these threads do not lock the canvas before starting these operations, the following thread collision scenario is possible: Thread 1 sets the pen color to red. The OS scheduler switches execution to thread 2. Thread 2 sets the pen color to blue and draws a circle. Execution switches to thread 1. Thread 1 draws a line. However, the line is not red; it is blue because thread 2 had the opportunity to slip in between the operations of thread 1.

Note also that it only takes one errant thread to cause problems. If thread 1 locks the canvas and thread 2 does not, the scenario just described is unchanged. Both threads must lock the canvas around their canvas operations to prevent that thread collision scenario.

SUMMARY

By now you've had a thorough introduction to threads and how to use them properly in the Delphi environment. You've learned several techniques for synchronizing multiple threads, and you've learned how to communicate between secondary threads and a Delphi application's primary thread. Additionally, you've seen examples of using threads within the context of a real-world file search application, you've gotten the lowdown on how to leverage threads in database applications, and you've learned about drawing to a TCanvas with multiple threads. In the next chapter, "Working with Files," you'll learn about a multitude of techniques for working with different types of files in Delphi.

WORKING WITH FILES

IN THIS CHAPTER

Working with files, directories, and drives is a common programming task that you'll undoubtedly have to do at some time. This chapter illustrates how to work with the different file types: text files, typed files, and untyped files. The chapter covers how to use a TFileStream to encapsulate file I/O and how to take advantage of one of Win32's nicest features, *memory-mapped files*. You'll create a TMemoryMappedFile class that you can use, which encapsulates some of the memory-mapped functionality, and you'll learn how to use this class to perform text searches in text files. This chapter also demonstrates some useful routines to determine available drives, walk directory trees to search for files, and obtain version information on files. At the end of this chapter, you'll have a strong feel for working with files, directories, and drives.

HARD-CORE TECHNIQUES

IN THIS CHAPTER

There comes a time when you must step off the beaten path to accomplish a particular goal. This chapter teaches you some advanced techniques that you can use in your Delphi applications. You get much closer to the Win32 API in this chapter than you do in most of the other chapters, and you explore some things that aren't obvious or aren't provided under VCL. You learn about concepts such as window procedures, multiple program instances, Windows hooks, and sharing Delphi and C++ code.

ADVANCED APPLICATION MESSAGE HANDLING

As discussed in Chapter 5, "Understanding Messages," a *window procedure* is a function that Windows calls whenever a particular window receives a message. Because the Application object contains a window, it has a window procedure that's called to receive all the messages sent to your application. The TApplication class even comes equipped with an OnMessage event that notifies you whenever one of these messages comes down the pike.

Well. . . not exactly.

TApplication.OnMessage fires only when a message is retrieved from the application's message queue (again, refer to Chapter 5 for a discussion of all this message terminology). Messages found in the application queue are typically those dealing with window management (WM_PAINT and WM_SIZE, for example) and those posted to the window by using an API function such as PostMessage(), PostAppMessage(), or Broadcast SystemMessage(). The problem arises when other types of messages are sent directly to the window procedure by Windows or by the SendMessage() function. When this occurs, the TApplication.OnMessage event never happens, and there's no way to know whether the message occurred based on this event.

Subclassing

To know when a message is sent to your application, you must replace the Application window's window procedure with your own. In your window procedure, you should do whatever processing or message handling you need to do before passing the message to the original window procedure. This process is known as *subclassing* a window.

You can use the SetWindowLong() Win32 API function with the GWL_WNDPROC constant to set a new window procedure function for a window. The window procedure function itself can have one of two formats: It can follow the API definition of a window procedure, or you can take advantage of some Delphi helper functions and make the window procedure a special method referred to as a *window method*.

> **CAUTION**
>
> A problem that can arise when you subclass the window procedure of a VCL window is that the handle of the window can be re-created beneath you—causing your application to fail. Beware of using this technique if there is a chance

> that the window handle of the window you are subclassing will be re-created.
> A safer technique is to use `Application.HookMainWindow()`, which is shown
> later in this chapter.

A Win32 API Window Procedure

An API window procedure must have the following declaration:

```
function AWndProc(Handle: hWnd; Msg, wParam, lParam: Longint):
   Longint; stdcall;
```

The `Handle` parameter identifies the destination window, the `Msg` parameter is the window message, and the `wParam` and `lParam` parameters contain additional message-specific information. This function returns a value that depends on the message received. Note carefully that this function must use the `stdcall` calling convention.

You can use the `SetWindowLong()` function to set the window procedure of `Application`'s window as shown here:

```
var
  WProc: Pointer;
begin
  WProc := Pointer(SetWindowLong(Application.Handle, GWL_WNDPROC,
    Integer(@NewWndProc)));
```

After this call, `WProc` will hold a pointer to the old window procedure. It's necessary to save this value because you must pass on any messages you don't handle yourself to the old window procedure using the `CallWindowProc()` API function. The following code gives you an idea of the implementation of the window procedure:

```
function NewWndProc(Handle: hWnd; Msg, wParam, lParam: Longint):
   Longint; stdcall;
begin
  { Check value of Msg, and perform whatever type of action you'd }
  { like depending on the value of the message.  For messages you }
  {don't explicitly handle, you must pass the message information }
  {on to the original window procedure as shown below: }
  Result := CallWindowProc(WProc, Application.Handle, Msg, wParam,
    lParam);
end;
```

Listing 13.1 shows the `ScWndPrc.pas` unit, which subclasses `Application`'s window procedure to handle a user-defined message called `DDGM_FOOMSG`.

LISTING 13.1. ScWndPrc.pas.

```
unit ScWndPrc;

interface

uses Forms, Messages;
```

continues

13

HARD-CORE
TECHNIQUES

LISTING 13.1. CONTINUED

```
const
  DDGM_FOOMSG = WM_USER;

implementation

uses Windows, SysUtils, Dialogs;
var
  WProc: Pointer;

function NewWndProc(Handle: hWnd; Msg, wParam, lParam: Longint): Longint;
  stdcall;
{ This is a Win32 API-level window procedure. It handles the messages }
{ received by the Application window. }
begin
  if Msg = DDGM_FOOMSG then
    { If it's our user-defined message, then alert the user. }
    ShowMessage(Format('Message seen by WndProc! Value is: $%x', [Msg]));
  { Pass message on to old window procedure }
  Result := CallWindowProc(WProc, Handle, Msg, wParam, lParam);
end;

initialization
  { Set window procedure of Application window. }
  WProc := Pointer(SetWindowLong(Application.Handle, gwl_WndProc,
    Integer(@NewWndProc)));
end.
```

CAUTION

Be sure to save the old window procedure returned by GetWindowLong(). If you don't call the old window procedure inside your subclassed window procedure for messages that you don't want to handle, you're likely to crash your application, and you might even crash the operating system.

A Delphi Window Method

Delphi provides a function called MakeObjectInstance() that bridges the gap between an API window procedure and a Delphi method. MakeObjectInstance() enables you to create a method of type TWndMethod to serve as the window procedure. MakeObjectInstance() is declared in the Forms unit as follows:

```
function MakeObjectInstance(Method: TWndMethod): Pointer;
```

TWndMethod is defined in the Forms unit as follows:

```
type
  TWndMethod = procedure(var Message: TMessage) of object;
```

The return value of MakeObjectInstance() is a Pointer to the address of the newly created window procedure. This is the value that you pass as the last parameter to

`SetWindowLong()`. You should free any window methods created with
`MakeObjectInstance()` by using the `FreeObjectInstance()` function.

As an illustration, the project called `WinProc.dpr` demonstrates both techniques
for subclassing the `Application` window procedure and its advantages over
`Application.OnMessage`. The main form for this project is shown in Figure 13.1.

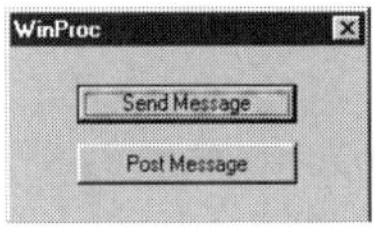

Figure 13.1.

*WinProc's main
form.*

Listing 13.2 shows the source code for `Main.pas`, the main unit for the WinProc project.

Listing 13.2. The source code for `Main.pas`.

```
unit Main;

interface

uses
  SysUtils, WinTypes, WinProcs, Messages, Classes, Graphics, Controls,
  Forms, Dialogs, StdCtrls;

type
  TMainForm = class(TForm)
    SendBtn: TButton;
    PostBtn: TButton;
    procedure SendBtnClick(Sender: TObject);
    procedure PostBtnClick(Sender: TObject);
    procedure FormCreate(Sender: TObject);
    procedure FormDestroy(Sender: TObject);
  private
    OldWndProc: Pointer;
    WndProcPtr: Pointer;
    procedure WndMethod(var Msg: TMessage);
    procedure HandleAppMessage(var Msg: TMsg; var Handled: Boolean);
  end;

var
  MainForm: TMainForm;

implementation
```

continues

13

HARD-CORE
TECHNIQUES

LISTING 13.2. CONTINUED

```
{$R *.DFM}

uses ScWndPrc;


procedure TMainForm.HandleAppMessage(var Msg: TMsg; var Handled: Boolean);
{ OnMessage handler for Application object. }
begin
  if Msg.Message = DDGM_FOOMSG then
    { if it's the user-defined message, then alert the user. }
    ShowMessage(Format('Message seen by OnMessage! Value is: $%x',
              ➥[Msg.Message]));
end;

procedure TMainForm.WndMethod(var Msg: TMessage);
begin
  if Msg.Msg = DDGM_FOOMSG then
    { if it's the user-defined message, then alert the user. }
    ShowMessage(Format('Message seen by WndMethod! Value is: $%x',
              [Msg.Msg]));
  with Msg do
    { Pass message on to old window procedure. }
    Result := CallWindowProc(OldWndProc, Application.Handle, Msg, wParam,
      lParam);
end;

procedure TMainForm.SendBtnClick(Sender: TObject);
begin
  SendMessage(Application.Handle, DDGM_FOOMSG, 0, 0);
end;

procedure TMainForm.PostBtnClick(Sender: TObject);
begin
  PostMessage(Application.Handle, DDGM_FOOMSG, 0, 0);
end;

procedure TMainForm.FormCreate(Sender: TObject);
begin
  Application.OnMessage := HandleAppMessage;      // set OnMessage handler
  WndProcPtr := MakeObjectInstance(WndMethod);    // make window proc
  { Set window procedure of application window. }
  OldWndProc := Pointer(SetWindowLong(Application.Handle, GWL_WNDPROC,
    Integer(WndProcPtr)));
end;

procedure TMainForm.FormDestroy(Sender: TObject);
begin
  { Restore old window procedure for Application window }
```

```
    SetWindowLong(Application.Handle, GWL_WNDPROC, Longint(OldWndProc));
    { Free our user-created window procedure }
    FreeObjectInstance(WndProcPtr);
  end;

end.
```

When SendBtn is clicked, the SendMessage() API function is used to send the message DDGM_FOOMSG to the Application's window handle. When PostBtn is clicked, the same message is posted to Application using the PostMessage() API function.

The HandleAppMessage() is assigned to handle the Application.OnMessage event. This procedure simply uses ShowMessage() to invoke a dialog box indicating that it sees a message. The OnMessage event is assigned in the OnCreate event handler for the main form.

Notice that the OnDestroy handler for the main form resets Application's window procedure to the original value (OldWndProc) before calling FreeObjectInstance() to free the procedure created with MakeProcInstance(). If the old window procedure isn't first reinstated, the effect would be that of "unplugging" the window procedure from an active window—effectively removing the window's capability to handle messages. That's bad news because doing so could potentially crash the application or the OS.

Just for kicks, the ScWndPrc unit shown earlier in this chapter is included in Main. This means that the Application window will be subclassed twice: once by ScWndPrc using the API technique and once by Main using the window method technique. There's absolutely no danger in doing this as long as you remember to use CallWindowProc() in the window procedure and method to pass messages down to the old window procedures.

When you run this application, you'll be able to see that the ShowMessage() dialog box is shown from both the window procedure and method no matter which button is pushed. What's more, you'll see that Application.OnMessage sees only the messages posted to the window.

HookMainWindow()

Another, perhaps more VCL-friendly, technique for intercepting messages meant for the Application window is TApplication's HookMainWindow() method. This method allows you to insert your own message handler at the top of the TApplication's WndProc() method to perform special message processing or prevent TApplication from processing certain messages. HookMainWindow() is defined as:

```
procedure HookMainWindow(Hook: TWindowHook);
```

The parameter for this method is of type `TWindowHook`, which is defined as:

```
type
  TWindowHook = function (var Message: TMessage): Boolean of object;
```

There isn't much to using this method; just call `HookMainWindow()`, passing your own method in the `Hook` parameter. This adds your method to a list of window hook methods that will be called prior to the normal message processing that occurs in `TApplication.WndProc()`. If a window hook method returns `True`, the message is considered handled, and the `WndProc()` method will immediately exit.

When you are through processing messages, call the `UnhookMainWindow()` method to remove your method from the window hook method list. This method is similarly defined as:

```
procedure UnhookMainWindow(Hook: TWindowHook);
```

Listing 13.3 shows the main form for a simple one-form VCL project that employs this technique, and Figure 13.2 shows this application in action.

LISTING 13.3. `Main.pas` FOR THE HookWnd PROJECT.

```
unit HookMain;

interface

uses
  Windows, Messages, SysUtils, Classes, Graphics, Controls, Forms, Dialogs,
  StdCtrls, ExtCtrls;

type
  THookForm = class(TForm)
    SendBtn: TButton;
    GroupBox1: TGroupBox;
    LogList: TListBox;
    DoLog: TCheckBox;
    ExitBtn: TButton;
    procedure SendBtnClick(Sender: TObject);
    procedure FormCreate(Sender: TObject);
    procedure FormDestroy(Sender: TObject);
    procedure ExitBtnClick(Sender: TObject);
  private
    function AppWindowHook(var Message: TMessage): Boolean;
  end;

var
  HookForm: THookForm;
```

```
implementation

{$R *.DFM}

procedure THookForm.FormCreate(Sender: TObject);
begin
  Application.HookMainWindow(AppWindowHook);
end;

procedure THookForm.FormDestroy(Sender: TObject);
begin
  Application.UnhookMainWindow(AppWindowHook);
end;

function THookForm.AppWindowHook(var Message: TMessage): Boolean;
const
  LogStr = 'Message ID: $%x, WParam: $%x, LParam: $%x';
begin
  Result := True;
  if DoLog.Checked then
    with Message do
      LogList.Items.Add(Format(LogStr, [Msg, WParam, LParam]));
end;

procedure THookForm.SendBtnClick(Sender: TObject);
begin
  SendMessage(Application.Handle, WM_NULL, 0, 0);
end;

procedure THookForm.ExitBtnClick(Sender: TObject);
begin
  Close;
end;

end.
```

13

HARD-CORE TECHNIQUES

FIGURE 13.2.

Spying on the Application *with the* HookWnd *project.*

PREVENTING MULTIPLE APPLICATION INSTANCES

Multiple instances means running more than one copy of your program simultaneously. The capability to run multiple instances of an application independently from one another is a feature provided by the Win32 operating system. As Win32 developers, we occasionally find that we need to prevent multiple instances of an application from running and allow only one copy of an application to run at any given time.

This is a fairly simple task in the 16-bit Windows world: The hPrevInst system variable can be used to determine whether multiple copies of an application are running simultaneously. If the value of hPrevInst is nonzero, another instance of the application is active. However, as explained in Chapter 3, "The Win32 API," Win32 provides a thick layer of R32 insulation between each process, which isolates each from the other. Because of this, the value for hPrevInst is always zero for Win32 applications.

Another technique that works for both 16-bit and 32-bit Windows is to use the FindWindow() API function to search for an already-active Application window. This solution has two disadvantages, however. First, FindWindow() allows you to search for a window based only on its class name or caption. Depending on the class name isn't a particularly robust solution because there's no guarantee that the class name of your form is unique throughout the system. Searching based on the form caption has obvious drawbacks in that you can't change the caption of the form while it runs (as with applications such as Delphi or Microsoft Word). The second drawback to FindWindow() is that it tends to be slow because it must iterate over all top-level windows.

The optimal solution for Win32, then, is to use some type of API object that's persistent across processes. As explained in Chapter 11, "Writing Multithreaded Applications," several of the thread-synchronization objects are persistent across multiple processes. Because of their simplicity of use, mutexes provide an ideal solution to this problem.

The first time an application is run, a mutex is created using the CreateMutex() API function. The lpName parameter of this function holds a unique string identifier. Subsequent instances of this application should try to open the mutex by name using the OpenMutex() function. OpenMutex() will succeed only when a mutex has already been created using the CreateMutex() function.

Additionally, when you attempt to run a second instance of these applications, the first instance of the application should come into focus. The most elegant approach to focusing the main form of the previous instance is to use a registered window message obtained by the RegisterWindowMessage() function to create a message identifier unique to your application. You then can have the initial instance of your application respond to this message by focusing itself. This approach is illustrated in Listing 13.4, which shows the source for the MultInst.pas unit, and Listing 13.5, OIMain.pas, which is the main unit of the OneInst project. The application is shown in all its glory in Figure 13.3.

LISTING 13.4. MultInst.pas.

```
unit multinst;
interface
uses Forms, Windows, Dialogs, SysUtils;
// The following declaration is necessary because of an error in
// the declaration of BroadcastSystemMessage() in the Windows unit
function BroadcastSystemMessage(Flags: DWORD; Recipients: PDWORD;
  uiMessage: UINT; wParam: WPARAM; lParam: LPARAM): Longint; stdcall;
  external 'user32.dll';
const
  MI_NO_ERROR          = 0;
  MI_FAIL_SUBCLASS     = 1;
  MI_FAIL_CREATE_MUTEX = 2;
{ Query this function to determine if error occurred in startup. }
{ Value will be one or more of the MI_* error flags. }
function GetMIError: Integer;
implementation
const
  UniqueAppStr : PChar = 'I am the Eggman!';
var
  MessageId: Integer;
  WProc: TFNWndProc = Nil;
  MutHandle: THandle = 0;
  MIError: Integer = 0;
function GetMIError: Integer;
begin
  Result := MIError;
end;
function NewWndProc(Handle: HWND; Msg: Integer; wParam, lParam: Longint):
  Longint; stdcall;
begin
  { If this is the registered message... }
  if Msg = MessageID then
  begin
    { if main form is minimized, normalize it }
    { set focus to application }
    if IsIconic(Application.Handle) then
    begin
      Application.MainForm.WindowState := wsNormal;
      Application.Restore;
    end;
    SetForegroundWindow(Application.MainForm.Handle);
  end
```

13

continues

LISTING 13.4. CONTINUED

```
  { Otherwise, pass message on to old window proc }
  else
    Result := CallWindowProc(WProc, Handle, Msg, wParam, lParam);
end;
procedure SubClassApplication;
begin
  { We subclass Application window procedure so that }
  { Application.OnMessage remains available for user. }
  WProc := TFNWndProc(SetWindowLong(Application.Handle, GWL_WNDPROC,
                               Longint(@NewWndProc)));
  { Set appropriate error flag if error condition occurred }
  if WProc = Nil then
    MIError := MIError or MI_FAIL_SUBCLASS;
end;
procedure DoFirstInstance;
begin
  SubClassApplication;
  MutHandle := CreateMutex(Nil, False, UniqueAppStr);
  if MutHandle = 0 then
    MIError := MIError or MI_FAIL_CREATE_MUTEX;
end;
procedure BroadcastFocusMessage;
{ This is called when there is already an instance running. }
var
  BSMRecipients: DWORD;
begin
  { Don't flash main form }
  Application.ShowMainForm := False;
  { Post message and inform other instance to focus itself }
  BSMRecipients := BSM_APPLICATIONS;
  BroadCastSystemMessage(BSF_IGNORECURRENTTASK or BSF_POSTMESSAGE,
    @BSMRecipients, MessageID, 0, 0);
  Application.Terminate;
end;
procedure InitInstance;
begin
  MutHandle := OpenMutex(MUTEX_ALL_ACCESS, False, UniqueAppStr);
  if MutHandle = 0 then
    { Mutex object has not yet been created, meaning that no previous }
    { instance has been created. }
    DoFirstInstance
  else
    BroadcastFocusMessage;
end;
initialization
  MessageID := RegisterWindowMessage(UniqueAppStr);
  InitInstance;
finalization
```

```
  if WProc <> Nil then
    { Restore old window procedure }
    SetWindowLong(Application.Handle, GWL_WNDPROC, LongInt(WProc));
end.
```

LISTING 13.5. OIMain.pas.

```
unit OIMain;
interface
uses
  Windows, Messages, SysUtils, Classes, Graphics, Controls, Forms, Dialogs,
  StdCtrls;
type
  TMainForm = class(TForm)
    Label1: TLabel;
    CloseBtn: TButton;
    procedure CloseBtnClick(Sender: TObject);
  private
    { Private declarations }
  public
    { Public declarations }
  end;
var
  MainForm: TMainForm;
implementation
uses MultInst;
{$R *.DFM}
procedure TMainForm.CloseBtnClick(Sender: TObject);
begin
  Close;
end;
end.
```

FIGURE 13.3.

The main form for the OneInst project.

USING BASM WITH DELPHI

Because Delphi is based on a true compiler, one benefit you receive is the capacity to write assembly code right in the middle of your Object Pascal procedures and functions. This capability is facilitated through Delphi's built-in assembler (BASM). Before you learn about BASM, you learn when to use assembly language in your Delphi programs.

It's great to have such a powerful tool at your disposal, but, like any good thing, BASM can be overdone. If you follow these simple BASM rules, you can write better, cleaner, and more portable code:

- Never use assembly language for something that can be done in Object Pascal. For example, you wouldn't write assembly-language routines to communicate through the serial ports because the Win32 API provides built-in functions for serial communications.

- Don't over-optimize your programs with assembly language. Hand-optimized assembly might run faster than Object Pascal code—but at the price of readability and maintainability. Object Pascal is a language that communicates algorithms so naturally that it's a shame to have that communication muddled by a bunch of low-level register operations. In addition, after all your assembler toils, you might be surprised to find out that Delphi's optimizing compiler often compiles code that executes faster than hand-written assembly code.

- Always comment your assembly code thoroughly. Your code will probably be read in the future by another programmer—or even by you—and lack of comments can make it difficult to understand.

- Don't use BASM to access machine hardware. Although Windows 95 will let you get away with this in most cases, Windows NT won't.

- Where possible, wrap your assembly language code in procedures or functions callable from Object Pascal. This will make your code not only easier to maintain but also easier to port to other platforms when the time comes.

NOTE

This section doesn't teach you assembler programming, but it shows you the Delphi spin on assembler if you're already familiar with the language.

Also, if you programmed in BASM with Delphi 1, bear in mind that in 32-bit Delphi, BASM is a whole new ball game. Because you must now write 32-bit assembly language, almost all your 16-bit BASM code will have to be rewritten for the new platform. The fact that BASM code can require so much care to maintain is yet another reason to minimize your use of BASM in applications.

How Does BASM Work?

Using assembly code in your Delphi applications is easier than you might think. In fact, it's so simple that it's scary. Just use the asm keyword followed by your assembly code and then an end. The following code fragment demonstrates how to use assembly code inline:

```
var
  i: integer;
begin
  i := 0;
  asm
    mov eax, i
    inc eax
    mov i, eax
  end;
  { i has incremented by one }
```

This snippet declares a variable i and initializes it to 0. It then moves the value of i into the eax register, increments the register by one, and moves the value of the eax register back into i. This illustrates not only how easy it is to use BASM, but, as the usage of the variable i shows, how easily you can access your Pascal variables from BASM.

Easy Parameter Access

Not only is it easy to access variables declared globally or locally to a procedure, it's just as easy to access variables passed into procedures, as the following code illustrates:

```
procedure Foo(I: integer);
begin
  { some code }
  asm
    mov eax, I
    inc eax
    mov I, eax
  end;
  { I has incremented by one }
  { some more code }
end;
```

The capability to access parameters by name is important because you don't have to reference variables passed into a procedure through the stack base pointer (ebp) register as you would in a normal assembly program. In a regular assembly language procedure, you would have to refer to the variable I as [ebp+4]—its offset from the stack's base pointer.

> **NOTE**
>
> When you use BASM to reference parameters passed into a procedure, remember that you can access those parameters by name, and you don't have to access them by their offset from the ebp register. Accessing by offset from ebp makes your code more difficult to maintain.

13

**HARD-CORE
TECHNIQUES**

var Parameters

Remember that when a parameter is declared as var in a function or procedure's parameter list, a pointer to that variable is passed instead of the value. This means that when you reference var parameters within a BASM block, you must take into account that the parameter is a 32-bit pointer to a variable and not a variable instance. To expand on the early sample snippet, the following example shows how you would increment the variable I if it were passed in as a var parameter:

```
procedure Foo(var I: integer);
begin
  { some code }
  asm
    mov eax, I
    inc dword ptr [eax]
  end;
  { I has now been incremented by one }
  { some more code }
end;
```

Register Calling Convention

Remember that the default calling convention for Object Pascal functions and procedures is register. Taking advantage of this method of parameter passing can help you to optimize your code. The register calling convention dictates that the first three 32-bit parameters are passed in the eax, edx, and ecx registers. This means that for the following function declaration:

```
function BlahBlah(I1, I2, I3: Integer): Integer;
```

you can count on the fact that the value of I1 is stored in eax, I2 in edx, and I3 in ecx. Consider the following method as another example:

```
procedure TSomeObject.SomeProc(S1, S2: PChar);
```

Here, the value of S1 will be passed in ecx, S2 in edx, and the implicit Self parameter will be passed in eax.

All-Assembly Procedures

Object Pascal enables you to write procedures and functions entirely in assembly language simply by beginning the function or procedure with the word asm rather than begin, as shown here:

```
function IncAnInt(I: Integer): Integer;
asm
  mov eax, I
  inc eax
end;
```

> **NOTE**
>
> It's no longer necessary to use the `assembler` directive from Delphi 1. That directive is simply ignored by the Delphi 4 compiler.

The preceding procedure accepts an integer variable `I` and increments it. Because the variable value is placed in the `eax` register, that's the value returned by the function. Table 13.1 shows how different types of data are returned from a function in Delphi.

TABLE 13.1. HOW VALUES ARE RETURNED FROM DELPHI FUNCTIONS.

Return Type	*Return Method*
`Char, Byte`	`al` register
`SmallInt, Word`	`ax` register
`Integer, LongWord, AnsiString,` `Pointer, class`	`eax` register
`Real48`	`eax` contains pointer to data on stack
`Int64`	`edx:eax` register pair
`Single, Double, Extended, Comp`	ST(0) on 8087's register stack

> **NOTE**
>
> `ShortStrings` are returned as a pointer to a string temporary on the stack.

Records

BASM provides a slick shortcut for accessing the fields of a record. You can access the fields of any record in a BASM block using the syntax of *Register.Type.Field*. For example, consider a record defined as follows:

```
type
  TDumbRec = record
    i: integer;
    c: char;
  end;
```

And a function that accepts a `TDumbRec` as a reference parameter as shown here:

```
procedure ManipulateRec(var DR: TDumbRec);
asm
  mov [eax].TDumbRec.i, 24
  mov [eax].TDumbRec.c, 's'
end;
```

Notice the shortcut syntax for accessing the fields of a record. The alternative would be to manually calculate the proper offset into the record to get or set the appropriate value. Use this technique wherever you use records in BASM, to make your BASM more resilient to potential changes to data types.

USING WINDOWS HOOKS

Windows *hooks* give programmers the means to control the occurrence and handling of system events. A hook offers perhaps the ultimate degree of power for an applications programmer because a hook enables the programmer to preview and modify system events and messages, and to prevent system events and messages from occurring systemwide.

Setting the Hook

A Windows hook is set using the `SetWindowsHookEx()` API function:

```
function SetWindowsHookEx(idHook: Integer; lpfn: TFNHookProc; hmod: HINST;
```

> **CAUTION**
>
> Use only the `SetWindowsHookEx()` function—not the `SetWindowsHook()` function—in your applications. `SetWindowsHook()`, which existed in Windows 3.x, is not implemented in the Win32 API.

```
  dwThreadID: DWORD): HHOOK; stdcall;
```

The `idHook` parameter describes the type of hook to be installed. This can be any one of the predefined hook constants shown in Table 13.2.

TABLE 13.2. WINDOWS HOOKS.

Hook Constant	Description
wh_CallWndProc	A window procedure filter. The hook procedure is called whenever a message is sent to a window procedure.
wh_CallWndProcRet	Installs a hook procedure that monitors messages after they've been processed by the destination window procedure.
wh_CBT	A computer-based training filter. The hook procedure is called before processing most window-management, mouse, and keyboard messages.

Hook Constant	Description
wh_Debug	A debugging filter. The hook function is called before any other Windows hook.
wh_GetMessage	A message filter. The hook function is called whenever a message is retrieved from the application queue.
wh_Hardware	A hardware message filter. The hook function is called whenever a hardware message is retrieved from the application queue.
wh_JournalPlayback	The hook function is called whenever a message is retrieved from the system queue. Typically used to insert system events into the queue.
wh_JournalRecord	The hook function is called whenever an event is requested from the system queue. Typically used to "record" system events.
wh_Keyboard	A keyboard filter. The hook function is called whenever a wm_KeyDown or wm_KeyUp message is retrieved from the application queue.
wh_Mouse	A mouse message filter. The hook function is called whenever a mouse message is retrieved from the application queue.
wh_MsgFilter	A special message filter. The hook function is called whenever an application's dialog box, menu, or message box is about to process a message.
wh_Shell	A shell application filter. The hook function is called when top-level windows are created and destroyed, and when the shell application needs to become active.
wh_SysMsgFilter	A system message filter. A MsgFilter that operates systemwide.

The lpfn parameter is the address of the callback function to act as the Windows hook function. This function is of type TFNHookProc, which is defined as follows:

```
TFNHookProc = function (code: Integer; wparam: WPARAM; lparam: LPARAM):
    LRESULT stdcall;
```

The contents of each of the hook function's parameters vary according to the type of hook installed; the parameters are documented in the Win32 API help.

The hMod parameter should be the value of hInstance in the EXE or DLL containing the hook callback.

The `dwThreadID` parameter identifies the thread with which the hook is to be associated. If this parameter is zero, the hook will be associated with all threads.

The return value is a hook handle that you must save in a global variable for later use.

Windows can have multiple hooks installed at one time, and it can even have the same type of hook installed multiple times.

Note also that some hooks operate with the restriction that they must be implemented from a DLL. Check the Win32 API documentation for details on each specific hook.

CAUTION

One serious limitation for system hooks is that new instances of the hook DLL are loaded into each process address space separately. Because of this, the hook DLL cannot communicate directly with the host application that set the hook. You have to go through messages or shared memory areas (such as the memory mapped files described in Chapter 12, "Working with Files") to communicate with the host application.

Using the Hook Function

The values of the hook function's `Code`, `wParam`, and `lParam` parameters vary depending on the type of hook installed, and they're documented in the Windows API help. These parameters all have one thing in common: Depending on the value of `Code`, you're responsible for calling the next hook in the chain.

To call the next hook, use the `CallNextHookEx()` API function:

```
Result := CallNextHookEx(HookHandle, Code, wParam, lParam);
```

CAUTION

When calling the next hook in the chain, don't call `DefHookProc()`. This is another unimplemented Windows 3.x function.

Note also that some hooks operate with the restriction that they must be implemented from a DLL. Check the Win 32 API documentation for details on each specific hook.

Using the Unhook Function

When you want to release the Windows hook is another old-style function:

```
UnhookWindowsHookEx(HookHandle);
```

Using SendKeys: A JournalPlayback Hook

If you come to Delphi from environments such as Visual Basic or Paradox for Windows, you might be familiar with a function called SendKeys(). SendKeys() enables you to pass it a string of characters that it then plays back as if they were typed from the keyboard, and all the keystrokes are sent to the active window. Because Delphi doesn't have a function like this built in, creating one proves a great opportunity to add a powerful feature to Delphi as well as to demonstrate how to implement a wh_JournalPlayback hook from within Delphi.

Deciding Whether to Use a JournalPlayback Hook

There are a number of reasons why a hook is the best way to send keystrokes to your application or another application. You might wonder, "Why not just post wm_KeyDown and wm_KeyUp messages?" The primary reason is that you might not know the handle of the window to which you want to post messages, or that the handle for that window might periodically change. And, of course, if you don't know the window handle, you can't send a message. Also, some applications call API functions to check the state of the keyboard in addition to looking at messages to obtain information on keystrokes.

Understanding How SendKeys Works

The declaration of the SendKeys() function looks like this:

```
function SendKeys(S: String): TSendKeyError; export;
```

The TSendKeyError return type is an enumerated type that indicates the error condition. It can be any one of the values shown in the following table:

Value	Meaning
sk_None	The function was successful.
sk_FailSetHook	The Windows hook couldn't be set.
sk_InvalidToken	An invalid token was detected in the string.
sk_UnknownError	Some other unknown but fatal error occurred.
sk_AlreadyPlaying	The hook is currently active, and keystrokes are already being played back.

S can include any alphanumeric character or @ for the Alt key, ^ for the Control key, or ~ for the Shift key. SendKeys() also enables you to specify special keyboard keys in curly braces, as depicted in the KeyDefs.pas unit in Listing 13.6.

13

HARD-CORE
TECHNIQUES

LISTING 13.6. KeyDefs.pas, SPECIAL KEY DEFINITIONS FOR SendKeys().

```
unit KeyDefs;

interface

uses Windows;

const
  MaxKeys = 24;
  ControlKey = '^';
  AltKey = '@';
  ShiftKey = '~';
  KeyGroupOpen = '{';
  KeyGroupClose = '}';

type
  TKeyString = String[7];

  TKeyDef = record
    Key: TKeyString;
    vkCode: Byte;
  end;

const
  KeyDefArray : array[1..MaxKeys] of TKeyDef = (
    (Key: 'F1';     vkCode: vk_F1),
    (Key: 'F2';     vkCode: vk_F2),
    (Key: 'F3';     vkCode: vk_F3),
    (Key: 'F4';     vkCode: vk_F4),
    (Key: 'F5';     vkCode: vk_F5),
    (Key: 'F6';     vkCode: vk_F6),
    (Key: 'F7';     vkCode: vk_F7),
    (Key: 'F8';     vkCode: vk_F8),
    (Key: 'F9';     vkCode: vk_F9),
    (Key: 'F10';    vkCode: vk_F10),
    (Key: 'F11';    vkCode: vk_F11),
    (Key: 'F12';    vkCode: vk_F12),
    (Key: 'INSERT'; vkCode: vk_Insert),
    (Key: 'DELETE'; vkCode: vk_Delete),
    (Key: 'HOME';   vkCode: vk_Home),
    (Key: 'END';    vkCode: vk_End),
    (Key: 'PGUP';   vkCode: vk_Prior),
    (Key: 'PGDN';   vkCode: vk_Next),
    (Key: 'TAB';    vkCode: vk_Tab),
    (Key: 'ENTER';  vkCode: vk_Return),
    (Key: 'BKSP';   vkCode: vk_Back),
    (Key: 'PRTSC';  vkCode: vk_SnapShot),
    (Key: 'SHIFT';  vkCode: vk_Shift),
    (Key: 'ESCAPE'; vkCode: vk_Escape));
```

```
function FindKeyInArray(Key: TKeyString; var Code: Byte): Boolean;

implementation

uses SysUtils;

function FindKeyInArray(Key: TKeyString; var Code: Byte): Boolean;
{ function searches array for token passed in Key, and returns the }
{ virtual key code in Code. }
var
  i: word;
begin
  Result := False;
  for i := Low(KeyDefArray) to High(KeyDefArray) do
    if UpperCase(Key) = KeyDefArray[i].Key then begin
      Code := KeyDefArray[i].vkCode;
      Result := True;
      Break;
    end;
end;

end.
```

After receiving the string, SendKeys() parses the individual key presses out of the string, and adds each of the key presses to a list in the form of message records containing wm_KeyUp and wm_KeyDown messages. These messages then are played back to Windows through a wh_JournalPlayback hook.

Creating Key Presses

After each key press is parsed out of the string, the virtual key code and message (the messages can be wm_KeyUp, wm_KeyDown, wm_SysKeyUp, or wm_SysKeyDown) are passed to a procedure called MakeMessage(). MakeMessage()creates a new message record for the key press and adds it to a list of messages called MessageList. The message record used here isn't the standard TMessage that you're familiar with, or even the TMsg record discussed in Chapter 5. This record is called a TEvent message, and it represents a system queue message. The definition is as follows:

```
type
  { Message Structure used in Journaling }
  PEventMsg = ^TEventMsg;
  TEventMsg = packed record
    message: UINT;
    paramL: UINT;
    paramH: UINT;
    time: DWORD;
    hwnd: HWND;
  end;
```

Table 13.3 shows the values for a TEventMsg's fields.

TABLE 13.3. VALUES FOR TEventMsg FIELDS.

TEventMsg *Field*	*Value*
message	The message constant. Can be wm_(Sys)KeyUp or wm_SysKeyDown for a keyboard message. Can be wm_xButtonUp, wm_xButtonDown, or wm_MouseMove for a mouse message.
paramL	If message is a keyboard message, this field holds the virtual key code. If message is a mouse message, wParam contains the x coordinate of the mouse cursor (in screen units).
paramH	If message is a keyboard message, this field holds the scan code of the key. If a mouse message, lParam contains the y coordinate of the mouse cursor.
time	The time, in system ticks, that the message occurred.
hwnd	Identifies the window to which the message is posted. This parameter isn't used for wh_JournalPlayback hooks.

Because the table in the KeyDefs unit maps only to the virtual key code, you must find a way to determine the scan code of the key given the virtual key code. Luckily, the Windows API provides a function called MapVirtualKey() that does just that. The following listing shows the source for the MakeMessage() procedure:

```
procedure MakeMessage(vKey: byte; M: Cardinal);
{ procedure builds a TEventMsg record that emulates a keystroke and }
{ adds it to message list }
var
  E: PEventMsg;
begin
  New(E);                              // allocate a message record
  with E^ do begin
    message := M;                      // set message field
    paramL := vKey;                    // vk code in ParamL
    paramH := MapVirtualKey(vKey, 0);  // scan code in ParamH
    time := GetTickCount;              // set time
    hwnd := 0;                         // ignored
  end;
  MessageList.Add(E);
end;
```

After the entire message list is created, the hook can be set to play back the key sequence. You do this through a procedure called StartPlayback(). StartPlayback() primes the pump by placing the first message from the list into a global buffer. It also initializes a global that keeps track of how many messages have been played and the flags that indicate the state of the Ctrl, Alt, and Shift keys. This procedure then sets the hook. StartPlayBack() is shown in the following listing:

```
procedure StartPlayback;
{ Initializes globals and sets the hook }
begin
  { grab first message from list and place in buffer in case we }
  { get an hc_GetNext before an hc_Skip }
MessageBuffer := TEventMsg(MessageList.Items[0]^);
  { initialize message count and play indicator }
  MsgCount := 0;
  { initialize Alt, Control, and Shift key flags }
  AltPressed := False;
  ControlPressed := False;
  ShiftPressed := False;
  { set the hook! }
  HookHandle := SetWindowsHookEx(wh_JournalPlayback, Play, hInstance, 0);
  if HookHandle = 0 then
    raise ESKSetHookError.Create('Couldn''t set hook')
  else
    Playing := True;
end;
```

As you might notice from the SetWindowsHookEx() call, Play is the name of the hook function. The declaration for Play is as follows:

```
function Play(Code: integer; wParam, lParam: Longint): Longint; stdcall;
```

The following table shows its parameters.

Value	*Meaning*
Code	A value of hc_GetNext indicates that you should prepare the next message in the list for processing. You do this by copying the next message from the list into your global buffer. A value of hc_Skip means that a pointer to the next message should be placed into the lParam parameter for processing. Any other value means that you should call CallNextHookEx() and pass on the parameters to the next hook in the chain.
wParam	Unused.
lParam	If Code is hc_Skip, you should place a pointer to the next TEventMsg record in the lParam.
Return value	Return zero if Code is hc_GetNext. If Code is hc_Skip, return the amount of time (in ticks) before this message should be processed. If zero is returned, the message is processed. Otherwise, the return value should be the return value of CallNextHookEx().

Listing 13.7 shows the complete source code to the SendKey.pas unit.

LISTING 13.7. THE SendKey.pas UNIT.

```pascal
unit SendKey;

interface

uses
 SysUtils, WinTypes, WinProcs, Messages, Classes, KeyDefs;

type
  { Error codes }
  TSendKeyError = (sk_None, sk_FailSetHook, sk_InvalidToken,
                   sk_UnknownError, sk_AlreadyPlaying);
  { first vk code to last vk code }
  TvkKeySet = set of vk_LButton..vk_Scroll;

  { exceptions }
  ESendKeyError = class(Exception);
  ESKSetHookError = class(ESendKeyError);
  ESKInvalidToken = class(ESendKeyError);
  ESKAlreadyPlaying = class(ESendKeyError);

function SendKeys(S: String): TSendKeyError;
procedure WaitForHook;
procedure StopPlayback;

var
  Playing: Boolean = False;

implementation

uses Forms;

type
  { a TList descendant that knows how to dispose of its contents }
  TMessageList = class(TList)
  public
    destructor Destroy; override;
  end;

const
  { valid "sys" keys }
  vkKeySet: TvkKeySet = [Ord('A')..Ord('Z'), vk_Menu, vk_F1..vk_F12];

destructor TMessageList.Destroy;
var
  i: longint;
```

```
begin
  { deallocate all the message records before discarding the list }
  for i := 0 to Count - 1 do
    Dispose(PEventMsg(Items[i]));
  inherited Destroy;
end;

var
  { variables global to the DLL }
  MsgCount: word = 0;
  MessageBuffer: TEventMsg;
  HookHandle: hHook = 0;
  MessageList: TMessageList = Nil;
  AltPressed, ControlPressed, ShiftPressed: Boolean;

procedure StopPlayback;
{ Unhook the hook, and clean up }
begin
  { if Hook is currently active, then unplug it }
  if Playing then
    UnhookWindowsHookEx(HookHandle);
  MessageList.Free;
  Playing := False;
end;

function Play(Code: integer; wParam, lParam: Longint): Longint; stdcall;
{ This is the JournalPlayback callback function.  It is called by Windows }
{ when Windows polls for hardware events.  The code parameter indicates what }
{ to do. }
begin
  case Code of

    hc_Skip: begin
    { hc_Skip means to pull the next message out of our list. If we }
    { are at the end of the list, it's okay to unhook the JournalPlayback }
    { hook from here. }
      { increment message counter }
      inc(MsgCount);
      { check to see if all messages have been played }
      if MsgCount >= MessageList.Count then
        StopPlayback
      else
      { copy next message from list into buffer }
      MessageBuffer := TEventMsg(MessageList.Items[MsgCount]^);
      Result := 0;
    end;

    hc_GetNext: begin
    { hc_GetNext means to fill the wParam and lParam with the proper }
```

continues

LISTING **13.7.** CONTINUED

```
  { values so that the message can be played back.  DO NOT unhook }
  { hook from within here.  Return value indicates how much time until }
  { Windows should playback message.  We'll return 0 so that it's }
  { processed right away. }
    { move message in buffer to message queue }
    PEventMsg(lParam)^ := MessageBuffer;
    Result := 0  { process immediately }
  end

  else
    { if Code isn't hc_Skip or hc_GetNext, then call next hook in chain }
    Result := CallNextHookEx(HookHandle, Code, wParam, lParam);
  end;
end;

procedure StartPlayback;
{ Initializes globals and sets the hook }
begin
  { grab first message from list and place in buffer in case we }
  { get a hc_GetNext before and hc_Skip }
  MessageBuffer := TEventMsg(MessageList.Items[0]^);
  { initialize message count and play indicator }
  MsgCount := 0;
  { initialize Alt, Control, and Shift key flags }
  AltPressed := False;
  ControlPressed := False;
  ShiftPressed := False;
  { set the hook! }
  HookHandle := SetWindowsHookEx(wh_JournalPlayback, Play, hInstance, 0);
  if HookHandle = 0 then
    raise ESKSetHookError.Create('Couldn''t set hook')
  else
    Playing := True;
end;

procedure MakeMessage(vKey: byte; M: Cardinal);
{ procedure builds a TEventMsg record that emulates a keystroke and }
{ adds it to message list }
var
  E: PEventMsg;
begin
  New(E);                               // allocate a message record
  with E^ do begin
    message := M;                       // set message field
    paramL := vKey;                     // vk code in ParamL
    paramH := MapVirtualKey(vKey, 0);   // scan code in ParamH
    time := GetTickCount;               // set time
    hwnd := 0;                          // ignored
  end;
  MessageList.Add(E);
end;
```

```
procedure KeyDown(vKey: byte);
{ Generates KeyDownMessage }
begin
  { don't generate a "sys" key if the control key is pressed (Windows }
  { quirk) }
  if AltPressed and (not ControlPressed) and  (vKey in vkKeySet) then
    MakeMessage(vKey, wm_SysKeyDown)
  else
    MakeMessage(vKey, wm_KeyDown);
end;

procedure KeyUp(vKey: byte);
{ Generates KeyUp message }
begin
  { don't generate a "sys" key if the control key is pressed (Windows }
  { quirk) }
  if AltPressed and (not ControlPressed) and (vKey in vkKeySet) then
    MakeMessage(vKey, wm_SysKeyUp)
  else
    MakeMessage(vKey, wm_KeyUp);
end;

procedure SimKeyPresses(VKeyCode: Word);
{ This function simulates keypresses for the given key, taking into }
{ account the current state of Alt, Ctrl, and Shift keys }
begin
  { press Alt key if flag has been set }
  if AltPressed then
    KeyDown(vk_Menu);
  { press Control key if flag has been set }
  if ControlPressed then
    KeyDown(vk_Control);
  { if shift is pressed, or shifted key and control is not pressed... }
  if (((Hi(VKeyCode) and 1) <> 0) and (not ControlPressed)) or ShiftPressed
➥then
    KeyDown(vk_Shift);    { ...press shift }
  KeyDown(Lo(VKeyCode));  { press key down }
  KeyUp(Lo(VKeyCode));    { release key }
  { if shift is pressed, or shifted key and control is not pressed... }
  if (((Hi(VKeyCode) and 1) <> 0) and (not ControlPressed)) or ShiftPressed
➥then
    KeyUp(vk_Shift);       { ...release shift }
  { if shift flag is set, reset flag }
  if ShiftPressed then begin
    ShiftPressed := False;
  end;
  { Release Ctrl key if flag has been set, reset flag }
  if ControlPressed then begin
    KeyUp(vk_Control);
    ControlPressed := False;
  end;
```

13

HARD-CORE
TECHNIQUES

continues

LISTING 13.7. CONTINUED

```
  { Release Alt key if flag has been set, reset flag }
  if AltPressed then begin
    KeyUp(vk_Menu);
    AltPressed := False;
  end;
end;

procedure ProcessKey(S: String);
{ This function parses each character in the string to create the message }
{ list }
var
  KeyCode: word;
  Key: byte;
  index: integer;
  Token: TKeyString;
begin
  index := 1;
  repeat
    case S[index] of

        KeyGroupOpen : begin
        { It's the beginning of a special token! }
          Token := '';
          inc(index);
          while S[index] <> KeyGroupClose do begin
            { add to Token until the end token symbol is encountered }
            Token := Token + S[index];
            inc(index);
            { check to make sure the token's not too long }
            if (Length(Token) = 7) and (S[index] <> KeyGroupClose) then
              raise ESKInvalidToken.Create('No closing brace');
          end;
          { look for token in array, Key parameter will }
          { contain vk code if successful }
          if not FindKeyInArray(Token, Key) then
            raise ESKInvalidToken.Create('Invalid token');
          { simulate keypress sequence }
          SimKeyPresses(MakeWord(Key, 0));
        end;

        AltKey : begin
          { set Alt flag }
          AltPressed := True;
        end;

        ControlKey : begin
          { set Control flag }
          ControlPressed := True;
        end;
```

```
        ShiftKey : begin
          { set Shift flag }
          ShiftPressed := True;
        end;

        else begin
        { A normal character was pressed }
          { convert character into a word where the high byte contains }
          { the shift state and the low byte contains the vk code }
          KeyCode := vkKeyScan(S[index]);
          { simulate keypress sequence }
          SimKeyPresses(KeyCode);
        end;
      end;
      inc(index);
  until index > Length(S);
end;

procedure WaitForHook;
begin
  repeat Application.ProcessMessages until not Playing;
end;

function SendKeys(S: String): TSendKeyError;
{ This is the one entry point.  Based on the string passed in the S  }
{ parameter, this function creates a list of keyup/keydown messages, }
{ sets a JournalPlayback hook, and replays the keystroke messages.   }
begin
  Result := sk_None;                         // assume success
  try
    if Playing then raise ESKAlreadyPlaying.Create('');
    MessageList := TMessageList.Create;  // create list of messages
    ProcessKey(S);                       // create messages from string
    StartPlayback;                       // set hook and play back messages
  except
    { if an exception occurs, return an error code, and clean up }
    on E:ESendKeyError do begin
      MessageList.Free;
      if E is ESKSetHookError then
        Result := sk_FailSetHook
      else if E is ESKInvalidToken then
        Result := sk_InvalidToken
      else if E is ESKAlreadyPlaying then
        Result := sk_AlreadyPlaying;
    end
    else
      { Catch-all exception handler }
      Result := sk_UnknownError;
  end;
end;

end.
```

Using SendKeys()

In this section, you'll create a small project that demonstrates the SendKeys() function. Start with a form that contains two TEdit components and several TButtons, as shown in Figure 13.4. This project is called TestSend.dpr.

FIGURE 13.4.

The TestSend main form.

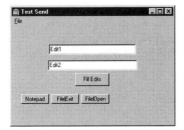

Listing 13.8 shows the source code for TestSend's main unit, Main.pas. This unit includes event handlers for the button-click events.

LISTING 13.8. THE SOURCE CODE FOR Main.pas.

```
unit Main;

interface

uses
  SysUtils, Windows, Messages, Classes, Graphics, Controls,
  Forms, Dialogs, StdCtrls, Menus;

type
  TForm1 = class(TForm)
    Edit1: TEdit;
    Edit2: TEdit;
    Button1: TButton;
    Button2: TButton;
    MainMenu1: TMainMenu;
    File1: TMenuItem;
    Open1: TMenuItem;
    Exit1: TMenuItem;
    Button4: TButton;
    Button3: TButton;
    procedure Button1Click(Sender: TObject);
    procedure Button2Click(Sender: TObject);
    procedure Open1Click(Sender: TObject);
    procedure Exit1Click(Sender: TObject);
    procedure Button4Click(Sender: TObject);
    procedure FormDestroy(Sender: TObject);
    procedure Button3Click(Sender: TObject);
```

```
    private
      { Private declarations }
    public
      { Public declarations }
    end;

var
  Form1: TForm1;

implementation

{$R *.DFM}

uses SendKey, KeyDefs;

procedure TForm1.Button1Click(Sender: TObject);
begin
  Edit1.SetFocus;                                // focus Edit1
  SendKeys('^{DELETE}I love...');                // send keys to Edit1
  WaitForHook;                                   // let keys playback
  Perform(wm_NextDlgCtl, 0, 0);                  // move to Edit2
  SendKeys('~delphi 4 ~developer''s ~guide!');   // send keys to Edit2
end;

procedure TForm1.Button2Click(Sender: TObject);
var
  H: hWnd;
  PI: TProcessInformation;
  SI: TStartupInfo;
begin
  FillChar(SI, SizeOf(SI), 0);
  SI.cb := SizeOf(SI);
  { Invoke notepad }
  if CreateProcess(nil, 'notepad', nil, nil, False, 0, nil, nil, SI, PI)
➥then
    begin
      { wait until notepad is ready to receive keystrokes }
      WaitForInputIdle(PI.hProcess, INFINITE);
      H := FindWindow('Notepad', nil);           // find notepad window
      if SetForegroundWindow(H) then             // bring it to front
        SendKeys('Hello from the SendKeys example!{ENTER}');  // send keys!
    end
    else
      MessageDlg(Format('Failed to invoke Notepad.  Error code %d',
                 [GetLastError]), mtError, [mbOk], 0);
end;

procedure TForm1.Open1Click(Sender: TObject);
begin
  ShowMessage('Open');
end;
```

13

HARD-CORE
TECHNIQUES

continues

LISTING 13.8. CONTINUED

```
procedure TForm1.Exit1Click(Sender: TObject);
begin
  Close;
end;

procedure TForm1.Button4Click(Sender: TObject);
begin
  WaitForInputIdle(GetCurrentProcess, INFINITE);
  SendKeys('@fx');
end;

procedure TForm1.FormDestroy(Sender: TObject);
begin
  WaitForHook;
end;

procedure TForm1.Button3Click(Sender: TObject);
begin
  WaitForInputIdle(GetCurrentProcess, INFINITE);
  SendKeys('@fo');
end;

end.
```

After you click Button1, SendKeys() is called, and the following key presses are sent: Shift+Delete to delete the contents of Edit1; "I love..." then is typed into Edit1; a tab character is sent, which moves the focus to Edit2, where Shift+D, "elphi 4 ", Shift+D, "eveloper's ", Shift+G, "uide!" is sent.

The OnClick handler for Button2 is also interesting. This method uses the CreateProcess() API function to invoke an instance of Notepad. It then uses the WaitForInputIdle() API function to pause until Notepad's process is ready for input. Finally, it types a message in the Notepad window.

USING C/C++ OBJ FILES

Delphi provides you with the capability for linking object (OBJ) files created using another compiler directly into your Delphi programs. You can link an object file into your Object Pascal code by using the $L or $LINK directives. The syntax for this is as follows:

```
{$L filename.obj}
```

After the object file is linked, you must define each function you want to call out of the object file in your Object Pascal code. Use the external directive to indicate that the

Pascal compiler should wait until link time to attempt to resolve the function name. For example, the following line of code defines an external function called `Foo` that neither takes nor returns any parameters:

```
procedure Foo; external;
```

Although this capability might seem powerful on the surface, it comes with a number of limitations that make this feature difficult to implement in many cases:

- Object Pascal can directly access only code, not data, contained in object files (although there is a trick to getting at data in an OBJ, which you'll see later). However, Pascal data can be accessed from object files.

- Object Pascal can't link with LIB (static library) files.

- Object files containing C++ classes will not link due to the implicit references to C++ RTL. Although it might be possible to resolve these references by pulling apart the C++ RTL into OBJs, it's generally more trouble than it's worth.

- Object files must be in the Intel OMF format. This is the output format of the Borland C++ compilers but not the Microsoft C++ compilers, which produce COFF-format OBJ files.

13

> **NOTE**
>
> One previously stifling limitation that has been addressed by the Delphi 3 compiler is the capability to resolve OBJ-to-OBJ references. In previous versions of Delphi, object files couldn't contain references to code or data stored in other object files. As of Delphi 3, this limitation was removed from the compiler.

Calling a Function

For example, say that you had a C++ object file called `ccode.obj` that includes a function with the following prototype:

```
int   __fastcall SAYHELLO(char * hellostr)
```

To call this function from a Delphi application, you must first link the object file into the EXE using either the `$L` or `$LINK` directive:

```
{$L ccode.obj}
```

After that, you must create an Object Pascal definition for the function as shown here:

```
function SayHello(Text: PChar): integer; external;
```

> **CAUTION**
>
> Notice the use of the __fastcall directive in C++, which serves to ensure that the calling conventions used in the C++ and Object Pascal code are the same. Heinous crash errors can occur if you don't correctly match calling conventions between the C++ prototype and the Object Pascal declaration, and calling convention problems are the most common for developers trying to share code between the two languages. To help clear things up, the following table shows the correspondence between Object Pascal and C++ calling convention directives.
>
> | Object Pascal | C++ |
> | --- | --- |
> | register* | __fastcall |
> | pascal | __pascal |
> | cdecl | __cdecl* |
> | stdcall | __stdcall |
>
> *Indicates the default calling convention for the language.

Name Mangling

By default, the C++ compiler will mangle the names of functions not explicitly declared using the extern "C" modifier. The Object Pascal compiler, of course, doesn't mangle the names of functions. For example, Delphi's TDUMP utility reveals the exported symbol name of the SAYHELLO function shown earlier in ccode.obj as @SAYHELLO$qqrpc, whereas the name of the imported function according to Object Pascal is SAYHELLO. (Object Pascal forces symbols to uppercase.)

On the surface, this would seem to be a problem: how can the Delphi linker resolve the external if the function name isn't even the same? The answer is that the Delphi linker simply ignores the mangled portion (the @ and everything after the $) of the symbol. But this can have some pretty nasty side effects.

The whole reason C++ mangles names is to allow function overloading (functions having the same names and different parameter lists). If you have a function that has several overloaded definitions and Delphi ignores the mangling portion of the symbol, you'll never know for sure whether Delphi is calling the overloaded function you want to call. Because of these complexities, we recommend that you don't attempt to call overloaded functions through object files.

Functions in a C++ source file (.CPP) will always be mangled unless the proto-types are combined with the extern "C" modifier or the proper command-line switch is used on the C++ compiler to suppress name mangling.

Sharing Data

As mentioned earlier, it's possible to access Delphi data from the object file. The first step is to declare a global variable in your Object Pascal source similar to the variable shown here (note the underscore):

```
var
  _GLOBALVAR: PChar = 'This is a Delphi String';
```

Note that although this variable is initialized, that isn't a requirement.

In the C++ module, declare a variable of the same name using the external modifier as shown here:

```
extern char * GLOBALVAR;
```

The default behavior of the Borland C++ compiler is to prepend external variables with an underscore when generating the external symbol (that is, GLOBALVAR becomes _GLOBALVAR). You can get around this in one of two ways:

- Use the command-line switch to disable the addition of the underscore (-u- with Borland C++ compilers).
- Place an underscore in front of the variable name in the Object Pascal code.

Although it's not possible to directly share data declared in an OBJ file with Object Pascal code, it is possible to trick Object Pascal into accessing OBJ-based data. The first step is to declare the data you want to export in your C++ code using the __export directive. For example, you would make a char array available for export like this:

```
char __export C_VAR[128];
```

Next (here comes part one of the trick), you declare this data as an external procedure in your Object Pascal code as follows (note, again, the underscore):

```
procedure _C_VAR; external;  // trick to import OBJ data
```

13

This will allow the linker to resolve references to _C_VAR in your Pascal code. Finally (here's the second part of the trick), you can use _C_VAR in your Pascal code as a pointer to the data. For example, the following code can be used to get the value of the array:

```
type
  PCharArray = ^TCharArray;
  TCharArray = array[0..127] of char;

function GetCArray: string;
var
  A: PCharArray;
begin
  A := PCharArray(@_C_VAR);
  Result := A^;
end;
```

And the following code can be used to set the value of the array:

```
procedure SetCArray(const S: string);
var
  A: PCharArray;
begin
  A := PCharArray(@_C_VAR);
  StrLCopy(A^, PChar(S), SizeOf(TCharArray));
end;
```

Using the Delphi RTL

It can be difficult to link an object file to your Delphi application if the object file contains references to the C++ RTL. This is because the C++ RTL generally lives in LIB files, and Delphi doesn't have the capability to link with LIB files.

How do you get around this problem? One way is to cut the definitions of the external functions you use out of the C++ RTL source code and place it in your object file. However, unless you're calling only one or two external functions, this type of solution will get mighty complex—not to mention the fact that your object file will become huge.

A more elegant solution to this problem is to create one or more header files that redeclare all the RTL functions you call using the external modifier and actually implement these functions inside your Object Pascal code. For example, let's say that you wanted to call the MessageBox() API function from your C++ code. Normally, this would require you to #include windows.h and link with the necessary Win32 libraries. However, redefining MessageBox() in your C++ code as follows:

```
extern "C" int __stdcall MessageBox(long, char *, char *, long);
```

will cause the Object Pascal linker to search for a function of its own called `MessageBox` when it builds the executable. Of course, there's a function of that name defined in the Windows unit. Now your application will happily compile and link without a hitch.

Listing 13.9 shows a complete example of everything we've talked about so far. It's a fairly simple C++ module called `ccode.cpp`.

LISTING 13.9. A SIMPLE C++ MODULE, `ccode.cpp`.

```cpp
#include "PasStng.h"

// globals
extern char * GLOBALVAR;

// exported data
char __export C_VAR[128];

//externals
extern "C" int __stdcall MessageBox(long, char *, char *, long);

// prototypes
int __fastcall SAYHELLO(char *);
int __fastcall SAYHELLO(int);

//functions
int __fastcall SAYHELLO(char * hellostr)
{
  char a[64];
  memset(a, 64, 0);
  strcat(a, hellostr);
  strcat(a, " from Borland C++");
  MessageBox(0, a, GLOBALVAR, 0);
  return 0;
}

int __fastcall SAYHELLO(int)
{
  return 0;
}
```

In addition to `MessageBox()`, notice the calls that this module makes to the `memset()` and `strcat()` C++ RTL functions. These functions are handled similarly in the `PasStng.h` header file, which contains some of the more common functions from the `string.h` header. This file is shown in Listing 13.10.

LISTING 13.10. PasStng.h.

```
// PasStng.h
// This module externalizes a portion of the string.h C++ RTL header so that
// the Object Pascal RTL can instead handle the calls.

#ifndef PASSTNG_H
#define PASSTNG_H

#ifndef _SIZE_T
#define _SIZE_T
typedef unsigned size_t;
#endif

#ifdef __cplusplus
extern "C" {
#endif

extern char * __cdecl strcat(char *dest, const char *src);
extern int __cdecl stricmp(const char *s1, const char *s2);
extern size_t __cdecl strlen(const char *s);
extern char * __cdecl strlwr(char *s);
extern char * __cdecl strncat(char *dest, const char *src, size_t maxlen);
extern void * __cdecl memcpy(void *dest, const void *src, size_t n);
extern int __cdecl strncmp(const char *s1, const char *s2, size_t  maxlen);
extern int __cdecl strncmpi(const char *s1, const char *s2, size_t n);
extern void * __cdecl memmove(void *dest, const void *src, size_t n);
extern char * __cdecl strncpy(char *dest, const char *src, size_t maxlen);
extern void * __cdecl memset(void *s, int c, size_t n);
extern int __cdecl strnicmp(const char *s1, const char *s2, size_t maxlen);
extern void __cdecl movmem(const void *src, void *dest, unsigned length);
extern void __cdecl setmem(void *dest, unsigned length, char value);
extern char * __cdecl stpcpy(char *dest, const char *src);
extern int __cdecl strcmp(const char *s1, const char *s2);
extern char * __cdecl strstr(char *s1, const char *s2);
extern int __cdecl strcmpi(const char *s1, const char *s2);
extern char * __cdecl strupr(char *s);
extern char * __cdecl strcpy(char *dest, const char *src);

#ifdef __cplusplus
}
#endif

#endif  // PASSTNG_H
```

Because these functions don't exist in the Object Pascal RTL, we can work around the problem by creating an Object Pascal unit to include in our project that maps these functions to their Object Pascal counterparts. This unit, PasStrng.pas, is shown in Listing 13.11.

LISTING 13.11. PasStrng.pas.

```pascal
unit PasStrng;
{ This unit maps some of the common String.h C++ RTL functions }
{ to their Object Pascal equivalent. }
{ Copyright (c) 1996,98 Steve Teixeira  }

interface

uses Windows;

function _strcat(Dest, Source: PChar): PChar; cdecl;
procedure _memset(P: Pointer; Count: Integer; value: DWORD); cdecl;
function _stricmp(P1, P2: PChar): Integer; cdecl;
function _strlen(P1: PChar): Integer; cdecl;
function _strlwr(P1: PChar): PChar; cdecl;
function _strncat(Dest, Source: PChar; MaxLen: Integer): PChar; cdecl;
function _memcpy(Dest, Source: Pointer; Len: Integer): Pointer;
function _strncmp(P1, P2: PChar; MaxLen: Integer): Integer; cdecl;
function _strncmpi(P1, P2: PChar; MaxLen: Integer): Integer; cdecl;
function _memmove(Dest, Source: Pointer; Len: Integer): Pointer;
function _strncpy(Dest, Source: PChar; MaxLen: Integer): PChar; cdecl;
function _strnicmp(P1, P2: PChar; MaxLen: Integer): Integer; cdecl;
procedure _movmem(Source, Dest: Pointer; MaxLen: Integer); cdecl;
procedure _setmem(Dest: Pointer; Len: Integer; Value: Char); cdecl;
function _stpcpy(Dest, Source: PChar): PChar; cdecl;
function _strcmp(P1, P2: PChar): Integer; cdecl;
function _strstr(P1, P2: PChar): PChar; cdecl;
function _strcmpi(P1, P2: PChar): Integer; cdecl;
function _strupr(P: PChar): PChar; cdecl;
function _strcpy(Dest, Source: PChar): PChar; cdecl;

implementation

uses SysUtils;

function _strcat(Dest, Source: PChar): PChar;
begin
  Result := SysUtils.StrCat(Dest, Source);
end;

function _stricmp(P1, P2: PChar): Integer;
begin
  Result := StrIComp(P1, P2);
end;

function _strlen(P1: PChar): Integer;
begin
  Result := SysUtils.StrLen(P1);
end;
```

continues

13

LISTING 13.11. CONTINUED

```
function _strlwr(P1: PChar): PChar;
begin
  Result := StrLower(P1);
end;

function _strncat(Dest, Source: PChar; MaxLen: Integer): PChar;
begin
  Result := StrLCat(Dest, Source, MaxLen);
end;

function _memcpy(Dest, Source: Pointer; Len: Integer): Pointer;
begin
  Move(Source^, Dest^, Len);
  Result := Dest;
end;

function _strncmp(P1, P2: PChar; MaxLen: Integer): Integer;
begin
  Result := StrLComp(P1, P2, MaxLen);
end;

function _strncmpi(P1, P2: PChar; MaxLen: Integer): Integer;
begin
  Result := StrLIComp(P1, P2, MaxLen);
end;

function _memmove(Dest, Source: Pointer; Len: Integer): Pointer;
begin
  Move(Source^, Dest^, Len);
  Result := Dest;
end;

function _strncpy(Dest, Source: PChar; MaxLen: Integer): PChar;
begin
  Result := StrLCopy(Dest, Source, MaxLen);
end;

procedure _memset(P: Pointer; Count: Integer; Value: DWORD);
begin
  FillChar(P^, Count, Value);
end;

function _strnicmp(P1, P2: PChar; MaxLen: Integer): Integer;
begin
  Result := StrLIComp(P1, P2, MaxLen);
end;

procedure _movmem(Source, Dest: Pointer; MaxLen: Integer);
```

```
begin
  Move(Source^, Dest^, MaxLen);
end;

procedure _setmem(Dest: Pointer; Len: Integer; Value: Char);
begin
  FillChar(Dest^, Len, Value);
end;

function _stpcpy(Dest, Source: PChar): PChar;
begin
  Result := StrCopy(Dest, Source);
end;

function _strcmp(P1, P2: PChar): Integer;
begin
  Result := StrComp(P1, P2);
end;

function _strstr(P1, P2: PChar): PChar;
begin
  Result := StrPos(P1, P2);
end;

function _strcmpi(P1, P2: PChar): Integer;
begin
  Result := StrIComp(P1, P2);
end;

function _strupr(P: PChar): PChar;
begin
  Result := StrUpper(P);
end;

function _strcpy(Dest, Source: PChar): PChar;
begin
  Result := StrCopy(Dest, Source);
end;

end.
```

13

**HARD-CORE
TECHNIQUES**

> **TIP**
>
> Using the technique shown here, you could externalize more of the C++ RTL
> and Win32 API into header files that map to Object Pascal units.

USING C++ CLASSES

Although it's impossible to use C++ classes contained in an object file, it's possible to get some limited use from C++ classes contained in DLLs. By "limited use," we mean that you'll be able to call the virtual functions exposed by the C++ class only from the Delphi side. This is possible because both Object Pascal and C++ follow the COM standard for virtual interfaces (see Chapter 23, "COM and ActiveX").

Listing 13.12 shows the source code for cdll.cpp, a C++ module that contains a class definition. Notice in particular the standalone functions—one of which creates and returns a reference to a new object, and another of which frees a given reference. These functions are the conduits through which we'll share the object between the languages.

LISTING 13.12. A C++ MODULE, cdll.cpp, THAT CONTAINS A CLASS DEFINITION.

```cpp
#include <windows.h>

// objects
class TFoo
{
  virtual int function1(char *);
  virtual int function2(int);
};

//member functions
int TFoo::function1(char * str1)
{
  MessageBox(NULL, str1, "Hello from C++ DLL", MB_OK);
  return 0;
}

int TFoo::function2(int i)
{
  return i * i;
}

#ifdef __cplusplus
extern "C" {
#endif

//prototypes
TFoo * __declspec(dllexport) ClassFactory(void);
void __declspec(dllexport) ClassKill(TFoo *);

TFoo * __declspec(dllexport) CLASSFACTORY(void)
{
  TFoo * Foo;
  Foo = new TFoo;
```

```
  return Foo;
}

void __declspec(dllexport) CLASSKILL(TFoo * Foo)
{
  delete Foo;
}

int WINAPI DllEntryPoint(HINSTANCE hinst, unsigned long reason, void*)
{
    return 1;
}

#ifdef __cplusplus
}
#endif
```

To use this object from a Delphi application, you must do two things. First, you must
import the functions that create and destroy class instances. Second, you must define a
virtual abstract Object Pascal class definition that wraps the C++ class. Here's how to do
that:

```
type
  TFoo = class
    function Function1(Str1: PChar): integer; virtual; cdecl; abstract;
    function Function2(i: integer): integer; virtual; cdecl; abstract;
  end;
function ClassFactory: TFoo; cdecl; external 'cdll.dll' name '_CLASSFACTORY';
procedure ClassKill(Foo: TFoo); cdecl; external 'cdll.dll' name '_CLASSKILL';
```

> **NOTE**
>
> When defining the Object Pascal wrapper for a C++ class, you don't need to
> worry about the names of the functions because they're unimportant in deter-
> mining how the function is called internally. Because all calls will be dispatched
> through the Virtual Method Table, the order in which the functions are
> declared is key. Make sure that the order of the functions is the same in both
> the C++ and Object Pascal definitions.

Listing 13.13 shows Main.pas, the main unit for the CallC.dpr project, which demonstrates all the C++ techniques shown so far in this chapter. The main form for this project
is shown in Figure 13.5.

LISTING 13.13. Main.pas.

```pascal
unit Main;

interface

uses
  Windows, Messages, SysUtils, Classes, Graphics, Controls, Forms, Dialogs,
  StdCtrls, ExtCtrls;

type
  TMainForm = class(TForm)
    Button1: TButton;
    Button2: TButton;
    FooData: TEdit;
    Button3: TButton;
    Button4: TButton;
    SetCVarData: TEdit;
    GetCVarData: TEdit;
    procedure Button1Click(Sender: TObject);
    procedure Button2Click(Sender: TObject);
    procedure Button3Click(Sender: TObject);
    procedure Button4Click(Sender: TObject);
  private
    { Private declarations }
  public
    { Public declarations }
  end;

var
  MainForm: TMainForm;
  _GlobalVar: PChar = 'This is a Delphi String';

implementation

uses PasStrng;

{$R *.DFM}

{$L ccode.obj}

type
  TFoo = class
    function Function1(Str1: PChar): integer; virtual; cdecl; abstract;
    function Function2(i: integer): integer; virtual; cdecl; abstract;
  end;

  PCharArray = ^TCharArray;
  TCharArray = array[0..127] of char;

// import from OBJ file:
```

```
function SayHello(Text: PChar): integer; external;
procedure SetCVar(Value: Integer); external;
procedure _C_VAR; external;  // trick to import OBJ data

// imports from DLL file:
function ClassFactory: TFoo; cdecl; external 'cdll.dll' name '_CLASSFACTORY';
procedure ClassKill(Foo: TFoo); cdecl; external 'cdll.dll' name '_CLASSKILL';

procedure TMainForm.Button1Click(Sender: TObject);
begin
  SayHello('hello world');
end;

procedure TMainForm.Button2Click(Sender: TObject);
var
  Foo: TFoo;
begin
  Foo := ClassFactory;
  Foo.Function1('huh huh, cool.');
  FooData.Text := IntToStr(Foo.Function2(10));
  ClassKill(Foo);
end;

function GetCArray: string;
var
  A: PCharArray;
begin
  A := PCharArray(@_C_VAR);
  Result := A^;
end;

procedure SetCArray(const S: string);
var
  A: PCharArray;
begin
  A := PCharArray(@_C_VAR);
  StrLCopy(A^, PChar(S), SizeOf(TCharArray));
end;

procedure TMainForm.Button3Click(Sender: TObject);
begin
  SetCArray(SetCVarData.Text);
end;

procedure TMainForm.Button4Click(Sender: TObject);
begin
  GetCVarData.Text := GetCArray;
end;

end.
```

13

FIGURE **13.5.**

*The main form for
the CallC project.*

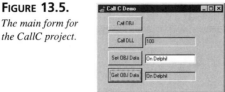

TIP

Although the technique demonstrated here does allow a limited means for communicating with C++ classes from Object Pascal, if you want to do this on a large scale, we recommend you use COM objects to communicate between languages as described in Chapter 23.

THUNKING

At some point in your development of Windows and Win32 applications, you'll need to call 16-bit code from a 32-bit application or even 32-bit code from a 16-bit application. This process is known as *thunking*. Although the different varieties of Win32 provide various facilities to make this possible, it remains one of the more difficult tasks to accomplish when developing Windows applications.

TIP

Aside from thunking, you should know that automation (described in Chapter 23) provides a reasonable alternative for crossing 16/32-bit boundaries. This capability is built into Automation's IDispatch interface.

Win32 provides three different types of thunking: universal, generic, and flat. Each of these techniques has its advantages and drawbacks:

- *Universal thunking* is available only under the Win32 platform. It allows 16-bit applications to load and call Win32 DLLs. Because this variety of thunking is supported only for Win32s, a platform not officially supported by Delphi, we won't devote any more discussion to this topic.

- *Generic thunking* enables 16-bit Windows applications to call Win32 DLLs under Windows 95 and Windows NT. This is the most flexible type of thunking because it's available on both major Win32 platforms and is API-based. We'll discuss this option in detail shortly.

• *Flat thunking* allows Win32 applications to call 16-bit DLLs and 16-bit applications to call Win32 DLLs. Unfortunately, this type of thunking is available only under Windows 95; it also requires the use of a thunk compiler to create object files, which must be linked to both the 32-bit and 16-bit sides. Because of the lack of portability and requirement for additional tools, we won't cover flat thunking here.

In addition, there's a way to share data between 32-bit and 16-bit processes by using the WM_COPYDATA Windows message. In particular, WM_COPYDATA provides a straightforward means for accessing 16-bit code from Windows NT, so we'll also cover that in this section.

Generic Thunking

Generic thunking is facilitated through a set of APIs that sit on both the 16-bit and 32-bit sides. These APIs are known as WOW16 and WOW32, respectively. From 16-bit land, WOW16 provides functions that allow you to load the Win32 DLL, get the address of functions in the DLL, and call those functions. The source code for the WOW16.pas unit is shown in Listing 13.14.

LISTING 13.14. WOW16.pas.

```
unit WOW16;
{ Unit which provides an interface to the 16-bit Windows on Win32 (WOW)  }
{ API from a 16-bit application running under Windows NT or Windows 95.  }
{ These functions allow you to call 32-bit DLLs from 16-bit applications. }
{ Copyright (c) 1996, 98 Steve Teixeira }
interface
uses WinTypes;
type
  THandle32 = Longint;
  DWORD = Longint;
{ Win32 module management.}
{ The following routines accept parameters that correspond directly  }
{ to the respective Win32 API function calls that they invoke. Refer }
{ to the Win32 reference documentation for more detail.              }
function LoadLibraryEx32W(LibFileName: PChar; hFile,
  dwFlags: DWORD): THandle32;
function FreeLibrary32W(LibModule: THandle32): BOOL;
function GetProcAddress32W(Module: THandle32; ProcName: PChar): TFarProc;
{ GetVDMPointer32W converts a 16-bit (16:16) pointer into a         }
{ 32-bit flat (0:32) pointer. The value of FMode should be 1 if     }
{ the 16-bit pointer is a protected mode address (the normal        }
{ situation in Windows 3.x) or 0 if the 16-bit pointer is real      }
```

continues

LISTING 13.14. CONTINUED

```
{ mode.                                                        }
{ NOTE:  Limit checking is not performed in the retail build   }
{ of Windows NT.  It is performed in the checked (debug) build }
{ of WOW32.DLL, which will cause 0 to be returned when the     }
{ limit is exceeded by the supplied offset.                    }
function GetVDMPointer32W(Address: Pointer; fProtectedMode: WordBool):
    ➡DWORD;
{ CallProc32W calls a proc whose address was retrieved by      }
{ GetProcAddress32W. The true definition of this function      }
{ actually allows for multiple DWORD parameters to be passed   }
{ prior to the ProcAddress parameter, and the nParams parameter }
{ should reveal the number of params passed prior to ProcAddress. }
{ The AddressConvert parameter is a bitmask which indicates which }
{ of the params are 16-bit pointers in need of conversion before }
{ the 32-bit function is called. Since this function doesn't lend }
{ itself to being defined in Object Pascal, you may want to use }
{ the simplified Call32BitProc function instead. }
function CallProc32W(Params: DWORD; ProcAddress, AddressConvert,
                     nParams: DWORD): DWORD;
{ Call32BitProc accepts a constant array of Longints as the parameter }
{ list for the function given by ProcAddress. This procedure is }
{ responsible for packaging the parameters into the correct format }
{ and calling the CallProc32W WOW function. }
function Call32BitProc(ProcAddress: DWORD; Params: array of Longint;
                       AddressConvert: Longint): DWORD;
{ Converts a 16-bit window handle to 32-bit for use by Windows NT. }
function HWnd16To32(Handle: hWnd): THandle32;
{ Converts a 32-bit window handle to 16-bit. }
function HWnd32To16(Handle: THandle32): hWnd;
implementation
uses WinProcs;
function HWnd16To32(Handle: hWnd): THandle32;
begin
  Result := Handle or $FFFF0000;
end;
function HWnd32To16(Handle: THandle32): hWnd;
begin
  Result := LoWord(Handle);
end;
function BitIsSet(Value: Longint; Bit: Byte): Boolean;
begin
  Result := Value and (1 shl Bit) <> 0;
end;
procedure FixParams(var Params: array of Longint; AddConv: Longint);
var
  i: integer;
begin
  for i := Low(Params) to High(Params) do
    if BitIsSet(AddConv, i) then
      Params[i] := GetVDMPointer32W(Pointer(Params[i]), True);
```

```
end;
function Call32BitProc(ProcAddress: DWORD; Params: array of Longint;
                       AddressConvert: Longint): DWORD;
var
  NumParams: word;
begin
  FixParams(Params, AddressConvert);
  NumParams := High(Params) + 1;
  asm
    les di, Params                { es:di -> Params }
    mov cx, NumParams             { loop counter = num params }
  @@1:
    push es:word ptr [di + 2]     { push hiword of param x }
    push es:word ptr [di]         { push loword of param x }
    add di, 4                     { skip to next param }
    loop @@1                      { iterate over all params }
    mov cx, ProcAddress.Word[2]   { cx = hiword of ProcAddress }
    mov dx, ProcAddress.Word[0]   { dx = loword of ProcAddress }
    push cx                       { push hi ProcAddress }
    push dx                       { push lo ProcAddress }
    mov ax, 0
    push ax                       { push dummy hi AddressConvert }
    push ax                       { push dummy lo AddressConvert }
    push ax                       { push hi NumParams }
    mov cx, NumParams
    push cx                       { push lo Number of Params }
    call CallProc32W              { call function }
    mov Result.Word[0], ax
    mov Result.Word[2], dx        { store return value }
  end
end;
{ 16-bit WOW functions }
function LoadLibraryEx32W;              external 'KERNEL' index 513;
function FreeLibrary32W;                external 'KERNEL' index 514;
function GetProcAddress32W;             external 'KERNEL' index 515;
function GetVDMPointer32W;              external 'KERNEL' index 516;
function CallProc32W;                   external 'KERNEL' index 517;
end.
```

All the functions in this unit are simply exports from the 16-bit kernel except for the
Call32BitProc() function, which employs some assembly code to allow the user to pass
a variable number of parameters in an array of Longint.

The WOW32 functions make up the WOW32.pas unit, which is shown in Listing 13.15.

LISTING 13.15. WOW32.pas.

```
unit WOW32;
interface
uses Windows;
//
// 16:16 -> 0:32 Pointer translation.
//
// WOWGetVDMPointer will convert the passed in 16-bit address
// to the equivalent 32-bit flat pointer.  If fProtectedMode
// is TRUE, the function treats the upper 16 bits as a selector
// in the local descriptor table.  If fProtectedMode is FALSE,
// the upper 16 bits are treated as a real-mode segment value.
// In either case the lower 16 bits are treated as the offset.
//
// The return value is 0 if the selector is invalid.
//
// NOTE:  Limit checking is not performed in the retail build
// of Windows NT.  It is performed in the checked (debug) build
// of WOW32.DLL, which will cause 0 to be returned when the
// limit is exceeded by the supplied offset.
//
function WOWGetVDMPointer(vp, dwBytes: DWORD; fProtectedMode: BOOL):
    Pointer; stdcall;
//
// The following two functions are here for compatibility with
// Windows 95.  On Win95, the global heap can be rearranged,
// invalidating flat pointers returned by WOWGetVDMPointer, while
// a thunk is executing.  On Windows NT, the 16-bit VDM is completely
// halted while a thunk executes, so the only way the heap will
// be rearranged is if a callback is made to Win16 code.
//
// The Win95 versions of these functions call GlobalFix to
// lock down a segment's flat address, and GlobalUnfix to
// release the segment.
//
// The Windows NT implementations of these functions do *not*
// call GlobalFix/GlobalUnfix on the segment, because there
// will not be any heap motion unless a callback occurs.
// If your thunk does call back to the 16-bit side, be sure
// to discard flat pointers and call WOWGetVDMPointer again
// to be sure the flat address is correct.
//
function WOWGetVDMPointerFix(vp, dwBytes: DWORD; fProtectedMode: BOOL):
    Pointer; stdcall;
procedure WOWGetVDMPointerUnfix(vp: DWORD); stdcall;
//
// Win16 memory management.
//
// These functions can be used to manage memory in the Win16
// heap.  The following four functions are identical to their
```

```
// Win16 counterparts, except that they are called from Win32
// code.
//
function WOWGlobalAlloc16(wFlags: word; cb: DWORD): word; stdcall;
function WOWGlobalFree16(hMem: word): word; stdcall;
function WOWGlobalLock16(hMem: word): DWORD; stdcall;
function WOWGlobalUnlock16(hMem: word): BOOL; stdcall;
//
// The following three functions combine two common operations in
// one switch to 16-bit mode.
//
function WOWGlobalAllocLock16(wFlags: word; cb: DWORD; phMem: PWord):
    DWORD; stdcall;
function WOWGlobalLockSize16(hMem: word; pcb: PDWORD): DWORD; stdcall;
function WOWGlobalUnlockFree16(vpMem: DWORD): word; stdcall;
//
// Yielding the Win16 nonpreemptive scheduler
//
// The following two functions are provided for Win32 code called
// via Generic Thunks which needs to yield the Win16 scheduler so
// that tasks in that VDM can execute while the thunk waits for
// something to complete.  These two functions are functionally
// identical to calling back to 16-bit code which calls Yield or
// DirectedYield.
//
procedure WOWYield16;
procedure WOWDirectedYield16(htask16: word);
//
// Generic Callbacks.
//
// WOWCallback16 can be used in Win32 code called
// from 16-bit (such as by using Generic Thunks) to call back to
// the 16-bit side.  The function called must be declared similarly
// to the following:
//
// function CallbackRoutine(dwParam: Longint): Longint; export;
//
// If you are passing a pointer, declare the parameter as such:
//
// function CallbackRoutine(vp: Pointer): Longint; export;
//
// NOTE: If you are passing a pointer, you'll need to get the
// pointer using WOWGlobalAlloc16 or WOWGlobalAllocLock16
//
// If the function called returns a word instead of a Longint, the
// upper 16 bits of the return value is undefined.  Similarly, if
// the function called has no return value, the entire return value
// is undefined.
```

continues

Listing 13.15. continued

```
//
// WOWCallback16Ex allows any combination of arguments up to
// WCB16_MAX_CBARGS bytes total to be passed to the 16-bit routine.
// cbArgs is used to properly clean up the 16-bit stack after calling
// the routine.  Regardless of the value of cbArgs, WCB16_MAX_CBARGS
// bytes will always be copied from pArgs to the 16-bit stack.  If
// pArgs is less than WCB16_MAX_CBARGS bytes from the end of a page,
// and the next page is inaccessible, WOWCallback16Ex will incur an
// access violation.
//
// If cbArgs is larger than the WCB16_MAX_ARGS which the running
// system supports, the function returns FALSE and GetLastError
// returns ERROR_INVALID_PARAMETER.  Otherwise the function
// returns TRUE and the DWORD pointed to by pdwRetCode contains
// the return code from the callback routine.  If the callback
// routine returns a WORD, the HIWORD of the return code is
// undefined and should be ignored using LOWORD(dwRetCode).
//
// WOWCallback16Ex can call routines using the PASCAL and CDECL
// calling conventions.  The default is to use the PASCAL
// calling convention.  To use CDECL, pass WCB16_CDECL in the
// dwFlags parameter.
//
// The arguments pointed to by pArgs must be in the correct
// order for the callback routine's calling convention.
// To call the routine SetWindowText,
//
// SetWindowText(Handle: hWnd; lpsz: PChar): Longint;
//
// pArgs would point to an array of words:
//
// SetWindowTextArgs: array[0..2] of word =
//     (LoWord(Longint(lpsz)), HiWord(Longint(lpsz)), Handle);
//
// In other words, the arguments are placed in the array in reverse
// order with the least significant word first for DWORDs and offset
// first for FAR pointers.  Further, the arguments are placed in the array
// in the order listed in the function prototype with the least
// significant word first for DWORDs and offset first for FAR pointers.
//
function WOWCallback16(vpfn16, dwParam: DWORD): DWORD; stdcall;
const
  WCB16_MAX_CBARGS = 16;
  WCB16_PASCAL     = $0;
  WCB16_CDECL      = $1;
function WOWCallback16Ex(vpfn16, dwFlags, cbArgs: DWORD; pArgs: Pointer;
                         pdwRetCode: PDWORD): BOOL; stdcall;
//
// 16 <--> 32 Handle mapping functions.
```

```
//
type
  TWOWHandleType = (
    WOW_TYPE_HWND,
    WOW_TYPE_HMENU,
    WOW_TYPE_HDWP,
    WOW_TYPE_HDROP,
    WOW_TYPE_HDC,
    WOW_TYPE_HFONT,
    WOW_TYPE_HMETAFILE,
    WOW_TYPE_HRGN,
    WOW_TYPE_HBITMAP,
    WOW_TYPE_HBRUSH,
    WOW_TYPE_HPALETTE,
    WOW_TYPE_HPEN,
    WOW_TYPE_HACCEL,
    WOW_TYPE_HTASK,
    WOW_TYPE_FULLHWND);
function WOWHandle16(Handle32: THandle; HandType: TWOWHandleType):
    word; stdcall;
function WOWHandle32(Handle16: word; HandleType: TWOWHandleType):
    THandle; stdcall;
implementation
const
  WOW32DLL = 'WOW32.DLL';
function WOWCallback16;            external WOW32DLL name 'WOWCallback16';
function WOWCallback16Ex;          external WOW32DLL name 'WOWCallback16Ex';
function WOWGetVDMPointer;         external WOW32DLL name 'WOWGetVDMPointer';
function WOWGetVDMPointerFix;      external WOW32DLL name
➡'WOWGetVDMPointerFix'
procedure WOWGetVDMPointerUnfix; external WOW32DLL name
➡'WOWGetVDMPointerUnfix'
function WOWGlobalAlloc16;         external WOW32DLL name 'WOWGlobalAlloc16'
function WOWGlobalAllocLock16;     external WOW32DLL name
➡'WOWGlobalAllocLock16';
function WOWGlobalFree16;          external WOW32DLL name 'WOWGlobalFree16';
function WOWGlobalLock16;          external WOW32DLL name 'WOWGlobalLock16';
function WOWGlobalLockSize16;      external WOW32DLL name
➡'WOWGlobalLockSize16';
function WOWGlobalUnlock16;        external WOW32DLL name
➡'WOWGlobalUnlock16';
function WOWGlobalUnlockFree16;    external WOW32DLL name
➡'WOWGlobalUnlockFree16';
function WOWHandle16;              external WOW32DLL name 'WOWHandle16';
function WOWHandle32;              external WOW32DLL name 'WOWHandle32';
procedure WOWYield16;             external WOW32DLL name 'WOWYield16';
procedure WOWDirectedYield16;     external WOW32DLL name
➡'WOWDirectedYield16';
end.
```

13

Hard-Core Techniques

To illustrate generic thunking, we'll create a small 32-bit DLL that will be called from a 16-bit executable. The 32-bit DLL project, `TestDLL.dpr`, is shown in Listing 13.16.

LISTING 13.16. TestDLL.dpr.

```
library TestDLL;
uses
  SysUtils, Dialogs, Windows, WOW32;
const
  DLLStr = 'I am in the 32-bit DLL. The string you sent is: "%s"';
function DLLFunc32(P: PChar; CallBackFunc: DWORD): Integer; stdcall;
const
  MemSize = 256;
var
  Mem16: DWORD;
  Mem32: PChar;
  Hand16: word;
begin
  { Show string P }
  ShowMessage(Format(DLLStr, [P]));
  { Allocate some 16-bit memory }
  Hand16 := WOWGlobalAlloc16(GMem_Share or GMem_Fixed or GMem_ZeroInit,
                             MemSize);
  { Lock the 16-bit memory }
  Mem16 := WOWGlobalLock16(Hand16);
  { Convert 16-bit pointer to 32-bit pointer.  Now they point to the }
  { same place. }
  Mem32 := PChar(WOWGetVDMPointer(Mem16, MemSize, True));
  { Copy string into 32-bit pointer }
  StrPCopy(Mem32, 'I REALLY love DDG!!');
  { Call back into the 16-bit app, passing 16-bit pointer }
  Result := WOWCallback16(CallBackFunc, Mem16);
  { clean up allocated 16-bit memory }
  WOWGlobalUnlockFree16(Mem16);
end;
exports
  DLLFunc32 name 'DLLFunc32' resident;
begin
end.
```

This DLL exports one function that takes a `PChar` and a callback function as parameters. The `PChar` is immediately displayed in a `ShowMessage()`. The callback function allows the function to call back into the 16-bit process, passing some specially allocated 16-bit memory.

The code for the 16-bit application, `Call32.dpr`, is shown in Listing 13.17. The main form is shown in Figure 13.6.

LISTING 13.17. Main.pas.

```pascal
unit Main;
{$C FIXED DEMANDLOAD PERMANENT}
interface
uses
  SysUtils, WinTypes, WinProcs, Messages, Classes, Graphics, Controls,
  Forms, Dialogs, StdCtrls;
type
  TMainForm = class(TForm)
    CallBtn: TButton;
    Edit1: TEdit;
    Label1: TLabel;
    procedure CallBtnClick(Sender: TObject);
  private
    { Private declarations }
  public
    { Public declarations }
  end;
var
  MainForm: TMainForm;
implementation
{$R *.DFM}
uses WOW16;
const
  ExeStr = 'The 32-bit DLL has called back into the 16-bit EXE. ' +
           'The string to the EXE is: "%s"';
function CallBackFunc(P: PChar): Longint; export;
begin
  ShowMessage(Format(ExeStr, [StrPas(P)]));
  Result := StrLen(P);
end;
procedure TMainForm.CallBtnClick(Sender: TObject);
var
  H: THandle32;
  R, P: Longint;
  AStr: PChar;
begin
  { load 32-bit DLL }
  H := LoadLibraryEx32W('TestDLL.dll', 0, 0);
  AStr := StrNew('I love DDG.');
  try
    if H > 0 then begin
      { Retrieve address of proc from 32-bit DLL }
      TFarProc(P) := GetProcAddress32W(H, 'DLLFunc32');
      if P > 0 then begin
        { Call proc in 32-bit DLL }
        R := Call32BitProc(P, [Longint(AStr), Longint(@CallBackFunc)], 1);
        Edit1.Text := IntToStr(R);
      end;
    end;
```

13

HARD-CORE
TECHNIQUES

continues

LISTING 13.17. CONTINUED

```
finally
  StrDispose(AStr);
  if H > 0 then FreeLibrary32W(H);
  end;
end;
end.
```

FIGURE 13.6.

The Call32 main form.

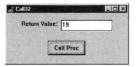

This application passes a 16-bit `PChar` and function address to the 32-bit DLL. The `CallBackFunc()` is eventually called by the 32-bit DLL, and in fact—if you look closely—the return value of `DLLFunc32()` is the value returned by `CallBackFunc()`.

WM_COPYDATA

Windows 95 supports flat thunks to call 16-bit DLLs from Win32 applications. Windows NT doesn't provide a means to directly call 16-bit code from a Win32 application. Given this limitation, the question that follows is: What's the best way to communicate data between 32-bit and 16-bit processes on NT? What's more, that leads us to another question: Is there an easy way to share data in such a way that it runs under both Windows 95 and NT?

The answer to both questions is `WM_COPYDATA`. The `WM_COPYDATA` Windows message provides a means for transferring binary data between processes—whether 32-bit or 16-bit processes. When a `WM_COPYDATA` message is sent to a window, the `wParam` of this message identifies the window passing the data, and the `lParam` holds a pointer to a `TCopyDataStruct` record. This record is defined as follows:

```
type
  PCopyDataStruct = ^TCopyDataStruct;
  TCopyDataStruct = packed record
    dwData: DWORD;
    cbData: DWORD;
    lpData: Pointer;
  end;
```

The `dwData` field holds 32 bits of user-defined information. `cbData` contains the size of the buffer pointed to by `lpData`. `lpData` is a pointer to a buffer of information you want to pass between applications. If you send this message between a 32-bit and a 16-bit application, Windows will automatically convert the lpData pointer from a 0:32 pointer to a 16:16 pointer, or vice versa. Additionally, Windows will ensure that the data pointed to by lpData is mapped into the receiving process's address space.

> **NOTE**
>
> WM_COPYDATA works great for relatively small amounts of information, but if you have a lot of information you must communicate across the 16/32-bit boundary, you might want to use automation. Automation is described in Chapter 23.

> **TIP**
>
> It should be clear that, although NT doesn't support direct usage of 16-bit DLLs from Win32 applications, you can create a 16-bit executable that encapsulates the DLL and can communicate with that executable by using WM_COPYDATA.

To show how WM_COPYDATA works, we'll create two projects, the first being a 32-bit application. This application will have a memo control into which you can type some text. Additionally, this application will provide a means for communicating with the second project, a 16-bit application, to transfer memo text. To provide a means whereby the two applications can begin communication, take the following steps:

1. Register a window message to obtain a unique message ID for interapplication communication.

2. Broadcast the message systemwide from the Win32 application. In the wParam of this message, store the handle to the main window of the Win32 application.

3. When the 16-bit application receives the broadcast message, it will answer by sending the registered message back to the sending application and pass its own main form's window handle as the wParam.

4. After receiving the response, the 32-bit application now has the handle to the main form of the 16-bit application. The 32-bit application can now send a WM_COPYDATA message to the 16-bit application so that the sharing can begin.

The code for the RegMsg.pas unit, which is shared by the two projects, is shown in Listing 13.18.

Listing 13.18. RegMsg.pas.

```
unit RegMsg;
interface
var
  DDGM_HandshakeMessage: Cardinal;
implementation
uses WinProcs;
const
  HandshakeMessageStr: PChar = 'DDG.CopyData.Handshake';
initialization
  DDGM_HandshakeMessage := RegisterWindowMessage(HandshakeMessageStr);
end.
```

The source code for `CopyMain.pas`, the source code for the 32-bit `CopyData.dpr` project, is shown in Listing 13.19. This is the unit that establishes the conversation and sends the data.

LISTING 13.19. CopyMain.pas.

```
unit CopyMain;
interface
uses
  Windows, Messages, SysUtils, Classes, Graphics, Controls, Forms, Dialogs,
  StdCtrls, ExtCtrls, Menus;
type
  TMainForm = class(TForm)
    DataMemo: TMemo;
    BottomPnl: TPanel;
    BtnPnl: TPanel;
    CloseBtn: TButton;
    CopyBtn: TButton;
    MainMenu1: TMainMenu;
    File1: TMenuItem;
    CopyData1: TMenuItem;
    N1: TMenuItem;
    Exit1: TMenuItem;
    Help1: TMenuItem;
    About1: TMenuItem;
    procedure CloseBtnClick(Sender: TObject);
    procedure FormResize(Sender: TObject);
    procedure About1Click(Sender: TObject);
    procedure CopyBtnClick(Sender: TObject);
  private
    { Private declarations }
  protected
    procedure WndProc(var Message: TMessage); override;
  public
    { Public declarations }
  end;
```

```
var
  MainForm: TMainForm;
implementation
{$R *.DFM}
uses AboutU, RegMsg;
var
  Recipients: DWORD = BSM_APPLICATIONS;
procedure TMainForm.WndProc(var Message: TMessage);
var
  DataBuffer: TCopyDataStruct;
  Buf: PChar;
  BufSize: Integer;
begin
  if Message.Msg = DDGM_HandshakeMessage then begin
    { Allocate buffer }
    BufSize := DataMemo.GetTextLen + (1 * SizeOf(Char));
    Buf := AllocMem(BufSize);
    { Copy memo to buffer }
    DataMemo.GetTextBuf(Buf, BufSize);
    try
      with DataBuffer do begin
        { Fill dwData with registered message as safety check }
        dwData := DDGM_HandshakeMessage;
        cbData := BufSize;
        lpData := Buf;
      end;
      { NOTE: WM_COPYDATA message must be *sent* }
      SendMessage(Message.wParam, WM_COPYDATA, Handle,
                ➥Longint(@DataBuffer));
    finally
      FreeMem(Buf, BufSize);
    end;
  end
  else
    inherited WndProc(Message);
end;
procedure TMainForm.CloseBtnClick(Sender: TObject);
begin
  Close;
end;
procedure TMainForm.FormResize(Sender: TObject);
begin
  BtnPnl.Left := BottomPnl.Width div 2 - BtnPnl.Width div 2;
end;
procedure TMainForm.About1Click(Sender: TObject);
begin
  AboutBox;
end;
procedure TMainForm.CopyBtnClick(Sender: TObject);
```

13

HARD-CORE TECHNIQUES

continues

LISTING 13.19. CONTINUED

```
begin
  { Call for any listening apps }
  BroadcastSystemMessage(BSF_IGNORECURRENTTASK or BSF_POSTMESSAGE,
                        @Recipients, DDGM_HandshakeMessage, Handle, 0);
end;
end.
```

The source for ReadMain.pas, the main unit for the 16-bit ReadData.dpr project, is shown in Listing 13.20. This is the unit that communicates with the CopyData project and receives the data buffer.

LISTING 13.20. ReadMain.pas.

```
unit Readmain;
interface
uses
  SysUtils, WinTypes, WinProcs, Messages, Classes, Graphics, Controls,
  Forms, Dialogs, Menus, StdCtrls;
{ The WM_COPYDATA Windows message is not defined in the 16-bit Messages }
{ unit, although it is available to 16-bit applications running under   }
{ Windows 95 or NT.  This message is discussed in the Win32 API online  }
{ help. }
const
  WM_COPYDATA = $004A;
type
  TMainForm = class(TForm)
    ReadMemo: TMemo;
    MainMenu1: TMainMenu;
    File1: TMenuItem;
    Exit1: TMenuItem;
    Help1: TMenuItem;
    About1: TMenuItem;
    procedure Exit1Click(Sender: TObject);
    procedure FormCreate(Sender: TObject);
    procedure About1Click(Sender: TObject);
  private
    procedure OnAppMessage(var M: TMsg; var Handled: Boolean);
    procedure WMCopyData(var M: TMessage); message WM_COPYDATA;
  end;
var
  MainForm: TMainForm;
implementation
{$R *.DFM}
uses RegMsg, AboutU;
type
  { The TCopyDataStruct record type is not defined in WinTypes unit, }
  { although it is available in the 16-bit Windows API when running  }
```

```
  { under Windows 95 and NT. The lParam of the WM_COPYDATA message   }
  { points to one of these. }
  PCopyDataStruct = ^TCopyDataStruct;
  TCopyDataStruct = record
    dwData: Longint;
    cbData: Longint;
    lpData: Pointer;
  end;
procedure TMainForm.OnAppMessage(var M: TMsg; var Handled: Boolean);
{ OnMessage handler for Application object. }
begin
  { The DDGM_HandshakeMessage message is received as a broadcast to    }
  { all applications.  The wParam of this message contains the handle  }
  { of the window which broadcast the message.  We respond by posting }
  { the same message back to the sender, with our handle in the wParam. }
  if M.Message = DDGM_HandshakeMessage then begin
    PostMessage(M.wParam, DDGM_HandshakeMessage, Handle, 0);
    Handled := True;
  end;
end;
procedure TMainForm.WMCopyData(var M: TMessage);
{ Handler for WM_COPYDATA message }
begin
  { Check wParam to ensure we know WHO sent us the WM_COPYDATA message }
  if PCopyDataStruct(M.lParam)^.dwData = DDGM_HandshakeMessage then
    { When WM_COPYDATA message is received, the lParam points to}
    ReadMemo.SetTextBuf(PChar(PCopyDataStruct(M.lParam)^.lpData));
end;
procedure TMainForm.Exit1Click(Sender: TObject);
begin
  Close;
end;
procedure TMainForm.FormCreate(Sender: TObject);
begin
  Application.OnMessage := OnAppMessage;
end;
procedure TMainForm.About1Click(Sender: TObject);
begin
  AboutBox;
end;
end.
```

Figure 13.7 shows the two applications working in harmony.

13

HARD-CORE TECHNIQUES

FIGURE 13.7.

Communicating with WM_COPYDATA.

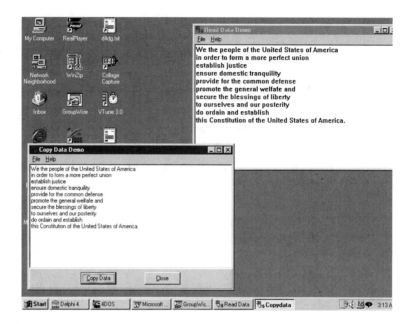

SUMMARY

Whew! This was an in-depth chapter! Step back for a moment and take a look at all you learned: subclassing window procedures, preventing multiple instances, windows hooks, BASM programming, using C++ object files, using C++ classes, thunking, and WM_COPYDATA. I don't know about you, but we've covered so much hacker stuff in this chapter that I'm hungry for Cheetos and Jolt Cola! Because we're on a roll with low-level programming, the next chapter, "Snooping System Information," details how to get inside the OS to obtain information about processes, threads, and modules.

SNOOPING SYSTEM INFORMATION

IN THIS CHAPTER

In this chapter, you'll learn how to create a full-featured utility, called SysInfo, that's designed to browse the vital parameters of your system. Through the course of developing this application, you'll learn how to employ rather lesser-known APIs to gain access to low-level, systemwide information on processes, threads, modules, heaps, drivers, and pages. This chapter also covers how Windows 95/98 and Windows NT obtain this information differently. Additionally, SysInfo provides you with techniques for obtaining information on free memory resources, Windows version information, environment variable settings, and a list of loaded modules. Not only do you learn to use these nuts-and-bolts API functions, but you also learn how to integrate this information into a functional and aesthetically pleasing user interface. Additionally, you learn which of the Windows 3.x API functions the Win32 functions in this chapter are designed to replace.

You need to get such information from Windows for several reasons. Of course, the hacker in each of us would argue that being able to snoop around the operating system's backyard like some kind of cyber-voyeur is its own reward. Perhaps you're writing a program that needs to access environment variables in order to find certain files. Maybe you need to determine which modules are loaded in order to remove modules from memory manually. Possibly you need to come up with a killer chapter for a book you're writing. See. . .lots of valid reasons exist!

InfoForm—OBTAINING GENERAL INFORMATION

To warm up, this section shows you how to obtain system information in an API that is consistent across Win32 versions. The code for this application will make a bit more sense if you learn about its user interface first. You'll learn about the user interface of this application a little bit backward, though, because we're going to explain one of the application's child forms first. This form (shown in Figure 14.1) is called InfoForm, and it's used to display various system and process settings, such as memory and hardware information, operating system (OS) version and directory information, and environment variables.

FIGURE 14.1.
The InfoForm
child form.

The contents of the form are quite simple. The form contains a THeaderListbox (a custom component covered in Chapter 21, "Writing Delphi Custom Components") and a TButton. To refresh your memory, the THeaderListbox control is a combination of a THeader control and a TListBox control. When the sections of the header are sized, the list box contents will also size appropriately. The TheaderListbox control, called InfoLB, displays the information mentioned earlier. The Close button dismisses the form.

Formatting the Strings

This application makes extensive use of the Format() function to format predefined strings with data retrieved from the OS at runtime. The strings that will be used are defined in a const section in the main unit as follows:

```
const
  { Memory status strings }
  SMemUse   = 'Memory in useq%d%%';
  STotMem   = 'Total physical memoryq$%.8x bytes';
  SFreeMem  = 'Free physical memoryq$%.8x bytes';
  STotPage  = 'Total page file memoryq$%.8x bytes';
  SFreePage = 'Free page file memoryq$%.8x bytes';
  STotVirt  = 'Total virtual memoryq$%.8x bytes';
  SFreeVirt = 'Free virtual memoryq$%.8x bytes';
  { OS version info strings }
  SOSVer    = 'OS Versionq%d.%d';
  SBuildNo  = 'Build Numberq%d';
  SOSPlat   = 'Platformq%s';
  SOSWin32s = 'Windows 3.1x running Win32s';
  SOSWin95  = 'Windows 95';
  SOSWinNT  = 'Windows NT';
  { System info strings }
  SProc     = 'Processor Arhitectureq%s';
  SPIntel   = 'Intel';
  SPageSize = 'Page Sizeq$%.8x bytes';
  SMinAddr  = 'Minimum Application Addressq$%p';
  SMaxAddr  = 'Maximum Application Addressq$%p';
  SNumProcs = 'Number of Processorsq%d';
  SAllocGra = 'Allocation Granularityq$%.8x bytes';
  SProcLevl = 'Processor Levelq%s';
  SIntel3   = '80386';
  SIntel4   = '80486';
  SIntel5   = 'Pentium';
  SIntel6   = 'Pentium Pro';
  SProcRev  = 'Processor Revisionq%.4x';
  { Directory strings }
  SWinDir   = 'Windows directoryq%s';
  SSysDir   = 'Windows system directoryq%s';
  SCurDir   = 'Current directoryq%s';
```

You're probably wondering about the conspicuous q in the middle of each of the strings. When displaying these strings, the DelimChar property of InfoLB is set to q, which means that the InfoLB component assumes that the character q defines the delimiter between each column in the list box.

There are three primary reasons for using Format() with predefined strings rather than individually formatting string literals:

- Because Format() accepts various types as parameters, you don't have to cloud your code with a bunch of varied calls to functions (such as IntToStr() or IntToHex()) that format different parameter types for display.

- Format() easily handles multiple data types. In this case, we use the %s and %d format strings to format string and numeric data, so it's more flexible.

- Keeping the strings in a separate location makes it easier to find, add, and change strings if necessary, so it's more maintainable.

> **NOTE**
>
> Use a double percent sign (%%) to display a single percent symbol in a formatted string.

Obtaining Memory Status

The first bit of system information you can obtain to place in `InfoLB` is the memory status obtained by the `GlobalMemoryStatus()` API call. `GlobalMemoryStatus()` is a procedure that accepts one `var` parameter of type `TMemoryStatus`, which is defined as follows:

```
type
  TMemoryStatus = record
    dwLength: DWORD;
    dwMemoryLoad: DWORD;
    dwTotalPhys: DWORD;
    dwAvailPhys: DWORD;
    dwTotalPageFile: DWORD;
    dwAvailPageFile: DWORD;
    dwTotalVirtual: DWORD;
    dwAvailVirtual: DWORD;
  end;
```

- The first field in this record, `dwLength`, describes the length of the `TMemoryStatus` record. You should initialize this value to `SizeOf(TMemoryStatus)` prior to calling `GlobalMemoryStatus()`. Doing this allows Windows to change the size of this record in future versions because it will be able to differentiate versions based on the value of the first field.

- `dwMemoryLoad` provides a number from `0` to `100` that's intended to give a general idea of memory usage. `0` means that no memory is being used, and `100` means that all memory is in use.

- `dwTotalPhys` indicates the total number of bytes of physical memory (the amount of RAM installed on the computer), and `dwAvailPhys` indicates how much of that total is currently unused.

- `dwTotalPageFile` indicates the total number of bytes that can be stored to hard disk page file(s). This number is not the same as the size of a page file on disk. `dwAvailPageFile` indicates how much of that total is available.

- `dwTotalVirtual` indicates the total number of bytes of usable virtual memory in the calling process. `dwAvailVirtual` indicates how much of this memory is available to the calling process.

The following code obtains the memory status and fills the list box with the status information:

```
procedure TInfoForm.ShowMemStatus;
var
  MS: TMemoryStatus;
begin
  InfoLB.DelimChar := 'q';
  MS.dwLength := SizeOf(MS);
  GlobalMemoryStatus(MS);
  with InfoLB.Items, MS do
  begin
    Clear;
    Add(Format(SMemUse, [dwMemoryLoad]));
    Add(Format(STotMem, [dwTotalPhys]));
    Add(Format(SFreeMem, [dwAvailPhys]));
    Add(Format(STotPage, [dwTotalPageFile]));
    Add(Format(SFreePage, [dwAvailPageFile]));
    Add(Format(STotVirt, [dwTotalVirtual]));
    Add(Format(SFreeVirt, [dwAvailVirtual]));
  end;
  InfoLB.Sections[0].Text := 'Resource';
  InfoLB.Sections[1].Text := 'Amount';
  Caption:= 'Memory Status';
end;
```

CAUTION

Don't forget to initialize the dwLength field of the TMemoryStatus structure before calling GlobalMemoryStatus().

Figure 14.2 shows `InfoForm` displaying memory status information at runtime.

FIGURE 14.2.

Viewing memory status information.

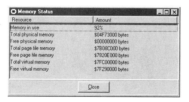

Getting the OS Version

You can find out what version of Windows and the Win32 OS you're running by making a call to the GetVersionEx() API function. GetVersionEx() accepts as its only parameter, a TOSVersionInfo record, by reference. This record is defined as follows:

```
type
  TOSVersionInfo = record
    dwOSVersionInfoSize: DWORD;
    dwMajorVersion: DWORD;
    dwMinorVersion: DWORD;
    dwBuildNumber: DWORD;
    dwPlatformId: DWORD;
    szCSDVersion: array[0..126] of AnsiChar; { Maintenance string for PSS
                                               usage }
  end;
```

- The dwOSVersionInfoSize field should be initialized to SizeOf(TOSVersionInfo) prior to calling GetVersionEx().

- dwMajorVersion indicates the major release number of the OS. In other words, if the OS version number is 4.0, the value of this field will be 4.

- dwMinorVersion indicates the minor release number of the OS. In other words, if the OS version number is 4.0, the value of this field will be 0.

- dwBuildNumber holds the build number of the OS in its low-order word.

- dwPlatformId describes the current Win32 platform. This parameter can have any one of the values in the following table:

Value	*Platform*
VER_PLATFORM_WIN32s	Win32s on Windows 3.1
VER_PLATFORM_WIN32_WINDOWS	Win32 on Windows 95
VER_PLATFORM_WIN32_NT	Windows NT

- szCSDVersion contains additional arbitrary OS information. This value is often an empty string.

The following procedure populates InfoLB with OS version information:

```
procedure TInfoForm.GetOSVerInfo;
var
  VI: TOSVersionInfo;
begin
  VI.dwOSVersionInfoSize := SizeOf(VI);
  GetVersionEx(VI);
  with InfoLB.Items, VI do
  begin
    Clear;
    Add(Format(SOSVer, [dwMajorVersion, dwMinorVersion]));
```

```
    Add(Format(SBuildNo, [LoWord(dwBuildNumber)]));
    case dwPlatformID of
      VER_PLATFORM_WIN32S: Add(Format(SOSPlat, [SOSWin32s]));
      VER_PLATFORM_WIN32_WINDOWS: Add(Format(SOSPlat, [SOSWin95]));
      VER_PLATFORM_WIN32_NT: Add(Format(SOSPlat, [SOSWinNT]));
    end;
  end;
end;
```

NOTE

In Windows 3.*x*, the `GetVersion()` function obtained similar version information. Because you're now in Win32 land, you should use the `GetVersionEx()` function; it provides more detailed information than `GetVersion()`.

Obtaining Directory Information

The OS uses the `Windows` and `System` directories extensively to store shared DLLs, drivers, applications, and INI files. Additionally, Win32 also maintains a current directory for each process. Throughout the course of writing Win32 applications, it's likely that you'll encounter a situation where you need to obtain the location of one of these directories. When this happens, you'll be in luck because three functions in the Win32 API enable you to obtain that directory information.

The functions `GetWindowsDirectory()`, `GetSystemDirectory()`, and `GetCurrentDirectory()` are straightforward. Each takes a pointer to a buffer in which to copy the directory string as the first parameter and the buffer size as the second parameter. The function copies into the buffer a null-terminated string containing the path. Hopefully, you can tell which directory each function returns by the name of the function. If not, well, let's just say we hope you don't rely on programming to eat.

This method uses a temporary array of `char` into which the directory information is stored. From there, the string is added to `InfoLB` as you can see for yourself in the code below:

```
procedure TInfoForm.GetDirInfo;
var
  S: array[0..MAX_PATH] of char;
begin
  { Get Windows directory }
  GetWindowsDirectory(S, SizeOf(S));
  InfoLB.Items.Add(Format(SWinDir, [S]));
  { Get Windows system directory }
  GetSystemDirectory(S, SizeOf(S));
  InfoLB.Items.Add(Format(SSysDir, [S]));
```

```
{ Get Current directory for current process }
GetCurrentDirectory(SizeOf(S), S);
InfoLB.Items.Add(Format(SCurDir, [S]));
end;
```

> **NOTE**
>
> The GetWindowsDir() and GetSystemDir() functions from the Windows 3.x API
> are unavailable under Win32.

Getting System Information

The Win32 API provides a procedure called GetSystemInfo() that in turn provides some very low-level details on the operating system. This procedure accepts one parameter of type TSystemInfo by reference, and it fills the record with the proper values. The TSystemInfo record is defined as follows:

```
type
  PSystemInfo = ^TSystemInfo;
  TSystemInfo = record
    case Integer of
      0: (
        dwOemId: DWORD);
      1: (
        wProcessorArchitecture: Word;
        wReserved: Word;
        dwPageSize: DWORD;
        lpMinimumApplicationAddress: Pointer;
        lpMaximumApplicationAddress: Pointer;
        dwActiveProcessorMask: DWORD;
        dwNumberOfProcessors: DWORD;
        dwProcessorType: DWORD;
        dwAllocationGranularity: DWORD;
        wProcessorLevel: Word;
        wProcessorRevision: Word);
  end;
```

- The dwOemId field is used for Windows 95. This value is always set to 0 or PROCESSOR_ARCHITECTURE_INTEL.

- Under NT, the wProcessorArchitecture portion of the variant record is used. This field describes the type of processor architecture under which you're currently running. Because Delphi is designed for Intel only, however, it's the only type that matters at this point. For the sake of completeness, this field can have any one of the following values:

```
PROCESSOR_ARCHITECTURE_INTEL
PROCESSOR_ARCHITECTURE_MIPS
PROCESSOR_ARCHITECTURE_ALPHA
PROCESSOR_ARCHITECTURE_PPC
```

- The wReserved field is unused at this time.

- The dwPageSize field holds the page size in kilobytes (KB) and specifies the granularity of page protection and commitment. On Intel *x*86 machines, this value is 4KB.

- lpMinimumApplicationAddress returns the lowest memory address accessible to applications and DLLs. Attempts to access a memory address below this value are likely to result in an access violation. lpMaximumApplicationAddress returns the highest memory address accessible to applications and DLLs. Attempts to access a memory address above this value are likely to result in an access violation.

- dwActiveProcessorMask returns a mask representing the set of processors configured into the system. Bit 0 represents the first processor, and bit 31 represents the 32nd processor. Wouldn't having 32 processors be cool? Because Windows 95/98 supports only one processor, only bit 0 will be set under that implementation of Win32.

- dwNumberOfProcessors also returns the number of processors in the system. We're not sure why Microsoft bothered to put both this and the preceding field in the TSystemInfo record, but here they are.

- The dwProcessorType field is no longer relevant. It was retained for backward compatibility. This field can have any one of the following values:

```
PROCESSOR_INTEL_386
PROCESSOR_INTEL_486
PROCESSOR_INTEL_PENTIUM
PROCESSOR_MIPS_R4000
PROCESSOR_ALPHA_21064
```

Of course, under Windows 95, only the PROCESSOR_INTEL_*x* values are possible, whereas all are valid under Windows NT.

- dwAllocationGranularity returns the allocation granularity upon which memory will be allocated. In previous implementations of Win32, this value was hard-coded as 64KB. It's possible, however, that other hardware architectures may require different values.

- The wProcessorLevel field specifies the system's architecture-dependent processor level. This field can hold a variety of values for different processors. For Intel processors, this parameter can have any of the values in the following table:

Value	Meaning
3	Processor is an 80386
4	Processor is an 80486
5	Processor is a Pentium

- wProcessorRevision specifies an architecture-dependent processor revision. Like wProcessorLevel, this field can hold a variety of values for different processors. For Intel architectures, this field holds a number in the format *xxyy*. For Intel 386 and 486 chips, *xx* + $0A is the stepping level and *yy* is the stepping (for example, 0300 is a D0 chip). For Intel Pentium or Cyrex/NextGen 486 chips, *xx* is the model number, and *yy* is the stepping (for example, 0201 is Model 2, Stepping 1).

The procedure used to obtain and add the formatted system information strings to InfoLB is as follows (note that this code is purposely slanted to display only Intel architecture information):

```
procedure TInfoForm.GetSysInfo;
var
  SI: TSystemInfo;
begin
  GetSystemInfo(SI);
  with InfoLB.Items, SI do
  begin
    Add(Format(SProc, [SPIntel]));
    Add(Format(SPageSize, [dwPageSize]));
    Add(Format(SMinAddr, [lpMinimumApplicationAddress]));
    Add(Format(SMaxAddr, [lpMaximumApplicationAddress]));
    Add(Format(SNumProcs, [dwNumberOfProcessors]));
    Add(Format(SAllocGra, [dwAllocationGranularity]));
    case wProcessorLevel of
      3: Add(Format(SProcLevl, [SIntel3]));
      4: Add(Format(SProcLevl, [SIntel4]));
      5: Add(Format(SProcLevl, [SIntel5]));
      6: Add(Format(SProcLevl, [SIntel6]));
    else Add(Format(SProcLevl, [IntToStr(wProcessorLevel)]));
    end;
  end;
end;
```

NOTE

The GetSystemInfo() function effectively replaces the GetWinFlags() function from the Windows 3.*x* API.

Figure 14.3 shows InfoForm displaying system information, including OS version and directory information, at runtime.

FIGURE **14.3.**

Viewing system information.

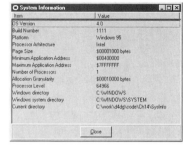

Checking Out the Environment

Obtaining the list of environment variables—things such as sets, path, and prompt—for the current process is an easy task, thanks to the GetEnvironmentStrings() API function. This function takes no parameters and returns a null-separated list of environment strings. The format of this list is a string, followed by a null, followed by a string, followed by a null, and so on until the entire string is terminated with a double null (#0#0). The following function is used in the SysInfo application to retrieve the output from the GetEnvironmentStrings() function and place it into the InfoLB:

```
procedure TInfoForm.ShowEnvironment;
var
  EnvPtr, SavePtr: PChar;
begin
  InfoLB.DelimChar := '=';
  EnvPtr := GetEnvironmentStrings;
  SavePtr := EnvPtr;
  InfoLB.Items.Clear;
  repeat
    InfoLB.Items.Add(StrPas(EnvPtr));
    inc(EnvPtr, StrLen(EnvPtr) + 1);
  until EnvPtr^ = #0;
  FreeEnvironmentStrings(SavePtr);
  InfoLB.Sections[0].Text := 'Environment Variable';
  InfoLB.Sections[1].Text := 'Value';
  Caption:= 'Current Environment';
end;
```

14

SNOOPING SYSTEM INFORMATION

> **NOTE**
>
> The ShowEnvironment() method takes advantage of Object Pascal's capability to perform pointer arithmetic on PChar-type strings. Notice how few lines of code are required to traverse the list of environment strings.

A couple of comments on this method are in order. First, notice that the DelimChar property of InfoLB is initially set to '='. Because each of the environment variable and value pairs are already separated by that character, it's very easy to display them properly in InfoLB. Also, when you're finished using the environment strings, you should call the FreeEnvironmentStrings() function to free the allocated block.

> **TIP**
>
> You can't obtain or set individual environment variables with the GetEnvironmentStrings() function. For getting and setting individual environment variables, see the GetEnvironmentVariable() and SetEnvironmentVariable() functions in the Win32 API help.

Figure 14.4 shows InfoForm environment strings at runtime.

FIGURE 14.4.

Viewing environment strings.

Listing 14.1 shows the entire source code for the InfoU.pas unit.

LISTING 14.1. THE SOURCE CODE FOR THE InfoU.pas UNIT.

```
unit InfoU;

interface

uses
  Windows, Messages, SysUtils, Classes, Graphics, Controls, Forms, Dialogs,
  HeadList, StdCtrls, ExtCtrls, SysMain;

type
  TInfoVariety = (ivMemory, ivSystem, ivEnvironment);

  TInfoForm = class(TForm)
    InfoLB: THeaderListbox;
    Panel1: TPanel;
    OkBtn: TButton;
  private
    procedure GetOSVerInfo;
    procedure GetSysInfo;
    procedure GetDirInfo;
  public
    procedure ShowMemStatus;
    procedure ShowSysInfo;
    procedure ShowEnvironment;
  end;

procedure ShowInformation(Variety: TInfoVariety);

implementation

{$R *.DFM}

procedure ShowInformation(Variety: TInfoVariety);
begin
  with TInfoForm.Create(Application) do
    try
      Font := MainForm.Font;
      case Variety of
        ivMemory: ShowMemStatus;
        ivSystem: ShowSysInfo;
        ivEnvironment: ShowEnvironment;
      end;
      ShowModal;
    finally
      Free;
    end;
end;
```

continues

14

SNOOPING
SYSTEM
INFORMATION

LISTING **14.1.** CONTINUED

```pascal
const
  { Memory status strings }
  SMemUse   = 'Memory in useq%d%%';
  STotMem   = 'Total physical memoryq$%.8x bytes';
  SFreeMem  = 'Free physical memoryq$%.8x bytes';
  STotPage  = 'Total page file memoryq$%.8x bytes';
  SFreePage = 'Free page file memoryq$%.8x bytes';
  STotVirt  = 'Total virtual memoryq$%.8x bytes';
  SFreeVirt = 'Free virtual memoryq$%.8x bytes';

  { OS version info strings }
  SOSVer    = 'OS Versionq%d.%d';
  SBuildNo  = 'Build Numberq%d';
  SOSPlat   = 'Platformq%s';
  SOSWin32s = 'Windows 3.1x running Win32s';
  SOSWin95  = 'Windows 95';
  SOSWinNT  = 'Windows NT';

  { System info strings }
  SProc     = 'Processor Arhitectureq%s';
  SPIntel   = 'Intel';
  SPageSize = 'Page Sizeq$%.8x bytes';
  SMinAddr  = 'Minimum Application Addressq$%p';
  SMaxAddr  = 'Maximum Application Addressq$%p';
  SNumProcs = 'Number of Processorsq%d';
  SAllocGra = 'Allocation Granularityq$%.8x bytes';
  SProcLevl = 'Processor Levelq%s';
  SIntel3   = '80386';
  SIntel4   = '80486';
  SIntel5   = 'Pentium';
  SIntel6   = 'Pentium Pro';
  SProcRev  = 'Processor Revisionq%.4x';

  { Directory strings }
  SWinDir   = 'Windows directoryq%s';
  SSysDir   = 'Windows system directoryq%s';
  SCurDir   = 'Current directoryq%s';

procedure TInfoForm.ShowMemStatus;
var
  MS: TMemoryStatus;
begin
  InfoLB.DelimChar := 'q';
  MS.dwLength := SizeOf(MS);
  GlobalMemoryStatus(MS);
  with InfoLB.Items, MS do
  begin
    Clear;
    Add(Format(SMemUse, [dwMemoryLoad]));
```

```
      Add(Format(STotMem, [dwTotalPhys]));
      Add(Format(SFreeMem, [dwAvailPhys]));
      Add(Format(STotPage, [dwTotalPageFile]));
      Add(Format(SFreePage, [dwAvailPageFile]));
      Add(Format(STotVirt, [dwTotalVirtual]));
      Add(Format(SFreeVirt, [dwAvailVirtual]));
    end;
    InfoLB.Sections[0].Text := 'Resource';
    InfoLB.Sections[1].Text := 'Amount';
    Caption:= 'Memory Status';
  end;

procedure TInfoForm.GetOSVerInfo;
var
  VI: TOSVersionInfo;
begin
  VI.dwOSVersionInfoSize := SizeOf(VI);
  GetVersionEx(VI);
  with InfoLB.Items, VI do
  begin
    Clear;
    Add(Format(SOSVer, [dwMajorVersion, dwMinorVersion]));
    Add(Format(SBuildNo, [LoWord(dwBuildNumber)]));
    case dwPlatformID of
      VER_PLATFORM_WIN32S: Add(Format(SOSPlat, [SOSWin32s]));
      VER_PLATFORM_WIN32_WINDOWS: Add(Format(SOSPlat, [SOSWin95]));
      VER_PLATFORM_WIN32_NT: Add(Format(SOSPlat, [SOSWinNT]));
    end;
  end;
end;

procedure TInfoForm.GetSysInfo;
var
  SI: TSystemInfo;
begin
  GetSystemInfo(SI);
  with InfoLB.Items, SI do
  begin
    Add(Format(SProc, [SPIntel]));
    Add(Format(SPageSize, [dwPageSize]));
    Add(Format(SMinAddr, [lpMinimumApplicationAddress]));
    Add(Format(SMaxAddr, [lpMaximumApplicationAddress]));
    Add(Format(SNumProcs, [dwNumberOfProcessors]));
    Add(Format(SAllocGra, [dwAllocationGranularity]));
    case wProcessorLevel of
      3: Add(Format(SProcLevl, [SIntel3]));
      4: Add(Format(SProcLevl, [SIntel4]));
      5: Add(Format(SProcLevl, [SIntel5]));
      6: Add(Format(SProcLevl, [SIntel6]));
```

14

SNOOPING
SYSTEM
INFORMATION

continues

LISTING **14.1.** CONTINUED

```
      else Add(Format(SProcLevl, [IntToStr(wProcessorLevel)]));
    end;
  end;
end;

procedure TInfoForm.GetDirInfo;
var
  S: array[0..MAX_PATH] of char;
begin
  { Get Windows directory }
  GetWindowsDirectory(S, SizeOf(S));
  InfoLB.Items.Add(Format(SWinDir, [S]));
  { Get Windows system directory }
  GetSystemDirectory(S, SizeOf(S));
  InfoLB.Items.Add(Format(SSysDir, [S]));
  { Get Current directory for current process }
  GetCurrentDirectory(SizeOf(S), S);
  InfoLB.Items.Add(Format(SCurDir, [S]));
end;

procedure TInfoForm.ShowSysInfo;
begin
  InfoLB.DelimChar := 'q';
  GetOSVerInfo;
  GetSysInfo;
  GetDirInfo;
  InfoLB.Sections[0].Text := 'Item';
  InfoLB.Sections[1].Text := 'Value';
  Caption:= 'System Information';
end;

procedure TInfoForm.ShowEnvironment;
var
  EnvPtr, SavePtr: PChar;
begin
  InfoLB.DelimChar := '=';
  EnvPtr := GetEnvironmentStrings;
  SavePtr := EnvPtr;
  InfoLB.Items.Clear;
  repeat
    InfoLB.Items.Add(StrPas(EnvPtr));
    inc(EnvPtr, StrLen(EnvPtr) + 1);
  until EnvPtr^ = #0;
  FreeEnvironmentStrings(SavePtr);
  InfoLB.Sections[0].Text := 'Environment Variable';
  InfoLB.Sections[1].Text := 'Value';
  Caption:= 'Current Environment';
end;

end.
```

PLATFORM-NEUTRAL DESIGN

SysInfo is designed to function under both Windows 95/98 and Windows NT, even though the different versions of Win32 have very different ways of accessing low-level information like processes and memory. The approach we took to enable platform-neutrality is to define an interface that contains methods that can obtain system information. This interface is then implemented for the two different operating systems. The interface is called IWin32Info, is pretty simple, and is shown here:

```
type
  IWin32Info = interface
    procedure FillProcessInfoList(ListView: TListView; ImageList:
    ➡TImageList);
    procedure ShowProcessProperties(Cookie: Pointer);
  end;
```

- FillProcessInfoList() is responsible for filling a TListView and TImageList with a list of running processes and their associated icon, if any.

- ShowProcessProperties() is called to obtain more information for a particular process selected in TListView.

In the SysInfo project, you'll find a unit called W95Info that contains a TWin95Info class that implements IWin32Info for Windows 95 using the ToolHelp32 API. Likewise, the project contains a WNTInfo unit with a TWinNTInfo class that takes advantage of PSAPI to implement IWin32Info. The following code segment, SysMain (which was taken from the project's main unit), shows how the proper class is created depending on the operating system:

```
if Win32Platform = VER_PLATFORM_WIN32_WINDOWS then
  FWinInfo := TWin95Info.Create
else if Win32Platform = VER_PLATFORM_WIN32_NT then
  FWinInfo := TWinNTInfo.Create
else
  raise Exception.Create('This application must be run on Win32');
```

WINDOWS 95/98: USING TOOLHELP32

ToolHelp32 is a collection of functions and procedures, part of the Win32 API, which enables you to see the status of some of the operation system's low-level operations. In particular, functions enable you to obtain information on all processes currently executing in the system and the threads, modules, and heaps that go with each of the processes. As you might guess, most of the information obtainable from ToolHelp32 is primarily used by applications that must look "inside" the OS, such as debuggers, although going through these functions gives even the average developer a better idea of how Win32 is put together.

14

NOTE

The ToolHelp32 API is available only under the Windows 95/98 implementation of Win32. This type of functionality would violate NT's robust process protection and security features. Therefore, applications that use ToolHelp32 functions will function only under Windows 95 and not Windows NT.

We say *ToolHelp32* to differentiate it from the 16-bit version of ToolHelp that was included in Windows 3.1*x*. Most of the functions in the previous version of ToolHelp no longer apply to Win32 and are therefore no longer supported. Also, under Windows 3.1*x*, the ToolHelp functions were physically located in a DLL called TOOLHELP.DLL, whereas ToolHelp32 functions reside in the kernel under Win32.

ToolHelp32 types and function definitions are located in the TlHelp32 unit, so be sure to have that in your uses clause when working with these functions. To ensure that you receive a solid overview, the application you build in this chapter uses every function defined in the TlHelp32 unit.

Figure 14.5 shows the main form for the SysInfo. The user interface consists primarily of TheaderListbox, a custom control explained in detail in Chapter 11, "Writing Multithreaded Applications." The list contains important information for a given process. By double-clicking a process in the list, you can obtain more detailed information about it. This detail is shown in a child form similar to the main form.

FIGURE 14.5.

SysInfo's *main form,* TMainForm.

Snapshots

Due to the multitasking nature of the Win32 environment, objects such as processes, threads, modules, and heaps are constantly being created, destroyed, and modified. Because the status of the machine is constantly in a state of flux, system information that might be meaningful now may have no meaning a second from now. For example, suppose you want to write a program to enumerate through all the modules loaded systemwide. Because the operating system might preempt the thread executing your program at any time in order to provide time slices to other threads in the system, modules theoretically can be created and destroyed even as you enumerate through them.

In this dynamic environment, it would make more sense if you could freeze the system in time for a moment in order to obtain such system information. Although ToolHelp32 doesn't provide a means for freezing the system in time, it does provide a function that enables you to take a snapshot of the system at a particular moment. `CreateToolhelp32Snapshot()` is that function and is declared as follows:

```
function CreateToolhelp32Snapshot(dwFlags, th32ProcessID: DWORD): THandle;
  stdcall;
```

- The `dwFlags` parameter indicates what type of information should be included in the snapshot. This parameter can have any one of the values shown in the following table:

Value	*Meaning*
TH32CS_INHERIT	Indicates that the snapshot handle will be inheritable.
TH32CS_SNAPALL	Equivalent to specifying the TH32CS_SNAPHEAPLIST, TH32CS_SNAPMODULE, TH32CS_SNAPPROCESS, and TH32CS_SNAPTHREAD values.
TH32CS_SNAPHEAPLIST	Includes the heap list of the specified Win32 process in the snapshot.
TH32CS_SNAPMODULE	Includes the module list of the specified Win32 process in the snapshot.
TH32CS_SNAPPROCESS	Includes the Win32 process list in the snapshot.
TH32CS_SNAPTHREAD	Includes the Win32 thread list in the snapshot.

- The `th32ProcessID` parameter identifies the process for which you want to obtain information. Pass zero in this parameter to indicate the current process. This parameter affects only module and heap lists, as they are process-specific. The process and thread lists provided by ToolHelp32 are systemwide.

- The `CreateToolhelp32Snapshot()` function returns the handle to a snapshot or −1 in case of an error. The handle returned works just as other Win32 handles do regarding the processes and threads for which it's valid.

14

SNOOPING
SYSTEM
INFORMATION

The following code creates a snapshot handle that contains information on all processes currently loaded systemwide (EToolHelpError is a programmer-defined exception):

```
var
  Snap: THandle;
begin
  Snap := CreateToolhelp32Snapshot(TH32CS_SNAPPROCESS, 0);
  if Snap = -1 then
    raise EToolHelpError.Create('CreateToolHelp32Snapshot failed');
end;
```

> **NOTE**
>
> When you're done using the handle, use the Win32 API CloseHandle() function to free resources associated with a handle created by CreateToolHelp32Snapshot().

Process Walking

Given a snapshot handle that includes process information, ToolHelp32 defines two functions that provide you with the capability of enumerating over (*walking*) processes. The functions, Process32First() and Process32Next(), are declared as follows:

```
function Process32First(hSnapshot: THandle;
    var lppe: TProcessEntry32): BOOL; stdcall;
function Process32Next(hSnapshot: THandle;
    var lppe: TProcessEntry32): BOOL; stdcall;
```

The first parameter to these functions, hSnapshot, is the snapshot handle returned by CreateToolHelp32Snapshot().

The second parameter, lppe, is a TProcessEntry32 record that's passed by reference. As you go through the enumeration, the functions will fill this record with information on the next process. The TProcessEntry32 record is defined as follows:

```
type
  TProcessEntry32 = record
    dwSize: DWORD;
    cntUsage: DWORD;
    th32ProcessID: DWORD;
    th32DefaultHeapID: DWORD;
    th32ModuleID: DWORD;
    cntThreads: DWORD;
    th32ParentProcessID: DWORD;
    pcPriClassBase: Longint;
    dwFlags: DWORD;
    szExeFile: array[0..MAX_PATH - 1] of Char;
  end;
```

- The dwSize field holds the size of the TProcessEntry32 record. This should be initialized to SizeOf(TProcessEntry32) prior to using the record.

- The cntUsage field indicates the reference count of the process. When the reference count is zero, the operating system will unload the process.

- The th32ProcessID field contains the identification number of the process.

- The th32DefaultHeapID field contains an identifier for the process's default heap. The ID has meaning only within ToolHelp32, and it can't be used with other Win32 functions.

- The thModuleID field identifies the module associated with the process. This field has meaning only within ToolHelp32 functions.

- The cntThreads field indicates how many threads of execution the process has started.

- The th32ParentProcessID identifies the parent process to this process.

- The pcPriClassBase field holds the base priority of the process. The operating system uses this value to manage thread scheduling.

- The dwFlags field is reserved; don't use it.

- The szExeFile field is a null-terminated string that contains the pathname and filename of the EXE or driver associated with the process.

After a snapshot containing process information has been taken, iterating over all processes is a matter of calling Process32First() and then calling Process32Next() until it returns False.

The process walking code is encapsulated in the TWin95Info class, which implements the IWin32Info interface. The following code listing shows the private Refresh() method of TWin95Info class, which iterates over the system processes and adds each to a list:

```
procedure TWin95Info.Refresh;
var
  PE: TProcessEntry32;
  PPE: PProcessEntry32;
begin
  FProcList.Clear;
  if FSnap > 0 then CloseHandle(FSnap);
  FSnap := CreateToolHelp32Snapshot(TH32CS_SNAPPROCESS, 0);
  if FSnap = -1 then
    raise Exception.Create('CreateToolHelp32Snapshot failed');
  PE.dwSize := SizeOf(PE);
  if Process32First(FSnap, PE) then         // get process
    repeat
      New(PPE);                             // create new PPE
      PPE^ := PE;                           // fill it
      FProcList.Add(PPE);                   // add it to list
    until not Process32Next(FSnap, PE);     // get next process
end;
```

14

SNOOPING
SYSTEM
INFORMATION

The Refresh()method is called by the FillProcessInfoList() method. As explained earlier, this method fills a TListView and TImageList with information on all the running processes, and it is shown here:

```
procedure TWin95Info.FillProcessInfoList(ListView: TListView;
  ImageList: TImageList);
var
  I: Integer;
  ExeFile: string;
  PE: TProcessEntry32;
  HAppIcon: HIcon;
begin
  Refresh;
  ListView.Columns.Clear;
  ListView.Items.Clear;
  for I := Low(ProcessInfoCaptions) to High(ProcessInfoCaptions) do
    with ListView.Columns.Add do
    begin
      if I = 0 then Width := 285
      else Width := 75;
      Caption := ProcessInfoCaptions[I];
    end;
  for I := 0 to FProcList.Count - 1 do
  begin
    PE := PProcessEntry32(FProcList.Items[I])^;
    HAppIcon := ExtractIcon(HInstance, PE.szExeFile, 0);
    try
      if HAppIcon = 0 then HAppIcon := FWinIcon;
      ExeFile := PE.szExeFile;
      if ListView.ViewStyle = vsList then
        ExeFile := ExtractFileName(ExeFile);
      // insert new item, set its caption, add subitems
      with ListView.Items.Add, SubItems do
      begin
        Caption := ExeFile;
        Data := FProcList.Items[I];
        Add(IntToStr(PE.cntThreads));
        Add(IntToHex(PE.th32ProcessID, 8));
        Add(IntToHex(PE.th32ParentProcessID, 8));
        if ImageList <> nil then
          ImageIndex := ImageList_AddIcon(ImageList.Handle, HAppIcon);
      end;
    finally
      if HAppIcon <> FWinIcon then DestroyIcon(HAppIcon);
    end;
  end;
end;
```

Figure 14.6 shows this code in action, displaying process information of a Windows 95 machine.

FIGURE 14.6.

*Viewing processes
under Windows 95.*

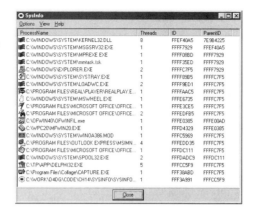

Not to be ignored is the code that obtains an icon for each process. Displaying the icon
along with the application name gives the application a more professional appearance
and a more native Windows feel. The `ExtractIcon()` API function from the `ShellAPI`
unit attempts to extract the icon from the application file. If `ExtractIcon()` fails,
`HWinIcon` is used instead. `HWinIcon` is the standard Windows icon, and it has been pre-
loaded in the `OnCreate` event handler for this form using the `LoadImage()` API function:

```
FWinIcon := LoadImage(0, IDI_WINLOGO, IMAGE_ICON, LR_DEFAULTSIZE,
  LR_DEFAULTSIZE, LR_DEFAULTSIZE or LR_DEFAULTCOLOR or LR_SHARED);
```

When the user double-clicks one of the processes in the main form (refer to Figure 14.6),
the `ShowProcessProperties()`method of `IWin32Info` is called, and the implementation
of this method passes the parameter on to a method in the `Detail95` unit called
`ShowProcessDetails()`:

```
procedure TWin95Info.ShowProcessProperties(Cookie: Pointer);
begin
  ShowProcessDetails(PProcessEntry32(Cookie));
end;
```

`ShowProcessDetails()` must take another snapshot with `CreateToolHelp32Snapshot()` in
order to obtain a snapshot of information for the selected process. This is done by passing
the `Cookie` parameter (which holds the process, ID in this case) to the chosen process as
the `th32ProcessID` field for `CreateToolHelp32Snapshot()`. The `TH32CS_SNAPALL` flag is

14

passed as the dwFlags parameter to put all the information into the snapshot as shown in the following snippet:

```
{ Create a snapshot for the current process }
FCurSnap := CreateToolhelp32Snapshot(TH32CS_SNAPALL, P^.th32ProcessID);
if FCurSnap = -1 then
  raise EToolHelpError.Create('CreateToolHelp32Snapshot failed');
```

The TDetailForm object displays only one list at a time. An enumerated type keeps track of which list is which:

```
type
  TListType = (ltThread, ltModule, ltHeap);
```

TDetailForm also maintains three separate TStringLists for each of the threads, modules, and heaps. These lists are defined as part of an array called DetailLists:

```
DetailLists: array[TListType] of TStringList;
```

Thread Walking

To walk a process's thread list, ToolHelp32 provides two functions similar to those for process walking: Thread32First() and Thread32Next(). These functions are declared as follows:

```
function Thread32First(hSnapshot: THandle;
  var lpte: TThreadEntry32): BOOL; stdcall;

function Thread32Next(hSnapshot: THandle;
  var lpte: TThreadENtry32): BOOL; stdcall;
```

In addition to the usual hSnapshot parameter, these functions also accept a parameter by reference of type TThreadEntry32. As for the process functions, the calling function fills in this record. The TThreadEntry32 record is defined as follows:

```
type
  TThreadEntry32 = record
    dwSize: DWORD;
    cntUsage: DWORD;
    th32ThreadID: DWORD;
    th32OwnerProcessID: DWORD;
    tpBasePri: Longint;
    tpDeltaPri: Longint;
    dwFlags: DWORD;
  end;
```

- dwSize is the size of the record, and it should be initialized to
  SizeOf(TThreadEntry32) prior to using the record.

- cntUsage is the reference count of the thread. When this value reaches zero, the thread is unloaded by the operating system.

- th32ThreadID is the identification number of the thread. This value has meaning only within the ToolHelp32 functions.

- th32OwnerProcessID is the identifier of the process that owns this thread. This ID can be used with other Win32 functions.

- tpBasePri is the base priority class of the thread. This value is the same for all threads of a given process. The possible values for this field are usually in the range of 4 through 24. The following table lists the meaning of each value:

Value	Meaning
4	Idle
8	Normal
13	High
24	Real time

- tpDeltaPri is the *delta* (change in) *priority* from tpBasePri. It's a signed number that, when combined with the base priority class, reveals the overall priority of the thread. The following table shows the constants defined for each possible value:

Constant	Value
THREAD_PRIORITY_IDLE	-15
THREAD_PRIORITY_LOWEST	-2
THREAD_PRIORITY_BELOW_NORMAL	-1
THREAD_PRIORITY_NORMAL	0
THREAD_PRIORITY_ABOVE_NORMAL	1
THREAD_PRIORITY_HIGHEST	2
THREAD_PRIORITY_TIME_CRITICAL	15

- dwFlags is currently reserved and shouldn't be used.

The WalkThreads() method of TDetailForm is used to walk the thread list. As the thread list is traversed, important information about the thread is added to the thread element of the DetailLists array. The code for this method is as follows:

```
procedure TWin95DetailForm.WalkThreads;
{ Uses ToolHelp32 functions to walk list of threads }
var
  T: TThreadEntry32;
begin
  DetailLists[ltThread].Clear;
  T.dwSize := SizeOf(T);
  if Thread32First(FCurSnap, T) then
    repeat
      { Make sure thread is for current process }
      if T.th32OwnerProcessID = FCurProc.th32ProcessID then
```

14

```
        DetailLists[ltThread].Add(Format(SThreadStr, [T.th32ThreadID,
          GetClassPriorityString(T.tpBasePri),
          GetThreadPriorityString(T.tpDeltaPri), T.cntUsage]));
    until not Thread32Next(FCurSnap, T);
end;
```

NOTE

The following line of code in the WalkThreads() method is important because ToolHelp32 thread lists are not process-specific:

`if T.th32OwnerProcessID = FCurProc.th32ProcessID then`

You must therefore do a manual comparison as you iterate through the threads to determine which threads are associated with the process in question.

Figure 14.7 shows the detail form with the thread list visible.

FIGURE 14.7.

Viewing Windows 95 threads in the detail form.

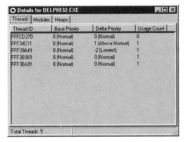

Module Walking

Module walking works much the same as process and thread walking. ToolHelp32 provides two functions that do the work: Module32First() and Module32Next(). These functions are declared as follows:

```
function Module32First(hSnapshot: THandle;
  var lpme: TModuleEntry32): BOOL; stdcall;

function Module32Next(hSnapshot: THandle;
  var lpme: TModuleEntry32): BOOL; stdcall;
```

Again, the snapshot handle is the first parameter to the functions. The second var parameter, lpme, is a TModuleEntry32 record. This record is defined as follows:

```
type
  TModuleEntry32 = record
    dwSize: DWORD;
    th32ModuleID: DWORD;
    th32ProcessID: DWORD;
    GlblcntUsage: DWORD;
    ProccntUsage: DWORD;
    modBaseAddr: PBYTE;
    modBaseSize: DWORD;
    hModule: HMODULE;
    szModule: array[0..MAX_MODULE_NAME32 + 1] of Char;
    szExePath: array[0..MAX_PATH - 1] of Char;
  end;
```

- dwSize is the size of the record, and it should be initialized to SizeOf(TModuleEntry32) prior to using the record.

- th32ModuleID is the identifier of the module. This value has meaning only with ToolHelp32 functions.

- th32ProcessID is the identifier of the process being examined. This value can be used with other Win32 functions.

- GlblcntUsage is the global reference count of the module.

- ProccntUsage is the reference count of the module within the context of the owning process.

- modBaseAddr is the base address of the module in memory. This value is valid only within the context of th32ProcessID's context.

- modBaseSize is the size in bytes of the module in memory.

- hModule is the module handle. This value is valid only within th32ProcessID's context.

- szModule is a null-terminated string containing the module name.

- szExepath is a null-terminated string containing the full path of the module.

The WalkModules() method of TDetailForm is very similar to its WalkThreads() method. As shown in the following code, this method traverses the module list and adds it to the module list portion of the DetailLists array:

```
procedure TWin95DetailForm.WalkModules;
{ Uses ToolHelp32 functions to walk list of modules }
var
  M: TModuleEntry32;
begin
  DetailLists[ltModule].Clear;
  M.dwSize := SizeOf(M);
  if Module32First(FCurSnap, M) then
```

```
    repeat
      DetailLists[ltModule].Add(Format(SModuleStr, [M.szModule,
    ➡M.ModBaseAddr,
        M.ModBaseSize, M.ProcCntUsage]));
    until not Module32Next(FCurSnap, M);
end;
```

Figure 14.8 shows the detail form with the module list visible.

FIGURE 14.8.

*Viewing Windows
95 modules in the
detail form.*

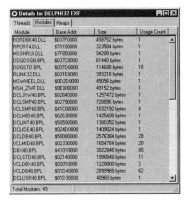

Heap Walking

Heap walking is slightly more complicated than the other types of enumeration you've learned about in this chapter. ToolHelp32 provides four functions that enable heap walking. The first two functions, `Heap32ListFirst()` and `Heap32ListNext()`, enable you to iterate over each of a process's heaps. The other two functions, `Heap32First()` and `Heap32Next()`, enable you to obtain more detailed information on all the blocks within an individual heap.

`Heap32ListFirst()` and `Heap32ListNext()` are defined as follows:

```
function Heap32ListFirst(hSnapshot: THandle;
  var lphl: THeapList32): BOOL; stdcall;

function Heap32ListNext(hSnapshot: THandle;
  var lphl: THeapList32): BOOL; stdcall;
```

Again, the first parameter is the customary snapshot handle. The second parameter, `lphl`, is a `THeapList32` record that's passed by reference. This record is defined as follows:

```
type
  THeapList32 = record
    dwSize: DWORD;
    th32ProcessID: DWORD;
    th32HeapID: DWORD;
    dwFlags: DWORD;
  end;
```

- dwSize is the size of the record, and it should be initialized to SizeOf(THeapList32) prior to using the record.

- th32ProcessID is the identifier of the owning process.

- th32HeapID is the identifier of the heap. This value has meaning only for the specified process and within ToolHelp32.

- dwFlags holds a flag that determines the heap type. The value of this field can be either HF32_DEFAULT, which means that the current heap is the process's default heap, or HF32_SHARED, which means that the current heap is a normal shared heap.

The Heap32First() and Heap32Next() functions are defined as follows:

```
function Heap32First(var lphe: THeapEntry32; th32ProcessID,
  th32HeapID: DWORD): BOOL; stdcall;

function Heap32Next(var lphe: THeapEntry32): BOOL; stdcall;
```

Notice that the parameter lists of these functions are a bit of a departure from the process, thread, module, and heap list enumeration functions that you've learned about in this chapter. These functions are designed to enumerate the blocks of a given heap in a given process rather than enumerating over some properties of just a process. When calling Heap32First(), the th32ProcessID and th32HeapID parameters should be set to the values of the field of the same name of the THeapList32 record filled by Heap32ListFirst() or Heap32ListNext(). The lphe var parameter of Heap32First() and Heap32Next() is of type THeapEntry32. This record contains descriptive information pertaining to the heap block, and is defined as follows:

```
type
  THeapEntry32 = record
    dwSize: DWORD;
    hHandle: THandle;        // Handle of this heap block
    dwAddress: DWORD;        // Linear address of start of block
    dwBlockSize: DWORD;      // Size of block in bytes
    dwFlags: DWORD;
    dwLockCount: DWORD;
    dwResvd: DWORD;
    th32ProcessID: DWORD;    // owning process
    th32HeapID: DWORD;       // heap block is in
  end;
```

14

- dwSize is the size of the record, and it should be initialized to SizeOf(THeapEntry32) prior to using the record.

- hHandle is the handle of the heap block.

- dwAddress is the linear address of the start of the heap block.

- dwBlockSize is the size in bytes of this heap block.

- dwFlags describes the type of heap block. This field can have any of the values shown in the following table:

Value	Meaning
LF32_FIXED	The memory block has a fixed (unmovable) location.
LF32_FREE	The memory block is not used.
LF32_MOVEABLE	The memory block location can be moved.

- dwLockCount is the lock count of the memory block. This value is increased by one every time the process calls GlobalLock() or LocalLock() on this block.

- dwResvd is reserved at this time and shouldn't be used.

- th32ProcessID is the identifier of the owning process.

- th32HeapID is the identifier of the heap to which the block belongs.

Because you must first walk the list of heap lists before you can walk the heap block list, the code for heap block walking is a bit—but not much—more complex than what you've seen so far. As you see in the TDetailForm.WalkHeaps() method that follows, the trick is to nest the Heap32First()/Heap32Next() loop within the Heap32ListFirst()/Heap32ListNext() loop. The method adds an additional level of complexity by adding a PHeapEntry32 record pointer to the objects in the heap list portion of the DetailLists array. This is done so that information on the heap is available later when viewing heap contents:

```
procedure TWin95DetailForm.WalkHeaps;
{ Uses ToolHelp32 functions to walk list of heaps }
var
  HL: THeapList32;
  HE: THeapEntry32;
  PHE: PHeapEntry32;
begin
  DetailLists[ltHeap].Clear;
  HL.dwSize := SizeOf(HL);
  HE.dwSize := SizeOf(HE);
  if Heap32ListFirst(FCurSnap, HL) then
    repeat
      if Heap32First(HE, HL.th32ProcessID, HL.th32HeapID) then
        repeat
```

```
        New(PHE);      // need to make copy of THeapList32 record so we
        PHE^ := HE;    // have enough info to view heap later
        DetailLists[ltHeap].AddObject(Format(SHeapStr, [HL.th32HeapID,
          Pointer(HE.dwAddress), HE.dwBlockSize,
          GetHeapFlagString(HE.dwFlags)]), TObject(PHE));
      until not Heap32Next(HE);
    until not Heap32ListNext(FCurSnap, HL);
  HeapListAlloc := True;
end;
```

Figure 14.9 shows the detail form with the heap block list visible.

FIGURE 14.9.

Viewing Windows 95 heap blocks in the detail form.

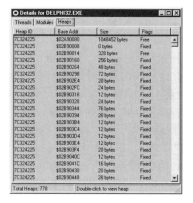

Heap Viewing

Up to this point, you've learned about every function in the ToolHelp32 API except for one: `ToolHelp32ReadProcessMemory()`. To make sure you finish this chapter with a warm, fuzzy feeling, you'll also learn about this function.

`ToolHelp32ReadProcessMemory()` is declared this way:

```
function Toolhelp32ReadProcessMemory(th32ProcessID: DWORD;
  lpBaseAddress: Pointer; var lpBuffer; cbRead: DWORD;
  var lpNumberOfBytesRead: DWORD): BOOL; stdcall;
```

This function is arguably the most powerful and definitely the most fun in ToolHelp32 because it actually allows you to peek into the memory space of another process. The parameters for this function are as follows:

- `th32ProcessID` is the identifier of the process whose memory you want to read. You can obtain this value by any of the ToolHelp32 enumeration functions. You can pass zero in this parameter to indicate the current process.

- `lpBaseAddress` is the linear address of the first byte of memory you want to read in process `th32ProcessID`. You need to use the right process with the right address because any given linear address is meaningful only to a particular process.

- `lpBuffer` is the buffer to which you want to copy process `th32ProcessID`'s memory. You must ensure that memory is allocated for this buffer.

- `cbRead` is the number of bytes to read from process `th32ProcessID`, starting at `lpBaseAddress`.

- `lpNumberOfBytesRead` is filled in by the function before it returns. This is the number of bytes actually read from process `th32ProcessID`.

Once the memory of a particular process is copied to a local buffer using this function, `SysInfo` shows another modal form, `HeapViewForm`, which formats the memory dump for viewing. To handle the formatting, `HeapViewForm` makes use of a custom component called `TddgMemView` for viewing a memory dump. Because discussing the internals of the `TddgMemView` control is off the topic for this chapter (and because the control isn't terribly complex), you can browse the source code for the control on this book's CD-ROM. The following method of `TDetailForm`, `DetailLBDblClick()`, is called when the user double-clicks in the `THeaderListbox` `DetailLB`:

```
procedure TWin95DetailForm.DetailLBDblClick(Sender: TObject);
{ This procedure is called when the user double clicks on an item }
{ in DetailLB.  If the current tab page is heaps, a heap view      }
{ form is presented to the user. }
var
  NumRead: DWORD;
  HE: THeapEntry32;
  MemSize: integer;
begin
  inherited;
  if DetailTabs.TabIndex = 2 then
  begin
    HE := PHeapEntry32(DetailLB.Items.Objects[DetailLB.ItemIndex])^;
    MemSize := HE.dwBlockSize;        // get heap size
    { if heap is too big, use ProcMemMaxSize }
    if MemSize > ProcMemMaxSize then MemSize := ProcMemMaxSize;
    ProcMem := AllocMem(MemSize);     // allocate a temp buffer
    Screen.Cursor := crHourGlass;
    try
      { Copy heap into temp buffer }
      if Toolhelp32ReadProcessMemory(FCurProc.th32ProcessID,
        Pointer(HE.dwAddress), ProcMem^, MemSize, NumRead) then
        { point HeapView control at temp buffer }
        ShowHeapView(ProcMem, MemSize)
      else
        MessageDlg(SHeapReadErr, mtInformation, [mbOk], 0);
    finally
```

```
      Screen.Cursor := crDefault;
      FreeMem(ProcMem, MemSize);
    end;
  end;
end;
```

This method first checks to see whether the current tab page is the heap list page. If so, it allocates a temporary buffer and passes it to the `ToolHelp32ReadProcessMemory()` function to be filled. After the buffer is filled, it is displayed in the `TddgMemView` control `HeapView`, and `HeapViewForm` is shown modally. When the form returns from the `ShowModal()` call, the buffer is freed. Figure 14.10 shows a heap view in action.

FIGURE 14.10.

Viewing the heap of another Windows 95 process.

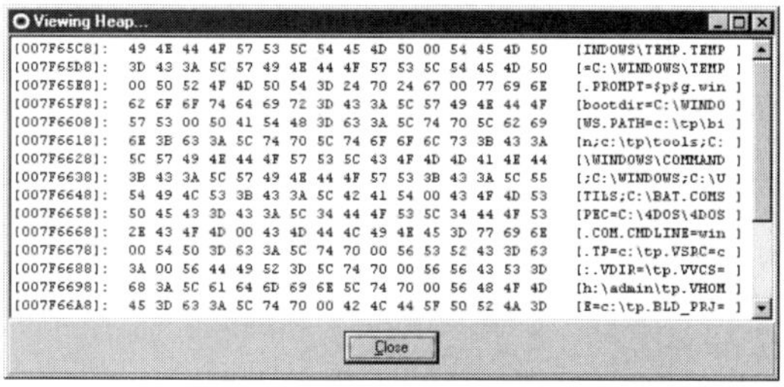

The Source

Listings 14.2 and 14.3 show the complete source for the `W95Info.pas` and `Detail95.pas` units respectively.

LISTING 14.2. `W95Info.pas`.

```pascal
unit W95Info;

interface

uses Windows, InfoInt, Classes, TlHelp32, Controls, ComCtrls;

type
  TWin95Info = class(TInterfacedObject, IWin32Info)
  private
    FProcList: TList;
    FWinIcon: HICON;
    FSnap: THandle;
    procedure Refresh;
```

continues

LISTING 14.2. CONTINUED

```
  public
    constructor Create;
    destructor Destroy; override;
    procedure FillProcessInfoList(ListView: TListView; ImageList:
      TImageList);
    procedure ShowProcessProperties(Cookie: Pointer);
  end;

implementation

uses ShellAPI, CommCtrl, SysUtils, Detail95;

const
  ProcessInfoCaptions: array[0..3] of string = (
    'ProcessName', 'Threads', 'ID', 'ParentID');

{ TProcList }

type
  TProcList = class(TList)
    procedure Clear; override;
  end;

procedure TProcList.Clear;
var
  I: Integer;
begin
  for I := 0 to Count - 1 do Dispose(PProcessEntry32(Items[I]));
  inherited Clear;
end;

{ TWin95Info }

constructor TWin95Info.Create;
begin
  FProcList := TProcList.Create;
  FWinIcon := LoadImage(0, IDI_WINLOGO, IMAGE_ICON, LR_DEFAULTSIZE,
    LR_DEFAULTSIZE, LR_DEFAULTSIZE or LR_DEFAULTCOLOR or LR_SHARED);
end;

destructor TWin95Info.Destroy;
begin
  DestroyIcon(FWinIcon);
  if FSnap > 0 then CloseHandle(FSnap);
  FProcList.Free;
  inherited Destroy;
end;
```

```
procedure TWin95Info.FillProcessInfoList(ListView: TListView;
  ImageList: TImageList);
var
  I: Integer;
  ExeFile: string;
  PE: TProcessEntry32;
  HAppIcon: HIcon;
begin
  Refresh;
  ListView.Columns.Clear;
  ListView.Items.Clear;
  for I := Low(ProcessInfoCaptions) to High(ProcessInfoCaptions) do
    with ListView.Columns.Add do
    begin
      if I = 0 then Width := 285
      else Width := 75;
      Caption := ProcessInfoCaptions[I];
    end;
  for I := 0 to FProcList.Count - 1 do
  begin
    PE := PProcessEntry32(FProcList.Items[I])^;
    HAppIcon := ExtractIcon(HInstance, PE.szExeFile, 0);
    try
      if HAppIcon = 0 then HAppIcon := FWinIcon;
      ExeFile := PE.szExeFile;
      if ListView.ViewStyle = vsList then
        ExeFile := ExtractFileName(ExeFile);
      // insert new item, set its caption, add subitems
      with ListView.Items.Add, SubItems do
      begin
        Caption := ExeFile;
        Data := FProcList.Items[I];
        Add(IntToStr(PE.cntThreads));
        Add(IntToHex(PE.th32ProcessID, 8));
        Add(IntToHex(PE.th32ParentProcessID, 8));
        if ImageList <> nil then
          ImageIndex := ImageList_AddIcon(ImageList.Handle, HAppIcon);
      end;
    finally
      if HAppIcon <> FWinIcon then DestroyIcon(HAppIcon);
    end;
  end;
end;

procedure TWin95Info.Refresh;
var
  PE: TProcessEntry32;
  PPE: PProcessEntry32;
```

14

SNOOPING
SYSTEM
INFORMATION

continues

LISTING 14.2. CONTINUED

```pascal
begin
  FProcList.Clear;
  if FSnap > 0 then CloseHandle(FSnap);
  FSnap := CreateToolHelp32Snapshot(TH32CS_SNAPPROCESS, 0);
  if FSnap = -1 then
    raise Exception.Create('CreateToolHelp32Snapshot failed');
  PE.dwSize := SizeOf(PE);
  if Process32First(FSnap, PE) then            // get process
    repeat
      New(PPE);                                // create new PPE
      PPE^ := PE;                              // fill it
      FProcList.Add(PPE);                      // add it to list
    until not Process32Next(FSnap, PE);        // get next process
end;

procedure TWin95Info.ShowProcessProperties(Cookie: Pointer);
begin
  ShowProcessDetails(PProcessEntry32(Cookie));
end;

end.
```

LISTING 14.3. Detail95.pas.

```pascal
unit Detail95;

interface

uses
  Windows, Messages, SysUtils, Classes, Graphics, Controls, Forms, Dialogs,
  StdCtrls, ComCtrls, HeadList, TlHelp32, Menus, SysMain, DetBase;

type
  TListType = (ltThread, ltModule, ltHeap);

  TWin95DetailForm = class(TBaseDetailForm)
    procedure DetailTabsChange(Sender: TObject);
    procedure FormCreate(Sender: TObject);
    procedure FormDestroy(Sender: TObject);
    procedure DetailLBDblClick(Sender: TObject);
  private
    FCurSnap: THandle;
    FCurProc: TProcessEntry32;
    DetailLists: array[TListType] of TStringList;
    ProcMem: PByte;
    HeapListAlloc: Boolean;
    procedure FreeHeapList;
    procedure ShowList(ListType: TListType);
```

```
    procedure WalkThreads;
    procedure WalkHeaps;
    procedure WalkModules;
  public
    procedure NewProcess(P: PProcessEntry32);
  end;

procedure ShowProcessDetails(P: PProcessEntry32);

implementation

{$R *.DFM}

uses ProcMem;

const
  { Array of strings which goes into the header of each respective list. }
  HeaderStrs: array[TListType] of TDetailStrings = (
      ('Thread ID', 'Base Priority', 'Delta Priority', 'Usage Count'),
      ('Module', 'Base Addr', 'Size', 'Usage Count'),
      ('Heap ID', 'Base Addr', 'Size', 'Flags'));

  { Array of strings which goes into the footer of each list. }
  ACountStrs: array[TListType] of string[31] = (
      'Total Threads: %d', 'Total Modules: %d', 'Total Heaps: %d');

  TabStrs: array[TListType] of string[7] = ('Threads', 'Modules', 'Heaps');

  SCaptionStr  = 'Details for %s';        // form caption
  SThreadStr   = '%x'#1'%s'#1'%s'#1'%d'; // id, base pri, delta pri, usage
  SModuleStr   = '%s'#1'$%p'#1'%d bytes'#1'%d'; // name, addr, size, usage
  SHeapStr     = '%x'#1'$%p'#1'%d bytes'#1'%s'; // ID, addr, size, flags
  SHeapReadErr = 'This heap is not accessible for read access.';

  ProcMemMaxSize = $7FFE;               // max size of heap view

procedure ShowProcessDetails(P: PProcessEntry32);
var
  I: TListType;
begin
  with TWin95DetailForm.Create(Application) do
    try
      for I := Low(TabStrs) to High(TabStrs) do
        DetailTabs.Tabs.Add(TabStrs[I]);
      NewProcess(P);
      Font := MainForm.Font;
      ShowModal;
    finally
      Free;
    end;
end;
```

continues

LISTING 14.3. CONTINUED

```pascal
function GetThreadPriorityString(Priority: DWORD): string;
{ Returns string describing thread priority }
begin
  case Priority of
    THREAD_PRIORITY_IDLE:          Result := '%d (Idle)';
    THREAD_PRIORITY_LOWEST:        Result := '%d (Lowest)';
    THREAD_PRIORITY_BELOW_NORMAL:  Result := '%d (Below Normal)';
    THREAD_PRIORITY_NORMAL:        Result := '%d (Normal)';
    THREAD_PRIORITY_ABOVE_NORMAL:  Result := '%d (Above Normal)';
    THREAD_PRIORITY_HIGHEST:       Result := '%d (Highest)';
    THREAD_PRIORITY_TIME_CRITICAL: Result := '%d (Time critical)';
  else
    Result := '%d (unknown)';
  end;
  Result := Format(Result, [Priority]);
end;

function GetClassPriorityString(Priority: DWORD): String;
{ returns string describing process priority class }
begin
  case Priority of
    4:  Result := '%d (Idle)';
    8:  Result := '%d (Normal)';
    13: Result := '%d (High)';
    24: Result := '%d (Real time)';
  else
    Result := '%d (non-standard)';
  end;
  Result := Format(Result, [Priority]);
end;

function GetHeapFlagString(Flag: DWORD): String;
{ Returns a string describing a heap flag }
begin
  case Flag of
    LF32_FIXED:    Result := 'Fixed';
    LF32_FREE:     Result := 'Free';
    LF32_MOVEABLE: Result := 'Moveable';
  end;
end;

procedure TWin95DetailForm.ShowList(ListType: TListType);
{ Shows appropriate thread, heap, or module list in DetailLB }
var
  i: Integer;
begin
  Screen.Cursor := crHourGlass;
  try
    with DetailLB do
```

```
    begin
      for i := 0 to 3 do
        Sections[i].Text := HeaderStrs[ListType, i];
      Items.Clear;
      Items.Assign(DetailLists[ListType]);
    end;
    DetailSB.Panels[0].Text := Format(ACountStrs[ListType],
      [DetailLists[ListType].Count]);
    if ListType = ltHeap then
      DetailSB.Panels[1].Text := 'Double-click to view heap'
    else
      DetailSB.Panels[1].Text := '';
  finally
    Screen.Cursor := crDefault;
  end;
end;

procedure TWin95DetailForm.WalkThreads;
{ Uses ToolHelp32 functions to walk list of threads }
var
  T: TThreadEntry32;
begin
  DetailLists[ltThread].Clear;
  T.dwSize := SizeOf(T);
  if Thread32First(FCurSnap, T) then
    repeat
      { Make sure thread is for current process }
      if T.th32OwnerProcessID = FCurProc.th32ProcessID then
        DetailLists[ltThread].Add(Format(SThreadStr, [T.th32ThreadID,
          GetClassPriorityString(T.tpBasePri),
          GetThreadPriorityString(T.tpDeltaPri), T.cntUsage]));
    until not Thread32Next(FCurSnap, T);
end;

procedure TWin95DetailForm.WalkModules;
{ Uses ToolHelp32 functions to walk list of modules }
var
  M: TModuleEntry32;
begin
  DetailLists[ltModule].Clear;
  M.dwSize := SizeOf(M);
  if Module32First(FCurSnap, M) then
    repeat
      DetailLists[ltModule].Add(Format(SModuleStr, [M.szModule,
        M.ModBaseAddr, M.ModBaseSize, M.ProcCntUsage]));
    until not Module32Next(FCurSnap, M);
end;
```

14

continues

LISTING 14.3. CONTINUED

```pascal
procedure TWin95DetailForm.WalkHeaps;
{ Uses ToolHelp32 functions to walk list of heaps }
var
  HL: THeapList32;
  HE: THeapEntry32;
  PHE: PHeapEntry32;
begin
  DetailLists[ltHeap].Clear;
  HL.dwSize := SizeOf(HL);
  HE.dwSize := SizeOf(HE);
  if Heap32ListFirst(FCurSnap, HL) then
    repeat
      if Heap32First(HE, HL.th32ProcessID, HL.th32HeapID) then
        repeat
          New(PHE);      // need to make copy of THeapList32 record so we
          PHE^ := HE;    // have enough info to view heap later
          DetailLists[ltHeap].AddObject(Format(SHeapStr, [HL.th32HeapID,
            Pointer(HE.dwAddress), HE.dwBlockSize,
            GetHeapFlagString(HE.dwFlags)]), TObject(PHE));
        until not Heap32Next(HE);
    until not Heap32ListNext(FCurSnap, HL);
  HeapListAlloc := True;
end;

procedure TWin95DetailForm.FreeHeapList;
{ Since special allocation of PHeapList32 objects are added to the list, }
{ these must be freed. }
var
  i: integer;
begin
  for i := 0 to DetailLists[ltHeap].Count - 1 do
    Dispose(PHeapEntry32(DetailLists[ltHeap].Objects[i]));
end;

procedure TWin95DetailForm.NewProcess(P: PProcessEntry32);
{ This procedure is called from the main form to show the detail }
{ form for a particular process. }
begin
  { Create a snapshot for the current process }
  FCurSnap := CreateToolhelp32Snapshot(TH32CS_SNAPALL, P^.th32ProcessID);
  if FCurSnap = -1 then
    raise Exception.Create('CreateToolHelp32Snapshot failed');
  HeapListAlloc := False;
  Screen.Cursor := crHourGlass;
  try
    FCurProc := P^;
    { Include module name in detail form caption }
    Caption := Format(SCaptionStr, [ExtractFileName(FCurProc.szExeFile)]);
    WalkThreads;                         // walk ToolHelp32 lists
```

```
    WalkModules;
    WalkHeaps;
    DetailTabs.TabIndex := 0;        // 0 = thread tab
    ShowList(ltThread);              // show thread page first
  finally
    Screen.Cursor := crDefault;
    if HeapListAlloc then FreeHeapList;
    CloseHandle(FCurSnap);           // close snapshot handle
  end;
end;

procedure TWin95DetailForm.DetailTabsChange(Sender: TObject);
{ OnChange event handler for tab set.  Sets visible list to jibe with tabs.
}
begin
  inherited;
  ShowList(TListType(DetailTabs.TabIndex));
end;

procedure TWin95DetailForm.FormCreate(Sender: TObject);
var
  LT: TListType;
begin
  inherited;
  { Dispose of lists }
  for LT := Low(TListType) to High(TListType) do
    DetailLists[LT] := TStringList.Create;
end;

procedure TWin95DetailForm.FormDestroy(Sender: TObject);
var
  LT: TListType;
begin
  inherited;
  { Dispose of lists }
  for LT := Low(TListType) to High(TListType) do
    DetailLists[LT].Free;
end;

procedure TWin95DetailForm.DetailLBDblClick(Sender: TObject);
{ This procedure is called when the user-double clicks on an item }
{ in DetailLB.  If the current tab page is heaps, a heap view     }
{ form is presented to the user. }
var
  NumRead: DWORD;
  HE: THeapEntry32;
  MemSize: integer;
begin
  inherited;
  if DetailTabs.TabIndex = 2 then
```

continues

Listing 14.3. CONTINUED

```
begin
  HE := PHeapEntry32(DetailLB.Items.Objects[DetailLB.ItemIndex])^;
  MemSize := HE.dwBlockSize;          // get heap size
  { if heap is too big, use ProcMemMaxSize }
  if MemSize > ProcMemMaxSize then MemSize := ProcMemMaxSize;
  ProcMem := AllocMem(MemSize);       // allocate a temp buffer
  Screen.Cursor := crHourGlass;
  try
    { Copy heap into temp buffer }
    if Toolhelp32ReadProcessMemory(FCurProc.th32ProcessID,
      Pointer(HE.dwAddress), ProcMem^, MemSize, NumRead) then
      { point HeapView control at temp buffer }
      ShowHeapView(ProcMem, MemSize)
    else
      MessageDlg(SHeapReadErr, mtInformation, [mbOk], 0);
  finally
    Screen.Cursor := crDefault;
    FreeMem(ProcMem, MemSize);
  end;
  end;
end;

end.
```

WINDOWS NT: PSAPI

As we mentioned earlier, the ToolHelp32 API does not exist under Windows NT. The Windows NT SDK, however, provides a DLL called PSAPI.DLL from which you can obtain the same types of information as with ToolHelp32, including the following:

- Running processes
- Modules loaded per process
- Loaded device drivers
- Process memory information
- Files memory mapped per process

Later versions of Windows NT include PSAPI.DLL, although you can redistribute this file if you want to deploy it to the users of your applications. Delphi provides an interface unit for this DLL called PSAPI.pas, which loads all its functions dynamically. Therefore, applications that use this unit will run on machines with or without PSAPI.DLL. (Of course, the functions won't work without PSAPI.DLL installed, but the application will run.)

The first step in obtaining process information using PSAPI is to call the
EnumProcesses(), which is defined as follows:

```
function EnumProcesses(lpidProcess: LPDWORD; cb: DWORD;
  var cbNeeded: DWORD): BOOL;
```

- lpidProcess is a pointer to an array of DWORDs that will be filled in with process
  IDs by the function.

- cb contains the number of DWORDs in the array passed in lpidProcess.

- Upon return, cbNeeded will hold the number of bytes copied into lpidProcess.
  The expression cbNeeded div SizeOf(DWORD) will provide the number of elements copied into the array, and therefore the number of running processes.

After calling this function, the array passed in lpidProcess will contain many process
IDs. Process IDs aren't particularly useful on their own, but you can pass a process ID to
the OpenProcess() API function in order to obtain a process handle. After you have a
process handle, you can call other PSAPI functions or even other Win32 API functions
that call for process handles.

PSAPI provides a similar function for obtaining information on loaded device drivers
called—we'll give you one guess—EnumDeviceDrivers(). This method is defined as the
following:

```
function EnumDeviceDrivers(lpImageBase: PPointer; cb: DWORD;
  var lpcbNeeded: DWORD): BOOL;
```

- lpImageBase is a pointer to an array of Pointers that will be filled with the base
  address of each device driver.

- cb contains the number of Pointers in the array passed in lpImageBase.

- Upon return, lpcbNeeded will hold the number of bytes copied to lpImageBase.

In the SysInfo project ID, a unit called WNTInfo.pas contains a class called TWinNTInfo
that implements IWin32Info. This class contains a private method called Refresh(),
which obtains process and device driver information:

```
procedure TWinNTInfo.Refresh;
var
  Count: DWORD;
  BigArray: array[0..$3FFF - 1] of DWORD;
begin
  // Get array of process IDs
  if not EnumProcesses(@BigArray, SizeOf(BigArray), Count) then
    raise Exception.Create(SFailMessage);
  SetLength(FProcList, Count div SizeOf(DWORD));
  Move(BigArray, FProcList[0], Count);
  // Get array of Driver addresses
  if not EnumDeviceDrivers(@BigArray, SizeOf(BigArray), Count) then
```

```
    raise Exception.Create(SFailMessage);
  SetLength(FDrvList, Count div SizeOf(DWORD));
  Move(BigArray, FDrvList[0], Count);
end;
```

This method initially passes a local called BigArray to EnumProcesses() and
EnumDeviceDrivers() and then moves the data from BigArray into dynamic arrays
called FProcList and FDrvList. The reason for this ungainly implementation of these
functions is that neither EnumProcesses() nor EnumDeviceDrivers() provides a means
for determining how many elements will be returned before allocating an array. We are
therefore stuck passing a large array (that we hope is large enough) to the methods and
copying the result to an appropriately sized dynamic array.

The FillProcessInfoList() method for TWinNTInfo calls into two helper methods:
FillProcesses() and FillDrivers() to fill the contents of the TListView on the main
form. FillProcesses() is shown in the following listing:

```
procedure TWinNTInfo.FillProcesses(ListView: TListView;
  ImageList: TImageList);
var
  I, Count: Integer;
  ProcHand: THandle;
  ModHand: HMODULE;
  HAppIcon: HICON;
  ModName: array[0..MAX_PATH] of char;
begin
  for I := Low(FProcList) to High(FProcList) do
  begin
    ProcHand := OpenProcess(PROCESS_QUERY_INFORMATION or PROCESS_VM_READ,
      False, FProcList[I]);
    if ProcHand > 0 then
      try
        EnumProcessModules(Prochand, @ModHand, 1, Count);
        if GetModuleFileNameEx(Prochand, ModHand, ModName,
        ➥SizeOf(ModName)) > 0 then
        begin
          HAppIcon := ExtractIcon(HInstance, ModName, 0);
          try
            if HAppIcon = 0 then HAppIcon := FWinIcon;
            with ListView.Items.Add, SubItems do
            begin
              Caption := ModName;                    // file name
              Data := Pointer(FProcList[I]);         // save ID
              Add(SProcName);                        // "process"
              Add(IntToStr(FProcList[I]));           // process ID
              Add('$' + IntToHex(ProcHand, 8));      // process handle
              // priority class
              Add(GetPriorityClassString(GetPriorityClass(ProcHand)));
              // icon
```

```
                if ImageList <> nil then
                    ImageIndex := ImageList_AddIcon(ImageList.Handle,
                    ➥HAppIcon);
                end;
            finally
                if HAppIcon <> FWinIcon then DestroyIcon(HAppIcon);
            end;
        end;
    finally
        CloseHandle(ProcHand);
    end;
  end;
end;
```

This method uses `OpenProcess()` to convert each process ID into a process handle. Several flags can be passed to this method in the first parameter, but for purposes of querying information with PSAPI, the `PROCESS_QUERY_INFORMATION` and `PROCESS_VM_READ` together work best. Given a process handle, the code then calls `EnumProcessModules()` to obtain the filename for the process. This method is defined as:

```
function EnumProcessModules(hProcess: THandle; lphModule: LPDWORD;
  cb: DWORD; var lpcbNeeded: DWORD): BOOL;
```

This method works in a manner similar to the other PSAPI functions: `hProcess` is a process handle, `lphModule` is a pointer to an array of module handles, `cb` indicates the number of elements in the array, and the final parameter returns the number of bytes copied to `lphModule`.

Because we are only interested in the primary module for this process right now, we only pass an array of one element. The first module returned by `EnumProcessModules()` is the primary module for the process. All the process information is then added to the `TListView` in a manner similar to that shown in `TWin95Info`.

`FillDrivers()` functions in a like manner, except that it uses the `GetDeviceDriverFileName()` method shown here:

```
function GetDeviceDriverFileName(ImageBase: Pointer; lpFileName: PChar;
  nSize: DWORD): DWORD;
```

This method takes the image base of the device driver as the first parameter, a pointer to a string buffer as the second parameter, and the size of the buffer in the last parameter. Upon successful return, `lpFileName` will contain the filename of the device driver. Our use of this method is shown in the following code listing:

```
procedure TWinNTInfo.FillDrivers(ListView: TListView;
  ImageList: TImageList);
var
  I: Integer;
  DrvName: array[0..MAX_PATH] of char;
```

```
begin
  for I := Low(FDrvList) to High(FDrvList) do
    if GetDeviceDriverFileName(FDrvList[I], DrvName, SizeOf(DrvName)) > 0
    ➡then
      with ListView.Items.Add do
      begin
        Caption := DrvName;
        SubItems.Add(SDrvName);
        SubItems.Add('$' + IntToHex(Integer(FDrvList[I]), 8));
      end;
end;
```

Figure 14.11 shows the SysInfo application running on a Windows NT 4.0 machine.

FIGURE 14.11.

Browsing Windows NT processes and drivers.

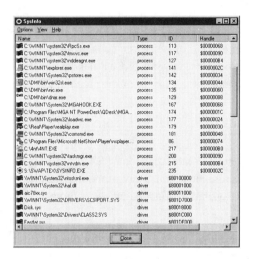

Like TWin95Info's implementation of ShowProcessProperties(), TWinNTInfo calls out to another unit to display a form containing more process information. In particular, the additional information pertains to process modules and memory usage. The method that does the work of obtaining this information resides in the TWinNTDetailForm class in the DetailNT unit, and it is shown in the following code:

```
procedure TWinNTDetailForm.NewProcess(ProcessID: DWORD);
const
  AddrMask = DWORD($FFFFF000);
var
  I, Count: Integer;
  ProcHand: THandle;
```

```
  WSPtr: Pointer;
  ModHandles: array[0..$3FFF - 1] of DWORD;
  WorkingSet: array[0..$3FFF - 1] of DWORD;
  ModInfo: TModuleInfo;
  ModName, MapFileName: array[0..MAX_PATH] of char;
begin
  ProcHand := OpenProcess(PROCESS_QUERY_INFORMATION or PROCESS_VM_READ,
    False, ProcessID);
  if ProcHand = 0 then
    raise Exception.Create('No information available for this
process/driver');
  try
    EnumProcessModules(ProcHand, @ModHandles, SizeOf(ModHandles), Count);
    for I := 0 to (Count div SizeOf(DWORD)) - 1 do
      if (GetModuleFileNameEx(ProcHand, ModHandles[I], ModName,
        SizeOf(ModName)) > 0) and GetModuleInformation(ProcHand,
        ModHandles[I], @ModInfo, SizeOf(ModInfo)) then
        with ModInfo do
          DetailLists[ltModules].Add(Format(SModuleStr, [ModName,
            lpBaseOfDll, SizeOfImage, EntryPoint]));
    if QueryWorkingSet(ProcHand, @WorkingSet, SizeOf(WorkingSet)) then
      for I := 1 to WorkingSet[0] do
      begin
        WSPtr := Pointer(WorkingSet[I] and AddrMask);
        GetMappedFileName(ProcHand, WSPtr, MapFileName,
        ➥SizeOf(MapFileName));
        DetailLists[ltMemory].Add(Format(SMemoryStr, [WSPtr,
          MemoryTypeToString(WorkingSet[I]), MapFileName]));
      end;
  finally
    CloseHandle(ProcHand);
  end;
end;
```

As you can see, this method makes calls to OpenProcess() and EnumProcessModules(), about which you've already learned. This method also calls a PSAPI function called QueryWorkingSet(), however, to obtain memory information for a process. This function is defined as

```
function QueryWorkingSet(hProcess: THandle; pv: Pointer; cb: DWORD): BOOL;
```

hProcess is the process handle. pv is a pointer to an array of DWORDs, and cb holds the number of elements in the array. Upon return, pv will point to an array of DWORDs. The upper 20 bits of this DWORD hold the base address of a memory page, and the lower 12 bits of each DWORD hold flags that indicate whether the page is readable, writable, executable, and so on.

14

SNOOPING SYSTEM INFORMATION

Figures 14.12 and 14.13 show module and memory details under Windows NT. Listings 14.4 and 14.5 show the WNTInfo.pas and DetailNT.pas units.

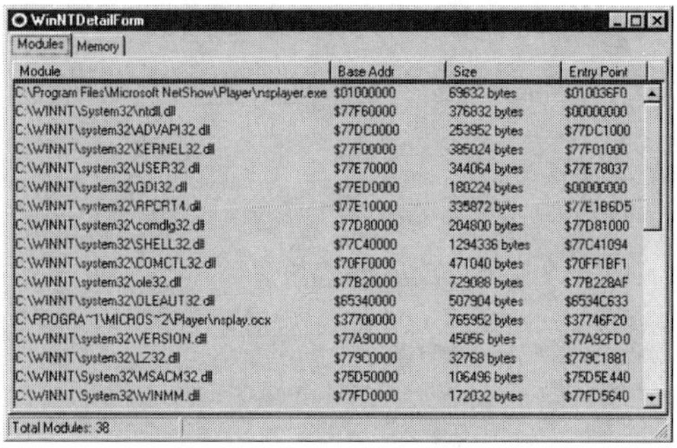

FIGURE 14.12.

Viewing Windows NT process modules.

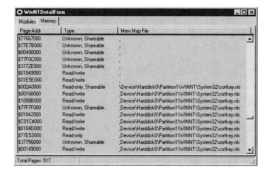

FIGURE 14.13.

Viewing Windows NT process memory details.

LISTING 14.4. WNTInfo.pas.

```
unit WNTInfo;

interface

uses InfoInt, Windows, Classes, ComCtrls, Controls;

type
  TWinNTInfo = class(TInterfacedObject, IWin32Info)
  private
    FProcList: array of DWORD;
    FDrvlist: array of Pointer;
```

```
    FWinIcon: HICON;
    procedure FillProcesses(ListView: TListView; ImageList: TImageList);
    procedure FillDrivers(ListView: TListView; ImageList: TImageList);
    procedure Refresh;
  public
    constructor Create;
    destructor Destroy; override;
    procedure FillProcessInfoList(ListView: TListView; ImageList:
        TImageList);
    procedure ShowProcessProperties(Cookie: Pointer);
  end;

implementation

uses SysUtils, PSAPI, ShellAPI, CommCtrl, DetailNT;

const
  SFailMessage = 'Failed to enumerate processes or drivers.  Make sure ' +
    'PSAPI.DLL is installed on your system.';
  SDrvName = 'driver';
  SProcname = 'process';
  ProcessInfoCaptions: array[0..4] of string = (
    'Name', 'Type', 'ID', 'Handle', 'Priority');

function GetPriorityClassString(PriorityClass: Integer): string;
begin
  case PriorityClass of
    HIGH_PRIORITY_CLASS: Result := 'High';
    IDLE_PRIORITY_CLASS: Result := 'Idle';
    NORMAL_PRIORITY_CLASS: Result := 'Normal';
    REALTIME_PRIORITY_CLASS: Result := 'Realtime';
  else
    Result := Format('Unknown ($%x)', [PriorityClass]);
  end;
end;

{ TWinNTInfo }

constructor TWinNTInfo.Create;
begin
  FWinIcon := LoadImage(0, IDI_WINLOGO, IMAGE_ICON, LR_DEFAULTSIZE,
    LR_DEFAULTSIZE, LR_DEFAULTSIZE or LR_DEFAULTCOLOR or LR_SHARED);
end;

destructor TWinNTInfo.Destroy;
begin
  DestroyIcon(FWinIcon);
  inherited Destroy;
end;
```

continues

LISTING 14.4. CONTINUED

```
procedure TWinNTInfo.FillDrivers(ListView: TListView;
  ImageList: TImageList);
var
  I: Integer;
  DrvName: array[0..MAX_PATH] of char;
begin
  for I := Low(FDrvList) to High(FDrvList) do
    if GetDeviceDriverFileName(FDrvList[I], DrvName, SizeOf(DrvName)) > 0
    ➥then
      with ListView.Items.Add do
      begin
        Caption := DrvName;
        SubItems.Add(SDrvName);
        SubItems.Add('$' + IntToHex(Integer(FDrvList[I]), 8));
      end;
end;

procedure TWinNTInfo.FillProcesses(ListView: TListView;
  ImageList: TImageList);
var
  I, Count: Integer;
  ProcHand: THandle;
  ModHand: HMODULE;
  HAppIcon: HICON;
  ModName: array[0..MAX_PATH] of char;
begin
  for I := Low(FProcList) to High(FProcList) do
  begin
    ProcHand := OpenProcess(PROCESS_QUERY_INFORMATION or PROCESS_VM_READ,
      False, FProcList[I]);
    if ProcHand > 0 then
      try
        EnumProcessModules(Prochand, @ModHand, 1, Count);
        if GetModuleFileNameEx(Prochand, ModHand, ModName,
SizeOf(ModName)) > 0 then
        begin
          HAppIcon := ExtractIcon(HInstance, ModName, 0);
          try
            if HAppIcon = 0 then HAppIcon := FWinIcon;
            with ListView.Items.Add, SubItems do
            begin
              Caption := ModName;                       // file name
              Data := Pointer(FProcList[I]);            // save ID
              Add(SProcName);                           // "process"
              Add(IntToStr(FProcList[I]));              // process ID
              Add('$' + IntToHex(ProcHand, 8));         // process handle
              // priority class
              Add(GetPriorityClassString(GetPriorityClass(ProcHand)));
```

```
                        // icon
                        if ImageList <> nil then
                          ImageIndex := ImageList_AddIcon(ImageList.Handle,
                                        HAppIcon);
                    end;
                finally
                    if HAppIcon <> FWinIcon then DestroyIcon(HAppIcon);
                end;
            end;
        finally
            CloseHandle(ProcHand);
        end;
    end;
end;

procedure TWinNTInfo.FillProcessInfoList(ListView: TListView;
  ImageList: TImageList);
var
  I: Integer;
begin
  Refresh;
  ListView.Columns.Clear;
  ListView.Items.Clear;
  for I := Low(ProcessInfoCaptions) to High(ProcessInfoCaptions) do
    with ListView.Columns.Add do
    begin
      if I = 0 then Width := 285
      else Width := 75;
      Caption := ProcessInfoCaptions[I];
    end;
  FillProcesses(ListView, ImageList);  // Add processes to listview
  FillDrivers(ListView, ImageList);    // Add device drivers to listview
end;

procedure TWinNTInfo.Refresh;
var
  Count: DWORD;
  BigArray: array[0..$3FFF - 1] of DWORD;
begin
  // Get array of process IDs
  if not EnumProcesses(@BigArray, SizeOf(BigArray), Count) then
    raise Exception.Create(SFailMessage);
  SetLength(FProcList, Count div SizeOf(DWORD));
  Move(BigArray, FProcList[0], Count);
  // Get array of Driver addresses
  if not EnumDeviceDrivers(@BigArray, SizeOf(BigArray), Count) then
    raise Exception.Create(SFailMessage);
  SetLength(FDrvList, Count div SizeOf(DWORD));
  Move(BigArray, FDrvList[0], Count);
end;
```

14

SNOOPING
SYSTEM
INFORMATION

continues

LISTING 14.4. CONTINUED

```
procedure TWinNTInfo.ShowProcessProperties(Cookie: Pointer);
begin
  ShowProcessDetails(DWORD(Cookie));
end;

end.
```

LISTING 14.5. DetailNT.pas.

```
unit DetailNT;

interface

uses
  Windows, Messages, SysUtils, Classes, Graphics, Controls, Forms,
  Dialogs, DetBase, ComCtrls, HeadList;

type
  TListType = (ltModules, ltMemory);

  TWinNTDetailForm = class(TBaseDetailForm)
    procedure FormCreate(Sender: TObject);
    procedure FormDestroy(Sender: TObject);
    procedure DetailTabsChange(Sender: TObject);
  private
    FProcHand: THandle;
    DetailLists: array[TListType] of TStringList;
    procedure ShowList(ListType: TListType);
  public
    procedure NewProcess(ProcessID: DWORD);
  end;

procedure ShowProcessDetails(ProcessID: DWORD);

implementation

uses PSAPI;

{$R *.DFM}

const
  TabStrs: array[0..1] of string[7] = ('Modules', 'Memory');

  { Array of strings that goes into the footer of each list. }
  ACountStrs: array[TListType] of string[31] = (
      'Total Modules: %d', 'Total Pages: %d');
```

```
  { Array of strings that goes into the header of each respective list. }
  HeaderStrs: array[TListType] of TDetailStrings = (
    ('Module', 'Base Addr', 'Size', 'Entry Point'),
    ('Page Addr', 'Type', 'Mem Map File', ''));

  SCaptionStr  = 'Details for %s';                  // form caption
  SModuleStr   = '%s'#1'$%p'#1'%d bytes'#1'$%p';    // name, addr, size,
entry pt
  SMemoryStr   = '$%p'#1'%s'#1'%s';                 // addr, type, mem map
                                                    // file

procedure ShowProcessDetails(ProcessID: DWORD);
var
  I: Integer;
begin
  with TWinNTDetailForm.Create(Application) do
    try
      for I := Low(TabStrs) to High(TabStrs) do
        DetailTabs.Tabs.Add(TabStrs[I]);
      NewProcess(ProcessID);
      ShowList(ltModules);
      ShowModal;
    finally
      Free;
    end;
end;

function MemoryTypeToString(Value: DWORD): string;
const
  TypeMask = DWORD($0000000F);
begin
  Result := '';
  case Value and TypeMask of
    1: Result := 'Read-only';
    2: Result := 'Executable';
    4: Result := 'Read/write';
    5: Result := 'Copy on write';
  else
    Result := 'Unknown';
  end;
  if Value and $100 <> 0 then
    Result := Result + ', Shareable';
end;

procedure TWinNTDetailForm.FormCreate(Sender: TObject);
var
  LT: TListType;
begin
  inherited;
  { Dispose of lists }
```

continues

LISTING 14.5. CONTINUED

```
  for LT := Low(TListType) to High(TListType) do
    DetailLists[LT] := TStringList.Create;
end;

procedure TWinNTDetailForm.FormDestroy(Sender: TObject);
var
  LT: TListType;
begin
  inherited;
  { Dispose of lists }
  for LT := Low(TListType) to High(TListType) do
    DetailLists[LT].Free;
end;

procedure TWinNTDetailForm.NewProcess(ProcessID: DWORD);
const
  AddrMask = DWORD($FFFFF000);
var
  I, Count: Integer;
  ProcHand: THandle;
  WSPtr: Pointer;
  ModHandles: array[0..$3FFF - 1] of DWORD;
  WorkingSet: array[0..$3FFF - 1] of DWORD;
  ModInfo: TModuleInfo;
  ModName, MapFileName: array[0..MAX_PATH] of char;
begin
  ProcHand := OpenProcess(PROCESS_QUERY_INFORMATION or PROCESS_VM_READ,
      False, ProcessID);
  if ProcHand = 0 then
    raise Exception.Create('No information available for this
process/driver');
  try
    EnumProcessModules(ProcHand, @ModHandles, SizeOf(ModHandles), Count);
    for I := 0 to (Count div SizeOf(DWORD)) - 1 do
      if (GetModuleFileNameEx(ProcHand, ModHandles[I], ModName,
        SizeOf(ModName)) > 0) and GetModuleInformation(ProcHand,
        ModHandles[I], @ModInfo, SizeOf(ModInfo)) then
        with ModInfo do
          DetailLists[ltModules].Add(Format(SModuleStr, [ModName,
            lpBaseOfDll, SizeOfImage, EntryPoint]));
    if QueryWorkingSet(ProcHand, @WorkingSet, SizeOf(WorkingSet)) then
      for I := 1 to WorkingSet[0] do
      begin
        WSPtr := Pointer(WorkingSet[I] and AddrMask);
        GetMappedFileName(ProcHand, WSPtr, MapFileName,
        ➥SizeOf(MapFileName));
        DetailLists[ltMemory].Add(Format(SMemoryStr, [WSPtr,
```

```
        MemoryTypeToString(WorkingSet[I]), MapFileName]));
      end;
  finally
    CloseHandle(ProcHand);
  end;
end;

procedure TWinNTDetailForm.ShowList(ListType: TListType);
var
  I: Integer;
begin
  Screen.Cursor := crHourGlass;
  try
    with DetailLB do
    begin
      for I := 0 to 3 do
        Sections[I].Text := HeaderStrs[ListType, i];
      Items.Clear;
      Items.Assign(DetailLists[ListType]);
    end;
      DetailSB.Panels[0].Text := Format(ACountStrs[ListType],
        [DetailLists[ListType].Count]);
  finally
    Screen.Cursor := crDefault;
  end;
end;

procedure TWinNTDetailForm.DetailTabsChange(Sender: TObject);
begin
  inherited;
  ShowList(TListType(DetailTabs.TabIndex));
end;

end.
```

14

SUMMARY

This chapter demonstrates techniques for accessing system information from within your Delphi programs. It focuses on the proper usage of the ToolHelp32 functions provided by Windows 95/98 and the PSAPI functions found on Windows NT. You learned how to use a few Win32 API functions to obtain other types of system information: including memory information, environment variables, and version information. Additionally, you learned how to incorporate the TListView, TImageList, THeaderListbox, and TddgMemView custom components into your applications. The next chapter, "Porting to Delphi 4," is found on the CD-ROM accompanying this book, and it discusses migrating your applications from previous versions of Delphi.

PORTING TO DELPHI 4

IN THIS CHAPTER

If you're upgrading to Delphi 4 from a previous version, this chapter is written for you. The first section of this chapter discusses the issues involved in moving from any version of Delphi to Delphi 4. In the second and third sections, you learn about the often subtle differences between the various 32-bit versions of Delphi, and how to take these differences into account as you migrate applications to Delphi 4. The fourth section of this chapter is intended to help those migrating 16-bit Delphi 1 applications to the 32-bit world of Delphi 4. Although Borland makes a concerted effort to ensure that your code is compatible between versions, it's understandable that some changes have to be made in the name of progress, and certain situations require code changes if applications are to compile and run properly under the latest version of Delphi.

MDI APPLICATIONS

IN THIS CHAPTER

The Multiple Document Interface, otherwise known as MDI, was introduced to Windows 2.0 in the Microsoft Excel spreadsheet program. MDI gave Excel users the ability to work on more than one spreadsheet at a time. Other uses of MDI included the Windows 3.1 Program Manager and File Manager programs. Borland Pascal for Windows is another MDI application.

During the development of Windows 95, many developers were under the impression that Microsoft was going to eliminate MDI capabilities. Much to their surprise, Microsoft kept MDI as part of Windows 95, and there has been no further word about any intention to get rid of it.

CAUTION

Microsoft has acknowledged that the Windows MDI implementation is flawed. It advised developers against continuing to build apps in the MDI model. Since then, Microsoft has returned to building MS apps in the MDI model, but does so without using the Windows MDI implementation. You can still use MDI, but be forewarned that Windows MDI implementation is still flawed, and Microsoft has no plans to fix those problems. What we present in this chapter is a safe implementation of the MDI model.

Handling events simultaneously between multiple forms might seem difficult. In traditional Windows programming, you needed knowledge of the Windows class MDICLIENT, MDI data structures, and the additional functions and messages specific to MDI. With Delphi 4, creating MDI applications is greatly simplified. When you finish this chapter, you will have a solid foundation for building MDI applications, which you can easily expand to include more advanced techniques.

SHARING INFORMATION WITH THE CLIPBOARD

IN THIS CHAPTER

Once upon a time, humankind struggled just to survive. People lived in dark caves, hunted for food with spears and rocks, and communicated with grunt-like sounds and hand motions. They worshipped fire because it gave them light under which they worked on their very slow computers. Computers back then could run only one application at a time due to hardware and software limitations. The only way to share information was to save it on disk and to pass the disk along for others to copy to their machines.

Nowadays, at least the equipment and software have improved. With operating systems such as Windows 95 and Windows NT, multiple applications can be run simultaneously, which makes life much easier and more productive for the computer user. One of the advantages gained from Windows is that information can be shared between applications on the same machine. Two of the earlier technologies for sharing information are the Win32 clipboard and Dynamic Data Exchange (DDE). You can make it possible for your users to copy information from one application to another application with little effort using either of these.

This chapter shows you how to use Delphi's encapsulation of the Win32 clipboard. Previous editions of this book covered DDE as well. However, with powerful inter-process communication technologies such as COM, we can't, in all good conscience, refer you back to a dead technology. Later, in Chapter 23, "COM and ActiveX," we'll discuss COM in greater depth. For simple implementations of sharing information between applications, the clipboard is still a very solid solution.

MULTIMEDIA PROGRAMMING WITH DELPHI

IN THIS CHAPTER

Delphi's TMediaPlayer component is proof that good things come in small packages. In the guise of this little component, Delphi encapsulates a great deal of the functionality of the Windows *Media Control Interface (MCI)*—the portion of the Windows API that provides control for multimedia devices.

Delphi makes multimedia programming so easy that the traditional and boring "Hello World" program may be a thing of the past. Why write Hello World to the screen when it's almost as easy to play a sound or video file that offers its greetings?

In this chapter, you learn how to write a simple yet powerful media player, and you even construct a fully functional audio CD player. This chapter explains the uses and nuances of the TMediaPlayer. Of course, your computer must be equipped with multimedia devices, such as a sound card and CD-ROM, for this chapter to be of real use to you.

TESTING AND DEBUGGING

IN THIS CHAPTER

Some programmers in the industry believe that the knowledge and application of good programming practice make the need for debugging expertise unnecessary. In reality, however, the two complement each other, and whoever masters both will reap the greatest benefits. This is especially true when multiple programmers are working on different parts of the same program. It's simply impossible to completely remove the possibility of human error.

A surprising number of people say, "My code compiles all right, so I don't have any bugs, right?" Wrong. There's no correlation between whether a program compiles and whether it has bugs; there's a big difference between code that is syntactically correct and code that is logically correct and bug free. Also, don't assume that because a particular piece of code worked yesterday or on another system, it's bug free. When it comes to hunting software bugs, everything should be presumed guilty until proven innocent.

During the development of any application, you should allow the compiler to help you as much as possible. You can do this in Delphi by enabling all the runtime error checking in Project | Options | Compiler (as shown in Figure 19.1) or by enabling the necessary directives in your code. Additionally, you should have the Show Hints and Show Warnings options enabled in that same dialog in order to receive more information on your code. It's common for a developer to spend needless hours trying to track down "that impossible bug," when he could have found the error immediately by simply employing these effective compiler-aided tools. (Of course, the authors would never be guilty of failing to remember to use these aids. You believe us, right?)

FIGURE 19.1.

The Compiler page of the Project Options dialog.

Table 19.1 describes the different runtime error options available through Delphi.

TABLE 19.1. DELPHI RUNTIME ERRORS.

Runtime Error	Directive	Function
Range Checking	{$R+}	Checks to ensure that you don't index an array or string beyond its bounds and that assignments

Runtime Error	Directive	Function
		don't assign a value to a scalar variable that's outside its range.
Stack Checking	{$S+}	Checks to ensure that you don't try to use more stack than you have available.
I/O Checking	{$I+}	Checks for input/output errors after every I/O call (ReadLn() and WriteLn(), for example). This almost always should be enabled.
Overflow Checking	{$Q+}	Checks to ensure that calculation results are not larger than the register size.

TIP

Keep in mind that each of these runtime errors exacts a performance penalty on your application. Therefore, once you're out of the debugging phase of development and are ready to ship a final product, you can improve performance by disabling some of the runtime errors. It's common practice for developers to disable all except I/O Checking for the final product.

19

TESTING AND DEBUGGING

COMPONENT-BASED DEVELOPMENT

PART

III

IN THIS PART

KEY ELEMENTS OF THE VISUAL COMPONENT LIBRARY

IN THIS CHAPTER

When Borland first introduced the Object Windows Library (OWL) with Turbo Pascal for Windows, it ushered in a drastic simplification over traditional Windows programming. OWL objects automated and streamlined many tedious tasks you otherwise were required to code yourself. No longer did you have to write huge case statements to capture messages or big chunks of code to manage Windows classes; OWL did this for you. However, you had to learn a new programming methodology—object-oriented programming.

The Visual Component Library (VCL), introduced in Delphi 1, was OWL's successor. It was based on an object model similar to OWL's in principle but radically different in implementation. The VCL in Delphi 4 is the same as its predecessors in Delphi 1, 2, and 3 with quite a few enhancements and additions.

The VCL is designed specifically to work within Delphi's visual environment. Instead of creating a window or dialog box and adding its behavior in code, you modify the behavioral and visual characteristics of components as you design your program visually.

The level of knowledge required about the VCL really depends on how you use it. First, you must realize that there are two types of Delphi developers: applications developers and visual component writers. *Applications developers* create complete applications by interacting with the Delphi visual environment (a concept nonexistent in many other frameworks). These people use the VCL to create their UI and other elements of their application such as database connectivity. *Component writers,* on the other hand, expand the existing VCL by developing more components. Such components are made available through third-party companies.

Whether you plan to create applications with Delphi or to create Delphi components, understanding the Visual Component Library is essential. An applications developer should know which properties, events, and methods are available for each component. Additionally, it is advantageous to fully understand the object model inherent in a Delphi application that is provided by the VCL. A common problem we see with Delphi developers is that they tend to fight the tool—a symptom of not understanding it completely. Component writers take this knowledge one step further to determine whether to write a new component or to extend an existing one by knowing how VCL handles window messages, internal notifications, component ownership, parenting/ownership issues, property editors, and so on.

This chapter introduces you to the Visual Component Library. It discusses the component hierarchy and explains the purpose of the key levels within the hierarchy. It also discusses the purposes of the common properties, methods, and events that appear at the different component levels. Finally, we complete this chapter by covering Runtime Type Information (RTTI).

WHAT IS A COMPONENT?

Components are the building blocks developers use to design the user interface and provide some nonvisual capability to their applications. As far as applications developers are concerned, a component is something developers get from the Component Palette and place on their forms. From there, they can manipulate the various properties and add event handlers to give the component a specific appearance or behavior. From the perspective of a component writer, components are objects in Object Pascal code. These objects can encapsulate the behavior of elements provided by the system (such as the standard Windows 95 controls). Other objects can introduce an entirely new visual or nonvisual element, in which case the component's code makes up the entire behavior of the component.

The complexity of components varies widely. Some components are simple; others encapsulate elaborate tasks. There's no limit to what a component can do or be made up of. You can have a simple component such as a TLabel, or a much more complex component that encapsulates the complete functionality of a spreadsheet.

The key to understanding the VCL is to know what types of components exist. You should understand the common elements of components. You should also understand the component hierarchy and the purpose of each level within the hierarchy. The following sections provide this information.

COMPONENT TYPES

There are four basic types of components you either use and/or create in Delphi: standard controls, custom controls, graphical controls, and nonvisual components.

> **NOTE**
>
> You'll often see the terms *component* and *control* used interchangeably, although they're not always the same. A *control* refers to a visual user-interface element. In Delphi, controls are always components because they descend from the TComponent class. *Components* are the objects whose basic behavior allows them to appear on the Component Palette and be manipulated in the form designer. Components are of the type TComponent and are not always controls— that is, they aren't always visual user-interface elements.

Standard Components

Delphi provides *standard components* that encapsulate the behavior of Windows 95 controls such as TRichEdit, TTrackBar, and TListView (to name a few). These components exist on the Win95 page of the Component Palette. These components are actually Object Pascal wrappers around the Windows 95 common controls. If you're an owner of the VCL source code, you can view Borland's method for wrapping these controls in the file ComCtrls.pas.

TIP

Having the source code to the VCL is essential to understanding the VCL, especially if you plan to write components. There probably is no better way to learn how to write components than to see how Borland has done it. If you don't have the Runtime Library (RTL), it's strongly recommended that you obtain it from Borland.

Custom Components

Custom components is a general term that refers to components that aren't part of the standard Delphi component library. In other words, these are components that either you or other programmers write and add to the existing set of components. We'll get more into designing custom components later in this chapter.

Graphical Components

Graphical components let you have or create visual controls that don't receive the input focus from the user. These components are useful when you want to display something to the user but don't want the component to use up Windows resources, as standard and custom components do. Graphical components don't use Windows resources because they require no window handle, which is also the reason that they can't get focus. Examples of graphical components are TLabel and TShape. Such components can't serve as container components either; that is, they can't own other components placed on top of them. Examples of graphical components are TImage, TBevel, and TPaintBox.

HANDLES

Handles are 32-bit numbers issued by Win32 that refer to certain object instances. The term *objects* here refers to Win32 objects and not Delphi objects. There are different types of objects under Win32: kernel objects, user objects, and GDI objects. Kernel objects apply to things such as events, file-mapping objects, and processes. User objects refer to window objects such as edit controls, list boxes, and buttons. GDI objects refer to bitmaps, brushes, fonts, and so on.

In the Win32 environment, every window has a unique handle. Many Windows API functions require a handle so that they know the window on which they are to perform the operation. Delphi encapsulates much of the Win32 API and performs handle management. If you want to use a Windows API function that requires a window handle, you must use descendants of TWinControl and TCustomControl, which both have a Handle property.

Nonvisual Components

As the name implies, *nonvisual components* don't have a visual characteristic. Such components give you the ability to encapsulate the functionality of an entity within an object and allow you to modify certain characteristics of that component through the Object Inspector at design time by modifying its properties and providing event handlers for its events. Examples of such components are TOpenDialog, TTable, and TTimer.

THE COMPONENT STRUCTURE

As mentioned earlier, components are Object Pascal classes that encapsulate the functionality and behavior of elements developers use to add visual and behavioral characteristics to their programs. All components have a certain structure. The following sections discuss the makeup of Delphi components.

> **NOTE**
>
> Understand the distinction between a component and a class. A component is a class that can be manipulated within the Delphi environment. A class is an Object Pascal structure, as explained in Chapter 2, "The Object Pascal Language."

Properties

Chapter 2 introduced you to properties. Properties give the user an interface to the component's internal storage fields. Using properties, the component user can modify or read storage field values. Typically, the user doesn't have direct access to component storage fields because they're declared in the private section of a component's class definition.

Properties—Storage Field Accessors

Properties provide access to storage fields by either accessing the storage fields directly or through *access methods*. Take a look at the following property definition:

```
TCustomEdit = class(TWinControl)
private
  FMaxLength: Integer;
protected
  procedure SetMaxLength(Value: Integer);
...
published
  property MaxLength: Integer read FMaxLength write SetMaxLength default 0;
...
end;
```

The property MaxLength is the access to the storage field FMaxLength. The parts of a property definition consist of the property name, the property type, a read declaration, a write declaration, and an optional default value. The read declaration specifies how the component's storage fields are read. The MaxLength property directly reads the value from the FMaxLength storage field. The write declaration specifies the method by which the storage fields are assigned values. For the property MaxLength, a writer access method SetMaxLength() is used to assign the value to the storage field FMaxLength. A property may also contain a reader access method in which case the MaxLength property would be declared as:

```
property MaxLength: Integer read GetMaxLength write SetMaxLength default 0;
```

The reader access method GetMaxLength() would be declared as:

```
function GetMaxLength: Integer;
```

Property Access Methods

Access methods take a single parameter of the same type as the property. The purpose of the write access method is to assign the value of the parameter to the internal storage field to which the property refers. The reason for using the method layer to assign values is to protect the storage field from receiving erroneous data as well as to perform various side effects, if required. For example, examine the implementation of the following SetMaxLength() method:

```
procedure TCustomEdit.SetMaxLength(Value: Integer);
begin
  if FMaxLength <> Value then
  begin
    FMaxLength := Value;
    if HandleAllocated then SendMessage(Handle, EM_LIMITTEXT, Value, 0);
  end;
end;
```

This method first checks to see that the component user isn't attempting to assign the same value as that which the property already holds. If not, it makes the assignment to the internal storage field `FMaxLength` and then calls the `SendMessage()` function to pass the `EM_LIMITTEXT` Windows message to the window that the `TCustomEdit` encapsulates. This message limits the amount of text that a user can enter into an edit control. Calling `SendMessage()` in the property's `write` access method is known as a *side effect* when assigning property values.

Side effects are any actions affected by the assignment of a value to a property. In assigning a value to the `MaxLength` property of `TCustomEdit`, the side effect is that the encapsulated edit control is given an entry limit. Side effects can be much more sophisticated than this.

One key advantage to providing access to a component's internal storage fields through properties is that the component writer can change the implementation of the field access without affecting the behavior for the component user.

A reader access method, for example, can change the type of the returned value to something different from the type of the storage field to which the property refers.

Another fundamental reason for the use of properties is to make modifications available to them during design time. When a property appears in the `published` section of a component's declaration, it also appears in the Object Inspector so that the component user can make modifications to this property.

You learn much more about properties and how to create them and their access methods in Chapter 21, "Writing Delphi Custom Components."

Types of Properties

The standard rules that apply to Object Pascal data types apply to properties as well. The important point about properties is that their types also determine how they're edited in the Object Inspector. Properties can be of the types shown in Table 20.1. For more detailed information, look up "properties" in the online help.

TABLE 20.1. PROPERTY TYPES.

Property Type	Object Inspector Treatment
Simple	Numeric, character, and string properties appear in the Object Inspector as numbers, characters, and strings, respectively. The user can type and edit the value of the property directly.

continues

TABLE 20.1. CONTINUED

Property Type	Object Inspector Treatment
Enumerated	Properties of enumerated types (including Boolean) display the value as defined in the source code. The user can cycle through the possible values by double-clicking the Value column. There's also a drop-down list that shows all possible values of the enumerated type.
Set	Properties of set types appear in the Object Inspector looking like a set. By expanding the set, the user can treat each element of the set as a Boolean value: True if the element is included in the set or False if it's not included.
Object	Properties that are themselves objects often have their own property editors. However, if the object that's a property also has published properties, the Object Inspector allows the user to expand the list of object properties and edit them individually. Object properties must descend from TPersistent.
Array	Array properties must have their own property editors. The Object Inspector has no built-in support for editing array properties.

Methods

Because components are objects, they can therefore have methods. You've already seen information on object methods in Chapter 2 (that information is not repeated here). The later section "The Visual Component Hierarchy" describes some of the key methods of the different component levels in the component hierarchy.

Events

Events are occurrences of an action, typically a system action such as clicking on a button control or pressing a key on a keyboard. Components contain special properties called *events*; component users can plug code into the event that executes when the event occurs.

Plugging Code into Events at Design Time

If you look at the events page of a TEdit component, you'll find events such as OnChange, OnClick, and OnDblClick. To component writers, events are really pointers to methods. When users of a component assign code to an event, they create an *event handler*. For example, when you double-click on an event in the Object Inspector's events page for a component, Delphi generates a method to which you add your code, such as the following code for the OnClick event of a TButton component:

```
TForm1 = class(TForm)
  Button1: Tbutton;
  procedure Button1Click(Sender: TObject);
end;
...
procedure TForm1.Button1Click(Sender: TObject);
begin
  { Event code goes here }
end;
```

This code is generated by Delphi.

Plugging Code into Events at Runtime

It becomes clear how events are method pointers when you assign an event handler to an event programmatically. For example, to link your own event handler to an OnClick event of a TButton component, you first declare and define the method you intend to assign to the button's OnClick event. This method might belong to the form that owns the TButton component, as shown here:

```
TForm1 = class(TForm)
  Button1: TButton;
...
private
  MyOnClickEvent(Sender: TObject); // Your method declaration
end;
...
{ Your method definition below }
procedure TForm1.MyOnClickEvent(Sender: TObject);
begin
  { Your code goes here }
end;
```

The preceding example shows a user-defined method MyOnClickEvent() that serves as the event handler for Button1.OnClick. The following line shows how you assign this method to the Button1.OnClick event in code, which is usually done in the form's OnCreate event handler:

```
procedure TForm1.FormCreate(Sender: TObject);
begin
  Button1.OnClick := MyOnClickEvent;
end;
```

This technique can be used to add different event handlers to events, based on various conditions in your code. Additionally, you can disable an event handler from an event by assigning nil to the event, as shown here:

```
Button1.OnClick := nil;
```

20

KEY ELEMENTS OF THE VCL

Assigning event handlers at runtime is essentially what happens when you create an event handler through Delphi's Object Inspector—except that Delphi generates the method declaration. You can't just assign any method to a particular event handler. Because event properties are method pointers, they have specific method signatures, depending on the type of event. For example, an `OnMouseDown` method is of the type `TMouseEvent`, a procedure definition shown here:

```
TMouseEvent = procedure (Sender: TObject; Button: TMouseButton; Shift:
  TShiftState; X, Y: Integer) of object;
```

Therefore, the methods that become event handlers for certain events must follow the same signature as the event types. They must contain the same type, number, and order of parameters.

Earlier, we said that events are properties. Like data properties, events refer to private data fields of a component. This data field is of the procedure type such as the `TMouseEvent`. Examine this code:

```
TControl = class(TComponent)
private
  FOnMouseDown: TMouseEvent;
protected
  property OnMouseDown: TMouseEvent read FOnMouseDown write FOnMouseDown;
public
end;
```

Recall the discussion of properties and how they refer to private data fields of a component. You can see how events, being properties, refer to private method pointer fields of a component.

You learn much more about creating events and event handlers in Chapter 21, "Writing Delphi Custom Components."

Streamability

One characteristic of components is that they must have the capability to be streamed. *Streaming* is a way to store a component and information regarding its properties' values to a file. Delphi's streaming capabilities take care of all this for you. In fact, the `.dfm` file created by Delphi is nothing more than a resource file containing the streamed information on the form and its components as an RCDATA resource. As a component writer, however, you must sometimes go beyond what Delphi can do automatically. The streaming mechanism of Delphi is explained in greater depth in Chapter 22, "Advanced Component Techniques."

Ownership

Components have the capability of owning other components. A component's owner is specified by its Owner property. When a component owns other components, a component is responsible for freeing the components it owns when it's destroyed. Typically, the form owns all components that appear on it. When you place a component on the form in the form designer, the form automatically becomes the component's owner. When you create a component at runtime, you must pass the ownership of the component to the component's Create constructor; it's assigned to the new component's Owner property. The following line shows how to pass the form's implicit Self variable to a TButton.Create() constructor, thus making the form the owner of the newly created component:

```
MyButton := TButton.Create(self);
```

When the form is destroyed, the TButton instance to which MyButton refers is also destroyed. This is handled internally in the VCL. Essentially, the form iterates through the components referred to by its Components array property (explained in more detail shortly) and destroys them.

It's possible to create a component without an owner by passing nil to the component's Create() method. However, when this is done, it's your responsibility to destroy the component programmatically. The following code shows this technique:

```
MyTable := TTable.Create(nil)
try
  { Do stuff with MyTable }
finally
  MyTable.Free;
end;
```

When using this technique, you should use a try...finally to ensure that you free up any allocated resources if an exception is raised. You wouldn't use this technique except in specific circumstances when it's impossible to pass an owner to the component.

Another property associated with ownership is the Components property. The Components property is an array property that maintains a list of all components belonging to that component. For example, to loop through all the components on a form to show their class name, execute the following code:

```
var
  i: integer;
begin
  for i := 0 to ComponentCount - 1 do
    ShowMessage(Components[i].ClassName);
end;
```

20

KEY ELEMENTS OF THE VCL

Obviously, you'll probably perform a more meaningful operation on these components. The preceding code merely illustrates the technique.

Parenthood

Not to be confused with ownership is the concept of parenthood. Components can be *parents* to other components. Only windowed components such as TWinControl descendants can serve as parents to other components. Parent components are responsible for calling the child component methods to force them to draw themselves. Parent components are responsible for the proper painting of child components. A component's parent is specified through its Parent property.

A component's parent doesn't necessarily have to be its owner. It's perfectly legal for a component to have different parents and owners.

THE VISUAL COMPONENT HIERARCHY

Remember from Chapter 2 that the abstract class TObject is the base class from which all classes descend.

Figure 20.1 shows a skeleton hierarchy of the VCL from the Delphi help file.

FIGURE 20.1.

The hierarchy of the Visual Component Library.

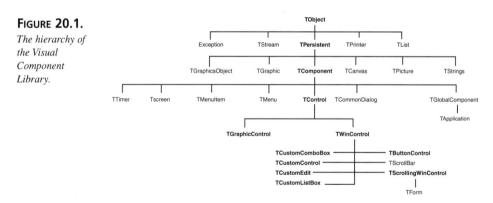

As a component writer, you don't descend your components directly from TObject. The VCL already has TObject class descendants from which your new components can be derived. These existing classes provide much of the functionality you require for your own components. Only when you create noncomponent classes do your classes descend from TObject.

TObject's Create() and Destroy() methods are responsible for allocating and deallocating memory for an object instance. In fact, the TObject.Create() constructor returns a reference to the object being created. TObject has several functions that return useful information about a specific object.

The VCL uses most of TObject's methods internally. You can obtain useful information about an instance of a TObject or TObject descendant such as the instance's class type, class name, and ancestor classes.

> **CAUTION**
>
> Use TObject.Free instead of TObject.Destroy. The free method calls destroy for you but first checks to see whether the object is nil before calling destroy. This method ensures that you won't generate an exception by attempting to destroy an invalid object.

The TPersistent Class

The TPersistent class descends directly from TObject. The special characteristic of TPersistent is that objects descending from it can read and write their properties from and to a stream after they are created. Because all components are descendants of TPersistent, they are all streamable. TPersistent defines no special properties or events, although it does define some methods that are useful to both the component user and writer.

TPersistent Methods

Table 20.2 lists some methods of interest defined by the TPersistent class.

TABLE 20.2. METHODS OF THE TPersistent CLASS.

Method	Purpose
Assign()	This public method allows a component to assign to itself the data associated with another component.
AssignTo()	This protected method is where TPersistent descendants must implement the VCL definition for AssignTo(). TPersistent itself raises an exception when this method is called. AssignTo() is where a component can assign its data values to another instance or class, the reverse of Assign().
DefineProperties()	This protected method allows component writers to define how the component stores extra or unpublished properties. This method is typically used to provide a way for a component to store data that is not of a simple data type such as binary data.

The streamability of components is described in greater depth in Chapter 12, "Working with Files." For now, it's enough to know that components can be stored and retrieved from a disk file by means of streaming.

The TComponent Class

The TComponent class descends directly from TPersistent. TComponent's special characteristics are that its properties can be manipulated at design time through the Object Inspector and that it can own other components.

Nonvisual components also descend from TComponent so that they inherit the capability to be manipulated at design time. A good example of a nonvisual TComponent descendant is the TTimer component. TTimers are not visual controls but are still available on the Component Palette.

TComponent defines several properties and methods of interest, as described in the following sections.

TComponent Properties

The properties defined by TComponent and their purposes are shown in Table 20.3.

TABLE 20.3. THE SPECIAL PROPERTIES OF TComponent.

Property Name	Purpose
Owner	Points to the component's owner.
ComponentCount	Holds the number of components that the component owns.
ComponentIndex	The position of this component in its owners list of components. The first component in this list has the value 0.
Components	A property array containing a list of components owned by this component. The first component in this list has the value 0.
ComponentState	This property holds the current state of a component of the type TComponentState. Additional information about TComponentState can be found in the online help and in Chapter 21.
ComponentStyle	Governs various behavioral characteristics of the component. csInheritable and csCheckPropAvail are two values that can be assigned to this property, both of which are explained in the online help.
Name	Holds the name of a component.
Tag	An integer property that has no defined meaning. This property should not be used by component writers—it is intended to be used by application writers. Because this value is an integer type, pointers to data structures—or even object instances—can be referred to by this property.
DesignInfo	Used by the form designer. Do not access this property.

`TComponent` Methods

`TComponent` defines several methods having to do with its capacity to own other components and to be manipulated on the form designer.

`TComponent` defines the component's `Create()` constructor, which was discussed earlier in this chapter. This constructor is responsible for creating an instance of the component and giving it an owner based on the parameter passed to it. Unlike `TObject.Create()`, `TComponent.Create()` is virtual. `TComponent` descendants that implement a constructor must declare the `Create()` constructor with the `override` directive. Although you can declare other constructors on a component class, `TComponent.Create()` is the only constructor VCL will use to create an instance of the class at design time and at runtime when loading component from a stream.

The `TComponent.Destroy()` destructor is responsible for freeing the component and any resources allocated by the component.

The `TComponent.Destroying()` method is responsible for setting a component and its owned components to a state indicating that they are being destroyed; the `TComponent.DestroyComponents()` method is responsible for destroying the components. You probably won't have to deal with these methods.

The `TComponent.FindComponent()` method is handy when you want to refer to a component for which you know only the name. Suppose that you know that the main form has a `TEdit` component named `Edit1`. When you don't have a reference to this component, you can retrieve a pointer to its instance by executing the following code:

```
EditInstance := FindComponent.('Edit1');
```

In this example, `EditInstance` is a `TEdit` type. `FindComponent()` will return `nil` if the name does not exist.

The `TComponent.GetParentComponent()` method retrieves an instance to the component's parent component. This method can return `nil` if there is no parent to a component.

The `TComponent.HasParent()` returns a Boolean value indicating whether the component has a parent component. Note that this method doesn't refer to whether this component has an owner.

The `TComponent.InsertComponent()` adds a component so that it's owned by the calling component; `TComponent.RemoveComponent()` removes an owned component from the calling component. You wouldn't normally use these methods because these methods are called automatically by the component's `Create()` constructor and `Destroy()` destructor.

The `TControl` Class

The `TControl` class defines many properties, methods, and events commonly used by visual components. For example, `TControl` introduces the capability for a control to display itself. The `TControl` class includes position properties such as `Top` and `Left`, as well as size properties such as `Width` and `Height`, which hold the horizontal and vertical sizes. Other properties include `ClientRect`, `ClientWidth`, and `ClientHeight`.

`TControl` also introduces properties regarding appearances and accessibility, such as `Visible`, `Enabled`, and `Color`. You can even specify a font for the text of a `TControl` through its `Font` property. This text is provided through the `TControl` properties `Text` and `Caption`.

`TControl` also introduces some standard events, such as the mouse events `OnClick`, `OnDblClick`, `OnMouseDown`, `OnMouseMove`, and `OnMouseUp`. It also introduces drag events such as `OnDragOver`, `OnDragDrop`, and `OnEndDrag`.

`TControl` itself isn't very useful at the `TControl` level. You'll never create descendants of `TControl`.

Another concept introduced by `TControl` is that it may have a parent component. Although `TControl` may have a parent, its parent must be a `TWinControl` (parent controls must be *windowed* controls). The `TControl` introduces the `Parent` property.

Most of Delphi's controls are derived from `TControl`'s descendants: `TWinControl` or `TGraphicControl`.

The `TWinControl` Class

Standard Windows controls descend from the class `TWinControl`. Standard controls are the user interface objects you see in most Windows applications. Items such as edit controls, list boxes, combo boxes, and buttons are examples of these controls. Because Delphi encapsulates the behavior of standard controls instead of using Windows API functions to manipulate them, you use the properties provided by each of the various control components.

The three basic characteristics of `TWinControl` objects are that they have a Windows handle, can receive input focus, and can be parents to other controls. You'll find that the properties, methods, and events belonging to `TWinControl` support focus changing, keyboard events, drawing of controls, and other functions required of `TWinControl`.

An applications developer primarily uses `TWinControl` descendants. A component writer must understand the `TCustomControl` descendant of `TWinControl`.

`TWinControl` **Properties**

`TWinControl` defines several properties applicable to changing the focus and appearance of the control.

The `TWinControl.Brush` property is used to draw the patterns and shapes of the control. We discussed this property in Chapter 8, "Graphics Programming with GDI and Fonts."

The `TWinControl.Controls` property is an array property that maintains a list of all controls to which the calling `TWinControl` is a parent.

The `TWinControl.ControlCount` property holds the count of controls to which it is a parent.

`TWinControl.Ctl3D` is a property that specifies whether to draw the control using a three-dimensional appearance.

The `TWinControl.Handle` property corresponds to the handle of the Windows object that the `TWinControl` encapsulates. This is the handle that you would pass to Win32 API functions requiring a window handle parameter.

`TWinControl.HelpContext` holds a help context number that corresponds to a help screen in a help file. This is used to provide context-sensitive help for individual controls.

`TWinControl.Showing` indicates whether a control is visible.

The `TWinControl.TabStop` property holds a Boolean value to determine whether a user can tab to the said control. The `TWinControl.TabOrder` property specifies where in the parent's list of tabbed controls the control exists.

`TWinControl` **Methods**

The `TWinControl` component also offers several methods that have to do with window creation, focus control, event dispatching, and positioning. There are too many methods to discuss in depth in this chapter; however, they are all documented in Delphi's online help. We'll list only those methods of particular interest in the following paragraphs.

Methods that relate to window creation, re-creation, and destruction apply mainly to component writers and are discussed in Chapter 21. These methods are `CreateParams()`, `CreateWnd()`, `CreateWindowHandle()`, `DestroyWnd()`, `DestroyWindowHandle()`, and `RecreateWnd()`.

Methods having to do with window focusing, positioning, and alignment are `CanFocus()`, `Focused()`, `AlignControls()`, `EnableAlign()`, `DisableAlign()`, and `ReAlign()`.

TWinControl Events

TWinControl introduces events for keyboard interaction and focus change. Keyboard events are OnKeyDown, OnKeyPress, and OnKeyUp. Focus-change events are OnEnter and OnExit. All these events are documented in Delphi's online help.

The TGraphicControl Class

TGraphicControls, unlike TWinControls, don't have a window handle and therefore can't receive input focus. They also can't be parents to other controls. TGraphicControls are used when you want to display something to the user on the form, but you don't want this control to function as a regular user-input control. The advantage of TGraphicControls is that they don't request a handle from Windows that uses up system resources. Additionally, not having a window handle means that TGraphicControls don't have to go through the convoluted Windows paint process. This makes drawing with TGraphicControls much faster than using the TWinControl equivalents.

TGraphicControls can respond to mouse events. Actually, the TGraphicControl parent processes the mouse message and sends it to its child controls.

TGraphicControl allows you to paint the control and therefore provides the property Canvas, which is of the type TCanvas. TGraphicControl also provides a Paint() method that its descendants must override.

The TCustomControl Class

You might have noticed that the names of some TWinControl descendants begin with TCustom, such as TCustomComboBox, TCustomControl, TCustomEdit, and TCustomListBox.

Custom controls have the same functionality as other TWinControl descendants, except that with specialized visual and interactive characteristics, custom controls provide you with a base from which you can derive and create your own customized components. You provide the functionality for the custom control to draw itself if you're a component writer.

Other Classes

Several classes aren't components but serve as supporting classes to the existing component. These classes are typically properties of other components and descend directly from TPersistent. Some of these classes are of the type TStrings, TCanvas, and TCollection.

The TStrings and TStringLists Classes

The TStrings abstract class gives you the capability to manipulate lists of strings that belong to a component such as a TListBox. TStrings doesn't actually maintain the memory for the strings (that's done by the native control that owns the TStrings class). Instead, TStrings defines the methods and properties to access and manipulate the control's strings without having to use the control's set of Win32 API functions and messages.

Notice that we said TStrings is an abstract class. This means that TStrings doesn't really implement the code required to manipulate the strings—it just defines the methods that must be there. It's up to the descendant components to implement the actual string-manipulation methods.

To explain this point further, some of the components and their TStrings properties are TListBox.Items, TMemo.Lines, and TComboBox.Items. Each of these properties is of the type TStrings. You might wonder, if their properties are TStrings, how you can call methods of these properties when these methods have yet to be implemented in code? Good question. The answer is that, even though these properties are defined as TStrings, the variable to which the property refers, TListBox.FItems for example, was instantiated as a descendant class. To clarify this, FItems is the private storage field for the Items property of TListBox:

```
TCustomListBox = class(TWinControl)
  private
    FItems: TStrings;
```

> **NOTE**
>
> Although the class type shown in the preceding code snippet is a TCustomListBox, the TListBox descends directly from TCustomListBox in the same unit and therefore has access to its private fields.

The unit STDCTRLS.PAS, which is part of the Delphi VCL, defines a descendant class TListBoxStrings, which is a descendant of TStrings. Listing 20.1 shows its definition.

LISTING 20.1. THE DECLARATION OF THE TListBoxStrings CLASS.

```
TListBoxStrings = class(TStrings)
  private
    ListBox: TCustomListBox;
  protected
    function Get(Index: Integer): string; override;
```

continues

LISTING 20.1. CONTINUED

```
    function GetCount: Integer; override;
    function GetObject(Index: Integer): TObject; override;
    procedure PutObject(Index: Integer; AObject: TObject); override;
    procedure SetUpdateState(Updating: Boolean); override;
  public
    function Add(const S: string): Integer; override;
    procedure Clear; override;
    procedure Delete(Index: Integer); override;
    procedure Insert(Index: Integer; const S: string); override;
end;
```

STDCTRLS.PAS then defines the implementation of each method of this descendant class. When TListBox creates its class instances for its FItems variable, it actually creates an instance of this descendant class and refers to it with the FItems property:

```
constructor TCustomListBox.Create(AOwner: TComponent);
begin
  inherited Create(AOwner);
  ...
  FItems := TListBoxStrings.Create;   // Note: an instance of
                                      // TListBoxStrings is created
  ...
end;
```

We want to make it clear that although the TStrings class defines its methods, it doesn't implement these methods to manipulate strings. The TStrings descendant class does implementation of these methods. This is important if you're a component writer because you must know how to perform this technique as the Delphi components did it. It is always good to refer to the VCL source code to see how Borland performs these techniques when you're unsure.

If you're not a component writer but want to manipulate a list of strings, you can use the TStringList class, another descendant of TStrings, with which you can instantiate a completely self-contained class. TStringList maintains a list of strings external to components. The best part is that TStringList is totally compatible with TStrings. This means that you can directly assign a TStringList instance to a control's TStrings property. The following code shows how you can create an instance of TStringList:

```
var
  MyStringList: TStringList;
begin
  MyStringList := TStringList.Create;
```

To add strings to this TStringList instance, do the following:

```
MyStringList.Add('Red');
MyStringList.Add('White');
MyStringList.Add('Blue');
```

If you want to add these same strings to both a TMemo component and a TListBox component, all you have to do is take advantage of the compatibility between the different components' TStrings properties and make the assignments in one line of code each:

```
Memo1.Lines.Assign(MyStringList);
ListBox1.Items.Assign(MyStringList);
```

You use the Assign() method to copy TStrings instances instead of making a direct assignment like Memo1.Lines := MyStringList.

Table 20.4 shows some common methods of TStrings classes.

TABLE 20.4. SOME COMMON TStrings METHODS.

TStrings *Method*	*Description*
Add(const S: String): Integer	Adds the string S to the string lists and returns the string's position in the list.
AddObject(const S: string; AObject: TObject): Integer	Appends both a string and an object to a string or string list object.
AddStrings(Strings: TStrings)	Copies strings from one TStrings to the end of its existing list of strings.
Assign(Source: TPersistent)	Replaces the existing strings with those specified by the Source parameter.
Clear	Removes all strings from the list.
Delete(Index: Integer)	Removes the string at the location specified by Index.
Exchange(Index1, Index2: Integer)	Switches the location of the two strings specified by the two index values.
IndexOf(const S: String): Integer	Returns the position of the string S on the list.
Insert(Index: Integer; const S: String)	Inserts the string S into the position in the list specified by Index.
Move(CurIndex, NewIndex: Integer)	Moves the string at the position CurIndex to the position NewIndex.
LoadFromFile(const FileName: String)	Reads the text file, FileName, and places its lines into the string list.
SaveToFile(const FileName: string)	Saves the string list to the text file, FileName.

20

The `TCanvas` Class

The `Canvas` property, of type `TCanvas`, is provided for windowed controls and represents the drawing surface of the control. `TCanvas` encapsulates what's called the *device context* of a window. It provides many of the functions and objects required for drawing to the window's surface. Chapter 8 went into detail about the `TCanvas` class.

RUNTIME TYPE INFORMATION

Back in Chapter 2, you were introduced to *Runtime Type Information (RTTI)*. This chapter delves much deeper into the RTTI innards that will allow you to take advantage of RTTI beyond what you get in the normal usage of the Object Pascal language. In other words, we're going to show you how to obtain type information on objects and data types much like the way the Delphi IDE obtains the same information.

So how does RTTI manifest itself? You'll see RTTI at work in at least two areas with which you normally work. The first place is right in the Delphi IDE as stated earlier. Through RTTI, the IDE magically knows everything about the object and components with which you work—see the Object Inspector. Actually, there's more to it than just RTTI, but for the sake of this discussion, we're covering only the RTTI aspect of this. The second area is in the runtime code that you write. Already, in Chapter 2, you read about the `is` and `as` operators.

Let's examine the `is` operator to illustrate typical usage of RTTI.

Suppose that you need to make all `TEdit` components read-only on a given form. This is simple enough—just loop through all components, use the `is` operator to determine whether the component is a `TEdit` class, and then set the `ReadOnly` property accordingly.

```
for i := 0 to ComponentCount - 1 do
    if Components[i] is TEdit then
      TEdit(Components[i]).ReadOnly := True;
```

A typical use case for the `as` operator would be to perform an action on the `Sender` parameter of an event handler where the handler is attached to several different components. Assuming that you know that all components are derived from a common ancestor whose property you want to access, the event handler can use the `as` operator to safely typecast `Sender` as the desired descendant, thus surfacing the wanted property.

```
procedure TForm1.ControlOnClickEvent(Sender: TObject);
var
  i: integer;
begin
  (Sender as TControl).Enabled := False;
end;
```

These examples of *type-safe* programming illustrate enhancements to the Object Pascal language that indirectly use RTTI. Now look at a problem that would call for direct usage of RTTI.

Suppose that you have a form containing both data aware and nondata-aware components. You need to perform some action on only the data-aware components. Certainly you could loop through the `Components` array for the form and test for each data-aware component type. However, this could get messy to maintain because you would have to test against every type of data-aware component. Also, you don't have a base class to test against that is common to only data-aware components. For instance, something like `TDataAwareControl` would have been nice, but it doesn't exist.

A clean way to determine whether a component is data aware, is to test for the existence of a `DataSource` property. You are sure that this property exists for all data-aware components. To do this, however, you need to use RTTI directly.

The following sections discuss RTTI in more depth to give you the background knowledge needed to solve problems such as that mentioned earlier.

The `TypInfo.pas` Unit—Definer of Runtime Type Information

Type information exists for any object (a descendant of `TObject`). This information exists in memory and is queried by the IDE and the Runtime Library to obtain information about objects. The `TypInfo.pas` unit defines the structures that allow you to query for type information. Some methods of `TObject` are repeated from Chapter 2 in the following table.

Function	Return Type	Returns
ClassName()	string	The name of the object's class
ClassType()	TClass	The object's type
InheritsFrom()	Boolean	Boolean to indicate whether class descends from a given class
ClassParent()	TClass	The object ancestor's type
InstanceSize()	word	The size in bytes of an instance
ClassInfo()	Pointer	A pointer to the object's in-memory RTTI

For now, we want to focus on the `ClassInfo()` function, which is defined as:

```
class function ClassInfo: Pointer;
```

This function returns a pointer to the RTTI for the calling class. The structure to which this pointer refers is of the type `PTypeInfo`. This type is defined in the `TypInfo.pas` unit as a pointer to a `TTypeInfo` structure. Both definitions are given in the following code as they appear in `TypInfo.pas`.

```
PPTypeInfo = ^PTypeInfo;
  PTypeInfo = ^TTypeInfo;
  TTypeInfo = record
    Kind: TTypeKind;
    Name: ShortString;
   {TypeData: TTypeData}
  end;
```

The commented field, `TypeData`, represents the actual reference to the type information for the given class. The type to which it actually refers depends on the value of the `Kind` field. `Kind` can be of any of the enumerated values defined in the `TTypeKind`.

```
TTypeKind = (tkUnknown, tkInteger, tkChar, tkEnumeration, tkFloat,
    tkString, tkSet, tkClass, tkMethod, tkWChar, tkLString, tkWString,
    tkVariant, tkArray, tkRecord, tkInterface);
```

You might take a look at the `TypInfo.pas` unit at this time to examine subtypes to some of the preceding enumerated values to get yourself familiar with them. For example, the `tkFloat` value can be further broken down into one of the following:

```
TFloatType = (ftSingle, ftDouble, ftExtended, ftComp, ftCurr);
```

Now you know that `Kind` determines to which type `TypeData` refers. The `TTypeData` structure is defined in `TypInfo.pas` as shown in Listing 20.2.

LISTING 20.2. THE `TTypeData` STRUCTURE.

```
PTypeData = ^TTypeData;
TTypeData = packed record
  case TTypeKind of
    tkUnknown, tkLString, tkWString, tkVariant: ();
    tkInteger, tkChar, tkEnumeration, tkSet, tkWChar: (
        OrdType: TOrdType;
        case TTypeKind of
          tkInteger, tkChar, tkEnumeration, tkWChar: (
            MinValue: Longint;
            MaxValue: Longint;
            case TTypeKind of
              tkInteger, tkChar, tkWChar: ();
              tkEnumeration: (
                BaseType: PPTypeInfo;
                NameList: ShortStringBase));
          tkSet: (
            CompType: PPTypeInfo));
    tkFloat: (FloatType: TFloatType);
    tkString: (MaxLength: Byte);
    tkClass: (
```

```
        ClassType: TClass;
        ParentInfo: PPTypeInfo;
        PropCount: SmallInt;
        UnitName: ShortStringBase;
      {PropData: TPropData});
  tkMethod: (
    MethodKind: TMethodKind;
    ParamCount: Byte;
    ParamList: array[0..1023] of Char
    {ParamList: array[1..ParamCount] of
      record
        Flags: TParamFlags;
        ParamName: ShortString;
        TypeName: ShortString;
      end;
      ResultType: ShortString});
  tkInterface: (
      IntfParent : PPTypeInfo; { ancestor }
      IntfFlags : TIntfFlagsBase;
      Guid : TGUID;
      IntfUnit : ShortStringBase;
    {PropData: TPropData});
  end;
```

As you can see, the `TTypeData` structure is really just a big variant record. If you're familiar with working with variant records, and pointers, you'll see that dealing with RTTI is simple. It just seems complex because it's an undocumented feature.

NOTE

Often, Borland doesn't document a feature because it might change between versions. When using features such as the undocumented RTTI, realize that your code might not be fully portable between versions of Delphi.

At this point, we're ready to demonstrate how to use these structures of RTTI to obtain type information.

Obtaining Type Information

To demonstrate how to obtain Runtime Type Information on an object, we've created a project whose main form is defined in Listing 20.3.

LISTING 20.3. MAIN FORM FOR `ClassInfo.dpr`.

```
unit MainFrm;

interface

uses
  Windows, Messages, SysUtils, Classes, Graphics, Controls, Forms,
  Dialogs, StdCtrls, ExtCtrls, DBClient, MidasCon, MConnect;

type

  TMainForm = class(TForm)
    pnlTop: TPanel;
    pnlLeft: TPanel;
    lbBaseClassInfo: TListBox;
    spSplit: TSplitter;
    lblBaseClassInfo: TLabel;
    pnlRight: TPanel;
    lblClassProperties: TLabel;
    lbPropList: TListBox;
    lbSampClasses: TListBox;
    procedure FormCreate(Sender: TObject);
    procedure lbSampClassesClick(Sender: TObject);
  private
    { Private declarations }
  public
    { Public declarations }
  end;

var
  MainForm: TMainForm;

implementation
uses TypInfo;

{$R *.DFM}

function CreateAClass(const AClassName: string): TObject;
{ This method illustrates how you can create a class from the class name.
  Note that this requires that you register the class using
  RegisterClasses() as shown in the initialization method of this unit. }
var
  C : TFormClass;
  SomeObject: TObject;
begin
  C := TFormClass(FindClass(AClassName));
  SomeObject := C.Create(nil);
```

```
    Result := SomeObject;
end;


procedure GetBaseClassInfo(AClass: TObject; AStrings: TStrings);
{ This method obtains some basic RTTI data from the given object and adds
  that information to the AStrings parameter. }
var
  ClassTypeInfo: PTypeInfo;
  ClassTypeData: PTypeData;
  EnumName: String;
begin
  ClassTypeInfo := AClass.ClassInfo;
  ClassTypeData := GetTypeData(ClassTypeInfo);
  with AStrings do
  begin
    Add(Format('Class Name:    %s', [ClassTypeInfo.Name]));
    EnumName := GetEnumName(TypeInfo(TTypeKind),
    ➥Integer(ClassTypeInfo.Kind));
    Add(Format('Kind:          %s', [EnumName]));
    Add(Format('Size:          %d', [AClass.InstanceSize]));
    Add(Format('Defined in:    %s.pas', [ClassTypeData.UnitName]));
    Add(Format('Num Properties: %d',[ClassTypeData.PropCount]));
  end;
end;

procedure GetClassAncestry(AClass: TObject; AStrings: TStrings);
{ This method retrieves the ancestry of a given object and adds the
  class names of the ancestry to the AStrings parameter. }
var
  AncestorClass: TClass;
begin
  AncestorClass := AClass.ClassParent;
  { Iterate through the Parent classes starting with Sender's
    Parent until the end of the ancestry is reached. }
  AStrings.Add('Class Ancestry');
  while AncestorClass <> nil do
  begin
    AStrings.Add(Format('    %s',[AncestorClass.ClassName]));
    AncestorClass := AncestorClass.ClassParent;
  end;
end;


procedure GetClassProperties(AClass: TObject; AStrings: TStrings);
{ This method retrieves the property names and types for the given object
  and adds that information to the AStrings parameter. }
var
  PropList: PPropList;
  ClassTypeInfo: PTypeInfo;
```

continues

20

KEY ELEMENTS OF
THE VCL

LISTING 20.3. CONTINUED

```
  ClassTypeData: PTypeData;
  i: integer;
  NumProps: Integer;
begin

  ClassTypeInfo := AClass.ClassInfo;
  ClassTypeData := GetTypeData(ClassTypeInfo);

  if ClassTypeData.PropCount <> 0 then
  begin
    // allocate the memory needed to hold the references to the TPropInfo
    // structures on the number of properties.
    GetMem(PropList, SizeOf(PPropInfo) * ClassTypeData.PropCount);
    try
      // fill PropList with the pointer references to the TPropInfo
      // structures
      GetPropInfos(AClass.ClassInfo, PropList);
      for i := 0 to ClassTypeData.PropCount - 1 do
        // filter out properties that are events ( method pointer
        // properties)
        if not (PropList[i]^.PropType^.Kind = tkMethod) then
          AStrings.Add(Format('%s: %s', [PropList[i]^.Name,
            ➥PropList[i]^.PropType^.Name]));

      // Now get properties that are events (method pointer properties)
      NumProps := GetPropList(AClass.ClassInfo, [tkMethod], PropList);
      if NumProps <> 0 then begin
        AStrings.Add('');
        AStrings.Add('    EVENTS   =============== ');
        AStrings.Add('');
      end;
      // Fill the AStrings with the events.
      for i := 0 to NumProps - 1 do
          AStrings.Add(Format('%s: %s', [PropList[i]^.Name,
            ➥PropList[i]^.PropType^.Name]));

    finally
      FreeMem(PropList, SizeOf(PPropInfo) * ClassTypeData.PropCount);
    end;
  end;

end;

procedure TMainForm.FormCreate(Sender: TObject);
begin
  // Add some example classes to the list box.
  lbSampClasses.Items.Add('TApplication');
  lbSampClasses.Items.Add('TButton');
  lbSampClasses.Items.Add('TForm');
```

```
    lbSampClasses.Items.Add('TListBox');
    lbSampClasses.Items.Add('TPaintBox');
    lbSampClasses.Items.Add('TMidasConnection');
    lbSampClasses.Items.Add('TFindDialog');
    lbSampClasses.Items.Add('TOpenDialog');
    lbSampClasses.Items.Add('TTimer');
    lbSampClasses.Items.Add('TComponent');
    lbSampClasses.Items.Add('TGraphicControl');
end;

procedure TMainForm.lbSampClassesClick(Sender: TObject);
var
  SomeComp: TObject;
begin
  lbBaseClassInfo.Items.Clear;
  lbPropList.Items.Clear;

  // Create an instance of the selected class.
  SomeComp := CreateAClass(lbSampClasses.Items[lbSampClasses.ItemIndex]);
  try
    GetBaseClassInfo(SomeComp, lbBaseClassInfo.Items);
    GetClassAncestry(SomeComp, lbBaseClassInfo.Items);
    GetClassProperties(SomeComp, lbPropList.Items);
  finally
    SomeComp.Free;
  end;
end;

initialization
begin
  RegisterClasses([TApplication, TButton, TForm, TListBox, TPaintBox,
    TMidasConnection, TFindDialog, TOpenDialog, TTimer, TComponent,
    TGraphicControl]);
end;

end.
```

This main form contains three list boxes. lbSampClasses contains class names for a few sample objects whose type information we'll retrieve. On selecting an object from lbSampClasses, lbBaseClassInfo will be populated with basic information about the selected object such as its size and ancestry. lbPropList will display the properties belonging to the selected object from lbSampClasses.

Three helper procedures are used to obtain class information:

GetBaseClassInfo()	Populates a string list with basic information about an object such as its type, size, defining unit, and number of properties

20

KEY ELEMENTS OF THE VCL

GetClassAncestry()   Populates a string list with the object names of a given object's ancestry

GetClassProperties()   Populates a string list with the properties and their types for a given class

Each procedure takes an object instance and a string list as parameters.

As the user selects one of the classes from lbSampClasses, its OnClick event, lbSampClassesClick(), calls a helper function, CreateAClass(), which creates an instance of a class given the name of the class type. It then passes the object instance and the appropriate TListBox.Items property to be populated.

TIP

The CreateAClass() function can be used to create any class by its name. However, as demonstrated, you must make sure that any classes passed to it have been registered by calling the RegisterClasses()procedure.

Obtaining Runtime Type Information for Objects

GetBaseClassInfo() passes the return value from TObject.ClassInfo() to the function GetTypeData(). GetTypeData() is defined in TypInfo.pas. Its purpose is to return a pointer to the TTypeData structure based on the class whose PTypeInfo structure was passed to it (see Listing 20.2). GetBaseClassInfo() simply refers to the various fields of both the TTypeInfo and TTypeData structures to populate the AStrings string list. Note the use of the function GetEnumName() to return the string for an enumerated type. This is also a function of RTTI defined in TypInfo.pas. Type information on enumerated types is discussed in a later section.

TIP

Use the GetTypeData()function defined in TypInfo.pas to return a pointer to the TTypeInfo structure for a given class. You must pass the result of TObject.ClassInfo() to GetTypeData().

TIP

You can use the GetEnumName()function to obtain the name of an enumeration value as a string. GetEnumValue() returns the enumeration value given its name.

Obtaining the Ancestry for an Object

The GetClassAncestry() procedure populates a string list with the class names of the given object's ancestry. This is a simple operation that uses the ClassParent() class procedure on the given object. ClassParent() will return a TClass reference to the given class's parent, or nil if the top of the ancestry is reached. GetClassAncestry() simply walks up the ancestry and adds each class name to the string list until the top is reached.

Obtaining Type Information on Object Properties

If an object has properties, its TTypeData.PropCount value will contain the number of properties it has. There are several approaches you can use to obtain the property information for a given class—we demonstrate two.

The GetClassProperties() procedure begins much like the previous two methods in that it passes the ClassInfo() result to GetTypeData() to obtain the reference to the TTypeData structure for the class. It then allocates memory for the PropList variable based on the value of ClassTypeData.PropCount. PropList is defined as the type PPropList. PPropList is defined in TypInfo.pas as

```
type
  PPropList = ^TPropList;
  TPropList = array[0..16379] of PPropInfo;
```

The TPropList array stores pointers to the TPropInfo data for each property. TPropInfo is defined in TypInfo.pas as:

```
  PPropInfo = ^TPropInfo;
  TPropInfo = packed record
    PropType: PPTypeInfo;
    GetProc: Pointer;
    SetProc: Pointer;
    StoredProc: Pointer;
    Index: Integer;
    Default: Longint;
    NameIndex: SmallInt;
    Name: ShortString;
  end;
```

TPropInfo is the Runtime Type Information for a property.

GetClassProperties() uses the GetPropInfos() function to fill this array with pointers to the RTTI information for all properties for the given object. It then loops through the array and writes out the name and type for the property by accessing that property's type information. Note the line:

```
if not (PropList[i]^.PropType^.Kind = tkMethod) then
```

This is used to filter out properties that are events (method pointers). We populate these properties last, which allows us to demonstrate an alternative method for retrieving property RTTI. In the final part of the `GetClassProperties()` method, we use the `GetPropList()` function to return the `TPropList` for properties of a specific type. In this case, we want only properties of the type, `tkMethod`. `GetPropList()` is also defined in `TypInfo.pas`. Refer to the source commentary for additional information.

TIP

Use `GetPropInfos()` when you want to retrieve a pointer to the property Runtime Type Information for *all* properties of a given object. Use `GetPropList()` if you want to retrieve the same information, except for properties of a specific type.

Figure 20.2 shows the output of the main form with Runtime Type Information for a selected class.

FIGURE 20.2.

Output of a class's Runtime Type Information.

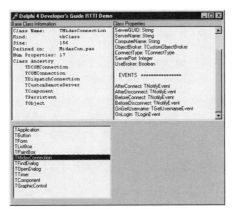

Checking for the Existence of a Property on an Object

Earlier we presented the problem of needing to check for the existence of a property for a given object. Specifically, we were referring to the `DataSource` property. Using functions defined in `TypInfo.pas`, we could write the following function to determine whether a control is data aware:

```
function IsDataAware(AComponent: TComponent): Boolean;
var
  PropInfo: PPropInfo;
begin
```

```
// Find the property named datasource.
PropInfo := GetPropInfo(AComponent.ClassInfo, 'DataSource');
Result := PropInfo <> nil;

// Double check, make sure it descends from TDataSource
if Result then
  if not ((PropInfo^.Proptype^.Kind = tkClass) and
(GetTypeData(PropInfo^.PropType^).ClassType.InheritsFrom(TDataSource)))
➡then
    Result := False;
end;
```

Here, we're using the `GetPropInfo()` function to return the `TPropInfo` pointer on a given property. This function returns `nil` if the property does not exist. As an additional check, we make sure that the property named `DataSource` is actually a descendant of `TDataSource`.

We also could have written this function more generically to check for the existence of any property by its name as:

```
function HasProperty(AComponent: TComponent; APropertyName: String):
  Boolean;
var
  PropInfo: PPropInfo;
begin
  PropInfo := GetPropInfo(AComponent.ClassInfo, APropertyName);
  Result := PropInfo <> nil;
end;
```

Note, however, that this works only on properties that are published. RTTI does not exist for unpublished properties.

Obtaining Type Information on Method Pointers

Runtime Type Information can be obtained on method pointers. For example, you can determine the type of method (procedure, function, and so on) and its parameters. Listing 20.4, demonstrates how to obtain Runtime Type Information for a selected group of methods.

LISTING 20.4. OBTAINING RUNTIME TYPE INFORMATION FOR METHODS.

```
unit MainFrm;

interface

uses
  Windows, Messages, SysUtils, Classes, Graphics, Controls, Forms,
```

continues

20

KEY ELEMENTS OF
THE VCL

LISTING 20.4. CONTINUED

```
  Dialogs, StdCtrls, ExtCtrls, DBClient, MidasCon, MConnect;

type

  TMainForm = class(TForm)
    lbSampMethods: TListBox;
    lbMethodInfo: TMemo;
    lblBasicMethodInfo: TLabel;
    procedure FormCreate(Sender: TObject);
    procedure lbSampMethodsClick(Sender: TObject);
  private
    { Private declarations }
  public
    { Public declarations }
  end;

var
  MainForm: TMainForm;

implementation
uses TypInfo, DBTables, Provider;

{$R *.DFM}

type
  // It is necessary to redefine this record as it is commented out in
  // typinfo.pas.

  PParamRecord = ^TParamRecord;
  TParamRecord = record
    Flags:     TParamFlags;
    ParamName: ShortString;
    TypeName:  ShortString;
  end;

procedure GetBaseMethodInfo(ATypeInfo: PTypeInfo; AStrings: TStrings);
{ This method obtains some basic RTTI data from the the TTypeInfo and adds
  that information to the AStrings parameter. }
var
  MethodTypeData: PTypeData;
  EnumName: String;
begin
  MethodTypeData := GetTypeData(ATypeInfo);
  with AStrings do
  begin
    Add(Format('Class Name:    %s', [ATypeInfo^.Name]));
    EnumName := GetEnumName(TypeInfo(TTypeKind),
    ➥Integer(ATypeInfo^.Kind));
```

```
      Add(Format('Kind:              %s', [EnumName]));
      Add(Format('Num Parameters: %d',[MethodTypeData.ParamCount]));
   end;
end;

procedure GetMethodDefinition(ATypeInfo: PTypeInfo; AStrings: TStrings);
{ This method retrieves the property info on a method pointer. We use this
   information to reconstruct the method definition. }
var
   MethodTypeData: PTypeData;
   MethodDefine:   String;
   ParamRecord:    PParamRecord;
   TypeStr:        ^ShortString;
   ReturnStr:      ^ShortString;
   i: integer;
begin
   MethodTypeData := GetTypeData(ATypeInfo);

   // Determine the type of method
   case MethodTypeData.MethodKind of
     mkProcedure:      MethodDefine := 'procedure ';
     mkFunction:       MethodDefine := 'function ';
     mkConstructor:    MethodDefine := 'constructor ';
     mkDestructor:     MethodDefine := 'destructor ';
     mkClassProcedure: MethodDefine := 'class procedure ';
     mkClassFunction:  MethodDefine := 'class function ';
   end;

   // point to the first parameter
   ParamRecord    := @MethodTypeData.ParamList;
   i := 1; // first parameter

   // loop through the method's parameters and add them to the string list
   // as they would be normally defined.
   while i <= MethodTypeData.ParamCount do
   begin
     if i = 1 then
       MethodDefine := MethodDefine+'(';

     if pfVar in ParamRecord.Flags then
       MethodDefine := MethodDefine+('var ');
     if pfconst in ParamRecord.Flags then
       MethodDefine := MethodDefine+('const ');
     if pfArray in ParamRecord.Flags then
       MethodDefine := MethodDefine+('array of ');
//   we won't do anything for the pfAddress but know that the Self
```

continues

20

LISTING 20.4. CONTINUED

```
//  parameter gets passed with this flag set.
{
    if pfAddress in ParamRecord.Flags then
      MethodDefine := MethodDefine+('*address* ');
}
    if pfout in ParamRecord.Flags then
      MethodDefine := MethodDefine+('out ');


    // Use pointer arithmetic to get the type string for the parameter.
    TypeStr := Pointer(Integer(@ParamRecord^.ParamName) +
      Length(ParamRecord^.ParamName)+1);

    MethodDefine := Format('%s%s: %s', [MethodDefine,
      ParamRecord^.ParamName, TypeStr^]);

    inc(i); // Increment the counter.

    // Go the the next parameter. Notice that use of pointer arithmetic to
    // get to the appropriate location of the next parameter.
    ParamRecord := PParamRecord(Integer(ParamRecord) + SizeOf(TParamFlags) +
      (Length(ParamRecord^.ParamName) + 1) + (Length(TypeStr^)+1));

    // if there are still parameters then setup
    if i <= MethodTypeData.ParamCount then
    begin
      MethodDefine := MethodDefine + '; ';
    end
    else
      MethodDefine := MethodDefine + ')';
  end;

  // If the method type is a function, it has a return value. This is also
  // placed in the method definition string. The return value will be at
  // the location following the last parameter.
  if MethodTypeData.MethodKind = mkFunction then
  begin
    ReturnStr := Pointer(ParamRecord);
    MethodDefine := Format('%s: %s;', [MethodDefine, ReturnStr^])
  end
  else
    MethodDefine := MethodDefine+';';

  // finally, add the string to the listbox.
  with AStrings do
  begin
```

```
      Add(MethodDefine)
   end;
end;

procedure TMainForm.FormCreate(Sender: TObject);
begin
   { Add some method types to the list box. Also, store the pointer to the
     RTTI data in listbox's Objects array }
   with lbSampMethods.Items do
   begin
     AddObject('TNotifyEvent', TypeInfo(TNotifyEvent));
     AddObject('TMouseEvent', TypeInfo(TMouseEvent));
     AddObject('TBDECallBackEvent', TypeInfo(TBDECallBackEvent));
     AddObject('TDataRequestEvent', TypeInfo(TDataRequestEvent));
     AddObject('TGetModuleProc', TypeInfo(TGetModuleProc));
     AddObject('TReaderError', TypeInfo(TReaderError));
   end;
end;

procedure TMainForm.lbSampMethodsClick(Sender: TObject);
begin
   lbMethodInfo.Lines.Clear;
   with lbSampMethods do
   begin
     GetBaseMethodInfo(PTypeInfo(Items.Objects[ItemIndex]),
     ➥lbMethodInfo.Lines);
     GetMethodDefinition(PTypeInfo(Items.Objects[ItemIndex]),
     ➥lbMethodInfo.Lines);
   end;
end;

end.
```

In Listing 20.4, we populate a list box, lbSampMethods, with some sample method names. We also store the reference to that method's RTTI in the Objects array of the list box. We do this by using the TypeInfo() function, which is a special function that can retrieve a pointer to Runtime Type Information for a given type identifier. When the user selects one of these methods, we use that RTTI data from the Objects array to retrieve and reconstruct the method definition from the information we have about the method and its parameters in the RTTI data. Refer to the listing's commentary for further information. Figure 20.3 shows this form's output when a method is selected.

FIGURE 20.3.

Output of a method's Runtime Type Information.

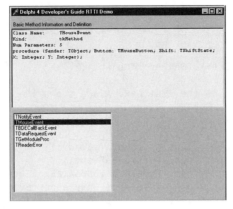

TIP

Use the `TypeInfo()` function to retrieve a pointer to the compiler generated Runtime Type Information for a given type identifier. For example, the following line retrieves a pointer to the RTTI for the `TButton` type:

```
TypeInfoPointer := TypeInfo(TButton);
```

Obtaining Type Information for Ordinal Types

We've already covered the more difficult pieces to RTTI. However, you can also obtain RTTI for ordinal types. The following sections illustrate how to obtain RTTI data on integer, enumerated, and set types.

Type Information for Integer Types

Obtaining type information for integer types is simple. Listing 20.5 illustrates this process.

LISTING 20.5. OBTAINING RUNTIME TYPE INFORMATION FOR INTEGERS.

```
procedure TForm1.Button1Click(Sender: TObject);
var
  OrdTypeInfo: PTypeInfo;
  OrdTypeData: PTypeData;

  TypeNameStr: String;
  TypeKindStr: String;
  MinVal, MaxVal: Integer;
```

```
begin
  ListBox1.Items.Clear;

  // Get the TTypeInfo pointer for the Integer type
  OrdTypeInfo := TypeInfo(Integer);
  // Get the TTypeData pointer
  OrdTypeData := GetTypeData(OrdTypeInfo);

  // Get the type name string
  TypeNameStr := OrdTypeInfo.Name;
  // Get the type kind string
  TypeKindStr := GetEnumName(TypeInfo(TTypeKind),
  ➥Integer(OrdTypeInfo^.Kind));

  // Get the minimum and maximum values for the type
  MinVal := OrdTypeData^.MinValue;
  MaxVal := OrdTypeData^.MaxValue;


  // Add the information to the memo
  with ListBox1.Items do
  begin
    Add('Type Name: '+TypeNameStr);
    Add('Type Kind: '+TypeKindStr);

    Add('Min Val: '+IntToStr(MinVal));
    Add('Max Val: '+IntToStr(MaxVal));
  end;
end;
```

Here, we use the TypeInfo() function to obtain a pointer to the TTypeInfo structure for
the Integer data type. We then pass that reference to the GetTypeData() function to
obtain a pointer to the TTypeData structure. We use both those structures to populate a
list box with the integer's RTTI. See the demo named IntegerRTTI.dpr in the directory
for this chapter on the CD for a more detailed demonstration.

Type Information for Enumerated Types

Obtaining RTTI for enumerated types is just as easy as it is for integers. In fact, you'll
see that Listing 20.6, is almost identical to Listing 20.5 with the exception of the additional for loop to show the values of the enumeration value.

LISTING 20.6. OBTAINING RTTI FOR AN ENUMERATED TYPE.

```
procedure TForm1.Button1Click(Sender: TObject);
var
  OrdTypeInfo: PTypeInfo;
  OrdTypeData: PTypeData;
```

continues

20

KEY ELEMENTS OF
THE VCL

LISTING 20.6. CONTINUED

```
  TypeNameStr: String;
  TypeKindStr: String;
  MinVal, MaxVal: Integer;
  i: integer;
begin
  ListBox1.Items.Clear;

  // Get the TTypeInfo pointer for the TBorderStyle type
  OrdTypeInfo := TypeInfo(TBorderStyle);
  // Get the TTypeData pointer
  OrdTypeData := GetTypeData(OrdTypeInfo);

  // Get the type name string
  TypeNameStr := OrdTypeInfo.Name;
  // Get the type kind string
  TypeKindStr := GetEnumName(TypeInfo(TTypeKind),
  ➥Integer(OrdTypeInfo^.Kind));

  // Get the minimum and maximum values for the type
  MinVal := OrdTypeData^.MinValue;
  MaxVal := OrdTypeData^.MaxValue;


  // Add the information to the memo
  with ListBox1.items do
  begin
    Add('Type Name: '+TypeNameStr);
    Add('Type Kind: '+TypeKindStr);

    Add('Min Val: '+IntToStr(MinVal));
    Add('Max Val: '+IntToStr(MaxVal));

    // Show the values and names of the enumerated types
    if OrdTypeInfo^.Kind = tkEnumeration then
      for i := MinVal to MaxVal do
        Add(Format(' Value: %d    Name: %s', [i, GetEnumName(OrdTypeInfo,
        ➥i)]));

  end;
end;
```

You'll find a more detailed demo, named EnumRTTI.dpr, on the CD in the directory for this chapter.

Type Information for Set Types

Obtaining RTTI for set types is only slightly more complex than the two previous techniques. Listing 20.7 is the main form for the project SetRTTI.dpr, which you'll find on the CD in the directory for this chapter.

LISTING 20.7. OBTAINING RTTI FOR SET TYPES.

```
unit MainFrm;

interface

uses
  Windows, Messages, SysUtils, Classes, Graphics, Controls, Forms,
  Dialogs, StdCtrls, Grids;

type
  TMainForm = class(TForm)
    lbSamps: TListBox;
    memInfo: TMemo;
    procedure FormCreate(Sender: TObject);
    procedure lbSampsClick(Sender: TObject);
  private
    { Private declarations }
  public
    { Public declarations }
  end;

var
  MainForm: TMainForm;

implementation
uses TypInfo, Buttons;

{$R *.DFM}


procedure TMainForm.FormCreate(Sender: TObject);
begin
  // Add some example enumerated types
  with lbSamps.Items do
  begin
    AddObject('TBorderIcons', TypeInfo(TBorderIcons));
    AddObject('TGridOptions', TypeInfo(TGridOptions));
  end;
end;

procedure GetTypeInfoForOrdinal(AOrdTypeInfo: PTypeInfo; AStrings:
➡TStrings);
var
//  OrdTypeInfo: PTypeInfo;
  OrdTypeData: PTypeData;

  TypeNameStr: String;
  TypeKindStr: String;
```

continues

LISTING 20.7. CONTINUED

```
  MinVal, MaxVal: Integer;
  i: integer;
begin

  // Get the TTypeData pointer
  OrdTypeData := GetTypeData(AOrdTypeInfo);

  // Get the type name string
  TypeNameStr := AOrdTypeInfo.Name;
  // Get the type kind string
  TypeKindStr := GetEnumName(TypeInfo(TTypeKind),
➡Integer(AOrdTypeInfo^.Kind));

  // Get the minimum and maximum values for the type
  MinVal := OrdTypeData^.MinValue;
  MaxVal := OrdTypeData^.MaxValue;


  // Add the information to the memo
  with AStrings do
  begin
    Add('Type Name: '+TypeNameStr);
    Add('Type Kind: '+TypeKindStr);


    // Call this function recursively to show the enumeration
    // values for this set type.
    if AOrdTypeInfo^.Kind = tkSet then
    begin
      Add('==========');
      Add('');
      GetTypeInfoForOrdinal(OrdTypeData^.CompType^, AStrings);
    end;

    // Show the values and names of the enumerated types belonging to the
    // set.
    if AOrdTypeInfo^.Kind = tkEnumeration then
    begin
      Add('Min Val: '+IntToStr(MinVal));
      Add('Max Val: '+IntToStr(MaxVal));

      for i := MinVal to MaxVal do
        Add(Format(' Value: %d   Name: %s', [i, GetEnumName(AOrdTypeInfo,
        ➡i)]));
    end;
  end;

end;
```

```
procedure TMainForm.lbSampsClick(Sender: TObject);
begin
  memInfo.Lines.Clear;
  with lbSamps do
    GetTypeInfoForOrdinal(PTypeInfo(Items.Objects[ItemIndex]),
    ↦memInfo.Lines);
end;
end.
```

In this demo, we set up two set types in a list box. We add the pointer to the TTypeInfo structures for these two types to the Objects array of the list box by using the TypeInfo() function. When the user selects one of the items in the list box, the GetTypeInfoForOrdinal() procedure is called passing both the PTypeInfo pointer and the memInfo.Lines property that is populated with the RTTI data.

The GetTypeInfoForOrdinal() procedure goes through the same steps you've already seen for getting the pointer to the type's TTypeData structure. This initial type information is stored to the TStrings parameter and then the GetTypeInfoForOrdinal() is called recursively, passing OrdTypeData^.CompType^, which refers to the enumerated data type for the set. This RTTI data is also added to the same TStrings property.

SUMMARY

This chapter introduced you to the Visual Component Library. We discussed the VCL hierarchy and the special characteristics of components at different levels in the hierarchy. We also covered Runtime Type Information in depth. This chapter prepared you for the following chapters, which cover component writing.

20

KEY ELEMENTS OF
THE VCL

WRITING DELPHI CUSTOM COMPONENTS

IN THIS CHAPTER

The ability to easily write custom components in Delphi 4 is a chief productivity advantage that you wield over other programmers. In most other environments, folks are stuck using the standard controls available through Windows or else have to use an entirely different set of complex controls that were developed by somebody else. Being able to incorporate your custom components into your Delphi applications means that you have complete control over the application's user interface. Custom controls give you the final say in your application's look and feel.

If your forte is component design, you will appreciate all the information this chapter has to offer. You will learn about all aspects of component design from concept to integration into the Delphi environment. You will also learn about the pitfalls of component design, as well as some tips and tricks to developing highly functional and extensible components.

Even if your primary interest is application development and not component design, you will get a great deal out of this chapter. Incorporating a custom component or two into your programs is an ideal way to spice up and enhance the productivity of your applications. Invariably, you will get caught in a situation while writing your application where, of all the components at your disposal, none is quite right for some particular task. That's where component design comes in. You will be able to tailor a component to meet your exact needs, and hopefully design it smart enough to use again and again in subsequent applications.

COMPONENT BUILDING BASICS

The following sections teach you the basic skills required to get you started in writing components. Then, we show you how to apply those skills by demonstrating how we designed some useful components.

Deciding Whether to Write a Component

Why go through the trouble of writing a custom control in the first place when it's probably less work to make do with an existing component or hack together something quick and dirty that "will do"? There are a number of reasons to write your own custom control:

- You want to design a new user-interface element that can be used in more than one application.
- You want to make your application more robust by separating its elements into logical object-oriented classes.
- You cannot find an existing Delphi component or ActiveX control that suits your needs for a particular situation.

Writing Delphi Custom Components

CHAPTER 21

513

21

WRITING DELPHI
CUSTOM
COMPONENTS

- You recognize a market for a particular component, and you want to create a component to share with other Delphi developers for fun or profit.

- You want to increase your knowledge of Delphi, VCL internals, and the Win32 API.

One of the best ways to learn how to create custom components is from the people who invented them. Delphi's VCL source code is an invaluable resource for component writers, and it is highly recommended for anyone who is serious about creating custom components. The VCL source code is included in the Client Server and Professional versions of Delphi.

Writing custom components can seem like a pretty daunting task, but don't believe the hype. Writing a custom component is only as hard or as easy as you make it. Components can be tough to write, of course, but you also can create very useful components fairly easily.

Component Writing Steps

Assuming that you have already defined a problem and have a component-based solution, here are the important points in creating a component—from concept to deployment.

- First, you need an idea for a useful and hopefully unique component.

- Next, sit down and map out the algorithm for how the component will work.

- Start with the preliminaries—don't jump right into the component. Ask yourself, "What do I need up front to make this component work?"

- Try to break up the construction of your component into logical portions. This will not only modularize and simplify the creation of the component, but it also will help you to write cleaner, more organized code. Design your component with the thought that someone else might try to create a descendant component.

- Test your component in a test project first. You will be sorry if you immediately add it to the Component Palette.

- Finally, add the component and an optional bitmap to the Component Palette. After a little fine-tuning, it will be ready for you to drop into your Delphi applications.

There are six basic steps to writing your Delphi component.

1. Deciding on an ancestor class.
2. Creating the Component Unit.
3. Adding properties, methods, and events to your new component.

4. Testing your component.

5. Registering your component with the Delphi environment.

6. Creating a help file for your component.

In this chapter, we'll discuss the first five steps as it is beyond the scope of this chapter to discuss writing help files. However, this does not mean that this step is any less important than the others. We recommend that you look into some of the third-party tools available that simplify writing help files. Also, Borland provides information on how to do this in their online help. Look up "Providing Help for Your Component" in the online help for more information.

Deciding on an Ancestor Class

In Chapter 20, "Key Elements of the Visual Component Library," we discussed the VCL hierarchy and the special purposes of the different classes at the different hierarchical levels. We wrote about four basic components from which your components will descend: standard controls, custom controls, graphical controls, and nonvisual components. For example, if you need to simply extend the behavior of an existing Win32 control like a TMemo, you'll be extending a standard control. If you need to define an entirely new component class, you'll be dealing with a custom control. Graphical controls let you create components that have a visual effect, but don't take up Win32 resources. Finally, if you want to create a component that can be edited from Delphi's Object Inspector but doesn't necessarily have a visual characteristic, you'll be creating a nonvisual component. Different VCL classes represent these different types of components. You might want to review Chapter 20 unless you're quite comfortable with these concepts. Table 21.1 gives you a quick reference.

TABLE 21.1. VCL CLASSES AS COMPONENT BASE CLASSES.

VCL Class	*Types of Custom Controls*
TObject	Although classes descending directly from TObject are not components, strictly speaking, they do merit mention. You will use TObject as a base class for many things that you don't need to work with at design time. A good example is the TIniFile object.
TComponent	A starting point for many nonvisual components. Its forte is that it offers built-in streaming capability to load and save itself in the IDE at design time.
TGraphicControl	Use this class when you want to create a custom component that has no window handle. TGraphicControl descendants are drawn on their parent's client surface, so they are easier on resources.

VCL Class	*Types of Custom Controls*
TWinControl	This is the base class for all components that require a window handle. It provides you with common properties and events specific to windowed controls.
TCustomControl	This class descends from TWinControl. It introduces the concepts of a canvas and a Paint() method to give you greater control over the component's appearance. Use this class for most of your window-handled custom component needs.
TCustom*ClassName*	The VCL contains several classes that do not publish all their properties but leave it up to descendant classes to do. This allows component developers to create "custom" components from the same base class and to publish only the predefined properties required for each customized class.
T*ComponentName*	An existing class such as TEdit, TPanel, or TScrollBox. Use an already established component as a base class for your class (such as TEdit), and custom components when you want to extend the behavior of TPanel, or an existing control, rather than create a new one from scratch. Most of your custom components will fall into this category.

It is extremely important that you understand these various classes and also the capabilities of the existing components. The majority of the time, you'll find that an existing component already provides most of the functionality you require of your new component. Only by knowing the capabilities of existing components will you be able to decide from which component to derive your new component. We can't inject this knowledge into your brain from this book. What we can do is to tell you that you must make every effort to learn about each component and class within Delphi's VCL, and the only way to do that is to use it, even if only experimentally.

Creating a Component Unit

When you have decided on a component from which your new component will descend, you can go ahead and create a unit for your new component. We're going to go through the steps of designing a new component in the next several sections. Because we want to focus on the steps, and not on component functionality, this component will do nothing other than to illustrate these necessary steps.

The component is appropriately named TddgWorthless. TddgWorthless will descend from TCustomControl and will therefore have both a window handle and the capability to paint itself. This component will also inherit several properties, methods, and events already belonging to TCustomControl.

The easiest way to get started is to use the Component Expert, shown in Figure 21.1, to create a component unit.

FIGURE 21.1.

The Component Expert.

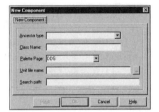

You invoke the Component Expert by selecting Component | New Component. In the Component Expert, you enter the component's ancestor class name, the component's class name, the palette page on which you want the component to appear, and the unit name for the component. When you select OK, Delphi automatically creates the component unit that has the component's type declaration and a register procedure. Listing 21.1 shows the unit created by Delphi.

LISTING 21.1. Worthless.pas, A SAMPLE DELPHI COMPONENT.

```
unit Worthless;
interface
uses
  Windows, Messages, SysUtils, Classes, Graphics, Controls, Forms,
Dialogs;
type
  TddgWorthless = class(TCustomControl)
  private
    { Private declarations }
  protected
    { Protected declarations }
  public
    { Public declarations }
  published
    { Published declarations }
  end;
procedure Register;
implementation
procedure Register;
begin
  RegisterComponents('DDG', [TddgWorthless]);
end;
end.
```

You can see that at this point TddgWorthless is nothing more than a skeleton component. In the following sections, you'll add properties, methods, and events to TddgWorthless.

Creating Properties

Chapter 20 discusses the use and advantages of using properties with your components. This section shows you how to add the various types of properties to your components.

Types of Properties

Table 20.1 in Chapter 20 listed the various property types. We're going to add properties of each of these types to the `TddgWorthless` component to illustrate the differences between each type. Each different type of property is edited a bit differently from the Object Inspector. You will examine each of these types and how they are edited.

Adding Simple Properties to Components

Simple properties refer to numbers, strings, and characters. They can be edited directly by the user from within the Object Inspector and require no special access method. Listing 21.2 shows the `TddgWorthless` component with three simple properties.

LISTING 21.2. SIMPLE PROPERTIES.

```
TddgWorthless = class(TCustomControl)
  private
    // Internal Data Storage
    FIntegerProp: Integer;
    FStringProp: String;
    FCharProp: Char;
published
    // Simple property types
    property IntegerProp: Integer read FIntegerProp write FIntegerProp;
    property StringProp: String read FStringProp write FStringProp;
    property CharProp: Char read FCharProp write FCharProp;
  end;
```

You should already be familiar with the syntax used here because it was discussed previously in Chapter 20. Here, you have your internal data storage for the component declared in the `private` section. The properties that refer to these storage fields are declared in the `published` section, meaning that when you install the component in Delphi, you can edit the properties in the Object Inspector.

NOTE

When writing components, the convention is to make private field names begin with the letter *F.* For components and types in general, give the object or type a name starting with the letter *T.* Your code will be much clearer if you follow these simple conventions.

Adding Enumerated Properties to Components

You can edit user-defined enumerated properties and Boolean properties in the Object Inspector by double-clicking in the Value section or by selecting the property value from a drop-down list. An example of such a property is the Align property that exists on most visual components. To create an enumerated property, you must first define the enumerated type as follows:

```
TEnumProp = (epZero, epOne, epTwo, epThree);
```

You then define the internal storage field to hold the value specified by the user. Listing 21.3 shows two enumerated property types for the TddgWorthless component.

LISTING 21.3. ENUMERATED PROPERTIES.

```
TddgWorthless = class(TCustomControl)
  private
    // Enumerated data types
    FEnumProp: TEnumProp;
    FBooleanProp: Boolean;
published
    property EnumProp: TEnumProp read FEnumProp write FEnumProp;
    property BooleanProp: Boolean read FBooleanProp write FBooleanProp;
  end;
```

We've excluded the other properties for illustrative purposes. If you were to install this component, its enumerated properties would appear in the Object Inspector as shown in Figure 21.2.

FIGURE 21.2.

The Object Inspector showing enumerated properties for TddgWorthless.

Adding Set Properties to Components

Set properties, when edited in the Object Inspector, appear as a set in Pascal syntax. An easier way to edit them is to expand the property in the Object Inspector. Each set item

Writing Delphi Custom Components

CHAPTER 21

519

21

WRITING DELPHI
CUSTOM
COMPONENTS

then works in the Object Inspector like a Boolean property. To create a set property for the `TddgWorthless` component, you must first define a set type as follows:

```
TSetPropOption = (poOne, poTwo, poThree, poFour, poFive);
TSetPropOptions = set of TSetPropOption;
```

Here, you first define a range for the set by defining an enumerated type, `TSetPropOption`. Then you define the set `TSetPropOptions`.

You can now add a property of `TSetPropOptions` to the `TddgWorthless` component as follows:

```
TddgWorthless = class(TCustomControl)
 private
   FOptions: TSetPropOptions;
published
   property Options: TSetPropOptions read FOptions write FOptions;
end;
```

Figure 21.3 shows how this property looks when expanded in the Object Inspector.

FIGURE 21.3.

The set property in the Object Inspector.

Adding Object Properties to Components

Properties can also be objects or other components. For example, the `TBrush` and `TPen` properties of a `TShape` component are also objects. When a property is an object, it can be expanded in the Object Inspector so its own properties can also be modified. Properties that are objects must be a descendant of `TPersistent` so that their published properties can be streamed and displayed in the Object Inspector.

To define an object property for the `TddgWorthless` component, you must first define an object that will serve as this property's type. This object is shown in Listing 21.4.

LISTING 21.4. TSomeObject DEFINITION.

```
TSomeObject = class(TPersistent)
  private
    FProp1: Integer;
    FProp2: String;
  public
    procedure Assign(Source: TPersistent)
  published
    property Prop1: Integer read FProp1 write FProp1;
    property Prop2: String read FProp2 write FProp2;
  end;
```

The TSomeObject class descends directly from TPersistent, although it doesn't have to. As long as the object from which the new class descends is, itself, a descendant of TPersistent, it can be used as another object's property.

We've given this class two properties of its own: Prop1 and Prop2, which are both simple property types. We've also added a procedure, Assign(), to TSomeObject, which we'll discuss momentarily.

Now, you can add a field of the type TSomeObject to the TddgWorthless component. However, because this property is an object, it must be created. Otherwise, when the user places a TddgWorthless component on the form, there won't be an instance of TSomeObject that the user can edit. Therefore, it is necessary to override the Create() constructor for TddgWorthless to create an instance of TSomeObject. Listing 21.5 shows the declaration of TddgWorthless with its new object property.

LISTING 21.5. ADDING OBJECT PROPERTIES.

```
TddgWorthless = class(TCustomControl)
private
  FSomeObject: TSomeObject;
  procedure SetSomeObject(Value: TSomeObject);
public
  constructor Create(AOwner: TComponent); override;
  destructor Destroy; override;
published
  property SomeObject: TSomeObject read FSomeObject write SetSomeObject;
end;
```

Notice that we've included the overridden Create() constructor and Destroy() destructor. Also, notice that we've declared a write access method, SetSomeObject(), for the SomeObject property. A write access method is often referred to as a *writer method*. Read access methods are called *reader methods*. If you recall from Chapter 20, writer methods must have one parameter of the same type as the property to which they belong. By convention, the name of the writer method usually begins with Set.

We've defined the TddgWorthless.Create() constructor as follows:

```
constructor TddgWorthless.Create(AOwner: TComponent);
begin
  inherited Create(AOwner);
  FSomeObject := TSomeObject.Create;
end;
```

Here, we first call the inherited Create() constructor and then create the instance of the TSomeObject class. Because Create() is called both when the user drops the component on the form at design time and when the application is run, you can be assured that FSomeObject will always be valid.

You must also override the Destroy() destructor to free the object before you free the TddgWorthless component. The code to do this follows.

```
destructor TddgWorthless.Destroy;
begin
  FSomeObject.Free;
  inherited Destroy;
end;
```

Now that we've shown how to create the instance of TSomeObject, consider what would happen if at runtime the user executes the following code:

```
var
  MySomeObject: TSomeObject;
begin
  MySomeObject := TSomeObject.Create;
  ddgWorthless.SomeObjectj := MySomeObject;
end;
```

If the TddgWorthless.SomeObject property were defined without a writer method like the following, when the user assigns their own object to the SomeObject field, the previous instance to which FSomeObject referred would be lost:

```
property SomeObject: TSomeObject read FSomeObject write FSomeObject;
```

If you recall from Chapter 2, "The Object Pascal Language," object instances are really pointer references to the actual object. When you make an assignment as shown in the preceding example, you refer the pointer to another object instance while the previous object instance still hangs around. When designing components, you want to avoid having to place conditions on your users when accessing properties. To prevent this pitfall, you foolproof your component by creating access methods for properties that are objects. These access methods can then ensure that no resources get lost when the user assigns new values to these properties. The access method for SomeObject does just that and is shown here:

```
procedure TddgWorthLess.SetSomeObject(Value: TSomeObject);
begin
  if Assigned(Value) then
    FSomeObject.Assign(Value);
end;
```

The SetSomeObject() method calls the FSomeObject.Assign(), passing it the new TSomeObject reference. TSomeObject.Assign() is implemented as follows:

```
procedure TSomeObject.Assign(Source: TPersistent);
begin
  if Source is TSomeObject then
  begin
    FProp1 := TSomeObject(Source).Prop1;
    FProp2 := TSomeObject(Source).Prop2;
    inherited Assign(Source);
  end;
end;
```

In TSomeObject.Assign(), you first ensure that the user has passed in a valid TSomeObject instance. If so, you then copy the property values from Source accordingly. This illustrates another technique you'll see throughout the VCL for assigning objects to other objects. If you have the VCL source code, you might take a look at the various Assign() methods such as TBrush and TShape to see how they are implemented. This would give you some ideas on how to implement them in your components.

CAUTION

Never make an assignment to a property in a property's writer method. For example, examine the following property declaration:

```
property SomeProp: integer read FSomeProp write SetSomeProp;
  ....
  procedure SetSomeProp(Value:integer);
  begin
    SomeProp := Value;  // This causes infinite recursion }
    end;
```

Because you are accessing the property itself (not the internal storage field), you cause the SetSomeProp() method to be called again, which results in a recursive loop. Eventually, the program will crash with a stack overflow. Always access the internal storage field in the writer methods of properties.

Writing Delphi Custom Components

CHAPTER 21

523

21

WRITING DELPHI
CUSTOM
COMPONENTS

Adding Array Properties to Components

Some properties lend themselves to being accessed as though they were arrays. That is, they contain a list of items that can be referenced with an index value. The actual items referenced can be of any object type. Examples of such properties are `TScreen.Fonts`, `TMemo.Lines`, and `TDBGrid.Columns`. Such properties require their own property editors. We will get into creating property editors later in the next chapter. Therefore, we won't get into detail on creating array properties that have a list of different object types until later. For now, we'll show a simple method for defining a property that can be indexed as though it were an array of items, yet contains no list at all.

You're going to put aside the `TddgWorthless` component for a moment and instead look at the `TddgPlanets` component. `TddgPlanets` contains two properties: `PlanetName` and `PlanetPosition`. `PlanetName` will be an array property that returns the name of the planet based on the value of an integer index. `PlanetPosition` won't use an integer index, but rather a string index. If this string is one of the planet names, the result will be the planet's position in the solar system.

For example, the following statement will display the string `"Neptune"` by using the `TddgPlanets.PlanetName` property:

```
ShowMessage(ddgPlanets.PlanetName[8]);
```

Compare the difference when the sentence `From the sun, Neptune is planet number: 8` is generated from the following statement:

```
ShowMessage('From the sun, Neptune is planet number: '+
  IntToStr(ddgPlanets.PlanetPosition['Neptune']));
```

Before we show you this component, we should list some key characteristics of array properties that differ from the other properties we've mentioned.

1. Array properties are declared with one or more index parameters. These indexes can be of any simple type. For example, the index may be an integer or it may be a string, but not a record or a class.

2. Both the `read` and `write` property access directives must be methods. They cannot be one of the component's fields.

3. If the array property is indexed by multiple index values, that is, the property represents a multidimensional array, the access method must include parameters for each index in the same order as defined by the property.

Now, we'll get to the actual component shown in Listing 21.6.

LISTING 21.6. `Planets.pas, TddgPlanets`—ILLUSTRATING ARRAY PROPERTIES.

```
unit planets;

interface

uses
  Classes, SysUtils;

type

  TddgPlanets = class(TComponent)
  private
    // Array property access methods
    function GetPlanetName(const AIndex: Integer): String;
    function GetPlanetPosition(const APlanetName: String): Integer;
  public
    { Array property indexed by an integer value. This will be the default
      array property.  }
    property PlanetName[const AIndex: Integer]: String
        read GetPlanetName; default;
    // Array property index by a string value
    property PlanetPosition[const APlantetName: String]: Integer
        read GetPlanetPosition;
  end;

implementation

const
  // Declare a constant array containing planet names
  PlanetNames: array[1..9] of String[7] =
    ('Mercury', 'Venus', 'Earth', 'Mars', 'Jupiter', 'Saturn',
     'Uranus', 'Neptune', 'Pluto');

function TddgPlanets.GetPlanetName(const AIndex: Integer): String;
begin
  { Return the name of the planet specified by Index. If Index is
    out of the range, then raise an exception }
  if (AIndex < 0) or (AIndex > 9) then
    raise Exception.Create('Wrong Planet number, enter a number 1-9')
  else
    Result := PlanetNames[AIndex];
end;

function TddgPlanets.GetPlanetPosition(const APlanetName: String):
Integer;
var
  i: integer;
begin
  Result := 0;
  i := 0;
```

```
  { Compare PName to each planet name and return the index of the
    appropriate position where PName appears in the constant array.
    Otherwise return zero. }
  repeat
    inc(i);
  until (i = 10) or (CompareStr(UpperCase(APlanetName),
      UpperCase(PlanetNames[i])) = 0);

  if i <> 10 then // A Planet name was found
    Result := i;
end;

end.
```

This component gives you an idea of how you would create an array property with both an integer and string being used as an index. Notice how the value returned from reading the property's value is based on the function return value and not a value from a storage field as is the case with the other properties. You can refer to the code's comments for additional explanation on this component.

Default Values

You can give a property a default value by assigning a value to the property in the component's constructor. Therefore, if you added the following statement to the constructor of the `TddgWorthless` component, its `FIntegerProp` property would always default to 100 when the component is first placed onto the form:

```
FIntegerProp := 100;
```

This is probably the best place to mention the `Default` and `NoDefault` directives for property declarations. If you've looked at Delphi's VCL source code, you've probably noticed that some property declarations contain a `Default` directive, as is the case with the `TComponent.FTag` property:

```
property Tag: Longint read FTag write FTag default 0;
```

Don't confuse this statement with the default value specified in the component's constructor that actually sets the property value. For example, change the declaration of the `IntegerProp` property for the `TddgWorthless` component to read as follows:

```
property IntegerProp: Integer read FIntegerProp write FIntegerProp default
➥100;
```

This statement does not set the value of the property to 100. This only affects whether the property value is saved when you save a form containing the `TddgWorthless` component. If `IntegerProp`'s value is not 100, the value will be saved to the DFM file.

Otherwise, it does not get saved (because 100 is what the property value will be in a newly constructed object prior to reading its properties from the stream). It is recommended that you use the Default directive whenever possible as it may speed up the load time of your forms. It is important that you realize that the Default directive does not set the value of the property. You must do that in the component's constructor as was shown previously.

The NoDefault directive is used to redeclare a property that specifies a default value, so that it will always be written to the stream regardless of its value. For example, you can redeclare your component to not specify a default value for the Tag property:

```
TSample = class(TComponent)
published
  property Tag NoDefault;
```

Note that you should never declare anything NoDefault unless you have a specific reason. An example of such a property is TForm.PixelsPerInch, which must always be stored so that scaling will work right at runtime. Also, string, floating point, and int64 type properties cannot declare default values.

To change a property's default value, you redeclare it by using the new default value (but no reader or writer methods).

Default Array Properties

You can declare an array property so that it is the default property for the component to which it belongs. This allows the component user to use the object instance as though it were an array variable. For example, using the TddgPlanets component, we declared the TddgPlanets.PlanetName property with the default keyword. By doing this, the component user is not required to use the property name, PlanetName, in order to retrieve a value. One simply has to place the index next to the object identifier. Thus, the following two lines of code will produce the same result:

```
ShowMessage(ddgPlanets.PlanetName[8]);
ShowMessage(ddgPlanets[8]);
```

Only one default array property can be declared for an object, and it cannot be overridden in descendants.

Creating Events

In Chapter 20, we introduced events and told you that events were special properties linked to code that gets executed whenever a particular action occurs. In this section, we're going to discuss events in more detail. We'll show you how events are generated and how you can define your own event properties for your custom components.

Writing Delphi Custom Components

CHAPTER 21

527

21

WRITING DELPHI
CUSTOM
COMPONENTS

Where Do Events Come From?

The general definition of an event is basically any type of occurrence that might result from user interaction, the system, or from code logic. The event is linked to some code that responds to that occurrence. The linkage of the event to code that responds to an event is called an *event property* and is provided in the form of a method pointer. The method to which an event property points is called an *event handler*.

For example, when the user presses the mouse button, a WM_MOUSEDOWN message is sent to the Win32 system. Win32 passes that message to the control for which the message was intended. This control can then respond to the message. The control can respond to this event by first checking to see if there is any code to execute. It does this by checking to see if the event property points to any code. If so, it executes that code, or rather, the event handler.

The OnClick event is just one of the standard event properties defined by Delphi. OnClick and other event properties each have a corresponding *event-dispatching method*. This method is typically a protected method of the component to which it belongs. This method performs the logic to determine whether the event property refers to any code provided by the user of the component. For the OnClick property, this would be the Click() method. Both the OnClick property and the Click() method are defined by TControl as follows:

```
TControl = class(TComponent)
private
  FOnClick: TNotifyEvent;
protected
  procedure Click; dynamic;
  property OnClick: TNotifyEvent read FOnClick write FOnClick;
end;
```

The TControl.Click() method follows:

```
procedure TControl.Click;
begin
  if Assigned(FOnClick) then FOnClick(Self);
end;
```

One bit of essential information that you must understand is that event properties are nothing more then method pointers. Notice that FOnClick property is defined to be a TNotifyEvent. TNotifyEvent is defined as

```
TNotifyEvent = procedure(Sender: TObject) of object;
```

This says that TNotifyEvent is a procedure that takes one parameter, Sender, which is of the type TObject. The directive, of object, is what makes this procedure become a method. This means that an additional *implicit* parameter that you do not see in the parameter list also gets passed to this procedure. This is the `Self` parameter that refers to the object to which this method belongs. When the `Click()` method of a component is called, it checks to see if `FOnClick` actually points to a method, and if so, calls that method.

As a component writer, you write all the code that defines your event, your event property, and your dispatching methods. The component user will provide the event handler when they use your component. Your event-dispatching method will check to see if the user has assigned any code to your event property and then execute it when code exists.

In Chapter 20, we discussed how event handlers are assigned to event properties either at runtime or at design time. In the following section, we show you how to create your own events, event properties, and dispatching methods.

Defining Event Properties

Before you define an event property, you need to determine whether you need a special event type. It helps to be familiar with the common event properties that exist in the Delphi VCL. Most of the time, you'll be able to have your component descend from one of the existing components and just use its event properties, or you might have to surface a protected event property. If you determine that none of the existing events meet your need, you can define your own.

Creating Your Own Events

As an example, consider the following scenario. Suppose you want a component that contains an event that gets called every half-minute based on the system clock. That is, it gets invoked on the minute and on the half-minute. Well, you can certainly use a `TTimer` component to check the system time and then perform some action whenever the time is at the minute or half-minute. But you might want to incorporate this code into your own component and then make that component available to your users so that all they have to do is to add code to your `OnHalfMinute` event.

The `TddgHalfMinute` component shown in Listing 21.7 illustrates how you would design such a component. More importantly, it shows how you would go about creating your own event type.

LISTING 21.7. `TddgHalfMinute`—EVENT CREATION.

```
unit halfmin;

interface
```

```
uses
  Windows, Messages, SysUtils, Classes, Graphics, Controls,
  Forms, Dialogs, ExtCtrls;

type
  { Define a procedure for the event handler. The event property will
    be of this procedure type. This type will take two parameters, the
    object that invoked the event and a TDateTime value to represent
    the time that the event occurred. For our component this will be
    every half-minute. }
  TTimeEvent = procedure(Sender: TObject; TheTime: TDateTime) of object;

  TddgHalfMinute = class(TComponent)
  private
    FTimer: TTimer;
    { Define a storage field to point to the user's event handler.
      The user's event handler must be of the procedural type
      TTimeEvent. }
    FOnHalfMinute: TTimeEvent;
    FOldSecond, FSecond: Word; // Variables used in the code
    { Define a procedure, FTimerTimer that will be assigned to
      FTimer.OnClick. This procedure must be of the type TNotifyEvent
      which is the type of TTimer.OnClick. }
    procedure FTimerTimer(Sender: TObject);
  protected
    { Define the dispatching method for the OnHalfMinute event. }
    procedure DoHalfMinute(TheTime: TDateTime); dynamic;
  public
    constructor Create(AOwner: TComponent); override;
    destructor Destroy; override;
  published
    // Define the actual property that will show in the Object Inspector
    property OnHalfMinute: TTimeEvent read FOnHalfMinute write
    ➥FOnHalfMinute;
  end;

implementation

constructor TddgHalfMinute.Create(AOwner: TComponent);
{ The Create constructor, creates the TTimer instanced for FTimer. It
  then sets up the various properties of FTimer, including its OnTimer
  event handler which is TddgHalfMinute's FTimerTimer() method. Notice
  that FTimer.Enabled is set to true only if the component is running
  and not while the component is in design mode. }
begin
  inherited Create(AOwner);
  // If the component is in design mode, do not enable FTimer.
```

continues

LISTING 21.7. CONTINUED

```pascal
  if not (csDesigning in ComponentState) then
  begin
    FTimer := TTimer.Create(self);
    FTimer.Enabled := True;
    // Set up the other properties, including the FTimer.OnTimer event
    // handler
    FTimer.Interval := 500;
    FTimer.OnTimer := FTimerTimer;
  end;
end;

destructor TddgHalfMinute.Destroy;
begin
  FTimer.Free;
  inherited Destroy;
end;

procedure TddgHalfMinute.FTimerTimer(Sender: TObject);
{ This method serves as the FTimer.OnTimer event handler and is assigned
  to FTimer.OnTimer at run-time in TddgHalfMinute's constructor.

  This method gets the system time, and then determines whether or not
  the time is on the minute, or on the half-minute. If either of these
  conditions are true, it calls the OnHalfMinute dispatching method,
  DoHalfMinute. }
var
  DT: TDateTime;
  Temp: Word;
begin
  DT := Now; // Get the system time.
  FOldSecond := FSecond; // Save the old second.
  // Get the time values, needed is the second value
  DecodeTime(DT, Temp, Temp, FSecond, Temp);

  { If not the same second when this method was last called, and if
    it is a half minute, call DoOnHalfMinute. }
  if FSecond <> FOldSecond then
    if ((FSecond = 30) or (FSecond = 0)) then
      DoHalfMinute(DT)
end;

procedure TddgHalfMinute.DoHalfMinute(TheTime: TDateTime);
{ This method is the dispatching method for the OnHalfMinute event.
  it checks to see if the user of the component has attached an
  event handler to OnHalfMinute and if so, calls that code. }
begin
  if Assigned(FOnHalfMinute) then
    FOnHalfMinute(Self, TheTime);
end;

end.
```

When creating your own events, you must determine what information you want to provide to users of your component as a parameter in the event handler. For example, when you create an event handler for the TEdit.OnKeyPress event, your event handler looks like the following code:

```
procedure TForm1.Edit1KeyPress(Sender: TObject; var Key: Char);
begin
end;
```

Not only do you get a reference to the object that caused the event, but you also get a Char parameter specifying the key that was pressed. Deep in the Delphi VCL, this event occurred as a result of a WM_CHAR Win32 message that drags along some additional information relating to the key pressed. Delphi takes care of extracting the necessary data and making it available to component users as event handler parameters. One of the nice things about the whole scheme is that it enables component writers to take information that might be somewhat complex to understand and make it available to component users in a much more understandable and easy-to-use format.

Notice the var parameter in the preceding Edit1KeyPress() method. You might be wondering why this method was not declared as a function that returns a Char type instead of a procedure. Although method types can be functions, you should not declare events as functions because it will introduce ambiguity; when you refer to a method pointer that is a function, you can't know whether you're referring to the function result or to the function pointer value itself. By the way, there is one function event in the VCL that slipped past the developers from the Delphi 1 days and now it must remain. This event is the TApplication.OnHelp event.

Looking at Listing 21.7, you'll see that we've defined a procedure type TOnHalfMinute as

```
TTimeEvent = procedure(Sender: TObject; TheTime: TDateTime) of object;
```

This procedure type defines the procedure type for the OnHalfMinute event handler. Here, we decided that we want the user to have a reference to the object causing the event to occur, and the TDateTime value of when the event occurred.

The FOnHalfMinute storage field is the reference to the user's event handler and is surfaced to the Object Inspector at design time through the OnHalfMinute property.

The basic functionality of the component uses a TTimer object to check the seconds value every half second. If the seconds value is 0 or 30, it invokes the DoHalfMinute() method, which is responsible for checking for the existence of an event handler and then calling it. Much of this is explained in the code's comments, which you should read over.

After installing this component to Delphi's Component Palette, you can place the component on the form and add the following event handler to the OnHalfMinute event:

```
procedure TForm1.ddgHalfMinuteHalfMinute(Sender: TObject; TheTime:
TDateTime);
begin
  ShowMessage('The Time is '+TimeToStr(TheTime));
end;
```

This should illustrate how your newly defined event type becomes an event handler.

Creating Methods

Adding methods to components is no different than adding methods to other objects. However, there are a few guidelines that you should always take into account when designing components.

No Interdependencies!

One of the key goals behind creating components is to simplify the use of the component for the end user. Therefore, you'll want to avoid any method interdependencies as much as possible. For example, you never want to force the user to have to call a particular method in order to use the component, and methods should not have to be called in any particular order. Also, methods called by the user should not place the component in a state that makes other events or methods invalid. Finally, you'll want to give your methods meaningful names so that the user doesn't have to try to guess what a method does.

Method Exposure

Part of designing a component is to know what methods to make private, public, or protected. You must take into account not only users of your component but also those who might use your component as an ancestor for yet another custom component. Table 21.2 will help you decide what goes where in your custom component.

TABLE 21.2. PRIVATE, PROTECTED, PUBLIC, OR PUBLISHED?

Directive	What Goes There?
Private	Instance variables and methods that you do not want the descendant type to be able to access or modify. Typically, you will give access to some private instance variables through properties that have read and write directives set in such a way as to help prevent the users from shooting themselves in the foot. Therefore, you want to avoid giving access to any methods that are property-implementation methods.

Writing Delphi Custom Components

CHAPTER 21

533

21

WRITING DELPHI
CUSTOM
COMPONENTS

Directive	What Goes There?
Protected	Instance variables, methods, and properties that you want descendant classes to be able to access and modify—but not users of your class. It is a common practice to place properties in the protected section of a base class for descendant classes to publish at their discretion.
Public	Methods and properties that you want to be accessible to any user of your class. If you have properties that you want to be accessible at runtime, but not at design time, this is the place to put them.
Published	Properties that you want to be placed on the Object Inspector at design time. Runtime Type Information is generated for all properties in this section.

Constructors and Destructors

When creating a new component, you have the option of overriding the ancestor component's constructor and defining your own. There are a few precautions that you should keep in mind when doing so.

Overriding Constructors

Always make sure to include the `override` directive when declaring a constructor on a `TComponent` descendant class as shown following:

```
TSomeComopnent = class(TComponent)
private
  { Private declarations }
protected
  { Protected declarations }
public
  constructor Create(AOwner: TComponent); override;
published
  { Published declarations }
end;
```

> **NOTE**
>
> The `Create()` constructor is made virtual at the `TComponent` level. Noncomponent classes have static constructors that are invoked from within the constructor of `TComponent` classes. Therefore, if you are creating a noncomponent, descendant class such as the following, the constructor cannot be overridden because it is not virtual:
>
> `TMyObject = class(TPersistant)`
>
> You simply redeclare the constructor in this instance.

Although not adding the override directive is syntactically legal, it can cause problems when using your component. This is because when you use the component (both at design time and at runtime), the nonvirtual constructor won't be called by code that creates the component through a class reference (such as the streaming system).

Also, be sure that you call the inherited constructor inside your constructor's code:

```
constructor TSomeComponent.Create(AOwner: TComponent);
begin
  inherited Create(AOwner);
  // Place your code here.
end;
```

Design-Time Behavior

Remember that your component's constructor is called whenever the component is created. This includes the component's design-time creation—when you place it on the form. You might want to prevent certain actions from occurring when the component is being designed. For example, in the TddgHalfMinute component, you created a TTimer component inside the component's constructor. Although it doesn't hurt to do this, it can be avoided by making sure that the TTimer is only created at runtime.

You can check the ComponentState property of a component to determine its current state. Table 21.3 lists the various component states as shown in Delphi 4's online help.

TABLE 21.3. COMPONENT STATE VALUES.

Flag	Component State
csAncestor	Set if the component was introduced in an ancestor form. Only set if csDesigning is also set.
csDesigning	Design mode, meaning it is in a form being manipulated by a form designer.
csDestroying	The component is about to be destroyed.
csFixups	Set if the component is linked to a component in another form that has not yet been loaded. This flag is cleared when all pending fixups are resolved.
csLoading	Loading from a filer object.
csReading	Reading its property values from a stream.
csUpdating	The component is being updated to reflect changes in an ancestor form. Only set if csAncestor is also set.
csWriting	Writing its property values to a stream.

Writing Delphi Custom Components

CHAPTER 21

535

21

WRITING DELPHI
CUSTOM
COMPONENTS

You will mostly use the `csDesigning` state to determine whether your component is in design mode. You can do this with the following statement:

```
inherited Create(AOwner);
if  csDesigning in ComponentState then
  { Do your stuff }
```

You should note that the `csDesigning` state is uncertain until after the inherited constructor has been called and the component is being created with an owner. This is almost always the case in the IDE form designer.

Overriding Destructors

The general guideline to follow when overriding destructors is to make sure you call the inherited destructor only after you free up resources allocated by your component, not before. The following code illustrates this:

```
destructor TMyComponent.Destroy;
begin
  FTimer.Free;
  MyStrings.Free;
  inherited Destroy;
end;
```

> **TIP**
>
> As a rule of thumb, when you override constructors, you usually call the inherited constructor first, and when you override destructors, you usually call the inherited destructor last. This ensures that the class has been set up before you modify it and that all dependent resources have been cleaned up before you dispose of a class.
>
> There are exceptions to this rule, but you generally should stick with it unless you have good reason not to.

Registering Your Component

Registering the component tells Delphi which component to place on the Component Palette. If you used the Component Expert to design your component, you don't have to do anything here because Delphi has already generated the code for you. However, if you are creating your component manually, you'll need to add the `Register()` procedure to your component's unit.

All you have to do is add the procedure `Register()` to the `interface` section of the component's unit.

The Register procedure simply calls the RegisterComponents() procedure for every component that you are registering in Delphi. The RegisterComponents() procedure takes two parameters: the name of the page on which to place the components and an array of component types. Listing 21.8 shows how to do this.

LISTING 21.8. REGISTERING COMPONENTS.

```
Unit MyComp;
interface
type
  TMyComp = class(TComponent)
  ...
  end;
  TOtherComp = class(TComponent)
  ...
  end;
procedure Register;
implementation
{ TMyComp methods }
{ TOtherCompMethods }
procedure Register;
begin
  RegisterComponents('DDG', [TMyComp, TOtherComp]);
end;
end.
```

The preceding code registers the components TMyComp and TOtherComp and places them on Delphi's Component Palette on a page labeled DDG.

THE COMPONENT PALETTE

In Delphi 1 and 2, Delphi maintained a single component library file that stored all components, icons, and editors for design-time usage. Although it was sometimes convenient to have everything dealing with design in one file, it could easily get unwieldy when many components were placed in the component library. Additionally, the more components you added to the palette, the longer it would take to rebuild the component library when adding new components.

Thanks to packages, introduced with Delphi 3, you can split up your components into several design packages. Although it's slightly more complex to deal with multiple files, this solution is significantly more configurable, and the time required to rebuild a package after adding a component is a fraction of the time it took to rebuild the component library.

Writing Delphi Custom Components

Chapter 21

537

21

WRITING DELPHI
CUSTOM
COMPONENTS

By default, new components are added to a package called DCLUSR40, but you can create and install new design packages using the File I New I Package menu item. The CD accompanying this book contains a prebuilt design package called Ddglib40.dpk (in the \SOURCE\COMPS subdirectory), which includes the components from this book. The runtime package is named Ddgstd40.dpk.

If your design-time support involves anything more than a call to RegisterComponents() (like property editors or component editors or expert registrations), you should move the Register() procedure and the stuff it registers into a separate unit from your component. The reason for this is that if you compile your all-in-one unit into a runtime package, and your all-in-one unit's Register procedure refers to classes or procedures that exist only in design-time IDE packages, your runtime package is unusable. Design-time support should be packaged separately from runtime material.

Testing the Component

Although it's very exciting when you finally write a component and are in the testing stages, don't get carried away by trying to add your component to the Component Palette before it has been debugged sufficiently. You should do all preliminary testing with your component by creating a project that creates and uses a dynamic instance of the component. The reason for this is that your component lives inside the IDE when it is used at design time. If your component contains a bug that corrupts memory, for example, it might crash the IDE as well. Listing 21.9 depicts a unit for testing the TddgExtendedMemo component that will be created later in this chapter. This project can be found on the CD in the project TestEMem.dpr.

LISTING 21.9. TESTING THE TddgExtendedMemo COMPONENT.

```
unit MainFrm;

interface

uses
  Windows, Messages, SysUtils, Classes, Graphics, Controls,
  Forms, Dialogs, StdCtrls, exmemo, ExtCtrls;

type

  TMainForm = class(TForm)
    btnCreateMemo: TButton;
    btnGetRowCol: TButton;
```

continues

LISTING 21.9. CONTINUED

```
    btnSetRowCol: TButton;
    edtColumn: TEdit;
    edtRow: TEdit;
    Panel1: TPanel;
    procedure btnCreateMemoClick(Sender: TObject);
    procedure btnGetRowColClick(Sender: TObject);
    procedure btnSetRowColClick(Sender: TObject);
  public
    EMemo: TddgExtendedMemo;  // Declare the component.
    procedure OnScroll(Sender: TObject);
  end;

var
  MainForm: TMainForm;

implementation

{$R *.DFM}

procedure TMainForm.btnCreateMemoClick(Sender: TObject);
begin
  { Dynamically create the component. Make sure to make the appropriate
    property assignments so that the component can be used normally.
    These assignments depend on the component being tested }
  if not Assigned(EMemo) then
  begin
    EMemo := TddgExtendedMemo.Create(self);
    EMemo.Parent := Panel1;
    EMemo.ScrollBars := ssBoth;
    EMemo.WordWrap := True;
    EMemo.Align := alClient;
    // Assign event handlers to untested events.
    EMemo.OnVScroll := OnScroll;
    EMemo.OnHScroll := OnScroll;
  end;
end;

{ Write whatever methods are required to test the run-time behavior
  of the component. This includes methods to access each of the
  new properties and methods belonging to the component.

  Also, create event handlers for user-defined events so that you can
  test them. Since you're creating the component at runtime, you
  have to manually assign the event handlers as was done in the
  above Create() constructor.
}
procedure TMainForm.btnGetRowColClick(Sender: TObject);
begin
  if Assigned(EMemo) then
```

```
    ShowMessage(Format('Row: %d   Column: %d', [EMemo.Row, EMemo.Column]));
  EMemo.SetFocus;
end;

procedure TMainForm.btnSetRowColClick(Sender: TObject);
begin
  if Assigned(EMemo) then
  begin
    EMemo.Row := StrToInt(edtRow.Text);
    EMemo.Column := StrToInt(edtColumn.Text);
    EMemo.SetFocus;
  end;
end;

procedure TMainForm.OnScroll(Sender: TObject);
begin
  MessageBeep(0);
end;

end.
```

Keep in mind that even testing the component at design time doesn't mean that your component is foolproof. Some design-time behavior can still raise havoc with the Delphi IDE, like not calling the inherited `Create()` constructor.

NOTE

You cannot assume that your component has been created and set up by the design-time environment. Your component must be fully usable after only the `Create()` constructor has executed. Therefore, you should not treat the `Loaded()` method as part of the component construction process. The `Loaded()` method is called only when the component is loaded from a stream—such as when it is placed in a form built at design time. `Loaded()` marks the end of the streaming process. If your component was simply created (not streamed), `Loaded()` is not called.

Providing a Component Icon

No custom component would be complete without its own icon for the Component Palette. To create one of these icons, use Delphi's Image Editor (or your favorite bitmap editor) to create a 24×24 bitmap on which you will draw the component's icon. This bitmap must be stored within a DCR file. A file with a `.dcr` extension is nothing more than a renamed RES file. Therefore, if you store your icon in a RES file, you can simply rename it to a DCR file.

> **TIP**
>
> Even if you have a 256 or higher color driver, save your Component Palette icon as a 16-color bitmap if you plan on releasing the component to others. Your 256-color bitmaps most likely will look awful on machines running 16-color drivers.

After you create the bitmap in the DCR file, give the bitmap the same name as the class name of your component—in ALL CAPS. Save the resource file as the same name as your component's unit with a `.dcr` extension. So if your component is named `TXYZComponent`, the bitmap name is `TXYZCOMPONENT`. If the component's unit name is `XYZCOMP.PAS`, name the resource file `XYZCOMP.DCR`. Place this file in the same directory as the unit, and when you recompile the unit, the bitmap automatically is linked into the component library.

SAMPLE COMPONENTS

The remaining sections of this chapter give some real examples of component creation. The components created here serve two primary purposes. First, they illustrate the techniques explained in the first part of this chapter. Secondly, you can actually use these components in your applications. You might even decide to extend their functionality to meet your needs.

Extending Win32 Component Wrapper Capabilities

In some cases you might want to extend the functionality of existing components, especially those components that wrap the Win32 control classes. We're going to show you how to do this by creating two components that extend the behavior of the `TMemo` control and the `TListBox` control.

TddgExtendedMemo—Extending the `TMemo` Component

Although the `TMemo` component is quite robust, there are a few features that it doesn't make available that would be useful. For starters, it's not capable of providing the caret position in terms of the row and column on which the caret sits. We'll extend the `TMemo` component to provide these as public properties.

Writing Delphi Custom Components

CHAPTER 21

541

21

WRITING DELPHI
CUSTOM
COMPONENTS

Additionally, it is sometimes convenient to perform some action whenever the user touches the TMemo's scrollbars. You'll create events to which the user can attach code whenever these scrolling events occur.

The source code for the TddgExtendedMemo component is shown in Listing 21.10.

LISTING 21.10. ExtMemo.pas, THE SOURCE FOR THE TddgExtendedMemo COMPONENT.

```
unit ExMemo;

interface

uses
  Windows, Messages, Classes, StdCtrls;

type

  TddgExtendedMemo = class(TMemo)
  private
    FRow: Longint;
    FColumn: Longint;
    FOnHScroll: TNotifyEvent;
    FOnVScroll: TNotifyEvent;
    procedure WMHScroll(var Msg: TWMHScroll); message WM_HSCROLL;
    procedure WMVScroll(var Msg: TWMVScroll); message WM_VSCROLL;
    procedure SetRow(Value: Longint);
    procedure SetColumn(Value: Longint);
    function GetRow: Longint;
    function GetColumn: Longint;
  protected
    // Event dispatching methods
    procedure HScroll; dynamic;
    procedure VScroll; dynamic;
  public
    property Row: Longint read GetRow write SetRow;
    property Column: Longint read GetColumn write SetColumn;
  published
    property OnHScroll: TNotifyEvent read FOnHScroll write FOnHScroll;
    property OnVScroll: TNotifyEvent read FOnVScroll write FOnVScroll;
  end;

procedure Register;

implementation

procedure TddgExtendedMemo.WMHScroll(var Msg: TWMHScroll);
begin
  inherited;
  HScroll;
end;
```

continues

LISTING 21.10. CONTINUED

```
procedure TddgExtendedMemo.WMVScroll(var Msg: TWMVScroll);
begin
  inherited;
  VScroll;
end;

procedure TddgExtendedMemo.HScroll;
{ This is the OnHScroll event dispatch method. It checks to see
  if OnHScroll points to an event handler and calls it if it does. }
begin
  if Assigned(FOnHScroll) then
    FOnHScroll(self);
end;

procedure TddgExtendedMemo.VScroll;
{ This is the OnVScroll event dispatch method. It checks to see
  if OnVScroll points to an event handler and calls it if it does. }
begin
  if Assigned(FOnVScroll) then
    FOnVScroll(self);
end;

procedure TddgExtendedMemo.SetRow(Value: Longint);
{ The EM_LINEINDEX returns the character position of the first
  character in the line specified by wParam. The Value is used for
  wParam in this instance. Setting SelStart to this return value
  positions the caret on the line specified by Value. }
begin
  SelStart := Perform(EM_LINEINDEX, Value, 0);
  FRow := SelStart;
end;

function TddgExtendedMemo.GetRow: Longint;
{ The EM_LINEFROMCHAR returns the line in which the character specified
  by wParam sits. If -1 is passed as wParam, the line number at which
  the caret sits is returned. }
begin
  Result := Perform(EM_LINEFROMCHAR, -1, 0);
end;

procedure TddgExtendedMemo.SetColumn(Value: Longint);
begin
  { Get the length of the current line using the EM_LINELENGTH
    message. This message takes a character position as WParam.
    The length of the line in which that character sits is returned. }
  FColumn := Perform(EM_LINELENGTH, Perform(EM_LINEINDEX, GetRow, 0), 0);
  { If the FColumn is greater than the value passed in, then set
    FColumn to the value passed in }
  if FColumn > Value then
```

```
    FColumn := Value;
  // Now set SelStart to the newly specified position
  SelStart := Perform(EM_LINEINDEX, GetRow, 0) + FColumn;
end;

function TddgExtendedMemo.GetColumn: Longint;
begin
  { The EM_LINEINDEX message returns the line index of a specified
    character passed in as wParam. When wParam is -1 then it
    returns the index of the current line. Subtracting SelStart from this
    value returns the column position }
  Result := SelStart - Perform(EM_LINEINDEX, -1, 0);
end;

end.
```

First, we'll discuss adding the capability to provide row and column information to TddgExtendedMemo. Notice that we've added two private fields to the component, FRow and FColumn. These fields will hold the row and column of the TddgExtendedMemo's caret position. Notice that we've also provided the Row and Column public properties. These properties are made public because there's really no use for them at design time. The Row and Column properties have both reader and writer access methods. For the Row property these access methods are GetRow() and SetRow(). The Column access methods are GetColumn() and SetColumn(). For all practical purposes, you probably could do away with the FRow and FColumn storage fields because the values for Row and Column are provided through access methods. However, we've left them there because it offers the opportunity to extend this component.

The four access methods make use of various EM_XXXX messages. The code comments explain what is going on in each method and how these messages are used to provide Row and Column information for the component.

The TddgExtendedMemo component also provides two new events: OnHScroll and OnVScroll. The OnHScroll event occurs whenever the user clicks the horizontal scroll-bar of the control. Likewise, the OnVScroll occurs when the user clicks the vertical scrollbar. To surface such events, you have to capture the WM_HSCROLL and WM_VSCROLL Win32 messages that are passed to the control whenever the user clicks either scrollbar. Thus, you've created the two message handlers: WMHScroll() and WMVScroll(). These two message handlers call the event-dispatching methods HScroll() and VScroll(). These methods are responsible for checking whether the component user has provided event handlers for the OnHScroll and OnVScroll events and then calling those event handlers. If you're wondering why we didn't just perform this check in the message handler methods, it's because often times you want to be able to invoke an event handler as a result of a different action, such as when the user changes the caret position.

You can install and use the TddgExtendedMemo with your applications. You might even consider extending this component; for example, whenever the user changes the caret position, a WM_COMMAND message is sent to the control's owner. The HiWord(wParam) carries a notification code indicating the action that occurred. This code would have the value of EN_CHANGE, which stands for edit-notification message change. It is possible to have your component subclass its parent and capture this message in the parent's window procedure. It can then automatically update the FRow and FColumn fields. Subclassing is an altogether different and advanced topic that is discussed later.

TddgTabbedListBox—Extending the TListBox Component

VCL's TListbox component is merely an Object Pascal wrapper around the standard Win32 API LISTBOX control. Although it does do a fair job encapsulating most of that functionality, there is a little bit of room for improvement. This section takes you through the steps in creating a custom component based on TListbox.

The Idea

The idea for this component, like most, was born out of necessity. A list box was needed with the capability to use tab stops (which is supported in the Win32 API, but not in a TListbox), and a horizontal scrollbar was needed to view strings that were longer than the list box width (also supported by the API but not a TListbox). This component will be called a TddgTabListbox.

The plan for the TddgTabListbox component isn't terribly complex: We did this by creating a TListbox descendant component containing the correct field properties, overridden methods, and new methods to achieve the desired behavior.

The Code

The first step in creating a scrollable list box with tab stops is to include those window styles in the TddgTabListbox's style when the listbox window is created. The window styles needed are lbs_UseTabStops for tabs and ws_HScroll to allow a horizontal scrollbar. Whenever you add window styles to a descendant of TWinControl, do so by overriding the CreateParams() method, as shown in the following code:

```
procedure TddgTabListbox.CreateParams(var Params: TCreateParams);
begin
  inherited CreateParams(Params);
  Params.Style := Params.Style or lbs_UseTabStops or ws_HScroll;
end;
```

CreateParams()

Whenever you need to modify any of the parameters—such as style or window class—that are passed to the CreateWindowEx() API function, you should do so in the CreateParams() method. CreateWindowEx() is the function used to create the window handle associated with a TWinControl descendant. By overriding CreateParams(), you can control the creation of a window on the API level.

CreateParams accepts one parameter of type TCreateParams, which follows:

```
TCreateParams = record
    Caption: PChar;
    Style: Longint;
    ExStyle: Longint;
    X, Y: Integer;
    Width, Height: Integer;
    WndParent: HWnd;
    Param: Pointer;
    WindowClass: TWndClass;
    WinClassName: array[0..63] of Char;
end;
```

As a component writer, you will override CreateParams() frequently—whenever you need to control the creation of a component on the API level. Make sure that you call the inherited CreateParams() first in order to fill up the Params record for you.

To set the tab stops, the TddgTabListbox performs an lb_SetTabStops message, passing the number of tab stops and a pointer to an array of tabs as the wParam and lParam. (These two variables will be stored in the class as FNumTabStops and FTabStops.) The only catch is that listbox tab stops are handled in a unit of measure called *dialog box units*. Because dialog box units don't make sense for the Delphi programmer, you will surface tabs only in pixels. With the help of the PixDlg.pas unit shown in Listing 21.11, you can convert back and forth between dialog box units and screen pixels in both the X and Y planes.

LISTING 21.11. THE SOURCE CODE FOR PixDlg.pas.

```
unit Pixdlg;

interface

function DialogUnitsToPixelsX(DlgUnits: word): word;
function DialogUnitsToPixelsY(DlgUnits: word): word;
```

continues

LISTING 21.11. CONTINUED

```pascal
function PixelsToDialogUnitsX(PixUnits: word): word;
function PixelsToDialogUnitsY(PixUnits: word): word;

implementation
uses WinProcs;

function DialogUnitsToPixelsX(DlgUnits: word): word;
begin
  Result := (DlgUnits * LoWord(GetDialogBaseUnits)) div 4;
end;

function DialogUnitsToPixelsY(DlgUnits: word): word;
begin
  Result := (DlgUnits * HiWord(GetDialogBaseUnits)) div 8;
end;

function PixelsToDialogUnitsX(PixUnits: word): word;
begin
  Result := PixUnits * 4 div LoWord(GetDialogBaseUnits);
end;

function PixelsToDialogUnitsY(PixUnits: word): word;
begin
  Result := PixUnits * 8 div HiWord(GetDialogBaseUnits);
end;

end.
```

When you know the tab stops, you can calculate the extent of the horizontal scrollbar. The scrollbar should extend at least to the end of the longest string in the listbox. Luckily, the Win32 API provides a function called GetTabbedTextExtent() that retrieves just the information you need. When you know the length of the longest string, you can set the scrollbar range by performing the lb_SetHorizontalExtent message, passing the desired extent as the wParam.

You also need to write message handlers for some special Win32 messages. In particular, you need to handle the messages that control inserting and deleting, because you need to be able to measure the length of any new string or know when a long string has been deleted. The messages you're concerned with are lb_AddString, lb_InsertString, and lb_DeleteString. Listing 21.12 contains the source code for the LbTab.pas unit, which contains the TddgTabListbox component.

LISTING 21.12. LbTab.pas, THE TddgTabbedListBox.

```pascal
unit Lbtab;

interface
```

```
uses
  SysUtils, Windows, Messages, Classes, Controls, StdCtrls;

type

  EddgTabListboxError = class(Exception);

  TddgTabListBox = class(TListBox)
  private
    FLongestString: Word;
    FNumTabStops: Word;
    FTabStops: PWord;
    FSizeAfterDel: Boolean;
    function GetLBStringLength(S: String): word;
    procedure FindLongestString;
    procedure SetScrollLength(S: String);
    procedure LBAddString(var Msg: TMessage); message lb_AddString;
    procedure LBInsertString(var Msg: TMessage); message lb_InsertString;
    procedure LBDeleteString(var Msg: TMessage); message lb_DeleteString;
  protected
    procedure CreateParams(var Params: TCreateParams); override;
  public
    constructor Create(AOwner: TComponent); override;
    procedure SetTabStops(A: array of word);
  published
    property SizeAfterDel: Boolean read FSizeAfterDel write FSizeAfterDel
    ➥default True;
  end;

implementation

uses PixDlg;

constructor TddgTabListBox.Create(AOwner: TComponent);
begin
  inherited Create(AOwner);
  FSizeAfterDel := True;
  { set tab stops to Windows defaults... }
  FNumTabStops := 1;
  GetMem(FTabStops, SizeOf(Word) * FNumTabStops);
  FTabStops^ := DialogUnitsToPixelsX(32);
end;

procedure TddgTabListBox.SetTabStops(A: array of word);
{ This procedure sets the listbox's tabstops to those specified
  in the open array of word, A.  New tabstops are in pixels, and must
  be in ascending order.  An exception will be raised if new tabs
  fail to set. }
```

continues

LISTING 21.12. CONTINUED

```pascal
var
  i: word;
  TempTab: word;
  TempBuf: PWord;
begin
  { Store new values in temps in case exception occurs in setting tabs }
  TempTab := High(A) + 1;      // Figure number of tabstops
  GetMem(TempBuf, SizeOf(A));  // Allocate new tabstops
  Move(A, TempBuf^, SizeOf(A));// copy new tabstops }
  { convert from pixels to dialog units, and... }
  for i := 0 to TempTab - 1 do
    A[i] := PixelsToDialogUnitsX(A[i]);
  { Send new tabstops to listbox.  Note that we must use dialog units. }
  if Perform(lb_SetTabStops, TempTab, Longint(@A)) = 0 then
  begin
    { if zero, then failed to set new tabstops, free temp
      tabstop buffer and raise an exception }
    FreeMem(TempBuf, SizeOf(Word) * TempTab);
    raise EddgTabListboxError.Create('Failed to set tabs.')
  end
  else begin
    { if nonzero, then new tabstops set okay, so
      Free previous tabstops }
    FreeMem(FTabStops, SizeOf(Word) * FNumTabStops);
    { copy values from temps... }
    FNumTabStops := TempTab;  // set number of tabstops
    FTabStops := TempBuf;     // set tabstop buffer
    FindLongestString;        // reset scrollbar
    Invalidate;               // repaint
  end;
end;

procedure TddgTabListBox.CreateParams(var Params: TCreateParams);
{ We must OR in the styles necessary for tabs and horizontal scrolling
  These styles will be used by the API CreateWindowEx() function. }
begin
  inherited CreateParams(Params);
  { lbs_UseTabStops style allows tabs in listbox
    ws_HScroll style allows horizontal scrollbar in listbox }
  Params.Style := Params.Style or lbs_UseTabStops or ws_HScroll;
end;

function TddgTabListBox.GetLBStringLength(S: String): word;
{ This function returns the length of the listbox string S in pixels }
var
  Size: Integer;
begin
  // Get the length of the text string
  Canvas.Font := Font;
```

Writing Delphi Custom Components

CHAPTER 21

549

21

WRITING DELPHI
CUSTOM
COMPONENTS

```
    Result := LoWord(GetTabbedTextExtent(Canvas.Handle, PChar(S),
        StrLen(PChar(S)), FNumTabStops, FTabStops^));
    // Add a little bit of space to the end of the scrollbar extent for
    // looks
    Size := Canvas.TextWidth('X');
    Inc(Result, Size);
end;

procedure TddgTabListBox.SetScrollLength(S: String);
{ This procedure resets the scrollbar extent if S is longer than the }
{ previous longest string                                            }
var
  Extent: Word;
begin
  Extent := GetLBStringLength(S);
  // If this turns out to be the longest string...
  if Extent > FLongestString then
  begin
    // reset longest string
    FLongestString := Extent;
    //reset scrollbar extent
    Perform(lb_SetHorizontalExtent, Extent, 0);
  end;
end;

procedure TddgTabListBox.LBInsertString(var Msg: TMessage);
{ This procedure is called in response to a lb_InsertString message.
  This message is sent to the listbox every time a string is inserted.
  Msg.lParam holds a pointer to the null-terminated string being
  inserted.  This will cause the scrollbar length to be adjusted if
  the new string is longer than any of the existing strings. }
begin
  inherited;
  SetScrollLength(PChar(Msg.lParam));
end;

procedure TddgTabListBox.LBAddString(var Msg: TMessage);
{ This procedure is called in response to a lb_AddString message.
  This message is sent to the listbox every time a string is added.
  Msg.lParam holds a pointer to the null-terminated string being
  added.  This Will cause the scrollbar length to be ajdusted if the
  new string is longer than any of the existing strings.}
begin
  inherited;
  SetScrollLength(PChar(Msg.lParam));
end;

procedure TddgTabListBox.FindLongestString;
var
```

continues

LISTING 21.12. CONTINUED

```
  i: word;
  Strg: String;
begin
  FLongestString := 0;
  { iterate through strings and look for new longest string }
  for i := 0 to Items.Count - 1 do
  begin
    Strg := Items[i];
    SetScrollLength(Strg);
  end;
end;

procedure TddgTabListBox.LBDeleteString(var Msg: TMessage);
{ This procedure is called in response to a lb_DeleteString message.
  This message is sent to the listbox everytime a string is deleted.
  Msg.wParam holds the index of the item being deleted.  Note that
  by setting the SizeAfterDel property to False, you can cause the
  scrollbar update to not occur.  This will improve performance
  if you're deleting often. }
var
  Str: String;
begin
  if FSizeAfterDel then
  begin
    Str := Items[Msg.wParam]; // Get string to be deleted
    inherited;                // Delete string
    { Is deleted string the longest? }
    if GetLBStringLength(Str) = FLongestString then
      FindLongestString;
  end
  else
    inherited;
end;

end.
```

One particular point of interest in this component is the `SetTabStops()` method, which accepts an open array of `word` as a parameter. This enables users to pass in as many tab stops as they want, for example:

```
ddgTabListboxInstance.SetTabStops([50, 75, 150, 300]);
```

If the text in the `listbox` extends beyond the viewable window, the horizontal scrollbar will appear automatically.

TddgRunButton—Creating Properties

If you wanted to run another executable program in 16-bit Windows, you could use the WinExec() API function. Although these functions still work in Win32, it is not the recommended approach. Now, you should use the CreateProcess() or ShellExecute() functions to launch another application. CreateProcess() can be a somewhat daunting task when needed just for that purpose. Therefore, we've provided the ProcessExecute() method, which we'll show in a moment.

To illustrate the use of ProcessExecute(), we've created the component TddgRunButton. All that is required of the user is to click the button and the application executes.

The TddgRunButton is an ideal example to illustrate creating properties, validating property values, and encapsulating complex operations. Additionally, we'll show you how to grab the application icon from an executable file and how to display it in the TddgRunButton at design time. One other thing; TddgRunButton descends from TSpeedButton. Because TSpeedButton contains certain properties that you don't want accessible at design time through the Object Inspector, we'll show you how you can hide (sort of) existing properties from the component user. Admittedly, this technique is not exactly the cleanest approach to use. Typically, you would create a component of your own if you want to take the purist approach—of which the authors are advocates. However, this is one of those instances where Borland, in all its infinite wisdom, did not provide an intermediate component in between TSpeedButton and TCustomControl (from which TSpeedButton descends), as Borland did with its other components. Therefore, the choice was either to roll our own component that pretty much duplicates the functionality you get from TSpeedButton, or borrow from TSpeedButton's functionality and hide a few properties that aren't applicable for your needs. We opted for the latter, but only out of necessity. However, this should clue you in to practice careful forethought as to how component writers might want to extend your own components.

The code to TddgRunButton is shown in Listing 21.13.

LISTING 21.13. RunBtn.pas, THE SOURCE TO THE TddgRunButton COMPONENT.

```
unit RunBtn;

interface

uses
  Windows, Messages, SysUtils, Classes, Graphics, Controls,
  Forms, Dialogs, StdCtrls, Buttons;
```

continues

LISTING 21.13. CONTINUED

```
type

  TCommandLine = type String;

  TddgRunButton = class(TSpeedButton)
  private
    FCommandLine: TCommandLine;
    // Hiding Properties from the Object Inspector
    FCaption: TCaption;
    FAllowAllUp: Boolean;
    FFont: TFont;
    FGroupIndex: Integer;
    FLayOut: TButtonLayout;
    procedure SetCommandLine(Value: TCommandLine);
  public
    constructor Create(AOwner: TComponent); override;
    procedure Click; override;
  published
    property CommandLine: TCommandLine read FCommandLine write
    ➥SetCommandLine;
    // Read only properties are hidden
    property Caption: TCaption read FCaption;
    property AllowAllUp: Boolean read FAllowAllUp;
    property Font: TFont read FFont;
    property GroupIndex: Integer read FGroupIndex;
    property LayOut: TButtonLayOut read FLayOut;
  end;

implementation
uses ShellAPI;

const
  EXEExtension = '.EXE';

function ProcessExecute(CommandLine: TCommandLine; cShow: Word): Integer;
{ This method encapsulates the call to CreateProcess() which creates
  a new process and its primary thread. This is the method used in
  Win32 to execute another application, This method requires the use
  of the TStartInfo and TProcessInformation structures. These structures
  are not documented as part of the Delphi 4 online help but rather
  the Win32 help as STARTUPINFO and PROCESS_INFORMATION.

  The CommandLine paremeter specifies the pathname of the file to
  execute.

  The cShow paremeter specifies one of the SW_XXXX constants which
  specifies how to display the window. This value is assigned to the
  sShowWindow field of the TStartupInfo structure. }
var
```

```
  Rslt: LongBool;
  StartUpInfo: TStartUpInfo;  // documented as STARTUPINFO
  ProcessInfo: TProcessInformation; // documented as PROCESS_INFORMATION
begin
  { Clear the StartupInfo structure }
  FillChar(StartupInfo, SizeOf(TStartupInfo), 0);
  { Initialize the StartupInfo structure with required data.
    Here, we assign the SW_XXXX constant to the wShowWindow field
    of StartupInfo. When specifying a value to this field the
    STARTF_USESHOWWINDOW flag must be set in the dwFlags field.
    Additional information on the TStartupInfo is provided in the Win32
    online help under STARTUPINFO. }
  with StartupInfo do
  begin
    cb := SizeOf(TStartupInfo); // Specify size of structure
    dwFlags := STARTF_USESHOWWINDOW or STARTF_FORCEONFEEDBACK;
    wShowWindow := cShow
  end;

  { Create the process by calling CreateProcess(). This function
    fills the ProcessInfo structure with information about the new
    process and its primary thread. Detailed information is provided
    in the Win32 online help for the TProcessInfo structure under
    PROCESS_INFORMATION. }
  Rslt := CreateProcess(PChar(CommandLine), nil, nil, nil, False,
    NORMAL_PRIORITY_CLASS, nil, nil, StartupInfo, ProcessInfo);
  { If Rslt is true, then the CreateProcess call was successful.
    Otherwise, GetLastError will return an error code representing the
    error which occurred. }
  if Rslt then
    with ProcessInfo do
    begin
      { Wait until the process is in idle. }
      WaitForInputIdle(hProcess, INFINITE);
      CloseHandle(hThread); // Free the hThread  handle
      CloseHandle(hProcess);// Free the hProcess handle
      Result := 0;          // Set Result to 0, meaning successful
    end
  else Result := GetLastError; // Set result to the error code.
end;

function IsExecutableFile(Value: TCommandLine): Boolean;
{ This method returns whether or not the Value represents a valid
  executable file by ensuring that its file extension is 'EXE' }
var
  Ext: String[4];
begin
  Ext := ExtractFileExt(Value);
  Result := (UpperCase(Ext) = EXEExtension);
end;
```

continues

LISTING 21.13. CONTINUED

```
constructor TddgRunButton.Create(AOwner: TComponent);
{ The constructor sets the default height and width properties
  to 45x45 }
begin
  inherited Create(AOwner);
  Height := 45;
  Width  := 45;
end;

procedure TddgRunButton.SetCommandLine(Value: TCommandLine);
{ This write access method sets the FCommandLine field to Value, but
  only if Value represents a valid executable file name. It also
  set the icon for the TddgRunButton to the application icon of the
  file specified by Value. }
var
  Icon: TIcon;
begin
  { First check to see that Value *is* an executable file and that
    it actually exists where specified. }
  if not IsExecutableFile(Value) then
    Raise Exception.Create(Value+' is not an executable file.');
  if not FileExists(Value) then
    Raise Exception.Create('The file: '+Value+' cannot be found.');

  FCommandLine := Value;  // Store the Value in FCommandLine

  { Now draw the application icon for the file specified by Value
    on the TddgRunButton icon. This requires us to create a TIcon
    instance to which to load the icon. It is then copied from this
    TIcon instance to the TddgRunButton's Canvas.

    We must use the Win32 API function ExtractIcon() to retrive the
    icon for the application. }
  Icon := TIcon.Create; // Create the TIcon instance
  try
    { Retrieve the icon from the application's file }
    Icon.Handle := ExtractIcon(hInstance, PChar(FCommandLine), 0);
    with Glyph do
    begin
      { Set the TddgRunButton properties so that the icon held by Icon
        can be copied onto it. }
      { First, clear the canvas. This is required in case another
        icon was previously drawn on the canvas }
      Canvas.Brush.Style := bsSolid;
      Canvas.FillRect(Canvas.ClipRect);
      { Set the Icon's width and height }
      Width := Icon.Width;
      Height := Icon.Height;
      Canvas.Draw(0, 0, Icon); // Draw the icon to TddgRunButton's Canvas
```

```
      end;
    finally
      Icon.Free; // Free the TIcon instance.
    end;
end;

procedure TddgRunButton.Click;
var
  WERetVal: Word;
begin
  inherited Click; // Call the inherited Click method
  { Execute the ProcessExecute method and check its return value.
    if the return value is <> 0 then raise an exception because
    an error occured. The error code is shown in the exception }
  WERetVal := ProcessExecute(FCommandLine, sw_ShowNormal);
  if WERetVal <> 0 then begin
    raise Exception.Create('Error executing program. Error Code:; '+
        IntToStr(WERetVal));
  end;
end;

end.
```

TddgRunButton has one property, CommandLine, which is defined to be of the type String. The private storage field for CommandLine is FCommandLine.

> | **TIP**
>
> It is worth discussing the special definition of TCommandLine. The syntax used is
>
> TCommandLine = type string;
>
> By defining TCommandLine as such, it tells the compiler to treat TCommandLine as a unique type—but still compatible with other string types. The new type will get its own runtime type information and thus can have its own property editor. This same technique can be used with other types as well, for example:
>
> TMySpecialInt = type Integer;
>
> We will show you how we use this so that you can create a property editor for the CommandLine property in the next chapter. We don't show this in this chapter because creating property editors is an advanced topic that we want to talk about later.

The write access method for CommandLine is SetCommandLine(). We've provided two helper functions: IsExecutableFile() and ProcessExecute().

IsExecutableFile() is a function that determines whether or not a filename passed to it is an executable file based on the file's extension.

Creating and Executing a Process

ProcessExecute() is a function that encapsulates the CreateProcess() Win32 API function that enables you to launch another application. The application to launch is specified by the CommandLine parameter, which holds the filename path. The second parameter contains one of the SW_XXXX constants that indicate how the process's main windows is to be displayed. Table 21.4 lists the various SW_XXXX constants and their meanings as explained in the online help.

TABLE 21.4. SW_XXXX CONSTANTS.

SW_XXXX *Constant*	*Meaning*
SW_HIDE	Hides the window. Another window will become active.
SW_MAXIMIZE	Displays the window as maximized.
SW_MINIMIZE	Minimizes the window.
SW_RESTORE	Displays a window in its size before it was maximized/minimized.
SW_SHOW	Displays a window in its current size/position.
SW_SHOWDEFAULT	Shows a window in the state specified by the TStartupInfo structure passed to CreateProcess().
SW_SHOWMAXIMIZED	Activates/displays the window as maximized.
SW_SHOWMINIMIZED	Activates/displays the window as minimized.
SW_SHOWMINNOACTIVE	Displays the window as minimized but the currently active window remains active.
SW_SHOWNA	Display the window in the current state. The currently active window remains active.
SW_SHOWNOACTIVATE	Displays the window in the most recent size/position. The currently active window remains active.
SW_SHOWNORMAL	Activates/displays the window in its more recent size/position. This position is restored if the window was previously maximized/minimized.

The ProcessExecute() is a handy utility function that you might want to keep around in a separate unit that may be shared by other applications.

TddgRunButton **Methods**

The TddgRunButton.Create() constructor simply sets a default size for itself after calling the inherited constructor.

The SetCommandLine() method, which is the writer access method for the CommandLine parameter, performs several steps. First, it determines whether the value being assigned to CommandLine is a valid executable filename. If not, it raises an exception.

If the entry is valid, it is assigned to the FCommandLine field. SetCommandLine() then extracts the icon from the application file and draws it to the TddgRunButton's canvas. The Win32 API function ExtractIcon() is used to do this. The technique used is explained in the commentary.

TddgRunButton.Click() is the event-dispatching method for the TSpeedButton.OnClick event. It is necessary to call the inherited Click() method that will invoke the OnClick event handler if assigned. After calling the inherited Click(), you call ProcessExecute() and examine its result value to determine if the call was successful. If not, an exception is raised.

TddgButtonEdit—CONTAINER COMPONENTS

Occasionally you might like to create a component that is composed of one or more other components. Delphi's TDBNavigator is a good example of such a component, as it consists of a TPanel and a number of TSpeedButton components. Specifically, this section illustrates this concept by creating a component that is a combination of a TEdit and a TSpeedButton component. We will call this component TddgButtonEdit.

Design Decisions

Considering that Object Pascal is based upon a single-inheritance object model, TddgButtonEdit will need to be a component in its own right, which must contain both a TEdit1 and a TSpeedButton. Furthermore, because it's necessary that this component contain windowed controls, it will need to be a windowed control itself. For these reasons, we chose to descend TddgButtonEdit from TWinControl. We created both the TEdit and TSpeedButton in TddgButtonEdit's constructor using the following code:

```
constructor TddgButtonEdit.Create(AOwner: TComponent);
begin
  inherited Create(AOwner);
  FEdit        := TEdit.Create(Self);
```

```
  FEdit.Parent := self;
  FEdit.Height := 21;

  FSpeedButton := TSpeedButton.Create(Self);
  FSpeedButton.Left := FEdit.Width;
  FSpeedButton.Height := 19; // two less then TEdit's Height
  FSpeedButton.Width  := 19;
  FSpeedButton.Caption := '...';
  FSpeedButton.Parent := Self;

  Width  := FEdit.Width+FSpeedButton.Width;
  Height := FEdit.Height;
end;
```

The challenge when creating a component that contains other components is surfacing the properties of the "inner" components from the container component. For example, the TddgButtonEdit will need a Text property. You also might want to be able to change the font for the text in the control, therefore, a Font property is needed. Finally, there needs to be an OnClick event for the button in the control. You wouldn't want to attempt to implement this yourself in the container component when it is already available from the inner components. The goal, then, is to surface the appropriate properties of the inner controls without rewriting the interfaces to these controls.

Surfacing Properties

This usually boils down to the simple but time-consuming task of writing reader and writer methods for each of the inner component properties you want to resurface through the container component. In the case of the Text property, for example, you might give the TddgButtonEdit a Text property with read and write methods:

```
TddgButtonEdit = class(TWinControl)
private
  FEdit: TEdit;
  protected
  procedure SetText(Value: String);
    function  GetText: String;
published
    property Text: String read GetText write SetText;
end;
```

The SetText() and GetText() methods directly access the Text property of the contained TEdit control, as shown following:

```
function TddgButtonEdit.GetText: String;
begin
  Result := FEdit.Text;
end;
```

```
procedure TddgButtonEdit.SetText(Value: String);
begin
  FEdit.Text := Value;
end;
```

Surfacing Events

In addition to properties, it's also quite likely that you might want to resurface events that exist in the inner components. For example, when the user clicks the mouse on the TSpeedButton control, you would want to surface its OnClick event. Resurfacing events is just as straightforward as resurfacing properties—after all, events are properties.

You need to first give the TddgButtonEdit its own OnClick event. For clarity, we named this event OnButtonClick. The read and write methods for this event simply redirect the assignment to the OnClick event of the internal TSpeedButton.

Listing 21.14 shows the TddgButtonEdit container component.

LISTING 21.14. TddgButtonEdit, A CONTAINER COMPONENT.

```
unit ButtonEdit;

interface

uses
  Windows, Messages, SysUtils, Classes, Graphics, Controls, Forms,
  Dialogs, StdCtrls, Buttons;

type
  TddgButtonEdit = class(TWinControl)
  private
    FSpeedButton: TSpeedButton;
    FEdit: TEdit;
  protected
    procedure WMSize(var Message: TWMSize); message WM_SIZE;
    procedure SetText(Value: String);
    function  GetText: String;
    function GetFont: TFont;
    procedure SetFont(Value: TFont);
    function GetOnButtonClick: TNotifyEvent;
    procedure SetOnButtonClick(Value: TNotifyEvent);
  public
    constructor Create(AOwner: TComponent); override;
    destructor  Destroy; override;
```

continues

LISTING 21.14. CONTINUED

```
published
  property Text: String read GetText write SetText;
  property Font: TFont read GetFont write SetFont;
  property OnButtonClick: TNotifyEvent read GetOnButtonClick
       write SetOnButtonClick;
end;

implementation

procedure TddgButtonEdit.WMSize(var Message: TWMSize);
begin
  inherited;
  FEdit.Width := Message.Width-FSpeedButton.Width;
  FSpeedButton.Left := FEdit.Width;
end;

constructor TddgButtonEdit.Create(AOwner: TComponent);
begin
  inherited Create(AOwner);
  FEdit        := TEdit.Create(Self);
  FEdit.Parent := self;
  FEdit.Height := 21;

  FSpeedButton := TSpeedButton.Create(Self);
  FSpeedButton.Left := FEdit.Width;
  FSpeedButton.Height := 19; // two less than TEdit's Height
  FSpeedButton.Width  := 19;
  FSpeedButton.Caption := '...';
  FSpeedButton.Parent := Self;

  Width  := FEdit.Width+FSpeedButton.Width;
  Height := FEdit.Height;
end;

destructor  TddgButtonEdit.Destroy;
begin
  FSpeedButton.Free;
  FEdit.Free;
  inherited Destroy;
end;

function TddgButtonEdit.GetText: String;
begin
  Result := FEdit.Text;
end;

procedure TddgButtonEdit.SetText(Value: String);
begin
  FEdit.Text := Value;
end;
```

Writing Delphi Custom Components

CHAPTER 21

561

21

WRITING DELPHI
CUSTOM
COMPONENTS

```
function TddgButtonEdit.GetFont: TFont;
begin
  Result := FEdit.Font;
end;

procedure TddgButtonEdit.SetFont(Value: TFont);
begin
  if Assigned(FEdit.Font) then
    FEdit.Font.Assign(Value);
end;

function TddgButtonEdit.GetOnButtonClick: TNotifyEvent;
begin
  Result := FSpeedButton.OnClick;
end;

procedure TddgButtonEdit.SetOnButtonClick(Value: TNotifyEvent);
begin
  FSpeedButton.OnClick := Value;
end;

end.
```

TddgDigitalClock—Creating Component Events

The TddgDigitalClock illustrates the process of creating and making available user-defined events. We will use the same technique discussed earlier when we illustrated creating events with the TddgHalfMinute component.

TddgDigitalClock descends from TPanel. We decided that TPanel was an ideal component from which TddgDigitalClock could descend because TPanel has the BevelXXXX properties. This enables you to give the TddgDigitalClock a pleasing visual appearance. Also, you can use the TPanel.Caption property to display the system time.

TddgDigitalClock contains the following events to which the user can assign code:

OnHour	Occurs on the hour, every hour.
OnHalfPast	Occurs on the half-hour.
OnMinute	Occurs on the minute.
OnHalfMinute	Occurs every 30 seconds, on the minute and on the half minute.
OnSecond	Occurs on the second.

TddgDigitalClock uses a TTimer component internally. Its OnTimer event handler performs the logic to paint the time information and to invoke the event-dispatching methods for the previously listed events accordingly. Listing 21.15 shows the source code for DdgClock.pas.

LISTING 21.15. DdgClock.pas—SOURCE FOR THE TddgDigitalClock COMPONENT.

```
unit DDGClock;
interface
uses
  Windows, Messages, Controls, Forms, SysUtils, Classes, ExtCtrls;

type
  { Declare an event type which takes the sender of the event, and
    a TDateTime variable as parameters }
  TTimeEvent = procedure(Sender: TObject; DDGTime: TDateTime) of object;

  TddgDigitalClock = class(TPanel)
  private
    { Data fields }
    FHour,
    FMinute,
    FSecond: Word;
    FDateTime: TDateTime;
    FOldMinute,
    FOldSecond: Word;
    FTimer: TTimer;
    { Event handlers }
    FOnHour: TTimeEvent;        // Occurs on the hour
    FOnHalfPast: TTimeEvent;    // Occurs every half-hour
    FOnMinute: TTimeEvent;      // Occurs on the minute
    FOnSecond: TTimeEvent;      // Occurs every second
    FOnHalfMinute: TTimeEvent;  // Occurs every 30 seconds
    { Data fields to hide }
    FCaption: TCaption;    // Used to hide the Caption property
    { Define OnTimer event handler for internal TTimer, FTimer }
    procedure TimerProc(Sender: TObject);
  protected
    { Override the Paint methods }
    procedure Paint; override;

    { Define the various event dispatching methods }
    procedure DoHour(Tm: TDateTime); dynamic;
    procedure DoHalfPast(Tm: TDateTime); dynamic;
    procedure DoMinute(Tm: TDateTime); dynamic;
    procedure DoHalfMinute(Tm: TDateTime); dynamic;
    procedure DoSecond(Tm: TDateTime); dynamic;
  public
    { Override the Create constructor and Destroy destructor }
    constructor Create(AOwner: TComponent); override;
    destructor Destroy; override;
  published
    { Define event properties }
```

```
    property OnHour: TTimeEvent read FOnHour write FOnHour;
    property OnHalfPast: TTimeEvent read FOnHalfPast write FOnHalfPast;
    property OnMinute: TTimeEvent read FOnMinute write FOnMinute;
    property OnHalfMinute: TTimeEvent read FOnHalfMinute
            write FOnHalfMinute;
    property OnSecond: TTimeEvent read FOnSecond write FOnSecond;
  end;

implementation

constructor TddgDigitalClock.Create(AOwner: TComponent);
begin
  inherited Create(AOwner); // Call the inherited constructor
  Height := 25; // Set default width and height properties
  Width := 120;
  BevelInner := bvLowered; // Set Default bevel properties
  BevelOuter := bvLowered;
  { Set the inherited Caption property to an empty string }
  inherited Caption := '';
  { Create the TTimer instance and set both its Interval property and
    OnTime event handler. }
  FTimer:= TTimer.Create(self);
  FTimer.interval:= 200;
  FTimer.OnTimer:= TimerProc;
end;

destructor TddgDigitalClock.Destroy;
begin
  FTimer.Free; // Free the TTimer instance.
  inherited Destroy; // Call inherited Destroy method
end;

procedure TddgDigitalClock.Paint;
begin
  inherited Paint; // Call the inherited Paint method
  { Now set the inherited Caption property to current time. }
  inherited Caption := TimeToStr(FDateTime);
end;

procedure TddgDigitalClock.TimerProc(Sender: TObject);
var
  HSec: Word;
begin
  { Save the old minute and second for later use }
  FOldMinute := FMinute;
  FOldSecond := FSecond;
  FDateTime := Now; // Get the current time.
  { Extract the individual time elements }
  DecodeTime(FDateTime, FHour, FMinute, FSecond, Hsec);
```

continues

LISTING 21.15. CONTINUED

```
refresh; // Redraw the component so that the new time is diaplayed.

  { Now call the event handlers depending on the time }
  if FMinute = 0 then
    DoHour(FDateTime);
  if FMinute = 30 then
    DoHalfPast(FDateTime);
  if (FMinute <> FOldMinute) then
    DoMinute(FDateTime);
  if FSecond <> FOldSecond then
    if ((FSecond = 30) or (FSecond = 0)) then
      DoHalfMinute(FDateTime)
    else
      DoSecond(FDateTime);
end;

{ The event dispatching methods below determine if component user has
  attached event handlers to the various clock events and calls them
  if they exist }

procedure TddgDigitalClock.DoHour(Tm: TDateTime);
begin
  if Assigned(FOnHour) then
    TTimeEvent(FOnHour)(Self, Tm);
end;

procedure TddgDigitalClock.DoHalfPast(Tm: TDateTime);
begin
  if Assigned(FOnHalfPast) then
    TTimeEvent(FOnHalfPast)(Self, Tm);
end;

procedure TddgDigitalClock.DoMinute(Tm: TDateTime);
begin
  if Assigned(FOnMinute) then
    TTimeEvent(FOnMinute)(Self, Tm);
end;

procedure TddgDigitalClock.DoHalfMinute(Tm: TDateTime);
begin
  if Assigned(FOnHalfMinute) then
    TTimeEvent(FOnHalfMinute)(Self, Tm);
end;

procedure TddgDigitalClock.DoSecond(Tm: TDateTime);
begin
  if Assigned(FOnSecond) then
    TTimeEvent(FOnSecond)(Self, Tm);
end;

end.
```

The logic behind this component is explained in the source commentary. The methods used are no different than those previously explained when we discussed creating events. TddgDigitalClock only adds more events and contains logic to determine when each event is invoked.

Adding Forms to the Component Palette

Adding forms to the Object Repository is a convenient way to give forms a starting point. But what if you develop a form that you reuse often that does not need to be inherited and does not require added functionality? Delphi 4 provides a way you can reuse your forms as components on the Component Palette. In fact, the TFontDialog and TOpenDialog components are examples of forms that are accessible from the Component Palette. Actually, these dialogs are not Delphi forms; these are dialogs provided by the CommDlg.dll. Nevertheless, the concept is the same.

To add forms to the Component Palette, you must wrap your form with a component to make it a separate, installable component. The process as described here uses a simple password dialog whose functionality will verify your password automatically. Although this is a very simple project, the purpose of this discussion is not to show you how to install a complex dialog as a component, but rather to show you the general method for adding dialog boxes to the Component Palette. The same method applies to dialog boxes of any complexity.

First, you must create the form that is going to be wrapped by the component. The form we used is defined in the file PwDlg.pas. This unit also shows a component wrapper for this form.

Listing 21.16 shows the unit defining the TPasswordDlg form and its wrapper component, TddgPasswordDialog.

LISTING 21.16. PwDlg.pas—TPasswordDlg FORM AND ITS COMPONENT WRAPPER TddgPasswordDialog.

```
unit PwDlg;

interface

uses Windows, SysUtils, Classes, Graphics, Forms, Controls, StdCtrls,
  Buttons;

type
```

continues

LISTING 21.16. CONTINUED

```
  TPasswordDlg = class(TForm)
    Label1: TLabel;
    Password: TEdit;
    OKBtn: TButton;
    CancelBtn: TButton;
  end;

  { Now declare the wrapper component. }
  TddgPasswordDialog = class(TComponent)
  private
    PassWordDlg: TPasswordDlg; // TPassWordDlg instance
    FPassWord: String;         // Place holder for the password
  public
    function Execute: Boolean; // Function to launch the dialog
  published
    property PassWord: String read FPassword write FPassword;
  end;

implementation
{$R *.DFM}

function TddgPasswordDialog.Execute: Boolean;
begin
  { Create a TPasswordDlg instance }
  PasswordDlg := TPasswordDlg.Create(Application);
  try
    Result := False;  // Initialize the result to false
    { Show the dialog and return true if the password
      is correct. }
    if PasswordDlg.ShowModal = mrOk then
      Result := PasswordDlg.Password.Text = FPassword;
  finally
    PasswordDlg.Free;  // Free instance of PasswordDlg
  end;
end;

end.
```

The TddgPasswordDialog is called a *wrapper* component because it wraps the form with a component that can be installed into Delphi 4's Component Palette.

TddgPasswordDialog descends directly from TComponent. You might recall from the last chapter that TComponent is the lowest-level class that can be manipulated by the Form Designer in the IDE. This class has two private variables: PasswordDlg of type TPasswordDlg and FPassWord of type string. PasswordDlg is the TPasswordDlg instance that this wrapper component displays. FPassWord is an *internal storage field* that holds a password string.

Writing Delphi Custom Components

CHAPTER 21

567

21

WRITING DELPHI
CUSTOM
COMPONENTS

FPassWord gets its data through the property PassWord. Thus, PassWord doesn't actually store data; rather, it serves as an interface to the storage variable FPassWord.

TddgPassWordDialog's Execute() creates a TPasswordDlg instance and displays it as a modal dialog box. When the dialog box terminates, the string entered in the password TEdit control is compared against the string stored in FPassword.

The code here is contained within a try..finally construct. The finally portion ensures that the TPasswordDlg is disposed of regardless of any error that might occur.

Using `TddgPasswordDialog`

After you have added TddgPasswordDialog to the Component Palette, you can create a project that uses it. As with any other component, you select it from the Component Palette and place it on your form. The project created in the preceding section contains a TddgPasswordDialog and one button whose OnClick event handler does the following:

```
procedure TForm1.Button1Click(Sender: TObject);
begin
  if ddgPasswordDialog.Execute then       // Launch the PasswordDialog
    ShowMessage('You got it!')            // Correct password
  else
    ShowMessage('Sorry, wrong answer!'); // Incorrect password
end;
```

The Object Inspector contains three properties for the TddgPasswordDialog component: Name, Password, and Tag. To use the component, you must set the Password property to some string value. When you run the project, TddgPasswordDialog prompts the user for a password and compares it against the password you entered for the Password property.

COMPONENT PACKAGES

Delphi 3 introduced a new feature called *packages*, which enable you to place portions of your application into separate modules that can be shared across multiple applications. Packages are similar to dynamic link libraries (DLLs) but differ in their usage. Packages are primarily used to store collections of components in a separate, shareable module (a Delphi Package Library, or .bpl file). As you or other developers create Delphi applications, the packages you create can be used by the application at runtime instead of being directly linked at compile/link time. Because the code for these units resides in the .bpl file rather than in your .exe or .dll, the size of your .exe or .dll can become very small.

Packages differ from DLLs in that they are specific to Delphi VCL; that is, applications written in other languages can't use packages created by Delphi (with the exception of

C++Builder). One of the reasons behind packages was to get around a limitation of Delphi 1 and 2. In these two prior versions of Delphi, the VCL added a minimum of 150KB to 200KB of code to every executable. Therefore, even if you were to separate a piece of your application into a DLL, both the DLL and the application would contain redundant code. This was especially a problem if you were providing a suite of applications on one machine. Packages allow you to reduce the footprint of your applications and provide a convenient way for you to distribute your component collections.

Why Use Packages?

There are several reasons why you might want to use packages. Three are discussed in the following sections.

Code Reduction

A primary reason behind using packages is to reduce the size of your applications and DLLs. Delphi already ships with several predefined packages that break up the VCL into logical groupings. In fact, you can choose to compile your application so that it assumes the existence of many of these Delphi packages.

A Smaller Distribution of Applications—Application Partitioning

You'll find that many applications are available over the Internet as full-blown applications, downloadable demos, or updates to existing applications. Consider the benefit of giving users the option of downloading smaller versions of the application when pieces of the application might already exist on their system, such as when they have a prior installation.

By partitioning your applications using packages, you also allow your users to obtain updates to only those parts of the application that they need. Note, however, that there are some versioning issues that you'll have to take into account. We'll cover versioning issues momentarily.

Component Containment

Probably one of the most common reasons for using packages is the distribution of third-party components. If you are a component vendor, you must know how to create packages. The reason for this is that certain design-time elements—such as component and property editors, wizards, and experts—are all provided by packages.

Why Not to Use Packages

You shouldn't use runtime packages unless you are sure that other applications will be using these packages. Otherwise, these packages will end up using more disk space than if you were to just compile the source code into your final executable. Why is this so? If you create a packaged application resulting in a code reduction from 200KB to roughly 30KB, it might seem like you've saved quite a bit of space. However, you still have to distribute your packages and possibly even the `Vcl40.dcp` package, which is almost 2MB in size. You can see that this isn't quite the saving you had hoped for. My point is that you should use packages to share code when that code will be used by multiple executables. Note that this only applies to runtime packages. If you are a component writer, you must provide a design package that contains the component you want to make available to the Delphi IDE.

Types of Packages

There are four types of packages available for you to create and use:

- **Runtime package**. Runtime packages contain code, components, and so on needed by an application at runtime. If you write an application that depends on a particular runtime package, the application won't run in the absence of that package.

- **Design package**. Design packages contain components, property/component editors, experts, and so on necessary for application design in the Delphi IDE. This type of package is used only by Delphi and is never distributed with your applications.

- **Runtime and design package**. A package that is both design- and runtime-enabled is typically used when there are no design-specific elements such as property/component editors and experts. You can create this type of package to simplify application development and deployment. However, if this package does contain design elements, its runtime use will carry the extra baggage of the design support in your deployed applications. We recommend creating both a design and runtime package to separate design-specific elements when they are present.

- **Neither runtime nor design package**. This rare breed of package is intended to be used only by other packages and is not intended to be referenced directly by an application or used in the design environment. This implies that packages can use or include other packages.

Package Files

Table 21.5 lists and describes the package-specific files based on their file extensions.

TABLE 21.5. PACKAGE FILES.

File Extension	File Type	Description
.dpk	Package source file	This file is created when you invoke the Package Editor. You can think of this as you might think of the .dpr file for a Delphi project.
.dcp	Runtime/Design package symbol file	This is the compiled version of the package that contains the symbol information for the package and its units. Additionally, there is header information required by the Delphi IDE.
.dcu	Compiled unit	A compiled version of a unit contained in a package. One .dcu file will be created for each unit contained in the package.
.bpl	Runtime/Design package library	This is the runtime or design package, equivalent to a Windows DLL. If this is a runtime package, you will distribute the file along with your applications (if they are enabled for runtime packages). If this file represents a design package, you will distribute it along with its runtime partner to programmers that will use it to write programs. Note that if you aren't distributing source code, you must distribute the corresponding .dcp files.

Package-Enable Your Delphi 4 Applications

Package-enabling your Delphi applications is easy. Simply check the Build with Runtime Packages check box found in the Project I Options dialog on the Packages page. The next time you build your application after this option is selected, your application will be linked dynamically to runtime packages instead of having units linked statically into your .exe or .dll. The result will be a much more svelte application (although bear in mind that you will have to deploy the necessary packages with your application).

Installing Packages into Delphi's IDE

Installing packages into the Delphi IDE is simple. You might need to do this if you obtain a third-party set of components. First, however, you need to place the package files in their appropriate location. Table 21.6 shows where package files are typically located.

TABLE 21.6. PACKAGE FILE LOCATIONS.

Package File	*Location*
Runtime packages (`*.bpl`)	Runtime package files should be placed in the `\Windows\System\` directory (Windows 95) or `\WinNT\System32\` directory (Windows NT).
Design packages (`*.bpl`)	Because it is possible that you will obtain several packages from various vendors, design packages should be placed in a common directory where they can be properly managed. For example, create a `\PKG` directory off your `\Delphi 4\` directory and place design packages in that location.
Package symbol files (`*.dcp`)	You can place package symbol files in the same location as design package files (`*.bpl`).
Compiled units (`*.dcu`)	You must distribute compiled units if you are distributing design packages. We recommend keeping DCUs from third-party vendors in a directory similar to the `\Delphi 4\Lib` directory. For example, you can create the directory `\Delphi 4\3PrtyLib` in which third-party components' `*.dcus` will reside. Your search path will have to point to this directory.

To install a package, you simple invoke the Packages page of the Project Options dialog by selecting Component | Install Packages from the Delphi 4 menu.

By selecting the Add button, you can select the specific `.bpl` file. Upon doing so, this file will become the selected file on the Project page. When you click OK, the new package is installed into the Delphi IDE. If this package contains components, you will see the new component page on the Component Palette along with any newly installed components.

Designing Your Own Packages

Before creating a new package, you'll need to decide on a few things. First, you need to know what type of package you're going to create (runtime, design, and so on). This will be based on one or more of the scenarios that we present momentarily. Second, you need to know what you intend on naming your newly created package and where you want to store the package project. Keep in mind that the directory where your deployed package exists will probably not be the same as where you create your package. Finally, you need to know which units your package will contain and which other packages your new package will require.

The Package Editor

Packages are most commonly created using the Package Editor, which you invoke by selecting the Packages icon from the New Items dialog. (Select File | New from the Delphi main menu.) You'll notice that the Package Editor contains two folders: Contains and Requires.

The Contains Folder

In the Contains folder, you specify units that need to be compiled into your new package. There are a few rules for placing units into the Contains page of a package:

- The package must not be listed in the contains clause of another package or uses clause of a unit within another package.

- The units listed in the contains clause of a package, either directly or indirectly (they exist in uses clauses of units listed in the package's contains clause), cannot be listed in the packages requires clause. This is because these units are already bound to the package when it is compiled.

- You cannot list a unit in a package's contains clause if it is already listed in the contains clause of another package used by the same application.

The Requires Page

In the Requires page, you specify other packages that are required by the new package. This is similar to the uses clause of a Delphi unit. In most cases, any packages you create will have VCL40—the package that hosts Delphi's standard VCL components—in its requires clause. The typical arrangement here, for example, is that you place all your components into a runtime package. Then you create a design package that includes the runtime package in its requires clause. There are a few rules for placing packages on the Requires page of another package:

- Avoid circular references: Package1 cannot have Package1 in its requires clause, nor can it contain another package that has Package1 in its requires clause.

- The chain of references must not refer back to a package previously referenced in the chain.

The Package Editor has a toolbar and context-sensitive menus. Refer to the Delphi 4 online help under "Package Editor" for an explanation of what these buttons do. We won't repeat that information here.

Package Design Scenarios

Earlier we said that you must know what type of package you want to create based on a particular scenario. In this section, we're going to present three possible scenarios in which you would use design and/or runtime packages.

Writing Delphi Custom Components

CHAPTER 21

573

21

WRITING DELPHI
CUSTOM
COMPONENTS

Scenario 1—Design and Runtime Packages for Components

The design and runtime packages for components scenario is the case if you are a component writer and one or both of the following conditions apply:

- You want Delphi programmers to be able to compile/link your components right into their applications or to distribute them separately along with their applications.

- You have a component package, and you don't want to force your users to have to compile design features (component/property editors and so on) into their application code.

Given this scenario, you would create both a design and runtime package. Figure 21.4 depicts this arrangement. As the figure illustrates, the design package (DdgLib40.dpk) encompasses both the design features (property and component editors) and the runtime package (DdgStd40.dpk). The runtime package (DdgStd40.dpk) includes only your components. This arrangement is accomplished by listing the runtime package into the requires section of the design package, as shown in Figure 21.4.

FIGURE 21.4.

Design packages hosts design elements and runtime packages.

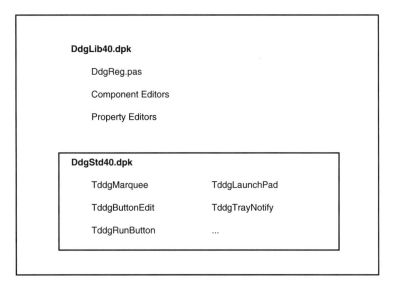

You must also apply the appropriate usage options for each package before compiling that package. You do this from the Package Options dialog. (You access the Package Options dialog by right-clicking within the Package Editor to invoke the local menu. Select Options to get to the dialog.) For the runtime package, DdgStd40.dpk, the usage option should be set to Runtime Only. This ensures that the package cannot be installed into the IDE as a design package (see the sidebar "Component Security" later in this

chapter). For the design package, DdgLib40.dpk, the usage option Design Time Only
should be selected. This enables users to install the package into the Delphi IDE, yet prevents them from using the package as a runtime package.

Adding the runtime package to the design package doesn't make the components contained in the runtime package available to the Delphi IDE yet. You must still register
your components with the IDE. As you already know, whenever you create a component,
Delphi automatically inserts a Register() procedure into the component unit, which in
turn calls the RegisterComponents() procedure. RegisterComponents() is the procedure that actually registers your component with the Delphi IDE when you install the
component. When working with packages, the recommended approach is to move the
Register() procedure from the component unit into a separate registration unit. This
registration unit registers all your components by calling RegisterComponents(). This
not only makes it easier for you to manage the registration of your components, but it
also prevents anyone from being able to install and use your runtime package illegally
because the components won't be available to the Delphi IDE.

As an example, the components used in this book are hosted by the runtime package
DdgStd40.dpk. The property editors, component editors, and registration unit
(DdgReg.pas) for our components exist in the design package DdgLib40.dpk.
DdgLib40.dpk also includes DdgStd40.dpk in its requires clause. Listing 21.17 shows
what our registration unit looks like.

LISTING 21.17. REGISTRATION UNIT FOR DELPHI 4 DEVELOPER'S GUIDE COMPONENTS.

```
unit DDGReg;

interface

procedure Register;

implementation

uses Classes, ExptIntf, DsgnIntf, TrayIcon, AppBars, ABExpt, Worthless,
  RunBtn, PwDlg, Planets, LbTab, HalfMin, DDGClock, ExMemo, MemView,
  Marquee, PlanetPE, RunBtnPE, CompEdit, DefProp, Wavez,
  WavezEd, LnchPad, LPadPE, Cards, ButtonEdit, Planet, DrwPnel;

procedure Register;
begin

  // Register the components.
  RegisterComponents('DDG',
  [ TddgTrayNotifyIcon, TddgDigitalClock, TddgHalfMinute, tddgButtonEdit,
    TddgExtendedMemo, TddgTabListbox, TddgRunButton, TddgLaunchPad,
```

Writing Delphi Custom Components

CHAPTER 21

575

21

WRITING DELPHI
CUSTOM
COMPONENTS

```
   TddgMemView, TddgMarquee, TddgWaveFile, TddgCard, TddgPasswordDialog,
   TddgPlanet, TddgPlanets, TddgWorthLess, TddgDrawPanel,
   TComponentEditorSample, TDefinePropTest]);


  // Register any property editors.
  RegisterPropertyEditor(TypeInfo(TRunButtons), TddgLaunchPad, '',
    TRunButtonsProperty);
  RegisterPropertyEditor(TypeInfo(TWaveFileString), TddgWaveFile,
    'WaveName', TWaveFileStringProperty);
  RegisterComponentEditor(TddgWaveFile, TWaveEditor);
  RegisterComponentEditor(TComponentEditorSample, TSampleEditor);
  RegisterPropertyEditor(TypeInfo(TPlanetName), TddgPlanet,
    'PlanetName', TPlanetNameProperty);
  RegisterPropertyEditor(TypeInfo(TCommandLine), TddgRunButton, '',
    TCommandLineProperty);


  // Register any custom modules, library experts.
  RegisterCustomModule(TAppBar, TCustomModule);
  RegisterLibraryExpert(TAppBarExpert.Create);

end;

end.
```

COMPONENT SECURITY

It is possible for someone to register your components, even though he has only your runtime package. He would do this by creating his own registration unit in which he would register your components. He would then add this unit to a separate package that would also have your runtime package in the `requires` clause. After he installs this new package into the Delphi IDE, your components will appear on the Component Palette. However, it is still not possible to compile any applications using your components because the required `*.dcu` files for your component units will be missing.

Package Distribution

When distributing your packages to component writers without the source code, you must distribute both compiled packages (DdgLib40.bpl and DdgStd40.bpl), both *.dcp files, and any compiled units (*.dcu) necessary to compile your components. Programmers using your components who want their applications' runtime packages enabled must distribute the DdgStd40.bpl package along with their applications and any other runtime package that they might be using.

Scenario 2—Design Package Only for Components

The design package only for components scenario is the case when you want to distribute components that you don't want to be distributed in runtime packages. In this case, you will include the components, component editors, property editors, component registration unit, and so on in one package file.

Package Distribution

When distributing your package to component writers without the source code, you must distribute the compiled package, DdgLib40.bpl, the DdgLib40.dcp file, and any compiled units (*.dcu) necessary to compile your components. Programmers using your components must compile your components into their applications. They will not be distributing any of your components as runtime packages.

Scenario 3—Design Features Only (No Components) IDE Enhancements

The design features only (no components) IDE enhancements scenario is the case if you are providing enhancements to the Delphi IDE, such as experts. For this scenario, you will register your expert with the IDE in your registration unit. The distribution for this scenario is simple; you only have to distribute the compiled *.bpl file.

Scenario 4—Application Partitioning

The application partitioning scenario is the case if you want to partition your application into logical pieces, each of which can be distributed separately. There are several reason why you might want to do this:

- This scenario is easier to maintain.
- Users can purchase only the needed functionality when they need it. Later, when they need added functionality, they can download the necessary package only, which will be much smaller than downloading the entire application.
- You can provide fixes (patches) to parts of the application more easily without requiring users to obtain a new version of the application altogether.

In this scenario, you will provide only the *.bpl files required by your application. This scenario is similar to the last with the difference being that instead of providing a package for the Delphi IDE, you will be providing a package for your own application. When partitioning your applications as such, you must pay attention to the issues regarding package versioning that we discuss in the next section.

Package Versioning

Package versioning is a topic that isn't well understood. You can think of package versioning in much the same way as you think of unit versioning. That is, any package that

Writing Delphi Custom Components

CHAPTER 21

577

21

WRITING DELPHI
CUSTOM
COMPONENTS

you provide for your application must be compiled using the same Delphi version used to compile the application. Therefore, you cannot provide a package written in Delphi 4 to be used by an application written in Delphi 3. The Inprise developers refer to the version of a package as a code base. So a package written in Delphi 4 has a code base of 4.0. This concept should influence the naming convention that you use for your package files.

Package Compiler Directives

There are some specific compiler directives that you can insert into the source code of your packages. Some of these directives are specific to units that are being packaged; others are specific to the package file. These directives are listed and described in Tables 21.7 and 21.8.

TABLE 21.7. COMPILER DIRECTIVES FOR UNITS BEING PACKAGED.

Directive	Meaning
`{$G}` or `{IMPORTEDDATA OFF}`	Use this when you want to prevent the unit from being packaged—when you want it to be linked directly to the application. Contrast this to the `{$WEAKPACKAGEUNIT}` directive, which allows a unit to be included in a package but whose code gets statically linked to the application.
`{$DENYPACKAGEUNIT}`	Same as `{$G}`.
`{$WEAKPACKAGEUNIT}`	See the section "More on the `{$WEAKPACKAGEUNIT}` Directive."

TABLE 21.8. COMPILER DIRECTIVES FOR THE PACKAGE `.dpk` FILE.

Directive	Meaning
`{$DESIGNONLY ON}`	Compiles package as a design-time only package.
`{$RUNONLY ON}`	Compiles package as a runtime only package.
`{$IMPLICITBUILD OFF}`	Prevents the package from being rebuilt later. Use this option when the package is not changed frequently.

More on the `{$WEAKPACKAGEUNIT}` Directive

The concept of a weak package is simple. Basically, it is used where your package may be referencing libraries (DLLs) that may not be present. For example, Vcl40 makes calls to the core Win32 API included with the Windows operating system. Many of these calls exist in DLLs that aren't present on every machine. These calls are exposed by units that contain the {$WEAKPACKAGEUNIT} directive. By including this directive, you keep the unit's source code in the package but place it into the DCP file rather than in the BPL file (think of a DCP as a DCU and a BPL as a DLL). Therefore, any references to functions of these weakly packaged units get statically linked to the application rather than dynamically referenced through the package.

The {$WEAKPACKAGEUNIT} directive is one that you will rarely use, if at all. It was created out of necessity by the Delphi developers to handle a specific situation. The problem exists if there are two components, each in a separate package and referencing the same interface unit of a DLL. When an application uses both of the components, this causes two instances of the DLL to be loaded, which raises havoc with initialization and global variable referencing. The solution was to provide the interface unit into one of the standard Delphi packages such as Vcl40.bpl. However, this raises the other problem for specialized DLLs that may not be present such as PENWIN.DLL. If Vcl40.bpl contains the interface unit for a DLL that isn't present, it will render Vcl40.bpl, and Delphi for that matter, unusable. The Delphi developers addressed this by allowing Vcl40.bpl to contain the interface unit in a single package, but to make it statically linked when used and not dynamically loaded whenever Vcl40 is used with the Delphi IDE.

As stated, you'll most likely never have to use this directive, unless you anticipate a similar scenario that the Delphi developers faced or if you want to make certain that a particular unit is included with a package but statically linked to the using application. A reason for the latter might be for optimization purposes. Note that any units that are weakly packaged cannot have global variables or code in their initialization/finalization sections. You must also distribute any *.dcu files for weakly packaged units along with your packages.

Package Naming Conventions

Earlier we said that the package versioning issue should influence how you name your packages. There isn't a set rule as to how you name your packages, but we suggest using a naming convention that incorporates the code base into the package's name. For example, the components for this book are contained in a runtime package whose name contains the 40 qualifier for Delphi 4.0 (DdgStd40.dpk). The same goes for the design package (DdgLib40.dpk). A preview version of the package would be DdgStd31.dpk. By using such a convention, you will prevent any confusion for your package users as to which version of the package they have and as to which version of the Delphi compiler applies to them. Note that our package name starts with a three-character author/

company identifier, followed by Std to indicate a runtime package and Lib to signify a design package. You can follow whatever naming convention you like. Just be consistent and use the recommended inclusion of the Delphi version into your package name.

SUMMARY

Knowing how components work is fundamental to understanding Delphi, and you work with many more custom components later in the book. Now that you can see what happens behind the scenes, components will no longer seem like just a black box. The next chapter goes beyond component creation into more advanced component building techniques.

ADVANCED COMPONENT TECHNIQUES

IN THIS CHAPTER

The last chapter broke into writing Delphi custom components, and it gave you a solid introduction to the basics. In this chapter, you learn how to take component writing to the next level by incorporating advanced design techniques into your Delphi custom components. This chapter provides examples of advanced techniques such as pseudo-visual components, detailed property editors, component editors, and collections.

PSEUDOVISUAL COMPONENTS

You've learned about visual components such as `TButton` and `TEdit`, and you've learned about nonvisual components such as `TTable` and `TTimer`. In this section, you'll also learn about a type of component that kind of falls in between visual and nonvisual components—we'll call these components *pseudovisual components*.

Extending Hints

Specifically, the pseudovisual component shown in this section is an extension of a Delphi pop-up hint window. We call this a pseudovisual component because it's not a component that's used visually from the Component Palette at design time, but it does represent itself visually at runtime in the body of pop-up hints.

Replacing the default style hint window in a Delphi application requires that you complete the following four steps:

1. Create a descendant of `THintWindow`.
2. Destroy the old hint window class.
3. Assign the new hint window class.
4. Create the new hint window class.

Creating a `THintWindow` Descendant

Before you write the code for a `THintWindow` descendant, you must first decide how you want your new hint window class to behave differently than the default one. In this case, you'll create an elliptical hint window rather than the default square one. This actually demonstrates another cool technique: creating nonrectangular windows! Listing 22.1 shows the `CoolHint.pas` unit, which contains the `THintWindow` descendant `TddgHintWindow`.

LISTING 22.1. `CoolHint.pas`.

```
unit CoolHint;

interface
```

```
uses Windows, Classes, Controls, Forms, Messages, Graphics;

type
  TddgHintWindow = class(THintWindow)
  private
    FRegion: THandle;
    procedure FreeCurrentRegion;
  public
    destructor Destroy; override;
    procedure ActivateHint(Rect: TRect; const AHint: string); override;
    procedure Paint; override;
    procedure CreateParams(var Params: TCreateParams); override;
  end;

implementation

destructor TddgHintWindow.Destroy;
begin
  FreeCurrentRegion;
  inherited Destroy;
end;

procedure TddgHintWindow.FreeCurrentRegion;
{ Regions, like other API objects, should be freed when you are  }
{ through using them.  Note, however, that you cannot delete a   }
{ region which is currently set in a window, so this method sets }
{ the window region to 0 before deleting the region object.      }
begin
  if FRegion <> 0 then begin        // if Region is alive...
    SetWindowRgn(Handle, 0, True);  // set win region to 0
    DeleteObject(FRegion);          // kill the region
    FRegion := 0;                   // zero out field
  end;
end;

procedure TddgHintWindow.ActivateHint(Rect: TRect; const AHint: string);
{ Called when the hint is activated by putting the mouse pointer }
{ above a control. }
begin
  with Rect do
    Right := Right + Canvas.TextWidth('WWWW');  // add some slop
  BoundsRect := Rect;
  FreeCurrentRegion;
  with BoundsRect do
    { Create a round rectangular region to display the hint window }
    FRegion := CreateRoundRectRgn(0, 0, Width, Height, Width, Height);
  if FRegion <> 0 then
    SetWindowRgn(Handle, FRegion, True);        // set win region
  inherited ActivateHint(Rect, AHint);          // call inherited
end;
```

continues

LISTING 22.1. CONTINUED

```
procedure TddgHintWindow.CreateParams(var Params: TCreateParams);
{ We need to remove the border created on the Windows API-level }
{ when the window is created. }
begin
  inherited CreateParams(Params);
  Params.Style := Params.Style and not ws_Border;  // remove border
end;

procedure TddgHintWindow.Paint;
{ This method gets called by the WM_PAINT handler.  It is }
{ responsible for painting the hint window. }
var
  R: TRect;
begin
  R := ClientRect;                    // get bounding rectangle
  Inc(R.Left, 1);                     // move left side slightly
  Canvas.Font.Color := clInfoText;    // set to proper color
  { paint string in the center of the round rect }
  DrawText(Canvas.Handle, PChar(Caption), Length(Caption), R,
        DT_NOPREFIX or DT_WORDBREAK or DT_CENTER or DT_VCENTER);
end;

initialization
  Application.ShowHint := False;      // destroy old hint window
  HintWindowClass := TDDGHintWindow;  // assign new hint window
  Application.ShowHint := True;       // create new hint window
end.
```

The overridden CreateParams() and Paint() methods are fairly straightforward. CreateParams() provides an opportunity to adjust the structure of the window styles before the hint window is created on an API level. In this method, the WS_BORDER style is masked out of the window class (using the not operation) in order to prevent a rectangular border from being drawn around the window. The Paint() method is responsible for rendering the window. In this case, the method must paint the hint's Caption property into the center of the caption window. The color of the text is set to clInfoText, which is the system-defined color of hint text.

An Elliptical Window

The ActivateHint() method contains the magic for creating the nonrectangular hint window. Well, it's not really magic. Actually, two API calls make it happen: CreateRoundRectRgn() and SetWindowRgn().

CreateRoundRectRgn() defines a rounded rectangular region within a particular window. A *region* is a special API object that allows you to perform special painting, hit testing, filling, and clipping in one area. In addition to `CreateRoundRectRgn()`, a number of other Win32 API functions create different types of regions, including the following:

- `CreateEllipticRgn()`
- `CreateEllipticRgnIndirect()`
- `CreatePolygonRgn()`
- `CreatePolyPolygonRgn()`
- `CreateRectRgn()`
- `CreateRectRgnIndirect()`
- `CreateRoundRectRgn()`
- `ExtCreateRegion()`

Additionally, the `CombineRgn()` function can be used to combine multiple regions into one complex region. All these functions are described in detail in the Win32 API online Help.

`SetWindowRgn()` is then called, passing the recently created region handle as a parameter. This function causes the operating system to take ownership of the region, and all subsequent drawing in the specified window will occur only within the region. Therefore, if the region defined is a rounded rectangle, painting will occur only within that rounded rectangular region.

> **CAUTION**
>
> You need to be aware of two side effects when using `SetWindowRgn()`. First, because only the portion of the window within the region is painted, your window probably won't have a frame or title bar. You must be prepared to provide the user with an alternative way to move, size, and close the window without the aid of a frame or title bar. Second, because the operating system takes ownership of the region specified in `SetWindowRgn()`, you must be careful not to manipulate or delete the region while it's in use. The `TddgHintWindow` component handles this by calling its `FreeCurrentRegion()` method before the window is destroyed or a new window is created.

Enabling the `THintWindow` Descendant

The initialization code for the `CoolHint` unit does the work of making the `TddgHintWindow` component the application-wide active hint window. Setting `Application.ShowHint` to `False` causes the old hint window to be destroyed. At that point, you must assign your `THintWindow` descendant class to the `HintWindowClass` global variable. Then, setting `Application.ShowHint` back to `True` causes a new hint window to be created—this time it will be an instance of your descendant class.

Figure 22.1 shows the `TddgHintWindow` component in action.

Deploying `TddgHintWindow`

Deploying this pseudovisual component is different than normal visual and nonvisual components. Because all the work for instantiating the component is performed in the `initialization` part of its unit, the component shouldn't be added to a design package for use on the Component Palette but merely added to the `uses` clause of one of the source files in your project.

ANIMATED COMPONENTS

Once upon a time while writing a Delphi application, we thought to ourselves, "This is a really cool application, but our About dialog is kind of boring. We need something to spice it up a little." Suddenly, a light bulb came on and an idea for a new component was born: We would create a scrolling credits marquee window to incorporate into our About dialogs.

The Marquee Component

Let's take a moment to analyze how the marquee component works. The marquee control is able to take a bunch of strings and scroll them across the component on command, like a real-life marquee. You'll use `TCustomPanel` as the base class for this `TddgMarquee` component, because it already has the basic built-in functionality you need, including a pretty 3D, beveled border.

`TddgMarquee` paints some text strings to a bitmap residing in memory and then copies portions of the memory bitmap to its own canvas to simulate a scrolling effect. It does this using the `BitBlt()` API function to copy a component-sized portion of the memory canvas to the component, starting at the top. Then, it moves down a couple of pixels on the memory canvas and copies that image to the control. It moves down again, copies again, and repeats the process over and over so that the entire contents of the memory canvas appear to scroll through the component. This logic is illustrated in Figure 22.2.

FIGURE 22.2.

How the
TddgMarquee
component works.

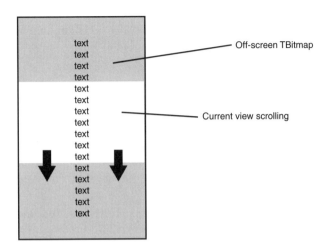

Off-screen TBitmap

Current view scrolling

Now is the time to identify any additional classes you might need to integrate into the
TddgMarquee component in order to bring it to life. There are really only two such class-
es. First, you need the TStringList class to hold all the strings you want to scroll.
Second, you must have a memory bitmap on which you can render all the text strings.
VCL's own TBitmap component will work nicely for this purpose.

Writing the Component

As with the previous components in this chapter, the code for TddgMarquee should be
approached with a logical plan of attack. In this case, break up the code work into reasonable parts. The TddgMarquee component can be divided into five major parts:

- The mechanism that renders the text onto the memory canvas
- The mechanism that copies the text from the memory canvas to the marquee win-
  dow
- The timer that keeps track of when and how to scroll the window to perform the
  animation
- The class constructor, destructor, and associated methods
- The finishing touches, such as various helper properties and methods

Drawing on an Offscreen Bitmap

When creating an instance of TBitmap, you need to know how big it must be to hold the
entire list of strings in memory. You do this by first figuring out how high each line of
text will be and then multiplying by the number of lines. To find the height and spacing
of a line of text in a particular font, use the GetTextMetrics() API function by passing
it the canvas's handle. The following is a TTextMetric record to be filled in by the function:

```
var
  Metrics: TTextMetric;
begin
  GetTextMetrics(Canvas.Handle, Metrics);
```

NOTE

The `GetTextMetrics()` API function modifies a `TTextMetric` record that contains a great deal of quantitative information about a device context's currently selected font. This function gives you information not only on font height and width, but also on whether the font is boldfaced, italicized, struck out, or even what the character set name is.

The `TextHeight()` method of TCanvas won't work here. That method only determines the height of a specific line of text rather than the spacing for the font in general.

The height of a character cell in the canvas's current font is given by the `tmHeight` field of the `Metric` record. If you add to that value the `tmInternalLeading` field—to allow for some space between lines—you get the height for each line of text to be drawn on the memory canvas:

```
LineHi := Metrics.tmHeight + Metrics.tmInternalLeading;
```

The height necessary for the memory canvas then can be determined by multiplying `LineHi` by the number of lines of text and adding that value to two times the height of the `TddgMarquee` control (to create the blank space at the beginning and end of the marquee). Suppose that the `TStringList` in which all the strings live is called `FItems`; now place the memory canvas dimensions in a `TRect` structure:

```
var
  VRect: TRect;
begin
  { VRect rectangle represents entire memory bitmap }
  with VRect do begin
    Top := 0;
    Left := 0;
    Right := Width;
    Bottom := LineHi * FItems.Count + Height * 2;
  end;
end;
```

After being instantiated and sized, the memory bitmap is initialized further by setting the font to match the `Font` property of `TddgMarquee`, filling the background with a color determined by the `Color` property of `TddgMarquee`, and setting the `Style` property of `Brush` to `bsClear`.

> **TIP**
>
> When you render text on TCanvas, the text background is filled with the current color of TCanvas.Brush. To cause the text background to be invisible, set TCanvas.Brush.Style to bsClear.

Most of the preliminary work is now in place, so it's time to render the text on the memory bitmap. As discussed in Chapter 8, "Graphics Programming with GDI and Fonts," there are a couple of ways to output text onto a canvas. The most straightforward way is to use TextOut() method of TCanvas; however, you have more control over the formatting of the text when you use the more complex DrawText() API function. Because it requires control over justification, TddgMarquee will use the DrawText() function. An enumerated type is ideal to represent the text justification:

```
type
  TJustification = (tjCenter, tjLeft, tjRight);
```

The following code shows the PaintLine() method for TddgMarquee, which makes use of DrawText() to render text onto the memory bitmap. In this method, FJust represents an instance variable of type TJustification. Here's the code:

```
procedure TddgMarquee.PaintLine(R: TRect; LineNum: Integer);
{ this method is called to paint each line of text onto MemBitmap }
const
  Flags: array[TJustification] of DWORD = (DT_CENTER, DT_LEFT, DT_RIGHT);
var
  S: string;
begin
  { Copy next line to local variable for clarity }
  S := FItems.Strings[LineNum];
  { Draw line of text onto memory bitmap }
  DrawText(MemBitmap.Canvas.Handle, PChar(S), Length(S), R,
    Flags[FJust] or DT_SINGLELINE or DT_TOP);
end;
```

Painting the Component

Now that you know how to create the memory bitmap and paint text onto it, the next step is learning how to copy that text to the TddgMarquee canvas.

The Paint() method of a component is invoked in response to a Windows WM_PAINT message. The Paint() method is what gives your component life; you use the Paint() method to paint, draw, and fill to determine the graphical appearance of your components.

22

ADVANCED
COMPONENT
TECHNIQUES

The job of `TddgMarquee.Paint()` is to copy the strings from the memory canvas to the canvas of `TddgMarquee`. This feat is accomplished by the `BitBlt()` API function, which copies the bits from one device context to another.

To determine whether `TddgMarquee` is currently running, `TddgMarquee` will maintain a Boolean instance variable called `FActive` that reveals whether the marquee's scrolling capability has been activated. Therefore, the `Paint()` method paints differently depending on whether the component is active:

```
procedure TddgMarquee.Paint;
{ this virtual method is called in response to a }
{ Windows paint message }
begin
  if FActive then
    { Copy from memory bitmap to screen }
    BitBlt(Canvas.Handle, 0, 0, InsideRect.Right, InsideRect.Bottom,
      MemBitmap.Canvas.Handle, 0, CurrLine, srcCopy)
  else
    inherited Paint;
end;
```

If the marquee is active, the component instead is painted by `BitBlt`ing a portion of the memory canvas onto the `TddgMarquee` canvas. Notice the `CurrLine` variable, which is passed as the next-to-last parameter to `BitBlt()`. The value of this parameter determines which portion of the memory canvas to transfer onto the screen. By continuously incrementing or decrementing the value of `CurrLine`, you can give `TddgMarquee` the appearance that the text is scrolling up or down.

Animating the Marquee

The visual aspects of the `TddgMarquee` component are now in place. The rest of the work involved in getting the component working is just hooking up the plumbing, so to speak. At this point, `TddgMarquee` requires some mechanism to change the value of `CurrLine` every so often and to repaint the component. This trick can be accomplished fairly easily using Delphi's `TTimer` component.

Before you can use `TTimer`, of course, you must create and initialize the class instance. `TddgMarquee` will have a `TTimer` instance called `FTimer`, and you'll initialize it in a procedure called `DoTimer`:

```
procedure DoTimer;
{ procedure sets up TddgMarquee's timer }
begin
  FTimer := TTimer.Create(Self);
  with FTimer do
  begin
```

```
    Enabled := False;
    Interval := TimerInterval;
    OnTimer := DoTimerOnTimer;
  end;
end;
```

In this procedure, `FTimer` is created, and it's disabled initially. Its `Interval` property then is assigned to the value of a constant called `TimerInterval`. Finally, the `OnTimer` event for `FTimer` is assigned to a method of `TddgMarquee` called `DoTimerOnTimer`. This is the method that will be called when an `OnTimer` event occurs.

> **NOTE**
>
> When assigning values to events in your code, you need to follow two rules:
>
> - The procedure you assign to the event must be a method of some object instance. It can't be a standalone procedure or function.
>
> - The method you assign to the event must accept the same parameter list as the event type. For example, the `OnTimer` event for `TTimer` is of type `TNotifyEvent`. Because `TNotifyEvent` accepts one parameter, `Sender`, of type `TObject`, any method you assign to `OnTimer` must also take one parameter of type `TObject`.

The `DoTimerOnTimer()` method is defined as follows:

```
procedure TddgMarquee.DoTimerOnTimer(Sender: TObject);
{ This method is executed in response to a timer event }
begin
  IncLine;
  { only repaint within borders }
  InvalidateRect(Handle, @InsideRect, False);
end;
```

In this method, a procedure named `IncLine()` is called; this procedure increments or decrements the value of `CurrLine` as necessary. Then the `InvalidateRect()` API function is called to "invalidate" (or repaint) the interior portion of the component. We chose to use `InvalidateRect()` rather than the `Invalidate()` method of `TCanvas` because `Invalidate()` causes the entire canvas to be repainted rather than just the portion within a defined rectangle, as is the case with `InvalidateRect()`. This method, because it doesn't continuously repaint the entire component, eliminates much of the flicker that would otherwise occur. Remember: Flicker is bad.

The `IncLine()` method, which updates the value of `CurrLine` and detects whether scrolling has completed, is defined as follows:

```
procedure TddgMarquee.IncLine;
{ this method is called to increment a line }
begin
  if not FScrollDown then         // if Marquee is scrolling upward
  begin
    { Check to see if marquee has scrolled to end yet }
    if FItems.Count * LineHi + ClientRect.Bottom -
      ScrollPixels  >= CurrLine then
      { not at end, so increment current line }
      Inc(CurrLine, ScrollPixels)
    else SetActive(False);
  end
  else begin                      // if Marquee is scrolling downward
    { Check to see if marquee has scrolled to end yet }
    if CurrLine >= ScrollPixels then
      { not at end, so decrement current line }
      Dec(CurrLine, ScrollPixels)
    else SetActive(False);
  end;
end;
```

The constructor for `TddgMarquee` is actually quite simple. It calls the inherited `Create()` method, creates a `TStringList` instance, sets up `FTimer`, and then sets all the default values for the instance variables. Once again, you must remember to call the inherited `Create()` in your components. Failure to do so means your components will miss out on important and useful functionality, such as handle and canvas creation, streaming, and Windows message response. The following code shows the `TddgMarquee` constructor, `Create()`:

```
constructor TddgMarquee.Create(AOwner: TComponent);
{ constructor for TddgMarquee class }

  procedure DoTimer;
  { procedure sets up TddgMarquee's timer }
  begin
    FTimer := TTimer.Create(Self);
    with FTimer do
    begin
      Enabled := False;
      Interval := TimerInterval;
      OnTimer := DoTimerOnTimer;
    end;
  end;

begin
  inherited Create(AOwner);
  FItems := TStringList.Create;  { instanciate string list }
  DoTimer;                       { set up timer }
  { set instance variable default values }
```

```
  Width := 100;
  Height := 75;
  FActive := False;
  FScrollDown := False;
  FJust := tjCenter;
  BevelWidth := 3;
end;
```

The TddgMarquee destructor is even simpler: The method deactivates the component by passing False to the SetActive() method, frees the timer and the string list, and then calls the inherited Destroy():

```
destructor TddgMarquee.Destroy;
{ destructor for TddgMarquee class }
begin
  SetActive(False);
  FTimer.Free;            // free allocated objects
  FItems.Free;
  inherited Destroy;
end;
```

TIP

As a rule of thumb, when you override constructors, you usually call inherited first, and when you override destructors, you usually call inherited last. This ensures that the class has been set up before you modify it and that all dependent resources have been cleaned up before you dispose of the class.

Exceptions to this rule exist; however, you should generally stick to it unless you have good reason not to.

The SetActive() method, which is called by both the IncLine() method and the destructor (in addition to serving as the writer for the Active property), serves as a vehicle that starts and stops the marquee scrolling up the canvas:

```
procedure TddgMarquee.SetActive(Value: Boolean);
{ called to activate/deactivate the marquee }
begin
  if Value and (not FActive) and (FItems.Count > 0) then
  begin
    FActive := True;                  // set active flag
    MemBitmap := TBitmap.Create;
    FillBitmap;                       // Paint Image on bitmap
    FTimer.Enabled := True;           // start timer
  end
  else if (not Value) and FActive then
```

```
  begin
    FTimer.Enabled := False;    // disable timer,
    if Assigned(FOnDone)        // fire OnDone event,
      then FOnDone(Self);
    FActive := False;           // set FActive to False
    MemBitmap.Free;             // free memory bitmap
    Invalidate;                 // clear control window
  end;
end;
```

An important feature TddgMarquee is lacking thus far is an event that tells the user when scrolling is complete. Never fear—this feature is very straightforward to add by way of an event: FOnDone. The first step to adding an event to your component is to declare an instance variable of some event type in the private portion of the class definition. You'll use the TNotifyEvent type for the FOnDone event:

```
FOnDone: TNotifyEvent;
```

The event should then be declared in the published part of the class as a property:

```
property OnDone: TNotifyEvent read FOnDone write FOnDone;
```

Recall that the read and write directives specify from which function or variable a given property should get or set its value.

Taking just these two small steps will cause an entry for OnDone to be displayed in the Events page of the Object Inspector at design time. The only other thing that needs to be done is to call the user's handler for OnDone (if a method is assigned to OnDone), as TddgMarquee demonstrates with this line of code in the Deactivate() method:

```
if Assigned(FOnDone) then FOnDone(Self); // fire OnDone event
```

This line basically reads, "If the component user has assigned a method to the OnDone event, call that method and pass the TddgMarquee class instance (Self) as a parameter."

Listing 22.2 shows the completed source code for the Marquee unit. Notice that TddgMarquee is a descendant of TCustomPanel, and therefore TddgMarquee must publish many of the properties provided by TCustomPanel.

LISTING 22.2. THE SOURCE CODE FOR Marquee.pas.

```
unit Marquee;

interface

uses
  SysUtils, Windows, Classes, Forms, Controls, Graphics,
  Messages, ExtCtrls, Dialogs;
```

```
const
  ScrollPixels = 3;      // num of pixels for each scroll
  TimerInterval = 50;    // time between scrolls in ms

type
  TJustification = (tjCenter, tjLeft, tjRight);

  EMarqueeError = class(Exception);

  TddgMarquee = class(TCustomPanel)
  private
    MemBitmap: TBitmap;
    InsideRect: TRect;
    FItems: TStringList;
    FJust: TJustification;
    FScrollDown: Boolean;
    LineHi : Integer;
    CurrLine : Integer;
    VRect: TRect;
    FTimer: TTimer;
    FActive: Boolean;
    FOnDone: TNotifyEvent;
    procedure SetItems(Value: TStringList);
    procedure DoTimerOnTimer(Sender: TObject);
    procedure MakeRects;
    procedure PaintLine(R: TRect; LineNum: Integer);
    procedure SetLineHeight;
    procedure SetStartLine;
    procedure IncLine;
    procedure SetActive(Value: Boolean);
  protected
    procedure Paint; override;
    procedure FillBitmap; virtual;
  public
    property Active: Boolean read FActive write SetActive;
    constructor Create(AOwner: TComponent); override;
    destructor Destroy; override;
  published
    property ScrollDown: Boolean read FScrollDown write FScrollDown;
    property Justify: TJustification read FJust write FJust default
    ➥tjCenter;
    property Items: TStringList read FItems write SetItems;
    property OnDone: TNotifyEvent read FOnDone write FOnDone;
    { Publish inherited properties: }
    property Align;
    property Alignment;
    property BevelInner;
    property BevelOuter;
    property BevelWidth;
```

continues

LISTING 22.2. CONTINUED

```
    property BorderWidth;
    property BorderStyle;
    property Color;
    property Ctl3D;
    property Font;
    property Locked;
    property ParentColor;
    property ParentCtl3D;
    property ParentFont;
    property Visible;
    property OnClick;
    property OnDblClick;
    property OnMouseDown;
    property OnMouseMove;
    property OnMouseUp;
    property OnResize;
  end;

implementation

constructor TddgMarquee.Create(AOwner: TComponent);
{ constructor for TddgMarquee class }

  procedure DoTimer;
  { procedure sets up TddgMarquee's timer }
  begin
    FTimer := TTimer.Create(Self);
    with FTimer do
    begin
      Enabled := False;
      Interval := TimerInterval;
      OnTimer := DoTimerOnTimer;
    end;
  end;

begin
  inherited Create(AOwner);
  FItems := TStringList.Create;  { instanciate string list }
  DoTimer;                       { set up timer }
  { set instance variable default values }
  Width := 100;
  Height := 75;
  FActive := False;
  FScrollDown := False;
  FJust := tjCenter;
  BevelWidth := 3;
end;

destructor TddgMarquee.Destroy;
{ destructor for TddgMarquee class }
```

```
begin
  SetActive(False);
  FTimer.Free;                // free allocated objects
  FItems.Free;
  inherited Destroy;
end;

procedure TddgMarquee.DoTimerOnTimer(Sender: TObject);
{ This method is executed in response to a timer event }
begin
  IncLine;
  { only repaint within borders }
  InvalidateRect(Handle, @InsideRect, False);
end;

procedure TddgMarquee.IncLine;
{ this method is called to increment a line }
begin
  if not FScrollDown then        // if Marquee is scrolling upward
  begin
    { Check to see if marquee has scrolled to end yet }
    if FItems.Count * LineHi + ClientRect.Bottom -
      ScrollPixels  >= CurrLine then
      { not at end, so increment current line }
      Inc(CurrLine, ScrollPixels)
    else SetActive(False);
  end
  else begin                     // if Marquee is scrolling downward
    { Check to see if marquee has scrolled to end yet }
    if CurrLine >= ScrollPixels then
      { not at end, so decrement current line }
      Dec(CurrLine, ScrollPixels)
    else SetActive(False);
  end;
end;

procedure TddgMarquee.SetItems(Value: TStringList);
begin
  if FItems <> Value then
    FItems.Assign(Value);
end;

procedure TddgMarquee.SetLineHeight;
{ this virtual method sets the LineHi instance variable }
var
  Metrics : TTextMetric;
begin
  { get metric info for font }
  GetTextMetrics(Canvas.Handle, Metrics);
```

continues

LISTING 22.2. CONTINUED

```pascal
  { adjust line height }
  LineHi := Metrics.tmHeight + Metrics.tmInternalLeading;
end;

procedure TddgMarquee.SetStartLine;
{ this virtual method initializes the CurrLine instance variable }
begin
  // initialize current line to top if scrolling up, or...
  if not FScrollDown then CurrLine := 0
  // bottom if scrolling down
  else CurrLine := VRect.Bottom - Height;
end;

procedure TddgMarquee.PaintLine(R: TRect; LineNum: Integer);
{ this method is called to paint each line of text onto MemBitmap }
const
  Flags: array[TJustification] of DWORD = (DT_CENTER, DT_LEFT, DT_RIGHT);
var
  S: string;
begin
  { Copy next line to local variable for clarity }
  S := FItems.Strings[LineNum];
  { Draw line of text onto memory bitmap }
  DrawText(MemBitmap.Canvas.Handle, PChar(S), Length(S), R,
    Flags[FJust] or DT_SINGLELINE or DT_TOP);
end;

procedure TddgMarquee.MakeRects;
{ procedure sets up VRect and InsideRect TRects }
begin
  { VRect rectangle represents entire memory bitmap }
  with VRect do
  begin
    Top := 0;
    Left := 0;
    Right := Width;
    Bottom := LineHi * FItems.Count + Height * 2;
  end;
  { InsideRect rectangle represents interior of beveled border }
  with InsideRect do
  begin
    Top := BevelWidth;
    Left := BevelWidth;
    Right := Width - (2 * BevelWidth);
    Bottom := Height - (2 * BevelWidth);
  end;
end;
```

```
procedure TddgMarquee.FillBitmap;
var
  y, i : Integer;
  Rect: TRect;
begin
  SetLineHeight;                 // set height of each line
  MakeRects;                     // make rectangles
  with Rect do
  begin
    Left := InsideRect.Left;
    Bottom := VRect.Bottom ;
    Right := InsideRect.Right;
  end;
  SetStartLine;
  MemBitmap.Width := Width;       // initialize memory bitmap
  with MemBitmap do
  begin
    Height := VRect.Bottom;
    with Canvas do
    begin
      Font := Self.Font;
      Brush.Color := Color;
      FillRect(VRect);
      Brush.Style := bsClear;
    end;
  end;
  y := Height;
  i := 0;
  repeat
    Rect.Top := y;
    PaintLine(Rect, i);
    { increment y by the height (in pixels) of a line }
    inc(y, LineHi);
    inc(i);
  until i >= FItems.Count;       // repeat for all lines
end;

procedure TddgMarquee.Paint;
{ this virtual method is called in response to a }
{ Windows paint message }
begin
  if FActive then
    { Copy from memory bitmap to screen }
    BitBlt(Canvas.Handle, 0, 0, InsideRect.Right, InsideRect.Bottom,
      MemBitmap.Canvas.Handle, 0, CurrLine, srcCopy)
  else
    inherited Paint;
end;
```

continues

Listing 22.2. CONTINUED

```
procedure TddgMarquee.SetActive(Value: Boolean);
{ called to activate/deactivate the marquee }
begin
  if Value and (not FActive) and (FItems.Count > 0) then
  begin
    FActive := True;              // set active flag
    MemBitmap := TBitmap.Create;
    FillBitmap;                   // Paint Image on bitmap
    FTimer.Enabled := True;       // start timer
  end
  else if (not Value) and FActive then
  begin
    FTimer.Enabled := False;    // disable timer,
    if Assigned(FOnDone)        // fire OnDone event,
      then FOnDone(Self);
    FActive := False;           // set FActive to False
    MemBitmap.Free;             // free memory bitmap
    Invalidate;                 // clear control window
  end;
end;

end.
```

> **TIP**
>
> Notice the `default` directive and value used with the `Justify` property of `TddgMarquee`. This use of `default` optimizes streaming of the component, which improves the component's design-time performance. You can give default values to properties of any ordinal type (`Integer`, `Word`, `Longint`, as well as enumerated types, for example), but you can't give them to nonordinal property types such as strings, floating-point numbers, arrays, records, and classes.
>
> You also need to initialize the default values for the properties in your constructor. Failure to do so will cause streaming problems.

Testing `TddgMarquee`

Although it's very exciting to finally have this component written and in the testing stages, don't get carried away by trying to add it to the Component Palette just yet. It has to be debugged first. You should do all preliminary testing with the component by creating a project that creates and uses a dynamic instance of the component. Listing 22.3 depicts the main unit for a project called `TestMarq`, which is used to test the `TddgMarquee` component. This simple project consists of a form that contains two buttons.

LISTING 22.3. THE SOURCE CODE FOR `Testu.pas`.

```pascal
unit Testu;

interface

uses
  SysUtils, WinTypes, WinProcs, Messages, Classes, Graphics, Controls,
  Forms, Dialogs, Marquee, StdCtrls, ExtCtrls;

type
  TForm1 = class(TForm)
    Button1: TButton;
    Button2: TButton;
    procedure FormCreate(Sender: TObject);
    procedure Button1Click(Sender: TObject);
    procedure Button2Click(Sender: TObject);
  private
    Marquee1: TddgMarquee;
    procedure MDone(Sender: TObject);
  public
    { Public declarations }
  end;

var
  Form1: TForm1;

implementation

{$R *.DFM}

procedure TForm1.MDone(Sender: TObject);
begin
  Beep;
end;

procedure TForm1.FormCreate(Sender: TObject);
begin
  Marquee1 := TddgMarquee.Create(Self);
  with Marquee1 do
  begin
    Parent := Self;
    Top := 10;
    Left := 10;
    Height := 200;
    Width := 150;
    OnDone := MDone;
    Show;
    with Items do
```

continues

LISTING 22.3. CONTINUED

```
  begin
    Add('Greg');
    Add('Peter');
    Add('Bobby');
    Add('Marsha');
    Add('Jan');
    Add('Cindy');
  end;
 end;
end;

procedure TForm1.Button1Click(Sender: TObject);
begin
  Marquee1.Active := True;
end;

procedure TForm1.Button2Click(Sender: TObject);
begin
  Marquee1.Active := False;
end;

end.
```

> **TIP**
>
> *Always* create a test project for your new components. *Never* try to do initial testing on a component by adding it to the Component Palette. By trying to debug a component that resides on the palette, not only will you waste time with a lot of gratuitous package rebuilding, but it's possible to crash the IDE as a result of a bug in your component.

Figure 22.3 shows the TestMarq project in action.

FIGURE 22.3.

Testing the
TddgMarquee
component.

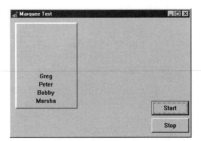

After you squash all the bugs you find in this program, it's time to add it to the Component Palette. As you may recall, doing so is easy: Simply choose Component | Install Component from the main menu and then fill in the unit filename and package name in the Install Component dialog. Choose OK and Delphi will rebuild the package to which the component was added and update the Component Palette. Of course, your component will need to expose a `Register()` procedure in order to be placed on the Component Palette. The `TddgMarquee` component is registered in the `DDGReg.pas` unit of the `DdgLib40` package on the software accompanying this book.

WRITING PROPERTY EDITORS

Chapter 21, "Writing Delphi Custom Components," shows how properties are edited in the Object Inspector for most of the common property types. The means by which a property is edited is determined by its *property editor*. Several predefined property editors are used for the existing properties. However, there may be a situation in which none of the predefined editors meets your needs, such as when you've created a custom property. Given this situation, you'll need to create your own editor for that property.

You can edit properties in the Object Inspector in two ways. One is to allow the user to edit the value as a text string. The other is to use a dialog that performs the editing of the property. In some cases, you'll want to allow both editing capabilities for a single property.

Here are the steps required for writing a property editor:

1. Create a descendant property editor object.
2. Edit the property as text.
3. Edit the property as a whole with a dialog (optional).
4. Specify the property editor's attributes.
5. Register the property editor.

The following sections cover each of these steps.

Creating a Descendant Property Editor Object

Delphi defines several property editors in the unit `DsgnIntf.pas`, all of which descend from the base class `TPropertyEditor`. When you create a property editor, your property editor must descend from `TPropertyEditor` or one of its descendants. Table 22.1 shows the `TPropertyEditor` descendants that are used with the existing properties.

TABLE 22.1. PROPERTY EDITORS DEFINED IN DsgnIntf.pas.

Property Editor	Description
TOrdinalProperty	Base class for all ordinal property editors, such as TIntegerProperty, TEnumProperty, TCharProperty, and so on.
TIntegerProperty	Default property editor for integer properties of all sizes.
TCharProperty	Property editor for properties that are a char type and a subrange of char; that is, 'A'..'Z'.
TEnumProperty	Default property for all user-defined enumerated types.
TFloatProperty	Default property editor for floating-point numeric properties.
TStringProperty	Default property editor for string type properties.
TSetElementProperty	Default property editor for individual set elements. Each element is treated as a independent Boolean element.
TSetProperty	Default property editor for set properties. The set expands into separate set elements for each element in the set.
TClassProperty	Default property editor for properties that are, themselves, objects.
TMethodProperty	Default property editor for properties that are method pointers— that is, events.
TComponentProperty	Default property editor for properties that refer to a component. This isn't the same as the TClassProperty editor. Instead, this editor allows the user to specify a component to which the property refers—that is, ActiveControl.
TColorProperty	Default property editor for properties of the type TColor.
TFontNameProperty	Default property editor for font names. This editor displays a drop-down list of fonts available on the system.
TFontProperty	Default property editor for properties of type TFont, which allows the editing of subproperties. TFontProperty allows the editing of subproperties because it derives from TClassProperty.

The property editor from which your property editor must descend depends on how the property is going to behave when it's edited. In some cases, for example, your property might require the same functionality as TIntegerProperty, but it might also require additional logic in the editing process. Therefore, it would be logical that your property editor descend from TIntegerProperty.

> **TIP**
>
> Bear in mind that there are cases when you don't need to create a property editor that depends on your property type. For example, subrange types are checked automatically (for example, 1..10 is checked for by TIntegerProperty), enumerated types get drop-down lists automatically, and so on. You should try to use type definitions instead of custom property editors because they're enforced by the language at compile time as well as by the default property editors.

Editing the Property as Text

The property editor has two basic purposes: One is to provide a means for the user to edit the property; this is obvious. The other not-so-obvious purpose is to provide the string representation of the property value to the Object Inspector so that it can be displayed accordingly.

When you create a descendant property editor class, you must override the GetValue() and SetValue() methods. GetValue() returns the string representation of the property value for the Object Inspector to display. SetValue() sets the value based on its string representation as it's entered in the Object Inspector.

As an example, examine the definition of the TIntegerProperty class type as it's defined in DsgnInfo.pas:

```
TIntegerProperty = class(TOrdinalProperty)
public
  function GetValue: string; override;
  procedure SetValue(const Value: string); override;
end;
```

Here, you see that the GetValue() and SetValue() methods have been overridden. The GetValue() implementation is as follows:

```
function TIntegerProperty.GetValue: string;
begin
  Result := IntToStr(GetOrdValue);
end;
```

Here's the SetValue() implementation:

```
procedure TIntegerProperty.SetValue(const Value: String);
var
  L: Longint;
begin
  L := StrToInt(Value);
```

```
  with GetTypeData(GetPropType)^ do
    if (L < MinValue) or (L > MaxValue) then
      raise EPropertyError.CreateResFmt(SOutOfRange, [MinValue,
      ➥MaxValue]);
  SetOrdValue(L);
end;
```

`GetValue()` returns the string representation of an integer property. The Object Inspector uses this value to display the property's value. `GetOrdValue()` is a method defined by `TPropertyEditor` and is used to retrieve the value of the property referenced by the property editor.

`SetValue()` takes the string value entered by the user and assigns it to the property in the correct format. `SetValue()` also performs some error checking to ensure that the value is within a specified range of values. This illustrates how you might perform error checking with your descendant property editors. The `SetOrdValue()` method assigns the value to the property referenced by the property editor.

`TPropertyEditor` defines several methods similar to `GetOrdValue()` for getting the string representation of various types. Additionally, `TPropertyEditor` contains the equivalent `Set` methods for setting the values in their respective format. `TPropertyEditor` descendants inherit these methods. These methods are used for getting and setting the values of the properties that the property editor references. Table 22.2 shows these methods.

TABLE 22.2. READ/WRITE PROPERTY METHODS FOR `TPropertyEditor`.

Property Type	Get *Method*	Set *Method*
Floating point	`GetFloatValue()`	`SetFloatValue()`
Event	`GetMethodValue()`	`SetMethodValue()`
Ordinal	`GetOrdValue()`	`SetOrdValue()`
String	`GetStrValue()`	`SetStrValue()`
Variant	`GetVarValue()`	`SetVarValue(), SetVarValueAt()`

To illustrate creating a new property editor, we'll have some more fun with the solar system introduced in the last chapter. This time, we've created a simple component, `TddgPlanet`, to represent a single planet. `TddgPlanet` contains the property `PlanetName`. Internal storage for `PlanetName` is going to be of type `Integer` and will hold the planet's position in the solar system. However, it will be displayed in the Object Inspector as the name of the planet.

So far this sounds easy, but here's the catch: We want to enable the user to type two values to represent the planet. He should be able to type the planet name as a string, such as **Venus** or **VENUS** or **VeNuS**. He should also be able to type the position of the planet in the solar system. So, for the planet Venus, the user would type the numeric value **2**.

The component TddgPlanet is as follows:

```
type
  TPlanetName = type Integer;

  TddgPlanet = class(TComponent)
  private
    FPlanetName: TPlanetName;
  published
    property PlanetName: TPlanetName read FPlanetName write FPlanetName;
  end;
```

As you can see, there's not much to this component. It has only one property: PlanetName of the type TPlanetName. Here, the special definition of TPlanetName is used so that it's given its own runtime type information, yet is still treated like an integer type.

This functionality doesn't come from the TddgPlanet component; rather, it comes from the property editor for the TPlanetName property type. This property editor is shown in Listing 22.4.

LISTING 22.4. PlanetPE.PAS, THE SOURCE CODE FOR TPlanetNameProperty.

```
unit PlanetPE;

interface

uses
  Windows, SysUtils, DsgnIntF;

type
  TPlanetNameProperty = class(TIntegerProperty)
  public
    function GetValue: string; override;
    procedure SetValue(const Value: string); override;
  end;

implementation

const
  { Declare a constant array containing planet names }
  PlanetNames: array[1..9] of String[7] =
    ('Mercury', 'Venus', 'Earth', 'Mars', 'Jupiter', 'Saturn',
     'Uranus', 'Neptune', 'Pluto');
```

continues

22

ADVANCED COMPONENT TECHNIQUES

LISTING 22.4. CONTINUED

```pascal
function TPlanetNameProperty.GetValue: string;
begin
  Result := PlanetNames[GetOrdValue];
end;

procedure TPlanetNameProperty.SetValue(const Value: String);
var
  PName: string[7];
  i, ValErr: Integer;
begin
  PName := UpperCase(Value);
  i := 1;
  { Compare the Value with each of the planet names in the PlanetNames
    array. If a match is found, the variable i will be less than 10 }
  while (PName <> UpperCase(PlanetNames[i])) and (i < 10) do
    inc(i);
  { If i is less than 10, a valid planet name was entered. Set the value
    and exit this procedure. }
  if i < 10 then  // A valid planet name was entered.
  begin
    SetOrdValue(i);
    Exit;
  end
  { If i was greater than 10, the user might have typed in a planet
    number, or an invalid planet name. Use the Val function to test if the
    user typed in a number, if an ValErr is non-zero, an invalid name was
    entered, otherwise, test the range of the number entered for (0 < i <
    10). }
  else begin
    Val(Value, i, ValErr);
    if ValErr <> 0 then
      raise Exception.Create(Format('Sorry, Never heard of the planet
        ➥%s.',
        [Value]));
    if (i <= 0) or (i >= 10) then
      raise Exception.Create('Sorry, that planet is not
        ➥in OUR solar system.');
    SetOrdValue(i);
  end;
end;

end.
```

First, we create our property editor, `TPlanetNameProperty`, which descends from
`TIntegerProperty`. By the way, it's necessary to include the `DsgnIntf` unit in the uses
clause of this unit.

We've defined an array of string constants to represent the planets in the solar system by their position from the sun. These strings will be used to display the string representation of the planet in the Object Inspector.

As stated earlier, we have to override the `GetValue()` and `SetValue()` methods. In the `GetValue()` method, we just return the string from the `PlanetNames` array, which is indexed by the property value. Of course, this value must be within the range of 1–9. We handle this by not allowing the user to enter a number out of that range in the `SetValue()` method.

`SetValue()` gets a string as it's entered from the Object Inspector. This string can either be a planet name or a number representing a planet's position. If a valid planet name or planet number is entered, as determined by the code logic, the value assigned to the property is specified by the `SetOrdValue()` method. If the user enters an invalid planet name or planet position, the code raises the appropriate exception.

That's all there is to defining a property editor. Well, not quite; it must still be registered before it becomes known to the property to which you want to attach it.

Registering the New Property Editor

You register a property editor by using the appropriately named procedure `RegisterPropertyEditor()`. This method is declared as follows:

```
procedure RegisterPropertyEditor(PropertyType: PTypeInfo;
  ComponentClass: TClass);
  const PropertyName: string; EditorClass: TPropertyEditorClass);
```

The first parameter, *PropertyType*, is a pointer to the runtime type information of the property being edited. This information is obtained by using the `TypeInfo()` function. *ComponentClass* is used to specify to which class this property editor will apply. *PropertyName* specifies the property name on the component, and the *EditorClass* parameter specifies the type of property editor to use. For the `TddgPlanet.PlanetName` property, this function looks like this:

```
RegisterPropertyEditor(TypeInfo(TPlanetName), TddgPlanet, 'PlanetName',
  TPlanetNameProperty);
```

TIP

While, for the purpose of illustration, this particular property editor is registered for use only with the `TddgPlanet` component and `'PlanetName'` property name, you might choose to be less restrictive in registering your custom property editors. By setting the `ComponentClass` parameter to `nil` and the `PropertyName` parameter to `' '`, your property editor will work for any component's property of type `TPlanetName`.

It is best to register the property editor in the registration unit for your components, which gets added to your design package. See DdgReg.pas where we register all the property editors for the components accompanying this book. Listing 22.5 shows Planet.pas.

LISTING 22.5. Planet.pas, THE TddgPlanet COMPONENT.

```
unit Planet;

interface

uses
  Classes, SysUtils;

type
  TPlanetName = type Integer;

  TddgPlanet = class(TComponent)
  private
    FPlanetName: TPlanetName;
  published
    property PlanetName: TPlanetName read FPlanetName write FPlanetName;
  end;

implementation

end.
```

TIP

Placing the property editor registration in the Register() procedure of the component unit will force all the property editor code to be linked in with your component when your component is put into a package. For complex components, the design-time tools may take up more code space than the components themselves. Although code size isn't much of an issue for a small component such as this, keep in mind that everything that's listed in the interface section of your component unit (such as the Register() procedure) as well as everything it touches (such as the property editor class type) will tag along with your component when it's compiled into a package. For this reason, you might want to perform registration of your property editor in a separate unit. Furthermore, some component writers choose to create both design-time and runtime packages for their components, where the property editors and other design-time tools reside only in the design-time package. You'll note that the packages containing this book's code do this using the DdgStd40.dpk runtime package and the DdgLib40.dpk design package.

Editing the Property as a Whole with a Dialog

Sometimes it's necessary to provide more editing capability than the in-place editing of the Object Inspector. This is when it becomes necessary to use a dialog as a property editor. An example of this would be the Font property for most Delphi components. Certainly, the makers of Delphi could have forced the user to type the font name and other font-related information. However, it would be unreasonable to expect the user to know this information. It's far easier to provide the user with a dialog where he or she can set these various attributes related to the font and see an example before selecting it.

To illustrate using a dialog to edit a property, we're going to extend the functionality of the TddgRunButton component created in the Chapter 21. Now the user will be able to click an ellipsis button in the Object Inspector for the CommandLine property, which will invoke an Open File dialog from which the user can select a file for TddgRunButton to represent.

Sample Dialog Property Editor: Extending TddgRunButton

The TddgRunButton component is shown in Listing 21.13 in Chapter 21. We won't show it again here, but there are a few things we want to point out. The TddgRunButton.CommandLine property is defined as a TCommandLine type with this definition:

```
TCommandLine = type string;
```

Again, this is a special declaration that attaches unique runtime type information to this special type. This allows you to define a property editor specific to the TCommandLine type. Additionally, because TCommandLine is treated as a string, the property editor for editing string properties still applies to the TCommandLine type as well.

Also, as we illustrate the property editor for the TCommandLine type, keep in mind that TddgRunButton already has included the necessary error checking of property assignments in the properties' access methods. Therefore, it isn't necessary to repeat this error checking in the property editor's logic.

Listing 22.6 shows the definition of the TCommandLineProperty property editor.

LISTING 22.6. RunBtnPE.pas, THE TCommandLineProperty EDITOR.

```
unit RunBtnPE;

interface

uses
  Windows, Messages, SysUtils, Classes, Graphics, Controls,
  Forms, Dialogs, StdCtrls, Buttons, DsgnIntF, TypInfo;
```

continues

LISTING 22.6. CONTINUED

```
type
  { Descend from the TStringProperty class so that this editor
    inherits the string property editing capabilities }
  TCommandLineProperty = class(TStringProperty)
    function GetAttributes: TPropertyAttributes; override;
    procedure Edit; override;
  end;

implementation

function TCommandLineProperty.GetAttributes: TPropertyAttributes;
begin
  Result := [paDialog]; // Display a dialog in the Edit method
end;

procedure TCommandLineProperty.Edit;
{ The Edit method displays a TOpenDialog from which the user obtains
  an executable file name that gets assigned to the property }
begin
  { Create the TOpenDialog }
  with TOpenDialog.Create(Application) do
    try
      { Show only executable files }
      Filter := 'Executable Files|*.EXE';
      { If the user selects a file, then assign it to the property. }
      if Execute then SetStrValue(FileName);
    finally
      Free // Free the TOpenDialog instance.
    end;
end;

end.
```

Examination of TCommandLineProperty shows that the property editor is very simple.
First, notice that it descends from TStringProperty so that the string-editing capabilities
are maintained. Therefore, in the Object Inspector, it isn't necessary to invoke the
dialog. The user can just type the command line directly. Also, we didn't override the
SetValue() or GetValue() methods because TStringProperty already handles this
correctly. However, it was necessary to override the GetAttributes() method in order
for the Object Inspector to know that this property is capable of being edited with a
dialog. GetAttributes() merits further discussion.

Specifying the Property Editor's Attributes

Every property editor must tell the Object Inspector how a property is to be edited and
what special attributes (if any) must be used when editing a property. Most of the time,

the inherited attributes from a descendant property editor will suffice. In certain circumstances, however, you must override the `GetAttributes()` method of `TPropertyEditor`, which returns a set of property attribute flags, `TPropertyAttributes`, that indicate special property-editing attributes. The various `TPropertyAttribute` flags are shown in Table 22.3.

TABLE 22.3. `TPropertyAttribute` FLAGS.

Attribute	How the Property Editor Works with the Object Inspector
paValueList	Returns an enumerated list of values for the property. The `GetValues()` method populates the list. A drop-down arrow button appears to the right of the property value. This applies to enumerated properties such as `TForm.BorderStyle` and `Integer const` groups such as `TColor` and `TCharSet`.
paSubProperties	Subproperties are displayed indented below the current property in outline format. `paValueList` must also be set. This applies to set properties and class properties such as `TOpenDialog.Options` and `TForm.Font`.
paDialog	An ellipsis button is displayed to the right of the property in the Object Inspector, which, when pressed, causes the property editor's `Edit()` method to invoke a dialog. This applies to properties such as `TForm.Font`.
paMultiSelect	Properties are displayed when more than one component is selected on the Form Designer, allowing the user to change the property values for multiple components at once. Some properties aren't appropriate for this capability, such as the `Name` property.
paAutoUpdate	`SetValue()` is called on each change made to the property. If this flag isn't set, `SetValue()` is called when the user presses Enter or moves off the property in the Object Inspector. This applies to properties such as `TForm.Caption`.
paSortList	The Object Inspector sorts the list returned by `GetValues()`.
paReadOnly	The property value can't be changed.
paRevertable	The property can be reverted to its original value. Some properties, such as nested properties, shouldn't be reverted. `TFont` is an example of this.

22

**ADVANCED
COMPONENT
TECHNIQUES**

> **NOTE**
>
> You should take a look at `DsgnIntf.pas` and examine which `TPropertyAttribute` flags are set for various property editors.

Setting the `paDialog` Attribute for `TCommandLineProperty`

Because TCommandLineProperty is to display a dialog, you must tell the Object Inspector to use this capability by setting the paDialog attribute in the TCommandLineProperty.GetAttributes() method. This will place an ellipsis button to the right of the CommandLine property value in the Object Inspector. When the user presses this button, the TCommandLineProperty.Edit() method will be called.

Registering the `TCommandLineProperty`

The final step required for implementing the TCommandLineProperty property editor is to register it using the RegisterProperyEditor() procedure discussed earlier in this chapter. This procedure was added to the Register() procedure in DDGReg.pas in the DdgLib40 package:

```
RegisterComponents('DDG', [TddgRunButton]);
  RegisterPropertyEditor(TypeInfo(TCommandLine), TddgRunButton,
    '', TCommandLineProperty);
```

Also, note that the units DsgnIntf and RunBtnPE had to be added to the uses clause.

COMPONENT EDITORS

Component editors extend the design-time behavior of your components by allowing you to add items to the local menu associated with a particular component and by allowing you to change the default action when a component is double-clicked in the Form Designer. You might already be familiar with component editors without knowing it if you've ever used the fields editor provided with the TTable, TQuery, and TStoredProc components.

TComponentEditor

You might not be aware of this, but a different component editor is created for each component that's selected in the Form Designer. The type of component editor created depends on the component's type, although all component editors descend from TComponentEditor. This class is defined in the DsgnIntf unit as follows:

```
type
  TComponentEditor = class(TInterfacedObject, IComponentEditor)
  private
    FComponent: TComponent;
    FDesigner: IFormDesigner;
  public
    constructor Create(AComponent: TComponent; ADesigner: IFormDesigner);
      virtual;
    procedure Edit; virtual;
    procedure ExecuteVerb(Index: Integer); virtual;
```

```
function GetIComponent: IComponent;
function GetDesigner: IFormDesigner;
function GetVerb(Index: Integer): string; virtual;
function GetVerbCount: Integer; virtual;
procedure Copy; virtual;
property Component: TComponent read FComponent;
property Designer: IFormDesigner read GetDesigner;
end;
```

Properties

The `Component` property of `TComponentEditor` is the instance of the component you're in the process of editing. Because this property is of the generic `TComponent` type, you must typecast the property in order to access fields introduced by descendant classes.

The `Designer` property is the instance of `TFormDesigner` that's currently hosting the application at design time. You'll find the complete definition for this class in the `DsgnIntf.pas` unit.

Methods

The `Edit()` method is called when the user double-clicks the component at design time. Often, this method will invoke some sort of design dialog. The default behavior for this method is to call `ExecuteVerb(0)` if `GetVerbCount()` returns a value of 1 or greater. You must call `Designer.Modified()` if you modify the component from this (or any) method.

The `GetVerbCount()` method is called to retrieve the number of items that are to be added to the local menu.

`GetVerb()` accepts an integer, `Index`, and returns a string containing the text that should appear on the local menu in the position corresponding to `Index`.

When an item is chosen from the local menu, the `ExecuteVerb()` method is called. This method receives the zero-based index of the item selected from the local menu in the `Index` parameter. You should respond by performing whatever action is necessary based on the verb the user selected from the local menu.

The `Paste()` method is called whenever the component is pasted to the Clipboard. Delphi places the component's resource (streamed) image on the Clipboard, but you can use this method to paste data on the Clipboard in a different type of format.

TDefaultEditor

If a custom component editor isn't registered for a particular component, that component will use the default component editor, `TDefaultEditor`. `TDefaultEditor` overrides the behavior of the `Edit()` method so that it searches the properties of the component and generates (or navigates to) the `OnCreate`, `OnChanged`, or `OnClick` event (whichever it finds first).

A Simple Component

Consider the following simple custom component:

```
type
  TComponentEditorSample = class(TComponent)
  protected
    procedure SayHello; virtual;
    procedure SayGoodbye; virtual;
  end;

procedure TComponentEditorSample.SayHello;
begin
  MessageDlg('Hello, there!', mtInformation, [mbOk], 0);
end;

procedure TComponentEditorSample.SayGoodbye;
begin
  MessageDlg('See ya!', mtInformation, [mbOk], 0);
end;
```

As you can see, this little guy doesn't do much: It's a nonvisual component that descends directly from TComponent, and it contains two methods, SayHello() and SayGoodbye(), that simply display message dialogs.

A Simple Component Editor

To make the component a bit more exiting, you'll create a component editor that calls into the component and executes its methods at design time. The minimum TComponentEditor methods that must be overridden are ExecuteVerb(), GetVerb(), and GetVerbCount(). The code for this component editor is as follows:

```
type
  TSampleEditor = class(TComponentEditor)
  private
    procedure ExecuteVerb(Index: Integer); override;
    function GetVerb(Index: Integer): string; override;
    function GetVerbCount: Integer; override;
  end;

procedure TSampleEditor.ExecuteVerb(Index: Integer);
begin
  case Index of
    0: TComponentEditorSample(Component).SayHello;    // call function
    1: TComponentEditorSample(Component).SayGoodbye;  // call function
  end;
end;

function TSampleEditor.GetVerb(Index: Integer): string;
```

```
begin
  case Index of
    0: Result := 'Hello';      // return hello string
    1: Result := 'Goodbye';    // return goodbye string
  end;
end;

function TSampleEditor.GetVerbCount: Integer;
begin
  Result := 2;      // two possible verbs
end;
```

The `GetVerbCount()` method returns 2, indicating that there are two different verbs the component editor is prepared to execute. `GetVerb()` returns a string for each of these verbs to appear on the local menu. The `ExecuteVerb()` method calls the appropriate method inside the component, based on the verb index it receives as a parameter.

Registering a Component Editor

Like components and property editors, component editors must also be registered with the IDE within a unit's `Register()` method. To register a component editor, call the aptly named `RegisterComponentEditor()` procedure, which is defined as follows:

```
procedure RegisterComponentEditor(ComponentClass: TComponentClass;
  ComponentEditor: TComponentEditorClass);
```

The first parameter to this function is the component type for which you want to register a component editor, and the second parameter is the component editor itself.

Listing 22.7 shows the `CompEdit.pas` unit, which includes the component, component editor, and registration calls. Figure 22.4 shows the local menu associated with the `TComponentEditorSample` component, and Figure 22.5 displays the result of selecting one of the verbs from the local menu.

LISTING 22.7. `CompEdit.pas`—THE `TComponentEditorSample` COMPONENT.

```
unit CompEdit;

interface

uses
  SysUtils, Windows, Messages, Classes, Graphics, Controls, Forms,
  Dialogs, DsgnIntf;

type
  TComponentEditorSample = class(TComponent)
  protected
```

continues

22

ADVANCED
COMPONENT
TECHNIQUES

LISTING 22.7. CONTINUED

```
  procedure SayHello; virtual;
  procedure SayGoodbye; virtual;
end;

TSampleEditor = class(TComponentEditor)
private
  procedure ExecuteVerb(Index: Integer); override;
  function GetVerb(Index: Integer): string; override;
  function GetVerbCount: Integer; override;
end;

implementation

{ TComponentEditorSample }

procedure TComponentEditorSample.SayHello;
begin
  MessageDlg('Hello, there!', mtInformation, [mbOk], 0);
end;

procedure TComponentEditorSample.SayGoodbye;
begin
  MessageDlg('See ya!', mtInformation, [mbOk], 0);
end;

{ TSampleEditor }

const
  vHello = 'Hello';
  vGoodbye = 'Goodbye';

procedure TSampleEditor.ExecuteVerb(Index: Integer);
begin
  case Index of
    0: TComponentEditorSample(Component).SayHello;    // call function
    1: TComponentEditorSample(Component).SayGoodbye;  // call function
  end;
end;

function TSampleEditor.GetVerb(Index: Integer): string;
begin
  case Index of
    0: Result := vHello;      // return hello string
    1: Result := vGoodbye;    // return goodbye string
  end;
end;
```

```
function TSampleEditor.GetVerbCount: Integer;
begin
  Result := 2;      // two possible verbs
end;

end.
```

FIGURE 22.4.

The local menu of
TComponent
EditorSample.

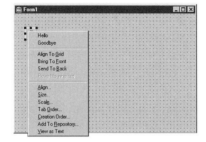

FIGURE 22.5.

*The result of
selecting a verb.*

STREAMING NONPUBLISHED COMPONENT DATA

Chapter 21 indicates that the Delphi IDE automatically knows how to stream the published properties of a component to and from a DFM file. What happens, however, when you have nonpublished data that you want to be persistent by keeping it in the DFM file? Fortunately, Delphi components provide a mechanism for writing and reading programmer-defined data to and from the DFM file.

Defining Properties

The first step in defining persistent nonpublished "properties" is to override a component's DefineProperties() method. This method is inherited from TPersistent, and it's defined as follows:

```
procedure DefineProperties(Filer: TFiler); virtual;
```

By default, this method handles reading and writing published properties to and from the DFM file. You can override this method, and, after calling inherited, you can call the TFiler method DefineProperty() or DefineBinaryProperty() once for each piece of data you want to become part of the DFM file. These methods are defined, respectively, as follows:

```
procedure DefineProperty(const Name: string; ReadData: TReaderProc;
    WriteData: TWriterProc; HasData: Boolean); virtual;

procedure DefineBinaryProperty(const Name: string; ReadData,
    WriteData: TStreamProc; HasData: Boolean); virtual;
```

DefineProperty() is used to make persistent standard data types such as strings, integers, Booleans, chars, floats, and enumerated types. DefineBinaryProperty() is used to provide access to raw binary data, such as a graphic or sound, written to the DFM file.

For both of these functions, the Name parameter identifies the property name that should be written to the DFM file. This doesn't have to be the same as the internal name of the data field you're accessing. The ReadData and WriteData parameters differ in type between DefineProperty() and DefineBinaryProperty(), but they serve the same purpose: These methods are called in order to write or read data to or from the DFM file. (We'll discuss these in more detail in just a moment.) The HasData parameter indicates whether the property has data that it needs to store.

The ReadData and WriteData parameters of DefineProperty() are of type TReaderProc and TWriterProc, respectively. These types are defined as follows:

```
type
  TReaderProc = procedure(Reader: TReader) of object;
  TWriterProc = procedure(Writer: TWriter) of object;
```

TReader and TWriter are specialized descendants of TFiler that have additional methods for reading and writing native types. Methods of these types provide the conduit between component data of these standard, native types and the DFM file.

The ReadData and WriteData parameters of DefineBinaryProperty() are of type TStreamProc, which is defined as follows:

```
type
  TStreamProc = procedure(Stream: TStream) of object;
```

Because TStreamProc type methods receive only TStream as a parameter, this allows you to read and write binary data very easily to and from the stream. Like the other method types described earlier, methods of this type provide the conduit between non-standard data and the DFM file.

An Example of DefineProperty()

In order to bring all this rather technical information together, Listing 22.8 shows the DefProp.pas unit. This unit illustrates the use of DefineProperty() by providing storage for two private data fields: a string and an integer.

LISTING 22.8. DefProp.pas—EXAMPLE USE OF DefineProperty().

```
unit DefProp;

interface

uses
  Windows, Messages, SysUtils, Classes, Graphics, Controls, Forms,
    Dialogs;

type
  TDefinePropTest = class(TComponent)
  private
    FString: String;
    FInteger: Integer;
    procedure ReadStrData(Reader: TReader);
    procedure WriteStrData(Writer: TWriter);
    procedure ReadIntData(Reader: TReader);
    procedure WriteIntData(Writer: TWriter);
  protected
    procedure DefineProperties(Filer: TFiler); override;
  public
    constructor Create(AOwner: TComponent); override;
  end;

implementation

constructor TDefinePropTest.Create(AOwner: TComponent);
begin
  inherited Create(AOwner);
  { Put data in private fields }
```

continues

LISTING 22.8. CONTINUED

```
  FString := 'The following number is the answer...';
  FInteger := 42;
end;

procedure TDefinePropTest.DefineProperties(Filer: TFiler);
begin
  inherited DefineProperties(Filer);
  { Define new properties and reader/writer methods }
  Filer.DefineProperty('StringProp', ReadStrData, WriteStrData,
    FString <> '');
  Filer.DefineProperty('IntProp', ReadIntData, WriteIntData, True);
end;

procedure TDefinePropTest.ReadStrData(Reader: TReader);
begin
  FString := Reader.ReadString;
end;

procedure TDefinePropTest.WriteStrData(Writer: TWriter);
begin
  Writer.WriteString(FString);
end;

procedure TDefinePropTest.ReadIntData(Reader: TReader);
begin
  FInteger := Reader.ReadInteger;
end;

procedure TDefinePropTest.WriteIntData(Writer: TWriter);
begin
  Writer.WriteInteger(FInteger);
end;

end.
```

CAUTION

Always use the `ReadString()` and `WriteString()` methods of `TReader` and `TWriter` to read and write string data. Never use the similar-looking `ReadStr()` and `WriteStr()` methods, because they'll corrupt your DFM file.

To demonstrate that the proof is in the pudding, Figure 22.6 shows a form containing a `TDefinePropTest` component, as text, in the Delphi Code Editor. Notice that the new properties have been written to the file.

FIGURE 22.6.

Viewing a form as text to see the properties.

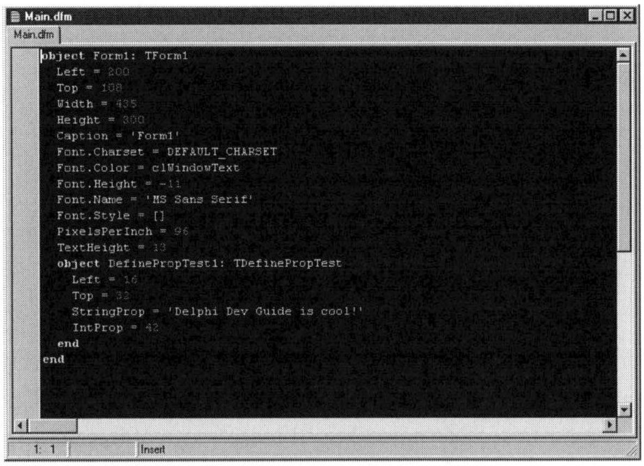

TddgWaveFile: An Example of DefineBinaryProperty()

We mentioned earlier that a good time to use `DefineBinaryProperty()` is when you need to store graphic or sound information along with a component. In fact, VCL uses this technique for storing images associated with components—the `Glyph` of a `TBitBtn`, for example, or the `Icon` of a `TForm`. In this section, you'll learn how to use this technique when storing the sound associated with the `TddgWaveFile` component.

> **NOTE**
>
> `TddgWaveFile` is quite a full-featured component, complete with a custom property, property editor, and component editor to allow you to play sounds at design time. You'll be able to pick through the code for all of this a little later in the chapter, but for now we're going to focus the discussion on the mechanism for storing the binary property.

The `DefineProperties()` method for `TddgWaveFile` is as follows:

```
procedure TddgWaveFile.DefineProperties(Filer: TFiler);
{ Defines binary property called "Data" for FData field. }
{ This allows FData to be read from and written to DFM file. }

  function DoWrite: Boolean;
  begin
```

22

ADVANCED
COMPONENT
TECHNIQUES

```
    if Filer.Ancestor <> nil then
      Result := not (Filer.Ancestor is TddgWaveFile) or
        not Equal(TddgWaveFile(Filer.Ancestor))
    else
      Result := not Empty;
  end;

begin
  inherited DefineProperties(Filer);
  Filer.DefineBinaryProperty('Data', ReadData, WriteData, DoWrite);
end;
```

This method defines a binary property called Data, which is read and written using the
component's ReadData() and WriteData() methods. Additionally, data is written only if
the return value of DoWrite() is True. (You'll learn more about DoWrite() in just a
moment.)

The ReadData() and WriteData() methods are defined as follows:

```
procedure TddgWaveFile.ReadData(Stream: TStream);
{ Reads WAV data from DFM stream. }
begin
  LoadFromStream(Stream);
end;

procedure TddgWaveFile.WriteData(Stream: TStream);
{ Writes WAV data to DFM stream }
begin
  SaveToStream(Stream);
end;
```

As you can see, there isn't much to these methods; they simply call the
LoadFromStream() and SaveToStream() methods, which are also defined by the
TddgWaveFile component. The LoadFromStream() method is as follows:

```
procedure TddgWaveFile.LoadFromStream(S: TStream);
{ Loads WAV data from stream S.  This procedure will free }
{ any memory previously allocated for FData. }
begin
  if not Empty then
    FreeMem(FData, FDataSize);
  FDataSize := 0;
  FData := AllocMem(S.Size);
  FDataSize := S.Size;
  S.Read(FData^, FDataSize);
end;
```

This method first checks to see whether memory has been previously allocated by testing
the value of the FDataSize field. If it's greater than zero, the memory pointed to by the
FData field is freed. At that point, a new block of memory is allocated for FData, and

FDataSize is set to the size of the incoming data stream. The contents of the stream are then read into the FData pointer.

The SaveToStream() method is much simpler; it's defined as follows:

```
procedure TddgWaveFile.SaveToStream(S: TStream);
{ Saves WAV data to stream S. }
begin
  if FDataSize > 0 then
    S.Write(FData^, FDataSize);
end;
```

This method writes the data pointed to by pointer FData to TStream S.

The local DoWrite() function inside the DefineProperties() method determines whether the Data property needs to be streamed. Of course, if FData is empty, there's no need to stream data. Additionally, you must take extra measures to ensure that your component works correctly with form inheritance: You must check to see whether the Ancestor property for Filer is non-nil. If it is and it points to an ancestor version of the current component, you must check to see whether the data you're about to write is different than the ancestor. If you don't perform these additional tests, a copy of the data (the wave file, in this case) will be written in each of the descendant forms, and changing the ancestor's wave file won't be copied to the descendant forms.

> **CAUTION**
>
> For the reasons just explained, DefineProperties() is one area where you'll find a distinct difference between 16- and 32-bit Delphi. For the most part, Borland tried to make form inheritance transparent to the component writer. This is one place where it couldn't be hidden. Although Delphi 1.0 components will function in Delphi 4, they won't be able to propagate updates in form inheritance without modification.

Figure 22.7 shows a view of the Delphi Code Editor displaying, as text, a form containing TddgWaveFile.

FIGURE 22.7.

Viewing the Data *property in the Code Editor.*

Listing 22.9 shows Wavez.pas, which includes the complete source code for the component. Listing 22.10, WavezEd.pas, shows the component's property editor and component editor.

LISTING 22.9. Wavez.pas—SOURCE CODE TO TddgWaveFile.

```
unit Wavez;

interface

uses
  SysUtils, Classes;

type
  { Special string "descendant" used to make a property editor. }
  TWaveFileString = type string;

  EWaveError = class(Exception);

  TWavePause = (wpAsync, wpsSync);
  TWaveLoop = (wlNoLoop, wlLoop);

  TddgWaveFile = class(TComponent)
  private
    FData: Pointer;
    FDataSize: Integer;
    FWaveName: TWaveFileString;
    FWavePause: TWavePause;
```

```
      FWaveLoop: TWaveLoop;
      FOnPlay: TNotifyEvent;
      FOnStop: TNotifyEvent;
      procedure SetWaveName(const Value: TWaveFileString);
      procedure WriteData(Stream: TStream);
      procedure ReadData(Stream: TStream);
    protected
      procedure DefineProperties(Filer: TFiler); override;
    public
      destructor Destroy; override;
      function Empty: Boolean;
      function Equal(Wav: TddgWaveFile): Boolean;
      procedure LoadFromFile(const FileName: String);
      procedure LoadFromStream(S: TStream);
      procedure Play;
      procedure SaveToFile(const FileName: String);
      procedure SaveToStream(S: TStream);
      procedure Stop;
    published
      property WaveLoop: TWaveLoop read FWaveLoop write FWaveLoop;
      property WaveName: TWaveFileString read FWaveName write SetWaveName;
      property WavePause: TWavePause read FWavePause write FWavePause;
      property OnPlay: TNotifyEvent read FOnPlay write FOnPlay;
      property OnStop: TNotifyEvent read FOnStop write FOnStop;
    end;

implementation

uses MMSystem, Windows;

{ TddgWaveFile }

destructor TddgWaveFile.Destroy;
{ Ensures that any allocated memory is freed }
begin
  if not Empty then
    FreeMem(FData, FDataSize);
  inherited Destroy;
end;

function StreamsEqual(S1, S2: TMemoryStream): Boolean;
begin
  Result := (S1.Size = S2.Size) and CompareMem(S1.Memory, S2.Memory,
  ➥S1.Size);
end;

procedure TddgWaveFile.DefineProperties(Filer: TFiler);
{ Defines binary property called "Data" for FData field. }
{ This allows FData to be read from and written to DFM file. }
```

continues

LISTING 22.9. CONTINUED

```
  function DoWrite: Boolean;
  begin
    if Filer.Ancestor <> nil then
      Result := not (Filer.Ancestor is TddgWaveFile) or
        not Equal(TddgWaveFile(Filer.Ancestor))
    else
      Result := not Empty;
  end;

begin
  inherited DefineProperties(Filer);
  Filer.DefineBinaryProperty('Data', ReadData, WriteData, DoWrite);
end;

function TddgWaveFile.Empty: Boolean;
begin
  Result := FDataSize = 0;
end;

function TddgWaveFile.Equal(Wav: TddgWaveFile): Boolean;
var
  MyImage, WavImage: TMemoryStream;
begin
  Result := (Wav <> nil) and (ClassType = Wav.ClassType);
  if Empty or Wav.Empty then
  begin
    Result := Empty and Wav.Empty;
    Exit;
  end;
  if Result then
  begin
    MyImage := TMemoryStream.Create;
    try
      SaveToStream(MyImage);
      WavImage := TMemoryStream.Create;
      try
        Wav.SaveToStream(WavImage);
        Result := StreamsEqual(MyImage, WavImage);
      finally
        WavImage.Free;
      end;
    finally
      MyImage.Free;
    end;
  end;
end;

procedure TddgWaveFile.LoadFromFile(const FileName: String);
{ Loads WAV data from FileName. Note that this procedure does }
```

```
{ not set the WaveName property. }
var
  F: TFileStream;
begin
  F := TFileStream.Create(FileName, fmOpenRead);
  try
    LoadFromStream(F);
  finally
    F.Free;
  end;
end;

procedure TddgWaveFile.LoadFromStream(S: TStream);
{ Loads WAV data from stream S.  This procedure will free }
{ any memory previously allocated for FData. }
begin
  if not Empty then
    FreeMem(FData, FDataSize);
  FDataSize := 0;
  FData := AllocMem(S.Size);
  FDataSize := S.Size;
  S.Read(FData^, FDataSize);
end;

procedure TddgWaveFile.Play;
{ Plays the WAV sound in FData using the parameters found in }
{ FWaveLoop and FWavePause. }
const
  LoopArray: array[TWaveLoop] of DWORD = (0, SND_LOOP);
  PauseArray: array[TWavePause] of DWORD = (SND_ASYNC, SND_SYNC);
begin
  { Make sure component contains data }
  if Empty then
    raise EWaveError.Create('No wave data');
  if Assigned(FOnPlay) then FOnPlay(Self);    // fire event
  { attempt to play wave sound }
  if not PlaySound(FData, 0, SND_MEMORY or PauseArray[FWavePause] or
                   LoopArray[FWaveLoop]) then
    raise EWaveError.Create('Error playing sound');
end;

procedure TddgWaveFile.ReadData(Stream: TStream);
{ Reads WAV data from DFM stream. }
begin
  LoadFromStream(Stream);
end;

procedure TddgWaveFile.SaveToFile(const FileName: String);
{ Saves WAV data to file FileName. }
var
  F: TFileStream;
```

22

**ADVANCED
COMPONENT
TECHNIQUES**

continues

LISTING 22.9. CONTINUED

```pascal
begin
  F := TFileStream.Create(FileName, fmCreate);
  try
    SaveToStream(F);
  finally
    F.Free;
  end;
end;

procedure TddgWaveFile.SaveToStream(S: TStream);
{ Saves WAV data to stream S. }
begin
  if not Empty then
    S.Write(FData^, FDataSize);
end;

procedure TddgWaveFile.SetWaveName(const Value: TWaveFileString);
{ Write method for WaveName property. This method is in charge of }
{ setting WaveName property and loading WAV data from file Value. }
begin
  if Value <> '' then begin
    FWaveName := ExtractFileName(Value);
    { don't load from file when loading from DFM stream }
    { because DFM stream will already contain data. }
    if (not (csLoading in ComponentState)) and FileExists(Value) then
      LoadFromFile(Value);
  end
  else begin
    { if Value is an empty string, that is the signal to free }
    { memory allocated for WAV data. }
    FWaveName := '';
    if not Empty then
      FreeMem(FData, FDataSize);
    FDataSize := 0;
  end;
end;

procedure TddgWaveFile.Stop;
{ Stops currently playing WAV sound }
begin
  if Assigned(FOnStop) then FOnStop(Self);  // fire event
  PlaySound(Nil, 0, SND_PURGE);
end;

procedure TddgWaveFile.WriteData(Stream: TStream);
{ Writes WAV data to DFM stream }
begin
  SaveToStream(Stream);
end;

end.
```

LISTING 22.10. WavezEd.pas—PROPERTY EDITOR FOR TddgWaveFile.WaveName.

```pascal
unit WavezEd;

interface

uses DsgnIntf;

type
  { Property editor for TddgWaveFile's WaveName property }
  TWaveFileStringProperty = class(TStringProperty)
  public
    procedure Edit; override;
    function GetAttributes: TPropertyAttributes; override;
  end;

  { Component editor for TddgWaveFile.  Allows user to play and stop }
  { WAV sounds from local menu in IDE. }
  TWaveEditor = class(TComponentEditor)
  private
    procedure EditProp(PropertyEditor: TPropertyEditor);
  protected
    procedure Edit; override;
    procedure ExecuteVerb(Index: Integer); override;
    function GetVerb(Index: Integer): string; override;
    function GetVerbCount: Integer; override;
  end;

implementation

uses TypInfo, Wavez, Classes, Controls, Dialogs;

const
  VerbCount = 2;
  VerbArray: array[0..VerbCount - 1] of string[7] = ('Play', 'Stop');

{ TWaveFileStringProperty }

procedure TWaveFileStringProperty.Edit;
{ Executed when user clicks the ellipsis button on the WavName   }
{ property in the Object Inspector.  This method allows the user }
{ to pick a file from an OpenDialog and sets the property value. }
begin
  with TOpenDialog.Create(nil) do
    try
      { Set up properties for dialog }
      Filter := 'Wav files|*.wav|All files|*.*';
      DefaultExt := '*.wav';
      { Put current value in the FileName property of dialog }
```

22

ADVANCED
COMPONENT
TECHNIQUES

continues

LISTING 22.10. CONTINUED

```
        FileName := GetStrValue;
        { Execute dialog and set property value if dialog is OK }
        if Execute then
          SetStrValue(FileName);
      finally
        Free;
      end;
end;

function TWaveFileStringProperty.GetAttributes: TPropertyAttributes;
{ Indicates the property editor will invoke a dialog. }
begin
  Result := [paDialog];
end;


{ TWaveEditor }

procedure TWaveEditor.Edit;
{ Called when user double-clicks on the component at design time. }
{ This method calls the GetComponentProperties method in order to }
{ invoke the Edit method of the WaveName property editor. }
var
  Components: TComponentList;
begin
  Components := TComponentList.Create;
  try
    Components.Add(Component);
    GetComponentProperties(Components, tkAny, Designer, EditProp);
  finally
    Components.Free;
  end;
end;

procedure TWaveEditor.EditProp(PropertyEditor: TPropertyEditor);
{ Called once per property in response to GetComponentProperties }
{ call.  This method looks for the WaveName property editor and  }
{ calls its Edit method. }
begin
  if PropertyEditor is TWaveFileStringProperty then begin
   `TWaveFileStringProperty(PropertyEditor).Edit;
    Designer.Modified;    // alert Designer to modification
  end;
end;

procedure TWaveEditor.ExecuteVerb(Index: Integer);
begin
  case Index of
    0: TddgWaveFile(Component).Play;
    1: TddgWaveFile(Component).Stop;
```

```
  end;
end;

function TWaveEditor.GetVerb(Index: Integer): string;
begin
  Result := VerbArray[Index];
end;

function TWaveEditor.GetVerbCount: Integer;
begin
  Result := VerbCount;
end;

end.
```

LISTS OF COMPONENTS: `TCollection` AND `TCollectionItem`

It's common for components to maintain or own a list of items such as data types, records, objects, or even other components. In some cases, it's suitable to encapsulate this list within its own object and then make this object a property of the owner component. An example of this arrangement is the `Lines` property of a `TMemo` component. `Lines` is a `TStrings` object type that encapsulates a list of strings. With this arrangement, the `TStrings` object is responsible for the streaming mechanism used to store its lines to the form file when the user saves the form.

What if you wanted to save a list of items such as components or objects that weren't already encapsulated by an existing class such as `TStrings`? Well, you could create a class that performs the streaming of the listed items and then make that a property of the owner component. Or, you could override the default streaming mechanism of the owner component so that it knows how to stream its list of items. However, a better solution would be to take advantage of the `TCollection` and `TCollectionItem` classes.

The `TCollection` class is an object used to store a list of `TCollectionItem` objects. `TCollection`, itself, isn't a component but rather a descendant of `TPersistent`. Typically, `TCollection` is associated with an existing component.

To use `TCollection` to store a list of items, you would derive a descendant class from `TCollection`, which you could call `TNewCollection`. `TNewCollection` will serve as a property type for a component. Then, you must derive a class from the `TCollectionItem` class, which you could call `TNewCollectionItem`. `TNewCollection` will maintain a list of `TNewCollectionItem` objects. The beauty of this is that data belonging to `TNewCollectionItem` that needs to be streamed only needs to be published by `TNewCollectionItem`. Delphi already knows how to stream published properties.

An example of where TCollection is used is with the TStatusBar component. TStatusBar is a TWinControl descendant. One of its properties is Panels. TStatusBar.Panels is of type TStatusPanels, which is a TCollection descendant and defined as follows:

```
type
  TStatusPanels = class(TCollection)
  private
    FStatusBar: TStatusBar;
    function GetItem(Index: Integer): TStatusPanel;
    procedure SetItem(Index: Integer; Value: TStatusPanel);
  protected
    procedure Update(Item: TCollectionItem); override;
  public
    constructor Create(StatusBar: TStatusBar);
    function Add: TStatusPanel;
    property Items[Index: Integer]: TStatusPanel read GetItem
        write SetItem; default;
  end;
```

TStatusPanels stores a list of TCollectionItem descendants, TStatusPanel, as defined here:

```
type
  TStatusPanel = class(TCollectionItem)
  private
    FText: string;
    FWidth: Integer;
    FAlignment: TAlignment;
    FBevel: TStatusPanelBevel;
    FStyle: TStatusPanelStyle;
    procedure SetAlignment(Value: TAlignment);
    procedure SetBevel(Value: TStatusPanelBevel);
    procedure SetStyle(Value: TStatusPanelStyle);
    procedure SetText(const Value: string);
    procedure SetWidth(Value: Integer);
  public
    constructor Create(Collection: TCollection); override;
    procedure Assign(Source: TPersistent); override;
  published
    property Alignment: TAlignment read FAlignment
      write SetAlignment default taLeftJustify;
    property Bevel: TStatusPanelBevel read FBevel
      write SetBevel default pbLowered;
    property Style: TStatusPanelStyle read FStyle write SetStyle
      default psText;
    property Text: string read FText write SetText;
    property Width: Integer read FWidth write SetWidth;
  end;
```

The TStatusPanel properties in the published section of the class declaration will automatically be streamed by Delphi. TStatusPanel takes a TCollection parameter in its Create() constructor, and it associates itself with that TCollection. Likewise, TStatusPanels takes the TStatusBar component in its constructor to which it associates itself. The TCollection engine knows how to deal with the streaming of TCollectionItem components and also defines some methods and properties for manipulating the items maintained in TCollection. You can look these up in the online help.

To illustrate how you might use these two new classes, we've created the TddgLaunchPad component. TddgLaunchPad will enable the user to store a list of TddgRunButton components, which we created in Chapter 21.

TddgLaunchPad is a descendant of the TScrollBox component. One of the properties of TddgLaunchPad is RunButtons, a TCollection descendant. RunButtons maintains a list of TRunBtnItem components. TRunBtnItem is a TCollectionItem descendant whose properties are used to create a TddgRunButton component, which is placed on TddgLaunchPad. In the following sections, we'll discuss how we created this component.

Defining the `TCollectionItem` Class: `TRunBtnItem`

The first step is to define the item to be maintained in a list. For TddgLaunchPad, this would be a TddgRunButton component. Therefore, each TRunBtnItem instance must associate itself with a TddgRunButton component. The following code shows a partial definition of the TRunBtnItem class:

```
type
  TRunBtnItem = class(TCollectionItem)
  private
    FCommandLine: String;    // Store the command line
    FLeft: Integer;          // Store the positional properties for the
    FTop: Integer;           //      TddgRunButton.
    FRunButton: TddgRunButton; // Reference to a TddgRunButton
    ...
  public
    constructor Create(Collection: TCollection); override;
  published
    { The published properties will be streamed }
    property CommandLine: String read FCommandLine write SetCommandLine;
    property Left: Integer read FLeft write SetLeft;
    property Top: Integer read FTop write SetTop;
  end;
```

Notice that TRunBtnItem keeps a reference to a TddgRunButton component, yet it only streams the properties required to build a TddgRunButton. At first you might think that because TRunBtnItem associates itself with a TddgRunButton, it could just publish the component and let the streaming engine do the rest. Well, this poses some problems with the streaming engine and how it handles the streaming of TComponent classes differently than TPersistent classes. The fundamental rule here is that the streaming system is responsible for creating new instances for every TComponent-derived class name it finds in a stream, whereas it assumes TPersistent instances already exist, and it does not attempt to instantiate new ones. Following this rule, we stream the information required of the TddgRunButton, and then we create the TddgRunButton in the TRunBtnItem constructor, which we'll illustrate shortly.

Defining the TCollection Class: TRunButtons

The next step is to define the object that will maintain this list of TRunBtnItem components. We already said that this object must be a TCollection descendant. We called this class TRunButtons; its definition is as follows:

```
type
  TRunButtons = class(TCollection)
  private
    FLaunchPad: TddgLaunchPad; // Keep a reference to the TddgLaunchPad
    function GetItem(Index: Integer): TRunBtnItem;
    procedure SetItem(Index: Integer; Value: TRunBtnItem);
  protected
    procedure Update(Item: TCollectionItem); override;
  public
    constructor Create(LaunchPad: TddgLaunchPad);
    function Add: TRunBtnItem;
    procedure UpdateRunButtons;
    property Items[Index: Integer]: TRunBtnItem read GetItem
      write SetItem; default;
  end;
```

TRunButtons associates itself with a TddgLaunchPad component that we'll show a bit later. It does this in its Create() constructor, which, as you can see, takes a TddgLaunchPad component as its parameter. Notice the various properties and methods that have been added to allow the user to manipulate the individual TRunBtnItem classes. In particular, the Items property is an array to the TRunBtnItem list.

The use of the TRunBtnItem and TRunButtons classes will become clearer as we discuss the implementation of the TddgLaunchPad component.

Implementing the TddgLaunchPad, TRunBtnItem, and TRunButtons Objects

The TddgLaunchPad component has a property of the type TRunButtons. Its implementation, as well as the implementation of TRunBtnItem and TRunButtons, is shown in Listing 22.11.

LISTING 22.11. LnchPad.pas ILLUSTRATES THE TddgLaunchPad IMPLEMENTATION.

```
unit LnchPad;

interface

uses
  Windows, Messages, SysUtils, Classes, Graphics, Controls,
  Forms, Dialogs, RunBtn, ExtCtrls;

type
  TddgLaunchPad = class;

  TRunBtnItem = class(TCollectionItem)
  private
    FCommandLine: string;    // Store the command line
    FLeft: Integer;          // Store the positional properties for the
    FTop: Integer;           // TRunButton.
    FRunButton: TRunButton;  // Reference to a TRunButton
    FWidth: Integer;         // Keep track of the width and height
    FHeight: Integer;
    procedure SetCommandLine(const Value: string);
    procedure SetLeft(Value: Integer);
    procedure SetTop(Value: Integer);
  public
    constructor Create(Collection: TCollection); override;
    destructor Destroy; override;
    procedure Assign(Source: TPersistent); override;
    property Width: Integer read FWidth;
    property Height: Integer read FHeight;
  published
    { The published properties will be streamed }
    property CommandLine: String read FCommandLine
      write SetCommandLine;
    property Left: Integer read FLeft write SetLeft;
    property Top: Integer read FTop write SetTop;
  end;

  TRunButtons = class(TCollection)
  private
    FLaunchPad: TddgLaunchPad; // Keep a reference to the TddgLaunchPad
    function GetItem(Index: Integer): TRunBtnItem;
    procedure SetItem(Index: Integer; Value: TRunBtnItem);
  protected
    procedure Update(Item: TCollectionItem); override;
  public
    constructor Create(LaunchPad: TddgLaunchPad);
    function Add: TRunBtnItem;
```

continues

22

ADVANCED
COMPONENT
TECHNIQUES

LISTING 22.11. CONTINUED

```
    procedure UpdateRunButtons;
    property Items[Index: Integer]: TRunBtnItem read
      GetItem write SetItem; default;
  end;

  TddgLaunchPad = class(TScrollBox)
  private
    FRunButtons: TRunButtons;
    TopAlign: Integer;
    LeftAlign: Integer;
    procedure SetRunButtons(Value: TRunButtons);
    procedure UpdateRunButton(Index: Integer);
  public
    constructor Create(AOwner: TComponent); override;
    destructor Destroy; override;
    procedure GetChildren(Proc: TGetChildProc; Root: TComponent);
    ➥override;
  published
    property RunButtons: TRunButtons read FRunButtons write SetRunButtons;
  end;

implementation

{ TRunBtnItem }

constructor TRunBtnItem.Create(Collection: TCollection);
{ This constructor gets the TCollection that owns this TRunBtnItem.  }
begin
  inherited Create(Collection);
  { Create an FRunButton instance. Make the launch pad the owner
    and parent. Then initialize its various properties. }
  FRunButton := TRunButton.Create(TRunButtons(Collection).FLaunchPad);
  FRunButton.Parent := TRunButtons(Collection).FLaunchPad;
  FWidth := FRunButton.Width;   // Keep track of the width and the
  FHeight := FRunButton.Height; //   height.
end;

destructor TRunBtnItem.Destroy;
begin
  FRunButton.Free;   // Destroy the TddgRunButton instance.
  inherited Destroy; // Call the inherited Destroy destructor.
end;

procedure TRunBtnItem.Assign(Source: TPersistent);
{ It is necessary to override the TCollectionItem.Assign method so that
  it knows how to copy from one TRunBtnItem to another. If this is done,
  then don't call the inherited Assign(). }
begin
  if Source is TRunBtnItem then
  begin
```

```
    { Instead of assigning the command line to the FCommandLine storage
      field, make the assignment to the property so that the accessor
      method will be called. The accessor method has some side-effects
      that we want to occur. }
    CommandLine := TRunBtnItem(Source).CommandLine;
    { Copy values to the remaining fields. Then exit the procedure. }
    FLeft := TRunBtnItem(Source).Left;
    FTop := TRunBtnItem(Source).Top;
    Exit;
  end;
  inherited Assign(Source);
end;

procedure TRunBtnItem.SetCommandLine(const Value: string);
{ This is the write accessor method for TRunBtnItem.CommandLine. It
  ensures that the private TddgRunButton instance, FRunButton, gets
  assigned the specified string from Value }
begin
  if FRunButton <> nil then
  begin
    FCommandLine := Value;
    FRunButton.CommandLine := FCommandLine;
    { This will cause the TRunButtons.Update method to be called
      for each TRunBtnItem }
    Changed(False);
  end;
end;

procedure TRunBtnItem.SetLeft(Value: Integer);
{ Access method for the TRunBtnItem.Left property. }
begin
  if FRunButton <> nil then
  begin
    FLeft := Value;
    FRunButton.Left := FLeft;
  end;
end;

procedure TRunBtnItem.SetTop(Value: Integer);
{ Access method for the TRunBtnItem.Top property }
begin
  if FRunButton <> nil then
  begin
    FTop := Value;
    FRunButton.Top := FTop;
  end;
end;

{ TRunButtons }
```

continues

LISTING 22.11. CONTINUED

```
constructor TRunButtons.Create(LaunchPad: TddgLaunchPad);
{ The constructor points FLaunchPad to the TddgLaunchPad parameter.
  LauchPad is the owner of this collection. It is necessary to keep
  a reference to LauchPad as it will be accessed internally. }
begin
  inherited Create(TRunBtnItem);
  FLaunchPad := LaunchPad;
end;


function TRunButtons.GetItem(Index: Integer): TRunBtnItem;
{ Access method for TRunButtons.Items which returns the TRunBtnItem
  instance. }
begin
  Result := TRunBtnItem(inherited GetItem(Index));
end;


procedure TRunButtons.SetItem(Index: Integer; Value: TRunBtnItem);
{ Access method for TRunButton.Items which makes the assignment to
  the specified indexed item. }
begin
  inherited SetItem(Index, Value)
end;


procedure TRunButtons.Update(Item: TCollectionItem);
{ TCollection.Update is called by TCollectionItems
  whenever a change is made to any of the collection items. This is
  initially an abstract method. It must be overridden to contain
  whatever logic is necessary when a TCollectionItem has changed.
  We use it to redraw the item by calling TddgLaunchPad.UpdateRunButton.}
begin
  if Item <> nil then
    FLaunchPad.UpdateRunButton(Item.Index);
end;


procedure TRunButtons.UpdateRunButtons;
{ UpdateRunButtons is a public procedure that we made available so that
  users of TRunButtons can force all run-buttons to be re-drawn. This
  method calls TddgLaunchPad.UpdateRunButton for each TRunBtnItem
  instance. }
var
  i: integer;
begin
  for i := 0 to Count - 1 do
    FLaunchPad.UpdateRunButton(i);
end;


function TRunButtons.Add: TRunBtnItem;
{ This method must be overridden to return the TRunBtnItem instance when
  the inherited Add method is called. This is done by typcasting the
  original result }
```

```
begin
  Result := TRunBtnItem(inherited Add);
end;


{ TddgLaunchPad }

constructor TddgLaunchPad.Create(AOwner: TComponent);
{ Initializes the TRunButtons instance and internal variables
  used for positioning of the TRunBtnItem as they are drawn }
begin
  inherited Create(AOwner);
  FRunButtons := TRunButtons.Create(Self);
  TopAlign := 0;
  LeftAlign := 0;
end;

destructor TddgLaunchPad.Destroy;
begin
  FRunButtons.Free;  // Free the TRunButtons instance.
  inherited Destroy; // Call the inherited destroy method.
end;

procedure TddgLaunchPad.GetChildren(Proc: TGetChildProc; Root:
TComponent);
{ Override GetChildren to cause TddgLaunchpad to ignore any TRunButtons
  that it owns since they do not need to be streamed in the context
  TddgLaunchPad. The information necessary for creating the TRunButton
  instances is already streamed as published properties of the
  TCollectionItem descendant, TRunBtnItem. This method prevents the
  TRunButton's from being streamed twice. }
var
  I: Integer;
begin
  for I := 0 to ControlCount - 1 do
    { Ignore the run buttons and the scrollbox }
    if not (Controls[i] is TRunButton) then
      Proc(TComponent(Controls[I]));
end;

procedure TddgLaunchPad.SetRunButtons(Value: TRunButtons);
{ Access method for the RunButtons property }
begin
  FRunButtons.Assign(Value);
end;

procedure TddgLaunchPad.UpdateRunButton(Index: Integer);
{ This method is responsible for drawing the TRunBtnItem instances.
  It ensures that the TRunBtnItem's do not extend beyond the width
  of the TddgLaunchPad. If so, it creates rows. This is only in effect
```

22

ADVANCED
COMPONENT
TECHNIQUES

continues

LISTING 22.11. CONTINUED

```
  as the user is adding/removing TRunBtnItems. The user can still
  resize the TddgLaunchPad so that it is smaller than the width of a
  TRunBtnItem }
begin
  { If the first item being drawn, set both positions to zero. }
  if Index = 0 then
  begin
    TopAlign := 0;
    LeftAlign := 0;
  end;
  { If the width of the current row of TRunBtnItems is more than
    the width of the TddgLaunchPad, then start a new row of TRunBtnItems.
}
  if (LeftAlign + FRunButtons[Index].Width) > Width then
  begin
    TopAlign := TopAlign + FRunButtons[Index].Height;
    LeftAlign := 0;
  end;
  FRunButtons[Index].Left := LeftAlign;
  FRunButtons[Index].Top := TopAlign;
  LeftAlign := LeftAlign + FRunButtons[Index].Width;
end;

end.
```

Implementing `TRunBtnItem`

The `TRunBtnItem.Create()` constructor creates an instance of `TRunButton`. Each `TRunBtnItem` in the collection will maintain its own `TddgRunButton` instance. The following two lines in `TRunBtnItem.Create()` require further explanation:

```
FRunButton := TRunButton.Create(TRunButtons(Collection).FLaunchPad);
FRunButton.Parent := TRunButtons(Collection).FLaunchPad;
```

The first line creates a `TddgRunButton` instance, `FRunButton`. The owner of `FRunButton` is `FLaunchPad`, which is a `TddgLaunchPad` component and a field of the `TCollection` object passed in as a parameter. It's necessary to use the `FLaunchPad` as the owner of `FRunButton` because neither a `TRunBtnItem` instance nor a `TRunButtons` object can be owners because they descend from `TPersistent`. Remember, an owner must be a `TComponent`.

We want to point out a problem that arises by making `FLaunchPad` the owner of `FRunButton`. By doing this, we effectively make `FLaunchPad` the owner of `FRunButton` at design time. The normal behavior of the streaming engine will cause Delphi to stream `FRunButton` as a component owned by the `FLaunchPad` instance when the user saves the form. This is not a desired behavior because FRunButton is already being created in the constructor of TRunBtnItem, based on the information that's also streamed in the context of TRunBtnItem. This is a vital tidbit of information. Later, you'll see how we prevent TddgRunButton components from being streamed by TddgLaunchPad in order to remedy this undesired behavior.

The second line assigns FLaunchPad as the parent to FRunButton so that FLaunchPad can take care of drawing FRunButton.

The TRunBtnItem.Destroy() destructor frees FRunButton before calling its inherited destructor.

Under certain circumstances, it becomes necessary to override the TRunBtnItem.Assign() method that's called. One such instance is when the application is first run and the form is read from the stream. It's in the Assign() method that we tell the TRunBtnItem instance to assign the streamed values of its properties to the properties of the component (in this case TRunButton) that it encompasses.

The other methods are simply access methods for the various properties of TRunBtnItem; they are explained in the code's comments.

Implementing TRunButtons

TRunButtons.Create() simply points FLaunchPad to the TddgLaunchPad parameter, LaunchPad, so that it can be referred to later.

TRunButtons.Update() is a method that's invoked whenever a change has been made to any of the TRunBtnItem instances. This method contains logic that should occur due to that change. We use it to call the method of TddgLaunchPad that redraws the TRunBtnItem instances. We've also added a public method, UpdateRunButtons(), to allow the user to force a redraw.

The remaining methods of TRunButtons are property access methods, which are explained in the code's comments in Listing 22.11.

Implementing TddgLaunchPad

The constructor and destructor for TddgLaunchPad are simple. TddgLaunchPad.Create() creates an instance of the TRunButtons object and passes itself as a parameter. TddgLaunchPad.Destroy() frees the TRunButtons instance.

The overriding of the TddgLaunchPad.GetChildren() method is important to note here. This is where we prevent the TddgRunButton instances stored by the collection from being streamed as owned components of TddgLaunchPad. Remember that this is necessary because they shouldn't be created in the context of the TddgLaunchPad object but rather in the context of the TRunBtnItem instances. Because no TddgRunButton compo-nents are passed to the Proc procedure, they won't be streamed or read from a stream.

The TddgLaunchPad.UpdateRunButton() method is where the TddgRunButton instances maintained by the collection are drawn. The logic in this code ensures that they never extend beyond the width of TddgLaunchPad. Because TddgLaunchPad is a descendant of TScrollBox, scrolling will occur vertically.

The other methods are simply property-access methods and are commented in the code in Listing 22.11.

Finally, we register the property editor for the TRunButtons collection class in this unit's Register() procedure. The next section discusses this property editor and illustrates how to edit a list of components from a dialog property editor.

Editing the List of TCollectionItem Components with a Dialog Property Editor

Now that we've defined the TddgLaunchPad component, the TRunButtons collection class, and the TRunBtnItem collection class, we must provide a way for the user to add TddgRunButton components to the TRunButtons collection. The best way to do this is through a property editor that manipulates the list maintained by the TRunButtons collection.

The property editor that we'll use is a dialog, as shown in Figure 22.8.

FIGURE 22.8.

The TddgLaunchPad-RunButtons *editor.*

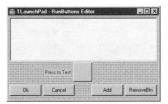

This dialog directly manipulates the TRunBtnItem components maintained by the RunButtons collection of TddgLaunchPad. The various CommandLine strings for each TddgRunButton enclosed in TRunBtnItem are displayed in PathListBox. A TddgRunButton component reflects the currently selected item in the list box to allow the user to test the selection. The dialog also contains buttons to allow the user to add or remove an item, accept the changes, and cancel the operation. As the user makes changes in the dialog, the changes are reflected on the TddgLaunchPad.

TIP

A convention for property editors is to include an Apply button to invoke changes on the form. We didn't show this here, but you might consider adding such a button to the RunButtons property editor as an exercise. To see how an Apply button works, take a look at the property editor for the Panels property of the TStatusBar component from the Win95 page of the Component Palette.

Figure 22.9 illustrates the TddgLaunchPad - RunButtons property editor with some items. It also shows the form's TddgLaunchPad component with the TddgRunButton components listed in the property editor.

FIGURE 22.9.

The TddgLaunchPad-RunButtons *property editor with* TRunBtnItem *components.*

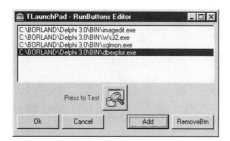

Listing 22.12 shows the source code for the TddgLaunchPad - RunButtons property editor and its dialog.

LISTING 22.12. LPadPE.pas, THE TRunButtons PROPERTY EDITOR.

```
unit LPadPE;

interface

uses
  Windows, Messages, SysUtils, Classes, Graphics, Controls, Forms,
  Dialogs, Buttons, RunBtn, StdCtrls, LnchPad, DsgnIntF, TypInfo,
  ExtCtrls;

type

  { First declare the editor dialog }
  TLaunchPadEditor = class(TForm)
```

continues

LISTING 22.12. CONTINUED

```
    PathListBox: TListBox;
    AddBtn: TButton;
    RemoveBtn: TButton;
    CancelBtn: TButton;
    OkBtn: TButton;
    Label1: TLabel;
    pnlRBtn: TPanel;
    procedure PathListBoxClick(Sender: TObject);
    procedure AddBtnClick(Sender: TObject);
    procedure RemoveBtnClick(Sender: TObject);
    procedure FormCreate(Sender: TObject);
    procedure FormDestroy(Sender: TObject);
    procedure CancelBtnClick(Sender: TObject);
  private
    TestRunBtn: TddgRunButton;
    FLaunchPad: TddgLaunchPad;    // To be used as a backup
    FRunButtons: TRunButtons; // Will refer to the actual TRunButtons
    Modified: Boolean;
    procedure UpdatePathListBox;
  end;

  { Now declare the TPropertyEditor descendant and override the
    required methods }
  TRunButtonsProperty = class(TPropertyEditor)
    function GetAttributes: TPropertyAttributes; override;
    function GetValue: string; override;
    procedure Edit; override;
  end;

{ This function will be called by the property editor. }
function EditRunButtons(RunButtons: TRunButtons): Boolean;

implementation

{$R *.DFM}

function EditRunButtons(RunButtons: TRunButtons): Boolean;
{ Instantiates the TLaunchPadEditor dialog which directly modifies
  the TRunButtons collection. }
begin
  with TLaunchPadEditor.Create(Application) do
    try
      FRunButtons := RunButtons; // Point to the actual TRunButtons
      { Copy the TRunBtnItems to the backup FLaunchPad, which will be
        used as a backup in case the user cancels the operation }
      FLaunchPad.RunButtons.Assign(RunButtons);
      { Draw the listbox with the list of TRunBtnItems. }
      UpdatePathListBox;
      ShowModal; // Display the form.
```

```
        Result := Modified;
      finally
        Free;
      end;
end;


{ TLaunchPadEditor }

procedure TLaunchPadEditor.FormCreate(Sender: TObject);
begin
  { Created the backup instances of TLaunchPad to be used if the user
    cancels editing the TRunBtnItems }
  FLaunchPad := TddgLaunchPad.Create(Self);

  // Create the TddgRunButton instance and align it to the
  // enclosing panel.
  TestRunBtn := TddgRunButton.Create(Self);
  TestRunBtn.Parent := pnlRBtn;

  TestRunBtn.Width  := pnlRBtn.Width;
  TestRunBtn.Height := pnlRBtn.Height;
end;

procedure TLaunchPadEditor.FormDestroy(Sender: TObject);
begin
  TestRunBtn.Free;
  FLaunchPad.Free; // Free the TLaunchPad instance.
end;

procedure TLaunchPadEditor.PathListBoxClick(Sender: TObject);
{ When the user clicks an item in the list of TRunBtnItems, make
  the test TRunButton reflect the currently selected item }
begin
  if PathListBox.ItemIndex > -1 then
    TestRunBtn.CommandLine := PathListBox.Items[PathListBox.ItemIndex];
end;

procedure TLaunchPadEditor.UpdatePathListBox;
{ Reinitializes the PathListBox so that it reflects the list of
  TRunBtnItems }
var
  i: integer;
begin
  PathListBox.Clear; // First clear the list box.
  for i := 0 to FRunButtons.Count - 1 do
    PathListBox.Items.Add(FRunButtons[i].CommandLine);
end;
```

continues

Listing 22.12. CONTINUED

```
procedure TLaunchPadEditor.AddBtnClick(Sender: TObject);
{ When the add button is clicked, launch a TOpenDialog to retrieve
  an executable filename and path. Then add this file to the
  PathListBox. Also, add a new FRunBtnItem. }
var
  OpenDialog: TOpenDialog;
begin
  OpenDialog := TOpenDialog.Create(Application);
  try
    OpenDialog.Filter := 'Executable Files¦*.EXE';
    if OpenDialog.Execute then
    begin
      { add to the PathListBox. }
      PathListBox.Items.Add(OpenDialog.FileName);
      FRunButtons.Add; // Create a new TRunBtnItem instance.
      { Set focus to the new item in PathListBox }
      PathListBox.ItemIndex := FRunButtons.Count - 1;
      { Set the command line for the new TRunBtnItem to that of the
        file name gotten as specified by PathListBox.ItemIndex }
      FRunButtons[PathListBox.ItemIndex].CommandLine :=
        PathListBox.Items[PathListBox.ItemIndex];
      { Invoke the PathListBoxClick event handler so that the test
        TRunButton will reflect the newly added item }
      PathListBoxClick(nil);
      Modified := True;
    end;
  finally
    OpenDialog.Free
  end;
end;

procedure TLaunchPadEditor.RemoveBtnClick(Sender: TObject);
{ Remove the selected path/filename from PathListBox as well as the
  corresponding TRunBtnItem from FRunButtons }
var
  i: integer;
begin
  i := PathListBox.ItemIndex;
  if i >= 0 then
  begin
    PathListBox.Items.Delete(i);  // Remove the item from the listbox
    FRunButtons[i].Free;          // Remove the item from the collection
    TestRunBtn.CommandLine := ''; // Erase the test run button
    Modified := True;
  end;
end;

procedure TLaunchPadEditor.CancelBtnClick(Sender: TObject);
{ When the user cancels the operation, copy the backup LaunchPad
```

```
     TRunBtnItems back to the original TLaunchPad instance. Then,
     close the form by setting ModalResult to mrCancel. }
begin
  FRunButtons.Assign(FLaunchPad.RunButtons);
  Modified := False;
  ModalResult := mrCancel;
end;


{ TRunButtonsProperty }

function TRunButtonsProperty.GetAttributes: TPropertyAttributes;
{ Tell the Object Inspector that the property editor will use a
  dialog. This will cause the Edit method to be invoked when the user
  clicks the ellipsis button in the Object Inspector. }
begin
  Result := [paDialog];
end;

procedure TRunButtonsProperty.Edit;
{ Invoke the EditRunButton() method and pass in the reference to the
  TRunButton's instance being edited. This reference can be obtain by
  using the GetOrdValue method. Then redraw the LaunchDialog by calling
  the TRunButtons.UpdateRunButtons method. }
begin
  if EditRunButtons(TRunButtons(GetOrdValue)) then
    Modified;
  TRunButtons(GetOrdValue).UpdateRunButtons;
end;

function TRunButtonsProperty.GetValue: string;
{ Override the GetValue method so that the class type of the property
  being edited is displayed in the Object Inspector. }
begin
  Result := Format('(%s)', [GetPropType^.Name]);
end;

end.
```

This unit first defines the TLaunchPadEditor dialog and then the TRunButtonsProperty property editor. We're going to discuss the property editor first because it's the property editor that invokes the dialog.

The TRunButtonsProperty property editor is not much different than the dialog property editor we showed earlier. Here, we override the GetAttributes(), Edit(), and GetValue() methods.

GetAttributes() simply sets the TPropertyAttributes return value to specify that this editor invokes a dialog. Again, this will place an ellipsis button on the Object Inspector.

The GetValue() method uses the GetPropType() function to return a pointer to the run-time type information for the property being edited. It returns the name field of this information that represents the property's type string. The string is displayed in the Object Inspector inside parentheses, which is a convention used by Delphi.

Finally, the Edit() method calls a function defined in this unit, EditRunButtons(). As a parameter, it passes the reference to the TRunButtons property by using the GetOrdValue function. When the function returns, the method UpdateRunButton() is invoked to cause RunButtons to be redrawn to reflect any changes.

The EditRunButtons() function creates the TLaunchPadEditor instance and points its FRunButtons field to the TRunButtons parameter passed to it. It uses this reference internally to make changes to the TRunButtons collection. The function then copies the TRunButtons collection of the property to an internal TddgLaunchPad component, FLaunchPad. It uses this instance as a backup in case the user cancels the edit operation.

Earlier we talked about the possibility of adding an Apply button to this dialog. To do so, you can edit the FLaunchPad component's RunButtons collection instance instead of directly modifying the actual collection. This way, if the user cancels the operation, nothing happens; if the user presses Apply or OK, the changes are invoked.

The form's Create() constructor creates the internal TddgLaunchPad instance. The Destroy() destructor ensures that it's freed when the form is destroyed.

PathListBoxClick() is the OnClick event handler for PathListBox. This method makes TestRunBtn (the test TRunButton) reflect the currently selected item in PathListBox, which displays a path to the executable file. The user can press this TddgRunButton instance to launch the application.

UpdatePathListBox() initializes PathListBox with the items in the collection.

AddButtonClick() is the OnClick event handler for the Add button. This event handler invokes a File Open dialog box to retrieve an executable filename from the user and adds this filename's path to PathListBox. AddButtonClick() also creates a TRunBtnItem instance in the collection and assigns the path to the TRunBtnItems.CommandLine property, which in turn does the same for the TddgRunButton component that TRunBtnItems encloses.

RemoveBtnClick() is the OnClick event handler for the Remove button. It removes the selected item from PathListBox as well as the TRunBtnItem instance from the collection.

CancelBtnClick() is the OnClick event handler for the Cancel button. It copies the backup collection from FLaunchPad to the actual TRunButtons collection and closes the form.

The TCollection and TCollectionItems objects are extremely useful and offer themselves to being used for a variety of purposes. Get to know them well, and next time you need to store a list of components, you'll already have a solution.

SUMMARY

This chapter let you in on some of the more advanced tricks and techniques for Delphi component design. Among other things, you learned about extending hints, animating components, component editors, property editors, and component collections. Armed with this information, as well as the more conventional information you learned in Chapter 21, you should be able to write a component to suit just about any of your programming needs. In the next chapter, "COM and ActiveX," we'll go even deeper into the world of component-based development.

22

ADVANCED
COMPONENT
TECHNIQUES

COM AND ACTIVEX

IN THIS CHAPTER

Robust support for COM, ActiveX, and Object Linking and Embedding (OLE) technologies is one of the marquee features of Delphi. However, all this new technology at your fingertips can be a bit perplexing, if not daunting. This chapter is designed to give you a complete overview of the technologies that make up COM, ActiveX, and OLE and help you leverage these technologies in your own applications. Traditionally, OLE technologies provide a method for sharing data among different applications, dealing primarily with linking or embedding data associated with one type of application to data associated with another application (such as embedding a spreadsheet into a word processor document). However, there's a lot more to OLE and ActiveX than word processor tricks.

In this chapter, you will first get a solid background in the basics of COM, ActiveX, and OLE, and then you will learn about Object Pascal and VCL, which support these technologies. You'll also learn about more advanced topics such as Automation, how to control Automation servers from your Delphi applications, and how to write Automation servers of your own. Finally, this chapter covers VCL's TOleContainer class, which encapsulates ActiveX containers. This chapter does not teach you everything there is to know about OLE and ActiveX—that could take volumes—but it covers all the important features of OLE and ActiveX, particularly as they apply to Delphi.

OLE BASICS

Before we jump into the topic at hand, it's important that you understand the basic concepts and terminology associated with the technology. This section introduces you to basic ideas and terms behind COM, ActiveX, and OLE.

The Component Object Model

The *Component Object Model* (COM) forms the foundation upon which OLE and ActiveX technology is built. COM defines an API and a binary standard for communication between objects that is independent of any particular programming language or (in theory) platform. COM objects are similar to the VCL objects you are familiar with, except that they have only methods and properties associated with them, not data fields.

A COM object consists of one or more *interfaces* (described in detail later in this chapter), which are essentially tables of functions associated with that object. You can call an interface's methods just like the methods of a Delphi object.

The component objects that you use can be implemented from any EXE or DLL, although the implementation is transparent to you as a user of the object because of a service provided by COM called *marshaling*. The COM marshaling mechanism handles all the intricacies of calling functions across process—and even machine—boundaries, which makes it possible to use a 32-bit object from a 16-bit application or access an object located on machine A from an application running on machine B. This intermachine communication is known as Distributed COM (DCOM) and is described in greater detail later in this chapter.

COM Versus ActiveX Versus OLE

"So, what's the difference between COM, OLE, and ActiveX, anyway?" That's one of the most common (and reasonable) questions developers ask as they get into this technology. It's a reasonable question because it seems that the purveyor of this technology, Microsoft, does little to clarify the matter. You've already learned that COM is the API and binary standard that forms the building blocks of the other technologies. In the old days (like 1995), OLE was the blanket term used to describe the entire suite of technologies built on the COM architecture. These days, OLE refers only to those technologies associated specifically with linking and embedding, such as containers, servers, in-place activation, drag-and-drop, and menu merging. In 1996, Microsoft embarked on an aggressive marketing campaign in an attempt to create brand recognition for the term *ActiveX*. ActiveX became the blanket term used to describe non-OLE technologies built on top of COM. ActiveX technologies include Automation (formerly called *OLE Automation*) controls, documents, containers, scripting, and several Internet technologies. Because of the confusion created by using the term ActiveX to describe everything short of the family pet, Microsoft has backed off a bit and now sometimes refers to non-OLE COM technologies simply as *COM-based*.

Those with a more cynical view of the industry might say that the term "OLE" became associated with adjectives like "slow" and "bloat," and marketing-savvy Microsoft needed a new term for those APIs on which it planned to base its future operating system and Internet technologies. Also amusing is the fact that Microsoft now claims OLE no longer stands for Object Linking and Embedding—it's just a word that is pronounced Oh-Lay.

Terminology

COM technologies bring with them a great deal of new terminology, so some terms are presented here before going any deeper into the guts of ActiveX and OLE.

Although an instance of a COM object is usually referred to simply as an *object*, the type that identifies that object is usually referred to as a *component class* or *coclass*. Therefore, to create an instance of a COM *object*, you must place the CLSID of the *COM class* you want to create.

The chunk of data that is shared between applications is referred to as an *OLE object*. Applications having the capability to contain OLE objects are referred to as *OLE containers*. Applications having the capability to have their data contained within an OLE container are called *OLE servers*.

A document that contains one or more OLE objects is usually referred to as a *compound document*. Although OLE objects can be contained within a particular document, full-scale applications that can be hosted within the context of another document are known as ActiveX documents.

As the name implies, an OLE object can be *linked* or *embedded* into a compound document. Linked objects are stored in a file on disk. With object linking, multiple containers— or even the server application—can link to the same OLE object on disk. When one application modifies the linked object, the modification is reflected in all the other applications maintaining a link to that object. Embedded objects are stored by the OLE container application. Only the container application is able to edit the OLE object. Embedding prevents other applications from accessing (and therefore modifying or corrupting) your data, but it does put the burden of managing the data on the container.

Another facet of ActiveX that you'll learn more about in this chapter is called *Automation*. Automation is a means by which you can allow applications (called *Automation controllers*) to manipulate objects associated with other applications or libraries (called an *Automation server*). Automation enables you to manipulate objects in another application, and, conversely, to expose elements of your application to other developers.

What's So Great About ActiveX?

The coolest thing about ActiveX is that it enables you to easily build the capability to manipulate many types of data into your applications. You might snicker at the word "easily," but it's true. It is much easier, for example, to give your application the capability to contain ActiveX objects than it is to build word processing, spreadsheet, or graphics-manipulation capabilities into your application.

ActiveX fits very well with Delphi's tradition of maximum code reuse. You don't have to write code to manipulate a particular kind of data if you already have an OLE server application that does the job. As complicated as OLE can be, it often makes more sense than the alternatives.

It also is no secret that Microsoft has a large investment in ActiveX technology, and serious developers for Windows 95, NT, and other upcoming operating systems will have to become familiar with using ActiveX in their applications. So, like it or not, COM is here for a while, and it behooves you, as a developer, to become comfortable with it.

OLE 1 Versus OLE 2

One of the primary differences between OLE objects associated with 16-bit OLE version 1 servers and those associated with OLE version 2 servers is in how they activate themselves. When you activate an object created with an OLE 1 server, the server application starts up, receives focus, and the OLE object appears in the server application ready for editing. When you activate an OLE 2 object, the OLE 2 server application becomes active "inside" your container application. This is known as *in-place activation* or *visual editing*.

When an OLE 2 object is activated, the menus and toolbars of the server application replace or merge with those of the client application, and a portion of the client application's window essentially becomes the window of the server application. This process is demonstrated in the sample application shown later in this chapter.

Structured Storage

OLE 2 defines a system for storing information on disk known as *structured storage*. This system basically does on a file level what DOS does on a disk level. A storage object is one physical file on a disk, but it equates with the DOS concept of a directory, and it is made up of multiple storages and streams. A storage equates to a subdirectory and a stream equates to a DOS file. You will often hear this implementation referred to as *compound files*.

Uniform Data Transfer

OLE 2 also has the concept of a data object, which is the basic object used to exchange data under the rules of uniform data transfer. *Uniform data transfer* (UDT) governs data transfers through the Clipboard, drag-and-drop, DDE, and OLE. Data objects allow for a greater degree of description about the kind of data they contain than previously was practical given the limitations of those transfer media. In fact, UDT is destined to replace DDE. A data object can be aware of its important properties such as size, color, or even what device it is designed to be rendered on, for example. Try doing that on the Windows Clipboard!

Threading Models

Every COM object operates in a particular threading model that dictates how an object can be manipulated in a multithreaded environment. When a COM server is registered, each of the COM objects contained in that server should register the threading model they support. For COM objects written in Delphi, the threading model chosen in the Automation, ActiveX control, or COM object wizards dictates how a control is registered. The COM threading models include

- Single. The entire COM server runs on a single thread.

- Apartment, also known as *single-threaded apartment* (STA). Each COM object executes within the context of its own thread, and multiple instances of the same type of COM object can execute within separate threads. As a result, any data that is shared between object instances (such as global variables) must be protected by thread synchronization objects when appropriate.

- Free, also known as *multithreaded apartment* (MTA). A client can call a method of an object on any thread at any time. This means that the COM object must protect even its own instance data from simultaneous access by multiple threads.

- Both. Both the Apartment and Free threading models are supported.

Keep in mind that merely selecting the desired threading model in the wizard doesn't guarantee that your COM object will be safe for that threading model. You must write the code to ensure that your COM servers operate correctly for the threading model you want to support. This most often includes using thread synchronization objects to protect access to global or instance data in your COM objects.

Looking Forward: COM+

In 1997, Microsoft announced plans for the next version of COM, which Microsoft calls *COM+*. At the time, COM+ plans were ambitious and called for the integration of type library-like functionality into C++ compilers, a new garbage-collected runtime environment for COM objects (and hence the deprecation of IUnknown's AddRef() and Release()), and the integration of several new features into the COM library. Later, Microsoft backed off on these grandiose plans for COM+ and indicated that COM+ would primarily be the integration of Microsoft Transaction Server (MTS) features into the COM library. As of this writing, no concrete spec or ship date for COM+ has been announced.

COM MEETS OBJECT PASCAL

Now that you understand the basic concepts and terms behind COM, ActiveX, and OLE, it's time to discuss how the concepts are implemented in Delphi. This section goes into more detail on COM and gives you a look at how it fits into the Object Pascal language and VCL.

Interfaces

COM defines a standard map for how an object's functions are laid out in memory. Functions are arranged in virtual tables (or *vtables*)—tables of function addresses identical to Delphi class virtual method tables (VMTs). The programming language description of each vtable is referred to as an *interface*.

Think of an interface as a facet of a particular class. Each facet represents a specific set of functions or procedures that you can use to manipulate the class. For example, a COM object that represents a bitmap image might support two interfaces: one containing methods that enable the bitmap to render itself to the screen or printer and another interface to manage storing and retrieving the bitmap to and from a file on disk.

There are really two parts to an interface: The first part is the interface definition, which consists of a collection of one or more function declarations in a specific order. The interface definition is shared between the object and the user of the object. The second part is the interface implementation, which is the actual implementation of the functions described in the interface declaration. The interface definition is like a contract between the COM object and a client of that object, a guarantee to the client that the object will implement specific methods in a specific order.

Introduced in Delphi 3, the interface keyword in Object Pascal enables you to easily define COM interfaces. An interface declaration is semantically similar to a class declaration with a few exceptions. Interfaces can consist only of properties and methods—no data. Because interfaces cannot contain data, their properties must write and read to and from methods. Most importantly, interfaces have no implementation, as they only define a contract.

IUnknown

Just as all Object Pascal classes implicitly descend from TObject, all COM interfaces (and therefore all Object Pascal interfaces) implicitly derive from IUnknown. IUnknown is defined in the System unit as follows:

```
type
  IUnknown = interface
    ['{00000000-0000-0000-C000-000000000046}']
    function QueryInterface(const IID: TGUID; out Obj): Integer; stdcall;
    function _AddRef: Integer; stdcall;
    function _Release: Integer; stdcall;
  end;
```

Aside from the use of the interface keyword, another obvious difference between an interface and class declaration that you will notice from the preceding listing is the presence of a Globally Unique Identifier, or *GUID*.

GLOBALLY UNIQUE IDENTIFIERS (GUIDS)

A GUID (pronounced goo-id) is a 128-bit integer used in COM to uniquely identify an interface, coclass, or other entity. Because of their large size and the hairy algorithm used to generate these numbers, GUIDs are almost guaranteed to be globally unique (hence the name!). GUIDs are generated using the CoCreateGUID() API function, and the algorithm employed by this function to generate new GUIDs combines information such as the current date and time, CPU clock sequence, network card number, and the balance of Bill Gates' bank accounts (okay, so we made up the last one). If you have a network card

continues

installed on a particular machine, a GUID generated on that machine is guaranteed to be unique because every network card has an internal ID, which is globally unique. If you don't have a network card, it will synthesize a close approximation using other hardware information.

Because there is no language type that holds something as large as 128 bits in size, GUIDs are represented by the TGUID record, which is defined as follows in the System unit:

```
type
  PGUID = ^TGUID;
  TGUID = record
    D1: LongWord;
    D2: Word;
    D3: Word;
    D4: array[0..7] of Byte;
  end;
```

Because it can be a pain to assign GUID values to variables and constants in this record format, Object Pascal also allows a TGUID to be represented as a string with the following format:

```
'{xxxxxxxx-xxxx-xxxx-xxxx-xxxxxxxxxxxx}'
```

Thanks to this, the following declarations are equivalent as far as the Delphi compiler is concerned:

```
MyGuid: TGUID = (

D1:$12345678;D2:$1234;D3:$1234;D4:($01,$02,$03,$04,$05,$06,$07,$08));

MyGuid: TGUID = '{12345678-1234-1234-12345678}';
```

In COM, every interface or class has an accompanying GUID, which uniquely defines that interface. In this way, two interfaces or classes having the same name defined by two different people will never conflict because their respective GUIDs will be different. When used to represent an interface, a GUID is normally referred to as an interface ID or *IID*. When used to represent a class, a GUID is referred to as a class ID or *CLSID*.

TIP

You can generate a new GUID in the Delphi IDE using the Ctrl+Shift+G keystroke in the Code Editor.

In addition to its IID, IUnknown declares three methods: QueryInterface(), _AddRef(), and _Release(). Because IUnknown is the base interface for COM, all interfaces must implement IUnknown and its methods. The _AddRef() method should be called when a client obtains and wants to use a pointer to a given interface, and a call to _AddRef() must have an accompanying call to _Release() when the client is finished using the interface. In this way, the object that implements the interfaces can maintain a count of clients that are keeping a reference to the object, or *reference count*. When the reference count reaches zero, the object should free itself from memory. The QueryInterface() function is used to query whether an object supports a given interface and, if so, to return a pointer to that interface. For example, suppose that object O supports two interfaces, I1 and I2, and you have a pointer to O's I1 interface. To obtain a pointer to O's I2 interface, you would call I1.QueryInterface().

> **NOTE**
>
> If you're an experienced COM developer, you may have noticed that the under-score in front of the _AddRef() and _Release() methods is not consistent with other COM programming languages or even with Microsoft's COM documenta-tion. Because Object Pascal is "IUnknown-aware," you won't normally call these methods directly (more on this in a moment), so the underscores exist primarily to make you think before calling these methods.

Because every interface in Delphi implicitly descends from IUnknown, every Delphi class that implements interfaces must also implement the three IUnknown methods. You can do this yourself manually, or you can let VCL do the dirty work for you by descending your class from TInterfacedObject, which implements IUnknown for you.

Using Interfaces

Chapter 2, "The Object Pascal Language," and Delphi's own *Object Pascal Language Guide* documentation cover the semantics of using interface instances, so we won't rehash that material here. Instead, we'll discuss how IUnknown is seamlessly integrated into the rules of Object Pascal.

When an interface variable is assigned a value, the compiler automatically generates a call to the interface's _AddRef() method so that the reference count of the object is incremented. When an interface variable falls out of scope or is assigned the value nil, the compiler automatically generates a call to the interface's _Release() method. Consider the following piece of code:

```
var
  I: ISomeInteface;
begin
  I := FunctionThatReturnsAnInterface;
  I.SomeMethod;
end;
```

Now take a look at the following code snippet, which shows the code you would type in bold and an approximate Pascal version of the code the compiler generates in normal font:

```
var
  I: ISomeInterface;
begin
  // interface is automatically initialized to nil
  I := nil;
  try
    // your code goes here
    I := FunctionThatReturnsAnInterface;
    // _AddRef() is called implicitly when I is assigned
    I._AddRef;
    I.SomeMethod;
  finally
    // implicit finally block ensures that the reference to the
    // interface is released
    if I <> nil I._Release;
  end;
end;
```

The Delphi compiler is also smart enough to know when to call `_AddRef()` and `_Release()` as interfaces are reassigned to other interface instances or are assigned the value `nil`. For example, consider the following code block:

```
var
  I: ISomeInteface;
begin
  // assign I
  I := FunctionThatReturnsAnInterface;
  I.SomeMethod;
  // reassign I
  I := OtherFunctionThatReturnsAnInterface;
  I.OtherMethod;
  // set I to nil
  I := nil;
end;
```

Again, a composite of the user-written (bold) and the approximate compiler-generated (normal) code is shown following:

```
var
  I: ISomeInterface;
begin
  // interface is automatically initialized to nil
  I := nil;
  try
    // your code goes here
    // assign I
    I := FunctionThatReturnsAnInterface;
    // _AddRef() is called implicitly when I is assigned
    I._AddRef;
    I.SomeMethod;
    // reassign I
    I._Release;
    I := OtherFunctionThatReturnsAnInterface;
    I._AddRef;
    I.OtherMethod;
    // set I to nil
    I._Release;
    I := nil;
  finally
    // implicit finally block ensures that the reference to the
    // interface is released
    if I <> nil I._Release;
  end;
end;
```

The preceding code sample also helps to illustrate why Delphi prepends the underscore to the AddRef() and Release() methods. Forgetting to increment or decrement the reference of an interface was one of the classic COM programming bugs in the pre-interface days. Delphi's interface support is designed to alleviate these problems by handling the housekeeping details for you, so there's rarely ever a reason to call these methods directly.

Because the compiler knows how to generate calls to AddRef() and Release(), wouldn't it make sense if the compiler had some inherent knowledge of the third IUnknown method, QueryInterface()? It would, and it does. Given an interface pointer for an object, you can use the as operator to "typecast" the interface to another interface supported by the COM object. We say "typecast" because this application of the as operator isn't really a typecast in the strict sense, but an internal call to the QueryInterface() method. The following code sample demonstrates this:

```
var
  I1: ISomeInterface;
  I2: ISomeOtherInterface;
begin
  // assign to I1
  I1 := FunctionThatReturnsAnInterface;
  // QueryInterface I1 for an I2 interface
  I2 := I1 as ISomeOtherInterface;
end;
```

23

**COM AND
ACTIVEX**

In the preceding example, if the object referenced by I1 doesn't support the ISomeOtherInterface interface, an exception will be raised by the as operator.

One additional language rule pertaining to interfaces is that an interface variable is assignment-compatible with an Object Pascal class that implements that interface. For example, consider the following interface and class declarations:

```
type
  IFoo = interface
    // definition of IFoo
  end;

  IBar = interface(IFoo)
    // definition of IBar
  end;

  TBarClass = class(TObject, IBar)
    // definition of TBarClass
  end;
```

Given the preceding declarations, the following code is correct:

```
var
  IB: IBar;
  TB: TBarClass;
begin
  TB := TBarClass.Create;
  try
    // obtain TB's IBar interface pointer:
    IB := TB;
    // use TB and IB
  finally
    IB := nil;  // expicitly release IB
    TB.Free;
  end;
end;
```

Although this feature seems to violate traditional Pascal assignment-compatibility rules, it does make interfaces feel more natural and easier to work with.

An important but non-obvious corollary to this rule is that interfaces are only assignment-compatible with classes that explicitly support the interface. For example, the TBarClass class defined earlier declares explicit support for the IBar interface. Because IBar descends from IFoo, conventional wisdom might indicate that TBarClass also directly supports IFoo. This is not the case, however, as the following code sample illustrates:

```
var
  IF: IFoo;
  TB: TBarClass;
```

```
begin
  TB := TBarClass.Create;
  try
    // compiler error raised on the next line because TBarClass
    // doesn't explicitly support IFoo.
    IF := TB;
    // use TB and IF
  finally
    IF := nil;  // expicitly release IF
    TB.Free;
  end;
end;
```

Interfaces and IIDs

Because the interface ID is declared as a part of an interface declaration, the Object Pascal compiler knows how to obtain IID from an interface. Therefore, you can pass an interface type to a procedure or function that requires a TIID or TGUID as a parameter. For example, suppose you have a function like this:

```
procedure TakesIID(const IID: TIID);
```

The following code is syntactically correct:

```
TakesIID(IUnknown);
```

This capability obviates the need for IID_*InterfaceType* constants defined for each interface type that you might be familiar with if you've done COM development in C++.

Method Aliasing

A problem that occasionally arises when you implement multiple interfaces in a single class is that there can be a collision of method names in two or more interfaces. For example, consider the following interfaces:

```
type
  IIntf1 = interface
    procedure AProc;
  end;

  IIntf2 = interface
    procedure AProc;
  end;
```

Given that each of the interfaces contains a method called AProc(), how can you declare a class that implements both interfaces? The answer is method aliasing. Method aliasing enables you to map a particular interface method to a method of a different name in a class. The following code example demonstrates how to declare a class that implements IIntf1 and IIntf2:

```
type
  TNewClass = class(TInterfacedObject, IIntf1, IIntf2)
  protected
    procedure IIntf2.AProc = AProc2;
    procedure AProc;   // binds to IIntf1.AProc
    procedure AProc2;  // binds to IIntf2.AProc
  end;
```

In the preceding declaration, the AProc() method of IIntf2 is mapped to a method with the name AProc(). Creating aliases in this way enables you to implement any interface on any class without fear of method name collisions.

The HResult Return Type

You might notice that the QueryInterface() method of IUnknown returns a result of type HResult. HResult is a very common return type for many ActiveX and OLE interface methods and COM API functions. HResult is defined in the System unit as a type LongWord. Possible HResult values are listed in the Windows unit (if you have the VCL source code, you find them under the heading { HRESULT value definitions }). An HResult value of S_OK or NOERROR (0) indicates success, whereas if the high bit of the HResult value is set, it indicates failure or some type of error condition. There are two functions in the Windows unit, Succeeded() and Failed(), which take an HResult as a parameter and return a BOOL indicating success or failure. The syntax for calling this method is

```
if Succeeded(FunctionThatReturnsHResult) then
  \\ continue as normal
```

```
if Failed(FunctionThatReturnsHResult) then
  \\ error condition code
```

Of course, checking the return value of every single function call can become tedious. Also, dealing with errors returned by functions undermines Delphi's exception handling methods for error detection and recovery. For these reasons, the ComObj unit defines a procedure called OleCheck() that converts HResult errors to exceptions. The syntax for calling this method is

```
OleCheck(FunctionThatReturnsHResult);
```

This procedure can be quite handy, and it will clean up your ActiveX code considerably.

COM OBJECTS AND CLASS FACTORIES

In addition to supporting one or more interfaces that descend from IUnknown and implementing reference counting for lifetime management, COM objects also have another special feature: They are created through special objects called *class factories*. Each COM class has an associated class factory, which is responsible for creating instances of that COM class. Class factories are special COM objects that support the IClassFactory interface. This interface is defined in the ActiveX unit as follows:

```
type
  IClassFactory = interface(IUnknown)
    ['{00000001-0000-0000-C000-000000000046}']
    function CreateInstance(const unkOuter: IUnknown; const iid: TIID;
      out obj): HResult; stdcall;
    function LockServer(fLock: BOOL): HResult; stdcall;
  end;
```

The CreateInstance() method is called to create an instance of the class factory's associated COM object. The unkOuter parameter of this method references the controlling IUnknown if the object is being created as a part of an aggregate (aggregation is explained a bit later). The iid parameter contains the IID of the interface by which you want to manipulate the object. Upon return, the obj parameter will hold a pointer to the interface indicated by iid.

The LockServer() method is called to keep a COM server in memory, even though no clients may be referencing the server. The fLock parameter, when True, should increment the server's lock count. When False, fLock should decrement the server's lock count. When the server's lock count is 0, and there are no clients referencing the server, COM will unload the server.

23

TComObject **and** TComObjectFactory

Delphi provides two classes that encapsulate COM objects and class factories, called respectively TComObject and TComObjectFactory. TComObject contains the necessary infrastructure for supporting IUnknown and for being created from a TComObjectFactory. Likewise, TComObjectFactory supports IClassFactory and has the capability to create TComObject objects. You can easily generate a COM object using the COM Object Wizard found on the ActiveX page of the New Items dialog. Listing 23.1 shows pseudocode for the unit generated by this wizard, which illustrates the relationship between these classes.

LISTING 23.1. COM SERVER UNIT PSEUDOCODE.

```
unit ComDemo;

interface

uses ComObj;

type
  TSomeComObject = class(TComObject, interfaces supported)
    class and interface methods declared here
  end;

implementation

uses ComServ;

TSomeComObject implementation here

initialization
  TComObjectFactory.Create(ComServer, TSomeComObject,
    CLSID_TSomeComObject, 'ClassName', 'Description');
end;
```

The `TComServer` descendant is declared and implemented like most VCL classes. What binds it to its corresponding `TComObjectFactory` object is the parameters passed to `TComObjectFactory`'s constructor `Create()`. The first constructor parameter is a `TComServer` object. You almost always will pass the global `ComServer` object declared in the `ComServ` unit in this parameter. The second parameter is the `TComObject` class you want to bind to the class factory. The third parameter is the CLSID of the `TComObject`'s COM class. The fourth and fifth parameters are the class name and description strings used to describe the COM class in the System Registry.

The `TComObjectFactory` instance is created in the initialization of the unit in order to ensure that the class factory will be available to create instances of the COM object as soon as the COM server is loaded. Exactly how the COM server is loaded depends on whether the COM server is an in-process server (a DLL) or an out-of-process server (an application).

In-Process COM Servers

In-process (or in-proc, for short) COM servers are DLLs that can create COM objects for use by their host application. This type of COM server is called in-process because, as a DLL, it resides in the same process as the calling application. An in-proc server must export four standard entry point functions:

```
function DllRegisterServer: HResult; stdcall;
function DllUnregisterServer: HResult; stdcall;
function DllGetClassObject (const CLSID, IID: TGUID; var Obj): HResult;
  stdcall;
function DllCanUnloadNow: HResult; stdcall;
```

Each of these functions is already implemented by the ComServ unit, so the only work to be done for your Delphi COM servers is to ensure that these functions are added to an exports clause in your project.

> **NOTE**
>
> A good example of a real-world application of in-process COM servers can be found in Chapter 24, "Extending the Windows Shell," which demonstrates how to create shell extensions.

DllRegisterServer()

The DllRegisterServer()function is called to register a COM server DLL with the System Registry. If you simply export this method from your Delphi application as described earlier, VCL will iterate over all of the COM objects in your application and register them with the System Registry. When a COM server is registered, it will make a key entry in the System Registry under HKEY_CLASSES_ROOT\CLSID\{xxxxxxxx-xxxx-xxxx-xxxx-xxxxxxxx} for each COM class, where the x's denote the CLSID of the COM class. For in-proc servers, an additional entry is created as a subkey of the preceding key called InProcServer32. The default value for this key is the full path to the in-proc server DLL. Figure 23.1 shows a COM server registered with the System Registry.

23

COM AND ACTIVEX

FIGURE 23.1.

A COM server as shown in the Registry Editor.

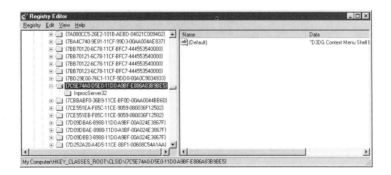

DllUnregisterServer()

The DllUnregisterServer() function's job is simply to undo what is done by the DllRegisterServer() function. When called, it should remove all the entries in the System Registry made by DllRegisterServer().

DllGetClassObject()

DllGetClassObject() is called by the COM engine in order to retrieve a class factory for a particular COM class. The CLSID parameter of this method is the CLSID of the type of COM class you want to create. The IID parameter holds the IID of the interface instance pointer you want to obtain for the class factory object (usually, IClassFactory's interface ID is passed here). Upon successful return, the Obj parameter contains a pointer to the class factory interface denoted by IID capable of creating COM objects of the class type denoted by CLSID.

DllCanUnloadNow()

DllCanUnloadNow() is called by the COM engine to determine whether or not the COM server DLL is capable of being unloaded from memory. If there are references to any COM object within the DLL, this function should return S_FALSE, indicating that the DLL should not be unloaded. If none of the DLL's COM objects are in use, this method should return S_TRUE.

> **TIP**
>
> Even after all references to an in-proc server's COM objects have been freed, COM may not necessarily call DllCanUnloadNow() to begin the process of releasing the in-proc server DLL from memory. If you want to ensure that all unused COM server DLLs have been released from memory, call the CoFreeUnusedLibraries() API function, which is defined in the ActiveX units as follows:
>
> ```
> procedure CoFreeUnusedLibraries; stdcall;
> ```

Creating an Instance of an In-Proc COM Server

To create an instance of a COM server in Delphi, use the CreateComObject() function, which is defined in the ComObj unit as follows:

```
function CreateComObject(const ClassID: TGUID): IUnknown;
```

The ClassID parameter holds the CLSID, which identifies the type of COM object you want to create. The return value of this function is the IUnknown interface of the requested COM object, or it raises an exception if the COM object cannot be created.

`CreateComObject()` is a wrapper around the `CoCreateInstance()` COM API function. Internally, `CoCreateInstance()` calls the `CoGetClassObject()` API function to obtain an `IClassFactory` for the specified COM object. `CoCreateInstance()` does this by looking in the registry for the COM class's `InProcServer32` entry in order to find the path to the in-proc server DLL, calling `LoadLibrary()` on the in-proc server DLL, and then calling the DLL's `DllGetClassObject()` function. After obtaining the `IClassFactory` interface pointer, `CoCreateInstance()` calls `IClassFactory.CreateInstance()` to create an instance of the specified COM class.

TIP

`CreateComObject()` can be inefficient if you need to create multiple objects from a class factory because it disposes of the `IClassFactory` interface pointer obtained by `CoGetClassObject()` after creating the requested COM object. In cases where you need to create multiple instances of the same COM object, you should call `CoGetClassObject()` directly and use `IClassFactory.CreateInstance()` to create multiple instances of the COM object.

NOTE

Before you can use any COM or OLE API functions, you must initialize the COM library using the `CoInitialize()` function. The single parameter to this function must be nil. To properly shut down the COM library, you should call the `CoUninitialize()` function as the last call to the OLE library. Calls are cumulative, so each call to `CoInitialize()` in your application must have a corresponding call to `CoUninitialize()`.

For applications, `CoInitialize()` is called automatically from `Application.Initialize()`, and `CoUninitialize()` is called automatically from the finalization of `ComObj`.

It's not necessary to call these functions from in-process libraries because their client applications are required to perform the initialization and uninitialization for the process.

Out-of-Process COM Servers

Out-of-process servers are executables that can create COM objects for use by other applications. Their name comes from the fact that they do not execute from within the same process of the client but instead are executables that operate within the context of their own process.

Registration

Like their in-proc cousins, out-of-process servers must also be registered with the System Registry. Out-of-process servers must make an entry under HKEY_CLASSES_ROOT\CLSID\ {xxxxxxxx-xxxx-xxxx-xxxx-xxxxxxxx} called LocalServer32, which identifies the full path name of the out-of-process server executable.

Delphi applications' COM servers are registered in the Application.Initialize() method, which is usually the first line of code in the application's project file. If the /regserver command-line switch is passed to your application, Application.Initialize() will register the COM classes with the System Registry and immediately terminate the application. Likewise, if the /unregserver command-line switch is passed, Application.Initialize() will unregister the COM classes with the System Registry and immediately terminate the application. If neither of these switches is passed, Application.Initialize() will register the COM classes with the System Registry and continue to run the application normally.

Creating an Instance of an Out-of-Proc COM Server

On the surface, the method for creating instances of COM objects from out-of-process servers is the same as for in-proc servers: just call ComObj's CreateComObject() function. Behind the scenes, however, the process is quite different. In this case, CoGetClassObject() looks for the LocalServer32 entry in the System Registry, and invokes the associated application using the CreateProcess() API function. When the out-of-proc server application is invoked, the server must register its class factories using the CoRegisterClassObject() COM API function. This function adds an IClassFactory pointer to COM's internal table of active registered class objects. CoGetClassObject() can then obtain the requested COM class's IClassFactory pointer from this table to create an instance of the COM object.

Aggregation

You know now that interfaces are the basic building blocks of COM and that inheritance is possible with interfaces. However, interfaces are entities without implementation. What happens, then, when you want to recycle the implementation of one COM object within another? COM's answer to this question is a concept called *aggregation*. Aggregation means that the containing (or outer) object creates the contained (or inner) object as part of its creation process, and the interfaces of the inner object are exposed by the outer. An object has to allow itself to operate as an aggregate by providing a means to forward all calls to its IUnknown methods to the containing object. For an example of aggregation within the context of VCL COM objects, you should take a look at the TAggregatedObject class in the AxCtrls unit.

DISTRIBUTED COM

Introduced with Windows NT 4, Distributed COM (or DCOM) provides a means for accessing COM objects located on other machines on a network. In addition to remote object creation, DCOM also provides security facilities allowing servers to specify which clients have rights to create instances of which servers and what operations they may perform. Windows NT 4 and Windows 98 have built-in DCOM capability, but Windows 95 requires an add-on available on Microsoft's Web site (`http://www.microsoft.com`) to serve as a DCOM client.

You can create remote COM objects using the `CreateRemoteComObject()`function, which is declared in the `ComObj` unit as follows:

```
function CreateRemoteComObject(const MachineName: WideString;
  const ClassID: TGUID): IUnknown;
```

The first parameter, `MachineName`, to this function is a string representing the network name of the machine containing the COM class. The `ClassID` parameter specifies the CLSID of the COM class to be created. The return value for this function is the `IUnknown` interface pointer for the COM object specified in `CLSID`. An exception will be raised if the object cannot be created.

`CreateRemoteComObject()` is a wrapper around the `CoCreateInstanceEx()` COM API function, which is an extended version of `CoCreateInstance()` that knows how to create objects remotely.

AUTOMATION

Automation (formerly known as OLE Automation) provides a means for applications or DLLs to expose programmable objects for use by other applications. Applications or DLLs that expose programmable objects are referred to as *Automation servers*. Applications that access and manipulate the programmable objects contained within Automation servers are known as *Automation controllers*. Automation controllers are able to program the Automation server using a macro-like language exposed by the server.

Among the chief advantages to using Automation in your applications is its language-independent nature. An Automation controller is able to manipulate a server regardless of the programming language used to develop either component. Additionally, because Automation is supported at the operating system level, the theory is that you'll be able to leverage future advancements in this technology by using Automation today. If these things sound good to you, then read on. What follows is information on creating Automation servers and controllers in Delphi.

> ### CAUTION
>
> If you have an Automation project from Delphi 2 that you want to migrate to
> Delphi 4, you should be forewarned that Automation in Delphi 4 is much differ-
> ent than in Delphi 2. In general, you shouldn't mix Delphi 2's Automation unit,
> OleAuto, with Delphi 3's ComObj or ComServ units. If you want to compile a
> Delphi 2 Automation project under Delphi 4, the OleAuto unit remains in the
> \Delphi 4\Delphi2 subdirectory for backward compatibility.

IDispatch

Automation objects are essentially COM objects that implement the IDispatch interface.
IDispatch is defined in the System unit as shown in the following:

```
type
  IDispatch = interface(IUnknown)
    ['{00020400-0000-0000-C000-000000000046}']
    function GetTypeInfoCount(out Count: Integer): Integer; stdcall;
    function GetTypeInfo(Index, LocaleID: Integer; out TypeInfo): Integer;
      stdcall;
    function GetIDsOfNames(const IID: TGUID; Names: Pointer;
      NameCount, LocaleID: Integer; DispIDs: Pointer): Integer; stdcall;
    function Invoke(DispID: Integer; const IID: TGUID; LocaleID: Integer;
      Flags: Word; var Params; VarResult, ExcepInfo, ArgErr: Pointer):
      Integer;
  end;
```

The first thing you should know is that you don't have to understand the ins and outs of
the IDispatch interface to take advantage of Automation in Delphi, so don't let this
complicated interface alarm you. You generally don't have to interact with this interface
directly because Delphi provides an elegant encapsulation Automation, but the description of IDispatch in this section should provide you with a good foundation for understanding Automation.

Central to the function of IDispatch is the Invoke() method, so we'll start here. When a
client obtains an IDispatch pointer for an Automation server, it can call the Invoke()
method to execute a particular method on the server. The DispID parameter of this
method holds a number, called a dispatch ID, which indicates which method on the
server should be invoked. The IID parameter is unused. The LocaleID parameter contains language information. The Flags parameter describes what kind of method is to be
invoked, whether it's a normal method or a put or get method for a property. The Params
property contains a pointer to an array of TDispParams, which holds the parameters
passed to the method. The VarResult parameter is a pointer to an OleVariant, which

will hold the return value of the method that is invoked. `ExcepInfo` is a pointer to a `TExcepInfo` record that will contain error information if `Invoke()` returns `DISP_E_EXCEPTION`. Finally, if `Invoke()` returns `DISP_E_TYPEMISMATCH` or `DISP_E_PARAMNOTFOUND`, the `ArgError` parameter is a pointer to an integer that will contain the index of the offending parameter in the `Params` array.

The `GetIDsOfName()` method of `IDispatch` is called to obtain the dispatch ID of one or more method names given strings identifying those methods. The `IID` parameter of this method is unused. The `Names` parameter points to an array of `PWideChar` method names. The `NameCount` parameter holds the number of strings in the `Names` array. `LocaleID` contains language information. The last parameter, `DispIDs`, is a pointer to an array of `NameCount` integers, which `GetIDsOfName()` will fill in with the dispatch IDs for the methods listed in the `Names` parameter.

`GetTypeInfo()` retrieves the type information (type information is described next) for the Automation object. The `Index` parameter represents the type of information to obtain and should normally be 0. The `LCID` parameter holds language information. Upon successful return, the `TypeInfo` parameter will hold an `ITypeInfo` pointer for the Automation object's type information.

The `GetTypeInfoCount()` method retrieves the number of type information interfaces supported by the Automation object in the `Count` parameter. Currently, `Count` will only contain two possible values: 0, meaning the Automation object doesn't support type information, and 1, meaning the Automation object does support type information.

Type Information

After spending a great deal of time carefully crafting an Automation server, it would be a shame if potential users of your server couldn't exploit its capabilities to the fullest because of lack of documentation on the methods and properties provided. Fortunately, Automation provides a means for helping avoid this problem by allowing developers to associate type information with Automation objects. This type information is stored in something called a *type library*, and an Automation server's type library can be linked to the server application or library as a resource or stored in an external file. Type libraries contain information about classes, interfaces, types, and other entities in a server. This information provides clients of the Automation server with the information needed to create instances of each of its classes and properly call methods on each interface.

Delphi generates type libraries for you when you add Automation objects to applications and libraries. Additionally, Delphi knows how to translate type library information into Object Pascal so that you can easily control Automation servers from your Delphi applications.

Late Versus Early Binding

The elements of Automation that you've learned about so far in this chapter deal with what's called *late binding*. Late binding is a fancy way to say that a method is called through IDispatch's Invoke() method. It's called late binding because the method call isn't resolved until runtime; at compile time, an Automation method call resolves into a call to IDispatch.Invoke() with the proper parameters, and at runtime, Invoke() executes the Automation method.

Early binding occurs when the Automation object exposes methods by means of a custom interface descending from IDispatch. This way, controllers can call Automation objects directly without going through IDispatch.Invoke(). Because the call is direct, this method is faster than late binding.

An Automation object that allows methods to be called both from Invoke() and directly from an IDispatch descendant interface is said to support a *dual interface*. Delphi-generated Automation objects always support dual interface, and Delphi controllers allow methods to be called both through Invoke() and directly through an interface.

Registration

Automation objects must make all the same registry entries as regular COM objects, but Automation servers also typically make an additional entry under HKEY_CLASSES_ROOT\CLSID\{xxxxxxxx-xxxx-xxxx-xxxx-xxxxxxxx} called ProgID, which provides a string identifier for the Automation class. Yet another Registry entry under HKEY_CLASSES_ROOT\(ProgID string) is made, which contains the CLSID of the Automation class in order to cross-reference back to the first Registry entry under CLSID.

Creating Automation Servers

Delphi makes it a fairly simple chore to create both out-of-process and in-process Automation servers. The process for creating an Automation server can be boiled down into four steps:

1. Create the application or DLL you want to automate. You can even use one of your existing applications as a starting point in order to spice it up with some automation. This is the only step where you'll see a real difference between creating in-process and out-of-process servers.

2. Create the Automation object and add it to your project. Delphi provides an Automation Object Expert to help this step go smoothly.

3. Add properties and methods to the Automation object by means of the type library. These are the properties and methods that will be exposed to Automation controllers.

4. Implement the methods generated by Delphi from your type library in your source code.

Creating an Out-of-Process Automation Server

The section walks you through the creation of a simple out-of-process Automation server. Start by creating a new project and placing a TShape and a TEdit component on the main form, as shown in Figure 23.2. Save this project as Srv.dpr.

FIGURE 23.2.

The main form of the Srv *project.*

Now add an Automation object to the project by selecting File I New from the main menu and choosing Automation Object from the ActiveX page of the New Items dialog, as shown in Figure 23.3. This will invoke the Automation Object Wizard shown in Figure 23.4.

FIGURE 23.3.

Adding a new Automation object.

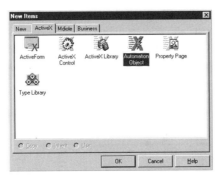

FIGURE 23.4.

*The Automation
Object Wizard.*

In the Class Name field of the Automation Object Wizard dialog, you should enter the name you want to give the COM class for this Automation object. The wizard will automatically prepend a T to the class name when creating the Object Pascal class for the Automation object and an I to the class name when creating the primary interface for the Automation object. The Instancing combo box in the wizard can hold any one of these three values:

Internal	This OLE object will be used internal to the application only, and it will not be registered with the System Registry. External processes cannot access Internal instanced Automation servers.
Single Instance	Each instance of the server can export only one instance of the OLE object. If a controller application requests another instance of the OLE object, Windows will start a new instance of the server application.
Multiple Instance	Each server instance can create and export multiple instances of the OLE object. In-process servers are always multiple-instance.

When you complete the Wizard dialog, Delphi will create a new type library for your project (if one doesn't already exist) and add an interface and a coclass to the type library. Additionally, the wizard will generate a new unit in your project that contains implementation of the Automation interface added to the type library. Figure 23.5 shows the type library editor immediately after dismissing the wizard dialog, and Listing 23.2 shows the implementation unit for the Automation object.

LISTING 23.2. AUTOMATION OBJECT IMPLEMENTATION UNIT.

```
unit Unit2;

interface
```

```
uses
  ComObj, Project1_TLB;

type
  TAutoTest = class(TAutoObject, IAutoTest)
  protected
  end;

implementation

uses ComServ;

initialization
  TAutoObjectFactory.Create(ComServer, TAutoTest, Class_AutoTest,
    ciMultiInstance);
end.
```

FIGURE 23.5.

*New Automation
project as seen
from the type
library editor.*

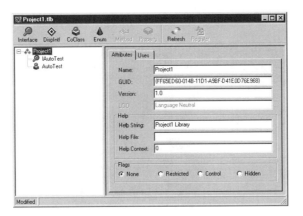

The Automation object, TAutoTest, is a class that descends from TAutoObject.
TAutoObject is the base class for all Automation servers. As you add methods to your
interface by using the type library editor, new method skeletons will be generated in this
unit that you will implement, forming the innards of your Automation object.

When the Automation object has been added to the project, you must add one or more properties or methods to the primary interface using the type library editor. For this project, the type library will contain properties to get and set the shape color, type, and the edit control's text. For good measure, you'll also add a method that displays the current status of those properties in a dialog. Figure 23.6 shows the completed type library for the Srv project. Note especially the enum added to the type library (whose values are shown in the right pane) to support the ShapeType property.

FIGURE 23.6.

The completed type library.

When the type library has been completed, all that is left to do is fill in the implementation for each of the method stubs created by the type library editor. This unit is shown in Listing 23.3.

LISTING 23.3. THE COMPLETED IMPLEMENTATION UNIT.

```
unit TestImpl;

interface

uses
  ComObj, ActiveX, Graphics, Srv_TLB;

type
  TAutoTest = class(TAutoObject, IAutoTest)
  protected
    function Get_EditText: WideString; safecall;
    function Get_ShapeColor: OLE_COLOR; safecall;
    function Get_ShapeType: TxShapeType; safecall;
    procedure Set_EditText(const Value: WideString); safecall;
    procedure Set_ShapeColor(ShapeColor: OLE_COLOR); safecall;
    procedure Set_ShapeType(Value: TxShapeType); safecall;
    procedure ShowInfo; safecall;
  end;

implementation

uses SysUtils, ComServ, ExtCtrls, ServMain, TypInfo, Dialogs;

function TAutoTest.Get_EditText: WideString;
begin
  Result := AutoTestForm.Edit1.Text;
end;

function TAutoTest.Get_ShapeType: TxShapeType;
begin
  Result := TxShapeType(AutoTestForm.Shape1.Shape);
end;

procedure TAutoTest.Set_EditText(const Value: WideString);
begin
  AutoTestForm.Edit1.Text := Value;
end;

procedure TAutoTest.Set_ShapeType(Value: TxShapeType);
begin
  AutoTestForm.Shape1.Shape := TShapeType(Value);
end;
```

continues

23

COM AND
ACTIVEX

LISTING 23.3. CONTINUED

```
function TAutoTest.Get_ShapeColor: OLE_COLOR;
begin
  Result := AutoTestForm.Shape1.Brush.Color;
end;

procedure TAutoTest.Set_ShapeColor(ShapeColor: OLE_COLOR);
begin
  AutoTestForm.Shape1.Brush.Color := ShapeColor;
end;

procedure TAutoTest.ShowInfo;
const
  SInfoStr = 'The Shape''s color is %s, and it''s shape is %s.'#13#10 +
    'The Edit''s text is "%s."';
begin
  with AutoTestForm do
    ShowMessage(Format(SInfoStr, [ColorToString(Shape1.Brush.Color),
      GetEnumName(TypeInfo(TShapeType), Ord(Shape1.Shape)), Edit1.Text]));
end;

initialization
  TAutoObjectFactory.Create(ComServer, TAutoTest, Class_AutoTest,
    ciMultiInstance);
end.
```

The uses clause for this unit contains a unit called `Srv_TLB`. This unit is the Object
Pascal translation of the project type library, and it is shown in Listing 23.4.

LISTING 23.4. `Srv_TLB`, THE TYPE LIBRARY FILE.

```
unit Srv_TLB;

// ********************************************************************** //
// WARNING                                                              //
// -------                                                              //
// The types declared in this file were generated from data read from a //
// Type Library. If this type library is explicitly or indirectly (via  //
// another type library referring to this type library) re-imported, or the //
// 'Refresh' command of the Type Library Editor activated while editing the //
// Type Library, the contents of this file will be regenerated and all  //
// manual modifications will be lost.                                   //
// ********************************************************************** //

// PASTLWTR : $Revision:   1.11.1.63  $
// File generated on 6/23/98 2:38:39 AM from Type Library described below.
```

```
// ********************************************************************* //
// Type Lib: C:\work\d4dg\code\Ch23\Automate\Srv.tlb
// IID\LCID: {17A05B84-0094-11D1-A9BF-F15F8BE883D4}\0
// Helpfile:
// HelpString: D4DG Srv Library
// Version:     1.0
// ********************************************************************* //

interface

uses Windows, ActiveX, Classes, Graphics, OleCtrls, StdVCL;

// *********************************************************************//
// GUIDS declared in the TypeLibrary. Following prefixes are used:    //
//   Type Libraries        : LIBID_xxxx                               //
//   CoClasses             : CLASS_xxxx                               //
//   DISPInterfaces        : DIID_xxxx                                //
//   Non-DISP interfaces   : IID_xxxx                                 //
// *********************************************************************//
const
  LIBID_Srv: TGUID = '{17A05B84-0094-11D1-A9BF-F15F8BE883D4}';
  IID_IAutoTest: TGUID = '{17A05B85-0094-11D1-A9BF-F15F8BE883D4}';
  CLASS_AutoTest: TGUID = '{17A05B86-0094-11D1-A9BF-F15F8BE883D4}';

// *********************************************************************//
// Declaration of Enumerations defined in Type Library               //
// *********************************************************************//
// TxShapeType constants
type
  TxShapeType = TOleEnum;
const
  stRectangle = $00000000;
  stSquare = $00000001;
  stRoundRect = $00000002;
  stRoundSquare = $00000003;
  stEllipse = $00000004;
  stCircle = $00000005;

type

// *********************************************************************//
// Forward declaration of interfaces defined in Type Library         //
// *********************************************************************//
  IAutoTest = interface;
  IAutoTestDisp = dispinterface;

// *********************************************************************//
// Declaration of CoClasses defined in Type Library                  //
// (NOTE: Here we map each CoClass to its Default Interface)          //
// *********************************************************************//
```

23

COM AND ACTIVEX

continues

LISTING 23.4. CONTINUED

```
  AutoTest = IAutoTest;


// *********************************************************************//
// Interface: IAutoTest
// Flags:      (4432) Hidden Dual OleAutomation Dispatchable
// GUID:       {17A05B85-0094-11D1-A9BF-F15F8BE883D4}
// *********************************************************************//
  IAutoTest = interface(IDispatch)
    ['{17A05B85-0094-11D1-A9BF-F15F8BE883D4}']
    function Get_ShapeType: TxShapeType; safecall;
    procedure Set_ShapeType(ShapeType: TxShapeType); safecall;
    function Get_ShapeColor: OLE_COLOR; safecall;
    procedure Set_ShapeColor(ShapeColor: OLE_COLOR); safecall;
    function Get_EditText: WideString; safecall;
    procedure Set_EditText(const EditText: WideString); safecall;
    procedure ShowInfo; safecall;
    property ShapeType: TxShapeType read Get_ShapeType write Set_ShapeType;
    property ShapeColor: OLE_COLOR read Get_ShapeColor write Set_ShapeColor;
    property EditText: WideString read Get_EditText write Set_EditText;
  end;

// *********************************************************************//
// DispIntf:  IAutoTestDisp
// Flags:      (4432) Hidden Dual OleAutomation Dispatchable
// GUID:       {17A05B85-0094-11D1-A9BF-F15F8BE883D4}
// *********************************************************************//
  IAutoTestDisp = dispinterface
    ['{17A05B85-0094-11D1-A9BF-F15F8BE883D4}']
    property ShapeType: TxShapeType dispid 1;
    property ShapeColor: OLE_COLOR dispid 2;
    property EditText: WideString dispid 3;
    procedure ShowInfo; dispid 4;
  end;

  CoAutoTest = class
    class function Create: IAutoTest;
    class function CreateRemote(const MachineName: string): IAutoTest;
  end;

implementation

uses ComObj;

class function CoAutoTest.Create: IAutoTest;
begin
  Result := CreateComObject(CLASS_AutoTest) as IAutoTest;
end;
```

```
class function CoAutoTest.CreateRemote(const MachineName: string): IAutoTest;
begin
  Result := CreateRemoteComObject(MachineName, CLASS_AutoTest) as IAutoTest;
end;

end.
```

Looking at this unit from the top down, first the GUID for the type library, LIBID_Srv, is declared. This GUID will be used when the type library is registered with the System Registry. Next, the values for the TxShapeType enumeration are listed. What's interesting about the enumeration is that the values are declared as constants rather than as an Object Pascal enumerated type. This is because type library enums are like C/C++ enums (and unlike Object Pascal) in that they don't have to start at the ordinal value zero or be sequential in value.

Next, in the Srv_TLB unit the IAutoTest interface is declared. In this interface declaration, you'll see the properties and methods you created in the type library editor. Additionally, you'll see the Get_*XXX* and Set_*XXX* methods generated as the read and write methods for each of the properties.

---

safecall

safecall is the default calling convention for methods entered into the type library editor, as you can see from the IAutoTest declaration earlier. safecall is actually more than a calling convention, as it implies two things: First, it means that the method will be called using the safecall calling convention. Second, it means that the method will be encapsulated so that it returns an HResult value to the caller. For example, suppose you have a method that looks like this in Object Pascal:

```
function Foo(W: WideString): Integer; safecall;
```

This method actually compiles to code that looks something like this:

```
function Foo(W: WideString; out RetVal: Integer): HResult; stdcall;
```

The advantage of safecall is that it catches all exceptions before they flow back into the caller. When an unhandled exception is raised in a safecall method, the exception is handled by the implicit wrapper and converted into an HResult, which is returned to the caller.

Next in Srv_TLB is the dispinterface declaration for the Automation object, IAutoTestDisp. A dispinterface signals to the caller that Automation methods may be executed by Invoke() but does not imply a custom interface through which methods can be executed. Although the IAutoTest interface can be used by development tools that support early-binding Automation, the IAutoTestDisp dispinterface can be used by tools that support late binding.

Finally, Srv_TLB declares a class called CoAutoTest, which makes creation of the Automation object easy; just call CoAutoTest.Create() to create an instance of the Automation object.

As mentioned earlier, you must run this application once to register it with the System Registry. Later in this chapter, you'll learn about the controller application used to manipulate this server.

Creating an In-Process Automation Server

Just as out-of-process servers start out as applications, in-process servers start out as DLLs. You can begin with an existing DLL or with a new DLL, which you can create by selecting DLL from the New Items dialog found under the File | New menu.

> **NOTE**
>
> If you're not familiar with DLLs, they are covered in depth in Chapter 9, "Dynamic Link Libraries." This chapter assumes that you have some knowledge of DLL programming.

As mentioned earlier, in order to serve as an in-process Automation server, a DLL must export four functions that are defined in the ComServ unit: DllGetClassObject(), DllCanUnloadNow(), DllRegisterServer(), and DllUnregisterServer(). Do this by adding these functions to the exports clause in your project file as shown in the project file, IPS.dpr, in Listing 23.5.

LISTING 23.5. THE IPS.dpr PROJECT.

```
library IPS;

uses
  ComServ;

exports
  DllRegisterServer,
  DllUnregisterServer,
  DllGetClassObject,
  DllCanUnloadNow;

begin
end.
```

The Automation object is added to the DLL project in the same manner as an executable project: through the Automation Object Wizard. For this project, you will add only one property and one method, as shown in the type library editor in Figure 23.7. The Object Pascal version of the type library, IPS_TLB, is shown in Listing 23.6.

FIGURE 23.7.

The IPS project in the type library editor.

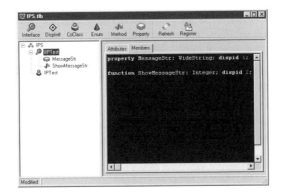

LISTING 23.6. THE IPS_TLB.pas PROJECT.

```
unit IPS_TLB;

// ******************************************************************** //
// WARNING
// -------
// The types declared in this file were generated from data read from a  //
// Type Library. If this type library is explicitly or indirectly (via   //
// another type library referring to this type library) re-imported, or the //
// 'Refresh' command of the Type Library Editor activated while editing the //
// Type Library, the contents of this file will be regenerated and all    //
// manual modifications will be lost.                                     //
// ******************************************************************** //

// PASTLWTR : $Revision:   1.11.1.63  $
// File generated on 6/23/98 2:46:46 AM from Type Library described below.

// ******************************************************************** //
// Type Lib: C:\work\d4dg\code\Ch23\Automate\IPS.tlb
// IID\LCID: {17A05B88-0094-11D1-A9BF-F15F8BE883D4}\0
// Helpfile:
// HelpString: Delphi 4 Developer\ Guide In-process Server demo
// Version:   1.0
// ******************************************************************** //
```

continues

LISTING 23.6. CONTINUED

```
interface

uses Windows, ActiveX, Classes, Graphics, OleCtrls, StdVCL;

// ********************************************************************//
// GUIDS declared in the TypeLibrary. Following prefixes are used:   //
//   Type Libraries    : LIBID_xxxx                                  //
//   CoClasses         : CLASS_xxxx                                  //
//   DISPInterfaces    : DIID_xxxx                                   //
//   Non-DISP interfaces: IID_xxxx                                   //
// ********************************************************************//
const
  LIBID_IPS: TGUID = '{17A05B88-0094-11D1-A9BF-F15F8BE883D4}';
  IID_IIPTest: TGUID = '{17A05B89-0094-11D1-A9BF-F15F8BE883D4}';
  CLASS_IPTest: TGUID = '{17A05B8A-0094-11D1-A9BF-F15F8BE883D4}';
type

// ********************************************************************//
// Forward declaration of interfaces defined in Type Library         //
// ********************************************************************//
  IIPTest = interface;
  IIPTestDisp = dispinterface;


// ********************************************************************//
// Declaration of CoClasses defined in Type Library                  //
// (NOTE: Here we map each CoClass to its Default Interface)          //
// ********************************************************************//
  IPTest = IIPTest;


// ********************************************************************//
// Interface: IIPTest
// Flags:     (4432) Hidden Dual OleAutomation Dispatchable
// GUID:      {17A05B89-0094-11D1-A9BF-F15F8BE883D4}
// ********************************************************************//
  IIPTest = interface(IDispatch)
    ['{17A05B89-0094-11D1-A9BF-F15F8BE883D4}']
    function Get_MessageStr: WideString; safecall;
    procedure Set_MessageStr(const Value: WideString); safecall;
    function ShowMessageStr: Integer; safecall;
    property MessageStr: WideString read Get_MessageStr write Set_MessageStr;
  end;

// ********************************************************************//
// DispIntf:  IIPTestDisp
// Flags:     (4432) Hidden Dual OleAutomation Dispatchable
// GUID:      {17A05B89-0094-11D1-A9BF-F15F8BE883D4}
// ********************************************************************//
```

```
  IIPTestDisp = dispinterface
    ['{17A05B89-0094-11D1-A9BF-F15F8BE883D4}']
    property MessageStr: WideString dispid 1;
    function ShowMessageStr: Integer; dispid 2;
  end;

implementation

uses ComObj;

end.
```

Clearly, this is a pretty simple Automation server, but it serves to illustrate the point. The
MessageStr property can be set to a value and then shown with the ShowMessageStr()
function. The implementation of the IIPTest interface resides in unit IPSMain.pas,
shown in Listing 23.7.

LISTING 23.7. THE IPSMain.pas UNIT.

```
unit IPSMain;

interface

uses
  ComObj, IPS_TLB;

type
  TIPTest = class(TAutoObject, IIPTest)
  private
    MessageStr: string;
  protected
    function Get_MessageStr: WideString; safecall;
    procedure Set_MessageStr(const Value: WideString); safecall;
    function ShowMessageStr: Integer; safecall;
  end;

implementation

uses Windows, ComServ;

function TIPTest.Get_MessageStr: WideString;
begin
  Result := MessageStr;
end;

function TIPTest.ShowMessageStr: Integer;
```

continues

LISTING 23.7. CONTINUED

```
begin
  MessageBox(0, PChar(MessageStr), 'Your string is...', MB_OK);
  Result := Length(MessageStr);
end;

procedure TIPTest.Set_MessageStr(const Value: WideString);
begin
  MessageStr := Value;
end;

initialization
  TAutoObjectFactory.Create(ComServer, TIPTest, Class_IPTest,
ciMultiInstance);
end.
```

As you learned earlier in this chapter, in-process servers are registered differently than
out-of-process servers; an in-process server's `DllRegisterServer()` function is called to
register it with the System Registry. The Delphi IDE makes this very easy: select Run |
Register ActiveX server from the main menu.

Creating Automation Controllers

Delphi makes it extremely easy to control Automation servers in your applications.
Delphi also gives you a great amount of flexibility in how you want to control
Automation servers—with options for early binding using interfaces or late binding
using `dispinterfaces` or `Variants`.

Controlling Out-of-Process Servers

The `Control` project is an Automation controller that demonstrates all three types of
Automation (interfaces, `dispinterface`, and `Variants`). `Control` is the controller for the
`Srv` Automation server application that you built earlier in this chapter, and the main
form for this project is shown in Figure 23.8.

When the Connect button is clicked, the Control application connects to the server in
several different ways with the following code:

```
FIntf := CoAutoTest.Create;
FDispintf := CreateComObject(Class_AutoTest) as IAutoTestDisp;
FVar := CreateOleObject('Srv.AutoTest');
```

FIGURE 23.8.

The main form for the Control *project.*

This code shows interface, dispinterface, and OleVariant variables each creating an instance of the Automation server in different ways. What's interesting about these different techniques is that they're almost totally interchangeable. For example, the following code is also correct:

```
FIntf := CreateComObject(Class_AutoTest) as IAutoTest;
FDispintf := CreateOleObject('Srv.AutoTest') as IAutoTestDisp;
FVar := CoAutoTest.Create;
```

Listing 23.8 shows the Ctrl unit, which contains the rest of the source code for the Automation controller. Notice that the application allows you to manipulate the server using either the interface, dispinterface, or OleVariant.

LISTING 23.8. THE Ctrl.pas UNIT.

```
unit Ctrl;

interface

uses
  Windows, Messages, SysUtils, Classes, Graphics, Controls, Forms,
  Dialogs, StdCtrls, ColorGrd, ExtCtrls, Srv_TLB, Buttons;

type
  TControlForm = class(TForm)
    CallViaRG: TRadioGroup;
```

continues

LISTING 23.8. CONTINUED

```
    ShapeTypeRG: TRadioGroup;
    GroupBox1: TGroupBox;
    GroupBox2: TGroupBox;
    Edit: TEdit;
    GroupBox3: TGroupBox;
    ConBtn: TButton;
    DisBtn: TButton;
    InfoBtn: TButton;
    ColorBtn: TButton;
    ColorDialog: TColorDialog;
    ColorShape: TShape;
    ExitBtn: TButton;
    TextBtn: TButton;
    procedure ConBtnClick(Sender: TObject);
    procedure DisBtnClick(Sender: TObject);
    procedure ColorBtnClick(Sender: TObject);
    procedure ExitBtnClick(Sender: TObject);
    procedure TextBtnClick(Sender: TObject);
    procedure InfoBtnClick(Sender: TObject);
    procedure ShapeTypeRGClick(Sender: TObject);
  private
    { Private declarations }
    FIntf: IAutoTest;
    FDispintf: IAutoTestDisp;
    FVar: OleVariant;
    procedure SetControls;
    procedure EnableControls(DoEnable: Boolean);
  public
    { Public declarations }
  end;

var
  ControlForm: TControlForm;

implementation

{$R *.DFM}

uses ComObj;

procedure TControlForm.SetControls;
// Initializes the controls to the current server values
begin
  case CallViaRG.ItemIndex of
    0:
      begin
```

```
            ColorShape.Brush.Color := FIntf.ShapeColor;
            ShapeTypeRG.ItemIndex := FIntf.ShapeType;
            Edit.Text := FIntf.EditText;
          end;
      1:
        begin
          ColorShape.Brush.Color := FDispintf.ShapeColor;
          ShapeTypeRG.ItemIndex := FDispintf.ShapeType;
          Edit.Text := FDispintf.EditText;
        end;
      2:
        begin
          ColorShape.Brush.Color := FVar.ShapeColor;
          ShapeTypeRG.ItemIndex := FVar.ShapeType;
          Edit.Text := FVar.EditText;
        end;
    end;
end;

procedure TControlForm.EnableControls(DoEnable: Boolean);
begin
  DisBtn.Enabled := DoEnable;
  InfoBtn.Enabled := DoEnable;
  ColorBtn.Enabled := DoEnable;
  ShapeTypeRG.Enabled := DoEnable;
  Edit.Enabled := DoEnable;
  TextBtn.Enabled := DoEnable;
end;

procedure TControlForm.ConBtnClick(Sender: TObject);
begin
  FIntf := CoAutoTest.Create;
  FDispintf := CreateComObject(Class_AutoTest) as IAutoTestDisp;
  FVar := CreateOleObject('Srv.AutoTest');
  EnableControls(True);
  SetControls;
end;

procedure TControlForm.DisBtnClick(Sender: TObject);
begin
  FIntf := nil;
  FDispintf := nil;
  FVar := Unassigned;
  EnableControls(False);
end;

procedure TControlForm.ColorBtnClick(Sender: TObject);
var
  NewColor: TColor;
```

continues

LISTING 23.8. CONTINUED

```
begin
  if ColorDialog.Execute then
  begin
    NewColor := ColorDialog.Color;
    case CallViaRG.ItemIndex of
      0: FIntf.ShapeColor := NewColor;
      1: FDispintf.ShapeColor := NewColor;
      2: FVar.ShapeColor := NewColor;
    end;
    ColorShape.Brush.Color := NewColor;
  end;
end;

procedure TControlForm.ExitBtnClick(Sender: TObject);
begin
  Close;
end;

procedure TControlForm.TextBtnClick(Sender: TObject);
begin
  case CallViaRG.ItemIndex of
    0: FIntf.EditText := Edit.Text;
    1: FDispintf.EditText := Edit.Text;
    2: FVar.EditText := Edit.Text;
  end;
end;

procedure TControlForm.InfoBtnClick(Sender: TObject);
begin
  case CallViaRG.ItemIndex of
    0: FIntf.ShowInfo;
    1: FDispintf.ShowInfo;
    2: FVar.ShowInfo;
  end;
end;

procedure TControlForm.ShapeTypeRGClick(Sender: TObject);
begin
  case CallViaRG.ItemIndex of
    0: FIntf.ShapeType := ShapeTypeRG.ItemIndex;
    1: FDispintf.ShapeType := ShapeTypeRG.ItemIndex;
    2: FVar.ShapeType := ShapeTypeRG.ItemIndex;
  end;
end;

end.
```

Another interesting thing this code illustrates is how easy it is to disconnect from an Automation server: interfaces and `dispinterfaces` can be set to `nil`, and `Variants` can be set to `Unassigned`. Of course, the Automation server will also be released when the `Control` application is closed, as a part of the normal finalization of these lifetime-managed types.

TIP

Interfaces will almost always perform better than `dispinterfaces` or `Variants`, so you should always use interfaces to control Automation servers when available.

`Variants` rank last in terms of performance because, at runtime, an Automation call through a `Variant` must call `GetIDsOfNames()` to convert a method name into a dispatch ID before it can execute the method with a call to `Invoke()`.

The performance of `dispinterfaces` is in between that of an interface and that of a `Variant`. "But why," you might ask, "is the performance different if `Variants` and `dispinterfaces` both use late binding?" The reason for this is that `dispinterfaces` take advantage of an optimization called *ID binding*. ID binding means that the dispatch IDs of methods are known at compile time, so the compiler doesn't need to generate a runtime call to `GetIDsOfName()` prior to calling `Invoke()`. Another, perhaps more obvious, advantage of `dispinterfaces` over `Variants` is that `dispinterfaces` allow use of CodeInsight for easier coding, whereas this is not possible using `Variants`.

23

COM AND ACTIVEX

Figure 23.9 shows the `Control` application controlling the `Srv` server.

FIGURE 23.9.

Automation controller and server.

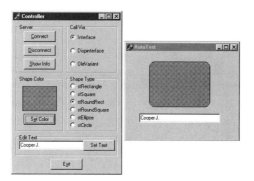

Controlling In-Process Servers

The technique for controlling an in-process server is no different than that for controlling
its out-of-process counterpart. Just keep in mind that the Automation controller is now
executing within your own process space. This means performance will be a bit better
than with out-of-process servers, but it also means that a crash in the Automation server
can take down your application.

Now you'll look at a controller application for the in-process Automation server created
earlier in this chapter. In this case, we'll use only the interface for controlling the server.
This is a pretty simple application, and Figure 23.10 shows the main form for the IPCtrl
project. The code in Listing 23.9 is IPCMain.pas, the main unit for the IPCtrl project.

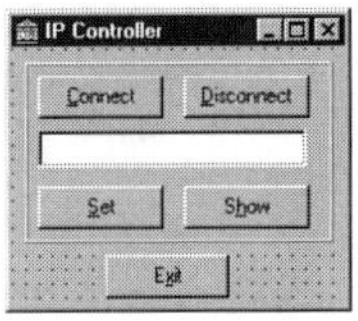

FIGURE 23.10.

The IPCtrl *project
main form.*

LISTING 23.9. THE IPCMain.pas UNIT.

```
unit IPCMain;

interface

uses
  Windows, Messages, SysUtils, Classes, Graphics, Controls, Forms,
  Dialogs, StdCtrls, ExtCtrls, IPS_TLB;

type
  TIPCForm = class(TForm)
    ExitBtn: TButton;
    Panel1: TPanel;
    ConBtn: TButton;
    DisBtn: TButton;
    Edit: TEdit;
    SetBtn: TButton;
    ShowBtn: TButton;
    procedure ConBtnClick(Sender: TObject);
    procedure DisBtnClick(Sender: TObject);
    procedure SetBtnClick(Sender: TObject);
    procedure ShowBtnClick(Sender: TObject);
    procedure ExitBtnClick(Sender: TObject);
  private
```

```
    { Private declarations }
    IPTest: IIPTest;
    procedure EnableControls(DoEnable: Boolean);
  public
    { Public declarations }
  end;

var
  IPCForm: TIPCForm;

implementation

uses ComObj;

{$R *.DFM}

procedure TIPCForm.EnableControls(DoEnable: Boolean);
begin
  DisBtn.Enabled := DoEnable;
  Edit.Enabled := DoEnable;
  SetBtn.Enabled := DoEnable;
  ShowBtn.Enabled := DoEnable;
end;

procedure TIPCForm.ConBtnClick(Sender: TObject);
begin
  IPTest := CreateComObject(CLASS_IPTest) as IIPTest;
  EnableControls(True);
end;

procedure TIPCForm.DisBtnClick(Sender: TObject);
begin
  IPTest := nil;
  EnableControls(False);
end;

procedure TIPCForm.SetBtnClick(Sender: TObject);
begin
  IPTest.MessageStr := Edit.Text;
end;

procedure TIPCForm.ShowBtnClick(Sender: TObject);
begin
  IPTest.ShowMessageStr;
end;

procedure TIPCForm.ExitBtnClick(Sender: TObject);
begin
  Close;
end;

end.
```

23

COM AND
ACTIVEX

Remember to ensure that the server has been registered prior to attempting to run IPCtrl. You can do this in several ways: using Run | Register ActiveX Server from the main menu while the IPS project is loaded, using the Windows RegSvr32.exe utility, or using the TRegSvr.exe tool that comes with Delphi. Figure 23.11 shows this project in action controlling the IPS server.

Figure 23.11.

The IPCtrl controlling the IPS server.

TOleContainer

Now that you have some ActiveX OLE background under your belt, take a look at Delphi's TOleContainer class. TOleContainer is located in the OleCntrs unit, and it encapsulates the complexities of an OLE Document and ActiveX Document container into an easily digestible VCL component.

> **Note**
>
> If you're familiar with using Delphi 1.0's TOleContainer component, you can pretty much throw that knowledge out the window. This component was redesigned from the ground up (as they say in the car commercials) for Delphi 2, so any knowledge you have of the Delphi 16-bit version of this component may not be applicable to the 32-bit version. Don't let that scare you, though; the 32-bit version of this component is of a much cleaner design, and you'll find that the code you must write to support the object is perhaps a quarter of what it used to be.

A Small Sample Application

Now let's jump right in and create an OLE container application. Create a new project and drop a TOleContainer (found on the System page of the Component Palette) on the form. Right-click on the object in the Form Designer and select Insert Object from the local menu. This invokes the Insert Object dialog box, as shown in Figure 23.12.

FIGURE 23.12.

The Insert Object dialog box.

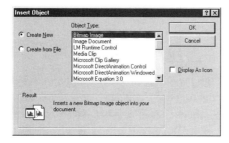

Embedding a New OLE Object

By default, the Insert Object dialog box contains the names of OLE server applications registered with Windows. To embed a new OLE object, you can select a server application from the Object Type list box. This causes the OLE server to execute in order to create a new OLE object to be inserted into the `TOleContainer`. When you close the server application, the `TOleContainer` object is updated with the embedded object. For this example, you will create a new MS Word 97 document, as shown in Figure 23.13.

FIGURE 23.13.

An embedded MS Word 97 document.

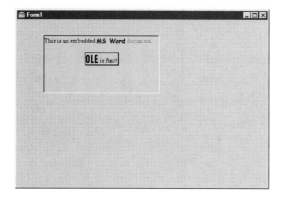

NOTE

An OLE object will not activate in place at design time. You will only be able to take advantage of the in-place activation capability of `TOleContainer` at runtime.

If you want to invoke the Insert Object dialog at runtime, you can call the `InsertObjectDialog()` method of `TOleContainer`, which is defined as follows:

```
function InsertObjectDialog: Boolean;
```

This function returns True if a new type of OLE object was successfully chosen from the dialog.

Embedding or Linking an Existing OLE File

To embed an existing OLE file into the TOleContainer, select the Create From File radio button on the Insert Object dialog box. This enables you to pick an existing file, as shown in Figure 23.14. After you choose the file, it behaves much the same as with a new OLE object.

FIGURE 23.14.

Inserting an object from a file.

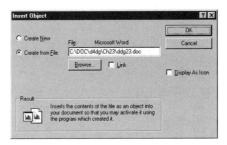

To embed a file at runtime, call the CreateObjectFromFile() method of TOleContainer, which is defined as follows:

```
procedure CreateObjectFromFile(const FileName: string; Iconic: Boolean);
```

To link (rather than embed) the OLE object, simply check the Link check box in the Insert Object dialog box shown in Figure 23.14. As described earlier, this creates a link from your application to the OLE file so that you can edit and view the same linked object from multiple applications.

To link to a file at runtime, call the CreateLinkToFile() method of TOleContainer, which is defined as follows:

```
procedure CreateLinkToFile(const FileName: string; Iconic: Boolean);
```

A Bigger Sample Application

Now that you have the basics of OLE and the TOleContainer class behind you, you will create a more sizable application that truly reflects the usage of OLE in realistic applications.

Start by creating a new project based on the MDI application template. The main form makes only a few modifications to the standard MDI template (see Figure 23.15).

FIGURE 23.15.

The MDI OLE Demo main window.

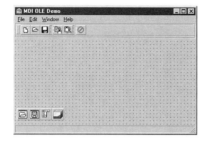

The MDI child form is shown in Figure 23.16. It is simply an `fsMDIChild` style form with a `TOleContainer` component aligned to `alClient`.

FIGURE 23.16.

The MDI OLE Demo child window.

Listing 23.10 shows `ChildWin.pas`, the source code unit for the MDI child form. Note that this unit is fairly standard except for the addition of the `OLEFileName` property and the associated method and `private` instance variable. This property stores the path and filename of the OLE file, and the property accessor sets the child form's caption to the filename.

LISTING 23.10. THE SOURCE CODE FOR `ChildWin.pas`.

```
unit Childwin;

interface

uses WinTypes, WinProcs, Classes, Graphics, Forms, Controls, OleCtnrs;

type
  TMDIChild = class(TForm)
    OleContainer: TOleContainer;
    procedure FormClose(Sender: TObject; var Action: TCloseAction);
```

continues

LISTING 23.10. CONTINUED

```
private
  FOLEFilename: String;
  procedure SetOLEFileName(const Value: String);
public
  property OLEFileName: String read FOLEFileName write SetOLEFileName;
end;

implementation

{$R *.DFM}

uses Main, SysUtils;

procedure TMDIChild.SetOLEFileName(const Value: String);
begin
  if Value <> FOLEFileName then begin
    FOLEFileName := Value;
    Caption := ExtractFileName(FOLEFileName);
  end;
end;

procedure TMDIChild.FormClose(Sender: TObject; var Action: TCloseAction);
begin
  Action := caFree;
end;

end.
```

Creating a Child Form

When a new MDI child form is created from the File | New menu of the
MDI OLE Demo application, the Insert Object dialog box is invoked using the
InsertObjectDialog() method mentioned earlier. Additionally, a caption is assigned
to the MDI child form using a global variable called NumChildren to provide a unique
number. The following code shows the main form's CreateMDIChild() method:

```
procedure TMainForm.FileNewItemClick(Sender: TObject);
begin
  inc(NumChildren);
  { create a new MDI child window }
  with TMDIChild.Create(Application) do
  begin
```

```
      Caption := 'Untitled' + IntToStr(NumChildren);
      { bring up insert OLE object dialog and insert into child }
      OleContainer.InsertObjectDialog;
  end;
end;
```

Saving to and Reading from Files

As discussed earlier in this chapter, OLE objects lend themselves to the capability of being written to and read from streams and, therefore, files. The TOleContainer component has methods called SaveToStream(), LoadFromStream(), SaveToFile(), and LoadFromFile(), which make saving an OLE object out to a file or stream very easy.

The MDIOLE application's main form contains methods for saving and opening OLE object files. The following code shows the FileOpenItemClick() method, which is called in response to choosing File | Open from the main form. In addition to loading a saved OLE object from a file specified by OpenDialog, this method also assigns the OleFileName field of the TMDIChild instance to the filename provided by OpenDialog. If an error occurs loading the file, the form instance is freed.

```
procedure TMainForm.FileOpenItemClick(Sender: TObject);
begin
  if OpenDialog.Execute then
    with TMDIChild.Create(Application) do
    begin
      try
        OleFileName := OpenDialog.FileName;
        OleContainer.LoadFromFile(OleFileName);
        Show;
      except
        Release;  // free form on error
        raise;    // reraise exception
      end;
    end;
end;
```

The following listing shows the code that handles the File | Save As and File | Save menu items. Note that the FileSaveItemClick() method invokes FileSaveAsItemClick() when the active MDI child does not have a name specified.

```
procedure TMainForm.FileSaveAsItemClick(Sender: TObject);
begin
  if (ActiveMDIChild <> nil) and (SaveDialog.Execute) then
    with TMDIChild(ActiveMDIChild) do
    begin
      OleFileName := SaveDialog.FileName;
      OleContainer.SaveToFile(OleFileName);
    end;
end;

procedure TMainForm.FileSaveItemClick(Sender: TObject);
begin
  if ActiveMDIChild <> nil then
    { if no name is assigned, then do a "save as" }
    if TMDIChild(ActiveMDIChild).OLEFileName = '' then
      FileSaveAsItemClick(Sender)
    else
      { otherwise save under current name }
      with TMDIChild(ActiveMDIChild) do
        OleContainer.SaveToFile(OLEFileName);
end;
```

Using the Clipboard to Copy and Paste

Thanks to the universal data-transfer mechanism described earlier, it is also possible to use the Windows Clipboard to transfer OLE objects. Again, the TOleContainer component automates these tasks to a great degree.

Copying an OLE object from a TOleContainer to the Clipboard, in particular, is a trivial task. Simply call the Copy() method:

```
procedure TMainForm.CopyItemClick(Sender: TObject);
begin
  if ActiveMDIChild <> nil then
    TMDIChild(ActiveMDIChild).OleContainer.Copy;
end;
```

After you think you have an OLE object on the Clipboard, only one additional step is required to properly read it out into a TOleContainer component. Prior to attempting to paste the contents of the Clipboard into a TOleContainer, you should first check the value of the CanPaste property to ensure that the data on the Clipboard is a suitable OLE object. After that, you can invoke the Paste Special dialog to paste the object into the TOleContainer by calling its PasteSpecialDialog() method as shown in the following code. The Paste Special dialog box is shown in Figure 23.17.

```
procedure TMainForm.PasteItemClick(Sender: TObject);
begin
  if ActiveMDIChild <> nil then
    with TMDIChild(ActiveMDIChild).OleContainer do
      { Before invoking dialog, check to be sure that there }
      { are valid OLE objects on the clipboard. }
      if CanPaste then PasteSpecialDialog;
end;
```

FIGURE 23.17.

The Paste Special dialog box.

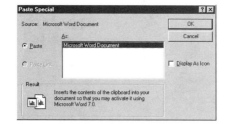

When the application is run, the server controlling the OLE object in the active MDI child merges with or takes control of the application's menu and toolbar. Figures 23.18 and 23.19 show OLE's in-place activation feature—the MDI OLE application is controlled by two different OLE servers.

FIGURE 23.18.

Editing an embedded Word 7 document.

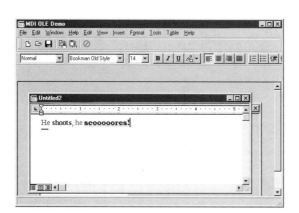

23

COM AND ACTIVEX

FIGURE 23.19.

Editing an embedded Paint graphic.

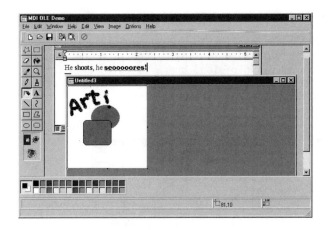

The complete listing for `Main.pas`, the MDI OLE application's main unit, is shown in Listing 23.11.

LISTING 23.11. THE SOURCE CODE FOR `Main.pas`.

```
unit Main;

interface

uses WinTypes, WinProcs, SysUtils, Classes, Graphics, Forms, Controls,
  Menus, StdCtrls, Dialogs, Buttons, Messages, ExtCtrls, ChildWin,
ComCtrls,
  ToolWin;

type
  TMainForm = class(TForm)
    MainMenu1: TMainMenu;
    File1: TMenuItem;
    FileNewItem: TMenuItem;
    FileOpenItem: TMenuItem;
    FileCloseItem: TMenuItem;
    Window1: TMenuItem;
    Help1: TMenuItem;
    N1: TMenuItem;
    FileExitItem: TMenuItem;
    WindowCascadeItem: TMenuItem;
    WindowTileItem: TMenuItem;
    WindowArrangeItem: TMenuItem;
```

```
        HelpAboutItem: TMenuItem;
        OpenDialog: TOpenDialog;
        FileSaveItem: TMenuItem;
        FileSaveAsItem: TMenuItem;
        Edit1: TMenuItem;
        PasteItem: TMenuItem;
        WindowMinimizeItem: TMenuItem;
        SaveDialog: TSaveDialog;
        CopyItem: TMenuItem;
        CloseAll1: TMenuItem;
        StatusBar: TStatusBar;
        CoolBar1: TCoolBar;
        ToolBar1: TToolBar;
        OpenBtn: TToolButton;
        SaveBtn: TToolButton;
        ToolButton3: TToolButton;
        CopyBtn: TToolButton;
        PasteBtn: TToolButton;
        ToolButton6: TToolButton;
        ExitBtn: TToolButton;
        ImageList1: TImageList;
        procedure FormCreate(Sender: TObject);
        procedure FileNewItemClick(Sender: TObject);
        procedure WindowCascadeItemClick(Sender: TObject);
        procedure UpdateMenuItems(Sender: TObject);
        procedure WindowTileItemClick(Sender: TObject);
        procedure WindowArrangeItemClick(Sender: TObject);
        procedure FileCloseItemClick(Sender: TObject);
        procedure FileOpenItemClick(Sender: TObject);
        procedure FileExitItemClick(Sender: TObject);
        procedure FileSaveItemClick(Sender: TObject);
        procedure FileSaveAsItemClick(Sender: TObject);
        procedure PasteItemClick(Sender: TObject);
        procedure WindowMinimizeItemClick(Sender: TObject);
        procedure FormDestroy(Sender: TObject);
        procedure HelpAboutItemClick(Sender: TObject);
        procedure CopyItemClick(Sender: TObject);
        procedure CloseAll1Click(Sender: TObject);
    private
        procedure ShowHint(Sender: TObject);
    end;

var
    MainForm: TMainForm;

implementation

{$R *.DFM}

uses About;
```

continues

LISTING 23.11. CONTINUED

```
var
  NumChildren: Cardinal = 0;

procedure TMainForm.FormCreate(Sender: TObject);
begin
  Application.OnHint := ShowHint;
  Screen.OnActiveFormChange := UpdateMenuItems;
end;

procedure TMainForm.ShowHint(Sender: TObject);
begin
  { Show hints on status bar }
  StatusBar.Panels[0].Text := Application.Hint;
end;

procedure TMainForm.FileNewItemClick(Sender: TObject);
begin
  inc(NumChildren);
  { create a new MDI child window }
  with TMDIChild.Create(Application) do
  begin
    Caption := 'Untitled' + IntToStr(NumChildren);
    { bring up insert OLE object dialog and insert into child }
    OleContainer.InsertObjectDialog;
  end;
end;

procedure TMainForm.FileOpenItemClick(Sender: TObject);
begin
  if OpenDialog.Execute then
    with TMDIChild.Create(Application) do
    begin
      try
        OleFileName := OpenDialog.FileName;
        OleContainer.LoadFromFile(OleFileName);
        Show;
      except
        Release;  // free form on error
        raise;    // reraise exception
      end;
    end;
end;

procedure TMainForm.FileCloseItemClick(Sender: TObject);
begin
  if ActiveMDIChild <> nil then
    ActiveMDIChild.Close;
```

```
end;

procedure TMainForm.FileSaveAsItemClick(Sender: TObject);
begin
  if (ActiveMDIChild <> nil) and (SaveDialog.Execute) then
    with TMDIChild(ActiveMDIChild) do
    begin
      OleFileName := SaveDialog.FileName;
      OleContainer.SaveToFile(OleFileName);
    end;
end;

procedure TMainForm.FileSaveItemClick(Sender: TObject);
begin
  if ActiveMDIChild <> nil then
    { if no name is assigned, then do a "save as" }
    if TMDIChild(ActiveMDIChild).OLEFileName = '' then
      FileSaveAsItemClick(Sender)
    else
      { otherwise save under current name }
      with TMDIChild(ActiveMDIChild) do
        OleContainer.SaveToFile(OLEFileName);
end;

procedure TMainForm.FileExitItemClick(Sender: TObject);
begin
  Close;
end;

procedure TMainForm.PasteItemClick(Sender: TObject);
begin
  if ActiveMDIChild <> nil then
    with TMDIChild(ActiveMDIChild).OleContainer do
      { Before invoking dialog, check to be sure that there }
      { are valid OLE objects on the clipboard. }
      if CanPaste then PasteSpecialDialog;
end;

procedure TMainForm.WindowCascadeItemClick(Sender: TObject);
begin
  Cascade;
end;

procedure TMainForm.WindowTileItemClick(Sender: TObject);
begin
  Tile;
end;

procedure TMainForm.WindowArrangeItemClick(Sender: TObject);
begin
  ArrangeIcons;
end;
```

23

**COM AND
ACTIVEX**

continues

LISTING 23.11. CONTINUED

```delphi
procedure TMainForm.WindowMinimizeItemClick(Sender: TObject);
var
  I: Integer;
begin
  { Must be done backwards through the MDIChildren array }
  for I := MDIChildCount - 1 downto 0 do
    MDIChildren[I].WindowState := wsMinimized;
end;

procedure TMainForm.UpdateMenuItems(Sender: TObject);
var
  DoIt: Boolean;
begin
  DoIt := MDIChildCount > 0;
  { only enable options if there are active children }
  FileCloseItem.Enabled := DoIt;
  FileSaveItem.Enabled := DoIt;
  CloseAll1.Enabled := DoIt;
  FileSaveAsItem.Enabled := DoIt;
  CopyItem.Enabled := DoIt;
  PasteItem.Enabled := DoIt;
  CopyBtn.Enabled := DoIt;
  SaveBtn.Enabled := DoIt;
  PasteBtn.Enabled := DoIt;
  WindowCascadeItem.Enabled := DoIt;
  WindowTileItem.Enabled := DoIt;
  WindowArrangeItem.Enabled := DoIt;
  WindowMinimizeItem.Enabled := DoIt;
end;

procedure TMainForm.FormDestroy(Sender: TObject);
begin
  Screen.OnActiveFormChange := nil;
end;

procedure TMainForm.HelpAboutItemClick(Sender: TObject);
begin
  with TAboutBox.Create(Self) do
  begin
    ShowModal;
    Free;
  end;
end;

procedure TMainForm.CopyItemClick(Sender: TObject);
begin
  if ActiveMDIChild <> nil then
```

```
      TMDIChild(ActiveMDIChild).OleContainer.Copy;
end;

procedure TMainForm.CloseAll1Click(Sender: TObject);
begin
  while ActiveMDIChild <> nil do
  begin
    ActiveMDIChild.Release;        // use Release, not Free!
    Application.ProcessMessages;   // let Windows take care of business
  end;
end;

end.
```

SUMMARY

That wraps up this chapter on COM, OLE, and ActiveX. This chapter provides a solid foundation in COM-based technologies, which should help you understand the goings-on behind the scenes. More importantly, the chapter provides you with some firsthand insight and information on how to make all this ActiveX stuff work for you in Delphi.

In addition to in-depth coverage of COM and Automation, you should be familiar with the workings of VCL's TOleContainer component. You'll find even more information on COM and ActiveX technologies in other areas of this book as well. Chapter 24, "Extending the Windows Shell," shows real-world examples of COM server creation, and Chapter 25, "Creating ActiveX Controls," discusses ActiveX control creation in Delphi.

23

**COM AND
ACTIVEX**

EXTENDING THE
WINDOWS SHELL

IN THIS CHAPTER

First introduced in Windows 95, the Windows shell is also supported on Windows NT 3.51 (and higher) and Windows 98. A far cry from Program Manager, the Windows shell includes some great features for extending the shell to meet your own needs. Problem is, many of these nifty extensible features are some of the most poorly documented subjects of Win32 development. This chapter is intended to give you the information and examples you need to tap into shell features such as tray-notification icons, application desktop toolbars, shell links, and shell extensions.

CREATING ACTIVEX CONTROLS

IN THIS CHAPTER

For many developers, the ability to easily create ActiveX controls is one of the most compelling features Delphi brings to the table. ActiveX is a standard for programming language-independent controls that can function in a variety of environments, including Delphi, C++Builder, Visual Basic, and Internet Explorer. These controls can be as simple as a static text control or as complex as a fully functional spreadsheet or word processor. Traditionally, ActiveX controls are quite complicated and difficult to write, but Delphi brings ActiveX control creation to the masses by allowing you to convert a relatively easy-to-create VCL component or form into an ActiveX control.

This chapter won't teach you everything there is to know about ActiveX controls—that would take a thick book in its own right. What this chapter will demonstrate is how ActiveX control creation works in Delphi and how to use the Delphi wizards and framework to make Delphi-created ActiveX controls work for you.

> **NOTE**
>
> ActiveX control creation capability is provided only with the Professional, Client/Server Suite, and Enterprise editions of Delphi.

WHY CREATE ACTIVEX CONTROLS?

As a Delphi developer, you may be completely happy with the capabilities of native VCL components and forms, and you might be wondering why you should even bother creating ActiveX controls. There are several reasons. First, if you are a professional component developer, the payoff can be huge; by converting your VCL controls into ActiveX controls, your potential market is not merely fellow Delphi and C++Builder developers but also users of practically any Win32 development tool. Even if you're not a component vendor, you can take advantage of ActiveX controls to add content and functionality to World Wide Web pages.

CREATING AN ACTIVEX CONTROL

Delphi's one-step wizards make creating an ActiveX control a simple process. However, as you'll soon learn, the wizard is just the beginning if you want your controls to really shine.

To help you become familiar with Delphi's ActiveX capabilities, Figure 25.1 shows the ActiveX page of the New Items dialog, which appears when you select File | New from the main menu. Many of the items shown here will be described as this chapter progresses.

FIGURE 25.1.

The ActiveX page of the New Items dialog.

The first icon in this dialog represents an ActiveForm (described later in this chapter), and you can click it to invoke a wizard that aids you in creating an ActiveForm. Note that ActiveForms are only slightly different than regular ActiveX controls, so we'll refer to both generically as *ActiveX controls* throughout this chapter.

Next you see the icon representing an ActiveX control. Clicking here will invoke the ActiveX Control Wizard, which we'll describe in the next section.

The third icon represents an ActiveX library. Click on this icon to create a new library project that exports the four ActiveX server functions described in Chapter 23, "COM and ActiveX." This can be used as a starting point before adding an ActiveX control to the project.

The Automation Object Wizard, represented by the next icon, is described in Chapter 15, "Porting to Delphi 4."

The next icon represents the COM Object Wizard. The wizard invoked by clicking this icon enables you to create a plain COM object. You learned about this wizard in Chapter 24, "Extending the Windows Shell," when you created shell extensions.

Clicking the icon at the far right enables you to add a property page to the current project. *Property pages* allow visual editing of ActiveX controls, and you'll see an example of creating a property page and integrating it into your ActiveX control project later in this chapter.

The final icon represents a type library; you can click it when you wish to add a type library to your project. Because the wizards for ActiveX controls and ActiveForms (as well as Automation objects) automatically add a type library to the project, you'll rarely use this option.

The ActiveX Control Wizard

Clicking the ActiveX Control icon on the ActiveX page of the New Items dialog will invoke the ActiveX Control Wizard, which is shown in Figure 25.2.

FIGURE 25.2.

*The ActiveX
Control Wizard.*

This wizard allows you to choose a VCL control class to encapsulate as an ActiveX control. Additionally, it allows you to specify the name of the ActiveX control class, the name of the file that will contain the implementation of the new ActiveX control, and the name of the project in which the ActiveX control will reside.

VCL Controls in the ActiveX Control Wizard

If you examine the list of VCL controls in the drop-down combo box in the ActiveX Control Wizard, you'll notice that not all VCL components are found in the list. A VCL control must meet three criteria in order to be listed in the wizard:

- The VCL control must reside in a currently installed design package (that is, it must be on the Component Palette).
- The VCL control must descend from TWinControl. Currently, nonwindowed controls cannot be encapsulated as ActiveX controls.
- The VCL control must not have been excluded from the list with the RegisterNonActiveX() procedure. RegisterNonActiveX() is described in detail in the Delphi online help.

Many standard VCL components are excluded from the list because they either don't make sense as ActiveX controls or would require significant work beyond the wizard's scope in order to function as ActiveX controls. TDBGrid is a good example of a VCL control that doesn't make sense as an ActiveX control; it requires another VCL class (TDataSource) as a property in order to function, and this isn't possible using ActiveX. TTreeView is an example of a control that would require significant work beyond the wizard to encapsulate as an ActiveX control because the TTreeView nodes would be difficult to represent in ActiveX.

NOTE

Although the ActiveX Control Wizard doesn't allow you to automatically generate an ActiveX control from a non-TWinControl, it is possible to write such a control by hand using the Delphi ActiveX (DAX) framework.

ActiveX Control Option

The lower portion of the ActiveX Control Wizard dialog allows you to set certain options that will become a part of the ActiveX control. These options consist of three check boxes:

- Include Design-Time License—When this option is selected, a license (LIC) file will be generated along with the control project. In order for other developers to use the generated ActiveX control in a development environment, they will need to have the LIC file in addition to the ActiveX control (OCX) file.

- Include Version Information—When selected, this option will cause a VersionInfo resource to be linked into the OCX file. In addition, the string file information in the VersionInfo resource includes a value called OleSelfRegister, which is set to 1. This setting is required for some older ActiveX control hosts, such as Visual Basic 4.0. You can edit a project's VersionInfo in the VersionInfo page of the Project Options dialog.

- Include About Box—Select this option in order to include an "About box" dialog with your ActiveX control. The About box is usually available in ActiveX container applications by selecting an option from a local right-click menu on the ActiveX control. The About box generated is a regular Delphi form that you can edit to your liking.

How VCL Controls Are Encapsulated

After you finish describing your control in the ActiveX Control Wizard and click the OK button, the wizard goes about the task of writing the wrapper to encapsulate the selected VCL control as an ActiveX control. The end result is an ActiveX library project that includes a working ActiveX control, but there's a lot of interesting stuff going on behind the scenes. Here's a description of the steps involved in encapsulating a VCL control as an ActiveX control:

1. The wizard determines what unit contains the VCL control. That unit is then handed to the compiler, and the compiler generates special symbolic information for the VCL control's properties, methods, and events.

2. A type library is created for the project. It contains an interface to hold properties and methods, a dispinterface to hold events, and a coclass to represent the ActiveX control.

3. The wizard iterates over all the symbol information for the VCL control, adding qualified properties and methods to the interface in the type library and qualified events to the dispinterface.

NOTE

The description of step 3 begs the following question: What constitutes a *qualified* property, method, or event for inclusion in the type library? In order to qualify for inclusion in the type library, properties must be of an Automation-compatible type, and the parameters and return values of the methods and events must also be of an Automation-compatible type. Recall from Chapter 23 that Automation-compatible types include `Byte`, `SmallInt`, `Integer`, `Single`, `Double`, `Currency`, `TDateTime`, `WideString`, `WordBool`, `PSafeArray`, `TDecimal`, `OleVariant`, `IUnknown`, `IDispatch`.

However, there are exceptions to this rule. In addition to Automation-compatible types, parameters of type `TStrings`, `TPicture`, and `TFont` are also permitted. For these types, the wizard will employ special adapter objects that allows them to be wrapped with an ActiveX-compatible `IDispatch` or `dispinterface`.

---

4. After all the qualifying properties, methods, and events have been added, the type library editor generates a file that's an Object Pascal translation of the type library contents.

5. The wizard then generates the implementation file for the ActiveX control. This implementation file contains a `TActiveXControl` object that implements the interface described in the type library. The wizard automatically writes *forwarders* for interface properties and methods. These forwarders forward method calls from the ActiveX control wrapper into the control and forward events from the VCL control out to the ActiveX control.

To help illustrate what we're describing here, we've provided the following listings. They belong to an ActiveX control project created from a `TMemo` VCL control. This project will be saved as `Memo.dpr`. Listing 25.1 shows the project file, Listing 25.2 shows the type library file, and Listing 25.3 shows the implementation file generated for the control. Figure 25.3 shows the contents of the type library editor.

FIGURE 25.3.

Memo, *as shown in the type library editor.*

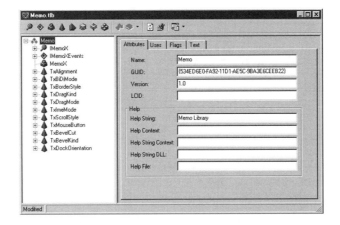

LISTING 25.1. THE PROJECT FILE, Memo.dpr.

```
library Memo;

uses
  ComServ,
  Memo_TLB in 'Memo_TLB.pas',
  MemoImpl in 'MemoImpl.pas' {MemoX: CoClass},
  About in 'About.pas' {MemoXAbout};

{$E ocx}

exports
  DllGetClassObject,
  DllCanUnloadNow,
  DllRegisterServer,
  DllUnregisterServer;

{$R *.TLB}

{$R *.RES}

begin
end.
```

LISTING 25.2. THE TYPE LIBRARY FILE, Memo_TLB.pas.

```
unit Memo_TLB;

// ************************************************************************ //
// WARNING                                                                 //
// -------                                                                 //
// The types declared in this file were generated from data read from a    //
```

continues

LISTING 25.2. CONTINUED

```
// Type Library. If this type library is explicitly or indirectly (via    //
// another type library referring to this type library) re-imported, or the //
// 'Refresh' command of the Type Library Editor activated while editing the //
// Type Library, the contents of this file will be regenerated and all     //
// manual modifications will be lost.                                       //
// ********************************************************************* //


// PASTLWTR : $Revision:    1.11.1.63  $
// File generated on 6/22/98 11:37:19 AM from Type Library described below.


// ********************************************************************* //
// Type Lib: C:\work\d4dg\code\Ch25\Memo\Memo.tlb
// IID\LCID: {0DB4686F-09C5-11D2-AE5C-00A024E3867F}\0
// Helpfile:
// HelpString: Memo Library
// Version:    1.0
// ********************************************************************* //


interface

uses Windows, ActiveX, Classes, Graphics, OleCtrls, StdVCL;


// *********************************************************************//
// GUIDS declared in the TypeLibrary. Following prefixes are used:    //
//   Type Libraries     : LIBID_xxxx                                  //
//   CoClasses          : CLASS_xxxx                                  //
//   DISPInterfaces     : DIID_xxxx                                   //
//   Non-DISP interfaces: IID_xxxx                                    //
// *********************************************************************//
const
  LIBID_Memo: TGUID = '{0DB4686F-09C5-11D2-AE5C-00A024E3867F}';
  IID_IMemoX: TGUID = '{0DB46870-09C5-11D2-AE5C-00A024E3867F}';
  DIID_IMemoXEvents: TGUID = '{0DB46872-09C5-11D2-AE5C-00A024E3867F}';
  CLASS_MemoX: TGUID = '{0DB46874-09C5-11D2-AE5C-00A024E3867F}';


// *********************************************************************//
// Declaration of Enumerations defined in Type Library               //
// *********************************************************************//
// TxAlignment constants
type
  TxAlignment = TOleEnum;
const
  taLeftJustify = $00000000;
  taRightJustify = $00000001;
  taCenter = $00000002;

// TxBiDiMode constants
type
  TxBiDiMode = TOleEnum;
```

```
const
  bdLeftToRight = $00000000;
  bdRightToLeft = $00000001;
  bdRightToLeftNoAlign = $00000002;
  bdRightToLeftReadingOnly = $00000003;

// TxBorderStyle constants
type
  TxBorderStyle = TOleEnum;
const
  bsNone = $00000000;
  bsSingle = $00000001;

// TxDragMode constants
type
  TxDragMode = TOleEnum;
const
  dmManual = $00000000;
  dmAutomatic = $00000001;

// TxImeMode constants
type
  TxImeMode = TOleEnum;
const
  imDisable = $00000000;
  imClose = $00000001;
  imOpen = $00000002;
  imDontCare = $00000003;
  imSAlpha = $00000004;
  imAlpha = $00000005;
  imHira = $00000006;
  imSKata = $00000007;
  imKata = $00000008;
  imChinese = $00000009;
  imSHanguel = $0000000A;
  imHanguel = $0000000B;

// TxScrollStyle constants
type
  TxScrollStyle = TOleEnum;
const
  ssNone = $00000000;
  ssHorizontal = $00000001;
  ssVertical = $00000002;
  ssBoth = $00000003;

// TxMouseButton constants
type
  TxMouseButton = TOleEnum;
const
  mbLeft = $00000000;
```

25

CREATING
ACTIVEX
CONTROLS

continues

LISTING 25.2. CONTINUED

```
  mbRight = $00000001;
  mbMiddle = $00000002;

type

// ***********************************************************************//
// Forward declaration of interfaces defined in Type Library            //
// ***********************************************************************//
  IMemoX = interface;
  IMemoXDisp = dispinterface;
  IMemoXEvents = dispinterface;

// ***********************************************************************//
// Declaration of CoClasses defined in Type Library                     //
// (NOTE: Here we map each CoClass to its Default Interface)             //
// ***********************************************************************//
  MemoX = IMemoX;


// ***********************************************************************//
// Interface: IMemoX
// Flags:      (4416) Dual OleAutomation Dispatchable
// GUID:       {0DB46870-09C5-11D2-AE5C-00A024E3867F}
// ***********************************************************************//
  IMemoX = interface(IDispatch)
    ['{0DB46870-09C5-11D2-AE5C-00A024E3867F}']
    function Get_Alignment: TxAlignment; safecall;
    procedure Set_Alignment(Value: TxAlignment); safecall;
    function Get_BiDiMode: TxBiDiMode; safecall;
    procedure Set_BiDiMode(Value: TxBiDiMode); safecall;
    function Get_BorderStyle: TxBorderStyle; safecall;
    procedure Set_BorderStyle(Value: TxBorderStyle); safecall;
    function Get_Color: OLE_COLOR; safecall;
    procedure Set_Color(Value: OLE_COLOR); safecall;
    function Get_Ctl3D: WordBool; safecall;
    procedure Set_Ctl3D(Value: WordBool); safecall;
    function Get_DragCursor: Smallint; safecall;
    procedure Set_DragCursor(Value: Smallint); safecall;
    function Get_DragMode: TxDragMode; safecall;
    procedure Set_DragMode(Value: TxDragMode); safecall;
    function Get_Enabled: WordBool; safecall;
    procedure Set_Enabled(Value: WordBool); safecall;
    function Get_Font: IFontDisp; safecall;
    procedure _Set_Font(const Value: IFontDisp); safecall;
    procedure Set_Font(var Value: IFontDisp); safecall;
    function Get_HideSelection: WordBool; safecall;
    procedure Set_HideSelection(Value: WordBool); safecall;
    function Get_ImeMode: TxImeMode; safecall;
    procedure Set_ImeMode(Value: TxImeMode); safecall;
```

```
function Get_ImeName: WideString; safecall;
procedure Set_ImeName(const Value: WideString); safecall;
function Get_MaxLength: Integer; safecall;
procedure Set_MaxLength(Value: Integer); safecall;
function Get_OEMConvert: WordBool; safecall;
procedure Set_OEMConvert(Value: WordBool); safecall;
function Get_ParentColor: WordBool; safecall;
procedure Set_ParentColor(Value: WordBool); safecall;
function Get_ParentCtl3D: WordBool; safecall;
procedure Set_ParentCtl3D(Value: WordBool); safecall;
function Get_ParentFont: WordBool; safecall;
procedure Set_ParentFont(Value: WordBool); safecall;
function Get_ReadOnly: WordBool; safecall;
procedure Set_ReadOnly(Value: WordBool); safecall;
function Get_ScrollBars: TxScrollStyle; safecall;
procedure Set_ScrollBars(Value: TxScrollStyle); safecall;
function Get_Visible: WordBool; safecall;
procedure Set_Visible(Value: WordBool); safecall;
function Get_WantReturns: WordBool; safecall;
procedure Set_WantReturns(Value: WordBool); safecall;
function Get_WantTabs: WordBool; safecall;
procedure Set_WantTabs(Value: WordBool); safecall;
function Get_WordWrap: WordBool; safecall;
procedure Set_WordWrap(Value: WordBool); safecall;
function GetControlsAlignment: TxAlignment; safecall;
procedure Clear; safecall;
procedure ClearSelection; safecall;
procedure CopyToClipboard; safecall;
procedure CutToClipboard; safecall;
procedure PasteFromClipboard; safecall;
procedure Undo; safecall;
procedure ClearUndo; safecall;
procedure SelectAll; safecall;
function Get_CanUndo: WordBool; safecall;
function Get_Modified: WordBool; safecall;
procedure Set_Modified(Value: WordBool); safecall;
function Get_SelLength: Integer; safecall;
procedure Set_SelLength(Value: Integer); safecall;
function Get_SelStart: Integer; safecall;
procedure Set_SelStart(Value: Integer); safecall;
function Get_SelText: WideString; safecall;
procedure Set_SelText(const Value: WideString); safecall;
function Get_Text: WideString; safecall;
procedure Set_Text(const Value: WideString); safecall;
function Get_DoubleBuffered: WordBool; safecall;
procedure Set_DoubleBuffered(Value: WordBool); safecall;
procedure FlipChildren(AllLevels: WordBool); safecall;
function DrawTextBiDiModeFlags(Flags: Integer): Integer; safecall;
function DrawTextBiDiModeFlagsReadingOnly: Integer; safecall;
procedure InitiateAction; safecall;
function IsRightToLeft: WordBool; safecall;
```

continues

25

CREATING
ACTIVEX
CONTROLS

LISTING 25.2. CONTINUED

```
  function UseRightToLeftAlignment: WordBool; safecall;
  function UseRightToLeftReading: WordBool; safecall;
  function UseRightToLeftScrollBar: WordBool; safecall;
  function Get_Cursor: Smallint; safecall;
  procedure Set_Cursor(Value: Smallint); safecall;
  function ClassNameIs(const Name: WideString): WordBool; safecall;
  procedure AboutBox; safecall;
  property Alignment: TxAlignment read Get_Alignment write Set_Alignment;
  property BiDiMode: TxBiDiMode read Get_BiDiMode write Set_BiDiMode;
  property BorderStyle: TxBorderStyle read Get_BorderStyle
    write Set_BorderStyle;
  property Color: OLE_COLOR read Get_Color write Set_Color;
  property Ctl3D: WordBool read Get_Ctl3D write Set_Ctl3D;
  property DragCursor: Smallint read Get_DragCursor write Set_DragCursor;
  property DragMode: TxDragMode read Get_DragMode write Set_DragMode;
  property Enabled: WordBool read Get_Enabled write Set_Enabled;
  property Font: IFontDisp read Get_Font write _Set_Font;
  property HideSelection: WordBool read Get_HideSelection
    write Set_HideSelection;
  property ImeMode: TxImeMode read Get_ImeMode write Set_ImeMode;
  property ImeName: WideString read Get_ImeName write Set_ImeName;
  property MaxLength: Integer read Get_MaxLength write Set_MaxLength;
  property OEMConvert: WordBool read Get_OEMConvert write Set_OEMConvert;
  property ParentColor: WordBool read Get_ParentColor write Set_ParentColor;
  property ParentCtl3D: WordBool read Get_ParentCtl3D write Set_ParentCtl3D;
  property ParentFont: WordBool read Get_ParentFont write Set_ParentFont;
  property ReadOnly: WordBool read Get_ReadOnly write Set_ReadOnly;
  property ScrollBars: TxScrollStyle read Get_ScrollBars
    write Set_ScrollBars;
  property Visible: WordBool read Get_Visible write Set_Visible;
  property WantReturns: WordBool read Get_WantReturns write Set_WantReturns;
  property WantTabs: WordBool read Get_WantTabs write Set_WantTabs;
  property WordWrap: WordBool read Get_WordWrap write Set_WordWrap;
  property CanUndo: WordBool read Get_CanUndo;
  property Modified: WordBool read Get_Modified write Set_Modified;
  property SelLength: Integer read Get_SelLength write Set_SelLength;
  property SelStart: Integer read Get_SelStart write Set_SelStart;
  property SelText: WideString read Get_SelText write Set_SelText;
  property Text: WideString read Get_Text write Set_Text;
  property DoubleBuffered: WordBool read Get_DoubleBuffered
    write Set_DoubleBuffered;
  property Cursor: Smallint read Get_Cursor write Set_Cursor;
  end;

// ********************************************************************//
// DispIntf:  IMemoXDisp
// Flags:     (4416) Dual OleAutomation Dispatchable
// GUID:      {0DB46870-09C5-11D2-AE5C-00A024E3867F}
// ********************************************************************//
```

```
IMemoXDisp = dispinterface
  ['{0DB46870-09C5-11D2-AE5C-00A024E3867F}']
  property Alignment: TxAlignment dispid 1;
  property BiDiMode: TxBiDiMode dispid 2;
  property BorderStyle: TxBorderStyle dispid 3;
  property Color: OLE_COLOR dispid -501;
  property Ctl3D: WordBool dispid 4;
  property DragCursor: Smallint dispid 5;
  property DragMode: TxDragMode dispid 6;
  property Enabled: WordBool dispid -514;
  property Font: IFontDisp dispid -512;
  property HideSelection: WordBool dispid 7;
  property ImeMode: TxImeMode dispid 8;
  property ImeName: WideString dispid 9;
  property MaxLength: Integer dispid 10;
  property OEMConvert: WordBool dispid 11;
  property ParentColor: WordBool dispid 12;
  property ParentCtl3D: WordBool dispid 13;
  property ParentFont: WordBool dispid 14;
  property ReadOnly: WordBool dispid 15;
  property ScrollBars: TxScrollStyle dispid 16;
  property Visible: WordBool dispid 17;
  property WantReturns: WordBool dispid 18;
  property WantTabs: WordBool dispid 19;
  property WordWrap: WordBool dispid 20;
  function GetControlsAlignment: TxAlignment; dispid 21;
  procedure Clear; dispid 22;
  procedure ClearSelection; dispid 23;
  procedure CopyToClipboard; dispid 24;
  procedure CutToClipboard; dispid 25;
  procedure PasteFromClipboard; dispid 27;
  procedure Undo; dispid 28;
  procedure ClearUndo; dispid 29;
  procedure SelectAll; dispid 31;
  property CanUndo: WordBool readonly dispid 33;
  property Modified: WordBool dispid 34;
  property SelLength: Integer dispid 35;
  property SelStart: Integer dispid 36;
  property SelText: WideString dispid 37;
  property Text: WideString dispid -517;
  property DoubleBuffered: WordBool dispid 39;
  procedure FlipChildren(AllLevels: WordBool); dispid 40;
  function DrawTextBiDiModeFlags(Flags: Integer): Integer; dispid 43;
  function DrawTextBiDiModeFlagsReadingOnly: Integer; dispid 44;
  procedure InitiateAction; dispid 46;
  function IsRightToLeft: WordBool; dispid 47;
  function UseRightToLeftAlignment: WordBool; dispid 52;
  function UseRightToLeftReading: WordBool; dispid 53;
  function UseRightToLeftScrollBar: WordBool; dispid 54;
  property Cursor: Smallint dispid 55;
  function ClassNameIs(const Name: WideString): WordBool; dispid 59;
```

25

CREATING
ACTIVEX
CONTROLS

continues

LISTING 25.2. CONTINUED

```
    procedure AboutBox; dispid -552;
  end;

// ********************************************************************//
// DispIntf:   IMemoXEvents
// Flags:      (0)
// GUID:       {0DB46872-09C5-11D2-AE5C-00A024E3867F}
// ********************************************************************//
  IMemoXEvents = dispinterface
    ['{0DB46872-09C5-11D2-AE5C-00A024E3867F}']
    procedure OnChange; dispid 1;
    procedure OnClick; dispid 2;
    procedure OnDblClick; dispid 3;
    procedure OnKeyPress(var Key: Smallint); dispid 9;
  end;


// ********************************************************************//
// OLE Control Proxy class declaration
// Control Name     : TMemoX
// Help String      : MemoX Control
// Default Interface: IMemoX
// Def. Intf. DISP? : No
// Event   Interface: IMemoXEvents
// TypeFlags        : (34) CanCreate Control
// ********************************************************************//
  TMemoXOnKeyPress = procedure(Sender: TObject; var Key: Smallint) of object;

  TMemoX = class(TOleControl)
  private
    FOnChange: TNotifyEvent;
    FOnClick: TNotifyEvent;
    FOnDblClick: TNotifyEvent;
    FOnKeyPress: TMemoXOnKeyPress;
    FIntf: IMemoX;
    function  GetControlInterface: IMemoX;
  protected
    procedure CreateControl;
    procedure InitControlData; override;
  public
    function GetControlsAlignment(out Value: TxAlignment): TxAlignment;
    procedure Clear;
    procedure ClearSelection;
    procedure CopyToClipboard;
    procedure CutToClipboard;
    procedure PasteFromClipboard;
    procedure Undo;
    procedure ClearUndo;
    procedure SelectAll;
```

```
procedure FlipChildren(AllLevels: WordBool);
function DrawTextBiDiModeFlags(Flags: Integer; out Value: Integer):
  Integer;
function DrawTextBiDiModeFlagsReadingOnly(out Value: Integer): Integer;
procedure InitiateAction;
function IsRightToLeft(out Value: WordBool): WordBool;
function UseRightToLeftAlignment(out Value: WordBool): WordBool;
function UseRightToLeftReading(out Value: WordBool): WordBool;
function UseRightToLeftScrollBar(out Value: WordBool): WordBool;
function ClassNameIs(const Name: WideString; out Value: WordBool):
  WordBool;
procedure AboutBox;
property  ControlInterface: IMemoX read GetControlInterface;
property CanUndo: WordBool index 33 read GetWordBoolProp;
property Modified: WordBool index 34 read GetWordBoolProp
  write SetWordBoolProp;
property SelLength: Integer index 35 read GetIntegerProp
  write SetIntegerProp;
property SelStart: Integer index 36 read GetIntegerProp
  write SetIntegerProp;
property SelText: WideString index 37 read GetWideStringProp
  write SetWideStringProp;
property Text: WideString index -517 read GetWideStringProp
  write SetWideStringProp;
property DoubleBuffered: WordBool index 39 read GetWordBoolProp
  write SetWordBoolProp;
published
  property Alignment: TOleEnum index 1 read GetTOleEnumProp
    write SetTOleEnumProp stored False;
  property BiDiMode: TOleEnum index 2 read GetTOleEnumProp
    write SetTOleEnumProp stored False;
  property BorderStyle: TOleEnum index 3 read GetTOleEnumProp
    write SetTOleEnumProp stored False;
  property Color: TColor index -501 read GetTColorProp
    write SetTColorProp stored False;
  property Ctl3D: WordBool index 4 read GetWordBoolProp
    write SetWordBoolProp stored False;
  property DragCursor: Smallint index 5 read GetSmallintProp
    write SetSmallintProp stored False;
  property DragMode: TOleEnum index 6 read GetTOleEnumProp
    write SetTOleEnumProp stored False;
  property Enabled: WordBool index -514 read GetWordBoolProp
    write SetWordBoolProp stored False;
  property Font: TFont index -512 read GetTFontProp write SetTFontProp
    stored False;
  property HideSelection: WordBool index 7 read GetWordBoolProp
    write SetWordBoolProp stored False;
  property ImeMode: TOleEnum index 8 read GetTOleEnumProp
    write SetTOleEnumProp stored False;
  property ImeName: WideString index 9 read GetWideStringProp
    write SetWideStringProp stored False;
```

25

CREATING
ACTIVEX
CONTROLS

continues

LISTING 25.2. CONTINUED

```
      property MaxLength: Integer index 10 read GetIntegerProp
        write SetIntegerProp stored False;
      property OEMConvert: WordBool index 11 read GetWordBoolProp
        write SetWordBoolProp stored False;
      property ParentColor: WordBool index 12 read GetWordBoolProp
        write SetWordBoolProp stored False;
      property ParentCtl3D: WordBool index 13 read GetWordBoolProp
        write SetWordBoolProp stored False;
      property ParentFont: WordBool index 14 read GetWordBoolProp
        write SetWordBoolProp stored False;
      property ReadOnly: WordBool index 15 read GetWordBoolProp
        write SetWordBoolProp stored False;
      property ScrollBars: TOleEnum index 16 read GetTOleEnumProp
        write SetTOleEnumProp stored False;
      property Visible: WordBool index 17 read GetWordBoolProp
        write SetWordBoolProp stored False;
      property WantReturns: WordBool index 18 read GetWordBoolProp
        write SetWordBoolProp stored False;
      property WantTabs: WordBool index 19 read GetWordBoolProp
        write SetWordBoolProp stored False;
      property WordWrap: WordBool index 20 read GetWordBoolProp
        write SetWordBoolProp stored False;
      property Cursor: Smallint index 55 read GetSmallintProp
        write SetSmallintProp stored False;
      property OnChange: TNotifyEvent read FOnChange write FOnChange;
      property OnClick: TNotifyEvent read FOnClick write FOnClick;
      property OnDblClick: TNotifyEvent read FOnDblClick write FOnDblClick;
      property OnKeyPress: TMemoXOnKeyPress read FOnKeyPress write FOnKeyPress;
    end;

procedure Register;

implementation

uses ComObj;

procedure TMemoX.InitControlData;
const
  CEventDispIDs: array [0..3] of DWORD = (
    $00000001, $00000002, $00000003, $00000009);
  CTFontIDs: array [0..0] of DWORD = (
    $FFFFFE00);
  CControlData: TControlData = (
    ClassID: '{0DB46874-09C5-11D2-AE5C-00A024E3867F}';
    EventIID: '{0DB46872-09C5-11D2-AE5C-00A024E3867F}';
    EventCount: 4;
    EventDispIDs: @CEventDispIDs;
    LicenseKey: nil;
    Flags: $0000002D;
```

```
    Version: 300;
    FontCount: 1;
    FontIDs: @CTFontIDs);
begin
  ControlData := @CControlData;
end;

procedure TMemoX.CreateControl;

  procedure DoCreate;
  begin
    FIntf := IUnknown(OleObject) as IMemoX;
  end;

begin
  if FIntf = nil then DoCreate;
end;

function TMemoX.GetControlInterface: IMemoX;
begin
  CreateControl;
  Result := FIntf;
end;

function TMemoX.GetControlsAlignment(out Value: TxAlignment): TxAlignment;
begin
  Result := ControlInterface.GetControlsAlignment;
end;

procedure TMemoX.Clear;
begin
  ControlInterface.Clear;
end;

procedure TMemoX.ClearSelection;
begin
  ControlInterface.ClearSelection;
end;

procedure TMemoX.CopyToClipboard;
begin
  ControlInterface.CopyToClipboard;
end;

procedure TMemoX.CutToClipboard;
begin
  ControlInterface.CutToClipboard;
end;

procedure TMemoX.PasteFromClipboard;
```

25

CREATING
ACTIVEX
CONTROLS

continues

LISTING 25.2. CONTINUED

```
begin
  ControlInterface.PasteFromClipboard;
end;

procedure TMemoX.Undo;
begin
  ControlInterface.Undo;
end;

procedure TMemoX.ClearUndo;
begin
  ControlInterface.ClearUndo;
end;

procedure TMemoX.SelectAll;
begin
  ControlInterface.SelectAll;
end;

procedure TMemoX.FlipChildren(AllLevels: WordBool);
begin
  ControlInterface.FlipChildren(AllLevels);
end;

function TMemoX.DrawTextBiDiModeFlags(Flags: Integer; out Value: Integer):
➡Integer;
begin
  Result := ControlInterface.DrawTextBiDiModeFlags(Flags);
end;

function TMemoX.DrawTextBiDiModeFlagsReadingOnly(out Value: Integer): Integer;
begin
  Result := ControlInterface.DrawTextBiDiModeFlagsReadingOnly;
end;

procedure TMemoX.InitiateAction;
begin
  ControlInterface.InitiateAction;
end;

function TMemoX.IsRightToLeft(out Value: WordBool): WordBool;
begin
  Result := ControlInterface.IsRightToLeft;
end;

function TMemoX.UseRightToLeftAlignment(out Value: WordBool): WordBool;
begin
  Result := ControlInterface.UseRightToLeftAlignment;
end;
```

```
function TMemoX.UseRightToLeftReading(out Value: WordBool): WordBool;
begin
  Result := ControlInterface.UseRightToLeftReading;
end;

function TMemoX.UseRightToLeftScrollBar(out Value: WordBool): WordBool;
begin
  Result := ControlInterface.UseRightToLeftScrollBar;
end;

function TMemoX.ClassNameIs(const Name: WideString; out Value: WordBool):
WordBool;
begin
  Result := ControlInterface.ClassNameIs(Name);
end;

procedure TMemoX.AboutBox;
begin
  ControlInterface.AboutBox;
end;

procedure Register;
begin
  RegisterComponents('ActiveX',[TMemoX]);
end;

end.
```

> **NOTE**
>
> If you examine the code in Listing 25.2 carefully, you'll notice that, in addition to type library information, `Memo_TLB.pas` also contains a class called `TMemoX`, which is the `TOleControl` wrapper for the ActiveX control. This enables you to add a Delphi-created ActiveX control to the palette simply by adding the generated *xxx_TLB* unit to a design package.

LISTING 25.3. THE IMPLEMENTATION FILE, `MemoImpl.pas`.

```
unit MemoImpl;

interface

uses
  Windows, ActiveX, Classes, Controls, Graphics, Menus, Forms, StdCtrls,
  ComServ, StdVCL, AXCtrls, Memo_TLB;
```

continues

25

LISTING 25.3. CONTINUED

```
type
  TMemoX = class(TActiveXControl, IMemoX)
  private
    { Private declarations }
    FDelphiControl: TMemo;
    FEvents: IMemoXEvents;
    procedure ChangeEvent(Sender: TObject);
    procedure ClickEvent(Sender: TObject);
    procedure DblClickEvent(Sender: TObject);
    procedure KeyPressEvent(Sender: TObject; var Key: Char);
  protected
    { Protected declarations }
    procedure DefinePropertyPages(DefinePropertyPage:
      TDefinePropertyPage); override;
    procedure EventSinkChanged(const EventSink: IUnknown); override;
    procedure InitializeControl; override;
    function ClassNameIs(const Name: WideString): WordBool; safecall;
    function DrawTextBiDiModeFlags(Flags: Integer): Integer; safecall;
    function DrawTextBiDiModeFlagsReadingOnly: Integer; safecall;
    function Get_Alignment: TxAlignment; safecall;
    function Get_BiDiMode: TxBiDiMode; safecall;
    function Get_BorderStyle: TxBorderStyle; safecall;
    function Get_CanUndo: WordBool; safecall;
    function Get_Color: OLE_COLOR; safecall;
    function Get_Ctl3D: WordBool; safecall;
    function Get_Cursor: Smallint; safecall;
    function Get_DoubleBuffered: WordBool; safecall;
    function Get_DragCursor: Smallint; safecall;
    function Get_DragMode: TxDragMode; safecall;
    function Get_Enabled: WordBool; safecall;
    function Get_Font: IFontDisp; safecall;
    function Get_HideSelection: WordBool; safecall;
    function Get_ImeMode: TxImeMode; safecall;
    function Get_ImeName: WideString; safecall;
    function Get_MaxLength: Integer; safecall;
    function Get_Modified: WordBool; safecall;
    function Get_OEMConvert: WordBool; safecall;
    function Get_ParentColor: WordBool; safecall;
    function Get_ParentCtl3D: WordBool; safecall;
    function Get_ParentFont: WordBool; safecall;
    function Get_ReadOnly: WordBool; safecall;
    function Get_ScrollBars: TxScrollStyle; safecall;
    function Get_SelLength: Integer; safecall;
    function Get_SelStart: Integer; safecall;
    function Get_SelText: WideString; safecall;
    function Get_Text: WideString; safecall;
    function Get_Visible: WordBool; safecall;
    function Get_WantReturns: WordBool; safecall;
```

```
      function Get_WantTabs: WordBool; safecall;
      function Get_WordWrap: WordBool; safecall;
      function GetControlsAlignment: TxAlignment; safecall;
      function IsRightToLeft: WordBool; safecall;
      function UseRightToLeftAlignment: WordBool; safecall;
      function UseRightToLeftReading: WordBool; safecall;
      function UseRightToLeftScrollBar: WordBool; safecall;
      procedure _Set_Font(const Value: IFontDisp); safecall;
      procedure AboutBox; safecall;
      procedure Clear; safecall;
      procedure ClearSelection; safecall;
      procedure ClearUndo; safecall;
      procedure CopyToClipboard; safecall;
      procedure CutToClipboard; safecall;
      procedure FlipChildren(AllLevels: WordBool); safecall;
      procedure InitiateAction; safecall;
      procedure PasteFromClipboard; safecall;
      procedure SelectAll; safecall;
      procedure Set_Alignment(Value: TxAlignment); safecall;
      procedure Set_BiDiMode(Value: TxBiDiMode); safecall;
      procedure Set_BorderStyle(Value: TxBorderStyle); safecall;
      procedure Set_Color(Value: OLE_COLOR); safecall;
      procedure Set_Ctl3D(Value: WordBool); safecall;
      procedure Set_Cursor(Value: Smallint); safecall;
      procedure Set_DoubleBuffered(Value: WordBool); safecall;
      procedure Set_DragCursor(Value: Smallint); safecall;
      procedure Set_DragMode(Value: TxDragMode); safecall;
      procedure Set_Enabled(Value: WordBool); safecall;
      procedure Set_Font(var Value: IFontDisp); safecall;
      procedure Set_HideSelection(Value: WordBool); safecall;
      procedure Set_ImeMode(Value: TxImeMode); safecall;
      procedure Set_ImeName(const Value: WideString); safecall;
      procedure Set_MaxLength(Value: Integer); safecall;
      procedure Set_Modified(Value: WordBool); safecall;
      procedure Set_OEMConvert(Value: WordBool); safecall;
      procedure Set_ParentColor(Value: WordBool); safecall;
      procedure Set_ParentCtl3D(Value: WordBool); safecall;
      procedure Set_ParentFont(Value: WordBool); safecall;
      procedure Set_ReadOnly(Value: WordBool); safecall;
      procedure Set_ScrollBars(Value: TxScrollStyle); safecall;
      procedure Set_SelLength(Value: Integer); safecall;
      procedure Set_SelStart(Value: Integer); safecall;
      procedure Set_SelText(const Value: WideString); safecall;
      procedure Set_Text(const Value: WideString); safecall;
      procedure Set_Visible(Value: WordBool); safecall;
      procedure Set_WantReturns(Value: WordBool); safecall;
      procedure Set_WantTabs(Value: WordBool); safecall;
      procedure Set_WordWrap(Value: WordBool); safecall;
      procedure Undo; safecall;
  end;
```

25

CREATING ACTIVEX CONTROLS

continues

LISTING 25.3. CONTINUED

```
implementation

uses ComObj, About;

{ TMemoX }

procedure TMemoX.DefinePropertyPages(DefinePropertyPage:
➥TDefinePropertyPage);
begin
  { Define property pages here.  Property pages are defined by calling
    DefinePropertyPage with the class id of the page.  For example,
      DefinePropertyPage(Class_MemoXPage); }
end;

procedure TMemoX.EventSinkChanged(const EventSink: IUnknown);
begin
  FEvents := EventSink as IMemoXEvents;
end;

procedure TMemoX.InitializeControl;
begin
  FDelphiControl := Control as TMemo;
  FDelphiControl.OnChange := ChangeEvent;
  FDelphiControl.OnClick := ClickEvent;
  FDelphiControl.OnDblClick := DblClickEvent;
  FDelphiControl.OnKeyPress := KeyPressEvent;
end;

function TMemoX.ClassNameIs(const Name: WideString): WordBool;
begin
  Result := FDelphiControl.ClassNameIs(Name);
end;

function TMemoX.DrawTextBiDiModeFlags(Flags: Integer): Integer;
begin
  Result := FDelphiControl.DrawTextBiDiModeFlags(Flags);
end;

function TMemoX.DrawTextBiDiModeFlagsReadingOnly: Integer;
begin
  Result := FDelphiControl.DrawTextBiDiModeFlagsReadingOnly;
end;

function TMemoX.Get_Alignment: TxAlignment;
begin
  Result := Ord(FDelphiControl.Alignment);
end;

function TMemoX.Get_BiDiMode: TxBiDiMode;
```

```
begin
  Result := Ord(FDelphiControl.BiDiMode);
end;

function TMemoX.Get_BorderStyle: TxBorderStyle;
begin
  Result := Ord(FDelphiControl.BorderStyle);
end;

function TMemoX.Get_CanUndo: WordBool;
begin
  Result := FDelphiControl.CanUndo;
end;

function TMemoX.Get_Color: OLE_COLOR;
begin
  Result := OLE_COLOR(FDelphiControl.Color);
end;

function TMemoX.Get_Ctl3D: WordBool;
begin
  Result := FDelphiControl.Ctl3D;
end;

function TMemoX.Get_Cursor: Smallint;
begin
  Result := Smallint(FDelphiControl.Cursor);
end;

function TMemoX.Get_DoubleBuffered: WordBool;
begin
  Result := FDelphiControl.DoubleBuffered;
end;

function TMemoX.Get_DragCursor: Smallint;
begin
  Result := Smallint(FDelphiControl.DragCursor);
end;

function TMemoX.Get_DragMode: TxDragMode;
begin
  Result := Ord(FDelphiControl.DragMode);
end;

function TMemoX.Get_Enabled: WordBool;
begin
  Result := FDelphiControl.Enabled;
end;
```

continues

25

CREATING
ACTIVEX
CONTROLS

LISTING 25.3. CONTINUED

```
function TMemoX.Get_Font: IFontDisp;
begin
  GetOleFont(FDelphiControl.Font, Result);
end;

function TMemoX.Get_HideSelection: WordBool;
begin
  Result := FDelphiControl.HideSelection;
end;

function TMemoX.Get_ImeMode: TxImeMode;
begin
  Result := Ord(FDelphiControl.ImeMode);
end;

function TMemoX.Get_ImeName: WideString;
begin
  Result := WideString(FDelphiControl.ImeName);
end;

function TMemoX.Get_MaxLength: Integer;
begin
  Result := FDelphiControl.MaxLength;
end;

function TMemoX.Get_Modified: WordBool;
begin
  Result := FDelphiControl.Modified;
end;

function TMemoX.Get_OEMConvert: WordBool;
begin
  Result := FDelphiControl.OEMConvert;
end;

function TMemoX.Get_ParentColor: WordBool;
begin
  Result := FDelphiControl.ParentColor;
end;

function TMemoX.Get_ParentCtl3D: WordBool;
begin
  Result := FDelphiControl.ParentCtl3D;
end;

function TMemoX.Get_ParentFont: WordBool;
begin
  Result := FDelphiControl.ParentFont;
end;
```

```
function TMemoX.Get_ReadOnly: WordBool;
begin
  Result := FDelphiControl.ReadOnly;
end;

function TMemoX.Get_ScrollBars: TxScrollStyle;
begin
  Result := Ord(FDelphiControl.ScrollBars);
end;

function TMemoX.Get_SelLength: Integer;
begin
  Result := FDelphiControl.SelLength;
end;

function TMemoX.Get_SelStart: Integer;
begin
  Result := FDelphiControl.SelStart;
end;

function TMemoX.Get_SelText: WideString;
begin
  Result := WideString(FDelphiControl.SelText);
end;

function TMemoX.Get_Text: WideString;
begin
  Result := WideString(FDelphiControl.Text);
end;

function TMemoX.Get_Visible: WordBool;
begin
  Result := FDelphiControl.Visible;
end;

function TMemoX.Get_WantReturns: WordBool;
begin
  Result := FDelphiControl.WantReturns;
end;

function TMemoX.Get_WantTabs: WordBool;
begin
  Result := FDelphiControl.WantTabs;
end;

function TMemoX.Get_WordWrap: WordBool;
begin
  Result := FDelphiControl.WordWrap;
end;
```

25

CREATING
ACTIVEX
CONTROLS

continues

LISTING 25.3. CONTINUED

```
function TMemoX.GetControlsAlignment: TxAlignment;
begin
 Result := TxAlignment(FDelphiControl.GetControlsAlignment);
end;

function TMemoX.IsRightToLeft: WordBool;
begin
  Result := FDelphiControl.IsRightToLeft;
end;

function TMemoX.UseRightToLeftAlignment: WordBool;
begin
  Result := FDelphiControl.UseRightToLeftAlignment;
end;

function TMemoX.UseRightToLeftReading: WordBool;
begin
  Result := FDelphiControl.UseRightToLeftReading;
end;

function TMemoX.UseRightToLeftScrollBar: WordBool;
begin
  Result := FDelphiControl.UseRightToLeftScrollBar;
end;

procedure TMemoX._Set_Font(const Value: IFontDisp);
begin
  SetOleFont(FDelphiControl.Font, Value);
end;

procedure TMemoX.AboutBox;
begin
  ShowMemoXAbout;
end;

procedure TMemoX.Clear;
begin
  FDelphiControl.Clear;
end;

procedure TMemoX.ClearSelection;
begin
  FDelphiControl.ClearSelection;
end;

procedure TMemoX.ClearUndo;
begin
  FDelphiControl.ClearUndo;
end;
```

```
procedure TMemoX.CopyToClipboard;
begin
  FDelphiControl.CopyToClipboard;
end;

procedure TMemoX.CutToClipboard;
begin
  FDelphiControl.CutToClipboard;
end;

procedure TMemoX.FlipChildren(AllLevels: WordBool);
begin
  FDelphiControl.FlipChildren(AllLevels);
end;

procedure TMemoX.InitiateAction;
begin
  FDelphiControl.InitiateAction;
end;

procedure TMemoX.PasteFromClipboard;
begin
  FDelphiControl.PasteFromClipboard;
end;

procedure TMemoX.SelectAll;
begin
  FDelphiControl.SelectAll;
end;

procedure TMemoX.Set_Alignment(Value: TxAlignment);
begin
  FDelphiControl.Alignment := TAlignment(Value);
end;

procedure TMemoX.Set_BiDiMode(Value: TxBiDiMode);
begin
  FDelphiControl.BiDiMode := TBiDiMode(Value);
end;

procedure TMemoX.Set_BorderStyle(Value: TxBorderStyle);
begin
  FDelphiControl.BorderStyle := TBorderStyle(Value);
end;

procedure TMemoX.Set_Color(Value: OLE_COLOR);
begin
  FDelphiControl.Color := TColor(Value);
end;
```

continues

LISTING 25.3. CONTINUED

```
procedure TMemoX.Set_Ctl3D(Value: WordBool);
begin
  FDelphiControl.Ctl3D := Value;
end;

procedure TMemoX.Set_Cursor(Value: Smallint);
begin
  FDelphiControl.Cursor := TCursor(Value);
end;

procedure TMemoX.Set_DoubleBuffered(Value: WordBool);
begin
  FDelphiControl.DoubleBuffered := Value;
end;

procedure TMemoX.Set_DragCursor(Value: Smallint);
begin
  FDelphiControl.DragCursor := TCursor(Value);
end;

procedure TMemoX.Set_DragMode(Value: TxDragMode);
begin
  FDelphiControl.DragMode := TDragMode(Value);
end;

procedure TMemoX.Set_Enabled(Value: WordBool);
begin
  FDelphiControl.Enabled := Value;
end;

procedure TMemoX.Set_Font(var Value: IFontDisp);
begin
  SetOleFont(FDelphiControl.Font, Value);
end;

procedure TMemoX.Set_HideSelection(Value: WordBool);
begin
  FDelphiControl.HideSelection := Value;
end;

procedure TMemoX.Set_ImeMode(Value: TxImeMode);
begin
  FDelphiControl.ImeMode := TImeMode(Value);
end;

procedure TMemoX.Set_ImeName(const Value: WideString);
begin
  FDelphiControl.ImeName := TImeName(Value);
end;
```

```
procedure TMemoX.Set_MaxLength(Value: Integer);
begin
  FDelphiControl.MaxLength := Value;
end;

procedure TMemoX.Set_Modified(Value: WordBool);
begin
  FDelphiControl.Modified := Value;
end;

procedure TMemoX.Set_OEMConvert(Value: WordBool);
begin
  FDelphiControl.OEMConvert := Value;
end;

procedure TMemoX.Set_ParentColor(Value: WordBool);
begin
  FDelphiControl.ParentColor := Value;
end;

procedure TMemoX.Set_ParentCtl3D(Value: WordBool);
begin
  FDelphiControl.ParentCtl3D := Value;
end;

procedure TMemoX.Set_ParentFont(Value: WordBool);
begin
  FDelphiControl.ParentFont := Value;
end;

procedure TMemoX.Set_ReadOnly(Value: WordBool);
begin
  FDelphiControl.ReadOnly := Value;
end;

procedure TMemoX.Set_ScrollBars(Value: TxScrollStyle);
begin
  FDelphiControl.ScrollBars := TScrollStyle(Value);
end;

procedure TMemoX.Set_SelLength(Value: Integer);
begin
  FDelphiControl.SelLength := Value;
end;

procedure TMemoX.Set_SelStart(Value: Integer);
begin
  FDelphiControl.SelStart := Value;
end;
```

continues

25

CREATING ACTIVEX CONTROLS

LISTING 25.3. CONTINUED

```pascal
procedure TMemoX.Set_SelText(const Value: WideString);
begin
  FDelphiControl.SelText := String(Value);
end;

procedure TMemoX.Set_Text(const Value: WideString);
begin
  FDelphiControl.Text := TCaption(Value);
end;

procedure TMemoX.Set_Visible(Value: WordBool);
begin
  FDelphiControl.Visible := Value;
end;

procedure TMemoX.Set_WantReturns(Value: WordBool);
begin
  FDelphiControl.WantReturns := Value;
end;

procedure TMemoX.Set_WantTabs(Value: WordBool);
begin
  FDelphiControl.WantTabs := Value;
end;

procedure TMemoX.Set_WordWrap(Value: WordBool);
begin
  FDelphiControl.WordWrap := Value;
end;

procedure TMemoX.Undo;
begin
  FDelphiControl.Undo;
end;

procedure TMemoX.ChangeEvent(Sender: TObject);
begin
  if FEvents <> nil then FEvents.OnChange;
end;

procedure TMemoX.ClickEvent(Sender: TObject);
begin
  if FEvents <> nil then FEvents.OnClick;
end;

procedure TMemoX.DblClickEvent(Sender: TObject);
begin
  if FEvents <> nil then FEvents.OnDblClick;
end;
```

```
procedure TMemoX.KeyPressEvent(Sender: TObject; var Key: Char);
var
  TempKey: Smallint;
begin
  TempKey := Smallint(Key);
  if FEvents <> nil then FEvents.OnKeyPress(TempKey);
  Key := Char(TempKey);
end;

initialization
  TActiveXControlFactory.Create(
    ComServer,
    TMemoX,
    TMemo,
    Class_MemoX,
    1,
    ' ',
    0,
    tmApartment);
end.
```

There's no doubt that Listings 25.1 through 25.3 contain a lot of code. Sometimes the sheer volume of code can make something appear daunting and difficult; however, if you look closely you'll see that there isn't any rocket science going on in these files. What's pretty nifty is that you now have a fully functional ActiveX control (including interface, type library, events) based on a memo control, and you're yet to write a line of code!

Note the helper functions that are used to convert back and forth between properties of IStrings and IFont to the native Delphi TStrings and TFont types. Each of these routines operates in a similar manner: They provide a bridge between an Object Pascal class and an Automation-compatible dispatch interface. Table 25.1 shows a list of VCL classes and their automation interface equivalents.

TABLE 25.1. VCL CLASSES AND THEIR CORRESPONDING AUTOMATION INTERFACES.

VCL Class	Automation Interface
TFont	IFont
TPicture	IPicture
TStrings	IStrings

> **NOTE**
>
> ActiveX defines the `IFont` and `IPicture` interfaces. However, the `IStrings` type is defined in VCL. Delphi provides a redistributable file named `StdVcl40.dll` that contains the type library that defines this interface. This library must be installed and registered on client machines in order for applications using an ActiveX control with `IStrings` properties to function properly.

The ActiveX Framework

The Delphi ActiveX framework (or DAX, for short) resides in the `AxCtrls` unit. An ActiveX control could be described as an Automation object on steroids, because it must implement the `IDispatch` interface (in addition to many others). Because of this fact, the DAX framework is similar to that of Automation objects, which you learned about in Chapter 23. `TActiveXControl` is a `TAutoObject` descendant that implements the interfaces required of an ActiveX control. The DAX framework works as a dual-object framework, where the ActiveX control portion contained in `TActiveXControl` communicates with a separate `TWinControl` class that contains the VCL control.

Like all COM objects, ActiveX controls are created from factories. DAX's `TActiveXControlFactory` serves as the factory for the `TActiveXControl` object. An instance of one of these factories is created in the `initialization` section of each control implementation file. The constructor for this class is defined as follows:

```
constructor TActiveXControlFactory.Create(ComServer: TComServerObject;
  ActiveXControlClass: TActiveXControlClass;
  WinControlClass: TWinControlClass; const ClassID: TGUID;
  ToolboxBitmapID: Integer; const LicStr: string; MiscStatus: Integer;
  ThreadingModel: TThreadingModel = tmSingle);
```

`ComServer` holds an instance of `TComServer`. Generally, the `ComServer` global declared in the `ComServ` unit is passed in this parameter.

`ActiveXControlClass` contains the name of the `TActiveXControl` descendant that's declared in the implementation file.

`WinControlClass` contains the name of the VCL `TWinControl` descendent that you want to encapsulate as an ActiveX control.

`ClassID` holds the CLSID of the control coclass as listed in the type library editor.

`ToolboxBitmapID` contains the resource identifier of the bitmap that should be used as the control's representation on the Component Palette.

LicStr holds the string that should be used as the control's license key string. If this is empty, the control is not licensed.

MiscStatus holds the OLEMISC_*XXX* status flags for the control. These flags are defined in the ActiveX unit. These OLEMISC flags are entered into the System Registry when the ActiveX control is registered. OLEMISC flags provide ActiveX control containers with information regarding various attributes of the ActiveX control. For example, there are OLEMISC flags that indicate how a control is painted or whether a control can contain other controls. These flags are fully documented in the Microsoft Developer's Network under the topic OLEMISC.

Finally, ThreadingModel identifies the threading model that this control will be registered as supporting. It's important to note that setting this parameter to some particular threading model doesn't guarantee that your control is safer for that particular model; it only affects how the control is registered. Building in thread safety is up to you as the developer. See Chapter 23 for a discussion of each of the threading models.

Simple Frame Controls

One of the OLEMISC_*XXX* flags is OLEMISC_SIMPLEFRAME, which will automatically be added if csAcceptsControls is included in the VCL control's ControlStyle set. This makes the ActiveX control a simple frame control capable of containing other ActiveX controls in an ActiveX container application. The TActiveXControl class contains the necessary message-handling infrastructure to make simple frame controls work correctly. Occasionally, the wizard will add this flag to a control that you do not wish to serve as a simple frame; in this case, it's okay to remove the flag from the class factory constructor call.

The Reflector Window

Some VCL controls require notification messages in order to properly function. For this purpose, DAX will create a reflector window whose job is to receive messages and forward them on to the VCL control. Standard VCL controls that require a reflector window will have the csReflector member included in their ControlStyle set. If you have a custom TWinControl that operates using notification messages, you should be sure to add this member to the ControlStyle set in the control's constructor.

Design Time Versus Runtime

VCL provides a simple means for determining whether a control is currently in design mode or run mode—by checking for the csDesigning member in the ComponentState set. Although you can make this distinction for ActiveX controls, it's not so straightforward.

It involves obtaining a pointer to the container's `IAmbientDispatch` dispinterface and checking the `UserMode` property on that dispinterface. You can use the following function for this purpose:

```
function IsControlRunning(Control: IUnknown): Boolean;
var
  OleObj: IOleObject;
  Site: IOleClientSite;
begin
  Result := True;
  // Get control's IOleObject pointer.  From that, get container's
  // IOleClientSite.  From that, get IAmbientDispatch.
  if (Control.QueryInterface(IOleObject, OleObj) = S_OK) and
    (OleObj.GetClientSite(Site) = S_OK) and (Site <> nil) then
    Result := (Site as IAmbientDispatch).UserMode;
end;
```

Control Licensing

We mentioned earlier in this chapter that the default DAX scheme for licensing involves an LIC file that should accompany the ActiveX control OCX file on development machines. As you saw earlier, the license string is one of the parameters to the ActiveX control's class factory constructor. When Include Design-Time License is selected in the wizard, this option will generate a GUID string that will be inserted into both the constructor call and the LIC file. (You're free to modify the string later if you so choose.) When the control is used at design time in a development tool, DAX will attempt to match the license string in the class factory with a string in the LIC file. If a match occurs, the control instance will be created. When an application that includes the licensed ActiveX control is compiled, the license string is embedded in the application, and the LIC file is not required to run the application.

The LIC file scheme for licensing is not the only one under the sun. For example, some developers find the use of an additional file cumbersome and prefer to store a license key in the Registry. Fortunately, DAX makes it very easy to implement an alternative licensing scheme such as this. The license check occurs in a `TActiveXControlFactory` method called `HasMachineLicense()`. By default, this method attempts to look up the licensing string in the LIC file, but you can have this method perform whatever check you wish to determine licensing. For example, Listing 25.4 shows a `TActiveXControlFactory` descendent that looks in the Registry for the license key.

LISTING 25.4. AN ALTERNATIVE SCHEME FOR LICENSING.

```
{ TRegLicAxControlFactory }

type
  TRegLicActiveXControlFactory = class(TActiveXControlFactory)
  protected
```

```
    function HasMachineLicense: Boolean; override;
  end;

function TRegLicActiveXControlFactory.HasMachineLicense: Boolean;
var
  Reg: TRegistry;
begin
  Result := True;
  if not SupportsLicensing then Exit;
  Reg := TRegistry.Create;
  try
    Reg.RootKey := HKEY_CLASSES_ROOT;
    // control is licensed if key is in registry
    Result := Reg.OpenKey('\Licenses\' + LicString, False);
  finally
    Reg.Free;
  end;
end;
```

A Registry file (REG) can be used to place the license key in the Registry on a licensed machine. This is shown in Listing 25.5.

LISTING 25.5. THE LICENSING REG FILE.

```
REGEDIT4

[HKEY_CLASSES_ROOT\Licenses\{C06EFEA0-06B2-11D1-A9BF-B18A9F703311}]
@= "Licensing info for DDG demo ActiveX control"
```

Property Pages

Property pages provide a means for modifying the properties of an ActiveX control through a custom dialog. A control's property pages are added as pages in a tabbed dialog that's created by ActiveX. Property page dialogs are usually invoked from a local right-click menu provided by the control's host container.

Standard Property Pages

DAX provides standard property pages for properties of type IStrings, IPicture, TColor, and IFont. The CLSIDs for these property pages are found in the AxCtrls unit. They are declared as follows:

```
const
  { Delphi property page CLSIDs }
  Class_DColorPropPage: TGUID = '{5CFF5D59-5946-11D0-BDEF-00A024D1875C}';
  Class_DFontPropPage: TGUID = '{5CFF5D5B-5946-11D0-BDEF-00A024D1875C}';
  Class_DPicturePropPage: TGUID = '{5CFF5D5A-5946-11D0-BDEF-00A024D1875C}';
  Class_DStringPropPage: TGUID = '{F42D677E-754B-11D0-BDFB-00A024D1875C}';
```

Using any of these property pages in your control is a simple matter: Just pass one of these CLSIDs to the `DefinePropertyPage()` procedural parameter in the `DefinePropertyPages()` method of your ActiveX control, as shown here:

```
procedure TMemoX.DefinePropertyPages(DefinePropertyPage:
➥TDefinePropertyPage);
begin
  DefinePropertyPage(Class_DColorPropPage);
  DefinePropertyPage(Class_DFontPropPage);
  DefinePropertyPage(Class_DStringPropPage);
end;
```

Figures 25.4 through 25.7 show each of the standard DAX property pages.

FIGURE 25.4.

DAX Colors property page.

FIGURE 25.5.

DAX Fonts property page.

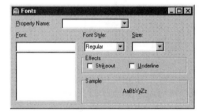

FIGURE 25.6.

DAX Strings property page.

FIGURE 25.7.

DAX Pictures property page.

Each of these property pages operates similarly: The combo box contains the names of each of the properties of the specified type. You just select the property name, set the value in the dialog, and then click OK to modify the selected property.

> **NOTE**
>
> If you want to use the standard DAX property pages, you must distribute `StdVc140.dll` along with your OCX file. As mentioned earlier in this chapter, this file contains the definition for `IStrings` as well as the `IProvider` and `IDataBroker` interfaces. Additionally, `StdVc140.dll` contains the implementation for each of the DAX property pages. You must also ensure that the OCX file and `StdVc140.dll` have been registered on the target machine.

Custom Property Pages

To help illustrate the creation of custom property pages, we'll create a control that's more interesting than the simple `Memo` control we've been working with so far. Listing 25.6 shows the implementation file for the `TCardX` ActiveX control. This control is an encapsulation of the playing card VCL control that comes from the `Cards` unit, which you'll find in the `\Code\Comps` subdirectory of the CD-ROM accompanying this book.

LISTING 25.6. CardImpl.pas.

```
unit CardImpl;

interface

uses
  Windows, ActiveX, Classes, Controls, Graphics, Menus, Forms, StdCtrls,
  ComServ, StdVCL, AXCtrls, AxCard_TLB, Cards;

type
  TCardX = class(TActiveXControl, ICardX)
  private
    { Private declarations }
    FDelphiControl: TCard;
    FEvents: ICardXEvents;
    procedure ClickEvent(Sender: TObject);
    procedure DblClickEvent(Sender: TObject);
    procedure KeyPressEvent(Sender: TObject; var Key: Char);
  protected
    { Protected declarations }
    procedure DefinePropertyPages(DefinePropertyPage:
      TDefinePropertyPage); override;
    procedure EventSinkChanged(const EventSink: IUnknown); override;
    procedure InitializeControl; override;
    function ClassNameIs(const Name: WideString): WordBool; safecall;
    function DrawTextBiDiModeFlags(Flags: Integer): Integer; safecall;
    function DrawTextBiDiModeFlagsReadingOnly: Integer; safecall;
```

continues

LISTING 25.6. CONTINUED

```
  function Get_BackColor: OLE_COLOR; safecall;
  function Get_BiDiMode: TxBiDiMode; safecall;
  function Get_Color: OLE_COLOR; safecall;
  function Get_Cursor: Smallint; safecall;
  function Get_DoubleBuffered: WordBool; safecall;
  function Get_DragCursor: Smallint; safecall;
  function Get_DragMode: TxDragMode; safecall;
  function Get_Enabled: WordBool; safecall;
  function Get_FaceUp: WordBool; safecall;
  function Get_ParentColor: WordBool; safecall;
  function Get_Suit: TxCardSuit; safecall;
  function Get_Value: TxCardValue; safecall;
  function Get_Visible: WordBool; safecall;
  function GetControlsAlignment: TxAlignment; safecall;
  function IsRightToLeft: WordBool; safecall;
  function UseRightToLeftAlignment: WordBool; safecall;
  function UseRightToLeftReading: WordBool; safecall;
  function UseRightToLeftScrollBar: WordBool; safecall;
  procedure FlipChildren(AllLevels: WordBool); safecall;
  procedure InitiateAction; safecall;
  procedure Set_BackColor(Value: OLE_COLOR); safecall;
  procedure Set_BiDiMode(Value: TxBiDiMode); safecall;
  procedure Set_Color(Value: OLE_COLOR); safecall;
  procedure Set_Cursor(Value: Smallint); safecall;
  procedure Set_DoubleBuffered(Value: WordBool); safecall;
  procedure Set_DragCursor(Value: Smallint); safecall;
  procedure Set_DragMode(Value: TxDragMode); safecall;
  procedure Set_Enabled(Value: WordBool); safecall;
  procedure Set_FaceUp(Value: WordBool); safecall;
  procedure Set_ParentColor(Value: WordBool); safecall;
  procedure Set_Suit(Value: TxCardSuit); safecall;
  procedure Set_Value(Value: TxCardValue); safecall;
  procedure Set_Visible(Value: WordBool); safecall;
  procedure AboutBox; safecall;
end;

implementation

uses ComObj, About, CardPP;

{ TCardX }

procedure TCardX.DefinePropertyPages(DefinePropertyPage:
TDefinePropertyPage);
begin
  DefinePropertyPage(Class_DColorPropPage);
  DefinePropertyPage(Class_CardPropPage);
end;
```

```
procedure TCardX.EventSinkChanged(const EventSink: IUnknown);
begin
  FEvents := EventSink as ICardXEvents;
end;

procedure TCardX.InitializeControl;
begin
  FDelphiControl := Control as TCard;
  FDelphiControl.OnClick := ClickEvent;
  FDelphiControl.OnDblClick := DblClickEvent;
  FDelphiControl.OnKeyPress := KeyPressEvent;
end;

function TCardX.ClassNameIs(const Name: WideString): WordBool;
begin
  Result := FDelphiControl.ClassNameIs(Name);
end;

function TCardX.DrawTextBiDiModeFlags(Flags: Integer): Integer;
begin
  Result := FDelphiControl.DrawTextBiDiModeFlags(Flags);
end;

function TCardX.DrawTextBiDiModeFlagsReadingOnly: Integer;
begin
  Result := FDelphiControl.DrawTextBiDiModeFlagsReadingOnly;
end;

function TCardX.Get_BackColor: OLE_COLOR;
begin
  Result := OLE_COLOR(FDelphiControl.BackColor);
end;

function TCardX.Get_BiDiMode: TxBiDiMode;
begin
  Result := Ord(FDelphiControl.BiDiMode);
end;

function TCardX.Get_Color: OLE_COLOR;
begin
  Result := OLE_COLOR(FDelphiControl.Color);
end;

function TCardX.Get_Cursor: Smallint;
begin
  Result := Smallint(FDelphiControl.Cursor);
end;
```

continues

25

CREATING
ACTIVEX
CONTROLS

Listing 25.6. CONTINUED

```
function TCardX.Get_DoubleBuffered: WordBool;
begin
  Result := FDelphiControl.DoubleBuffered;
end;

function TCardX.Get_DragCursor: Smallint;
begin
  Result := Smallint(FDelphiControl.DragCursor);
end;

function TCardX.Get_DragMode: TxDragMode;
begin
  Result := Ord(FDelphiControl.DragMode);
end;

function TCardX.Get_Enabled: WordBool;
begin
  Result := FDelphiControl.Enabled;
end;

function TCardX.Get_FaceUp: WordBool;
begin
  Result := FDelphiControl.FaceUp;
end;

function TCardX.Get_ParentColor: WordBool;
begin
  Result := FDelphiControl.ParentColor;
end;

function TCardX.Get_Suit: TxCardSuit;
begin
  Result := Ord(FDelphiControl.Suit);
end;

function TCardX.Get_Value: TxCardValue;
begin
  Result := Ord(FDelphiControl.Value);
end;

function TCardX.Get_Visible: WordBool;
begin
  Result := FDelphiControl.Visible;
end;
```

```
function TCardX.GetControlsAlignment: TxAlignment;
begin
 Result := TxAlignment(FDelphiControl.GetControlsAlignment);
end;

function TCardX.IsRightToLeft: WordBool;
begin
  Result := FDelphiControl.IsRightToLeft;
end;

function TCardX.UseRightToLeftAlignment: WordBool;
begin
  Result := FDelphiControl.UseRightToLeftAlignment;
end;

function TCardX.UseRightToLeftReading: WordBool;
begin
  Result := FDelphiControl.UseRightToLeftReading;
end;

function TCardX.UseRightToLeftScrollBar: WordBool;
begin
  Result := FDelphiControl.UseRightToLeftScrollBar;
end;

procedure TCardX.FlipChildren(AllLevels: WordBool);
begin
  FDelphiControl.FlipChildren(AllLevels);
end;

procedure TCardX.InitiateAction;
begin
  FDelphiControl.InitiateAction;
end;

procedure TCardX.Set_BackColor(Value: OLE_COLOR);
begin
  FDelphiControl.BackColor := TColor(Value);
end;

procedure TCardX.Set_BiDiMode(Value: TxBiDiMode);
begin
  FDelphiControl.BiDiMode := TBiDiMode(Value);
end;

procedure TCardX.Set_Color(Value: OLE_COLOR);
```

continues

25

LISTING 25.6. CONTINUED

```
begin
  FDelphiControl.Color := TColor(Value);
end;

procedure TCardX.Set_Cursor(Value: Smallint);
begin
  FDelphiControl.Cursor := TCursor(Value);
end;

procedure TCardX.Set_DoubleBuffered(Value: WordBool);
begin
  FDelphiControl.DoubleBuffered := Value;
end;

procedure TCardX.Set_DragCursor(Value: Smallint);
begin
  FDelphiControl.DragCursor := TCursor(Value);
end;

procedure TCardX.Set_DragMode(Value: TxDragMode);
begin
  FDelphiControl.DragMode := TDragMode(Value);
end;

procedure TCardX.Set_Enabled(Value: WordBool);
begin
  FDelphiControl.Enabled := Value;
end;

procedure TCardX.Set_FaceUp(Value: WordBool);
begin
  FDelphiControl.FaceUp := Value;
end;

procedure TCardX.Set_ParentColor(Value: WordBool);
begin
  FDelphiControl.ParentColor := Value;
end;

procedure TCardX.Set_Suit(Value: TxCardSuit);
begin
  FDelphiControl.Suit := TCardSuit(Value);
end;

procedure TCardX.Set_Value(Value: TxCardValue);
```

```
begin
  FDelphiControl.Value := TCardValue(Value);
end;

procedure TCardX.Set_Visible(Value: WordBool);
begin
  FDelphiControl.Visible := Value;
end;

procedure TCardX.ClickEvent(Sender: TObject);
begin
  if FEvents <> nil then FEvents.OnClick;
end;

procedure TCardX.DblClickEvent(Sender: TObject);
begin
  if FEvents <> nil then FEvents.OnDblClick;
end;

procedure TCardX.KeyPressEvent(Sender: TObject; var Key: Char);
var
  TempKey: Smallint;
begin
  TempKey := Smallint(Key);
  if FEvents <> nil then FEvents.OnKeyPress(TempKey);
  Key := Char(TempKey);
end;

procedure TCardX.AboutBox;
begin
  ShowCardXAbout;
end;

initialization
  TActiveXControlFactory.Create(ComServer, TCardX, TCard, Class_CardX,
    1, '', 0, tmApartment);
end.
```

This unit is essentially what was generated by the wizard, except for the two lines of code shown in the `DefinePropertyPages()` method. In this method, you can see that we employ the standard VCL Color property page in addition to a custom property page whose CLSID is defined as `Class_CardPropPage`. This property page was created by selecting the Property Page item from the ActiveX page of the New Items dialog. Figure 25.8 shows this property page in the Form Designer, and Listing 25.7 shows the source code for this property page.

25

FIGURE 25.8.

A property page in the Form Designer.

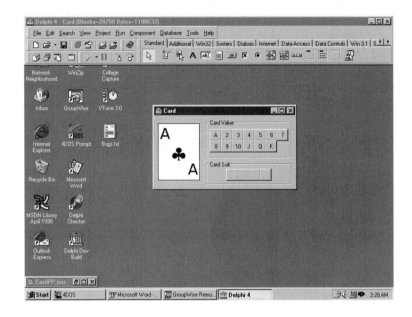

LISTING 25.7. THE PROPERTY PAGE UNIT, CardPP.pas.

```
unit CardPP;

interface

uses SysUtils, Windows, Messages, Classes, Graphics, Controls, StdCtrls,
  ExtCtrls, Forms, ComServ, ComObj, StdVcl, AxCtrls, Buttons, Cards,
  AxCard_TLB;

type
  TCardPropPage = class(TPropertyPage)
    Card1: TCard;
    ValueGroup: TGroupBox;
    SpeedButton1: TSpeedButton;
    SpeedButton2: TSpeedButton;
    SpeedButton3: TSpeedButton;
    SpeedButton4: TSpeedButton;
    SpeedButton5: TSpeedButton;
    SpeedButton6: TSpeedButton;
    SpeedButton7: TSpeedButton;
    SpeedButton8: TSpeedButton;
    SpeedButton9: TSpeedButton;
    SpeedButton10: TSpeedButton;
    SpeedButton11: TSpeedButton;
    SpeedButton12: TSpeedButton;
    SuitGroup: TGroupBox;
    SpeedButton13: TSpeedButton;
```

```
      SpeedButton14: TSpeedButton;
      SpeedButton15: TSpeedButton;
      SpeedButton16: TSpeedButton;
      SpeedButton17: TSpeedButton;
      procedure FormCreate(Sender: TObject);
      procedure SpeedButton1Click(Sender: TObject);
    protected
      procedure UpdatePropertyPage; override;
      procedure UpdateObject; override;
    end;

const
  Class_CardPropPage: TGUID = '{C06EFEA1-06B2-11D1-A9BF-B18A9F703311}';

implementation

{$R *.DFM}

procedure TCardPropPage.UpdatePropertyPage;
var
  i: Integer;
  AValue, ASuit: Integer;
begin
  // get suit and value
  AValue := OleObject.Value;
  ASuit := OleObject.Suit;
  // set card correctly
  Card1.Value := TCardValue(AValue);
  Card1.Suit := TCardSuit(ASuit);
  // set correct value speedbutton
  with ValueGroup do
    for i := 0 to ControlCount - 1 do
      if (Controls[i] is TSpeedButton) and
         (TSpeedButton(Controls[i]).Tag = AValue) then
         TSpeedButton(Controls[i]).Down := True;
  // set correct suit speedbutton
  with SuitGroup do
    for i := 0 to ControlCount - 1 do
      if (Controls[i] is TSpeedButton) and
         (TSpeedButton(Controls[i]).Tag = ASuit) then
         TSpeedButton(Controls[i]).Down := True;
end;

procedure TCardPropPage.UpdateObject;
var
  i: Integer;
```

continues

25

CREATING
ACTIVEX
CONTROLS

LISTING 25.7. CONTINUED

```
begin
  // set correct value speedbutton
  with ValueGroup do
    for i := 0 to ControlCount - 1 do
      if (Controls[i] is TSpeedButton) and TSpeedButton(Controls[i]).Down
      ➡then
      begin
        OleObject.Value := TSpeedButton(Controls[i]).Tag;
        Break;
      end;
  // set correct suit speedbutton
  with SuitGroup do
    for i := 0 to ControlCount - 1 do
      if (Controls[i] is TSpeedButton) and TSpeedButton(Controls[i]).Down
      ➡then
      begin
        OleObject.Suit := TSpeedButton(Controls[i]).Tag;
        Break;
      end;
end;

procedure TCardPropPage.FormCreate(Sender: TObject);
const
  // ordinal values of "suit" characters in Symbol font:
  SSuits: PChar = #167#168#169#170;
var
  i: Integer;
begin
  // set up captions of suit speedbuttons using high
  // characters in Symbol font
  with SuitGroup do
    for i := 0 to ControlCount - 1 do
      if Controls[i] is TSpeedButton then
        TSpeedButton(Controls[i]).Caption := SSuits[i];
end;

procedure TCardPropPage.SpeedButton1Click(Sender: TObject);
begin
  if Sender is TSpeedButton then
  begin
    with TSpeedButton(Sender) do
    begin
      if Parent = ValueGroup then
        Card1.Value := TCardValue(Tag)
      else if Parent = SuitGroup then
        Card1.Suit := TCardSuit(Tag);
    end;
    Modified;
  end;
end;
```

```
initialization
  TActiveXPropertyPageFactory.Create(
    ComServer,
    TCardPropPage,
    Class_CardPropPage);
end.
```

You must communicate with the ActiveX control from the property page using its OleObject field. OleObject is a Variant that holds a reference to the control's IDispatch interface. The UpdatePropertyPage() and UpdateObject() methods are generated by the wizard. UpdatePropertyPage() is called when the property page is invoked. In this method, you must set the contents of the page to match the current values of the ActiveX control as indicated in the OleObject property. UpdateObject() will be called when the user clicks the OK or Apply button in the Property Page dialog. In this method, you should use the OleObject property to set the ActiveX control properties to those indicated by the property page.

In this example, the property page allows you to edit the suit or value of the TCardX ActiveX control. As you modify the suit or value using speedbuttons in the dialog, a TCard VCL control residing on the property page is changed to reflect the current suit and value. Notice also that when a speedbutton is clicked, the property page's Modified() procedure is called to set the modified flag of the Property Page dialog. This enables the Apply button on the dialog.

This property page is shown in action in Figure 25.9.

FIGURE 25.9.

The Card property page in action.

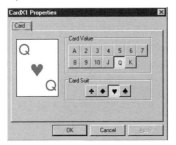

ACTIVEFORMS

Functionally, ActiveForms work very much the same as the ActiveX controls you learned about earlier in this chapter. The primary difference is that the VCL control upon which you base an ActiveX control doesn't really change after you run the wizard, whereas the whole point of an ActiveForm is that it changes constantly as it's manipulated in the designer. Because the ActiveForm's wizard and framework is essentially the same as the ones for ActiveX controls, we won't rehash that material. Instead, let's focus on some interesting things you can do with ActiveForms.

Adding Properties to ActiveForms

One problem with ActiveForms is that their representation in the type library consists of "flat" interfaces rather than the nested components you're familiar with in VCL. This means that if you have a form with several buttons, they cannot easily be addressed in the VCL manner of `ActiveForm.Button.ButtonProperty` as an ActiveForm. Instead, the easiest way to accomplish this is to surface the button properties in question as properties of the ActiveForm itself. The DAX framework makes adding properties to ActiveForms a pretty painless process; you just need to follow a couple of steps. Here's what's required to publish the `Caption` property of a button on an ActiveForm:

1. Add a new published property to the ActiveForm declaration in the implementation file. This property will be called `ButtonCaption`, and it will have reader and writer methods that modify the `Caption` of the button.

2. Add a new property of the same name to the ActiveForm's interface in the type library. Delphi will automatically write the skeletons for the reader and writer methods for this property, and you must implement them by reading and writing the ActiveForm's `ButtonCaption` property.

The implementation file for this component is shown in Listing 25.8.

LISTING 25.8. ADDING PROPERTIES TO ACTIVEFORMS.

```
unit AFImpl;

interface

uses
  Windows, Messages, SysUtils, Classes, Graphics, Controls, Forms,
Dialogs,
  ActiveX, AxCtrls, AFrm_TLB, StdCtrls;

type
  TActiveFormX = class(TActiveForm, IActiveFormX)
    Button1: TButton;
  private
    { Private declarations }
    FEvents: IActiveFormXEvents;
    procedure ActivateEvent(Sender: TObject);
    procedure ClickEvent(Sender: TObject);
```

```
    procedure CreateEvent(Sender: TObject);
    procedure DblClickEvent(Sender: TObject);
    procedure DeactivateEvent(Sender: TObject);
    procedure DestroyEvent(Sender: TObject);
    procedure KeyPressEvent(Sender: TObject; var Key: Char);
    procedure PaintEvent(Sender: TObject);
    function GetButtonCaption: string;
    procedure SetButtonCaption(const Value: string);
  protected
    { Protected declarations }
    procedure DefinePropertyPages(DefinePropertyPage:
      TDefinePropertyPage); override;
    procedure EventSinkChanged(const EventSink: IUnknown); override;
    function Get_Active: WordBool; safecall;
    function Get_AutoScroll: WordBool; safecall;
    function Get_AutoSize: WordBool; safecall;
    function Get_AxBorderStyle: TxActiveFormBorderStyle; safecall;
    function Get_BiDiMode: TxBiDiMode; safecall;
    function Get_Caption: WideString; safecall;
    function Get_Color: OLE_COLOR; safecall;
    function Get_Cursor: Smallint; safecall;
    function Get_DoubleBuffered: WordBool; safecall;
    function Get_DropTarget: WordBool; safecall;
    function Get_Enabled: WordBool; safecall;
    function Get_Font: IFontDisp; safecall;
    function Get_HelpFile: WideString; safecall;
    function Get_KeyPreview: WordBool; safecall;
    function Get_PixelsPerInch: Integer; safecall;
    function Get_PrintScale: TxPrintScale; safecall;
    function Get_Scaled: WordBool; safecall;
    function Get_Visible: WordBool; safecall;
    procedure _Set_Font(const Value: IFontDisp); safecall;
    procedure AboutBox; safecall;
    procedure Set_AutoScroll(Value: WordBool); safecall;
    procedure Set_AutoSize(Value: WordBool); safecall;
    procedure Set_AxBorderStyle(Value: TxActiveFormBorderStyle); safecall;
    procedure Set_BiDiMode(Value: TxBiDiMode); safecall;
    procedure Set_Caption(const Value: WideString); safecall;
    procedure Set_Color(Value: OLE_COLOR); safecall;
    procedure Set_Cursor(Value: Smallint); safecall;
    procedure Set_DoubleBuffered(Value: WordBool); safecall;
    procedure Set_DropTarget(Value: WordBool); safecall;
    procedure Set_Enabled(Value: WordBool); safecall;
    procedure Set_Font(var Value: IFontDisp); safecall;
    procedure Set_HelpFile(const Value: WideString); safecall;
    procedure Set_KeyPreview(Value: WordBool); safecall;
    procedure Set_PixelsPerInch(Value: Integer); safecall;
    procedure Set_PrintScale(Value: TxPrintScale); safecall;
    procedure Set_Scaled(Value: WordBool); safecall;
    procedure Set_Visible(Value: WordBool); safecall;
```

25

CREATING
ACTIVEX
CONTROLS

continues

LISTING 25.8. CONTINUED

```
  function Get_ButtonCaption: WideString; safecall;
  procedure Set_ButtonCaption(const Value: WideString); safecall;
public
  { Public declarations }
  procedure Initialize; override;
published
  property ButtonCaption: string read GetButtonCaption
    write SetButtonCaption;
end;

implementation

uses ComObj, ComServ, About1;

{$R *.DFM}

{ TActiveFormX }

procedure TActiveFormX.DefinePropertyPages(DefinePropertyPage:
TDefinePropertyPage);
begin
  { Define property pages here.  Property pages are defined by calling
    DefinePropertyPage with the class id of the page.  For example,
      DefinePropertyPage(Class_ActiveFormXPage); }
end;

procedure TActiveFormX.EventSinkChanged(const EventSink: IUnknown);
begin
  FEvents := EventSink as IActiveFormXEvents;
end;

procedure TActiveFormX.Initialize;
begin
  inherited Initialize;
  OnActivate := ActivateEvent;
  OnClick := ClickEvent;
  OnCreate := CreateEvent;
  OnDblClick := DblClickEvent;
  OnDeactivate := DeactivateEvent;
  OnDestroy := DestroyEvent;
  OnKeyPress := KeyPressEvent;
  OnPaint := PaintEvent;
end;

function TActiveFormX.Get_Active: WordBool;
begin
  Result := Active;
end;
```

```
function TActiveFormX.Get_AutoScroll: WordBool;
begin
  Result := AutoScroll;
end;

function TActiveFormX.Get_AutoSize: WordBool;
begin
  Result := AutoSize;
end;

function TActiveFormX.Get_AxBorderStyle: TxActiveFormBorderStyle;
begin
  Result := Ord(AxBorderStyle);
end;

function TActiveFormX.Get_BiDiMode: TxBiDiMode;
begin
  Result := Ord(BiDiMode);
end;

function TActiveFormX.Get_Caption: WideString;
begin
  Result := WideString(Caption);
end;

function TActiveFormX.Get_Color: OLE_COLOR;
begin
  Result := OLE_COLOR(Color);
end;

function TActiveFormX.Get_Cursor: Smallint;
begin
  Result := Smallint(Cursor);
end;

function TActiveFormX.Get_DoubleBuffered: WordBool;
begin
  Result := DoubleBuffered;
end;

function TActiveFormX.Get_DropTarget: WordBool;
begin
  Result := DropTarget;
end;

function TActiveFormX.Get_Enabled: WordBool;
begin
  Result := Enabled;
end;
```

continues

25

CREATING
ACTIVEX
CONTROLS

LISTING 25.8. CONTINUED

```
function TActiveFormX.Get_Font: IFontDisp;
begin
  GetOleFont(Font, Result);
end;

function TActiveFormX.Get_HelpFile: WideString;
begin
  Result := WideString(HelpFile);
end;

function TActiveFormX.Get_KeyPreview: WordBool;
begin
  Result := KeyPreview;
end;

function TActiveFormX.Get_PixelsPerInch: Integer;
begin
  Result := PixelsPerInch;
end;

function TActiveFormX.Get_PrintScale: TxPrintScale;
begin
  Result := Ord(PrintScale);
end;

function TActiveFormX.Get_Scaled: WordBool;
begin
  Result := Scaled;
end;

function TActiveFormX.Get_Visible: WordBool;
begin
  Result := Visible;
end;

procedure TActiveFormX._Set_Font(const Value: IFontDisp);
begin
  SetOleFont(Font, Value);
end;

procedure TActiveFormX.AboutBox;
begin
  ShowActiveFormXAbout;
end;

procedure TActiveFormX.Set_AutoScroll(Value: WordBool);
begin
  AutoScroll := Value;
end;
```

```
procedure TActiveFormX.Set_AutoSize(Value: WordBool);
begin
  AutoSize := Value;
end;

procedure TActiveFormX.Set_AxBorderStyle(Value: TxActiveFormBorderStyle);
begin
  AxBorderStyle := TActiveFormBorderStyle(Value);
end;

procedure TActiveFormX.Set_BiDiMode(Value: TxBiDiMode);
begin
  BiDiMode := TBiDiMode(Value);
end;

procedure TActiveFormX.Set_Caption(const Value: WideString);
begin
  Caption := TCaption(Value);
end;

procedure TActiveFormX.Set_Color(Value: OLE_COLOR);
begin
  Color := TColor(Value);
end;

procedure TActiveFormX.Set_Cursor(Value: Smallint);
begin
  Cursor := TCursor(Value);
end;

procedure TActiveFormX.Set_DoubleBuffered(Value: WordBool);
begin
  DoubleBuffered := Value;
end;

procedure TActiveFormX.Set_DropTarget(Value: WordBool);
begin
  DropTarget := Value;
end;

procedure TActiveFormX.Set_Enabled(Value: WordBool);
begin
  Enabled := Value;
end;

procedure TActiveFormX.Set_Font(var Value: IFontDisp);
begin
  SetOleFont(Font, Value);
end;
```

continues

LISTING 25.8. CONTINUED

```
procedure TActiveFormX.Set_HelpFile(const Value: WideString);
begin
  HelpFile := String(Value);
end;

procedure TActiveFormX.Set_KeyPreview(Value: WordBool);
begin
  KeyPreview := Value;
end;

procedure TActiveFormX.Set_PixelsPerInch(Value: Integer);
begin
  PixelsPerInch := Value;
end;

procedure TActiveFormX.Set_PrintScale(Value: TxPrintScale);
begin
  PrintScale := TPrintScale(Value);
end;

procedure TActiveFormX.Set_Scaled(Value: WordBool);
begin
  Scaled := Value;
end;

procedure TActiveFormX.Set_Visible(Value: WordBool);
begin
  Visible := Value;
end;

procedure TActiveFormX.ActivateEvent(Sender: TObject);
begin
  if FEvents <> nil then FEvents.OnActivate;
end;

procedure TActiveFormX.ClickEvent(Sender: TObject);
begin
  if FEvents <> nil then FEvents.OnClick;
end;

procedure TActiveFormX.CreateEvent(Sender: TObject);
begin
  if FEvents <> nil then FEvents.OnCreate;
end;

procedure TActiveFormX.DblClickEvent(Sender: TObject);
begin
  if FEvents <> nil then FEvents.OnDblClick;
end;
```

```
procedure TActiveFormX.DeactivateEvent(Sender: TObject);
begin
  if FEvents <> nil then FEvents.OnDeactivate;
end;

procedure TActiveFormX.DestroyEvent(Sender: TObject);
begin
  if FEvents <> nil then FEvents.OnDestroy;
end;

procedure TActiveFormX.KeyPressEvent(Sender: TObject; var Key: Char);
var
  TempKey: Smallint;
begin
  TempKey := Smallint(Key);
  if FEvents <> nil then FEvents.OnKeyPress(TempKey);
  Key := Char(TempKey);
end;

procedure TActiveFormX.PaintEvent(Sender: TObject);
begin
  if FEvents <> nil then FEvents.OnPaint;
end;

function TActiveFormX.GetButtonCaption: string;
begin
  Result := Button1.Caption;
end;

procedure TActiveFormX.SetButtonCaption(const Value: string);
begin
  Button1.Caption := Value;
end;

function TActiveFormX.Get_ButtonCaption: WideString;
begin
  Result := ButtonCaption;
end;

procedure TActiveFormX.Set_ButtonCaption(const Value: WideString);
begin
  ButtonCaption := Value;
end;

initialization
  TActiveFormFactory.Create(ComServer, TActiveFormControl, TActiveFormX,
    Class_ActiveFormX, 1, '', OLEMISC_SIMPLEFRAME or
OLEMISC_ACTSLIKELABEL,
    tmApartment);
end.
```

ACTIVEX ON THE WEB

An ideal use for ActiveForms is as a vehicle for delivering small applications over the World Wide Web. Smaller ActiveX controls are also useful for enhancing the appearance and usefulness of Web pages. However, in order to get the most out of Delphi-written ActiveX controls on the Web, you need to know a few things about control streaming, safety, and communication with the browser.

Communicating with the Web Browser

Because ActiveX controls can run within the context of a Web browser, it makes sense that Web browsers expose functions and interfaces that allow ActiveX controls to manipulate them. Most of these functions and interfaces are located in the UrlMon unit (that's Jamaican Web talk). Among the simplest of these functions are the HlinkXXX() functions, which cause the browser to hyperlink to different locations. For example, the HlinkGoForward() and HlinkGoBack() functions cause the browser to travel forward or back in its location stack. The HlinkNavigateString() function causes the browser to travel to a specified URL. These functions are defined in UrlMon as follows:

```
function HlinkGoBack(pUnk: IUnknown): HResult; stdcall;
function HlinkGoForward(pUnk: IUnknown): HResult; stdcall;
function HlinkNavigateString(pUnk: IUnknown; szTarget: PWideChar): HResult;
  stdcall;
```

The pUnk parameter for each of these functions is the IUnknown for the ActiveX control. In the case of ActiveX controls, you can pass *Control* as IUnknown in this parameter. In the case of ActiveForms, you should pass IUnknown(VclComObject) in this parameter. The szTarget parameter of HlinkNavigateString() represents the URL you want to use.

A more ambitious task would be to use the URLDownloadToFile() function to download a file from the server to the local machine. This method is defined in UrlMon as follows:

```
function URLDownloadToFile(p1: IUnknown; p2: PChar; p3: PChar; p4: DWORD;
  p5: IBindStatusCallback): HResult; stdcall;
```

Helpful parameter names, eh? p1 represents the IUnknown for the ActiveX control, similar to the pUnk parameter of the HlinkXXX() functions. p2 holds the URL of the file to be downloaded. p3 is the name of the local file that will be filled with the data of the file specified by p2. p4 must be set to 0, and p5 holds an optional IBindStatusCallback interface pointer. This interface can be used to obtain incremental information on the file as it downloads.

Listing 25.9 shows the implementation file for an ActiveForm that implements these methods. It also demonstrates a simple example of implementing the `IBindStatusCallback` interface.

LISTING 25.9. AN ACTIVEFORM THAT USES UrlMon FUNCTIONS.

```
unit UrlTestMain;

interface

uses
  Windows, Messages, SysUtils, Classes, Graphics, Controls, Forms,
  Dialogs, ActiveX, AxCtrls, UrlTest_TLB, UrlMon, StdCtrls, MPlayer,
  ExtCtrls, ComCtrls;

type
  TUrlTestForm = class(TActiveForm, IUrlTestForm, IBindStatusCallback)
    GroupBox1: TGroupBox;
    Label1: TLabel;
    Label2: TLabel;
    Label3: TLabel;
    MediaPlayer1: TMediaPlayer;
    Panel1: TPanel;
    Button1: TButton;
    StatusPanel: TPanel;
    ProgressBar1: TProgressBar;
    ServerName: TEdit;
    StaticText1: TStaticText;
    procedure Label1Click(Sender: TObject);
    procedure Label2Click(Sender: TObject);
    procedure Label3Click(Sender: TObject);
    procedure Button1Click(Sender: TObject);
  private
    { Private declarations }
    FEvents: IUrlTestFormEvents;
    procedure ActivateEvent(Sender: TObject);
    procedure ClickEvent(Sender: TObject);
    procedure CreateEvent(Sender: TObject);
    procedure DblClickEvent(Sender: TObject);
    procedure DeactivateEvent(Sender: TObject);
    procedure DestroyEvent(Sender: TObject);
    procedure KeyPressEvent(Sender: TObject; var Key: Char);
    procedure PaintEvent(Sender: TObject);
  protected
    { IBindStatusCallback }
    function OnStartBinding(dwReserved: Longint; pib: IBinding): HResult;
      stdcall;
    function GetPriority(out pnPriority: Longint): HResult; stdcall;
```

continues

25

LISTING 25.9. CONTINUED

```pascal
    function OnLowResource(reserved: Longint): HResult; stdcall;
    function OnProgress(ulProgress: Longint; ulProgressMax: Longint;
      ulStatusCode: Longint; szStatusText: PWideChar): HResult; stdcall;
    function OnStopBinding( hRes: HResult; szError: PWideChar ): HResult;
      stdcall;
    function GetBindInfo(out grfBINDF: Longint; var pbindinfo: TBindInfo):
      HResult; stdcall;
    function OnDataAvailable(grfBSCF: Longint; dwSize: Longint;
      var pformatetc: TFormatEtc; var pstgmed: TSTGMEDIUM): HResult;
      stdcall;
    function OnObjectAvailable(const iid: TGUID; const punk: IUnknown):
      HResult; stdcall;
    { UrlTestForm }
    procedure EventSinkChanged(const EventSink: IUnknown); override;
    procedure Initialize; override;
    function Get_Active: WordBool; safecall;
    function Get_AutoScroll: WordBool; safecall;
    function Get_AxBorderStyle: TxActiveFormBorderStyle; safecall;
    function Get_Caption: WideString; safecall;
    function Get_Color: OLE_COLOR; safecall;
    function Get_Cursor: Smallint; safecall;
    function Get_DropTarget: WordBool; safecall;
    function Get_Enabled: WordBool; safecall;
    function Get_Font: IFontDisp; safecall;
    function Get_HelpFile: WideString; safecall;
    function Get_KeyPreview: WordBool; safecall;
    function Get_PixelsPerInch: Integer; safecall;
    function Get_PrintScale: TxPrintScale; safecall;
    function Get_Scaled: WordBool; safecall;
    function Get_Visible: WordBool; safecall;
    function Get_WindowState: TxWindowState; safecall;
    procedure Set_AutoScroll(Value: WordBool); safecall;
    procedure Set_AxBorderStyle(Value: TxActiveFormBorderStyle); safecall;
    procedure Set_Caption(const Value: WideString); safecall;
    procedure Set_Color(Color: OLE_COLOR); safecall;
    procedure Set_Cursor(Value: Smallint); safecall;
    procedure Set_DropTarget(Value: WordBool); safecall;
    procedure Set_Enabled(Value: WordBool); safecall;
    procedure Set_Font(const Font: IFontDisp); safecall;
    procedure Set_HelpFile(const Value: WideString); safecall;
    procedure Set_KeyPreview(Value: WordBool); safecall;
    procedure Set_PixelsPerInch(Value: Integer); safecall;
    procedure Set_PrintScale(Value: TxPrintScale); safecall;
    procedure Set_Scaled(Value: WordBool); safecall;
    procedure Set_Visible(Value: WordBool); safecall;
    procedure Set_WindowState(Value: TxWindowState); safecall;
  public
    { Public declarations }
  end;
```

```pascal
implementation

uses ComObj, ComServ;

{$R *.DFM}

{ TUrlTestForm.IBindStatusCallback }

function TUrlTestForm.OnStartBinding(dwReserved: Longint; pib: IBinding):
  HResult;
begin
  Result := S_OK;
end;

function TUrlTestForm.GetPriority(out pnPriority: Longint): HResult;
begin
  Result := S_OK;
end;

function TUrlTestForm.OnLowResource(reserved: Longint): HResult;
begin
  Result := S_OK;
end;

function TUrlTestForm.OnProgress(ulProgress: Longint; ulProgressMax:
  Longint; ulStatusCode: Longint; szStatusText: PWideChar): HResult;
begin
  Result := S_OK;
  ProgressBar1.Max := ulProgressMax;
  ProgressBar1.Position := ulProgress;
  StatusPanel.Caption := szStatusText;
end;

function TUrlTestForm.OnStopBinding(hRes: HResult; szError: PWideChar ):
  HResult;
begin
  Result := S_OK;
  if hRes = S_OK then
  begin
    MediaPlayer1.FileName := 'c:\temp\testavi.avi';
    MediaPlayer1.Open;
    MediaPlayer1.Play;
  end;
end;

function TUrlTestForm.GetBindInfo(out grfBINDF: Longint;
  var pbindinfo: TBindInfo): HResult;
begin
  Result := S_OK;
end;
```

25

continues

LISTING 25.9. CONTINUED

```pascal
function TUrlTestForm.OnDataAvailable(grfBSCF: Longint; dwSize: Longint;
  var pformatetc: TFormatEtc; var pstgmed: TSTGMEDIUM): HResult;
begin
  Result := S_OK;
end;

function TUrlTestForm.OnObjectAvailable(const iid: TGUID;
  const punk: IUnknown): HResult;
begin
  Result := S_OK;
end;

{ TUrlTestForm }

procedure TUrlTestForm.EventSinkChanged(const EventSink: IUnknown);
begin
  FEvents := EventSink as IUrlTestFormEvents;
end;

procedure TUrlTestForm.Initialize;
begin
  OnActivate := ActivateEvent;
  OnClick := ClickEvent;
  OnCreate := CreateEvent;
  OnDblClick := DblClickEvent;
  OnDeactivate := DeactivateEvent;
  OnDestroy := DestroyEvent;
  OnKeyPress := KeyPressEvent;
  OnPaint := PaintEvent;
end;

function TUrlTestForm.Get_Active: WordBool;
begin
  Result := Active;
end;

function TUrlTestForm.Get_AutoScroll: WordBool;
begin
  Result := AutoScroll;
end;

function TUrlTestForm.Get_AxBorderStyle: TxActiveFormBorderStyle;
begin
  Result := Ord(AxBorderStyle);
end;

function TUrlTestForm.Get_Caption: WideString;
begin
  Result := WideString(Caption);
end;
```

```
function TUrlTestForm.Get_Color: OLE_COLOR;
begin
  Result := Color;
end;

function TUrlTestForm.Get_Cursor: Smallint;
begin
  Result := Smallint(Cursor);
end;

function TUrlTestForm.Get_DropTarget: WordBool;
begin
  Result := DropTarget;
end;

function TUrlTestForm.Get_Enabled: WordBool;
begin
  Result := Enabled;
end;

function TUrlTestForm.Get_Font: IFontDisp;
begin
  GetOleFont(Font, Result);
end;

function TUrlTestForm.Get_HelpFile: WideString;
begin
  Result := WideString(HelpFile);
end;

function TUrlTestForm.Get_KeyPreview: WordBool;
begin
  Result := KeyPreview;
end;

function TUrlTestForm.Get_PixelsPerInch: Integer;
begin
  Result := PixelsPerInch;
end;

function TUrlTestForm.Get_PrintScale: TxPrintScale;
begin
  Result := Ord(PrintScale);
end;

function TUrlTestForm.Get_Scaled: WordBool;
begin
  Result := Scaled;
end;
```

25

CREATING
ACTIVEX
CONTROLS

continues

LISTING 25.9. CONTINUED

```pascal
function TUrlTestForm.Get_Visible: WordBool;
begin
  Result := Visible;
end;

function TUrlTestForm.Get_WindowState: TxWindowState;
begin
  Result := Ord(WindowState);
end;

procedure TUrlTestForm.Set_AutoScroll(Value: WordBool);
begin
  AutoScroll := Value;
end;

procedure TUrlTestForm.Set_AxBorderStyle(Value: TxActiveFormBorderStyle);
begin
  AxBorderStyle := TActiveFormBorderStyle(Value);
end;

procedure TUrlTestForm.Set_Caption(const Value: WideString);
begin
  Caption := TCaption(Value);
end;

procedure TUrlTestForm.Set_Color(Color: OLE_COLOR);
begin
  Self.Color := Color;
end;

procedure TUrlTestForm.Set_Cursor(Value: Smallint);
begin
  Cursor := TCursor(Value);
end;

procedure TUrlTestForm.Set_DropTarget(Value: WordBool);
begin
  DropTarget := Value;
end;

procedure TUrlTestForm.Set_Enabled(Value: WordBool);
begin
  Enabled := Value;
end;

procedure TUrlTestForm.Set_Font(const Font: IFontDisp);
begin
  SetOleFont(Self.Font, Font);
end;
```

```
procedure TUrlTestForm.Set_HelpFile(const Value: WideString);
begin
  HelpFile := String(Value);
end;

procedure TUrlTestForm.Set_KeyPreview(Value: WordBool);
begin
  KeyPreview := Value;
end;

procedure TUrlTestForm.Set_PixelsPerInch(Value: Integer);
begin
  PixelsPerInch := Value;
end;

procedure TUrlTestForm.Set_PrintScale(Value: TxPrintScale);
begin
  PrintScale := TPrintScale(Value);
end;

procedure TUrlTestForm.Set_Scaled(Value: WordBool);
begin
  Scaled := Value;
end;

procedure TUrlTestForm.Set_Visible(Value: WordBool);
begin
  Visible := Value;
end;

procedure TUrlTestForm.Set_WindowState(Value: TxWindowState);
begin
  WindowState := TWindowState(Value);
end;

procedure TUrlTestForm.ActivateEvent(Sender: TObject);
begin
  if FEvents <> nil then FEvents.OnActivate;
end;

procedure TUrlTestForm.ClickEvent(Sender: TObject);
begin
  if FEvents <> nil then FEvents.OnClick;
end;

procedure TUrlTestForm.CreateEvent(Sender: TObject);
begin
  if FEvents <> nil then FEvents.OnCreate;
end;
```

continues

25

CREATING ACTIVEX CONTROLS

LISTING 25.9. CONTINUED

```
procedure TUrlTestForm.DblClickEvent(Sender: TObject);
begin
  if FEvents <> nil then FEvents.OnDblClick;
end;

procedure TUrlTestForm.DeactivateEvent(Sender: TObject);
begin
  if FEvents <> nil then FEvents.OnDeactivate;
end;

procedure TUrlTestForm.DestroyEvent(Sender: TObject);
begin
  if FEvents <> nil then FEvents.OnDestroy;
end;

procedure TUrlTestForm.KeyPressEvent(Sender: TObject; var Key: Char);
var
  TempKey: Smallint;
begin
  TempKey := Smallint(Key);
  if FEvents <> nil then FEvents.OnKeyPress(TempKey);
  Key := Char(TempKey);
end;

procedure TUrlTestForm.PaintEvent(Sender: TObject);
begin
  if FEvents <> nil then FEvents.OnPaint;
end;

procedure TUrlTestForm.Label1Click(Sender: TObject);
begin
  HLinkNavigateString(IUnknown(VCLComObject), 'http://www.inprise.com');
end;

procedure TUrlTestForm.Label2Click(Sender: TObject);
begin
  HLinkGoForward(IUnknown(VCLComObject));
end;

procedure TUrlTestForm.Label3Click(Sender: TObject);
begin
  HLinkGoBack(IUnknown(VCLComObject));
end;

procedure TUrlTestForm.Button1Click(Sender: TObject);
begin
  // Note: you may have to change the name of the AVI file shown in the
  // first parameter to Format to another AVI file which resides on your
  // server.
```

```
    URLDownloadToFile(IUnknown(VCLComObject),
      PChar(Format('http://%s/delphi3.avi', [ServerName.Text])),
      'c:\temp\testavi.avi', 0, Self);
end;

initialization
  TActiveFormFactory.Create(ComServer, TActiveFormControl, TUrlTestForm,
    Class_UrlTestForm, 1, '', OLEMISC_SIMPLEFRAME or
OLEMISC_ACTSLIKELABEL,
    tmApartment);
end.
```

The URLDownloadToFile() example downloads an AVI file from the server and plays it in a TMediaPlayer. Note that this example expects to find a file called delphi3.avi in the root of the server, so you may need to change the code depending on what AVI files you have on your machine. Figure 25.10 shows this ActiveForm in action inside of Internet Explorer.

FIGURE 25.10.

The ActiveForm running in Internet Explorer.

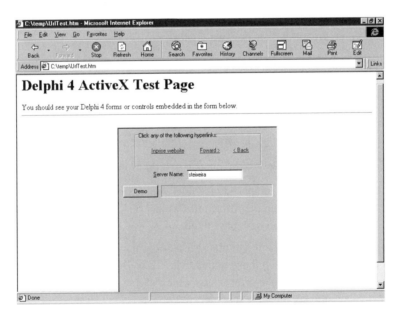

Web Deployment

The Delphi IDE contains a very convenient feature that helps you deploy your ActiveX projects over the Web. This option is accessible when you're editing an ActiveX project from Project | Web Deployment Options from the main menu. The main page of this dialog is shown in Figure 25.11.

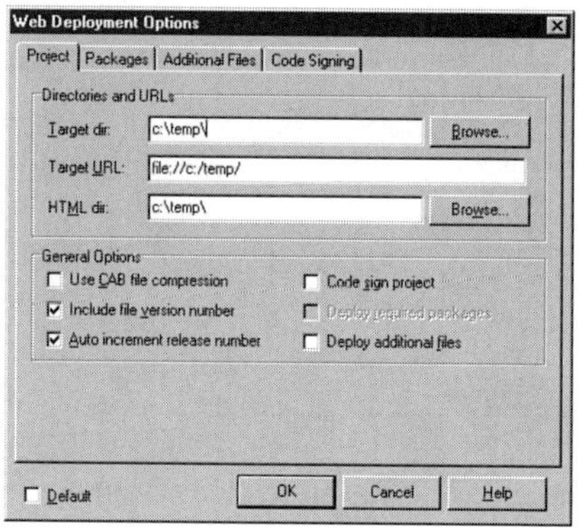

FIGURE 25.11.

The Project page of the Web Deployment Options dialog.

The Project Page

On the Project page, Target Dir represents the pathname to which you want to deploy the ActiveX project. Note that this assumes you're able to map a drive to your Web server—the contents of the edit control must be a regular or UNC pathname. Note also that you should not type in a filename, just a path.

Target URL is the URL that references the same directory specified in Target Dir. This must be a valid URL that uses a standard URL prefix (`http://`, `file://`, `ftp://`, and so on). Again, do not include a filename here, just a pathname URL.

HTML Dir is another pathname that dictates where the generated HTML file will be copied. Typically, this is the same as Target Dir.

This dialog also enables you to choose several project deployment options:

- Use CAB File Compression—Selecting this option will cause your OCX file to be compressed using the Microsoft Cabinet (CAB) format. This is recommended for controls you plan to deploy to clients who use low-bandwidth Web links.
- Include File Version Number—This option indicates whether or not to include a version number in the generated HTML or INF file. Doing so is recommended, because it provides a means by which users can avoid downloading the control if they already have the most recent version.
- Auto Increment Release Number—When checked, this option causes the release number portion of your `VersionInfo` resources to be automatically incremented after deployment.
- Code Sign Project—If you have an Authenticode certificate for digitally signing code, you can let the IDE do the work for you while deploying your project.

- Deploy Required Packages—If your project is built with packages, simply checking this box will automatically include packages used by your project in the file deployment set.
- Deploy Additional Files—By checking this box, you can add files shown on the Additional Files page to your file deployment set.

Packages and Additional Files

The Packages page and Additional Files page are shown in Figures 25.12 and 25.13. The only difference between the pages is that the Packages page is filled automatically based on the packages used by the project, and files are added to and removed from the Additional Files page by you.

FIGURE 25.12.

The Packages page.

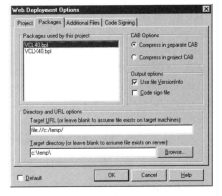

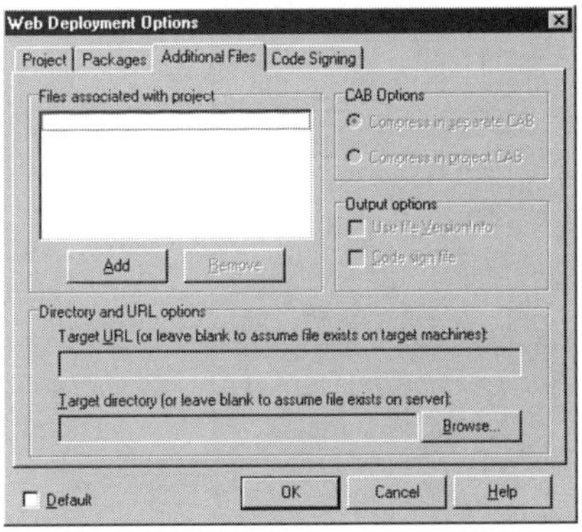

FIGURE 25.13.

The Additional Files page.

25

CREATING
ACTIVEX
CONTROLS

When you choose to use CAB compression on the Project page, the CAB Options group of the Packages and Additional Files pages enable you to select whether you want the file compressed with the OCX or in a separate CAB file. It's generally more efficient to compress each file in its own CAB, because then the user won't have to download files that they potentially already have installed on their machine. Here are some other options you should be familiar with:

- If Use File VersionInfo is selected, the deployment engine will determine whether the selected file has `VersionInfo` and, if so, will stamp the version number contained in `VersionInfo` in the INF file.

- Code Sign File allows you to specify whether you want to add an Authenticode signature to the selected file.

- The Target URL edit will default to the same location as the target URL from the Project page. This is the URL from which the file can be downloaded. If you're assuming that the client of your ActiveX control already has this file installed, leave this value blank.

- The Target Directory edit allows you to specify the directory to which the particular file should be copied. Leave this blank if the file already exists on the server and should not be recopied to the server.

Code Signing

The Code Signing page, shown in Figure 25.14, allows you to specify the location of the certificate file and private key file associated with your certificate. In addition, you can specify a title for your application, a URL for your application or company, the type of encryption you want to use, and whether or not to time stamp your certificate. It's recommended that you choose to time stamp as you code sign so that the signature will remain valid even after your certificate expires.

FIGURE 25.14.

The Code Signing page.

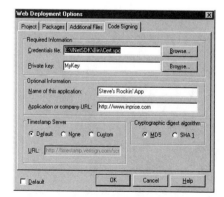

General Tips

If you make an error on the Project page, your control will usually appear on the Web page as a box with a red X in the upper-left corner. If this happens, you should check the generated HTM file and the INF file (if you're deploying multiple files) for errors. The most common problem is an incorrect URL specified for the control.

SUMMARY

That about sums it up for the topic of creating ActiveX controls and ActiveForms in Delphi. This chapter provides a lot of insight into the inner workings of the ActiveX wizards to help you work within and extend the Delphi ActiveX framework for your benefit. This chapter also builds on the COM and ActiveX knowledge you gained in the previous two chapters—you're well on your way to becoming an expert ActiveX programmer. Now it's time to change gears. The next chapter focuses on using Delphi's OpenTools API to get inside the IDE.

USING DELPHI'S OPEN TOOLS API

IN THIS CHAPTER

Have you ever thought to yourself, "Delphi is great, but why doesn't the IDE perform this little task that I'd like it to?" If you have, then have no fear. The Open Tools API is for you. The Delphi Open Tools API provides you with the ability to create your own tools that work closely with Delphi's IDE. In this chapter, you'll learn about the different interfaces that make up the Open Tools API, how to use the interfaces, and also how to leverage your newly found expertise to write a fully featured expert.

DATABASE DEVELOPMENT

PART
IV

IN THIS PART

WRITING DESKTOP DATABASE APPLICATIONS

IN THIS CHAPTER

In this chapter, you'll learn the art and science of accessing external database files from your Delphi applications. If you're new to database programming, we do assume a bit of database knowledge, but this chapter will get you started on the road to creating high-quality database applications. If database applications are "old hat" to you, you'll benefit from the chapter's demonstration of Delphi's spin on database programming. In this chapter, you first learn about data sets and techniques for manipulating them, and later you learn how to work with tables and queries specifically. Along the way, this chapter outlines the important points you need to know to be a productive Delphi database developer.

Delphi 4 ships with version 5.0 of the Borland Database Engine (BDE), which offers you the capability to communicate with Paradox, dBASE, Access, FoxPro, ODBC, ASCII text, and SQL server databases all in much the same manner. The Standard edition of Delphi provides connections to file-based Paradox, dBASE, Access, FoxPro, and ASCII text formats. The Delphi Professional package adds connectivity to Local InterBase and ODBC data sources. Delphi Client/Server Suite builds upon Delphi Professional, adding high-performance SQL server connections for InterBase, Microsoft SQL Server, Oracle, Informix, Sybase SQL Server, and DB2. The topics discussed pertain primarily to using Delphi with file-based data, such as Paradox and dBASE tables. This chapter also serves as a primer for the next chapter, "Developing Client/Server Applications."

WORKING WITH DATA SETS

A *data set* is a collection of rows and columns of data. Each *column* is of some homogeneous data type, and each *row* is made up of a collection of data of each column data type. Additionally, a column is also known as a *field*, and a row is sometimes called a *record*. VCL (Visual Component Library) encapsulates a data set into an abstract component called TDataSet. TDataSet introduces many of the properties and methods necessary for manipulating and navigating a data set.

To help keep the nomenclature clear and to cover some of the basics, the following list explains some of the common database terms that are used in this and other database-oriented chapters:

- A *data set* is a collection of discrete data records. Each record is made up of multiple fields. Each field can contain a different type of data (integer number, string, decimal number, graphic, and so on). Data sets are represented by VCL's abstract TDataset class.

- A *table* is a special type of data set. A table is generally a file containing records that are physically stored on a disk somewhere. VCL's TTable class encapsulates this functionality.

- A *query* is also a special type of data set. Think of queries as "memory tables" that are generated by special commands that manipulate some physical table or set of tables. VCL has a TQuery class to handle queries.

- A *database* refers to a directory on a disk (when dealing with non-server data such as Paradox and dBASE files) or a SQL database (when dealing with SQL servers). A database can contain multiple tables. As you may have guessed, VCL also has a TDatabase class.

- An *index* defines rules by which a table is ordered. To have an index on a particular field in a table means to sort its records based on the value that field holds for each record. The TTable component contains properties and methods that help you manipulate indexes.

> **NOTE**
>
> We mentioned earlier that this chapter assumes a bit of database knowledge. This chapter is not intended to be a primer on database programming, and we expect that you're already familiar with the items in this list. If terms such as *database*, *table*, and *index* sound foreign to you, you might want to obtain an introductory text on database concepts.

VCL Database Architecture

During the development of Delphi 3, VCL's database architecture was significantly overhauled in order to open the data set architecture to allow non-BDE data sets to more easily be used within Delphi. At the root of this architecture is the base TDataSet class. TDataSet is a component that provides an abstract representation of data set records and fields. A number of methods of TDataSet can be overridden in order to create a component that communicates with some particular physical data format. Following this formula, VCL's TBDEDataSet descends from TDataSet and serves as the base class for data sources that communicate via the BDE. If you'd like to learn how to create a TDataSet descendant to plug some type of custom data into this architecture, you'll find an example in Chapter 29, "Extending Database VCL."

BDE Data Access Components

The Data Access page of the Component Palette contains the VCL components you'll use to access and manage BDE data sets. These are shown in Figure 27.1. VCL represents data sets with three components: TTable, TQuery, and TStoredProc. These components all descend directly from the TDBDataSet component, which descends from TBDEDataSet (which, in turn, descends from TDataSet). As mentioned earlier, TDataSet is an abstract component that encapsulates data set management, navigation, and manipulation. TBDEDataSet is an abstract component that represents a BDE-specific data set. TDBDataSet introduces concepts such as BDE databases and sessions (these are explained in detail in the next chapter). Throughout the rest of this chapter, we'll refer to this type of BDE-specific data set simply as a *data set*.

FIGURE 27.1.

The Data Access page of the Component Palette.

As their names imply, TTable is a component that represents the structure and data contained within a database table, and TQuery is a component representing the set of data returned from a SQL query operation. TStoredProc encapsulates a stored procedure on a SQL server. In this chapter, for simplicity's sake, we use the TTable component when discussing data sets. Later, the TQuery component is covered in detail.

Opening a Data Set

Before you can do any nifty manipulation of your data set, you must first open it. To open a data set, simply call its Open() method, as shown in this example:

```
Table1.Open;
```

This is equivalent, by the way, to setting a data set's Active property to True:

```
Table1.Active := True;
```

There's slightly less overhead in the latter method, because the Open() method ends up setting the Active property to True. However, the overhead is so minimal that it's not worth worrying about.

Once the data set has been opened, you're free to manipulate it, as you'll see in just a moment. When you finish using the data set, you should close it by calling its Close() method, like this:

```
Table1.Close;
```

Alternatively, you could close it by setting its Active property to False, like this:

```
Table1.Active := False;
```

> **TIP**
>
> When you're communicating with SQL servers, a connection to the database must be established when you first open a data set in that database. When you close the last data set in a database, your connection is terminated. Opening and closing these connections involves a certain amount of overhead. Therefore, if you find that you open and close the connection to the database often, use a TDatabase component instead to maintain a connection to a SQL server's database throughout many open and close operations. The TDatabase component is explained in more detail in the next chapter.

Navigating Data Sets

TDataSet provides some simple methods for basic record navigation. The First() and Last() methods move you to the first and last records in the data set, respectively, and the Next() and Prior() methods move you either one record forward or back in the data set. Additionally, the MoveBy() method, which accepts an Integer parameter, moves you a specified number of records forward or back.

> **NOTE**
>
> One of the big, but less obvious, benefits of using the BDE is that it allows navigable SQL tables and queries. SQL data generally is not navigable—you can move forward through the rows of a query but not backward. Unlike ODBC, BDE makes SQL data navigable.

BOF, EOF, and Looping

BOF and EOF are Boolean properties of TDataSet that reveal whether the current record is the first or last record in the data set. For example, you might need to iterate through each record in a data set until reaching the last record. The easiest way to do so would be to employ a while loop to keep iterating over records until the EOF property returns True, as shown here:

```
Table1.First;                        // go to beginning of data set
while not Table1.EOF do              // iterate over table
begin
  // do some stuff with current record
  Table1.Next;                       // move to next record
end;
```

> **CAUTION**
>
> Be sure to call the `Next()` method inside your `while-not-EOF` loop or else your application will get caught in an endless loop.

Avoid using a `repeat..until` loop to perform actions on a data set. The following code may look OK on the surface, but bad things may happen if you try to use it on an empty data set, because the `DoSomeStuff()` procedure will always execute at least once, regardless of whether or not the data set contains records.

```
repeat
  DoSomeStuff;
  Table1.Next;
until Table1.EOF;
```

Because the `while-not-EOF` loop performs the check up front, you won't encounter such a problem with this construct.

Bookmarks

Bookmarks enable you to save your place in a data set so that you can come back to the same spot at a later time. Bookmarks are very easy to use in Delphi because you only have one property to remember.

Delphi represents a bookmark as a type `TBookmarkStr`. `TTable` has a property of this type called `Bookmark`. When you read from this property, you obtain a bookmark, and when you write to this property, you go to a bookmark. When you find a particularly interesting place in a data set that you'd like to be able to get back to easily, here's the syntax to use:

```
var
  BM: TBookmarkStr;
begin
  BM := Table1.Bookmark;
```

When you want to return to the place in the data set you marked, just do the reverse—set the `Bookmark` property to the value you obtained earlier by reading the `Bookmark` property:

```
Table1.Bookmark := BM;
```

`TBookmarkStr` is defined as an `AnsiString`, so memory is automatically managed for bookmarks (you never have to free them). If you'd like to clear an existing bookmark, just set it to an empty string:

```
BM := '';
```

Note that `TBookmarkStr` is an `AnsiString` for storage convenience. You should consider it an opaque data type and not depend on the implementation because the bookmark data is completely determined by BDE and the underlying data layers.

> **NOTE**
>
> Delphi 4 still supports `GetBookmark()`,`GotoBookmark()`, and `FreeBookmark()` from Delphi 1.0. However, because the 32-bit Delphi technique is a bit cleaner and less prone to error, you should use this newer technique unless you have to maintain compatibility with 16-bit projects.

Navigational Example

You'll now create a small project that incorporates the `TDataSet` navigational methods and properties you just learned. This project will be called `Navig8`, and the main form for this project is shown in Figure 27.2.

FIGURE 27.2.

The `Navig8` *project's main form.*

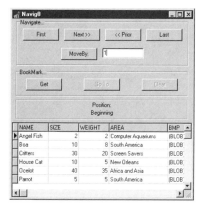

To display the data contained in a `TTable` object, this project will employ the `TDBGrid` component. The process of "wiring" a data-aware control such as the `TDBGrid` component to a data set requires several steps. The following list covers the steps for displaying `Table1`'s data in `DBGrid1`:

1. Set `Table1`'s `DatabaseName` property to an existing alias or directory. Use the `DBDEMOS` alias if you installed Delphi's sample programs.

2. Choose a table from the list presented in `Table1`'s `TableName` property.

3. Drop a `TDataSource` component on the form and wire it to `TTable` by setting `DataSource1`'s data set property to `Table1`. `TDataSource` serves as a conduit between data sources and controls; it's explained in more detail earlier in the chapter.

4. Wire the TDBGrid component to the TDataSource component by setting DBGrid1's DataSource property to DataSource1.

5. Open the table by setting Table1's Active property to True.

6. Poof! You now have data in the grid control.

TIP

A shortcut for picking components from the drop-down list provided for the data set and DataSource properties is to double-click the area to the right of the property name in the Object Inspector. This sets the property value to the first item in the drop-down list.

The source code for main unit of Navig8, called Nav.pas, is shown in Listing 27.1.

LISTING 27.1. THE SOURCE CODE FOR Nav.pas.

```
unit Nav;

interface

uses
  SysUtils, Windows, Messages, Classes, Controls, Forms, StdCtrls,
  Grids, DBGrids, DB, DBTables, ExtCtrls;

type
  TForm1 = class(TForm)
    Table1: TTable;
    DataSource1: TDataSource;
    DBGrid1: TDBGrid;
    GroupBox1: TGroupBox;
    GetButton: TButton;
    GotoButton: TButton;
    ClearButton: TButton;
    GroupBox2: TGroupBox;
    FirstButton: TButton;
    LastButton: TButton;
    NextButton: TButton;
    PriorButton: TButton;
    MoveByButton: TButton;
    Edit1: TEdit;
    Panel1: TPanel;
    PosLbl: TLabel;
    Label1: TLabel;
    procedure FirstButtonClick(Sender: TObject);
    procedure LastButtonClick(Sender: TObject);
    procedure NextButtonClick(Sender: TObject);
```

```
      procedure PriorButtonClick(Sender: TObject);
      procedure MoveByButtonClick(Sender: TObject);
      procedure DataSource1DataChange(Sender: TObject; Field: TField);
      procedure GetButtonClick(Sender: TObject);
      procedure GotoButtonClick(Sender: TObject);
      procedure ClearButtonClick(Sender: TObject);
    private
      BM: TBookmarkStr;
    public
      { Public declarations }
    end;

var
  Form1: TForm1;

implementation

{$R *.DFM}

procedure TForm1.FirstButtonClick(Sender: TObject);
begin
  Table1.First;        // Go to first record in table
end;

procedure TForm1.LastButtonClick(Sender: TObject);
begin
  Table1.Last;         // Go to last record in table
end;

procedure TForm1.NextButtonClick(Sender: TObject);
begin
  Table1.Next;         // Go to next record in table
end;

procedure TForm1.PriorButtonClick(Sender: TObject);
begin
  Table1.Prior;        // Go to prior record in table
end;

procedure TForm1.MoveByButtonClick(Sender: TObject);
begin
  // Move a specified number of record forward or back in the table
  Table1.MoveBy(StrToInt(Edit1.Text));
end;

procedure TForm1.DataSource1DataChange(Sender: TObject; Field: TField);
begin
  // Set caption appropriately, depending on state of Table1 BOF/EOF
  if Table1.BOF then PosLbl.Caption := 'Beginning'
  else if Table1.EOF then PosLbl.Caption := 'End'
```

27

continues

LISTING 27.1. CONTINUED

```delphi
  else PosLbl.Caption := 'Somewheres in between';
end;

procedure TForm1.GetButtonClick(Sender: TObject);
begin
  BM := Table1.Bookmark;        // Get a bookmark
  GotoButton.Enabled := True;   // Enable/disable proper buttons
  GetButton.Enabled := False;
  ClearButton.Enabled := True;
end;

procedure TForm1.GotoButtonClick(Sender: TObject);
begin
  Table1.Bookmark := BM;        // Go to the bookmark position
end;

procedure TForm1.ClearButtonClick(Sender: TObject);
begin
  BM := '';                     // clear the bookmark
  GotoButton.Enabled := False;  // Enable/disable appropriate buttons
  GetButton.Enabled := True;
  ClearButton.Enabled := False;
end;

end.
```

This example illustrates quite well the fact that you can use Delphi's database classes to do quite a lot of database manipulation in your programs with very little code.

Note that you should initially set the Enabled properties of GotoButton and FreeButton to False, because you can't use them until a bookmark is allocated. The FreeButtonClick() and GetButtonClick() methods ensure that the proper buttons are enabled, depending on whether or not a bookmark has been set.

Most of the other procedures in this example are one-liners, although one method that does require some explanation is TForm1.DataSource1DataChange(). This method is wired to DataSource1's OnDataChange event, which fires every time a field value changes (for example, when you move from one record to another). This event checks to see if you're at the beginning, in the middle, or at the end of a data set; it then changes the label's caption appropriately. You'll learn more about the TTable and TDataSource events a bit later in this chapter.

BOF AND EOF

You may notice that when you run the `Navig8` project, `PosLbl`'s caption indicates that you're at the beginning of the data set, which makes sense. However, if you move to the next record and back again, `PosLbl`'s caption isn't aware that you're at the first record. Notice, however, that `PosLbl.Caption` does indicate `BOF` if you click the Prior button once more. Note that the same holds true for `EOF` if you try this at the end of the data set. Why?

The reason is that the BDE cannot be sure you're at the beginning or end of the data set any more, because another user of the table (if it's a networked table) or even another process within your program could have added a record to the beginning or end of the table in the time it took you to move from the first to the second record and then back again.

With that in mind, `BOF` can only be `True` under one of the following circumstances:

- You just opened the data set.
- You just called the data set's First() method.
- A call to TDataSet.Prior() failed, indicating that there are no prior records.

Likewise, `EOF` can only be `True` under the following circumstances:

- You opened an empty data set.
- You just called the data set's `Last()` method.
- A call to `TDataSet.Next()` failed, indicating that there are no more records.

A subtle but important piece of information that you can garner from this list is that you know a data set is empty when both `BOF` and `EOF` are `True`.

TDataSource

A `TDataSource` component was used in that last example, so let's digress for a moment to discuss this very important object. `TDataSource` is the conduit that enables data access components such as `TTables` to connect to data controls such as `TDBEdit` and `TDBLookupCombo` components. In addition to being the interface between data sets and data-aware controls, `TDataSource` contains a couple of handy properties and events that make your life easier when manipulating data.

The `State` property of `TDataSource` reveals the current state of the underlying data set. The value of `State` tells you whether the data set is currently inactive or in Insert, Edit, SetKey, or CalcFields mode, for example. The `State` property of `TDataSet` is explained in more detail later in this chapter. The `OnStateChange` event fires whenever the value of this property changes.

The `OnDataChange` event of `TDataset` is executed whenever the data set becomes active or a data-aware control informs the data set that something has changed.

The `OnUpdateData` event occurs whenever a record is posted or updated. This is the event that causes data-aware controls to change their value based on the contents of the table. You can respond to the event yourself to keep track of such changes within your application.

Working with Fields

Delphi enables you to access the fields of any data set through the `TField` object and its descendants. Not only can you get and set the value of a given field of the current record of a data set, but you can also change the behavior of a field by modifying its properties. You can also modify the data set itself by changing visual order of fields, removing fields, or even creating new calculated or lookup fields.

Field Values

It's very easy to access field values from Delphi. `TDataSet` provides a default array property called `FieldValues[]` that returns the value of a particular field as a Variant. Because `FieldValues[]` is the default array property, you don't need to specify the property name to access the array. For example, the following piece of code assigns the value of `Table1`'s `CustName` field to `String S`:

```
S := Table1['CustName'];
```

You could just as easily store the value of an integer field called `CustNo` in an integer variable called `I`:

```
I := Table1['CustNo'];
```

A powerful corollary to this is the capability to store the values of several fields into a Variant array. The only catches are that the Variant array index must be zero-based and the Variant array contents should be `varVariant`. The following code demonstrates this capability:

```
const
  AStr = 'The %s is of the %s category and its length is %f in.';
var
  VarArr: Variant;
  F: Double;
begin
  VarArr := VarArrayCreate([0, 2], varVariant);
```

```
  { Assume Table1 is attached to Biolife table }
  VarArr := Table1['Common_Name;Category;Length_In'];
  F := VarArr[2];
  ShowMessage(Format(AStr, [VarArr[0], VarArr[1], F]));
end;
```

Delphi 1.0 programmers will note that the FieldValues[] technique is much easier than the previous technique for accessing field values. That technique (which still works in Delphi 4 for backward compatibility) involves using TDataset's Fields[] array property or FieldsByName() function to access individual TField objects associated with the data set. The TField component provides information about a specific field.

Fields[] is a zero-based array of TField objects, so Fields[0] returns a TField representing the first logical field in the record. FieldsByName() accepts a string parameter that corresponds to a given field name in the table; therefore, FieldsByName('OrderNo') would return a TField component representing the OrderNo field in the current record of the data set.

Given a TField object, you can retrieve or assign the field's value using one of the TField properties shown in Table 27.1.

TABLE 27.1. PROPERTIES TO ACCESS TField VALUES.

Property	*Return Type*
AsBoolean	Boolean
AsFloat	Double
AsInteger	Longint
AsString	String
AsDateTime	TDateTime
Value	Variant

If the first field in the current data set is a string, you can store its value in the String variable S, like this:

```
S := Table1.Fields[0].AsString;
```

The following code sets the integral variable I to contain the value of the 'OrderNo' field in the current record of the table:

```
I := Table1.FieldsByName('OrderNo').AsInteger;
```

Field Data Types

If you want to know the type of a field, look at TField's DataType property, which indicates the data type with respect to the database table (irrespective of a corresponding Object Pascal type). The DataType property is of TFieldType, and TFieldType is defined as

```
type
  TFieldType = (ftUnknown, ftString, ftSmallint, ftInteger, ftWord,
    ftBoolean, ftFloat, ftCurrency, ftBCD, ftDate, ftTime, ftDateTime,
    ftBytes, ftVarBytes, ftAutoInc, ftBlob, ftMemo, ftGraphic, ftFmtMemo,
    ftParadoxOle, ftDBaseOle, ftTypedBinary, ftCursor, ftFixedChar,
    ftWideString, ftLargeint, ftADT, ftArray, ftReference, ftDataSet);
```

There are descendants of TField designed to work specifically with many of the preceding data types. These are covered a bit later in this chapter.

Field Names and Numbers

To find the name of a specified field, use TField's FieldName property. For example, the following code places the name of the first field in the current table in the String variable S:

```
var
  S: String;
begin
  S := Table1.Fields[0].FieldName;
end;
```

Likewise, you can obtain the number of a field you know only by name by using the FieldNo property. The following code stores the number of the OrderNo field in the Integer variable I:

```
var
  I: integer;
begin
  I := Table1.FieldsByName('OrderNo').FieldNo;
end;
```

> **NOTE**
>
> To determine how many fields a data set contains, use TDataset's FieldList property. FieldList represents a flattened view of all the nested fields in a table containing fields that are abstract data types (ADTs).
>
> For backward compatibility, the FieldCount property still works, but it will skip over any ADT fields.

Manipulating Field Data

Here's a three-step process for editing one or more fields in the current record.

1. Call the data set's Edit() method to put the data set into Edit mode.

2. Assign new values to the fields of your choice.

3. Post the changes to the data set either by calling the Post() method or by moving to a new record, which will automatically post the edit.

For instance, a typical record edit looks like this:

```
Table1.Edit;
Table1['Age'] := 23;
Table1.Post;
```

> **TIP**
>
> Sometimes you work with data sets that contain read-only data. Examples of this would include a table located on a CD-ROM drive or a query with a non-live result set. Before attempting to edit data, you can determine whether the data set contains read-only data before you try to modify it by checking the value of the CanModify property. If CanModify is True, you have the green light to edit the data set.

Along the same lines as editing data, you can insert or append records to a data set in much the same way:

1. Call the data set's Insert() or Append() methods to put the data set into Insert or Append mode.

2. Assign values to the data set's fields.

3. Post the new record to the data set either by calling Post() or by moving to a new record, which forces a post to occur.

> **NOTE**
>
> When you are in Edit, Insert, or Append mode, keep in mind that your changes will always post when you move off the current record. Therefore, be careful when you use the Next(), Prior(), First(), Last(), and MoveBy() methods while editing records.

If at some point, before your additions or modifications to the data set are posted, you want to abandon your changes, you can do so by calling the `Cancel()` method. For instance, the following code cancels the edit before changes are posted to the table:

```
Table1.Edit;
Table1['Age'] := 23;
Table1.Cancel;
```

`Cancel()` undoes changes to the data set, takes the data set out of Edit, Append, or Insert mode, and puts it back into Browse mode.

To round out the set of `TDataSet`'s record manipulation method, the `Delete()` method removes the current record from the data set. For example, the following code deletes the last record in the table:

```
Table1.Last;
Table1.Delete;
```

The Fields Editor

Delphi gives you a great degree of control and flexibility when working with data set fields through the Fields Editor. You can view the Fields Editor for a particular data set in the Form Designer, either by double-clicking the `TTable`, `TQuery`, or `TStoredProc` or by selecting Fields Editor from the data set's local menu. The Fields Editor window enables you to determine which of a data set's fields you want to work with and create new calculated or lookup fields. You can use a local menu to accomplish these tasks. The Fields Editor window with its local menu deployed is shown in Figure 27.3.

FIGURE 27.3.

The Fields Editor's local menu.

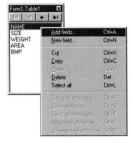

To demonstrate the usage of the Fields Editor, open a new project and drop a `TTable` component onto the main form. Set `Table1`'s `DatabaseName` property to `DBDEMOS` (this is the alias that points to the Delphi sample tables) and set the `TableName` property to `ORDERS.DB`. To provide some visual feedback, also drop a `TDataSource` and `TDBGrid` component on the form. Hook `DataSource1` to `Table1`, and hook `DBGrid1` to `DataSource1`. Now set `Table1`'s `Active` property to `True`, and you'll see `Table1`'s data in the grid.

Adding Fields

Invoke the Fields Editor by double-clicking `Table1`, and you'll see the Fields Editor window, as shown in Figure 27.3. Let's say you want to limit your view of the table to only a few fields. Select Add Fields from the Fields Editor local menu. This will invoke the Add Fields dialog. Highlight the `OrderNo`, `CustNo`, and `ItemsTotal` fields in this dialog and click OK. The three selected fields will now be visible in the Fields Editor and in the grid.

Delphi creates `TField` descendant objects, which map to the data set fields you select in the Fields Editor. For example, for the three fields mentioned in the preceding paragraph, Delphi adds the following declarations of `TField` descendants to the source code for your form:

```
Table1OrderNo: TFloatField;
Table1CustNo: TFloatField;
Table1ItemsTotal: TCurrencyField;
```

Notice that the name of the field object is the concatenation of the `TTable` name and the field name. Because these fields are created in code, you can also access `TField` descendant properties and methods in your code, rather than solely at design time.

`TField` Descendants

Let's digress for just a moment on the topic of `TField`s. There are one or more different `TField` descendant objects for each field type (field types are described in the "Field Data Types" section earlier in this chapter). Each of these field types also maps to an Object Pascal data type. Table 27.2 shows the different `TField` descendants, their field types, and the Object Pascal type to which they equate.

TABLE 27.2. TField DESCENDANTS AND THEIR FIELD TYPES.

TField *Descendant*	*Field Type*	*Object Pascal Type*
TStringField	ftString	String
TIntegerField	ftInteger	Integer
TSmallIntField	ftSmallInt	SmallInt
TWordField	ftWord	Word
TAutoIncField	ftAutoInc	Integer
TFloatField	ftFloat	Double
TCurrencyField	ftCurrency	Currency
TBCDField	ftBCD	Double

continues

27

WRITING DESKTOP
DATABASE
APPLICATIONS

TABLE 27.2. TField DESCENDANTS AND THEIR FIELD TYPES.

TField *Descendant*	*Field Type*	*Object Pascal Type*
TBooleanField	ftBoolean	Boolean
TDateTimeField	ftDateTime	TDateTime
TDateField	ftDate	TDateTime
TTimeField	ftTime	TDateTime
TBytesField	ftBytes	*none*
TVarBytesField	ftVarBytes	*none*
TBlobField	ftBlob	*none*
TMemoField	ftMemo	*none*
TGraphicField	ftGraphic	*none*

As Table 27.2 shows, Blob field types are special in that they don't map directly to native Object Pascal types. Blob fields are discussed in more detail later in this chapter.

Fields and the Object Inspector

When you select a field in the Fields Editor, you can access the properties and events associated with that TField descendant object in the Object Inspector. This feature enables you to modify field properties such as minimum and maximum values, display formats, and whether the field is required as well as whether it's read-only. Some of these properties, such as ReadOnly, are obvious in their purpose, but some aren't quite as intuitive. Some of the less intuitive properties are covered later in this chapter. Figure 27.4 shows the OrderNo field focused in the Object Inspector.

FIGURE 27.4.

Editing a field's properties.

Switch to the Events page of the Object Inspector and you'll see that there are also events associated with field objects. The events OnChange, OnGetText, OnSetText, and OnValidate are all well-documented in the online help. Simply click to the left of the event in the Object Inspector and press F1. Of these, OnChange is probably the most common to use. It enables you to perform some action whenever the contents of the field change (moving to another record or adding a record, for example).

Calculated Fields

You can also add calculated fields to a data set using the Fields Editor. Let's say, for example, you wanted to add a field that figures the wholesale total for each entry in the ORDERS table, and the wholesale total was 32 percent of the normal total. Select New Field from the Fields Editor local menu, and you'll be presented with the New Field dialog, as shown in Figure 27.5. Enter the name, WholesaleTotal, for the new field in the Name edit control. The type of this field is Currency, so enter that in the Type edit control. Make sure the Calculated radio button is selected in the Field Type group; then press OK. Now the new field will show up in the grid, but it won't yet contain any data.

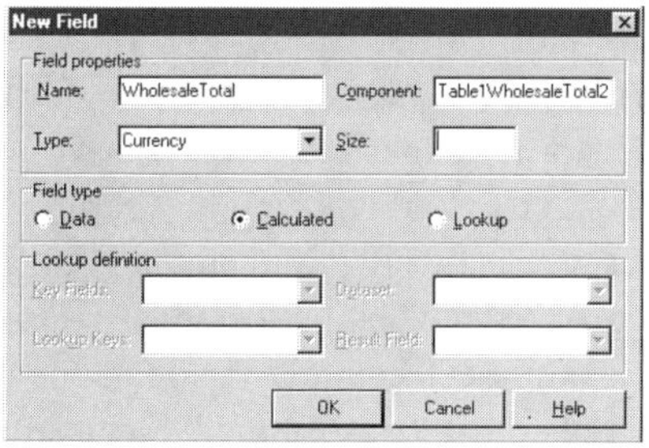

FIGURE 27.5.

Adding a calculated field with the New Field dialog.

To cause the new field to become populated with data, you must assign a method to Table1's OnCalcFields event. The code for this event simply assigns the value of the WholesaleTotal field to be 32 percent of the value of the existing SalesTotal field. This method, which handles Table1.OnCalcFields, is shown here:

```
procedure TForm1.Table1CalcFields(DataSet: TDataSet);
begin
  DataSet['WholesaleTotal'] := DataSet['ItemsTotal'] * 0.68;
end;
```

Figure 27.6 shows that the WholesaleTotal field in the grid now contains the correct data.

FIGURE 27.6.

The calculated field has been added to the table.

Lookup Fields

Lookup fields enable you to create fields in a data set that actually look up their value from another data set. To illustrate this, you'll add a lookup field to the current project. The CustNo field of the ORDERS table doesn't mean anything to someone who doesn't have all the customer numbers memorized. You can add a lookup field to Table1 that looks into the CUSTOMER table and then based on the customer number, retrieves the name of the current customer.

First, you should drop in a second TTable object, setting its DatabaseName property to DBDEMOS and its TableName property to CUSTOMER. This is Table2. Then you once again select New Field from the Fields Editor local menu to invoke the New Field dialog. This time you'll call the field CustName, and the field type will be a String. The size of the string is 15 characters. Don't forget to select the Lookup button in the Field Type radio group. The Dataset control in this dialog should be set to Table2—the data set you wish to look into. The Key Fields and Lookup Keys controls should be set to CustNo—this is the common field upon which the lookup will be performed. Finally, the Result field should be set to Contact—this is the field you want displayed. Figure 27.7 shows the New Field dialog for the new lookup field. The new field will now display the correct data, as shown in the completed project in Figure 27.8.

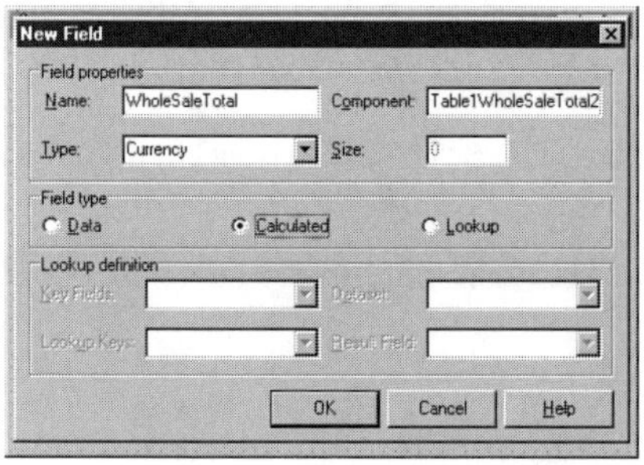

FIGURE 27.7.

Adding a lookup field with the New Field dialog.

FIGURE 27.8.

Viewing the table containing a lookup field.

Drag-and-Drop Fields

Another less obvious feature of the Fields Editor is that it enables you to drag fields from its Fields list box and drop them onto your forms. We can easily demonstrate this feature by starting a new project that contains only a `TTable` on the main form. Assign `Table1.DatabaseName` to DBDEMOS and assign `Table1.TableName` to BIOLIFE.DB. Invoke the Fields Editor for this table and add all the fields in the table to the Fields Editor list box. You can now drag one or more of the fields at a time from the Fields Editor window and drop them on your main form.

You'll notice a couple of cool things happening here: First, Delphi senses what kind of field you're dropping onto your form and creates the appropriate data-aware control to display the data (that is, a `TDBEdit` is created for a string field, whereas a `TDBImage` is created for a graphic field). Second, Delphi checks to see if you have a `TDataSource` object connected to the data set; it hooks to an existing one if available or creates one if needed. Figure 27.9 shows the result of dragging and dropping the fields of the BIOLIFE table onto a form.

FIGURE 27.9.

Dragging and dropping fields on a form.

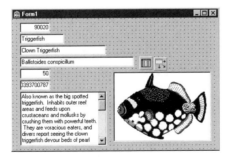

Working with BLOB Fields

A BLOB (Binary Large Object) field is a field that is designed to contain an indeterminate amount of data. A BLOB field in one record of a data set may contain three bytes of data, whereas the same field in another record of that data set may contain 3K bytes. Blobs are most useful for holding large amounts of text, graphic images, or raw data streams such as OLE objects.

`TBlobField` and Field Types

As discussed earlier, VCL includes a `TField` descendant called `TBlobField`, which encapsulates a BLOB field. `TBlobField` has a `BlobType` property of type `TBlobType`, which indicates what type of data is stored in the BLOB field. `TBlobType` is defined in the `DBTables` unit as follows:

```
TBlobType = ftBlob..ftTypedBinary;
```

All these field types and the type of data associated with these field types are listed in Table 27.3.

TABLE 27.3. `TBlobField` FIELD TYPES.

Field Type	Type of Data
ftBlob	Untyped or user-defined data
ftMemo	Text
ftGraphic	Windows bitmap
ftFmtMemo	Paradox formatted memo
ftParadoxOle	Paradox OLE object
ftDBaseOLE	dBASE OLE object
ftTypedBinary	Raw data representation of an existing type

You'll find that most of the work you need to do in getting data in and out of `TBlobField` components can be accomplished by loading or saving the BLOB to a file or by using a `TBlobStream`. `TBlobStream` is a specialized descendant of `TStream` that uses the BLOB field inside the physical table as the stream location. To demonstrate these techniques for interacting with `TBlobField` components, you'll create a sample application.

NOTE

If you ran the Setup program on the CD-ROM accompanying this book, it should have set up a BDE alias that points to the \Data subdirectory of the directory in which you installed the software. In this directory, you can find the tables used in the applications throughout this book. Several of the examples on the CD-ROM expect the DDGData alias.

BLOB Field Sample

This project creates an application that enables the user to store WAV files in a database table and play them directly from the table. Start the project by creating a main form with the components shown in Figure 27.10. The `TTable` component can map to the `Wavez` table in the `DDGUtils` alias or your own table of the same structure. The structure of the table is as follows:

Field Name	Field Type	Size
WaveTitle	Character	25
FileName	Character	25
Wave	BLOB	

FIGURE 27.10.

Main form for Wavez, *the BLOB field example.*

The Add button is used to load a WAV file from disk and add it to the table. The method assigned to the `OnClick` event of the Add button is shown here:

```
procedure TMainForm.sbAddClick(Sender: TObject);
begin
  if OpenDialog.Execute then
  begin
    tblSounds.Append;
    tblSounds['FileName'] := ExtractFileName(OpenDialog.FileName);
    tblSoundsWave.LoadFromFile(OpenDialog.FileName);
    edTitle.SetFocus;
  end;
end;
```

The code first attempts to execute `OpenDialog`. If it's successful, `tblSounds` is put into Append mode, the `FileName` field is assigned a value, and the `Wave` BLOB field is loaded from the file specified by `OpenDialog`. Notice that `TBlobField`'s `LoadFromFile` method is very handy here, and the code is very clean for loading a file into a BLOB field.

Similarly, the Save button saves the current WAV sound found in the `Wave` field to an external file. The code for this button is as follows:

```
procedure TMainForm.sbSaveClick(Sender: TObject);
begin
  with SaveDialog do
  begin
    FileName := tblSounds['FileName'];      // initialize file name
```

```
    if Execute then                         // execute dialog
      tblSoundsWave.SaveToFile(FileName); // save blob to file
  end;
end;
```

There's even less code here. SaveDialog is initialized with the value of the FileName field. If SaveDialog's execution is successful, tblSoundsWave's SaveToFile method is called to save the contents of the BLOB field to the file.

The handler for the Play button does the work of reading the WAV data from the BLOB field and passing it to the PlaySound() API function to be played. The code for this handler, shown in the following code, is a bit more complex than the code shown thus far:

```
procedure TMainForm.sbPlayClick(Sender: TObject);
var
  B: TBlobStream;
  M: TMemoryStream;
begin
  B := TBlobStream.Create(tblSoundsWave, bmRead); // create blob stream
  Screen.Cursor := crHourGlass;                    // wait hourglass
  try
    M := TMemoryStream.Create;                      // create memory stream
    try
      M.CopyFrom(B, B.Size);      // copy from blob to memory stream
      // Attempt to play sound. Raise exception if something goes wrong
      Win32Check(PlaySound(M.Memory, 0, SND_SYNC or SND_MEMORY));
    finally
      M.Free;
    end;
  finally
    Screen.Cursor := crDefault;
    B.Free;                                         // clean up
  end;
end;
```

The first thing this method does is to create an instance of TBlobStream, B, using the tblSoundsWave BLOB field. The first parameter passed to TBlobStream.Create() is the BLOB field object, and the second parameter indicates how you want to open the stream. Typically, you'll use bmRead for read-only access to the BLOB stream or bmReadWrite for read/write access.

TIP

The data set must be in Edit, Insert, or Append mode to open a TBlobStream with bmReadWrite privilege.

An instance of `TMemoryStream`, `M`, is then created. At this point, the cursor shape is changed to an hourglass to let the user know that the operation may take a couple of seconds. The stream `B` is then copied to the stream `M`. The function used to play a WAV sound, `PlaySound()`, requires a filename or a memory pointer as its first parameter. `TBlobStream` doesn't provide pointer access to the stream data, but `TMemoryStream` does through its `Memory` property. Given that, you can successfully call `PlaySound()` to play the data pointed at by `M.Memory`. Once the function is called, it cleans up by freeing the streams and restoring the cursor. The complete code for the main unit of this project is shown in Listing 27.2.

LISTING 27.2. THE MAIN UNIT FOR THE Wavez PROJECT.

```
unit Main;

interface

uses
  Windows, Messages, SysUtils, Classes, Graphics, Controls, Forms,
  Dialogs, ExtCtrls, DBCtrls, DB, DBTables, StdCtrls, Mask, Buttons,
  ComCtrls;

type
  TMainForm = class(TForm)
    tblSounds: TTable;
    dsSounds: TDataSource;
    tblSoundsWaveTitle: TStringField;
    tblSoundsWave: TBlobField;
    edTitle: TDBEdit;
    edFileName: TDBEdit;
    Label1: TLabel;
    Label2: TLabel;
    OpenDialog: TOpenDialog;
    tblSoundsFileName: TStringField;
    SaveDialog: TSaveDialog;
    pnlToobar: TPanel;
    sbPlay: TSpeedButton;
    sbAdd: TSpeedButton;
    sbSave: TSpeedButton;
    sbExit: TSpeedButton;
    Bevel1: TBevel;
    dbnNavigator: TDBNavigator;
    stbStatus: TStatusBar;
    procedure sbPlayClick(Sender: TObject);
    procedure sbAddClick(Sender: TObject);
    procedure sbSaveClick(Sender: TObject);
    procedure sbExitClick(Sender: TObject);
    procedure FormCreate(Sender: TObject);
```

continues

LISTING 27.2. CONTINUED

```pascal
  private
    procedure OnAppHint(Sender: TObject);
  end;

var
  MainForm: TMainForm;

implementation

{$R *.DFM}

uses MMSystem;

procedure TMainForm.sbPlayClick(Sender: TObject);
var
  B: TBlobStream;
  M: TMemoryStream;
begin
  B := TBlobStream.Create(tblSoundsWave, bmRead); // create blob stream
  Screen.Cursor := crHourGlass;                   // wait hourglass
  try
    M := TMemoryStream.Create;                    // create memory stream
    try
      M.CopyFrom(B, B.Size);        // copy from blob to memory stream
      // Attempt to play sound.  Show error box if something goes wrong
      Win32Check(PlaySound(M.Memory, 0, SND_SYNC or SND_MEMORY));
    finally
      M.Free;
    end;
  finally
    Screen.Cursor := crDefault;
    B.Free;                                       // clean up
  end;
end;

procedure TMainForm.sbAddClick(Sender: TObject);
begin
  if OpenDialog.Execute then
  begin
    tblSounds.Append;
    tblSounds['FileName'] := ExtractFileName(OpenDialog.FileName);
    tblSoundsWave.LoadFromFile(OpenDialog.FileName);
    edTitle.SetFocus;
  end;
end;
```

```
procedure TMainForm.sbSaveClick(Sender: TObject);
begin
  with SaveDialog do
  begin
    FileName := tblSounds['FileName'];     // initialize file name
    if Execute then                        // execute dialog
      tblSoundsWave.SaveToFile(FileName);  // save blob to file
  end;
end;

procedure TMainForm.sbExitClick(Sender: TObject);
begin
  Close;
end;

procedure TMainForm.FormCreate(Sender: TObject);
begin
  Application.OnHint := OnAppHint;
end;

procedure TMainForm.OnAppHint(Sender: TObject);
begin
  stbStatus.SimpleText := Application.Hint;
end;

end.
```

Refreshing the Data Set

If there's one thing you can count on when you create database applications, it's that data contained in a data set is in a constant state of flux. Records will constantly be added to, removed from, and modified in your data set, particularly in a networked environment. Because of this, you may occasionally need to reread the data set information from disk or memory to update the contents of your data set.

You can update your data set using TDataset's Refresh() method. It functionally does about the same thing as using Close() and then Open() on the data set, but Refresh() is a bit faster.

SQL tables and queries must have a unique index before the BDE will attempt a Refresh() operation. This is because Refresh() tries to preserve the current record, if possible. This means that the BDE has to use Seek() to go to the current record at some point, which is practical only on a SQL data set if a unique index is available.

CAUTION

When Refresh() is called, it can create some unexpected side effects for the users of your program. For example, if User 1 is viewing a record on a networked table, and that record has been deleted by User 2, a call to Refresh() will cause User 1 to see the record disappear for no apparent reason. The fact that data could be changing beneath the user is something you need to keep in mind when you call this function.

Altered States

At some point, you may need to know whether a table is in Edit mode or Append mode, or even if it's active. You can obtain this information by inspecting TDataset's State property. The State property is of type TDataSetState, and it can have any one of the values shown in Table 27.4.

TABLE 27.4. VALUES FOR TDataSet.State.

Value	Meaning
dsBrowse	The data set is in Browse (normal) mode.
dsCalcFields	The OnCalcFields event has been called, and a record value calculation is in progress.
dsEdit	The data set is in Edit mode. This means the Edit() method has been called, but the edited record has not yet been posted.
dsInactive	The data set is closed.
dsInsert	The data set is in Insert mode. This typically means that Insert() has been called but changes haven't been posted.
dsSetKey	The data set is in SetKey mode, meaning that SetKey() has been called but GotoKey() hasn't yet been called.
dsUpdateNew	The data set is in the processes of committing a delayed update to the underlying table.
dsUpdateOld	The data set is in the process of canceling a delayed update and returning the data to its original value.
dsFilter	The data set is currently processing a record filter, lookup, or some other operation that requires a filter.

Filters

Filters enable you to do simple data set searching or filtering using only Object Pascal code. The primary advantage of using filters is that they don't require an index or any other preparation on the data sets with which they are used. Of course, filters are still a bit slower than index-based searching (which is covered later in this chapter), but they are still very usable in almost any type of application.

Filtering a Data Set

One of the more common uses of Delphi's filtering mechanism is to limit a view of a data set to some specific records only. This is a simple two-step process:

1. Assign a procedure to the data set's `OnFilterRecord` event. Inside of this procedure, you should write code that accepts records based on the values of one or more fields.

2. Set the data set's `Filtered` property to `True`.

As an example, Figure 27.11 shows a form containing `TDBGrid`, which displays an unfiltered view of Delphi's `CUSTOMER` table.

FIGURE 27.11.

An unfiltered view of the CUSTOMER *table.*

In step 1, you write a handler for the table's `OnFilterRecord` event. In this case, we'll accept only records whose `Company` field starts with the letter S. The code for this procedure is shown here:

```
procedure TForm1.Table1FilterRecord(DataSet: TDataSet;
  var Accept: Boolean);
var
  FieldVal: String;
begin
  FieldVal := DataSet['Company'];  // Get the value of the Company field
  Accept := FieldVal[1] = 'S';     // Accept record if field starts with 'S'
end;
```

After following step 2 and setting the table's `Filtered` property to `True`, you can see in Figure 27.12 that the grid displays only those records that meet the filter criteria.

FIGURE 27.12.

A filtered view of the CUSTOMER table.

CustNo	Company	Addr1
1351	Sight Diver	1 Neptune Lane
2163	SCUBA Heaven	PO Box Q-8874
2165	Shangri-La Sports Center	PO Box D-5495
3051	San Pablo Dive Center	1701-D N Broadway
5163	Safari Under the Sea	PO Box 7456

FindFirst/FindNext

`TDataSet` also provides methods called `FindFirst()`,`FindNext()`,`FindPrior()`, and `FindLast()` that employ filters to find records that match a particular search criteria. All these functions work on unfiltered data sets by calling that data set's `OnFilterRecord` event handler. Based on the search criteria in the event handler, these functions will find the first, next, previous, or last match, respectively. Each of these functions accepts no parameters and returns a Boolean, which indicates whether a match was found.

Locating a Record

Not only are filters useful for defining a subset view of a particular data set, but they can also be used to search for records within a data set based on the value of one or more fields. For this purpose, `TDataSet` provides a method called `Locate()`. Once again, because `Locate()` employs filters to do the searching, it will work irrespective of any index applied to the data set. The `Locate()` method is defined as follows:

```
function Locate(const KeyFields: string; const KeyValues: Variant;
  Options: TLocateOptions): Boolean;
```

The first parameter, `KeyFields`, contains the name of the field(s) on which you want to search. The second parameter, `KeyValues`, holds the field value(s) you want to locate. The third and last parameter, `Options`, allows you to customize the type of search you want to perform. This parameter is of type `TLocateOptions`, which is a set type defined in the `DB` unit as follows:

```
type
  TLocateOption = (loCaseInsensitive, loPartialKey);
  TLocateOptions = set of TLocateOption;
```

If the set includes the `loCaseInsensitive` member, a case-insensitive search of the data will be performed. If the set includes the `loPartialKey` member, the values contained in `KeyValues` will match even if they are substrings of the field value.

Locate() will return True if it finds a match. For example, to search for the first occurrence of the value 1356 in the CustNo field of Table1, use the following syntax:

```
Table1.Locate('CustNo', 1356, []);
```

> **TIP**
>
> You should use Locate() whenever possible to search for records, because it will always attempt to use the fastest method possible to find the item, switching indexes temporarily if necessary. This makes your code independent of indexes, and if you determine that you no longer need an index on a particular field, or if adding one will make your program faster, you can make that change on the data without having to recode the application.

USING TTable

This section describes the common properties and methods of the TTable component and how to use them. In particular, you learn how to search for records, filter records using ranges, and create tables. This section also contains a discussion of TTable events.

Searching for Records

When you need to search for records in a table, VCL provides several methods to help you out. When you're working with dBASE and Paradox tables, Delphi assumes that the fields on which you search are indexed. For SQL tables, the performance of your search will suffer if you search on unindexed fields.

Say, for example, you have a table that's keyed on field 1, which is numeric, and on field 2, which is alphanumeric. You can search for a specific record based on those two criteria in one of two ways: using the FindKey() technique or the SetKey()..GotoKey() technique.

FindKey()

TTable's FindKey() method enables you to search for a record matching one or more keyed fields in one function call. FindKey() accepts an array of const (the search criteria) as a parameter and returns True when it's successful. For example, the following code causes the data set to move to the record where the first field in the index has the value 123 and the second field in the index contains the string Hello:

```
if not Table1.FindKey([123, 'Hello']) then MessageBeep(0);
```

If a match is not found, FindKey() returns False and the computer beeps.

SetKey()..GotoKey()

Calling TTable's SetKey() method puts the table in a mode that prepares its fields to be loaded with values representing search criteria. Once the search criteria have been established, use the GotoKey() method to do a top-down search for a matching record. The previous example can be rewritten with SetKey()..GotoKey(), as follows:

```
with Table1 do begin
  SetKey;
  Fields[0].AsInteger := 123;
  Fields[1].AsString := 'Hello';
  if not GotoKey then MessageBeep(0);
end;
```

The Closest Match

Similarly, you can use FindNearest() or the SetKey..GotoNearest methods to search for a value in the table that is the closest match to the search criteria. To search for the first record where the value of the first indexed field is closest to (greater than or equal to) 123, use the following code:

```
Table1.FindNearest([123]);
```

Once again, FindNearest() accepts an array of const as a parameter that contains the field values for which you want to search.

To search using the longhand technique provided by SetKey()..GotoNearest(), you can use this code:

```
with Table1 do begin
  SetKey;
  Fields[0].AsInteger := 123;
  GotoNearest;
end;
```

If the search is successful and the table's KeyExclusive property is set to False, the record pointer will be on the first matching record. If KeyExclusive is True, the current record will be the one immediately following the match.

TIP

If you want to search on the indexed fields of a table, use FindKey() and FindNearest()—rather than SetKey()..GotoX()—whenever possible because you type less code and leave less room for human error.

Which Index?

All these searching methods assume that you're searching under the table's primary index. If you want to search using a secondary index, you need to set the table's `IndexName` parameter to the desired index. For instance, if your table had a secondary index on the `Company` field called `ByCompany`, the following code would enable you to search for the company Unisco:

```
with Table1 do begin
  IndexName := 'ByCompany';
  SetKey;
  FieldValues['Company'] := 'Unisco';
  GotoKey;
end;
```

> **NOTE**
>
> Keep in mind that some overhead is involved in switching indexes while a table is opened. You should expect a delay of a second or more when you set the `IndexName` property to a new value.

Ranges enable you to filter a table so that it contains only records with field values that fall within a certain scope you define. Ranges work similar to key searches, and as with searches, there are several ways to apply a range to a given table—either using the `SetRange()` method, or the manual `SetRangeStart()`, `SetRangeEnd()`, and `ApplyRange()`methods.

> **CAUTION**
>
> If you are working with dBASE or Paradox tables, ranges only work with indexed fields. If you're working with SQL data, performance will suffer greatly if you don't have an index on the ranged field.

SetRange()

Like `FindKey()`and `FindNearest()`, `SetRange()` enables you to perform a fairly complex action on a table with one function call. `SetRange()` accepts two `array of const` variables as parameters: the first represents the field values for the start of the range, and the second represents the field values for the end of the range. As an example, the following code filters through only those records where the value of the first field is greater than or equal to 10 but less than or equal to 15:

```
Table1.SetRange([10], [15]);
```

ApplyRange()

To use the `ApplyRange()` method of setting a range, follow these steps:

1. Call the `SetRangeStart()` method and then modify the `Fields[]` array property of the table to establish the starting value of the keyed field(s).

2. Call the `SetRangeEnd()` method and modify the `Fields[]` array property once again to establish the ending value of the keyed field(s).

3. Call `ApplyRange()` to establish the new range filter.

The preceding range example could be rewritten using this technique:

```
with Table1 do begin
  SetRangeStart;
  Fields[0].AsInteger := 10;      // range starts at 10
  SetRangeEnd;
  Fields[0].AsInteger := 15;      // range ends at 15
  ApplyRange;
end;
```

> **TIP**
>
> Use `SetRange()` whenever possible to filter records—your code will be less prone to error when doing so.

To remove a range filter from a table and restore the table to the state it was in before you called `ApplyRange()` or `SetRange()`, just call TTable's `CancelRange()` method.

```
Table1.CancelRange;
```

Master/Detail Tables

Very often, when programming databases, you'll find situations where the data to be managed lends itself to being broken up into multiple tables that relate to one another. The classic example is a customer table with one record per customer information and an orders table with one record per order. Because every order would have to be made by one of the customers, a natural relationship forms between the two collections of data. This is called a *one-to-many* relationship, because one customer may have many orders (the customer table being the master and the orders table being the detail).

Delphi makes it easy to create these types of relationships between tables. In fact, it's all handled at design time through the Object Inspector; therefore, it's not even necessary for you to write any code. Start with an empty project and add two each of a `TTable`, `TDataSource`, and `TDBGrid` component. `DBGrid1` will hook to `Table1` via `DataSource1`, and `DBGrid2` hooks to `Table2` via `DataSource2`. Using the `DBDEMOS` alias as the `DatabaseName`, `Table1` hooks to the `CUSTOMER.DB` table, and `Table2` hooks to the `ORDERS.DB` table. Your form should look like the one shown in Figure 27.13.

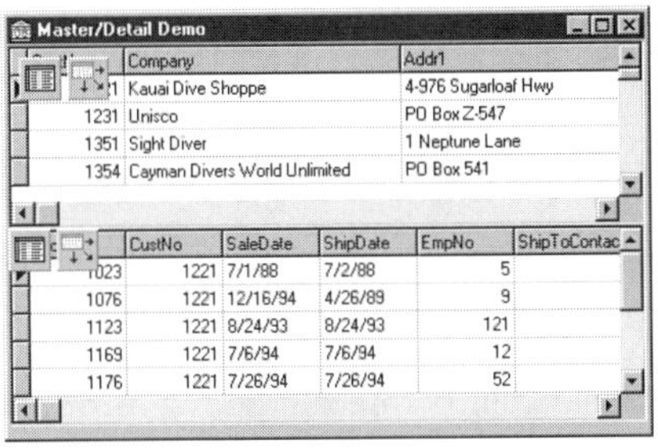

FIGURE 27.13.

The master/detail main form in progress.

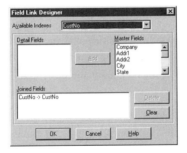

You now have two unrelated tables sharing the same form. Once you've come this far, the only thing left to do is to create the relationship between the tables using the `MasterSource` and `MasterFields` properties of the detail table. `Table2`'s `MasterSource` property should be set to `DataSource1`. When you attempt to edit the `MasterFields` property, you are presented with a property editor called the Field Link Designer. This is shown in Figure 27.14.

FIGURE 27.14.

The Field Link Designer.

In this dialog, you specify which common fields relate the two tables to one another. The field the two tables have in common is `CustNo`—a numeric identifier that represents a customer. Because the `CustNo` field is not a part of the `ORDERS` table's primary index, you'll need to switch to a secondary index that does include the `CustNo` field. You can do that using the Available Indexes drop-down list in the Field Link Designer. Once you've switched to the `CustNo` index, you can then select the `CustNo` field from both the Detail Fields and Master Fields list boxes and click the Add button to create a link between the tables. Click OK to dismiss the Field Link Designer.

You'll now notice that as you move through the records in `Table1`, the view of `Table2` will be limited to only those records that share the same value in the `CustNo` field as `Table1`. The behavior is shown in the finished application in Figure 27.15.

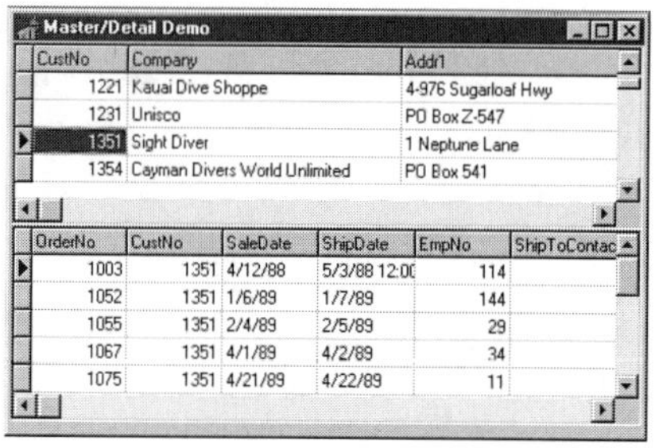

FIGURE 27.15.

*Master/detail
demo program.*

TTable Events

TTable provides you with events that occur before and after a record in the table is deleted, edited, and inserted, whenever a modification is posted or canceled, and whenever the table is opened or closed. This is so that you have full control of your database application. The nomenclature for these events is Before*XXX* and After*XXX*, where *XXX* stands for Delete, Edit, Insert, Open, and so on. These events are fairly self-explanatory, and you'll use them in the database applications in Parts II, "Advanced Techniques," and III, "Component-Based Development," of this book.

TTable's OnNewRecord event fires every time a new record is posted to the table. It's ideal to do various housekeeping tasks in a handler for this event. An example of this would be to keep a running total of records added to a table.

The OnCalcFields event occurs whenever the table cursor is moved off the current record or the current record changes. Adding a handler for the OnCalcFields event enables you to keep a calculated field current whenever the table is modified.

Creating a Table in Code

Instead of creating all your database tables up front (using the Database Desktop, for example) and deploying them with your application, a time will come when you'll need your program to have the capability to create local tables for you. When this need arises, once again VCL has you covered. TTable contains the CreateTable() method, which enables you to create tables on disk. Simply follow these steps to create a table:

1. Create an instance of TTable.

2. Set the DatabaseName property of the table to a directory or existing alias.

3. Give the table a unique name in the TableName property.

4. Set the TableType property to indicate what type of table you want to create. If you set this property to ttDefault, the table type will correspond to the extension of the name provided in the TableName property (for example, DB stands for Paradox, and DBF stands for dBASE).

5. Use `Add()` method for `TTable.FieldDefs` to add fields to the table. The `Add()` method takes four parameters:

   - A string indicating the field name.

   - A `TFieldType` variable indicating the field type.

   - A `word` parameter that represents the size of the field. Note that this parameter is only valid for types such as String and Memo, where the size may vary. Fields such as Integer and Date are always the same size, so this parameter doesn't apply to them.

   - A Boolean parameter that dictates whether or not this is a required field. All required fields must have a value before a record can be posted to a table.

6. If you want the table to have an index, use the `Add()` method of `Table.IndexDefs` to add indexed fields. `IndexDefs.Add()` takes the following three parameters:

   - A string that identifies the index.

   - A string that matches the field name to be indexed. Composite key indexes (indexes on multiple fields) can be specified as a semicolon-delimited list of field names.

   - A set of `TIndexOptions` that determines the index type.

7. Call `TTable.CreateTable()`.

The following code creates a table with Integer, String, and Float fields with an index on the Integer field. The table is called `FOO.DB`, and it will live in the `C:\TEMP` directory:

```
begin
  with TTable.Create(Self) do begin      // create TTable object
    DatabaseName := 'c:\temp';           // point to directory or alias
    TableName := 'FOO';                  // give table a name
    TableType := ttParadox;              // make a Paradox table
    with FieldDefs do begin
      Add('Age', ftInteger, 0, True);    // add an integer field
      Add('Name', ftString, 25, False);  // add a string field
      Add('Weight', ftFloat, 0, False);  // add a floating-point field
    end;
    { create a primary index on the Age field... }
    IndexDefs.Add('', 'Age', [ixPrimary, ixUnique]);
    CreateTable;                         // create the table
  end;
end;
```

> **NOTE**
>
> As mentioned earlier, `TTable.CreateTable()` works only for local tables. For SQL tables, you should use a technique that employs `TQuery` (this is shown in the next chapter).

DATA MODULES

Data modules enable you to keep all your database rules and relationships in one central location to be shared across projects, groups, or enterprises. Data modules are encapsulated by VCL's TDataModule component. Think of TDataModule as an invisible form on which you can drop data access components to be used throughout a project. Creating a TDataModule instance is simple: Select File | New from the main menu and then select Data Module from the Object Repository.

The simple justification for using TDataModule over just putting data access components on a form is that it's easier to share the same data across multiple forms and units in your project. In a more complex situation, you would have an arrangement of multiple TTable, TQuery, and/or TStoredProc components. You might have relationships defined between the components and perhaps rules enforced on the field level, such as minimum/maximum values or display formats. Perhaps this assortment of data access components models the business rules of your enterprise. After taking great pains to set up something so impressive, you wouldn't want to have to do it again for another application, would you? Of course you wouldn't. In such cases, you would want to save your data module to the Object Repository for later use. If you work in a team environment, you might even want to keep the Object Repository on a shared network drive for the use of all the developers on your team.

In the example that follows, you'll create a simple instance of a data module so that many forms have access to the same data. In the database applications shown in several of the later chapters, you'll build more complex relationships into data modules.

SEARCH, RANGE, AND FILTER DEMO

Now it's time to create a sample application to help drive home some of the key concepts that were covered in this chapter. In particular, this application will demonstrate the proper use of filters, key searches, and range filters in your applications. This project, called SRF, contains multiple forms; the main form consists mainly of a grid for browsing a table, and other forms demonstrate the different concepts mentioned earlier. Each of these forms will be explained in turn.

The Data Module

Although we're starting a bit out of order, the data module for this project will be covered first. This data module, called DM, contains only a TTable and a TDataSource component. The TTable, called Table1, is hooked to the CUSTOMERS.DB table in the DBDEMOS alias. The TDataSource, DataSource1, is wired to Table1. All the data-aware controls in this project will use DataSource1 as their DataSource. DM is contained in a unit called DataMod, and it's shown in its design-time state in Figure 27.16.

FIGURE 27.16.

DM, *the data module.*

The Main Form

The main form for SRF, appropriately called MainForm, is shown in Figure 27.17. This form is contained in a unit called Main. As you can see, it contains a TDBGrid control, DBGrid1, for browsing a table, and it contains a radio button that enables you to switch between different indexes on the table. DBGrid1, as explained earlier, is hooked to DM.DataSource1 as its DataSource.

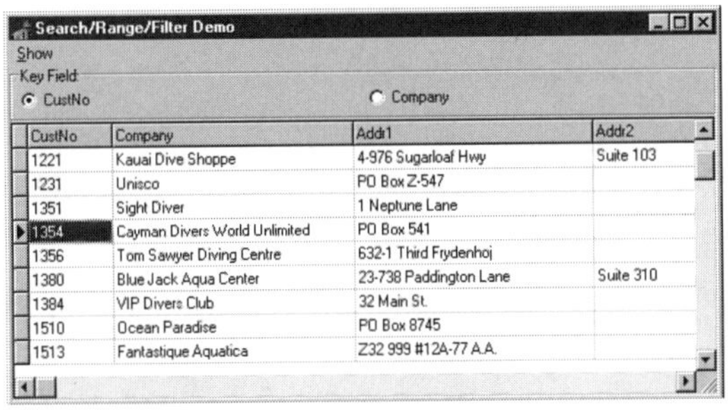

FIGURE 27.17.

MainForm *in the* SRF *project.*

NOTE

In order for DBGrid1 to be able to hook to DM.DataSource1 at design time, the DataMod unit must be in the uses clause of the Main unit. The easiest way to do this is to bring up the Main unit in the Code Editor and select File | Use Unit from the main menu. You'll then be presented with a list of units in your project from which you can select DataMod. You must do this for each of the units from which you want to access the data contained within DM.

The radio group, called RGKeyField, is used to determine which of the table's two indexes is currently active. The code attached to the OnClick event for RGKeyField is shown here:

```
procedure TMainForm.RGKeyFieldClick(Sender: TObject);
begin
  case RGKeyField.ItemIndex of
    0: DM.Table1.IndexName := '';            // primary index
    1: DM.Table1.IndexName := 'ByCompany';   // secondary, by company
  end;
end;
```

MainForm also contains a TMainMenu component, MainMenu1, which enables you to open and close each of the other forms. The items on this menu are Key Search, Range, Filter, and Exit. The Main unit, in its entirety, is shown in Listing 27.3.

LISTING 27.3. THE SOURCE CODE FOR MAIN.PAS.

```
unit Main;

interface

uses
  SysUtils, Windows, Messages, Classes, Graphics, Controls,
  Forms, Dialogs, StdCtrls, ExtCtrls, Grids, DBGrids, DB, DBTables,
  Buttons, Mask, DBCtrls, Menus;

type
  TMainForm = class(TForm)
    DBGrid1: TDBGrid;
    RGKeyField: TRadioGroup;
    MainMenu1: TMainMenu;
    Forms1: TMenuItem;
    KeySearch1: TMenuItem;
    Range1: TMenuItem;
    Filter1: TMenuItem;
    N1: TMenuItem;
    Exit1: TMenuItem;
    procedure RGKeyFieldClick(Sender: TObject);
    procedure KeySearch1Click(Sender: TObject);
    procedure Range1Click(Sender: TObject);
    procedure Filter1Click(Sender: TObject);
    procedure Exit1Click(Sender: TObject);
  private
    { Private declarations }
  public
    { Public declarations }
  end;

var
  MainForm: TMainForm;

implementation

uses DataMod, KeySrch, Rng, Fltr;

{$R *.DFM}

procedure TMainForm.RGKeyFieldClick(Sender: TObject);
begin
  case RGKeyField.ItemIndex of
```

```
      0: DM.Table1.IndexName := '';          // primary index
      1: DM.Table1.IndexName := 'ByCompany'; // secondary, by company
  end;
end;

procedure TMainForm.KeySearch1Click(Sender: TObject);
begin
  KeySearch1.Checked := not KeySearch1.Checked;
  KeySearchForm.Visible := KeySearch1.Checked;
end;

procedure TMainForm.Range1Click(Sender: TObject);
begin
  Range1.Checked := not Range1.Checked;
  RangeForm.Visible := Range1.Checked;
end;

procedure TMainForm.Filter1Click(Sender: TObject);
begin
  Filter1.Checked := not Filter1.Checked;
  FilterForm.Visible := Filter1.Checked;
end;

procedure TMainForm.Exit1Click(Sender: TObject);
begin
  Close;
end;

end.
```

The Range Form

RangeForm is shown in Figure 27.18. RangeForm is located in a unit called Rng. This form enables you to set a range on the data displayed in MainForm to limit the view of the table. Depending on the active index, the items you specify in the Range Start and Range End edit controls can be either numeric (the primary index) or text (the secondary index). Listing 27.4 shows the source code for RNG.PAS.

FIGURE 27.18.

The RangeForm *form.*

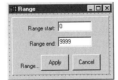

LISTING 27.4. THE SOURCE CODE FOR RNG.PAS.

```pascal
unit Rng;

interface

uses
  Windows, Messages, SysUtils, Classes, Graphics, Controls, Forms,
  Dialogs, StdCtrls, ExtCtrls;

type
  TRangeForm = class(TForm)
    Panel1: TPanel;
    Label2: TLabel;
    StartEdit: TEdit;
    Label1: TLabel;
    EndEdit: TEdit;
    Label7: TLabel;
    ApplyButton: TButton;
    CancelButton: TButton;
    procedure ApplyButtonClick(Sender: TObject);
    procedure CancelButtonClick(Sender: TObject);
  private
    { Private declarations }
    procedure ToggleRangeButtons;
  public
    { Public declarations }
  end;

var
  RangeForm: TRangeForm;

implementation

uses DataMod;

{$R *.DFM}

procedure TRangeForm.ApplyButtonClick(Sender: TObject);
begin
  { Set range of records in dataset from StartEdit's value to EndEdit's }
  { value.  Strings are again implicitly converted to numerics.        }
  DM.Table1.SetRange([StartEdit.Text], [EndEdit.Text]);
  ToggleRangeButtons;                    // enable proper buttons
end;

procedure TRangeForm.CancelButtonClick(Sender: TObject);
begin
  DM.Table1.CancelRange;                 // remove set range
  ToggleRangeButtons;                    // enable proper buttons
end;
```

```
procedure TRangeForm.ToggleRangeButtons;
begin
  { Toggle the enabled property of the range buttons }
  ApplyButton.Enabled := not ApplyButton.Enabled;
  CancelButton.Enabled := not CancelButton.Enabled;
end;

end.
```

> **NOTE**
>
> Pay close attention to the following line of code from the Rng unit:
>
> ```
> DM.Table1.SetRange([StartEdit.Text], [EndEdit.Text]);
> ```
>
> You might find it strange that although the keyed field can be of either Numeric type or Text type, you're always passing strings to the SetRange() method. Delphi allows this because SetRange(), FindKey(), FindNearest() will perform the conversion from String to Integer, or vice versa, automatically.
>
> What this means to you is that you should not bother calling IntToStr() or StrToInt() in these situations—it will be taken care of for you.

The Key Search Form

KeySearchForm, contained in the KeySrch unit, provides a means for the user of the application to search for a particular key value in the table. The form enables the user to search for a value in one of two ways. First, when the Normal radio button is selected, the user can search by typing text into the Search For edit control and pressing the Exact or Nearest button to find an exact match or closest match in the table. Second, when the Incremental radio button is selected, the user can perform an incremental search on the table every time he or she changes the text in the Search For edit control. The form is shown in Figure 27.19. The code for the KeySrch unit is shown in Listing 27.5.

FIGURE 27.19.

The KeySearchForm *form.*

LISTING 27.5. THE SOURCE CODE FOR KeySrch.PAS.

```
unit KeySrch;

interface

uses
  Windows, Messages, SysUtils, Classes, Graphics, Controls, Forms,
  Dialogs, StdCtrls, ExtCtrls;

type
  TKeySearchForm = class(TForm)
    Panel1: TPanel;
    Label3: TLabel;
    SearchEdit: TEdit;
    RBNormal: TRadioButton;
    Incremental: TRadioButton;
    Label6: TLabel;
    ExactButton: TButton;
    NearestButton: TButton;
    procedure ExactButtonClick(Sender: TObject);
    procedure NearestButtonClick(Sender: TObject);
    procedure RBNormalClick(Sender: TObject);
    procedure IncrementalClick(Sender: TObject);
  private
    procedure NewSearch(Sender: TObject);
  end;

var
  KeySearchForm: TKeySearchForm;

implementation

uses DataMod;

{$R *.DFM}

procedure TKeySearchForm.ExactButtonClick(Sender: TObject);
begin
  { Try to find record where key field matches SearchEdit's Text value. }
  { Notice that Delphi handles the type conversion from the string     }
  { edit control to the numeric key field value.                       }
  if not DM.Table1.FindKey([SearchEdit.Text]) then
    MessageDlg(Format('Match for "%s" not found.', [SearchEdit.Text]),
               mtInformation, [mbOk], 0);
end;

procedure TKeySearchForm.NearestButtonClick(Sender: TObject);
begin
  { Find closest match to SearchEdit's Text value.  Note again the }
```

```
  { implicit type conversion.                                         }
  DM.Table1.FindNearest([SearchEdit.Text]);
end;

procedure TKeySearchForm.NewSearch(Sender: TObject);
{ This is the method which is wired to the SearchEdit's OnChange }
{ event whenever the Incremental radio is selected. }
begin
  DM.Table1.FindNearest([SearchEdit.Text]); // search for text
end;

procedure TKeySearchForm.RBNormalClick(Sender: TObject);
begin

  ExactButton.Enabled := True;    // enable search buttons
  NearestButton.Enabled := True;
  SearchEdit.OnChange := Nil;     // unhook the OnChange event
end;

procedure TKeySearchForm.IncrementalClick(Sender: TObject);
begin
  ExactButton.Enabled := False;        // disable search buttons
  NearestButton.Enabled := False;
  SearchEdit.OnChange := NewSearch;    // hook the OnChange event
  NewSearch(Sender);                   // search current text
end;

end.
```

The code for the KeySrch unit should be fairly straightforward to you. You might notice that, once again, we can safely pass text strings to the FindKey() and FindNearest() methods with the knowledge that they will do the right thing with regard to type conversion. You might also appreciate the small trick that's employed to switch to and from incremental searching on the fly. This is accomplished by either assigning a method to or assigning Nil to the OnChange event of the SearchEdit edit control. When assigned a handler method, the OnChange event will fire whenever the text in the control is modified. By calling FindNearest() inside that handler, an incremental search can be performed as the user types.

The Filter Form

The purpose of FilterForm, found in the Fltr unit, is two-fold. First, it enables the user to filter the view of the table to a set where the value of the State field matches that of the current record. Second, this form enables the user to search for a record where the value of any field in the table is equal to some value he or she has specified. This form is shown in Figure 27.20.

FIGURE 27.20.

The FilterForm
form.

The record-filtering functionality actually involves very little code. First, the state of the checkbox labeled Filter on this State (called cbFiltered) determines the setting of DM.Table1's Filtered property. This is accomplished with the following line of code attached to cbFiltered.OnClick:

```
DM.Table1.Filtered := cbFiltered.Checked;
```

When DM.Table1.Filtered is True, Table1 filters records using the following OnFilterRecord method, which is actually located in the DataMod unit:

```
procedure TDM.Table1FilterRecord(DataSet: TDataSet;
  var Accept: Boolean);
begin
  { Accept record as a part of the filter if the value of the State }
  { field is the same as that of DBEdit1.Text.                      }
  Accept := Table1State.Value = FilterForm.DBEdit1.Text;
end;
```

To perform the filter-based search, the Locate() method of TTable is employed:

```
DM.Table1.Locate(CBField.Text, EValue.Text, LO);
```

The field name is taken from a combo box called CBField. The contents of this combo box are generated in the OnCreate event of this form using the following code to iterate through the fields of Table1:

```
procedure TFilterForm.FormCreate(Sender: TObject);
var
  i: integer;
begin
  with DM.Table1 do begin
    for i := 0 to FieldCount - 1 do
      CBField.Items.Add(Fields[i].FieldName);
  end;
end;
```

> **TIP**
>
> The preceding code will only work when DM is created prior to this form. Otherwise, any attempts to access DM before it's created will probably result in an Access Violation error. To make sure that the data module, DM, is created prior to any of the child forms, we manually adjusted the creation order of the forms in the Auto-Create forms list on the Forms page of the Project Options dialog (found under Options | Project on the main menu).
>
> The main form must, of course, be the first one created, but other than that, this little trick ensures that the data module gets created prior to any other form in the application.

The complete code for the `Fltr` unit is shown in Listing 27.6.

LISTING 27.6. THE SOURCE CODE FOR Fltr.pas.

```
unit Fltr;

interface

uses
  Windows, Messages, SysUtils, Classes, Graphics, Controls, Forms,
  Dialogs, StdCtrls, Buttons, Mask, DBCtrls, ExtCtrls;

type
  TFilterForm = class(TForm)
    Panel1: TPanel;
    Label4: TLabel;
    DBEdit1: TDBEdit;
    cbFiltered: TCheckBox;
    Label5: TLabel;
    SpeedButton1: TSpeedButton;
    SpeedButton2: TSpeedButton;
    SpeedButton3: TSpeedButton;
    SpeedButton4: TSpeedButton;
    Panel2: TPanel;
    EValue: TEdit;
    LocateBtn: TButton;
    Label1: TLabel;
    Label2: TLabel;
    CBField: TComboBox;
    MatchGB: TGroupBox;
    RBExact: TRadioButton;
    RBClosest: TRadioButton;
    CBCaseSens: TCheckBox;
```

continues

LISTING 27.6. CONTINUED

```
    procedure cbFilteredClick(Sender: TObject);
    procedure FormCreate(Sender: TObject);
    procedure LocateBtnClick(Sender: TObject);
    procedure SpeedButton1Click(Sender: TObject);
    procedure SpeedButton2Click(Sender: TObject);
    procedure SpeedButton3Click(Sender: TObject);
    procedure SpeedButton4Click(Sender: TObject);
  end;

var
  FilterForm: TFilterForm;

implementation

uses DataMod, DB;

{$R *.DFM}

procedure TFilterForm.cbFilteredClick(Sender: TObject);
begin
  { Filter table if checkbox is checked }
  DM.Table1.Filtered := cbFiltered.Checked;
end;

procedure TFilterForm.FormCreate(Sender: TObject);
var
  i: integer;
begin
  with DM.Table1 do begin
    for i := 0 to FieldCount - 1 do
      CBField.Items.Add(Fields[i].FieldName);
  end;
end;

procedure TFilterForm.LocateBtnClick(Sender: TObject);
var
  LO: TLocateOptions;
begin
  LO := [];
  if not CBCaseSens.Checked then Include(LO, loCaseInsensitive);
  if RBClosest.Checked then Include(LO, loPartialKey);
  if not DM.Table1.Locate(CBField.Text, EValue.Text, LO) then
    MessageDlg('Unable to locate match', mtInformation, [mbOk], 0);
end;

procedure TFilterForm.SpeedButton1Click(Sender: TObject);
begin
  DM.Table1.FindFirst;
end;
```

```
procedure TFilterForm.SpeedButton2Click(Sender: TObject);
begin
  DM.Table1.FindNext;
end;

procedure TFilterForm.SpeedButton3Click(Sender: TObject);
begin
  DM.Table1.FindPrior;
end;

procedure TFilterForm.SpeedButton4Click(Sender: TObject);
begin
  DM.Table1.FindLast;
end;

end.
```

TQuery AND TStoredProc: THE OTHER DATA SETS

Although these components aren't discussed in detail until the next chapter, this section is intended to introduce you to the TQuery and TStoredProc components as TDataSet descendants and siblings of TTable.

TQuery

The TQuery component enables you to use SQL to obtain specific data sets from one or more tables. Delphi enables you to use the TQuery component with both file-oriented server data (that is, Paradox and dBASE) and SQL server data. After assigning the DatabaseName property of TQuery to an alias or directory, you can enter into the SQL property the lines of SQL code you want to execute against the given database. For example, if Query1 were hooked to the DBDEMOS alias, the following code would retrieve all records in the BIOLIFE table where the Length (cm) field is greater than 100:

```
select * from BIOLIFE where BIOLIFE."Length (cm)" > 100
```

Like other data sets, the query will execute when its Active property is set to True or when its Open() method is called. If you want to perform a query that doesn't return a result set (an insert into query, for example), you should use Execute() rather than Open() to invoke the query.

Another important property of TQuery is RequestLive. The RequestLive property indicates whether or not the result set returned is editable. Set this property to True when you want to edit the data returned by a query.

In the next chapter, you'll learn more about TQuery features such as parameterized queries and SQL optimization.

TStoredProc

The TStoredProc component provides you with a means to execute stored procedures on a SQL server. Because this is a server-specific feature, and certainly not for database beginners, we'll save the explanation of this component for the next chapter.

TEXT FILE TABLES

Delphi provides limited support for using text file tables in your applications. Text tables must consist of two files: a data file, which must end in a .txt extension, and a schema file, which must end in an .sch extension. Each file must have the same name (that is, FOO.TXT and FOO.SCH). The data file can be of fixed length or delimited. The schema file tells the BDE how to interpret the data file by providing information such as field name, sizes, and types.

The Schema File

The format of a schema file is similar to that of a Windows INI file. The section name is the same as that of the table (minus the extension). Table 27.5 shows the items and possible item values for a schema file.

TABLE 27.5. SCHEMA FILE ITEMS AND VALUES.

Item	Possible Values	Meaning
FILETYPE	VARYING	Each field in the file can occupy a variable amount of space. Fields are separated with a special character, and strings are delimited with a special character.
	FIXED	Each field can be found at a specific offset from the beginning of the line.
CHARSET	*(many)*	Specifies which language driver to use. Most commonly, this will be set to ASCII.
DELIMITER	*(any char)*	Specifies which character is to be used as a delimiter for CHAR fields. Used for VARYING tables only.
SEPARATOR	*(any char)*	Specifies which character is to be used as a field separator. Used for VARYING tables only.

Using the information shown in Table 27.5, the schema file must have an entry for each field in the table. Each entry will be in the following form:

```
FieldX = Field Name, Field Type, Size, Decimal Places, Offset
```

The syntax in the preceding example is explained in the following list:

- *X* represents the field number, from one to the total number of fields.
- *Field Name* can be any string identifier. Do not use quotes or string delimiters.
- *Field Type* can be any one of the values listed in Table 27.6.

TABLE 27.6. TEXT TABLE FIELD TYPES.

Type	Meaning
CHAR	A character or string field
BOOL	A Boolean (T or F)
DATE	A date in the format specified in the BDE Config Tool
FLOAT	A 64-bit floating-point number
LONGINT	A 32-bit integer
NUMBER	A 16-bit integer
TIME	A time in the format specified in the BDE Config Tool
TIMESTAMP	A date and time in the format specified in the BDE Config Tool

- *Size* refers to the total number of characters or units. This value must be less than or equal to 20 for numeric fields.
- *Decimal Places* only has meaning for FLOAT fields. It specifies the number of digits after the decimal.
- *Offset* is used only for FIXED tables. It specifies the character position where a particular field begins.

Now, here's a sample schema file for a fixed table called PasAdv:

```
[PASADV]
FILETYPE = FIXED
CHARSET = ascii
Field1 = EmpNo,LONGINT,04,00,00
Field2 = Name,CHAR,15,00,05
Field3 = CubeNo,CHAR,05,00,21
Field4 = PhoneExt,LONGINT,04,00,27
Field5 = Height,FLOAT,05,02,32
```

27

WRITING DESKTOP
DATABASE
APPLICATIONS

Here's a schema file for a VARYING version of a similar table called PasAdv2:

```
[PASADV2]
FILETYPE = VARYING
CHARSET = ascii
DELIMITER = "
SEPARATOR = ,
Field1 = EmpNo,LONGINT,04,00,00
Field2 = Name,CHAR,15,00,00
Field3 = CubeNo,CHAR,05,00,00
Field4 = PhoneExt,LONGINT,04,00,00
Field5 = Height,FLOAT,05,02,00
```

CAUTION

The BDE is very picky about the format of a schema file. If you have one misplaced character or misspelled word, the BDE may not be able to recognize your data at all. If you're having problems getting at your data, scrutinize your schema file.

The Data File

The data file should be a fixed-length (FIXED) or delimited (VARYING) file that contains one record per line. A sample data file for PasAdv can be shown as this:

```
2093 Charlie Calvert C2121 1234 6.0
2610 Scott Frolich   E2126 5678 5.11
2900 Heather Latham  C2221 9012 5.10
3265 Xavier Pacheco  C0001 3456 5.6
0007 Jason Sprenger  F3169 7890 6.0
1001 Matt Stave      C3456 0987 5.9
2611 Steve Teixeira  E2127 6543 6.5
```

A similar data file for PasAdv2 would look like this:

```
2093,"Charlie Calvert","C2121",1234,6.0
2610,"Scott Frolich","E2126",5678,5.11
2900,"Heather Latham","C2221",9012,5.10
3265,"Xavier Pacheco","C0001",3456,5.6
0007,"Jason Sprenger","F3169",7890,6.0
1001,"Matt Stave","C3456",0987,5.9
2611,"Steve Teixeira","E2127",6543,6.5
```

Using the Text Table

You can use text tables with TTable components much like any other database type. Set the table's DatabaseName property to the alias or directory containing the TXT and SCH files. Set the TableType property to ttASCII. Now you should be able to view all available text tables by clicking the drop-down button on the TableName property. Select one of the tables into the property, and you'll be able to view the fields by hooking up a TDataSource and a TDBGrid. Figure 27.21 shows a form browsing the PasAdv table.

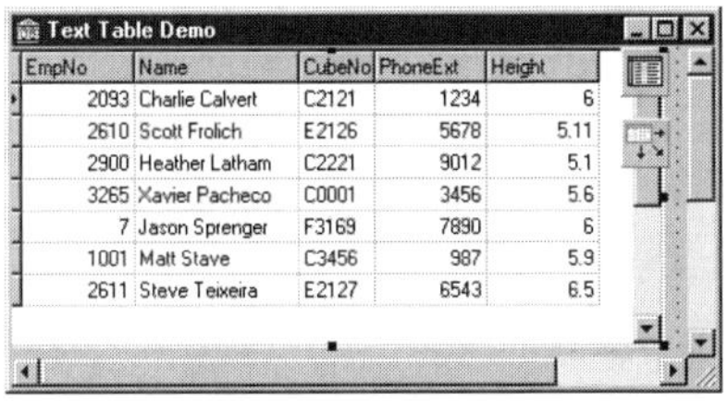

FIGURE 27.21.

Browsing a text table.

EmpNo	Name	CubeNo	PhoneExt	Height
2093	Charlie Calvert	C2121	1234	6
2610	Scott Frolich	E2126	5678	5.11
2900	Heather Latham	C2221	9012	5.1
3265	Xavier Pacheco	C0001	3456	5.6
7	Jason Sprenger	F3169	7890	6
1001	Matt Stave	C3456	987	5.9
2611	Steve Teixeira	E2127	6543	6.5

> **NOTE**
>
> If all the fields in your text table appear to be cramped into one field, the BDE is having problems reading your schema file.

Limitations

Borland never intended for text files to be used in lieu of proper database formats. Because of the limitations inherent in text files, we (the authors) seriously advise against using text file tables for anything other than importing data to and exporting data from real database formats. Here's a list of limitations to keep in mind when working with text tables:

- Indexes are not supported, so you can't use any TTable method that requires an index.
- You cannot use a TQuery component with a text table.
- Deleting records is not supported.
- Inserting records is not supported. Attempts to insert a record will cause the new record to be appended to the end of the table.
- Referential integrity is not supported.
- BLOB data types are not supported.
- Editing is not supported on VARYING tables.
- Text tables are always opened with exclusive access. You should, therefore, open your text tables in code rather than during design time.

Text Table Import

As mentioned earlier, about the only reasonable use for text tables is in converting them to a real database format. With that in mind, what follows is a set of step-by-step instructions for using a TBatchMove component to copy a table from text format to a Paradox table. Assume a form containing two TTable objects and one TBatchMove component. The TTable object that represents the text table is called TextTbl, and the TTable object that represents the target Paradox table is called PDoxTbl. The TBatchMove component is called BM.

1. Hook TextTbl to the text table you want to import (as described earlier).

2. Set the DatabaseName property of PDoxTbl to the target alias or directory. Set the TableName property to the desired table name. Set the TableType property to ttParadox.

3. Set the Source property of BM to TextTbl. Set the Destination property to PDoxTbl. Set the Mode property to batCopy.

4. Right click BM and select Execute from the local menu.

5. Voilà! You have just copied your text table to a Paradox table.

CONNECTING WITH ODBC

It's a given that the BDE can only provide native support for a limited subset of databases in the world. What happens, then, when your situation requires that you connect to a database type—such as Btrieve, for example—that's not directly supported by the BDE? Can you still use Delphi? Of course. The BDE provides an ODBC socket so that you can use an ODBC (Open Database Connectivity) driver to access databases not directly supported by the BDE; the capability to take advantage of this feature is built into the Professional and Client/Server Suite editions of Delphi. ODBC is a standard developed by Microsoft for product-independent database driver support.

Where to Find an ODBC Driver

The best place to obtain an ODBC driver is through the vendor who distributes the database format you want to access. When you do venture out to obtain an ODBC driver, bear in mind that there's a difference between 16- and 32-bit ODBC drivers, and that Delphi 4 requires the 32-bit drivers. In addition to the vendor of your particular database, there are a number of vendors who produce ODBC drivers for many different types of databases. In particular, you can obtain ODBC drivers for Access, Excel, SQL Server, and FoxPro from Microsoft. These drivers are available either in their ODBC Driver Pack, or you can often find them on the MS Developer Network CD-ROMs.

CAUTION

Not all ODBC drivers are created equal! Many ODBC drivers are "brain dead-ened" to work with only one particular software package or to have their functionality otherwise limited. Examples of these types of drivers are the ones that ship with the MS Office products (which are intended to work only with MS Office). Make sure that the ODBC driver you purchase is certified for application development, not just to work with some existing package.

ODBC Example: Connecting to MS Access

Assuming you have obtained the necessary 32-bit ODBC driver from Microsoft or another vendor, this section takes you step by step from configuring the driver to making it work with a Delphi TTable object. Although Access is directly supported by the BDE, that's beside the point—this section is intended to serve as an example of using the BDE's ODBC socket. This demonstration assumes that you do not yet have an Access database on your hard disk, and it takes you through the steps for creating one:

1. Install the driver using the vendor-provided disk. Once it's installed, run the Windows Control Panel, and you should see an icon for 32bit ODBC, as shown in Figure 27.22. Double-click the icon and you'll be presented with the ODBC Data Source Administrator dialog, as shown in Figure 27.23.

FIGURE 27.22.

The Windows Control Panel containing the 32-bit ODBC icon.

FIGURE 27.23.

*The ODBC
Data Source
Administrator
dialog.*

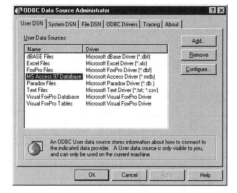

2. Click the Add button in the ODBC Data Source Administrator dialog, and you'll be presented with the Create New Data Source dialog, as shown in Figure 27.24. From this dialog, select Microsoft Access Driver (*.mdb) and click Finish.

FIGURE 27.24.

*The Create New
Data Source
dialog.*

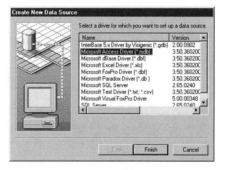

3. You'll now be presented with a dialog similar to the ODBC Microsoft Access 97 Setup dialog shown in Figure 27.25. You can give the data source any name and description you choose. In this case, we'll call it AccessDB, and the description will read DDG Test For Access.

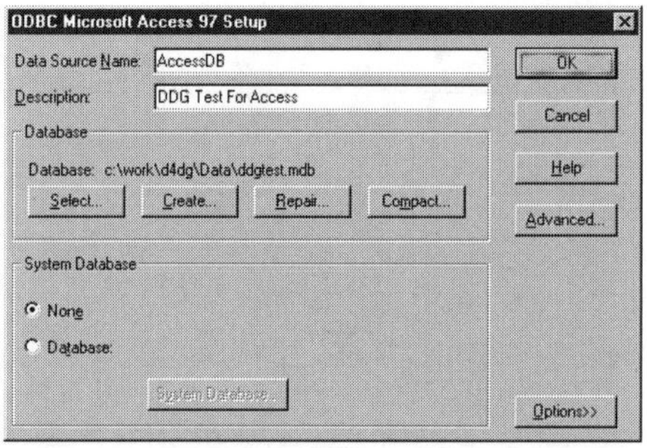

FIGURE 27.25.

*The ODBC
Microsoft Access
97 Setup dialog.*

4. Click the Create button in the ODBC Microsoft Access 97 Setup dialog, and you'll be presented with the New Database dialog, where you can choose a name for your new database and a directory in which to store the database file. Click the OK button after you choose a file and path. Figure 27.25 shows the ODBC Microsoft Access 97 Setup dialog with steps 3 and 4 completed. Click OK to dismiss this dialog and then click Close to dismiss the ODBC Data Source Administrator dialog. The data source is now configured, and you're ready to create a BDE alias that maps to this data source.

5. Close all applications that use the BDE. Run the BDE Administrator tool that comes with Delphi and change to the Configuration page on the left pane. Expand the Drivers branch of the tree view, right-click ODBC, and select New from the local menu. This will invoke the New ODBC Driver dialog. Driver Name can be anything you like. For the sake of this example, we'll use `ODBC_Access`. ODBC Driver Name will be Microsoft Access Driver (*.mdb) (the same driver name as step 2). Default Data Source Name should come up automatically as `AccessDB` (the same name as step 3). The completed dialog is shown in Figure 27.26. Select OK, and you'll return to the BDE Administrator main window.

27

WRITING DESKTOP
DATABASE
APPLICATIONS

FIGURE 27.26.

*The completed
New ODBC
Driver dialog.*

6. Change to the Databases page in the left pane of the BDE Administrator and select Object | New from the main menu. This will invoke the New Database Alias dialog. In this dialog, select `ODBC_Access` (from step 5) as the Database Driver Name and click OK. You can then give the alias any name you like—we'll use `Access` in this case. The completed alias is shown in Figure 27.27. Select OK to dismiss the dialog and then select Object | Apply from the BDE Administrator main window. The alias has now been created, and you may now close the BDE Administrator tool. The next step is to create a table for the database.

FIGURE 27.27.

*The new Access
alias in BDE
Administrator.*

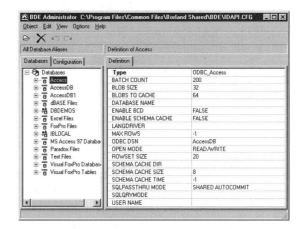

7. You'll use the Database Desktop application that ships with Delphi to create tables for your Access database. Select File | New | Table from the main menu, and you'll be presented with the Create Table dialog. Choose ODBC_Access (same as steps 5 and 6) as the table type, and the Create ODBC_Access Table dialog will come up.

8. Assuming you're familiar with creating tables in Database Desktop (if you're not, refer to the Delphi documentation), the Create ODBC_Access Table dialog works the same as the "create table" dialogs for other database types. For demonstration purposes, add one field of type CHAR and one of type INTEGER. Figure 27.28 shows the completed dialog.

FIGURE 27.28.

*The completed
Create
ODBC_Access
Table dialog.*

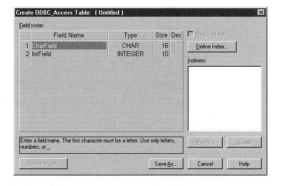

9. Click the Save As button, and you'll be prompted with the Save Table As dialog. In this dialog, first set the Alias to Access (from step 6). At this point, you'll be presented with a database login dialog—just click OK to dismiss the dialog, because no user name or password have been specified. Now give the table a name (do not use an extension) in the File Name edit control. We'll use TestTable in this case.

Click OK, and the table will be stored to the database. You're now ready to access this database with Delphi.

> **NOTE**
>
> MS Access tables that comprise a database are stored in one MDB file. Although this is in contrast to Paradox and dBASE, which store each table as a separate file, it is similar to SQL server databases.

10. Create a new project in Delphi. The main form should contain one each of a TTable, TDataSource, and TDBGrid component. DBGrid1 hooks to Table1 via DataSource1. Select Access (from steps 6 and 9) into Table1's DatabaseName property. Click on Table1's TableName property, and you'll be presented with a login dialog. Simply click the OK button (no password has been configured) and you can choose an available table from the Access database. Because TestTable is the only table you created, choose that table. Now set Table1's Active property to True, and you'll see the field names appear in DBGrid1. Run the application, and you'll be able to edit the table. Figure 27.29 shows the completed application.

FIGURE 27.29.

Browsing an ODBC table in Delphi.

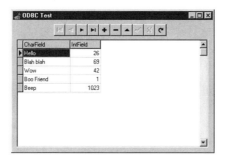

27

WRITING DESKTOP
DATABASE
APPLICATIONS

SUMMARY

After reading this chapter, you should be ready for just about any type of non-SQL database programming with Delphi. You learned the ins and outs of Delphi's TDataSet component, which is the ancestor of the TTable, TQuery, and TStoredProc components. You also learned techniques for manipulating TTable objects, how to manage fields, and how to work with text tables. As you've seen, VCL offers a pretty tight object-oriented wrapper around the procedural BDE.

The next chapter, "Developing Client/Server Applications," focuses a bit more on client/server technology and using related VCL classes such as TQuery and TStoredProc components.

DEVELOPING CLIENT/SERVER APPLICATIONS

IN THIS CHAPTER

So what's all this hoopla about "client/server"? It seems that everyone, these days, is either using or developing some sort of client/server system. Unless you've invested the time to understand what client/server is all about, it's easy to become confused over what exactly client/server is and what it offers you that other technologies do not.

If you're a Delphi developer, it wouldn't be a surprise if you've been overwhelmed with all this client/server rhetoric. Delphi 4 is, after all, a client/server development environment. However, that doesn't mean that everything you develop with Delphi is client/server. Nor does it mean that just because an application accesses data from a client/server database, such as Oracle, Microsoft SQL, or Interbase, that it's a client/server application.

This chapter discusses the elements that make up a client/server system. It compares client/server development to traditional desktop or mainframe database development. It also illustrates reasons for using a client/server solution. It discusses how Delphi 4 provides the capability to develop client/server (three-tier) applications. We also point out some pitfalls desktop database developers fall into when moving to client/server.

WHY CLIENT/SERVER?

A typical example of when you might consider a client/server solution would be the following: Imagine that you are responsible for a departmental-level application that accesses data residing on a LAN or file server. Various people within your department may use this application. As this data becomes of greater use to your department, other applications are created to make use of this data.

Suppose this data becomes of interest to other departments within your company. Now, additional applications will have to be built for these departments. This may also require you to move the data to a database server to make it more globally available. As the data becomes of greater interest companywide, it becomes important that decision makers are able to access it through a means that not only gets them the data quickly, but also presents the data such that it actually helps in the decision-making process.

The global availability of this data creates several problems inherent in desktop database access across network connections. Two of these problems may be excessive network traffic (creating a bottleneck in data retrieval) and data security.

This is a simplified example, yet it does illustrate a situation in which one might consider the need for a client/server solution. A client/server solution would

- Allow departmental access to the data, allowing departments to process only the part of the business for which they're responsible

- Provide data access to decision makers efficiently in the way it should be presented
- Enhance centralized control by MIS of maintaining data integrity while placing less emphasis on centralized control of data analysis and use
- Enforce data integrity rules for the entire database
- Provide better division of labor between the client and the server (each performs the tasks for which it is best suited)
- Be able to use the advanced data integrity capabilities provided by most database servers
- Reduce network traffic because subsets of data are returned to the client, as opposed to entire tables as is the case with desktop databases

Keep in mind that this list is not all-inclusive. As you get into the rest of the chapter, you will see additional benefits to moving to a client/server-based system.

It's also necessary to mention that making the move to client/server isn't always the right thing to do. As a developer, you must ensure that you've performed a thorough analysis of your user requirements to determine whether or not client/server is what you need. One consideration you must take into account is that client/server systems are costly. This cost includes network software, the server O/S, database server, and hardware capable of housing such software. Additionally, there will be a significant learning period if users are unfamiliar with the server O/S and database server software.

CLIENT/SERVER ARCHITECTURE

The typical client/server architecture is one in which the front end, or end user—the *client*—accesses and processes data from a remote machine—the *server*. There is no "true" definition of client/server. However, one can think of it as if the server provides a service and the client requests a service from the server. There may be many clients that request such services from the same server. It is up to the server to decide how to process such requests. Also, there may be more than just the client and server to a client/server system. We will discuss this further in the section covering three-tier systems.

In a client/server environment, the server handles much more than just data distribution. In fact, the server more than likely performs the bulk of the business logic. It also governs how the data is to be accessed and manipulated by the client. The client applications really only serve as a means to present data to or extract data from the end user. The following subsections explain in more detail the responsibilities of the client and the server. Additionally, we'll talk about "business rules," which are the governing rules for client access to server data.

The Client

The client can be either a GUI or non-GUI application. Delphi 4 allows you to develop both the client and any middle layer application servers in three-tier models. The database server is most likely developed using an RDBMS such as Oracle or Interbase.

Client applications provide the interface for users needing to manipulate data on the server end. Through the client, services are requested of the server. A typical service might be, for example, adding a customer, adding an order, or printing a report. Here the client simply makes the request and provides any necessary data. The server carries the responsibility of processing the request. This doesn't mean that the client is not capable of performing any of the logic. It's entirely possible that the client can carry out most, if not all, of the business logic in the entire application. In this case, this is what we refer to as a *fat client*.

SCALABLE APPLICATIONS

You'll often hear the term *scalability* when referring to client/server development with Delphi. What exactly is scalability? Well, to some it means the ability to easily access server databases using Delphi's powerful database features. Or, it can mean to rapidly increase the number of users and demands on a system with no or minimal effect on performance. To others, it means magically turning a desktop application into a client application by simply changing an `Alias` in your application. Unfortunately, the latter is not really true. Sure, you can change an `Alias` property and suddenly access data from a server database. However, this doesn't turn your application into a client application. A key advantage to client/server is that you can take advantage of the powerful features offered by the server. It would be impossible to take advantages of these features if your application is designed using desktop database methods.

The Server

The server provides the services to the client. It essentially waits for the client to make a request and then processes that request. A server must be capable of processing multiple requests from multiple clients and also must be capable of prioritizing these requests. More than likely, the server will run continuously to allow constant access to its services.

> **NOTE**
>
> A client doesn't necessarily have to reside on a different machine than the server. Often, the background tasks performed on the data may well reside on the same server machine.

Business Rules

What exactly are business rules? In short, business rules are the governing procedures that dictate how clients access data on the server. These rules are implemented in programming code on the client, the server, or both. In Delphi 4, business rules are implemented in the form of Object Pascal code. On the server side, business rules are implemented in the form of SQL stored procedures, triggers, and other database objects native to server databases. In three-tier models, business rules can be implemented in the middle tier. We will discuss these objects later in the chapter.

It is important that you understand that business rules define how the entire system will behave. Without business rules, you have nothing more than data residing on one machine and a GUI application on another and no method for connecting the two.

At some point in the design phase of developing your system, you must decide what processes must exist in your system. Take an inventory system, for example. Here, typical processes would be tasks like placing an order, printing an invoice, adding a customer, ordering a part, and so on. As stated earlier, these rules are implemented in Object Pascal code on the client or on a middle tier. These rules may also be SQL code on the server, or a combination of all three. When the majority of rules are placed on the server, we refer to this as a "fat server." When most of the rules exist on the client, this is called a "fat client." When the rules exist on the middle tier, we can still refer to this as a fat server as well. How much and what type of control is required over the data determine what side the business rules should exist on.

> **NOTE**
>
> You'll often see *three-tier* referred to as *n-tier* or *multitier*. The terms *n-tier* and *multitier* are each something of a misnomer. In a three-tier model, you typically have one or more clients, business logic, and the database server. The business logic may very well be split into many pieces on several different machines or even application servers. It seems a bit absurd when you start to refer to this as a 10-, 15-, or even 25-tier system. We prefer to think of the business logic or middle tier as a single tier regardless of how many boxes and application servers it requires.

28

DEVELOPING CLIENT/SERVER APPLICATIONS

Fat Client, Fat Server, Middle Tier: Where Do Business Rules Belong?

The decision about where you want the business rules to exist, or how you want to separate business rules between the server and clients, depends on several factors. Some of these factors may include data security, data integrity, centralized control, and proper distribution of work.

Data Security Concerns

Security concerns come into play when you want to provide limited access to various parts of the data or to various tasks that may be performed on the data. This is done through user access privileges to various database objects such as views and stored procedures. We will discuss these objects later in this chapter. By using access privileges to database objects, you can restrict a user's access to only those parts of the data that he or she needs. Privileges and stored procedures exist on the server.

One very important concept to remember is that client/server databases are designed so that a wide range of client applications and tools can access them. Although you may have limited access to data as defined in the coding logic of your client application, nothing prevents a user from using another tool to view or edit tables within your database. By making database access accessible only through views and stored procedures, you can prevent unauthorized access to your data. This also plays an important role in maintaining data integrity, as discussed in the next section.

Data Integrity Concerns

Data integrity refers to the correctness and completeness of the data on the server. Unless you take the necessary measures to protect the data, it is possible that this data may get corrupted. Examples of data corruption are placing an order on a nonexistent or depleted product, changing the quantity of a product on an order without adjusting the cost, or deleting a customer with an outstanding balance.

So how do you protect data integrity? One way is to limit the type of operations that can be performed on the data through stored procedures. Another way is by placing the bulk of the business logic on the server or on the middle layer. For example, suppose that in an inventory system, you have a client application that contains most of the business logic. In the client application, the procedure to delete a customer might be smart enough to look at the server data to determine whether or not a customer has an outstanding balance. This is fine for the client application. However, because this logic exists only with the client and not with the server, there's nothing to prevent a user from loading Database Desktop or some other client tool and deleting a customer directly from the table. To prevent this, you revoke access to the customer table to all users. You then provide a stored procedure on the server that takes care of deleting the user but only after making the necessary checks. Because nobody has access to the tables directly, all users are forced to use the stored procedure.

This is only one way that a business rule existing on the server can protect data integrity. The same thing can be accomplished by placing the necessary checks in triggers or by providing views to only the data the users need access to. It's important to remember that data on the server is there so that many departments through different applications can access it. The more business rules that exist on the server, the more control you have over protecting the data.

Centralized Control of Data

Another benefit to having the business logic on the server, or on another layer in a three-tier setup, is that MIS can implement updates to this business logic without affecting the operation of the client applications. That means that if additional code were to be added to any stored procedures, this change is transparent to the clients as long as the client interfaces to the server aren't affected by the change. This makes life for MIS much easier and benefits the company overall because MIS can do its job better.

Work Distribution

By placing business rules on the server, or by separating them on various middle tiers, MIS can more easily perform the tasks of dividing up responsibilities to specific departments while still maintaining the integrity/security of the server data. This allows departments to share the same data, yet manipulate only that data necessary to accomplish their particular objectives. This distribution of work is accomplished by granting access to only those stored procedures and other database objects necessary for a particular department.

As an example, we'll use the inventory system again. To be more specific, let's say this is an inventory system for an automotive parts warehouse. Here, several people need to access the same data but for different purposes. A cashier must be able to process invoices, add and remove customers, and change customer information. Warehouse personnel must be able to add new parts to the database as well as order new parts. Accounting personnel must be able to perform their part of the system as well. It's not likely that warehouse personnel will have to run a monthly budget report. Nor is it likely that accounting personnel will have to change customer address information. By creating these business rules on the server, it's possible to grant access based on the needs of a person or department. Here, cashier personnel will have access to customer/invoice rules. Warehouse personnel will have access to business rules specific to their needs, whereas accounting personnel can access accounting-related data.

Distribution of work refers not only to dividing up work among various clients, but also to determining what work would best be performed on a client as opposed to the server or middle layers. As a developer, you must evaluate various strategies that might allow you to assign CPU-intensive operations to the fast client machines, thus relieving the server so that it can perform less intensive operations. Of course, in deciding which strategies to employ, you must also consider which business rules would be violated, and whether or not this approach poses any security risks.

CLIENT/SERVER MODELS

You often hear of client/server systems falling under one of two models. These are the two-tiered model and three-tiered model, as shown in Figures 28.1 and 28.2, respectively.

FIGURE 28.1.

The two-tiered client/server model.

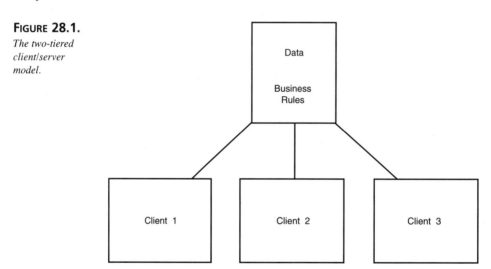

The Two-Tiered Model

Figure 28.1 illustrates what is referred to as a *two-tiered* client/server model. This model is probably the most common as it follows the same schema as desktop database design. Additionally, many client/server systems being built today have evolved out of existing desktop database applications that stored their data on shared file servers. The migration of systems built around network-shared Paradox or dBASE files up to SQL servers is based on the hope of improved performance, security, and reliability.

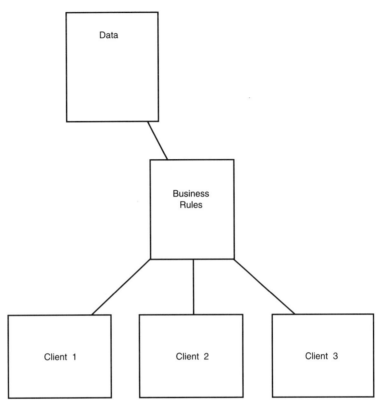

FIGURE 28.2.
The three-tiered client/server model.

Under this model, the data resides on the server, and client applications exist on the client machine. The business logic, or business rules, exist on either the client or the server or both.

The Three-Tiered Model

Figure 28.2 shows the *three-tiered* client/server model. Here, the client is the user interface to the data. The remote database server is where the data resides. The client application makes requests to access or modify the data through an application server or Remote Data Broker. It is typically the Remote Data Broker where the business rules exist.

By distributing the client, server, and business rules on separate machines, designers can more effectively optimize data access and maintain data integrity for other applications in the entire system. Delphi 4 adds powerful capabilities for developing three-tier architectures with the MIDAS technology.

> ## MIDAS—MULTITIER DISTRIBUTED APPLICATION SERVICES SUITE
>
> Borland's MIDAS technology is included with the Delphi 4 Client/Server and Enterprise versions only. This technology is a suite of highly advanced components, servers, and core technologies for your three-tier application development. Chapter 31, "MIDAS Development," discusses this technology in more depth.

CLIENT/SERVER VERSUS DESKTOP DATABASE DEVELOPMENT

If you're coming from a background of designing desktop databases, it's important that you understand the differences between desktop database and client/server database development. This next section presents some of the key differences between the two.

Set-Oriented Versus Record-Oriented Data Access

One of the most often misunderstood concepts in client/server development has to do with client/server databases being *set-oriented* versus *record-oriented*. What this means is that client applications do not work with tables directly as do desktop databases. Instead, client applications work with subsets of the data.

The way this works is that the client application requests rows from the server, which are made up of fields from a table or a combination of several tables. These requests are made using Structured Query Language (SQL).

By using SQL, clients are able to limit the number of records that may be returned from the server. Clients use SQL statements to query the server for a result set, which may consist of a subset of the data on a server. This is an important point to note because when accessing desktop databases over a network, the entire table is sent to the calling application across the network. The larger the table, the more this weighs on network traffic. This differs from client/servers in that only the requested records are transferred across the network, placing fewer requirements on the network.

This difference also affects the navigability of SQL data sets. Concepts such as *first, last, next*, and *previous* record are foreign to SQL-based data sets. This is especially true when you think that result sets may consist of rows made up of several tables. Many SQL servers provide "scrollable cursors," which are navigable pointers on a SQL result set. However, this is not the same as the desktop navigability, which directly navigates through the actual table. You will see later in the section entitled "TTable or TQuery" how these concepts affect the way you design your client applications with Delphi 4.

Data Security

SQL databases handle security issues differently than do desktop databases. They offer the same password security measures on the overall database access, but they also offer a mechanism to restrict user access to specific database objects like views, tables, stored procedures, and so on. We will discuss more about these objects later in this chapter. What this means is that user access can be defined on the server based on the user's need to view the data.

Typically, SQL databases allow you to GRANT or REVOKE privileges to a user, or a group of users. Therefore, it is possible to define a group of users in SQL databases. These privileges may refer to any of the already mentioned database objects.

Record-Locking Methods

Locking is a mechanism used to allow concurrent SQL transactions for many users on the same database. Several locking levels exist, and servers differ as to which level they use.

Table-level locking restricts you from modifying tables that may be involved in an ongoing transaction. Although this method allows for parallel processing, it is slow because users typically need to share the same tables.

An improved locking technique is *page-level* locking. Here, the server locks certain blocks on data on the disk. These are referred to as *pages*. As one transaction is performing an operation on a given page, other transactions are restricted from updating data on that same page. Typically, data is spread over several hundreds of pages, so multiple transactions occurring on the same page are not common.

Some servers offer *record-level* locking, which imposes a lock on a specific row in a database table. However, this results in large overhead in maintaining the locking information.

Desktop databases use what is referred to as *pessimistic* or *deterministic* locking. This means that you are restricted from making changes to table records that are currently being modified by another user. When an attempt to access such a record is made, you will receive an error message indicating that you cannot access that record until the previous user has freed it.

SQL databases operate on a concept known as *optimistic* locking. With this technique, you aren't restricted from accessing a record that was previously accessed by another user. You can edit and then request the server to save this record. However, before a record is saved, it is compared with the server copy, which may have been updated by another user in the time that you were viewing/editing it on the client end. This will result in an error indicating that the record was modified since you initially received it. As a developer, you must take this into account when designing your client application. Client/server applications must be more reactive to this type of occurrence, which is not the case with their desktop counterparts.

Data Integrity

With SQL databases, you have the opportunity to employ more robust integrity constraints with your server data. Although desktop databases have data integrity constraints built into the database, you must define any business rules in the context of the application's code. In contrast, SQL databases allow you to define these rules on the server end. This gives you the benefit of not only requiring all client applications to use the same set of business rules, but also centralizing the maintenance of these rules.

Integrity constraints are defined when you create the tables on the server. We will show you some samples of this later in the chapter in the section "Creating the Table." Such constraints include validity, uniqueness, and referential constraints.

As stated earlier, integrity constraints can also be defined in the context of the SQL stored procedures. Here, for example, you can check to see if a customer has the proper credit limit before processing an order. You can see how such rules enforce the integrity of the data.

Transaction Orientation

SQL databases are transaction-oriented. This means that changes to data aren't made directly to the tables as they are in desktop databases. Instead, the client applications request that the server make these changes, and the server implements this batch of operations in a single transaction.

In order for any changes to the data to be final, the transaction as a whole must be *committed*. If any of the operations within the transaction fail, the entire transaction may be *rolled back*, in other words, aborted.

Transactions preserve the consistency of the data on the server. Let's go back to our inventory example. When an order is made, an ORDER table must be updated to reflect the order. Additionally, the PARTS table must reflect the reduced number of parts based on the order. If, for some reason, the system failed in between the update to the ORDERS table and the update to the PARTS table, the data would not correctly reflect the actual number of parts on hand. By encapsulating this entire operation within a transaction, none of the tables affected within the transaction would be updated until the entire transaction is committed.

Transactions can be controlled at the server level or at the client level within your Delphi 4 application. We will illustrate this later in the chapter in the section "Transaction Control."

> **NOTE**
>
> Some desktop databases do support transactions, such as Paradox 7.

SQL: ITS ROLE IN CLIENT/SERVER DEVELOPMENT

SQL is an industry standard database-manipulation command set that is used with applications programming environments such as Delphi. SQL is not a language in and of its own. That is, you can't go to the local software store and buy a box of SQL. Instead, SQL is part of the server database.

SQL gained great acceptance as a database query language throughout the '80s and '90s, and today it has become the standard for working with client/server databases across networked environments. Delphi enables you to use SQL through its components. SQL gives you the advantage of viewing your data in the way that only SQL commands will generate, which also gives you much more flexibility than its record-oriented counterpart.

SQL allows you to control the server data by providing the following functionality:

- *Data definition*—SQL lets you define the structures of your tables—the data types of the fields within the tables as well as the referential relationships of certain fields to fields in other tables.

- *Data retrieval*—Client applications use SQL to request from the server whatever data they require. SQL also lets clients define what data to retrieve and how that data is to be retrieved, such as the sorting order, and what fields are retrieved.

- *Data integrity*—SQL lets you protect the integrity of the data by using various integrity constraints either defined as part of the table or separately from the table as stored procedures or other database objects.

- *Data processing*—SQL allows clients to update, add, or delete data from the server. This can be as part of a simple SQL statement passed to the server, or as a stored procedure that exists on the server.

- *Security*—SQL allows you to protect the data by letting you define user access privileges, views, and restricted access to various database objects.

- *Concurrent access*—SQL manages the concurrent access of data such that users using the system simultaneously don't interfere with each other.

In short, SQL is the primary tool for the development and manipulation of client/server data.

DELPHI CLIENT/SERVER DEVELOPMENT

So how does Delphi 4 fit into this client/server environment? Delphi 4 provides you with database object components that encapsulate the functionality of the Borland Database Engine (BDE). This allows you to build database applications without having to know all of the functions of the BDE. Additionally, data-aware components communicate with the database access components. This makes it easy to build user interfaces for database applications. The SQL Links provide native drivers to servers such as Oracle, Sybase, Informix, Microsoft SQL Server, DB2, and Interbase. You can also access data from other databases through ODBC. In the sections to follow, we will use both a client/server database—Interbase—and Delphi 4 database components to illustrate various techniques in designing client/server applications.

Delphi 4 includes MIDAS. See the sidebar "MIDAS Multitier Distributed Application Services Suite" earlier in the chapter or refer to Chapter 31 for more information. Finally, Delphi also gives you the ability to create distributed applications using the Common Object Request Broker Architecture (CORBA). The CORBA specification was adopted by the Object Management Group. This technology gives you the ability to create object-oriented distributed applications. You'll find information on how Delphi 4 handles CORBA in the online help under "Writing CORBA Applications." We simply don't have enough space in this book to provide an adequate discussion of the CORBA technology. This is a topic that merits a book of its own.

THE SERVER: DESIGNING THE BACK END

When designing an application to be built around a client/server environment, quite a bit of planning has to take place before you actually begin coding. Part of this planning process involves defining the business rules for the application. That means deciding which tasks are to be performed on the server and which on the client. Then, you have to decide on table structures and relationships between fields, data types, and user security. In order to accomplish all of this, you should be thoroughly familiar with the database objects on the server end.

For illustration purposes, we'll explain these concepts using Interbase. Interbase is a server database that ships with Delphi. It allows you to create standalone client/server applications that adhere to the ANSI entry-level SQL-92 standard. To use Interbase, you must be familiar with the Windows ISQL program, which ships with Delphi.

> **NOTE**
>
> It is beyond the scope of this book to cover Interbase's implementation of SQL, or any aspect of Interbase for that matter. We are merely using Interbase as a means to discuss client/server application development, which is convenient because the local version of Interbase ships with Delphi 4. Much of what we discuss applies to other implementations of SQL in other server databases except when it relates to server-specific features.

Database Objects

Interbase uses a Data Definition Language (DDL) to define the various database objects that maintain information about the structure of the database and the data. These objects are also referred to as *metadata*. In the following sections, we describe the various objects that make up the metadata and show examples of how such metadata is defined. Keep in mind that most SQL-based databases consist of similar database objects with which you store information about data.

> **NOTE**
>
> Powerful data-modeling tools such as Erwin and RoboCase allow you to graphically design your databases using standard data-modeling methodologies. This is something to consider before you start creating your 200-table system by hand.

Defining Tables

As far as table structure and functionality are concerned, Interbase tables are much like the tables described in Chapter 27, "Writing Desktop Database Applications." That is, they contain an unordered set of rows, each having a certain number of *columns*.

Data Types

Columns can be of any of the available data types, as shown in Table 28.1.

TABLE 28.1. INTERBASE DATA TYPES.

Name	Size	Range/Precision
BLOB	variable	No limit, 64KB segment size
CHAR(n)	n characters	1 to 32767 bytes

continues

TABLE 28.1. CONTINUED

Name	Size	Range/Precision
DATE	64 bits	Jan 1, 100–Dec 11, 5941
DECIMAL (precision, scale)	variable	prec—1 to 15 scale—1 to 15
DOUBLE PRECISION	64 bits (platform-dependent)	1.7×10^{-308} to 1.7×10^{308}
FLOAT	32 bits	3.4×10^{-38} to 3.4×10^{38}
INTEGER	32 bits	-2,147,483,648 to 2,147,483,648
NUMERIC (precision, scale)	variable	-32768 to 32767
SMALLINT	16 bits	1 to 32767
VARCHAR(n)	n characters	1 to 32765

Field types may also be defined with domains in Interbase. We will discuss this shortly in the section "Using Domains."

Creating the Table

You use the CREATE TABLE statement to create the table, its columns, and whatever integrity constraints you want applied to each column. Listing 28.1 shows how you would create an Interbase table.

LISTING 28.1. TABLE CREATION IN INTERBASE.

```
/* Domain definitions */
CREATE DOMAIN FIRSTNAME AS VARCHAR(15);
CREATE DOMAIN LASTNAME AS VARCHAR(20);
CREATE DOMAIN DEPTNO AS CHAR(3)
        CHECK (VALUE = '000' OR (VALUE > '0' AND VALUE <= '999')
            OR VALUE IS NULL);
CREATE DOMAIN JOBCODE AS VARCHAR(5)
        CHECK (VALUE > '99999');
CREATE DOMAIN JOBGRADE AS SMALLINT
        CHECK (VALUE BETWEEN 0 AND 6);
CREATE DOMAIN SALARY AS NUMERIC(15, 2)
        DEFAULT 0 CHECK (VALUE > 0);

/* Table: EMPLOYEE, Owner: SYSDBA */
CREATE TABLE EMPLOYEE (
        EMP_NO EMPNO NOT NULL,
        FIRST_NAME FIRSTNAME NOT NULL,
        LAST_NAME LASTNAME NOT NULL,
        PHONE_EXT VARCHAR(4),
        HIRE_DATE DATE DEFAULT 'NOW' NOT NULL,
```

```
           DEPT_NO DEPTNO NOT NULL,
           JOB_CODE JOBCODE NOT NULL,
           JOB_GRADE JOBGRADE NOT NULL,
           JOB_COUNTRY COUNTRYNAME NOT NULL,
           SALARY SALARY NOT NULL,
           FULL_NAME COMPUTED BY (last_name ¦¦ ', ' ¦¦ first_name),
PRIMARY KEY (EMP_NO));
```

The first section of Listing 28.1 shows a series of CREATE DOMAIN statements, which we'll explain shortly. The second section of Listing 28.1 creates a table named EMPLOYEE with the rows specified. Each row definition is followed by the row type and possibly the NOT NULL clause. The NOT NULL clause indicates that a value is required for that row. You will also see that we've specified a primary key on the EMP_NO field by using the PRIMARY KEY clause. Specifying a primary key not only ensures the uniqueness of the field, but also creates an *index* on that field. Indexes speed up data retrieval.

Indexes

Indexes can also be created explicitly by using the CREATE INDEX statement. Indexes are based on one or more columns of a table. For example, the following SQL statement would create an index on the last and first names of an employee:

```
CREATE INDEX IDX_EMPNAME ON EMPLOYEE (LAST_NAME, FIRST_NAME);
```

Computed Columns

The FULL_NAME field is a computed field. Computed columns are based on a certain expression in the COMPUTED BY clause. The example in Listing 28.1 uses the COMPUTED BY clause to concatenate the last name and first name, separated by a comma. You can create many variations of computed columns to suit your needs. You should refer to your server documentation to see what capabilities are available for computed columns.

Foreign Keys

You can also specify a foreign key constraint on certain fields. For example, the field DEPT_NO is defined as

```
DEPT_NO DEPTNO NOT NULL
```

The type DEPT_NO is defined by its domain. It's okay if you don't understand this for now. Just assume that the field has been given a valid definition like CHAR(3). To ensure that this field references another field in another table, add the FOREIGN KEY clause to the table definition as shown following with some of the fields excluded for illustration:

```
CREATE TABLE EMPLOYEE (
        EMP_NO EMPNO NOT NULL,
        DEPT_NO DEPTNO NOT NULL
        FIRST_NAME FIRSTNAME NOT NULL,
        LAST_NAME LASTNAME NOT NULL,
PRIMARY KEY (EMP_NO),
FOREIGN KEY (DEPT_NO) REFERENCES DEPARTMENT (DEPT_NO));
```

Here, the FOREIGN KEY clause ensures that the value in the DEPT_NO field of the table
EMPLOYEE is the same as a value in the DEPT_NO column in the table DEPARTMENT. Foreign
keys also result in an index being created for a column.

Default Values

You can use the DEFAULT clause to specify a default value for a certain field. For example, notice the definition for HIRE_DATE, which uses the DEFAULT clause to specify a
default value for this field:

```
HIRE_DATE DATE DEFAULT 'NOW' NOT NULL,
```

Here the default value to be assigned to this field comes from the result of the NOW function, an Interbase function that returns the current date.

Using Domains

Notice the list of domain definitions that appears before the CREATE TABLE statement.
Domains are customized column definitions. By using domains, you can define table
columns with complex characteristics that can be used by other tables in the same database. For example, Listing 28.1 shows the domain definition for FIRSTNAME as

```
CREATE DOMAIN FIRSTNAME VARCHAR(15);
```

Any other table that uses FIRSTNAME as one of its field definitions will inherit the same
data type, VARCHAR(15). If you find the need to redefine FIRSTNAME later on, any table
defining a field of this type inherits the new definition.

You can add constraints to domain definitions as with column definitions. Take, for
example, the domain definition for JOBCODE, which ensures that its value is greater than
99999:

```
CREATE DOMAIN JOBCODE AS VARCHAR(5)
        CHECK (VALUE > '99999');
```

You'll also see that the domain JOBGRADE ensures that the value is between 0 and 6:

```
CREATE DOMAIN JOBGRADE AS SMALLINT
        CHECK (VALUE BETWEEN 0 AND 6);
```

The examples provided here are just a mere glimpse of what type of integrity constraints you can place on table definitions. This also varies depending on which type of server you intend to use. It would be to your advantage to be thoroughly familiar with the various techniques provided by your server.

Defining the Business Rules with Views, Stored Procedures, and Triggers

Earlier in the chapter, we talked about business rules—the database logic that defines how data is accessed and processed. Three database objects that allow you to define business rules are *views*, *stored procedures*, and *triggers*, which we discuss in the following sections.

Defining Views

A view is a valuable database object that allows you to create a customized result set consisting of clusters of columns from one or more tables in a database. This "virtual table" can have operations performed on it as though it were a real table. This allows you to define the subset of data that a particular user (or group of users) requires in addition to restricting their access to the rest of the data.

To create a view, you would use the CREATE VIEW statement. In InterBase, there are basically three ways to construct a view:

- A horizontal subset of a single table's rows. For example, the following view displays all of the fields of an EMPLOYEE table with the exception of the SALARY column, which may apply only to management personnel:

```
CREATE VIEW EMPLOYEE_LIST AS
    SELECT EMP_NO, FIRST_NAME, LAST_NAME, PHONE_EXT, FULL_NAME
    FROM EMPLOYEE;
```

- A subset of rows and columns from a single table. The following example shows a view of employees that are executives based on salaries above 100,000 dollars:

```
CREATE VIEW EXECUTIVE_LIST AS
    SELECT EMP_NO, FIRST_NAME, LAST_NAME, PHONE_EXT, FULL_NAME
    FROM EMPLOYEE WHERE SALARY >= 100,000;
```

- A subset of rows and columns from more than one table. The following view shows a subset of the EMPLOYEE table along with two columns from the JOB table. As far as the client application is concerned, the returned rows/columns belong to a single table:

```
CREATE VIEW ENTRY_LEVEL_EMPL AS
  SELECT JOB_CODE, JOB_TITLE, FIRST_NAME, LAST_NAME.
  FROM JOB, EMPLOYEE
  WHERE JOB.JOB_CODE = EMPLOYEE.JOB_CODE AND SALARY < 15000;
```

28

Many operations can be applied to views. Some views are read-only, whereas others can be updated. This depends on certain criteria specific to the server you are using.

Defining Stored Procedures

You can think of a stored procedure as a standalone routine that is run on the server, which is invoked from the client applications. Stored procedures are created with the CREATE PROCEDURE statement. There are essentially two types of stored procedures:

- *Select procedures* return a result set of rows consisting of selected columns from one or more tables, or a view.

- *Executable procedures* don't return a result set, but perform some type of logic on the server side against the server data.

The syntax for defining each type of procedure is the same and consists of a *header* and a *body*.

The stored procedure header consists of a procedure name, an optional list of parameters, and an optional list of output parameters. The body consists of an optional list of local variables and the block of SQL statements that perform the actual logic. This block is enclosed within a BEGIN..END block. The stored procedure can also nest blocks.

A SELECT Stored Procedure

Listing 28.2 illustrates a simple SELECT stored procedure.

LISTING 28.2. A SELECT STORED PROCEDURE.

```
CREATE PROCEDURE CUSTOMER_SELECT(
iCOUNTRY         VARCHAR(15)
)
RETURNS(
CUST_NO          INTEGER,
CUSTOMER         VARCHAR(25),
STATE_PROVINCE   VARCHAR(15),
COUNTRY          VARCHAR(15),
POSTAL_CODE      VARCHAR(12)
)
AS
BEGIN
  FOR SELECT
    CUST_NO,
    CUSTOMER,
    STATE_PROVINCE,
    COUNTRY,
    POSTAL_CODE
  FROM customer WHERE COUNTRY = :iCOUNTRY
  INTO
```

```
    :CUST_NO,
    :CUSTOMER,
    :STATE_PROVINCE,
    :COUNTRY,
    :POSTAL_CODE
 DO
  SUSPEND;
END
 ^
```

This procedure takes an iCOUNTRY string as a parameter and returns the specified rows of the CUSTOMER table where the country matches that of the iCOUNTRY parameter. The code that accomplishes this uses a FOR SELECT..DO statement that retrieves multiple rows. This statement functions just like a regular SELECT statement except that it retrieves one row at a time and places the specified column values into the variables specified with the INTO statement. So, to execute this statement from the Windows ISQL, you would enter the following statement:

```
SELECT * FROM CUSTOMER_SELECT("USA");
```

Later, we'll show you how to execute this stored procedure from a Delphi 4 application.

An Executable Stored Procedure

Listing 28.3 illustrates a simple executable stored procedure.

LISTING 28.3. EXECUTABLE STORED PROCEDURE.

```
CREATE PROCEDURE ADD_COUNTRY(
iCOUNTRY          VARCHAR(15),
iCURRENCY         VARCHAR(10)
)
AS
BEGIN
  INSERT INTO COUNTRY(COUNTRY, CURRENCY)
  VALUES (:iCOUNTRY, :iCURRENCY);
  SUSPEND;
END
 ^
```

This procedure adds a new record to the COUNTRY table by issuing an INSERT statement with the data passed into the procedure through parameters. This procedure does not return a result set and would be executed by using the EXECUTE PROCEDURE statement in the Windows ISQL as shown following:

```
EXECUTE PROCEDURE ADD_COUNTRY("Mexico", "Peso");
```

28

Enforcing Data Integrity Through Stored Procedures

Earlier we stated that stored procedures are a way of enforcing data integrity on the server, rather than the client. With the stored procedure logic, you can test for integrity rules and raise an error if the client is requesting an illegal operation. As an example, Listing 28.4 performs a "ship order" operation and performs the necessary checks to ensure that the operation is valid. If not, the procedure aborts after raising an exception.

LISTING 28.4. SHIP ORDER STORED PROCEDURE.

```
CREATE EXCEPTION ORDER_ALREADY_SHIPPED "Order status is 'shipped.'";
CREATE EXCEPTION CUSTOMER_ON_HOLD "This customer is on hold.";
CREATE EXCEPTION CUSTOMER_CHECK "Overdue balance -- can't ship.";

CREATE PROCEDURE SHIP_ORDER (PO_NUM CHAR(8))
AS

 DECLARE VARIABLE ord_stat CHAR(7);
 DECLARE VARIABLE hold_stat CHAR(1);
 DECLARE VARIABLE cust_no INTEGER;
 DECLARE VARIABLE any_po CHAR(8);
BEGIN
/* First retrieve the order status,
    customer hold information, and the customer no.,
    which will be for tests later in the procedure.
    These values are stored in the
    local variables defined above. */

 SELECT s.order_status, c.on_hold, c.cust_no
 FROM sales s, customer c
 WHERE po_number = :po_num
 AND s.cust_no = c.cust_no
 INTO :ord_stat, :hold_stat, :cust_no;

 /* Check if the purchase order has been already shipped. If so, raise an
    exception and terminate the procedure */

 IF (ord_stat = "shipped") THEN
 BEGIN
  EXCEPTION order_already_shipped;
  SUSPEND;
 END

 /* Check if the Customer is on hold. If so, raise an exception and
    terminate the procedure */

 ELSE IF (hold_stat = "*") THEN
 BEGIN
```

```
  EXCEPTION customer_on_hold;
  SUSPEND;
END

/* If there is an unpaid balance on orders shipped over 2 months ago,
   put the customer on hold, raise an exception, and terminate the
   procedure */

FOR SELECT po_number
 FROM sales
 WHERE cust_no = :cust_no
 AND order_status = "shipped"
 AND paid = "n"
 AND ship_date < 'NOW' - 60
 INTO :any_po
DO
BEGIN
 EXCEPTION customer_check;

 UPDATE customer
 SET on_hold = "*"
 WHERE cust_no = :cust_no;

 SUSPEND;
END

/* If we've made it to this point, everything checks out so ship the
   order.*/
UPDATE sales
SET order_status = "shipped", ship_date = 'NOW'
WHERE po_number = :po_num;

 SUSPEND;
END
 ^
```

You'll notice in Listing 28.4 that the procedure illustrates another feature of Interbase's DDL—*exceptions*. Exceptions in Interbase are much like exceptions in Delphi 4. They are named error messages that are raised from within the stored procedure when an error occurs. When an exception is raised, it returns the error message to the calling application and terminates the execution of the stored procedure. It is possible, however, to handle the exception within the stored procedure and to allow the procedure to continue processing.

Exceptions are created with the CREATE EXCEPTION statement shown in Listing 28.4. To raise an exception within a stored procedure, you would use the syntax shown in the following example:

```
EXCEPTION ExceptionName;
```

In Listing 28.4, we define three exceptions that are raised in the stored procedure under various circumstances. The procedure's commentary explains the process that occurs. The main thing to keep in mind is that these checks are being performed within the stored procedure. Therefore, any client application that executes this procedure would have the same integrity constraints enforced.

Defining Triggers

Triggers are basically stored procedures except that they occur upon a certain event and are not invoked directly from the client application nor from within another stored procedure. A trigger event occurs during a table *update*, *insert,* or *delete* operation.

Like stored procedures, triggers can make use of exceptions, thus allowing you to perform various data integrity checks during any of the previously mentioned operations on a particular table. Triggers offer you the following benefits:

- Data integrity enforcement—only valid data can be inserted into a table.
- Improved maintenance—any changes made to the trigger would be reflected by all applications using the table to which the trigger is applied.
- Automatic tracking of table modifications. The trigger can log various events that occur on the tables.
- Automatic notification of table changes through event alerters.

Triggers consist of a *header* and a *body* just as stored procedures do. The trigger header contains the trigger name, the table name to which the trigger applies, and a statement indicating when a trigger is invoked. The trigger body contains an optional list of local variables and the block of SQL statements that perform the actual logic enclosed between a BEGIN..END block like the stored procedure.

Triggers are created with the CREATE TRIGGER statement. Listing 28.5 illustrates a trigger in Interbase that stores a history of salary changes to employees.

LISTING 28.5. A TRIGGER EXAMPLE.

```
CREATE TRIGGER SALARY_CHANGE_HISTORY FOR EMPLOYEE
AFTER UPDATE AS
BEGIN
  IF (old.SALARY <> new.SALARY) THEN
    INSERT INTO SALARY_HISTORY (
       EMP_NO,
       CHANGE_DATE,
       UPDATER_ID,
       OLD_SALARY,
       PERCENT_CHANGE)
```

```
VALUES
    old.EMP_NO,
    "now",
    USER,
    old.SALARY,
    (new.SALARY - old.SALARY) * 100 / old.SALARY);
END
```

Let's examine this example more closely. The header contains the statement:

```
CREATE TRIGGER SALARY_CHANGE_HISTORY FOR EMPLOYEE
AFTER UPDATE AS
```

First, the CREATE TRIGGER statement creates a trigger with the name SALARY_CHANGE_HISTORY. Then, the statement FOR EMPLOYEE tells to what table the trigger is to be applied; in this case, this is the EMPLOYEE table. The AFTER UPDATE statement says that the trigger is to be fired after updates to the EMPLOYEE table. This statement could have read BEFORE UPDATE, which would specify to fire the trigger before changes are made to the table.

Triggers aren't only for updating tables. The following portions of the trigger header can be used in the definition of triggers:

AFTER UPDATE	Fire trigger after the table is updated.
AFTER INSERT	Fire trigger after a record has been inserted into the table.
AFTER DELETE	Fire trigger after a record is deleted from the table.
BEFORE UPDATE	Fire trigger before updating a record in the table.
BEFORE INSERT	Fire trigger before inserting a new record into the table.
BEFORE DELETE	Fire trigger before deleting a record from the table.

Following the AS clause in the trigger definition is the trigger body, which consists of SQL statements that form the trigger logic. In the example in Listing 28.5, a comparison is done between the old and new salary. If a difference exists, a record is added to the SALARY_HISTORY table indicating the change.

You'll notice that the example makes reference to the identifiers old and new. These context variables refer to the current and previous values of a row being updated. Old is not used during a record insert, and New is not used during a record delete.

You'll see triggers used more extensively in Chapter 32, "Inventory Manager: Client/Server Development," which covers an Interbase client/server application.

Privileges/Access Rights to Database Objects

In client/server databases, users are granted access to or are restricted from accessing data on the server. These *access privileges* can be applied to tables, stored procedures, and views. Privileges are granted by using the GRANT statement, which will be illustrated in a moment. First, Table 28.2 illustrates the various SQL access privileges available to Interbase and most SQL servers.

TABLE 28.2. SQL ACCESS PRIVILEGES.

Privilege	Access
ALL	User can select, insert, update, and delete data; see other access rights. ALL also grants execute rights on stored procedures.
SELECT	User can read data.
DELETE	User can delete data.
INSERT	User can write new data.
UPDATE	User can edit data.
EXECUTE	User can execute or call a stored procedure.

Granting Access to Tables

To grant user access to a table, you must use the GRANT statement, which must include the following information:

- The access privilege
- The table, stored procedure, or view name to which the privilege is applied
- The username who is being granted this access

By default, in Interbase only the creator of a table has access to that table and has the ability to grant access to other users. Some examples of granting access follow. You can refer to your Interbase documentation for more information.

The following statement grants UPDATE access on the EMPLOYEE table to the user with the username JOHN:

```
GRANT SELECT ON EMPLOYEE TO JOHN;
```

The following statement grants read and edit access on the EMPLOYEE table to the users JOHN and JANE:

```
GRANT SELECT, UPDATE on EMPLOYEE to JOHN, JANE;
```

You can see that you can grant access to a list of users as well. If you want to grant all privileges to a user, use the ALL privilege in your GRANT statement:

```
GRANT ALL ON EMPLOYEE TO JANE;
```

By the preceding statement, the user JANE will have SELECT, UPDATE, and DELETE access on the table EMPLOYEE.

It is also possible to grant privileges to specific columns in a table as illustrated below:

```
GRANT SELECT, UPDATE (CONTACT, PHONE) ON CUSTOMERS TO PUBLIC;
```

This statement grants read and edit access on the fields CONTACT and PHONE in the CUSTOMERS table to all users by using the PUBLIC keyword, which specifies all users.

You must also grant privileges to stored procedures that require access to certain tables. For example, the following example grants read and update access on the customer's table to the stored procedure UPDATE_CUSTOMER:

```
GRANT SELECT, UPDATE ON CUSTOMERS TO PROCEDURE UPDATE_CUSTOMER;
```

The variations on the GRANT statement apply to stored procedures as well.

Granting Access to Views

For the most part, when GRANT is used against a view, SQL treats this just as it would when using GRANT against a table. However, you must be sure that the user to whom you are granting UPDATE, INSERT, or DELETE privileges also has the same privileges on the underlying tables to which the view refers. A WITH CHECK OPTION statement used when creating a view ensures that the fields to be edited can be seen through the view before the operation is attempted. It is recommended that modifiable views be created with this option.

Granting Access to Stored Procedures

For users or stored procedures to execute other stored procedures, you must grant them EXECUTE access to the stored procedure to be executed. The following example illustrates how you would grant access to a list of users and stored procedures requiring EXECUTE access to another stored procedure:

```
GRANT EXECUTE ON EDIT_CUSTOMER TO MIKE, KIM, SALLY, PROCEDURE
ADD_CUSTOMER;
```

Here, the users MIKE, KIM, and SALLY as well as the stored procedure ADD_CUSTOMER can execute the stored procedure EDIT_CUSTOMER.

28

DEVELOPING CLIENT/SERVER APPLICATIONS

Revoking Access to Users

To revoke user access to a table or stored procedure, you must use the REVOKE statement, which must include

- The access privilege to revoke
- The table name/stored procedure to which the revocation is applied
- The username whose privilege is being revoked

REVOKE looks like the GRANT statement syntactically. The following example shows how you would revoke access to a table.

```
REVOKE UPDATE, DELETE ON EMPLOYEE TO JANE, TOM;
```

THE CLIENT: DESIGNING THE FRONT END

In the following sections, we'll discuss the Delphi 4 database components and how to use them to access a client/server database. We'll discuss various methods on how to perform common tasks efficiently with these components.

Using the TDatabase Component

The TDatabase component gives you more control over your database connections. This includes

- Creating a persistent database connection
- Overriding the default server logins
- Creating application-level BDE aliases
- Controlling transactions and specifying transaction isolation levels

Tables 28.3 and 28.4 are brief references to TDatabase's properties and methods. For more detailed descriptions, you'll want to refer to the Delphi online help or documentation. We'll show you how to use some of these properties and methods in this and later chapters.

TABLE 28.3. TDatabase PROPERTIES.

Property	*Purpose*
AliasName	An existing BDE alias defined with the BDE Configuration utility. This property cannot be used in conjunction with the DriverName property.
Connected	A Boolean property to determine whether the TDatabase component is linked to a database.

Property	*Purpose*
DatabaseName	Defines an application-specific alias. Other TDataset components (TTable, TQuery, TStoredProc) use this property's value for their AliasName property.
DatasetCount	The number of TDataset components that are linked to the TDatabase component.
Datasets	An array referring to all TDataset components linked to the TDatabase component.
DriverName	Name of a BDE driver such as Oracle, dBASE, Interbase, and so on. This property cannot be used in conjunction with the AliasName property.
Handle	Used to make direct calls to the Borland Database Engine (BDE) API.
IsSQLBased	A Boolean property to determine whether or not the connected database is SQL-based. This value is False if the Driver property holds STANDARD.
KeepConnection	A Boolean property to determine if the TDatabase maintains a connection to the database when no TDatasets are open. This property is used for efficiency reasons because connecting to some SQL servers can take quite a while.
Locale	Identifies the language driver used with the TDatabase component. This is used primarily for direct BDE calls.
LoginPrompt	Determines how the TDatabase component handles user logins. If this property is set to True, a default login dialog will be displayed. If this property is set to False, the login parameters must be provided in code in the TDataBase.OnLogin event.
Name	The name of the component as referenced by other components.
Owner	The owner of the TDatabase component.
Params	Holds the parameters required to connect to the server database. Default parameters are set using the BDE configuration utility but may be customized here.
Tag	A longint property used to store any integer value.
Temporary	A Boolean property indicating whether the TDatabase component was created as a result of no TDatabase component being present when a TTable, TQuery, or TStoredProc was opened.
TransIsolation	Determines the transaction isolation level for the server.

Table 28.4 lists TDataBase's methods.

28

DEVELOPING
CLIENT/SERVER
APPLICATIONS

TABLE 28.4. TDataBase METHODS.

Method	Purpose
Close	Closes the TDatabase connection and all linked TDataset components.
CloseDatasets	Closes all linked TDataset components linked to the TDatabase component. This does not necessarily close the TDatabase connection.
Commit	Commits all changes to the database within a transaction. The transaction must have been established with a call to StartTransaction.
Create	Allocates memory and creates an instance of a TDatabase component.
Destroy	Deallocates memory and destroys the TDatabase instance.
Free	Performs the same as Destroy except that it first determines whether or not the TDatabase is set to nil before calling destroy.
Open	Connects the TDatabase component to the server database. Setting the Connected property to True automatically calls this method.
RollBack	Rolls back or cancels a transaction, thus canceling any changes made to the server since the last call to StartTransaction.
StartTransaction	Begins a transaction with the isolation level specified by the TransIsolation property. Modifications made to the server are not committed until a call to the Commit method is made. To cancel changes, you must call the RollBack method.

Application-Level Connections

One reason for using a TDatabase component with your project is to provide an application-level alias for the entire project. This differs from a BDE-level alias in that the alias name provided by the TDatabase component is available only to your project. This application-level alias may be shared among other projects by placing the TDatabase on a sharable TDataModule. The TDataModule can be made sharable by placing it where other developers can add it to their projects or by placing it into the Object Repository.

You specify the application-level alias by assigning a value to the TDataBase.DatabaseName property. The BDE alias that specifies the server database to which the TDatabase component is connected is specified by the TDatabase.AliasName property.

Security Control

The TDatabase component allows you to control user access to server data in how it handles the login process. During the login process, a user must provide a valid username and password to gain access to vital data. By default, there is a standard login dialog that is invoked when connected to a server database.

There are several ways you might want to handle logins. First, you can override the login altogether and allow users to gain access to data without having to log in at all. Second, you can provide a different login dialog so that you can perform your own validity checks if necessary before passing the username and password to the server for normal checks. Finally, you might want to allow users to log off and log in again without shutting down the application. The following sections illustrate all three techniques.

Automatic Login—Preventing the Login Dialog

To prevent the login dialog from displaying when launching an application, you must set the following TDataBase properties:

AliasName	Set to an existing BDE alias that was defined with the BDE Configuration utility. This is the same value typically used as the Alias property value for TTable and TQuery components.
DatabaseName	Set to an application-level alias that will be seen by TDataset descendant components (TTable, TQuery, TStoredProc) within the current application. These components will use this value as their Alias property value.
LoginPrompt	Set to False. This causes the TDatabase component to look to its Params property to find the username and password.
Params	Specify the username and password here. To do this, you must invoke the String List Editor for this property to set the values.

After you have set the TDatabase properties accordingly, you must link all TTable, TQuery, and TStoredProc components to the TDatabase by placing the TDatabase.DatabaseName property value as their Alias property value. This value will appear in the drop-down list of aliases when you select the drop-down list in the Object Inspector.

Now, when you set the TDatabase.Connected property to True, your application will connect to the server without prompting you for a username and password because it will use those values defined in the Params property. The same will be true when running the application.

You'll find a small example illustrating this on the accompanying CD as NoLogin.dpr.

Providing a Customized Login Dialog

In certain cases, you might want to present your users with a more customized login dialog. For example, you may want to prompt your users for additional information other than just username and password from the same dialog. Perhaps you just want a more appealing dialog at program startup than that provided by the default login. Whatever the situation, the process is fairly simple.

Basically, you can disable the default login dialog by setting the TDatabase. LoginPrompt property to True. However, this time you won't provide the username and password through the Params property. Instead, you create an event handler for the TDatabase.OnLogin event. This event handler is called whenever the TDatabase. Connected property is set to True and the TDatabase.LoginPrompt property is set to True.

The following function instantiates a custom login form and assigns the user's username and password back to the calling application:

```
function GetLoginParams(ALoginParams: TStrings): word;
var
  LoginForm: TLoginForm;
begin
  LoginForm := TLoginForm.Create(Application);
  try
    Result := LoginForm.ShowModal;
    if Result = mrOK then
    begin
      ALoginParams.Values['USER NAME'] := LoginForm.edtUserName.Text;
      ALoginParams.Values['PASSWORD'] := LoginForm.edtPassWord.Text;
    end;
  finally
    LoginForm.Free;
  end;
end;
```

The TDataBase.OnLogin event handler would invoke the preceding procedure as illustrated below. You'll find this sample project on the accompanying CD as LOGIN.DPR.

```
procedure TMainForm.dbMainLogin(Database: TDatabase;
  LoginParams: TStrings);
begin
  GetLoginParams(LoginParams);
end;
```

Logoff During a Current Session

You can also provide functionality for your users to be able to log off and log in again perhaps as different users without having to shut down the application. To do this, again you set up the TDatabase component so that it does not invoke the default login dialog. Therefore, you must override its OnLogin event handler. Also, you must set TDataBase.LoginPrompt to True so that the event handler will be invoked. The process requires the use of some variables to hold the username and password as well as a Boolean variable to indicate either a successful or unsuccessful login attempt. Also, you must provide two methods, one to perform the login logic, and another to perform the logoff logic. Listing 28.6 illustrates a project that performs this logic.

LISTING 28.6. LOGIN/LOGOFF LOGIC EXAMPLE.

```
unit MainFrm;

interface

uses
  Windows, Messages, SysUtils, Classes, Graphics, Controls,
  Forms, Dialogs, StdCtrls, Grids, DBGrids, DB, DBTables;

type
  TMainForm = class(TForm)
    dbMain: TDatabase;
    tblEmployee: TTable;
    dsEmployee: TDataSource;
    dgbEmployee: TDBGrid;
    btnLogon: TButton;
    btnLogOff: TButton;
    procedure btnLogonClick(Sender: TObject);
    procedure dbMainLogin(Database: TDatabase; LoginParams: TStrings);
    procedure btnLogOffClick(Sender: TObject);
    procedure FormCreate(Sender: TObject);
    procedure FormDestroy(Sender: TObject);
  public
    TempLoginParams: TStringList;
    LoginSuccess: Boolean;
  end;

var
  MainForm: TMainForm;

implementation
uses LoginFrm;

{$R *.DFM}

procedure TMainForm.btnLogonClick(Sender: TObject);
begin
  // Get the new login params.
  if GetLoginParams(TempLoginParams) = mrOk then
  begin
    // Disconnect the TDatabase component
    dbMain.Connected := False;
    try
      { Attempt to reconnect the TDatabase component. This will invoke
        the DataBase1Login event handler which will set the LoginParams
        with the current username and password. }
      dbMain.Connected := True;
      tblEmployee.Active := True;
      LoginSuccess := True;
```

continues

28

DEVELOPING CLIENT/SERVER APPLICATIONS

LISTING 28.6. CONTINUED

```
    except
      on EDBEngineError do
      begin
        //If login failed, specify a failed login and reraise the
        // exception
        LoginSuccess := False;
        Raise;
      end;
    end;
  end;
end;

procedure TMainForm.dbMainLogin(Database: TDatabase;
  LoginParams: TStrings);
begin
  LoginParams.Assign(TempLoginParams);
end;

procedure TMainForm.btnLogOffClick(Sender: TObject);
begin
  { Disconnect the TDatabase component and set the UserName
    and password variables to empty strings }
  dbMain.Connected := False;
  TempLoginParams.Clear;
end;

procedure TMainForm.FormCreate(Sender: TObject);
begin
  TempLoginParams := TStringList.Create;
end;

procedure TMainForm.FormDestroy(Sender: TObject);
begin
  TempLoginParams.Free;
end;

end.
```

In Listing 28.6, you see that the main form has two fields: TempLoginParams and LoginSuccess. The TempLoginParams holds the user's username and password. The btnLogonClick() method is the logic for the login process, whereas the btnLogOffClick() event handler is the logic for the logoff process. The dbMainLogin() method is the OnLogin event handler for dbMain. The code logic is explained in the code commentary. You should also notice that this project uses the same TLoginForm used in the previous example. You'll find this example in the project LogOnOff.dpr on the accompanying CD.

Transaction Control

Earlier in this chapter, we spoke of transactions. We mentioned how transactions allow a series of changes to the database to be committed as a whole to ensure database consistency.

Transaction processing can be handled from Delphi 4 client applications by making use of the TDatabase properties and methods specific to transactions. The following section explains how to perform transaction processing from within your Delphi 4 application.

Implicit Versus Explicit Transaction Control

Delphi 4 handles transactions either implicitly or explicitly. By default, transactions are handled implicitly.

Implicit transactions are transactions that are started and committed on a row-by-row basis. This means whenever you call a Post method or when Post is called automatically in VCL code. Because such transactions occur on a row-by-row basis, this increases network traffic, which may lead to efficiency problems.

Explicit transactions are handled in one of two ways. The first method is whenever you call the StartTransaction(), Commit(), or RollBack() methods of TDataBase. The other method is by using pass-through SQL statements within a TQuery component, which we explain momentarily. Explicit transaction control is the recommended approach to use because it provides for less network traffic and safer code.

Handling Transactions

Back in Table 28.4, you saw three methods of TDatabase that deal specifically with transactions: StartTransaction(), Commit(), and RollBack().

StartTransaction() begins a transaction using the isolation level specified by the TDatabase.TransIsolation property. Any changes made to the server after StartTransaction() is called will fall within the current transaction.

If all changes to the server were successful, a call to TDatabase.Commit() is made in order to finalize all changes at once. Otherwise, if an error occurs, TDatabase.RollBack() is invoked to cancel any changes made.

The typical example of where transaction processing comes in handy has to do with the inventory example. Given an ORDER table and an INVENTORY table, whenever an order is made, a new record must be added to the ORDER table. Likewise, the INVENTORY table must be updated to reflect the new item count on hand for the part or parts just ordered. Now suppose that a user enters an order with a system in which transactions were not present. The ORDER table gets its new record, but just before the INVENTORY table gets updated, a power failure occurs. The database would be in an inconsistent state because the INVENTORY table would not accurately reflect the items on hand. Transaction processing would circumvent this problem by ensuring that both table modifications are successful before finalizing any changes to the database. Listing 28.7 illustrates how this might look in Delphi 4 code.

LISTING 28.7. TRANSACTION PROCESSING.

```
dbMain.StartTransaction;
  try
    spAddOrder.ParamByName('ORDER_NO').AsInteger := OrderNo;
    { Make other Parameter assignments and then execute the stored
      procedure to add the new order record to the ORDER table.}
    spAddOrder.ExecProc;
    { Iterate through all the parts ordered and update the
      INVENTORY table to reflect the # of parts on hand }
    for i := 0 to PartList.Count - 1 do
    begin
      spReduceParts.ParamByName('PART_NO').AsInteger :=
        PartRec(PartList.Objects[i]).PartNo;
      spReduceParts.ParamByName('NUM_SOLD').AsInteger :=
        PartRec(PartList.Objects[i]).NumSold;
      spReduceParts.ExecProc;
    end;
    // Commit the changes to both the ORDER and INVENTORY tables.
    dbMain.Commit;
  except
    // If we get here, an error occurred. Cancel all changes.
    dbMain.RollBack;
    raise;
  end;
```

This code is a simplistic example of how to use transaction processing to ensure database consistency. It uses two stored procedures, one to add the new order record and another to update the INVENTORY table with the new data. Keep in mind that this is just a code snippet to illustrate the transaction processing with Delphi. This logic could probably be handled better on the server side.

In some cases, the type of transaction processing that must happen might depend on server-specific features. Given this situation, you would have to use a TQuery component to pass the server-specific SQL code, which requires that you set the SQL pass-through mode accordingly.

SQL Pass-through Mode

The SQL pass-through mode specifies how Delphi 4 database applications and the Borland Database Engine (BDE) share connections to database servers. The BDE connections are those used in Delphi methods that make BDI API calls. The pass-through mode is set in the BDE Configuration Utility. The three settings for the pass-through mode are as follows:

SHARED AUTOCOMMIT	Transactions are handled on a row-by-row basis. This method is more closely related to that of desktop data-bases. In the client/server world, this causes heavy net-work traffic and is not the recommended approach. However, this is the default setting for Delphi 4 applica-tions.
SHARED NOAUTOCOMMIT	Delphi 4 applications must explicitly start, commit, and cancel transactions using the TDatabase.StartTransaction(), Commit(), and RollBack() methods.
NOT SHARED	The BDE and TQuery components issuing pass-through SQL statements do not share the same connections. This means that the SQL code is not restricted to BDE capa-bilities and may consist of server-specific features.

If you are not using pass-through SQL but want more control over your transaction pro-cessing, set the pass-through mode to SHARED NOAUTOCOMMIT and handle the transaction processing yourself. In most cases, this should suit your needs. Just keep in mind that in multiuser environments where the same rows get updated often, conflicts may occur.

Isolation Levels

Isolation levels determine how transactions see data that is being accessed from other transactions. The TDatabase.TransIsolation property determines what isolation level a particular transaction will use. There are three isolation levels to which you can assign the TransIsolation property:

tiDirtyRead	The lowest isolation level. Transactions using this isolation level can read uncommitted changes from other transac-tions.
tiReadCommitted	The default isolation level. Transactions using this isolation level can read only committed changes by other transac-tions.
tiRepeatableRead	This is the highest isolation level. Transactions using this isolation level cannot read changes to previously read data made by other transactions.

The support for the isolation levels listed here may vary on different servers. Delphi 4 will always use the next highest isolation level if a specific isolation level is not supported.

TTable or TQuery

A common misunderstanding is the idea that developing front-end client applications is the same as or similar to developing desktop database applications.

Where you'll see this frame of thinking manifest itself is in how or when one uses TTable versus TQuery components for database access. In the following paragraphs, we'll discuss some of the merits and faults of using a TTable component, and when it should and should not be used. You'll see why you're most often better off using a TQuery component.

Can TTable Components Do SQL?

TTable components are great for accessing data in a desktop environment. They are designed to perform the tasks that desktop databases require such as manipulation of the entire table, navigation forward and backward through a table, or even going to a specific record in the table. These concepts, however, are foreign to SQL database servers. Relational databases are designed to be accessed in sets of data. SQL databases do not know the concepts of "next," "previous," and "last" record—something that TTable is good at. Although some SQL databases provide "scrollable cursors," this is not a standard and typically applies only to the result set. Additionally, some servers don't provide bidirectional scrolling.

The key point to make when comparing TTable components against SQL databases is that ultimately, the commands issued through TTable must be converted to SQL code that the SQL database can understand. Not only does this limit how you can access the server, but it also weighs heavily on efficiency.

To demonstrate the inherent weakness of using TTable to access large datasets, consider the process of opening a TTable just to retrieve a few records. The time it takes for a TTable to open a SQL table is directly proportional to the number of fields and the amount of metadata (index definitions and so on) attached to the SQL table. When you issue a command such as the following against a SQL table, the BDE sends a series of SQL commands to the server to first retrieve information about the table's columns, indexes, and so on:

```
Table1.Open;
```

Then it issues a SELECT statement to build a result set consisting of all the columns and rows from the table. This is where the time it takes to open a table might also be proportional to the size of the SQL table (the number of rows). Even though only the amount of rows necessary to populate the data-aware components are returned to the client, an entire result set is being built in response to the query. This process occurs whenever the

TTable is opened. On extremely large tables, typical with client/server databases, this single operation can take up to 20 seconds. Keep in mind that some SQL servers such as Sybase and Microsoft SQL don't allow a client to abort the retrieval of a result set. This is where the table's size affects the select duration. Oracle, Interbase, and Informix all enable you to abort a result set without this considerable penalty.

Despite the disadvantages to using TTables with a client application, they are typically fine for accessing small tables on the server. You have to test your applications to determine if the performance hit is unacceptable.

> **NOTE**
>
> MIDAS handles the returning of data packets a bit differently. You'll want to read about this in Chapter 31.

Issuing FindKey and FindNearest Against SQL Databases

Although TTable is capable of looking up records using the FindKey()method, it has its limitations when using this against a SQL database. First, TTable can only perform FindKey against an indexed field or fields if you're performing a search based on values from multiple fields. TQuery is not faced with this limitation because you perform the record search through SQL. It's true that TTable.FindKey results in a SELECT statement against the server table. However, the result set will consist of all fields of the table even though you may have only selected certain fields from the TTable component's Fields Editor.

Achieving the functionality of FindNearest() with SQL code is not as straightforward as using a TTable, yet it's not impossible. The following SQL statement almost accomplishes the TTable.FindNearest() functionality:

```
SELECT * FROM EMPLOYEES
  WHERE NAME >= "CL"
  ORDER BY NOMENCLATURE
```

Here the result set returns the record either *at* the position searched for or directly after where it *should be*. The problem here is that this result set returns *all* the records after the position searched on. To be more accurate so that the result set will consist of only one record, you can do the following:

```
SELECT * FROM EMPLOYEES
  WHERE NAME = (SELECT MIN(NAME) FROM EMPLOYEES
  WHERE NAME >= "CL")
```

Here you use a nested SELECT. In a nested SELECT statement, the inner statement returns its result set to the outer SELECT. The outer SELECT then uses this result set to process its statement. In the inner query in this example, you use the SQL aggregate function MIN() to return the lowest value in the column NAME on the table EMPLOYEES. This single-row single-column result set is then used in the outer query to retrieve the remaining rows.

The point is that you give yourself much more flexibility and efficiency by maximizing SQL capabilities and using the TQuery component. By using TTable, you only limit what you're able to do against the server data.

Using the TQuery Component

In the previous chapter, you were introduced to the TQuery component and shown how you can use it to retrieve result sets of rows in tables. We're going to get into a bit more detail on TQuery in the following sections. We'll illustrate how to create dynamic SQL statements at runtime, and how to pass parameters to queries, as well as how to improve TQuery performance by setting certain property values.

There are basically two types of queries for which you'll use TQuery: those that return result sets and those that don't return a result set. For queries returning a result set, you use the TQuery.Open()method. The TQuery.ExecSQL() method is used where a result set is not returned.

Dynamic SQL

Dynamic SQL means that you can modify your SQL statements at runtime based on various conditions. When you invoke the String List Editor for the TQuery.SQL property and enter a statement like the following, you are entering a static SQL statement:

```
SELECT * FROM EMPLOYEE WHERE COUNTRY = "USA"
```

This statement won't vary unless you completely replace it at runtime.

To make this statement dynamic, you would enter the following into the SQL property:

```
SELECT * FROM CUSTOMER WHERE COUNTRY = :iCOUNTRY;
```

In this statement, instead of hard-coding the value on which to search, we've provided a placeholder, or a parameter whose value can be specified later. This variable is named iCountry and follows the colon in the SELECT statement. Its name was chosen at random. Now, you can search on any country by providing the country string to search on.

There are several ways to provide values for a parameterized query. One way is to use the property editor for the TQuery.Params property. Another is to provide that value at runtime. You can also provide the value from another dataset through a TDataSource component.

Providing TQuery Parameters Through the Params Property Editor

When you invoke the TQuery.Params property editor, the Parameter Name list displays the parameters for a given query. For each parameter listed, you must select a type from the Data Type drop-down combo. The value field is where you can specify an initial value for the parameter if you like. You can also select NULL check box to set the parameter's value to NULL. When you select OK, the query will prepare its parameters, which binds them to their types (see the sidebar on "Preparing Queries"). When you invoke TQuery.Open(), a result set will be returned to the TQuery.

PREPARING QUERIES

When a SQL statement is sent to the server, the server must parse, validate, compile, and execute the statement. This happens every time you send a SQL statement to the server. You can improve performance by allowing the server to perform the preliminary steps of parsing, validating, and compiling by "preparing" the SQL statement before having the server execute it. This is especially advantageous when using a query repetitively in a loop, by calling TQuery.Prepare() before entering the loop as shown in the following code:

```
Query1.Prepare; // First prepare the query.
try
  { Enter a loop to execute a query numerous times }
  for i := 1 to 100 do begin
    { provide the parameters for the query }
    Query1.ParamByName('SomeParam').AsInteger := i;
    Query1.ParamByName('SomeOtherParam').AsString := SomeString;
    Query1.Open;  // Open the query.
    try
      { Use the result set of Query1 here. }
    finally
      Query1.Close; // Close the query.
    end;
  end;
finally
  Query1.Unprepare; // Call unprepare to free up resouces
end;
```

Prepare() only needs to be called once before its repetitive use. You can also change the values of the query parameters after the first call to Prepare() without having to call Prepare() again. However, if you change the SQL statement itself, you must call Prepare() again before reusing it. A call to Prepare() must be matched with a call to TQuery.UnPrepare() to release the resources allocated by Prepare().

continues

> Queries get prepared when you select the OK button on the Params property
> editor, or when you call the TQuery.Prepare() method as shown in the preced-
> ing code. It is also recommended that you call Prepare() once in the form's
> OnCreate event handler and UnPrepare() in the form's OnDestroy event handler
> for those queries whose SQL statements won't change. It is not necessary to
> prepare your SQL queries, but it's certainly beneficial to do so.

Providing TQuery Parameters Using the Params Property

The TQuery component has a zero-based array of TParam objects, each representing parameters of the SQL statement in the TQuery.SQL property. For example, take a look at the
following SQL statement:

```
INSERT INTO COUNTRY (
   NAME,
   CAPITAL,
   POPULATION)
VALUES(
   :NAME,
   :CAPITAL,
   :POPULATION)
```

To use the Params property to provide values for the parameters :NAME, :CAPITAL, and
:POPULATION, you would issue the following statement:

```
with Query1 do begin
   Params[0].AsString := 'Peru';
   Params[1].AsString := 'Lima"
   Params[2].AsInteger := 22,000,000;
end;
```

The values provided would be bound to the parameters in the SQL statement. Keep in
mind that the order of the parameters in the SQL statement dictates their position in the
Params property.

Providing TQuery Parameters Using the ParamByName Method

In addition to the Params property, the TQuery component has the
ParamByName()method. The ParamByName() method enables you to assign values to the
SQL parameters by their name rather than by their position in the SQL statement. This
enhances code readability but isn't as efficient as the positional method because Delphi
must resolve the parameters being references.

To use the ParamByName() method to provide value for the preceding INSERT query, you
would use the following code:

```
with Query1 do begin
  ParamByName('COUNTRY').AsString := 'Peru';
  ParamByName('CAPITAL').AsString := 'Lima';
  ParamByName('POPULATION').AsInteger := 22,000,000;
end;
```

You should see that this code is a bit clearer as to what parameters you are providing values for.

Providing TQuery Parameters Using Another Data Set

The parameters provided to a TQuery component can also be obtained from another TDataset such as a TQuery or TTable. This creates a master-detail relationship between the two data sets. To do this, you must link a TDataSource component to the master data set. The name of this TDataSource is assigned to the DataSource property of the detail TQuery component. When the query is executed, Delphi checks to see if there is any value assigned to the TQuery.DataSource property. If so, it will look for column names of the DataSource that match parameter names in the SQL statement and will then bind them.

As an example, consider the following SQL statement:

```
SELECT * FROM SALARY_HISTORY
  WHERE EMP_NO = :EMP_NO
```

Here, you need a value for the parameter named EMP_NO. First you assign the TDataSource that refers to the master TTable component to the TQuery's DataSource property. Delphi will then search for a field named EMP_NO in the table to which the TTable refers and will bind the value of that column to the TQuery's parameter for the current row. This is illustrated in the example found in the project LnkQuery.dpr on the accompanying CD.

Using the Format Function to Design Dynamic SQL Statements

Now that we've shown you how to use parameterized queries, it might seem reasonable that either of the following SQL statements would be valid:

```
SELECT * FROM PART ORDER BY :ORDERVAL;
SELECT * FROM :TABLENAME
```

Unfortunately, you cannot replace certain words in a SQL statement such as column names and table names. SQL servers just don't support this capability. So how do you go about putting this type of flexibility into your dynamic SQL statements? You do this by constructing your SQL statements at design time by using the Format() function.

If you have any experience programming in C or C++, you'll find that the Format() function is much like C's Printf() function. See the sidebar on the Format() function.

> ## USING THE Format() FUNCTION
>
> Use the Format() function to customize strings that vary depending on values provided by *format specifiers*. Format specifiers are placeholders where strings of a specified type will be inserted into a given string. These specifiers consist of a percent symbol (%) and a *type specifier*. The following list illustrates some type specifiers:
>
> c   Specifies a char type
>
> d   Specifies an integer type
>
> f   Specifies a float type
>
> p   Specifies a pointer type
>
> s   Specifies a string type
>
> For example, in the string "My name is %s and I'm %d years old.", you see two format specifiers. The %s specifier indicates that a string is to be inserted in its place. The %d specifier indicates that an integer is to be inserted in its place. To construct the string, here's how to use the Format() function:
>
> S := Format('My name is %s and I'm %d years old.", ['Xavier', 32]);
>
> The Format() function takes the source string and an open array of arguments to replace the format specifiers. It returns the resulting string. You'll find detailed information on the Format() function in Delphi 4's online help.

Therefore, to construct SQL statements with the flexibility to modify field names or table names, you can use the Format() function as illustrated in the following code samples.

Listing 28.8 illustrates how you would use the Format() function to allow the user to pick the fields by which to sort the result set of a query. The list of fields exist in a list box, and the code is actually the OnClick event of that list box. You'll find this demo in the project OrderBy.dpr on the accompanying CD.

LISTING 28.8. USING Format() TO SPECIFY SORTING COLUMN.

```
procedure TMainForm.lbFieldsClick(Sender: TObject);
{ Define a constant string from which the SQL string will be built }
const
   SQLString = 'SELECT * FROM PARTS ORDER BY %s';
begin
  with qryParts do
  begin
    Close;      // Make sure the query is closed.
    SQL.Clear; // Clear any previous SQL statement.
    { Now add the new SQL statement constructed with the format
      function }
```

```
    SQL.Add(Format(SQLString, [lbFields.Items[lbFields.ItemIndex]]));
    Open;   { Now open Query1 with the new statement }
  end;
end;
```

To populate the list box in Listing 28.8 with the field names in the parts table, we performed the following in the form's `OnCreate` event handler:

```
tblParts.Open;
try
  tblParts.GetFieldNames(lbFields.Items);
finally
  tblParts.Close;
end;
```

`Table1` is linked to the `PARTS.DB` table.

This next example in Listing 28.9 illustrates how to pick a table on which to perform a `SELECT` statement. The code is practically the same as that presented in Listing 28.8 except that the format string is different and the form's `OnCreate` event handler retrieves a list of table names in the given session rather than a list of fields for a single table.

First, a list of table names is obtained:

```
procedure TMainForm.FormCreate(Sender: TObject);
begin
{  First, get a list of table names for the user to select }
  Session.GetTableNames(dbMain.DatabaseName, '', False, False,
    lbTables.Items);
end;
```

Then, the `lbTables.OnClick` event handler is used to select the table on which to perform a `SELECT` query as shown in Listing 28.9.

LISTING 28.9. USING `Format()` TO SPECIFY A TABLE TO SELECT.

```
procedure TMainForm.lbTablesClick(Sender: TObject);
{ Define a constant string from which the SQL string will be built }
const
   SQLString = 'SELECT * FROM %s';
begin
  with qryMain do
  begin
    Close;      // Make sure the query is closed.
    SQL.Clear; // Clear any previous SQL statement.
    { Now add the new SQL statement constructed with the format
      function }
    SQL.Add(Format(SQLString, [lbTables.Items[lbTables.ItemIndex]]));
    Open;   { Now open Query1 with the new statement }
  end;
end;
```

This demo is provided in the project `SelTable.dpr` on the accompanying CD.

28

DEVELOPING
CLIENT/SERVER
APPLICATIONS

Retrieving the Result Set Values of a Query Through TQuery

When a query operation returns a result set, you can access the values of the columns in that result set by using the TQuery component as though it were an array whose field names are indexes into this array. For example, suppose you have a TQuery whose SQL property contains the following SQL statement:

```
SELECT * FROM CUSTOMER
```

You would retrieve the values of the columns as shown in Listing 28.10, which shows code for the project, ResltSet.dpr, on the accompanying CD.

LISTING 28.10. RETRIEVING THE FIELDS OF A TQuery RESULT SET.

```
procedure TMainForm.dsCustomerDataChange(Sender: TObject; Field: TField);
begin
  with lbCustomer.Items do
  begin
    Clear;
    Add(VarToStr(qryCustomer['CustNo']));
    Add(VarToStr(qryCustomer['Company']));
    Add(VarToStr(qryCustomer['Addr1']));
    Add(VarToStr(qryCustomer['City']));
    Add(VarToStr(qryCustomer['State']));
    Add(VarToStr(qryCustomer['Zip']));
    Add(VarToStr(qryCustomer['Country']));
    Add(VarToStr(qryCustomer['Phone']));
    Add(VarToStr(qryCustomer['Contact']));
  end;
end;
```

In the preceding code you use the default data-set method, FieldValues(), to access the field values of qryCustomer. Because FieldValues() is the default data-set method, it is not necessary to specify the method name explicitly as shown following:

```
Add(VarToStr(qryCustomer.FieldValues['Contact']));
```

CAUTION

The function FieldValues() returns a variant field type. If a field were to contain a NULL value, an attempt to get the field's value with FieldValue() would result in an EVariantError exception. Therefore, Delphi provides the VarToStr() function, which converts NULL string values to an empty string. Equivalent functions for other data types are not provided. However, you can construct your own as shown following for integer types:

```
function VarToInt(const V: Variant): Integer;
begin
  if TVarData(V).VType <> varNull then
    Result := V
  else
```

```
 Result := 0;
end;
```

Be careful, however, when you resave the data. A NULL value in a SQL database is a valid value. If you were to replace that value with an empty string, which is not the same as NULL, you could destroy the integrity of the data. You'll have to come up with a runtime solution to this, such as testing for NULL and storing some predefined string to represent the NULL value.

You can also retrieve the field values from a TQuery using the TQuery.Fields property. The Fields property is used in the same way as the TQuery.Params property except that it refers to the columns in the result set. Similarly, TQuery has the FieldByName() method, which functions like the ParamByName() method.

The UniDirectional Property

To optimize access to a database, the TQuery component has the UniDirectional property. This applies to databases that support *bidirectional cursors*. Bidirectional cursors enable you to move forward and backward through the query's result set. By default, this property is False. Therefore, when you have components like the TDBGrid component linked to a database that does not support bidirectional movement, Delphi emulates this movement by buffering records on the client side. This can take up a lot of resources on the client end rather quickly. Therefore if you plan to only move forward through a result set, or if you plan to go through the result set only once, set UniDirectional to True.

Live Result Sets

By default, TQuery returns read-only result sets. You can specify for TQuery to return a modifiable result set by changing the TQuery.RequestLive property to True. However, certain restrictions apply to doing this, as shown in the following lists.

For queries returning result sets from dBASE or Paradox tables, these restrictions apply:

- Uses local SQL Syntax (information provided in online help)
- Uses only a single table
- SQL statement does not use an ORDER BY clause
- SQL statement does not use aggregate functions like SUM or AVG
- SQL statement does not use calculated fields
- Comparisons in the WHERE clause may consist only of column names to scalar types

28

DEVELOPING
CLIENT/SERVER
APPLICATIONS

For queries using pass-through SQL from a server table, these restrictions apply:

- Uses a single table
- SQL statement does not use an ORDER BY clause
- SQL statement does not use aggregate functions like SUM or AVG

To determine whether or not a query can be modified, you can check the TQuery.CanModify property.

Cached Updates

TDataSets contain a CachedUpdate property, which allows you to turn any query or stored procedure into an updateable view. This means the changes to the data set are written to a temporary buffer on the client instead of writing these changes to the server. These changes can then be sent to the server by calling the ApplyUpdates() method for the TQuery or TStoredProc component. Cached updates allow optimization of the updates and remove much of the lock contention on the server. You might refer to Chapter 13 of *Delphi 4 Database Application Developer's Guide*, which is dedicated to working with cached updates.

Executing Stored Procedures

Delphi's TStoredProc and TQuery components are both capable of executing stored procedures on the server. The following sections explain how to use both components to perform stored procedure execution.

Using the TStoredProc Component

The TStoredProc component enables you to execute stored procedures on the server. Depending on the server, it can return either a singleton or multiple result set. TStoredProc may also execute stored procedures that return no data at all. To execute server stored procedures, the following TStoredProc properties must be set accordingly:

DataBaseName	The name of the database that contains the stored procedure. This is usually the DataBaseName property for the TDatabase component referring to this server database.
StoredProcName	The name of the stored procedure to execute.
Params	This contains the input and output parameters defined by the stored procedure. The order is also based on the definition of the stored procedure on the server.

TStoredProc Input and Output Parameters

You provide input and output parameters through the TStoredProc.Params property. Like TQuery, the parameters must be *prepared* with default data types. This can be done either at design time through the Parameters Editor, or at runtime as will be illustrated.

To prepare parameters using the Parameters Editor, you right-click the `TStoredProc` component to invokes the Parameters Editor.

The Parameters Name list box shows a list of the input and output parameters for the stored procedure. Note that you must have already selected a `StoredProcName` from the server for any parameter to display. For each parameter, you specify a data type in the Data Type drop-down combo. You can also specify an initial value, or a NULL value as with the `TQuery` component. When you select the OK button, the parameters will be prepared.

You can also prepare the `TStoredProc`'s parameters at runtime by executing the `TStoredProc.Prepare()` method. This functions just like the `Prepare()` method for the `TQuery` component discussed earlier.

Executing Non-Result-Set Stored Procedures

To illustrate executing a stored procedure that does not return a result set, see Listing 28.11, which shows an Interbase stored procedure that adds a record to a COUNTRY table.

LISTING 28.11. INSERT COUNTRY STORED PROCEDURE IN INTERBASE.

```
CREATE PROCEDURE ADD_COUNTRY(
iCOUNTRY          VARCHAR(15),
iCURRENCY         VARCHAR(10)
)
AS
BEGIN
  INSERT INTO COUNTRY(COUNTRY, CURRENCY)
  VALUES (:iCOUNTRY, :iCURRENCY);
  SUSPEND;
END
  ^
```

To execute this stored procedure from Delphi, you would first set up the `TStoredProc` component with the appropriate values for the properties specified earlier. This includes specifying the parameter types from the Parameters Editor. The Delphi code to run this stored procedure is presented in Listing 28.12.

LISTING 28.12. EXECUTING A STORED PROCEDURE THROUGH `TStoredProc`.

```
with spAddCountry do
  begin
    ParamByName('iCOUNTRY').AsString := edtCountry.Text;
    ParamByName('iCURRENCY').AsString := edtCurrency.Text;
    ExecProc;
```

continues

LISTING 28.12. CONTINUED

```
    edtCountry.Text := '';
    edtCurrency.Text := '';
    tblCountries.Refresh;
  end;
```

Here, you first assign the values from two TEdits to the TStoredProc parameters through the ParamByName() method. Then you call the TStoredProc.ExecProc() function, which executes the stored procedure. You'll find a sample that illustrates this code in the project AddCntry.dpr.

> **NOTE**
>
> To run the AddCntry.dpr project, you must use the BDECFG32.EXE utility to set up a new alias named "DDGIB." This alias must point the file \CODE\DATA\ DDGIB.GDB, which exists on the CD-ROM accompanying this book. Refer to the documentation the BDECFG32 utility for further information.

Getting a Stored Procedure Result Set from TQuery

It is also possible to execute a stored procedure using a pass-through SQL statement with a TQuery component. This is necessary in some cases as with Interbase, which doesn't support stored procedures that must be called with a SELECT statement. For example, a stored procedure that returns result sets can be called just as though it were a table. Take a look at Listing 28.13, which is an Interbase stored procedure that returns a list of employees from an EMPLOYEE table belonging to a particular department. The department is specified by the input parameter iDEPT_NO.

LISTING 28.13. GET_EMPLOYEES_BY_DEPT STORED PROCEDURE.

```
CREATE PROCEDURE GET_EMPLOYEES_IN_DEPT (
iDEPT_NO            CHAR(3))
RETURNS(
EMP_NO             SMALLINT,
FIRST_NAME         VARCHAR(15),
LAST_NAME          VARCHAR(20),
DEPT_NO            CHAR(3),
HIRE_DATE          DATE)
AS
BEGIN
  FOR SELECT
    EMP_NO,
    FIRST_NAME,
    LAST_NAME,
```

```
     DEPT_NO,
     HIRE_DATE
   FROM EMPLOYEE
   WHERE DEPT_NO = :iDEPT_NO
   INTO
     :EMP_NO,
     :FIRST_NAME,
     :LAST_NAME,
     :DEPT_NO,
     :HIRE_DATE
   DO
     SUSPEND;
END ^
```

To execute this stored procedure from within Delphi 4, you need to use a `TQuery` component with the following `SQL` property:

```
SELECT * FROM GET_EMPLOYEES_IN_DEPT(
:iDEPT_NO)
```

Notice that this statement uses the `SELECT` statement as though the procedure were a table. The difference, as you can see, is that you must also provide the input parameter `iDEPT_NO`.

We've created a sample project, `Emp_Dept.dpr`, that illustrates executing the preceding stored procedure.

`qryGetEmployees` is the `TQuery` component that executes the stored procedure shown in Listing 28.13. It gets its parameter from `qryDepartment`, which performs a simple `SELECT` statement on the `DEPARTMENT` table in the database. `qryGetEmployees` is linked to `dbgEmployees`, which shows a scrollable list of departments. When the user scrolls through `dbgDepartment`, this invokes `dsDepartment`'s `OnDataChange` event handler. We should mention that `dsDepartment` is linked to `qryDepartment`. This event handler executes the code shown in Listing 28.14, which sets the parameter for `qryGetEmployees` and retrieves its output result set.

LISTING 28.14. DataSource1's OnChange EVENT HANDLER.

```
procedure TMainForm.dsDepartmentDataChange(Sender: TObject; Field:
TField);
begin
  with qryGetEmployees do
  begin
   Close;
   ParamByName('iDEPT_NO').AsString := qryDepartment['DEPT_NO'];
   Open;
  end;
end;
```

So why would you want to retrieve this information through a stored procedure rather than a simple statement on a table? Consider that there may be several people at different levels within a department who need access to the information provided. If these people had direct access to the table, they would be able to see sensitive information such as an employee's salary. By restricting access to a table, but providing the "need to know" information through stored procedures and views, you not only establish good security measures, but you also create a more maintainable set of business rules for the database.

SUMMARY

This chapter presented you with quite a bit of information about client/server development. We first discussed the elements that make up a client/server system. We compared client/server development to traditional desktop database development methodologies. We also introduced you to various techniques using Delphi 4 and Interbase that should have you well on your way to developing client/server projects.

EXTENDING DATABASE VCL

IN THIS CHAPTER

Out of the box, Visual Component Library (VCL)'s database architecture is equipped to communicate primarily by means of the Borland Database Engine (BDE)—feature-rich and reliable database middleware. What's more, VCL serves as a kind of insulator between you and your databases—allowing you to access different types of databases in much the same manner. Although all this adds up to reliability, scalability, and ease of use, there is a downside: database-specific features provided both within and outside the BDE are generally not provided for in the VCL database framework. This chapter provides you with the insight you'll need to extend VCL by communicating directly with the BDE and other data sources to obtain database functionality not otherwise available in Delphi.

USING THE BDE

When you're writing applications that make direct calls to the BDE, there are a few rules of thumb to keep in mind. This section presents the general information you need to get into the BDE API from your Delphi applications.

The BDE Unit

All BDE functions, types, and constants are defined in the BDE unit. This unit will need to be in the uses clause of any unit from which you want to make BDE calls. Additionally, the interface portion of the BDE unit is available in the BDE.INT file, which you'll find in the ..\Delphi 4\Doc directory. You can use this file as a reference to the functions and records available to you.

> **TIP**
>
> For additional assistance on programming the BDE API, take a look at the BDE32.hlp help file provided in your BDE directory (the default path for this directory is \Program Files\Borland\Common Files\BDE). This file contains detailed information on all BDE API functions and very good examples in both Object Pascal and C.

Check()

All BDE functions return a value of type DBIRESULT, which indicates the success or failure of the function call. Rather than going through the cumbersome process of checking the result of every BDE function call, Delphi defines a procedure called Check(), which accepts a DBIRESULT as a parameter. This procedure will raise an exception when the DBIRESULT indicates any value except success. The following code shows how to, and how not to, make a BDE function call:

```
// !!Don't do this:
var
  Rez: DBIRESULT;
  A: array[0..dbiMaxUserNameLen] of char;
begin
  Rez := dbiGetNetUserName(A);   // make BDE call
  if Rez <> DBIERR_NONE then     // handle error
    // handle error here
  else begin
    // continue with function
  end;
end;

// !!Do do this:
var
  A: array[0..dbiMaxUserNameLen] of char;
begin
  { Handle error and make BDE call at one time. }
  { Exception will be raised in case of error.   }
  Check(dbiGetNetUserName(A));
  // continue with functon
end;
```

Cursors and Handles

Many BDE functions accept as parameters handles to cursors or databases. Roughly speaking, a cursor handle is a BDE object that represents a particular set of data positioned at some particular row in that data. The data type of a cursor handle is hDBICur. Delphi surfaces this concept as the current record in a particular table, query, or stored procedure. The Handle property of TTable, TQuery, and TStoredProc holds this cursor handle. Remember to pass the Handle of one of these objects to any BDE function that requires an hDBICur.

Some BDE functions also require a handle to a database. A BDE database handle is of type hDBIDb, and it represents some particular open database—either a local or networked directory in the case of dBASE or Paradox, or a server database file in the case of a SQL server database. You can obtain this handle from a TDatabase through its Handle property. If you are not connecting to a database using a TDatabase object, the DBHandle property of a TTable, TQuery, and TStoredProc also contains this handle.

Synching Cursors

It's been established that an open Delphi data set has the concept of a current record, whereas the underlying BDE maintains the concept of a cursor that points to some particular record in a data set. Because of the way Delphi performs record caching to optimize performance, sometimes the Delphi current record is not in sync with the underlying BDE cursor. Normally, this is not a problem because this behavior is business as usual for VCL's database framework. However, if you want to make a direct call to a BDE function that expects a cursor as a parameter, you need to ensure that Delphi's current cursor position is synchronized with the underlying BDE cursor. It might sound like a daunting task, but it's actually quite easy to do. Simply call the `UpdateCursorPos()` method of a `TDataSet` descendant to perform this synchronization.

In a similar vein, after making a BDE call that modifies the position of the underlying cursor, you need to inform VCL that it needs to resynchronize its own current record position with that of the BDE. To do this, you must call the `CursorPosChanged()` method of `TDataSet` descendants immediately after calling into the BDE. The following code demonstrates how to use these cursor synchronization functions:

```
procedure DoSomethingWithTable(T: TTable);
begin
  T.UpdateCursorPos;
  // call BDE function(s) which modifies cursor position
  T.CursorPosChanged;
end;
```

DBASE TABLES

dBASE tables have a number of useful capabilities that are not directly supported by Delphi. These features include, among other things, the maintenance of a unique physical record number for each record, the capability to "soft-delete" records (delete records without removing them from the table), the capability to undelete soft-deleted records, and the capability to pack a table to remove soft-deleted records. In this section, you'll learn about the BDE functions involved in performing these actions, and you'll create a `TTable` descendant called `TdBaseTable` that incorporates these features.

Physical Record Number

dBASE tables maintain a unique physical record number for each record in a table. This number represents a record's physical position relative to the beginning of the table (regardless of any index currently applied to the table). To obtain a physical record number, you must call the BDE's `dbiGetRecord()` function, which is defined as follows:

```
function DbiGetRecord(hCursor: hDBICur; eLock: DBILockType;
    pRecBuff: Pointer; precProps: pRECProps): DBIResult stdcall;
```

`hCursor` is the cursor handle. Usually, this is the `Handle` property of the `TDataSet` descendant.

`eLock` is an optional request for the type of lock to place on the record. This parameter is of type `DBILockType`, which is an enumerated type defined as follows:

```
type
  DBILockType = (
    dbiNOLOCK,              // No lock (Default)
    dbiWRITELOCK,           // Write lock
    dbiREADLOCK);           // Read lock
```

In this case you don't want to place a lock on the record because you're not intending to modify the record content; so, `dbiNOLOCK` is the appropriate choice.

`pRecBuff` is a pointer to a record buffer. Because you want to obtain only the record properties and not the data, you should pass `Nil` for this parameter.

`pRecProps` is a pointer to a `RECProps` record. This record is defined as follows:

```
type
  pRECProps = ^RECProps;
  RECProps = packed record      // Record properties
    iSeqNum        : Longint;   // When Seq# supported only
    iPhyRecNum     : Longint;   // When Phy Rec#s supported only
    iRecStatus     : Word;      // Delayed Updates Record Status
    bSeqNumChanged : WordBool;  // Not used
    bDeleteFlag    : WordBool;  // When soft delete supported only
  end;
```

As you can see, you can obtain a variety of information from this record. In this case, you're concerned only with the `iPhyRecNum` field, which is valid only in the case of dBASE and FoxPro tables.

Putting this all together, the following code shows a method of `TdBaseTable` that returns the physical record of the current record:

```
function TdBaseTable.GetRecNum: Longint;
{ Returns the physical record number of the current record. }
var
  RP: RECProps;
begin
  UpdateCursorPos;             // update BDE from Delphi
  { Get current record properties }
  Check(dbiGetRecord(Handle, dbiNOLOCK, Nil, @RP));
  Result := RP.iPhyRecNum;     // return value from properties
end;
```

Viewing Deleted Records

Viewing records that have been soft-deleted in a dBASE table is as easy as one BDE API call. The function to call is `dbiSetProp()`, which is a very powerful function that enables you to modify the different properties of multiple types of BDE objects. For a complete description of this function and how it works, your best bet is to check out the "properties—getting and setting" topic in the BDE help. This function is defined as follows:

```
function DbiSetProp(hObj: hDBIObj; iProp: Longint;
  iPropValue: Longint): DBIResult stdcall;
```

The hObj parameter holds a handle to some type of BDE object. In this case, it will be a cursor handle.

The iProp parameter will contain the identifier of the property to be set. You'll find a complete list of these in the aforementioned topic in the BDE help. For purposes of enabling or disabling the view of deleted records, use the curSOFTDELETEON identifier.

iPropValue is the new value for the given property. In this case, it's a Boolean value—0 meaning off and 1 meaning on.

The following code shows the SetViewDeleted() method of TdBaseTable:

```
procedure TdBaseTable.SetViewDeleted(Value: Boolean);
{ Allows the user to toggle between viewing and not viewing }
{ deleted records. }
begin
  { Table must be active }
  if Active and (FViewDeleted <> Value) then begin
    DisableControls;     // avoid flicker
    try
      { Magic BDE call to toggle view of soft deleted records }
      Check(dbiSetProp(hDBIObj(Handle), curSOFTDELETEON, Longint(Value)));
    finally
      Refresh;           // update Delphi
      EnableControls;    // flicker avoidance complete
    end;
    FViewDeleted := Value
  end;
end;
```

This method first performs a test to ensure that the table is open and that the value to be set is different than the value the FViewDeleted field in the object already contains. It then calls DisableControls() to avoid flicker of any data-aware controls attached to the table. The dbiSetProp() function is called next—notice the necessary typecast of the hDBICur Handle parameter to an hDBIObj. Think of hDBIObj as an untyped handle to some type of BDE object. After that, the data set is refreshed and any attached controls re-enabled.

TIP

Whenever you use DisableControls() to suspend a data set's connection to data-aware controls, you should always use a try..finally block to ensure that the subsequent call to EnableControls() takes place whether or not an error occurs.

Testing for a Deleted Record

When viewing a data set that includes deleted records, you probably will need to determine as you navigate through the data set which records are deleted and which aren't. Actually, you've already learned how to perform this check. You can obtain this information using the `dbiGetRecord()` function that you used to obtain the physical record number. The following code shows this procedure. The only material difference between this procedure and `GetRecNum()` is the checking of the `bDeletedFlag` field rather than the `iPhyRecNo` field of the `RECProps` record.

```
function TdBaseTable.GetIsDeleted: Boolean;
{ Returns a boolean indicating whether or not the current record }
{ has been soft deleted. }
var
  RP: RECProps;
begin
  if not FViewDeleted then      // don't bother if they aren't viewing
    Result := False             // deleted records
  else begin
    UpdateCursorPos;            // update BDE from Delphi
    { Get current record properties }
    Check(dbiGetRecord(Handle, dbiNOLOCK, Nil, @RP));
    Result := RP.bDeleteFlag;  // return flag from properties
  end;
end;
```

Undeleting a Record

So far, you've learned how to view deleted records and determine whether a record has been deleted, and, of course, you already know how to delete a record. The only other thing you need to learn regarding record deletion is how to undelete a record. Fortunately, the BDE makes this an easy task thanks to the `dbiUndeleteRecord()` function, which is defined as follows:

```
function DbiUndeleteRecord(hCursor: hDBICur): DBIResult stdcall;
```

The lone parameter is a cursor handle for the current data set. Using this function, you can create an `UndeleteRecord()` method for `TdBaseTable`:

```
procedure TdBaseTable.UndeleteRecord;
begin
  if not IsDeleted then
    raise EDatabaseError.Create('Record is not deleted');
  Check(dbiUndeleteRecord(Handle));
  Refresh;
end;
```

Packing a Table

To remove soft-deleted records from a dBASE table, that table must go through a process called *packing*. For this, the BDE provides a function called `dbiPackTable()`, which is defined as follows:

```
function DbiPackTable(hDb: hDBIDb; hCursor: hDBICur;
    pszTableName: PChar; pszDriverType: PChar;
    bRegenIdxs: Bool): DBIResult stdcall;
```

`hDb` is a handle to a database. You should pass the `DBHandle` property of a `TDataSet` descendant or the `Handle` property of a `TDatabase` component in this parameter.

`hCursor` is a cursor handle. You should pass the `Handle` property of a `TDataSet` descendant in this parameter. You may also pass `Nil` if you want to instead use the `pszTableName` and `pszDriverType` parameters to identify the table.

`pszTableName` is a pointer to a string containing the name of the table.

`pszDriverType` is a pointer to a string representing the driver type of the table. If `hCursor` is `Nil`, this parameter must be set to `szDBASE`. As a side note, it's unusual that this parameter is required because this function is supported only for dBASE tables—but we don't make the rules, we just play by them.

`bRegenIdxs` indicates whether you want to rebuild all out-of-date indexes associated with the table.

Here is the `Pack()` method for the `TdBaseTable` class:

```
procedure TdBaseTable.Pack(RegenIndexes: Boolean);
{ Packs the table in order to removed soft deleted records }
{ from the file. }
const
  SPackError = 'Table must be active and opened exclusively';
begin
  { Table must be active and opened exclusively }
  if not (Active and Exclusive) then
    raise EDatabaseError.Create(SPackError);
  try
    { Pack the table }
    Check(dbiPackTable(DBHandle, Handle, Nil, Nil, RegenIndexes));
  finally
    { update Delphi from BDE }
    CursorPosChanged;
    Refresh;
  end;
end;
```

The complete listing of the `TdBaseTable` object is provided in Listing 29.1 later in this chapter.

PARADOX TABLES

Paradox tables don't have as many nifty features, such as soft deletion, but they do carry the concept of a record number and table pack. In this section, you'll learn how to extend a `TTable` to perform these Paradox-specific tasks and to create a new `TParadoxTable` class.

Sequence Number

Paradox tables do not have the concept of a physical record number in the dBASE sense. They do, however, maintain the concept of a sequence number for each record in a table. The sequence number differs from the physical record number in that the sequence number is dependent on whatever index is currently applied to the table. The sequence number of a record is the order in which the record appears based on the current index.

The BDE makes it easy to obtain a sequence number using the `dbiGetSeqNo()` function, which is defined as follows:

```
function DbiGetSeqNo(hCursor: hDBICur; var iSeqNo: Longint): DBIResult
➥stdcall;
```

`hCursor` is a cursor handle for a Paradox table, and the `iSeqNo` parameter will be filled in with the sequence number of the current record. The following code shows the `GetRecNum()` function for `TParadoxTable`:

```
cfunction TParadoxTable.GetRecNum: Longint;
{ Returns the sequence number of the current record. }
begin
  UpdateCursorPos;            // update BDE from Delphi
  { Get sequence number of current record into Result }
  Check(dbiGetSeqNo(Handle, Result));
end;
```

Table Packing

Table packing in Paradox has a different meaning than in dBASE because Paradox does not support soft deletion of records. When a record is deleted in Paradox, the record is removed from the table, but a "hole" is left in the database file where the record used to be. To compress these holes left by deleted records and make the table smaller and more efficient, you must pack the table.

Unlike with dBASE tables, there is no obvious BDE function you can use to pack a Paradox table. Instead, you must use `dbiDoRestructure()` to restructure the table and specify that the table should be packed as it's restructured. `dbiDoRestructure()` is defined as follows:

```
function DbiDoRestructure(hDb: hDBIDb; iTblDescCount: Word;
    pTblDesc: pCRTblDesc; pszSaveAs, pszKeyviolName,
    pszProblemsName: PChar; bAnalyzeOnly: Bool): DBIResult stdcall;
```

hDb is the handle to a database. However, because this function will not work when Delphi has the table open, you will not be able to use the DBHandle property of a TDataSet. To overcome this, the sample code (shown a bit later) that uses this function demonstrates how to create a temporary database.

iTblDescCount is the number of table descriptors. This parameter must be set to 1 because the current version of the BDE supports only one table descriptor per call.

pTblDesc is a pointer to a CRTblDesc record. This is the record that identifies the table and specifies how the table is to be restructured. This record is defined as follows:

```
type
  pCRTblDesc = ^CRTblDesc;
  CRTblDesc = packed record       // Create/Restruct Table descr
    szTblName    : DBITBLNAME;     // TableName incl. optional path & ext
    szTblType    : DBINAME;        // Driver type (optional)
    szErrTblName : DBIPATH;        // Error Table name (optional)
    szUserName   : DBINAME;        // User name (if applicable)
    szPassword   : DBINAME;        // Password (optional)
    bProtected   : WordBool;       // Master password supplied in szPassword
    bPack        : WordBool;       // Pack table (restructure only)
    iFldCount    : Word;           // Number of field defs supplied
    pecrFldOp    : pCROpType;      // Array of field ops
    pfldDesc     : pFLDDesc;       // Array of field descriptors
    iIdxCount    : Word;           // Number of index defs supplied
    pecrIdxOp    : pCROpType;      // Array of index ops
    pidxDesc     : PIDXDesc;       // Array of index descriptors
    iSecRecCount : Word;           // Number of security defs supplied
    pecrSecOp    : pCROpType;      // Array of security ops
    psecDesc     : pSECDesc;       // Array of security descriptors
    iValChkCount : Word;           // Number of val checks
    pecrValChkOp : pCROpType;      // Array of val check ops
    pvchkDesc    : pVCHKDesc;      // Array of val check descs
    iRintCount   : Word;           // Number of ref int specs
    pecrRintOp   : pCROpType;      // Array of ref int ops
    printDesc    : pRINTDesc;      // Array of ref int specs
    iOptParams   : Word;           // Number of optional parameters
    pfldOptParams: pFLDDesc;       // Array of field descriptors
    pOptData     : Pointer;        // Optional parameters
  end;
```

For Paradox table packing, it's only necessary to specify values for the szTblName, szTblType, and bPack fields.

pszSaveAs is an optional string pointer that identifies the destination table if it is different than the source table.

pszKeyviolName is an optional string pointer that identifies the table to send records that cause key violations during the restructure.

pszProblemsName is an optional string pointer that identifies the table to send records that cause problems during the restructure.

bAnalyzeOnly is unused.

The following code shows the Pack() method of TParadoxTable. You can see from the code how the CRTblDesc record is initialized and how the temporary database is created using the dbiOpenDatabase() function. Also note the finally block, which ensures that the temporary database is cleaned up after use.

```
procedure TParadoxTable.Pack;
var
  TblDesc: CRTblDesc;
  TempDBHandle: HDBIDb;
  WasActive: Boolean;
begin
  { Initialize TblDesc record }
  FillChar(TblDesc, SizeOf(TblDesc), 0); // fill with 0s
  with TblDesc do begin
    StrPCopy(szTblName, TableName);      // set table name
    StrCopy(szTblType, szPARADOX);       // set table type
    bPack := True;                       // set pack flag
  end;
  { Store table active state.  Must close table to pack. }
  WasActive := Active;
  if WasActive then Close;
  try
    { Create a temporary database.  Must be read-write/exclusive }
    Check(dbiOpenDatabase(PChar(DatabaseName), Nil, dbiREADWRITE,
        dbiOpenExcl, Nil, 0, Nil, Nil, TempDBHandle));
    try
      { Pack the table }
      Check(dbiDoRestructure(TempDBHandle, 1, @TblDesc, Nil, Nil, Nil,
          False));
    finally
      { Close the temporary database }
      dbiCloseDatabase(TempDBHandle);
    end;
  finally
    { Reset table active state }
    Active := WasActive;
  end;
end;
```

Listing 29.1 shows the DDGTbls unit in which the TdBaseTable and TParadoxTable objects are defined.

LISTING 29.1. THE DDGTbls.pas UNIT.

```pascal
unit DDGTbls;

interface

uses DB, DBTables, BDE;

type
  TdBaseTable = class(TTable)
  private
    FViewDeleted: Boolean;
    function GetIsDeleted: Boolean;
    function GetRecNum: Longint;
    procedure SetViewDeleted(Value: Boolean);
  protected
    function CreateHandle: HDBICur; override;
  public
    procedure Pack(RegenIndexes: Boolean);
    procedure UndeleteRecord;
    property IsDeleted: Boolean read GetIsDeleted;
    property RecNum: Longint read GetRecNum;
    property ViewDeleted: Boolean read FViewDeleted write SetViewDeleted;
  end;

  TParadoxTable = class(TTable)
  private
  protected
    function CreateHandle: HDBICur; override;
    function GetRecNum: Longint;
  public
    procedure Pack;
    property RecNum: Longint read GetRecNum;
  end;

implementation

uses SysUtils;

{ TdBaseTable }

function TdBaseTable.GetIsDeleted: Boolean;
{ Returns a boolean indicating whether the current record }
{ has been soft deleted. }
var
  RP: RECProps;
begin
  if not FViewDeleted then      // don't bother if they aren't viewing
    Result := False             // deleted records
  else begin
    UpdateCursorPos;            // update BDE from Delphi
```

```
      { Get current record properties }
      Check(dbiGetRecord(Handle, dbiNOLOCK, Nil, @RP));
      Result := RP.bDeleteFlag;  // return flag from properties
  end;
end;

function TdBaseTable.GetRecNum: Longint;
{ Returns the physical record number of the current record. }
var
  RP: RECProps;
begin
  UpdateCursorPos;            // update BDE from Delphi
  { Get current record properties }
  Check(dbiGetRecord(Handle, dbiNOLOCK, Nil, @RP));
  Result := RP.iPhyRecNum;    // return value from properties
end;

function TdBaseTable.CreateHandle: HDBICur;
{ Overridden from ancestor in order to perform a check to }
{ ensure that this is a dBASE table. }
var
  CP: CURProps;
begin
  Result := inherited CreateHandle;      // do inherited
  if Result <> Nil then begin
    { Get cursor properties and raise exception if the }
    { table isn't using the dBASE driver. }
    Check(dbiGetCursorProps(Result, CP));
    if not (CP.szTableType = szdBASE) then
      raise EDatabaseError.Create('Not a dBASE table');
  end;
end;

procedure TdBaseTable.Pack(RegenIndexes: Boolean);
{ Packs the table in order to removed soft deleted records }
{ from the file. }
const
  SPackError = 'Table must be active and opened exclusively';
begin
  { Table must be active and opened exclusively }
  if not (Active and Exclusive) then
    raise EDatabaseError.Create(SPackError);
  try
    { Pack the table }
    Check(dbiPackTable(DBHandle, Handle, Nil, Nil, RegenIndexes));
  finally
    { update Delphi from BDE }
    CursorPosChanged;
    Refresh;
  end;
end;
```

29

EXTENDING
DATABASE VCL

continues

LISTING 29.1. CONTINUED

```
procedure TdBaseTable.SetViewDeleted(Value: Boolean);
{ Allows the user to toggle between viewing and not viewing }
{ deleted records. }
begin
  { Table must be active }
  if Active and (FViewDeleted <> Value) then begin
    DisableControls;      // avoid flicker
    try
      { Magic BDE call to toggle view of soft deleted records }
      Check(dbiSetProp(hdbiObj(Handle), curSOFTDELETEON, Longint(Value)));
    finally
      Refresh;            // update Delphi
      EnableControls;     // flicker avoidance complete
    end;
    FViewDeleted := Value
  end;
end;

procedure TdBaseTable.UndeleteRecord;
begin
  if not IsDeleted then
    raise EDatabaseError.Create('Record is not deleted');
  Check(dbiUndeleteRecord(Handle));
  Refresh;
end;

function TParadoxTable.CreateHandle: HDBICur;
{ Overridden from ancestor in order to perform a check to }
{ ensure that this is a Paradox table. }
var
  CP: CURProps;
begin
  Result := inherited CreateHandle;      // do inherited
  if Result <> Nil then begin
    { Get cursor properties and raise exception if the }
    { table isn't using the Paradox driver. }
    Check(dbiGetCursorProps(Result, CP));
    if not (CP.szTableType = szPARADOX) then
      raise EDatabaseError.Create('Not a Paradox table');
  end;
end;

function TParadoxTable.GetRecNum: Longint;
{ Returns the sequence number of the current record. }
begin
  UpdateCursorPos;              // update BDE from Delphi
  { Get sequence number of current record into Result }
  Check(dbiGetSeqNo(Handle, Result));
end;
```

```
procedure TParadoxTable.Pack;
var
  TblDesc: CRTblDesc;
  TempDBHandle: HDBIDb;
  WasActive: Boolean;
begin
  { Initialize TblDesc record }
  FillChar(TblDesc, SizeOf(TblDesc), 0); // fill with 0s
  with TblDesc do begin
    StrPCopy(szTblName, TableName);      // set table name
    szTblType := szPARADOX;              // set table type
    bPack := True;                       // set pack flag
  end;
  { Store table active state.  Must close table to pack. }
  WasActive := Active;
  if WasActive then Close;
  try
    { Create a temporary database.  Must be read-write/exclusive }
    Check(dbiOpenDatabase(PChar(DatabaseName), Nil, dbiREADWRITE,
        dbiOpenExcl, Nil, 0, Nil, Nil, TempDBHandle));
    try
      { Pack the table }
      Check(dbiDoRestructure(TempDBHandle, 1, @TblDesc, Nil, Nil, Nil,
          False));
    finally
      { Close the temporary database }
      dbiCloseDatabase(TempDBHandle);
    end;
  finally
    { Reset table active state }
    Active := WasActive;
  end;
end;
end.
```

Limiting TQuery Result Sets

Here's a classic SQL programming *faux pas*: your application issues a SQL statement to the server that returns a result set consisting of a gazillion rows, thereby making the application user wait forever for the query to return and tying up precious server and network bandwidth. Conventional SQL wisdom dictates that one shouldn't issue queries that are so general that they cause so many records to be fetched. However, this is sometimes unavoidable, and TQuery doesn't seem to help matters much, as it doesn't provide a means for restricting the number of records in a result set to be fetched from the server. Fortunately, the BDE does provide this capability, and it's not very difficult to surface in a TQuery descendant.

The BDE API call that performs this magic is the catch-all DbiSetProp() function, which was explained earlier in this chapter. In this case, the first parameter to DbiSetProp() is the cursor handle for the query, the second parameter must be curMAXROWS, and the final parameter should be set to the maximum number of rows to which you want to restrict the result set.

The ideal place to make the call to this function is in the PrepareCursor() method of TQuery, which is called immediately after the query is opened. Listing 29.2 shows the ResQuery unit, in which the TRestrictedQuery component is defined.

LISTING 29.2. THE ResQuery.pas UNIT.

```
unit ResQuery;

interface

uses
  Windows, Messages, SysUtils, Classes, Graphics, Controls, Forms,
  Dialogs, DB, DBTables, BDE;

type
  TRestrictedQuery = class(TQuery)
  private
    FMaxRowCount: Longint;
  protected
    procedure PrepareCursor; override;
  published
    property MaxRowCount: Longint read FMaxRowCount write FMaxRowCount;
  end;

procedure Register;

implementation

procedure TRestrictedQuery.PrepareCursor;
begin
  inherited PrepareCursor;
  if FMaxRowCount > 0 then
    Check(DbiSetProp(hDBIObj(Handle), curMAXROWS, FMaxRowCount));
end;

procedure Register;
begin
  RegisterComponents('DDG', [TRestrictedQuery]);
end;

end.
```

You can limit the result set of a query by simply setting the MaxRowCount property to a value greater than zero. To further illustrate the point, Figure 29.1 shows the result of a query restricted to three rows as shown in SQL Monitor.

FIGURE 29.1.

A restricted query viewed from SQL Monitor.

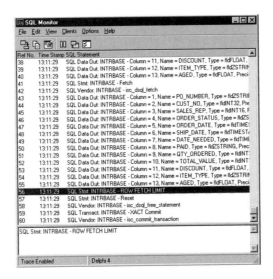

BDE Miscellany

Through our development of database applications, we've found a few common development tasks that could serve to be automated a bit. Some of these miscellaneous tasks include performing SQL aggregate functions on a table, copying tables, and obtaining a list of Paradox users for a particular session.

SQL Aggregate Functions

Generally speaking, SQL aggregate functions are functions that are built into the SQL language which perform some arithmetic operation on one or more columns from one or more rows. Some common examples of this are sum(), which adds columns from multiple rows; avg(), which calculates the average value of columns from multiple rows; min(), which finds the minimum value of columns in multiple rows; and max(), which (as you might guess) determines the maximum value of columns within multiple rows.

Aggregate functions such as these can sometimes be inconvenient to use in Delphi. For example, if you're working with TTables to access data, using these functions involves creating a TQuery, formulating the correct SQL statement for the table and column in question, executing the query, and obtaining the result from the query. Clearly this is a process crying out to be automated. The code in Listing 29.3 is just that.

LISTING 29.3. AUTOMATING SQL AGGREGATE FUNCTIONS.

```
type
  TSQLAggFunc = (safSum, safAvg, safMin, safMax);

const
  // SQL aggregate functions
  SQLAggStrs: array[TSQLAggFunc] of string = (
    'select sum(%s) from %s',
    'select avg(%s) from %s',
    'select min(%s) from %s',
    'select max(%s) from %s');

function CreateQueryFromTable(T: TTable): TQuery;
// returns a query hooked to the same database and session as the give
// table
begin
  Result := TQuery.Create(nil);
  try
    Result.DatabaseName := T.DatabaseName;
    Result.SessionName := T.SessionName;
  except
    Result.Free;
    Raise;
  end;
end;

function DoSQLAggFunc(T: TTable; FieldNames: string;
  Func: TSQLAggFunc): Extended;
begin
  with CreateQueryFromTable(T) do
  begin
    try
      SQL.Add(Format(SQLAggStrs[Func], [FieldNames, T.TableName]));
      Open;
      Result := Fields[0].AsFloat;
    finally
      Free;
    end;
  end;
end;

function SumField(T: TTable; Field: String): Extended;
begin
  Result := DoSQLAggFunc(T, Field, safSum);
end;

function AvgField(T: TTable; Field: String): Extended;
begin
  Result := DoSQLAggFunc(T, Field, safAvg);
end;
```

```
function MinField(T: TTable; Field: String): Extended;
begin
  Result := DoSQLAggFunc(T, Field, safMin);
end;

function MaxField(T: TTable; Field: string): Extended;
begin
  Result := DoSQLAggFunc(T, Field, safMax);
end;
```

As you can see from the listing, each of the individual aggregate function wrappers call into the `DoSQLAggFun()` function. In this function, the `CreateQueryFromTable()` function creates and returns a `TQuery` component that uses the same database and session as the `TTable` passed in the `T` parameter. The proper SQL string is then formatted from an array of strings, the query is executed, and the query's result is returned from the function.

Quick Table Copy

If you want to make a copy of a table, traditional wisdom might dictate a few different courses of action. The first might be to use the Win32 API's `CopyFile()` function to physically copy the table file(s) from one location to another. Another option is to use a `TBatchMove` component to copy one `TTable` to another. Yet another option is to use `TTable`'s `BatchMove()` method to perform the copy.

However, there are problems with each of these traditional alternatives: A brute-force file copy using the `CopyFile()` API function may not work if the table files are open by another process or user, and it certainly will not work if the table exists within some type of database file on a SQL server. A file copy might become a very complex task if you consider that you may also have to copy associated index, BLOB, or value files. The use of `TBatchMove` would solve these problems, but only if you submit to the disadvantage of the complexity involved in using this component. An additional drawback is the fact that the batch move process is much slower than a direct file copy. Using `TTable.BatchMove()` does help to alleviate the issue of complexity in performing the table copy, but it does not overcome the performance shortcomings inherent in the batch move process.

Fortunately, the BDE developers also recognized this issue, and there is a BDE API function that provides the best of both worlds: speed and ease of use. The function in question is `DbiCopyTable()`, and it is declared as shown following:

```
function DbiCopyTable (          { Copy one table to another }
      hDb        : hDBIDb;       { Database handle }
      bOverWrite : Bool;         { True, to overwrite existing file }
```

```
   pszSrcTableName : PChar;         { Source table name }
   pszSrcDriverType : PChar;        { Source driver type }
   pszDestTableName : PChar         { Destination table name }
 ): DBIResult stdcall;
```

Because the BDE API function can't deal directly with VCL TTable components, the following procedure wraps DbiCopyTable() into a nifty routine to which you can pass a TTable and a destination table name.

```
procedure QuickCopyTable(T: TTable; DestTblName: string; Overwrite:
Boolean);
// Copies TTable T to an identical table with name DestTblName.
// Will overwrite existing table with name DestTblName if Overwrite is
// True.
var
  DBType: DBINAME;
  WasOpen: Boolean;
  NumCopied: Word;
begin
  WasOpen := T.Active;          // save table active state
  if not WasOpen then T.Open;   // ensure table is open
  // Get driver type string
  Check(DbiGetProp(hDBIObj(T.Handle), drvDRIVERTYPE, @DBType,
    SizeOf(DBINAME), NumCopied));
  // Copy the table
  Check(DbiCopyTable(T.DBHandle, Overwrite, PChar(T.TableName), DBType,
    PChar(DestTblName)));
  T.Active := WasOpen;          // restore active state
end;
```

NOTE

For local databases (Paradox, dBASE, Access, and FoxPro), all files associated with the table—index and BLOB files, for example—are copied to the destination table. For tables residing in a SQL database, only the table will be copied, and it is up to you to ensure that the necessary indexes and other elements are applied to the destination table.

Paradox Session Users

If your application uses Paradox tables, you may come across a situation where you need to determine which users are currently using a particular Paradox table. You can accomplish this with the DbiOpenUserList() BDE API function. This function provides a BDE cursor for a list of users for the current session. The following procedure demonstrates how to use this function effectively:

```
procedure GetPDoxUsersForSession(Sess: TSession; UserList: TStrings);
// Clears UserList and adds each user using the same netfile as session
// Sess to the list.  If Sess = nil, then procedure works for default
// net file.
var
  WasActive: Boolean;
  SessHand: hDBISes;
  ListCur: hDBICur;
  User: UserDesc;
begin
  if UserList = nil then Exit;
  UserList.Clear;
  if Assigned(Sess) then
  begin
    WasActive := Sess.Active;
    if not WasActive then Sess.Open;
    Check(DbiStartSession(nil, SessHand, PChar(Sess.NetFileDir)));
  end
  else
    Check(DbiStartSession(nil, SessHand, nil));
  try
    Check(DbiOpenUserList(ListCur));
    try
      while DbiGetNextRecord(ListCur, dbiNOLOCK, @User, nil) = DBIERR_NONE
        do UserList.Add(User.szUserName);
    finally
      DbiCloseCursor(ListCur);  // close "user list table" cursor
    end;
  finally
    DbiCloseSession(SessHand);
    if Assigned(Sess) then Sess.Active := WasActive;
  end;
end;
```

The interesting thing about the `DbiOpenUserList()` function is that it creates a cursor for a table that is manipulated in the same manner as any other BDE table cursor. In this case, `DbiGetNextRecord()` is called repeatedly until the end of the table is reached. The record buffer for this table follows the format of the `UserDesc` record, which is defined in the BDE unit as follows:

```
type
  pUSERDesc = ^USERDesc;
  USERDesc = packed record         { User description }
    szUserName   : DBIUSERNAME;    { User Name }
    iNetSession  : Word;           { Net level session number }
    iProductClass: Word;           { Product class of user }
    szSerialNum  : packed array [0..21] of Char; { Serial number }
  end;
```

Each call to `DbiGetNextRecord()` fills a `UserDesc` record called `User`, and the `szUserName` field of that record is added to the `UserList` `TStrings`.

> **Tip**
>
> Note the use of the `try..finally` resource protection blocks in the `GetPDoxUsersForSession()` procedure. These ensure that both the BDE resources associated with the session and cursor are properly released.

Writing Data-Aware VCL Controls

Chapter 21, "Writing Delphi Custom Components," and Chapter 22, "Advanced Component Techniques," provided you with thorough coverage of component-building techniques and methodologies. One large topic that wasn't covered, however, is data-aware controls. Actually, there isn't much more to creating a data-aware control than there is to creating a regular VCL control, but a typical data-aware component is different in four key respects:

- Data-aware controls maintain an internal data link object. A descendant of `TDataLink`, this object provides the means by which the control communicates with a `TDataSource`. For data-aware controls that connect to a single field of a data set, this is usually a `TFieldDataLink`. The control should handle the `OnDataChange` event of the data link in order to receive notifications when the field or record data has changed.

- Data-aware controls must handle the `CM_GETDATALINK` message. The typical response to this message is to return the data link object in the message's `Result` field.

- Data-aware controls should surface a property of type `TDataSource` so the control can be connected to a data source by which it will communicate with a data set. By convention, this property is called `DataSource`. Controls that connect to a single field should also surface a string property to hold the name of the field to which it is connected. By convention, this property is called `DataField`.

- Data-aware controls should override the `Notification()` method of `TComponent`. By overriding this method, the data-aware control can be notified if the data source component connected to the control has been deleted from the form.

A Data-Aware WAV Player

To demonstrate the creation of a simple data-aware control, Listing 29.4 shows the `DBSound` unit. This unit contains the `TDBWavPlayer` component, a component that plays WAV sounds from a BLOB field in a data set.

LISTING 29.4. THE DBSound.pas UNIT.

```pascal
unit DBSound;

interface

uses Windows, Messages, Classes, SysUtils, Controls, Buttons, DB,
➡DBTables;

type
  EDBWavError = class(Exception);

  TDBWavPlayer = class(TSpeedButton)
  private
    FAutoPlay: Boolean;
    FDataLink: TFieldDataLink;
    FDataStream: TMemoryStream;
    FExceptOnError: Boolean;
    procedure DataChange(Sender: TObject);
    function GetDataField: string;
    function GetDataSource: TDataSource;
    function GetField: TField;
    procedure SetDataField(const Value: string);
    procedure SetDataSource(Value: TDataSource);
    procedure CMGetDataLink(var Message: TMessage); message
    ➡CM_GETDATALINK;
    procedure CreateDataStream;
    procedure PlaySound;
    procedure Notification(AComponent: TComponent; Operation: TOperation);
      override;
  protected
    procedure Click; override;
  public
    constructor Create(AOwner: TComponent); override;
    destructor Destroy; override;
    property Field: TField read GetField;
  published
    property AutoPlay: Boolean read FAutoPlay write FAutoPlay default
    ➡False;
    property ExceptOnError: Boolean read FExceptOnError write
    ➡FExceptOnError;
    property DataField: string read GetDataField write SetDataField;
    property DataSource: TDataSource read GetDataSource write
    ➡SetDataSource;
  end;

procedure Register;

implementation
```

continues

LISTING 29.4. CONTINUED

```
uses MMSystem;

const
  // Error strings
  SNotBlobField = 'Field "%s" is not a blob field';
  SPlaySoundErr = 'Error attempting to play sound';

constructor TDBWavPlayer.Create(AOwner: TComponent);
begin
  inherited Create(AOwner);               // call inherited
  FDataLink := TFieldDataLink.Create;     // create field data link
  FDataLink.OnDataChange := DataChange;   // get data link notifications
  FDataStream := TMemoryStream.Create;    // create worker memory stream
end;

destructor TDBWavPlayer.Destroy;
begin
  FDataStream.Free;
  FDataLink.Free;
  FDataLink := Nil;
  inherited Destroy;
end;

procedure TDBWavPlayer.Click;
begin
  inherited Click; // do default behavior
  PlaySound;       // play the sound
end;

procedure TDBWavPlayer.CreateDataStream;
// creates memory stream from wave file in blob field
var
  BS: TBlobStream;
begin
  // make sure it's a blob field
  if not (Field is TBlobField) then
    raise EDBWavError.CreateFmt(SNotBlobField, [DataField]);
  // create a blob stream
  BS := TBlobStream.Create(TBlobField(Field), bmRead);
  try
    // copy from blob stream to memory stream
    FDataStream.SetSize(BS.Size);
    FDataStream.CopyFrom(BS, BS.Size);
  finally
    BS.Free;  // free blob stream
  end;
end;
```

```
procedure TDBWavPlayer.PlaySound;
// plays wave sound loaded in memory stream
begin
  // make sure we are hooked to a dataset and field
  if (DataSource <> nil) and (DataField <> '') then
  begin
    // make sure data stream is created
    if FDataStream.Size = 0 then CreateDataStream;
    // Play the sound in the memory stream, raise exception on error
    if (not MMSystem.PlaySound(FDataStream.Memory, 0, SND_ASYNC or
    ➥SND_MEMORY))
      and FExceptOnError then
      raise EDBWavError.Create(SPlaySoundErr);
  end;
end;

procedure TDBWavPlayer.DataChange(Sender: TObject);
// OnChange handler FFieldDataLink.DataChange
begin
  // deallocate memory occupied by previous wave file
  with FDataStream do if Size <> 0 then SetSize(0);
  // if AutoPlay is on, then play the sound
  if FAutoPlay then PlaySound;
end;

procedure TDBWavPlayer.Notification(AComponent: TComponent;
  Operation: TOperation);
begin
  inherited Notification(AComponent, Operation);
  // do some required housekeeping
  if (Operation = opRemove) and (FDataLink <> nil) and
    (AComponent = FDataSource) then DataSource := nil;
end;

function TDBWavPlayer.GetDataSource: TDataSource;
begin
  Result := FDataLink.DataSource;
end;

procedure TDBWavPlayer.SetDataSource(Value: TDataSource);
begin
  FDataLink.DataSource := Value;
  if Value <> nil then Value.FreeNotification(Self);
end;

function TDBWavPlayer.GetDataField: string;
begin
  Result := FDataLink.FieldName;
end;
```

29

EXTENDING
DATABASE VCL

continues

LISTING 29.4. CONTINUED

```
procedure TDBWavPlayer.SetDataField(const Value: string);
begin
  FDataLink.FieldName := Value;
end;

function TDBWavPlayer.GetField: TField;
begin
  Result := FDataLink.Field;
end;

procedure TDBWavPlayer.CMGetDataLink(var Message: TMessage);
begin
  Message.Result := Integer(FDataLink);
end;

procedure Register;
begin
  RegisterComponents('DDG', [TDBWavPlayer]);
end;

end.
```

This component is a TSpeedButton descendant which, when pressed, can play a WAV sound residing in a database BLOB field. The AutoPlay property can also be set to True, which will cause the sound to play every time the user navigates to a new record in the table. When this property is set, it might also make sense to set the Visible property of the component to False so a button doesn't appear visually on the form.

In the FDataLink.OnChange handler, DataChange(), the component works by extracting the BLOB field using a TBlobStream and copying the BLOB stream to a memory stream, FDataStream. When the sound is in a memory stream, you can play it using the PlaySound() Win32 API function.

EXTENDING TDataSet

One of the marquee features of the database VCL is the abstract TDataSet, which provides the capability to manipulate non-BDE data sources within the database VCL framework.

In the Olden Days...

In previous versions of Delphi, the VCL database architecture was closed, such that it was very difficult to manipulate non-BDE data sources using VCL components. Figure 29.2 illustrates the BDE-centric data-set architecture found in Delphi 1 and 2.

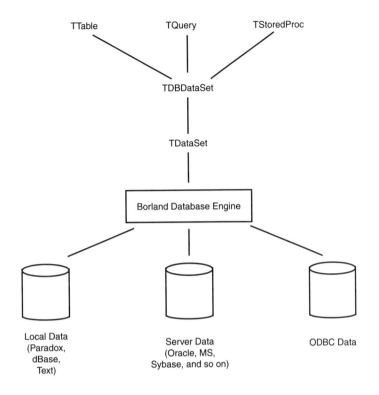

FIGURE 29.2.

*Delphi 1 and 2
VCL data-set
architecture.*

As Figure 29.2 shows, TDataSet is essentially hard-coded for the BDE, and there is no room in this architecture for non-BDE data sources. Developers wanting to use non-BDE data sources within VCL had two choices: 1) create a DLL that looks to VCL like the BDE but talks to a different type of data, or 2) throw TDataSet out the window, and write your own data set class and data-aware controls. Clearly, either of these options involves a very significant amount of work, and neither is a particularly elegant solution. Something had to be done.

Modern Times

Recognizing these issues and the strong customer demand for easier access to non-BDE data sources, the Delphi development team made it a priority to extend VCL's data-set architecture in Delphi 3. The idea behind the new architecture was to make the TDataSet class an abstraction of a VCL data set and to move the BDE-specific data-set code into the new TBDEDataSet class. Figure 29.3 provides an illustration of this new architecture.

FIGURE 29.3.
Delphi 3 and 4 VCL data-set architecture.

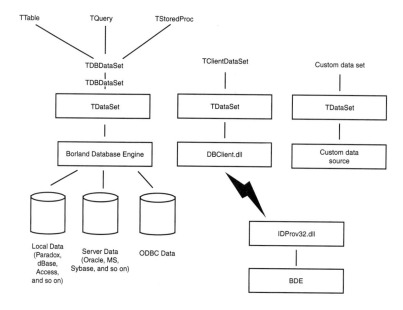

When you understand how TDataSet was uncoupled from the BDE, the challenge becomes how to employ this concept to create a TDataSet descendant that manipulates some type of non-BDE data. And we're not using the term *challenge* loosely; creating a functional TDataSet descendant is not a task for the faint of heart. This is a fairly demanding task that requires familiarity with VCL database architecture and component writing.

> **TIP**
>
> Delphi provides two examples of creating a TDataSet descendant, one very simple and one very complicated. The simple example is the TTextDataSet class found in the TextData unit in the \Delphi 4\Demos\Db\TextData directory. This example encapsulates TStringList as a one-field data set. The complex example is the TBDEDataSet class found in the DbTables unit in the VCL source. As mentioned earlier, this class maps VCL's data-set architecture to the BDE.

Creating a TDataSet Descendant

Most data-set implementations will fall in between TTextDataSet and TBDEDataSet in terms of complexity. To provide an example of this, we will demonstrate how to create a TDataSet descendant that manipulates an Object Pascal file of record (for a description of file of record, see Chapter 12, "Working With Files"). The following record and file type will be used for this example:

```
type
  // arbitary-length array of char used for name field
  TNameStr = array[0..31] of char;

  // this record info represents the "table" structure:
  PDDGData = ^TDDGData;
  TDDGData = record
    Name: TNameStr;
    Height: Double;
    ShoeSize: Integer;
  end;

  // Pascal file of record which holds "table" data:
  TDDGDataFile = file of TDDGData;
```

An Object Pascal `file of record` can be a convenient and efficient way to store information, but the format is inherently limited by its inability to insert records into or delete records from the middle of the file. For this reason, we will use a two-file scheme to track our "table" information: the first, *data file*, being the `file of record`; and the second, *index file*, maintaining a list of integers that represent seek values into the first file. This means that a record's position in the data file doesn't necessarily coincide with its position in the data set. A record's position in the data set is controlled by the order of the index file; the first integer in the index file contains the seek value of the first record in the data file, the second integer in the index file contains the next seek value into the data file, and so on.

In this section we will discuss what's necessary to create a TDataSet descendant called TDDGDataSet, which communicates to this `file of record`.

TDataSet Abstract Methods

TDataSet, being an abstract class, is useless until you override the methods necessary for manipulation of some particular type of data set. In particular, you must at least override each of TDataSet's 23 abstract methods and perhaps some optional methods. For the sake of discussion, we've divided them into six logical groupings: record buffer methods, navigational methods, bookmark methods, editing methods, miscellaneous methods, and optional methods.

The following listing shows an edited version of TDataSet as it is defined in Db.pas. For clarity, only the methods mentioned thus far are shown, and the methods are categorized based on the logical groupings we discussed.

```
type
  TDataSet = class(TComponent)
  { ... }
  protected
```

```
{ Record buffer methods }
  function AllocRecordBuffer: PChar; virtual; abstract;
  procedure FreeRecordBuffer(var Buffer: PChar); virtual; abstract;
  procedure InternalInitRecord(Buffer: PChar); virtual; abstract;
  function GetRecord(Buffer: PChar; GetMode: TGetMode; DoCheck:
➥Boolean):
    TGetResult;
    virtual; abstract;
  function GetRecordSize: Word; virtual; abstract;
  function GetFieldData(Field: TField; Buffer: Pointer): Boolean;
➥override;
  procedure SetFieldData(Field: TField; Buffer: Pointer); virtual;
➥abstract;
{ Bookmark methods }
  function GetBookmarkFlag(Buffer: PChar): TBookmarkFlag; override;
  procedure SetBookmarkFlag(Buffer: PChar; Value: TBookmarkFlag);
➥override;
  procedure GetBookmarkData(Buffer: PChar; Data: Pointer); override;
  procedure SetBookmarkData(Buffer: PChar; Data: Pointer); override;
  procedure InternalGotoBookmark(Bookmark: Pointer); override;
  procedure InternalSetToRecord(Buffer: PChar); override;
{ Navigational methods }
  procedure InternalFirst; virtual; abstract;
  procedure InternalLast; virtual; abstract;
{ Editing methods }
  procedure InternalAddRecord(Buffer: Pointer; Append: Boolean);
    virtual; abstract;
  procedure InternalDelete; virtual; abstract;
  procedure InternalPost; virtual; abstract;
{ Miscellaneous methods }
  procedure InternalClose; virtual; abstract;
  procedure InternalHandleException; virtual; abstract;
  procedure InternalInitFieldDefs; virtual; abstract;
  procedure InternalOpen; virtual; abstract;
  function IsCursorOpen: Boolean; virtual; abstract;
{ optional methods }
  function GetRecordCount: Integer; virtual;
  function GetRecNo: Integer; virtual;
  procedure SetRecNo(Value: Integer); virtual;
{ ... }
end;
```

Record Buffer Methods

You must override a number of methods that deal with record buffers. Actually, VCL does a pretty good job of hiding the gory details of its record buffer implementation; TDataSet will create and manage groups of buffers, so your job is primarily to decide what goes in the buffers and to move data between different buffers. Because it's a requirement for all `TDataSet` descendants to implement bookmarks, we will store bookmark information after the record data in the record buffer. The record we will use to describe bookmark information is as follows:

```
type
  // Bookmark information record to support TDataset bookmarks:
  PDDGBookmarkInfo = ^TDDGBookmarkInfo;
  TDDGBookmarkInfo = record
    BookmarkData: Integer;
    BookmarkFlag: TBookmarkFlag;
  end;
```

The `BookmarkData` field will represent a simple seek value into the data file. The `BookmarkFlag` field is used to determine whether the buffer contains a valid bookmark, and it will contain special values when the data set is positioned on the BOF and EOF cracks.

> **NOTE**
>
> Keep in mind that this implementation of bookmarks and record buffers is specific to this solution. If you were creating a `TDataSet` descendant to manipulate some other type of data, you might choose to implement your record buffer or bookmarks differently. For example, the data source you are trying to encapsulate may natively support bookmarks.

Before examining the record-buffer-specific methods, first take a look at the constructor for the `TDDGDataSet` class:

```
constructor TDDGDataSet.Create(AOwner: TComponent);
begin
  FIndexList := TIndexList.Create;
  FRecordSize := SizeOf(TDDGData);
  FBufferSize := FRecordSize + SizeOf(TDDGBookmarkInfo);
  inherited Create(AOwner);
end;
```

This constructor does three important things: First, it creates the `TIndexList` object. This list object is used as the index file described earlier to maintain order in the data set. Next, the `FRecordSize` and `FBufferSize` fields are initialized. `FRecordSize` holds the size of the data record, and `FBufferSize` represents the total size of the record buffer, data record size plus the size of the bookmark information record. Finally, this method calls the inherited constructor to perform the default `TDataSet` setup.

The following are `TDataSet` methods that deal with record buffers that must be overridden in a descendant. All of these except `GetFieldData()` are declared as abstract in the base class:

```
function AllocRecordBuffer: PChar; override;
procedure FreeRecordBuffer(var Buffer: PChar); override;
procedure InternalInitRecord(Buffer: PChar); override;
function GetRecord(Buffer: PChar; GetMode: TGetMode;
  DoCheck: Boolean): TGetResult; override;
function GetRecordSize: Word; override;
function GetFieldData(Field: TField; Buffer: Pointer): Boolean; override;
procedure SetFieldData(Field: TField; Buffer: Pointer); override;
```

AllocRecordBuffer()

The `AllocRecordBuffer()`method is called to allocate memory for a single record buffer. In this implementation of this method, the `AllocMem()` function is used to allocate enough memory to hold both the record data and the bookmark data:

```
function TDDGDataSet.AllocRecordBuffer: PChar;
begin
  Result := AllocMem(FBufferSize);
end;
```

FreeRecordBuffer()

As you might expect, `FreeRecordBuffer()` must free the memory allocated by the `AllocRecordBuffer()` method. It is implemented using the `FreeMem()` procedure as shown following:

```
procedure TDDGDataSet.FreeRecordBuffer(var Buffer: PChar);
begin
  FreeMem(Buffer);
end;
```

InternalInitRecord()

The `InternalInitRecord()` method is called to initialize a record buffer. In this method, you can do things like set default field values or perform some type of initialization of custom record buffer data. In this case, we simply zero-initialize the record buffer:

```
procedure TDDGDataSet.InternalInitRecord(Buffer: PChar);
begin
  FillChar(Buffer^, FBufferSize, 0);
end;
```

GetRecord()

The primary function of the `GetRecord()` method is to retrieve the record data for either the previous, current, or next record in the data set. The return value of this function is of type `TGetResult`, which is defined in the Db unit as follows:

```
TGetResult = (grOK, grBOF, grEOF, grError);
```

The meaning of each of the enumerations is pretty much self-explanatory: grOk means success, grBOF means the data set is at the beginning, grEOF means the data set is at the end, and grError means an error has occurred.

The implementation of this method is as follows:

```
function TDDGDataSet.GetRecord(Buffer: PChar; GetMode: TGetMode;
  DoCheck: Boolean): TGetResult;
var
  IndexPos: Integer;
begin
 if FIndexList.Count < 1 then
    Result := grEOF
  else begin
    Result := grOk;
    case GetMode of
      gmPrior:
        if FRecordPos <= 0 then
        begin
          Result := grBOF;
          FRecordPos := -1;
        end
        else
          Dec(FRecordPos);
      gmCurrent:
        if (FRecordPos < 0) or (FRecordPos >= RecordCount) then
          Result := grError;
      gmNext:
        if FRecordPos >= RecordCount-1 then
          Result := grEOF
        else
          Inc(FRecordPos);
    end;
    if Result = grOk then
    begin
      IndexPos := Integer(FIndexList[FRecordPos]);
      Seek(FDataFile, IndexPos);
      BlockRead(FDataFile, PDDGData(Buffer)^, 1);
      with PDDGBookmarkInfo(Buffer + FRecordSize)^ do
      begin
        BookmarkData := FRecordPos;
        BookmarkFlag := bfCurrent;
      end;
    end
    else if (Result = grError) and DoCheck then
      DatabaseError('No records');
  end;
end;
```

The FRecordPos field tracks the current record position in the data set. You'll notice that FRecordPos is incremented or decremented as appropriate when GetRecord() is called to obtain the next or previous record. If FRecordPos contains a valid record number, FRecordPos is used as an index into FIndexList. The number at that index is a seek value into the data file, and the record data is read from that position in the data file into the buffer specified by the Buffer parameter.

GetRecord() also has one additional job: When the DoCheck parameter is True, and grError is the potential return value, an exception should be raised.

GetRecordSize()

The GetRecordSize() method should return the size, in bytes, of the record data portion of the record buffer. Be careful not to return the size of the entire record buffer; just return the size of the data portion. In this implementation, we return the value of the FRecordSize field.

```
function TDDGDataSet.GetRecordSize: Word;
begin
  Result := FRecordSize;
end;
```

GetFieldData()

The GetFieldData() method is responsible for copying data from the active record buffer (as provided by the ActiveBuffer property) into a field buffer. This is accomplished most expediently using the Move() procedure. You can differentiate which field to copy using Field's Index or Name properties. Also, be sure to copy from the correct offset into ActiveBuffer because ActiveBuffer contains a complete record's data, and Buffer only holds one field's data.

```
function TDDGDataSet.GetFieldData(Field: TField; Buffer: Pointer):
Boolean;
begin
  Result := True;
  case Field.Index of
    0:
      begin
        Move(ActiveBuffer^, Buffer^, Field.Size);
        Result := PChar(Buffer)^ <> #0;
      end;
    1: Move(PDDGData(ActiveBuffer)^.Height, Buffer^, Field.DataSize);
    2: Move(PDDGData(ActiveBuffer)^.ShoeSize, Buffer^, Field.DataSize);
  end;
end;
```

Both this method and `SetFieldData()` can become much more complex if you want to support more advanced features such as calculated fields and filters.

SetFieldData()

The purpose of `SetFieldData()` is inverse to that of `GetFieldData()`; `SetFieldData()` copies data from a field buffer into the active record buffer. As you can see from the following code, the implementations of these two methods are very similar:

```
procedure TDDGDataSet.SetFieldData(Field: TField; Buffer: Pointer);
begin
  case Field.Index of
    0: Move(Buffer^, ActiveBuffer^, Field.Size);
    1: Move(Buffer^, PDDGData(ActiveBuffer)^.Height, Field.DataSize);
    2: Move(Buffer^, PDDGData(ActiveBuffer)^.ShoeSize, Field.DataSize);
  end;
  DataEvent(deFieldChange, Longint(Field));
end;
```

After copying the data, the `DataEvent()` method is called to signal that a field has changed and fire the `OnChange` event of the field.

Bookmark Methods

We mentioned earlier that bookmark support is required for `TDataSet` descendants. The following abstract methods of `TDataSet` are overridden to provide this support:

```
function GetBookmarkFlag(Buffer: PChar): TBookmarkFlag; override;
procedure SetBookmarkFlag(Buffer: PChar; Value: TBookmarkFlag); override;
procedure GetBookmarkData(Buffer: PChar; Data: Pointer); override;
procedure SetBookmarkData(Buffer: PChar; Data: Pointer); override;
procedure InternalGotoBookmark(Bookmark: Pointer); override;
procedure InternalSetToRecord(Buffer: PChar); override;
```

For `TDDGDataSet`, you'll see that the implementations of these methods revolve mostly around manipulating the bookmark information tacked onto the end of the record buffer.

GetBookmarkFlag() and SetBookmarkFlag()

Bookmark flags are used internally by `TDataSet` to determine whether a particular record is the first or last in the data set. For this purpose, you must override the `GetBookmarkFlag()` and `SetBookmarkFlag()` methods. The `TDDGDataSet` implementation of these methods reads from and writes to the record buffer to keep track of this information:

```
function TDDGDataSet.GetBookmarkFlag(Buffer: PChar): TBookmarkFlag;
begin
  Result := PDDGBookmarkInfo(Buffer + FRecordSize)^.BookmarkFlag;
end;
```

```
procedure TDDGDataSet.SetBookmarkFlag(Buffer: PChar; Value:
➥TBookmarkFlag);
begin
  PDDGBookmarkInfo(Buffer + FRecordSize)^.BookmarkFlag := Value;
end;
```

GetBookmarkData() and SetBookmarkData()

The GetBookmarkData() and SetBookmarkData() methods provide a means for TDataSet to manipulate a record's bookmark data without repositioning the current record. Shown following, these methods are implemented in a manner similar to the methods described in the preceding example:

```
procedure TDDGDataSet.GetBookmarkData(Buffer: PChar; Data: Pointer);
begin
  PInteger(Data)^ := PDDGBookmarkInfo(Buffer + FRecordSize)^.BookmarkData;
end;

procedure TDDGDataSet.SetBookmarkData(Buffer: PChar; Data: Pointer);
begin
  PDDGBookmarkInfo(Buffer + FRecordSize)^.BookmarkData := PInteger(Data)^;
end;
```

InternalGotoBookmark()

The InternalGotoBookmark() method is called to reposition the current record to that represented by the Bookmark parameter. Because a bookmark value is the same as the record number for TDDGDataSet, the implementation of this method is straightforward:

```
procedure TDDGDataSet.InternalGotoBookmark(Bookmark: Pointer);
begin
  FRecordPos := Integer(Bookmark);
end;
```

InternalSetToRecord()

InternalSetToRecord() is similar to InternalGotoBookmark() except that it receives as a parameter a record buffer instead of a bookmark value. The job of this method is to position the data set to the record provided in the Buffer parameter. This implementation of a record buffer contains the bookmark information because the bookmark value is the same as the record position—so the implementation of this method is a one-liner:

```
procedure TDDGDataSet.InternalSetToRecord(Buffer: PChar);
begin
  // bookmark value is the same as an offset into the file
  FRecordPos := PDDGBookmarkInfo(Buffer + FRecordSize)^.Bookmarkdata;
end;
```

Navigational Methods

You must override several abstract navigational methods in `TDataSet` in order to position the data set on the first or last record:

```
procedure InternalFirst; override;
procedure InternalLast; override;
```

The implementations of these methods are quite simple; `InternalFirst()` sets the `FRecordPos` value to -1 (the BOF crack value), and `InternalLast()` sets the record position to the record count. Because the record index is zero-based, the count is 1 greater than the last index (the EOF crack).

```
procedure TDDGDataSet.InternalFirst;
begin
  FRecordPos := -1;
end;

procedure TDDGDataSet.InternalLast;
begin
  FRecordPos := FIndexList.Count;
end;
```

Editing Methods

Three abstract `TDataSet` methods must be overridden in order to allow for the editing, appending, inserting, and deleting of records:

```
procedure InternalAddRecord(Buffer: Pointer; Append: Boolean); override;
procedure InternalDelete; override;
procedure InternalPost; override;
```

InternalAddRecord()

`InternalAddRecord()` is called when a record is inserted or appended to the data set. The `Buffer` parameter points to the record buffer to be added to the data set, and the `Append` parameter is `True` when a record is being appended and `False` when a record is being inserted. The `TDDGDataSet` implementation of this method seeks to the end of the data file, writes the record data to the file, and then adds or inserts the data file seek value into the appropriate position in the index list.

```
procedure TDDGDataSet.InternalAddRecord(Buffer: Pointer; Append: Boolean);
var
RecPos: Integer;
begin
  Seek(FDataFile, FileSize(FDataFile));
  BlockWrite(FDataFile, PDDGData(Buffer)^, 1);
  if Append then
  begin
```

```
    FIndexList.Add(Pointer(FileSize(FDataFile) - 1));
    InternalLast;
  end
  else begin
    if FRecordPos = -1 then RecPos := 0
    else RecPos := FRecordPos;
    FIndexList.Insert(RecPos, Pointer(FileSize(FDataFile) - 1));
  end;
  FIndexList.SaveToFile(FIdxName);
end;
```

InternalDelete()

The `InternalDelete()` method deletes the current record from the data set. Because it's not practical to remove a record from the middle of the data file, the current record is deleted from the index list. This, in effect, orphans the deleted record in the data file by removing the index entry for a data record.

```
procedure TDDGDataSet.InternalDelete;
begin
  FIndexList.Delete(FRecordPos);
  if FRecordPos >= FIndexList.Count then Dec(FRecordPos);
end;
```

> **NOTE**
>
> This method of deletion means that the data file will not shrink in size even as records are deleted (similar to dBASE files). If you intend to use this type of data set for commercial work, a good addition would be a file-pack method, which removes orphaned records from the data file.

InternalPost()

The `InternalPost()` method is called by `TDataSet.Post()`. In this method, you should write the data from the active record buffer to the data file. You'll note that the implementation of this method is quite similar to that of `InternalAddRecord()`.

```
procedure TDDGDataSet.InternalPost;
var
  RecPos, InsPos: Integer;
begin
  if FRecordPos = -1 then
    RecPos := 0
  else begin
    if State = dsEdit then RecPos := Integer(FIndexList[FRecordPos])
    else RecPos := FileSize(FDataFile);
  end;
```

```
  Seek(FDataFile, RecPos);
  BlockWrite(FDataFile, PDDGData(ActiveBuffer)^, 1);
  if State <> dsEdit then
  begin
    if FRecordPos = -1 then InsPos := 0
    else InsPos := FRecordPos;
    FIndexList.Insert(InsPos, Pointer(RecPos));
  end;
  FIndexList.SaveToFile(FIdxName);
end;
```

Miscellaneous Methods

Several other abstract methods must be overridden in order to create a working TDataSet descendant. These are general housekeeping methods, and because these methods can't be pigeonholed into a particular category, we'll call them miscellaneous methods. These methods are as follows:

```
procedure InternalClose; override;
procedure InternalHandleException; override;
procedure InternalInitFieldDefs; override;
procedure InternalOpen; override;
function IsCursorOpen: Boolean; override;
```

InternalClose()

InternalClose() is called by TDataSet.Close(). In this method, you should deallocate all resources associated with the data set that were allocated by InternalOpen() or that were allocated throughout the course of using the data set. In this implementation, the data file is closed, and we ensure that the index list has been persisted to disk. Additionally, the FRecordPos is set to the BOF crack, and the data file record is zeroed out.

```
procedure TDDGDataSet.InternalClose;
begin
  if TFileRec(FDataFile).Mode <> 0 then
    CloseFile(FDataFile);
  FIndexList.SaveToFile(FIdxName);
  FIndexList.Clear;
  if DefaultFields then
    DestroyFields;
  FRecordPos := -1;
  FillChar(FDataFile, SizeOf(FDataFile), 0);
end;
```

InternalHandleException()

InternalHandleException() is called if an exception is raised while this component is being read from or written to a stream. Unless you have a specific need to handle these exceptions, you should implement this method as follows:

```
procedure TDDGDataSet.InternalHandleException;
begin
  // standard implementation for this method:
  Application.HandleException(Self);
end;
```

InternalInitFieldDefs()

It is in the `InternalInitFieldDefs()` method that you should define the fields contained in the data set. This is done by instantiating `TFieldDef` objects, passing the `TDataSet`'s `FieldDefs` property as the `Owner`. In this case, three `TFieldDef` objects are created, representing the three fields in this data set.

```
procedure TDDGDataSet.InternalInitFieldDefs;
begin
  // create FieldDefs which map to each field in the data record
  FieldDefs.Clear;
  TFieldDef.Create(FieldDefs, 'Name', ftString, SizeOf(TNameStr), False,
➥1);
  TFieldDef.Create(FieldDefs, 'Height', ftFloat, 0, False, 2);
  TFieldDef.Create(FieldDefs, 'ShoeSize', ftInteger, 0, False, 3);
end;
```

InternalOpen()

The `InternalOpen()` method is called by `TDataSet.Open()`. In this method, you should open the underlying data source, initialize any internal fields or properties, create the field defs if necessary, and bind the field defs to the data. Our implementation of this method opens the data file, loads the index list from a file, initializes the `FRecordPos` field and the `BookmarkSize` property, and creates and binds the field defs. You'll see from the following code that this method also gives the user a chance to create the database files if they aren't found on disk.

```
procedure TDDGDataSet.InternalOpen;
var
  HFile: THandle;
begin
  // make sure table and index files exist
  FIdxName := ChangeFileExt(FTableName, feDDGIndex);
  if not (FileExists(FTableName) and FileExists(FIdxName)) then
  begin
    if MessageDlg('Table or index file not found.  Create new table?',
      mtConfirmation, [mbYes, mbNo], 0) = mrYes then
    begin
      HFile := FileCreate(FTableName);
      if HFile = INVALID_HANDLE_VALUE then
        DatabaseError('Error creating table file');
      FileClose(HFile);
      HFile := FileCreate(FIdxName);
```

```
      if HFile = INVALID_HANDLE_VALUE then
        DatabaseError('Error creating index file');
      FileClose(HFile);
    end
    else
      DatabaseError('Could not open table');
  end;
  // open data file
  FileMode := fmShareDenyNone or fmOpenReadWrite;
  AssignFile(FDataFile, FTableName);
  Reset(FDataFile);
  try
    FIndexList.LoadFromFile(FIdxName); // initialize index TList from file
    FRecordPos := -1;                  // initial record pos before BOF
    BookmarkSize := SizeOf(Integer);   // initialize bookmark size for VCL
    InternalInitFieldDefs;             // initialize FieldDef objects
    // Create TField components when no persistent fields have been
    // created
    if DefaultFields then CreateFields;
    BindFields(True);                  // bind FieldDefs to actual data
  except
    CloseFile(FDataFile);
    FillChar(FDataFile, SizeOf(FDataFile), 0);
    raise;
  end;
end;
```

NOTE

Any resources allocations made in `InternalOpen()` should be freed in
`InternalClose()`.

IsCursorOpen()

The `IsCursorOpen()` method is called internal to `TDataSet` while the data set is being
opened in order to determine whether data is available even though the data set is inactive. The `TDDGData` implementation of this method returns `True` only if the data file has
been opened.

```
function TDDGDataSet.IsCursorOpen: Boolean;
begin
  // "Cursor" is open if data file is open.  File is open if FDataFile's
  // Mode includes the FileMode in which the file was open.
  Result := TFileRec(FDataFile).Mode <> 0;
end;
```

> **TIP**
>
> The preceding method illustrates an interesting feature of Object Pascal: a *file of record* or untyped file can be typecast to a TFileRec in order to obtain low-level information about the file. TFileRec is described in the online help.

Optional Record Number Methods

If you want to take advantage of TDBGrid's capability to scroll relative to the cursor position in the data set, you must override three methods:

```
function GetRecordCount: Integer; override;
function GetRecNo: Integer; override;
procedure SetRecNo(Value: Integer); override;
```

Although this feature makes sense for this implementation, in many cases this capability isn't practical or even possible. For example, if you are working with a huge amount of data, it might not be practical to obtain a record count, or if you are communicating with a SQL server, this information may not even be available.

This TDataSet implementation is fairly simple, and these methods are appropriately straightforward to implement:

```
function TDDGDataSet.GetRecordCount: Integer;
begin
  Result := FIndexList.Count;
end;

function TDDGDataSet.GetRecNo: Integer;
begin
  UpdateCursorPos;
  if (FRecordPos = -1) and (RecordCount > 0) then
    Result := 1
  else
    Result := FRecordPos + 1;
end;

procedure TDDGDataSet.SetRecNo(Value: Integer);
begin
  if (Value >= 0) and (Value <= FIndexList.Count-1) then
  begin
    FRecordPos := Value - 1;
    Resync([]);
  end;
end;
```

TDDGDataSet

Listing 29.5 shows the DDG_DS unit, which contains the complete implementation of the TDDGDataSet unit.

LISTING 29.5. THE DDG_DS.pas UNIT.

```
unit DDG_DS;

interface

uses Windows, Db, Classes, DDG_Rec;

type

  // Bookmark information record to support TDataset bookmarks:
  PDDGBookmarkInfo = ^TDDGBookmarkInfo;
  TDDGBookmarkInfo = record
    BookmarkData: Integer;
    BookmarkFlag: TBookmarkFlag;
  end;

  // List used to maintain access to file of record:
  TIndexList = class(TList)
  public
    procedure LoadFromFile(const FileName: string); virtual;
    procedure LoadFromStream(Stream: TStream); virtual;
    procedure SaveToFile(const FileName: string); virtual;
    procedure SaveToStream(Stream: TStream); virtual;
  end;

  // Specialized DDG TDataset descendant for our "table" data:
  TDDGDataSet = class(TDataSet)
  private
    function GetDataFileSize: Integer;
  public
    FDataFile: TDDGDataFile;
    FIdxName: string;
    FIndexList: TIndexList;
    FTableName: string;
    FRecordPos: Integer;
    FRecordSize: Integer;
    FBufferSize: Integer;
    procedure SetTableName(const Value: string);
  protected
    { Mandatory overrides }
    // Record buffer methods:
    function AllocRecordBuffer: PChar; override;
    procedure FreeRecordBuffer(var Buffer: PChar); override;
```

continues

LISTING 29.5. CONTINUED

```
  procedure InternalInitRecord(Buffer: PChar); override;
  function GetRecord(Buffer: PChar; GetMode: TGetMode;
    DoCheck: Boolean): TGetResult; override;
  function GetRecordSize: Word; override;
  procedure SetFieldData(Field: TField; Buffer: Pointer); override;
  // Bookmark methods:
  procedure GetBookmarkData(Buffer: PChar; Data: Pointer); override;
  function GetBookmarkFlag(Buffer: PChar): TBookmarkFlag; override;
  procedure InternalGotoBookmark(Bookmark: Pointer); override;
  procedure InternalSetToRecord(Buffer: PChar); override;
  procedure SetBookmarkFlag(Buffer: PChar; Value: TBookmarkFlag);
➥override;
  procedure SetBookmarkData(Buffer: PChar; Data: Pointer); override;
  // Navigational methods:
  procedure InternalFirst; override;
  procedure InternalLast; override;
  // Editing methods:
  procedure InternalAddRecord(Buffer: Pointer; Append: Boolean);
➥override;
  procedure InternalDelete; override;
  procedure InternalPost; override;
  // Misc methods:
  procedure InternalClose; override;
  procedure InternalHandleException; override;
  procedure InternalInitFieldDefs; override;
  procedure InternalOpen; override;
  function IsCursorOpen: Boolean; override;
  { Optional overrides }
  function GetRecordCount: Integer; override;
  function GetRecNo: Integer; override;
  procedure SetRecNo(Value: Integer); override;
public
  constructor Create(AOwner: TComponent); override;
  destructor Destroy; override;
  function GetFieldData(Field: TField; Buffer: Pointer): Boolean;
➥override;

  // Additional procedures
  procedure EmptyTable;
published
  property Active;
  property TableName: string read FTableName write SetTableName;
  property BeforeOpen;
  property AfterOpen;
  property BeforeClose;
  property AfterClose;
  property BeforeInsert;
  property AfterInsert;
  property BeforeEdit;
```

```
    property AfterEdit;
    property BeforePost;
    property AfterPost;
    property BeforeCancel;
    property AfterCancel;
    property BeforeDelete;
    property AfterDelete;
    property BeforeScroll;
    property AfterScroll;
    property OnDeleteError;
    property OnEditError;

    // Additional Properties
    property DataFileSize: Integer read GetDataFileSize;
  end;

procedure Register;

implementation

uses BDE, DBTables, SysUtils, DBConsts, Forms, Controls, Dialogs;

const
  feDDGTable = '.ddg';
  feDDGIndex = '.ddx';
  // note that file is not being locked!

{ TIndexList }

procedure TIndexList.LoadFromFile(const FileName: string);
var
  F: TFileStream;
begin
  F := TFileStream.Create(FileName, fmOpenRead or fmShareDenyWrite);
  try
    LoadFromStream(F);
  finally
    F.Free;
  end;
end;

procedure TIndexList.LoadFromStream(Stream: TStream);
var
  Value: Integer;
begin
  while Stream.Position < Stream.Size do
  begin
    Stream.Read(Value, SizeOf(Value));
    Add(Pointer(Value));
  end;
```

29

EXTENDING
DATABASE VCL

continues

LISTING 29.5. CONTINUED

```
  ShowMessage(IntToStr(Count));
end;

procedure TIndexList.SaveToFile(const FileName: string);
var
  F: TFileStream;
begin
  F := TFileStream.Create(FileName, fmCreate or fmShareExclusive);
  try
    SaveToStream(F);
  finally
    F.Free;
  end;
end;

procedure TIndexList.SaveToStream(Stream: TStream);
var
  i: Integer;
  Value: Integer;
begin
  for i := 0 to Count - 1 do
  begin
    Value := Integer(Items[i]);
    Stream.Write(Value, SizeOf(Value));
  end;
end;

{ TDDGDataSet }

constructor TDDGDataSet.Create(AOwner: TComponent);
begin
  FIndexList := TIndexList.Create;
  FRecordSize := SizeOf(TDDGData);
  FBufferSize := FRecordSize + SizeOf(TDDGBookmarkInfo);
  inherited Create(AOwner);
end;

destructor TDDGDataSet.Destroy;
begin
  inherited Destroy;
  FIndexList.Free;
end;

function TDDGDataSet.AllocRecordBuffer: PChar;
begin
  Result := AllocMem(FBufferSize);
end;
```

```pascal
procedure TDDGDataSet.FreeRecordBuffer(var Buffer: PChar);
begin
  FreeMem(Buffer);
end;

procedure TDDGDataSet.InternalInitRecord(Buffer: PChar);
begin
  FillChar(Buffer^, FBufferSize, 0);
end;

function TDDGDataSet.GetRecord(Buffer: PChar; GetMode: TGetMode;
  DoCheck: Boolean): TGetResult;
var
  IndexPos: Integer;
begin
  if FIndexList.Count < 1 then
    Result := grEOF
  else begin
    Result := grOk;
    case GetMode of
      gmPrior:
        if FRecordPos <= 0 then
        begin
          Result := grBOF;
          FRecordPos := -1;
        end
        else
          Dec(FRecordPos);
      gmCurrent:
        if (FRecordPos < 0) or (FRecordPos >= RecordCount) then
          Result := grError;
      gmNext:
        if FRecordPos >= RecordCount-1 then
          Result := grEOF
        else
          Inc(FRecordPos);
    end;
    if Result = grOk then
    begin
      IndexPos := Integer(FIndexList[FRecordPos]);
      Seek(FDataFile, IndexPos);
      BlockRead(FDataFile, PDDGData(Buffer)^, 1);
      with PDDGBookmarkInfo(Buffer + FRecordSize)^ do
      begin
        BookmarkData := FRecordPos;
        BookmarkFlag := bfCurrent;
      end;
    end
```

continues

29

EXTENDING
DATABASE VCL

LISTING 29.5. CONTINUED

```
    else if (Result = grError) and DoCheck then
      DatabaseError('No records');
  end;
end;

function TDDGDataSet.GetRecordSize: Word;
begin
  Result := FRecordSize;
end;

function TDDGDataSet.GetFieldData(Field: TField; Buffer: Pointer):
➥Boolean;
begin
  Result := True;
  case Field.Index of
    0:
      begin
        Move(ActiveBuffer^, Buffer^, Field.Size);
        Result := PChar(Buffer)^ <> #0;
      end;
    1: Move(PDDGData(ActiveBuffer)^.Height, Buffer^, Field.DataSize);
    2: Move(PDDGData(ActiveBuffer)^.ShoeSize, Buffer^, Field.DataSize);
  end;
end;

procedure TDDGDataSet.SetFieldData(Field: TField; Buffer: Pointer);
begin
  case Field.Index of
    0: Move(Buffer^, ActiveBuffer^, Field.Size);
    1: Move(Buffer^, PDDGData(ActiveBuffer)^.Height, Field.DataSize);
    2: Move(Buffer^, PDDGData(ActiveBuffer)^.ShoeSize, Field.DataSize);
  end;
  DataEvent(deFieldChange, Longint(Field));
end;

procedure TDDGDataSet.GetBookmarkData(Buffer: PChar; Data: Pointer);
begin
  PInteger(Data)^ := PDDGBookmarkInfo(Buffer + FRecordSize)^.BookmarkData;
end;

function TDDGDataSet.GetBookmarkFlag(Buffer: PChar): TBookmarkFlag;
begin
  Result := PDDGBookmarkInfo(Buffer + FRecordSize)^.BookmarkFlag;
end;

procedure TDDGDataSet.InternalGotoBookmark(Bookmark: Pointer);
begin
  FRecordPos := Integer(Bookmark);
end;
```

```
procedure TDDGDataSet.InternalSetToRecord(Buffer: PChar);
begin
  // bookmark value is the same as an offset into the file
  FRecordPos := PDDGBookmarkInfo(Buffer + FRecordSize)^.Bookmarkdata;
end;

procedure TDDGDataSet.SetBookmarkData(Buffer: PChar; Data: Pointer);
begin
  PDDGBookmarkInfo(Buffer + FRecordSize)^.BookmarkData := PInteger(Data)^;
end;

procedure TDDGDataSet.SetBookmarkFlag(Buffer: PChar; Value:
TBookmarkFlag);
begin
  PDDGBookmarkInfo(Buffer + FRecordSize)^.BookmarkFlag := Value;
end;

procedure TDDGDataSet.InternalFirst;
begin
  FRecordPos := -1;
end;

procedure TDDGDataSet.InternalInitFieldDefs;
begin
  // create FieldDefs which map to each field in the data record
  FieldDefs.Clear;
  TFieldDef.Create(FieldDefs, 'Name', ftString, SizeOf(TNameStr), False,
➥1);
  TFieldDef.Create(FieldDefs, 'Height', ftFloat, 0, False, 2);
  TFieldDef.Create(FieldDefs, 'ShoeSize', ftInteger, 0, False, 3);
end;

procedure TDDGDataSet.InternalLast;
begin
  FRecordPos := FIndexList.Count;
end;

procedure TDDGDataSet.InternalClose;
begin
  if TFileRec(FDataFile).Mode <> 0 then
    CloseFile(FDataFile);
  FIndexList.SaveToFile(FIdxName);
  FIndexList.Clear;
  if DefaultFields then
    DestroyFields;
  FRecordPos := -1;
  FillChar(FDataFile, SizeOf(FDataFile), 0);
end;
```

continues

LISTING 29.5. CONTINUED

```pascal
procedure TDDGDataSet.InternalHandleException;
begin
  // standard implementation for this method:
  Application.HandleException(Self);
end;

procedure TDDGDataSet.InternalDelete;
begin
  FIndexList.Delete(FRecordPos);
  if FRecordPos >= FIndexList.Count then Dec(FRecordPos);
end;

procedure TDDGDataSet.InternalAddRecord(Buffer: Pointer; Append: Boolean);
var
  RecPos: Integer;
begin
  Seek(FDataFile, FileSize(FDataFile));
  BlockWrite(FDataFile, PDDGData(Buffer)^, 1);
  if Append then
  begin
    FIndexList.Add(Pointer(FileSize(FDataFile) - 1));
    InternalLast;
  end
  else begin
    if FRecordPos = -1 then RecPos := 0
    else RecPos := FRecordPos;
    FIndexList.Insert(RecPos, Pointer(FileSize(FDataFile) - 1));
  end;
  FIndexList.SaveToFile(FIdxName);
end;

procedure TDDGDataSet.InternalOpen;
var
  HFile: THandle;
begin
  // make sure table and index files exist
  FIdxName := ChangeFileExt(FTableName, feDDGIndex);
  if not (FileExists(FTableName) and FileExists(FIdxName)) then
  begin
    if MessageDlg('Table or index file not found.  Create new table?',
      mtConfirmation, [mbYes, mbNo], 0) = mrYes then
    begin
      HFile := FileCreate(FTableName);
      if HFile = INVALID_HANDLE_VALUE then
        DatabaseError('Error creating table file');
      FileClose(HFile);
      HFile := FileCreate(FIdxName);
      if HFile = INVALID_HANDLE_VALUE then
        DatabaseError('Error creating index file');
```

```
        FileClose(HFile);
      end
      else
        DatabaseError('Could not open table');
    end;
    // open data file
    FileMode := fmShareDenyNone or fmOpenReadWrite;
    AssignFile(FDataFile, FTableName);
    Reset(FDataFile);
    try
      FIndexList.LoadFromFile(FIdxName); // initialize index TList from file
      FRecordPos := -1;                  // initial record pos before BOF
      BookmarkSize := SizeOf(Integer);   // initialize bookmark size for VCL
      InternalInitFieldDefs;             // initialize FieldDef objects
      // Create TField components when no persistent fields have been
      // created
      if DefaultFields then CreateFields;
      BindFields(True);                  // bind FieldDefs to actual data
    except
      CloseFile(FDataFile);
      FillChar(FDataFile, SizeOf(FDataFile), 0);
      raise;
    end;
  end;

procedure TDDGDataSet.InternalPost;
var
  RecPos, InsPos: Integer;
begin
  if FRecordPos = -1 then
    RecPos := 0
  else begin
    if State = dsEdit then RecPos := Integer(FIndexList[FRecordPos])
    else RecPos := FileSize(FDataFile);
  end;
  Seek(FDataFile, RecPos);
  BlockWrite(FDataFile, PDDGData(ActiveBuffer)^, 1);
  if State <> dsEdit then
  begin
    if FRecordPos = -1 then InsPos := 0
    else InsPos := FRecordPos;
    FIndexList.Insert(InsPos, Pointer(RecPos));
  end;
  FIndexList.SaveToFile(FIdxName);
end;

function TDDGDataSet.IsCursorOpen: Boolean;
begin
  // "Cursor" is open if data file is open.  File is open if FDataFile's
```

continues

LISTING 29.5. CONTINUED

```
  // Mode includes the FileMode in which the file was open.
  Result := TFileRec(FDataFile).Mode <> 0;
end;

function TDDGDataSet.GetRecordCount: Integer;
begin
  Result := FIndexList.Count;
end;

function TDDGDataSet.GetRecNo: Integer;
begin
  UpdateCursorPos;
  if (FRecordPos = -1) and (RecordCount > 0) then
    Result := 1
  else
    Result := FRecordPos + 1;
end;

procedure TDDGDataSet.SetRecNo(Value: Integer);
begin
  if (Value >= 0) and (Value <= FIndexList.Count-1) then
  begin
    FRecordPos := Value - 1;
    Resync([]);
  end;
end;

procedure TDDGDataSet.SetTableName(const Value: string);
begin
  CheckInactive;
  FTableName := Value;
  if ExtractFileExt(FTableName) = '' then
    FTableName := FTableName + feDDGTable;

  FIdxName := ChangeFileExt(FTableName, feDDGIndex);

end;

procedure Register;
begin
  RegisterComponents('DDG', [TDDGDataSet]);
end;


function TDDGDataSet.GetDataFileSize: Integer;
begin
  Result := FileSize(FDataFile);
end;
```

```
procedure TDDGDataSet.EmptyTable;
var
  HFile: THandle;
begin
  Close;

  DeleteFile(FTableName);
  HFile := FileCreate(FTableName);
  FileClose(HFile);

  DeleteFile(FIdxName);
  HFile := FileCreate(FIdxName);
  FileClose(HFile);

  Open;
end;

end.
```

SUMMARY

This chapter demonstrated how to extend your Delphi database applications to incorporate features that aren't encapsulated by VCL. Additionally, you learned some of the rules and processes for making direct calls into the BDE from Delphi applications. You also learned the specifics for extending the behavior of TTable with regard to dBASE and Paradox tables. Finally, you went step by step through the challenging process of creating a working TDataSet descendant. In the next chapter, "Internet-Enabling Your Applications with WebBroker," you'll learn how to create server-side applications for the Web and deliver data to Web clients in real-time.

29

EXTENDING DATABASE VCL

INTERNET-ENABLING YOUR APPLICATIONS WITH WEBBROKER

by Nick Hodges

IN THIS CHAPTER

The Internet's popularity has exploded, and its use by computer owners has become almost a given. The technology that makes the Internet work is deceptively simple, and as a result, many business organizations are using the technology to create *intranets*— small Web networks accessible only to those within a given organization. Intranets are proving to be an inexpensive and highly effective way to leverage an organization's information systems. As new technologies arrive, the intranet is even being expanded to the "extranet"—a network that allows limited access, but isn't limited to an organization's boundaries.

All of this, of course, makes programming for the Internet and intranet a very important arrow in a programmer's quiver. As you might expect, Delphi makes programming for the Internet/intranet a very straightforward task. Delphi lets you bring its full power to the Web by

- Encapsulating the *Hypertext Transfer Protocol* (*HTTP*) in easily accessible objects
- Providing an application framework around the application programming interfaces (APIs) of the most popular and powerful Web servers
- Providing a RAD approach to building Web server extensions

With Delphi and its WebBroker components, you can easily build Web server extensions that provide customized, dynamic *Hypertext Markup Language* (HTML) pages that include access to data from virtually any source.

> **TIP**
>
> The WebBroker components are provided as a part of Delphi Client/Server Suite and Delphi Enterprise. If you are a Delphi Professional user, you can purchase the WebBroker components as a separate add-on. Visit the Inprise Web site (`http://www.inprise.com`) for more information.

The basic technology that makes the Web possible is quite simple. The two agents in the process, the Web client and the Web server, must establish a communications link and pass information to and from each other. The client requests information and the server provides it. Of course, the client and the server have to agree on how to communicate and what form the information they share will take. They do this across the Web with nothing more than an ASCII byte stream. The client sends a text request and gets a text answer back. The Web client knows little about what takes place on the server and the client, allowing for cross-platform communication, normally by means of the TCP/IP protocol.

The standard method of communicating used on the Web is the Hypertext Transfer Protocol (HTTP). A *protocol* is simply an agreement about a way of doing business, and HTTP is a protocol designed to pass information from the client to the server in the form of a request, and from the server to the client in the form of a response. It does so by formatting information as a byte stream of ASCII characters and sending it between the two agents. The HTTP protocol itself is both flexible and powerful. When used in concert with Hypertext Markup Language (HTML), it can quickly and easily provide Web pages to a browser.

An HTTP request might look like this:

```
GET /mysite/webapp.dll/dataquery?name=CharlieTuna&company=Borland HTTP/1.0
Connection: Keep-Alive
User-Agent: Mozilla/3.0b4Gold (WinNT; I)
Host: www.mysite.com:1024
Accept: image/gif, image/x-xbitmap, image/jpeg, image/pjpeg, */*
```

HTTP is *stateless*, which means that the server has no knowledge of the state of the client and the communication between the server and the client ends when the request has been satisfied. This makes creating database applications using HTTP somewhat problematic, as many database applications rely on the client having access to a live data set. State information can be stored through the use of *cookies*—pieces of information that are stored on the client as a result of the HTTP response. Cookies are discussed later in the chapter.

ISAPI, NSAPI, AND CGI WEB SERVER EXTENSIONS

Web servers are the engines that make the Web function. They provide all the content to Web browsers, whether that content is HTML pages, Java applets, or ActiveX controls. Web servers are the tools that provide responses to a client's request. Many different Web servers are available for use on any of the different popular platforms.

The Common Gateway Interface

The first Web servers would merely retrieve and return an existing, static HTML page. Web site managers could provide nothing more in a Web site than the pages that were present on the server at the time of the request. Soon, however, it became clear that a higher level of interaction between client and server was required, and the *Common Gateway Interface (CGI)* was developed as a result. CGI allowed the Web server to launch a separate process based on input from the user, work on that information, and return a dynamically created Web page to the client. A CGI program could do any type of data manipulation that the programmer required, and could return any sort of page that HTML would allow.

Standard CGI applications work by reading from STDIN, writing to STDOUT, and reading environmental variables. WinCGI works by storing the request parameters in a file, launching the WinCGI application, reading and processing the data in the file, and then writing an HTML file, which is then returned by the Web server. Suddenly, the Web took a large step forward, as servers could provide tailored, unique responses to users' requests.

However, CGI and WinCGI applications have some drawbacks. Each request must launch its own process on the server, so multiple requests can easily tie up even a moderately busy server. The task of creating a file, launching a separate process, executing the process, and then writing and returning yet another file is relatively slow.

ISAPI and NSAPI

The major Web server vendors, Microsoft and Netscape, saw the weaknesses inherent in CGI programming, but they also saw the advantages of dynamic Web creation. Thus, instead of using a separate process for each request, each company wrote APIs for its Web servers that allowed Web server extensions to be run as *dynamic link libraries* (DLLs). DLLs can be loaded once and then respond to any number of requests. They run as part of the Web server process, executing their code in the same memory space as the Web server itself. Instead of having to pass information back and forth as files, Web server extensions can simply pass the information back and forth inside the same memory space. This allows for faster, more efficient, and less resource-intensive Web applications.

Microsoft provides the rather simple and straightforward *Internet Server Application Programming Interface* (ISAPI) with its Internet Information Server (IIS), and Netscape provides the more complex *Netscape Application Programming Interface* (NSAPI) with its family of Web servers.

Delphi provides access to both APIs through the NSAPI.PAS and ISAPI.PAS units. To run the applications in this chapter, you have to be running the IIS server, a Netscape server, or one of a number of shareware or freeware servers that meet the ISAPI specification.

TIP

If you don't currently have a Web server installed, you can download the Microsoft Personal Web Server from their Web site (http://www.microsoft.com). It's freeware and is ISAPI-compliant. It will run all the examples in this chapter.

CREATING WEB APPLICATIONS WITH DELPHI

Delphi's WebBroker components make developing Internet/intranet applications easy. The following sections discuss these components and how they allow you to focus on the content of your Web servers without having to worry about the details of HTTP communications protocols.

TWebModule and TWebDispatcher

If you select File I New from the Delphi menu, the New Items dialog box appears. Select the Web Server Application icon to open a wizard that will allow you to select the type of Web server extension. The three choices are ISAPI/NSAPI, CGI, and Win-CGI applications. This chapter deals with the ISAPI/NSAPI application type. The construction of the CGI server extensions is done in almost the same manner, and the ISAPI applications are easier to deal with and run.

After you select the application type, Delphi creates a project based on a TWebModule. The main project itself is a DLL, and the main unit contains the TWebModule. TWebModule is a descendant of TDataModule, and it contains all the logic needed to receive the HTTP request and respond to it. A TWebModule can accept only nonvisual controls, just like its ancestor. You can use all the database controls, as well as the controls on the Internet page of the Component Palette that produce HTML, to produce content in a TWebModule. This allows you to add business rules for your Web-based application in the same manner as you can with TDataModule in regular applications.

The TWebModule has an Actions property, which contains a collection of TWebActionItems. A TWebActionItem allows you to execute code based on a given request. Each TWebActionItem has its own name; when a client makes a request based on that name, your code is executed and the appropriate response is given.

> **NOTE**
>
> You can create a Web server application with one of your existing data modules. The TWebModule has as one of its fields the TWebDispatcher class. This class is included on the Component Palette as the TWebDispatcher component. If you replace the default TWebModule in your Web server application with an existing data module by using the Project Manager, you can drop a TWebDispatcher component on it and it will become a Web server application. The TWebDispatcher component on the Internet page of the Component Palette adds all the functionality encapsulated in the TWebModule. So if you have all your business rules wrapped up in an existing TDataModule, making those rules available to your Web applications is as easy as point-and-click. A TDataModule with a TWebDispatcher component is functionally equivalent to a TWebModule. The only difference is that you access the HTTP actions through the TWebDispatcher component and not the TDataModule itself.

Select the TWebModule so that its properties are displayed in the Object Inspector. Select the Actions property and either double-click it or select the property editor with the small ellipsis (...) button. This will bring up the WebModule Actions dialog box. Click the New button and select the resulting WebActionItem in the property editor that appears. The Action item's properties will then be displayed in the Object Inspector. Go to the PathInfo property and enter /test. Then go to the Events page in the Object Inspector and double-click the OnAction event to create a new event handler. It will look like this:

```
procedure TWebModule1.WebModule1WebActionItem1Action(Sender: TObject;
  Request: TWebRequest; Response: TWebResponse; var Handled: Boolean);
begin
end;
```

This event handler contains all the information about the request that generated this action and the means to respond to it. The client's request information is contained in the

Request parameter, which is of type TWebRequest. The Response parameter is of type TWebResponse, and it's used to send the necessary information back to the client. Within this event handler, you can write any code necessary to respond to the request, including file manipulation, database actions, or anything else needed to send an HTML page back to the client.

Before you get into the depths of the TWebModule, a simple example will demonstrate the basics of how a Web server application works. The simplest way to create an HTML page that responds to the client's request is to build the HTML on-the-fly. You can do this easily by using a TStringList. After the HTML is placed into the TStringList, it can easily be assigned to the Content property of the Response parameter. Content is a string, and it's used to hold the HTML that is to be returned to the client. This is the only property of Response that must be filled, as it contains the data to be displayed. If it's left blank, the client's browser will report that the requested document is empty. Listing 30.1 shows the code that you must add to the test action item event handler.

LISTING 30.1. THE WebModule1WebActionItem1Action EVENT HANDLER.

```
procedure TWebModule1.WebModule1WebActionItem1Action(Sender: TObject;
  Request: TWebRequest; Response: TWebResponse; var Handled: Boolean);
var
   Page: TStringList;
begin
   Page := TStringList.Create;
   try
     with Page do
     begin
         Add('<HTML>');
         Add('<HEAD>');
      Add('<TITLE>Web Server Application -- Basic Sample</TITLE>');
         Add('</HEAD>');
         Add('<BODY>');
         Add('<B>This page was created on the fly by Delphi</B><P>');
         Add('<HR>');
         Add('See how easy it was to create a page on the fly with
         ➥Delphi''s Web Extensions?');
         Add('</BODY>');
         Add('</HTML>');
     end;
         Response.Content := Page.Text;
   finally
     Page.Free;
   end;
   Handled := True;
end;
```

Save the project as SAMPLE1, compile it, and place the resulting SAMPLE1.DLL in the default directory for your ISAPI- or NSAPI-capable Web server. Then, point your browser to the following location:

```
<default dir>/sample1.dll/test
```

You should see the expected Web page in your browser, as shown in Figure 30.1.

FIGURE 30.1.

A sample Web page.

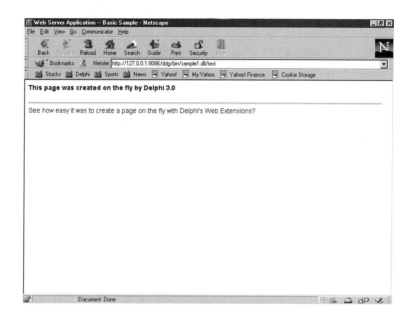

NOTE

If you take the code from the CD-ROM and place it on your computer, maintaining the same directory structure as on the CD-ROM, you can easily set your Web server up to access the HTML and the DLLs to run all the sample applications from this chapter. Simply create a virtual Web server directory for the root directory, and an ISAPI-capable directory that points to the \bin directory. Then, you can open up the INDEX.HTM file in the root directory, giving you access to all of the sample code.

Note that the result of the project's compilation is a DLL that conforms to the ISAPI specification. The project's source code reveals the following:

```
library Sample1;
uses
  HTTPApp,
  ISAPIApp,
```

```
  Unit1 in 'Unit1.pas' {WebModule1: TWebModule};
{$R *.RES}
exports
  GetExtensionVersion,
  HttpExtensionProc,
  TerminateExtension;
begin
  Application.Initialize;
  Application.CreateForm(TWebModule1, WebModule1);
  Application.Run;
end.
```

Note the three exported routines. These three, `GetExtensionVersion`, `HttpExtensionProc`, and `TerminateExtension`, are the only three procedures required by the ISAPI specification. In addition to meeting the ISAPI requirements, this application and all like it will also work with NSAPI-based servers.

CAUTION

Like a typical application, your ISAPI application uses a global `Application` object. However, unlike a regular application, this project doesn't use the `Forms` unit. Instead, the `HTTPApp` unit contains an `Application` variable declared as type `TWebApplication`. It handles all the special calls needed to be able to hook into an ISAPI- or NSAPI-capable Web server. As a result, you should never try to add the `Forms` unit to an ISAPI-based Web server extension, as this may confuse the compiler into using the wrong `Application` variable.

This simple project illustrates how easy it is to build a Web server application and provide a response to a client's request by using Delphi. This is a relatively simple example, creating HTML dynamically in code. However, as you will soon see, Delphi provides the tools to respond in much more complex and interesting ways. Before looking at what Delphi can do in this regard, we'll delve a little deeper into the workings of a Web server application in the following section.

TWebRequest and TWebResponse

`TWebRequest` and `TWebResponse` are abstract classes that encapsulate the HTTP protocol. `TWebRequest` provides access to all the information passed to the server by the client, and `TWebResponse` contains properties and methods that allow you to respond in any of the multiple ways that the HTTP protocol allows. Both of these classes are declared in the `HTTPAPP.pas` unit. ISAPI- and NSAPI-based Web applications actually use `TISAPIResponse` and `TISAPIRequest`, which are descendants of the abstract classes and are declared in ISAPIAPP.PAS. The power of polymorphism allows Delphi to pass the TISAPIxxx classes to the TWebxxx parameters of the OnAction event handler in TWebModule.

TISAPIRequest contains all the information passed by a client when making a request for a Web page. You can gather information about the client from the request. Many of the properties may be blank for any given request, as not all fields are completed for every HTTP request. The RemoteHost and RemoteAddr properties contain the IP address of the requesting machine. The UserAgent property contains information about the browser that the client is using. The Accept property includes a listing of the types of graphics that the user's browser can display. The Referer property contains the URL for the page that the user clicked to create the request. If cookie information is present (cookies are discussed later in the chapter), it's contained in the Cookie property. Multiple Cookies can be more easily accessed by the CookieFields array. If any parameters were passed with the request, they'll all be contained in a single string inside the Query property. They'll also be broken out into an array in the QueryFields property.

NOTE

When passing parameters to a URL, they normally follow a question mark (?) after the URL's name. Multiple parameters are separated by an ampersand (&) and if the parameters contain spaces, a plus sign (+) is substituted for the spaces. Thus, a valid set of parameters might look like this inside an HTML page:

```
<A HREF="http://www.someplace.com/ISAPIApp?Param1=This+
➥Parameter&Param2=That+Parameter">Some Link</A>
```

Most of the information for a TISAPIRequest is revealed in properties, but the class makes public many of the functions used to fill those properties, allowing you to access the data directly if you want. TISAPIRequest contains other properties than those discussed here, but these are the main ones that you should be interested in. All of these properties can be used in your OnAction event handler to determine the type of response that your Web server application will provide. If you want to include information about the user's IP address and the type of browser he or she is using in your response, that information is available to you.

You can see what a TISAPIRequest looks like by running the following project in your Web server. Create a new Web server application, bring up the Actions property editor by double-clicking the Actions property in the Object Inspector, and create a new TWebActionItem with the PathInfo set to http. Go to the Internet page on the Component Palette and drop a TPageProducer (discussed later in this chapter) on the WebModule, and add the code shown in Listing 30.2 to the /http OnAction event handler.

LISTING 30.2. THE OnAction EVENT HANDLER.

```
procedure TWebModule1.WebModule1Actions0Action(Sender: TObject;
  Request: TWebRequest; Response: TWebResponse; var Handled: Boolean);
var
  Page: TStringList;
begin
  Page := TStringList.Create;
  try
    with Page do
    begin
        Add('<HTML>');
        Add('<HEAD>');
      Add('<TITLE>Web Server Extensions THTTPRequest Demo</TITLE>');
        Add('</HEAD>');
        Add('<BODY>');
        Add('<H3><FONT="RED">This page displays the properties
    ➥of the HTTP request that asked for it.</FONT></H3>');
Add('<P>');

        Add('Method = ' + Request.Method + '<BR>');
        Add('ProtocolVersion = ' + Request.ProtocolVersion + '<BR>');
        Add('URL = ' + Request.URL + '<BR>');
        Add('Query = ' + Request.Query + '<BR>');
        Add('PathInfo = ' + Request.PathInfo + '<BR>');
        Add('PathTranslated = ' + Request.PathTranslated + '<BR>');
        Add('Authorization = ' + Request.Authorization + '<BR>');
        Add('CacheControl = ' + Request.CacheControl + '<BR>');
        Add('Cookie = ' + Request.Cookie + '<BR>');
        Add('Date = ' + FormatDateTime ('mmm dd, yyyy hh:mm',
            ➥Request.Date) + '<BR>');
        Add('Accept = ' + Request.Accept + '<BR>');
        Add('From = ' + Request.From + '<BR>');
        Add('Host = ' + Request.Host + '<BR>');
        Add('IfModifiedSince = ' + FormatDateTime ('mmm dd, yyyy hh:mm',
            ➥Request.IfModifiedSince) + '<BR>');
        Add('Referer = ' + Request.Referer + '<BR>');
        Add('UserAgent = ' + Request.UserAgent + '<BR>');
        Add('ContentEncoding = ' + Request.ContentEncoding + '<BR>');
        Add('ContentType = ' + Request.ContentType + '<BR>');
        Add('ContentLength = ' + IntToStr(Request.ContentLength) +
            ➥'<BR>');
        Add('ContentVersion = ' + Request.ContentVersion + '<BR>');
        Add('Content = ' + Request.Content + '<BR>');
        Add('Connection = ' + Request.Connection + '<BR>');
        Add('DerivedFrom = ' + Request.DerivedFrom + '<BR>');
        Add('Expires = ' + FormatDateTime ('mmm dd, yyyy hh:mm',
            ➥ Request.Expires) + '<BR>');
Add('Title = ' + Request.Title + '<BR>');
        Add('RemoteAddr = ' + Request.RemoteAddr + '<BR>');
        Add('RemoteHost = ' + Request.RemoteHost + '<BR>');
```

continues

30

INTERNET-
ENABLING YOUR
APPLICATIONS

LISTING 30.2. CONTINUED

```
            Add('ScriptName = ' + Request.ScriptName + '<BR>');
            Add('ServerPort = ' + IntToStr(Request.ServerPort) + '<BR>');

            Add('</BODY>');
            Add('</HTML>');
        end;
          PageProducer1.HTMLDoc := Page;
          Response.Content := PageProducer1.Content;
      finally
        Page.Free;
      end;
    Handled := True;
end;
```

Point your Web browser to http://<your server>/project1.dll/http; when you view this application, it will show you all the values of the HTTP fields passed to the server in the request from your browser.

Of course, every request should have a proper response, and so Delphi defines the TISAPIResponse class to allow you to return information to the requesting client. The most important property of TISAPIResponse is the Content property. This is the property that will contain the HTML code to be displayed for the client.

TISAPIResponse contains a number of additional properties that can be set by your application. You can pass version information in the Version property. You can tell the client when the information being passed back was last modified with the LastModified property. You can pass information about the content itself with the ContentEncoding, ContentType, and ContentVersion properties. The StatusCode property allows you to return error codes and other status codes to the client.

TIP

Most browsers react in specific ways to certain StatusCodes. You can check the HTTP specification at the Web site http://www.w3.org for the specific status codes.

The real power of TISAPIResponse comes in its methods. Rather than wait for the OnAction event handler to finish, you can direct your Web server application to immediately return a response with the SendResponse method. You can send any sort of data back to the client using the SendStream method. And if your application decides to send the client somewhere other than the response provided by the application itself, it can do so using the SendRedirect method. SendRedirect is discussed later in the chapter in the section "Redirecting to a Different Web Site."

DYNAMIC HTML PAGES WITH HTML CONTENT PRODUCERS

Of course, building HTML code dynamically isn't the most efficient way to provide Web pages, so Delphi provides a number of tools to make building HTML pages much easier, more efficient, and customizable. `TCustomContentProducer` is an abstract class that provides the basic functionality for handling and manipulating HTML pages. `TPageProducer`, `TDataSetTableProducer`, and `TQueryTableProducer` descend from it. When used together, and with either existing or dynamically created HTML, these classes allow you to create a site based on dynamic HTML pages, including data in tables, hyperlinks, and the full range of HTML capabilities. These controls won't actually create HTML for you, but they make the management of HTML and the dynamic creation of Web pages based on parameters and other inputs quite simple.

TPageProducer

`TPageProducer` is used for the manipulation of straight HTML code. It uses customized HTML tags, replacing them with the proper content. You create, either at design time or runtime, an HTML template that contains special tags that aren't usable by standard HTML. The `TPageProducer` can then find these tags and replace them with the appropriate information. The tags can contain parameters for passing information. You can even replace one custom tag with another, allowing you to link page producers together, causing a "daisy chain" effect that allows you to define a dynamic Web page based on differing inputs.

These dynamic tags look just like regular HTML tags, but because they're not standard HTML tags, they're ignored by the client's browser. Such a tag looks like this:

```
<#CustomTag Param1=SomeValue "Param2=Some Value with Spaces">
```

The tag should be surrounded by the less-than (<) and greater-than (>) brackets, and the tag's name must begin with a pound sign (#). The tag name must be a valid Pascal identifier. Parameters with spaces must be entirely surrounded by quotes.

Delphi provides a number of predefined tag names. None of the values have any special action associated with them; rather, they're defined only for convenience and code clarity. For example, you're not required to use the `tgLink` custom tag for a link, but it makes sense—and is clearer in your HTML templates—if you do so. Note that you could define all your custom tags as you want, and they'll all become `tgCustom` values. Table 30.1 shows the predefined tag values.

TABLE 30.1. PREDEFINED TAG VALUES.

Name	Value	Tag Conversion Value
Custom	TgCustom	A user-defined or unidentified tag. It can be converted to any user-defined value.
Link	TgLink	This tag should be converted to an anchor value. This is normally a hypertext link or a bookmark value (`<A>..</A>`).
Image	TgImage	This tag should be converted to an image tag (`<IMG SRC=...>`).
Table	TgTable	This tag should be replaced with an HTML table (`<TABLE>..</TABLE>`).
ImageMap	TgImageMap	This tag should be replaced with an image map. An image map defines links based on hot zones within an image (`<MAP>...</MAP>`).
Object	TgObject	This tag should be replaced with code that calls an ActiveX control.
Embed	TgEmbed	This tag should be converted to a tag that refers to a Netscape-compliant add-in DLL.

Using the `TPageProducer` component is rather straightforward. You can assign HTML code to the component in either the `HTMLDoc` or `HTMLFile` property. Whenever the `Content` property is assigned to another variable (usually the `TISAPIResponse.Content` property), it scans the given HTML, calling the `OnHTMLTag` event whenever a custom tag is found in the HTML. The `OnHTMLTag` event handler looks like this:

```
procedure TWebModule1.PageProducer1HTMLTag(Sender: TObject; Tag: TTag;
  const TagString: String; TagParams: TStrings; var ReplaceText: String);
begin
end;
```

The `Tag` parameter contains the type of tag found (refer to Table 30.1). The `TagString` parameter holds the value of the whole tag itself. The `TagParams` parameter is an indexed list of each parameter, including the parameter name, the equal sign (=), and the value itself. The `ReplaceText` parameter is a string variable that you'll fill with the new value that will replace the tag. The entire tag, including the angle brackets (< and >), is replaced in the HTML code with whatever value is passed back in this parameter.

You can assign an HTML template to the `TPageProducer` in one of two ways. You can create the HTML at runtime as a string and pass it to the `HTMLDoc` property, or you can assign an existing HTML file to the `HTMLFile` property. This allows you to build HTML on-the-fly or to use existing templates that you've prepared ahead of time.

For example, suppose you have an HTML file called `MYPAGE.HTM` with the following HTML code:

```
<HTML>
<HEAD>
    <TITLE>My Cool Homepage</TITLE>
</HEAD>
<BODY>
Howdy <#Name>!  Thanks for stopping by my web site!
</BODY>
</HTML>
```

You can then assign the following code to the `PageProducer.OnHTMLTag` event handler:

```
procedure TWebModule1.PageProducer1HTMLTag(Sender: TObject; Tag: TTag;
  const TagString: String; TagParams: TStrings; var ReplaceText: String);
begin
    case Tag of
        tgCustom: if TagString = 'Name' then ReplaceText := 'Partner';
    end;
end;
```

This results in the following HTML code:

```
<HTML>
<HEAD>
    <TITLE>My Cool Homepage</TITLE>
</HEAD>
<BODY>
Howdy Partner!  Thanks for stopping by my web site!
</BODY>
</HTML>
```

Suppose that you used this code with the `OnAction` event in a `WebModule` like this:

```
procedure TWebModule1.WebModule1WebActionItem1Action(Sender: TObject;
  Request: TWebRequest; Response: TWebResponse; var Handled: Boolean);
begin
    PageProducer1.HTMLFile := 'MYPAGE.HTM';
    Response.Content := PageProducer1.Content;
end;
```

The newly created page would be sent back to the client when requested. When the `PageProducer.Content` property is called, it makes the given replacement of text for every tag it finds, calling the `OnHTMLTag` event handler for each one. More complex pages might have numerous entries in the `case` statement, replacing various different custom tags with large chunks of HTML, links to other pages, graphics, tables, and so on.

`TCustomPageProducers` can also be linked together in a chain. You can use two of them to produce a single page. For example, you might have a basic HTML template that holds standard header and footer code, along with custom tags that define some general values for the page and the location of the main body of the page. You might pass this through one page producer, replacing general data tags with standard information. You might replace the main body tag with customized code that contains more custom tags. The result could then be passed to another TPageProducer, which would replace those specific tag values with the appropriate information.

TDataSetTableProducer and TQueryTableProducer

In addition to regular HTML documents, Delphi provides the TDataSetTableProducer to allow you to easily and powerfully create HTML tables based on a given data set. TDataSetTableProducer allows you to fully customize all characteristics of the table, within the limits set by HTML. This class can function to a large degree as a TDBGrid because you can format individual cells, rows, and columns. You can access data from any data set available to your system, whether local or remote. This allows you to build enterprise-level Web sites that access data from virtually any source.

The TDataSetTableProducer behaves a bit differently than the other database controls in that it accesses data directly from a TDataSet descendant rather than through a TDataSource. It has a DataSet property that can be set at design time to any TDataSet descendant found in the same TWebModule, or at runtime to any dynamically created value. After the DataSet property has been set, you can access and configure the TDataSetTableProducer to display any of the columns of the given data set as desired. The TableAttributes property allows you to set the general characteristics of the table, again within the confines of the HTML specification.

The Header and Footer properties are of type TStrings and allow you to add HTML code before and after the table itself. You can use these properties in conjunction with your own dynamically created HTML or with HTML from a TPageProducer. For instance, if the main feature of a page is the table, you might use the Header and Footer properties to fill in the basic structure of the HTML page. If the table isn't the main focus of the page, you might choose to use a custom TTag in a TPageProducer to place the table in the appropriate place. Either way, you can use the TDataSetTableProducer to create data-based Web pages.

The Columns, RowAttributes, and TableAttributes properties are where customizing is done for the table to be produced. The Columns property hides a very powerful component editor that you can use to set most of the component's attributes.

> **TIP**
>
> Double-click the component itself or the `Columns` property in the Object Inspector to invoke the `Columns` property editor.

The `Caption` and `CaptionAlign` properties determine how the caption of the table will be shown. The `Caption` is the text displayed either above or below the table, serving to explain the table's contents. The `DataSet` property (`Query` in the `TQueryTableProducer`) determines the data to be used in the table.

Other than the way they access data, the `TDataSetTableProducer` and the `TQueryTableProducer` function identically. They have the same properties and are configured the same way. Because of this, you'll create a table that's the result of a simple join and use the `TQueryTableProducer` in an example to see how they both work.

Start a new Web application, and drop a `TQueryTableProducer` from the Internet page of the Component Palette and a `TQuery` and a `TSession` from the Data Access Palette page onto the `TWebModule`. Set the `QueryTableProducer1.DataSet` property to `Query1`, and the `Query1.DatabaseName` to DBDEMOS. Save the project as TABLEEX.DPR. Then set the `Query1.SQL` property as follows:

```
SELECT CUSTNO, ORDERNO, COMPANY, AMOUNTPAID, ITEMSTOTAL FROM CUSTOMER,
➥ORDERS WHERE
    CUSTOMER.CUSTNO = ORDERS.CUSTNO
    AND
    ORDERS.AMOUNTPAID <> ORDERS.ITEMSTOTAL
```

This will produce a small, joined table that has all the customers from the CUSTOMER.DB table in the standard DBDemos alias who haven't yet paid all their orders in full. You can then build a table that shows this data, and highlight the amount owed. Set `Query1.Active` to `True` so that the data will be displayed in the `Columns` editor.

> **NOTE**
>
> All Web server applications that will be handling data and using Delphi's data components need to have a `TSession` included in the WebModule. Web Server applications can be accessed many times concurrently, and Delphi will run each ISAPI or NSAPI server application in a separate thread for each request. As a result, your application needs to have its own, unique session when talking to the BDE. A `TSession` in your application ensures that each thread has its own session and doesn't conflict with other threads trying to access the same data. All you need to do is make sure that there's a `TSession` present in your project—Delphi takes care of the rest.

TIP

When you're building Web extension applications, the `TWebApplication.CacheConnections` property can speed up your application. Each time a client makes a request of your ISAPI or NSAPI application, a new thread is spawned to handle your request, in the process creating a new instance of your `TWebModule`. Normally, each thread is executed for a single connection, and the `TWebModule` is destroyed when that connection is closed. If `CacheConnections` is set to `True`, each thread is preserved and reused as needed. New threads are only created when a cached thread is not available. This will speed performance by saving the execution time for creating a `TWebModule` request every time. However, you have to be really careful, as `TWebModule.OnCreate` is called only once for each cached thread. When a cached thread is finished, it remains in the state it was at completion. This might cause problems the next time the thread is used, depending on what happens in your `OnCreate` event. If you depend on `OnCreate` to initialize variables or perform other initialization actions, you may not want to use cached connections.

You can check the current number of unused, cached connections with the `TWebApplication.InactiveCount` property. `TWebApplication.ActiveCount` will tell you the number of active connections. These two properties may help you determine a good value for `TWebApplication.MaxConnections`, which limits the total number of connections that the `TWebModule` can handle at once. An exception will be raised if `ActiveCount` ever exceeds `MaxConnections`.

Next, set the `Caption` property to `Delinquent Customers`. This will create what appears to be a rather unimpressive title in the component editor, but this will be fixed at run-time.

Double-click `QueryTableProducer1` to invoke the `Columns` component editor. In the upper left of the component editor, you can set the general properties for the table as a whole. The lower half of the editor contains an HTML control that will display the table as it's currently configured. The upper right contains the controls to determine which fields of the database will be included in the table and how those fields will be displayed.

TIP

It might be a good idea to resize the `Columns` property editor in order to accommodate your table, especially if it will contain a number of columns.

In the upper left of the window, set the `Border` value to 1 so that you'll be able to see the border of the table in the component editor as it's built. Set the `CellPadding` value to 2 to provide a bit of spacing between the border and the text. If you want to add a little color to the table, set the `BgColor` property to `Aqua`. This will cause the default background color of the table to be aqua. Note that this is the default color—setting the background color for a row or a column will override this value. In addition, `Column` color settings take precedence over `Row` color settings.

Finally, click the `Add` button in the upper-right corner of the window four times. This will create four `THTMLTableColumn` items in the editor. A table column will be displayed for each one in the HTML control in the lower half of the editor. Selecting one of the `THTMLTableColumns` in the editor will cause its properties to be displayed in the Object Inspector.

Select the first `THTMLTableColumn` item and set its `FieldName` property to `CUSTNO`. Notice that the `Fields` property has gathered up the fields that resulted from the SQL done in `Query1` and made them available here. Select `CustNo`, `Company`, and `AmountOwed` as the `FieldName` for the remaining three `THTMLTableColumn` items.

Setting the `FieldName` value causes the table to create column headers with the same values as the field names. However, database field names often don't make nice table column headings, so you can change their values using the `Title` property. `Title` is a compound property, and one of its subproperties is `Caption`. Set the `Title.Caption` properties of the four columns to `Cust #`, `Order #`, `Company`, and `Amount Owed`, respectively. `Amount Owed` isn't quite what the fourth column currently represents, but you'll customize the output for this column a little later. The `Title` property also allows you to customize the vertical and horizontal alignment, as well as the color of the column header cell.

> **NOTE**
>
> The `TTHMLTableColumn`, like other table-related classes, has a `Custom` property. This property lets you enter a string value for the given item in the table. This value will be entered directly in the HTML tag that defines the given table element. `Custom` items might include HTML cell, row, or column modifiers not included in the properties of the class, or proprietary HTML extensions. Microsoft Internet Explorer includes a number of table-formatting extensions that allow you to customize the frames of the table. If you want to add these capabilities, make the entry in the `Custom` property in the form of *paramname=value*. You can add multiple parameters separated by spaces.

That covers the basic properties for the table that you can set at runtime. Now we'll discuss the events associated with the TQueryTableProducer that allow you to customize the table at runtime. The OnCreateContent occurs prior to any HTML being generated. It contains the Continue parameter, a Boolean value that you can set. If your application determines that for some reason the table shouldn't be generated, you can set this parameter to False, and no more processing will be done; a call to the Content property will return an empty string. It might be used to do such things as prepare the query, set the TQueryTableProducer.MaxRows property, or any other processing that you need to do before actually displaying the table.

For instance, in the current example, the application will need to step through each record in the Query as the table is drawn. To ensure that as the table is built the query is pointing to the proper record, the application has to manually increment the cursor in the query each time a new row is started. To do that, the query has to start at the beginning, as does the TQueryTableProducer. Therefore, a call to Query1.First in the OnCreateContent event handler ensures that the query and the HTML table are in sync with each other. Therefore, add the following code to the event handler for QueryTableProducer1.OnCreateContent:

```
procedure TWebModule1.QueryTableProducer1CreateContent(Sender: TObject;
  var Continue: Boolean);
begin
    QueryTableProducer1.MaxRows := Query1.RecordCount;
    Query1.First;
    Continue := True;
end;
```

The OnGetTableCaption event allows you to format the table's caption however you want. Double-clicking on the event in the Object Inspector yields this event handler:

```
procedure TWebModule1.QueryTableProducer1GetTableCaption(Sender: TObject;
  var Caption: String; var Alignment: THTMLCaptionAlignment);
begin
end;
```

The Caption parameter is a variable parameter that will hold the end result of your caption. You can manipulate this parameter as you please, including adding HTML tags to size, color, and format the font of the table's caption. You can use the Alignment parameter to determine whether the caption is aligned at the top or the bottom of the table.

Create an OnGetTableCaption for the example that you've been working on by double-clicking it in the Object Inspector. Enter the following code to format the table's Caption in order to make it stand out a bit more on the page (this change won't be reflected on the HTML table shown in the Columns property editor):

```
procedure TWebModule1.QueryTableProducer1GetTableCaption(Sender: TObject;
  var Caption: String; var Alignment: THTMLCaptionAlignment);
begin
  ➥Caption := '<B><FONT SIZE="+2" COLOR="RED">Delinquent
  ➥Accounts</FONT></B>';
  Alignment := caTop;
end;
```

The `OnFormatCell` event can be used to change the appearance of an individual cell. In this example, you can add code to highlight the `Amount Owed` cell of any company that hasn't paid its bill in full. This gets a little trickier than with the regular grids, as the `TQueryTableProducer` only provides you with string values. However, as mentioned earlier, you can use the `CellRow` and `CellColumn` parameters to move the cursor of the `TQuery` along as the table is built, gathering the proper data and making calculations as each row is processed.

The `OnFormatCell` event handler passes you the information about the current cell being formatted in the `CellRow` and `CellColumn` parameters. These are both zero-based. The rest of the parameters are variable parameters to which you can assign values, depending on your application's logic. You can adjust the horizontal and vertical alignment of the data in the cell with the `Align` and `VAlign` parameters. You can pass additional `Custom` parameters for the cell in the `CustomAttrs` parameter, and of course you can alter the actual text of the cell with the `CellData` parameter.

The `CellData` parameter is of type `string`, which limits your ability to process it in its native format. If the data were actually stored in the database as an integer, you'd have to call `StrtoInt` to convert it back to a usable number. The following code illustrates how you might gather the actual `TField` values for the given cell. Perhaps future versions of Delphi will pass the `TField` value into the `OnFormatCell` event handler in addition to or in place of the string value. Add the code in Listing 30.3 to the `OnFormatCell` event handler for the `TQueryTableProducer`.

LISTING 30.3. THE `OnFormatCell` EVENT HANDLER.

```
procedure TWebModule1.QueryTableProducer1FormatCell(Sender: TObject;
  CellRow, CellColumn: Integer; var BgColor: THTMLBgColor;
  var Align: THTMLAlign; var VAlign: THTMLVAlign; var CustomAttrs,
  CellData: String);
var
  Owed, Paid, Total: Currency;
begin
    if CellRow = 0 then Exit; // Don't process the header row
    if CellColumn = 3 then //if the column is the Amount Owed Column
    begin
```

continues

LISTING 30.3. CONTINUED

```
        //Calculate the amount that the company owes
        Paid := Query1.FieldByName('AmountPaid').AsCurrency;
        Total := Query1.FieldByName('ItemsTotal').AsCurrency;
        Owed := Total - Paid;
        //Set CellData to amount owed
        CellData := FormatFloat('$0.00', Owed);
        //if it is greater than zero, then highlight the cell.
        if Owed > 0 then
        begin
            BgColor := 'RED';
        end;
        Query1.Next; //Advance the query since we came to the end of a
                    // row
    end;
end;
```

Then, add the following strings to the `TQueryTableProducer.Header` property:

```
<HTML>
<HEAD>
    <TITLE>Delinquent Accounts</TITLE>
</HEAD>
<BODY>
<CENTER><H2>Big Shot Widgets</H2></CENTER>
<P>
The Accounts highlighted in red are late in paying:
<P>
```

and this to the `TQueryTableProducer.Footer` property:

```
<P>
<I>This information is to be kept in the strictest confidence</I><P>
<B><I>Copyright 1997 by BigShotWidgets</I></B><P>
</BODY>
</HTML>
```

This will cause the table to be placed between these two sets of HTML code, causing a complete page to be created when the Content property of `TQueryTableProducer` is called in the following code.

Finally, go back to the main `TWebModule` of your application and add a single `Action`, setting its `PathInfo` to `/TestTable`. In its `OnAction` event handler, add the following code:

```
procedure TWebModule1.WebModule1WebActionItem1Action(Sender: TObject;
  Request: TWebRequest; Response: TWebResponse; var Handled: Boolean);
begin
    Response.Content := QueryTableProducer1.Content;
end;
```

Then compile the project and make sure that the resulting DLL is accessible by your Web server. Now, if you call the URL `http://<your server>/tableex.dll/TestTable`, you'll see the table with the header and footer text, and the positive amounts owed highlighted in red, as shown in Figure 30.2.

FIGURE 30.2.

A table-based Web page.

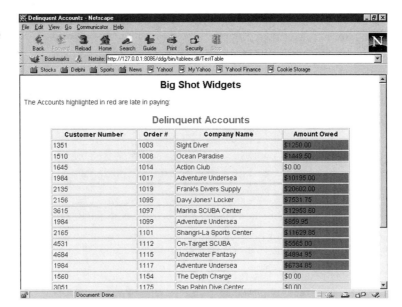

MAINTAINING STATE WITH COOKIES

The HTTP protocol is a powerful tool, but one of its weaknesses is that it's stateless. This means that after an HTTP conversation has been completed, neither the client nor the server has any memory at all that the conversation even took place, much less what it was about. This can present a number of problems for applications that run across the Web, as the server isn't able to remember important things like passwords, data, record positions, and so on that have been sent to the client. Database applications are particularly affected as they often rely on the client knowing which record is the current record back on the server.

The HTTP protocol provides a basic method for writing information on the client's machine to allow the server to get information about the client from previous HTTP exchanges. Called by the curious name *cookies*, they allow the server to write state information into a file on the client's hard drive and to recall that information at a subsequent HTTP request. This greatly increases a server's capabilities with respect to dynamic Web pages.

Cookies are no more than a text value in the form of *CookieName=CookieValue*. A cookie should not include semicolons or commas. The user can refuse to accept cookies, so no application should ever assume that a cookie will be present. Cookies are becoming more and more prevalent as Web sites get more and more sophisticated. If you're a Netscape user, you might be surprised by what you find in your COOKIES.TXT file. Internet Explorer users might peek into the \WINDOWS\COOKIES folder. If you want to track cookies as they're set on your machine, both of these browsers allow you to approve individual cookie settings within their security preference settings.

Managing cookies in Delphi is, pardon the pun, a piece of cake. The THTTPRequest and THTTPResponse classes encapsulate the handling of cookies quite cleanly, allowing you to easily control how cookie values are set on a client's machine, and to read what cookies have been previously set.

The work of setting a cookie is all done in the TWebResponse.SetCookieField method. Here you can pass a TStrings descendant full of cookie values, along with the restrictions placed on the cookies.

The SetCookieField method is declared as follows in the HTTPAPP unit:

```
procedure SetCookieField(Values: TStrings; const ADomain, APath: string;
➥AExpires: TDateTime; ASecure: Boolean);
```

The Values parameter is a TStrings descendant (you'll probably use a TStringList) that holds the actual string values of the cookies. You can pass multiple cookies in the Values parameter.

The ADomain parameter allows you to define in which domain the given cookies are relevant. If no domain value is passed, the cookie will be passed to every server to which a client makes a request. Normally, a Web application will set its own domain here, so that only the pertinent cookies are returned. The client will examine the existing cookie values and return those cookies that match the given criteria.

For example, if you pass widgets.com in the ADomain parameter, all future requests to a server in the widgets.com domain will pass along the cookie value set with that domain value. The cookie value won't be passed to other domains. If the client requests big.widgets.com or small.widgets.com, the cookie will be passed. Only hosts within the domain can set cookie values for that domain, avoiding all sorts of potential for mischief.

The APath parameter allows you to set a subset of URLs within the domain where the cookie is valid. The APath parameter is a subset of the ADomain parameter. If the server domain matches the ADomain parameter, the APath parameter is checked against the current path information of the requested domain. If the APath parameter matches the pathname information in the client request, the cookie is considered valid.

For example, continuing the preceding example, if APath contained the value /nuts, the cookie would be valid for a request to widgets.com/nuts and any further paths, such as widgets.com/nuts/andbolts.

The AExpires parameter determines how long a cookie should remain valid. You can pass any TDateTime value in this parameter. Because the client could be anywhere in the world, this value needs to be based on the GMT time zone. If you want a cookie to be valid for ten days, pass Now + 10 as a value.

If you want to delete a cookie, pass a date value that's in the past, and that will invalidate the cookie. Note that a cookie may become invalid and not be passed, but that doesn't necessarily mean that the data is actually removed from the client's machine.

The final parameter, ASecure, is a Boolean value that determines whether the cookie can be passed over nonsecure channels. A True value means that the cookie can only be passed over the HTTP-Secure protocol or a Secure Sockets Layer network. For normal use, this parameter should be set to False.

You Web server application receives cookies sent by the client in the TWebRequest.CookieFields property. This parameter is a TStrings descendant that holds the values in an indexed array. The strings are the complete cookie value in *param=value* form. They can be accessed like any other TStrings value. The cookies are also passed as a single string in the TWebRequest.Cookie property, but normally you wouldn't want to manipulate them here. You can assign the cookies directly to an existing TStrings object with the TWebRequest.ExtractCookieFields method.

A simple example can illustrate the ease with which Delphi deals with cookies. First, add the WebUtils unit to your uses clause. The WebUtils unit is included on the CD-ROM accompanying this book. Then create a new Web server application and give it two Actions, one named SetCookie and the other GetCookie. Set the code in the OnAction event for SetCookie to the following code:

```
procedure TWebModule1.WebModule1WebActionItem1Action(Sender: TObject;
  Request: TWebRequest; Response: TWebResponse; var Handled: Boolean);
var
  List: TStringList;
begin
  List := TStringList.Create;
  try
    List.Add('LastVisit=' + FormatDateTime('mm/dd/yyyy hh:mm:ss', Now));
    Response.SetCookieField(List, '', '', Now + 10, False);
    Response.Content := 'Cookie set -- ' + Response.Cookies[0].Name;
  finally
    List.Free;
  end;
```

```
    Handled := True;
end;
```

The `OnAction` code for `GetCookie` should be as follows:

```
procedure TWebModule1.WebModule1WebActionItem2Action(Sender: TObject;
  Request: TWebRequest; Response: TWebResponse; var Handled: Boolean);
var
  Params: TParamsList;
begin
    Params := TParamsList.Create;
    try
      Params.AddParameters(Request.CookieFields);
      Response.Content := 'You last set the cookie on ' +
      ➥Params['LastVisit'];
    finally
      Params.Free;
    end;
end;
```

Set up a Web page that calls the following two URLs:

```
http://<your server>/project1.dll/SetCookie
http://<your server>/project1.dll/GetCookie
```

NOTE

The `TParamsList` class is part of the `WebUtils` unit included on the CD-ROM. It's a class that automatically parses out parameters from a `TStrings` descendant and allows you to index them by the parameter's name. For instance, `TWebResponse` gathers all the cookies passed in an HTTP response and places them in the `CookieFields` property, which is a `TStrings` descendant. The cookies are in the form *CookieName=CookieValue*. `TParamsList` takes these values, parses them, and indexes them by the parameter name. Thus, the preceding parameter could be accessed with `MyParams['`*CookieName*`']`, which would return *CookieValue*. You can use this class, or you can use the Values property found in the `TStrings` class included in the VCL.

Set the cookie by calling for the first URL from a Web page in the same directory as the DLL. This will set a cookie on the client machine that lasts for ten days and contains the date and time that the request was made in a cookie called `LastVisit`. If you have your Web browser set to accept cookies, it should ask you to confirm the writing of the cookie. Then call the `GetCookie` action to read the cookie, and you should see the date and time that you last called the `SetCookie` action.

Cookies can contain any information that can be stored in a string. Cookies can be as big as 4KB, and a client can store as many as 300 cookies. Any individual server or domain is limited to 20 cookies. Cookies are powerful but, as you can see, you should try to limit their use. They certainly can't be used to store large amounts of data on a client's machine.

Very often, you will want to store more information about a user than can be stored in a cookie. Sometimes you'll want to keep track of a user's preferences, address, personal information, or even items in a user's "grocery cart" that are to be purchased from your e-commerce site. This information can easily become rather voluminous. Rather than try to store all of this information in the cookie itself, it is often better to encode user information into a cookie rather than storing the information as is. For instance, in order to store a collection of user preferences that are really Boolean values, you might store them in binary format inside the cookie. So a cookie value of '1001' might mean that the user does want further email updates, doesn't want his or her email address given to other users, doesn't want to be added to your list server, and does want to join your online discussion groups. You can use characters or numbers to further encode even more data about a user in a cookie.

You can also store a user identification value in a cookie that uniquely identifies a user. You can then retrieve that value from the cookie and use it to look up the user's data in a database. That way you would be able to minimize the amount of data stored on the user's computer and maximize your control over the information that you maintain about a user.

Cookies can thus be a powerful and easy way to maintain data about your users between individual HTTP sessions.

REDIRECTING TO A DIFFERENT WEB SITE

Often, a given URL may want to change the destination of a user's request. A Web application may want to process some data based on a request, and then serve back a page that may vary depending on the nature of the request or a database entry. Web advertising does this frequently. Often an ad graphic will point to another URL within the domain where it appears, but clicking it takes the user to the advertiser's home page. Along the way, data is gathered about the request, and then the client is handed off to the advertiser's page. Frequently, the HTML code for the advertisement's graphic will contain parameters that describe the ad to the server. The server can log that information, and then pass the client on to the proper page. This technique is called *redirection*, and it can be very useful for a number of tasks.

Delphi's TWebResponse class includes a method called SendRedirect. It takes a single string as a parameter that should contain the full address of the site to which the client should be redirected. The method is declared as follows:

```
procedure SendRedirect(const URI: string); virtual; abstract;
```

SendRedirect is declared as an abstract method in HTTPAPP.PAS, and defined in ISAPI-APP.PAS.

A Web server could easily process an HTTP request that includes parameters, and then pass that request to a site named by one of those parameters. For instance, if a cool GIF file is on a page, and the whole graphic is wrapped up as a hyperlink, the URL assigned to it might look something like this:

```
<A
HREF="http://www.somecoolplace.com/transfer?www.borland.com&
➥coolgif.gif&borland"> <IMG SRC="coolgif.gif"></A>
```

Given that information, an OnAction event in a Web server application named /transfer might look like the following code fragment:

```
procedure TWebModule1.WebModule1WebActionItem3Action(Sender: TObject;
  Request: TWebRequest; Response: TWebResponse; var Handled: Boolean);
begin
 {Process Request.QueryFields[1] perhaps placing it in a database.
  It holds the name of the GIF file that caused the user to click on it.
  You might want to track the GIFs that are the most effective.
  Then you can keep track of how many hits a particular company is
  getting from your site by tracking the company name that is getting
  requested in the Request.QueryFields[2] parameter}
  //Then, you can call this to send the user on his merry way...
  Response.SendRedirect(Request.QueryFields[0]);
end;
```

By using this technique, you can create a generic transfer application that processes every advertisement on a site. Of course, there may be other reasons for calling SendRedirect than just advertising. You can use SendRedirect whenever you want to keep track of specific URL requests and any data that might be associated with a particular hyperlink. Simply gather the data from the QueryFields property and then call SendRedirect as needed.

RETRIEVING INFORMATION FROM HTML FORMS

HTML-based forms are growing in use with the growth of the Internet and intranet. It's not a surprise that Delphi makes gathering information from forms easy. This chapter doesn't cover the details of creating an HTML-based form and the controls that go with it, but rather deals with how Delphi handles the forms and their data.

On the CD-ROM in the back of this book is a straightforward guest book application that gathers the input from an HTML form and makes entries into a database table. Opening the INDEX.HTM file in your browser can access the application. The HTML form for the guest book, GUEST.HTM, uses the following line to define the form and the action to take when the user clicks the Submit button:

```
<form method="post" action="guestbk.dll/form">
```

This code causes the form to "post" its data when asked to do so, and to call the given DLL OnAction event. The form allows the user to enter his or her name, email address, home town, and comments. When the user clicks the Submit button, that information is gathered up and passed to the Web application.

The Action with the name /form then receives the data in the Request.ContentFields, in the form of standard HTTP parameters. ContentFields is a TStrings descendant that holds the contents of the submitted form. The application contains a TTable named GBTable that's referenced by the GBDATA alias. You'll need to create this alias and point it to the /GBDATA directory where the Paradox tables reside in order to run the guest book. Listing 30.4 shows the code that receives the content of the form and enters it into the database.

LISTING 30.4. CODE FOR RETRIEVING CONTENT OF A FORM.

```
var
   MyPage: TStringList;
   ParamsList: TParamsList;
begin
    begin
        ParamsList := TParamsList.Create;
        try try
          ParamsList.AddParameters(Request.ContentFields);
          GBTable.Open;
          GBTable.Append;
          GBTable.FieldByName('Name').Value :=
ParamsList['fullnameText'];
          GBTable.FieldByName('EMail').Value := ParamsList['emailText'];
          GBTable.FieldByName('WhereFrom').Value :=
ParamsList['wherefromText'];
GBTable.FieldByName('Comments').Value := ParamsList['commentsTextArea'];
          GBTable.FieldByName('FirstTime').Value :=
          ➥(CompareStr(ParamsList['firstVisitCheck'], 'on') = 0);
          GBTable.FieldByName('DateTime').Value := Now;
          GBTable.Post;
        except
            Response.Content := 'An Error occurred in processing your
            ➥data.';
            Handled := True;
```

continues

LISTING 30.4. CONTINUED

```
          end;
        finally
          ParamsList.Free;
          GBTable.Close;
        end;
    end;
```

The code first inserts the `ContentFields` property into a `TParamsList`. It then opens the `GBTable` and inserts the data from the form into the appropriate fields. The code in Listing 30.4 is relatively straightforward.

The next portion of the code, shown in Listing 30.5, creates an HTML response that thanks the user for making an entry. It uses some of the data from the form to address the user by name, and confirms the user's email address.

LISTING 30.5. CODE FOR CREATING AN HTML RESPONSE.

```
MyPage := TStringList.Create;
  ParamsList := TParamsList.Create;
    try
      with MyPage do
      begin
        Add('<HTML>');
        Add('<HEAD><TITLE>Guest Book Demo Page</TITLE></HEAD>');
        Add('<BODY>');
        Add('<H2>Delphi Guest Book Demo</H2><HR>');
        ParamsList.AddParameters(Request.ContentFields);
        Add('<H3>Hello <FONT COLOR="RED">'+ ParamsList['fullnameText']
          ➥+'</FONT> from '+ParamsList['wherefromText']+'!</H3><P>');
        Add('Thanks for visiting my homepage and making
          ➥an entry into my Guestbook.<P>');
        Add('If we need to e-mail you, we will use this address -- <B>'
          ➥+ParamsList['emailText']+'</B>');
        Add('<HR></BODY>');
        Add('</HTML>');
      end;
     PageProducer1.HtmlDoc := MyPage;
    finally
      MyPage.Free;
      ParamsList.Free;
    end;
    Response.Content := PageProducer1.Content;
    Handled := True;
```

Finally, the application provides a summary of all guest book entries in the `/entries` Action.

DATA STREAMING

Most of the data that you will be providing to clients by HTTP requests will probably be HTML-based pages. However, there may be a time when you want to send other types of data in response to a user's request. Sometimes you might want to provide different graphics or sound based upon a user's input. You may have a special data format that you want to send down the pipe to a user that can be specially handled by the client's browser. For instance, Netscape provides a plug-in architecture that allows developers to write extensions to the Navigator Browser to handle any type of data. RealAudio, Shockwave, and other types of data streaming are examples of Netscape plug-ins that can extend the power of the client's browser.

Whatever the type of data you want to transmit, Delphi makes it easy to stream data back to a client. The `TWebResponse.SendStream` method along with the `TWebResponse.ContentStream` property enable you to send any type of data back to the client by loading it into a Delphi stream class. Of course, you'll need to let the client's browser know what type of data is being sent, so you'll need to set the `TWebResponse.ContentType` property as well. Setting this string value to an appropriate MIME type will allow the browser to properly handle the incoming data. For instance, if you want to stream a Windows WAV file, you'd set the `ContentType` property to `'audio/wav'`.

> **NOTE**
>
> MIME stands for Multipurpose Internet Mail Extensions. MIME Extensions were developed to allow clients and servers to pass data by email that was more complex than the standard text passed in most emails. Browsers and the HTTP protocol have adapted MIME extensions to allow you to pass almost any sort of data from a Web server to a Web browser. Your Web browser contains a rather large list of these MIME types, and associates a particular application or plug-in with each MIME type. When the browser gets that type, it looks up which application should be used to handle that particular MIME type and passes the data to it.

Using streams allows you to pass any type of data from virtually any source on your Web server's machine. You can pass data from files that reside on your server or anywhere on your network, from Windows resources built into your ISAPI DLL or other DLLs available to your ISAPI DLL, or you can even construct the data on-the-fly and send it to the client. There's really no limit to how or what you can send, as long as your client's browser knows what to do with the data.

Now construct a simple Web application that illustrates what can be done. You'll set up a Web page that displays images from various sources. The application will process the image data as needed and return it to the client as requested. This will be surprisingly easy, as Delphi provides numerous different stream classes that make gathering data into a stream very easy, and of the ISAPI extension classes make sending that data a snap as well.

Data Streaming Example

To build the data streaming example, select File | New from the main menu and choose Web Server Application from the resulting dialog. This will give you a TWebModule. Go to the Web Module, select it, and then go to the Object Inspector. Double-click on the Actions property and create three actions called /file, /bitmap, and /resource.

Select the /file action, go to the Object Inspector, and select the Events page. Create an OnAction event and then add the following code to the event handler:

```
procedure TWebModule1.WebModule1WebActionItem2Action(Sender: TObject;
  Request: TWebRequest; Response: TWebResponse; var Handled: Boolean);
var
  FS: TFileStream;
begin
    FS := TFileStream.Create(JPEGFilename, fmOpenRead);
    try
      Response.ContentType := 'image/jpeg';
      Response.ContentStream := FS;
      Response.SendResponse;
      Handled := True;
    finally
      FS.Free;
    end;
end;
```

The preceding code is pretty straightforward. If you set up the code from the CD on your computer as described earlier, there should be a JPEG file called TESTIMG.JPG in the \bin directory. The OnAction event handler creates a TFileStream that loads that file. It then sets the proper MIME type to tell the client browser that a JPEG file is coming and assigns the TFileStream to the Response.ContentStream property. The data is then returned to the client by calling the Response.SendResponse method. As a result, in the accompanying HTML file, there should be a picture of a rose on the provided HTML page.

Note

In the HTML that displays this JPEG file in your browser, you can simply place the reference to the Web application's Action directly in the IMG tag like so:

```
<IMG SRC="../bin/streamex.dll/file" BORDER=0>
```

The streaming examples can be displayed by means of the INDEX.HTM page in the \STREAMS directory

The application is able to find the JPEG file because when it was created, it set the JPEGFilename variable as follows:

```
procedure TWebModule1.WebModule1Create(Sender: TObject);
var
  Path: array[0..MAX_PATH - 1] of Char;
  PathStr: string;
begin
  SetString(PathStr, Path, GetModuleFileName(HInstance, Path,
  ➥SizeOf(Path)));
  JPEGFilename := ExtractFilePath(PathStr) + 'TESTIMG.JPG';
end;
```

The /bitmap action will load a different image, but in a totally different way. The code for this action is a bit more complicated and should look like this:

```
procedure TWebModule1.WebModule1WebActionItem3Action(Sender: TObject;
  Request: TWebRequest; Response: TWebResponse; var Handled: Boolean);
var
  BM: TBitmap;
  JPEGImage: TJPEGImage;
begin
    BM := TBitmap.Create;
    JPEGImage := TJPEGImage.Create;
    try
      BM.Handle := LoadBitmap(hInstance, 'ATHENA');
      JPEGImage.Assign(BM);
      Response.ContentStream := TMemoryStream.Create;
      JPEGImage.SaveToStream(Response.ContentStream);
      Response.ContentStream.Position := 0;
      Response.SendResponse;
      Handled := True;
    finally
      BM.Free;
      JPEGImage.Free;
    end;
end;
```

It takes a bit more work to get a bitmap converted to a JPEG and streamed out to the client. A TBitmap is used to grab the bitmap out of the resource file. A TJPEGImage from the JPEG unit is created and will convert the bitmap to a JPEG file.

The TBitmap class is created, and then the Windows API call LoadBitmap is used to grab the bitmap from the resource named 'ATHENA'. LoadBitmap returns the bitmap's handle, which is assigned to the Handle property. The bitmap itself is then immediately assigned to the TJPEGImage. The Assign method is overloaded and contains the smarts to convert the bitmap to a JPEG.

Next comes a nice example of polymorphism. The Response.ContentStream is declared as a TStream, an abstract class. Because of the power of polymorphism, you can create it as any type of TStream descendant that you like. In this case, it is created as a TMemoryStream and used to hold the JPEG with the TJPEGImage.SaveToStream method. Now the JPEG is in a stream and can be sent out. An important but easy-to-forget step is to return the position of the stream to zero after saving the JPEG into it. If this is not done, the stream will be positioned at the end, and no data will be streamed out to the client. After all of that is completed, the Response.SendResponse method is called to send out the data stored in the stream. The result in this case is the bust of Athena from Delphi's About Box.

Another way to load a JPEG is by using a resource entry. You can load a JPEG into a *.RES file using the following code in a *.RC file and then compiling it using BRCC32.EXE. If you load it as RCDATA, you can use the TResourceStream class to easily load it and send it to the client browser. TResourceStream is a very powerful class that will load a resource from either the EXE file itself or a resource located in an external DLL file. The /resource action illustrates how to do this, loading the JPEG from the resource named 'JPEG' that is compiled into the EXE:

```
procedure TWebModule1.WebModule1WebActionItem4Action(Sender: TObject;
  Request: TWebRequest; Response: TWebResponse; var Handled: Boolean);
begin
  Response.ContentStream := TResourceStream.Create(hInstance,
  ➥'JPEG', RT_RCDATA);
  Response.ContentType := 'image/jpeg';
  Response.SendResponse;
  Handled := True;
end;
```

This code sends the data to the client a little differently. It's much more straightforward, and is again a nice example of polymorphism in action. A TResourceStream is created and assigned to the ContentStream property. Because the TResourceStream's constructor loads the resource into the stream, no further action needs to be taken on the stream, and a simple call to Response.SendResponse sends the data down the stream.

The final example streams out a WAV file that is stored as an RCDATA resource. This example uses the `Response.SendStream` method to send out a stream created within the method. This illustrates yet another way of sending stream data. You can create a stream, manipulate and modify it as needed, and send it directly back to the client with the `SendStream` method. This `Action` should cause your browser to play a WAV file of a dog barking.

```
procedure TWebModule1.WebModule1WebActionItem1Action(Sender: TObject;
  Request: TWebRequest; Response: TWebResponse; var Handled: Boolean);
var
  RS: TResourceStream;
begin
    RS := TResourceStream.Create(hInstance, 'BARK', RT_RCDATA);
    try
      Response.ContentType := 'audio/wav';
      Response.SendStream(RS);
      Handled := True;
    finally
      RS.Free;
    end;
end;
```

SUMMARY

This chapter shows you how to build Web server extensions using the ISAPI/NSAPI extensions. This information is easily transferable to the CGI applications that Delphi produces. We discussed the HTTP protocol and how Delphi encapsulates it in its `TWebRequest` and `TWebResponse` classes. We showed you how to build applications using the `TWebModule` and its `OnAction` events with dynamic HTML. We then illustrated custom HTML documents with the `TContentPageProducer` descendants. We also discussed accessing data and building HTML tables using the `TQueryTableProducer`. Finally, we discussed how to handle cookies and the content of HTML forms. In the next chapter, we'll get back to a database-centric way of thinking as you learn about the MIDAS multitier technology.

MIDAS DEVELOPMENT

by Louis Kleiman

IN THIS CHAPTER

MIDAS is an acronym for Middle-Tier Distributed Application Services. It is a group of technologies that allows development of multitier applications based on open standards. Delphi has always encouraged developers to design applications that implement three (or more) logical tiers based on its separation of data access and manipulation from data presentation. In version 3, however, Delphi introduced tools that permit the *physical* separation of these tiers across a network. The benefits of implementing such an architecture are many. These benefits depend on the system requirements and the implementation strategies chosen. However, they commonly center on issues of application distribution and maintenance, code reuse among separate development teams, and client platform flexibility. The topics presented in this chapter are based on real-world development efforts and will help you design and develop successful multitier or distributed applications.

DISTRIBUTED APPLICATION BASICS

The client/server architectures of the recent past no longer meet the needs of modern applications. As the number of users increases, distributing megabytes of application and support files to each and every user's computer and configuring each and every copy of those files is far too demanding. The Web gives a vast community access to your programs, but this community may have only a modem with which to access your code. Thus, what you distribute to your users must be small and as configuration-free as possible. It is exactly this philosophy that drives the design of the Delphi distributed application development tools.

The basic parts and major components involved in a Delphi distributed application are shown in Figure 31.1. The T...Connection indicates any of the family of components that provide connections to remote data modules. Currently this list of components includes TDCOMConnection, TCorbaConnection, TSocketConnection, and TOLEEnterpriseConnection. TRemoteServer and TMidasConnection are also available but provided primarily for compatibility with applications developed using Delphi 3. The newer connection components have property names that clearly indicate their purpose and do not have to incur the overhead of any unused connection types.

Note that as multiple clients connect to a single executable application server, a *remote data module* instance is created for each client. To be more precise, a remote data module instance is created for each T...Connection instance connected to that application server. Thus, if the remote data module is multithreaded, each remote data module should contain its own TDatabase and associated TSession component. In addition, the TSession should have AutoSessionName set to True. In this way, each remote data module instance will operate safely within its own thread.

FIGURE 31.1.

*The parts of a
Delphi distributed
application.*

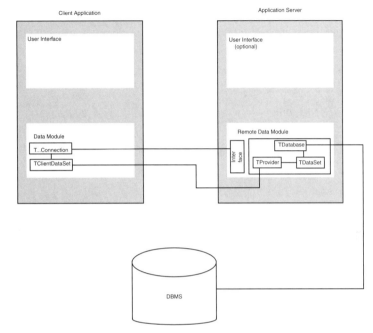

If you want to provide statistics from your application server, you can easily do so by
displaying the desired values as text or even as sophisticated graphs within the main
form of the application server. Be careful, however, to put proper threading precautions
in place when you are updating the components in the main form from the remote data
module. Also be aware that excessive time spent monitoring a process can adversely
affect the performance of that process.

A SIMPLE MIDAS APPLICATION

The Delphi documentation, online help, and demonstration programs all provide examples of simple MIDAS applications. This section explains the operation of the various
pieces of a Delphi distributed application.

Building the Application Server

In any Delphi database application, it is usually beneficial to place and configure the
data-access components prior to creating the user interface. Similarly, in a distributed
application, you should start by developing the middle tier or application server pieces.
After creating a new application, you should add a remote data module to the application
by selecting Remote Data Module from the Multitier page in the Delphi Object

Repository. You will be asked for a class name, instancing options, and a threading model for this remote data module. It is far more important that you decide on a class name correctly now than it is to decide on the instancing or threading options because the final two options can be changed easily later on, whereas the class name has many ramifications.

Our example of a simple MIDAS application is provided on the CD. Given a class name of EmployeeData and a project named AppServer, the following items will be created:

- An IDataBroker descendant interface named IEmployeeData defined in AppServer_TLB.pas (see Listing 31.1).

- A dispinterface named IEmployeeDataDisp defined in AppServer_TLB.pas (see Listing 31.1).

- A TRemoteDataModule descendant named TEmployeeData defined in rdmEmployee.pas (see Listing 31.2).

LISTING 31.1. AppServer_TLB.pas.

```
unit AppServer_TLB;

// ********************************************************************//
// WARNING                                                          //
// -------                                                          //
// The types declared in this file were generated from data read from a //
// Type Library. If this type library is explicitly or indirectly (via  //
// another type library referring to this type library) re-imported,    //
// or the 'Refresh' command of the Type Library Editor activated while  //
// editing the Type Library, the contents of this file will be          //
// regenerated and all manual modifications will be lost.               //
// ********************************************************************//


// ********************************************************************//
// HelpString: AppServer Library
// Version:    1.0
// ********************************************************************//

interface

uses Windows, ActiveX, Classes, Graphics, OleCtrls, StdVCL;

// ********************************************************************//
// GUIDS declared in the TypeLibrary. Following prefixes are used:    //
```

```
//    Type Libraries     : LIBID_xxxx                                    //
//    CoClasses          : CLSID_xxxx                                    //
//    DISPInterfaces     : DIID_xxxx                                     //
//    Non-DISP interfaces: IID_xxxx                                      //
// ********************************************************************//
const
  LIBID_AppServer: TGUID = '{621EB4E5-DE29-11D1-A88B-0060978F02D2}';
  IID_IEmployeeData: TGUID = '{621EB4E6-DE29-11D1-A88B-0060978F02D2}';
  CLASS_EmployeeData: TGUID = '{621EB4E8-DE29-11D1-A88B-0060978F02D2}';


// ********************************************************************//
// Forward declaration of interfaces defined in Type Library          //
// ********************************************************************//
type
  IEmployeeData = interface;
  IEmployeeDataDisp = dispinterface;


// ********************************************************************//
// Declaration of CoClasses defined in Type Library                   //
// (NOTE: Here we map each CoClass to it's Default Interface           //
// ********************************************************************//
  EmployeeData = IEmployeeData;

  IEmployeeData = interface(IDataBroker)
    ['{621EB4E6-DE29-11D1-A88B-0060978F02D2}']
    function Get_qryEmployee: IProvider; safecall;
    property qryEmployee: IProvider read Get_qryEmployee;
  end;

// Dispinterface declaration for dual interface IEmployeeData

  IEmployeeDataDisp = dispinterface
    ['{621EB4E6-DE29-11D1-A88B-0060978F02D2}']
    property qryEmployee: IProvider readonly dispid 1;
  end;

  CoEmployeeData = class
    class function Create: IEmployeeData;
    class function CreateRemote(const MachineName: string): IEmployeeData;
  end;

implementation

uses ComObj;
```

continues

LISTING 31.1. CONTINUED

```
class function CoEmployeeData.Create: IEmployeeData;
begin
  Result := CreateComObject(CLASS_EmployeeData) as IEmployeeData;
end;

class function CoEmployeeData.CreateRemote(const MachineName: string):
➥IEmployeeData;
begin
  Result := CreateRemoteComObject(MachineName, CLASS_EmployeeData) as
  ➥IEmployeeData;
end;

end.
```

LISTING 31.2. rdmEmployee.pas.

```
unit rdmEmployee;

interface

uses
  Windows, Messages, SysUtils, Classes, Graphics, Controls, Forms,
  Dialogs, ComServ, ComObj, VCLCom, StdVcl, BdeProv, DataBkr, DBClient,
  AppServer_TLB, DBTables, Db;

type
  TEmployeeData = class(TRemoteDataModule, IEmployeeData)
    Database1: TDatabase;
    qryEmployee: TQuery;
    Session1: TSession;
  private
    { Private declarations }
  public
    { Public declarations }
  protected
    function Get_qryEmployee: IProvider; safecall;
  end;

var
  EmployeeData: TEmployeeData;

implementation

{$R *.DFM}

function TEmployeeData.Get_qryEmployee: IProvider;
begin
```

```
    Result := qryEmployee.Provider;
end;

initialization
  TComponentFactory.Create(ComServer, TEmployeeData,
    Class_EmployeeData, ciMultiInstance, tmBoth);
end.
```

The final two parameters passed to `TComponentFactory.Create()` in the initialization section of `rdmEmployee.pas` (see Listing 32.2) reflect the instancing options and threading model you selected in the wizard. We will discuss the instancing option later in this chapter, but for now leave it set to the default `ciMultiInstance`. The threading model is a new option for Delphi 4 and should be changed with some knowledge of what its effects are.

- `Single` will create a server that operates entirely on a single thread. Thus, a request by one client will block other clients from obtaining access to the server until the first response is completed.

- `Apartment` is the threading model required by the Microsoft Transaction Server. It dictates that object methods may only be called from the thread in which the object was created. This makes server object design a bit easier because the object doesn't have to worry about serializing access to its own instance data.

- `Free` is a multithreaded model in which requests from one client do not block requests from other clients. Using free threading, a client may call any method on an object at any time from any thread. This means that the server object is responsible for serializing access to its data.

- `Both` is a combination of `Apartment` and `Free`.

After the wizard has been completed and Delphi has finished generating code, you will see what appears to be a standard data module. Looking at the code in Listing 32.2 will show you that the class declaration for this data module is different from the standard data module.

This declaration defines a descendant of `TRemoteDataModule` (which, in turn, descends from `TDataModule`) that implements the `IEmployeeData` interface defined by the wizard. You will come back to this interface later so that you can add some custom functionality to this remote data module.

You may now place a `TSession`, a `TDatabase`, and a `TQuery` component in this remote data module. As described earlier, the `TSession.AutoSessionName` should be `True`, and the `TDatabase.HandleShared` should also be set to `True`. The database component should be configured to log in to the database automatically (we will discuss security a bit later). After the query is written and tied to the database, you should also name the query component. Take great care in naming this component because you are about to export this query from the remote data module and define interface members based on its current name. This exporting is most easily accomplished by right-clicking on the query and choosing Export…from Data Module. When you select this item from the context menu, it may seem as if nothing has happened. But in fact, Delphi has made the difficult task of creating a new interface member property with an accessor method that yields the appropriate value as easy as a click of the mouse.

If you now select View | Type Library from the Delphi menu, you will see the interface you are defining for the remote data module. Drilling into this interface shows the magically created property that reflects your exported query. This property is of type IProvider. This IProvider interface is called upon by the ClientDataSet component in the client application to get data and metadata from the application server. It is also used to ship data changes from the client to the application server. The implementation of the behavior exhibited by the IProvider interface is made by a TProvider instance in the application server. This TProvider instance is either implicitly created by the data set or explicitly created by the developer dropping a TProvider or TDataSetProvider component in the remote data module.

There is no need to write code to open or close the query; this code is built into TProvider. In fact, make sure that the exported data sets are not active when you save the application server project. This will ensure that your application server wastes no time opening unneeded data sets when creating new instances of the remote data module.

Run the application server to register its type library and make it available for use to clients.

Building the Client

The client is built using traditional Delphi development techniques and only a few new components. Our example uses a data module named EmployeeDataModule. You use a new Delphi 4 component to connect this client data module to the AppServer project you built in the last section. This new component is TDCOMConnection, and it appears on the MIDAS page of the Component Palette. After you place this component in the data module, you set its ServerName property. Delphi will scan the Registry to find any known servers. If you drop down the selection list in the object inspector, you will see AppServer.EmployeeData as an option. Thus, the TDCOMConnection component provides a connection to a remote data module within an application server.

TClientDataSet is the first component displayed in the MIDAS page of the Component Palette. You drop a TClientDataSet into the data module and set its RemoteServer to the `TDCOMConnection` you just configured. The `ProviderName` property of the `TClientDataSet` is your hook into the application server's providers. Dropping down the list of providers in the Object Inspector may give a surprising result—the server launches! The reason for this is that Delphi is trying to determine the list of providers that this server has available to a client. To find this list, Delphi must fire up an instance of the server and ask it what it knows. You select `qryEmployee` to tie this `ClientDataSet` to the appropriate query in the server. If you select the `TDCOMConnection` component, you will notice that its `Connected` property is set to `True`. Setting it back to `False` will cause the server to shut down. You then place a `TDataSource` into the data module and set its `DataSet` property to the `TClientDataSet`. We won't get involved in a war over the proper placement of `TDataSource` components. Some folks think they belong in the data module, and some think they should be in the form. We say put them wherever it makes sense based on the situation at hand. In this case, we like them in the data module.

Now go back to the main form of this Client project and link it to the data module (choose File|Use Unit from the Delphi menu). You place a `TDBGrid` and a `TDBNavigator` on the form. Plug these components into the `TDataSource` just discussed. Set the `Active` property of the `TClientDataSet` to `True` and voilà. The server cranks up, gets some data from the DBMS, feeds it to the provider that sends the data to the client data set, and presto! You are a multitier developer.

Now it's time to bring this whole thing into the real world and do some master-detail relationships, some security, some custom method calls to the middle tier, and maybe a few other tricks.

Saving Your Changes

So far, you have looked at data coming from a middle tier. But if you can't put data in, you won't have anything to look at! The process of taking changes (updates, inserts, or deletes) from the client and applying them to the database is called *resolving*. When changes are made to the data in a `TClientDataSet`, a change log is created into a property called `Delta` as long as the `LogChanges` property is set to `True`. (If you use a client data set in a situation where the data will not be edited or if you don't need to keep an edit log, set `LogChanges` to `False` to conserve resources.) This `Delta` property will be sent back to the middle tier upon calling `TClientDataSet.ApplyUpdates()`. This method takes a single parameter that indicates the number of errors that will be tolerated by the application server during the resolution process. If all goes well, the provider will apply the changes to the database and the `ClientDataSet` will issue a `MergeChangeLog()`. This method basically clears out the `Delta` property and applies all the changes to the local Data image in the client data set.

> **NOTE**
>
> MergeChangeLog() is called automatically by ApplyUpdates(). Because there is no call to apply updates when you are editing local data using the client data set, you will need to call MergeChangeLog()yourself in a single-tier application.

You will commonly see the parameter for ApplyUpdates()set to -1. This indicates that the provider should stop when it encounters any error, but MergeChangeLog()will not be called if an error is raised on the middle tier or the back-end database. Thus, your Delta will remain intact, and you can try to apply the updates again after correcting any problems. If the ApplyUpdates() parameter is set to anything greater than -1, the application server will stop when the indicated number of errors has been reached, and any successfully applied rows will be removed from the change log.

If any errors are encountered, a data packet with information describing the situation surrounding the errors will be sent back by the provider. This data packet contains rows that the provider tried unsuccessfully to resolve to the database. The OnReconcileError() event will be called for each row in the error packet. You may interrogate and/or manipulate three versions of each row. These versions can be found through three different properties of the fields contained in the DataSet parameter passed to the OnReconcileError event. These properties are OldValue, NewValue, and CurValue and correspond to the field values before any editing, after editing, and the current values in the database, respectively. To determine how the error is handled, set the value of the Action parameter to any of the allowed values documented in the help for the TClientDataSet. OnReconcileError()event. It is very important that you not change the row on which the client data set is positioned.

The Delphi repository contains a form on the Dialog page that can make short work of handling this possibly complex error-handling situation. The Reconcile Error Dialog will present the user with the different row versions and ask for the appropriate action to take.

DISTRIBUTED MASTER-DETAIL RELATIONSHIPS

Prior to Delphi 4, managing master-detail relationships in a distributed environment could prove to be somewhat difficult. The reason for this difficulty revolves around the fact that the application server doesn't know exactly what is happening in the client, and master-detail relationships require that the server know the "state" of the client. In particular, if the client asks the server for detail rows, the server must know what master row the client is currently on so that the proper rows are returned. Thus, custom work had to be done to make sure that the client passed the necessary master key field values to the application server. Applying any updates, managing scrolling back to rows that had already been visited, and other buffer management issues were also tricky.

In the project group named "Master Detail" under the Chapter 31 directory on the CD accompanying this book, you will see an example of a major advance in the way that master-detail relationships are handled in a distributed environment. This advance involves a new capability of the Delphi 4 `TClientDataSet` called nested data sets. In the `MasterDetailServer`, there is a single data module (`urdmEmployee.pas`) that defines a master-detail relationship between `Employee` and `Salary_History` data by means of the typical method of a parameterized detail query whose `DataSource` property points to the data source for the master Employee query. When this basic setup has been accomplished, all that remains to be done is to export the master query from the data module. Note that the detail data set does not have to be exported.

Next you step over to the client. You have only one client data set because you have only one exported provider from the application server. However, you have two `TDataSource` components and two grids on your form in which you want to display information. How do you get data into your second data source? The beginning of the answer lies in the following line of code:

```
dsSalaryHistory.DataSet := cdsEmployeeqrySalaryHistory.NestedDataSet;
```

When the application server is constructing a data packet to send to your client, it first creates fields in the data packet for the fields in the data set being provided. It then scans through any data sets that are defined as details to the one that has been exported and creates data packets for them. This recursive process executes until all detail data sets have been read into packets. (You can control the fields and detail data sets included in the data packets by creating persistent field objects using the standard Delphi fields editor for the `TDataSet` being exported.) The detail packets are then appended to the master row to which they correspond and wrapped in a new class of field called a `TDataSetField`. Thus, you now have fields that contain entire data sets within them, and you can access this nested data set by using the `TDataSetField.NestedDataSet` property.

A few other added capabilities hook into these nested data sets. First, the `TDBGrid` has been enhanced to allow displaying a nested data set in a floating window. This window will appear when you click the Edit button for the grid column containing the nested data set. Second, there are some very sophisticated resolution capabilities that allow you to ship an entire complex of nested data set updates back to the middle tier and, magically, the updates will be made to all the appropriate tables. We will discuss updates later in this chapter.

You need to be a bit careful here. When the client asks for a master row, the application server will wrap up all of the detail rows it knows about and send the entire bundle back to the client to be displayed and/or edited. You need to ensure that by fetching a single master row you aren't implicitly gathering up thousands of detail rows (or more) and saturating the application server and/or the network. You can control when the fetching of these detail rows occurs if you put your own TProvider component into the remote data module and add poFetchDetailsOnDemand to the value of its Options property. You will also need to change the TClientDataSet.FetchOnDemand to True and use the TClientDataSet.FetchDetails method to retrieve the nested data sets.

THE BRIEFCASE MODEL: TAKE THE DATA AND RUN

Inprise often speaks of the "briefcase model" that the client data set supports. What this refers to is the ability of the client data set to stream its data to/from disk while you are disconnected from the original source of the data using the SaveToFile() and LoadFromFile() methods. This ability even applies to nested details. This means that in a single data file you can now store as many data sets as you want. And because fewer distribution files usually means fewer maintenance headaches, this may be a beneficial side effect of nested data sets. It should be noted here that the field and index definitions for a client data set can now be made persistent through the StoreDefs property. If this property is set to True and the client data set has been opened and hooked up to a provider at design time, the field and index definitions will be stored in the DFM file containing the client data set. Thus, creating an empty TClientDataSet at runtime involves nothing more than a call to the CreateDataSet() method. If StoreDefs is False, you must create the field and index definitions manually before calling CreateDataSet.

The ability of the client data set to stream data to and from disk means that it can be used as a lightweight database any time one is needed. Lookup tables, user-specific data, and simple database applications are all applications that lend themselves to this small, fast, and flexible data storage mechanism. Although it does not support SQL or multiuser access, the client data set does implement filters, indices, calculated fields, BLOBs, master-detail relationships, and an expression-based aggregation mechanism. At less than 200KB, the dbclient.dll support file that it requires represents a small price to pay for a lot of useful functionality. Chapter 33, "Client Tracker: MIDAS Development," presents a sample application that makes use of the briefcase model.

CONNECTION POOLING: ONE SOLUTION FOR A FEW PROBLEMS

In the world of distributed database applications, "connection pooling" is a buzzword that is little understood, but often asked for. This section presents a connection-pooling mechanism and analyzes its pros and cons in different situations. The work presented here comes straight from the keyboard of Josh Dahlby. Josh is one of the great minds behind the MIDAS architecture and an invaluable member of the Delphi R&D team.

The term "connection pooling" refers to the creation of a pool of database connections created by an application server. The size of this pool can be controlled so as to limit the growth of a variety of resources. These resources include not only database connections (which may each cost a set amount of money depending on the licensing arrangement with the database vendor), but also application server memory, processor utilization, and others, depending on the application. So really, connection pooling is a specific form of the more general *resource* pooling.

The general idea behind any such resource pooling is to make the server appear bigger than it actually is by allowing a single resource to serve more than one client. A typical MIDAS application will progress through three phases as it runs. First, the client will ask the application server for data. Second, the client will, with or without user intervention, process that data. Third, the client will call upon the server to resolve the manipulated data to the DBMS. During the second phase, you have an obvious opportunity to let the application server switch to serving another client while the original client performs work on its own. You must be careful, though. The original client must not expect that the application server be in the same state in which it was left when a second service request is made. This lack of assumption of state is called *stateless operation*. A stateless interaction between client and server is completely self-describing. It contains all the information necessary to completely perform the requested operation.

Unfortunately, stateless operation is not the norm in a MIDAS application. When a client data set is tied to a provider through its `ProviderName` property, it will fetch rows from the provider in increments specified by the `PacketRows` property of `TClientDataSet`. If the user asks to see a row that the client has not yet fetched, data packet requests will be made of the provider until the client need is fulfilled. These requests for subsequent packets do not include any information that tells the application server what row to start sending. They assume that the data set giving data to the provider has a cursor positioned in the proper place. Thus, any manipulation of that cursor position will cause the client data set to fetch a packet that is out of sequence. So, while you are relying on that cursor position, you cannot let another client use your server resource.

The resolving process is, by design, stateless. So most of the issues surrounding stated operations relate to the example illustrated earlier. You have two options to solve the stated fetching problem. You can either get all of the data in your first request, or you can lock other clients out of your resource until you are done.

It's time to look at a pooling mechanism and discuss how to combat these problems.

The Pooler example in the Chapter 31 directory on the CD accompanying this book shows a wonderful way in which pooling can be implemented. The pooler object itself is defined in `Pooler.pas` (see Listing 31.3).

LISTING 31.3. `Pooler.pas`—`TPooler`.

```
unit Pooler;

interface

uses
  ComObj, ActiveX, Server_TLB, Classes, SyncObjs, Windows;

type
  TPooler = class(TAutoObject, IPooledRDM)
  protected
    { IDataBroker }
    function GetProviderNames: OleVariant; safecall;
    { IPooledRDM }
    function Select(const SQLStr: WideString) : OleVariant; safecall;

    function LockRDM: IPooledRDM;
    procedure UnlockRDM(Value: IPooledRDM);
  end;

  TPoolManager = class(TObject)
  private
    FRDMList: TList;
    FMaxCount: Integer;
    FTimeout: Integer;
    FCriticalSection: TCriticalSection;
    FSemaphore: THandle;

    function GetLock(Index: Integer): Boolean;
    procedure ReleaseLock(Index: Integer; var Value: IPooledRDM);
    function CreateNewInstance: IPooledRDM;
  public
    constructor Create;
    destructor Destroy; override;
    function LockRDM: IPooledRDM;
    procedure UnlockRDM(var Value: IPooledRDM);
```

```
    property Timeout: Integer read FTimeout;
    property MaxCount: Integer read FMaxCount;
  end;

  PRDM = ^TRDM;
  TRDM = record
    Intf: IPooledRDM;
    InUse: Boolean;
  end;

var
  PoolManager: TPoolManager;

implementation

uses ComServ, SrvrDM, SysUtils, ThrddCF;

constructor TPoolManager.Create;
begin
  FRDMList := TList.Create;
  FCriticalSection := TCriticalSection.Create;
  FTimeout := 5000;
  FMaxCount := 2;
  FSemaphore := CreateSemaphore(nil, FMaxCount, FMaxCount, nil);
end;

destructor TPoolManager.Destroy;
var
  i: Integer;
begin
  FCriticalSection.Free;
  for i := 0 to FRDMList.Count - 1 do
  begin
    PRDM(FRDMList[i]).Intf := nil;
    FreeMem(PRDM(FRDMList[i]));
  end;
  FRDMList.Free;
  CloseHandle(FSemaphore);
  inherited Destroy;
end;

function TPoolManager.GetLock(Index: Integer): Boolean;
begin
  FCriticalSection.Enter;
  try
    Result := not PRDM(FRDMList[Index]).InUse;
    if Result then
      PRDM(FRDMList[Index]).InUse := True;
```

continues

LISTING 31.3. CONTINUED

```
  finally
    FCriticalSection.Leave;
  end;
end;

procedure TPoolManager.ReleaseLock(Index: Integer; var Value: IPooledRDM);
begin
  FCriticalSection.Enter;
  try
    PRDM(FRDMList[Index]).InUse := False;
    Value := nil;
    ReleaseSemaphore(FSemaphore, 1, nil);
  finally
    FCriticalSection.Leave;
  end;
end;

function TPoolManager.CreateNewInstance: IPooledRDM;
var
  p: PRDM;
begin
  FCriticalSection.Enter;
  try
    New(p);
    p.Intf := RDMFactory.CreateComObject(nil) as IPooledRDM;
    p.InUse := True;
    FRDMList.Add(p);
    Result := p.Intf;
  finally
    FCriticalSection.Leave;
  end;
end;

function TPoolManager.LockRDM: IPooledRDM;
var
  i: Integer;
begin
  Result := nil;
  if WaitForSingleObject(FSemaphore, Timeout) = WAIT_FAILED then
    raise Exception.Create('Server too busy');
  for i := 0 to FRDMList.Count - 1 do
  begin
    if GetLock(i) then
    begin
      Result := PRDM(FRDMList[i]).Intf;
      Exit;
    end;
  end;
  if FRDMList.Count < MaxCount then
```

```
      Result := CreateNewInstance;
    if Result = nil then { This shouldn't happen because of the sempahore
                          locks }
      raise Exception.Create('Unable to lock RDM');
  end;

procedure TPoolManager.UnlockRDM(var Value: IPooledRDM);
var
  i: Integer;
begin
  for i := 0 to FRDMList.Count - 1 do
  begin
    if Value = PRDM(FRDMList[i]).Intf then
    begin
      ReleaseLock(i, Value);
      break;
    end;
  end;
end;

function TPooler.GetProviderNames: OleVariant;
var
  TestValet: IPooledRDM;
begin
  TestValet := LockRDM;
  try
    Result := TestValet.GetProviderNames;
  finally
    UnlockRDM(TestValet);
  end;
end;

function TPooler.Select(const SQLStr: WideString) : OleVariant;
var
  RDM: IPooledRDM;
begin
  RDM := LockRDM;
  try
    Result := RDM.Select(SQLStr);
  finally
    UnlockRDM(RDM);
  end;
end;

function TPooler.LockRDM: IPooledRDM;
begin
  Result := PoolManager.LockRDM;
end;
```

continues

LISTING 31.3. CONTINUED

```
procedure TPooler.UnlockRDM(Value: IPooledRDM);
begin
  PoolManager.UnlockRDM(Value);
end;

initialization
  PoolManager := TPoolManager.Create;
  TThreadedAutoObjectFactory.Create(ComServer, TPooler, Class_Pooler,
  ➥ciMultiInstance);
finalization
  PoolManager.Free;
end.
```

TPooler descends from TAutoObject and implements the interface of the remote data module. This means that it looks to the outside world as if the Pooler object were a remote data module, but, in fact, it is an empty shell that forwards any requests it receives to a real remote data module. The Pooler object uses a PoolManager to maintain a list of remote data modules that only it knows about. When a request comes in, the pooler finds an idle data module in the list, or creates one if it is within its resource bounds (set by the TPoolManager.Create() constructor to a value of 2), or raises an exception indicating it is too busy. It locks a remote data module by setting the InUse flag, passes the request to the remote data module, and unlocks the entry in the list.

The beauty of this design (thanks to Josh) is that neither the client nor the remote data module knows anything about the presence of a pooler except for the fact that the client maintains a stateless relationship with the application server. The client requesting all the rows for its client data set in a single operation accomplishes this stateless relationship. Although this example uses a custom method to perform its data requests, the same result could be implemented by means of a client data set whose PacketRecords property is set to –1.

You'll find a sample client (Client.dpr) and server (Server.dpr) on the CD under Ch31 that demonstrates the use of the TPooler object.

INSTANCING: HOW MANY SERVERS WOULD YOU LIKE?

We spoke earlier about the instancing option you are allowed to choose in the wizard that creates a remote data module. Because the pooler utilizes a nonstandard value for this option, we will discuss the implications of the different instancing choices here.

The instancing choice you make will affect the call that creates the COM object factory for your application server. There are three valid choices: ciInternal, ciSingleInstance, and ciMultiInstance. The default is ciMultiInstance because the default modus operandi for a MIDAS application server is to create a new remote data module instance for each client connection, and that is how a factory initialized using this value operates. The ciSingleInstance option creates one instance for all incoming connections to share. This implementation can be useful in situations where a single middle-tier instance is holding data that many clients should be sharing. An invoice number generator, for example, could be implemented using a factory operating in ciSingleInstance mode. The pooler uses ciInternal instancing for the remote data module because the outside world does not see the remote data modules directly. These remote data modules are only visible inside the COM server.

CALLBACKS: THE CLIENT IS NOW A SERVER

Here again, we must give credit where it is due. Much of the groundwork for this section comes from work done by Tom Stickle, a member of the outstanding Inprise Field Systems Engineering team. Tom created the notification example included here, which provides a base upon which the other examples are built.

If you are familiar with a Windows callback, you already understand the basic concept we are discussing here. But the mechanism we use to implement callbacks goes far beyond the basic function callbacks used by Windows. Our callbacks are callback *interfaces*. By registering an interface to an object in your client with your server, you give the server the information it needs to implement a callback to the client. A callback is a mechanism by which your server can ask the client to provide information or perform a task. Because our callbacks are based on interfaces, we have the ability to call functions as well as to interrogate and manipulate property values on the client from our server.

Listings 31.4 and 31.5 illustrate the two sides of a callback mechanism. The entire working example can be found in the CD directory for this chapter.

LISTING 31.4. CLIENT CODE TO REGISTER AND UNREGISTER A CALLBACK INTERFACE.

```
TAClient = class(TForm)
    MIDASConnection1: TMIDASConnection;
    Edit1: TEdit;
    procedure FormCreate(Sender: TObject);
    procedure FormDestroy(Sender: TObject);
  private
    ANotification: IANotification;
...
```

continues

LISTING 31.4. CONTINUED

```
procedure TAClient.FormCreate(Sender: TObject);
begin
  ANotification := TANotification.Create;
  MidasConnection1.Connected := True;
  MidasConnection1.AppServer.AddNotify(ANotification);
end;

procedure TAClient.FormDestroy(Sender: TObject);
begin
  MidasConnection1.AppServer.RemoveNotify(ANotification);
end;
```

LISTING 31.5. SERVER CODE TO REGISTER, UNREGISTER, AND CALL A CLIENT INTERFACE.

```
var
  NotifyServer: TNotifyServer;
  InterfaceList : TList;

procedure TNotifyServer.AddNotify(Intf: IDispatch);
begin
  InterfaceList.Add(Pointer(Intf));
  Intf._AddRef;     { Prevent it from auto-releasing }
end;

procedure TNotifyServer.RemoveNotify(Intf: IDispatch);
begin
  InterfaceList.Remove(Pointer(Intf));
  Intf._Release;    { Garbage Collection }
end;

procedure TNotifyServer.NotifyAll(const Msg: WideString);
var
  I : Integer;
  AVariant: OleVariant;
begin
  if not Assigned(InterfaceList) then Exit;
  for I := 0 to InterfaceList.count - 1 do
    begin
      AVariant := (IDispatch(InterfaceList[I]));
      AVariant.Notify(Msg);
    end;
end;
```

Registering an interface refers to the process of creating an interface class on the client and passing it to a function on the server. In Listing 31.4, the call to AddNotify() in the client's FormCreate() demonstrates how easy it can be to register a callback interface with a remote object. This function on the server accepts the interface to the client and saves it in a TList to be used later. In Listing 31.5, the server is building a list of clients that want to be notified when an event occurs on the application server (see the implementation of AddNotify() in Listing 31.5). When the server wants the client to perform some action, all that needs to be done is to invoke the call on the interface as if it were the remote object. This call is shown in the body of the for loop in the implementation of the server's AddNotify() procedure. When the client wants to remove the possibility of being touched by means of a callback, it needs to ask the server to remove its interface from the list of notifications. In this case, our client asks that it be unregistered when the client form is destroyed.

All that you need to do now is to create this interface in your client. You start the process of enabling your client to accept callbacks by adding a new OLE Automation object to the client project by choosing File|New, choosing the ActiveX page of the gallery, and choosing Automation Object. The one-screen wizard that appears asks questions similar to the ones the Remote Data Module wizard asked earlier, but you are going to choose different responses this time because the rules are different. The instancing type you are going to use this time is Internal. Objects created using Internal instancing cannot be created at the request of another process. Because you will be controlling when the interface object is created, and you will be passing this interface to a remote object, the Internal model fits well. Single threading will work just fine because your notification load will be light. If you opt to make a multithreaded client that will respond to multiple callbacks at the same time, remember to use proper threading protection mechanisms when dealing with calls to VCL components.

You now have a client with an OLE Automation server inside it, but that server has an empty interface. Use the Type Library Editor that Delphi presents you after running the wizard (or use View|Type Library) to add one method to this interface. This method is called Notify() in the preceding example, and it takes a single input parameter of type WideString. This interface now gives a remote process the capability to call the client as if it were a server. The possible uses for this architecture are many—from security, to event notification and broadcasting, to any other situation in which a server needs to control or interrogate a client. Although this callback mechanism was only supported using DCOM and OLE Enterprise in Delphi 3, Delphi 4 adds callback support for the socket server running over plain TCP/IP.

SECURITY

Security means many different things to different application developers. In a distributed database application, security can take on even more meanings than just the data and user interface restrictions you put on applications of the recent past. Now you may, in fact, want to put in place object-level security with the possibility of granting access on a method or attribute level to the various objects within the system. This section discusses the database security issues that surround the techniques presented to this point.

In the simple MIDAS application presented at the beginning of this chapter, if you do not provide a username and password to the application server, that server will ask you for the information to log in to the database when the client first asks for data. Because it is probable that the client application is far away from the application, this presents a bad situation. When you try to start up your client, a dialog box appears on a server that is sitting in a closet somewhere asking you for a username and password.

The TDCOMConnection component has a shell of a login process that is described in the Delphi help for TDispatchConnection.LoginPrompt. This shell does provide a sequence of events and a login dialog into which the user can enter the appropriate information. It does not, however, provide a mechanism to get this user information to the application server. Because we have already edited a few type libraries, we will leave it to you to build an interface member(s) that permits you to pass the login information to the application server. The appropriate code that uses these interface members should be written into the OnLogin event for the TRemoteServer descendant.

There is an alternative to the client's proactively pushing this login information to the application server, though. If the client defines an interface that provides login information, this interface may be used by the server as a callback using the techniques just discussed. In this way, the server may challenge the client for user information only when necessary, no state is presumed by the client or server, and the security model is controlled in great part by the application server. This leads to a more flexible security implementation, and one that can operate with a variety of application server implementations including the pooler presented earlier.

SUMMARY

In this chapter, we have shown how the Delphi client/server components interact to provide distributed application development. We have also shown some atypical uses and architectures for these components. But we have in no way exhausted the uses for this technology. Open your mind to a vision of objects that are all clients to and servers for each other—a software system composed of objects all cooperating to solve the problem at hand. Once again, Delphi has raised the roof on what we as software developers can do.

When the software development world moved to objects, developers realized that up-front software design had become much more critical than in the days of procedural coding. Now that the move to distributed objects is underway, we as developers must realize that failing to perform extensive analysis and design will doom a project that intends to implement a distributed architecture.

Distributed application development is the future of software. The tools that Delphi provides bring this complex and powerful development paradigm to the world of Rapid Application Development (RAD). But there is a danger here that RAD can start to stand for *Rushed* Application Development. You need to make sure that you think about how the objects in a system are going to interact, how they will react to changes, and how they will be maintained and deployed.

The distributed application development tools that Delphi provides give you great power and flexibility. Just remember that with power must come responsibility.

RAPID DATABASE APPLICATION DEVELOPMENT

PART V

INVENTORY MANAGER: CLIENT/SERVER DEVELOPMENT

IN THIS CHAPTER

This chapter illustrates how to design a database application using the concepts discussed in Chapter 28, "Developing Client/Server Applications." Here, we illustrate techniques for developing a two-tier client/server application. In this application we've divided up the application logic, or business rules, between both the client and the server. We also illustrate how to centralize data access in a data module, thus allowing us to completely separate the user interface from the database logic.

In Chapter 4, "Application Frameworks and Design Concepts," we introduced you to a framework for forms that could be created independently or as child windows to another control. In this chapter, we use that framework for our user interface.

The database back end used is Local InterBase. The application is designed around a typical auto-parts business model. This business model requires the application to keep track of three primary sets of data:

Product Inventory	This includes the quantities of each item in the inventory and how much each item is worth.
Sales	This set contains information on items sold and to which customer these items were sold.
Customer	This set contains information such as name and address.

This is by no means a full-blown inventory manager application. The purpose of this chapter is to focus on the techniques of client/server development. We've provided a complete working application to illustrate that focus.

The chapter is divided into three parts. The first part, "Designing the Back End," discusses the design of the back end. This includes the database objects you learned about in Chapter 28. The second part, "Centralizing Database Access—The Business Rules," discusses how to use Delphi's TDataModule to centralize database access. Finally, the third part, "Designing the User Interface," discusses the design of the actual user interface for the inventory application.

CLIENT TRACKER: MIDAS DEVELOPMENT

IN THIS CHAPTER

In Chapter 32, "Inventory Manager: Client/Server Development," we discussed techniques for developing two-tier applications. In this chapter, we'll create a three-tier application using the MIDAS technology presented in Chapter 31, "MIDAS Development." The focus of this chapter is to illustrate the simplicity of using the MIDAS components as well as the briefcase model for offsite work.

The application we'll develop lends itself to the briefcase model. This application is a client tracker or manager. Often, sales reps perform much of their work offsite, possibly travelling to several different locations. The client list that these sales reps work with might be critical to both the reps and their parent company. Therefore, this client information should probably reside at the company site. How, then, can the sales rep make use of this data without having to rely on a network connection? Also, how can the sales rep update the company data with newer information that he or she is likely to get at the client's site?

TClientDataSet makes it possible to create briefcase applications with its implementation of *internal caching*. This allows the sales reps to download the data or even a subset of the data with which they can work offsite. Later, when they return to home base, they can upload any changes made to the database. In this chapter, we'll build a simple client management tool that illustrates this approach to building briefcase applications.

DESIGNING THE SERVER APPLICATION

The server application is designed using the same procedure discussed in Chapter 31. Here, you'll see our TRemoteDataModule, CustomerRemoteDataModule, containing TSession, TDataBase, and TQuery components. The TSession component, ssnCust, is provided to handle multi-instancing issues (its AutoSessionName property is set to True). DbCust, the TDataBase component, provides the client connection to the database and prevents the login dialog from displaying. QryCust, the TQuery component, returns the result set to the client table. We use the same Customer table presented in the last chapter.

Listing 33.1 shows the source code for the remote data module.

LISTING 33.1. CustRDM.pas—CustomerRemoteDataModule.

```
unit CustRDM;

interface

uses
  Windows, Messages, SysUtils, Classes, Graphics, Controls, Forms,
  Dialogs, ComServ, ComObj, VCLCom, StdVcl, BdeProv, DataBkr, DBClient,
  CustServ_TLB, Db, DBTables;
```

```
type

  TFilterType = (ftNone, ftCity, ftState);

  TCustomerRemoteDataModule = class(TRemoteDataModule,
      ICustomerRemoteDataModule)
    ssnCust: TSession;
    dbCust: TDatabase;
    qryCust: TQuery;
  private
    FFilterStr: String;
    FFilterType: TFilterType;
  public
    { Public declarations }
  protected
    function Get_qryCust: IProvider; safecall;
    procedure FilterByCity(const ACity: WideString; out Data: OleVariant);
      safecall;
    procedure FilterByState(const AStateStr: WideString; out Data:
        OleVariant); safecall;
    procedure NoFilter(out Data: OleVariant); safecall;
  end;

var
  CustomerRemoteDataModule: TCustomerRemoteDataModule;

implementation

{$R *.DFM}

function TCustomerRemoteDataModule.Get_qryCust: IProvider;
begin
  Result := qryCust.Provider;
end;

procedure TCustomerRemoteDataModule.FilterByCity(const ACity: WideString;
  out Data: OleVariant);
begin
  FFilterType  := ftCity;
  FFilterStr   := ACity;
  qryCust.Close;
  qryCust.SQL.Clear;
  qryCust.SQL.Add(Format('select * from CUSTOMER where CITY = "%s"',
  ➥[ACity]));
  qryCust.Open;
  Data := qryCust.Provider.Data;
end;
```

continues

LISTING 33.1. CONTINUED

```
procedure TCustomerRemoteDataModule.FilterByState(
  const AStateStr: WideString; out Data: OleVariant);
begin
  FFilterType  := ftState;
  FFilterStr   := AStateStr;
  qryCust.Close;
  qryCust.SQL.Clear;
  qryCust.SQL.Add(Format('select * from CUSTOMER where STATE = "%s"',
    [AStateStr]));
  qryCust.Open;
  Data := qryCust.Provider.Data;
end;

procedure TCustomerRemoteDataModule.NoFilter(out Data: OleVariant);
begin
  FFiltertype := ftNone;
  qryCust.Close;
  qryCust.SQL.Clear;
  qryCust.SQL.Add('select * from CUSTOMER');
  qryCust.Open;
  Data := qryCust.Provider.Data;
end;

initialization
  TComponentFactory.Create(ComServer, TCustomerRemoteDataModule,
    Class_CustomerRemoteDataModule, ciMultiInstance, tmSingle);
end.
```

Listing 33.1 shows three methods that were added to TCustomerDataModule. These methods were actually added to the interface ICustomerRemoteDateModule through the Type Library Editor, which in turn created the implementation methods for the TCustomerRemoteDataModule class (see Figure 33.1). In the Type Library Editor, we defined the methods and their parameters and then added the code to each implementation method created by Delphi. You can examine the source code for the type library in the file CustServ_TLB.pas.

The methods FilterByCity() and FilterByState() are used to allow the client to download a subset of the entire table. This makes sense because it might not be necessary to download the entire client list when the sales rep is traveling to a single location. Both of these methods take a string parameter that's used to specify the filter value. NoFilter() removes any filtering applied to the table.

These methods cause server-side filtering in that they provide a way to limit the records returned to the client. Alternatively, the user may want to perform filtering on the client side. That is, the sales rep may want to access the entire result set but have the ability to filter out desired records as needed. We'll illustrate both techniques.

FIGURE 33.1.

The Type Library Editor.

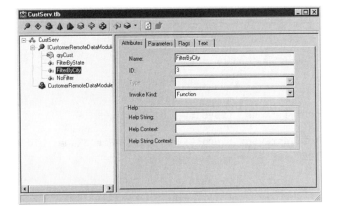

DESIGNING THE CLIENT APPLICATION

The client application contains a data module and a main form. We'll discuss the data module first.

Client Data Module

The data module for the Client Tracker application illustrates several techniques. First, it illustrates how to implement the briefcase model. Second, it shows how to make its mode (online/offline) persistent. In other words, when the user shuts down the application, it will recall its state when executed again. This prevents the application from attempting to attach to the server when the client is running it offline. We also illustrate how to perform client-side filtering. When the user is online, the application performs server-side filtering. When the user is offline, filtering is performed on the client end. Listing 33.2 shows the source code for `CustomerDataModule`.

LISTING 33.2. `CustDM.pas`—`CustomerDataModule`.

```
unit CustDM;

interface

uses
  Windows, Messages, SysUtils, Classes, Graphics, Controls, Forms,
    Dialogs, DBClient, MConnect, Db;

const
  cFileName        = 'CustData.cds';
```

continues

LISTING 33.2. CONTINUED

```
cRegIniFile      = 'Software\DDG Client App';
cRegSection      = 'Startup Config';
cRegOnlineIdent  = 'Run Online';

type

  TFilterType = (ftNone, ftByCity, ftByState);

  TAddErrorToClientEvent = procedure(const AFieldName, OldStr, NewStr,
    CurStr, ErrMsg: String) of Object;


  TCustomerDataModule = class(TDataModule)
    cdsCust: TClientDataSet;
    dcomCust: TDCOMConnection;
    cdsCustCUSTOMER_ID: TIntegerField;
    cdsCustFNAME: TStringField;
    cdsCustLNAME: TStringField;
    cdsCustCREDIT_LINE: TSmallintField;
    cdsCustWORK_ADDRESS: TStringField;
    cdsCustALT_ADDRESS: TStringField;
    cdsCustCITY: TStringField;
    cdsCustSTATE: TStringField;
    cdsCustZIP: TStringField;
    cdsCustWORK_PHONE: TStringField;
    cdsCustALT_PHONE: TStringField;
    cdsCustCOMMENTS: TMemoField;
    cdsCustCOMPANY: TStringField;
    procedure CustomerDataModuleCreate(Sender: TObject);
    procedure cdsCustReconcileError(DataSet: TClientDataSet;
      E: EReconcileError; UpdateKind: TUpdateKind;
      var Action: TReconcileAction);
    procedure CustomerDataModuleDestroy(Sender: TObject);
    procedure cdsCustFilterRecord(DataSet: TDataSet; var Accept: Boolean);
  private
    FFilterType: TFilterType;
    FFilterStr: String;
    FOnAddErrorToClient: TAddErrorToClientEvent;

    function GetOnline: Boolean;
    procedure SetOnline(const Value: Boolean);
    { Private declarations }
  protected
    function GetChangeCount: Integer;

  public
    procedure EditClient;
    procedure AddClient;
    procedure SaveClient;
```

```
        procedure CancelClient;
        procedure DeleteClient;
        procedure ApplyUpdates;
        procedure CancelUpdates;
        procedure First;
        procedure Previous;
        procedure Next;
        procedure Last;
        function IsBOF: Boolean;
        function IsEOF: Boolean;

        procedure FilterByState;
        procedure FilterByCity;
        procedure NoFilter;

        property ChangeCount: Integer read GetChangeCount;
        property Online: Boolean read GetOnline write SetOnline;

        property OnAddErrorToClient: TAddErrorToClientEvent
            read FOnAddErrorToClient
          write FOnAddErrorToClient;

    end;

var
  CustomerDataModule: TCustomerDataModule;

implementation
uses MainCustFrm, Registry;

{$R *.DFM}

procedure TCustomerDataModule.AddClient;
begin
  cdsCust.Insert;
end;

procedure TCustomerDataModule.ApplyUpdates;
begin
  cdsCust.ApplyUpdates(-1);
end;

procedure TCustomerDataModule.CancelClient;
begin
  cdsCust.Cancel;
end;

procedure TCustomerDataModule.CancelUpdates;
begin
  cdsCust.CancelUpdates;
end;
```

continues

LISTING 33.2. CONTINUED

```
procedure TCustomerDataModule.DeleteClient;
begin
  if MessageDlg('Are you sure you want to delete the current record?',
  mtConfirmation, [mbYes, mbNo], 0) = mrYes then
      cdsCust.Delete;
end;

procedure TCustomerDataModule.EditClient;
begin
  cdsCust.Edit;
end;

function TCustomerDataModule.IsBOF: Boolean;
begin
  Result := cdsCust.Bof;
end;

function TCustomerDataModule.IsEOF: Boolean;
begin
  Result := cdsCust.Eof;
end;

procedure TCustomerDataModule.First;
begin
  cdsCust.First;
end;

procedure TCustomerDataModule.Last;
begin
  cdsCust.Last;
end;

procedure TCustomerDataModule.Next;
begin
  cdsCust.Next;
end;

procedure TCustomerDataModule.Previous;
begin
  cdsCust.Prior;
end;

procedure TCustomerDataModule.SaveClient;
begin
  cdsCust.Post;
end;

procedure TCustomerDataModule.cdsCustReconcileError(
  DataSet: TClientDataSet; E: EReconcileError; UpdateKind: TUpdateKind;
  var Action: TReconcileAction);
```

```
{ If an error occurs, update the appropriate TListview on the main form
  with the error data.  }
var
  CurStr, NewStr, OldStr: String;
  i: integer;
  V: Variant;

procedure SetString(V: Variant; var S: String);
{ We must test for a null value on V, which would be returned if the
  table field was null. This is necessary because we can't typcast null
  as a string. }
begin

  if VarIsNull(V) then
    S := EmptyStr
  else
    S := String(V);
end;


begin
  for i := 0 to DataSet.FieldCount - 1 do
  begin

    V := DataSet.Fields[i].NewValue;
    SetString(V, NewStr);

    V := DataSet.Fields[i].CurValue;
    SetString(V, CurStr);

    V := DataSet.Fields[i].OldValue;
    SetString(V, OldStr);

    if NewStr <> CurStr then
      if Assigned(FOnAddErrorToClient) then
        FOnAddErrorToClient(DataSet.Fields[i].FieldName, OldStr, NewStr,
        CurStr, E.Message)
  end;
  //Update record and remove changes from the change log.
  Action := raRefresh;
end;

function TCustomerDataModule.GetChangeCount: Integer;
begin
  Result := cdsCust.ChangeCount;
end;

function TCustomerDataModule.GetOnline: Boolean;
begin
  Result := dcomCust.Connected;
end;
```

continues

LISTING 33.2. CONTINUED

```
procedure TCustomerDataModule.SetOnline(const Value: Boolean);
{ It seems to me that the result set from the server
  should take precedence over what's in file referred to by
  FileName. }
begin

  if Value = True then
  begin
    dcomCust.Connected := True;

    if cdsCust.ChangeCount > 0 then begin
      ShowMessage('Your changes must be applied before going online');
      cdsCust.ApplyUpdates(-1);
    end;
    cdsCust.Refresh;

  end
  else begin
    cdsCust.FileName := cFileName;
    dcomCust.Connected := False;
  end;
end;

procedure TCustomerDataModule.CustomerDataModuleCreate(Sender: TObject);
{ Determine if the user last left the application online or offline and
  re-launch the application in that same mode. }
var
  RegIniFile: TRegIniFile;
  IsOnline: Boolean;
begin
  RegIniFile := TRegIniFile.Create(cRegIniFile);
  try
    IsOnline := RegIniFile.ReadBool(cRegSection, cRegOnlineIdent, True);
  finally
    RegIniFile.Free;
  end;

  if IsOnline then
  begin
    dcomCust.Connected := True;
    cdsCust.Open;
  end
  else begin
    cdsCust.FileName := cFileName;
    cdsCust.Open;
  end;

end;
```

```pascal
procedure TCustomerDataModule.CustomerDataModuleDestroy(Sender: TObject);
{ Save the online/offline status of the application to the registry. When
  the user runs the application again, it will launch as it was last
  brought down. }
var
  RegIniFile: TRegIniFile;
begin
  RegIniFile := TRegIniFile.Create(cRegIniFile);
  try
    RegIniFile.WriteBool(cRegSection, cRegOnlineIdent, Online);
  finally
    RegIniFile.Free;
  end;
end;

procedure TCustomerDataModule.FilterByCity;
{ If we're online, let the server apply the filter so that we retrieve
  only the records we want. Otherwise, apply the filter to the
  in-memory result set of cdsCust. }
var
  CityStr: String;
  Data: OleVariant;
begin
  InputQuery('Filter on City', 'Enter City: ', CityStr);
  FFilterStr := CityStr;

  if Online then
  begin
    dcomCust.AppServer.FilterByCity(CityStr, Data);

//    cdsCust.Data := Data;
    cdsCust.Refresh;
  end
  else begin
    FFilterType     := ftByCity;
    cdsCust.Filtered := True;
    cdsCust.Refresh;
  end;
end;

procedure TCustomerDataModule.FilterByState;
{ If we're online, let the server apply the filter so that we
  retrieve only the records we want. Otherwise, apply the filter to the
  in-memory result set of cdsCust. }
var
  StateStr: String;
  Data: OleVariant;
```

continues

LISTING 33.2. CONTINUED

```
begin
  InputQuery('Filter on State', 'Enter State: ', StateStr);
  FFilterStr := StateStr;

  if Online then
  begin
    dcomCust.AppServer.FilterByState(StateStr, Data);

//    cdsCust.Data := Data;
    cdsCust.Refresh;
  end
  else begin
    FFilterType      := ftByState;
    cdsCust.Filtered := True;
    cdsCust.Refresh;
  end;
end;

procedure TCustomerDataModule.NoFilter;
{ If we're online, let the server apply the filter so that we retrieve
  only the records we want. Otherwise, apply the filter to the
  in-memory result set of cdsCust. }
var
  Data: OleVariant;
begin

  if Online then
  begin
    dcomCust.AppServer.NoFilter(Data);

//    cdsCust.Data := Data;
    cdsCust.Refresh;
  end
  else begin
    FFilterType      := ftNone;
    cdsCust.Filtered := False;
    cdsCust.Refresh;
  end;
end;

procedure TCustomerDataModule.cdsCustFilterRecord(DataSet: TDataSet;
  var Accept: Boolean);
```

```
begin
  case FFilterType of
    ftByCity:  Accept := DataSet.FieldByName('CITY').AsString =
    ➡FFilterStr;
    ftByState: Accept := DataSet.FieldByName('STATE').AsString =
    ➡FFilterStr;
    ftNone:  Accept := True;
  end;
end;

end.
```

Initial Wiring

Most of the methods you see in Listing 33.2 are simple methods that perform navigation or manipulation on the client data set, cdsCust. Notice that we provide a method on the data module to expose an operation on cdsCust rather than to allow any forms to access it directly. Here, we're just adhering to strict OOP methodologies. Although this isn't necessary in Delphi, we do so for consistency and to enforce centralization of database logic.

CustomerDataModule contains a TDCOMConnection, dcomCust, and the TClientDataSet, cdsCust. DcomCust is connected to the server application through its ServerName property, which is set to CustServ.CustomerRemoteDataModule.

CdsCust is linked to qryCust on the remote data module in its ProviderName property. That takes care of the wiring necessary to get a MIDAS application's server and client up and running. However, to get the most out of this technology, some code needs to be written.

Error Reconciliation

After the client application passes changes back to the server, errors may occur (especially in the briefcase model, where it's possible that another user has modified a given record). The error can be handled on the server or on the client. If it's handled on the client, the server passes error information back to the client through the OnReconcileError handler of TClientDataSet. In this event handler, several options are available that we'll discuss momentarily. The OnReconcileError property refers to a TReconcileErrorEvent method, which is defined as follows:

```
TReconcileErrorEvent = procedure(DataSet: TClientDataSet; E:
➡EReconcileError; UpdateKind: TUpdateKind; var Action: TReconcileAction)
➡of object;
```

The DataSet parameter refers to the data set on which the error occurred.

EReconcileError is an exception class for client data set errors. You can use this class as you would any exception class. UpdateKind can be any of the values specified in Table 33.1. This information comes from Delphi's online help.

TABLE 33.1. THE TUpdateKind VALUES.

TUpdateKind *Value*	*Meaning*
ukModify	The cached update to the record is a modification to the record's contents.
ukInsert	The cached update is the insertion of a new record.
ukDelete	The cached update is the deletion of a record.

The Action parameter is of type TReconcileAction. By setting the Action parameter to raRefresh, the client application cancels any changes made by the user and refreshes its copy of the result so that it's the same as the server's copy. This is what is done in the example. Other options for the Action property may be set to those shown in Table 33.2, which comes from Delphi's online help (where you can also refer for further information on error reconciliation).

TABLE 33.2. THE TReconcileAction VALUES.

TReconcileAction *Value*	*Meaning*
raSkip	Skips updating the record that raised the error condition and leaves the unapplied changes in the change log.
raAbort	Aborts the entire reconcile operation.
raMerge	Merges the updated record with the record on the server.
raCorrect	Replaces the current updated record with the value of the record in the event handler.
raCancel	Backs out all changes for this record, reverting to the original field values.
raRefresh	Backs out all changes for this record, replacing it with the current values from the server.

Within the OnReconcileError handler, you can refer to the OldValue, NewValue, and CurValue properties for each field of the client data set. These are discussed in Chapter 31.

The OnReconcileError event handler for cdsCust, cdsCustReconcileError(), takes care of retrieving the new, old, and current values of any field for which an error has been passed back to the client upon an update. It then invokes the method referred to by

FOnAddErrorToClient. FOnAddErrorToClient is a method pointer of type TAddErrorToClientEvent that's defined at the top of Listing 33.2. You'll see in our discussion of the application's main form, MainCustForm, how we implement a TAddErrorToClientEvent method and assign it to FOnAddErrorToClient. Again, this is another example of how we try to keep the data module independent of the user interface elements.

Online and Offline Data Manipulation

We've provided a Boolean property, Online, whose reader and writer methods take care of putting the client in either its online or offline state. The method that does this is SetOnline().

SetOnline() sets dcomCust.Connected to True if the user is going online (that is, connecting to the server). If the user was previously offline, any pending changes are applied to the server database. Errors will result in the cdsCust.OnReconcileError event handler that's executed. If the user is going offline, dcomCust.Connected is set to False. CdsCust will still work with its in-memory copy of the data. In fact, because a filename is specified in cdsCust.FileName, the data can be stored locally to a flat file.

GetOnline() just returns True if the user is online.

> **NOTE**
>
> TClientDataSet.FileName is specific to Delphi 4. If you're running Delphi 3, you can accomplish the same thing by invoking the SaveToFile() and LoadFromFile() methods of TClientDataSet.

Online and Offline Persistence

The OnCreate and OnDestroy event handlers for CustomerDataModule ensure that the client application is run in the same mode (online or offline) as when it was last closed. This is done by storing its state in the system Registry, which is checked every time the application runs. The constants defined at the top of Listing 33.2 specify the Registry section and keys.

Filtering Records

CustomerDataModule allows the user to filter out certain records based on the client's city or state of residence. Client-side filtering occurs when the status of the application is offline. When the client is online, the server is allowed to perform the filtering. One thing to note is that when the client issues a filter while online, when he or she goes offline, only those records that were part of the filter are saved locally to the client's machine.

The `FilterByCity()` and `FilterByState()` methods call the `FilterbyCity()` and `FilterbyState()` methods of the application server discussed earlier. These methods are called only if the user is online. If the user is offline, filtering is done via the `Filter` property and the `OnFilterRecord` event handler of `TClientDataSet`.

Client Main Form

The main form for the client application is very straightforward. It is shown in Listing 33.3.

LISTING 33.3. `MainCustFrm.pas—TMainCustForm`.

```pascal
unit MainCustFrm;

interface

uses
  Windows, Messages, SysUtils, Classes, Graphics, Controls, Forms,
  Dialogs, DBNAVSTATFRM, Db, StdCtrls, DBCtrls, Mask, ComCtrls, Menus,
  ImgList, ToolWin, DBMODEFRM, Grids, DBGrids;

type

  TMainCustForm = class(TDBNavStatForm)
    pcClients: TPageControl;
    dsClientDetail: TTabSheet;
    lblFirstName: TLabel;
    lblLastName: TLabel;
    lblCreditLine: TLabel;
    lblWorkAddress: TLabel;
    lblAltAddress: TLabel;
    lblCity: TLabel;
    lblState: TLabel;
    lblZipCode: TLabel;
    lblWorkPhone: TLabel;
    lblAltPhone: TLabel;
    lblCompany: TLabel;
    dbeFirstName: TDBEdit;
    dbeLastName: TDBEdit;
    dbeCreditLine: TDBEdit;
    dbeWorkAddress: TDBEdit;
    dbeAltAddress: TDBEdit;
    dbeCity: TDBEdit;
    dbeState: TDBEdit;
    dbeZipCode: TDBEdit;
    dbeWorkPhone: TDBEdit;
    dbeAltPhone: TDBEdit;
    dbeCompany: TDBEdit;
```

```
      tsComments: TTabSheet;
      dbmComments: TDBMemo;
      dsClients: TDataSource;
      SaveDialog1: TSaveDialog;
      OpenDialog1: TOpenDialog;
      mmiSave: TMenuItem;
      N3: TMenuItem;
      mmiApplyUpdates: TMenuItem;
      mmiCancelUpdates: TMenuItem;
      mmiMode: TMenuItem;
      mmiOffline: TMenuItem;
      mmiOnline: TMenuItem;
      tsErrors: TTabSheet;
      lvClient: TListView;
      mmiExit: TMenuItem;
      mmiFilter: TMenuItem;
      mmiByState: TMenuItem;
      mmiByCity: TMenuItem;
      mmiNoFilter: TMenuItem;
      tsClientList: TTabSheet;
      DBGrid1: TDBGrid;
      procedure sbAcceptClick(Sender: TObject);
      procedure sbCancelClick(Sender: TObject);
      procedure sbInsertClick(Sender: TObject);
      procedure sbEditClick(Sender: TObject);
      procedure sbDeleteClick(Sender: TObject);
      procedure sbFirstClick(Sender: TObject);
      procedure sbPrevClick(Sender: TObject);
      procedure sbNextClick(Sender: TObject);
      procedure sbLastClick(Sender: TObject);
      procedure FormCreate(Sender: TObject);
      procedure mmiOnlineClick(Sender: TObject);
      procedure mmiApplyUpdatesClick(Sender: TObject);
      procedure mmiCancelUpdatesClick(Sender: TObject);
      procedure dsClientsDataChange(Sender: TObject; Field: TField);
      procedure Exit1Click(Sender: TObject);
      procedure mmiExitClick(Sender: TObject);
      procedure mmiByStateClick(Sender: TObject);
      procedure mmiByCityClick(Sender: TObject);
      procedure mmiNoFilterClick(Sender: TObject);
    private
      procedure SetControls;
      procedure GoToOnlineMode;
      procedure GoToOfflineMode;

    public
      procedure AddErrorToClient(const aFieldName, aOldValue, aNewValue,
        aCurValue, aErrorStr: String);
    end;
```

continues

33

CLIENT TRACKER: MIDAS DEVELOPMENT

LISTING 33.3. CONTINUED

```
var
  MainCustForm: TMainCustForm;

implementation

uses CustDM;

{$R *.DFM}

procedure TMainCustForm.AddErrorToClient(const aFieldName, aOldValue,
    aNewValue,
  aCurValue, aErrorStr: String);
{ This method is used to add a TListItem to the TListView, aLV. The items
  added here give an indication of the errors that occur when performing
  updates to the server data. }
var
  NewItem: TListItem;
begin
  NewItem := lvClient.Items.Add;
  NewItem.Caption := aFieldName;
  NewItem.SubItems.Add(aOldValue);
  NewItem.SubItems.Add(aNewValue);
  NewItem.SubItems.Add(aCurValue);
  NewItem.SubItems.Add(aErrorStr);
end;

procedure TMainCustForm.SetControls;
begin
  // Ensure that the navigational buttons are set according to the form's
  // mode.
  sbFirst.Enabled := not CustomerDataModule.IsBof;
  sbLast.Enabled  := not CustomerDataModule.IsEof;
  sbPrev.Enabled  := not CustomerDataModule.IsBof;
  sbNext.Enabled  := not CustomerDataModule.IsEof;

  // synchronize the navigational menu items with the speedbuttons.
  mmiFirst.Enabled    := sbFirst.Enabled;
  mmiLast.Enabled     := sbLast.Enabled;
  mmiPrevious.Enabled := sbPrev.Enabled;
  mmiNext.Enabled     := sbNext.Enabled;

  // Set other menus accordingly

  mmiApplyUpdates.Enabled  := mmiOnline.Checked and (FormMode = fmBrowse)
    and CustomerDataModule.ChangeCount > 0);
  mmiCancelUpdates.Enabled := mmiOnline.Checked and (FormMode = fmBrowse)
    and CustomerDataModule.ChangeCount > 0);
```

```
    mmiOnline.Checked   := CustomerDataModule.Online;
    mmiOffline.Checked := not mmiOnline.Checked;

    stbStatusBar.Panels[0].Text := Format('Changed Records: %d',
      [CustomerDataModule.ChangeCount]);

    if CustomerDataModule.Online then
      stbStatusBar.Panels[2].Text := 'Working Online'
    else
      stbStatusBar.Panels[2].Text := 'Working Offline'

end;

procedure TMainCustForm.sbAcceptClick(Sender: TObject);
begin
  inherited;
  CustomerDataModule.SaveClient;
  SetControls;
end;

procedure TMainCustForm.sbCancelClick(Sender: TObject);
begin
  inherited;
  CustomerDataModule.CancelClient;
  SetControls;
end;

procedure TMainCustForm.sbInsertClick(Sender: TObject);
begin
  inherited;
  CustomerDataModule.AddClient;
  SetControls;
end;

procedure TMainCustForm.sbEditClick(Sender: TObject);
begin
  inherited;
  CustomerDataModule.EditClient;
  SetControls;
end;

procedure TMainCustForm.sbDeleteClick(Sender: TObject);
begin
  inherited;
  CustomerDataModule.DeleteClient;
  SetControls;
end;
```

continues

LISTING 33.3. CONTINUED

```
procedure TMainCustForm.sbFirstClick(Sender: TObject);
begin
  inherited;
  CustomerDataModule.First;
  SetControls;
end;

procedure TMainCustForm.sbPrevClick(Sender: TObject);
begin
  inherited;
  CustomerDataModule.Previous;
  SetControls;
end;

procedure TMainCustForm.sbNextClick(Sender: TObject);
begin
  inherited;
  CustomerDataModule.Next;
  SetControls;
end;

procedure TMainCustForm.sbLastClick(Sender: TObject);
begin
  inherited;
  CustomerDataModule.Last;
  SetControls;
end;

procedure TMainCustForm.FormCreate(Sender: TObject);
begin
  inherited;
  CustomerDataModule.OnAddErrorToClient := AddErrorToClient;
  SetControls;

  // Make these guys refer to each other so that they reset the other
  mmiOnline.Tag := Longint(mmiOffline);
  mmiOffline.Tag := Longint(mmiOnline);
end;

procedure TMainCustForm.GoToOnlineMode;
begin
  CustomerDataModule.Online := True;
  SetControls;
end;

procedure TMainCustForm.GoToOfflineMode;
begin
  CustomerDataModule.Online := False;
  SetControls;
end;
```

```
procedure TMainCustForm.mmiOnlineClick(Sender: TObject);
var
  mi: TMenuItem;
begin
  inherited;
  mi := Sender as TMenuItem;

  if not mi.Checked then
  begin

    mi.Checked := not mi.Checked;
    TMenuItem(mi.Tag).Checked := not mi.Checked;

    if mi = mmiOnline then
    begin
      if mi.Checked then
        GoToOnlineMode
      else
        GoToOffLineMode
    end

    else begin
      if mi.Checked then
        GoToOfflineMode
      else
        GoToOnlineMode
    end;
  end;
end;

procedure TMainCustForm.mmiApplyUpdatesClick(Sender: TObject);
begin
  inherited;
  CustomerDataModule.ApplyUpdates;
  SetControls;
end;

procedure TMainCustForm.mmiCancelUpdatesClick(Sender: TObject);
begin
  inherited;
  CustomerDataModule.CancelUpdates;
  SetControls;
end;

procedure TMainCustForm.dsClientsDataChange(Sender: TObject;
  Field: TField);
begin
  inherited;
  SetControls;
end;
```

continues

LISTING 33.3. CONTINUED

```
procedure TMainCustForm.Exit1Click(Sender: TObject);
begin
  inherited;
  Close;
end;

procedure TMainCustForm.mmiExitClick(Sender: TObject);
begin
  inherited;
  Close;
end;

procedure TMainCustForm.mmiByStateClick(Sender: TObject);
begin
  inherited;
  CustomerDataModule.FilterByState;
end;

procedure TMainCustForm.mmiByCityClick(Sender: TObject);
begin
  inherited;
  CustomerDataModule.FilterByCity;
end;

procedure TMainCustForm.mmiNoFilterClick(Sender: TObject);
begin
  inherited;
  CustomerDataModule.NoFilter;
end;

end.
```

Most of the methods for `TMainCustForm` call the methods of `CustomerDataModule`.

Notice the `AddErrorToClient()` method. This method serves as the `OnAddErrorToClient` property of `CustomerDataModule`. The `OnCreate` event handler of `TMainCustForm` assigns this method to the data module's property. `AddErrorToClient()` adds any events to the `TListView` control on the main form for the user to examine. This `TListView` control displays the field name, old value, new value, and current values for the error. It also displays the error string.

The simple `SetControls()` method handles setting up various controls on the form. It ensures that controls are enabled or disabled when appropriate. The rest of the methods are discussed in the commentary in the source code.

SUMMARY

Although the Client Tracker is a simple application, most of the wiring necessary for creating 3-tier applications is shown in this example. You might also find that you need to use some other specifics such as callbacks or connection pooling, as discussed in Chapter 31. The point is this: Developing three-tier applications using MIDAS is not harder than developing two-tier or even desktop database applications.

DDG BUG REPORTING TOOL—DESKTOP APPLICATION DEVELOPMENT

IN THIS CHAPTER

This chapter discusses techniques for developing desktop database applications. The DDG bug reporting application illustrates several methods to take into consideration, in particular, how to design an application that may be deployed to the Internet. In this demo, we also illustrate several techniques or tricks to get around some sticky issues when separating the user interface from the data manipulation routines.

Because of Delphi's ease of use, developing database applications is simple. However, it's also easy to overlook issues that may end up biting you later when you want to extend the application's basic functionality. In this chapter, we will show you how to take this into account when creating your database applications.

GENERAL APPLICATION REQUIREMENTS

The general requirements for the DDG bug reporting application are discussed in the following section. Be aware that our intentions were not to actually design a deployable bug reporting tool. Rather, we use a real-world need to illustrate the techniques discussed in this chapter. Therefore, we left out functionality that you might expect from this application so as not to cloud our techniques with application logic.

Web-Ready—May Be Deployed to the World Wide Web

The bug reporting application must be designed in such a manner as to minimize the development effort to make its functionality available on the World Wide Web. This means that the user interface must be completely—not almost completely—separated from the database logic. In essence, you should be able to attach different user interfaces to the database logic. In fact, you'll see that in Chapter 35, "DDG Bug Reporting Tool: Using WebBroker," when we make our application available through Web pages.

User Data Entry/Logon

The bug reporting application contains a table with users that can log on to the system. These users can report the existence of bugs by using this application. Users can also add other users to the bug reporting application. For this version of the application, it is not required that the users be able to edit or delete user information.

Users log on to the bug reporting tool by providing a user name, which is stored in the Users.db table. This logon is only for the process of obtaining the UserID, which is needed to manipulate reported bugs—this is not a security measure.

Bug Manipulation, Browsing, and Filtering

Users can add, edit, and delete bug information. Users can provide the necessary field information to each bug. For example, the user can enter the date the bug is reported, to whom the bug is assigned its status, a summary, details, and the affected source. The user entering the bug is added automatically.

Bug Actions

Users can add actions (notes) to an existing bug report. Users can browse actions previously entered by themselves or by other users. This is a handy way to track the bug correction progress and for interested parties to pass notes back and forth about the bug.

Other U/I Functionality

The application must make use of techniques necessary to make the user interface easy to understand and use. Features such as lookup fields and "friendly" display labels will be used where necessary.

THE DATA MODEL

The data model for the bug reporting application is shown in Figure 34.1. The tables in the model consist of

IDs	The IDs table serves as the key generation table and keeps track of the next available key for the Users, Bugs, and Actions tables.
Users	The Users table stores users that are added to the bug reporting system.
Bugs	The Bugs table stores the general information about bugs.
Actions	The Actions table stores notes on bugs. Each bug may have several notes.
Status	The Status table is a lookup table to assign a specific status to each bug.

FIGURE 34.1.

Bug reporting application data model.

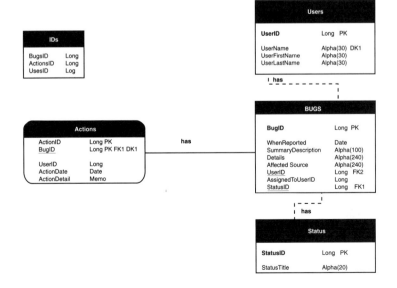

DEVELOPING THE DATA MODULE

The data module is the central piece to the bug reporting application. It is through the data module that all database manipulation is handled. The user interface uses the data module's functionality through public methods and properties. No direct reference to data-access components is made from any user interface element except where necessary from the Object Inspector. An example of directly accessing a data-access component would be in the DataSet property for the TDataSource component that resides on U/I forms.

> **NOTE**
>
> When developing applications in which you want to separate data logic from the user interface, the placement of the TDataSource component is not of grave concern. We chose to place it on the U/I forms rather than the data module because we feel that it has more to do with user interface versus data access. This, however, is a preference, and you may choose to do otherwise for whatever reason.

Listing 34.1 shows the source code to the bug application's data module.

LISTING 34.1. THE TDDGBugsDataModule.

```
unit DDGBugsDM;

interface

uses
  Windows, Messages, SysUtils, Classes, Graphics, Controls, Forms,
  Dialogs, Db, DBTables, HTTPApp, DBWeb;

type

  EUnableToObtainID = class(Exception);

  TDDGBugsDataModule = class(TDataModule)
    dbDDGBugs: TDatabase;
    tblBugs: TTable;
    tblUsers: TTable;
    tblStatus: TTable;
    tblActions: TTable;
    tblBugsBugID: TIntegerField;
    tblBugsWhenReported: TDateField;
    tblBugsSummaryDescription: TStringField;
```

```
    tblBugsDetails: TStringField;
    tblBugsAffectedSource: TStringField;
    tblBugsUserID: TIntegerField;
    tblBugsStatusID: TIntegerField;
    dsUsers: TDataSource;
    dsStatus: TDataSource;
    tblIDs: TTable;
    tblBugsUserNameLookup: TStringField;
    tblBugsAssignedToLookup: TStringField;
    tblUsersUserID: TIntegerField;
    tblUsersUserName: TStringField;
    tblUsersUserFirstName: TStringField;
    tblUsersUserLastName: TStringField;
    tblBugsAssignedToUserID: TIntegerField;
    dsBugs: TDataSource;
    wbdpBugs: TWebDispatcher;
    dstpBugs: TDataSetTableProducer;
    procedure DDGBugsDataModuleCreate(Sender: TObject);
    procedure tblBugsBeforePost(DataSet: TDataSet);
    procedure tblBugsFilterRecord(DataSet: TDataSet; var Accept: Boolean);
    procedure tblUsersBeforePost(DataSet: TDataSet);
    procedure tblBugsAfterInsert(DataSet: TDataSet);
    procedure wbdpBugswaShowAllBugsAction(Sender: TObject;
      Request: TWebRequest; Response: TWebResponse; var Handled: Boolean);
    procedure wbdpBugswaIntroAction(Sender: TObject; Request: TWebRequest;
      Response: TWebResponse; var Handled: Boolean);
    procedure wbdpBugswaUserNameAction(Sender: TObject;
      Request: TWebRequest; Response: TWebResponse; var Handled: Boolean);
    procedure wbdpBugswaVerifyUserNameAction(Sender: TObject;
      Request: TWebRequest; Response: TWebResponse; var Handled: Boolean);
  private
    FLoginUserID: Integer;
    FLoginUserName: String;

    function GetFilterOnUser: Boolean;
    procedure SetFilterOnUser(const Value: Boolean);
    function GetNumBugs: Integer;
  protected
    procedure PostAction(Sender: TObject; Action: TStrings);
  public

    // Bugs Methods
    procedure FirstBug;
    procedure LastBug;
    procedure NextBug;
    procedure PreviousBug;
    function IsLastBug: Boolean;
    function IsFirstBug: Boolean;
    function IsBugsTblEmpty: Boolean;
```

34

DESKTOP
APPLICATION
DEVELOPMENT

continues

LISTING 34.1. CONTINUED

```delphi
    procedure InsertBug;
    procedure DeleteBug;
    procedure EditBug;
    procedure SaveBug;
    procedure CancelBug;
    procedure SearchForBug;

    // User Functions
  {$IFNDEF DDGWEBBUGS}
    procedure AddUser;
  {$ENDIF}

    procedure PostUser(Sender: TObject);
    function GetUserFLName(AUserID: Integer): String;

    // Action Methods

  {$IFNDEF DDGWEBBUGS}
    procedure AddAction;
  {$ENDIF}

    procedure GetActions(AActions: TStrings);

    // Id Generation
    function GetDataSetID(const AFieldName: String): Integer;
    function GetNewBugID: Integer;
    function GetNewUserID: Integer;
    function GetNewActionID: Integer;

    // Login Function
    function Login: Boolean;

    // Exposed properties

    property LoginUserID: Integer read FLoginUserID;
    property FilterOnUser: Boolean read GetFilterOnUser write
➥SetFilterOnUser;
    property NumBugs: Integer read GetNumBugs;
  end;

var
  DDGBugsDataModule: TDDGBugsDataModule;

implementation

{$IFNDEF DDGWEBBUGS}
uses UserFrm, ActionFrm;
{$ENDIF}

{$R *.DFM}
```

```
// Helper functions.

function IsInteger(IntVal: String): Boolean;
var
  v, code: Integer;
begin
  val(IntVal, v, code);
  Result := code = 0;
end;

procedure MemoFromStrings(AMemoField: TMemoField; AStrings: TStrings);
var
  Stream: TMemoryStream;
begin
  Stream := TMemoryStream.Create;
  try
    AStrings.SaveToStream(Stream);
    Stream.Seek(0, soFromBeginning);
    AMemoField.LoadFromStream(Stream);
  finally
    Stream.Free;
  end;
end;

procedure StringsFromMemo(AStrings: TStrings; AMemoField: TMemoField);
var
  Stream: TMemoryStream;
begin
  Stream := TMemoryStream.Create;
  try
    AMemoField.SaveToStream(Stream);
    Stream.Seek(0, soFromBeginning);
    AStrings.LoadFromStream(Stream);
  finally
    Stream.Free;
  end;
end;

// Internal methods

function TDDGBugsDataModule.GetFilterOnUser: Boolean;
begin
  Result := tblBugs.Filtered;
end;

procedure TDDGBugsDataModule.SetFilterOnUser(const Value: Boolean);
begin
 tblBugs.Filtered := Value;
end;
```

continues

LISTING 34.1. CONTINUED

```
function TDDGBugsDataModule.GetNumBugs: Integer;
begin
  Result := tblBugs.RecordCount;
end;

// Identifier methods

function TDDGBugsDataModule.GetDataSetID(const AFieldName: String):
➥Integer;
const
  MaxAttempts = 50;
var
  Attempts: Integer;
  NextID: Integer;
begin
  tblIDs.Active := True;
  // Try fifty times if until this works or raise an exception
  Attempts := 0;
  while Attempts <= MaxAttempts do
  begin
    try
      Inc(Attempts);
      // If another user has the table in edit mode, an error occurs here.
      tblIDs.Edit;
      // If we reach the Break statement, we are successful. Break out of
      // loop.
      Break;
    except
      on EDBEngineError do
      begin
        // Do some delay
        Continue;
      end;
    end;
  end;

  if tblIDs.State = dsEdit then
  begin
    // Increment the value obtained from the table and restore the new
    // value to the table for the next record.
    NextID := tblIDs.FieldByName(AFieldName).AsInteger;
    tblIDs.FieldByName(AFieldName).AsInteger := NextID + 1;
    TblIDs.Post;
    Result := NextID;
  end
  else
    Raise EUnableToObtainID.Create('Cannot create unique ID');
end;
```

```
function TDDGBugsDataModule.GetNewActionID: Integer;
begin
  Result := GetDataSetID('ActionsID');
end;

function TDDGBugsDataModule.GetNewBugID: Integer;
begin
  Result := GetDataSetID('BugsID');
end;

function TDDGBugsDataModule.GetNewUserID: Integer;
begin
  Result := GetDataSetID('UsersID');
end;

// Initialization/Login methods.

procedure TDDGBugsDataModule.DDGBugsDataModuleCreate(Sender: TObject);
begin
  { These tables are opened in the proper order so the master-detail
    relationship does not fail.}
  dbDDGBugs.Connected := True;
  tblUsers.Active   := True;
  tblStatus.Active  := True;
  tblBugs.Active    := True;
  tblActions.Active := True;
end;

function TDDGBugsDataModule.Login: Boolean;
var
  UserName: String;
begin
  InputQuery('Login', 'Enter User Name: ', UserName);
  Result := tblUsers.Locate('UserName', UserName, []);
  if Result then
  begin
    FLoginUserID   := tblUsers.FieldByName('UserID').AsInteger;
    FLoginUserName := tblUsers.FieldByName('UserName').AsString;
  end;
end;

// Bug methods.

procedure TDDGBugsDataModule.FirstBug;
begin
  tblBugs.First;
end;
```

continues

LISTING 34.1. CONTINUED

```
procedure TDDGBugsDataModule.LastBug;
begin
  tblBugs.Last;
end;

procedure TDDGBugsDataModule.NextBug;
begin
  tblBugs.Next;
end;

procedure TDDGBugsDataModule.PreviousBug;
begin
  tblBugs.Prior;
end;

function TDDGBugsDataModule.IsLastBug: Boolean;
begin
  Result := tblBugs.Eof;
end;

function TDDGBugsDataModule.IsFirstBug: Boolean;
begin
  Result := tblBugs.Bof;
end;

function TDDGBugsDataModule.IsBugsTblEmpty: Boolean;
begin
  // If RecordCount is zero, there are not bugs in the table.
  Result := tblBugs.RecordCount = 0;
end;

procedure TDDGBugsDataModule.InsertBug;
begin
  tblBugs.Insert;
end;

procedure TDDGBugsDataModule.DeleteBug;
var
  Qry: TQuery;
  BugID: Integer;
begin
  if MessageDlg('Delete Action?', mtConfirmation, [mbYes, mbNo], 0) =
➥mrYes then
  begin
    BugID := tblBugs.FieldByName('BugID').AsInteger;
    // Use a dynamically created TQuery component to perform these
    // operations.
    Qry := TQuery.Create(self);
    try
```

```
      dbDDGBugs.StartTransaction;
      try
        // First delete any action belonging to this bug.
        Qry.DatabaseName := dbDDGBugs.DataBaseName;
        Qry.SQL.Add(Format('DELETE FROM ACTIONS WHERE BugID = %d',
        ➥[BugID]));
        Qry.ExecSQL;

        // Now delete bug from the bugs table.
        Qry.SQL.Clear;
        Qry.SQL.Add(Format('DELETE FROM BUGS WHERE BugID = %d', [BugID]));
        Qry.ExecSQL;

        tblBugs.Refresh;
        tblActions.Refresh;

        dbDDGBugs.Commit;
      except
        dbDDGBugs.Rollback;
        raise;
      end;
    finally
      Qry.Free;
    end;
  end;
end;

procedure TDDGBugsDataModule.EditBug;
begin
  tblBugs.Edit;
end;

procedure TDDGBugsDataModule.SaveBug;
begin
  tblBugs.Post;
end;

procedure TDDGBugsDataModule.CancelBug;
begin
  tblBugs.Cancel;
end;

procedure TDDGBugsDataModule.SearchForBug;
var
  BugStr: String;
begin
  InputQuery('Search for bug', 'Enter bug ID: ', BugStr);
  if IsInteger(BugStr) then
    if not tblBugs.Locate('BugID', StrToInt(BugStr), []) then
      MessageDlg('Bug not found.', mtInformation, [mbOK], 0);
end;
```

continues

34

DESKTOP
APPLICATION
DEVELOPMENT

LISTING 34.1. CONTINUED

```
// User methods.

{$IFNDEF DDGWEBBUGS}
procedure TDDGBugsDataModule.AddUser;
begin
  tblUsers.Insert;
  try
    if NewUserForm(PostUser) = mrCancel then
      tblUsers.Cancel;
  except
    // An error occurred. Put the table to browse mode and reraise the
    // exception
    tblUsers.Cancel;
    raise;
  end;
end;
{$ENDIF}

procedure TDDGBugsDataModule.PostUser(Sender: TObject);
begin
  if tblUsers.State = dsInsert then
    tblUsers.FieldByName('UserID').AsInteger := GetNewUserID;
  tblUsers.Post;
end;

function TDDGBugsDataModule.GetUserFLName(AUserID: Integer): String;
begin
  // Returns the first and last name concatenated.
  if tblUsers.Locate('UserID', AUserID, []) then
    Result := Format('%s %s',
[tblUsers.FieldByName('UserFirstName').AsString,
      tblUsers.FieldByName('UserLastName').AsString])
  else
    Result := EmptyStr;
end;

{$IFNDEF DDGWEBBUGS}
procedure TDDGBugsDataModule.AddAction;
begin
  NewActionForm(PostAction);
end;
{$ENDIF}

procedure TDDGBugsDataModule.GetActions(AActions: TStrings);
var
  Action: TStringList;
  ActionUserId: Integer;
```

```
begin
  Action := TStringList.Create;
  try
    with tblActions do
    begin
      tblActions.First;
      while not Eof do
      begin
        Action.Clear;
        ActionUserID := FieldByName('UserID').AsInteger;
        StringsFromMemo(Action, TMemoField(FieldByName('ActionDetail')));
        AActions.Add(Format('Action Added on: %s',
            [FormatDateTime('mmm dd, yyyy',
          FieldByName('ActionDate').AsDateTime)]));
        AActions.Add(Format('Action Added by: %s',
            [GetUserFLName(ActionUserID)]));
        AActions.Add(EmptyStr);
        AActions.AddStrings(Action);
        AActions.Add('=============================');
        AActions.Add(EmptyStr);
        tblActions.Next;
      end; // while
    end; // with
  finally
    Action.Free;
  end;
end;

procedure TDDGBugsDataModule.PostAction(Sender: TObject; Action:
➥TStrings);
var
  BugID: Integer;
begin
  tblActions.Insert;
  try
    BugID := tblBugs.FieldByName('BugID').AsInteger;
    tblActions.FieldByName('ActionID').AsInteger      := GetNewActionID;
    tblActions.FieldByName('BugID').AsInteger         := BugID;
    tblActions.FieldByName('UserID').AsInteger        := LoginUserID;
    tblActions.FieldByName('ActionDate').AsDateTime   := Date;
    MemoFromStrings(TMemoField(tblActions.FieldByName('ActionDetail')),
    ➥Action);
    tblActions.Post;
  except
    tblActions.Cancel;
    raise;
  end;
end;
```

34

DESKTOP
APPLICATION
DEVELOPMENT

continues

LISTING 34.1. CONTINUED

```
// Event Handlers

procedure TDDGBugsDataModule.tblBugsBeforePost(DataSet: TDataSet);
begin
  if tblBugs.State = dsInsert then
    tblBugs.FieldByName('BugID').AsInteger := GetNewBugID;
end;

procedure TDDGBugsDataModule.tblBugsFilterRecord(DataSet: TDataSet;
  var Accept: Boolean);
begin
  Accept := tblBugs.FieldByName('UserID').AsInteger = FLoginUserID;
end;

procedure TDDGBugsDataModule.tblUsersBeforePost(DataSet: TDataSet);
begin
  if tblUsers.State = dsInsert then
    tblUsers.FieldByName('UserID').AsInteger := GetNewUserID;
end;

procedure TDDGBugsDataModule.tblBugsAfterInsert(DataSet: TDataSet);
begin
  tblBugs.FieldByName('UserID').AsInteger := FLoginUserID;
  tblBugs.FieldByName('UserNameLookup').AsString := FLoginUserName;
end;

end.
```

In order to support the logging in of a user, we had to modify the project file as shown in Listing 34.2.

LISTING 34.2. PROJECT FILE FOR BUG REPORTING APPLICATION.

```
program DDGBugs;

uses
  Forms,
  Dialogs,
  ChildFrm in '..\ObjRepos\CHILDFRM.pas' {ChildForm},
  DBModeFrm in '..\ObjRepos\DBMODEFRM.pas' {DBModeForm},
  DBNavStatFrm in '..\ObjRepos\DBNAVSTATFRM.pas' {DBNavStatForm},
  MainFrm in 'MainFrm.pas' {MainForm},
  UserFrm in 'UserFrm.pas' {UserForm},
  ActionFrm in 'ActionFrm.pas' {ActionForm},
  DDGBugsDM in '..\Shared\DDGBugsDM.pas' {DDGBugsDataModule: TDataModule};

{$R *.RES}
```

```
begin
  Application.Initialize;
  Application.CreateForm(TDDGBugsDataModule, DDGBugsDataModule);
  if DDGBugsDataModule.Login then
  begin
    Application.CreateForm(TMainForm, MainForm);
    Application.Run;
  end
  else
    MessageDlg('Invalid Login', mtError, [mbOk], 0);
end.
```

Application Initialization and Login

You'll see in Listing 34.2 that we moved the TDDGBugsDataModule so that it is created first. Then we call its Login() method, which determines whether or not the application execution continues. It makes this determination based on whether the user name entered actually exists in the Users.db table, as shown in the TDDGBugsDataModule.Login() method in Listing 34.1.

Generating IDs

The bug reporting application uses the Paradox database as the back end. In doing so, we also acquire a slight anomaly that we must get around. This anomaly has to do with the Paradox auto-increment fields. Although Paradox's auto-increment fields can supposedly allow you to use them as key fields, they are highly unreliable. Our experience has been that they can easily become out of sync with foreign keys. We opted to avoid their use and create our own keys based on the values contained in the IDs.db table.

The IDs.db table stores the next available integer value for the Bugs, Users, and Action keys. The TDDGBugsDataModule.GetDataSetID() method ensures that only one user is able to put the specific key field of the tblIDs table into Edit mode. This will ensure that no two users get identical key values when inserting records. GetDataSetID() is made generic for the three types of keys by passing in the field name for the key value desired. Therefore, this method can be used to obtain keys for Bugs, Users, and Actions. In fact, this method is called by the GetNewActionID(), GetNewBugID(), and GetNewUserID() methods. These three methods may be called whenever posting a record to one of these tables. You do so in the BeforePost event handlers for the tblBugs and tblUsers tables and in the PostAction() method for the tblActions table.

Bug Manipulation Routines

The bug manipulation routines are those methods declared under the comment // Bug Methods. Most of these functions are self-explanatory—especially the navigation method, which we won't go into. The method `DeleteBug()` contains most of the code for the bug manipulation routines. This method ensures that any actions belonging to a bug get deleted before the bug record is deleted. We'll discuss actions shortly. Here, we're using the transaction functionality of `TDatabase` to wrap this operation in a transaction. This will ensure that no data is lost if an error occurs. Note that to perform transaction processing against a local database such as Paradox, you must set the `TransIsolation` property of the `TDatabase` component to `tiDirtyRead` as we have so done.

Browsing/Filtering Bugs

The user is able to browse all bugs in the database or just those bugs belonging to him or her. This is made possible through the use of the `Filtered` property of the `tblBugs` component. When `tblBugs.Filtered` is `True`, the `tblBugs.OnFilterRecord` is invoked for each record. Here, you display a record only if its `UserID` field is that of the user logged on as indicated by the global field `FLoginUserID`. Notice how you surface the `Filtered` property of the `tblBugs` table to the user interface. Instead of allowing the user interface to directly access the `tblBugs.Filtered` property, you surface this property through the `TDDGBugsDataModule.FilterOnUser` property. This property's writer method, `SetFilterOnUser()`, performs the assignment to the `tblBugs.Filtered` property. Now, you can't actually enforce the rule that forms can't directly access properties of components that reside on `TDatamodules` because the VCL isn't using strict OOP visibility rules.

Adding Users

Adding users is done through the `TDDGBugsDataModule.AddUser()` and `TDDGBugsDataModule.PostUser()` methods. The `AddUser()` method invokes a simple dialog with which you add the user data. Note how the `PostUser()` method is passed to the `NewUserForm()` function, which invokes the user form. This illustrates how you can avoid having to make a form invoked by a data module refer right back to that data module. The reason this problem presented itself is because we're protecting the data module components from external access. There are probably a number of ways we might have accomplished this—this just happens to be the one we chose. `NewUserFrom()` invokes the form defined in the `UserFrm.pas` unit shown in Listing 34.3.

LISTING 34.3. `UserFrm.pas`—THE USER FORM.

```
unit UserFrm;

interface

uses
  Windows, Messages, SysUtils, Classes, Graphics, Controls, Forms,
  Dialogs, StdCtrls, Mask, DBCtrls;
```

```
type

  TUserForm = class(TForm)
    lblUserName: TLabel;
    dbeUserName: TDBEdit;
    lblFirstName: TLabel;
    dbeFirstName: TDBEdit;
    lblLastName: TLabel;
    dbeLastName: TDBEdit;
    btnOK: TButton;
    btnCancel: TButton;
    procedure btnOKClick(Sender: TObject);
  private
    FPostUser: TNotifyEvent;
  public
    { Public declarations }
  end;

function NewUserForm(APostUser: TNotifyEvent): Word;

implementation
uses dbTables;
{$R *.DFM}

function NewUserForm(APostUser: TNotifyEvent): Word;
var
  UserForm: TUserForm;
begin
  UserForm := TUserForm.Create(Application);
  try
    UserForm.FPostUser := APostUser;
    Result := UserForm.ShowModal;
  finally
    UserForm.Free;
  end;
end;

procedure TUserForm.btnOKClick(Sender: TObject);
begin
  if dbeUserName.Text = EmptyStr then begin
    MessageDlg('A user name is required.', mtWarning, [mbOK], 0);
    dbeUserName.SetFocus;
    ModalResult := mrNone;
  end
  else begin
    try
      FPostUser(self);
    except
      on EDBEngineError do
      begin
```

continues

LISTING 34.3. CONTINUED

```
        MessageDlg('User name already exists.', mtWarning, [mbOK], 0);
        dbeUserName.SetFocus;
        ModalResult := mrNone;
      end;
    end;
  end;
end;

end.
```

As shown in Listing 34.3, NewUserForm() instantiates the TUserForm and displays it. Notice that you assign the APostUser parameter to the FPostUser field that is of the type TNotifyEvent. By declaring FPostUser as a method pointer (TNofityEvent), you can assign the PostUser() method from TDDGBugDataModule to FPostUser because PostUser() matches the definition of TNotifyEvent. This concept is covered in Chapter 20, "Key Elements of the Visual Component Library," and Chapter 21, "Writing Delphi Custom Components," which deal with component writing.

When the user clicks the OK button, btnOkClick() is invoked. Provided a user name was entered, the TDDGBugDataModule.PostUser() method (referred to by FPostUser) is invoked, which should save the user record (see PostUser() in Listing 34.1). If an error occurs in PostUser(), the user name already exists in the database. This illustrates another advantage to passing the PostUser() method to the TUserForm. The TUserForm can handle an error raised in the data module. This concept is not that different from developing components. You develop the data module such that it is completely self-contained. You also allow users of the data module to handle any errors raised within the data module.

Adding Actions

Actions are basically notes that are optionally attached to each bug. Anybody can add an action to a bug. The TDDGBugsDataModule.AddAction() method calls the NewActionForm(), which obtains the action data from the user and adds it to the database. NewActionForm() is defined in ActionFrm.pas, shown in Listing 34.4.

LISTING 34.4. ActionFrm.pas—THE ACTION FORM.

```
unit ActionFrm;

interface

uses
```

```
Windows, Messages, SysUtils, Classes, Graphics, Controls, Forms,
Dialogs, StdCtrls;

type

  TPostActionEvent = procedure (Sender: TObject; Action: TStrings) of
  ➥Object;

  TActionForm = class(TForm)
    memAction: TMemo;
    lblAction: TLabel;
    btnOK: TButton;
    btnCancel: TButton;
    procedure btnOKClick(Sender: TObject);
  private
    FPostAction: TPostActionEvent;
  public
    { Public declarations }
  end;


procedure NewActionForm(APostAction: TPostActionEvent);

implementation
{$R *.DFM}

procedure NewActionForm(APostAction: TPostActionEvent);
var
  ActionForm: TActionForm;
begin
  ActionForm := TActionForm.Create(Application);
  try
    ActionForm.FPostAction := APostAction;
    ActionForm.ShowModal;
  finally
    ActionForm.Free;
  end;
end;

procedure TActionForm.btnOKClick(Sender: TObject);
begin
  if Assigned(FPostAction) then
    FPostAction(Self, memAction.Lines);
end;

end.
```

34

DESKTOP APPLICATION DEVELOPMENT

Much like NewUserForm(), the NewActionForm() method takes a method pointer as a
parameter. This time, we defined our own method type of TPostActionEvent that takes a

`TObject` and the `TStrings` object containing the action text. When the user clicks the OK button, the `btnOKClick()` event is invoked, which in turn invokes `TDDGBugsDataSource.PostAction()` to add the action to the database (`FPostAction` refers to `PostAction()`).

You can refer to the source commentary for additional information on the data module. Later, you'll see how to add code to this data module to share it with another application—an ISAPI server that Web-enables the bug program.

DEVELOPING THE USER INTERFACE

In this section, we will discuss the development of the user interface for this application. We will also point out some preparations you can make for Web deployment of this application.

The Main Form

The user interface basically refers to the methods of the data module. We have a single form interface consisting of three pages. The first page allows the user to add, edit, and view the bug information. The second page is for browsing actions. The third page allows the user to view a grid that contains either all bugs or only the (logged-in) user's bugs. Figures 34.2, 34.3, and 34.4 show the three pages for the main form.

FIGURE 34.2.
Bug Information page.

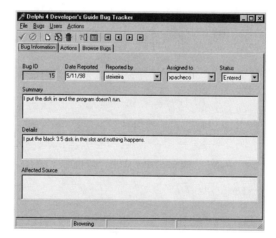

FIGURE 34.3.

Actions page.

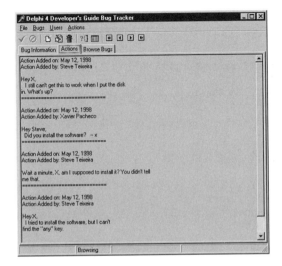

FIGURE 34.4.

Browse Bugs page.

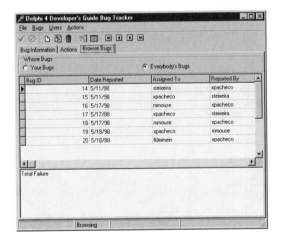

34

LISTING 34.5.   TMainForm.

```
unit MainFrm;

interface

uses
  Windows, Messages, SysUtils, Classes, Graphics, Controls, Forms,
  Dialogs, DBNAVSTATFRM, Menus, ImgList, ComCtrls, ToolWin, StdCtrls,
  DBCtrls, Db, Mask, dbModeFrm, ActnList, Grids, DBGrids, ExtCtrls;
```

continues

LISTING 34.5. CONTINUED

```
type

  TMainForm = class(TDBNavStatForm)
    pcMain: TPageControl;
    tsBugInformation: TTabSheet;
    tsActions: TTabSheet;
    lblBugID: TLabel;
    dbeBugID: TDBEdit;
    dsBugs: TDataSource;
    lblDateReported: TLabel;
    lblSummary: TLabel;
    lblDetails: TLabel;
    lblAffectedSource: TLabel;
    lblReportedBy: TLabel;
    lblAssignedTo: TLabel;
    lblStatus: TLabel;
    dbmSummary: TDBMemo;
    dbmDetails: TDBMemo;
    dbmAffectedSource: TDBMemo;
    tsBrowseBugs: TTabSheet;
    rgWhoseBugs: TRadioGroup;
    dbgBugs: TDBGrid;
    dbmSummary2: TDBMemo;
    memAction: TMemo;
    dblcAssignedTo: TDBLookupComboBox;
    dblcStatus: TDBLookupComboBox;
    dbeDateReported: TDBEdit;
    mmiFile: TMenuItem;
    mmiExit: TMenuItem;
    mmiUsers: TMenuItem;
    mmiAddUser: TMenuItem;
    mmiActions: TMenuItem;
    mmiAddActionToBug: TMenuItem;
    dblcReportedBy: TDBLookupComboBox;
    procedure FormCreate(Sender: TObject);
    procedure sbFirstClick(Sender: TObject);
    procedure sbPreviousClick(Sender: TObject);
    procedure sbNextClick(Sender: TObject);
    procedure sbLastClick(Sender: TObject);
    procedure sbSearchClick(Sender: TObject);
    procedure FormCloseQuery(Sender: TObject; var CanClose: Boolean);
    procedure sbAcceptClick(Sender: TObject);
    procedure sbCancelClick(Sender: TObject);
    procedure sbInsertClick(Sender: TObject);
    procedure sbEditClick(Sender: TObject);
    procedure sbDeleteClick(Sender: TObject);
    procedure sbBrowseClick(Sender: TObject);
    procedure rgWhoseBugsClick(Sender: TObject);
    procedure mmiExitClick(Sender: TObject);
```

```
    procedure mmiAddUserClick(Sender: TObject);
    procedure mmiAddActionToBugClick(Sender: TObject);
    procedure dsBugsDataChange(Sender: TObject; Field: TField);
  private
    procedure SetActionStatus;

  protected
  public
    { Public declarations }
  end;

var
  MainForm: TMainForm;

implementation

uses DDGBugsDM;

{$R *.DFM}

{ TMainForm }

procedure TMainForm.SetActionStatus;
begin
  mmiFirst.Enabled := not DDGBugsDataModule.IsFirstBug;
  mmiLast.Enabled  := not DDGBugsDataModule.IsLastBug;
  mmiNext.Enabled  := not DDGBugsDataModule.IsLastBug;
  mmiPrevious.Enabled := not DDGBugsDataModule.IsFirstBug;
  mmiDelete.Enabled := not DDGBugsDataModule.IsBugsTblEmpty;

  sbFirst.Enabled := mmiFirst.Enabled;
  sbLast.Enabled  := mmiLast.Enabled;
  sbNext.Enabled  := mmiNext.Enabled;
  sbPrev.Enabled  := mmiPrevious.Enabled;
  sbDelete.Enabled := mmiDelete.Enabled;

  // User cannot add users or actions when adding/editing a bug.
  mmiUsers.Enabled := FormMode = fmBrowse;
  mmiActions.Enabled := (FormMode = fmBrowse) and
    (DDGBugsDataModule.NumBugs <> 0);

  { disable the browsing of bug records when the user is editing or adding
    a new bug. }
  dbgBugs.Enabled      := FormMode = fmBrowse;
  rgWhoseBugs.Enabled := FormMOde = fmBrowse;

end;
```

continues

34

DESKTOP
APPLICATION
DEVELOPMENT

LISTING 34.5. CONTINUED

```
procedure TMainForm.FormCreate(Sender: TObject);
begin
  inherited;
  SetActionStatus;
end;

procedure TMainForm.sbFirstClick(Sender: TObject);
begin
  inherited;
  DDGBugsDataModule.FirstBug;
  SetActionStatus;
end;

procedure TMainForm.sbPreviousClick(Sender: TObject);
begin
  inherited;
  DDGBugsDataModule.PreviousBug;
  SetActionStatus;
end;

procedure TMainForm.sbNextClick(Sender: TObject);
begin
  inherited;
  DDGBugsDataModule.NextBug;
  SetActionStatus;
end;

procedure TMainForm.sbLastClick(Sender: TObject);
begin
  inherited;
  DDGBugsDataModule.LastBug;
  SetActionStatus;
end;

procedure TMainForm.sbSearchClick(Sender: TObject);
begin
  inherited;
  DDGBugsDataModule.SearchForBug;
end;

procedure TMainForm.FormCloseQuery(Sender: TObject; var CanClose:
➥Boolean);
var
  Rslt: word;
begin
  inherited;
  if not (FormMode = fmBrowse) then
  begin
    rslt := MessageDlg('Save changes?', mtConfirmation, mbYesNoCancel, 0);
```

```
      case rslt of
        mrYes:
          begin
            DDGBugsDataModule.SaveBug;
            FormMode := fmBrowse;
            CanClose := True;
          end;
        mrNo:
          begin
            DDGBugsDataModule.CancelBug;
            FormMode := fmBrowse;
            CanClose := True;
          end;
        mrCancel:
          CanClose := False;
      end;
    end;
end;

procedure TMainForm.sbAcceptClick(Sender: TObject);
begin
  inherited;
  DDGBugsDataModule.SaveBug;
  SetActionStatus;
end;

procedure TMainForm.sbCancelClick(Sender: TObject);
begin
  inherited;
  DDGBugsDataModule.CancelBug;
  SetActionStatus;
end;

procedure TMainForm.sbInsertClick(Sender: TObject);
begin
  inherited;
  DDGBugsDataModule.InsertBug;
  SetActionStatus;
end;

procedure TMainForm.sbEditClick(Sender: TObject);
begin
  inherited;
  DDGBugsDataModule.EditBug;
  SetActionStatus;
end;
```

continues

34

DESKTOP
APPLICATION
DEVELOPMENT

LISTING 34.5. CONTINUED

```
procedure TMainForm.sbDeleteClick(Sender: TObject);
begin
  inherited;
  DDGBugsDataModule.DeleteBug;
  SetActionStatus;
end;

procedure TMainForm.sbBrowseClick(Sender: TObject);
begin
  inherited;
  DDGBugsDataModule.CancelBug;
  SetActionStatus;
end;

procedure TMainForm.rgWhoseBugsClick(Sender: TObject);
begin
  inherited;
  DDGBugsDataModule.FilterOnUser := rgWhoseBugs.ItemIndex = 0;
end;

procedure TMainForm.mmiExitClick(Sender: TObject);
begin
  inherited;
  Close;
end;

procedure TMainForm.mmiAddUserClick(Sender: TObject);
begin
  inherited;
  DDGBugsDataModule.AddUser;
end;

procedure TMainForm.mmiAddActionToBugClick(Sender: TObject);
begin
  inherited;
  DDGBugsDataModule.AddAction;
  dsBugsDataChange(nil, nil);
end;

procedure TMainForm.dsBugsDataChange(Sender: TObject; Field: TField);
begin
  inherited;
  // A new bug is being displayed so clear the action list and
  // retrieve the actions for the newly displayed bug.
  memAction.Lines.Clear;
  DDGBugsDataModule.GetActions(memAction.Lines);
end;

end.
```

The TMainForm descends from TDBNavStatForm that you created back in Chapter 4, "Application Frameworks and Design Concepts," and exists in your Object Repository. TDBNavStatForm contains functionality to update the speed buttons and status bar based on the form's mode (Add, Edit, Browse). Most of the methods simply call the corresponding data module methods.

Note that you set the dsBugs.AutoEdit property to False, thus preventing the user from inadvertently placing the table into edit mode. You want to have the user explicitly set the Bugs table to Edit or Insert mode by clicking the appropriate buttons or menu items.

This form is uncomplicated. SetActionStatus() simply enables/disables buttons and menus based on various conditions. FormCloseQuery() ensures that the user saves or cancels any pending edit or insert.

Other User Interface Issues

From the data module, we've controlled how field labels are displayed by adding the fields to the TTable object and specifying a friendlier label in the Object Inspector. The same can be done for TDBGrids by modifying the Title property of the TDBGrid.Columns property. We've used both methods to control the labels displayed to the user.

PREPARING FOR WEB ENABLEMENT

We stated earlier that this application was to have a Web-enabled version of itself. To make this possible, we need to remove any reference to any forms from within the TDDGBugsDataModule. Using conditional compilation directives that you'll see in the DDGBugsDM.pas unit does this. For example, notice the following code:

```
{$IFNDEF DDGWEBBUGS}
  procedure AddUser;
{$ENDIF}
```

The {$IFNDEF} condition ensures that the AddUser() method is compiled into the application only if the DDBWEBBUGS conditional is not defined, which is the case for this application.

SUMMARY

In this chapter we discussed techniques for developing desktop database applications. We emphasized separating the user interface from the data manipulation routines. This will make the transition of converting your application to a Web-enabled version easier. The next chapter illustrates how to do just that.

34

DESKTOP
APPLICATION
DEVELOPMENT

DDG BUG REPORTING
TOOL: USING WEBBROKER

IN THIS CHAPTER

The last chapter, "DDG Bug Reporting Tool—Desktop Application Development," demonstrated various techniques for designing desktop database applications. One consideration we discussed was how to develop an application that you plan to deploy to the World Wide Web. In this chapter, we're going to deploy the last chapter's application, a simple bug reporting tool, to the World Wide Web as an ISAPI server. As stated in the previous chapter, this effort should require minimal modifications to code already written. We'll use the techniques covered in Chapter 30 "Internet-Enabling Your Applications with WebBroker." Therefore, we won't go into any detail on topics covered in that chapter. If you feel you need to review that chapter, you might do so before reading on.

THE PAGE LAYOUT

The layout, or flow, of this Web-based bug reporting tool is illustrated in Figure 35.1.

FIGURE 35.1.
The flow for the Web-based bug reporting tool.

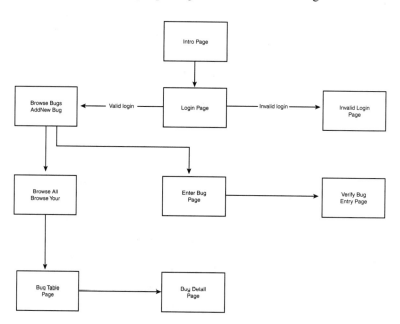

You can see from the page layout that this application is really a subset of the functionality presented in Chapter 34. As an exercise, feel free to expand on the techniques demonstrated in this chapter to provide the full functionality presented in the previous chapter.

The following sections explain the code used to develop the pages. You'll notice in this example that all pages are created at runtime—that is, no predefined HTML documents are loaded. There weren't any compelling reasons why we chose this method instead of writing some HTML documents that are loaded by the WebBroker components. You can certainly use the latter approach for your applications.

CHANGES TO THE DATA MODULE

Our intent here is to use much of the functionality and components that we used to design the TDDGBugsDataModule from the last chapter. We mainly want to add functionality to that data module and to minimize any changes that could potentially break its use in the original non-Web-based application. We accomplish this by avoiding making changes to already existing methods. We also recompile and test the original application to further verify that the previous application is left intact.

Note that we didn't have to create a separate Web module; rather, we just added the TWebDispatcher component to the existing TDataModule. This allows us to use TDataModule as we had already designed it.

For this Web-based version of the bug reporting tool, we've added four more components to TDDGBugsDataModule: TWebDispatcher, TDataSetTableProducer, TPageProducer, and TSession. We'll use these components throughout the code.

We should also mention the purpose of the TSession component. The ISAPI server DLL can potentially be accessed by multiple clients, meaning that multiple people might try to hit the database simultaneously through this single DLL instance. This DLL will operate within a single process space. Therefore, each client that attempts to hit the server requires a separate, dedicated Web module. These separate Web modules are created at runtime and are handled in their own unique thread. This also necessitates each database connection getting its own TSession component in order to prevent database connections from conflicting with each other when multiple clients hit the database. By setting the TSession.AutoSessionName property of the TSession component to True, we ensure that each TSession instance is also given its own unique name.

Note that adding a TSession component to the Web module or to TDataModule is not required when writing a WinCGI or CGI server because these are compiled to separate applications that operate in their own process spaces.

SETTING UP THE TDataSetTableProducer COMPONENT: dstpBugs

The data module's TDataSetTableProducer component, dstpBugs, is attached to the TTable component, tblBugs. Much like configuring a TDBGrid, we've modified the dstpBugs.Columns property to specify titles other than the default (see Figure 35.2). These are the titles that will show up in the Web page table. We've also modified the dstpBugs.TableAttributes property to allow for a one-pixel wide border that will give the table a three-dimensional appearance on most Web browsers.

FIGURE 35.2.

Editing the Columns *property for* dstpBugs.

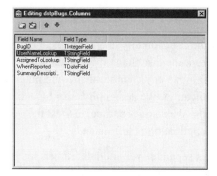

SETTING UP THE TWebDispatcher COMPONENT: wbdpBugs

Figure 35.3 shows the Actions editor used to add several TWebActionItems to wbdpBugs. We'll get into the details of each of these actions as well as how they present the user with access to the bug application through the Web.

FIGURE 35.3.

Editing the Actions *property for* wbdpBugs.

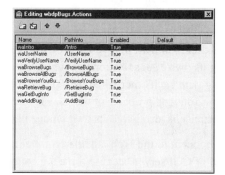

SETTING UP THE TPageProducer COMPONENT: pprdBugs

If you bring up the pprdBugs.HTMLDoc property, you'll notice that it's empty. This property is manipulated at runtime, programmatically. We'll use this same instance of TPageProducer in two different situations, as you'll see when we discuss the code.

CODING THE DDGWebBugs ISAPI SERVER— ADDING TActionItems

All the functionality of the Web bug reporting tool is provided through the TWebDispatcher component's TActionItems. Table 35.1 shows the purpose of each TActionItem instance. We'll discuss each of these separately.

TABLE 35.1. THE PURPOSE OF THE TActionItem INSTANCES.

TActionItem	*Purpose*
waIntro	Displays an initial introductory page to the user.
waUserName	Prompts the user to enter a username.
waVerifyUserName	Invoked from waUserName.OnAction. Verifies the username entered by the user.
waBrowseBugs	Displays two selections to the user: browse all bugs or browse user's bugs only.
waBrowseAllBugs	Displays a table containing all bugs in the database.
waBrowseYourBugs	Displays a table containing bugs belonging to the user.
waRetrieveBug	Displays detail information on the bugs.
waGetBugInfo	Provides the input page to which the user enters new bug information.
waAddBug	Adds the new bug to the table and displays a verification screen.

In the following sections, we'll show the individual listing for each method added to the DDBBugsDM.pas unit instead of showing the entire listing.

Helper Routines

The AddHeader() procedure, shown in Listing 35.1, is used to add a standard header to the Web bug pages consisting of the page title and header. Also, the background image to use is specified here. Note that the location of this background image is dependant on the Web server. You'll most likely have to modify this statement, depending on your system, to be able to find the image. AddFooter(), shown in Listing 35.2, is used to add the standard footer information, including the copyright statement.

LISTING 35.1. TDDGBugsDataModule.AddHeader().

```
procedure AddHeader(AWebPage: TStringList);
// Adds a standard header to each web page.
begin
  with AWebPage do
  begin
    Add('<HTML>');
    Add('<HEAD>');
    Add('<BODY BACKGROUND=''/samples/images/backgrnd.gif''">');
    Add('<TITLE>Delphi 4 Developer''s Guide Bug Demo</Title>');
    Add('<CENTER>');
    Add('<P>');
    Add('<FONT SIZE=6>Delphi 4 Developer''s Guide Bug Demo</font>');
    Add('</CENTER>');
    Add('</HEAD>');
  end;
end;
```

LISTING 35.2. TDDGBugsDataModule.AddFooter().

```
procedure AddFooter(AWebPage: TStringList);
// Adds the standard footer information to each web page.
begin
  with AWebPage do
  begin
    Add('<BR><BR>Copyright (c) 1998, Delphi 4 Developer''s Guide.');
    Add('</BODY>');
    Add('</HTML>');
  end;
end;
```

The Introduction Page

The introduction page is shown in Figure 35.4. It's created by the waIntro.OnAction event handler, wbdpBugswaIntroAction(), shown in Listing 35.3.

LISTING 35.3. TDDGBugsDataModule.wbdpBugswaIntroAction().

```
procedure TDDGBugsDataModule.wbdpBugswaIntroAction(Sender: TObject;
  Request: TWebRequest; Response: TWebResponse; var Handled: Boolean);
// Introductory page for the web demo.
var
  WebPage: TStringList;
begin
  WebPage := TStringList.Create;
  try
    AddHeader(WebPage);
    with WebPage do
```

```
    begin
      Add('<BODY>');
      Add('<H1>Introduction</H1>');
      Add('<P>Welcome to the Delphi 4 Developer''s Guide Bug
➡Demonstration.');
      Add('<BR>This demo, illustrates how to web enable an existing
➡application.');
      Add('<BR>To test the demo, just click on the logon
➡link and follow the pages');
      Add('<BR>to add bugs, or just to browse existing bugs.');
      Add('</P>');
      Add('<A href="../DDGWebBugs.dll/UserName">Login to DDG Bug
➡Demo</A>');
      AddFooter(WebPage);
      Response.Content :=  WebPage.Text;
      Handled := True;
    end;
  finally
    WebPage.Free;
  end;
end;
```

FIGURE 35.4.

The Introduction page.

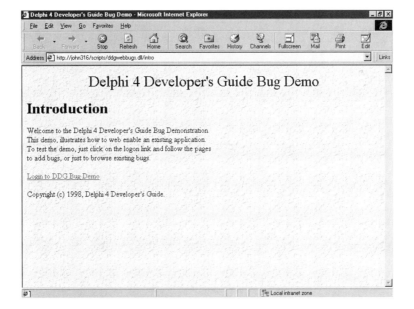

You'll notice that in each instance where a Web page is generated, we pass WebPage to the AddHeader() and AddFooter() procedures. The introduction page is straightforward enough. It simply contains a link to the TWebAction, waUserName.

USING
WEBBROKER

Obtaining and Verifying the User Login Name

Figure 35.5 shows the page generated by TDDGBugsDataModule.
wbdpBugswaUserNameAction() (see Listing 35.4). This is basically an HTML form
used to obtain the username. This page will invoke the TDDGBugsDataModule.
wbdpBugswaVerifyUserNameAction() event handler (see Listing 35.5).

FIGURE 35.5.

*Obtaining the
username.*

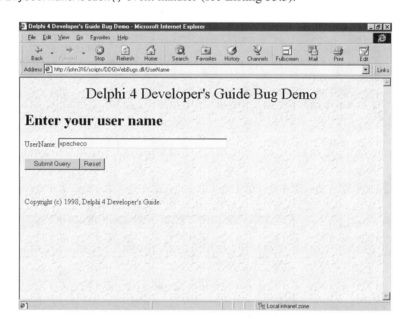

LISTING 35.4. TDDGBugsDataModule.wbdpBugswaUserNameAction().

```
procedure TDDGBugsDataModule.wbdpBugswaUserNameAction(Sender: TObject;
  Request: TWebRequest; Response: TWebResponse; var Handled: Boolean);
// This page prompts the user for the username.
var
  WebPage: TStringList;
begin
  WebPage := TStringList.Create;
  try
    AddHeader(WebPage);
    with WebPage do
    begin
      Add('<BODY>');
      Add('<H1>Enter your user name</H1>');
      Add('<FORM action="../DDGWebBugs.dll/VerifyUserName"
➥method="GET">');
      Add('<p>UserName: <INPUT type="text" name="UserName" maxlength="30"
➥size="50"></P>');
      Add('<p><INPUT type="SUBMIT"><INPUT type="RESET"></p>');
```

```
      Add('</FORM>');
      AddFooter(WebPage);
      Response.Content :=  WebPage.Text;
      Handled := True;
    end;
  finally
    WebPage.Free;
  end;
end;
```

LISTING 35.5. `TDDGBugsDataModule.wbdpBugswaVerifyUserNameAction()`.

```
procedure TDDGBugsDataModule.wbdpBugswaVerifyUserNameAction(
  Sender: TObject; Request: TWebRequest; Response: TWebResponse;
  var Handled: Boolean);
{ This page takes the name entered by the user. The information is saved
  and passed back to the client as a cookie. Additional information is
  also passed back as a cookie that will be used later for adding bugs
  from the Web. }

var
  WebPage: TStringList;
  CookieList: TStringList;
  UserName: String;
  UserFName,
  UserLName: String;
  UserID: Integer;
  ValidLogin: Boolean;

procedure BuildValidLoginPage;
begin
  AddHeader(WebPage);
  with WebPage do
  begin
    Add('<BODY>');
    Add(Format('<H1>User name, %s verified. User ID is: %d</H1>',
      [Request.QueryFields.Values['UserName'], UserID]));
    Add('<BR><BR><A href="../DDGWebBugs.dll/BrowseBugs">Browse Bug
➡List</A>');
    Add('<BR><A href="../DDGWebBugs.dll/GetBugInfo">Add a New Bug</A>');
    AddFooter(WebPage);
  end;
end;

procedure BuildInValidLoginPage;
begin
  AddHeader(WebPage);
  with WebPage do
```

continues

LISTING 35.5. CONTINUED

```
begin
  Add('<BODY>');
  Add(Format('<H1>User name, %s is not a valid user.</H1>',
    [Request.QueryFields.Values['UserName']]));
  AddFooter(WebPage);
  end;
end;

begin

  UserName := Request.QueryFields.Values['UserName'];

  // The login will be valid if the username exists in the Users.db.
  ValidLogin := tblUsers.Locate('UserName', UserName, []);

  WebPage := TStringList.Create;
  try

    if ValidLogin then
    begin

      // Retrieve the UserID and the user's first and last name
      UserID := tblUsers.FieldByName('UserID').AsInteger;
      UserFName := tblUsers.FieldByName('UserFirstName').AsString;
      UserLName := tblUsers.FieldByName('UserLastName').AsString;

      CookieList := TSTringList.Create;
      try

        // Store the user's information as cookies.
        CookieList.Add('UserID='+IntToStr(UserID));
        CookieList.Add('UserName='+UserName);
        CookieList.Add('UserFirstName='+UserFName);
        CookieList.Add('UserLastName='+UserLName);

        Response.SetCookieField(CookieList, '', '', Now + 1, False);
      finally
        CookieList.Free;
      end;
      BuildValidLoginPage;
    end
    else begin
      UserID := -1;
      BuildInvalidLoginPage;
    end;

    Response.Content :=  WebPage.Text;
    Handled := True;
```

```
  finally
    WebPage.Free;
  end;

end;
```

WbdpBugswaVerifyUserNameAction() performs several actions. First, it verifies that the username entered represents a valid user in the tblUsers table. If the username is valid, the BuildValidLoginPage() procedure is called; otherwise, BuildInvalidLoginPage() is called.

If the logon is valid, the user's first and last name and user ID is retrieved from tblUsers. Then, these items are returned as cookies back to the client. Future requests to the Web bug server will pass these values back to the server. We'll make use of these values in generating other pages. Finally, BuildValidLoginPage() is called. It constructs a page containing links for browsing bugs or adding new bugs. If the login is invalid, BrowseInvalidLoginPage() is called. It simply presents a message indicating the invalid login.

Assuming the user has entered a valid login, he or she has the option to browse bugs or to enter a new bug.

BROWSING BUGS

If the user chooses to browse bugs, he or she is presented with a page that provides the options for browsing all bugs in the database or just browsing those bugs the user has entered. This page is constructed in TDDGBugsDataModule.wbdpBugswaBrowseBugsAction() and is shown in Listing 35.6.

LISTING 35.6. TDDGBugsDataModule.wbdpBugswaBrowseBugsAction().

```
procedure TDDGBugsDataModule.wbdpBugswaBrowseBugsAction(Sender: TObject;
  Request: TWebRequest; Response: TWebResponse; var Handled: Boolean);
{ This page gives the user the option of browsing all bugs or just bugs
  entered by him/her. }
var
  WebPage: TStringList;
begin
  WebPage := TStringList.Create;
  try
    AddHeader(WebPage);
    with WebPage do
    begin
      Add('<BODY>');
      Add('<H1>Browse Option</H1>');
```

continues

LISTING 35.6. CONTINUED

```
        Add('<BR><BR><A href="../DDGWebBugs.dll/BrowseAllBugs">
➡Browse All Bugs</A>');
        Add('<BR><A href="../DDGWebBugs.dll/BrowseYourBugs">
➡Browse Your Bugs</A>');
        AddFooter(WebPage);
        Response.Content :=  WebPage.Text;
        Handled := True;
      end;
    finally
      WebPage.Free;
    end;

end;
```

Browsing All Bugs

The option to browse all bugs invokes the
TDDGBugsDataModule.wbdpBugswaBrowseAllBugsAction() event handler, as shown in
Listing 35.7.

LISTING 35.7. TDDGBugsDataModule.wbdpBugswaBrowseBugsAction().

```
procedure TDDGBugsDataModule.wbdpBugswaBrowseAllBugsAction(Sender:
➡TObject;
  Request: TWebRequest; Response: TWebResponse; var Handled: Boolean);
{ This page prepares the TPageProducer component for browsing all bugs.
  The standard header and footer is applied to this page, but a tag is
  used to add the table to the page.   }
var
  WebPage: TStringList;
begin
  WebPage := TStringList.Create;
  try
    AddHeader(WebPage);
    WebPage.Add('<BODY>');
    WebPage.Add('<H1>Browsing all Bugs</H1>');
    WebPage.Add('<#TABLE>');
    AddFooter(WebPage);

    pprdBugs.HTMLDoc.Clear;
    pprdBugs.HTMLDoc.AddStrings(WebPage);

    { As a result of the line below, the OnHTMLTag event handler for
      pprdBugs will be invoked. }
    Response.Content := pprdBugs.Content;
```

```
    Handled := True;
  finally
    WebPage.Free;
  end;
end;
```

This event handler makes use of the TPageProducer component pprdBugs. The functionality needed from this component is its capability to use tags within the HTML content.
In particular, we want to use the #TABLE tag. We added the standard header and footer to
the Web page. However, instead of assigning WebPage to Response.Content, we assign
WebPage to the pprdBugs.HTMLDoc property. Then, we assign pprdBugs.Content to
Response.Content. This causes the pprdBugs.OnHTMLTag event to be invoked. This
event is shown in Listing 35.8. as TDDGBugsDataModule.pprdBugsHTMLTag().

LISTING 35.8. TDDGBugsDataModule.pprdBugsHTMLTag().

```
procedure TDDGBugsDataModule.pprdBugsHTMLTag(Sender: TObject; Tag: TTag;
  const TagString: String; TagParams: TStrings; var ReplaceText: String);
begin
  if Tag = tgTable then begin
    with dstpBugs do
    begin
      DataSet.Open;
      ReplaceText := dstpBugs.Content;
      DataSet.Close;
    end;
  end;
end;
```

This simple event handler assigns the dstpBugs.Content property, which refers to the
table, to the pprdBugs.ReplaceText property, which will replace the #TABLE tag with the
table contents. The resulting page is shown in Figure 35.6. It displays the bugs entered
by all users.

Browsing User-Entered Bugs

If the user chooses to browse his or her own bugs, a page containing a table with only
the bugs he or she has entered is presented to the user. The
TDDGBugsDataModule.wbdpBugswaBrowseYourBugsAction() event handler constructs
this page (see Listing 35.9).

FIGURE 35.6.

A list of bugs entered by all users.

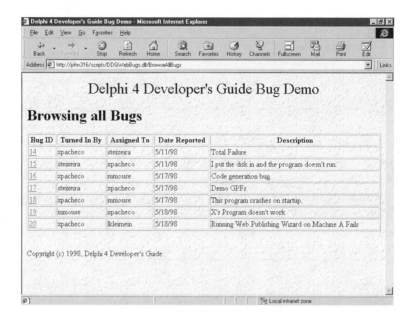

LISTING 35.9. TDDGBugsDataModule.wbdpBugswaBrowseYourBugsAction().

```
procedure TDDGBugsDataModule.wbdpBugswaBrowseYourBugsAction(
  Sender: TObject; Request: TWebRequest; Response: TWebResponse;
  var Handled: Boolean);
{ This page prepares the TPageProducer component for browsing bugs which
  belong to the user. The standard header and footer is applied to this
page,
  but a tag is used to add the table to the page.    }
var
  WebPage: TStringList;
  UserID: Integer;
  UserFName,
  UserLName: String;
begin
  WebPage := TStringList.Create;
  try
    AddHeader(WebPage);
    WebPage.Add('<BODY>');

    // Retrieve the user ID which is stored in the cookie.
    UserID   := StrToInt(Request.CookieFields.Values['UserID']);
    UserFName := Request.CookieFields.Values['UserFirstName'];
    UserLName := Request.CookieFields.Values['UserLastName'];

    WebPage.Add(Format('<H1>Browsing Bugs Entered by %s %s</H1>',
      [UserFName, UserLName]));
```

```
    WebPage.Add('<#TABLE>');
    pprdBugs.HTMLDoc.Clear;
    pprdBugs.HTMLDoc.AddStrings(WebPage);

    AddFooter(WebPage);

    // Make sure the table is now filtered by the UserID
    FLoginUserID := UserID;
    FilterOnUser := True;

    Response.Content := pprdBugs.Content;

    Handled := True;
  finally
    WebPage.Free;
  end;

end;
```

As was the case with the event handler for browsing all bugs, the standard header and
footer needs to be added to this page. Also, the UserID, UserFirstName, and
UserLastName cookies are retrieved from the Request.CookieFields property.
UserFirstName and UserLastName are used to display the user's name on the Web page.
UserID is assigned FLoginUserID. Then the FilterOnUser property is set to True. If you
recall from the previous chapter, by setting the FilterOnUser property to True, its
SetFilterOnUser() writer method is invoked, which in turn sets tblBugs.Filtered to
True. This causes the OnFilterRecord event handler for tblBugs,
tblBugsFilterRecord(), to be called for each record in the data set. This event executes
the following line of code:

```
Accept := tblBugs.FieldByName('UserID').AsInteger = FLoginUserID;
```

You can see that the filter applied depends on the value contained in the FLoginUserID
field. This explains why the value of UserID from the cookie field needs to be assigned
to FLoginUserID.

Finally, the pprdBugs.Content property is assigned to Response.Content. Again, this
will cause the pprdBugs.OnHTMLTag event to be invoked.

Formatting Table Cells and Displaying Bug Detail

DstpBugs contains the OnFormatCell event handler TDDGBugsDataModule.
dstpBugsFormatCell(). This event handler converts the displayed BugID to
an HTML link, which displays the detail information for that bug. TDDGBugsDataModule.
wbdpBugswaRetrieveBugAction() is the event handler that actually displays this bug
information. Both of these event handlers are shown in Listing 35.10.

35

USING
WEBBROKER

LISTING 35.10. THE EVENT HANDLERS FOR DISPLAYING BUG DETAIL.

```
procedure TDDGBugsDataModule.dstpBugsFormatCell(Sender: TObject; CellRow,
  CellColumn: Integer; var BgColor: THTMLBgColor; var Align: THTMLAlign;
  var VAlign: THTMLVAlign; var CustomAttrs, CellData: String);
{ Convert the BugID cell of the table to a link which invokes the page to
  display the bug detail. }
begin
  if (CellColumn = 0) and not (CellRow = 0) then
    CellData := Format('<A href="../DDGWebBugs.dll/RetrieveBug?
➡BugID=%s">%s</A>',
      [CellData, CellData]);
end;

procedure TDDGBugsDataModule.wbdpBugswaRetrieveBugAction(Sender: TObject;
  Request: TWebRequest; Response: TWebResponse; var Handled: Boolean);
{ View the bug detail information. }
var
  BugID: Integer;
  WebPage: TStringList;

procedure GetBug;
begin
  if tblBugs.Locate('BugID', BugID, []) then
    with tblBugs do
    begin
      WebPage.Add(Format('Bug ID:        %d', [BugID]));
      WebPage.Add(Format('<BR>Reported By:  %s',
        [FieldByName('UserNameLookup').AsString]));
      WebPage.Add(FormatDateTime('"<BR>Reported On:"   mmm dd, yyyy',
        FieldByName('WhenReported').AsDateTime));
      WebPage.Add(Format('<BR>Assigned To:  %s',
        [FieldByName('AssignedToLookup').AsString]));
      WebPage.Add(Format('<BR>Status:       %s',
        [FieldByName('StatusTitle').AsString]));
      WebPage.Add(Format('<BR>Summary:      %s',
        [FieldByName('SummaryDescription').AsString]));
      WebPage.Add(Format('<BR>Details:      %s',
        [FieldByName('Details').AsString]));
      WebPage.Add('<BR>');
      WebPage.Add('<BR>');

      GetActions(WebPage);
    end;
end;

begin
  BugID := StrToInt(Request.QueryFields.Values['BugID']);

  WebPage := TStringList.Create;
  try
```

```
    AddHeader(WebPage);
    with WebPage do
    begin
      Add('<BODY>');
      Add('<H1>Bug Detail</H1>');
      GetBug;
      AddFooter(WebPage);
      Response.Content :=  WebPage.Text;
      Handled := True;
    end;
  finally
    WebPage.Free;
  end;

end;
```

ADDING A NEW BUG

The user has the option of adding a new bug to the database. The following sections discuss the pages that retrieve the bug data from the user and display the bug information back to the user once the bug has been entered.

Retrieving the Bug Data

The event handler TDDGBugsDataModule.wbdpBugswaGetBugInfoAction(), shown in Listing 35.11, generates the page used to retrieve the new bug information from the user. This page basically creates an HTML form that contains the appropriate controls to allow the user to enter the proper bug information. Figure 35.7 shows the resulting page from this event handler.

LISTING 35.11. TDDGBugsDataModule.wbdpBugswaGetBugInfoAction().

```
procedure TDDGBugsDataModule.wbdpBugswaGetBugInfoAction(Sender: TObject;
  Request: TWebRequest; Response: TWebResponse; var Handled: Boolean);
{ Prepares the page to retrieve new bug information from the user. }
var
  WebPage: TStringList;

procedure AddAssignToNames;
{ Adds a drop down list to the HTML Page of Assign to users }
begin

  WebPage.Add('<BR>Assign To:');
  WebPage.Add('<BR><SELECT name="AssignTo"><BR>');

  with tblUsers do
```

continues

LISTING 35.11. CONTINUED

```
begin
  First;
  while not Eof do
  begin
    WebPage.Add(Format('<OPTION>%s %s - %s',
      [FieldByName('UserFirstName').AsString,
      FieldByName('UserLastName').AsString,
      FieldByName('UserName').AsString]));
    tblUsers.Next;
  end;
  WebPage.Add('</SELECT>');
  end;
end;

procedure AddStatusTitles;
{ Adds a drop down list to the HTML Page of bug status items }
begin
  WebPage.Add('<BR>Status:');
  WebPage.Add('<BR><SELECT name="Status"><BR>');

  with tblStatus do
  begin
    First;
    while not Eof do
    begin
      WebPage.Add(Format('<OPTION>%s',
➥[FieldByName('StatusTitle').AsString]));
      tblStatus.Next;
    end;
    WebPage.Add('</SELECT>');
  end;
end;

begin
  WebPage := TStringList.Create;
  try
    AddHeader(WebPage);
    with WebPage do
    begin
      Add('<BODY>');
      Add('<H1>Add New Bug</H1>');
      Add('<FORM action="../DDGWebBugs.dll/AddBug"
➥method="GET">');
      Add('<BR>Summary Description:<BR><INPUT type="text"
➥name="Summary" maxlength="100" size="50">');
      Add('<BR>Details:<BR><TEXTAREA name="Details"
➥rows=5 cols=50> </TEXTAREA>');

      AddAssignToNames;
      AddStatusTitles;
```

```
        Add('<p><INPUT type="SUBMIT"><INPUT type="RESET"></p>');
        Add('</FORM>');
        AddFooter(WebPage);
        Response.Content :=  WebPage.Text;
        Handled := True;
      end;
  finally
    WebPage.Free;
  end;
end;
```

FIGURE 35.7.

The bug entry page.

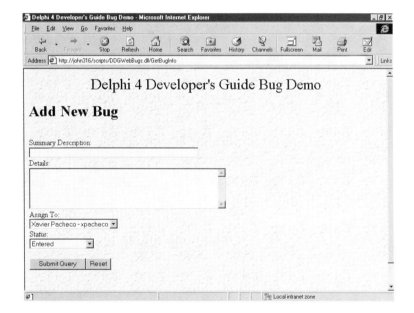

The two helper functions AddAssignToNames() and AddStatusTitle() create combo boxes from which the user can select values for the bug. Unlike using Delphi data-aware controls that can automatically assign the selected lookup values to the new record, this assignment has to be made manually, as you'll see in the event handler that adds the new bug to the database.

Verifying Bug Insertion

The event handler TDDGBugsDataModule.wbdpBugswaAddBugAction() is shown in Listing 35.12.

LISTING 35.12. TDDGBugsDataModule.wbdpBugswaAddBugAction().

```
procedure TDDGBugsDataModule.wbdpBugswaAddBugAction(Sender: TObject;
  Request: TWebRequest; Response: TWebResponse; var Handled: Boolean);
{ Adds the Bug to the database. Uses the cookies returned by the client
  to display information about the user. }
var
  SummaryStr,
  DetailsStr,
  AssignToStr,
  StatusStr: String;
  WebPage: TStringList;
  UserID: Integer;
  UserName: String;
  UserFName,
  UserLName: String;
  AssignedToUserName: String;
  PostSucceeded: boolean;

function GetAssignedToID: Integer;
var
  PosIdx: Integer;
begin
  PosIdx := Pos('-', AssignToStr);
  AssignedToUserName := Copy(AssignToStr, PosIdx+2, 100);
  tblUsers.Locate('UserName', AssignedToUserName, []);
  Result := tblUsers.FieldByName('UserID').AsInteger;
end;

function GetStatusID: Integer;
begin
  tblStatus.Locate('StatusTitle', StatusStr, []);
  Result := tblStatus.FieldByName('StatusID').AsInteger;
end;

procedure DoPostSuccessPage;
begin
  with WebPage do
  begin
    Add(Format('<H1>Thank you %s %s, your bug has been added.</H1>',
        [UserFName, UserLName]));
    Add(FormatDateTime('"<BR><BR>Bug Entered on:"  mmm dd, yyyy', Date));
    Add(Format('<BR>Bug Assigned to: %s', [AssignedToUserName]));
    Add(Format('<BR>Details: %s', [DetailsStr]));
    Add(Format('<BR>Status: %s', [StatusStr]));
  end;
end;

procedure DoPostFailPage;
begin
  WebPage.Add('<BR>Bug Entry failed.');
end;
```

```
begin

  // Retrieve the fields inserted.
  SummaryStr  := Request.QueryFields.Values['Summary'];
  DetailsStr  := Request.QueryFields.Values['Details'];
  AssignToStr := Request.QueryFields.Values['AssignTo'];
  StatusStr   := Request.QueryFields.Values['Status'];


  // Retrieve the cookie fields.
  UserID    := StrToInt(Request.CookieFields.Values['UserID']);
  UserName  := Request.CookieFields.Values['UserName'];
  UserFName := Request.CookieFields.Values['UserFirstName'];
  UserLName := Request.CookieFields.Values['UserLastName'];

  // Necessary for the AfterInsert event handler.
  FLoginUserID   := UserID;
  FLoginUserName := UserName;

  InsertBug;
  try
    tblBugs.FieldByName('SummaryDescription').AsString := SummaryStr;
    tblBugs.FieldByName('WhenReported').AsDateTime := Date;
    tblBugs.FieldByName('Details').AsString := DetailsStr;
    tblBugs.FieldByName('AssignedToUserID').AsInteger := GetAssignedToID;
    tblBugs.FieldByName('StatusID').AsInteger := GetStatusID;
    tblBugs.Post;
    PostSucceeded := True;

  except
    tblBugs.Cancel;
    PostSucceeded := False;
  end;

  WebPage := TStringList.Create;
  try
    AddHeader(WebPage);
    with WebPage do
    begin
      Add('<BODY>');

      if PostSucceeded then
        DoPostSuccessPage
      else
        DoPostFailPage;

      AddFooter(WebPage);
      Response.Content :=  WebPage.Text;
      Handled := True;
    end;
  finally
    WebPage.Free;
  end;

end;
```

This event handler first retrieves all the values entered by the user from the bug entry page shown in Figure 35.7. It also retrieves the cookie fields entered previously. The two lines of code

```
// Necessary for the AfterInsert event handler.
FLoginUserID   := UserID;
FLoginUserName := UserName;
```

are required for the AfterInsert event handler for tblBugs, which performs as follows:

```
tblBugs.FieldByName('UserID').AsInteger := FLoginUserID;
tblBugs.FieldByName('UserNameLookup').AsString := FLoginUserName;
```

Finally, the new bug is inserted into tblBugs. If the insertion succeeds, the Web page is constructed by calling DoPostSuccessPage(); otherwise, DoPostFailPage() is called. DoPostSuccessPage() simply presents the bug data back to the user, whereas DoPostFailPage() displays a fail notification.

Recall that data-aware look-up controls aren't used to obtain valid entries for the AssignToUserID and StatusID fields for tblBugs. Our bug entry page provides the user with the strings that represent these items in the drop-down combo boxes. In order to add the proper look-up index values to tblBugs, a search is performed on the strings selected by the user against both tblUsers and tblStatus. Note that a bit of string manipulation is required for the AssignToUserID field in order to extract the proper string with which to perform the search (see the GetAssignToID() method).

SUMMARY

This chapter covers deploying Web database applications. In this chapter, we demonstrated how, if properly designed, an existing application can be deployed to the Web with few modifications to the existing code (with the exception of adding code specific to the Web). In fact, most of what we presented here has more to do with the construction of the HTML documents rather than database manipulation. You might consider modifying this demo to extend its functionality, as well as move the HTML construction code to actual HTML files.

Error Messages and Exceptions

IN THIS APPENDIX

One difference between good software and great software is that although good software runs well, great software runs well and *fails* well. In Delphi programs, errors that are detected at runtime usually are reported and handled as exceptions. This allows your code the opportunity to respond to problems and recover (by backing up and trying another approach) or at least to "degrade gracefully" (free allocated resources, close files, and display an error message) instead of just crashing and making a mess of your system. Most exceptions in Delphi programs are raised and handled completely within the program; very few runtime errors actually will bring a Delphi program to a screeching halt.

This appendix lists the most common error messages that a Delphi application can report and provides field notes to help you find the cause of an error condition. Because each component you add to your Delphi environment often has its own set of error messages, this list can never be complete, so we'll focus on the most common or most insidious error messages you're likely to face while developing and debugging your Delphi applications.

BDE Error Codes

When working with the Borland Database Engine, occasionally you'll receive an error dialog box indicating that some error has occurred in the Engine. Most commonly, this happens when a customer or client installs your software on their machine and they have some configuration problems with their machine that you're trying to track down. Typically, the aforementioned error dialog box provides you with a hexadecimal error code as the description of the error. The question is how to turn that number into a meaningful error message. That's easy: Look it up in the following table. Table B.1 lists all the possible BDE error codes and the BDE error strings associated with each error code.

Suggested Reading

IN THIS APPENDIX

DELPHI PROGRAMMING

- *The Tomes of Delphi 3: Win32 Graphical API*, by John Ayres, David Bowden, Larry Diehl, Phil Dorcas, Kenneth Harrison, Rod Mathes, Ovias Reza, and Mike Tobin (Wordware Publishing, Inc., 1998).
- *The Tomes of Delphi 3: Win32 Core API*, by John Ayres, David Bowden, Larry Diehl, Phil Dorcas, Kenneth Harrison, Rod Mathes, Ovias Reza, and Mike Tobin (Wordware Publishing, Inc., 1998).
- *Delphi 2 Unleashed*, by Charlie Calvert (Sams Publishing, 1996).
- *Delphi Developer's Handbook*, by Marco Cantu, Tim Gooch, and John F. Lam (Sybex, 1998).
- *Hidden Paths of Delphi 3*, by Ray Lischner (Informant Press, 1997).
- *Secrets of Delphi 2*, by Ray Lischner (Waite Group Press, 1996).

COMPONENT DESIGN

- *Developing Custom Delphi 3 Components*, by Ray Konopka (Coriolis Group Books, 1997).
- *Delphi Component Design*, by Danny Thorpe (Addison-Wesley, 1997).

WINDOWS PROGRAMMING

- *Advanced Windows,* 3rd Ed., by Jeffrey Richter (Microsoft Press, 1997).

OBJECT-ORIENTED PROGRAMMING

- *Object-Oriented Analysis and Design with Applications*, 2nd Ed., by Grady Booch (Addison-Wesley, 1994).
- *Design Patterns: Elements of Reusable Object-Oriented Software*, by Erich Gamma, Richard Helm, Ralph Johnson, and John Vlissides (Addison-Wesley, 1995).

SOFTWARE PROJECT MANAGEMENT, USER INTERFACE DESIGN

- *About Face: The Essentials of User Interface Design*, by Alan Cooper (IDG Books, 1995).
- *Rapid Development*, by Steve McConnell (Microsoft Press, 1996).
- *Software Project Survival Guide*, by Steve McConnell (Microsoft Press, 1998).
- *Code Complete*, by Steve McConnell (Microsoft Press, 1993).

COM/ACTIVEX/OLE

- *Essential COM*, by Don Box (Addison-Wesley, 1998).
- *Inside OLE*, 2nd Ed., by Kraig Brockschmidt (Microsoft Press, 1995).

INDEX

Note: Pages with the prefix "CD:" are located on the CD-ROM.

SYMBOLS

A

U

Sams Teach Yourself JBuilder 2 in 21 Days

—Don Doherty

Sams Teach Yourself JBuilder 2 in 21 Days is in the format of the other best-selling *Sams Teach Yourself* books. This book presents information on JBuilder 2 and teaches you how to use it to develop. JBuilder 2 is Borland International's updated graphical development environment that uses the Java programming language and is compatible with Sun's JDK 1.2. Because JBuilder's programming language is Java, this book also teaches you how to program with Java within the JBuilder development environment, touching on Java fundamentals and the object-oriented approach. It doesn't assume that you already know Java.

JBuilder has built an excellent reputation in the Java development market in the tradition of Delphi and C++Builder. With its updated capabilities and release timed with Sun's JDK 1.2, it should gain even more ground in version 2.

Price: $39.99 USA/$57.95 CAN

ISBN: 0-672-31318-9

Beginning–Intermediate

700 pages

Charlie Calvert's Delphi 4 Unleashed

—Charlie Calvert

Charlie Calvert's Delphi 4 Unleashed is an all-new edition, written by one of the most well-known and respected developers in the Borland and Delphi communities. This advanced reference provides programmers with the information they need to build high-end Delphi applications and components compatible with ActiveX and Java. This book tells programmers what the manuals don't—and how to make Delphi 4 really work for them. Calvert brings the newest technologies and features of Delphi into focus and shows programmers how to use them. These features include building and integrating components with Java, using ActiveX, Internet-enabling applications, and building Internet and intranet applications. This book also covers Delphi's Multitier Distributed Applications Services Suite (MIDAS) and how it works with Delphi and the client/server architecture and enterprisewide development.

Price: $49.99 USA/$71.95 CAN

ISBN: 0-672-31285-9

Advanced–Expert

1,000 pages

Sams Teach Yourself Borland C++Builder 3 in 21 Days

—Kent Reisdorph

The drag-and-drop power of Borland C++Builder 3 is yours to command with *Sams Teach Yourself Borland C++Builder 3 in 21 Days*. In no time, you'll be able to rapidly build programs from reusable ActiveX controls, Java Beans, and Delphi components. Using the methods taught in this book, you can increase your productivity and leverage your knowledge of C++ 3 and Delphi to develop mainstream applications. The proven, step-by-step techniques of the *Sams Teach Yourself* series show you how to accomplish specific tasks with this powerful new programming interface. This is a key revision to an already-successful Borland Press book, with 30 percent new and updated content by a well-known author in the Borland development community.

Stop programming C++ the old-fashioned way and start tapping into the visual programming power of Borland C++Builder 3! It has a large potential customer base, and most developers are predicted to upgrade within 6 months of the product release.

Price: $39.99 USA/$57.95 CAN
ISBN: 0-672-31266-2

Beginning–Intermediate
832 pages

Charlie Calvert's C++Builder 3 Unleashed

—Charlie Calvert

Charlie Calvert's C++Builder 3 Unleashed teaches you how to use object-oriented programming to maximize your code reusability, develop Web applications by incorporating ActiveX and Internet functions into your programs, employ property editors to check your documents, and create updated, dynamic links between documents with OLE. You will also learn about implementing the new multimedia features to program 2D and 3D graphics, writing multimedia instructions for Windows with DirectX, connecting to your corporate data with scalable database tools, and developing C++ programs visually with drag-and-drop methods. Finally, this book covers how to Internet-enable client/server applications for your entire network.

Price: $59.99 USA/$85.95 CAN
ISBN: 0-672-31265-4

Intermediate–Advanced
1,200 pages

Add to Your Sams Library Today with the Best Books for Programming, Operating Systems, and New Technologies

To order, visit our Web site at www.mcp.com or fax us at

1-800-835-3202

ISBN	Quantity	Description of Item	Unit Cost	Total Cost
0-672-31318-9		Sams Teach Yourself JBuilder 2 in 21 Days	$39.99	
0-672-31285-9		Charlie Calvert's Delphi 4 Unleashed	$49.99	
0-672-31266-2		Sams Teach Yourself Borland C++Builder 3 in 21 Days	$39.99	
0-672-31265-4		Charlie Calvert's C++Builder 3 Unleashed	$59.99	
		Shipping and Handling: See information below.		
		TOTAL		

Shipping and Handling

Standard	$5.00
2nd Day	$10.00
Next Day	$17.50
International	$40.00

201 W. 103rd Street, Indianapolis, Indiana 46290   1-800-835-3202 — Fax

Book ISBN 0-672-31284-0

WHAT'S ON THE CD-ROM

The companion CD-ROM contains all the authors' source code, samples from the book, and some third-party software products.

WINDOWS NT 3.5.1 INSTALLATION INSTRUCTIONS

1. Insert the CD-ROM into your CD-ROM drive.
2. From File Manager or Program Manager, choose Run from the File menu.
3. Type `<drive>\AUTORUN.EXE` and press Enter, where `<drive>` corresponds to the drive letter of your CD-ROM. For example, if your CD-ROM is drive D:, type `D:\AUTORUN.EXE` and press Enter.
4. Follow the onscreen instructions to finish the installation.

WINDOWS 95 AND WINDOWS NT 4 INSTALLATION INSTRUCTIONS

1. Insert the CD-ROM into your CD-ROM drive.
2. From the Windows 95 desktop, double-click the My Computer icon.
3. Double-click the icon representing your CD-ROM drive.
4. Double-click the icon titled `AUTORUN.EXE` to run the installation program.
5. Follow the onscreen instructions to finish the installation.

> **NOTE**
>
> If Windows 95 is installed on your computer and you have the AutoPlay feature enabled, the `AUTORUN.EXE` program starts automatically whenever you insert the disc into your CD-ROM drive.